# Lecture Notes in Computer Science 16800

The series Lecture Notes in Computer Science (LNCS), including its subseries Lecture Notes in Artificial Intelligence (LNAI) and Lecture Notes in Bioinformatics (LNBI), has established itself as a medium for the publication of new developments in computer science and information technology research, teaching, and education.

LNCS enjoys close cooperation with the computer science R & D community, the series counts many renowned academics among its volume editors and paper authors, and collaborates with prestigious societies. Its mission is to serve this international community by providing an invaluable service, mainly focused on the publication of conference and workshop proceedings and postproceedings. LNCS commenced publication in 1973.

Nadia Heninger · Mike Rosulek
Editors

# Advances in Cryptology – CRYPTO 2026

## 46th Annual International Cryptology Conference
## Santa Barbara, CA, USA, August 17–20, 2026
## Proceedings, Part I

Springer

*Editors*
Nadia Heninger
University of California, San Diego
La Jolla, CA, USA

Mike Rosulek
Oregon State University
Corvallis, OR, USA

ISSN 0302-9743 ISSN 1611-3349 (electronic)
Lecture Notes in Computer Science
ISBN 978-3-032-35366-5 ISBN 978-3-032-35367-2 (eBook)
https://doi.org/10.1007/978-3-032-35367-2



This Springer imprint is published by the registered company Springer Nature Switzerland AG
The registered company address is: Gewerbestrasse 11, 6330 Cham, Switzerland

# Preface

These are the proceedings of the 46th Annual International Cryptology Conference (Crypto 2026). The conference was held in Santa Barbara, California, USA from August 17–20, 2026, and organized by the International Association for Cryptologic Research (IACR).

We received 781 submissions, a record number for an IACR conference. 29 papers were desk-rejected without review, for violations of anonymity or formatting requirements. The remaining papers continued to the formal peer-review process.

Each paper was assigned two "early" reviewers and one "late" reviewer. The reviewing process was double-blind. Based on the consensus of the early reviews and ensuing discussions, 323 papers were rejected, in most cases without a third review. The remaining papers received their assigned third review and were evaluated further.

After thorough deliberation and discussion, we accepted 193 papers. 20 of these papers were accepted subject to mild editorial revisions. Two pairs of these papers were deemed to be so closely related that each pair was merged into a single paper. Two accepted papers were voluntarily withdrawn by the authors. The final result of the process is the program you see presented in these proceedings, consisting of 189 papers. This far surpasses the previous record (156) for an IACR conference.

We recruited the assistance of 11 area chairs; their names are listed below. They led discussions on papers, wrangled reviewers, advised on strategic decisions, and generally helped the review process run smoothly.

Our program committee was comprised of 90 additional domain experts in cryptology, assembled from across the world. We have the utmost gratitude to our PC members for providing insightful and constructive feedback despite the heavy reviewing workload.

In consultation with the area chairs, two outstanding papers were selected for awards: *An attack on the CFS scheme and on TII McEliece challenges* by Magali Bardet, Axel Lemoine, and Jean-Pierre Tillich was awarded best paper. *CORAL: Faster Isogeny Group Action for Post-Quantum NIKE* by Andrea Basso, Giacomo Borin, Ryan Rueger, and Sina Schaeffler was selected as best paper authored by early-career researchers (all authors were students or postdocs at the time of submission).

Following the precedent from the previous year's Crypto conference, authors were given the option of presenting their work in person at the conference, or remotely and asynchronously via uploaded video.

In addition to the contributed papers, Crypto 2026 featured the IACR distinguished lecture by Joan Daemen, several pre-conference workshops on various topics, and a rump session program of short, often irreverent talks.

We are grateful to Kevin McCurley for all the work he has put into maintaining and customizing the IACR's instantiation of the HotCRP review software, and his prompt technical support. We would also like to thank the Crypto 2026 general chair Mayank Varia for coordinating with us and organizing the conference itself. We are also grateful to the IACR Board of Directors as a whole for their ongoing volunteer service to the field.

June 2026

Nadia Heninger
Mike Rosulek

# Organization

## General Chair

| | |
|---|---|
| Mayank Varia | Boston University, USA |

## Program Co-chairs

| | |
|---|---|
| Nadia Heninger | University of California, San Diego, USA |
| Mike Rosulek | Oregon State University, USA |

## Area Chairs

| | |
|---|---|
| Martin R. Albrecht | Kings College London & SandboxAQ, UK |
| Joseph Bonneau | New York University, USA |
| Henry Corrigan-Gibbs | UC Berkeley, USA |
| Dana Dachman-Soled | University of Maryland, College Park, USA |
| Léo Perrin | Inria, France |
| Ron Rothblum | Technion, Israel |
| Patrick Schaumont | Worcester Polytechnic Institute, USA |
| Ben Smith | Inria & École Polytechnique, France |
| Stefano Tessaro | University of Washington, USA |
| Vinod Vaikuntanathan | MIT, USA |
| Muthuramakrishnan Venkitasubramaniam | Georgetown University & Ligero, Inc., USA |

## Program Committee

| | |
|---|---|
| Damiano Abram | University of Edinburgh, UK |
| Henry Bambury | ENS PSL, France |
| Amos Beimel | Ben-Gurion University, Israel |
| Alexander Block | University of Illinois, Chicago, USA |
| Maxime Bombar | University of Bordeaux, France |
| Christina Boura | IRIF, Université Paris Cité, France |
| Elette Boyle | Reichman University, Israel & NTT Research, USA |

| | |
|---|---|
| Pierre Briaud | University of Limoges, France |
| Sofía Celi | Brave, Portugal |
| Mingjie Chen | KU Leuven, Belgium |
| Jung Hee Cheon | Seoul National University & CryptoLab, South Korea |
| Miranda Christ | Columbia University, USA |
| Kai-Min Chung | Academia Sinica, Taiwan |
| Ran Cohen | Reichman University, Israel |
| Daniel Collins | New York University, USA & Hebrew University, Israel |
| Simone Colombo | King's College London, UK |
| Geoffroy Couteau | CNRS, IRIF, Université Paris Cité, France |
| Pratish Datta | NTT Research, USA |
| Amit Deo | Zama, France |
| Itai Dinur | Ben-Gurion University, Israel |
| Martin Ekerå | KTH Royal Institute of Technology & Swedish NCSA, Sweden |
| Thomas Espitau | PQShield, France |
| Rachit Garg | New York University, USA |
| Sanjam Garg | UC Berkeley, USA |
| Rosario Gennaro | City College - CUNY, USA |
| Ashrujit Ghoshal | Indian Institute of Technology Madras, India |
| Aarushi Goel | Rutgers University, USA |
| Lorenzo Grassi | TU Eindhoven, Netherlands |
| Paul Grubbs | University of Michigan, USA |
| Mohammad Hajiabadi | University of Waterloo, Canada |
| Shai Halevi | AWS Cryptography, USA |
| David Heath | University of Illinois Urbana-Champaign, USA |
| Julius Hermelink | MPI-SP, Germany |
| Kathrin Hövelmanns | TU Eindhoven, Netherlands |
| Tetsu Iwata | Nagoya University, Japan |
| Joseph Jaeger | Georgia Tech University, USA |
| Sam Jaques | University of Waterloo, Canada |
| Matthias Kannwischer | Chelpis Quantum Tech, Taiwan |
| Shuichi Katsumata | PQShield & AIST, Japan |
| Elena Kirshanova | TII, UAE |
| Russell W. F. Lai | Aalto University, Finland |
| Eysa Lee | Barnard College, USA |
| Wei-Kai Lin | University of Virginia, USA |
| Patrick Longa | Microsoft Research, USA |
| Julian Loss | Ruhr University Bochum, Germany |
| Yiping Ma | UC Berkeley, USA |

| | |
|---|---|
| Hemanta Maji | Purdue University, USA |
| Surya Mathialagan | NTT Research, USA |
| Bart Mennink | Maastricht University, Netherlands |
| Pierre Meyer | Aarhus University, Denmark |
| Travis Morrison | Virginia Tech, USA |
| Tamer Mour | Bocconi University, Italy |
| Wilson Nguyen | New York University, USA |
| Claudio Orlandi | Aarhus University, Denmark |
| Omkant Pandey | Stony Brook University, USA |
| Omer Paneth | Tel Aviv University, Israel |
| Charalampos Papamanthou | Yale University, USA |
| Octavio Perez-Kempner | NTT Social Informatics Laboratories, Japan |
| Edoardo Persichetti | Florida Atlantic University, USA |
| Krzysztof Pietrzak | IST Austria, Austria |
| Bertram Poettering | IBM Research, Switzerland |
| Mariana Raykova | Google, USA |
| Doreen Riepel | CISPA, Germany |
| Mélissa Rossi | CryptoExperts, France |
| Lawrence Roy | Aarhus University, Denmark |
| Markku-Juhani Saarinen | Tampere University, Finland |
| Maria Corte-Real Santos | ENS Lyon, France |
| John Schanck | Mozilla, USA |
| Nicolas Sendrier | Inria, France |
| Daniel Smith-Tone | NIST & University of Louisville, USA |
| Akshayaram Srinivasan | University of Toronto, Canada |
| Alin Tomescu | Aptos Labs, USA |
| Ni Trieu | Arizona State University, USA |
| Eliad Tsfadia | Bar-Ilan University, Israel |
| Nirvan Tyagi | University of Washington, USA |
| Prashant Nalini Vasudevan | National University of Singapore, Singapore |
| Fernando Virdia | University of Surrey, UK |
| Alexandre Wallet | PQ Shield, France |
| Qingju Wang | Télécom Paris, France |
| Zhedong Wang | Shanghai Jiao Tong University, China |
| Mor Weiss | Bar-Ilan University, Israel |
| Weiqiang Wen | Télécom Paris, France |
| Chenkai Weng | Arizona State University, USA |
| Daniel Wichs | Northeastern University & NTT Research, USA |
| Ivy K. Y. Woo | Aalto University, Finland |
| David Wu | University of Texas, Austin, USA |
| Chaoping Xing | Shanghai Jiao Tong University, China |
| Jiayu Xu | Oregon State University, USA |

Sophia Yakoubov — Aarhus University, Denmark
Takashi Yamakawa — NTT Social Informatics Laboratories & Kyoto University, Japan

## Additional Reviewers

Aaron Kaiser
Aayush Jain
Abel Laval
Abhiram Kothapali
Abhishek Jain
Abishanka Saha
Aditi Partap
Aditya Gulati
Aditya Hegde
Adria Gascon
Adrien Siproudhis
Afonso Arriaga
Afonso Li
Akash Shah
Akhil Bandarupalli
Akin Ünal
Akinori Hosoyamada
Akshaya Kumar
Akshima
Alain Couvreur
Alain Passelègue
Albert Garreta
Albert Yu
Aleksei Udovenko
Aleksi Kalsta
Alessandro Budroni
Alex Davidson
Alex Lombardi
Alex B. Grilo
Alexander Bienstock
Alexander Hoover
Alexander Karening
Alexander Poremba
Alexandre Camelin
Alexis Korb
Alice Pellet-Mary
Alireza Shirzad
Amit Behera
Ananya Appan
Anasuya Acharya
Anat Paskin-Cherniavsky
Anders Kallesøe
André Chailloux
Andre Esser
André Schrottenloher
Andrea Basso
Andrea Flamini
Andrew Huang
Anirban Chakrabarti
Aniruddha Biswas
Anirudh Chandramouli
Antoine Bak
Antoine Joux
Antoine Mesnard
Antonio Flórez-Gutiérrez
Anubhav Baweja
Aparna Gupte
Arasu Arun
Archisman Dutta
Ariel Gabizon
Arka Rai Choudhuri
Aron Van Baarsen
Aurel Page
Aurélien Boeuf
Aurore Guillevic
Avantika Agarwal
Axel Lemoine
Aymen Boudguiga
Aysan Nishaburi
Baiyu Li
Bar Alon
Bart van Vulpen
Bas Westerbaan
Beatrice Biasioli
Ben Curtis
Benedikt Wagner

Benjamin Benčina
Benjamin Dowling
Benoit Libert
Berenika Richterová
Bernardo David
Bhagya Wimalasiri
Bhaskar Roberts
Blake Holman
Boyang Chen
Brady Testa
Brice Minaud
Caleb Geren
Calvin Abou Haidar
Camryn Steckel
Carles Padro
Cas Korporaal
Cavit Özbay
Cecilia Boschini
Chad Sharp
Changmin Lee
Changrui Mu
Charles Bouillaguet
Charles Olivier-Anclin
Charlotte Hoffmann
Chase Fickes
Chaya Ganesh
Chelsea Komlo
Chen Yuan
Chenzhi Zhu
Chethan Kamath
Chris Brzuska
Christian Knabenhans
Christian Majenz
Christof Beierle
Christoph Egger
Christoph Günther
Chun Guo
Clémence Bouvier
Clémence Chevignard
Clément Dell'aiera
Clément Ducros
Clement Hoffmann
Cody Freitag
Cong Ling
Cong Zhang
Corentin Jeudy
Craig Gidney
Cristina Onete
Cruz Barnum
Cyrius Nugier
Dachao Wang
Damien Stehlé
Daniel Augot
Daniel Escudero
Daniel Gardham
Daniel Jost
Daniel Pöllmann
David Balbás
David Richardson
Debasmita Chakraborty
Deep Inder Mohan
Dennis Funke
Derek Yen
Diego Aranha
Dimitris Kolonelos
Dimitris Mouris
Dipayan Das
Divya Ravi
Dominique Schröder
Dung Bui
Dustin Moody
Eamonn W. Postlethwaite
Eik List
Elahe Sadeghi
Elena Micheli
Elena Pagnin
Eli Goldin
Elisa Pioldi
Elisabeth Krahmer
Elisaweta Masserova
Emiel Wiedijk
Enrico Sorbera
Er-Cheng Tang
Erik Mårtensson
Erik Pohle
Erkan Tairi
Ertem Nusret Tas
Eshan Chattopadhyay
Ethan Mook
Eunsang Lee

Fabian Regen
Fabio Banfi
Fabio Campos
Fabrice Benhamouda
Fang Song
Fatima Elsheimy
Felix Rohrbach
Fermi Ma
Florian Tousnakhoff
Floyd Zweydinger
Francesco Migliaro
Francisco Rodríguez-Henríquez
François Gérard
Frederik Vercauteren
Freeman Slaughter
Fuchun Lin
Fukang Liu
Fuyuki Kitagawa
Gabriel Dettling
Gabriel Zaid
Gabrielle De Micheli
Gaëtan Leurent
Gal Arnon
Ganyuan Cao
Garrett Greiner
Gaspard Anthoine
Geng Wang
Georg Land
George Lu
Giacomo Borin
Gil Segev
Gilad Asharov
Giulio Malavolta
Gora Adj
Gregor Seiler
Guilhem Niot
Guillaume Hanrot
Guru-Vamsi Policharla
Gustavo Banegas
Gustavo Xavier Delerue Marinho Alves
Gyeongwon Cha
Hadas Zeilberger
Hamidreza Khoshakhlagh
Hanlin Liu
Hannah Keller
Hany Farid
Hanyu Luo
Hao Lin
Haolin Liu
Haoxiang Jin
Haoxing Lin
Haruhisa Kosuge
Harun Kir
Helger Lipmaa
Hendrik Waldner
Himanshu Vashishth
Ho Nguyen Pham
Hongqing Liu
Hovav Shacham
Hrithik Nandi
Hugo Beguinet
Hugo Krawczyk
Hugues Randriambololona
Hyeongmin Choe
Ignacio Amores
Ignacio Cascudo
Ilan Komargodski
Ilaria Chillotti
Ioana Boureanu
Ioannis Kaklamanis
Isaac Canales Martínez
Itay Shalit
Ivan Damgård
Jacob Schuldt
Jad Silbak
Jade Nardi
Jae Hong Seo
Jaehyung Kim
Jai Hyun Park
Jake Januzelli
Jakob Burkhardt
Jakub Klemsa
James Bartusek
James Bell-Clark
James Hulett
Jan Bormet
Jan Niklas Siemer
Janno Siim
Jason LeGrow
Jaspal Singh

Javier Verbel
Jean-Francois Biasse
Jean-Pierre Tillich
Jeff Champion
Jeongeun Park
Jeremiah Blocki
Jeremias Mechler
Jesko Dujmovic
Jessica Chen
Jesús-Javier Chi-Domínguez
Ji Luo
Jiahui Liu
Jiangtao Li
Jiaqi Cheng
Jiaxin Guan
Jiaxin Pan
Jiayi Kang
Jielong Zhang
Jim Choncholas
Jincheol Ha
Jinwei Zheng
Jinye He
Jinyeong Seo
Jiwon Kim
Joel Gärtner
Johanna Loyer
Johannes Mono
Jonas Janneck
Jonathan Bootle
Jonathan Levin
Jooyoung Lee
Jorge Chavez Saab
Jose Salazar
Joseph Carolan
Joseph Slote
Jouni Mauri
Jovan Komatovic
Julia Guskind
Julia Hesse
Julian Nowakowski
Julian Thomas
Julien Devevey
June Lee
Junichi Tomida
Jure Sternad
Justin Raizes
Kaartik Bhushan
Kabir Tomer
Kai Hu
Kamilla Nazirkhanova
Kanav Gupta
Kaoru Takemure
Karn Seth
Katharina Boudgoust
Kazuki Yamamura
Kazuma Ohara
Kecheng Shi
Keegan Ryan
Keewoo Lee
Keisuke Hara
Keitaro Hashimoto
Kel Zin Tan
Kelong Cong
Kelsey Melissaris
Kevin Carrier
Kevin Choi
Kevin Yeo
Kostas Papagiannopoulos
Krijn Reijnders
Ky Nguyen
LaKyah Tyner
Lalita Devadas
Lars Ran
Laura Luzzi
Lea Thiemt
Lena Heimberger
Lennart Braun
Léo Ducas
Leo Orshansky
Leonardo Errati
Lewis Glabush
Li Quan
Liam Eagen
Lin Jiao
Lior Rotem
Loïc Masure
Lola-Baie Mallordy
Long Chen
Lorenzo Martinico
Loris Bergerat

Louis Tremblay Thibault
Luca Campa
Lucas Piske
Lucas Xia
Luciano Maino
Luowen Qian
Madalina Bolboceanu
Mahimna Kelkar
Mahshid Riahinia
Manasi Shingane
Marc Gourjon
Marc Houben
Marcel Keller
Marcel Nageler
Marcel Tiepelt
Mari Muurman
María Naya-Plasencia
Mario Marhuenda Beltrán
Marios Georgiou
Mark Zhandry
Markus Krausz
Markus Schofnegger
Marloes Venema
Martijn Stam
Martin Roetteler
Marvin Beckmann
Massimo Battaglioni
Matan Hamilis
Mátè Horvath
Mathieu Ballandras
Matteo Scarlata
Matthew Gray
Matthew Prest
Matthias Meijers
Matthijs Bosch
Maxwell Cartor
Maya Farber Brodsky
Megan Chen
Meng Hao
Michael Klooß
Michael Reichle
Michael Rosenberg
Michael Schott
Michael Walter
Michał Osadnik
Michele Battagliola
Michele Orrù
Michiel Verbauwhede
Miguel Cueto Noval
Mihir Bellare
Mike Hamburg
Mikhail Mikhail Kudinov
Mikito Nanashima
Mingyuan Wang
Minki Hhan
Minsik Kang
Miran Kim
Miro Haller
Mirza Ahad Baig
Mohammed Barhoush
Morten Øygarden
Mustafa Khairallah
Nada Ali
Naman Kumar
Nathan Keller
Neekon Vafa
Ngoc Khanh Nguyen
Nicholas Spooner
Nicolas Aragon
Nicolas Bon
Nicolas Resch
Nikhil Pappu
Nikhil Vanjani
Nikita Machine
Nikolas Melissaris
Nikos Skoumios
Nils Fleischhacker
Niv Gilboa
Noam Mazor
Ojaswi Acharya
Oleksiy Klurman
Olga Sanina
Olivier Bernard
Olivier Ruatta
Omar Renawi
Or Lasri
Or Sheffet
Or Zamir
Oriol Farras
Orr Dunkelman

Orr Paradise
Paola de Perthuis
Pascal Sasdrich
Patrick Derbez
Patrick Steuer
Paul Gerhart
Paul Hermouet
Paul Lou
Pedro Branco
Péter Kutas
Peter Pessl
Peter Rindal
Peter Scholl
Phi-Hung Le
Phillip Gajland
Phillipp Schoppmann
Phong Nguyen
Phuoc Pham
Phuong Hoa Nguyen
Pierpaolo Della Monica
Pierre Galissant
Pierre Pebereau
Pouyan Forghani
Pradeep Mishra
Pranav Arunachalaramanan
Pranjal Agarwal
Pratik Soni
Pratyush Mishra
Qi Pang
Qiang Tang
Quang Dao
Quoc Huy Vu
Quynh Dang
Rafael del Pino
Rahmi El Mechri
Rahul Satish
Rasoul Akhavan Mahdavi
Ratnakar Medepalli
Ravi Kishore
Ray Neiheiser
Renas Bacho
Riana Pfefferkorn
Ricardo Rodriguez Reveco
Riccardo Schiavoni
Riddhi Ghosal
Rishav Gupta
Ritam Bhaumik
Robert Primas
Robert Schädlich
Roberto Parisella
Robin Geelen
Rohit Chatterjee
Rohit Sinha
Roman Langrehr
Roy Stracovsky
Ruben Niederhagen
Runzhi Zeng
Rutchathon Chairattana-Apirom
Ryad Benadjila
Ryann Cartor
Ryo Nishimaki
Saachi Mutreja
Sabrina Kunzweiler
Saikumar Yadugiri
Sam Frengley
Sam Gunn
Samin Nooripoor
Santanu Sarkar
Saroja Erabelli
Saswata Mukherjee
Satvinder Singh
Scott Fluhrer
Scott Griffy
Sebastian Kolby
Sebastian Verschoor
Sebastian A. Spindler
Seonhong Min
Serge Vaudenay
Seyoon Ragavan
Shafik Nassar
Shahram Rasoolzadeh
Sherman S. M. Chow
Shibam Ghosh
Shiduo Zhang
Shih-Han Hung
Shiyu Li
Shogo Yamada
Shoichi Hirose
Shota Yamada
Siddharth Agarwal

Sihang Pu
Sikhar Patranabis
Silvia Ritsch
Simon Gerhalter
Simon Holmgaard Kamp
Son Nguyen
Songsong Li
Sriram Sridhar
Srivatsan Sridhar
Stanislas Pawlak
Stanislav Peceny
Stanislaw Jarecki
Steven Galbraith
Subhadeep Banik
Subham Das
Sunyeop Kim
Supartha Podder
Sven Schäge
Swagata Sasmal
Tabitha Ogilvie
Taiga Hiroka
Takahiro Matsuda
Tako Boris Fouotsa
Tal Malkin
Tal Moran
Tal Rabin
Tapas Pal
Thales Paiva
Thomas Debris-Alazard
Thomas Pornin
Thomas Prest
Tianxin Tang
Tianyao Gu
Tianyu Zhang
Tomer Solomon
Tomoki Moriya
Tomoyuki Morimae
Tran Ngo
Tyge Tiessen
Vahid Jahandideh
Valentin Vasseur
Valerie Gilchrist
Valerio Cini
Valerio Coletti
Varun Madathil
Varun Maram
Varun Narayanan
Vedad Hadžić
Venkata Koppula
Venkitesh
Victor Dyseryn
Victor Normand
Viet Tung Hoang
Vincent Hwang
Vir Pathak
Virginie Lallemand
Ward Beullens
Weidan Ji
Weijie Wang
Wenhao Wang
Wenhao Zhang
Wenwen Xia
Wessel Van Woerden
Will Mahaney
William Wang
William Youmans
Wouter Castryck
Xavier Bonnetain
Xiang Liu
Xiangyu Liu
Xianhui Xianhui
Xiao Liang
Xiao Wang
Xicheng Wan
Xingyu Yan
Xinpeng Yang
Xinxin Gong
Xinyu Mao
Xuan Thanh Do
Yanbo Chen
Yang Yu
Yanghong Xu
Yann Rotella
Yanqi Gu
Yanxue Jia
Yao Ching Hsieh
Yao-Ting Lin
Yasar Plueckebaum
Yashvanth Kondi
Yevhen Perehuda

Yi-Fu Lai
Yibin Yang
Yifan Song
Yincen Chen
Ying-Teng Chen
Yixin Shen
Yizhi Huang
Yizhou Yao
Yongha Son
Yonglin Hao
Yongsoo Song
Yongwoo Lee
Yosuke Todo
Youssef El Housni
Yu Sasaki
Yu Shen
Yu Yu
Yu-Hsuan Huang
Yuange Li
Yuanmi Chen
Yuhao Jia
Yuhao Tang
Yun Lu
Yunhao Wang
Yunqi Li
Yuriy Polyakov
Yusuke Naito
Yusuke Sakai
Yuval Efron
Yuval Ishai
Zachary DeStefano
Zehua Shang
Zeyu Liu
Zhe Li
Zhengzhong Jin
Zhenzhen Bao
Zihan Hu
Ziyang Jin
Ziyi Guan
Zoë Ruha Bell
Zonghang Du
Zvika Brakerski

# Contents

## Foundations

## Obfuscation and Functional Encryption

# Foundations

# Pseudo-Equilibria, Or: How to Stop Worrying About Crypto and Just Analyze the Game

Alexandros Psomas[1(✉)], Athina Terzoglou[1], Yu Wei[2], and Vassilis Zikas[2]

[1] Purdue University, West Lafayette, IN, USA
{apsomas,aterzogl}@purdue.edu
[2] Georgia Institute of Technology, Atlanta, GA, USA
{ywei368,vzikas}@gatech.edu

**Abstract.** We revisit the problem of a game theorist analyzing a game that uses cryptographic protocols. Ideally, the game theorist should be able to ignore all implementation details of the cryptographic protocols and abstract them as ideal, implementation-independent primitives, in a way that conclusions in the "ideal world" can be faithfully transferred to the "real world," where real protocols are implemented by cryptography. Achieving this goal is crucial, as the game theorist cannot—and should not be expected to—grapple with the full complexity of cryptographic implementations. This is particularly relevant in the era of Web3, where the widespread adoption of distributed ledgers has created a pressing need for a common language that bridges cryptography and game theory. We propose a new solution concept: the *pseudo-Nash equilibrium*. Informally, a (poly-time) strategy profile is a pseudo-Nash equilibrium if no (poly-time) player observes a noticeable, i.e., non-negligible, (expected) utility gain by playing a different (poly-time) strategy. Pseudo-Nash is substantially simpler and more accessible to game theorists than any existing notion that attempted to address the mismatch in the (asymptotic) cryptographic method and game theory. We prove, in a very general sense, that Nash equilibria in games that use idealized, unbreakable cryptography correspond naturally to pseudo-Nash equilibria when idealized cryptography is instantiated with actual protocols (under state-of-the-world assumptions). Our translation is not only conceptually simpler than existing approaches, but also more general: it does not require tuning or restricting utility functions in the game with idealized cryptography to accommodate idiosyncrasies of cryptographic implementations. In other words, pseudo-Nash equilibria allow us to separately and seamlessly study game-theoretic and cryptographic aspects.

## 1 Introduction

(Distributed) cryptography and game theory both study interactions among agents. Cryptography traditionally takes an adversarial approach; protection


N. Heninger and M. Rosulek (Eds.): CRYPTO 2026, LNCS 16800, pp. 3–34, 2026.
https://doi.org/10.1007/978-3-032-35367-2_1

is demanded against the worst-case (mis)behavior of the agents. Game theory takes the view that agents are selfish and aim to optimize their own utility. The widespread adoption of blockchain protocols has set a stage where both viewpoints are invaluable, as decentralized systems must be both strategically robust and cryptographically secure.

However, while the interaction of the two fields has been fruitful, we believe it is fair to say that a universally adopted model that allows for the two fields to interact seamlessly has yet to emerge. Arguably, the most ambitious goal would be a model such that game theorists can work in an "ideal world" that completely ignores all implementation details of cryptographic protocols (i.e., treats cryptographic primitives as black boxes that provide a certain functionality), but such that game-theoretic solution concepts, e.g., equilibria, naturally carry over to the "real-world," where cryptographic primitives are replaced by their (imperfect) implementations. Such a model, by design, would also allow cryptographers to implement cryptographic primitives without worrying about downstream effects on game-theoretic predictions. Simply put, our work attempts to answer the following question: *Is this ambitious goal attainable?*

### 1.1 Our Contributions

Unfortunately, the answer to the aforementioned question is, in general, "no." This is because cryptographic protocols provide guarantees only under assumptions. There are, broadly speaking, two types of assumptions cryptographic protocols require. The first type is *state-of-the-world* assumptions; examples of this type are computational hardness, ideal obfuscation, secure hardware, and access to certain ideal functionalities or setups, which are common assumptions in the design of cryptographic protocols like encryption, digital signatures, commitments, MPC, etc. The second type is *behavioral* assumptions (e.g., "honest majority"), which are assumptions about the parties that implement the protocol at hand. The reason we cannot have a model that seamlessly abstracts away all cryptographic details, but is faithful to game-theoretic solution concepts, is because of this second type. Many central solution concepts in game theory, e.g., Nash equilibria, are predictions about players' behavior. Therefore, intuitively, it is not possible to ignore elements of a game that only work under specific player behavior. In the full version [40, Example B.1], we present a concrete example, where the behavioral assumption of "honest majority" fails to ensure stability against rational agents (in the context of a blockchain game).

We note that such an example is neither meant to exclude the possibility of designing a protocol that achieves a desired specification under assumptions about the utility of rational agents, nor is it intended as a claimed contribution of our work. Rather, its goal is to provide an abstract perspective on the challenges of combining cryptography and game theory, tailored to the mindset of a game theorist who wishes to use cryptography in their solution. Indeed, the study of rational cryptography has yielded several novel ways in which specific tasks, like secret sharing or function evaluation, can be achieved under specific rationality assumptions, e.g., parties/agents being selfish but curious [20,23,26,34,37,38] (preferring to learn the secret while others do not). What the above example reaffirms is that although a cryptographic proof considers worst-case adversaries, i.e., makes all attacks by such adversaries ineffective, a cryptographic security (proof) of a protocol under behavioral assumptions (like honest majority) does not render it a stable solution against arbitrary rational agents. In fact, even in the context of the above example, numerous works [3,6,9,14–16,18,19,24,36,41,42] show how, under several different classes of blockchain protocols, there are several ways that miners can alter their behavior in the protocol to manipulate timestamps, their rewards in the underlying cryptocurrency, or even the value of the cryptocurrency itself. Thus, the existence of these counterexamples is well-known (but perhaps not articulated using the ideal vs real-world perspective we take in this work).

Since our goal is unattainable in general, the next question is whether it is attainable under conditions. And, given our discussion so far, a natural condition would be to use cryptographic protocols under state-of-the-world assumptions. Our next observation is that standard game-theoretic solution concepts do not quite work. In fact, similar counterexamples have been motivating the drive to revised notions of equilibria [21,25,28,29,31,32] (see Sect. 1.2 for details). In the full version [40, Example B.2 and Section C.1], we demonstrate a simple "Guessing game" to illustrate how negligible-probability deviations (i.e., brute-forcing a cryptographic commitment) can alter Nash and $\epsilon$-Nash. This occurs because attempting to break crypto on the side is weakly preferred to not doing so since it offers a potential utility gain, however small. This phenomenon can be amplified when exploiting outcomes with very large utility that occur with negligible probability. Even though such examples rule out the Nash equilibrium (and $\epsilon$-Nash) as a general "plug-and-play" solution concept, it seems intuitively possible to fix the issue by slightly changing the rules. So, for example, we could "assume-away" the undesirable actions (e.g., players' attempts to break cryptography). However, assuming away cryptographic attacks is problematic: what does it formally mean to assume away that a player "attempts to guess a secret value"?

Perhaps more troubling, transitioning from a world of ideal cryptographic implementations (the "ideal world") to a world with real, imperfect implementations (the "real world") can result in two games with qualitatively different equilibria and approximate equilibria. In the full version [40, Example B.3], we provide such an example in the context of second-price auctions. In such cases, the real-world equilibrium is not just the ideal strategy with a side attempt to "break crypto", but rather the incentive to exploit cryptographic implementations derails the intended mechanism design. We demonstrate that while bidding truthfully is a Nash equilibrium in the ideal world, the real-world Nash equilibrium shifts to non-truthful bidding in order to exploit negligible-probability events.

All our examples so far paint a bleak picture, at least for Nash and $\epsilon$-Nash equilibria. Yet, a Nash equilibrium in an ideal game (where, e.g., agents do not attempt to break crypto, because it is impossible to do so) seems like the "correct" prediction of how agents will behave in the corresponding real games. But, if these strategies are not Nash or $\epsilon$-Nash equilibria in the real game, then what are they? In a nutshell, a key contribution of our paper is to propose, analyze, and showcase a new solution concept—the *pseudo-Nash equilibrium*—that allows us to reconcile this gap.[1]

**Pseudo-Equilibria.** Let us recall the classical notion of Nash equilibrium (NE): A strategy profile $s = (s_1, s_2, \ldots, s_n)$ is a Nash equilibrium if, for every agent $i$, the expected utility of $i$ when playing strategy $s_i$ is at least her utility when deviating to strategy $s_i'$ (when all other agents' strategies remain fixed). The above definition makes no assumption about the efficiency of strategies in $s$. However, in games that use cryptography, it is important to exclude strategies that require inefficient (e.g., super-polynomial in the cryptographic security parameter) computation. Indeed, allowing players this amount of computation makes breaking cryptography a feasible strategy for them. A strawman approach to solve the above conundrum is to require strategies to be polynomial-time computable. It is, however, not hard to verify that such a simple patch cannot be the solution: First, by doing so, one necessarily changes the description of the game, resulting in restricted and often complicated stability definitions that require hard-wiring cryptographic security parameters into the game—or, transitioning from simple standard games to game-families parameterized by the security parameter. Such a choice might seem natural to a cryptographer, but it substantially dilutes our goal of delivering a stability notion that is friendly to economists and game theorists with little exposure to cryptographic definitions.

Second, and more importantly, the above modification does not even solve the problem. To see why, one can look at the Guessing Game ([40, Example B.2]): Even for a polynomial bounded player, brute-forcing the cryptographic primitive is still the best response. In fact, on a more technical note, one would need to actually bound the player's reasoning (or rationality) to be polynomial time. To do so, one would need to consider such reasoning as part of the player's strategy, which is known to lead to cumbersome definitions.

Another strawman approach, which takes care of the above issues, would be to define pseudo-equilibrium as a strategy whose utility profile is (computationally) indistinguishable from a real equilibrium. This, however, is also quite problematic: first, in classical equilibrium definitions, one is interested in expected utilities. However, two random variables that are computationally indistinguishable may not have the same expectation. For example, consider a game where the utility random variables induced by two strategies are $U_1 = \{0 \text{ w.p. } 1-\epsilon \;\&\; 1 \text{ w.p. } \epsilon\}$ and $U_2 = \{0 \text{ w.p. } 1-\epsilon \;\&\; -1 \text{ w.p. } \epsilon\}$. These two random

[1] We note that the term Pseudo-Nash Equilibrium was previously defined in the context of sequential games [10], with very low adoption, in a definition irrelevant to indistinguishability. Given the wide adoption of the term pseudo-random for distributions indistinguishable from random, and the intuition of our notion, which is aimed at capturing strategies indistinguishable from Nash, we find the name Pseudo-Nash appropriate for it.

variables are computationally indistinguishable for negligible $\epsilon$, but the expected value of $U_1$ is positive, whereas that of $U_2$ is negative. Furthermore, two random variables with the same expectation but completely different support (e.g., $U_1 = \{1 \text{ w.p. } 1/2 \ \& \ -1 \text{ w.p. } 1/2\}$ and $U_2 = \{10 \text{ w.p. } 1/2 \ \& \ -10 \text{ w.p. } 1/2\}$). These are equivalent for a game theorist, but are clearly distinguishable.

Finally, defining pseudo-equilibrium, e.g., pseudo-Nash, as being indistinguishable from Nash, would restrict this notion to games where their idealized-crypto variant can be shown to have a Nash equilibrium. This approach, which is implicit in [30], substantially reduces the applicability of pseudo-equilibrium and makes the notion applicable only with respect to such games, which again makes it less accessible to non-crypto-savvy domain experts.

In this work, we take a different approach, which makes the fact that pseudo-Nash is indistinguishable from Nash (when such Nash exists) a consequence of the definition, rather than the definition itself. First, we observe that, intuitively, a necessary condition for "strange" strategies not to emerge as profitable deviations in any game (e.g., the "real game") is that events that occur with negligible probability (e.g., "break crypto") should be ignored. In other words, the condition "deviations should not improve expected utility" in the definition of Nash should be replaced; we should instead focus on different (statistical) properties of the utilities of strategies. Specifically, we build on the intuition that a player should be indifferent between two computationally indistinguishable utilities, since no PPT observer can reliably tell them apart. Hence, a deviation whose benefit arises only on negligible-probability events should not affect strategic preferences. Our definition of a pseudo-equilibrium formalizes this intuition.

We begin by attempting to replace "larger expectation" in the definition of Nash with the concept of indistinguishability. Recall that two random variables $X$ and $Y$ are $\epsilon$-indistinguishable, if, for any distinguisher $\mathcal{D}$, $|\Pr[\mathcal{D}(X) = 1] - \Pr[\mathcal{D}(Y) = 1]| \leq \epsilon$. A first observation is that in the context of a game, where the random variables $X$ and $Y$ naturally correspond to utilities of strategies (e.g. a strategy and a deviation), this definition overlooks a crucial point: Nash equilibrium relies on comparing (the utility of) different strategies to see if one is better than (i.e., dominates) the other. (In)distinguishability, however, does not allow us to take such a decision: if a strategy $s$ is a lot better than a strategy $s'$, we should be able to distinguish them, but the existence of such a distinguisher does not help us decide which strategy we should render dominant.

A straightforward remedy is to drop the absolute value from the previous definition. Adjusting to our game-theoretic goals, perhaps we should define a strategy $s$, whose utility is distributed according to a random variable $X$, to be "$\epsilon$-preferred" to a strategy $s'$, whose utility is distributed according to a random variable $Y$, if, for any distinguisher $\mathcal{D}$, $\Pr[\mathcal{D}(Y) = 1] - \Pr[\mathcal{D}(X) = 1] \leq \epsilon$. Hence, when $X$ is a lot "better" than $Y$, we allow for distinguishers that pick $X$ much more often. Yet, this definition also has an issue, albeit a more nuanced one.

Concretely, requiring the above *for all* distinguishers implies requiring it for the best one, i.e., the one that maximizes $\Pr[\mathcal{D}(Y) = 1] - \Pr[\mathcal{D}(X) = 1]$. Intuitively, $\mathcal{D}$ can be seen as implementing the best statistical test. However, the outcome of this best distinguisher might have a weak (or no) dependence on the expectations of $X$ and $Y$. This makes it challenging (and in some cases, impossible) to connect a notion based on this distinguisher to standard game theory concepts that only look at the expectation of (the outcome) of strategies. Thus, the corresponding equilibrium notion would not necessarily be implied by Nash equilibrium in standard games, diverging from our goal to find a version of Nash (satisfying the same intuitive stability properties) that is cryptography-friendly.

Nonetheless, the above intuition is on the right track. The key is to identify a statistical test (i.e., distinguisher) whose decision approximately follows the relation of the expectations, i.e., the test should favor strategy $X$ when the expectation of $X$ is greater than that of $Y$. This brings us to our (informal) definition of a pseudo-equilibrium, where instead of considering arbitrary distinguishers, we focus on a specific distinguisher that compares the sample means of the two random variables. As we will show, this distinguisher tells us all we need to decide which strategy should be preferred. The following (informal) definition uses the following standard notation from game theory: for any strategy profile $s = (s_1, s_2, \dots, s_n)$ (i.e., where each player $i$ plays $s_i$) we denote by $(s; s_{-i})$ the strategy profile in which player $i$ plays $s$, and every player $j \neq i$ plays $s_j$.

**Definition 1 (Pseudo-Nash (informal)).** *Let $s = (s_1, s_2, \dots, s_n)$ be a strategy profile, and let $U_i = U_i(s; s_{-i})$ be the random variable that indicates the utility of player i under strategy s, when all other players' strategies are given by $s_{-i}$. Then, s is an $(m, \epsilon)$-pseudo-Nash equilibrium, if for all players i, and deviations $s'$ with utility random variable $U_i' = U_i'(s'; s_{-i})$,*

$$\Pr\left[\frac{1}{m}\sum_{j=1}^{m} U_i'^{(j)} \geq \frac{1}{m}\sum_{j=1}^{m} U_i^{(j)}\right] - \Pr\left[\frac{1}{m}\sum_{j=1}^{m} U_i^{(j)} \geq \frac{1}{m}\sum_{j=1}^{m} U_i'^{(j)}\right] \leq \epsilon,$$

*where $U_i^{(j)}$ and $U_i'^{(j)}$ are i.i.d. samples from $U_i, U_i'$ respectively.*

The connection between the above definition and our discussion of distinguishers/tests is evident: It can be thought of as a distinguisher who observes the utility from $m$ independent executions of the game under strategy profiles $(s; s_{-i})$ and $(s'; s_{-i})$, and compares their empirical means to make its decision of dominance. This also hints towards the fact (which we prove) that the definition of pseudo-Nash equilibrium is robust against negligible-probability events. Indeed, rather than reasoning about the expected utility of each strategy (as in Nash equilibrium), players reason based on the empirical mean of $m$ samples; as long as $m$ is polynomial, negligible events are unlikely to be observed. This allows for the invariance of negligible events in strategic behavior. Note that the notions of negligible and polynomial are only meaningful in parameterized games. The formal definition of pseudo-Nash (Definition 8) captures how the notion seamlessly applies to such games (as well as all classical normal form games from the game theory literature). In a nutshell, the definition of pseudo-Nash (Definition 8) is the first notion that achieves all the following desired properties, simultaneously:

1. *Simplicity*: Our notion does not require any knowledge from cryptography, and can be defined for any game. This is in contrast to state-of-the-art proposals for crypto-friendly equilibria, e.g., [32], which require special and complicated classes of games. See Sect. 1.2 and [40, Appendix D] for more.
2. *Compatibility with Game Theory*: In standard (non-parameterized) games, pseudo-Nash equilibrium is well-defined and is equivalent to Nash equilibrium.
3. *Indistinguishability/Compatibility with cryptography*: The replacement of random variables with computationally indistinguishable ones does not affect our notion of dominance.
4. *Unrestricted utilities*: Unlike many existing attempts to devise a notion of equilibrium for computational games which require restrictions on the utility, (e.g., [32] assumes utilities of low probability events which are polynomial in a parameter of the game) a pseudo-equilibrium is not sensitive to the magnitude of the utility of low probability events.

In the technical part of this paper, we prove the above properties and present examples from the literature along with simple games, which showcase our notion and highlight its benefits over prior proposals. Most importantly, for the natural class of normal-form games that corresponds to games using cryptography—*computational games*—we can prove a general ideal-crypto-replacement theorem:

**Theorem 1 (Informal).** *Consider any (ideal) computation game* $\mathcal{G}^{\mathcal{I}}$ *using ideal cryptographic primitives. Consider the (real) computation game* $\mathcal{G}^{\mathcal{R}}$ *where the ideal primitive is replaced by its cryptographic implementation—secure under a state-of-the-world assumption. If a strategy* $s^{\mathcal{I}}$ *is a Nash or pseudo-Nash equilibrium in* $\mathcal{G}^{\mathcal{I}}$*, then the corresponding strategy* $s^{\mathcal{R}}$*—where ideal cryptography is replaced with real cryptography—is a pseudo-Nash equilibrium in* $\mathcal{G}^{\mathcal{R}}$*.*

We note that, in addition to having all the above desirable properties, pseudo-Nash also has a rather intuitive interpretation, which reinforces our claim that it is the natural notion for the games we aim to capture, and beyond. Recall that we are interested in equilibrium for players whose reasoning is computationally limited. The definition of pseudo-Nash captures the perception—from the perspective of a player who can only think of at most $m$ iterations of the game—of whether deviating from $s_i$ dominates $s_i$ (within some error $\epsilon$.) We thus conjecture that our notion might have connections to prospect theory [35,43]; investigating such connections is, in our opinion, an outstanding research direction.

### 1.2 Related Work

Several works have attempted to use game theory within cryptographic protocols (typically MPC or its special cases, e.g., [11,20,23,26,34,37,38]). The idea of such *game-theoretic cryptography* models is to incorporate incentives into the parties' misbehavior by treating them as rational agents acting according to some (partially) known preferences. A cryptographic protocol execution induces a sequential game among these agents/parties and is considered "secure" if they have no incentive to deviate, i.e., if it induces a game-theoretic equilibrium. Notably, several of these works have highlighted mismatches between the tools used in the two disciplines. For example, [37] shows that under standard equilibrium definitions, cryptography cannot be used in certain games in which privacy is important for the utility, e.g., games where selfish parties want to learn a common function on their inputs but prefer to be the only one who learns it. Most interestingly, a frequent reason for impossibilities has been rooted in the idea that it might be a best response for the adversary to try to break cryptography. Similarly, several works have used cryptographic primitives to improve game theory and mechanism design solutions (e.g., [5,12,17,39,44]), e.g., by relying on commitments to force consistency between different stages of the game.

Most relevant to our goals, several works have attempted to resolve mismatches between cryptography and game theory [21,25,28,29,31,32]. The standard approach in this area has been to either adapt the utility to account for computational complexity and asymptotics, e.g., by allocating a cost on computational steps [28], or develop new definitions of stability grounded in cryptography. Such definitions typically change the nature of the game, e.g., by transitioning from a simple, single game to a parameterized sequence of (usually more complex) games, in order to accommodate asymptotic reasoning, and define an equilibrium notion on top of this sequence. As such, they have typically been much more cumbersome compared to their (arguably simple and intuitive) game-theoretic analogues, such as Nash or subgame-perfect equilibria. We conjecture that this might be a reason why these new definitions, despite their evident novelty—and even support for replacing ideal cryptography with its cryptographic implementation [21,28,31]—have not been widely adopted by economists or game theorists, who are not necessarily familiar with theoretical computer science and cryptography idiosyncrasies. In contrast, our goal is to give such researchers a convenient tool to incorporate cryptography in their game analysis, without worrying about the aforementioned artifacts.

In order to understand the novelty and potential of the notion of pseudo-equilibrium, it is worth contrasting it with the notion of *computational Nash* in extensive form games [32], which, to the best of our knowledge, is the state-of-the-art among equilibrium definitions that allow using cryptography within game-theory arguments.[2] In a nutshell, the notion of computational Nash [32] defines a new class of (sequences of) games, termed *Computable Uniform Sequence of Games*, which embodies the idea that cryptographic protocols can be viewed as extensive-form games, where adversarial faults correspond to deviations. In such a game definition, one needs to carefully define properties of the history, utility, and players' moves to ensure they are polynomially computable—in fact, probabilistic polynomial-time, in short PPT. As discussed below, this makes the notion of computational Nash applicable only to games that fit such a description. The above complexity makes analyzing computational Nash directly a particularly

[2] We focus here on [32] but our reasoning and comparison applies to most proposed notions of equilibrium for games using cryptography, as long as they do not modify the underlying utility, e.g., by assuming that computation costs [28].

challenging task. In fact, this is acknowledged in [32], which offers a blueprint for finding computational Nash, which, as will become apparent below, can only be used when we are analyzing a game that is derived by replacing idealized cryptography in a sequential game with real cryptography. The core idea of this methodology is to "reverse-engineer" the cryptographic simulation paradigm to establish a mapping of the game using cryptography to the idealized-cryptography game. The details of this mapping are not relevant to our treatment, and the actual definition and its connection to the simulation paradigm have already been established in [32]. However, for readers who might be questioning whether the notion of pseudo-Nash is an important step in the direction of devising tools for non-crypto-experts to reason about games involving cryptography, we find it useful to contrast our notion to the above definition.

In addition to the evident difference in complexity of the definitions, there are several qualitative and quantitative arguments in favor of pseudo-NE compared to CNE: First, as discussed above, CNE can only be defined for a very restricted class of games; and even for this class, to make the analysis tractable one would typically require that the game itself is derived from an idealized-cryptography game, and even then, the analysis would need some degree of familiarity with advanced cryptographic reasoning (e.g., the simulation paradigm). In contrast, pseudo-NE is defined for any game. For the special class of games that use cryptography, we equip it with an automatic translation theorem that ensures that one can replace idealized cryptography with real-world cryptography. Second, the existence of a Nash equilibrium does not necessarily imply the existence of CNE in contrast to pseudo-NE (see [40, Sections C.1 and C.3]). Third, CNE is sensitive to the magnitude of the utilities of different events. For example, negligible events with huge (exponential) utility make the reasoning from [32] inapplicable and, as we demonstrate, eliminate the possibility of CNE. This is in contrast to pseudo-NE, which, by definition, renders negligible events irrelevant. This distinction makes a big difference in the analysis of classical rational-cryptography games, e.g., rational secret sharing [26]; see also the full version [40, Section C.3]. We note that this third distinction may seem somewhat esoteric, as in traditional game theory, it is reasonable to assume that utilities are constant. This is, however, not the case: first, when dealing with parameterized games that use asymptotic cryptography, it is reasonable to assume that the utilities depend on the underlying parameter. In this case, it is unclear why one should limit this dependency to be polynomial. In fact, there are natural games (even without using cryptography) in which utility would be exponential in a specific parameter (e.g., the size of the player's strategies): Imagine a version of the guessing game ([40, Example B.2]) where the leader (Player 1) chooses a $\kappa$-bit string; then the follower (Player 2) attempts to guess the leader's choice; every bit he guesses correctly doubles his reward. It is straightforward to show that the unique Nash equilibrium has both players choose uniformly at random. However, one can show that the above strategy cannot be proven to be CNE (and the aforementioned blueprint to prove CNE from [32] does not help here, since there is no ideal cryptography). In contrast, we can show that the Nash strategy is also pseudo-NE. In fact, as discussed in Sect. 3 we view pseudo-NE as the natural extension of Nash to such parameterized games; furthermore, our ideal-to-real theorem can be used to directly prove that replacing in the pseudo-NE of this game random coins with pseudo-random coins yields another pseudo-NE.

## 2 Preliminaries

Our goal is to develop tools that can be used by game-theorists and cryptographers alike, with little to no exposure to the other field's reasoning and advanced tools. Our results offer a seamless translation from games with idealized cryptography to games with real cryptography. Given these goals, in Sects. 2.1 (resp. Sect. 2.2,) below, we outline the basic definitions and tools from the cryptographic (resp. game theory) literature that a game theorist (resp. cryptographer) needs to understand the translation. Such an exposition is useful for the paper to serve its goal, but a CRYPTO reviewer is welcome to skip Sects. 2.1.

### 2.1 Cryptography Notation and Definitions

State-of-the-world assumptions that are typical in cryptography rely on asymmetries that (are assumed to) exist in certain problems. E.g., one-way functions are, intuitively, easy to compute and hard to invert, pseudo-random generators are efficiently computable length-expanding deterministic algorithms but their output on random inputs is hard to distinguish from samples from a random distribution, etc. However, "hardness" of a problem does not make it impossible to solve; in fact, most cryptographic hardness assumptions only apply to hardness on average (i.e., on random inputs). As such, a cryptographic statement would typically embrace the idea that the adversary might with "tiny" probability violate its claimed security (by violating the underlying assumption).

Capturing "tiny" in a way that allows for cryptographic proofs is tricky. For example, in an encryption scheme, we would want that the adversary has a tiny probability of recovering information about the plaintext. But if the key is small, say 5 bits, then with probability $2^{-5} = 1/32$ the adversary can guess it and recover the whole plaintext. As such, the notion of tiny is defined to correspond to "eventually tiny," i.e., for cryptographic keys whose size is larger than some value $\kappa_0$, usually referred to as the *security parameter*. This gives rise to the following notion of *negligibility* aimed at capturing the above intuition of eventually tiny:

**Definition 2.** *A function $\delta : \mathbb{N} \rightarrow \mathbb{R}$ is negligible if for every constant $c$ there exists a $\kappa_c \in \mathbb{N}$ such that for all $\kappa \geq \kappa_c$ it holds $\delta(\kappa) < \frac{1}{\kappa^c}$.*

Most cryptographic security definitions compare a cryptographic construction, that typically involves a key, to an ideal primitive, that the construction is supposed to securely realize. Security requires that the random variable that corresponds to the outcome of an execution of the cryptographic construction cannot be distinguished from the random variable that corresponds to the outcome of an invocation of the ideal primitive (we defer details of such a definition to Sect. 5). As such, the notion of (computational) indistinguishability is deeply rooted in the cryptographic method (and as we shall see, will be the key in defining a crypto-friendly notion of stability in games that use cryptography). We shortly define computational indistinguishability.

For a random variable $X$ and a randomized algorithm $\mathcal{D}$ with a binary output, that can draw a sample from the probability distribution $P_X$ of $X$, we denote by $\mathcal{D}^X(x)$ the random variable which corresponds to the outcome of $\mathcal{D}$ on input an $x$ sampled from $X$. We also denote by $1^\kappa$ the unary representation of $\kappa$, i.e., the string consisting of $\kappa$ ones.

**Definition 3 (Computational Indistinguishability).** *Let* $X = \{X_\kappa\}_{\kappa\in\mathbb{N}}$, $Y = \{Y_\kappa\}_{\kappa\in\mathbb{N}}$ *be a pair of ensembles of random variables.* $X$ *is computationally indistinguishable from* $Y$, *denoted by* $X \cong Y$, *if there exists a negligible function* $\mathtt{negl}(\cdot) : \mathbb{N} \to [0,1]$ *such that for every probabilistic polynomial time (PPT) algorithm* $\mathcal{D}$ *with a binary output, called the* distinguisher, *the following holds:*

$$|\Pr[\mathcal{D}(X_\kappa; 1^\kappa) = 1] - \Pr[\mathcal{D}(Y_\kappa; 1^\kappa) = 1]| \leq \mathtt{negl}(\kappa).$$

We will also use the standard closure of computational indistinguishability under taking polynomially many independent samples [22]. Namely, if $X \cong Y$, then for every constant $c \in \mathbb{N}$, the joint distributions of $\kappa^c$ i.i.d. samples from $X_\kappa$ and from $Y_\kappa$ are computationally indistinguishable (by a hybrid argument).

The quantity $|\Pr[\mathcal{D}(X_\kappa; 1^\kappa) = 1] - \Pr[\mathcal{D}(Y_\kappa; 1^\kappa) = 1]|$ is often referred to as the *distinguishing advantage* of $\mathcal{D}$ in distinguishing $X_\kappa$ from $Y_\kappa$, as it captures, intuitively, how similar $X_\kappa$ and $Y_\kappa$ look to $\mathcal{D}$. In fact, it is not hard to see that if we do not restrict $\mathcal{D}$ to be PPT, i.e., if we take the distinguishing advantage of the best (even inefficient) distinguisher, then this will be equal to the standard *statistical distance* between the $X_\kappa$ and $Y_\kappa$. For the curious reader, we note in passing that providing $\mathcal{D}$ the input $1^\kappa$ is to ensure that it runs in time polynomial in $\kappa$, which is needed to avoid trivial counter-examples of rendering cryptographic constructions secure because the distinguisher does not have sufficient time to parse $X_\kappa$ (see [22] for a detailed discussion).

### 2.2 Game Theory Notations and Definitions

We define the notion of pseudo-equilibrium on standard normal form games. We denote by $\mathcal{G}([n], \mathcal{N}, U)$ a game with $n$ players and with action set $\mathcal{N} = \mathcal{N}_1 \times \ldots \times \mathcal{N}_n$. For a mixed strategy profile $s \in \mathcal{N}$ we are interested in the utility random variable $U_i(s_i, s_{-i})$ of player $i \in [n]$, where $s_i$ denotes the strategy of player $i$ and $s_{-i}$ the strategies of all other players. In such games, the Nash equilibrium is defined as usual:

**Definition 4 (Nash Equilibrium).** *A strategy profile* $s = (s_1, \ldots, s_n)$ *is a Nash equilibrium (NE) of a game* $\mathcal{G}$ *if, for all* $i \in [n]$ *and for all deviating strategies* $\hat{s}_i$ *it holds* $\mathbb{E}[U_i(s)] \geq \mathbb{E}[U_i(\hat{s}_i, s_{-i})]$.

A common relaxation of NE to an approximate notion, called $\epsilon$-Nash, allows for strategies that are suboptimal at most $\epsilon$ (additive) factor.

**Definition 5 ($\epsilon$-Nash Equilibrium).** *A strategy profile $s = (s_1, \ldots, s_n)$ is an $\epsilon$-Nash equilibrium ($\epsilon$-NE) of a game $\mathcal{G}$ for some $\epsilon \geq 0$ if, for all $i \in [n]$ and for all deviating strategies $\hat{s}_i$ it holds $\mathbb{E}[U_i(s)] \geq \mathbb{E}[U_i(\hat{s}_i, s_{-i})] - \epsilon$.*

Looking ahead in the technical part of our paper, we remark that our notion of pseudo-equilibrium will allow us to seamlessly extend the above classical notions also to parameterized games—like the guessing game ([40, Example B.2]), modified so that player one has a variable-size input (or input that depends on a cryptographic security parameter) and the utilities depend on this size.

## 3 Empirical Dominance and Pseudo-Nash Equilibrium

We introduce a new notion of ordering random variables with respect to their empirical means. We say that a random variable $X$ $(m, \delta)$-empirically means dominates $Y$ if the empirical mean of $X$ tends to be higher than $Y$. Formally,

**Definition 6 (Empirical Mean Dominance).** *Let $X, Y$ be a pair of random variables. Then $X$ $(m, \delta)$*-**empirical mean dominates***(EM-dominates) $Y$, denoted by $X \underset{m,\delta}{\gtrsim} Y$, for $m \in \mathbb{N}^+$ and $\delta \in [0,1]$:*

$$\Pr\left[\frac{1}{m}\sum_{j=1}^{m} Y^{(j)} \geq \frac{1}{m}\sum_{j=1}^{m} X^{(j)}\right] - \Pr\left[\frac{1}{m}\sum_{j=1}^{m} X^{(j)} \geq \frac{1}{m}\sum_{j=1}^{m} Y^{(j)}\right] \leq \delta$$

*where $X^{(j)}, Y^{(j)}$ are i.i.d. samples from $X, Y$ respectively.*

As the name suggests, our goal is to use empirical dominance to compare (mixed) strategies, $s$ and $\hat{s}$, in normal-form games. In this context, the random variables $X$ and $Y$ will indicate the utilities of $s$ and $\hat{s}$, respectively in the game.[3] In order to account for computational considerations and enable cryptographic reasoning, we make the following restriction on empirical dominance.

**Definition 7 (Computational Mean Dominance).** *Let $X = \{X_\kappa\}_{\kappa \in \mathbb{N}}$, $Y = \{Y_\kappa\}_{\kappa \in \mathbb{N}}$ be a pair of random variable ensembles. Then $X$* **computational** *mean dominates $Y$, denoted by $X \gtrsim Y$, if for all constants $c \geq 1$, there exist constants $\hat{c} > c$, $\kappa_0 > 0$ such that for all $\kappa \geq \kappa_0$:*

$$\Pr\left[\frac{1}{\kappa^{\hat{c}}}\sum_{j=1}^{\kappa^{\hat{c}}} {Y_\kappa}^{(j)} \geq \frac{1}{\kappa^{\hat{c}}}\sum_{j=1}^{\kappa^{\hat{c}}} {X_\kappa}^{(j)}\right] - \Pr\left[\frac{1}{\kappa^{\hat{c}}}\sum_{j=1}^{\kappa^{\hat{c}}} {X_\kappa}^{(j)} \geq \frac{1}{\kappa^{\hat{c}}}\sum_{j=1}^{\kappa^{\hat{c}}} {Y_\kappa}^{(j)}\right] < \frac{1}{\kappa^{c}}$$

*where $X_\kappa^{(j)}, Y_\kappa^{(j)}$ are i.i.d. samples from $X_\kappa, Y_\kappa$ respectively.*

[3] Note that we mean the actual utility that players receive when they play these strategies rather than expected utility.

As discussed in the introduction, the intuitive interpretation of the above $X \gtrsim Y$ dominance definition is as follows. Consider a distinguisher who uses the empirical means of $X$ and $Y$ as a statistical test to decide whether or not the expected value of $X$ is above the expected value of $Y$. As long as this distinguisher takes at most polynomially many—i.e., $\kappa^{\hat{c}}$ for some constant $\hat{c}$—samples of $X$ and $Y$, with all but negligible —eventually diminishing faster than $1/k^c$ for any $c$—probability, he will decide that $X$ dominates $Y$.

In the context of analyzing games, the parameter $\kappa$ in the above ensembles corresponds to the size of the game's description, which is a natural input to any distinguisher performing the above statistical test. As such the above notion applies to comparing two strategies $s$ and $\hat{s}$ in standard (fixed) games similarly to Definition 6, by setting $X_\kappa = X_1$ and $Y_\kappa = Y_1$, for all $k \in \mathbb{N}$, where $X_1$ and $Y_1$ are the utilities of the two strategy profiles, $s$ and $\hat{s}$, respectively. In fact, somewhat surprisingly, as we prove in Lemmas 1 and 2, restricting the notion of empirical dominance as above yields a definition equivalent to standard dominance of expectations, something which is not true otherwise. Looking ahead this will render our pseudo-Nash notion equivalent to Nash in such games, which in our opinion is the ultimate "sanity check" for any such notion.

Most interestingly for the goals of our paper, by incorporating ensembles into the definition, we are now able to reason about parameterized games—think of the guessing game from our introduction where the size of the input string is a parameter and affects the utility (e.g., the more bits of player 1's input that player 2 guesses the higher his utility). We believe that pseudo-Nash is the natural adaptation of classical Nash to such games. Most importantly, it means that we can now seamlessly capture games using cryptography by simply making the security parameter (in unary notation, $1^\kappa$) part of the game description.

Given the above notion of dominance, we can now define our notion of pseudo-Nash equilibrium. Similar to Nash equilibrium, a strategy profile is a pseudo-equilibrium if for all players, the random variable (ensembles) that corresponds to their utility dominates all other utility random variables that come from a unilateral deviation. Formally, we define pseudo-equilibrium.

**Definition 8 (Pseudo-equilibrium).** *A computational pseudo-equilibrium of a (possibly parameterized) game $\mathcal{G}([n], \mathcal{N}, U)$ is a strategy profile $s = (s_1, \cdots, s_n) \in \mathcal{N}$ that for all $i \in [n]$ and for all $\hat{s}_i \in \mathcal{N}_i$, the utility random variable (ensemble) of player $i$ according to $s_i$, $U_i(s_i, s_{-i}) = \{U_i^\kappa(s)\}_{\kappa \in \mathbb{N}}$, computationally EM dominates the utility variable (ensemble) of player $i$ according to $\hat{s}_i$, $U_i(\hat{s}_i, s_{-i}) = \{U_i^\kappa((\hat{s}_i, s_{-i}))\}_{\kappa \in \mathbb{N}}$. That is, $s$ is a computational pseudo-equilibrium if $\forall i \in [n], \forall \hat{s}_i \in \mathcal{N}_i : U_i(s_i, s_{-i}) \gtrsim U_i(\hat{s}_i, s_{-i})$.*

## 3.1 Equivalence to Nash for Standard Games

In this section, we show that for standard fixed description (i.e., non-parameterized) games, our pseudo-equilibrium notion is equivalent to Nash equilibrium.

**Theorem 2.** *For a normal-form game $\mathcal{G}([n], \mathcal{N}, U)$, with bounded utilities, a strategy profile $s = (s_1, \ldots, s_n)$ is a Nash equilibrium if, and only if, it is a pseudo-Nash equilibrium (Definition 8).*

The proof relies on three technical lemmas relating computational mean dominance to expected utility comparisons for bounded-support random variables. Full proofs appear in Sect. A.

**Lemma 1.** *Let $X, Y$ be two random variables with bounded support $R$ such that $\mathbb{E}[X] > \mathbb{E}[Y]$. Then $X$ computationally dominates $Y$, $X \gtrsim Y$ (Definition 7).*

**Lemma 2.** *Let $X, Y$ be two random variables with bounded support $R$ such that $\mathbb{E}[X] = \mathbb{E}[Y]$. Then $X$ computationally dominates $Y$, $X \gtrsim Y$, and $Y$ computationally dominates $X$, $Y \gtrsim X$, according to Definition 7.*

**Lemma 3.** *Let $X, Y$ be two random variables with bounded support $R$. If $X$ computationally dominates $Y$, according to Definition 7, then $\mathbb{E}[X] \geq \mathbb{E}[Y]$.*

*Proof (Proof of Theorem 2).* Given the above three lemmas, the proof of Theorem 2 proceeds as follows:
We will show each direction separately.

( $\Longrightarrow$ ) **Nash Implies Pseudo.** We want to show that a Nash equilibrium also satisfies Definition 8. That is, there exists a $\kappa_0$ such that for all $\kappa \geq \kappa_0$ and for all players $i$ and for all alternative strategies $\hat{s}_i$ :

$$\Pr\left[\frac{1}{\kappa^{4c}}\sum_{j=1}^{\kappa^{4c}} U_i^{(j)}(\hat{s}_i; s_{-i}) > \frac{1}{\kappa^{4c}}\sum_{j=1}^{\kappa^{4c}} U_i^{(j)}(s)\right] - \Pr\left[\frac{1}{\kappa^{4c}}\sum_{j=1}^{\kappa^{4c}} U_i^{(j)}(s) > \frac{1}{\kappa^{4c}}\sum_{j=1}^{\kappa^{4c}} U_i^{(j)}(\hat{s}_i; s_{-i})\right] \leq \frac{1}{\kappa^c}$$

Since the strategy profile $s = (s_1, \ldots, s_n)$ is a Nash equilibrium, we have for all $i \in [n]$ and for every unilateral deviation $\hat{s}_i \in \mathcal{N}_i$ of player $i$ the $\mathbb{E}[U_i(s_i; s_{-i})] \geq \mathbb{E}[U_i(\hat{s}_i; s_{-i})]$. Let us define $\Delta = \min_{i, \hat{s}_i}\{\mathbb{E}[U_i(s_i; s_{-i})] - \mathbb{E}[U_i(\hat{s}_i; s_{-i})]\} \geq 0$. By construction of the game, the utilities are bounded, i.e., for all strategy profiles $U_i(\cdot) \in [a, b]$. Let $R = |b - a|$ be the range. Consider player $i$ and the deviating strategy $\hat{s}_i$ that minimizes the difference in expectation $\Delta$.

*Case 1:* $\Delta > 0$. In this case, we can directly apply Lemma 1, to show that $U_i(s_i; s_{-i}) \gtrsim U_i(\hat{s}; s_{-i})$.

*Case 2:* $\Delta = 0$ In this case we can directly apply Lemma 2

( $\Longleftarrow$ ) **Pseudo Implies Nash.** Assume that the strategy profile $s = (s_1, \ldots, s_n)$ is a pseudo-Nash equilibrium. By definition, for every player $i \in [n]$, for every unilateral deviation $\hat{s}_i \in \mathcal{N}_i$, for every constant $c$there exists a sample size $\kappa_0$ such that for all $\kappa \geq \kappa_0$ the following holds:

$$\Pr\left[\frac{1}{\kappa^{4c}}\sum_{j=1}^{\kappa^{4c}} U_i{}^{(j)}(\hat{s}_i; s_{-i}) > \frac{1}{\kappa^{4c}}\sum_{j=1}^{\kappa^{4c}} U_i^{(j)}(s)\right] - \Pr\left[\frac{1}{\kappa^{4c}}\sum_{j=1}^{\kappa^{4c}} U_i{}^{(j)}(s) > \frac{1}{\kappa^{4c}}\sum_{j=1}^{\kappa^{4c}} U_i^{(j)}(\hat{s}_i; s_{-i})\right] \leq \frac{1}{\kappa^c}$$

where $U_i^{(j)}(s_i, s_{-i})$ and $U_i^{(j)}(\hat{s}_i, s_{-i})$ denotes $j^{\text{th}}$ independent sample from the corresponding utility random variables. By Lemma 3, this condition implies that for every $i \in [n]$ and every deviation $\hat{s}_i \in \mathcal{N}_i$,

$$\mathbb{E}\left[U_i(s_i; s_{-i})\right] \geq \mathbb{E}\left[U_i(\hat{s}_i; s_{-i})\right],$$

which is exactly the Nash equilibrium condition. □

### 3.2 Beyond Nash for Parameterized Games

Recall that our goal is to define a notion of stability for games using cryptography, which eliminates unnatural Nash equilibria (e.g., brute-forcing crypto). The above equivalence theorem makes one wonder, if Nash is equivalent to pseudo-Nash, how can our notion provide more stability if it collapses to the very concept it seeks to improve? The resolution is that equivalence between Nash and pseudo-Nash does not hold in parametrized games (i.e., games where the utility depends on the security parameter $\kappa$). As a sanity check, we describe two ensembles $X = \{X_\kappa\}_{\kappa \in \mathbb{N}}, Y = \{Y_\kappa\}_{\kappa \in \mathbb{N}}$ for which $\mathbb{E}[Y_\kappa] > \mathbb{E}[X_\kappa]$ for all $\kappa$; but, the empirical mean of $Y_\kappa$ does not converge to its expectation with polynomial samples in $\kappa$, which would make the two equilibrium notions distinct.

Consider the following two random variable ensembles $X = \{X_\kappa\}_{\kappa \in \mathbb{N}}$, and $Y = \{Y_\kappa\}_{\kappa \in \mathbb{N}}$. Let $X_\kappa = \{0 \text{ w.p. } 1/2, 2 \text{ w.p. } 1/2\}$ and $Y_\kappa = \{0 \text{ w.p. } 1 - 1/2^\kappa, 2^{2\kappa} \text{ w.p. } 1/2^\kappa\}$. It is immediate that $\mathbb{E}[X_\kappa] = 1$ and $\mathbb{E}[Y_\kappa] = 2^\kappa$, hence $\mathbb{E}[X_\kappa] < \mathbb{E}[Y_\kappa]$ for all $\kappa$. However, we will show that $X$ computationally EM dominates $Y$, $X \gtrsim Y$. Intuitively, the probability that $\sum_{j=1}^{\kappa^c} Y_\kappa > 0$ is negligible. On the other hand, the probability that $\sum_{j=1}^{\kappa^c} X_\kappa = 0$ is also negligible.

To show that $X$ computationally dominates $Y$ we need to show that for all $c \geq 1$ there exists a $\hat{c} > c$ and a $\kappa_0$ such that for all $\kappa \geq \kappa_0$:

$$\Pr\left[\frac{1}{\kappa^{\hat{c}}}\sum_{j=1}^{\kappa^{\hat{c}}} Y_\kappa{}^{(j)} > \frac{1}{\kappa^{\hat{c}}}\sum_{j=1}^{\kappa^{\hat{c}}} X_\kappa{}^{(j)}\right] - \Pr\left[\frac{1}{\kappa^{\hat{c}}}\sum_{j=1}^{\kappa^{\hat{c}}} X_\kappa{}^{(j)} > \frac{1}{\kappa^{\hat{c}}}\sum_{j=1}^{\kappa^{\hat{c}}} Y_\kappa{}^{(j)}\right] \leq \frac{1}{\kappa^c} \quad (1)$$

Rearranging the LHS of Eq. (1)

$$\Pr\left[\frac{1}{\kappa^{\hat{c}}}\sum_{j=1}^{\kappa^{\hat{c}}} Y_\kappa{}^{(j)} > \frac{1}{\kappa^{\hat{c}}}\sum_{j=1}^{\kappa^{\hat{c}}} X_\kappa{}^{(j)}\right] - \Pr\left[\frac{1}{\kappa^{\hat{c}}}\sum_{j=1}^{\kappa^{\hat{c}}} X_\kappa{}^{(j)} > \frac{1}{\kappa^{\hat{c}}}\sum_{j=1}^{\kappa^{\hat{c}}} Y_\kappa{}^{(j)}\right]$$
$$= \Pr\left[\frac{1}{\kappa^{\hat{c}}}\sum_{j=1}^{\kappa^{\hat{c}}} Y_\kappa{}^{(j)} > \frac{1}{\kappa^{\hat{c}}}\sum_{j=1}^{\kappa^{\hat{c}}} X_\kappa{}^{(j)}\right] - \left(1 - \Pr\left[\frac{1}{\kappa^{\hat{c}}}\sum_{j=1}^{\kappa^{\hat{c}}} Y_\kappa{}^{(j)} \geq \frac{1}{\kappa^{\hat{c}}}\sum_{j=1}^{\kappa^{\hat{c}}} X_\kappa{}^{(j)}\right]\right)$$
$$= 2\Pr\left[\frac{1}{\kappa^{\hat{c}}}\sum_{j=1}^{\kappa^{\hat{c}}} Y_\kappa{}^{(j)} > \frac{1}{\kappa^{\hat{c}}}\sum_{j=1}^{\kappa^{\hat{c}}} X_\kappa{}^{(j)}\right] + \Pr\left[\frac{1}{\kappa^{\hat{c}}}\sum_{j=1}^{\kappa^{\hat{c}}} Y_\kappa{}^{(j)} = \frac{1}{\kappa^{\hat{c}}}\sum_{j=1}^{\kappa^{\hat{c}}} X_\kappa{}^{(j)}\right] - 1$$

To show that $X$ dominates $Y$ we will upper bound the probabilities separately. We will show that both probabilities are negligible and therefore the difference is negative, thus strictly less than $\frac{1}{\kappa^c}$.

First,

$$\Pr\left[\frac{1}{\kappa^{\hat{c}}}\sum_{j=1}^{\kappa^{\hat{c}}} Y_\kappa{}^{(j)} > \frac{1}{\kappa^{\hat{c}}}\sum_{j=1}^{\kappa^{\hat{c}}} X_\kappa{}^{(j)}\right] = 1 - \Pr\left[\forall j \in [\kappa^{\hat{c}}] : Y_\kappa^{(j)} = 0\right]$$
$$= 1 - \left(1 - \frac{1}{2^\kappa}\right)^{\kappa^{\hat{c}}} \leq 1 - 1 + \frac{\kappa^{\hat{c}}}{2^\kappa} \leq \mathtt{negl}(\kappa)$$

Next,

$$\Pr\left[\frac{1}{\kappa^{\hat{c}}}\sum_{j=1}^{\kappa^{\hat{c}}} Y_\kappa{}^{(j)} = \frac{1}{\kappa^{\hat{c}}}\sum_{j=1}^{\kappa^{\hat{c}}} X_\kappa{}^{(j)}\right] = \Pr\left[\forall j \in [\kappa^{\hat{c}}] : Y_\kappa^{(j)} = 0\right] \Pr\left[\forall j \in [\kappa^{\hat{c}}] : X_\kappa^{(j)} = 0\right]$$
$$\leq \Pr\left[\forall j \in [\kappa^{\hat{c}}] : X_\kappa^{(j)} = 0\right] = \frac{1}{2^{\kappa^{\hat{c}}}} \leq \mathtt{negl}(\kappa)$$

That concludes the example that demonstrates a random variable dominates a random variable with much higher expected utility.

## 4 Properties of Pseudo-Nash and Crypto-Friendliness

The previous section demonstrated that computational mean dominance (and pseudo-Nash) "plays well" with game theory. In this section, we demonstrate that they also play well with cryptography, developing the basic tools that will allow us to prove our main theorem (stability-preserving ideal to real cryptography transition). More concretely, we will show that the definition of computational mean dominance (Definition 7) is compatible with computational indistinguishability (Definition 3). The following results show that: (i) if two random variables are computationally indistinguishable then we have bidirectional dominance (Lemma 4) (ii) if a random variable $X$ dominates a random variable $Y$

then changing either with an indistinguishable one will not affect the dominance (Proposition 1 for replacing the dominating ensemble; Proposition 2 for replacing the dominated ensemble.) Conceptually, these results formalize the intuition that negligible-probability events should not affect incentives. In particular, Lemma 4 shows that a player should be indifferent between two computationally indistinguishable utility ensembles, since no PPT observer given polynomially many samples can reliably tell them apart. Consequently, a deviation that improves utility only on a negligible-probability event should not affect preferences. This is captured by Proposition 1 and 2 showing that computational mean dominance is invariant under replacing either the dominating or dominated ensemble by a computationally indistinguishable one, even if the replacement changes the expected utility by a large amount.

First, we show that if two ensembles of random variables $X = \{X_\kappa\}_{\kappa\in\mathbb{N}}$, $Y = \{Y_\kappa\}_{\kappa\in\mathbb{N}}$ are computationally indistinguishable, then we have bidirectional computational empirical mean dominance.

**Lemma 4.** *Let $X = \{X_\kappa\}_{\kappa\in\mathbb{N}}$, $Y = \{Y_\kappa\}_{\kappa\in\mathbb{N}}$ be a pair of random variable ensembles such that $X$ and $Y$ are computationally indistinguishable. Then $X$ computationally-EM dominates $Y$, and $Y$ computationally-EM dominates $X$. That is $X \cong Y \implies X \gtrsim Y \,\&\, Y \gtrsim X$.*

*Proof.* We prove this lemma by contradiction. Assume that for two computationally indistinguishable random variables ensembles $X$ and $Y$, the bidirectional dominance does not hold. Since $X \gtrsim Y$ and $Y \gtrsim X$ are symmetric, without loss of generality, we assume that $\neg(X \gtrsim Y)$ holds. Then we can construct a probabilistic polynomial-time (PPT) distinguisher that distinguishes $X$ from $Y$ with a non-negligible advantage.

By definition, $\neg(X \gtrsim Y)$ implies that there exists a constant $c$ such that for all $\hat{c} > c$, we set $\hat{c} = 4c$, and for all $\kappa_0$ there exists a $\kappa \geq \kappa_0$ such that:

$$\Pr\left[\frac{1}{\kappa^{4c}}\sum_{j=1}^{\kappa^{4c}} Y_\kappa{}^{(j)} > \frac{1}{\kappa^{4c}}\sum_{j=1}^{\kappa^{4c}} X_\kappa{}^{(j)}\right] - \Pr\left[\frac{1}{\kappa^{4c}}\sum_{j=1}^{\kappa^{4c}} X_\kappa{}^{(j)} > \frac{1}{\kappa^{4c}}\sum_{j=1}^{\kappa^{4c}} Y_\kappa{}^{(j)}\right] \geq \frac{1}{\kappa^{c}} \tag{2}$$

Consistent with the cryptographic literature, we assume that the distinguisher is non-uniform (i.e., can take a polynomial advice, which in our case will be the constant $c$ guaranteed to exist from the above observation). We consider the distinguisher $\mathcal{D}_1 : \{0,1\}^* \to \{0,1,\perp\}$ (Fig. 1), that takes as input the running time token $1^\kappa$ and $\kappa^{4c}$ i.i.d. samples from $Z_\kappa$, where $Z_\kappa$ is equally likely distributed according to $X_\kappa$ or $Y_\kappa$. The distinguisher then outputs (i) $\{0,1\}$ that indicates whether the samples were drawn from $X_\kappa$ or $Y_\kappa$ respectively (ii) $\perp$, which represents that $\mathcal{D}_1$ chooses to abort from making a guess.

First, we analyze the performance of the distinguisher $\mathcal{D}_1$ when the samples are drawn from $X_\kappa$.

$$\begin{aligned}
&\Pr\left[\mathcal{D}_1(X_\kappa^{(1)},\cdots,X_\kappa^{(\kappa^{4c})};1^\kappa)=0\right]-\Pr\left[\mathcal{D}_1(X_\kappa^{(1)},\cdots,X_\kappa^{(\kappa^{4c})};1^\kappa)=1\right]\\
&=\Pr\left[\overline{X}'_\kappa<\overline{X}_\kappa\right]-\Pr\left[\overline{X}'_\kappa>\overline{X}_\kappa\right]\\
&=0. \qquad (3)
\end{aligned}$$

Where $\overline{X}'_\kappa$ and $\overline{X}_\kappa$ are independent copies of the empirical mean random variable of $X_\kappa$ with $\kappa^{4c}$ samples. The last equality holds due to symmetry.

Similarly, we obtain the following when $\mathcal{D}_1$ has access to $Y$.

$$\begin{aligned}
&\Pr\left[\mathcal{D}_1(Y_\kappa^{(1)},\cdots,Y_\kappa^{(\kappa^{4c})};1^\kappa)=1\right]-\Pr\left[\mathcal{D}_1(Y_\kappa^{(1)},\cdots,Y_\kappa^{(\kappa^{4c})};1^\kappa)=0\right]\\
&=\Pr\left[\overline{Y}_\kappa>\overline{X}_\kappa\right]-\Pr\left[\overline{X}_\kappa>\overline{Y}_\kappa\right]\\
&=\Pr\left[\frac{1}{\kappa^{4c}}\sum_{j=1}^{\kappa^{4c}}{Y_\kappa}^{(j)}>\frac{1}{\kappa^{4c}}\sum_{j=1}^{\kappa^{4c}}{X_\kappa}^{(j)}\right]-\Pr\left[\frac{1}{\kappa^{4c}}\sum_{j=1}^{\kappa^{4c}}{X_\kappa}^{(j)}>\frac{1}{\kappa^{4c}}\sum_{j=1}^{\kappa^{4c}}{Y_\kappa}^{(j)}\right]\\
&\qquad \text{(From Equation (2))}\\
&\geq\frac{1}{\kappa^c}. \qquad (4)
\end{aligned}$$

Summing up Inequality (3) and Inequality (4), we get

$$\begin{aligned}
&\left(\Pr\left[\mathcal{D}_1(X_\kappa^{(1)},\cdots,X_\kappa^{(\kappa^{4c})};1^\kappa)=0\right]-\Pr\left[\mathcal{D}_1(Y_\kappa^{(1)},\cdots,Y_\kappa^{(\kappa^{4c})};1^\kappa)=0\right]\right)\\
&+\left(\Pr\left[\mathcal{D}_1(Y_\kappa^{(1)},\cdots,Y_\kappa^{(\kappa^{4c})};1^\kappa)=1\right]-\Pr\left[\mathcal{D}_1(X_\kappa^{(1)},\cdots,X_\kappa^{(\kappa^{4c})};1^\kappa)=1\right]\right)\geq\frac{1}{\kappa^c},
\end{aligned}$$

The final inequality implies that the distinguishing advantage of the distinguisher is at least $\frac{1}{2\kappa^c}$, which is non-negligible.

From the existence of the distinguisher $\mathcal{D}_1$, we have that there exists a PPT distinguisher $\mathcal{D}_2$ that can distinguish $X_\kappa$ from $Y_\kappa$ with non-negligible advantage, even when given only a single sample from either $X_\kappa$ or $Y_\kappa$. This result follows from a standard result in the cryptographic literature [22]. The existence of $\mathcal{D}_2$ implies that $\neg(X \cong Y)$ and we reach a contradiction. □

**Proposition 1.** *Let* $X = \{X_\kappa\}_{\kappa\in\mathbb{N}}, \hat{X} = \{\hat{X}_\kappa\}_{\kappa\in\mathbb{N}}, Y = \{Y_\kappa\}_{\kappa\in\mathbb{N}}$ *be random variable ensembles, such that* $X, \hat{X}$ *are computationally indistinguishable. Then* $X$ *computationally dominates* $Y$ *if, and only if,* $\hat{X}$ *computationally dominates* $Y$*. That is, if* $X \cong \hat{X}$ *then* $X \gtrsim Y \Leftrightarrow \hat{X} \gtrsim Y$*.*

*Proof.* We prove the forward direction; the reverse direction follows by swapping $X$ and $\hat{X}$. Assume $X \gtrsim Y$ and $X \cong \hat{X}$ but $\neg(\hat{X} \gtrsim Y)$. We will derive a contradiction by constructing a PPT distinguisher.

**Distinguisher $\mathcal{D}_1(1^\kappa)$**

1. $\mathcal{D}_1$ gets $c$ as its advice.
2. Compute the empirical mean of $\kappa^{4c}$ i.i.d. samples from $Z$.
   Let $\overline{Z} = \frac{1}{\kappa^{4c}} \sum_{i=1}^{\kappa^{4c}} Z^{(i)}$,
3. Compute the empirical mean of $\kappa^{4c}$ i.i.d. samples from $X_\kappa$.
   Let $\overline{X} = \frac{1}{\kappa^{4c}} \sum_{i=1}^{\kappa^{4c}} X_\kappa^{(i)}$,
4. If $\overline{Z} > \overline{X}$, output 1; If $\overline{Z} < \overline{X}$, output 0; Otherwise output $\perp$.

**Fig. 1.** Distinguisher $\mathcal{D}_1$ for $X, Y$

From $X \gtrsim Y$ we have that for all constants $c_1 \geq 1$, there exists a constant $d_1 > c_1$ and $\kappa_1$ such that for all $\kappa \geq \kappa_1$,

$$\Pr\left[\frac{1}{\kappa^{d_1}} \sum_{j=1}^{\kappa^{d_1}} Y_\kappa{}^{(j)} > \frac{1}{\kappa^{d_1}} \sum_{j=1}^{\kappa^{d_1}} X_\kappa{}^{(j)}\right] - \Pr\left[\frac{1}{\kappa^{d_1}} \sum_{j=1}^{\kappa^{d_1}} X_\kappa{}^{(j)} > \frac{1}{\kappa^{d_1}} \sum_{j=1}^{\kappa^{d_1}} Y_\kappa{}^{(j)}\right] < \frac{1}{\kappa^{c_1}} \tag{5}$$

Similarly, from $\neg(\hat{X} \gtrsim Y)$ we have that there exists a constant $c_2 \geq 1$ such that for all $d_2 > c_2$ and $\kappa_2$ there exists $\kappa \geq \kappa_2$ with

$$\Pr\left[\frac{1}{\kappa^{d_2}} \sum_{j=1}^{\kappa^{d_2}} Y_\kappa{}^{(j)} > \frac{1}{\kappa^{d_2}} \sum_{j=1}^{\kappa^{d_2}} \hat{X}_\kappa^{(j)}\right] - \Pr\left[\frac{1}{\kappa^{d_2}} \sum_{j=1}^{\kappa^{d_2}} \hat{X}_\kappa^{(j)} > \frac{1}{\kappa^{d_2}} \sum_{j=1}^{\kappa^{d_2}} Y_\kappa{}^{(j)}\right] \geq \frac{1}{\kappa^{c_2}} \tag{6}$$

First, we fix the polynomial sample size used by the distinguisher. Let $c_2 \geq 1$ be the constant guaranteed by Eq. (6), and set $c_1 := c_2 + 1$. Since Eq. (5) holds for all constants, there exists a constant $d > c_1$ and a threshold $\kappa_1$ such that Eq. (5) holds for all $\kappa \geq \kappa_1$ when using this $d$. Because $d > c_1 > c_2$, we may also instantiate the quantifier over $d_2 > c_2$ in Eq. (6) with the same exponent $d$. We therefore fix this $d$ and let the distinguisher use $\kappa^d$ samples throughout.

Next, we show that the PPT distinguisher $\mathcal{D}$ in Fig. 2 has a non-negligible advantage of distinguishing between $X$ and $\hat{X}$. Consistent with the cryptographic literature, we assume that the distinguisher is non-uniform (i.e., can take a polynomial advice, which in our case will be the constant $d$ guaranteed to exist from the above observation). That is, there exists a polynomial $\texttt{poly}(\cdot)$ that for all $\kappa_0$ there exists a $\kappa \geq \kappa_0$ :

$$\left|\Pr\left[\mathcal{D}(X_\kappa^{(1)}, \cdots, X_\kappa^{(\kappa^d)}; 1^\kappa) = 1\right] - \Pr\left[\mathcal{D}(\hat{X}_\kappa^{(1)}, \cdots, \hat{X}_\kappa^{(\kappa^d)}; 1^\kappa) = 1\right]\right| \geq \frac{1}{\texttt{poly}(\kappa)}.$$

To lower-bound the distinguishing advantage of $\mathcal{D}$, we must ensure that for every $\kappa_0$ there exists $\kappa \geq \kappa_0$ for which both (5) and (6) hold (with our fixed

**Distinguisher $\mathcal{D}(1^\kappa)$**

1. $\mathcal{D}$ gets $d$ as its advice.
2. Compute the empirical mean of $\kappa^d$ i.i.d. samples from $Z_\kappa$.
   Let $\overline{Z} = \frac{1}{\kappa^d} \sum_{i=1}^{\kappa^d} Z_\kappa^{(i)}$,
3. Compute the empirical mean of $\kappa^d$ i.i.d. samples from $Y_\kappa$.
   Let $\overline{Y} = \frac{1}{\kappa^d} \sum_{i=1}^{\kappa^d} Y_\kappa^{(i)}$,
4. If $\overline{Z} > \overline{Y}$, output 1; If $\overline{Z} < \overline{Y}$, output 0; Otherwise output $\perp$.

**Fig. 2.** Distinguisher $\mathcal{D}$ for $X, \hat{X}$

constants). Let $\kappa_1$ be the threshold from (5), and define $\kappa_2 := \max\{\kappa_0, \kappa_1\}$. By (6), there exists $\kappa \geq \kappa_2$ such that (6) holds. For this same $\kappa$, we also have $\kappa \geq \kappa_1$, hence (5) holds as well. By the construction of the distinguisher, when $\mathcal{D}$ is given samples from $X$ we have that,

$$\begin{aligned}
&\Pr\left[\mathcal{D}(X_\kappa^{(1)}, \cdots, X_\kappa^{(\kappa^d)}; 1^\kappa) = 1\right] - \Pr\left[\mathcal{D}(X_\kappa^{(1)}, \cdots, X_\kappa^{(\kappa^d)}; 1^\kappa) = 0\right] \\
&= \Pr\left[\frac{1}{\kappa^d}\sum_{j=1}^{\kappa^d} X_\kappa{}^{(j)} > \frac{1}{\kappa^d}\sum_{j=1}^{\kappa^d} Y_\kappa{}^{(j)}\right] - \Pr\left[\frac{1}{\kappa^d}\sum_{j=1}^{\kappa^d} Y_\kappa{}^{(j)} > \frac{1}{\kappa^d}\sum_{j=1}^{\kappa^d} X_\kappa{}^{(j)}\right] \\
&\geq -\frac{1}{\kappa^{c_1}} \qquad \text{(From Equation (5))}
\end{aligned} \tag{7}$$

On the other hand. When the distinguisher has access to samples from $\hat{X}$, we have

$$\begin{aligned}
&\Pr\left[\mathcal{D}(\hat{X}_\kappa^{(1)}, \cdots, \hat{X}_\kappa^{(\kappa^d)}; 1^\kappa) = 0\right] - \Pr\left[\mathcal{D}(\hat{X}_\kappa^{(1)}, \cdots, \hat{X}_\kappa^{(\kappa^d)}; 1^\kappa) = 1\right] \\
&= \Pr\left[\frac{1}{\kappa^d}\sum_{j=1}^{\kappa^d} Y_\kappa{}^{(j)} > \frac{1}{\kappa^d}\sum_{j=1}^{\kappa^d} \hat{X}_\kappa^{(j)}\right] - \Pr\left[\frac{1}{\kappa^d}\sum_{j=1}^{\kappa^d} \hat{X}_\kappa^{(j)} > \frac{1}{\kappa^d}\sum_{j=1}^{\kappa^d} Y_\kappa{}^{(j)}\right] \\
&\geq \frac{1}{\kappa^{c_2}} \qquad \text{(From Eq. (6))}
\end{aligned} \tag{8}$$

Summing up Inequality (7) and Inequality (8), we have

$$\left(\Pr\left[\mathcal{D}(\hat{X}_\kappa^{(1)},\cdots,\hat{X}_\kappa^{(\kappa^d)};1^\kappa)=0\right]-\Pr\left[\mathcal{D}(X_\kappa^{(1)},\cdots,X_\kappa^{(\kappa^d)};1^\kappa)=0\right]\right)$$
$$+\left(\Pr\left[\mathcal{D}(X_\kappa^{(1)},\cdots,X_\kappa^{(\kappa^d)};1^\kappa)=1\right]-\Pr\left[\mathcal{D}(\hat{X}_\kappa^{(1)},\cdots,\hat{X}_\kappa^{(\kappa^d)};1^\kappa)=1\right]\right)$$
$$\geq \frac{1}{\kappa^{c_2}}-\frac{1}{\kappa^{c_1}},$$

From the last inequality, we see the distinguishing advantage of $\mathcal{D}$ is at least $\frac{1}{2}(\frac{1}{\kappa^{c_2}}-\frac{1}{\kappa^{c_1}})$. Notice that for $c_1 > c_2$ there exists a $\texttt{poly}(\cdot)$ such that $\frac{1}{2}(\frac{1}{\kappa^{c_2}}-\frac{1}{\kappa^{c_1}}) \geq 1/\texttt{poly}(\kappa)$. However, we know that such a distinguisher $\mathcal{D}$ cannot exist by definition (Definition 3). Therefore, we conclude that $\hat{X}\gtrsim Y$. □

The proof of the following proposition follows the exact same reasoning as Proposition 1, with only minor modifications.

**Proposition 2.** *Let* $X = \{X_\kappa\}_{\kappa\in\mathbb{N}}, Y = \{Y_\kappa\}_{\kappa\in\mathbb{N}}, \hat{Y} = \{\hat{Y}_\kappa\}_{\kappa\in\mathbb{N}}$ *be random variable ensembles, such that* $Y, \hat{Y}$ *are computationally indistinguishable. Then* $X$ *computationally dominates* $Y$ *if, and only if,* $X$ *computationally dominates* $\hat{Y}$*. That is, if* $Y \cong \hat{Y}$ *then* $X\gtrsim Y \Leftrightarrow X\gtrsim\hat{Y}$*.*

## 5 Pseudo-Nash in Games that Involve Cryptography

In this section, we prove our main theorem, allowing us to translate (pseudo-) Nash equilibria in games that use idealized cryptography into pseudo-Nash in a game where the idealized cryptography is replaced by a (computationally secure) cryptographic protocol.

We start with a brief overview of basic concepts from the literature, defining the security of cryptographic protocols. We have included some intuition and concrete examples in Sect. 5.1, below, for any interested reader who is unfamiliar with the simulation-based paradigm. The contents of the following subsection would likely be considered common knowledge within the cryptographic protocols community (and can be safely skipped by a cryptographer), but will help a game theorist understand how to use our result.

### 5.1 Add'l Preliminaries on Cryptographic (Composable) Security

For clarity, we use multi-party cryptographic protocols as our running example, where parties wish to perform some joint computation securely. The common methodology to design and analyze such protocols can be outlined as follows:

1. Define the model of computation that specifies the possible actions by the parties, and the ways in which parties can interact with one another.

2. Specify the goal that the cryptographic protocol aims to achieve. This can be done either by describing properties that the protocol should have, e.g., for encryption, an attacker who observes the ciphertext should gain no information about the plaintext; or by specifying an idealized primitive, which in the cryptographic literature is called the ideal functionality, that embodies the goal that we are aiming to achieve. Consider, for example, the case of cryptographic commitments: a sender (the *committer*) with some input $x$ can run an interactive protocol with a receiver (the *verifier*) such that the following properties are satisfied:
   (a) (hiding) At the end of the above protocol, the receiver has not learned anything about $x$.
   (b) (binding) The sender is "committed" to his input, i.e., there is a way to convince the receiver that $x$ was the sender's original input, but there is no way to lie that his input was some $x' \neq x$.

   The above security goals are embodied by a simple commitment functionality, which upon receiving an input $x$ from the sender records it and informs the receiver that some input was received (without leaking anything about it); and once the input has been recorded and the receiver has been informed about it, the sender can instruct the functionality to reveal it to the receiver. It is easy to verify that the interaction of a protocol with the above functionality satisfies the security properties of a commitment.
3. Specify the protocol, i.e., define the actions, and prove that it satisfies a cryptographic security definition (as discussed below).

SIMULATION-BASED SECURITY. We use the notion of *simulation-based security* as the security definition for cryptographic protocols. In addition to being the standard security definition in modern cryptographic protocols analysis, simulation-based security is also suitable for our goal of seamlessly using cryptography within game theory, due to the composition theorems that it comes equipped with. In a nutshell, such theorems allow us to replace, within a bigger protocol, idealized cryptographic primitives with their cryptographic implementations, without destroying their security properties. This might sound very close to our main theorem. Therefore, it is worth here noticing a highly relevant difference between the standard approaches taken by cryptography and game theory to frame and reason about the (mis)behavior of parties in protocols and games, respectively: In particular, cryptography assumes that the adversary might corrupt several parties in a coordinated manner as opposed to rationality which is common in game theory. We note in passing that there are notable refinements of the cryptographic model to allow for capturing non-coordinated definitions [1]; similarly, game-theoretic stability notions that allow coordination have been proposed (see [27] for a nice survey.)

We can use any composable (simulation-based) security cryptographic framework, e.g., [2,7,8] but for this exposition, we will focus on Canetti's Universal Composability (UC) framework [8] which is the most broadly adopted in the modern literature.

The model of computation in UC models (the strategies of the) parties as interactive Turing machines (ITMs).[4] These are Turing machines—a standard theoretical abstraction of computing devices—with dedicated input and output tapes (corresponding to I/O interface) and communication tapes that can be connected to other ITMs' communication tapes: If two ITMs $M_1$ and $M_2$ have connected (linked) communication tapes, then $M_1$ can write to its communication tape shared with $M_2$ so that $M_2$ can read it and vice versa.

An interactive protocol among $n$ parties can be described as a vector $\pi = (\pi_1, \ldots, \pi_n)$ of $n$ ITM's, where the $i$th ITM, $\pi_i$, describes the (interactive) strategy of the $i$-th party (this can be thought of as a machine that specifies all possible reactions of an agent in an extensive form game). For simplicity, we will assume that the $n$ parties' ITMs are not connected to one another; instead, when in the protocol we want to have Party $i$ send a message to Party $j$, we will assume that they are both connected to another ITM (corresponding to a communication channel between them) that is linked to both of them.

Given the above model, a party that deviates from the protocol can be captured as a party that replaces its protocol-prescribed ITM with a different one. The actual cryptographic security definition considers situations where several parties might deviate in a coordinated (by an adversary) manner. However, for the purpose of this work—since we only consider Nash equilibrium with rational players—it suffices to discuss the definition restricted to any one of the parties being corrupted (and deviating).

The security definition of a cryptographic protocol is given as follows: First, we specify the ideal goal by means of an ideal functionality $\mathcal{F}$ (also an ITM), which as in Step 1, above, embodies the idealized version of our protocols goals, e.g., in the example above, a commitment functionality, which is an ITM with the behavior discussed above, that has communication tapes linked with the committer and the verifier. Then the definition of what it means for a protocol $\Pi$ which, recall, is a profile of ITMs—to *securely realize* $\mathcal{F}$ against a single corruption is devised by comparing an execution of the protocol (the so-called *real world*) to an ideal invocation of the functionality $\mathcal{F}$ (the so-called ideal world). In a nutshell, we require that there exists no distinguisher (also an ITM) that distinguishes an ideal-world execution from a real-world execution with better than negligible probability. (In the context of UC security, a distinguisher is also called the *environment* as it defines the protocol's input/output interfaces.)

In a nutshell, a cryptographic protocol securely realizes an idealized cryptographic functionality $\mathcal{F}$, if any deviation in the real world can be mapped to an indistinguishable deviation in the ideal world so that the input/output behavior of the two worlds remains indistinguishable.

A bit more formally, consider a distinguisher $\mathcal{D}$ who chooses inputs to the protocols ITMs and gets to observe their outputs. For any such $\mathcal{D}$, denote by $V^{\mathcal{D},Real}_{\pi=(\pi_1,\ldots,\pi_n)}$ the random variable corresponding to the view of $\mathcal{D}$ when inter-

[4] In UC, the parties are in fact *instances* of ITMs, simulated by a single, larger ITM which is the environment. For sake of accessibility to the broader computer science and game theory audience, we refer to them as ITMs here.

acting with the protocol. (This view includes $\mathcal{D}$'s own input and randomness, the security parameter, and all inputs and outputs to the ITMs in $\pi$.) Similarly, $V^{\mathcal{D},\mathcal{F},Ideal}_{(\phi_1,\ldots,\phi_n)}$ corresponds to the view of $\mathcal{D}$ in an ideal invocation of $\mathcal{F}$, where each $\phi_i$ is the "dummy" ITM that simply forwards inputs from $\mathcal{D}$ to $\mathcal{F}$ and hands any received inputs back to $\mathcal{D}$. Note that all ITMs involved in the above definition (including $\mathcal{D}$) are assumed to be probabilistic polynomial time (PPT).

We then say that protocol $\pi$, is secure if there exists an ITM $\mathsf{Sim}$, called the *simulator*, such that for any $i \in [n]$, and any PPT ITM $\pi'_i$ the view $V^{D,Real}_{(\pi'_i,\pi_{-i})}$ of $D$ when interacting with $\pi$ where party $i$ plays $\pi'_i$ instead of $\pi_i$ is (computationally) indistinguishable from the view $V^{D,Ideal}_{(\mathsf{Sim}(\pi'_i),\phi_{-i})}$ of $D$ in an ideal invocation where party $i$ plays the simulator's strategy (instead of the "dummy" one).

## 5.2 Normal Form Computational Games

Combining the above definition—which allows to replace deviations in the cryptographic protocols with indistinguishable deviations in the idealized-crypto setting—with Proposition 1 already hints towards the proof of our main theorem. However, we still need to formally define games among ITMs which will allow us to use cryptography. We do so in the following:

**Definition 9 (Normal Form Computational Game).** *A real normal form computational game $\mathcal{G}$ consists of the following:*

- *$[n] = \{1, \cdots, n\}$ is the set of players in the game. $\Omega$ is the set of all possible outcomes of the game. $\kappa$ is the security parameter.*
- *Players' strategies are interactive, probabilistic polynomial time (PPT) Turing machines. We use $\mathcal{N}_i = \{1, 2, \cdots\}$ to index these strategies/machines. That is, player $i$ chooses strategy $s \in \mathcal{N}_i$ means that she is playing using the $s^{th}$ Turing machine. This Turing machine receives a single input: the security parameter, written in unary: $1^\kappa$. We write $s_i^\kappa$ for the strategy/Turing machine chosen by player $i$, executed with input $1^\kappa$. Let $\mathcal{N} = \mathcal{N}_1 \times \ldots \times \mathcal{N}_n$.*
- *The Turing machines chosen by the players can be linked via one or more Turing machines, which are fixed and part of the game description. (These will correspond to ideal functionalities, or simple communication channels.) The security parameter $\kappa$ is written on the input tape of all ITMs in the game. All players simultaneously pick their strategies (Turing machine $s_i \in \mathcal{N}_i$ for every player $i$), and these Turing machines interact with each other according to the rules of the game, and a single outcome $\omega \in \Omega$ is selected (and learned by the players).*
- *$U_i : \Omega \to \mathbb{R}$ is the random variable that indicates the utility of player $i$. We slightly overload notation and write $U_i^\kappa(s)$ for the utility of player $i$ when the strategy profile is $s = (s_1, \ldots, s_n)$ and the security parameter is $\kappa$. We write $U_i^\kappa(\hat{s}_i; s_{-i})$ when player $i$ unilaterally deviates to $\hat{s}_i$ and the rest play according to $s_{-i}$, and assume $U_i^\kappa$ is efficiently computable in $\kappa$.*

### 5.3 Cryptographic Pseudo-Nash

In this subsection, we formalize how pseudo-equilibria in a game that uses an ideal functionality $\mathcal{F}$ automatically translate to pseudo-equilibria in the corresponding game where $\mathcal{F}$ is replaced by a cryptographic implementation $\Pi$.

**Definition 10 (Game implementation).** *Let $\mathcal{G}^{\mathcal{F}}([n], \mathcal{N}^{\mathcal{F}}, U)$ be a normal-form computational game in which strategies may invoke an ideal functionality $\mathcal{F}$. Let $\Pi$ be a protocol that securely realizes $\mathcal{F}$. The* implementation *of $\mathcal{G}^{\mathcal{F}}$ with $\Pi$, denoted $\mathcal{G}^{\Pi}([n], \mathcal{N}^{\Pi}, U)$, is defined by a mapping $\mathsf{Comp}_i : \mathcal{N}_i^{\mathcal{F}} \to \mathcal{N}_i^{\Pi}$ for each player $i$, where $\mathsf{Comp}_i(\sigma_i)$ executes $\sigma_i$ while replacing each call to $\mathcal{F}$ with an invocation of $\Pi$. The outcome space $\Omega$ and utilities $U_i : \Omega \to \mathbb{R}$ are the same in $\mathcal{G}^{\mathcal{F}}$ and $\mathcal{G}^{\Pi}$, and utilities are evaluated on the induced outcome distribution.*

**Theorem 3.** *Let $\mathcal{F}$ be an ideal functionality and $\Pi$ be a protocol that securely realizes $\mathcal{F}$ against a single corruption. Let $\mathcal{G}^{\mathcal{F}}([n], \mathcal{N}^{\mathcal{F}}, U)$ be a computational game with access to $\mathcal{F}$, and $\mathcal{G}^{\Pi}([n], \mathcal{N}^{\Pi}, U)$ be its implementation with $\Pi$ (Definition 10). If $\sigma \in \mathcal{N}^{\mathcal{F}}$ is a computational pseudo-Nash equilibrium (Definition 8) of $\mathcal{G}^{\mathcal{F}}$, then the corresponding strategy profile $s = (\mathsf{Comp}(\sigma_1), \ldots, \mathsf{Comp}(\sigma_n)) \in \mathcal{N}^{\Pi}$ is a computational pseudo-Nash equilibrium of $\mathcal{G}^{\Pi}$.*

*Proof.* Let $U_i(\sigma_i, \sigma_{-i})$ be the utility random variable ensemble of player $i$ when players playing strategy $\sigma_i$ in $\mathcal{G}^{\mathcal{F}}$. Similarly, let $U_i(s_i, s_{-i}) = \{U_i^{\kappa}\left((s_i^*, s_{-i}^*)\right)\}_{\kappa \in \mathbb{N}}$ be the utility random variable ensemble of player $i$ when players playing strategy $s_i$ in $\mathcal{G}^{\Pi}$. For ease of notation, we always use $\sigma$ to denote strategy profiles in $\mathcal{G}^{\mathcal{F}}$ and $s$ for strategy profiles in $\mathcal{G}^{\Pi}$.

We prove the theorem by contradiction. Suppose that $s = (s_1, \ldots, s_n)$ is not a computational pseudo-Nash equilibrium in $\mathcal{G}^{\Pi}$. By Definition 8, this implies there exists a player $i$ and unilateral deviation $\hat{s}_i \in \mathcal{N}^{\Pi}$ in $\mathcal{G}^{\Pi}$ such that the utility ensemble of $s$ does not computationally mean dominate the utility ensemble of the deviation, $\neg(U_i(s_i, s_{-i}) \gtrsim U_i(\hat{s}_i, s_{-i}))$, let $\hat{s} = (\hat{s}_i, s_{-i})$. This means that strategy $\hat{s}_i$ has observably better utility for player $i$. Towards the contradiction, we will show that if such a strategy exists in the real game $\mathcal{G}^{\Pi}$ then there exists a strategy in the ideal game $\mathcal{G}^{\mathcal{F}}$ that also has observably better utility. By definition, this implies that $\sigma$ is not a pseudo-equilibrium profile.

By the simulation-based security of $\Pi$, for every PPT unilateral deviation $\hat{s}_i$ in the real game $G_{\Pi}$ there exists a PPT ideal-world strategy (simulator) $\mathsf{Sim}(\hat{s}_i)$ such that the real execution under $(\hat{s}_i, s_{-i})$ is simulated in the ideal game under $(\mathsf{Sim}(\hat{s}_i), \sigma_{-i})$. More formally, fix any PPT distinguisher $\mathcal{D}$. For any strategy profile $t$ in the real game $\mathcal{G}^{\Pi}$ (resp., $\tau$ in the ideal game $\mathcal{G}^{\mathcal{F}}$), let $V_t^{\mathcal{D},Real}$ (resp., $V_\tau^{\mathcal{D},Ideal}$) denote the random variable corresponding to $\mathcal{D}$'s view in the execution induced by that profile. In particular, $V_{(\hat{s}_i,s_{-i})}^{\mathcal{D},Real}$ is $\mathcal{D}$'s view in the real execution where player $i$ deviates to $\hat{s}_i$, and $V_{(\mathsf{Sim}(\hat{s}_i),\sigma_{-i})}^{\mathcal{D},Ideal}$ is $\mathcal{D}$'s view in the corresponding ideal execution where player $i$ follows $\mathsf{Sim}(\hat{s}_i)$ Similarly, $V_{(s_i,s_{-i})}^{\mathcal{D},Real}$ and $V_{(\sigma_i,\sigma_{-i})}^{\mathcal{D},Ideal}$ denote $\mathcal{D}$'s views under the honest profiles in the real and ideal executions. Thus,

$$V_{(\hat{s}_i,s_{-i})}^{\mathcal{D},Real} \cong V_{(\mathsf{Sim}(\hat{s}_i),\sigma_{-i})}^{\mathcal{D},Ideal} \quad \text{and} \quad V_{(s_i,s_{-i})}^{\mathcal{D},Real} \cong V_{(\sigma_i,\sigma_{-i})}^{\mathcal{D},Ideal}.$$

From the indistinguishability of the views, we get that the corresponding utility ensembles are also indistinguishable, since $U_i$ can be efficiently computed from $\mathcal{D}$'s view. That is

$$U_i(\hat{s}_i, s_{-i}) \cong U_i(\mathsf{Sim}(\hat{s}_i), \sigma_{-i}) \qquad \text{and} \qquad U_i(s_i, s_{-i}) \cong U_i(\sigma_i, \sigma_{-i}).$$

Next, we apply the invariance of computational mean dominance under indistinguishable replacements. Given that $\neg(U_i(s_i, s_{-i}) \gtrsim U_i(\hat{s}_i, s_{-i}))$, we substitute the real deviation with its ideal counterpart. From Proposition 2 we get $\neg\left(U_i(s_i, s_{-i}) \gtrsim U_i(\mathsf{Sim}(\hat{s}_i), \sigma_{-i})\right)$. Similarly, we substitute the real honest execution with the ideal honest execution. Then, by applying Proposition 1, we get $\neg\left(U_i(\sigma_i, \sigma_{-i}) \gtrsim U_i(\mathsf{Sim}(\hat{s}_i), \sigma_{-i})\right)$.

The last statement implies that $\hat{\sigma}_i = \mathsf{Sim}(\hat{s}_i)$ is a unilateral deviation in the ideal game $\mathcal{G}^{\mathcal{F}}$ that violates the pseudo-Nash condition for $\sigma$, contradicting that $\sigma$ is a computational pseudo-Nash equilibrium in $G_{\mathcal{F}}$ Therefore, our assumption was false, and $s$ is a computational pseudo-Nash equilibrium in $\mathcal{G}^{\Pi}$. □

**Acknowledgments.** The authors would like to thank Joel Alwen and Georgios Amanatidis for their interesting discussions and their input in the early stages of this project. Vassilis Zikas was supported in part by NSF Awards No. 2448339 and No. 2531010, JPMorgan Chase, Halcyon Futures, the Stellar Development Foundation, and Sunday Group, Inc. Yu Wei was supported in part by NSF Awards No. 2448339 and No. 2531010, Halcyon Futures, and Sunday Group, Inc. Alexandros Psomas and Athina Terzoglou were supported in part by NSF CAREER Award CCF-2144208 and research awards from Halcyon Futures, Google, and Supra. Work was done in part while Vassilis Zikas and Alexandros Psomas were visiting the Simons Institute for the Theory of Computing, UC Berkeley.

## A Missing Proofs

*Proof (Proof of Lemma* 1*).* Let us define $\Delta = \mathbb{E}[X] - \mathbb{E}[Y] > 0$. We want to show that $X \gtrsim Y$, according to Definition 7. That is, for all constants $c \geq 1$, there exists a $\hat{c} > c$, which we set to $\hat{c} = 4c$, and a $\kappa_0 > 0$ such that for all $\kappa \geq \kappa_0$:

$$\Pr\left[\frac{1}{\kappa^{4c}}\sum_{j=1}^{\kappa^{4c}} Y_\kappa{}^{(j)} \geq \frac{1}{\kappa^{4c}}\sum_{j=1}^{\kappa^{4c}} X_\kappa{}^{(j)}\right] - \Pr\left[\frac{1}{\kappa^{4c}}\sum_{j=1}^{\kappa^{4c}} X_\kappa{}^{(j)} \geq \frac{1}{\kappa^{4c}}\sum_{j=1}^{\kappa^{4c}} Y_\kappa{}^{(j)}\right] < \frac{1}{\kappa^c} \tag{9}$$

where $X_\kappa^{(j)}, Y_\kappa^{(j)}$ are i.i.d. samples from $X_\kappa, Y_\kappa$ respectively.

Since $X$ and $Y$ are random variables (that is $X_\kappa = X$ and $Y_\kappa = Y$ for all $\kappa$), Eq. (9) is reduced to:

$$\Pr\left[\frac{1}{\kappa^{4c}}\sum_{j=1}^{\kappa^{4c}} Y^{(j)} \geq \frac{1}{\kappa^{4c}}\sum_{j=1}^{\kappa^{4c}} X^{(j)}\right] - \Pr\left[\frac{1}{\kappa^{4c}}\sum_{j=1}^{\kappa^{4c}} X^{(j)} \geq \frac{1}{\kappa^{4c}}\sum_{j=1}^{\kappa^{4c}} Y^{(j)}\right] < \frac{1}{\kappa^c} \tag{10}$$

For a fixed $\kappa$ and constant $c$, define the empirical averages and apply Hoeffding's inequality [33], for any $\epsilon > 0$ we have

$$\Pr\left[\left|\frac{1}{\kappa^{4c}}\sum_{j=1}^{\kappa^{4c}} X^{(j)} - \mathbb{E}[X]\right| \geq \epsilon\right] \leq 2\exp\left(-\frac{2\kappa^{4c}\epsilon^2}{R^2}\right)$$

and

$$\Pr\left[\left|\frac{1}{\kappa^{4c}}\sum_{j=1}^{\kappa^{4c}} Y^{(j)} - \mathbb{E}[Y]\right| \geq \epsilon\right] \leq 2\exp\left(-\frac{2\kappa^{4c}\epsilon^2}{R^2}\right)$$

For ease of notation, let us define for fixed but arbitrary $\kappa, c$:

$$\overline{X} = \frac{1}{\kappa^{4c}}\sum_{j=1}^{\kappa^{4c}} X^{(j)} \quad \text{and} \quad \overline{Y} = \frac{1}{\kappa^{4c}}\sum_{j=1}^{\kappa^{4c}} Y^{(j)}$$

Set $\epsilon = \Delta/4$. We consider the following two events, $\overline{X} \geq \mathbb{E}[X] - \Delta/4$ and $\overline{Y} \leq \mathbb{E}[Y] + \Delta/4$. When both events occur we have that $\overline{X} - \overline{Y} \geq \mathbb{E}[X] - \Delta/4 - (\mathbb{E}[Y] + \Delta/4) \geq \Delta/2 > 0$

$$\begin{aligned}
\Pr\left[\overline{X} > \overline{Y}\right] &\geq \Pr\left[\left(\overline{X} \geq \mathbb{E}[X] - \Delta/4\right) \;\&\; \left(\overline{Y} \leq \mathbb{E}[Y] + \Delta/4\right)\right] \\
&= \Pr\left[\left(\overline{X} \geq \mathbb{E}[X] - \Delta/4\right)\right] \cdot \Pr\left[\left(\overline{Y} \leq \mathbb{E}[Y] + \Delta/4\right)\right] \\
&\geq \left(1 - 2\exp\left(-\frac{2\kappa^{4c}(\Delta/4)^2}{R^2}\right)\right)\left(1 - 2\exp\left(-\frac{2\kappa^{4c}(\Delta/4)^2}{R^2}\right)\right) \\
&\geq 1 - 4\exp\left(-\frac{\kappa^{4c}\Delta^2}{8R^2}\right)
\end{aligned}$$

To conclude the proof, we need to show that there exists a $\kappa_0$ such that for all $\kappa \geq \kappa_0$ and for all $c \geq 1$ Eq. (10) holds. We can see that it suffices to find the number of samples required to obtain $\Pr\left[\overline{X} > \overline{Y}\right] \geq \frac{1}{2}$. That is because $\Pr\left[\overline{Y} > \overline{X}\right] - \Pr\left[\overline{X} > \overline{Y}\right] \leq 0 \leq \frac{1}{\kappa^c}$ Thus, we need

$$4\exp\left(-\frac{\kappa^{4c}\Delta^2}{8R^2}\right) \leq \frac{1}{2} \Leftrightarrow -\frac{\kappa^{4c}\Delta^2}{8R^2} + \ln 4 \leq -\ln 2 \Leftrightarrow \kappa^{4c} \geq \frac{8R^2}{\Delta^2}\ln 8$$

Thus, since $c \geq 1$ it suffices to set $\kappa_0 = \left(\frac{8R^2}{\Delta^2}\ln 8\right)^{1/4}$.

□

*Proof (Proof of Lemma 2).* For two random variables $X, Y$ with $\mathbb{E}[X] = \mathbb{E}[Y]$, we want to show that $X \gtrsim Y$ and $Y \gtrsim X$. Since $X \gtrsim Y$ and $Y \gtrsim X$ are symmetric, without loss of generality we will show that $X \gtrsim Y$. That is, for all constants $c \geq 1$, there exist $\hat{c} > c$ and a $\kappa_0 > 0$ such that for all $\kappa \geq \kappa_0$:

$$\Pr\left[\frac{1}{\kappa^{\hat{c}}}\sum_{j=1}^{\kappa^{\hat{c}}} Y^{(j)} \geq \frac{1}{\kappa^{\hat{c}}}\sum_{j=1}^{\kappa^{\hat{c}}} X^{(j)}\right] - \Pr\left[\frac{1}{\kappa^{\hat{c}}}\sum_{j=1}^{\kappa^{\hat{c}}} X^{(j)} \geq \frac{1}{\kappa^{\hat{c}}}\sum_{j=1}^{\kappa^{\hat{c}}} Y^{(j)}\right] < \frac{1}{\kappa^c} \quad (11)$$

where $X^{(j)}, Y^{(j)}$ are i.i.d. samples from $X, Y$ respectively.

We will consider the random variable $Z = X - Y$. By linearity of expectations we have that $\mathbb{E}[Z] = \mathbb{E}[X] - \mathbb{E}[Y] = 0$. For some fixed but arbitrary $\kappa, \hat{c}$ let the empirical mean of $Z$ with $\kappa^{\hat{c}}$ i.i.d. samples be

$$\overline{Z}_{\kappa,\hat{c}} = \frac{1}{\kappa^{\hat{c}}} \sum_{j=1}^{\kappa^{\hat{c}}} Z^{(j)} = \frac{1}{\kappa^{\hat{c}}} \sum_{j=1}^{\kappa^{\hat{c}}} \left( X^{(j)} - Y^{(j)} \right).$$

Since the random variable $Z$ has finite support, we know that its moments are also finite. Let $\sigma^2 = \mathbb{E}\left[Z^2\right] < \infty$ and $\rho = \mathbb{E}\left[|Z|^3\right] < \infty$. If $\sigma^2 = 0$, then $X$ and $Y$ are constants. Since $\mathbb{E}[X] = \mathbb{E}[Y]$, they are the same constant, and their empirical means are always equal, satisfying the computational condition trivially. If $\sigma^2 > 0$, by the BerryâĂŞEsseen theorem [4,13], considering the cumulative distribution function (CDF) $F_{\kappa,c}(\cdot)$ of $\frac{\overline{Z}_{\kappa,\hat{c}}\sqrt{\kappa^{\hat{c}}}}{\sigma}$ and the CDF of normal distribution $\Phi(\cdot)$ we have that for a $C < 0.47$:

$$\sup_{x \in \mathbb{R}} |F_{\kappa,c}(x) - \Phi(x)| \leq \frac{C\rho}{\sigma^3 \sqrt{\kappa^{\hat{c}}}} \tag{12}$$

To satisfy Eq. (11) we show that for all constants $c$ and a $\hat{c} > c$ there exists $\kappa_0$ such that for all $\kappa \geq \kappa_0$ we have $\Pr\left[\overline{Z}_{\kappa,\hat{c}} < 0\right] - \Pr\left[\overline{Z}_{\kappa,\hat{c}} > 0\right] < \frac{1}{\kappa^c}$. Notice that we can remove the event that $\overline{Z}_{\kappa,\hat{c}} = 0$ from both probabilities without changing their difference. From Eq. (12) we have that $\Pr\left[\overline{Z}_{\kappa,c} < 0\right] \leq \Pr\left[\overline{Z}_{\kappa,c} \leq 0\right] \leq \frac{C\rho}{\sigma^3\sqrt{\kappa^{\hat{c}}}} + \Phi(0) = \frac{C\rho}{\sigma^3\sqrt{\kappa^{\hat{c}}}} + \frac{1}{2}$. We can easily show that

$$\Pr\left[\overline{Z}_{\kappa,\hat{c}} > 0\right] = 1 - \Pr\left[\overline{Z}_{\kappa,\hat{c}} \leq 0\right] \geq 1 - \left(\frac{1}{2} + \frac{C\rho}{\sigma^3 \kappa^{2c}}\right) = \frac{1}{2} - \frac{C\rho}{\sigma^3 \kappa^{2c}}$$

Plugging these inequalities in to Eq. (11) we get:

$$\Pr\left[\overline{Z}_{\kappa,\hat{c}} < 0\right] - \Pr\left[\overline{Z}_{\kappa,\hat{c}} > 0\right] \leq \frac{1}{2} + \frac{C\rho}{\sigma^3\sqrt{\kappa^{\hat{c}}}} - \left(\frac{1}{2} - \frac{C\rho}{\sigma^3\sqrt{\kappa^{\hat{c}}}}\right) \leq \frac{2C\rho}{\sigma^3\sqrt{\kappa^{\hat{c}}}}$$

Therefore, we want that for all $c \geq 1$

$$\frac{2C\rho}{\sigma^3\sqrt{\kappa^{\hat{c}}}} < \frac{1}{\kappa^c} \implies \kappa^{\frac{\hat{c}}{2}-c} > \frac{2C\rho}{\sigma^3}$$

By selecting $\hat{c} = 2c + 2$, we get that

$$\kappa > \frac{2C\rho}{\sigma^3}$$

That concludes the proof. □

*Proof (Proof of Lemma 3).* We prove by contradiction. By the fact that $X \gtrsim Y$ we have that for all constants $c \geq 1$, there exist $\hat{c} > c$ and a $\kappa_0 > 0$ such that for all $\kappa \geq \kappa_0$:

$$\Pr\left[\frac{1}{\kappa^{\hat{c}}}\sum_{j=1}^{\kappa^{\hat{c}}} Y^{(j)} \geq \frac{1}{\kappa^{\hat{c}}}\sum_{j=1}^{\kappa^{\hat{c}}} X^{(j)}\right] - \Pr\left[\frac{1}{\kappa^{\hat{c}}}\sum_{j=1}^{\kappa^{\hat{c}}} X^{(j)} \geq \frac{1}{\kappa^{\hat{c}}}\sum_{j=1}^{\kappa^{\hat{c}}} Y^{(j)}\right] < \frac{1}{\kappa^c} \quad (13)$$

where $X^{(j)}, Y^{(j)}$ are i.i.d. samples from $X, Y$ respectively.

For the rest of the proof, it suffices to set $\hat{c} = 4c$. For ease of notation, let us define for fixed but arbitrary $\kappa, c$ the empirical mean random variable of $X, Y$:

$$\overline{X} = \frac{1}{\kappa^{4c}}\sum_{j=1}^{\kappa^{4c}} X^{(j)} \quad \text{and} \quad \overline{Y} = \frac{1}{\kappa^{4c}}\sum_{j=1}^{\kappa^{4c}} Y^{(j)}$$

Assume that $\mathbb{E}[Y] > \mathbb{E}[X]$. Let $\Delta = \mathbb{E}[Y] - \mathbb{E}[X] > 0$ We will show that for all $c \geq 1$ there exists a $\kappa_1$ such that for all $\kappa \geq \kappa_1$ Eq. (13) does not hold. Notice that Lemma 1 does not directly contradict Eq. (13) since the lemma implies $\Pr\left[\overline{Y} > \overline{X}\right] - \Pr\left[\overline{X} > \overline{Y}\right] \geq \frac{1}{\kappa^c}$. We need to show a tighter bound.

Towards the contradiction, we will show that $\Pr\left[\overline{Y} > \overline{X}\right] - \Pr\left[\overline{X} > \overline{Y}\right] \geq \frac{2}{\kappa^c} \geq \frac{1}{\kappa^c}$. Following the same steps as in Lemma 1.

By Hoeffding's inequality, for any $\epsilon > 0$ we have:

$$\Pr\left[\left|\overline{X} - \mathbb{E}[X]\right| \geq \epsilon\right] \leq 2\exp\left(-\frac{2\kappa^{4c}\epsilon^2}{R^2}\right)$$

and

$$\Pr\left[\left|\overline{Y} - \mathbb{E}\left[\overline{Y}\right]\right| \geq \epsilon\right] \leq 2\exp\left(-\frac{2\kappa^{4c}\epsilon^2}{R^2}\right)$$

Setting $\epsilon = \Delta/4$, we have that,

$$\begin{aligned}\Pr\left[\overline{Y} > \overline{X}\right] &\geq \Pr\left[\overline{Y} \geq \mathbb{E}[Y] - \Delta/4\right] \cdot \Pr\left[\overline{X} \leq \mathbb{E}[X] + \Delta/4\right] \\ &\geq \left(1 - 2\exp\left(-\frac{\kappa^{4c}\Delta^2}{8R^2}\right)\right)^2 \geq 1 - 4\exp\left(-\frac{\kappa^{4c}\Delta^2}{8R^2}\right)\end{aligned}$$

To obtain a tighter to contradict Eq. (13) bound we need to find a $\kappa_0$ such that for all $\kappa \geq \kappa_0$ and for all $c$ the $\Pr\left[\overline{Y} > \overline{X}\right] \geq 1/2 + 1/\kappa^c$. That implies $\Pr\left[\overline{X} > \overline{Y}\right] \leq 1/2 - 1/\kappa^c$. Combining the two we get that $\Pr\left[\overline{X} > \overline{Y}\right] - \Pr\left[\overline{Y} > \overline{X}\right] \leq -\frac{2}{\kappa^c}$ which directly contradicts Eq. (13). We can find the number of samples required by

$$\Pr\left[\overline{Y} > \overline{X}\right] \geq 1 - 4\exp\left(-\frac{\kappa^{4c}\Delta^2}{8R^2}\right) \geq 1/2 + \frac{1}{\kappa^c} \Leftrightarrow 4\exp\left(-\frac{\kappa^{4c}\Delta^2}{8R^2}\right) \leq \frac{1}{2} - \frac{1}{\kappa^c}$$

We can easily see that $4\exp\left(-\frac{\kappa^{4c}\Delta^2}{8R^2}\right)$ is a decreasing function of $\kappa$ that goes to 0 as $\kappa$ goes to infinity. On the other hand $\frac{1}{2}-\frac{1}{\kappa^c}$ is an increasing function of $\kappa$ that goes to $1/2$ as $\kappa$ goes to infinity. Furthermore, because of the monotonicity, if the inequality holds for some constant $c$ it also holds for all $c' > c$. Thus, it suffices to show it for $c = 1$. Finally, to show there exists a $\kappa_0$, consider any constant $\epsilon \in (1/2)$ such that $4\exp\left(-\frac{\kappa^4\Delta^2}{8R^2}\right) < \epsilon$ and $\epsilon < 1/2 - 1/\kappa$. Since we want both to be satisfied simultaneously we get

$$\kappa_0 > \max\left\{\frac{8R^2}{\Delta^2}\ln\left(\frac{4}{\epsilon}\right), \frac{2}{1-2\epsilon}\right\}.$$

That concludes the proof of Lemma 3.

□

## References

1. Alwen, J., Katz, J., Maurer, U., Zikas, V.: Collusion-preserving computation. In: Safavi-Naini, R., Canetti, R. (eds.) CRYPTO 2012. LNCS, vol. 7417, pp. 124–143. Springer, Heidelberg (2012). https://doi.org/10.1007/978-3-642-32009-5_9
2. Backes, M., Pfitzmann, B., Waidner, M.: A general composition theorem for secure reactive systems. In: Naor, M. (ed.) TCC 2004. LNCS, vol. 2951, pp. 336–354. Springer, Heidelberg (2004). https://doi.org/10.1007/978-3-540-24638-1_19
3. Bahrani, M., Weinberg, S.M.: Undetectable selfish mining. In: Proceedings of the 25th ACM Conference on Economics and Computation, pp. 1017–1044 (2024)
4. Berry, A.C.: The accuracy of the gaussian approximation to the sum of independent variates. Trans. Am. Math. Soc. **49**(1), 122–136 (1941)
5. Bradford, P.G., Park, S., Rothkopf, M.H., Park, H.: Protocol completion incentive problems in cryptographic vickrey auctions. Electron. Commer. Res. **8**(1–2), 57–77 (2008)
6. Brown-Cohen, J., Narayanan, A., Psomas, A., Weinberg, S.M.: Formal barriers to longest-chain proof-of-stake protocols. In: Proceedings of the 2019 ACM Conference on Economics and Computation, pp. 459–473. (2019)
7. Canetti, R.: Security and composition of multiparty cryptographic protocols. J. Cryptol. **13**(1), 143–202 (2000)
8. Canetti, R.: Universally composable security. J. ACM **67**(5) (2020). https://doi.org/10.1145/3402457
9. Carlsten, M., Kalodner, H., Weinberg, S.M., Narayanan, A.: On the instability of bitcoin without the block reward. In: Proceedings of the 2016 ACM SIGSAC Conference on Computer and Communications Security, pp. 154–167 (2016)
10. Chou, C., Geanakoplos, J.: On finitely repeated games and pseudo-nash equilibria. Cowles Foundation Discussion Papers 777, Cowles Foundation for Research in Economics, Yale University (1985). https://doi.org/None. https://ideas.repec.org/p/cwl/cwldpp/777.html
11. Dodis, Y., Halevi, S., Rabin, T.: A cryptographic solution to a game theoretic problem. In: Bellare, M. (ed.) CRYPTO 2000. LNCS, vol. 1880, pp. 112–130. Springer, Heidelberg (2000). https://doi.org/10.1007/3-540-44598-6_7

12. Essaidi, M., Ferreira, M.V., Weinberg, S.M.: Credible, strategyproof, optimal, and bounded expected-round single-item auctions for all distributions. In: Innovations in Theoretical Computer Science Conference (2022)
13. Esseen, C.G.: On the Liapunov limit error in the theory of probability. Ark. Mat. Astr. Fys. **28**, 1–19 (1942)
14. Eyal, I., Sirer, E.G.: Majority is not enough: bitcoin mining is vulnerable. Commun. ACM **61**(7), 95–102 (2018)
15. Ferreira, M.V., Ganesh, A., Hourigan, J., Huh, H., Weinberg, S.M., Yu, C.: Computing optimal manipulations in cryptographic self-selection proof-of-stake protocols. In: Proceedings of the 25th ACM Conference on Economics and Computation, pp. 676–702 (2024)
16. Ferreira, M.V., Hahn, Y.L.S., Weinberg, S.M., Yu, C.: Optimal strategic mining against cryptographic self-selection in proof-of-stake. In: Proceedings of the 23rd ACM Conference on Economics and Computation, pp. 89–114 (2022)
17. Ferreira, M.V., Weinberg, S.M.: Credible, truthful, and two-round (optimal) auctions via cryptographic commitments. In: Proceedings of the 21st ACM Conference on Economics and Computation, pp. 683–712 (2020)
18. Ferreira, M.V., Weinberg, S.M.: Proof-of-stake mining games with perfect randomness. In: Proceedings of the 22nd ACM Conference on Economics and Computation, pp. 433–453 (2021)
19. Fiat, A., Karlin, A., Koutsoupias, E., Papadimitriou, C.: Energy equilibria in proof-of-work mining. In: Proceedings of the 2019 ACM Conference on Economics and Computation, pp. 489–502. (2019)
20. Fuchsbauer, G., Katz, J., Naccache, D.: Efficient rational secret sharing in standard communication networks. In: Micciancio, D. (ed.) TCC 2010. LNCS, vol. 5978, pp. 419–436. Springer, Heidelberg (2010). https://doi.org/10.1007/978-3-642-11799-2_25
21. Garay, J.A., Katz, J., Maurer, U., Tackmann, B., Zikas, V.: Rational protocol design: cryptography against incentive-driven adversaries. In: FOCS, pp. 648–657. IEEE Computer Society (2013)
22. Goldreich, O.: Foundations of Cryptography: Volume1, Basic Tools. Cambridge University Press, Cambridge (2003)
23. Gordon, S.D., Katz, J.: Rational secret sharing, revisited. In: De Prisco, R., Yung, M. (eds.) SCN 2006. LNCS, vol. 4116, pp. 229–241. Springer, Heidelberg (2006). https://doi.org/10.1007/11832072_16
24. Goren, G., Spiegelman, A.: Mind the mining. In: Proceedings of the 2019 ACM Conference on Economics and Computation, pp. 475–487. ACM, Phoenix (2019)
25. Gradwohl, R., Livne, N., Rosen, A.: Sequential rationality in cryptographic protocols. ACM Trans. Econ. Comput. (TEAC) **1**(1), 1–38 (2013)
26. Halpern, J., Teague, V.: Rational secret sharing and multiparty computation. In: Proceedings of the Thirty-Sixth Annual ACM Symposium on Theory of Computing, pp. 623–632. ACM, Chicago (2004)
27. Halpern, J.Y.: Beyond nash equilibrium: solution concepts for the 21st century. In: Baras, J.S., Katz, J., Altman, E. (eds.) GameSec 2011. LNCS, vol. 7037, pp. 1–3. Springer, Heidelberg (2011). https://doi.org/10.1007/978-3-642-25280-8_1
28. Halpern, J.Y., Pass, R.: Algorithmic rationality: game theory with costly computation. J. Econ. Theory **156**, 246–268 (2015)
29. Halpern, J.Y., Pass, R.: Sequential equilibrium in games of imperfect recall. In: KR, pp. 278–287. ACM (2016)
30. Halpern, J.Y., Pass, R.: Sequential equilibrium in computational games. ACM Trans. Econ. Comput. (TEAC) **7**(2), 1–19 (2019)

31. Halpern, J.Y., Pass, R., Seeman, L.: Not just an empty threat: subgame-perfect equilibrium in repeated games played by computationally bounded players. In: Liu, T.-Y., Qi, Q., Ye, Y. (eds.) WINE 2014. LNCS, vol. 8877, pp. 249–262. Springer, Cham (2014). https://doi.org/10.1007/978-3-319-13129-0_20
32. Halpern, J.Y., Pass, R., Seeman, L.: Computational extensive-form games. In: Proceedings of the 2016 ACM Conference on Economics and Computation, pp. 681–698. ACM, Maastricht (2016)
33. Hoeffding, W.: Probability inequalities for sums of bounded random variables. J. Am. Stat. Assoc. **58**(301), 13–30 (1963)
34. Izmalkov, S., Micali, S., Lepinski, M.: Rational secure computation and ideal mechanism design. In: 46th Annual IEEE Symposium on Foundations of Computer Science (FOCS'05), pp. 585–594. IEEE, IEEE Computer Society, Pittsburgh (2005)
35. Kahneman, D., Tversky, A.: Prospect theory: an analysis of decision under risk. Econometrica **47**(2), 263–291 (1979). http://www.jstor.org/stable/1914185
36. Kiayias, A., Koutsoupias, E., Kyropoulou, M., Tselekounis, Y.: Blockchain mining games. In: Proceedings of the 2016 ACM Conference on Economics and Computation, pp. 365–382. ACM, Maastricht (2016)
37. Kol, G., Naor, M.: Games for exchanging information. In: Proceedings of the Fortieth Annual ACM Symposium on Theory of Computing, pp. 423–432. ACM, Victoria (2008)
38. Lepinksi, M., Micali, S., Shelat, A.: Collusion-free protocols. In: Proceedings of the Thirty-Seventh Annual ACM Symposium on Theory of Computing, pp. 543–552. ACM, Baltimore (2005)
39. Nurmi, H., Salomaa, A.: Cryptographic protocols for Vickrey auctions. Group Decis. Negot. **2**(4), 363–373 (1993)
40. Psomas, A., Terzoglou, A., Wei, Y., Zikas, V.: Pseudo-equilibria, or: How to stop worrying about crypto and just analyze the game. arXiv preprint arXiv:2506.22089 (2025)
41. Sapirshtein, A., Sompolinsky, Y., Zohar, A.: Optimal selfish mining strategies in bitcoin. In: Grossklags, J., Preneel, B. (eds.) FC 2016. LNCS, vol. 9603, pp. 515–532. Springer, Heidelberg (2017). https://doi.org/10.1007/978-3-662-54970-4_30
42. Tsabary, I., Eyal, I.: The gap game. In: Proceedings of the 2018 ACM SIGSAC conference on Computer and Communications Security, pp. 713–728. ACM, Toronto (2018)
43. Tversky, A., Kahneman, D.: Advances in prospect theory: cumulative representation of uncertainty. J. Risk Uncertainty **5**(4), 297–323 (1992). https://EconPapers.repec.org/RePEc:kap:jrisku:v:5:y:1992:i:4:p:297-323
44. Tyagi, N., Arun, A., Freitag, C., Wahby, R., Bonneau, J., Mazières, D.: Riggs: decentralized sealed-bid auctions. In: Proceedings of the 2023 ACM SIGSAC Conference on Computer and Communications Security, pp. 1227–1241. ACM, Copenhagen (2023)

# Security Amplification via Robust Indistinguishability Combiners

Benny Applebaum[1], Nir Bitansky[2], and Nathan Geier[1(✉)]

[1] Tel Aviv University, Tel Aviv, Israel
nathangeier.cs@gmail.com
[2] New York University, New York, USA

**Abstract.** A robust combiner for a cryptographic primitive $P$ takes multiple candidate constructions of $P$ and produces a secure construction of $P$ provided that sufficiently many of the candidates are secure. A closely related notion is that of a security amplifier, where given a weakly secure construction of $P$, we aim to obtain a (strongly) secure one. Intuitively, one may expect that any robust combiner should act as an amplifier by thinking of "good randomness" as inducing secure instances, and of "bad randomness" as inducing insecure instances. Formalizing this intuition, however, has turned out to be challenging. Despite significant progress, general results remain limited and confined either to specific primitives or only to the statistical setting.

We establish a new framework of *robust indistinguishability combiners*, which greatly extends the class of combiners covered by prior work, and prove that they inherently act as security amplifiers. Our results extend to the computational setting, provided that the combiner makes a *single query* to each candidate. The new framework allows us to rederive previously known amplification results in a simplified manner, as well as prove new amplification results that have so far been out of reach.

As our main application, we present the first *security amplifier for functional encryption*, resolving an open question that first arose in constructions of indistinguishability obfuscation, and for which a gap was discovered in previous proofs. Our amplifier transforms a weak scheme with any constant indistinguishability error into one with full negligible security.

**Keywords:** Security amplification · Robust combiners · Functional encryption

## 1 Introduction

*Security amplification* is a fundamental goal in cryptography: given a cryptographic primitive that is weakly secure in some sense, we would like to make it

A full version of this work is available in the Cryptology ePrint Archive, Report 2026/1121 [5].


N. Heninger and M. Rosulek (Eds.): CRYPTO 2026, LNCS 16800, pp. 35–66, 2026.
https://doi.org/10.1007/978-3-032-35367-2_2

strongly secure. It provides a method to guarantee constructions remain secure even if their underlying components exhibit weaknesses, for example due to physical side-channel leakage, an unproven mathematical assumption that turns out to only partially hold, or advances in technology and the computational power of adversaries. It also allows researchers to simplify the task of constructing advanced primitives by letting them aim merely for weak security. Foundational examples of security amplification include Yao's amplification of weak one-way functions (OWFs) and Yao's XOR lemma for amplifying unpredictability [23,49]. This line of research has been extended to public-key encryption (PKE) [19,30,37] and key-agreement (KE) [29], weakly verifiable puzzles [15], oblivious transfer (OT) [16,17,48], non-interactive zero knowledge (NIZK) [8–10,24], and many others.

The notion of *robust combiners* [27,28] is closely related, yet distinct. A $(k, n)$-robust combiner is a construction that takes $n$ candidate schemes and guarantees security as long as at least $k$ of them are secure. Such combiners are typically built using simple secret-sharing techniques, or more sophisticated tools such as secure multiparty computation (MPC) [7,26].

The existence of an amplifier usually implies the existence of a combiner, as one can construct a weakly secure scheme by executing a randomly selected candidate, and then amplify this resulting scheme. Indeed, this is true for all the amplifiers mentioned above. But *does a combiner imply an amplifier*? Such a theorem would be extremely valuable, as amplifiers are typically significantly more challenging to construct and analyze, and often incur substantial additional computational overhead. Moreover, for some primitives only a combiner is known to exist, most notably indistinguishability obfuscation [2,20] and functional encryption [34].

To illustrate the relation between combiners and amplifiers, let us review two classical examples that will be used across the introduction.

*Direct Product.* Given $n$ candidate one-way functions $f_1, \ldots, f_n$, it is straightforward to show that the mapping $(x_1, \ldots, x_n) \mapsto (f_1(x_1), \ldots, f_n(x_n))$ is one-way provided that at least one of the functions is one-way. Thus, the direct product yields a robust combiner. Demonstrating that the same construction also serves as an amplifier is considerably more subtle (see Sect. 2.3 of [22]).

*The XOR Lemma.* Suppose we are given $n$ weakly unpredictable bits $b_1, \ldots, b_n$. Trivially, XOR is a robust combiner: if at least one bit is uniformly distributed, then so is their XOR. However, analyzing the amplification properties of this combiner in the setting where the bits are only computationally weakly unpredictable turns out to be highly nontrivial [23,49]. Furthermore, extending the XOR lemma to bit-strings reveals an inherent barrier to any general combiner-is-amplifier theorem. While the combiner guarantee remains unchanged, amplification may fail for certain parameter regimes. In particular, if all strings are "almost random" except that their first bit is fixed to 0, XOR-based amplification fails dramatically. This underscores the distinction between the inherently "all-or-nothing" nature of combiners and the "consistent small leakage" phenomenon that may arise for weak candidates.

*Secret-Sharing-Based Amplification for Encryption Schemes.* Suppose we are given a public-key encryption scheme with both privacy and correctness error. Concretely, assume that any two encryptions cannot be efficiently distinguished with advantage better than 0.1, and that (honest) decryption fails with probability 0.1 for every message. The problem of amplifying privacy and correctness was studied by [19,30], who obtained amplification results for bit encryption.

For large message spaces, a natural approach is to secret-share the message $m$ into $n$ shares $m_1, \dots, m_n$ using a $t$-out-of-$n$ threshold scheme, say with $t = 0.5n$, that tolerates a 0.2-fraction of corrupted shares (e.g., Shamir's scheme based on Reed-Solomon codes). It is straightforward to show that this yields negligible decryption error. Intuitively, security should follow from the "combining" properties of the scheme. However, no formal analysis of this approach appears to be available in the literature. Indeed, [19] mention a similar idea and note that while the argument goes through for weak *information-theoretic* security, "it is not clear how to carry it through in the computational setting".

Given the above discussion, we ask:

> Is it possible to prove a general theorem that allows us to argue that a given combiner is also an amplifier?

Ideally, such a theorem would lead to new amplifiers, or, at the very least, provide a unified proof for all the above examples, possibly with sub-optimal parameters.

*Related Work: Neutralizing Constructions.* The potential for combiners to function as amplifiers was explored in [36,40,41] through the framework of *neutralizing constructions*. In this framework, a *specification* of a cryptographic primitive is modeled as an ideal "random system" $I$, which can be viewed as a randomized stateful oracle. (For example, in the context of pseudorandom functions, $I$ may be taken to be a truly random function.) Syntactically, a neutralizing construction $C$ is another system that is given oracle access to $n$ candidate constructions $\vec{S} = (S_1, \dots, S_n)$ over some input/output space.

Such a vector of candidates is said to be *$k$-ideal* with respect to a vector of ideal systems $\vec{I} = (I_1, \dots, I_n)$ if at least $k$ out of the $n$ candidates $\vec{S}$ are ideal. The neutralizing property asserts that for every $k$-ideal vector of candidates, the combined construction $C^{\vec{S}}$ behaves *exactly as if all $n$ candidates were ideal*; that is, $C^{\vec{S}} \equiv C^{\vec{I}}$.

It is shown in [36,40,41] that *neutralization implies amplification*: if each candidate is "close" to ideal, then the combined outcome is "close" to the ideal combined distribution $C^{\vec{I}}$. The notion of closeness is defined in [36,40] in an information-theoretic sense (namely, via statistical distance), and is extended in [41] to computational indistinguishability in the special case $k = 1$.

The latter extension yields several elegant amplification theorems. For example, in the case of pseudorandom functions, one can take the ideal oracle to be a truly random function and observe that the XOR construction provides a neutralizing combiner for $k = 1$. More generally, this framework is well suited to "random primitives," such as pseudorandom generators (PRGs), pseudorandom functions (PRFs), and pseudorandom permutations (PRPs). However, it becomes overly restrictive when applied to other cryptographic primitives.

*Limitations of Neutralizing Constructions.* We illustrate this point using secret-sharing based amplification for weak encryption. Ideally, one would like to analyze this construction via the neutralizing-to-amplifier theorem, but it is unclear how to define the appropriate ideal oracle. A natural candidate is a "simulator" that encrypts a fixed message, e.g., the all-zero message. Then, a $k$-ideal vector includes $k$ oracles that ignore their input message and use the weak scheme to encrypt zeros instead. However, this approach fails for two reasons. First, the real encryption is only computationally indistinguishable from the simulation, and the existing theorems do not accommodate this type of approximation when $k > 1$. Second, and more importantly: even in the case $k = 1$, the resulting combiner does not qualify as a "neutralizing construction" with respect to this ideal oracle, despite being a valid combiner. To see this, suppose one of the bad candidates outputs some "recognizable" ciphertext, e.g., reveals its entire input or outputs some fixed string. Then it becomes easy to distinguish between the setting in which all candidates are ideal and the setting in which only one is ideal, violating the neutralizing property.

Indeed, the neutralizing property implicitly requires hiding both which candidate fails and the nature of the failure. In the context of encryption, this is an overkill: we do not need an encryption of $x$ using a $k$-ideal vector $\vec{S}$ to be indistinguishable from an encryption of $x$ using $n$ ideal systems, that is, $C^{\vec{S}}(x) \approx C^{\vec{I}}(x)$. Rather, it suffices to guarantee indistinguishability between encryptions of $x$ and $x'$ whenever a $k$-ideal vector $\vec{S}$ is used, that is, $C^{\vec{S}}(x) \approx C^{\vec{S}}(x')$. For more advanced primitives with simulation-based security, such as NIZK, this distinction becomes even more apparent, since a weak simulator may simply output $\perp$ with some failure probability. In this case, distinguishing between an execution using $n$ (weak) simulators and, say, $n/2$ becomes overwhelmingly easy for most natural combiners.

*Indistinguishability Combiners Are Amplifiers.* The above discussion motivates our new generalized "indistinguishability combiner" notion, requiring indistinguishability between inputs/modes to hold whenever a sufficient number of candidates is ideal. This notion extends the notion of neutralizing constructions and captures all the examples discussed so far, as well as a broad class of known combiners for cryptographic primitives with indistinguishability-based security such as PKE, KA, OT, NIZK, and even OWFs (see the full version). We show that indistinguishability combiners inherently act as amplifiers for statistically weak candidates. Furthermore, we extend this result to the computational setting under the restriction that the combiner makes a single query to each candidate, and guarantees indistinguishability even if the non-ideal candidates are inefficient.

*Security Amplification for Functional Encryption.* As a main application, we employ our theorem to achieve unconditional security amplification for functional encryption (FE), a central cryptographic tool for enabling computation over encrypted inputs, first introduced by [45] and formalized by [12,43]. FE amplification was first studied by [1,3] under the assumption of subexponentially secure LWE, and was later extended to the unconditional setting by Jain et al. [33]. However, a gap was subsequently discovered in their proofs [32], rendering all existing amplification results invalid. We resolve this open problem by taking a fundamentally different approach to the security analysis, using our combiner-is-amplifier theorem. Our construction follows a similar design, refining and improving their implicit FE combiner.

We proceed with a detailed overview of our results.

### 1.1 Our Results

Our first contribution is definitional and conceptual: we introduce a new framework for *indistinguishability combiners* (iC) that overcomes the limitations of existing notions. Roughly speaking, $(s, \varepsilon)$-indistinguishability (i.e., $\varepsilon$-indistinguishability against circuits of size $s$) is guaranteed between inputs/modes whenever at least $k$ out of the $n$ candidates are "ideal". (By taking $s = \infty$, this definition also captures statistical indistinguishability.) The actual definition may at first appear somewhat technical and non-intuitive, but we will later explain how to adapt it to different settings (see Example 1 below).

An indistinguishability combiner consists of two $n$-oracle-aided algorithms $(C_0^{(\cdot)}, C_1^{(\cdot)})$. Its security guarantee, parameterized by $(s, \varepsilon, k, n)$ and a vector of "ideal" oracles $\vec{I} = (I_1, \ldots, I_n)$, is the following: For every $k$-ideal vector of $n$ candidates $\vec{S} = (S_1, \ldots, S_n)$, the distributions

$$C_0^{\vec{S}} \quad \text{and} \quad C_1^{\vec{S}} \tag{1}$$

are $(s, \varepsilon)$-indistinguishable. (Recall that a vector is $k$-ideal if there exists a subset $T \subseteq [n]$ of size at least $k$ for which $S_i$ behaves identically to $I_i$ for all $i \in T$.) Importantly, the indistinguishability requirement (1) uses the same $k$-ideal oracles $\vec{S}$ over different input distributions, and does not compare directly to the all-ideal oracles as in the case of neutralizing constructions ($C^{\vec{S}} \equiv C^{\vec{I}}$). Nevertheless, neutralizing constructions fit naturally within this framework: one may let $C_0^{\vec{S}}$ execute $C^{\vec{S}}$ normally, while $C_1^{\vec{S}}$ ignores its oracle access and directly implements the ideal functionality $C^{\vec{I}}$. Under this choice, indistinguishability of the two modes is precisely the standard neutralization requirement, showing that our formulation strictly generalizes the traditional one. As we shall see, this seemingly minor reformulation turns out to be surprisingly powerful.

We utilize this definition dynamically: in the analysis of a proposed amplifier, after fixing a weak candidate, a security game and an adversary, the combiner's definition is tailored to them. For example, a (non-adaptive) challenge chosen by the adversary can be embedded into the combiner as hardcoded non-uniform advice. Moreover, as we will later see, the definition of the ideal oracle is often based on the concrete (weak) implementation of the primitive and even on a fixed adversary.

We first show that in the setting where the underlying candidates are statistically close to ideal (to some secure construction), any indistinguishability combiner acts as an amplifier, even if the guaranteed indistinguishability is merely computational. (See Theorem 1 for formal statement).

**Informal Theorem 1 (iCombiner is Statistical Amplifier).** *Let* $(C_0^{(\cdot)}, C_1^{(\cdot)})$ *be an* $(s, \varepsilon, k, n)$ *indistinguishability combiner with respect to ideal oracles* $\vec{I}$. *Let* $\vec{R} = (R_1, \ldots, R_n)$ *be a vector of candidates where each* $R_i$ *is* statistically $\delta$*-close to ideal* $I_i$ *for* $\delta < 0.5$. *Then,* $C_0^{\vec{R}}$ *and* $C_1^{\vec{R}}$ *are* $(s,\ \delta' + \varepsilon')$*-indistinguishable for*

$$\delta' := \binom{n}{k-1}(2\delta)^{n-k+1}, \quad \textit{and} \quad \varepsilon' := \varepsilon \cdot \min\left(\binom{n}{k}, (1-2\delta)^{-k}\right).$$

Some remarks are in order.

- Recall that $\delta < 0.5$ is an inherent limitation of any general combiner-is-amplifier theorem, as demonstrated by the XOR example for weakly random strings whose first bit is fixed to 0.
- Note that $\delta'$ can be upper-bounded by $\delta' \leq (2\delta \cdot en/(n-k+1))^{n-k+1}$; this looser bound is often useful for a large $k$. For example, for $k = n/2$, we get that $\delta' \leq (4e\delta)^{n/2}$.
- If the combiner is imperfect with $\varepsilon > 0$, in order to ensure the error term $\varepsilon'$ does not blow up, we usually want $\binom{n}{k}$ to be polynomial in the security parameter $\lambda$ (e.g., $k < n = O(\log \lambda)$ or $k = O(1), n = \lambda$) or $\delta$ to be small enough (e.g., $\delta < 0.4/k$).

Next, we extend the above result to the setting where candidates are merely computationally close to ideal, provided the combiner makes a single, non-adaptive query to each candidate. By doing so, we implicitly limit the security notion to being "non-adaptive". (See the full version for a detailed discussion of the model's limitations and for some extensions.) We note that even if the combiner makes multiple queries, as long as they are non-adaptive, we can usually view it as a single-query combiner with batch queries (potentially increasing the indistinguishability error).

**Informal Theorem 2 (iCombiner is Computational Amplifier).** *Given an* $(s, \varepsilon, k, n)$ single-query *indistinguishability combiner* $(C_0^{(\cdot)}, C_1^{(\cdot)})$ *and candidates* $\vec{R} = (R_1, \ldots, R_n)$ *where each* $R_i$ *is* computationally $(s, \delta)$*-close to ideal for* $\delta < 0.5$, $C_0^{\vec{R}}$ *and* $C_1^{\vec{R}}$ *are* $(s \cdot \gamma^2 - \max_{b \in \{0,1\}} \mathrm{size}(C_b^{\vec{R}}),\ \delta' + \varepsilon' + n\gamma)$*-indistinguishable for any "slackness" parameter* $\gamma \in (0,1)$, *with*

$$\delta' := \binom{n}{k-1}(2\delta)^{n-k+1}, \quad \varepsilon' := \varepsilon \cdot \min\left(\binom{n}{k}, (1-2\delta)^{-k}\right).$$

Intuitively, the slackness parameter $\gamma$ represents the precision with which our reduction estimates probabilities. Higher precision (smaller $\gamma$) requires a longer running time (proportional to $1/\gamma^2$), creating a trade-off. A formal version of the theorem appears as Theorem 2.

*Example 1 (Secret-Sharing-Based Amplification of Weak Encryption).* With the aid of Informal Theorem 2, we analyze the previously described secret-sharing based amplifier for encryption. Let $n$ take the role of the security parameter. Given a message $m$, the amplifier $C$ secret-shares it into $n$ shares $m_1, \ldots, m_n$, queries its $n$ oracles $\vec{R} = (R_1, \ldots, R_n)$ (each an encryption scheme with an independent key) on the corresponding shares, and outputs the ciphertexts $R_1(m_1), \ldots, R_n(m_n)$. Suppose we use a $(t = 0.5n)$-out-of-$n$ secret-sharing scheme that is robust against a 0.2-fraction of errors. Correctness amplification is immediate using Chernoff. For security: Our goal is to show that for every pair of messages $x_0, x_1$, the corresponding ciphertext distributions $C_0^{\vec{R}} := C(x_0)$ and $C_1^{\vec{R}} := C(x_1)$ are computationally indistinguishable even if $R_i$ is instantiated with weakly-secure encryption scheme.

We apply Informal Theorem 2 as follows. Define the $i$-th ideal oracle by $I_i(m_i) := R_i(\mathbf{0})$, namely, an oracle that ignores its input share and outputs an encryption of the all-zero message under the $i$-th scheme. For these choices, $(C_0^{(\cdot)}, C_1^{(\cdot)})$ is a single-query $(k = n - t + 1)$-out-of-$n$ *perfect* indistinguishability combiner with parameters $s = \infty$ and $\varepsilon = 0$. Indeed, for every $k$-ideal vector of oracles $\vec{S}$, the output distribution of $C$ depends only on $< t$ shares (corresponding to bad candidates) and hence becomes independent of the input message $x_b$. We now consider the case in which each $R_i$ is instantiated with a $(\delta = 0.1)$-private encryption scheme. Then the real and ideal oracles are $\delta$-indistinguishable by polynomial-size adversaries, and the theorem yields $\delta' \leq 2^n \cdot 0.2^{n/2} \leq 2^{-\Omega(n)}$ and $\varepsilon' = 0$. Consequently, $C_0^{\vec{R}}$ and $C_1^{\vec{R}}$ cannot be efficiently distinguished with non-negligible advantage (better than $2^{-\Omega(n)} + \alpha(n)$ for an arbitrary inverse polynomial $\alpha(\cdot)$), establishing the security of the amplifier.[1] $\diamond$

Additional examples appear in the full version.

Finally, as our main application, we obtain the first unconditional security amplification result for functional encryption. To this end, we construct a new FE combiner, building on and extending the techniques of [33], and then apply the combiner-to-amplifier theorem (Theorem 2).

**Informal Theorem 3 (See Theorems 5 and 6).** *For any constant $\delta < 1/(6e)$, any $\delta$-weak functional encryption scheme can be unconditionally amplified to full security, achieving negligible (resp., subexponential) error provided the base scheme is weakly secure against polynomial-size (resp., subexponential-size) adversaries.*

The above implies FE amplification starting with any constant error, as we can reduce it to any smaller constant using nesting as observed by [33].

[1] If the base scheme is (subexp, $\delta$)-secure, we can reduce the distinguishing advantage to 1/subexp as well.

**Informal Corollary 1.** *For any constant $\delta < 1$, any $\delta$-weak functional encryption scheme can be unconditionally amplified to full security, achieving negligible (resp., subexponential) error provided the base scheme is weakly secure against polynomial-size (resp., subexponential-size) adversaries.*

*Computational Theorem Limitations.* Let us briefly point out the two limitations of our computational combiner-is-amplifier theorem: First, we view each candidate as a randomized function that can be accessed at most once. In particular, this only allows us to accommodate weakly selective security (and not adaptive security). For some primitives, such as CPA-secure public-key encryption, this may not be sufficient for direct amplification; although in the case of PKE (as well as some other cases) selective security can be later upgraded to (adaptive) CPA security. Second, the combiner must guarantee indistinguishability even when the non-ideal candidates are inefficient. For a detailed discussion of these limitations and potential extensions, see the full version.

### 1.2 Organization

A full version of this work is available in the Cryptology ePrint Archive, Report 2026/1121 [5]. In Sect. 2, we provide a technical overview of our techniques. Section 3 introduces the necessary preliminaries. Sections 4 and 5 present our core amplification theorems for the statistically close and computationally close oracle models, respectively. Finally, in Sect. 6, we apply this framework to the amplification of functional encryption.

## 2 Technical Overview

The idea that robust combiners should act as natural security amplifiers is quite intuitive. For the sake of this discussion, let us focus on $(1, n)$ combiners. Say we are given such a combiner $C$ and a candidate $R$ that is $\delta$-close to ideal $I$, then one might hope $C^{\vec{R}}$ achieves $\delta^n$ security. This intuition relies on the assumption that with probability $1 - \delta$ the real candidate behaves ideally and otherwise fails, or more formally that $R \equiv (1-\delta)I+\delta F$ for some residual "failure" candidate $F$. However, standard notions of closeness such as statistical distance (maximal distinguishing advantage) do not offer us that guarantee. Specifically, conditioning on an "agreement event" could bias the behavior of the ideal system. To demonstrate this, let us get back to the XOR-amplification example from the introduction. Consider $R \equiv (0, U_{m-1})$ and $I \equiv U_m$, where $U_m \leftarrow \{0,1\}^m$ and $\equiv$ denotes equality in distribution. Then $R \overset{\mathsf{s}}{\approx}_{0.5} I$ (i.e., their statistical distance is 0.5), yet we cannot write $R \equiv 0.5I + 0.5F$ for any distribution $F$, since strings starting with 1 have positive mass under $I$ but zero mass under $R$. Indeed, as already mentioned, in the case that $C$ is the XOR combiner, we do not achieve any amplification at all.

Although the above argument does not go through as stated, the underlying intuition can be formalized with a more careful coupling-based analysis. It is well known that if random variables $R$ and $I$ satisfy $R \overset{\mathsf{s}}{\approx}_\delta I$, then there exists a joint distribution $(X, Y)$ with marginals $R, I$ such that $\Pr[X = Y] = 1 - \delta$. Lanzenberger and Maurer [36] proved that this fundamental property generalizes to the setting of random systems. Another way to interpret it is that we can write $R \equiv (1-\delta)S + \delta R'$ and $I \equiv (1-\delta)S + \delta I'$ for some shared system $S$ and residual failure systems $R', I'$. We refer to this below as *the system decomposition lemma.*

### 2.1 The Statistical Setting

Using the above lemma in the setting of $(k, n)$ combiners, we decompose the systems one by one. Specifically, replacing the last system $R_n$ with ideal $I_n$ results in a $(k-1, n-1)$ combiner, and replacing it with one of the failure systems $R'_n, I'_n$ results in a $(k, n-1)$ combiner. (We do not replace with $S_n$ as it cancels out.) Explicitly, for $b \in \{0, 1\}$, we have

$$C_b^{\vec{R}_n} \equiv (1-\delta) \cdot C_b^{\vec{R}_{n-1}, S_n} + \delta \cdot C_b^{\vec{R}_{n-1}, R'_n},$$
$$C_b^{\vec{R}_{n-1}, I_n} \equiv (1-\delta) \cdot C_b^{\vec{R}_{n-1}, S_n} + \delta \cdot C_b^{\vec{R}_{n-1}, I'_n},$$

yielding the following upper bound on $\Delta(C_0^{\vec{R}_n}, C_1^{\vec{R}_n})$:

$$\Delta(C_0^{\vec{R}_{n-1}, I_n}, C_1^{\vec{R}_{n-1}, I_n}) + \delta \cdot \Delta(C_0^{\vec{R}_{n-1}, R'_n}, C_1^{\vec{R}_{n-1}, R'_n}) + \delta \cdot \Delta(C_0^{\vec{R}_{n-1}, I'_n}, C_1^{\vec{R}_{n-1}, I'_n}),$$

and the recurrence relation $\Delta(k, n) \leq \Delta(k-1, n-1) + 2\delta \cdot \Delta(k, n-1)$, for the absolute value of distinguishing between $(C_0^{(\cdot)}, C_1^{(\cdot)})$. For the base cases, $k = 0$ means we have satisfied the sufficient ideal systems requirement, so we can use the security guarantee of the combiner $\Delta(0, n) = \varepsilon$. On the other hand, $k = n$ means we are out of options and need to switch all remaining systems to ideal. A simple hybrid argument gives us $\vec{R} \overset{\mathsf{s}}{\approx}_{n \cdot \delta} \vec{I}$, yielding $\Delta(n, n) = 2n \cdot \delta + \varepsilon$ due to

$$C_0^{\vec{R}_n} \overset{\mathsf{s}}{\approx}_{n \cdot \delta} C_0^{\vec{I}_n} \overset{\mathsf{s}}{\approx}_{\varepsilon} C_1^{\vec{I}_n} \overset{\mathsf{s}}{\approx}_{n \cdot \delta} C_1^{\vec{R}_n}.$$

Finally, using Pascal's rule $\binom{n}{k} = \binom{n-1}{k-1} + \binom{n-1}{k}$ and $2\delta < 1$, we derive $\delta'(k, n) \leq \binom{n}{k-1}(2\delta)^{n-k+1}$ and $\varepsilon'(k, n) \leq \binom{n}{k}\varepsilon$. In the full proof, we improve these bounds with a tight analysis of the recurrence relation by counting grid paths, and a tighter bound than the hybrid argument's $n \cdot \delta$. We also derive another upper bound $\varepsilon'(k, n) \leq \varepsilon(1 - 2\delta)^{-k}$, which is useful if $\binom{n}{k}$ is too large and $\delta$ is small enough.

*Comparison with Prior Techniques.* We note that our proof technique extends to neutralizing constructions, where in fact we could shave a factor 2 off $\delta'$ due to the base case $(n, n)$ switching between $\vec{R}$ and $\vec{I}$ only once. In comparison, the bound of [36, Theorem 3] for $\delta'(k, n)$ is slightly tighter than ours, with the simplified bound above being the leading term in both cases. For example, for

$(k,n) = (2,3)$, the simplified bound is $6\delta^2$, our tighter bound is $6\delta^2 - 2\delta^3$ and their tighter bound is $6\delta^2 - 3\delta^3$. Furthermore, they are able to capture weaker neutralizing constructions where non-ideal systems must be real. On the other hand, their proof is more complex and their theorem is limited to the case where the combiner is *perfect*, i.e., the combiner's error $\varepsilon$ is assumed to be zero. Indeed, the technique from [36] seems unsuitable for dealing with a non-zero error $\varepsilon > 0$ (which is crucial for computational constructions).

Let us illustrate this point with an overview of the technique used for the simpler case $k = 1$, introduced by [40] (see also [46, Section 4.2.1]) and extended to $k > 1$ by [36] using a related approach with similar limitations. The idea is to use the XOR lemma to argue that for $R, I$ with $R \overset{\mathsf{s}}{\approx}_\delta I$, the following oracles are $\delta^n$-close: in $\vec{S}_{\text{Odd}}$ each candidate is randomly chosen to be real/ideal conditioned on the total number of ideal oracles being odd, and $\vec{S}_{\text{Even}}$ is similarly defined. Since $\vec{S}_{\text{Odd}}$ always contains at least one ideal candidate, according to the definition of a $(1,n)$ neutralizing construction, we have $C^{\vec{S}_{\text{Odd}}} \equiv C^{\vec{I}}$. As for $\vec{S}_{\text{Even}}$, the only case where there is no ideal candidate is the all-real $\vec{R}$, occurring with probability $2^{-n+1}$. We conclude that $C^{\vec{I}} \overset{\mathsf{s}}{\approx}_{\delta^n} (1-2^{-n+1}) \cdot C^{\vec{I}} + 2^{-n+1} \cdot C^{\vec{R}}$, and hence $C^{\vec{I}} \overset{\mathsf{s}}{\approx}_{(2\delta)^n/2} C^{\vec{R}}$. However, if we try to add an error $\varepsilon$ to the security guarantee, it is multiplied by a factor $2^n$, which could very well make it greater than 1. In comparison, our $\varepsilon'$ bound grows at most by a factor $\min(n, 1/(1-2\delta))$ for $k = 1$, which is just some constant for any constant $\delta < 0.5$.

## 2.2 The Computational Setting

To extend the combiner-is-amplifier theorem to the computational setting, we must address two weaknesses in the underlying hypothesis: (1) the combiner itself guarantees only computational security (provided that $k$ candidates are secure); and (2) the weak candidates are only computationally close to ideal. We observe that the first item can be handled with no change to the proof, by considering the distinguishing advantage of a specific adversary $D$ over $(C_0^{\vec{R}}, C_1^{\vec{R}})$. The second item requires additional care and is addressed using the hardcore lemma, as explained below.

We briefly mention that, to the best of our knowledge, item (1) has not been studied in the neutralizing constructions literature. Moreover, as discussed above, the techniques of [36] are generally not suitable for accommodating a nonzero error, even in the statistical case. For (2), Maurer and Tessaro [41] proved a tight neutralizing bound of $(2\delta)^n/2$ for the special case $k = 1$, and extended their result to computationally weak cc-stateless candidates.[2] However, as we will see, this result imposes a strong requirement on the indistinguishability properties of the underlying primitives, specifically indistinguishability under multiple queries.

[2] The system selects a fixed query-response behavior upfront, and maintains no history.

*The Hardcore Lemma.* A central tool for extending statistical bounds to the computational setting is the Hardcore Lemma [29,31]. Impagliazzo [31] originally introduced the lemma to structure mild hardness of decision problems into a dense "hard core" set of inputs, and Holenstein later provided a uniform and tighter proof [29]. We utilize the hardcore lemma here in its indistinguishability formulation [9,42]. This formulation can be viewed as the computational analogue of coupling. Recall that for statistically close random variables $R \overset{\mathsf{s}}{\approx}_\delta I$, coupling guarantees that we can write $R \equiv (1-\delta)S + \delta R'$ and $I \equiv (1-\delta)S + \delta I'$. The hardcore lemma provides a similar guarantee for computationally close random variables $R \overset{\mathsf{c}}{\approx}_\delta I$, but with a relaxation: instead of a single identical core, the random variables decompose into two distinct but computationally indistinguishable cores $S_R$ and $S_I$. Explicitly, this allows us to write $R \equiv (1-\delta)S_R + \delta R'$ and $I \equiv (1-\delta)S_I + \delta I'$, where $S_R \overset{\mathsf{c}}{\approx} S_I$. In particular, as observed by [9], for the hybrid $H := (1-\delta)S_I + \delta R'$ we have $R \overset{\mathsf{c}}{\approx} H \overset{\mathsf{s}}{\approx}_\delta I$. Getting back to the setting of indistinguishability combiners, this allows us to reduce the computational setting to the statistical setting; that is, we first obtain the statistical bound for $\vec{H}$ and $\vec{I}$, and then switch to $\vec{R}$ which is indistinguishable under efficient transformations.

A significant hurdle is that the hardcore lemma *fails for general interactive systems* because the reduction requires rewinding, which is incompatible with stateful interaction [25]. Tessaro [47] generalized the lemma to cc-stateless systems (where rewinding is not an issue), but their technique inherently requires the systems to be $\delta$-indistinguishable under many queries. This may be natural for primitives like PRFs or PRPs, but for general cryptographic primitives weakness is often quantified with respect to "one-shot" security games.[3] We observe that the hybrid methodology above can be extended to the single-query setting, because if for every query $q \in \mathcal{Q}$ we have $R(q) \overset{\mathsf{c}}{\approx}_\delta I(q)$, then we can invoke the random variable version to obtain $R(q) \overset{\mathsf{c}}{\approx} H(q) \overset{\mathsf{s}}{\approx}_\delta I(q)$, and define the single-query system $H$ accordingly. Some care is needed here, though, because $H$ may very well be an inefficient system. Still, we observe that for single-query systems $R \overset{\mathsf{c}}{\approx} H$, the hybrid argument $\vec{R} \overset{\mathsf{c}}{\approx} \vec{H}$ still works even if only $\vec{R}$ is efficient, intuitively because we can fix the queries and their responses one by one as non-uniform advice. This $\vec{R} \leftrightarrow \vec{H}$ switching technique allows us to generalize the statistical bound to the computational single-query setting. Intuitively, the fact that $H$ may be inefficient relates to the fact that our combiner must withstand inefficient "bad" candidates (that are explainable by the base real/ideal systems).

## 2.3 FE Amplification

Finally, we demonstrate the usefulness of our single-query combiner-is-amplifier theorem by obtaining the first unconditional security amplification for functional encryption. To be more precise, the underlying combiner is computational,

3 This reflects the goal of amplifying the weakest qualitative guarantee that can be lifted into a standard security notion.

assuming OWFs, but since weak FE implies OWFs we do not require any additional assumption.

*Functional Encryption.* Roughly speaking, a functional encryption scheme allows us to encrypt messages $\mathsf{CT} \leftarrow \mathsf{FE.Enc}(x)$ and generate functional keys $\mathsf{FSK}_f \leftarrow \mathsf{FE.Keygen}(f)$ for functional decryption $f(x) \leftarrow \mathsf{FE.Dec}(\mathsf{FSK}_f, \mathsf{CT})$. (Our technique is oblivious to whether the underlying weak FE is public key or secret key, hence we omit that.) We require *single-key security*,[4] meaning that given two messages $x$ and $x'$ such that $f(x) = f(x')$, an adversary cannot tell encryptions of $x$ and $x'$ apart, even if they are given $\mathsf{FSK}_f$—we refer to this as IND-security. An alternative security notion is that $(\mathsf{CT}, \mathsf{FSK}_f)$ can be simulated given only $(f, f(x))$—we refer to this as SIM-security. Our amplifier constructs an IND-secure FE given a weak SIM-secure FE, and we rely on the fact that these two definitions are essentially equivalent (see the full version).

A crucial property in FE applications is *succinctness*—the complexity of the encryption algorithm must not scale with the circuit size $|f|$. In fact, without succinctness, FE can be constructed from a plain encryption scheme [44] (and in particular can be easily amplified). Therefore, it is essential that the constructed amplifier preserves succinctness.

*Limitations of Existing FE Combiners.* In order to use our combiner-is-amplifier theorem, we need an FE combiner. FE combiners are studied explicitly in [34] and implicitly in [33].[5] Both works employ MPC-based techniques in the form of *homomorphic secret sharing* (HSS) [13,14]. However, we cannot use these combiners directly in our theorem for several reasons. First, the combiner of [34] sends multiple queries to each candidate. In addition, the amplifier construction presented in [33] does not induce a proper combiner with negligible error for a constant $\delta$. More importantly, we require our combiner to remain secure even against *inefficient bad candidates*, which necessitates a stronger "semi-malicious" privacy notion from the underlying MPC (or HSS) protocol. To address these limitations, we present a new FE combiner that builds on the HSS-based approach of [33,34], while introducing several important modifications.

*Homomorphic Secret Sharing (HSS).* Roughly speaking, we require the following (somewhat non-standard) variant of an $n$-party HSS scheme. Given an input $x$, a sharing algorithm $\mathsf{HSS.Share}(x)$ splits $x$ into $n$ shares $(x_1, \ldots, x_n)$, each of size $|x| \cdot \mathrm{poly}(\lambda)$. Intuitively, each of these shares will be given to an *HSS party*. Given a public target function $f$, the procedure $\mathsf{HSS.Eval}(f, i, \cdot)$ generates, for every party $i \in [n]$, a local processing function $f_i$ of size $|f| \cdot \mathrm{poly}(\lambda)$. Each $f_i$ is applied to the corresponding local share, producing an output share $y_i = f_i(x_i)$. Finally, given all the output shares $(y_1, \ldots, y_n)$, the value $f(x)$ can be recovered

[4] The literature contains additional notions of FE, such as *collusion-resistant* FE. We focus on the single key notion for its simplicity and the fact that it is already expressive enough to imply all other common notions of FE.

[5] While the construction of [33] lacks a proof that it serves as an amplifier, it does seem to work as a combiner.

by applying a decoder $\mathsf{HSS.Dec}(y_1, \ldots, y_n)$. Unlike the standard setting of HSS, we impose no "simplicity" requirement on the decoder. However, note that the shares are independent of the target function, and their size depends only on the security parameter.

Just like in standard secret-sharing (or MPC protocols), security is parameterized with a threshold $t \in [n]$, and we require that the shares $x_T = (x_i)_{i \in T}$ of any $t$-bounded corrupted subset $T \subseteq [n]$ should be independent of $x$. Moreover, just like in standard MPC protocols, we should be able to jointly simulate $x_T$ together with the outputs of the "honest" parties $y_{\overline{T}} = (y_i)_{i \notin T}$ based on $f$ and the output $f(x)$. We refer to this notion of security as *t-out-of-n privacy.* Jumping ahead, we will soon see that a somewhat stronger notion of security is needed.

*HSS-Based Amplification.* The above notion of HSS naturally gives rise to an FE amplifier, analogous to the SS-based combiner used for standard encryption schemes. Specifically, given a weak FE candidate $\mathsf{FE}^w$, the encryption algorithm $\mathsf{CT} \leftarrow \mathsf{FE.Enc}(x)$ first computes shares $(x_1, \ldots, x_n) \leftarrow \mathsf{HSS.Share}(x)$ and then encrypts each share independently as $\mathsf{CT}_i \leftarrow \mathsf{FE.Enc}_i^w(x_i)$ under $\mathsf{FE}^w$, using fresh keys. The functional-key generation $\mathsf{FSK}_f \leftarrow \mathsf{FE.Keygen}(f)$ proceeds by computing $\mathsf{FSK}_{f_i} \leftarrow \mathsf{FE.Keygen}_i^w(f_i)$ for functions defined as $f_i := \mathsf{HSS.Eval}(f, i, \cdot)$. Finally, functional decryption $y \leftarrow \mathsf{FE.Dec}(\mathsf{FSK}_f, \mathsf{CT})$ evaluates $y_i \leftarrow \mathsf{FE.Dec}_i^w(\mathsf{FSK}_{f_i}, \mathsf{CT}_i)$ and reconstructs the output as $y := \mathsf{HSS.Dec}(y_1, \ldots, y_n)$. Correctness follows directly from the correctness of the weak FE and HSS. Succinctness relies on the fact that the HSS function and share sizes grow only by a factor polynomial in the security parameter.

The main idea of the security analysis is as follows. We are given a weak FE candidate, a function $f$, and inputs $x, x'$ such that $f(x) = f(x') = y$. We define a single-query indistinguishability combiner that, given either $x$ or $x'$, first shares it as $(x_1, \ldots, x_n)$, and then sends to each oracle $i$ the query $(x_i, y_i)$, where $y_i = f_i(x_i)$. The real oracle $R_i(x_i, y_i)$ ignores $y_i$ and returns $(\mathsf{CT}_i, \mathsf{FSK}_{f_i})$, namely an encryption of $x_i$ together with a functional key for $f_i$. The ideal oracle $I_i(x_i, y_i)$ ignores $x_i$ and returns a simulated ciphertext and functional key pair, as produced by the weak FE simulator $\mathsf{FE.Sim}^w(f_i, y_i)$. By the security of the weak FE scheme, the real and ideal oracles are $\delta$-computationally close. Thus, to invoke our main theorem and obtain amplification, it remains to show that the above construction forms a secure combiner with respect to the ideal oracles.

At a high level, we show that if at least $k = n - t + 1$ of the oracles are "good"—namely, behave ideally (like the simulator) and therefore depend only on $y_i$—then computational indistinguishability is preserved between using $x$ or $x'$ as input. Indeed, for any $t$-subset of bad oracles $T \subseteq [n]$, we can use the HSS simulator to simulate $x_T$ and $y_{[n]} = (y_i)_{i \in [n]}$ (based on the output $y = f(x)$ and the function $f$), and then feed $(x_i, y_i)$ to "bad" oracles $i \in T$ and $(\perp, y_i)$ to "good" oracles $i \notin T$.

However, some care is required, since the combining property must hold even when the "bad" candidates are *inefficient* and the simulation security is only *computational.* To address this, we strengthen the privacy guarantees of the underlying HSS so that security holds even against *computationally unbounded* corrupted parties. Concretely, it suffices to require that the corresponding shares $x_T \leftarrow \mathsf{HSS.Share}(x)$ are distributed independently of $x$, and that the simulator operates correctly for any *semi-malicious* choice of shares $x_T$. Specifically, the simulation $(y_1, \ldots, y_n) \leftarrow \mathsf{HSS.Sim}(f, y, T, x_T)$ should succeed for any fixed valid (i.e., in the support) choice of shares $x_T$ provided to the bad candidates. In our amplification proof, this property allows us to arbitrarily fix the inputs and outputs of the "bad" oracles and treat them as non-uniform advice.[6] For a high-level comparison detailing how our use of the hardcore lemma avoids the simulation flaw of prior work [33], see Remark 3.

*Constructing HSS.* We construct the required HSS primitive using a combination of 3-party-local multiparty randomized encoding (MPRE) [6] and an elegant virtualization technique from [33]. We now describe the construction.

For a target function $f$ and a parameter $m$, we first define an $m$-party functionality $f^{\oplus}(z_1, \ldots, z_m)$, in which each party $i \in [m]$ provides an additive share $z_i$ of an input $z$. The functionality reconstructs $z$ and outputs $f(z)$ to all parties. We then construct a 3-party-local MPRE for $f^{\oplus}$.

At a high level, $f^{\oplus}$ is "encoded" by a functionality $\hat{f}((z_1, r_1), \ldots, (z_m, r_m))$ that takes as input each party's share $z_i$ together with private randomness $r_i$. Given a sample from $\hat{f}(\vec{z}, \vec{r})$ (for uniformly random $r_i$'s), one can efficiently recover $f^{\oplus}(\vec{z})$. Conversely, given $f^{\oplus}(\vec{z})$, one can simulate $\hat{f}(\vec{z}, \vec{r})$ along with the local views $(z_i, r_i)_{i \in T}$ for any strict subset $T \subsetneq [m]$ of the parties. (In fact, we will require a semi-malicious notion of security here as well.) The MPRE $\hat{f}$ is 3-party local, meaning that it can be decomposed into functions $\{\hat{f}_{i,j,k}\}_{i,j,k \in [m]}$, where each $\hat{f}_{i,j,k}$ depends only on inputs from parties $i, j, k$. We construct such an MPRE from one-way functions using standard techniques.

Next, for appropriate choices of $t$ and $n$ (discussed below), we construct a $t$-out-of-$n$ HSS using the virtualization technique of [33]. We begin by splitting the input $x$ into $m$ additive shares $z_1, \ldots, z_m$, and use the MPRE to define $m$ virtual MPRE parties, where the $i$th party holds $(z_i, r_i)$. Then, we group the $m$ MPRE parties into $n$ subsets $S_1, \ldots, S_n \subseteq [m]$, each representing an HSS party $S_j$ that "contains" all MPRE parties indexed by $S_j$. Accordingly, the share of the $j$th HSS party is $(z_i, r_i)_{i \in S_j}$, and its local computation $f_j$ corresponds to the MPRE computations $(\hat{f}_{i_1,i_2,i_3})_{i_1,i_2,i_3 \in S_j}$ over all triples $(i_1, i_2, i_3)$ contained in $S_j$.

The subsets are required to satisfy two combinatorial properties: (1) for correctness, every triple $\{i_1, i_2, i_3\}$ must be covered by some subset $S_j$; and (2) for privacy (parameterized by $t \in [n]$), the union of any $t$ subsets should not cover

[6] Note that although the corrupted HSS parties may be computationally unbounded, the simulation itself is only required to be computational. Put differently, $x_T$ (and $y_T$) are statistically independent of $x$, whereas the joint distribution $(x_T, (y_i)_{i \in [n]})$ is only computationally indistinguishable with respect to $x$. This non-standard combination of information-theoretic and computational security is a central ingredient in our amplification result.

all elements of $[m]$. In [33], a randomized construction of such subsets is used, but it incurs an error that is too large for our setting.[7]

To address this, we provide two explicit deterministic constructions of subsets that incur no error. The first achieves $t = n/3$ at the cost of taking $m$ to be exponential in $n$, forcing $n$ to be logarithmic in the security parameter $\lambda$. In the second construction, we settle for $t = \Theta(n^{1/3})$, which allows $m$ to be polynomial in $n$ and thus $n$ can be taken to be $\text{poly}(\lambda)$. Instantiating our combiner with the first construction yields our main FE amplifier, which achieves full security with negligible error. Finally, by combining both amplifiers, we extend our results to the subexponential security regime. For further details, see the full version.

## 3 Preliminaries

For $n \in \mathbb{N}$, we denote by $[n]$ the set $\{1, \dots, n\}$. For a sequence $(x_1, \dots, x_n)$ and a subset $V \subseteq [n]$, we denote by $x_V$ the subsequence corresponding to indices in $V$. For a distribution $X$ over a finite set $\mathcal{X}$, we use $x \leftarrow X$ to denote the result of sampling according to $X$, and $x \leftarrow \mathcal{X}$ to denote a uniformly random sample from the set.

We adopt standard cryptographic notation, including polynomial bounds, negligible functions, and size-bounded circuit families, to define statistical and computational indistinguishability (denoted by $\overset{\mathsf{s}}{\approx}$ and $\overset{\mathsf{c}}{\approx}$) for random variables and ensembles. For more details, see the full version.

### 3.1 Finite Discrete Systems

In this paper, we focus on finite discrete systems. Our formalism is essentially equivalent to the standard characterization of random systems using sequences of conditional distributions [39], and our classification is based on [38]. We emphasize that our framework aims to capture the external *behavior* of a system, not its implementation. A reader already comfortable with the notion of a system may skip to Sect. 3.2.

*Formalizing Interactive Systems.* We characterize external interaction using three types of systems: *resources*, *distinguishers*, and *converters*. In a nutshell:

- *Resources* abstract randomized stateful (possibly inefficient) algorithms: Given an input, the algorithm updates its internal state and samples an output based on a probability distribution that depends on the internal state.
- *Distinguishers* abstract randomized oracle-aided algorithms with a binary output. When the oracles are instantiated with a resource, the algorithm defines a probability distribution over 0/1 values.

[7] Specifically, for amplifying a constant $\delta$, we must take $n = O(\log \lambda)$ to ensure the term $\varepsilon'$ in our combiner-is-amplifier theorem remains small. For this choice of $n$, the probabilistic construction of [33] yields a non-negligible indistinguishability error of $\varepsilon = 1/\text{poly}(\lambda)$.

- *Converters* abstract oracle-aided randomized stateful (possibly inefficient) algorithms. Given an input, the algorithm makes a series of calls to its oracles while updating its internal state, and generates an output. By instantiating the oracles with resources, the converter simplifies into a resource.

We denote by $\mathcal{X}, \mathcal{Y}$ the spaces for incoming and outgoing messages. We always assume these are finite sets that include the special symbol $\perp$: if a resource accepts at most $h \in \mathbb{N}$ queries any subsequent queries are assumed to return $\perp$, and similarly, any invalid queries (not in input space) are assumed to return $\perp$. See more notational conventions below.

We model systems using alternating trees, which naturally capture the back-and-forth of stateful interaction: each alternating level represents a shift between queries and responses, and every node corresponds to a partial transcript. We defer the formal definitions to the full version.

*Notational Conventions.*

1. Interaction: Given a distinguisher $D$, an $n$-oracle-aided converter $C$, and $n$ resources $\vec{S} = (S_1, \ldots, S_n)$, we denote the execution of $D$ and $C^{\vec{S}}$ by $D(C^{\vec{S}})$ rather than $D^{C^{\vec{S}}}$ for notational convenience.
2. Terminology: We may refer to a resource simply as a system, and to an $n$-oracle-aided converter simply as an $n$-oracle-aided system.
3. Alphabets: In the above, it is possible to consider distinct input and output spaces for every resource, or even for every individual node in the tree. However, for the sake of simplicity, we choose to consider a single universal input space $\mathcal{X}$ and output space $\mathcal{Y}$, which can be viewed as the union of all sub-spaces. Furthermore, throughout most of the paper, we do not explicitly mention the sets $(\mathcal{X}, \mathcal{Y})$ and also omit the upper bound $h$ on the number of rounds (when irrelevant).
4. Convex Combinations: Given systems $S_0, S_1$ and $p \in [0,1]$, we denote by $(1-p)S_0 + pS_1$ the system equivalent to sampling $b \leftarrow \mathrm{Ber}(p)$ and using $S_b$. Furthermore, for a set $\mathcal{X}$ and given an ensemble of systems $\{S_x\}_{x \in \mathcal{X}}$ with a random variable $X$ over $\mathcal{X}$, we denote by $S_X$ the system equivalent to sampling $x \leftarrow X$ and using $S_x$.
5. Implementation: For a resource $S$, we define $\mathrm{size}(S)$ as the size of the smallest circuit realizing it. We allow circuits to receive advice sampled from arbitrary distributions, as we deal with indistinguishability where the best such advice can later be fixed. For a converter $C^{(\cdot)}$, we define $\mathrm{size}(C^{(\cdot)})$ as the size of its oracle-aided circuit. We define the composed size $\mathrm{size}(C^{\vec{S}})$ as the size of the circuit obtained by replacing the oracle gates in $C^{(\cdot)}$ with the circuits realizing $\vec{S}$, capturing the actual cost of the combined implementation rather than the minimal circuit size of the resulting resource.
   We may sometimes abuse notation and associate an implementation with the system it realizes, feeding it to a distinguisher or a converter.

**Definition 1 (Statistical Distance of Systems).** *For $\delta \in [0,1]$, we say that two systems $R$ and $I$ are $\delta$ statistically close, denoted $R \overset{s}{\approx}_\delta I$, if for every (unbounded adaptive) distinguisher $D$ we have*

$$\left|\mathbb{E}\left[D^R - D^I\right]\right| \leq \delta.$$

*If $\delta = 0$, we write $R \equiv I$.*

**Lemma 1 (System Decomposition Lemma, Reinterpretation of [36, Theorem 2]).** *For any finite discrete systems $R$ and $I$ with statistical distance $\delta \in [0,1]$, there exist systems $S, R', I'$ such that*

$$R \equiv (1-\delta)S + \delta R',$$
$$I \equiv (1-\delta)S + \delta I'.$$

In [36], randomized systems are modeled as probability distributions over deterministic systems. To be more accurate, since this representation is not unique, randomized systems are in fact seen as equivalence classes over these distributions. It is shown that the maximal distinguishing advantage between two random systems is equal to the minimal statistical distance between distributions in their equivalence classes. Then, standard coupling of probability distributions implies the above.

### 3.2 Indistinguishability Combiners

**Definition 2 (Indistinguishability Combiner).** *For finite sets $(\mathcal{X}, \mathcal{Y})$, $\varepsilon \in [0,1]$, $k, n \subset \mathbb{N}$ with $k \leq n$, an $(\varepsilon, k, n)$ indistinguishability combiner with respect to ideal $(\mathcal{Y}, \mathcal{X})$-systems $\vec{I} = (I_1, \ldots, I_n)$ against an $(\mathcal{X}, \mathcal{Y})$-distinguisher class $\mathcal{D}$, is a pair of n-oracle-aided $(\mathcal{X}, \mathcal{Y})$-systems $(C_0^{(\cdot)}, C_1^{(\cdot)})$ such that for all $(\mathcal{Y}, \mathcal{X})$-systems $\vec{S} = (S_1, \ldots, S_n)$:*

$$|\{i \in [n] \mid S_i \equiv I_i\}| \geq k \implies \forall D \in \mathcal{D}: \left|\mathbb{E}\left[D(C_0^{\vec{S}}) - D(C_1^{\vec{S}})\right]\right| \leq \varepsilon.$$

*For $s \in \mathbb{N}$, an $(s, \varepsilon, k, n)$ indistinguishability combiner is an $(\varepsilon, k, n)$ indistinguishability combiner against the distinguisher class $\mathcal{D}$ induced by s-sized oracle-aided circuits. If $\mathcal{D}$ consists of all (unbounded adaptive) distinguishers, we say the combiner is* statistically *secure. Furthermore, if $\varepsilon = 0$, we say the combiner is* perfect.

*Remark 1.* While the above definition may seem too restrictive at first since it targets a specific choice for the ideal systems $\vec{I}$, typically the same combiner $(C_0^{(\cdot)}, C_1^{(\cdot)})$ satisfies it with respect to any ideal $\vec{I}$ in some "good class" of systems.

# 4 The Statistically Close Oracle Model

In this section, we show that any indistinguishability combiner is inherently an amplifier for statistically weak candidates. We emphasize that, although the candidate systems are required to be statistically close to ideal, the theorem applies even when the combiner itself only guarantees indistinguishability against a computationally bounded class of distinguishers.

**Theorem 1 (Indistinguishability Combiners Are Amplifiers).** *For $\varepsilon \in [0,1]$, $\delta \in (0, 0.5)$, $k, n \in \mathbb{N}$, given an $(\varepsilon, k, n)$ indistinguishability combiner $(C_0^{(\cdot)}, C_1^{(\cdot)})$ with respect to ideal systems $\vec{I} = (I_1, \ldots, I_n)$ against a distinguisher class $\mathcal{D}$, let $\vec{R} = (R_1, \ldots, R_n)$ be a tuple of $n$ real systems such that $\forall i \in [n] : R_i \overset{\mathsf{s}}{\approx}_\delta I_i$. Then, we have*

$$\forall D \in \mathcal{D} : \left| \mathbb{E}\left[ D(C_0^{\vec{R}}) - D(C_1^{\vec{R}}) \right] \right| \leq \delta' + \varepsilon', \tag{2}$$

*where*

$$\delta' := (2\delta)^{n-k+1} \cdot \sum_{j=1}^{k} \binom{n}{k-j} (-\delta)^{j-1} \leq \binom{n}{k-1} (2\delta)^{n-k+1},$$

$$\varepsilon' := \varepsilon \cdot \sum_{i=0}^{n-k} \binom{i+k-1}{i} (2\delta)^i \leq \varepsilon \cdot \min\left( \binom{n}{k}, (1-2\delta)^{-k} \right).$$

*Proof.* Let us denote by $\Delta(k,n) = \Delta_{\varepsilon,\delta}(k,n)$ the worst-case upper bound on Eq. (2). That is, for every $(\varepsilon, k, n)$ combiner with respect to some ideal systems and distinguisher class, and for any real systems such that each is $\delta$-close statistically to ideal, $\Delta(k,n)$ bounds the distinguishing advantage of said class when the real systems are used. Our proof proceeds by deriving a recurrence relation for $\Delta(k,n)$ and solving it combinatorially using the boundary conditions $k = 0$ and $k = n$.

Fix any distinguisher $D \in \mathcal{D}$, and let $\Delta^D C^{\vec{R}} := \mathbb{E}\left[ D(C_0^{\vec{R}}) - D(C_1^{\vec{R}}) \right]$. By the system decomposition lemma (Lemma 1), for all $i \in [n]$, there exist systems $S_i, R'_i, I'_i$ such that

$$R_i \equiv (1-\delta) S_i + \delta R'_i,$$
$$I_i \equiv (1-\delta) S_i + \delta I'_i.$$

Then, we have

$$\Delta^D C^{\vec{R}} = (1-\delta) \Delta^D C^{\vec{R}_{n-1}, S_n} + \delta \Delta^D C^{\vec{R}_{n-1}, R'_n},$$
$$\Delta^D C^{\vec{R}_{n-1}, I_n} = (1-\delta) \Delta^D C^{\vec{R}_{n-1}, S_n} + \delta \Delta^D C^{\vec{R}_{n-1}, I'_n},$$

which together imply that

$$\Delta^D C^{\vec{R}} = \Delta^D C^{\vec{R}_{n-1}, I_n} + \delta \Delta^D C^{\vec{R}_{n-1}, R'_n} - \delta \Delta^D C^{\vec{R}_{n-1}, I'_n},$$
$$\left| \Delta^D C^{\vec{R}} \right| \leq \left| \Delta^D C^{\vec{R}_{n-1}, I_n} \right| + \delta \left( \left| \Delta^D C^{\vec{R}_{n-1}, R'_n} \right| + \left| \Delta^D C^{\vec{R}_{n-1}, I'_n} \right| \right).$$

Observe that by fixing the last system to ideal $I_n$ we obtain an $(\varepsilon,\ k-1,\ n-1)$ combiner with respect to $\vec{I}_{n-1}$ against the same distinguisher class, and for $\vec{R}_{n-1}$ we still have that $\forall i \in [n-1] : R_i \overset{\mathsf{s}}{\approx}_\delta I_i$. Similarly, fixing the last system to $R'_n$ or $I'_n$ results in an $(\varepsilon,\ k,\ n-1)$ combiner. Hence, we derive the recurrence relation

$$\Delta(k,n) \leq \Delta(k-1,n-1) + 2\delta \cdot \Delta(k,n-1).$$

For the base cases: (1) $\Delta(0,n) \leq \varepsilon$ since enough ideal systems are used and we can invoke the combiner's guarantee. (2) $\Delta(n,n) \leq 2(1-(1-\delta)^n) + \varepsilon$ by using a standard product bound $\vec{R} \overset{\mathsf{s}}{\approx}_{1-(1-\delta)^n} \vec{I}$ since with probability $(1-\delta)^n$ we get the shared system $\vec{S}$, and thus

$$C_0^{\vec{R}} \overset{\mathsf{s}}{\approx}_{1-(1-\delta)^n} C_0^{\vec{I}} \overset{\mathsf{s}}{\approx}_\varepsilon C_1^{\vec{I}} \overset{\mathsf{s}}{\approx}_{1-(1-\delta)^n} C_1^{\vec{R}}.$$

Structurally, it is more convenient to separate the base cases into a main term and an error term. Specifically, we define:

$$\begin{aligned}
&\delta'(0,n) := 0, \quad \delta'(n,n) := 2(1-(1-\delta)^n),\\
&\delta'(k,n) := \delta'(k-1,n-1) + 2\delta \cdot \delta'(k,n-1),\\
&\varepsilon'(0,n) := \varepsilon, \quad \varepsilon'(n,n) := \varepsilon,\\
&\varepsilon'(k,n) := \varepsilon'(k-1,n-1) + 2\delta \cdot \varepsilon'(k,n-1).
\end{aligned}$$

Since the sum $\delta'(k,n) + \varepsilon'(k,n)$ bounds the base cases and exactly matches the recurrence relation, we obtain the upper bound $\Delta(k,n) \leq \delta'(k,n) + \varepsilon'(k,n)$.

The simpler (and somewhat looser) upper bounds of

$$\delta'(k,n) < \binom{n}{k-1}(2\delta)^{n-k+1} \qquad \text{and} \qquad \varepsilon'(k,n) \leq \binom{n}{k}\varepsilon,$$

are immediately derived using Pascal's rule $\binom{n}{k} = \binom{n-1}{k-1} + \binom{n-1}{k}$ with $2\delta \leq 1$, noting for $\delta'(n,n)$ that $1-(1-\delta)^n \leq n\delta$ (union bound). For the second simplified bound of $\varepsilon'(k,n) \leq \varepsilon \cdot (1-2\delta)^{-k}$, we observe that

$$(1-2\delta)^{-(k-1)} + 2\delta(1-2\delta)^{-k} = (1-2\delta)^{-k}(1-2\delta+2\delta) = (1-2\delta)^{-k}.$$

In the full version, we proceed to derive the exact closed-form solutions for both $\delta'$ and $\varepsilon'$.

## 5 The Computationally Close Oracle Model

In this section, we generalize the combiner-is-amplifier theorem to the computational setting. To do so, we restrict the underlying real and ideal candidates to be single-round systems. That is, the combiner makes at most one query to each candidate oracle over the entire execution. Formally, this is captured by switching from general interactive systems to randomized functions (over finite domain and codomain), where any subsequent queries to an oracle are answered with $\bot$. Importantly, since the ideal system is modeled as a randomized function, the notion is limited to non-adaptive cryptographic games. For a detailed discussion of these limitations, see the full version.

As noted in the introduction, one can emulate the case of multiple non-adaptive queries by a single-query combiner with batch queries (potentially increasing the indistinguishability error). Extensions to the adaptive setting are discussed in the full version.

**Definition 3 (Single-Query Indistinguishability Combiner).** *For finite sets $(\mathcal{X}, \mathcal{Y})$ and randomized functions $F_1^*, \ldots, F_n^* : \mathcal{X} \to \mathcal{Y}$, we say that $(C_0^{(\cdot)}, C_1^{(\cdot)})$ is a single-query indistinguishability combiner with respect to $\vec{F^*}$ if it is an indistinguishability combiner with respect to $\vec{I} = (I_1, \ldots, I_n)$, where $I_i$ is the single-round system induced by $F_i^*$.*

### 5.1 Useful Lemmas

First, we introduce some lemmas that are useful in generalizing statistical bounds to the computational setting (regardless of combiners). Their proofs are deferred to the full version.

**Lemma 2 (Hybrid Indistinguishability Lemma** [9,42]**).** *Let $X_0$ and $X_1$ be random variables, and let $\delta, \varepsilon \in (0,1)$ and $s \in \mathbb{N}$.*
*Define $s' := \frac{s \cdot \varepsilon^2}{128(\log|\mathrm{Im}(X_0)| + \log|\mathrm{Im}(X_1)| + 1)}$. Assume that*

$$X_0 \overset{\mathsf{c}}{\approx}_{s,\delta} X_1.$$

*Then there exists a hybrid distribution $X'$ such that*

$$X_0 \overset{\mathsf{c}}{\approx}_{s',\varepsilon(1-\delta)} X' \overset{\mathsf{s}}{\approx}_{\delta} X_1.$$

Note that the first indistinguishability is computational and the second is statistical. The above lemma generalizes to randomized functions $F_0$ and $F_1$ where indistinguishability is guaranteed for every input choice $x$. In order to obtain the generalized HIL version, we simply apply the random-variable version on every possible input.

**Lemma 3 (Generalized Hybrid Indistinguishability Lemma).** *Let $F_0$ and $F_1$ be two randomized functions from $\mathcal{X}$ to $\mathcal{Y}$, and let $\delta, \varepsilon \in (0,1)$ and $s \in \mathbb{N}$. Define $s' := \frac{s \cdot \varepsilon^2}{128(\log|\mathrm{Im}(F_0)| + \log|\mathrm{Im}(F_1)| + 1)}$. Assume that*

$$F_0 \overset{\mathsf{c}}{\approx}_{s,\delta} F_1.$$

*Then there exists a hybrid randomized function $F'$ such that*

$$F_0 \overset{\mathsf{c}}{\approx}_{s',\varepsilon(1-\delta)} F' \overset{\mathsf{s}}{\approx}_{\delta} F_1.$$

**Lemma 4 (Single-Query Hybrid Argument).** *Let $s, n \in \mathbb{N}$ and $\varepsilon \in (0,1)$ be given, and let $\vec{F} = (F_1, \ldots, F_n)$ and $\vec{F}' = (F'_1, \ldots, F'_n)$ be tuples (direct product) of $n$ randomized functions from $\mathcal{X}$ to $\mathcal{Y}$, such that*

$$\forall i \in [n] : F_i \overset{\mathsf{c}}{\approx}_{s,\varepsilon} F'_i.$$

*Then, for every $s'$-sized distinguisher $D$ that makes at most one query to each oracle, we have*

$$\left| \mathbb{E}\left[ D^{\vec{F}} - D^{\vec{F}'} \right] \right| \leq \varepsilon n,$$

*for*

$$s' := s - \min \operatorname{size}(\vec{F}, \vec{F}').$$

### 5.2 The Amplification Theorem

Below, by $\max_{b \in \{0,1\}} \operatorname{size}(C_b^{\vec{F}})$, we denote the circuit size needed to implement the oracle-aided $C_0^{(\cdot)}, C_1^{(\cdot)}$ plus the implementation cost of the oracles $\vec{F}$ themselves. Also, we denote by $\gamma$ the computational slackness parameter—the closer we want to get to the statistical bound, the more we pay in circuit size.

**Theorem 2 (Single-Query Indistinguishability Combiners Are Computational Amplifiers).** *For $\varepsilon, \gamma \in [0,1]$, $\delta \in (0, 0.5)$, $k, n, s_c, s_f \in \mathbb{N}$, given a single-query $(s_c, \varepsilon, k, n)$ indistinguishability combiner $(C_0^{(\cdot)}, C_1^{(\cdot)})$ with respect to ideal functions $\vec{F}^* = (F_1^*, \ldots, F_n^*)$, let $\vec{F} = (F_1, \ldots, F_n)$ be a tuple of $n$ real functions such that $\forall i \in [n] : F_i \overset{\mathsf{c}}{\approx}_{s_f,\delta} F_i^*$. Then for every $s$-sized distinguisher $D$, we have*

$$\left| \mathbb{E}\left[ D(C_0^{\vec{F}}) - D(C_1^{\vec{F}}) \right] \right| \leq \delta' + \varepsilon' + 2n\gamma,$$

*where*

$$\delta' := (2\delta)^{n-k+1} \cdot \sum_{j=1}^{k} \binom{n}{k-j} (-\delta)^{j-1} \leq \binom{n}{k-1} (2\delta)^{n-k+1},$$

$$\varepsilon' := \varepsilon \cdot \sum_{i=0}^{n-k} \binom{i+k-1}{i} (2\delta)^i \leq \varepsilon \cdot \min\left( \binom{n}{k}, (1-2\delta)^{-k} \right),$$

$$s' := \frac{s_f \cdot \gamma^2}{128(\max_i(\log|\operatorname{Im}(F_i)| + \log|\operatorname{Im}(F_i^*)|) + 1)},$$

$$s := \min\left( s_c,\ s' - \max_{b \in \{0,1\}} \operatorname{size}(C_b^{\vec{F}}) \right).$$

*Proof.* Let $\vec{F}' = (F'_1, \ldots, F'_n)$ be the hybrid functions guaranteed by the generalized hybrid indistinguishability lemma (Lemma 3) such that $\forall i \in [n] : F_i \overset{\mathsf{c}}{\approx}_{s',\gamma}$

$F_i' \overset{\mathsf{s}}{\approx}_\delta F_i^*$. Next, using the triangle inequality and the single-query hybrid argument (Lemma 4) we get that

$$\begin{aligned}
&\left|\mathbb{E}\left[D(C_0^{\vec{F}}) - D(C_1^{\vec{F}})\right]\right| \leq \\
&\left|\mathbb{E}\left[D(C_0^{\vec{F}'}) - D(C_1^{\vec{F}'})\right]\right| + \\
&\left|\mathbb{E}\left[D(C_0^{\vec{F}}) - D(C_0^{\vec{F}'})\right]\right| + \\
&\left|\mathbb{E}\left[D(C_1^{\vec{F}}) - D(C_1^{\vec{F}'})\right]\right| \leq \\
&\left|\mathbb{E}\left[D(C_0^{\vec{F}'}) - D(C_1^{\vec{F}'})\right]\right| + 2 \cdot n\gamma,
\end{aligned}$$

since the induced distinguisher between $\vec{F}$ and $\vec{F}'$ using either $C_0^{(\cdot)}$ or $C_1^{(\cdot)}$ is small enough:

$$s + \max_{b \in \{0,1\}} \text{size}(C_b^{\vec{F}}) \leq s'.$$

Finally, using that $\forall i \in [n] : F_i' \overset{\mathsf{s}}{\approx}_\delta F_i^*$, we apply the result for statistically close oracles (Theorem 1):

$$\left|\mathbb{E}\left[D(C_0^{\vec{F}'}) - D(C_1^{\vec{F}'})\right]\right| \leq \delta' + \varepsilon'.$$

That is, we view $\vec{F}'$ and $\vec{F}^*$ as the real and ideal single-round systems (all further queries answered with $\perp$), and $\mathcal{D}$ is the class of $s \leq s_c$-sized distinguishers.

## 6 Amplification of Functional Encryption

In this section, we use our single-query combiner-is-amplifier theorem to achieve security amplification for weak FE schemes with sufficiently small constant indistinguishability error. We first construct a single-query FE combiner using homomorphic secret sharing, then apply our main theorem. We note that we cannot use the existing FE combiner due to [34], as it sends many queries to each candidate. Also, the amplifier construction presented in [33] does not induce a proper combiner with negligible error for a constant $\delta$ due to a randomized choice of sets that we fix. Of even greater significance, we need a stronger semi-malicious privacy notion, since our combiner must be secure against inefficient "bad" candidates.

### 6.1 Weak Functional Encryption

Below we describe a variant that is known in the literature as single-key, weakly selective secure, weakly compact PKFE [21].

**Definition 4 (Functional Encryption).** *A functional encryption scheme* $\mathsf{FE}$, *for a function class* $\mathcal{F}$ *(represented by Boolean circuits) and message space* $\{0,1\}^*$, *consists of four PPT algorithms* ($\mathsf{FE.Setup}$, $\mathsf{FE.Keygen}$, $\mathsf{FE.Enc}$, $\mathsf{FE.Dec}$) *with the following syntax:*

- $(\mathsf{MPK}, \mathsf{MSK}) \leftarrow \mathsf{FE.Setup}(1^\lambda, 1^p)$: *takes as input the unary representation of the security parameter and a size bound* $\lambda, p \in \mathbb{N}$, *and outputs the master public key (for encryption) and master secret key (for functional-key generation).*
- $\mathsf{FSK}_f \leftarrow \mathsf{FE.Keygen}(\mathsf{MSK}, f)$: *takes as input the master secret key and a function* $f \in \mathcal{F}$, *and outputs a (secret) functional key.*
- $\mathsf{CT} \leftarrow \mathsf{FE.Enc}(\mathsf{MPK}, x)$: *takes as input the master public key and a message* $x \in \{0,1\}^*$, *and outputs a ciphertext.*
- $y \leftarrow \mathsf{FE.Dec}(\mathsf{FSK}_f, \mathsf{CT})$: *takes as input a functional key and a ciphertext, and outputs a message.*

*We next define the relevant properties:*

- *Correctness: for all* $\lambda, p, \ell \in \mathbb{N}$, *message* $x \in \{0,1\}^\ell$ *and function* $f \in \mathcal{F}$ *with domain* $\{0,1\}^\ell$ *and size* $|f| \leq p$, *we have*
$$\Pr[\mathsf{FE.Dec}(\mathsf{FSK}_f, \mathsf{CT}) = f(x)] = 1,$$
*over* $(\mathsf{MPK}, \mathsf{MSK}) \leftarrow \mathsf{FE.Setup}(1^\lambda, 1^p)$, $\mathsf{FSK}_f \leftarrow \mathsf{FE.Keygen}(\mathsf{MSK}, f)$, $\mathsf{CT} \leftarrow \mathsf{FE.Enc}(\mathsf{MPK}, x)$.
- $\varepsilon$*-SIM-Security: there exists a PPT simulator* $\mathsf{FE.Sim}$ *such that for all* $\{x, f, p\}_\lambda$ *with* $|f| \leq p = \mathrm{poly}(\lambda)$ *we have*
$$(\mathsf{MPK},\ \mathsf{FSK}_f,\ \mathsf{CT}) \overset{\mathsf{c}}{\approx}_{\varepsilon(\lambda)} \mathsf{FE.Sim}(1^\lambda,\ 1^p,\ f,\ f(x)),$$
*over* $(\mathsf{MPK}, \mathsf{MSK}) \leftarrow \mathsf{FE.Setup}(1^\lambda, 1^p)$, $\mathsf{FSK}_f \leftarrow \mathsf{FE.Keygen}(\mathsf{MSK}, f)$, $\mathsf{CT} \leftarrow \mathsf{FE.Enc}(\mathsf{MPK}, x)$.
- $\varepsilon$*-IND-Security: for every* $\{x_0, x_1, f, p\}_\lambda$ *with* $|x_0| = |x_1|, f(x_0) = f(x_1)$ *and* $|f| \leq p = \mathrm{poly}(\lambda)$, *we have*
$$(\mathsf{MPK},\ \mathsf{FSK}_f,\ \mathsf{CT}_0) \overset{\mathsf{c}}{\approx}_{\varepsilon(\lambda)} (\mathsf{MPK},\ \mathsf{FSK}_f,\ \mathsf{CT}_1),$$
*over* $(\mathsf{MPK}, \mathsf{MSK}) \leftarrow \mathsf{FE.Setup}(1^\lambda, 1^p)$, $\mathsf{FSK}_f \leftarrow \mathsf{FE.Keygen}(\mathsf{MSK}, f)$, $\mathsf{CT}_b \leftarrow \mathsf{FE.Enc}(\mathsf{MPK}, x_b)$.
- *Succinctness: for every* $\lambda, p, \ell \in \mathbb{N}$, *the circuit size of* $\mathsf{FE.Enc}(\mathsf{MPK}, \cdot)$, *over* $\{0,1\}^\ell$ *where* $(\mathsf{MPK}, \mathsf{MSK}) \leftarrow \mathsf{FE.Setup}(1^\lambda, 1^p)$, *is upper bounded by* $p^{1-c} \cdot \mathrm{poly}(\lambda, \ell)$ *for some universal constant* $0 < c \leq 1$. *If* $c = 1$, *we say that the scheme is fully succinct.*

*Remark 2.* We note that the literature contains several common variants of FE, to which our results also extend (either directly or by amplifying our weaker version, then lifting). We choose to focus on weak FE because: (1) it is relatively simple, (2) its connection to other notions of FE is well understood, and (3) it is sufficient (in its subexponentially hard version) for the construction of indistinguishability obfuscation. We briefly address how our results generalize for these notions (for more elaboration, see the full version):

- **From Weak to Strong FE:** The weak notion of FE we address, in its fully secure version (i.e., post amplification), can be upgraded to a strong notion of FE that is both *adaptively secure* and *resistant to unbounded collusion* [35].
- **Indistinguishability Obfuscation:** A main application of FE is the construction of indistinguishability obfuscation (IO) [4,11]. For this application, weak FE is sufficient,[8] but it is required that the FE has a subexponentially small indistinguishability error. Our amplifier can reach this level of indistinguishability, assuming that the weak FE we start from is (weakly) indistinguishable against adversaries of subexponential size (see Theorem 6).
- **Secret Key FE:** We focus on public-key FE, which is somewhat more common. Our proof for weak public-key FE can be easily adapted to weak secret-key FE.

## 6.2 Homomorphic Secret Sharing

Below we describe a special variant of HSS, a notion first introduced in [13,14]. In the following, we assume that a functionality $f$ is given as a Boolean circuit. An efficiently computable functionality $f = \{f\}_\lambda$ is a (non-uniform) family of circuits of size $s(\lambda) \leq \text{poly}(\lambda)$ over $\ell(\lambda) \leq \text{poly}(\lambda)$ input bits. The construction is parametrized by some functions $t(\lambda), n(\lambda)$.[9] For ease of reading, we sometimes omit the dependency on $\lambda$ and simply write $s, \ell$ and $t, n$. In the full version we show how to instantiate semi-malicious HSS assuming OWFs, for any $t \leq \text{poly}(\lambda)$ and $n \geq \binom{3t}{3}$, or for $n \geq 3t$ if $t = O(\log(\lambda))$.

**Definition 5 (Homomorphic Secret Sharing).** *A homomorphic secret sharing scheme* $\mathsf{HSS}$ *consists of three PPT algorithms* $(\mathsf{HSS.Share}, \mathsf{HSS.Eval}, \mathsf{HSS.Dec})$ *with the following syntax:*

- $(x_1, \ldots, x_n) \leftarrow \mathsf{HSS.Share}(1^\lambda, x)$*: takes as input the unary representation of the security parameter* $\lambda \in \mathbb{N}$ *and an input* $x \in \{0,1\}^\ell$*. The sharing algorithm outputs* $n$ *shares, each of size* $\ell' = \ell \cdot \text{poly}(\lambda)$*.*
- $y_i := \mathsf{HSS.Eval}(1^\lambda, f, i, x_i)$*: deterministic; takes as input the unary representation of the security parameter* $\lambda \in \mathbb{N}$*, a functionality* $f$ *where* $s$ *and* $\ell$ *denote the circuit size of* $f$ *and the input length, an index* $i \in [n]$ *and a share* $x_i \in \{0,1\}^{\ell'}$*. The evaluation's circuit complexity is* $s' = s \cdot \text{poly}(\lambda)$*, and it outputs an output share* $y_i$*.*

[8] In fact, an even weaker notion of FE, in which a single function is known at setup time, is sufficient. Our amplification theorem readily extends to this weaker version.
[9] We parametrize combiners with a lower bound on the number of good candidates $k$, and secure computation with an upper bound on the number of malicious parties $t$.

- $y := \mathsf{HSS.Dec}(1^\lambda, f, y_1, \ldots, y_n)$: *deterministic; the decoder takes as input the unary representation of the security parameter* $\lambda \in \mathbb{N}$, *a functionality* $f$ *and an* $n$*-tuple* $(y_1, \ldots, y_n)$ *(supposedly output shares in the image of the evaluator).*

*The* HSS *should satisfy the following properties:*

- *Perfect Correctness: for every security parameter* $\lambda \in \mathbb{N}$, *every functionality* $f$ *with input length* $\ell$, *and every input* $x \in \{0,1\}^\ell$:

$$\Pr\left[\mathsf{HSS.Dec}(1^\lambda, f, y_1, \ldots, y_n) = f(x)\right] = 1,$$

*over* $(x_1, \ldots, x_n) \leftarrow \mathsf{HSS.Share}(1^\lambda, x)$, $\forall i \in [n] : y_i := \mathsf{HSS.Eval}(1^\lambda, f, i, x_i)$.
- *Semi-Malicious* $t$*-Privacy:*
  1. HSS.Share *is* $t$*-wise input-independent, namely for every security parameter* $\lambda \in \mathbb{N}$, *input* $x \in \{0,1\}^\ell$ *and subset* $T \subseteq [n]$ *of size* $|T| < t$:[10]

$$(x_i)_{i \in T} \equiv (x_i^*)_{i \in T},$$

  *over* $(x_i)_{i \in [n]} \leftarrow \mathsf{HSS.Share}(1^\lambda, x)$ *and* $(x_i^*)_{i \in [n]} \leftarrow \mathsf{HSS.Share}(1^\lambda, 0^\ell)$.
  2. *There exists an efficient randomized simulator* HSS.Sim *such that for every ensemble* $\{f, x, T, x_T\}_\lambda$, *where* $f$ *is a function with input length* $\ell$, $x \in \{0,1\}^\ell$, $T \subseteq [n]$ *with* $|T| < t$ *and* $x_T$ *are valid shares* $(x_i)_{i \in T} \in \mathsf{Supp}(\mathsf{HSS.Share}(1^\lambda, x)_T)$:

$$(y_1, \ldots, y_n) \overset{\mathsf{c}}{\approx} \mathsf{HSS.Sim}(1^\lambda, f, T, x_T, f(x)),$$

  *over conditional input sharing* $(x_1, \ldots, x_n) \leftarrow (\mathsf{HSS.Share}(1^\lambda, x) \mid x_T)$ *and the randomness of the simulator, where* $\forall i \in [n] : y_i := \mathsf{HSS.Eval}(1^\lambda, f, i, x_i)$.

### 6.3 The Amplifier

The construction of our FE amplifier is described in Fig. 1. To show IND-security, given $x, x', f$, our goal is to define a related single-query indistinguishability combiner $(C_{x,f}^{(\cdot)}, C_{x',f}^{(\cdot)})$ w.r.t. some ideal $\vec{F}^*$, such that for some real $\vec{F}'$ with $\forall i : F_i' \overset{\mathsf{c}}{\approx}_\delta F_i^*$, plugging $\vec{F}'$ into the combiner results in distributions identical to $(\mathsf{MPK}, \mathsf{FSK}_f, \mathsf{CT})$ and $(\mathsf{MPK}, \mathsf{FSK}_f, \mathsf{CT}')$ given by the FE amplifier (up to output formatting). The combiner is defined in Fig. 2, and the real/ideal functionalities are essentially chosen to be the weak FE and the weak simulator. Their formal definitions and the proofs of the theorems in this section appear in the full version.

[10] This can be relaxed to a small statistical distance

Given a weak SIM-secure functional encryption scheme $\mathsf{FE}^w$ and a $(t,n)$-$\mathsf{HSS}$, the construction works as follows:

$(\mathsf{MPK},\mathsf{MSK}) \leftarrow \mathsf{FE.Setup}(1^\lambda, 1^p)$

1. For all $i \in [n]$, call $(\mathsf{MPK}_i,\mathsf{MSK}_i) \leftarrow \mathsf{FE.Setup}^w(1^\lambda, 1^{p'})$, where $p' \leq p \cdot \mathrm{poly}(\lambda)$ is the corresponding upper bound of $\mathsf{HSS.Eval}$.
2. Output $\mathsf{MPK} := (\mathsf{MPK}_1, \ldots, \mathsf{MPK}_n)$, $\mathsf{MSK} := (\mathsf{MSK}_1, \ldots, \mathsf{MSK}_n)$.

$\mathsf{CT} \leftarrow \mathsf{FE.Enc}(\mathsf{MPK}, x)$

1. Share $(x_1, \ldots, x_n) \leftarrow \mathsf{HSS.Share}(1^\lambda, x)$.
2. For all $i \in [n]$, call $\mathsf{CT}_i \leftarrow \mathsf{FE.Enc}^w(\mathsf{MPK}_i, x_i)$.
3. Output $\mathsf{CT} := (\mathsf{CT}_1, \ldots, \mathsf{CT}_n)$.

$\mathsf{FSK}_f \leftarrow \mathsf{FE.Keygen}(\mathsf{MSK}, f)$

1. For all $i \in [n]$, let $f_i := \mathsf{HSS.Eval}(1^\lambda, f, i, \cdot)$ and call $\mathsf{FSK}_{f_i} \leftarrow \mathsf{FE.Keygen}^w(\mathsf{MSK}_i, f_i)$.
2. Output $\mathsf{FSK}_f := (\mathsf{FSK}_{f_1}, \ldots, \mathsf{FSK}_{f_n})$.

$y \leftarrow \mathsf{FE.Dec}(\mathsf{FSK}_f, \mathsf{CT})$

1. For all $i \in [n]$, call $y_i \leftarrow \mathsf{FE.Dec}^w(\mathsf{FSK}_{f_i}, \mathsf{CT}_i)$.
2. Output $y := \mathsf{HSS.Dec}(1^\lambda, f, y_1, \ldots, y_n)$.

**Fig. 1.** FE Amplifier

**Theorem 3.** *Given a* $(t,n)$-$\mathsf{HSS}$ *and* $\{x, x', f\}_\lambda$ *such that* $f : \{0,1\}^\ell \to \{0,1\}^m$, $x, x' \in \{0,1\}^\ell$, $f(x) = f(x')$ *and* $|f| \leq \mathrm{poly}(\lambda)$, *the n-oracle-aided pair* $\left\{C^{(\cdot)}_{x,f}, C^{(\cdot)}_{x',f}\right\}_\lambda$ *described in Fig. 2, is a* (poly, negl, $n-t+1$, $n$) *indistinguishability combiner w.r.t. any ideal* $\left\{\vec{F}^*\right\}_\lambda$ *such that* $\mathrm{size}(\vec{F}^*) \leq \mathrm{poly}(\lambda)$ *and each* $F^*_i(\cdot,\cdot)$ *ignores its first input.*

**Theorem 4.** *Let* $\mathsf{FE}^w$ *be a* $\delta$*-SIM-secure functional encryption scheme for* $\delta < 0.5$. *Then the scheme* $\mathsf{FE}$ *described in Fig. 1, instantiated with an* $(n/3, n)$-$\mathsf{HSS}$ *for* $n := 3\lceil \log \lambda \rceil$, *is a* $(\delta' + \mathrm{negl})$*-IND-secure functional encryption scheme where* $\delta' := \binom{n}{n/3}(2\delta)^{n/3} \leq (3e \cdot 2\delta)^{n/3}$.

In the theorem below, we employ a generic transformation from IND-security to SIM-security, as formalized in [18]. This transformation utilizes trapdoor circuits based on SKE/OWFs.

**Informal Lemma 1.** *Given a* $\delta$*-IND-secure functional encryption scheme, we can construct a* $(\delta + \mathrm{negl})$*-SIM-secure functional encryption scheme.*

We refer to the full version for a complete presentation of this transformation.

The single-query indistinguishability combiner $C^{(\cdot)}_{x,f}$, given a $(t,n)$-$\mathsf{HSS}$ and $\forall i \in [n] : f_i := \mathsf{HSS.Eval}(1^\lambda, f, i, \cdot)$, is defined below. (The corresponding $C^{(\cdot)}_{x',f}$ is identically defined.)

$z \leftarrow C^{\vec{F}}_{x,f}$

1. Share $(x_1, \ldots, x_n) \leftarrow \mathsf{HSS.Share}(1^\lambda, x)$.
2. For all $i \in [n]$, call
$$z_i \leftarrow F_i\left(x_i,\ f_i(x_i)\right).$$
3. Output $z := (z_1, \ldots, z_n)$.

**Fig. 2.** Combiner $\left(C^{(\cdot)}_{x,f}, C^{(\cdot)}_{x',f}\right)$

**Theorem 5.** *Assuming the existence of a $\delta$-IND-secure functional encryption scheme for some constant $\delta < 1/(6e)$, there also exists a* negl-*IND-secure functional encryption scheme.*

*Proof.* First, we note that weak FE implies OWFs which in turn imply SKE and an $(n/3, n)$-$\mathsf{HSS}$ for $n := 3\lceil \log \lambda \rceil$. We use the IND-security to SIM-security transformation (Lemma 1) to go from $\delta$-IND-secure FE to $(\delta + \text{negl})$-SIM-secure FE. Next, we use the FE amplifier (Theorem 4) to obtain a (1/poly)-IND-secure FE, as $(3e \cdot 2\delta) < 1$ and $n = \Omega(\log \lambda)$. We repeat this process once again: first the IND-security to SIM-security transformation to obtain a (1/poly)-SIM-secure FE, followed by the FE amplifier resulting in a negl-IND-secure FE.

Using similar ideas, along with a "heavier" combiner via $(\lambda^{c/3}, 5\lambda^c)$-HSS, we can generalize the above to the subexp setting. For more information, see the full version.

**Theorem 6.** *Assuming the existence of a $\delta$-IND-secure subexp functional encryption scheme for some constant $\delta < 1/(6e)$, there also exists a* (1/subexp)-*IND-secure subexp functional encryption scheme.*

We note without proof that for any constant $\delta < 1$, we can amplify $\delta$-IND-secure FE to any smaller constant (such as $1/(6e)$) by nesting, as pointed out in [33].

**Corollary 1.** *Assuming the existence of a $\delta$-IND-secure functional encryption scheme for some constant $\delta < 1$, there also exists a* negl-*IND-secure functional encryption scheme.*

**Corollary 2.** *Assuming the existence of a $\delta$-IND-secure subexp functional encryption scheme for some constant $\delta < 1$, there also exists a* (1/subexp)-*IND-secure subexp functional encryption scheme.*

*Remark 3.* At a high level, let us outline how our handling of the hardcore lemma differs from the approach taken by [33]. The main challenge with the hardcore lemma is that the hardcore event, namely the conditioning of randomness on the "shared distribution" (coupling analog), depends on the secret input. In particular, even though the FE simulator does not initially depend on any input $x$, once we condition on the hardcore event $(\mathsf{MPK}, \mathsf{FSK}_f, \mathsf{CT}_x) \mid H_E \overset{c}{\approx} \mathsf{FE.Sim}(f, y) \mid H_S$, the randomness chosen for the simulator $H_S$ becomes dependent on $x$, and so does its output. Similarly, conditioning on the hardcore event not occurring $\overline{H_S}$ also creates a dependency on $x$.

Jain et al. [33] tried to simulate the hardcore event by hiding $x$ inside a strong commitment and then using a leakage simulation lemma to simulate an inefficient transformation that breaks the commitment and then samples from the hardcore event. However, this approach failed because eventually they had to change the underlying committed value $x$, which fundamentally requires changing the leakage simulator as well. They implicitly assumed a single leakage simulator could work for both values, but because the required output distribution depends on the hidden secret, evaluating such a simulator inherently violates the commitment's hiding property.

Instead, we (1) employ a $(t, n)$ semi-malicious HSS, ensuring that the inputs of fewer than $t$ "bad" instances (where the hardcore event failed) are challenge-independent. Hence, no information is leaked and simulation is unnecessary. (2) We carefully analyze the impact of (small) leakage from "good" instances using the general combiner-is-amplifier theorem. In particular, the term $\delta' := \binom{n}{k-1}(2\delta)^{n-k+1}$ can be viewed as quantifying a penalty for the possible leakage, compared to the "idealized" bound of $\sum_{i=0}^{k-1} \binom{n}{i}\delta^{n-i}(1-\delta)^i$.

**Acknowledgments.** We thank Eliran Kachlon for helpful discussions at early stages of this project. We thank Aayush Jain for bringing the problem of FE amplification to our attention and for initial discussions that motivated this work. B. A. and N. G. are supported by Israel Science Foundation (ISF) grant no. 2805/21 and by the European Union (ERC-2022-ADG) under grant agreement no.101097959 NFITSC.

**Disclosure of Interests.** The authors have no competing interests to declare that are relevant to the content of this article.

## References

1. Ananth, P., Jain, A., Lin, H., Matt, C., Sahai, A.: Indistinguishability obfuscation without multilinear maps: new paradigms via low degree weak pseudorandomness and security amplification. In: Boldyreva, A., Micciancio, D. (eds.) CRYPTO 2019. LNCS, vol. 11694, pp. 284–332. Springer, Cham (2019). https://doi.org/10.1007/978-3-030-26954-8_10
2. Ananth, P., Jain, A., Naor, M., Sahai, A., Yogev, E.: Universal constructions and robust combiners for indistinguishability obfuscation and witness encryption. In: Robshaw, M., Katz, J. (eds.) CRYPTO 2016. LNCS, vol. 9815, pp. 491–520. Springer, Heidelberg (2016). https://doi.org/10.1007/978-3-662-53008-5_17

3. Ananth, P., Jain, A., Sahai, A.: Indistinguishability obfuscation without multilinear maps: iO from LWE, bilinear maps, and weak pseudorandomness. Cryptology ePrint Archive, Report 2018/615 (2018). https://eprint.iacr.org/2018/615
4. Ananth, P., Jain, A.: Indistinguishability obfuscation from compact functional encryption. In: Gennaro, R., Robshaw, M. (eds.) CRYPTO 2015. LNCS, vol. 9215, pp. 308–326. Springer, Heidelberg (2015). https://doi.org/10.1007/978-3-662-47989-6_15
5. Applebaum, B., Bitansky, N., Geier, N.: Security amplification via robust indistinguishability combiners. Cryptology ePrint Archive, Paper 2026/1121 (2026). https://eprint.iacr.org/2026/1121
6. Applebaum, B., Brakerski, Z., Tsabary, R.: Perfect secure computation in two rounds. In: Beimel, A., Dziembowski, S. (eds.) TCC 2018. LNCS, vol. 11239, pp. 152–174. Springer, Cham (2018). https://doi.org/10.1007/978-3-030-03807-6_6
7. Applebaum, B., Kachlon, E.: How to share an NP statement or combiners for zero-knowledge proofs. In: Kalai, Y.T., Kamara, S.F. (eds.) CRYPTO 2025, Part VII. LNCS, vol. 16006, pp. 480–513. Springer, Cham (2025). https://doi.org/10.1007/978-3-032-01907-3_16
8. Applebaum, B., Kachlon, E.: NIZK amplification via leakage-resilient secure computation. In: Kalai, Y.T., Kamara, S.F. (eds.) CRYPTO 2025, Part VII. LNCS, vol. 16006, pp. 462–479. Springer, Cham (2025). https://doi.org/10.1007/978-3-032-01907-3_15
9. Bitansky, N., Geier, N.: Amplification of non-interactive zero knowledge, revisited. In: Reyzin, L., Stebila, D. (eds.) CRYPTO 2024, Part IX. LNCS, vol. 14928, pp. 361–390. Springer, Cham (2024). https://doi.org/10.1007/978-3-031-68400-5_11
10. Bitansky, N., Kamath, C., Paneth, O., Rothblum, R.D., Vasudevan, P.N.: Batch proofs are statistically hiding. In: Mohar, B., Shinkar, I., O'Donnell, R. (eds.) 56th ACM STOC, pp. 435–443. ACM Press (2024). https://doi.org/10.1145/3618260.3649775
11. Bitansky, N., Vaikuntanathan, V.: Indistinguishability obfuscation from functional encryption. In: Guruswami, V. (ed.) 56th FOCS, pp. 171–190. IEEE Computer Society Press (2015). https://doi.org/10.1109/FOCS.2015.20
12. Boneh, D., Sahai, A., Waters, B.: Functional encryption: definitions and challenges. In: Ishai, Y. (ed.) TCC 2011. LNCS, vol. 6597, pp. 253–273. Springer, Heidelberg (2011). https://doi.org/10.1007/978-3-642-19571-6_16
13. Boyle, E., Gilboa, N., Ishai, Y.: Breaking the circuit size barrier for secure computation under DDH. In: Robshaw, M., Katz, J. (eds.) CRYPTO 2016. LNCS, vol. 9814, pp. 509–539. Springer, Heidelberg (2016). https://doi.org/10.1007/978-3-662-53018-4_19
14. Boyle, E., Gilboa, N., Ishai, Y., Lin, H., Tessaro, S.: Foundations of homomorphic secret sharing. In: Karlin, A.R. (ed.) ITCS 2018, vol. 94, pp. 21:1–21:21. LIPIcs (2018). https://doi.org/10.4230/LIPIcs.ITCS.2018.21
15. Canetti, R., Halevi, S., Steiner, M.: Hardness amplification of weakly verifiable puzzles. In: Kilian, J. (ed.) TCC 2005. LNCS, vol. 3378, pp. 17–33. Springer, Heidelberg (2005). https://doi.org/10.1007/978-3-540-30576-7_2
16. Crépeau, C., Kilian, J.: Weakening security assumptions and oblivious transfer. In: Goldwasser, S. (ed.) CRYPTO 1988. LNCS, vol. 403, pp. 2–7. Springer, New York (1990). https://doi.org/10.1007/0-387-34799-2_1
17. Damgård, I., Kilian, J., Salvail, L.: On the (im)possibility of basing oblivious transfer and bit commitment on weakened security assumptions. In: Stern, J. (ed.) EUROCRYPT 1999. LNCS, vol. 1592, pp. 56–73. Springer, Heidelberg (1999). https://doi.org/10.1007/3-540-48910-X_5

18. De Caro, A., Iovino, V., Jain, A., O'Neill, A., Paneth, O., Persiano, G.: On the achievability of simulation-based security for functional encryption. In: Canetti, R., Garay, J.A. (eds.) CRYPTO 2013. LNCS, vol. 8043, pp. 519–535. Springer, Heidelberg (2013). https://doi.org/10.1007/978-3-642-40084-1_29
19. Dwork, C., Naor, M., Reingold, O.: Immunizing encryption schemes from decryption errors. In: Cachin, C., Camenisch, J.L. (eds.) EUROCRYPT 2004. LNCS, vol. 3027, pp. 342–360. Springer, Heidelberg (2004). https://doi.org/10.1007/978-3-540-24676-3_21
20. Fischlin, M., Herzberg, A., Bin-Noon, H., Shulman, H.: Obfuscation combiners. In: Robshaw, M., Katz, J. (eds.) CRYPTO 2016. LNCS, vol. 9815, pp. 521–550. Springer, Heidelberg (2016). https://doi.org/10.1007/978-3-662-53008-5_18
21. Garg, S., Srinivasan, A.: Single-key to multi-key functional encryption with polynomial loss. In: Hirt, M., Smith, A. (eds.) TCC 2016. LNCS, vol. 9986, pp. 419–442. Springer, Heidelberg (2016). https://doi.org/10.1007/978-3-662-53644-5_16
22. Goldreich, O.: The Foundations of Cryptography - Volume 1: Basic Techniques. Cambridge University Press (2001). https://doi.org/10.1017/CBO9780511546891. http://www.wisdom.weizmann.ac.il/%7Eoded/foc-vol1.html
23. Goldreich, O., Nisan, N., Wigderson, A.: On Yao's XOR-lemma. In: Goldreich, O. (ed.) Studies in Complexity and Cryptography. Miscellanea on the Interplay between Randomness and Computation. LNCS, vol. 6650, pp. 273–301. Springer, Heidelberg (2011). https://doi.org/10.1007/978-3-642-22670-0_23
24. Goyal, V., Jain, A., Sahai, A.: Simultaneous amplification: the case of non-interactive zero-knowledge. In: Boldyreva, A., Micciancio, D. (eds.) CRYPTO 2019. LNCS, vol. 11693, pp. 608–637. Springer, Cham (2019). https://doi.org/10.1007/978-3-030-26951-7_21
25. Halevi, S., Rabin, T.: Degradation and amplification of computational hardness. In: Canetti, R. (ed.) TCC 2008. LNCS, vol. 4948, pp. 626–643. Springer, Heidelberg (2008). https://doi.org/10.1007/978-3-540-78524-8_34
26. Harnik, D., Ishai, Y., Kushilevitz, E., Nielsen, J.B.: OT-combiners via secure computation. In: Canetti, R. (ed.) TCC 2008. LNCS, vol. 4948, pp. 393–411. Springer, Heidelberg (2008). https://doi.org/10.1007/978-3-540-78524-8_22
27. Harnik, D., Kilian, J., Naor, M., Reingold, O., Rosen, A.: On robust combiners for oblivious transfer and other primitives. In: Cramer, R. (ed.) EUROCRYPT 2005. LNCS, vol. 3494, pp. 96–113. Springer, Heidelberg (2005). https://doi.org/10.1007/11426639_6
28. Herzberg, A.: On tolerant cryptographic constructions. In: Menezes, A. (ed.) CT-RSA 2005. LNCS, vol. 3376, pp. 172–190. Springer, Heidelberg (2005). https://doi.org/10.1007/978-3-540-30574-3_13
29. Holenstein, T.: Key agreement from weak bit agreement. In: Gabow, H.N., Fagin, R. (eds.) 37th ACM STOC, pp. 664–673. ACM Press (2005). https://doi.org/10.1145/1060590.1060689
30. Holenstein, T., Renner, R.: One-way secret-key agreement and applications to circuit polarization and immunization of public-key encryption. In: Shoup, V. (ed.) CRYPTO 2005. LNCS, vol. 3621, pp. 478–493. Springer, Heidelberg (2005). https://doi.org/10.1007/11535218_29
31. Impagliazzo, R.: Hard-core distributions for somewhat hard problems. In: 36th FOCS, pp. 538–545. IEEE Computer Society Press (1995). https://doi.org/10.1109/SFCS.1995.492584
32. Jain, A.: Author's note on "Amplifying the Security of Functional Encryption, Unconditionally". Personal website (2026). https://sites.google.com/view/aayushjain/home

33. Jain, A., Korb, A., Manohar, N., Sahai, A.: Amplifying the security of functional encryption, unconditionally. In: Micciancio, D., Ristenpart, T. (eds.) CRYPTO 2020. LNCS, vol. 12170, pp. 717–746. Springer, Cham (2020). https://doi.org/10.1007/978-3-030-56784-2_24
34. Jain, A., Manohar, N., Sahai, A.: Combiners for functional encryption, unconditionally. In: Canteaut, A., Ishai, Y. (eds.) EUROCRYPT 2020. LNCS, vol. 12105, pp. 141–168. Springer, Cham (2020). https://doi.org/10.1007/978-3-030-45721-1_6
35. Kitagawa, F., Nishimaki, R., Tanaka, K., Yamakawa, T.: Adaptively secure and succinct functional encryption: improving security and efficiency, simultaneously. In: Boldyreva, A., Micciancio, D. (eds.) CRYPTO 2019. LNCS, vol. 11694, pp. 521–551. Springer, Cham (2019). https://doi.org/10.1007/978-3-030-26954-8_17
36. Lanzenberger, D., Maurer, U.: Coupling of random systems. In: Pass, R., Pietrzak, K. (eds.) TCC 2020. LNCS, vol. 12552, pp. 207–240. Springer, Cham (2020). https://doi.org/10.1007/978-3-030-64381-2_8
37. Lin, H., Tessaro, S.: Amplification of chosen-ciphertext security. In: Johansson, T., Nguyen, P.Q. (eds.) EUROCRYPT 2013. LNCS, vol. 7881, pp. 503–519. Springer, Heidelberg (2013). https://doi.org/10.1007/978-3-642-38348-9_30
38. Maurer, U., Renner, R.: Abstract cryptography. In: Chazelle, B. (ed.) ICS 2011, pp. 1–21. Tsinghua University Press (2011)
39. Maurer, U.: Indistinguishability of random systems. In: Knudsen, L.R. (ed.) EUROCRYPT 2002. LNCS, vol. 2332, pp. 110–132. Springer, Heidelberg (2002). https://doi.org/10.1007/3-540-46035-7_8
40. Maurer, U., Pietrzak, K., Renner, R.: Indistinguishability amplification. In: Menezes, A. (ed.) CRYPTO 2007. LNCS, vol. 4622, pp. 130–149. Springer, Heidelberg (2007). https://doi.org/10.1007/978-3-540-74143-5_8
41. Maurer, U., Tessaro, S.: Computational indistinguishability amplification: tight product theorems for system composition. In: Halevi, S. (ed.) CRYPTO 2009. LNCS, vol. 5677, pp. 355–373. Springer, Heidelberg (2009). https://doi.org/10.1007/978-3-642-03356-8_21
42. Maurer, U., Tessaro, S.: A hardcore lemma for computational indistinguishability: security amplification for arbitrarily weak PRGs with optimal stretch. In: Micciancio, D. (ed.) TCC 2010. LNCS, vol. 5978, pp. 237–254. Springer, Heidelberg (2010). https://doi.org/10.1007/978-3-642-11799-2_15
43. O'Neill, A.: Definitional issues in functional encryption. Cryptology ePrint Archive, Report 2010/556 (2010). https://eprint.iacr.org/2010/556
44. Sahai, A., Seyalioglu, H.: Worry-free encryption: functional encryption with public keys. In: Al-Shaer, E., Keromytis, A.D., Shmatikov, V. (eds.) ACM CCS 2010, pp. 463–472. ACM Press (2010). https://doi.org/10.1145/1866307.1866359
45. Sahai, A., Waters, B.: Fuzzy identity-based encryption. In: Cramer, R. (ed.) EUROCRYPT 2005. LNCS, vol. 3494, pp. 457–473. Springer, Heidelberg (2005). https://doi.org/10.1007/11426639_27
46. Tessaro, S.: Computational indistinguishability amplification. Ph.D. thesis, ETH Zurich, Zürich, Switzerland (2010). https://doi.org/10.3929/ETHZ-A-006183893. https://hdl.handle.net/20.500.11850/72847

47. Tessaro, S.: Security amplification for the cascade of arbitrarily weak PRPs: tight bounds via the interactive hardcore lemma. In: Ishai, Y. (ed.) TCC 2011. LNCS, vol. 6597, pp. 37–54. Springer, Heidelberg (2011). https://doi.org/10.1007/978-3-642-19571-6_3
48. Wullschleger, J.: Oblivious-transfer amplification. In: Naor, M. (ed.) EUROCRYPT 2007. LNCS, vol. 4515, pp. 555–572. Springer, Heidelberg (2007). https://doi.org/10.1007/978-3-540-72540-4_32
49. Yao, A.C.C.: Theory and applications of trapdoor functions (extended abstract). In: 23rd FOCS, pp. 80–91. IEEE Computer Society Press (1982). https://doi.org/10.1109/SFCS.1982.45

# A Unifying Umbrella for Circular-Secure Cryptographic Primitives

Fuyuki Kitagawa[1(✉)] and Takahiro Matsuda[2]

[1] NTT Social Informatics Laboratories, Tokyo, Japan
fuyuki.kitagawa@ntt.com

[2] National Institute of Advanced Industrial Science and Technology (AIST), Tokyo, Japan
t-matsuda@aist.go.jp

**Abstract.** The main message of this paper is that several seemingly different circular-style primitives are *existentially equivalent*. In particular, somewhat surprisingly, we show that hinting PRGs (Koppula and Waters, CRYPTO 2019) are equivalent to secret-key encryption (SKE) schemes satisfying key-dependent-message (KDM) security. As a conceptual centerpiece, we introduce *key-dependent-shift (KDS) security* for weak pseudorandom functions (PRFs), and show that they serve as a convenient hub connecting these primitives. We also show that KDS secure weak PRFs imply other cryptographic primitives with circular-style security, such as linear-resistant PRGs (Hajiabadi et al., ITC 2023) and hinting weak PRFs (Alamati and Patranabis, ASIACRYPT 2022), all of which are thus existentially equivalent to KDM secure SKE and hinting PRGs as well. Hence, KDS secure weak PRFs can be thought of as a unifying umbrella for circular-secure cryptographic primitives. As another application of our new notion, we show that KDS security enables new constructions of public-key encryption (PKE) satisfying randomness-dependent-message (RDM) security and correlated-product secure trapdoor functions (TDFs). Our key technical contribution is a generic construction of KDS secure weak PRFs from any KDM secure SKE.

**Keywords:** Circular security · KDM-security · Hinting PRG · RDM security · Correlated-product secure TDF

## 1 Introduction

### 1.1 Backgrounds

*Weak Pseudorandom Functions.* A pseudorandom function (PRF) [12] is a keyed function $\mathsf{PRF} : \{0,1\}^n \times \{0,1\}^m \to \{0,1\}^\ell$ such that, for polynomially many adversarially chosen inputs $\mathsf{x}_i$, the outputs $\mathsf{PRF}(\mathsf{k}, \mathsf{x}_i)$ are computationally indistinguishable from uniform, where $\mathsf{k} \xleftarrow{\mathsf{r}} \{0,1\}^n$.[1] An important variant is a *weak*

[1] For a set $S$, "$x \xleftarrow{\mathsf{r}} S$" denotes that $x$ is picked uniformly at random from $S$.


N. Heninger and M. Rosulek (Eds.): CRYPTO 2026, LNCS 16800, pp. 67–96, 2026.
https://doi.org/10.1007/978-3-032-35367-2_3

PRF [22], where pseudorandomness is required only when the inputs are sampled uniformly at random. Despite being weaker than standard PRFs, weak PRFs already suffice for many applications, including secret-key encryption (SKE).

*Key-Dependent-Shift Security.* We introduce a circular-style notion for weak PRFs that we call *key-dependent-shift (KDS) security.* Fix a function family $\mathcal{F} = \{f : \{0,1\}^n \to \{0,1\}^\ell\}$. Informally, KDS security for $\mathcal{F}$ guarantees that for polynomially many independent samples $\mathsf{x}_i \xleftarrow{\mathsf{r}} \{0,1\}^m$,

$$\mathsf{PRF}(\mathsf{k}, \mathsf{x}_i) \oplus f_i(\mathsf{k})$$

is computationally indistinguishable from uniform, where $\mathsf{k} \xleftarrow{\mathsf{r}} \{0,1\}^n$ and each $f_i \in \mathcal{F}$ is chosen by an adversary. We show that KDS secure weak PRFs provide a unifying abstraction behind several circular-style primitives.

### 1.2 Our Results

The main message of this paper is that several seemingly different circular-style primitives are *existentially equivalent.* In particular, somewhat surprisingly, we show that *hinting PRGs* [21] *are equivalent to SKE satisfying key-dependent-message (KDM) security* [7]. As a conceptual centerpiece, we introduce KDS secure weak PRFs and show that they serve as a convenient hub connecting these primitives. The key technical step is a generic construction of KDS secure weak PRFs from any KDM secure SKE. Moreover, KDS security also enables new constructions of PKE satisfying randomness-dependent-message (RDM) security [5,6,16] and correlated-product secure trapdoor functions (TDFs) [24].

*Construction (KDM ⇒ KDS).* As stated above, we show that KDS secure weak PRFs can be constructed from any KDM secure SKE. Formally, we prove the following theorem.

**Theorem 1 (Informal).** *Assuming that there exists a SKE scheme satisfying KDM security for projection functions, there exists a KDS secure weak PRF for any functions computable by a-priori bounded polynomial-size circuits.*

Projection functions are elementary functions such that each output bit depends on at most a single bit of an input. Since projection-KDM secure SKE can be based on a number of concrete assumptions, including the learning-with-errors (LWE) and learning-parity-with noise (LPN) assumptions [4], computational Diffie–Hellman (CDH) and factoring assumptions [8], and even a group-action based assumption [1], we obtain KDS secure weak PRFs under each of these assumptions.

*Consequences of KDS Security.* We obtain the following consequences of KDS secure weak PRFs.

**Hinting PRG and Its Friends:** A hinting PRG [21] is a public-parameter-model PRG that stretches a seed $\mathsf{s} = (\mathsf{s}_1, \ldots, \mathsf{s}_n) \in \{0,1\}^n$ into $n+1$ $\lambda$-bit outputs $(\mathsf{y}_0, \mathsf{y}_1, \ldots, \mathsf{y}_n) \in (\{0,1\}^\lambda)^{n+1}$. It guarantees that the *hinting* distribution $\big(\mathsf{y}_0, (\mathsf{y}_{i,0}, \mathsf{y}_{i,1})_{i\in[n]}\big)$ is computationally indistinguishable from uniform, where $\mathsf{s} \xleftarrow{r} \{0,1\}^n$, $(\mathsf{y}_0, \mathsf{y}_{1,\mathsf{s}_1}, \ldots, \mathsf{y}_{n,\mathsf{s}_n}) \leftarrow \mathsf{HPRG}(\mathsf{pp}, \mathsf{s})$, and $\mathsf{y}_{i,1-\mathsf{s}_i} \xleftarrow{r} \{0,1\}^\lambda$ for each $i \in [n]$.

Koppula and Waters [21] introduced hinting PRGs and showed how to generically transform any CPA secure public-key encryption (PKE) scheme into a CCA secure one using a hinting PRG. Subsequently, hinting PRGs have been used in constructions of trapdoor functions (TDFs) [11,20], non-interactive CCA secure commitments [9,10], anamorphic PKE [23], and more.

We show that KDS secure weak PRFs for projection functions imply hinting PRGs. We also show that KDS secure weak PRFs for projection functions imply variants of a hinting PRG called a functional hinting PRG, and their "weak-PRF-analogues" called a hinting weak PRF and a functional hinting weak PRF that were introduced and studied in [2].

**Linear-Resistant PRG:** A PRG $\mathsf{G}$ is said to satisfy *linear resistance* if, for every $\mathbb{F}_2$-linear function $f$, the distribution of

$$\mathsf{G}(\mathsf{x}) \oplus f(\mathsf{x})$$

is computationally indistinguishable from uniform, where $\mathsf{x} \xleftarrow{r} \{0,1\}^n$. Hajiabadi, Khazaei, and Vahdini [14] introduced linear-resistant PRGs and showed that they can be used to realize randomness-recoverable secret sharing for monotone span programs.

A KDS secure weak PRF for linear functions immediately yields a linear-resistant PRG in the public-randomness model, where $\mathsf{G}$ takes a uniformly chosen public parameter $\mathsf{pp}$ together with $\mathsf{x}$ as input. Such a linear-resistant PRG still suffices for the randomness-recoverable secret-sharing application.

**Public-Coin KDM Secure SKE:** We can construct a CPA secure SKE scheme from a weak PRF via the standard construction, where a ciphertext encrypting a plaintext $\mathsf{m}$ is of the form

$$\Big(\mathsf{x},\ \mathsf{PRF}(\mathsf{k}, \mathsf{x}) \oplus \mathsf{m}\Big).$$

The encryption algorithm uses only public coins (randomness) $\mathsf{x}$. This public-coin property implies several appealing features, such as resilience to randomness leakage and randomness-recoverability. We show that this construction becomes KDM secure if the underlying weak PRF is KDS secure. This SKE scheme is KDM secure with respect to the same class of functions for which the underlying weak PRF is KDS secure.

**Correlation RDM Secure PKE:** Let $\mathcal{F}$ be a function family. A PKE scheme is said to satisfy randomness-dependent-message (RDM) security with respect to $\mathcal{F}$ ($\mathcal{F}$-RDM security) if, for every $f \in \mathcal{F}$, the ciphertext $\mathsf{Enc}(\mathsf{pk}, f(\mathsf{r}); \mathsf{r})$ is computationally indistinguishable from an encryption of a fixed message such as $0 \cdots 0$. Following Hajiabadi and Kapron [13], we consider a strengthened notion that we call *correlation $\mathcal{F}$-RDM security.* Correlation $\mathcal{F}$-RDM

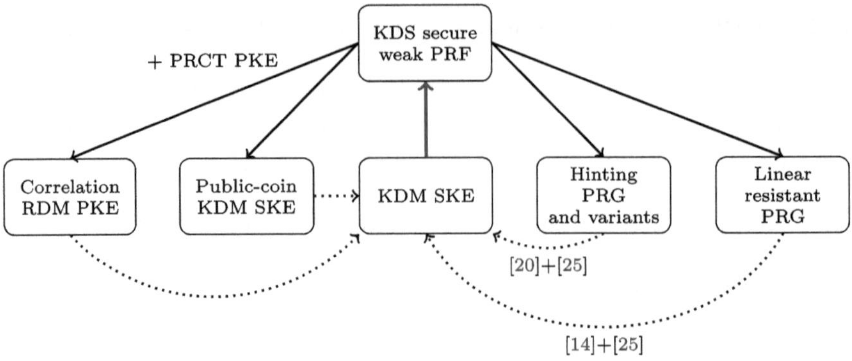


**Fig. 1.** Equivalence of circular secure primitives

security guarantees that, a-priori unbounded number (denoted by $q$) of RDM ciphertexts generated by using the same randomness $\mathsf{r}$, namely,

$$\mathsf{Enc}(\mathsf{pk}_1, f_1(\mathsf{r}); \mathsf{r}), \ldots, \mathsf{Enc}(\mathsf{pk}_q, f_q(\mathsf{r}); \mathsf{r}),$$

are computationally indistinguishable from encryptions of a fixed message, where $\mathsf{pk}_1, \ldots, \mathsf{pk}_q$ are independently generated public keys. Correlation $\mathcal{F}$-RDM secure PKE can also be seen as a generalization of correlated-product secure TDFs [24].
We show how to realize correlation $\mathcal{F}$-RDM secure PKE by combining a $\mathcal{F}$-KDS secure weak PRF with pseudorandom-ciphertext PKE.

*Corollaries and Instantiations.* We obtain several corollaries from the above results.

**Existential Equivalence:** Hinting PRGs and linear-resistant PRGs both imply one-time KDM secure SKE for projection functions [14,20], which in turn implies multi-time KDM secure SKE for all polynomial-time computable functions [25]. Furthermore, projection-KDM secure SKE can also be constructed from a circular-secure bit-SKE scheme [19], namely, an SKE scheme that can securely encrypt each bit of its secret key and thus satisfies arguably one of the weakest and simplest forms of KDM security. Combining these implications with our results, we show that KDM secure SKE and its public-coin variant, hinting PRG, linear-resistant PRG, and KDS secure weak PRF are all existentially equivalent. We can also prove that correlation RDM secure PKE implies KDM secure SKE,[2] which means these two primitives are existentially equivalent under the existence of pseudorandom-ciphertext PKE. We summarize these relations in Fig. 1.

[2] See Remark 1 for this implication.

**New Circular Secure PRGs:** Combining the above equivalence with the fact that KDM secure SKE can be realized from the LPN assumption [4], we obtain the first construction of a hinting PRG based on LPN. We also obtain the first realizations of linear-resistant PRGs based on a variety of assumptions that imply KDM secure SKE. In particular, Hajiabadi et al. [14] left open the problem of constructing linear-resistant PRGs without relying on the random oracle heuristic, which is resolved by our results.

**New RDM Secure PKE and Correlated Product Secure TDF:** Birrell, Chung, Pass, and Telang [6] argued that it is difficult to achieve RDM secure PKE that encrypts arbitrarily long messages using only short encryption randomness. Prior to our work, achieving RDM secure PKE with short randomness relied on deterministic encryption [5] or lossy trapdoor functions [6,16]. This left open the existence of such schemes under the LPN assumption and under group-action-based assumptions.

Our correlation RDM security notion guarantees that arbitrarily long messages can be securely encrypted using a single short randomness. Since both of the building blocks of our correlation RDM secure PKE can be instantiated from the LPN assumption [3,4,26] and from group-action-based assumptions [1,2], we obtain the first PKE schemes satisfying a form of RDM security with short randomness from each of these two assumptions.

Moreover, these correlation RDM secure PKE schemes also yield the first correlated-product secure TDFs from the LPN assumption and from group-action-based assumptions. We further highlight that our LPN-based TDF is the first TDF that is secure for uniformly random inputs. Previous LPN-based TDFs [18,20] are proved secure only when part of the input is drawn from a Bernoulli distribution. Security under uniformly random inputs is required in applications where some inputs are derived from randomness-extractors, such as [17].

### 1.3 Technical Overview

*KDS Secure Weak PRF from KDM Secure SKE.* We define SKE as a tuple consisting only of the encryption algorithm $\mathsf{SEnc}$ and the decryption algorithm $\mathsf{SDec}$, for which the key generation just chooses a secret key $\mathsf{k}$ uniformly at random from a binary space. We also require that the message space and the ciphertext space be respectively binary spaces $\{0,1\}^m$ and $\{0,1\}^\ell$ for some $m$ and $\ell$. In our construction of a KDS secure weak PRF, we utilize a new security notion for SKE that we call *pseudorandomness of ciphertexts against the receiver (receiver-PRCT security).* The notion guarantees that a ciphertext is computationally indistinguishable from uniform even given a secret key (hence the name of the security notion), as long as the plaintext is chosen uniformly at random, that is, $(\mathsf{k}, \mathsf{SEnc}(\mathsf{k}, \mathsf{m}))$ and $(\mathsf{k}, \mathsf{x})$, where $\mathsf{k} \xleftarrow{r} \{0,1\}^n$, $\mathsf{m} \xleftarrow{r} \{0,1\}^m$, and $\mathsf{x} \xleftarrow{r} \{0,1\}^\ell$, are computationally indistinguishable.

A weak PRF satisfying KDS security with respect to a function family $\mathcal{F}$ can be easily realized from SKE satisfying receiver-PRCT security and $\mathcal{F}$-KDM security[3] simultaneously.

We use a SKE scheme $\mathcal{E} = (\mathsf{SEnc}, \mathsf{SDec})$ with the key space $\{0,1\}^n$, the message space $\{0,1\}^m$, and the ciphertext space $\{0,1\}^\ell$, and construct weak PRF $\mathsf{PRF} : \{0,1\}^n \times \{0,1\}^\ell \to \{0,1\}^m$. The construction is highly simple: given a key $\mathsf{k}$ and an input $\mathsf{x}$, PRF outputs $\mathsf{SDec}(\mathsf{k}, \mathsf{x})$. We argue its KDS security as follows. Let $f \in \mathcal{F}$. Consider the distribution of

$$\left(\mathsf{x},\ \mathsf{PRF}(\mathsf{k},\mathsf{x}) \oplus f(\mathsf{k})\right) = \left(\mathsf{x},\ \mathsf{SDec}(\mathsf{k},\mathsf{x}) \oplus f(\mathsf{k})\right),$$

where $\mathsf{k} \xleftarrow{\mathsf{r}} \{0,1\}^n$ and $\mathsf{x} \xleftarrow{\mathsf{r}} \{0,1\}^\ell$. From the receiver-PRCT security of $\mathcal{E}$, it is computationally indistinguishable from

$$\left(\mathsf{x} = \mathsf{SEnc}(\mathsf{k}, f(\mathsf{k}) \oplus u),\ u\right),$$

where $u \xleftarrow{\mathsf{r}} \{0,1\}^m$. Note that we use the invariance $\mathsf{SDec}(\mathsf{k},\mathsf{x}) \oplus f(\mathsf{k}) = f(\mathsf{k}) \oplus u \oplus f(\mathsf{k}) = u$. From the $\mathcal{F}$-KDM security of $\mathcal{E}$, it is computationally indistinguishable from $\left(\mathsf{x} = \mathsf{SEnc}(\mathsf{k}, v), u\right)$, where $v \xleftarrow{\mathsf{r}} \{0,1\}^m$. The final distribution is computationally indistinguishable from a uniform tuple again from receiver-PRCT security of $\mathcal{E}$.[4] We can prove that the arguments go through in the multiple-sample setting and complete the proof of the KDS security of PRF.

To connect a KDS secure weak PRF with KDM secure SKE, we have to show that we can generically add receiver-PRCT security to any KDM secure SKE. We show that this is possible by extending the universal KDM amplification technique proposed by Waters and Wichs [25] using the notion of blind garbled circuits [8].

*Hinting PRG from KDS Secure Weak PRF.* We use a weak PRF $\mathsf{PRF} : \{0,1\}^n \times \{0,1\}^m \to (\{0,1\}^\lambda)^{2n+1}$ satisfying KDS security with respect to selector functions of the following form: A selector function $\mathsf{sel}[(\Delta_{i,v})_{i\in[n],v\in\{0,1\}}]$ has $2n$ $\lambda$-bit strings $(\Delta_{i,v})_{i\in[n],v\in\{0,1\}}$ hardwired, and on input $\mathsf{k} = (\mathsf{k}_1, \ldots, \mathsf{k}_n) \in \{0,1\}^n$ outputs $(0^\lambda, w_{1,0}, w_{1,1}, \ldots, w_{n,0}, w_{n,1}) \in (\{0,1\}^\lambda)^{2n+1}$ such that $w_{1,\mathsf{k}_1} = \cdots = w_{n,\mathsf{k}_n} = 0^\lambda$, and $w_{i,1-\mathsf{k}_i} = \Delta_{i,1-\mathsf{k}_i}$ for all $i \in [n]$. A selector function can be realized by a projection function.

We construct a hinting PRG HPRG that maps an $n$-bit seed to $n+1$ $\lambda$-bit outputs as follows. We set the public parameter as a randomly chosen string $\mathsf{x} \xleftarrow{\mathsf{r}} \{0,1\}^m$. The evaluation algorithm, on input $\mathsf{k} = (\mathsf{k}_1, \ldots, \mathsf{k}_n) \in \{0,1\}^n$, computes $(\mathsf{y}_0, \mathsf{y}_{1,0}, \mathsf{y}_{1,1}, \ldots, \mathsf{y}_{n,0}, \mathsf{y}_{n,1}) \leftarrow \mathsf{PRF}(\mathsf{k}, \mathsf{x})$, where each block is $\lambda$-bit long, and outputs $(\mathsf{y}_0, \mathsf{y}_{1,\mathsf{k}_1}, \ldots, \mathsf{y}_{n,\mathsf{k}_n})$. The reduction attacking the KDS secure weak PRF submits a selector function $\mathsf{sel}[(\Delta_{i,v})_{i\in[n],v\in\{0,1\}}]$ for randomly chosen

[3] Informally, a SKE scheme is $\mathcal{F}$-KDM secure if it can securely encrypt plaintexts of the form $f(\mathsf{k})$, where $f \in \mathcal{F}$ and $\mathsf{k}$ is a secret key. For the formal definition, see Sect. 2.2.

[4] This step can be done with the standard pseudorandom ciphertext property as well.

$\Delta_{i,v} \leftarrow \{0,1\}^\lambda$ as a KDS query, and is given $\mathsf{x} \xleftarrow{r} \{0,1\}^m$ and $\mathsf{Y} \in (\{0,1\}^\lambda)^{2n+1}$ that is either chosen uniformly at random, or

$$\begin{aligned}\mathsf{Y} &= \mathsf{PRF}(\mathsf{k},\mathsf{x}) \oplus \mathsf{sel}[(\Delta_{i,v})_{i\in[n],v\in\{0,1\}}](\mathsf{k}) \\ &= \Big(\mathsf{y}_0,\ \mathsf{y}_{1,0} \oplus w_{1,0},\ \mathsf{y}_{1,1} \oplus w_{1,1}, \cdots,\ \mathsf{y}_{n,0} \oplus w_{n,0},\ \mathsf{y}_{n,1} \oplus w_{n,1}\Big),\end{aligned}$$

where $(\mathsf{y}_0, \mathsf{y}_{1,0}, \mathsf{y}_{1,1}, \ldots, \mathsf{y}_{n,0}, \mathsf{y}_{n,1}) \leftarrow \mathsf{PRF}(\mathsf{k},\mathsf{x})$. We see that $\mathsf{y}_{i,\mathsf{k}_i} \oplus w_{i,\mathsf{k}_i} = \mathsf{y}_{i,\mathsf{k}_i}$ and $\mathsf{y}_{i,1-\mathsf{k}_i} \oplus w_{i,1-\mathsf{k}_i} = \mathsf{y}_{i,\mathsf{k}_i} \oplus \Delta_{i,1-\mathsf{k}_i}$ for each $i \in [n]$. Since $\mathsf{y}_{i,\mathsf{k}_i} \oplus \Delta_{i,1-\mathsf{k}_i}$ is distributed uniformly at random, the above distribution is identical to the hinting distribution of HPRG. Thus, the security of HPRG is reduced to that of PRF.

*Correlation RDM Secure PKE via KDS Secure Weak PRF.* Garg, Hajiabadi, Malavolta, and Ostrovsky [11] showed how to construct TDFs from pseudorandom-ciphertext PKE and hinting PRGs. At a technical level, they built a gadget that encodes a hinting PRG seed $\mathsf{k} = (\mathsf{k}_1, \ldots, \mathsf{k}_n) \in \{0,1\}^n$ in an invertible way using the output blocks $(\mathsf{y}_1, \ldots, \mathsf{y}_n)$, with $\mathsf{y}_0$ serving as hardcore bits.

In our construction of correlation RDM secure PKE, we instead use a KDS secure weak PRF whose output is of the form $(\mathsf{y}_0, \mathsf{y}_{1,0}, \mathsf{y}_{1,1}, \ldots, \mathsf{y}_{n,0}, \mathsf{y}_{n,1}) \leftarrow \mathsf{PRF}(\mathsf{k},\mathsf{x})$ as above, and the encryption randomness is simply the PRF key $\mathsf{k}$. The public and secret keys follow the evaluation and inversion keys in [11], except that the public key additionally contains a uniformly random PRF input $\mathsf{x} \xleftarrow{r} \{0,1\}^m$.

To encrypt a randomness-dependent message $f(\mathsf{k})$, we first compute $(\mathsf{y}_0, \mathsf{y}_{1,0}, \mathsf{y}_{1,1}, \ldots, \mathsf{y}_{n,0}, \mathsf{y}_{n,1}) \leftarrow \mathsf{PRF}(\mathsf{k},\mathsf{x})$. We then encode $\mathsf{k}$ into the gadget of [11] by using $(\mathsf{y}_{1,\mathsf{k}_1}, \ldots, \mathsf{y}_{n,\mathsf{k}_n})$ in place of the output of a hinting PRG, and mask $f(\mathsf{k})$ using $\mathsf{y}_0$.

Following the proof strategy of [11], we reach a hybrid in which an adversary's view can be simulated from

$$\mathsf{PRF}(\mathsf{k},\mathsf{x}) \oplus \Big(f(\mathsf{k}),\ \mathsf{sel}[(\Delta_{i,v})_{i\in[n],v\in\{0,1\}}](\mathsf{k})\Big),$$

where the XOR is performed component-wise. This distribution is computationally indistinguishable from uniform by the KDS security of the weak PRF, which guarantees that $f(\mathsf{k})$ is hidden from the adversary. Moreover, the multi-instance nature of KDS security allows us to complete the proof even in the correlation RDM setting.

## 2 Preliminaries

In this section, we review the basic notation and the definitions of main cryptographic primitives.

*Basic Notation.* For $n \in \mathbb{N}$, we define $[n] := \{1, \ldots, n\}$. For strings $x$ and $y$, "$|x|$" denotes the bit-length of $x$, $x \leftarrow y$ denotes the assignment of $y$ to $x$, "$x \| y$" denotes the concatenation $x$ and $y$, and "$(x \stackrel{?}{=} y)$" is the operation that returns 1 if $x = y$ and 0 otherwise. For a discrete finite set $S$, "$|S|$" denotes its size, and "$x \stackrel{r}{\leftarrow} S$" denotes choosing an element $x$ uniformly at random from $S$. For a probabilistic (resp. deterministic) algorithm $\mathsf{M}$, "$y \stackrel{r}{\leftarrow} \mathsf{M}(x)$" (resp. "$y \leftarrow \mathsf{M}(x)$") denote $\mathsf{M}$ takes $x$ as input, and outputs $y$. In particular, if $\mathsf{M}$ is probabilistic and we need to specify the randomness $r$ used in $\mathsf{M}$, we write "$y \leftarrow \mathsf{M}(x; r)$". If furthermore $\mathcal{O}$ is a function or an algorithm, then "$\mathsf{M}^{\mathcal{O}}$" means that $\mathsf{M}$ has oracle access to $\mathcal{O}$. A function $\epsilon(\lambda) : \mathbb{N} \rightarrow [0, 1]$ is said to be *negligible* if $\epsilon(\lambda) = \lambda^{-\omega(1)}$. The character "$\lambda$" always denotes a security parameter. "PPT" stands for *probabilistic polynomial time.*

### 2.1 Weak Pseudorandom Function

Let $\ell = \ell(\lambda)$, $m = m(\lambda)$ and $n = n(\lambda)$ be polynomials, and let $\mathsf{wPRF} : \{0,1\}^n \times \{0,1\}^m \rightarrow \{0,1\}^\ell$ be an efficiently computable function.

We say that $\mathsf{wPRF}$ is a *secure weak pseudorandom function (weak PRF)*, if for all PPT adversaries $\mathcal{A}$,

$$\mathsf{Adv}^{\mathtt{wPRF}}_{\mathsf{wPRF},\mathcal{A}}(\lambda) := 2 \cdot \left| \Pr\left[ \begin{array}{l} \mathsf{k} \stackrel{r}{\leftarrow} \{0,1\}^n;\ b \stackrel{r}{\leftarrow} \{0,1\}; \\ b' \stackrel{r}{\leftarrow} \mathcal{A}^{\mathcal{O}_{\mathtt{wPRF}}(\$)}(1^\lambda) \end{array} : b' = b \right] - \frac{1}{2} \right|$$

is negligible, where $\mathcal{O}_{\mathtt{wPRF}}(\$)$ is the oracle that, upon a query, picks $\mathsf{x} \stackrel{r}{\leftarrow} \{0,1\}^m$ and $\mathsf{y}_0 \stackrel{r}{\leftarrow} \{0,1\}^\ell$, computes $y_1 \leftarrow \mathsf{wPRF}(\mathsf{k}, \mathsf{x})$, and returns $(\mathsf{x}, \mathsf{y}_b)$.

Weak PRFs can be constructed from any one-way function [12,15].

### 2.2 Secret-Key Encryption

A secret-key encryption (SKE) scheme $\mathcal{E}$ consists of the two PPT algorithms $(\mathsf{SEnc}, \mathsf{SDec})$ with the following syntax:

| | |
|---|---|
| **Encryption:** | $\mathsf{ct} \stackrel{r}{\leftarrow} \mathsf{SEnc}(\mathsf{sk}, \mathsf{m})$ |
| **Decryption:** | $\mathsf{m} \,/\, \bot \leftarrow \mathsf{SDec}(\mathsf{sk}, \mathsf{ct})$ |

where $\mathsf{SDec}$ is deterministic, $\mathsf{sk}$ is a secret key, and $\mathsf{ct}$ is a ciphertext encrypting a plaintext $\mathsf{m}$ under $\mathsf{sk}$.

For simplicity, we assume that the security parameter $\lambda$ determines the secret key space $\mathcal{K}$, plaintext space $\mathcal{M}$, and ciphertext space $\mathcal{C}$, and each element in each space has the same bit length.

We require that for all $\mathsf{sk}$ and $\mathsf{m}$, we have $\mathsf{SDec}(\mathsf{sk}, \mathsf{SEnc}(\mathsf{sk}, \mathsf{m})) = \mathsf{m}$.

*Pseudorandomness of Ciphertexts (PRCT Security).* Let $\mathcal{E} = (\mathsf{SEnc}, \mathsf{SDec})$ be a SKE scheme whose secret key space is $\mathcal{K}$, plaintext space is $\mathcal{M}$, and ciphertext space is $\mathcal{C}$. We say that $\mathcal{E}$ is *PRCT secure*, if for all PPT adversaries $\mathcal{A}$,

$$\mathsf{Adv}^{\mathtt{PRCT}}_{\mathcal{E},\mathcal{A}}(\lambda) := 2 \cdot \left| \Pr\left[ \mathsf{sk} \xleftarrow{r} \mathcal{K};\ b \xleftarrow{r} \{0,1\};\ b' \xleftarrow{r} \mathcal{A}^{\mathcal{O}_{\mathtt{PRCT}}(\cdot)}(1^\lambda) : b' = b \right] - \frac{1}{2} \right|$$

is negligible, where $\mathcal{O}_{\mathtt{PRCT}}(\cdot)$ denotes the encryption oracle that takes a plaintext $\mathsf{m} \in \mathcal{M}$ as input, computes $\mathsf{ct}_1 \xleftarrow{r} \mathsf{SEnc}(\mathsf{sk}, \mathsf{m})$, picks $\mathsf{ct}_0 \xleftarrow{r} \mathcal{C}$, and returns $\mathsf{ct}_b$.

In this paper, we will use the well-known SKE scheme $\mathcal{E}_{\mathtt{wPRF}} = (\mathsf{SEnc}_{\mathtt{PRF}}, \mathsf{SDec}_{\mathtt{wPRF}})$ based on a weak PRF $\mathsf{wPRF} : \{0,1\}^n \times \{0,1\}^m \to \{0,1\}^\ell$, which is constructed as follows: Given a secret key $\mathsf{sk} \in \{0,1\}^n$, a plaintext $\mathsf{m} \in \{0,1\}^\ell$, and a randomness $\mathsf{r} \in \{0,1\}^m$, $\mathsf{SEnc}(\mathsf{sk}, \mathsf{m}; \mathsf{r})$ outputs $\mathsf{ct} = (\mathsf{r}, \mathsf{wPRF}(\mathsf{sk}, \mathsf{r}) \oplus \mathsf{m})$ as a ciphertext; Given a secret key $\mathsf{sk} \in \{0,1\}^\lambda$ and a ciphertext $\mathsf{ct} = (\mathsf{r}, \mathsf{y})$, $\mathsf{SDec}(\mathsf{sk}, \mathsf{ct})$ outputs $\mathsf{wPRF}(\mathsf{sk}, \mathsf{r}) \oplus \mathsf{y}$ as the decryption result. It is well-known that if $\mathsf{wPRF}$ is a secure weak PRF, then $\mathcal{E}_{\mathtt{wPRF}}$ is PRCT secure.

*Key-Dependent Message (KDM) Security.* Let $\mathcal{E} = (\mathsf{SEnc}, \mathsf{SDec})$ be a SKE scheme whose secret key space is $\mathcal{K}$ and plaintext space is $\mathcal{M}$, and let $\mathcal{F}$ be a family of functions whose domain is $\mathcal{K}$ and range is $\mathcal{M}$. We say that $\mathcal{E}$ is *$\mathcal{F}$-KDM secure* if for all PPT adversaries $\mathcal{A}$,

$$\mathsf{Adv}^{\mathcal{F}\text{-}\mathtt{KDM}}_{\mathcal{E},\mathcal{A}}(\lambda) := 2 \cdot \left| \Pr\left[ \mathsf{sk} \xleftarrow{r} \mathcal{K};\ b \xleftarrow{r} \{0,1\};\ b' \xleftarrow{r} \mathcal{A}^{\mathcal{O}_{\mathtt{KDM}}(\cdot,\cdot)}(1^\lambda) : b' = b \right] - \frac{1}{2} \right|$$

is negligible, where $\mathcal{O}_{\mathtt{KDM}}(\cdot)$ denotes the KDM-encryption oracle that takes two functions $(f_0, f_1) \in \mathcal{F}^2$ as input, and returns $\mathsf{ct} \xleftarrow{r} \mathsf{SEnc}(\mathsf{sk}, f_b(\mathsf{sk}))$.

We also say that $\mathcal{E}$ satisfies *one-time $\mathcal{F}$-KDM security* if for all PPT adversaries $\mathcal{A}$, $\mathsf{Adv}^{\mathtt{OT}\text{-}\mathcal{F}\text{-}\mathtt{KDM}}_{\mathcal{E},\mathcal{A}}(\lambda)$ is negligible, where $\mathsf{Adv}^{\mathtt{OT}\text{-}\mathcal{F}\text{-}\mathtt{KDM}}_{\mathcal{E},\mathcal{A}}(\lambda)$ is defined in the same way as $\mathsf{Adv}^{\mathcal{F}\text{-}\mathtt{KDM}}_{\mathcal{E},\mathcal{A}}(\lambda)$, except that $\mathcal{A}$ is allowed to make only a single KDM-encryption query.

In this paper, we will treat KDM-secure SKE schemes whose secret key space $\mathcal{K}$ and plaintext space $\mathcal{M}$ are of the form $\mathcal{K} = \{0,1\}^{\ell_{\mathsf{sk}}}$ and $\mathcal{M} = \{0,1\}^{\ell_{\mathsf{m}}}$, respectively, for some polynomials $\ell_{\mathsf{sk}} = \ell_{\mathsf{sk}}(\lambda)$ and $\ell_{\mathsf{m}} = \ell_{\mathsf{m}}(\lambda)$. The function families for KDM security that we will specifically treat are as follows:

- $\mathcal{P}$ *(Projection functions):* A function is said to be a projection function if each of its output bits depends on at most a single bit of its input. We denote by $\mathcal{P}$ the family of projection functions.
- $\mathcal{L}$ *(Affine functions):* A function $f : \{0,1\}^{\ell_{\mathsf{sk}}} \to \{0,1\}^{\ell_{\mathsf{m}}}$ is said to be an affine function if there exists a $\ell_{\mathsf{sk}}$-by-$\ell_{\mathsf{m}}$ matrix $\mathsf{A} \in \{0,1\}^{\ell_{\mathsf{sk}} \times \ell_{\mathsf{m}}}$ and a vector $\mathsf{b} \in \{0,1\}^{\ell_{\mathsf{m}}}$ such that $f(\mathsf{x}) = \mathsf{x} \cdot \mathsf{A} + \mathsf{b}$ holds for all $\mathsf{x} = (\mathsf{x}_1, \dots, \mathsf{x}_{\ell_{\mathsf{sk}}}) \in \{0,1\}^{\ell_{\mathsf{sk}}}$, where the arithmetic is performed over the finite field $\mathbb{F}_2$ of order 2. We denote by $\mathcal{L}$ the family of affine functions.
- $\mathcal{B}_s$ *(Circuits of a-priori bounded size):* We denote by $\mathcal{B}_s$, where $s = s(\lambda)$ is a polynomial, the function family each of whose members can be described by a circuit of size $s$.

Note that we have $\mathcal{P} \subseteq \mathcal{L}$. Furthermore, if $s$ is sufficiently large, we have $\mathcal{P} \subseteq \mathcal{B}_s$ and $\mathcal{L} \subseteq \mathcal{B}_s$.

### 2.3 Hinting PRG

Here, we recall the definition of a hinting PRG introduced in [21].

Let $n = n(\lambda)$ be a polynomial. A hinting PRG $\mathcal{H}$ with seed length $n$ consists of the two PPT algorithms $(\mathsf{HSetup}, \mathsf{HPRG})$ with the following syntax[5]:

$$\begin{array}{rcl}\textbf{Parameter Setup:} & \mathsf{pp} & \xleftarrow{\mathsf{r}} \mathsf{HSetup}(1^\lambda) \\ \textbf{Computation:} & (\mathsf{y}_0, \mathsf{y}_1, \ldots, \mathsf{y}_n) & \leftarrow \mathsf{HPRG}(\mathsf{pp}, \mathsf{s} \in \{0,1\}^n)\end{array}$$

where $\mathsf{HPRG}$ is deterministic, $\mathsf{pp}$ is a public parameter, $\mathsf{s} \in \{0,1\}^n$ is an input (seed), and $(\mathsf{y}_0, \mathsf{y}_1, \ldots, \mathsf{y}_n) \in (\{0,1\}^\lambda)^{n+1}$ is an output (and $y_i \in \{0,1\}^\lambda$ ($i \in \{0\} \cup [n]$) represents the $i$-th block of the output).

We say that $\mathcal{H}$ is a *secure hinting PRG* if for all PPT adversaries $\mathcal{A}$,

$$\mathsf{Adv}^{\mathtt{HPRG}}_{\mathcal{H},\mathcal{A}}(\lambda) := 2 \cdot \left| \Pr\left[ \begin{array}{l} \mathsf{pp} \xleftarrow{\mathsf{r}} \mathsf{HSetup}(1^\lambda); \\ \mathsf{s} = (\mathsf{s}_1, \ldots, \mathsf{s}_n) \xleftarrow{\mathsf{r}} \{0,1\}^n; \\ (\mathsf{y}_0, \mathsf{y}_1, \ldots, \mathsf{y}_n) \leftarrow \mathsf{HPRG}(\mathsf{pp}, \mathsf{s}); \\ \forall i \in [n] : \mathsf{y}_{i,\mathsf{s}_i} \leftarrow \mathsf{y}_i; \\ \forall i \in [n] : \mathsf{y}_{i,1-\mathsf{s}_i} \xleftarrow{\mathsf{r}} \{0,1\}^\lambda; \\ \mathsf{Y}_1 \leftarrow (\mathsf{y}_0, (\mathsf{y}_{i,0}, \mathsf{y}_{i,1})_{i \in [n]}); \\ \mathsf{Y}_0 \xleftarrow{\mathsf{r}} \{0,1\}^\lambda \times (\{0,1\}^\lambda \times \{0,1\}^\lambda)^n; \\ b \xleftarrow{\mathsf{r}} \{0,1\};\ b' \xleftarrow{\mathsf{r}} \mathcal{A}(\mathsf{pp}, \mathsf{Y}_b) \end{array} : b' = b \right] - \frac{1}{2} \right|$$

is negligible.

### 2.4 Linear-Resistant PRG

Here, we give the definition of a linear-resistant PRG introduced by Hajiabadi et al. [14], where unlike [14], we allow it to use a public parameter.

Let $m = m(\lambda)$ and $n = n(\lambda)$ be polynomials with $n < m$.

A linear-resistant PRG $\mathcal{LR}$ with seed length $n$ and output length $m$ consists of the two PPT algorithms $(\mathsf{LRSetup}, \mathsf{LRPRG})$ with the following syntax:

$$\begin{array}{rl}\textbf{Parameter Setup:} & \mathsf{pp} \xleftarrow{\mathsf{r}} \mathsf{LRSetup}(1^\lambda) \\ \textbf{Computation:} & \mathsf{y} \leftarrow \mathsf{LRPRG}(\mathsf{pp}, \mathsf{s} \in \{0,1\}^n)\end{array}$$

[5] Unlike the original paper [21], we adopt the syntax such that all the output blocks $(\mathsf{y}_0, \mathsf{y}_1, \ldots, \mathsf{y}_n)$ are computed in one-shot (exactly as done in a standard PRG). Furthermore, we only treat a hinting PRG such that the length of each output block is $\lambda$-bit (when $\mathsf{pp}$ is setup with the security parameter $\lambda$). This is without loss of generality, since if we want the length of some output block $\mathsf{y}_i$ to be longer, we can apply a (standard) PRG to $\mathsf{y}_i$ for stretching it securely.

where $\mathsf{LRPRG}$ is deterministic, $\mathsf{pp}$ is a public parameter, $\mathsf{s} \in \{0,1\}^n$ is an input (seed), and $\mathsf{y} \in \{0,1\}^m$ is an output.

We say that $\mathcal{LR}$ is a *secure linear-resistant PRG* if for all PPT adversaries $\mathcal{A} = (\mathcal{A}_1, \mathcal{A}_2)$,

$$\mathsf{Adv}^{\mathtt{LRPRG}}_{\mathcal{LR},\mathcal{A}}(\lambda) := 2 \cdot \left| \Pr\left[ \begin{array}{l} (f \in \mathcal{L}, \mathsf{st}) \xleftarrow{r} \mathcal{A}_1(1^\lambda); \\ \mathsf{pp} \xleftarrow{r} \mathsf{LRSetup}(1^\lambda); \\ \mathsf{s} \xleftarrow{r} \{0,1\}^n; \\ \mathsf{y}_1 \leftarrow \mathsf{LRPRG}(\mathsf{pp}, \mathsf{s}) \oplus f(\mathsf{s}); \\ \mathsf{y}_0 \xleftarrow{r} \{0,1\}^m;\ b \xleftarrow{r} \{0,1\}; \\ b' \xleftarrow{r} \mathcal{A}_2(\mathsf{pp}, \mathsf{y}_b, \mathsf{st}) \end{array} : b' = b \right] - \frac{1}{2} \right|$$

is negligible, where $\mathcal{L}$ denotes the family of affine functions (see Sect. 2.2 for its definition).

## 2.5 Public-Key Encryption

A public-key encryption (PKE) scheme consists of the three PPT algorithms $(\mathsf{KG}, \mathsf{Enc}, \mathsf{Dec})$ with the following syntax:

| | |
|---|---|
| **Key Generation:** | $(\mathsf{pk}, \mathsf{sk}) \xleftarrow{r} \mathsf{KG}(1^\lambda)$ |
| **Encryption:** | $\mathsf{ct} \xleftarrow{r} \mathsf{Enc}(\mathsf{pk}, \mathsf{m})$ |
| **Decryption:** | $\mathsf{m} / \bot \leftarrow \mathsf{Dec}(\mathsf{sk}, \mathsf{ct})$ |

where $\mathsf{Dec}$ is deterministic, $(\mathsf{pk}, \mathsf{sk})$ is a public/secret key pair, and $\mathsf{ct}$ is a ciphertext of a plaintext $\mathsf{m}$ under $\mathsf{pk}$. For simplicity, we assume that $\lambda$ determines the plaintext space $\mathcal{M}$, the encryption randomness space $\mathcal{R}$, and the ciphertext space $\mathcal{C}$, and each element in each space has the same bit length.

Let $\epsilon : \mathbb{N} \to [0,1]$. We say that a PKE scheme $\Pi = (\mathsf{KG}, \mathsf{Enc}, \mathsf{Dec})$ is $\epsilon$-*almost all-keys correct* if we have

$$\mathsf{Err}_\Pi(\lambda) := \Pr_{(\mathsf{pk},\mathsf{sk}) \xleftarrow{r} \mathsf{KG}(1^\lambda)} [\exists (\mathsf{m}, \mathsf{r}) \in \mathcal{M} \times \mathcal{R} : \mathsf{Dec}(\mathsf{sk}, \mathsf{Enc}(\mathsf{pk}, \mathsf{m}; \mathsf{r})) \neq \mathsf{m}] \leq \epsilon(\lambda).$$

(A key pair $(\mathsf{pk}, \mathsf{sk})$ under which incorrect decryption could occur is called *erroneous.*) Furthermore, we just say that $\Pi$ is *correct* (resp. *almost-all-keys correct*) if $\mathsf{Err}_\Pi(\lambda)$ is zero (resp. negligible).

*Pseudorandomness of Ciphertexts (PRCT Security).* We say that a PKE scheme $\Pi$ satisfies *pseudorandomness of ciphertexts (PRCT security)*, if for all PPT adversaries $\mathcal{A}$,

$$\mathsf{Adv}^{\mathtt{PRCT}}_{\Pi,\mathcal{A}}(\lambda) := 2 \cdot \left| \Pr\left[ \begin{array}{l} (\mathsf{pk}, \mathsf{sk}) \xleftarrow{r} \mathsf{KG}(1^\lambda);\ b \xleftarrow{r} \{0,1\}; \\ b' \xleftarrow{r} \mathcal{A}^{\mathcal{O}_{\mathtt{PRCT}}(\cdot)}(\mathsf{pk}) \end{array} : b' = b \right] - \frac{1}{2} \right|$$

is negligible, where $\mathcal{O}_{\mathtt{PRCT}}(\cdot)$ denotes the encryption oracle that takes a plaintext $\mathsf{m} \in \mathcal{M}$ as input, computes $\mathsf{ct}_1 \xleftarrow{r} \mathsf{Enc}(\mathsf{pk}, \mathsf{m})$, picks $\mathsf{ct}_0 \xleftarrow{r} \mathcal{C}$, and returns $\mathsf{ct}_b$.

### 2.6 Garbled Circuits

A (circuit) garbling scheme $\mathcal{G}$ consists of the three PPT algorithms $(\mathsf{Garble}, \mathsf{GEval}, \mathsf{GSim})$ with the following syntax:

| | | |
|---|---|---|
| **Garbling:** | $(\widetilde{C}, (\mathsf{L}_{i,v})_{i\in[n],v\in\{0,1\}})$ | $\xleftarrow{r} \mathsf{Garble}(1^\lambda, C)$ |
| **Evaluation:** | $\mathsf{y}$ | $\leftarrow \mathsf{GEval}(\widetilde{C}, (\mathsf{L}'_i)_{i\in[n]})$ |
| **Simulator (for Security):** | $(\widetilde{C}, (\mathsf{L}'_i)_{i\in[n]})$ | $\xleftarrow{r} \mathsf{GSim}(1^\lambda, \mathsf{y})$ |

where $\mathsf{GEval}$ is deterministic, $C : \{0,1\}^n \to \{0,1\}^m$ is (the description of) a circuit, $\widetilde{C}$ is a garbled circuit, $\mathsf{L}_{i,v} \in \{0,1\}^\lambda$ $(i \in [n], v \in \{0,1\})$ and $\mathsf{L}'_i \in \{0,1\}^\lambda$ $(i \in [n])$ are input labels for evaluating $\widetilde{C}$, and $\mathsf{y} \in \{0,1\}^m$ is an evaluation result.

For simplicity, we assume that the security parameter $\lambda$ determines the size $s = s(\lambda)$, the input length $n = n(\lambda)$, and the output length $m = m(\lambda)$ of circuits that can be treated by $\mathcal{G}$, and that the length of each input label is $\lambda$.

We require that for all $\lambda \in \mathbb{N}$, all circuits $C$ with input length $n = n(\lambda)$, and all inputs $\mathsf{x} = (\mathsf{x}_1, \ldots, \mathsf{x}_n) \in \{0,1\}^n$, the following holds: If $(\widetilde{C}, (\mathsf{L}_{i,v})_{i\in[n],v\in\{0,1\}}) \xleftarrow{r} \mathsf{Garble}(1^\lambda, C)$, then we have $\mathsf{GEval}(\widetilde{C}, (\mathsf{L}_{i,\mathsf{x}_i})_{i\in[n]}) = C(x)$.

*Simulation Security.* A standard security notion for a garbling scheme is *simulation security* defined using the simulator $\mathsf{GSim}$. The formal definition is as follows.

We say that a garbling scheme $\mathcal{G} = (\mathsf{Garble}, \mathsf{GEval}, \mathsf{GSim})$ satisfies *simulation security* if for all PPT adversaries $\mathcal{A} = (\mathcal{A}_1, \mathcal{A}_2)$,

$$\mathsf{Adv}^{\mathtt{Sim}}_{\mathcal{G},\mathcal{A}}(\lambda) := 2 \cdot \left| \Pr\left[\begin{array}{l} (C, \mathsf{x} = (\mathsf{x}_1, \ldots, \mathsf{x}_n), \mathsf{st}) \xleftarrow{r} \mathcal{A}_1(1^\lambda); \\ (\widetilde{C}_1, (\mathsf{L}_{i,v})_{i\in[n],v\in\{0,1\}}) \xleftarrow{r} \mathsf{Garble}(1^\lambda, C); \\ \mathsf{Labels}_1 \leftarrow (\mathsf{L}_{i,\mathsf{x}_i})_{i\in[n]}; \\ (\widetilde{C}_0, \mathsf{Labels}_0) \xleftarrow{r} \mathsf{GSim}(1^\lambda, C(\mathsf{x})); \\ b \xleftarrow{r} \{0,1\};\ b' \xleftarrow{r} \mathcal{A}_2(\widetilde{C}_b, \mathsf{Labels}_b, \mathsf{st}) \end{array} : b' = b \right] - \frac{1}{2} \right|$$

is negligible.

*Blindness.* Brakerski et al. [8] introduced *blindness* as a security notion for a garbling scheme. Informally, it guarantees that the output of the simulator $\mathsf{GSim}$ is pseudorandom when it is fed with a random input. In this paper, we will treat a garbling scheme satisfying blindness, and thus we recall its formal definition below.

We say that a garbling scheme $\mathcal{G} = (\mathsf{Garble}, \mathsf{GEval}, \mathsf{GSim})$ satisfies *blindness* if for all PPT adversaries $\mathcal{A}$,

$$\mathsf{Adv}^{\mathtt{Blind}}_{\mathcal{G},\mathcal{A}}(\lambda) := 2 \cdot \left| \Pr\left[\begin{array}{l} \mathsf{y} \xleftarrow{r} \{0,1\}^m; \\ (\widetilde{C}_1, \mathsf{Labels}_1) \xleftarrow{r} \mathsf{GSim}(1^\lambda, \mathsf{y}); \\ \widetilde{C}_0 \xleftarrow{r} \{0,1\}^{|\widetilde{C}_1|};\ \mathsf{Labels}_0 \xleftarrow{r} (\{0,1\}^\lambda)^n; \\ b \xleftarrow{r} \{0,1\};\ b' \xleftarrow{r} \mathcal{A}(\widetilde{C}_b, \mathsf{Labels}_b) \end{array} : b' = b \right] - \frac{1}{2} \right|$$

is negligible.

Brakerski et al. [8] showed a construction of a garbling scheme satisfying both simulation security and blindness, using a (standard) PRG as a building block. Hence, a garbling scheme satisfying both security notions exist if a one-way function exists [15].

# 3 Key-Dependent-Shift Secure Weak PRF

In this section, we formally define *key-dependent-shift (KDS) security* for a weak PRF.

**Definition 1 (Key-Dependent-Shift Secure Weak PRF).** *Let* $\ell = \ell(\lambda)$, $m = m(\lambda)$, *and* $n = n(\lambda)$ *be polynomials. Let* $\mathsf{KwPRF} : \{0,1\}^n \times \{0,1\}^m \to \{0,1\}^\ell$ *be an efficiently computable function. Let* $\mathcal{F}$ *be a family of functions from* $\{0,1\}^n$ *to* $\{0,1\}^\ell$.

*We say that* KwPRF *is a* $\mathcal{F}$-KDS secure weak PRF, *if for all PPT adversaries* $\mathcal{A}$,

$$\mathsf{Adv}^{\mathcal{F}\text{-KDS-wPRF}}_{\mathsf{KwPRF},\mathcal{A}}(\lambda) := 2 \cdot \left| \Pr\left[ \begin{array}{l} \mathsf{k} \xleftarrow{r} \{0,1\}^n;\ b \xleftarrow{r} \{0,1\}; \\ b' \xleftarrow{r} \mathcal{A}^{\mathcal{O}_{\mathtt{KDS\text{-}wPRF}}(\cdot)}(1^\lambda) \end{array} : b' = b \right] - \frac{1}{2} \right|$$

*is negligible, where* $\mathcal{O}_{\mathtt{KDS\text{-}wPRF}}(\cdot)$ *is the oracle that takes a function* $f \in \mathcal{F}$ *as input, and proceeds as follows:*

1. *Pick* $\mathsf{x} \xleftarrow{r} \{0,1\}^m$.
2. *Compute* $\mathsf{y}_1 \xleftarrow{r} \mathsf{KwPRF}(\mathsf{k}, \mathsf{x}) \oplus f(\mathsf{k})$.
3. *Pick* $\mathsf{y}_0 \xleftarrow{r} \{0,1\}^\ell$.
4. *Return* $(\mathsf{x}, \mathsf{y}_b)$.

*Function Families for KDS Security.* In this paper, we will treat the same function families as those considered for KDM security for SKE listed in Sect. 2.2, namely, the family of projection functions $\mathcal{P}$, the family of affine functions $\mathcal{L}$, and the family of functions that can be computed by size-$s$ circuits $\mathcal{B}_s$.

## 3.1 Applications

Here, we give applications of a KDS secure weak PRF: Hinting PRGs, linear-resistant PRGs, and public-coin KDM secure SKE. Its application to correlation RDM secure PKE will be presented in Sect. 4. In the full version, we will also show how to realize variants of hinting PRG called functional hinting PRG, hinting weak PRF, and functional hinting weak PRF [2] using a KDS secure weak PRF.

$\mathsf{HSetup}(1^\lambda)$ :
  Return $\mathsf{pp} \xleftarrow{r} \{0,1\}^m$.

$\mathsf{HPRG}(\mathsf{pp}, \mathsf{s})$ :
  Parse $\mathsf{s}$ as $(\mathsf{s}_1, \ldots, \mathsf{s}_n) \in \{0,1\}^n$.
  $(\mathsf{y}_0, (\mathsf{y}_{i,0}, \mathsf{y}_{i,1})_{i \in [n]}) \leftarrow \mathsf{KwPRF}(\mathsf{s}, \mathsf{pp})$
  Return $\mathsf{y} \leftarrow (\mathsf{y}_0, \mathsf{y}_{1,\mathsf{s}_1}, \ldots, \mathsf{y}_{n,\mathsf{s}_n})$.

$\mathsf{LRSetup}(1^\lambda)$ :
  Return $\mathsf{pp} \xleftarrow{r} \{0,1\}^m$.

$\mathsf{LRPRG}(\mathsf{pp}, \mathsf{s})$ :
  Return $\mathsf{y} \leftarrow \mathsf{KwPRF}(\mathsf{s}, \mathsf{pp})$.

$\mathsf{SEnc}(\mathsf{sk}, \mathsf{m}; \mathsf{r})$ :
  $\mathsf{y} \leftarrow \mathsf{KwPRF}(\mathsf{sk}, \mathsf{r}) \oplus \mathsf{m}$
  Return $\mathsf{ct} \leftarrow (\mathsf{r}, \mathsf{y})$.

$\mathsf{SDec}(\mathsf{sk}, \mathsf{ct} = (\mathsf{r}, \mathsf{y}))$ :
  Return $\mathsf{m} \leftarrow \mathsf{KwPRF}(\mathsf{sk}, \mathsf{r}) \oplus \mathsf{y}$.

**Fig. 2.** Applications of a KDS secure weak PRF KwPRF: Hinting PRG $\mathcal{H}$ (left-top), linear-resistant PRG $\mathcal{LR}$ (left-bottom), and public-coin KDM secure SKE $\mathcal{E}$ (right).

*Hinting PRG.* Let $\mathsf{KwPRF} : \{0,1\}^n \times \{0,1\}^m \rightarrow \{0,1\}^{(2n+1)\cdot\lambda}$ be a $\mathcal{P}$-KDS secure weak PRF, for some polynomials $n = n(\lambda)$ and $m = m(\lambda)$. We identify the output space $\{0,1\}^{(2n+1)\cdot\lambda}$ with $\{0,1\}^\lambda \times (\{0,1\}^\lambda \times \{0,1\}^\lambda)^n$.

Using KwPRF, we construct a hinting PRG $\mathcal{H} = (\mathsf{HSetup}, \mathsf{HPRG})$ as in Fig. 2 (left-top).

The following theorem guarantees that $\mathcal{H}$ constructed as above is indeed a secure hinting PRG.

**Theorem 2.** *If* KwPRF *is a $\mathcal{P}$-KDS secure weak PRF, then $\mathcal{H}$ is a secure hinting PRG.*

*Proof of Theorem* 2. Let $\mathcal{A}$ be an arbitrary PPT adversary that attacks the hinting PRG security of $\mathcal{H}$. Using $\mathcal{A}$, we consider the following PPT reduction algorithm $\mathcal{B}$ that attacks the $\mathcal{P}$-KDS security of KwPRF.

$\mathcal{B}^{\mathcal{O}_{\mathsf{KDS\text{-}wPRF}}(\cdot)}(1^\lambda)$: $\mathcal{B}$ picks $\Delta_{1,0}, \Delta_{1,1}, \ldots, \Delta_{n,0}, \Delta_{n,1} \xleftarrow{r} \{0,1\}^\lambda$, and define a projection function $g \in \mathcal{P}$ that computes the selector function $\mathsf{sel}[(\Delta_{i,v})_{i \in [n], v \in \{0,1\}}] : \{0,1\}^n \rightarrow (\{0,1\}^\lambda)^{2n+1}$ that has $2n$ $\lambda$-bit values hardwired, and on input $\mathsf{s} = (\mathsf{s}_1, \ldots, \mathsf{s}_n) \in \{0,1\}^n$, outputs $(w_0, w_{1,0}, w_{1,1}, \ldots, w_{n,0}, w_{n,1}) \in (\{0,1\}^\lambda)^{2n+1}$ so that $w_0 = w_{1,\mathsf{s}_1} = \cdots = w_{n,\mathsf{s}_n} = 0^\lambda$, and $w_{i,1-\mathsf{s}_i} = \Delta_{i,1-\mathsf{s}_i}$ for all $i \in [n]$. (Recall that a selector function can be computed by a projection function.) Then, $\mathcal{B}$ submits a query $g \in \mathcal{P}$ to the oracle $\mathcal{O}_{\mathsf{KDS\text{-}wPRF}}$, and receives the answer $(\mathsf{pp}, \mathsf{Y}) \in \{0,1\}^m \times (\{0,1\}^\lambda)^{2n+1}$, where $\mathsf{Y} = (\mathsf{y}_0, (\mathsf{y}_{i,0}, \mathsf{y}_{i,1})_{i \in [n]})$. Then, $\mathcal{B}$ runs $b' \xleftarrow{r} \mathcal{A}(\mathsf{pp}, \mathsf{Y})$, sets $\beta' \leftarrow b'$, and terminates with output $\beta'$.

The above completes the description of $\mathcal{B}$.

Let $\beta \in \{0,1\}$ be the challenge bit in $\mathcal{B}$'s $\mathcal{P}$-KDS security experiment regarding KwPRF, and let $\mathsf{s} = (\mathsf{s}_1, \ldots, \mathsf{s}_n) \in \{0,1\}^n$ be the key for KwPRF chosen in $\mathcal{B}$'s experiment. It is straightforward to see that if $\beta = 1$ and thus $\mathsf{Y} = \mathsf{KwPRF}(\mathsf{s}, \mathsf{pp}) \oplus g(\mathsf{s})$, then $\mathcal{A}$ simulates the hinting PRG security experiment with $b = 1$ perfectly for $\mathcal{A}$. (In particular, for all $i \in [n]$, $\mathsf{y}_{i,\mathsf{s}_i}$ is directly the $(i, \mathsf{s}_i)$-th output block of $\mathsf{KwPRF}(\mathsf{s}, \mathsf{pp})$ itself, while $\mathsf{y}_{i,1-\mathsf{s}_i}$ looks like a truly random string due to the XOR with $\Delta_{i,1-\mathsf{s}_i}$ that is chosen randomly.) On the other hand, if $\beta = 0$ and thus $\mathsf{Y}$ is just a random value in $(\{0,1\}^\lambda)^{2n+1}$, then $\mathcal{B}$ simulates the hinting PRG security experiment with $b = 0$ perfectly for $\mathcal{A}$. Therefore, $\mathcal{B}$ is simulating the hinting PRG security experiment perfectly for $\mathcal{A}$ so that $\mathcal{A}$'s challenge bit is that of $\mathcal{B}$'s. Since $\mathcal{B}$ uses $\mathcal{A}$'s output as it is, we have $\mathsf{Adv}^{\mathtt{HPRG}}_{\mathcal{H},\mathcal{A}}(\lambda) = \mathsf{Adv}^{\mathcal{P}\text{-}\mathtt{KDS}\text{-}\mathtt{wPRF}}_{\mathsf{KwPRF},\mathcal{B}}(\lambda)$, which is negligible by our assumption that $\mathsf{KwPRF}$ is a $\mathcal{P}$-KDS secure weak PRF. Hence, $\mathcal{H}$ is a secure hinting PRG. □ (**Theorem** 2)

*Linear-Resistant PRG (in the Public-Parameter Model).* Let $\mathsf{KwPRF} : \{0,1\}^n \times \{0,1\}^m \to \{0,1\}^\ell$ be a $\mathcal{L}$-KDS secure weak PRF, for some polynomials $n = n(\lambda)$, $m = m(\lambda)$, and $\ell = \ell(\lambda)$ with $n < \ell$.

Using $\mathsf{KwPRF}$, we construct a linear resistant PRG $\mathcal{LR} = (\mathsf{LRSetup}, \mathsf{LRPRG})$ as in Fig. 2 (left-bottom).

The following theorem guarantees that $\mathcal{LR}$ constructed as above is indeed a secure linear-resistant PRG.

**Theorem 3.** *If* $\mathsf{KwPRF}$ *is a* $\mathcal{L}$*-KDS secure weak PRF, then* $\mathcal{LR}$ *is a secure linear-resistant PRG.*

*Proof of Theorem* 3. Let $\mathcal{A} = (\mathcal{A}_1, \mathcal{A}_2)$ be an arbitrary PPT adversary that attacks the linear-resistant PRG security of $\mathcal{LR}$. Using $\mathcal{A}$, we consider the following PPT reduction algorithm $\mathcal{B}$ that attacks the $\mathcal{L}$-KDS security of $\mathsf{KwPRF}$.

$\mathcal{B}^{\mathcal{O}_{\mathtt{KDS\text{-}wPRF}}(\cdot)}(1^\lambda)$: $\mathcal{B}$ runs $(f \in \mathcal{L}, \mathsf{st}) \xleftarrow{r} \mathcal{A}_1(1^\lambda)$. Then, $\mathcal{B}$ submits a query $f \in \mathcal{L}$ to the oracle $\mathcal{O}_{\mathtt{KDS\text{-}wPRF}}$, and receives the answer $(\mathsf{pp}, \mathsf{y}) \in \{0,1\}^m \times \{0,1\}^\ell$. Then, $\mathcal{B}$ runs $b' \leftarrow \mathcal{A}_2(\mathsf{pp}, \mathsf{y}, \mathsf{st})$, sets $\beta' \leftarrow b'$, and terminates with output $\beta'$.

The above completes the description of $\mathcal{B}$.

Let $\beta \in \{0,1\}$ be the challenge bit in $\mathcal{B}$'s $\mathcal{L}$-KDS security experiment regarding $\mathsf{KwPRF}$, and let $\mathsf{s} \in \{0,1\}^n$ be the key for $\mathsf{KwPRF}$ chosen in $\mathcal{B}$'s experiment. It is straightforward to see that if $\beta = 1$ and thus $\mathsf{y} = \mathsf{KwPRF}(\mathsf{s}, \mathsf{pp}) \oplus f(\mathsf{s})$, then $\mathcal{A}$ simulates the linear-resistant PRG security experiment with $b = 1$ perfectly for $\mathcal{A}$. On the other hand, if $\beta = 0$ and thus $\mathsf{y}$ is just a random value in $\{0,1\}^\ell$, then $\mathcal{B}$ simulates the linear-resistant PRG security experiment with $b = 0$ perfectly for $\mathcal{A}$. Therefore, $\mathcal{B}$ is simulating the linear-resistant PRG security experiment perfectly for $\mathcal{A}$ so that $\mathcal{A}$'s challenge bit is that of $\mathcal{B}$'s. Since $\mathcal{B}$ uses $\mathcal{A}$'s output as it is, we have $\mathsf{Adv}^{\mathtt{LRPRG}}_{\mathcal{LR},\mathcal{A}}(\lambda) = \mathsf{Adv}^{\mathcal{L}\text{-}\mathtt{KDS}\text{-}\mathtt{wPRF}}_{\mathsf{KwPRF},\mathcal{B}}(\lambda)$, which is negligible by our assumption that $\mathsf{KwPRF}$ is a $\mathcal{L}$-KDS secure weak PRF. Hence, $\mathcal{LR}$ is a secure linear-resistant PRG. □ (**Theorem** 3)

*Public-Coin KDM Secure SKE.* Let $s = s(\lambda)$ be a polynomial. Let $\mathcal{F} \in \{\mathcal{P}, \mathcal{L}, \mathcal{B}_s\}$. Let $\mathsf{KwPRF} : \{0,1\}^n \times \{0,1\}^m \to \{0,1\}^\ell$ be a $\mathcal{F}$-KDS secure weak PRF, for some polynomials $n = n(\lambda)$, $m = m(\lambda)$, and $\ell = \ell(\lambda)$.

Using $\mathsf{KwPRF}$, we construct a SKE scheme $\mathcal{E} = (\mathsf{SEnc}, \mathsf{SDec})$ such that its key space is $\{0,1\}^n$, its plaintext space is $\{0,1\}^\ell$, and the encryption randomness space is $\{0,1\}^m$, as in Fig. 2 (right). Note that this construction is exactly the weak-PRF-based SKE scheme $\mathcal{E}_{\mathtt{wPRF}}$ recalled in Sect. 2.2, except that the underlying (standard) weak PRF $\mathsf{wPRF}$ is replaced with the KDS-secure weak PRF $\mathsf{KwPRF}$.

The following theorem guarantees that the SKE scheme $\mathcal{E}$ constructed as above satisfies $\mathcal{F}$-KDM security.

**Theorem 4.** *Let $s = s(\lambda)$ be a polynomial. Let $\mathcal{F} \in \{\mathcal{P}, \mathcal{L}, \mathcal{B}_s\}$. If $\mathsf{KwPRF}$ is a $\mathcal{F}$-KDS secure weak PRF, then the SKE scheme $\mathcal{E}$ satisfies $\mathcal{F}$-KDM security.*

*Proof of Theorem* 4. Let $\mathcal{A}$ be an arbitrary PPT adversary that attacks the $\mathcal{F}$-KDM security of the SKE scheme $\mathcal{E}$. Let $\mathtt{SUC}$ denote the event that $\mathcal{A}$ succeeds in guessing the challenge bit (i.e. $b' = b$ occurs) in the $\mathcal{F}$-KDM security experiment regarding $\mathcal{E}$.

Using $\mathcal{A}$, we consider the following PPT reduction algorithm $\mathcal{B}$ that attacks the $\mathcal{F}$-KDS security of $\mathsf{KwPRF}$.

$\mathcal{B}^{\mathcal{O}_{\mathtt{KDS\text{-}wPRF}}(\cdot)}(1^\lambda)$: $\mathcal{B}$ picks $b \xleftarrow{\mathsf{r}} \{0,1\}$, and runs $\mathcal{A}(1^\lambda)$.

For a KDM-encryption query $(f_0, f_1) \in \mathcal{F}^2$ from $\mathcal{A}$, $\mathcal{B}$ submits a query $f_b \in \mathcal{F}$ to the oracle $\mathcal{O}_{\mathtt{KDS\text{-}wPRF}}$, and receives the answer $(\mathsf{r}, \mathsf{y}) \in \{0,1\}^m \times \{0,1\}^\ell$, and returns a ciphertext $\mathsf{ct} = (\mathsf{r}, \mathsf{y})$ to $\mathcal{A}$.

When $\mathcal{A}$ teminates with output $b'$, $\mathcal{B}$ sets $\beta' \leftarrow (b' \stackrel{?}{=} b)$, and terminates with output $\beta'$.

The above completes the description of $\mathcal{B}$.

Let $\beta \in \{0,1\}$ be the challenge bit in $\mathcal{B}$'s $\mathcal{F}$-KDS security experiment regarding $\mathsf{KwPRF}$, and let $\mathsf{sk} \in \{0,1\}^n$ be the key for $\mathsf{KwPRF}$ chosen in $\mathcal{B}$'s experiment. It is straightforward to see that if $\beta = 1$ and thus $\mathsf{y} = \mathsf{KwPRF}(\mathsf{sk}, \mathsf{r}) \oplus f_b(\mathsf{sk})$ is returned from $\mathcal{B}$'s oracle $\mathcal{O}_{\mathtt{KDS\text{-}wPRF}}$ as the answer to $\mathcal{B}$'s query $f_b$, then the ciphertext $\mathsf{ct} = (\mathsf{r}, \mathsf{y})$ returned to $\mathcal{A}$ as the answer to a KDM-encryption query $(f_0, f_1)$ is exactly $\mathsf{SEnc}(\mathsf{sk}, f_b(\mathsf{sk}); \mathsf{r})$, and thus $\mathcal{B}$ simulates the $\mathcal{F}$-KDM security experiment perfectly for $\mathcal{A}$ so that $\mathcal{A}$'s challenge bit is $b$ (chosen by $\mathcal{B}$). Since $\mathcal{B}$ outputs $\beta' = 1$ only when $b' = b$ occurs, we have $\Pr[\beta' = 1 | \beta = 1] = \Pr[\mathtt{SUC}]$. On the other hand, if $\beta = 0$ and thus a random value $\mathsf{y} \in \{0,1\}^\ell$ is returned from $\mathcal{B}$'s oracle $\mathcal{O}_{\mathtt{KDS\text{-}wPRF}}$ as the answer to $\mathcal{B}$'s query $f_b$, then the ciphertext $\mathsf{ct} = (\mathsf{r}, \mathsf{y})$ returned to $\mathcal{A}$ as the answer to a KDM-encryption query $(f_0, f_1)$ is independent of $b$, and thus $\mathcal{A}$'s view contains no information on $b$. Hence, no matter what value $b'$ is output by $\mathcal{A}$, the probability that $b' = b$ occurs (and thus $\mathcal{B}$ outputs $\beta' = 1$) is exactly $1/2$, namely, we have $\Pr[\beta' = 1 | \beta = 0] = 1/2$.

Combining the arguments so far, we have

$$\begin{aligned}\mathsf{Adv}^{\mathcal{F}\text{-}\mathtt{KDS\text{-}wPRF}}_{\mathsf{KwPRF},\mathcal{B}}(\lambda) &= \left|\Pr[\beta' = 1 | \beta = 1] - \Pr[\beta' = 1 | \beta = 0]\right| \\ &= \left|\Pr[\mathtt{SUC}] - \frac{1}{2}\right| = \frac{1}{2} \cdot \mathsf{Adv}^{\mathcal{F}\text{-}\mathtt{KDM}}_{\mathcal{E},\mathcal{A}}(\lambda).\end{aligned}$$

This implies $\mathsf{Adv}^{\mathcal{F}\text{-KDM}}_{\mathcal{E},\mathcal{A}}(\lambda) = 2 \cdot \mathsf{Adv}^{\mathcal{F}\text{-KDS-wPRF}}_{\mathsf{KwPRF},\mathcal{B}}(\lambda)$, which is negligible by our assumption that $\mathsf{KwPRF}$ is a $\mathcal{F}$-KDS secure weak PRF. Hence, the SKE scheme $\mathcal{E}$ satisfies $\mathcal{F}$-KDM security. □ (**Theorem** 4)

## 4 Correlation RDM Secure PKE via KDS Secure Weak PRF

In this section, as another application of a KDS secure weak PRF, we show how to construct a randomness-dependent-message (RDM) secure PKE scheme [6,13, 16]. We first define RDM security for PKE. Following Hajiabadi and Kapron [13], we consider the correlated version of the definition.

*Correlation RDM Security.* Let $\Pi = (\mathsf{KG}, \mathsf{Enc}, \mathsf{Dec})$ be a PKE scheme whose encryption randomness space is $\{0,1\}^n$ and plaintext space is $\{0,1\}^m$, and let $\mathcal{F}$ be a family of functions whose domain is $\{0,1\}^n$ and range is $\{0,1\}^m$. We say that $\Pi$ satisfies *correlation $\mathcal{F}$-RDM security* if for all PPT adversaries $\mathcal{A}$,

$$\mathsf{Adv}^{\mathcal{F}\text{-CRDM}}_{\Pi,\mathcal{A}}(\lambda) := 2 \cdot \left| \Pr\left[ \begin{array}{l} b \xleftarrow{r} \{0,1\};\ \mathsf{r} \xleftarrow{r} \{0,1\}^n; \\ b' \xleftarrow{r} \mathcal{A}^{\mathcal{O}_{\mathtt{CRDM}}(\cdot,\cdot)}(1^\lambda); \end{array} : b' = \mathrm{b} \right] - \frac{1}{2} \right|$$

is negligible, where $\mathcal{O}_{\mathtt{CRDM}}(\cdot,\cdot)$ is the oracle that takes two functions $(f_0, f_1) \in \mathcal{F}^2$ as input, and proceeds as follows:

1. Generate $(\mathsf{pk}, \mathsf{sk}) \xleftarrow{r} \mathsf{KG}(1^\lambda)$.
2. Compute $\mathsf{ct} \leftarrow \mathsf{Enc}(\mathsf{pk}, f_b(\mathsf{r}); \mathsf{r})$.
3. Return $(\mathsf{pk}, \mathsf{ct})$.

*Remark 1.* We provide some remarks on our definition of correlation RDM security.

- The definition of [13] is recovered by restricting to the bit-circular case, where each RDM function outputs a single bit of $\mathsf{r}$. Our definition also implies correlated-product secure TDFs [24] if the function family $\mathcal{F}$ contains the identity function.
- A PKE scheme satisfying correlation $\mathcal{F}$-RDM security implies a $\mathcal{F}$-KDM secure SKE scheme. Consider the following SKE scheme based on a PKE scheme $\Pi = (\mathsf{KG}, \mathsf{Enc}, \mathsf{Dec})$. The key-generation algorithm samples $\mathsf{r} \leftarrow \{0,1\}^n$ as a secret key. To encrypt a one-bit message $\beta \in \{0,1\}$ under key $\mathsf{r}$, it generates $(\mathsf{pk}, \mathsf{sk}) \leftarrow \mathsf{KG}(1^\lambda)$ and outputs the ciphertext $(\mathsf{pk}, \mathsf{Enc}(\mathsf{pk}, \beta; \mathsf{r}))$. Decryption is done by computing $\mathsf{Enc}(\mathsf{pk}, 0; \mathsf{r})$ and $\mathsf{Enc}(\mathsf{pk}, 1; \mathsf{r})$ and comparing them with the second component of the ciphertext. The $\mathcal{F}$-KDM security of this SKE scheme follows directly from the correlation $\mathcal{F}$-RDM security of $\Pi$.
- Our notion does not capture the setting where the RDM function $f$ depends on the current public key used for computing the challenge ciphertext $\mathsf{Enc}(\mathsf{pk}, f(\mathsf{r}); \mathsf{r})$ (although $f$ may depend on public keys obtained from previous queries). Thus, our notion is incomparable to that of Birrell et al. [6], which allows fully public-key-dependent RDM functions but does not consider the correlation setting.

$\mathsf{RKG}(1^\lambda)$ :
- $(\mathsf{pk}, \mathsf{sk}) \xleftarrow{r} \mathsf{KG}(1^\lambda)$
- $\mathsf{A} \xleftarrow{r} \{0,1\}^{3\lambda}$; $\mathsf{B} \xleftarrow{r} \{0,1\}^{m}$; $\mathsf{C}_1, \ldots, \mathsf{C}_n \xleftarrow{r} \{0,1\}^{\ell_{\mathsf{ct}}}$
- $\mathsf{rpk} \leftarrow (\mathsf{pk}, \mathsf{A}, \mathsf{B}, (\mathsf{C}_i)_{i\in[n]})$; $\mathsf{rsk} \leftarrow (\mathsf{sk}, \mathsf{A}, \mathsf{B})$
- Return $(\mathsf{rpk}, \mathsf{rsk})$.

$\mathsf{REnc}(\mathsf{rpk}, \mathsf{m}; \mathsf{x} = (\mathsf{x}_1, \ldots, \mathsf{x}_n) \in \{0,1\}^n)$ :
- Parse $\mathsf{rpk}$ as $(\mathsf{pk}, \mathsf{A}, \mathsf{B}, (\mathsf{C}_i)_{i\in[n]})$.
- $(\mathsf{r}_0, (\mathsf{r}_{i,0}, \mathsf{r}_{i,1})_{i\in[n]}) \leftarrow \mathsf{KwPRF}(\mathsf{x}, \mathsf{B})$
- $\forall i \in [n]$ :
  - $\mathsf{ct}_{i,\mathsf{x}_i} \leftarrow \mathsf{Enc}(\mathsf{pk}, \mathsf{A}; \mathsf{r}_{i,\mathsf{x}_i})$
  - $\mathsf{ct}_i \leftarrow \begin{cases} \mathsf{ct}_{i,0} & \text{if } \mathsf{x}_i = 0 \\ \mathsf{ct}_{i,1} \oplus \mathsf{C}_i & \text{if } \mathsf{x}_i = 1 \end{cases}$
- $\mathsf{z} \leftarrow \mathsf{r}_0 \oplus \mathsf{m}$
- Return $\mathsf{rct} \leftarrow (\mathsf{z}, (\mathsf{ct}_i)_{i\in[n]})$.

$\mathsf{RDec}(\mathsf{rsk}, \mathsf{rct})$ :
- Parse $\mathsf{rsk}$ as $(\mathsf{sk}, \mathsf{A}, \mathsf{B})$.
- Parse $\mathsf{rct}$ as $(\mathsf{z}, (\mathsf{ct})_{i\in[n]})$.
- $\forall i \in [n]$ :
  - $\mathsf{x}_i \leftarrow \begin{cases} 0 & \text{if } \mathsf{Dec}(\mathsf{sk}, \mathsf{ct}_i) = \mathsf{A} \\ 1 & \text{otherwise} \end{cases}$
- $\mathsf{x} \leftarrow (\mathsf{x}_1, \ldots, \mathsf{x}_n)$
- $(\mathsf{r}_0, (\mathsf{r}_{i,0}, \mathsf{r}_{i,1})_{i\in[n]}) \leftarrow \mathsf{KwPRF}(\mathsf{x}, \mathsf{B})$
- Return $\mathsf{m} \leftarrow \mathsf{z} \oplus \mathsf{r}_0$.

**Fig. 3.** The RDM secure PKE scheme $\Pi_{\mathsf{RDM}}$ based on a PRCT secure PKE scheme and a KDS secure weak PRF.

*Construction.* Our construction is based on the TDF construction by Garg et al. [11] who showed, among other things, how to construct a TDF from the combination of a PRCT-secure PKE scheme and a hinting PRG.

Formally, our correlation RDM secure PKE scheme is constructed as follows: Consider the following ingredients:

- Let $\ell_{\mathsf{m}} = \ell_{\mathsf{m}}(\lambda)$ be a polynomial that represents the length of a plaintext that we wish to encrypt by the PKE scheme constructed here.
- Let $\Pi = (\mathsf{KG}, \mathsf{Enc}, \mathsf{Dec})$ be a PKE scheme such that, when the security parameter is $\lambda$, the plaintext space is $\{0,1\}^{3\lambda}$, the encryption randomness space is $\{0,1\}^{\lambda}$, and the ciphertext space is $\{0,1\}^{\ell_{\mathsf{ct}}}$ for some polynomial $\ell_{\mathsf{ct}} = \ell_{\mathsf{ct}}(\lambda)$.
- Let $\mathsf{KwPRF} : \{0,1\}^n \times \{0,1\}^m \to \{0,1\}^{\ell_{\mathsf{m}}+2n\lambda}$ be a KDS-secure[6] weak PRF, for some polynomials $n = n(\lambda)$ and $m = m(\lambda)$. We will identify the output space with $\{0,1\}^{\ell_{\mathsf{m}}} \times (\{0,1\}^{\lambda} \times \{0,1\}^{\lambda})^n$.

Using these primitives as building blocks, our correlation RDM secure PKE scheme $\Pi_{\mathsf{RDM}} = (\mathsf{RKG}, \mathsf{REnc}, \mathsf{RDec})$ is constructed as in Fig. 3. The plaintext space and encryption random space of $\Pi_{\mathsf{RDM}}$ are $\{0,1\}^{\ell_{\mathsf{m}}}$ and $\{0,1\}^n$, respectively.

$\Pi_{\mathsf{RDM}}$ satisfies almost-all-keys correctness, as stated below. Its proof is essentially the same as that for the TDF in [11], but we give a formal proof in the full version for completeness.

**Theorem 5.** *If the PKE scheme $\Pi$ satisfies correctness, then the PKE scheme $\Pi_{\mathsf{RDM}}$ satisfies $(n+1) \cdot 2^{-\lambda}$-almost-all-keys correctness.*

The correlation RDM security of $\Pi_{\mathsf{RDM}}$ is guaranteed by the following theorem.

[6] The function family with respect to which KwPRF is KDS secure will affect with respect to what function family the PKE scheme $\Pi_{\mathsf{RDM}}$ constructed here is RDM secure. See Theorem 6 below.

**Theorem 6.** *If the PKE scheme $\Pi$ satisfies PRCT security, then the following holds:*

- *Let $\mathcal{F} \in \{\mathcal{P}, \mathcal{L}\}$. If* KwPRF *is a $\mathcal{F}$-KDS secure weak PRF, then the PKE scheme $\Pi_{\mathtt{RDM}}$ satisfies correlation $\mathcal{F}$-RDM security.*
- *Let $s = s(\lambda)$ be an arbitrary polynomial, and let $p = p(\lambda) = O(n\lambda)$ be the size of the circuit computing the selector function that will appear in the proof. If* KwPRF *is a $\mathcal{B}_{s+p}$-KDS secure weak PRF, then the PKE scheme $\Pi_{\mathtt{RDM}}$ satisfies correlation $\mathcal{B}_s$-RDM security.*

*Proof of Theorem* 6. Since the proofs for both of the items are essentially the same, we mainly show the proof for the second item (i.e. correlation $\mathcal{B}_s$-RDM security of $\Pi_{\mathtt{RDM}}$), and briefly explain how the first item (i.e. correlation $\mathcal{F}$-RDM security of $\Pi_{\mathtt{RDM}}$ for $\mathcal{F} \in \{\mathcal{P}, \mathcal{L}\}$) can be proved.

Let $\mathcal{A}$ be an arbitrary PPT adversary that attacks the correlation $\mathcal{B}_s$-RDM security of the PKE scheme $\Pi_{\mathtt{RDM}}$, and let $q$ denote the number of queries to $\mathcal{O}_{\mathtt{CRDM}}(\cdot,\cdot)$ made by $\mathcal{A}$. We will show that for this $\mathcal{A}$, there exist PPT adversaries $\mathcal{B}$ and $\mathcal{B}'$ that satisfy

$$\mathsf{Adv}^{\mathcal{B}_s\text{-}\mathtt{CRDM}}_{\Pi_{\mathtt{RDM}},\mathcal{A}}(\lambda) \le 2q \cdot \mathsf{Adv}^{\mathtt{PRCT}}_{\Pi,\mathcal{B}}(\lambda) + 2 \cdot \mathsf{Adv}^{\mathcal{B}_{s+p}\text{-}\mathtt{KDS}\text{-}\mathtt{wPRF}}_{\mathsf{KwPRF},\mathcal{B}'}(\lambda), \tag{1}$$

which will ensure that $\mathcal{A}$'s advantage is negligible by our assumption that $\Pi$ satisfies PRCT security and KwPRF is a $\mathcal{B}_{s+p}$-KDS secure weak PRF, and hence imply the second item of the theorem.

Our proof is via a sequence of games argument using five games. In the following, let $\mathtt{SUC}_t$ denote the event that $\mathcal{A}$ succeeds in guessing the challenge bit (i.e. $b' = b$ occurs) in Game $t \in [5]$.

**Game 1:** This is the correlation $\mathcal{B}_s$-RDM security experiment regarding $\Pi_{\mathtt{RDM}}$. Specifically, the description of Game 1 is as follows:

1. Pick $b \xleftarrow{r} \{0,1\}$ and $\mathsf{x} = (\mathsf{x}_1, \dots, \mathsf{x}_n) \xleftarrow{r} \{0,1\}^n$.
2. Run $\mathcal{A}^{\mathcal{O}_{\mathtt{CRDM}}(\cdot,\cdot)}(1^\lambda)$. Then, $\mathcal{A}$ starts making queries to its oracle $\mathcal{O}_{\mathtt{CRDM}}(\cdot,\cdot)$. Each query $(f_0, f_1) \in (\mathcal{B}_s)^2$ from $\mathcal{A}$ is answered as follows. For making it easier to describe the subsequent games, we change the ordering of the operations for how the public/secret key pair $(\mathsf{rpk}, \mathsf{rsk})$ and the ciphertext $\mathsf{rct}$ are generated, so that the distribution of the oracle's answer $(\mathsf{rpk}, \mathsf{rct})$ is identical to that in the original correlation $\mathcal{B}_s$-RDM security experiment.
   (a) Compute $(\mathsf{pk}, \mathsf{sk}) \xleftarrow{r} \mathsf{KG}(1^\lambda)$.
   (b) Pick $\mathsf{A} \xleftarrow{r} \{0,1\}^{3\lambda}$.
   (c) Pick $\mathsf{B} \xleftarrow{r} \{0,1\}^m$, compute $(\mathsf{y}_0, (\mathsf{y}_{i,0}, \mathsf{y}_{i,1})_{i\in[n]}) \leftarrow \mathsf{KwPRF}(\mathsf{x}, \mathsf{B})$, and set $\mathsf{r}_0 \leftarrow \mathsf{y}_0$ and $\mathsf{r}_{i,\mathsf{x}_i} \leftarrow \mathsf{y}_{i,\mathsf{x}_i}$ for all $i \in [n]$.
   (d) Pick $\mathsf{r}_{1,1-\mathsf{x}_1}, \dots, \mathsf{r}_{n,1-\mathsf{x}_n} \xleftarrow{r} \{0,1\}^\lambda$.[7]
   (e) For all $i \in [n]$, do the following:

[7] The values $\{\mathsf{r}_{i,1-\mathsf{x}_i}\}_{i\in[n]}$ are not used in Game 1. Looking ahead, these will be used from Game 3.

i. Compute $\mathsf{ct}_{i,\mathsf{x}_i} \leftarrow \mathsf{Enc}(\mathsf{pk}, \mathsf{A}; \mathsf{r}_{i,\mathsf{x}_i})$.
ii. Pick $\mathsf{C}_i \xleftarrow{\mathsf{r}} \{0,1\}^{\ell_{\mathsf{ct}}}$.
iii. Set $\mathsf{ct}_i \leftarrow \begin{cases} \mathsf{ct}_{i,0} & \text{if } \mathsf{x}_i = 0 \\ \mathsf{ct}_{i,1} \oplus \mathsf{C}_i & \text{if } \mathsf{x}_i = 1 \end{cases}$.

(f) Set $\mathsf{z} \leftarrow \mathsf{r}_0 \oplus f_b(\mathsf{x})$.
(g) Return $\mathsf{rpk} \leftarrow (\mathsf{pk}, \mathsf{A}, \mathsf{B}, (\mathsf{C}_i)_{i\in[n]})$ and $\mathsf{rct} \leftarrow (\mathsf{z}, (\mathsf{ct}_i)_{i\in[n]})$ to $\mathcal{A}$.

3. At some point, $\mathcal{A}$ terminates with output $b'$.

It is straightforward to see that an answer $(\mathsf{rpk}, \mathsf{rct})$ from $\mathcal{O}_{\mathtt{CRDM}}(\cdot,\cdot)$ are generated in exactly the same way as in the original security game regarding $\Pi_{\mathtt{RDM}}$. Hence, we have

$$\mathsf{Adv}^{\mathcal{B}_s\text{-}\mathtt{CRDM}}_{\Pi_{\mathtt{RDM}},\mathcal{A}}(\lambda) = 2 \cdot \left|\Pr[\mathtt{SUC}_1] - \frac{1}{2}\right|. \tag{2}$$

**Game 2:** Same as Game 1, except that the value $\mathsf{C}_i \in \{0,1\}^{\ell_{\mathsf{ct}}}$ for every $i \in [n]$ that appears in the computation of $(\mathsf{rpk}, \mathsf{rct})$ by the oracle $\mathcal{O}_{\mathtt{CRDM}}$ as the response to $\mathcal{A}$'s query $(f_0, f_1) \in (\mathcal{B}_s)^2$, is generated as follows:

1. Pick $\mathsf{ct}_{i,1-\mathsf{x}_i} \xleftarrow{\mathsf{r}} \{0,1\}^{\ell_{\mathsf{ct}}}$.
2. Set $\mathsf{C}_i \leftarrow \mathsf{ct}_{i,0} \oplus \mathsf{ct}_{i,1}$.

Note that by this change, for all $i \in [n]$, $\mathsf{ct}_i$ in $\mathsf{rct}$ now always satisfies $\mathsf{ct}_i = \mathsf{ct}_{i,0}$ (regardless of $\mathsf{x}_i = 0$ or $\mathsf{x}_i = 1$) in Game 2.
In Game 2, for all $i \in [n]$, $\mathsf{ct}_{i,1-\mathsf{x}_i}$ works as the key (mask) of the one-time pad encryption, and makes $\mathsf{C}_i$ distributed uniformly at random in $\{0,1\}^{\ell_{\mathsf{ct}}}$, which is exactly how this value in Game 1 is distributed. Consequently, $\mathcal{A}$'s view in Game 2 is distributed identically to that in Game 1, which implies

$$\Pr[\mathtt{SUC}_1] = \Pr[\mathtt{SUC}_2]. \tag{3}$$

**Game 3:** Same as Game 2, except that for every $i \in [n]$ the value $\mathsf{ct}_{i,1-\mathsf{x}_i}$ that appears in the computation of $(\mathsf{rpk}, \mathsf{rct})$ by the oracle $\mathcal{O}_{\mathtt{CRDM}}$ as the response to $\mathcal{A}$'s query $(f_0, f_1) \in (\mathcal{B}_s)^2$, is generated as $\mathsf{ct}_{i,1-\mathsf{x}_i} \leftarrow \mathsf{Enc}(\mathsf{pk}, \mathsf{A}; \mathsf{r}_{i,1-\mathsf{x}_i})$.
Note that the values $\mathsf{r}_{i,1-\mathsf{x}_i}$ are not used in Game 2, and each of them is chosen uniformly at random. Hence, applying a query-wise hybrid argument, we can straightforwardly construct a PPT reduction algorithm $\mathcal{B}$ attacking the PRCT security of $\Pi$, such that

$$\left|\Pr[\mathtt{SUC}_2] - \Pr[\mathtt{SUC}_3]\right| = q \cdot \mathsf{Adv}^{\mathtt{PRCT}}_{\Pi,\mathcal{B}}(\lambda). \tag{4}$$

**Game 4:** Same as Game 3, except that the values $(\mathsf{r}_{i,0}, \mathsf{r}_{i,1})_{i\in[n]}$ that appear in the computation of $(\mathsf{rpk}, \mathsf{rct})$ by the oracle $\mathcal{O}_{\mathtt{CRDM}}$ as the response to $\mathcal{A}$'s query $(f_0, f_1) \in (\mathcal{B}_s)^2$ are generated as follows:

1. Pick $\Delta_{1,0}, \Delta_{1,1}, \ldots, \Delta_{n,0}, \Delta_{n,1} \xleftarrow{\mathsf{r}} \{0,1\}^{\lambda}$.
2. Define the selector function $\mathsf{sel}[(\Delta_{i,v})_{i\in[n],v\in\{0,1\}}] : \{0,1\}^n \to (\{0,1\}^{\lambda} \times \{0,1\}^{\lambda})^n$ that has $2n$ $\lambda$-bit strings $(\Delta_{i,v})_{i\in[n],v\in\{0,1\}}$ hardwired, and on input $\mathsf{x} = (\mathsf{x}_1, \ldots, \mathsf{x}_n) \in \{0,1\}^n$, outputs $(w_{i,0}, w_{i,1})_{i\in[n]} \in (\{0,1\}^{\lambda} \times \{0,1\}^{\lambda})^n$ where $w_{i,\mathsf{x}_i} = 0^{\lambda}$ and $w_{i,1-\mathsf{x}_i} = \Delta_{i,1-\mathsf{x}_i}$ hold for all $i \in [n]$.

3. Set $(\mathsf{r}_{i,0}, \mathsf{r}_{i,1})_{i \in [n]} \leftarrow (\mathsf{y}_{i,0}, \mathsf{y}_{i,1})_{i \in [n]} \oplus \mathsf{sel}[(\Delta_{i,b})_{i \in [n], b \in \{0,1\}}](\mathsf{x})$. (Here, the XOR is computed component-wise.)

By this change, in Game 4, the oracle $\mathcal{O}_{\mathtt{CRDM}}$ computes the answer to each query $(f_0, f_1) \in (\mathcal{B}_s)^2$ from $\mathcal{A}$ as follows:

1. Compute $(\mathsf{pk}, \mathsf{sk}) \xleftarrow{\mathsf{r}} \mathsf{KG}(1^\lambda)$.
2. Pick $\mathsf{A} \xleftarrow{\mathsf{r}} \{0,1\}^{3\lambda}$.
3. Pick $\Delta_{1,0}, \Delta_{1,1}, \ldots, \Delta_{n,0}, \Delta_{n,1} \xleftarrow{\mathsf{r}} \{0,1\}^\lambda$.
4. Pick $\mathsf{B} \xleftarrow{\mathsf{r}} \{0,1\}^m$, and compute

$$(\mathsf{z}, (\mathsf{r}_{i,0}, \mathsf{r}_{i,1})_{i \in [n]}) \leftarrow \mathsf{KwPRF}(\mathsf{x}, \mathsf{B}) \oplus (f_b(\mathsf{x}), \mathsf{sel}[(\Delta_{i,v})_{i \in [n], v \in \{0,1\}}](\mathsf{x})),$$

   where the XOR is computed component-wise.
5. For all $i \in [n]$, do the following:
   (a) Compute $\mathsf{ct}_{i,0} \leftarrow \mathsf{Enc}(\mathsf{pk}, \mathsf{A}; \mathsf{r}_{i,0})$ and $\mathsf{ct}_{i,1} \leftarrow \mathsf{Enc}(\mathsf{pk}, \mathsf{A}; \mathsf{r}_{i,1})$.
   (b) Set $\mathsf{C}_i \leftarrow \mathsf{ct}_{i,0} \oplus \mathsf{ct}_{i,1}$.
   (c) Set $\mathsf{ct}_i \leftarrow \mathsf{ct}_{i,0}$.
6. Return $\mathsf{rpk} \leftarrow (\mathsf{pk}, \mathsf{A}, \mathsf{B}, (\mathsf{C}_i)_{i \in [n]})$ and $\mathsf{rct} \leftarrow (\mathsf{z}, (\mathsf{ct}_i)_{i \in [n]})$ to $\mathcal{A}$.

In Game 4, for all $i \in [n]$, $\Delta_{i,1-\mathsf{x}_i}$ works as the key (mask) of the one-time pad encryption, and makes $\mathsf{r}_{i,1-\mathsf{x}_i}$ distributed uniformly at random in $\{0,1\}^\lambda$, which is exactly how this value in Game 3 is distributed. On the other hand, since $\mathsf{r}_{i,\mathsf{x}_i} = \mathsf{y}_{i,\mathsf{x}_i} \oplus 0^\lambda = \mathsf{y}_{i,\mathsf{x}_i}$ holds in Game 4, its value is unchanged and thus generated identically to that in Game 3. Hence, $\mathcal{A}$'s view in Game 4 is distributed identically to that in Game 3, which implies

$$\Pr[\mathtt{SUC}_3] = \Pr[\mathtt{SUC}_4]. \tag{5}$$

**Game 5:** Same as Game 4, except that the values $(\mathsf{z}, (\mathsf{r}_{i,0}, \mathsf{r}_{i,1})_{i \in [n]})$ that appear in the computation of $(\mathsf{rpk}, \mathsf{rct})$ by the oracle $\mathcal{O}_{\mathtt{CRDM}}$ as the response to $\mathcal{A}$'s query $(f_0, f_1) \in \mathcal{B}_s^2$, are picked from $\{0,1\}^{\ell_\mathsf{m}} \times (\{0,1\}^\lambda \times \{0,1\}^\lambda)^n$ uniformly at random.

Since the answers from the oracle $\mathcal{O}_{\mathtt{CRDM}}$ now contains no information of $b$, $\mathcal{A}$'s view is independent of $b$ in Game 5. Hence, we have

$$\Pr[\mathtt{SUC}_5] = \frac{1}{2}. \tag{6}$$

Also, we can construct a PPT reduction algorithm $\mathcal{B}'$ attacking the $\mathcal{B}_{s+p}$-KDS security of $\mathsf{KwPRF}$, such that

$$\left|\Pr[\mathtt{SUC}_4] - \Pr[\mathtt{SUC}_5]\right| = \mathsf{Adv}^{\mathcal{B}_{s+p}\text{-}\mathtt{KDS}\text{-}\mathtt{wPRF}}_{\mathsf{KwPRF},\mathcal{B}'}(\lambda). \tag{7}$$

Hence, Eqs. (2) to (7), together with the triangle inequality, imply Eq. (1). This completes the proof of the second item in the theorem statement.

Finally, we briefly explain how $\mathcal{P}$-KDS (resp. $\mathcal{L}$-KDS) security of $\mathsf{KwPRF}$ leads to the correlation $\mathcal{P}$-RDM (resp. $\mathcal{L}$-RDM) security of the PKE scheme $\Pi_{\mathtt{RDM}}$. In the above proof, the KDS function $g$ that the reduction algorithm $\mathcal{B}'$ (attacking the $\mathcal{B}_{s+p}$-KDS security of $\mathsf{KwPRF}$) uses is of the form $g(\mathsf{x}) :=$

$(f_b(\mathsf{x}), \mathsf{sel}[(\Delta_{i,v})_{i\in[n],v\in\{0,1\}})(\mathsf{x}))$. Thus, if each pair of functions $(f_0, f_1)$ queried by $\mathcal{A}$ is a pair of projection functions (resp. affine functions), then the function used by the reduction algorithm $\mathcal{B}'$ as its query to the oracle $\mathcal{O}_{\mathtt{KDS\text{-}wPRF}}$ is also a projection function (resp. an affine function). Hence, the first item in the theorem statement can also be established. □ (**Theorem** 6)

# 5 Constructing a KDS Secure Weak PRF from KDM Secure SKE

In this section, we show that a KDS secure weak PRF can be constructed by using any (one-time) $\mathcal{P}$-KDM secure SKE. Our KDS secure weak PRF is built in two modular steps, using a SKE scheme with a new security notion that we call *pseudorandomness of ciphertexts against the receiver (receiver-PRCT security, for short)*, as an intermediate building block.

Specifically, first, in Sect. 5.1 we formally introduce the new security notion for SKE called receiver-PRCT security. Then, as the first step in our construction, we show in Sect. 5.2 how to construct a SKE scheme that satisfies KDM security and receiver-PRCT security simultaneously, by using a weak PRF and a garbling scheme, and assuming the existence a one-time $\mathcal{P}$-KDM secure SKE scheme. The construction here relies on the KDM-amplification construction by Waters and Wichs [25]. Finally, as the second step in our construction, we show in Sect. 5.3 how to construct a KDS secure weak PRF from a SKE scheme that satisfies KDM security and receiver-PRCT security simultaneously.

## 5.1 New Security Notion for SKE: Pseudorandomness of Ciphertexts Against the Receiver (Receiver-PRCT Security)

In this section, we give the formal definition of receiver-PRCT security for SKE. As the name suggests, this security notion guarantees that a ciphertext encrypting a random plaintext cannot be distinguished from a random element in the ciphertext space, even by the legitimate receiver of the ciphertext who holds a secret key.

The formal definition is as follows.

Let $\mathcal{E} = (\mathsf{SEnc}, \mathsf{SDec})$ be a SKE scheme whose secret key space is $\mathcal{K}$, plaintext space is $\mathcal{M}$, and ciphertext space is $\mathcal{C}$. We say that $\mathcal{E}$ satisfies *receiver-PRCT security* if for all PPT adversaries $\mathcal{A}$,

$$\mathsf{Adv}^{\mathtt{R\text{-}PRCT}}_{\mathcal{E},\mathcal{A}}(\lambda) := 2 \cdot \left| \Pr\left[ \begin{array}{l} \mathsf{sk} \xleftarrow{r} \mathcal{K};\ \mathsf{m} \xleftarrow{r} \mathcal{M};\ \mathsf{ct}_1 \xleftarrow{r} \mathsf{SEnc}(\mathsf{sk}, \mathsf{m}) \\ \mathsf{ct}_0 \xleftarrow{r} \mathcal{C};\ b \xleftarrow{r} \{0,1\};\ b' \xleftarrow{r} \mathcal{A}(\mathsf{sk}, \mathsf{ct}_b) \end{array} : b' = b \right] - \frac{1}{2} \right|$$

is negligible.

### 5.2 Constructing a SKE Scheme Satisfying KDM Security and Receiver-PRCT Security

Waters and Wichs [25] showed that for any polynomial $s = s(\lambda)$, we can construct a $\mathcal{B}_s$-KDM secure scheme, by using a SKE scheme satisfying pseudorandomness of ciphertexts (PRCT security) and a garbling scheme satisfying simulation security as building blocks, and assuming the existence of a (one-time) $\mathcal{P}$-KDM secure SKE scheme.

In this section, we show that if the underlying PRCT-secure SKE scheme is instantiated with the weak PRF-based SKE scheme (recalled in Sect. 2.2) and the underlying garbling scheme satisfies *blindness* [8] (in addition to simulation security), then the KDM-secure SKE scheme resulting from the Waters-Wichs construction also satisfies receiver-PRCT security.

We now formally describe the intermediate SKE construction that achieves the desired properties. Consider the following ingredients:

- Let $\mathsf{wPRF} : \{0,1\}^\lambda \times \{0,1\}^\lambda \to \{0,1\}^\lambda$ be a weak PRF.
- Let $\mathcal{G} = (\mathsf{Garble}, \mathsf{GEval}, \mathsf{GSim})$ be a garbling scheme.
- Let $\mathcal{E} = (\mathsf{SEnc}, \mathsf{SDec})$ be a one-time $\mathcal{P}$-KDM secure SKE scheme whose secret key space is $\{0,1\}^n$ for some polynomial $n = n(\lambda)$ and whose plaintext space is $\{0,1\}^{n+n\cdot\lambda}$. (This KDM secure SKE scheme is not directly used as a building block, but is necessary to *exist* for proving the KDM security of the Waters-Wichs construction. See Theorem 7.)
- Let $\ell_m = \ell_m(\lambda)$ be an arbitrary polynomial that represents the length of a plaintext that we wish to encrypt.

Using them, the SKE scheme $\mathcal{E}'_p = (\mathsf{SEnc}', \mathsf{SDec}')$ proposed by Waters and Wichs [25], in which its underlying PRCT-secure SKE scheme is instantiated with the weak PRF-based SKE scheme, is constructed as in Fig. 4.

The constructed SKE scheme $\mathcal{E}'_p$ is parameterized by a polynomial $p = p(\lambda)$, which will be adjusted so that we can conduct the proof of its KDM security. (See Theorem 7 below.) The secret key space of $\mathcal{E}'_p$ is $\{0,1\}^{n+n\cdot\lambda}$, and its plaintext space is $\{0,1\}^{\ell_m}$.

It was shown in [25] that $\mathcal{E}'_p$ satisfies correctness, based on the correctness of the buliding blocks. Furthermore, it was shown to satisfy KDM security as follows[8]:

**Theorem 7** ([25]). *Assume that* $\mathsf{wPRF}$ *is a secure weak PRF, the garbling scheme* $\mathcal{G}$ *satisfies simulation security, and the SKE scheme* $\mathcal{E}$ *(which is used only in the proof) satisfies one-time* $\mathcal{P}$*-KDM security. Then, for any polynomial* $s = s(\lambda)$*, there exists a corresponding polynomial* $p = p(\lambda)$ *(that depends on* $s$ *and*

[8] Waters and Wichs [25] actually showed that their SKE construction achieves multi-key variant of KDM security (i.e. KDM security in the presence of multiple secret keys), which is stronger than KDM security in the single key setting treated in this paper. However, we do not recall this more general result since KDM security in the single key setting is sufficient for our purpose.

$\mathsf{SEnc}'(\mathsf{sk} \in \{0,1\}^{n+n\cdot\lambda}, \mathsf{m} \in \{0,1\}^{\ell_\mathsf{m}})$ :
Parse $\mathsf{sk}$ as $(\mathsf{z}, (\mathsf{k}_i)_{i\in[n]}) \in \{0,1\}^n \times (\{0,1\}^\lambda)^n$.
Parse $\mathsf{z}$ as $(\mathsf{z}_1, \ldots, \mathsf{z}_n) \in \{0,1\}^n$.
Let $C_\mathsf{m} : \{0,1\}^n \to \{0,1\}^{\ell_\mathsf{m}}$ be a constant circuit with size $p$ such that $\forall \mathsf{x} \in \{0,1\}^n : C_\mathsf{m}(\mathsf{x}) = \mathsf{m}$.
$(\widetilde{C}, (\mathsf{L})_{i\in[n],v\in\{0,1\}}) \xleftarrow{\mathsf{r}} \mathsf{Garble}(1^\lambda, C_\mathsf{m})$.
$\forall i \in [n]$ :
$\mathsf{r}_{i,0}, \mathsf{r}_{i,1}, \mathsf{ct}_{i,1-\mathsf{z}_i} \xleftarrow{\mathsf{r}} \{0,1\}^\lambda$
$\mathsf{ct}_{i,\mathsf{z}_i} \leftarrow \mathsf{wPRF}(\mathsf{k}_i, \mathsf{r}_{i,\mathsf{z}_i}) \oplus \mathsf{L}_{i,\mathsf{z}_i}$
Return $\mathsf{CT} \leftarrow (\widetilde{C}, (\mathsf{r}_{i,v}, \mathsf{ct}_{i,v})_{i\in[n],v\in\{0,1\}})$.

$\mathsf{SDec}'(\mathsf{sk} \in \{0,1\}^{n+n\cdot\lambda}, \mathsf{CT})$ :
Parse $\mathsf{sk}$ as $(\mathsf{z}, (\mathsf{k}_i)_{i\in[n]}) \in \{0,1\}^n \times (\{0,1\}^\lambda)^n$.
Parse $\mathsf{z}$ as $(\mathsf{z}_1, \ldots, \mathsf{z}_n) \in \{0,1\}^n$.
Parse $\mathsf{CT}$ as $(\widetilde{C}, (\mathsf{r}_{i,v}, \mathsf{ct}_{i,v})_{i\in[n],v\in\{0,1\}})$.
$\forall i \in [n]$ :
$\mathsf{L}'_i \leftarrow \mathsf{wPRF}(\mathsf{k}_i, \mathsf{r}_{i,\mathsf{z}_i}) \oplus \mathsf{ct}_{i,\mathsf{z}_i}$.
Return $\mathsf{m} \leftarrow \mathsf{GEval}(\widetilde{C}, (\mathsf{L}'_i)_{i\in[n]})$.

**Fig. 4.** The SKE scheme $\mathcal{E}'_p$ proposed by Waters and Wichs [25], in which the underlying PRCT secure SKE scheme is instantiated with the weak PRF-based SKE scheme.

*the complexity of the algorithms of $\mathcal{E}$) such that the SKE scheme $\mathcal{E}'_p$ satisfies $\mathcal{B}_s$-KDM security. (Hence, adjusting the polynomial $s$ appropriately, $\mathcal{E}'_p$ also satisfies $\mathcal{P}$-KDM security and $\mathcal{L}$-KDM security as well.)*

We now show that $\mathcal{E}'_p$ satisfies receiver-PRCT security as well.

**Theorem 8.** *Let $p = p(\lambda) \geq \max\{n, \ell_\mathsf{m}\}$ be an arbitrary polynomial. If the garbling scheme $\mathcal{G}$ satisfies simulation security and blindness simultaneously, then the SKE scheme $\mathcal{E}'_p$ satisfies receiver-PRCT security.*

*Proof of Theorem* 8. Let $\mathcal{A}$ be an arbitrary PPT adversary that attacks the receiver-PRCT security of $\mathcal{E}'_p$. We will show that for this $\mathcal{A}$, there exist PPT adversaries $\mathcal{B}$ and $\mathcal{B}'$ that satisfy

$$\mathsf{Adv}^{\mathtt{R\text{-}PRCT}}_{\mathcal{E}'_p,\mathcal{A}}(\lambda) \leq \mathsf{Adv}^{\mathtt{Sim}}_{\mathcal{G},\mathcal{B}}(\lambda) + \mathsf{Adv}^{\mathtt{Blind}}_{\mathcal{G},\mathcal{B}'}(\lambda), \tag{8}$$

which will ensure that $\mathcal{A}$'s advantage is negligible by our assumption that $\mathcal{G}$ satisfies simulation security and blindness simultaneously, and hence imply the theorem.

Our proof is via a sequence of games argument using four games. In the following, let $\mathtt{T}_t$ denote the event that $\mathcal{A}$ outputs $b' = 1$ in Game $t \in [4]$.

**Game 1:** This is the receiver-PRCT security experiment with the challenge bit $b = 1$.
Specifically, the description of Game 1 is as follows:
1. Pick $\mathsf{sk} = (\mathsf{z} = (\mathsf{z}_1, \ldots, \mathsf{z}_n), (\mathsf{k}_i)_{i\in[n]}) \xleftarrow{\mathsf{r}} \{0,1\}^n \times (\{0,1\}^\lambda)^n$.

2. Pick $\mathsf{m} \xleftarrow{r} \{0,1\}^{\ell_\mathsf{m}}$.
3. Let $C_\mathsf{m} : \{0,1\}^n \to \{0,1\}^{\ell_\mathsf{m}}$ be a constant circuit with size $p$ such that $\forall \mathsf{x} \in \{0,1\}^n : C_\mathsf{m}(\mathsf{x}) = \mathsf{m}$.
4. Compute $(\widetilde{C}, (\mathsf{L}_{i,v})_{i\in[n],v\in\{0,1\}}) \xleftarrow{r} \mathsf{Garble}(1^\lambda, C_\mathsf{m})$.
5. For all $i \in [n]$, do the following:
   (a) Pick $\mathsf{r}_{i,0}, \mathsf{r}_{i,1}, \mathsf{ct}_{i,1-\mathsf{z}_i} \xleftarrow{r} \{0,1\}^\lambda$.
   (b) Compute $\mathsf{ct}_{i,\mathsf{z}_i} \leftarrow \mathsf{wPRF}(\mathsf{k}_i, \mathsf{r}_{i,\mathsf{z}_i}) \oplus \mathsf{L}_{i,\mathsf{z}_i}$.
6. Set $\mathsf{CT} \leftarrow (\widetilde{C}, (\mathsf{r}_{i,v}, \mathsf{ct}_{i,v})_{i\in[n],v\in\{0,1\}})$.
7. Run $b' \xleftarrow{r} \mathcal{A}(\mathsf{sk}, \mathsf{CT})$.

Looking ahead, Game 4 will correspond to the receiver-PRCT security experiment with the challenge bit $b = 0$. That is, we have

$$\mathsf{Adv}^{\mathtt{R\text{-}PRCT}}_{\mathcal{E}'_p,\mathcal{A}}(\lambda) = \Big|\Pr[\mathrm{T}_1] - \Pr[\mathrm{T}_4]\Big|. \tag{9}$$

**Game 2:** Same as Game 1, except that $\widetilde{C}$ and $\{\mathsf{L}_{i,\mathsf{z}_i}\}_{i\in[n]}$ are generated by $(\widetilde{C}, (\mathsf{L}_{i,\mathsf{z}_i})_{i\in[n]}) \xleftarrow{r} \mathsf{GSim}(1^\lambda, \mathsf{m})$.
Note that the labels $\{\mathsf{L}_{i,1-\mathsf{z}_i}\}_{i\in[n]}$ are not at all used in Game 1. Hence, we can straightforwardly construct a PPT reduction algorithm $\mathcal{B}$ attacking the simulation security of $\mathcal{G}$, such that

$$\Big|\Pr[\mathrm{T}_1] - \Pr[\mathrm{T}_2]\Big| = \mathsf{Adv}^{\mathtt{Sim}}_{\mathcal{G},\mathcal{B}}(\lambda). \tag{10}$$

**Game 3:** Same as Game 2, except that $\widetilde{C}$ and $\{\mathsf{L}_{i,\mathsf{z}_i}\}_{i\in[n]}$ are replaced with truly random strings of the same length as the corresponding values in Game 2, respectively.

In Game 2, the input to $\mathsf{GSim}$, i.e. $\mathsf{m} \in \{0,1\}^{\ell_\mathsf{m}}$, is chosen uniformly at random. Hence, we can again straightforwardly construct a PPT reduction algorithm $\mathcal{B}'$ attacking the blindness of $\mathcal{G}$, such that

$$\Big|\Pr[\mathrm{T}_2] - \Pr[\mathrm{T}_3]\Big| = \mathsf{Adv}^{\mathtt{Blind}}_{\mathcal{G},\mathcal{B}'}(\lambda). \tag{11}$$

**Game 4:** Same as Game 3, except that for all $i \in [n]$, $\mathsf{ct}_{i,\mathsf{z}_i} \in \{0,1\}^\lambda$ is chosen uniformly at random.
In Game 3, $\mathsf{ct}_{i,\mathsf{z}_i}$ is computed as $\mathsf{ct}_{i,\mathsf{z}_i} = \mathsf{wPRF}(\mathsf{k}_i, \mathsf{r}_{i,\mathsf{z}_i}) \oplus \mathsf{L}_{i,\mathsf{z}_i}$, and $\mathsf{L}_{i,\mathsf{z}_i}$ is chosen uniformly at random (independently of any other values). Hence, for all $i \in [n]$, $\mathsf{L}_{i,\mathsf{z}_i}$ works as the key (mask) of the one-time pad encryption, and makes $\mathsf{ct}_{i,\mathsf{z}_i}$ look like a truly random string in $\{0,1\}^\lambda$. Consequently, $\mathcal{A}$'s view in Game 4 is distributed identically to that in Game 3, which implies

$$\Pr[\mathrm{T}_3] = \Pr[\mathrm{T}_4]. \tag{12}$$

In Game 4, all the values in $\mathcal{A}$'s view $(\mathsf{sk}, \mathsf{CT} = (\widetilde{C}, (\mathsf{r}_{i,v}, \mathsf{ct}_{i,v})_{i\in[n],v\in\{0,1\}}))$ are just truly random strings, which is exactly how these values are generated in the receiver-PRCT security experiment with the challenge bit $b = 0$. (Thus, we indeed obtain Eq. (9).)

Hence, Eqs. (9) to (12), together with the triangle inequality, imply Eq. (8).
□ (**Theorem** 8)

### 5.3 Constructing a KDS Secure Weak PRF

In this section, we show how to construct a KDS secure weak PRF from a SKE scheme that satisfies KDM security and receiver-PRCT security simultaneously.

Let $\mathcal{E} = (\mathsf{SEnc}, \mathsf{SDec})$ be a SKE scheme whose secret key space is $\{0,1\}^n$, plaintext space is $\{0,1\}^{\ell_\mathsf{m}}$, and ciphertext space is $\{0,1\}^{\ell_\mathsf{ct}}$, for some polynomials $n = n(\lambda)$, $\ell_\mathsf{m} = \ell_\mathsf{m}(\lambda)$, and $\ell_\mathsf{ct} = \ell_\mathsf{ct}(\lambda)$. For simplicity, we assume that $\mathsf{SDec}(\mathsf{sk}, \mathsf{ct})$ always returns a string in $\{0,1\}^{\ell_\mathsf{m}}$ as long as $\mathsf{sk} \in \{0,1\}^n$ and $\mathsf{ct} \in \{0,1\}^{\ell_\mathsf{ct}}$.[9]

Using $\mathcal{E}$ as a building block, our KDS secure weak PRF $\mathsf{KwPRF} : \{0,1\}^n \times \{0,1\}^{\ell_\mathsf{ct}} \to \{0,1\}^{\ell_\mathsf{m}}$ is defined by

$$\forall (\mathsf{k}, \mathsf{x}) \in \{0,1\}^n \times \{0,1\}^{\ell_\mathsf{ct}} : \quad \mathsf{KwPRF}(\mathsf{k}, \mathsf{x}) := \mathsf{SDec}(\mathsf{k}, \mathsf{x}).$$

The KDS security of $\mathsf{KwPRF}$ is guaranteed by the following theorem.

**Theorem 9.** *If the SKE scheme $\mathcal{E}$ satisfies receiver-PRCT security, then the following holds:*

- *Let $\mathcal{F} \in \{\mathcal{P}, \mathcal{L}\}$. If the SKE scheme $\mathcal{E}$ additionally satisfies $\mathcal{F}$-KDM security, then* $\mathsf{KwPRF}$ *is a $\mathcal{F}$-KDS secure weak PRF.*
- *Let $s = s(\lambda)$ be an arbitrary polynomial. If the SKE scheme $\mathcal{E}$ additionally satisfies $\mathcal{B}_{s+\ell_\mathsf{m}}$-KDM security, then* $\mathsf{KwPRF}$ *is a $\mathcal{B}_s$-KDS secure weak PRF.*

*Proof of Theorem* 9. Since the proofs for both of the items are essentially the same, we mainly show the proof for the second item (i.e. $\mathcal{B}_s$-KDS security of $\mathsf{KwPRF}$), and briefly explain how the first item (i.e. $\mathcal{F}$-KDS security of $\mathsf{KwPRF}$ for $\mathcal{F} \in \{\mathcal{P}, \mathcal{L}\}$) can be proved.

Let $s = s(\lambda)$ be an arbitrary polynomial. Let $\mathcal{A}$ be an arbitrary PPT adversary that attacks the $\mathcal{B}_s$-KDS security of $\mathsf{KwPRF}$ and makes $q$ queries to the oracle $\mathcal{O}_{\texttt{KDS-wPRF}}(\cdot)$. We will show that for this $\mathcal{A}$, there exist PPT adversaries $\mathcal{B}$ and $\mathcal{B}'$ that satisfy

$$\mathsf{Adv}^{\mathcal{B}_s\texttt{-KDS-wPRF}}_{\mathsf{KwPRF},\mathcal{A}}(\lambda) \le 2q \cdot \mathsf{Adv}^{\texttt{R-PRCT}}_{\mathcal{E},\mathcal{B}}(\lambda) + 2 \cdot \mathsf{Adv}^{\mathcal{B}_{s+\ell_\mathsf{m}}\texttt{-KDM}}_{\mathcal{E},\mathcal{B}'}(\lambda), \tag{13}$$

which will ensure that $\mathcal{A}$'s advantage is negligible by our assumption that $\mathcal{E}$ satisfies receiver-PRCT security and $\mathcal{B}_{s+\ell_\mathsf{m}}$-KDM security simultaneously, and hence imply the second item of the theorem.

Our proof is via a sequence of games argument using four games. In the following, let $\texttt{SUC}_t$ denote the event that $\mathcal{A}$ succeeds in guessing the challenge bit (i.e. $b' = b$ occurs) in Game $t \in [4]$.

**Game 1:** This is the $\mathcal{B}_s$-KDS security experiment regarding $\mathsf{KwPRF}$.

Specifically, the description of Game 1 is as follows:

[9] This requirement on $\mathsf{SDec}$ is without loss of generality, since if the output of $\mathsf{SDec}$ does not follow this requirement, we can replace it with some fixed value $\mathsf{m}_0 \in \{0,1\}^{\ell_\mathsf{m}}$. (Note that this modification does no harm to correctness, KDM security, and receiver-PRCT security of the original SKE scheme).

1. Pick $\mathsf{k} \xleftarrow{r} \{0,1\}^n$ and $b \xleftarrow{r} \{0,1\}$.
2. Run $\mathcal{A}^{\mathcal{O}_{\mathtt{KDS\text{-}wPRF}}(\cdot)}(1^\lambda)$. Then, $\mathcal{A}$ starts making queries to its oracle $\mathcal{O}_{\mathtt{KDS\text{-}wPRF}}(\cdot)$. Each query $f \in \mathcal{B}_s$ from $\mathcal{A}$ is answered as follows:
   (a) Pick $\mathsf{x} \xleftarrow{r} \{0,1\}^{\ell_{\mathsf{ct}}}$.
   (b) Compute $\mathsf{y}_1 \leftarrow \mathsf{SDec}(\mathsf{k}, \mathsf{x}) \oplus f(\mathsf{k})$.
   (c) Pick $\mathsf{y}_0 \xleftarrow{r} \{0,1\}^{\ell_{\mathsf{m}}}$.
   (d) Return $(\mathsf{x}, \mathsf{y}_b)$.
3. At some point, $\mathcal{A}$ terminates with output $b'$.

By definition, we have

$$\mathsf{Adv}_{\mathsf{KwPRF},\mathcal{A}}^{\mathcal{B}_s\text{-}\mathtt{KDS\text{-}wPRF}}(\lambda) = 2 \cdot \left|\Pr[\mathtt{SUC}_1] - \frac{1}{2}\right|. \tag{14}$$

**Game 2:** Same as Game 1, except that $\mathsf{x} \in \{0,1\}^{\ell_{\mathsf{ct}}}$ and $\mathsf{y}_1 \in \{0,1\}^{\ell_{\mathsf{m}}}$ that appear in the computation by the oracle $\mathcal{O}_{\mathtt{KDS\text{-}wPRF}}$ as the response to $\mathcal{A}$'s query $f \in \mathcal{B}_s$, are generated as follows:
1. Pick $\mathsf{y} \xleftarrow{r} \{0,1\}^{\ell_{\mathsf{m}}}$.
2. Compute $\mathsf{y}_1 \leftarrow \mathsf{y} \oplus f(\mathsf{k})$.
3. Compute $\mathsf{x} \xleftarrow{r} \mathsf{SEnc}(\mathsf{k}, \mathsf{y})$.

Comparing the way $\mathsf{x}$ and $\mathsf{y}_1$ are generated in Game 2 and that in Game 1 and applying a query-wise hybrid argument, we can straightforwardly construct a PPT reduction algorithm $\mathcal{B}$ attacking the receiver-PRCT security of $\mathcal{E}$, such that

$$\left|\Pr[\mathtt{SUC}_1] - \Pr[\mathtt{SUC}_2]\right| = q \cdot \mathsf{Adv}_{\mathcal{E},\mathcal{B}}^{\mathtt{R\text{-}PRCT}}(\lambda). \tag{15}$$

**Game 3:** Same as Game 2, except that $\mathsf{y}_1 \in \{0,1\}^{\ell_{\mathsf{m}}}$ and $\mathsf{y} \in \{0,1\}^{\ell_{\mathsf{m}}}$ that appear in the computation by the oracle $\mathcal{O}_{\mathtt{KDS\text{-}wPRF}}$ as the response to $\mathcal{A}$'s query $f \in \mathcal{B}_s$, are generated as follows:
1. Pick $\mathsf{y}_1 \xleftarrow{r} \{0,1\}^{\ell_{\mathsf{m}}}$.
2. Compute $\mathsf{y} \leftarrow \mathsf{y}_1 \oplus f(\mathsf{k})$.

The distribution of $(\mathsf{y}, \mathsf{y}_1)$ in Game 3 and that in Game 2 are clearly identical, and thus we have

$$\Pr[\mathtt{SUC}_2] = \Pr[\mathtt{SUC}_3]. \tag{16}$$

**Game 4:** Same as Game 3, except that $\mathsf{x}$ that appears in the computation by the oracle $\mathcal{O}_{\mathtt{KDS\text{-}wPRF}}$ as the response to $\mathcal{A}$'s query $f \in \mathcal{B}_s$, is generated as $\mathsf{x} \xleftarrow{r} \mathsf{SEnc}(\mathsf{k}, 1^{\ell_{\mathsf{m}}})$.

Notice that in Game 3, given $\mathsf{y}_1 \in \{0,1\}^{\ell_{\mathsf{m}}}$, the "plaintext" $\mathsf{y} = \mathsf{y}_1 \oplus f(\mathsf{k})$ encrypted in the "ciphertext" $\mathsf{x}$, can be computed by a circuit with size $s + \ell_{\mathsf{m}}$ (since $f$ can be computed by a size-$s$ circuit and XORing with $\mathsf{y}_1 \in \{0,1\}^{\ell_{\mathsf{m}}}$ can be realized by $\ell_{\mathsf{m}}$ XOR gates), using the "secret key" $\mathsf{k} \in \{0,1\}^n$ as an input. Hence, we can again straightforwardly construct a PPT reduction algorithm $\mathcal{B}'$ attacking the $\mathcal{B}_{s+\ell_{\mathsf{m}}}$-KDM security of $\mathcal{E}$, such that

$$\left|\Pr[\mathtt{SUC}_3] - \Pr[\mathtt{SUC}_4]\right| = \mathsf{Adv}_{\mathcal{E},\mathcal{B}'}^{\mathcal{B}_{s+\ell_{\mathsf{m}}}\text{-}\mathtt{KDM}}(\lambda). \tag{17}$$

In Game 4, $\mathsf{x}$ and $\mathsf{y}_1$ generated as an answer (to $\mathcal{A}$'s query $f \in \mathcal{B}_s$) by the oracle $\mathcal{O}_{\mathtt{KDS\text{-}wPRF}}$ are generated independently. Furthermore, already in Game 3,

$\mathsf{y}_1$ and $\mathsf{y}_0$ are just independent random strings and thus distributed identically. Hence, the challenge bit $b$ is information-theoretically hidden from $\mathcal{A}$'s view in Game 4, which implies

$$\Pr[\mathtt{SUC}_4] = \frac{1}{2}. \tag{18}$$

Hence, Eqs. (14) to (18), together with the triangle inequality, imply Eq. (13). This completes the proof of the second item in the theorem statement.

Finally, we briefly explain how $\mathcal{P}$-KDM (resp. $\mathcal{L}$-KDM) security of the SKE scheme $\mathcal{E}$ leads to the $\mathcal{P}$-KDS (resp. $\mathcal{L}$-KDS security) of $\mathsf{KwPRF}$. At this point, it should be obvious from the above proof that if $\mathcal{A}$'s query $f$ is a projection function (resp. an affine function), then the functions used by the reduction algorithm $\mathcal{B}'$ as its KDM-encryption queries are also projection functions (resp. affine functions). Hence, the first item in the theorem statement can also be established. □ **(Theorem** 9)

**Acknowledgement.** This work was partially supported by JST K Program JPMJKP24U3 and JST CREST JPMJCR22M1.

## References

1. Alamati, N., De Feo, L., Montgomery, H., Patranabis, S.: Cryptographic group actions and applications. In: Moriai, S., Wang, H. (eds.) ASIACRYPT 2020, Part II. LNCS, vol. 12492, pp. 411–439. Springer, Cham (2020). https://doi.org/10.1007/978-3-030-64834-3_14
2. Alamati, N., Patranabis, S.: Cryptographic primitives with hinting property. In: Agrawal, S., Lin, D. (eds.) ASIACRYPT 2022, Part I. LNCS, vol. 13791, pp. 33–62. Springer, Cham (2022). https://doi.org/10.1007/978-3-031-22963-3_2
3. Alekhnovich, M.: More on average case vs approximation complexity. In: 44th FOCS, pp. 298–307. IEEE Computer Society Press (2003). https://doi.org/10.1109/SFCS.2003.1238204
4. Applebaum, B., Cash, D., Peikert, C., Sahai, A.: Fast cryptographic primitives and circular-secure encryption based on hard learning problems. In: Halevi, S. (ed.) CRYPTO 2009. LNCS, vol. 5677, pp. 595–618. Springer, Heidelberg (2009). https://doi.org/10.1007/978-3-642-03356-8_35
5. Bellare, M., et al.: Hedged public-key encryption: how to protect against bad randomness. In: Matsui, M. (ed.) ASIACRYPT 2009. LNCS, vol. 5912, pp. 232–249. Springer, Heidelberg (2009). https://doi.org/10.1007/978-3-642-10366-7_14
6. Birrell, E., Chung, K.M., Pass, R., Telang, S.: Randomness-dependent message security. In: Sahai, A. (ed.) TCC 2013. LNCS, vol. 7785, pp. 700–720. Springer, Heidelberg (2013). https://doi.org/10.1007/978-3-642-36594-2_39
7. Black, J., Rogaway, P., Shrimpton, T.: Encryption-scheme security in the presence of key-dependent messages. In: Nyberg, K., Heys, H. (eds.) SAC 2002. LNCS, vol. 2595, pp. 62–75. Springer, Heidelberg (2003). https://doi.org/10.1007/3-540-36492-7_6
8. Brakerski, Z., Lombardi, A., Segev, G., Vaikuntanathan, V.: Anonymous IBE, leakage resilience and circular security from new assumptions. In: Nielsen, J.B., Rijmen, V. (eds.) EUROCRYPT 2018, Part I. LNCS, vol. 10820, pp. 535–564. Springer, Cham (2018). https://doi.org/10.1007/978-3-319-78381-9_20

9. Garg, R., Khurana, D., Lu, G., Waters, B.: Black-box non-interactive non-malleable commitments. In: Canteaut, A., Standaert, F.-X. (eds.) EUROCRYPT 2021, Part III. LNCS, vol. 12698, pp. 159–185. Springer, Cham (2021). https://doi.org/10.1007/978-3-030-77883-5_6
10. Garg, R., Khurana, D., Lu, G., Waters, B.: On non-uniform security for black-box non-interactive CCA commitments. In: Hazay, C., Stam, M. (eds.) EUROCRYPT 2023, Part I. LNCS, vol. 14004, pp. 173–204. Springer, Cham (2023). https://doi.org/10.1007/978-3-031-30545-0_7
11. Garg, S., Hajiabadi, M., Malavolta, G., Ostrovsky, R.: How to build a trapdoor function from an encryption scheme. In: Tibouchi, M., Wang, H. (eds.) ASIACRYPT 2021, Part III. LNCS, vol. 13092, pp. 220–249. Springer, Cham (2021). https://doi.org/10.1007/978-3-030-92078-4_8
12. Goldreich, O., Goldwasser, S., Micali, S.: How to construct random functions (extended abstract). In: 25th FOCS. pp. 464–479. IEEE Computer Society Press (1984). https://doi.org/10.1109/SFCS.1984.715949
13. Hajiabadi, M., Kapron, B.M.: Reproducible circularly-secure bit encryption: applications and realizations. In: Gennaro, R., Robshaw, M. (eds.) CRYPTO 2015, Part I. LNCS, vol. 9215, pp. 224–243. Springer, Heidelberg (2015). https://doi.org/10.1007/978-3-662-47989-6_11
14. Hajiabadi, M., Khazaei, S., Vahdani, B.: Randomness recoverable secret sharing schemes. In: Chung, K.M. (ed.) ITC 2023. LIPIcs, vol. 267, pp. 12:1–12:25. Schloss Dagstuhl (2023). https://doi.org/10.4230/LIPIcs.ITC.2023.12
15. Håstad, J., Impagliazzo, R., Levin, L.A., Luby, M.: A pseudorandom generator from any one-way function. SIAM J. Comput. **28**(4), 1364–1396 (1999)
16. Hemenway, B., Ostrovsky, R.: Building injective trapdoor functions from oblivious transfer. Electron. Colloquium Comput. Complex. **TR10-127** (2010). https://eccc.weizmann.ac.il/report/2010/127
17. Hohenberger, S., Koppula, V., Waters, B.: Chosen ciphertext security from injective trapdoor functions. In: Micciancio, D., Ristenpart, T. (eds.) CRYPTO 2020, Part I. LNCS, vol. 12170, pp. 836–866. Springer, Cham (2020). https://doi.org/10.1007/978-3-030-56784-2_28
18. Kiltz, E., Masny, D., Pietrzak, K.: Simple chosen-ciphertext security from low-noise LPN. In: Krawczyk, H. (ed.) PKC 2014. LNCS, vol. 8383, pp. 1–18. Springer, Heidelberg (2014). https://doi.org/10.1007/978-3-642-54631-0_1
19. Kitagawa, F., Matsuda, T.: Circular security is complete for KDM security. In: Moriai, S., Wang, H. (eds.) ASIACRYPT 2020, Part I. LNCS, vol. 12491, pp. 253–285. Springer, Cham (2020). https://doi.org/10.1007/978-3-030-64837-4_9
20. Kitagawa, F., Matsuda, T., Tanaka, K.: CCA security and trapdoor functions via key-dependent-message security. In: Boldyreva, A., Micciancio, D. (eds.) CRYPTO 2019, Part III. LNCS, vol. 11694, pp. 33–64. Springer, Cham (2019). https://doi.org/10.1007/978-3-030-26954-8_2
21. Koppula, V., Waters, B.: Realizing chosen ciphertext security generically in attribute-based encryption and predicate encryption. In: Boldyreva, A., Micciancio, D. (eds.) CRYPTO 2019, Part II. LNCS, vol. 11693, pp. 671–700. Springer, Cham (2019). https://doi.org/10.1007/978-3-030-26951-7_23
22. Naor, M., Reingold, O.: Synthesizers and their application to the parallel construction of pseudo-random functions. J. Comput. Syst. Sci. **58**(2), 336–375 (1999). https://doi.org/10.1006/JCSS.1998.1618
23. Persiano, G., Phan, D.H., Yung, M.: Public-key anamorphism in (CCA-secure) public-key encryption and beyond. In: Reyzin, L., Stebila, D. (eds.) CRYPTO 2024,

Part II. LNCS, vol. 14921, pp. 422–455. Springer, Cham (2024). https://doi.org/10.1007/978-3-031-68379-4_13
24. Rosen, A., Segev, G.: Chosen-ciphertext security via correlated products. In: Reingold, O. (ed.) TCC 2009. LNCS, vol. 5444, pp. 419–436. Springer, Berlin, Heidelberg (2009). https://doi.org/10.1007/978-3-642-00457-5_25
25. Waters, B., Wichs, D.: Universal amplification of KDM security: from 1-key circular to multi-key KDM. In: Handschuh, H., Lysyanskaya, A. (eds.) CRYPTO 2023, Part II. LNCS, vol. 14082, pp. 674–693. Springer, Cham (2023). https://doi.org/10.1007/978-3-031-38545-2_22
26. Yu, Yu., Zhang, J.: Cryptography with auxiliary input and trapdoor from constant-noise LPN. In: Robshaw, M., Katz, J. (eds.) CRYPTO 2016, Part I. LNCS, vol. 9814, pp. 214–243. Springer, Heidelberg (2016). https://doi.org/10.1007/978-3-662-53018-4_9

# On the Complexity of Interactive Arguments

Idan Baril[1(✉)] and Iftach Haitner[1,2]

[1] Tel-Aviv University, Tel Aviv, Israel
idan@baril.co.il
[2] Stellar Development Foundation, San Francisco, USA

**Abstract.** We study the minimal hardness assumptions required for constructing *interactive arguments* for NP, focusing on *succinct* arguments—where the prover's total communication is smaller than the witness size—and on *relaxed* forms of *zero knowledge*, such as *witness indistinguishability.* Known constructions of succinct arguments rely on various types of *collision-resistant hash functions*, *indistinguishability obfuscation*, *hardness of discrete logarithm*, and *lattice-based assumptions*, while known constructions of witness-indistinguishable arguments require *one-way functions (OWFs).* This suggests that succinct witness-indistinguishable interactive arguments require OWFs, or equivalently, that the existence of such arguments implies that of OWFs.

Nevertheless, we prove that, at least as far as fully black-box reductions are concerned, interactive arguments do not imply OWFs. Specifically, we consider *assumption-dependent* fully black-box reductions from OWFs to succinct witness-indistinguishable interactive arguments *and* an additional hardness assumption $\mathsf{G}$ (e.g., NP $\not\subseteq$ P/poly). Such a reduction is a pair $(f, \mathsf{R})$ of (oracle-aided) function $f$ and algorithm $\mathsf{R}$ such that, for any succinct witness-indistinguishable interactive argument $\Pi = (\mathsf{P}, \mathsf{V})$ and any inverter $\mathsf{Inv}$ of $f^{\Pi}$, the algorithm $\mathsf{R}^{\Pi,\mathsf{Inv}}$ breaks *either* the soundness of $\Pi$ *or* the assumption $\mathsf{G}$. We prove that the existence of such a reduction implies a black-box reduction from OWFs to $\mathsf{G}$ *alone*. Namely, beyond what is implied by $\mathsf{G}$, succinct witness-indistinguishable interactive arguments have no black-box implications for the existence of OWFs.

## 1 Introduction

In an *interactive argument for* NP, the prover, holding the witness, interacts with the verifier to convince it of the validity of a statement given as a common input. We require the protocol to be *sound*: even a malicious *efficient* prover cannot make the verifier accept a false statement, except with negligible probability.[1]

In *succinct* interactive arguments for NP, the prover gets a witness $w$ as a private input, and the total number of bits it sends is significantly smaller than $|w|$,

[1] Interactive arguments are a relaxation of *interactive proofs*, where soundness is required to hold against *arbitrary* malicious provers.


N. Heninger and M. Rosulek (Eds.): CRYPTO 2026, LNCS 16800, pp. 97–126, 2026.
https://doi.org/10.1007/978-3-032-35367-2_4

to the extreme of being poly-logarithmic in $|w|$. Succinct interactive arguments are cornerstones of modern cryptography, enabling applications such as verifiable computation, cf., [26], where a computationally bounded client delegates work to a powerful server while maintaining assurance of the result's validity. While non-succinct (non-interactive) arguments trivially exist for any NP language—the prover simply sends the witness it receives as private input to the verifier—this does not seem to be the case for succinct arguments; known constructions of succinct interactive arguments for NP are based on *collision-resistant hash functions* [35], *multi-collision resistant hash functions* [36], *indistinguishability obfuscation* [43], *hardness of discrete logarithm* [8], and lattice-based assumptions [3]. This state of affairs raises the question of whether succinct interactive arguments for NP can be based on *weaker* assumptions, for example, the existence of one-way functions? And the following complementary question, which is in the focus of this paper,

> Are one-way functions *required* for building *succinct* interactive arguments for NP?

An interactive argument is *witness indistinguishable* if, after the interaction, the verifier cannot tell which witness the prover used. It is *witness hiding* if, after the interaction, the verifier cannot compute any function of the witness used by the prover better than it could without the interaction. While all known constructions of witness indistinguishable and witness hiding arguments use one-way functions, cf., Goldreich et al. [24], unlike in the case of *zero knowledge*, it is not known that one-way functions are necessary. This raises the following question,

> Are one-way functions *necessary* for constructing *witness-indistinguishable* and *witness-hiding* interactive arguments for NP?

### 1.1 Our Results

We study the existence of *fully black-box reductions* from one-way functions (OWFs) to interactive arguments. It is easy to see that, unless one proves that $\mathrm{P} \neq \mathrm{NP}$, reductions from one-way functions to the existence of succinct interactive arguments do *not* exist; if $\mathrm{P} = \mathrm{NP}$, then one-way functions do not exist, but non-interactive arguments do exist (the verifier decides the language by itself). Hence, a reduction from one-way functions to the existence of interactive arguments (of any type) would establish that $\mathrm{P} \neq \mathrm{NP}$. Therefore, the right type of reductions to consider is from one-way functions to interactive arguments *together with* an additional hardness assumption, e.g., $\mathrm{NP} \not\subseteq \mathrm{P/poly}$. Such reductions would enable, for instance, to prove that one-way functions are necessary for building succinct or witness-indistinguishable interactive arguments for *hard-to-decide languages*.[2] To formalize such reductions, we naturally capture

[2] Similar types of reductions were used by Ostrovsky and Wigderson [41] and Hirahara and Nanashima [31] to prove that the existence of one-way functions is necessary for building *zero-knowledge proofs* for hard-to-decide languages. See more details in Section 1.3.

hardness assumptions using interactive games between a *player* and a (possibly inefficient) *challenger*,[3] and consider the following type of *assumption-dependent* reductions.

**Definition 1 (Assumption-dependent, fully black-box reductions from OWFs to interactive arguments, informal).** *An* assumption-dependent, fully black-box reduction from OWFs to interactive arguments for an NP-relation $\mathcal{R}$, *with respect to* a game $\mathsf{G}$, *is a poly-time, oracle-aided function* $f$ *and a* PPT, *oracle-aided algorithm* $\mathsf{R}$, *such that for every efficient interactive argument* $(\mathsf{P}, \mathsf{V})$ *and any efficient* $\mathsf{Inv}$ *that inverts* $f^{\mathsf{P},\mathsf{V}}$ *with non-negligible probability,* $\mathsf{R}^{(\mathsf{P},\mathsf{V}),\mathsf{Inv}}$ *breaks the soundness of* $(\mathsf{P}, \mathsf{V})$, *with respect to* $\mathcal{R}$, or *wins the game* $\mathsf{G}$, *with non-negligible probability.*

That is, if $f$ is not one-way then either the interactive argument $(\mathsf{P}, \mathsf{V})$ is not sound or the game $\mathsf{G}$ is not hard. We make the following remarks:

- The one-way function $f$ treats the interactive argument parties as oracles, but might depend *arbitrarily* on the game $\mathsf{G}$.
- The security proof $\mathsf{R}$ treats both the interactive argument and an adversary inverting $f$ as oracles.
- We only require the reduction to work given access to an *efficient* interactive argument and an efficient inverter, where "efficient" stands for non-uniform poly-time algorithms.[4]

For such reductions, we prove the following result.

**Theorem 1 (Informal).** *If there exists an assumption-dependent, fully black-box reduction from OWFs to interactive arguments for an* NP*-relation* $\mathcal{R}$, *with respect to a game* $\mathsf{G}$, *then there exists a black-box reduction from OWFs to* $\mathsf{G}$. *Moreover, the above holds even if the reduction only needs to work when the interactive argument oracle is perfect zero knowledge.*

Namely, if one can use the soundness of an interactive argument (succinct or not), together with the hardness of a game $\mathsf{G}$ to construct one-way functions, then one could also use *only* the hardness of $\mathsf{G}$ for this task. Moreover, since being perfect zero knowledge implies being perfect witness indistinguishable and witness hiding, the above holds also for reductions from one-way functions to witness-indistinguishable/hiding arguments. For the same reason, the above captures black-box reductions to zero-knowledge arguments with *inefficient simulators* (in which the efficient reduction does not get oracle access to the inefficient

---

[3] Our actual definition, see Section 2.5, allows more complex games than such interactive protocols, and captures a larger set of hardness assumptions, such as $\mathrm{NP} \not\subseteq \mathrm{P/poly}$.

[4] Most separation results for fully black-box reductions exploit the fact that the reduction under consideration is required to work given access to *any* instantiation of the hardness assumption and the adversary. Requiring the reduction to succeed only given access to *efficient* entities simplifies the reduction's task, and thus makes lower bounds on such reductions, such as the ones we present here, more insightful.

simulator). However, Theorem 1 does *not* address reductions that get an oracle access to the zero-knowledge simulator.[5] Theorem 1 naturally extends to *auxiliary-input* one-way functions.

### 1.2 Our Technique

Fix an assumption-dependent, fully black-box reduction $(f, \mathsf{R})$ with respect to NP-relation $\mathcal{R}$ and a game $\mathsf{G}$. Our approach is to give a construction of an efficient non-interactive argument $\Pi$,[6] and an efficient (no oracle) function $g$, such that inverting $g$ implies the inversion of $f^{\Pi} := f^{\mathsf{P},\mathsf{V}}$. Hence, for any inverter $\mathsf{Inv}$ of $g$, it holds that $\mathsf{R}^{\Pi,\mathsf{Inv}}$ either breaks the soundness of $\Pi$, or wins the game $\mathsf{G}$. By carefully constructing the argument $\Pi$, we prove that the former does not hold, and conclude that $\mathsf{R}^{\Pi,\mathsf{Inv}}$ wins the game $\mathsf{G}$. Finally, by letting $\mathsf{R}$ emulate $\Pi$ internally (recall that $\Pi$ is efficient), we get an efficient algorithm $\widehat{R}$ such that $\widehat{R}^{\mathsf{Inv}}$ wins the game $\mathsf{G}$. Namely, we construct a (black-box) reduction from the one-wayness of $g$ to the hardness of $\mathsf{G}$. (We ignore the zero-knowledge part for now, and address it in Section 1.2.2.)

Given the above blueprint, the main challenge is to construct the desired argument $\Pi$. We start with a simple approach, explain its shortcomings, and gradually develop the actual argument. Throughout, we assume without loss of generality that $f$ only makes valid queries $(\phi, w) \in \mathcal{R}$ to the prover (by design, our prover returns $\perp$ on invalid queries). We also assume for simplicity that both $f$ and $\mathsf{R}$ are *length-preserving*: on inputs of length $n$, the function $f$ queries the interactive argument $\Pi$ only on instances of length $n$, and the reduction $\mathsf{R}$ queries $\Pi$ and the potential adversary $\mathsf{Inv}$ only on inputs of this length. In Section 1.2.1, we explain how to handle arbitrary reductions.

*The Unpredictable-Function Argument.* When considering interactive arguments for an NP-relation $\mathcal{R}$ to be given as oracles to the reduction, the first thing that might come to mind is to use an *unpredictable function*. That is, consider the following argument $\Pi_h = (\mathsf{P}_h, \mathsf{V}_h)$.

**Prover $\mathsf{P}_h$.** On input $(\phi, w)$: If $(\phi, w) \notin \mathcal{R}$, return $\perp$. Return $h(\phi)$.
**Verifier $\mathsf{V}_h$.** On input $(\phi, \pi)$: Accept if and only if $\pi = h(\phi)$.

Here, $h \colon \{0,1\}^n \to \{0,1\}^{\ell(n)}$ is sampled from a family of $t(n)$-wise independent hash functions, where $t(n) \in \mathrm{poly}(n)$ is larger than the query complexity of $f$ and $\mathsf{R}$, and $\ell(n) \in \omega(\log n)$. While the above argument uses shared randomness (i.e., $h$), it can later be replaced with fixed non-uniform advice. Clearly, the above argument is perfectly complete (for any fixing of $h$). The problem is that we do not know how to prove that an inverter $\mathsf{Inv}$ of $f^{\Pi_h}$, cannot be used by the

[5] This is mandatory, since there *are* black-box reductions from zero-knowledge arguments and hardness of NP, to one-way functions. See Footnote 2 and 1.3.

[6] Using non-interactive arguments in our proof stipulates that the black-box reduction cannot benefit from the low round complexity of the argument.

reduction R to break the soundness of $\Pi_h$,[7] and our proof strategy does not go through.[8]

**Prover** $\mathsf{P}_h$**.** On input $(\phi, w)$: If $(\phi, w) \notin \mathcal{R}$, return $\perp$.
1. Let $z \leftarrow \mathsf{stInv}(\phi)$.
2. If $\mathsf{qry}(z) = \phi$, return "check". Otherwise, return $h(\phi)$.

**Verifier** $\mathsf{V}_h$**.** On input $(\phi, \pi)$: If $\pi \neq$ "*check*", accept if and only if $\pi = h(\phi)$. Otherwise:
1. Let $z \leftarrow \mathsf{stInv}(\phi)$.
2. Accept if and only if $\mathsf{qry}(z) = \phi$.

*Separately answering f-generated queries.* The crux of our approach is modifying the above argument so that it no longer uses $h$ on "inputs generated by $f$". By doing so, we are guaranteed that an inverter of $f^{\Pi_h}$ will not be useful in breaking the soundness of $\Pi_h$, overcoming the shortcoming of the first construction of $\Pi_h$. As a first simple case, assume that the function $f$ makes only a single query $(\phi, w)$ to the prover $\mathsf{P}_h$ (and none to the verifier), and let $\mathsf{qry}$ denote the function that maps $x \in \{0,1\}^n$ to the first part of the query (i.e., the statement part). A key observation is that we can assume without loss of generality that $\mathsf{qry}$ is *not* one-way; if it is one-way, let $g := \mathsf{qry}$ and let $\widehat{R}$ be the reduction that does nothing. Since $g$ is one-way, there is no efficient $\mathsf{Inv}$ that inverts it. Thus, $\widehat{R}$ is a valid reduction to the security of $\mathsf{G}$, and the pair $(g, \widehat{R})$ concludes the proof. For the same reason, we can assume that $\mathsf{qry}$ is not even weakly one-way.[9] This leads to the following interactive argument. Let $\mathsf{stInv}$ be a *strong inverter* of $\mathsf{qry}$: it finds a preimage of $\mathsf{qry}$ with all but negligible probability (since, by assumption, $\mathsf{qry}$ is not weakly one-way, such an $\mathsf{stInv}$ exists).

That is, the prover lets the verifier *decide by itself* on instances generated by $f$. The key observation is that when called by $f$, it will almost always be the case that the prover identifies the query as such, and will return "check". Hence, the function $f$ (effectively) *gets no access to* $h$. Let $g$ be the efficient function that on input $x$, emulates $f(x)$ while answering all $\mathsf{P}_h$ queries with "check", and let $\mathsf{Inv}$ be an inverter of $g$. Namely, $g$ captures the behavior of $f$, but under simulated oracle answers that avoid access to $h$. Since the output distributions of $g$ and $f^{\Pi_h}$ are statistically close, $\mathsf{Inv}$ also inverts $f^{\Pi_h}$. The point is that being (effectively) *independent of* $h$, algorithm $\mathsf{R}^{\mathsf{Inv},\Pi_h}$ cannot break the soundness of $\Pi_h$, and thus it must win $\mathsf{G}$. Hence, the function $g$ and the reduction $\widehat{R}$, which acts like R while emulating the calls to $\Pi_h$ internally, establish the proof.

---

[7] While the query complexity of $f$ and R is smaller than $t$, the information returned by $\mathsf{Inv}$ might be used by R to break the unpredictability of $h$, thus breaking the soundness of $\Pi_h$.

[8] Interestingly, if we use a truly random function for $h$, i.e., a random oracle, then one can prove that $\mathsf{R}^{\Pi_h,\mathsf{Inv}}$ *cannot* break the soundness of $\Pi_h$. It is unclear, however, how to define the efficient one-way function $g$ with respect to such an inefficient argument.

[9] Weak one-way functions can be amplified, in a fully black-box manner, to full-fledged one-way functions, and the same argument as above would apply.

*Multiple Prover-Queries.* The above naturally extends to the case where $f$ makes *multiple* queries to $\mathsf{P}$ (but no queries to $\mathsf{V}$). Define the function $\mathsf{qry}(x,i)$ to output the $i^{\text{th}}$ query made by $f^{\mathsf{P}_h}(x)$, while answering its previous $\mathsf{P}_h$-queries with "check". Define the function $g$ analogously to $\mathsf{qry}$ while outputting $f$'s (final) output (and not its $i^{\text{th}}$ query). Finally, let $\mathsf{stInv}$ be a strong inverter of $\mathsf{qry}$. By construction, the output distributions of $g$ and $f^{\Pi_h}$ are close, and a similar proof to the one in the single-query case goes through.

*Verifier Queries.* We finally explain how to handle queries made by $f$ to the verifier $\mathsf{V}_h$. For the above construction, allowing verifier queries would give the function $f$ access to an inverter of its query function $\mathsf{qry}$. This would yield a recursive definition of $\mathsf{qry}$, rendering the argument inefficient for a function $f$ of super-constant query complexity. We handle this problem by using a second hash function $h^{\mathsf{C}}$ for the "easy" (i.e., $f$-generated) queries, preventing $f$ from making verifier queries for which it does not already know the answer.

We define the argument $\Pi$ using a query function $\mathsf{qry}$ that on input $(x,i)$ outputs the statement part of the $i^{\text{th}}$ query made by $f(x)$, while answering $f$'s oracle queries as follows:

**$\mathsf{P}$-query** $(\phi,\cdot)$**.** Answer $h^{\mathsf{C}}(\phi)$.
**$\mathsf{V}$-query** $(\phi,\pi)$**.** Answer 1 if and only if $\pi = h^{\mathsf{C}}(\phi)$.

Let $\mathsf{stInv}$ be an efficient, strong inverter of $\mathsf{qry}$. (Note that $\mathsf{qry}$ is clearly efficient.)

**Prover** $\mathsf{P}_{h^{\mathsf{C}},h^{\mathsf{T}}}$**.** On input $(\phi,w)$: If $(\phi,w)\notin\mathcal{R}$, return $\perp$.
1. Let $z \leftarrow \mathsf{stInv}(\phi)$.
2. If $\mathsf{qry}(z)=\phi$, return $h^{\mathsf{C}}(\phi)$. Otherwise, return $h^{\mathsf{T}}(\phi)$.

**Verifier** $\mathsf{V}_{h^{\mathsf{C}},h^{\mathsf{T}}}$**.** On input $(\phi,\pi)$:
1. If $\pi = h^{\mathsf{T}}(\phi)$, accept. Otherwise,
2. Let $z \leftarrow \mathsf{stInv}(\phi)$.
3. Accept if and only if $\pi = h^{\mathsf{C}}(\phi)$ and $\mathsf{qry}(z)=\phi$.

That is, on $f$-generated queries, the prover returns $h^{\mathsf{C}}(\phi)$, and the verifier checks that $\pi = h^{\mathsf{C}}(\phi)$. Define the function $g$ analogously to $\mathsf{qry}$ while outputting $f$'s (final) output. By construction, the output distributions of $g$ and $f^{\Pi_{h^{\mathsf{C}},h^{\mathsf{T}}}}$ are close, and a similar proof to the one in the prover-only queries case goes through.

**1.2.1 Handling Arbitrary Reductions.** When considering arbitrary reductions, the function $f$ can query $\Pi$ (i.e., the prover and verifier) on queries of arbitrary length. Hence, we no longer can instruct the query function $\mathsf{qry}$ to return $h^{\mathsf{C}}(\phi)$ on all prover-queries of the form $(\phi,\cdot)$; if the query $(\phi,w)$ has length $n' \leftarrow \log n$ (where $n$ is the input length of $f$), then in terms of $n'$, the function $f$ has invested *exponential time* in generating it, and the prover will use the function $h^{\mathsf{T}}$ on such queries. So to closely mimic the real query function of $f$, the query function $\mathsf{qry}$ has to also use $h^{\mathsf{T}}$, and our proof strategy breaks down.

The solution is to change $\Pi$ to use a different pair of hash functions $(h^{\mathsf{C}},h^{\mathsf{T}})$ according to the length of $\phi$. In addition, we instruct $\mathsf{P}$ and $\mathsf{V}$ to try, on input

$(\phi, \cdot)$, to invert the query function, which now is using $h^{\mathsf{T}}$, on *all* inputs of length $n^{1/c}, \ldots, n^c$, for an appropriate choice of $c \in \mathbb{N}$, and for $n \leftarrow |\phi|$. Proving the above turned out to be rather subtle, and constitutes the most technically challenging part of the paper.

**1.2.2 Zero Knowledge.** Note that the interactive arguments we considered above are *perfect* zero-knowledge. Indeed, on input $\phi$, the simulator simply acts as the prover $\mathsf{P}$ would on input $(\phi, w)$, after verifying that $(\phi, w) \in \mathcal{R}$. Consequently, our implication—that any fully black-box reduction from one-way functions to interactive arguments (possibly combined with $\mathsf{G}$) yields a reduction from one-way functions to $\mathsf{G}$ alone—continues to hold even if the reduction $(f, \mathsf{R})$ is only required to work when the interactive arguments are *perfect* zero-knowledge.

As a sanity check, observe that if $\mathsf{R}$ was given access to the simulator of $\Pi$, it could use this access to break the soundness of $\Pi$. However, our definition of fully black-box reductions does not permit such access.

### 1.3 Related Work

We briefly survey work related to our result.

*Black-Box Limitations.* The use of black-box limitations in cryptography was initiated in the seminal work of [33], showing a *black-box separation* between key-agreement protocols and one-way functions.[10] Subsequent work established black-box limitations on constructions of other primitives, such as collision-resistant hash functions [45] and oblivious transfer [20]. Our proof technique resembles the so-called *meta-reductions*, cf., [12,30], where one shows that the oracle gates used by the black-box proof of security (i.e., $\mathsf{R}$ in our case) can be *emulated* efficiently.

*Constructing One-Way Functions.* One-way functions are known to be implied by the existence of many other primitives and hardness assumptions, e.g., pseudorandom generators, cf., [32]. Among them, the most relevant results are the construction of one-way functions from the existence of *zero-knowledge (ZK)* proofs/arguments for (all) NP together with the assumption that NP is hard. [41] pioneered this direction by constructing auxiliary-input one-way functions assuming ZK-proofs (or arguments) for NP and NP $\not\subseteq$ BPP. More recently, [31] (see also [37]), improved this result by showing the existence of (standard) one-way functions, assuming ZK-arguments for NP and NP $\not\subseteq$ *i.o.*P/poly.[11] The

[10] A black-box a separation presents a "world" in which the assumption, e.g., OWFs, exist but the desired primitive, e.g., *key agreement*, does not. Black-box separations are more informative than fully black-box reductions; they can be used, for instance, to refute the existence of a two-part black-box construction in which the second part uses an adversary of the first part, if such exists (see [42] for an example of such a construction), where fully black-box reduction cannot.

[11] The class *i.o.*P/poly contains all languages that can be solved by poly-size circuits, for infinitely many $n$'s.

above constructions are *assumption-dependent fully black-box reductions from one-way functions to ZK proofs/arguments, the zero-knowledge simulator, and the relevant hardness assumption* (under the natural adaptation of Definition 1 to zero-knowledge protocols).

*Succinct Arguments.* The feasibility of succinct interactive arguments was established by [35], who constructed such arguments for all NP assuming the existence of collision-resistant hash functions. More recently, [36] showed a construction from multi-collision resistant hash functions. Succinct (zero-knowledge) arguments were also constructed using stronger assumptions, such as *discrete logarithm* [8] and lattice-based assumptions [3] (see also [1,5,9–11]).

For succinct *non*-interactive arguments (SNARGs), [19] proved that (certain types of) SNARGs cannot be black-box reduced to a falsifiable assumption (as defined by [40]). Following this barrier, SNARGs were constructed using non-falsifiable assumptions, such as indistinguishability obfuscation (io) [43] and the generic group model [27] (see also [4,13,38,44]). The barrier was also bypassed by considering more restricted languages, specifically by constructing SNARGs for P from falsifiable assumptions such as *bilinear groups* [34] and *learning with errors (LWE)* [16]. Recently, [15] constructed a SNARG for NC assuming average-case hardness against bounded-space computation, an assumption that is not known to imply one-way functions. On a different vein, [29] proved that, assuming the randomized exponential time hypothesis (rETH) holds, certain types of SNARGs constructions in the *random-oracle model (ROM)* cannot be "very concise".

*Succinct Arguments and One-Way Functions.* Wee [46] gave the first indication that succinct interactive arguments might not imply the existence of one-way functions. He presented an oracle-world in which one-way functions do not exist, but there exist a succinct, two-round interactive argument for a specific (oracle-aided) hard language. A limitation of his result, however, is that since the interactive argument he constructed is tailored to the specific (oracle-aided) language, the result does not address black-box reductions that apply the assumed interactive arguments to a well-crafted language, such as the ones used by [31]. In addition, Wee [46]'s world does contain auxiliary-information one-way functions[12], so it cannot rule out reductions from such to succinct arguments.

*Succinct Proofs.* Succinctness was also studied in the context of interactive proofs (i.e., soundness should hold against unbounded provers). [25] analyzed the complexity of interactive proofs with succinct (referred there as *laconic*) provers. They showed that any language admitting an interactive proof where the prover sends at most $c(n)$ bits is decidable in probabilistic time $O(2^{c(n)})$. Thus, (sufficiently) succinct interactive proofs are unlikely to exist for all NP.

[12] Actually, it contains even a stronger variant of one-way functions: non-uniform functions, i.e., computed by poly-circuits, that are one way against uniform adversaries, i.e., against algorithms.

*Witness Indistinguishability and Witness Hiding.* Goldreich et al. [23] constructed the first zero-knowledge (ZK) proof for NP, and thus witness indistinguishable (WI) and witness hiding (WH), assuming the existence of one-way functions.[13] Feige et al. [18] constructed non-interactive ZK proof using *trapdoor permutations*. Dwork and Naor [17] relaxed the required assumption for non-interactive witness indistinguishable arguments (NIWIs) to *verifiable PRGs*. Groth et al. [28] constructed NIWIs from *bi-linear groups*, and Bitansky and Paneth [7] have done it assuming *indistinguishability obfuscation*. Finally, Bitansky et al. [6] showed that statistically sound batch proofs for a language $\mathcal{L}$ imply that $\mathcal{L}$ has a statistically witness indistinguishable proof.

**1.3.1 Paper Organization.** Section 2 contains definitions and background material used in the paper. The formal statement of our result and its proof, are given in Section 3. Some parts of the proof are omitted due to lack of space, and can be found in [2].

## 2 Preliminaries

### 2.1 Notation

We use calligraphic letters to denote sets, uppercase for random variables, lowercase for integers and functions, and boldface for vectors. All logarithms are base 2. For $n \in \mathbb{N}$, let $[n] := \{1, \ldots, n\}$. For a vector $\mathbf{x} := (x_1, \ldots, x_n)$ and $j \leq n$, let $(\mathbf{x})_j := x_j$ and let $(\mathbf{x})_{\leq j} := (x_1, \ldots, x_j)$. We naturally extend this notation to strings as well. For a distribution $\mathcal{X}$, let $x \overset{\mathrm{R}}{\leftarrow} \mathcal{X}$ denote the process of sampling $x$ according to $\mathcal{X}$. Similarly, for a set $\mathcal{S}$, $s \overset{\mathrm{R}}{\leftarrow} \mathcal{S}$ stands for the process of sampling $s$ uniformly from $\mathcal{S}$. For two distributions $\mathcal{X}$ and $\mathcal{Y}$, let $\mathrm{SD}(\mathcal{X}, \mathcal{Y})$ denote their *statistical distance* (also known as, variation distance). Let poly stand for the set of all (integer) polynomials. We sometimes abuse notation and treat poly as an arbitrary polynomial. A function $f(n)$ is *negligible* if for every $p \in \mathrm{poly}$ there exists $n_0 \in \mathbb{N}$ such that $f(n) < 1/p(n)$ for all $n > n_0$. We write $f(n) \leq \mathrm{neg}(n)$ to denote that $f(n)$ is negligible. For an NP-relation $\mathcal{R}$, let $\mathcal{L}_{\mathcal{R}}$ be the language $\{x \colon \exists w \text{ s.t } (x, w) \in \mathcal{R}\}$. We use PPT to denote *probabilistic polynomial time* and PPTM to denote PPT machines, i.e., algorithms. A circuit family $\mathsf{C} = \{\mathsf{C}_n\}_{n \in \mathbb{N}}$ is *of size* $p$ if $|\mathsf{C}_n| \leq p(n)$ for every $n \in \mathbb{N}$.

### 2.2 Many-wise Independent Hashing

**Definition 2 (Many-wise Independent Hash).** *A function-family* $\mathcal{H} = \{h \colon \mathcal{X} \to \mathcal{Y}\}$ *is* $t$-wise independent, *if for any distinct inputs* $x_1, \ldots, x_t \in \mathcal{X}$ *and any values* $y_1, \ldots, y_t \in \mathcal{Y}$:

$$\Pr_{h \overset{R}{\leftarrow} \mathcal{H}} [h(x_1) = y_1 \wedge \cdots \wedge h(x_t) = y_t] = 1/|\mathcal{Y}|^t.$$

[13] More precisely, their construction used commitments, which were later shown by [39] to be implied by one-way functions.

**Definition 3 (Efficient function ensemble).** *A function-family ensemble* $\mathcal{H} = \{\mathcal{H}_n = \{h \colon \mathcal{X}_n \to \mathcal{Y}_n\}\}_{n\in\mathbb{N}}$ *is* efficient, *if sampling* $h \stackrel{R}{\leftarrow} \mathcal{H}_n$ *and computing* $h(x)$ *for* $h \in \mathcal{H}_n$ *and* $x \in \mathcal{X}_n$*, can be done in time* $\operatorname{poly}(\log|\mathcal{X}_n|)$.

**Fact 2** ([14]). *For every* $t, \ell \in \operatorname{poly}$*, there exists an efficient,* $t$*-wise independent, function-family ensemble* $\{\mathcal{H}_n = \{h \colon \{0,1\}^n \to \{0,1\}^{\ell(n)}\}\}_{n\in\mathbb{N}}$.

### 2.3 One-way Functions

Since we deal with "lower bounds", we focus on *infinitely often, i.o,* one-way functions.[14]

**Definition 4 (Infinitely often one-way functions (OWF)).**
*A poly-time function* $f \colon \{0,1\}^* \to \{0,1\}^*$ *is* i.o one-way *if for any* PPTM $\mathsf{A}$*:*

$$\Pr_{\substack{x \stackrel{R}{\leftarrow} \{0,1\}^n \\ y \leftarrow f(x)}} \left[\mathsf{A}(1^n, y) \in f^{-1}(y)\right] \leq \operatorname{neg}(n) \tag{1}$$

*for infinitely many* $n \in \mathbb{N}$*. The function* $f$ *is* i.o weakly one-way *if for any* PPTM $\mathsf{A}$*:*

$$\Pr_{\substack{x \stackrel{R}{\leftarrow} \{0,1\}^n \\ y \leftarrow f(x)}} \left[\mathsf{A}(1^n, y) \in f^{-1}(y)\right] \leq 1 - 1/\operatorname{poly}(n) \tag{2}$$

*for infinitely many* $n \in \mathbb{N}$*. The function* $f$ *is* non-uniform i.o one-way *if* (1) *holds with respect to non-uniform poly-time algorithms (i.e., poly-size circuit family).* Non-uniform i.o weak one-way functions *are analogously defined.*

We omit $1^n$ from $\mathsf{A}$'s input list when clear from the context. When clear from the context, we denote a (length-regular) function $f \colon \{0,1\}^* \to \{0,1\}^*$ that maps $n$-bit strings to $p(n)$-bit strings, by $f \colon \{0,1\}^n \to \{0,1\}^{p(n)}$.

**Definition 5 (Strong inversion).** *A function* $f \colon \{0,1\}^* \to \{0,1\}^*$ *is* strongly invertible *if for every* $t \in \operatorname{poly}$ *there exists a* PPTM $\mathsf{A}$ *such that:*

$$\Pr_{\substack{x \stackrel{R}{\leftarrow} \{0,1\}^n \\ y \leftarrow f(x)}} \left[\mathsf{A}(1^n, y) \in f^{-1}(y)\right] \geq 1 - 1/t(n).$$

*for* all $n \in \mathbb{N}$.

Note that if i.o weak one-way functions do not exist, every poly-time function is strongly invertible.

[14] Since a OWF is also an i.o OWF, showing limitations on (assumption dependent) black-box reductions from i.o OWFs to interactive arguments, is a more insightful result.

**2.3.1 Weak to Strong One-way Functions.** We use the following variant of [47]'s one-way functions amplification, implicit in [21].

**Lemma 1 (Weak to strong one-way functions).** *For every poly-time* $f_{\mathsf{w}}$*,* $\alpha \in (0, 1)$ *and* $\varepsilon \geq 1/\text{poly}$*, there exist poly-time* $f$ *and oracle-aided algorithm* $\mathsf{R}$ *such that the following holds: for any algorithm* $\mathsf{A}$ *such that*

$$\Pr_{\substack{x \xleftarrow{R} \{0,1\}^n \\ y \leftarrow f(x)}} \left[\mathsf{A}(1^n, y) \in f^{-1}(y)\right] > \varepsilon(n)$$

*for every* $n \in \mathbb{N}$*, it holds that*

$$\Pr_{\substack{x \xleftarrow{R} \{0,1\}^n \\ y = f_{\mathsf{w}}(x)}} \left[\mathsf{R}^{\mathsf{A}}(1^n, y) \in f_{\mathsf{w}}^{-1}(y)\right] > \alpha$$

*for every* $n \in \mathbb{N}$*.*

Lemma 1 holds, under the natural extension, for non-uniform and auxiliary-input one-way functions.

### 2.4 Interactive Arguments

We use the standard definition of interactive arguments for NP relations.

**Definition 6 (Interactive argument).** *An* interactive argument for an NP-relation $\mathcal{R}$ *is a pair of* PPT *algorithms* $(\mathsf{P}, \mathsf{V})$ *such that the following holds:*

**Completeness.** *For all* $(\phi, w) \in \mathcal{R}$*:* $\Pr\left[(\mathsf{P}(\phi, w), \mathsf{V})(\phi) = 1\right] = 1$.[15]
**Soundness.** *For any* PPT $\widehat{P}$ *and* $\phi \notin \mathcal{L}_{\mathcal{R}}$*:* $\Pr\left[(\widehat{P}, \mathsf{V})(\phi) = 1\right] \leq \text{neg}(|\phi|)$.

*The* prover is $\ell$-bit, *if for any* $(\phi, w) \in \mathcal{R}$*,* $\mathsf{P}(\phi, w)$ *sends at most* $\ell(|\phi|)$ *bits. The interactive argument is* laconic, *if the prover is* $\ell(n) \in O(\log(n))$*-bit. The interactive argument is* non uniform, *if* $\mathsf{P}$ *and* $\mathsf{V}$ *are non-uniform: receive non-uniform advice* $z_n$ *for common input of length* $n$*.*

**2.4.1 Zero Knowledge and Witness Hiding.** We consider the following strong variants of perfect zero knowledge, witness indistinguishability, and witness hiding interactive arguments. In particular, all definitions below apply to *unbounded* cheating verifiers.[16] Let $\text{View}_{\mathsf{V}^*, \mathsf{P}(w)}(\phi)$ denote $\mathsf{V}^*$'s view in a random execution of $(\mathsf{P}(w), \mathsf{V}^*)(\phi)$.

---

[15] While standard definitions usually allow completeness $1 - \text{neg}(|\phi|)$, requiring perfect completeness only strengthens our results.

[16] Since we care about separation results, considering the strongest variants of these definitions is more informative.

**Definition 7 (Perfect zero knowledge).** *An interactive argument* $(\mathsf{P},\mathsf{V})$ *for an* NP*-relation* $\mathcal{R}$ *is* perfect zero knowledge, *if for any probabilistic t-time verifier* $\mathsf{V}^*$ *there exists a probabilistic* $\text{poly}(t)$*-time simulator* $\mathsf{S}$ *such that for any* $(\phi, w) \in \mathcal{R}$*, the distributions* $\mathsf{S}(\phi)$ *and* $\text{View}_{\mathsf{V}^*,\mathsf{P}(w)}(\phi)$ *are* identical. *The argument is* zero knowledge with a non-uniform simulator *if its simulator is non uniform, i.e., computed by a poly-size circuit.*

**Definition 8 (Perfect witness indistinguishability).** *An interactive argument* $(\mathsf{P},\mathsf{V})$ *for an* NP*-relation* $\mathcal{R}$ *is* perfect witness indistinguishable, *if for any probabilistic verifier* $\mathsf{V}^*$ *and* $(\phi, w_1, w_2)$ *with* $(\phi, w_1), (\phi, w_2) \in \mathcal{R}$*, the distributions* $\text{View}_{\mathsf{V}^*,\mathsf{P}(w_1)}(\phi)$ *and* $\text{View}_{\mathsf{V}^*,\mathsf{P}(w_2)}(\phi)$ *are* identical.

**Definition 9 (Perfect witness hiding).** *An interactive argument* $(\mathsf{P},\mathsf{V})$ *for an* NP*-relation* $\mathcal{R}$ *is* perfect witness hiding, *if for any probabilistic verifier* $\mathsf{V}^*$*, function* $h$*, instance* $\phi \in \mathcal{L}(\mathcal{R})$ *and distribution* $W$ *over* $\{w : (\phi, w) \in \mathcal{R}\}$*, it holds that* $\Pr_{w \stackrel{R}{\leftarrow} W}[(\mathsf{P}(w), \mathsf{V}^*)(\phi) = h(w)] \leq 2^{-\operatorname{H}_\infty(h(W))}$.

The proofs of the following facts are immediate.

**Fact 3.** *A perfect zero-knowledge interactive argument (with a non-uniform simulator) for an* NP*-relation* $\mathcal{R}$ *is perfect witness hiding for* $\mathcal{R}$.

**Fact 4.** *A perfect witness-hiding interactive argument for an* NP*-relation* $\mathcal{R}$ *is perfect witness indistinguishable for* $\mathcal{R}$.

## 2.5 Games

We capture hardness assumptions using the following notion of games.

**Definition 10 (Games).** *A* game $\mathsf{G}$ *is a pair of a (possibly inefficient)* challenger $\mathsf{C}$ *and a family of sets* $\mathcal{I} = \{\mathcal{I}^k = \{i_n^k \in \{0,1\}^n\}_{n \in \mathbb{N}}\}_{k \in \mathbb{N}}$. *Player* $\mathsf{P}$ wins the game Gwith probability $\varepsilon$, *if for* all $k \in \mathbb{N}$, *it holds that*

$$\Pr\left[(\mathsf{P},\mathsf{C})(1^n, i_n^k) = 1\right] \geq \varepsilon(n)$$

*for infinitely many* $n$.

Namely, the player is required to succeed with probability at least $\varepsilon$, for infinitely many $n$, given any set $\mathcal{I}^k$ in the family. The above definition of games encompasses standard falsifiable assumptions, such as the hardness of inverting one-way functions, but also models more complex assumptions, such as the soundness of an interactive argument, and even assumptions like $\text{NP} \not\subseteq \text{P/poly}$, see below.

**2.5.1 Three Games of Interest.** We exemplify the above notion of games using three games of interest.

*Inverting One-Way Functions.* The following game captures the hardness of inverting a function.

**Definition 11 (The game $\mathsf{G}_f^{\mathsf{OWF}}$).** *For a function $f\colon \{0,1\}^* \to \{0,1\}^*$, the game $\mathsf{G}_f^{\mathsf{OWF}}$ is the pair $(\mathsf{C}, \emptyset)$, where on input $1^n$ the challenger $\mathsf{C}$ samples $x \xleftarrow{R} \{0,1\}^n$, sends $y \leftarrow f(x)$ to the player, and outputs 1 if the player answers back with $x' \in f^{-1}(y)$.*

It is easy to verify that $f$ is one-way if and only if no PPTM wins the game $\mathsf{G}_f^{\mathsf{OWF}}$ with non-negligible probability.

*Soundness of an Interactive Argument.* The following game captures the soundness of an interactive argument $(\cdot, \mathsf{V})$ with respect to a language $\mathcal{L}$.

**Definition 12 (The game $\mathsf{G}_{\mathsf{V},\mathcal{L}}$).** *For a* PPTM $\mathsf{V}$ *and language $\mathcal{L} \subseteq \{0,1\}^*$, the game $\mathsf{G}_{\mathsf{V},\mathcal{L}}$ is the pair $(\mathsf{C}, \emptyset)$, where the player first sends $x \in \{0,1\}^n$, and $\mathsf{C}(1^n)$ then run $\mathsf{V}(x)$. The challenger $\mathsf{C}$ outputs 1 if $\mathsf{V}$ accepts the interaction and $x \in \{0,1\}^n \setminus \mathcal{L}$.*

It is easy to verify that the argument $(\cdot, \mathsf{V})$ is sound for the language $\mathcal{L}$, if and only if no PPTM wins the game $\mathsf{G}_{\mathsf{V},\mathcal{L}}$ with non-negligible probability.

*Deciding* NP. The following game captures the hardness of NP.

**Definition 13 (The game $\mathsf{G}^{\mathrm{NP}}$).** *The game $\mathsf{G}^{\mathrm{NP}}$ is the pair $(\mathsf{C}, \mathcal{I})$, where $i_n^k$ is the $n$-bit binary representation of* $\min\{k, 2^n - 1\}$. *On input $(1^n, x)$, the player sends $b \in \{0,1\}$, and the challenger $\mathsf{C}$ accepts if and only if $b = 1_{\mathrm{SAT}}(x)$.*

It is easy to verify that the assumption $\mathrm{P} \neq \mathrm{NP}$ is equivalent to the assumption that no poly-time player wins the game $\mathsf{G}^{\mathrm{NP}}$ with probability one. The assumption $\mathrm{NP} \not\subseteq \mathrm{P/poly}$ [resp., $\mathrm{NP} \not\subseteq \mathrm{BPP}$] is equivalent to the assumption that no poly-size [resp., PPT] player wins the game $\mathsf{G}^{\mathrm{NP}}$ with non-negligible probability.

## 3 Emulating Assumption-Dependent Reductions to Interactive Arguments

In this section, we define assumption-dependent, fully black-box reductions from one-way functions to interactive arguments and present our main result, showing that the existence of such a reduction implies a reduction from non-uniform one-way functions to the underlying game alone.

In Section 3.1, we formally define assumption-dependent fully black-box reductions from OWFs to succinct interactive arguments. In Section 3.2, we state our main result regarding such reductions. As a warm-up, we prove in Section 3.3 a simplified variant of Theorem 5. A full proof of Theorem 5 is given in Section 3.4. Finally, in ??, we explain how to extend our result to reductions from auxiliary-input one-way functions.

### 3.1 Assumption-Dependent Reductions

In this section, we formally define assumption-dependent, fully black-box reductions from one-way functions to interactive arguments.

**Definition 14 (Assumption-dependent fully black-box reductions from OWFs to interactive arguments).**
*An* assumption-dependent fully black-box reduction from OWFs to non-uniform, $\ell$-bit interactive arguments for an NP-relation $\mathcal{R}$ *with respect to* a game $\mathsf{G}$, *is an oracle-aided, poly-time, non-uniform pair of a function $f$ and a probabilistic algorithm* $\mathsf{R}$, *such that the following holds for any non-uniform $\ell$-bit interactive argument* $(\mathsf{P}, \mathsf{V})$ *for $\mathcal{R}$:*

1. $f^{(\mathsf{P},\mathsf{V})}$ *maps $n$-bit strings to $n$-bit strings.*
2. *There exists* $p \in \text{poly}$ *such that for any* $t \in \text{poly}$ *and any non-uniform poly-time* $\mathsf{Inv}$ *that inverts* $f^{(\mathsf{P},\mathsf{V})}$ *with probability* $1/t(n)$ *for all $n$, it holds that* $\mathsf{R}^{(\mathsf{P},\mathsf{V}),\mathsf{Inv}}(1^{t(n)}, 1^n)$ *wins either the game* $\mathsf{G}_{\mathsf{V},\mathcal{L}_\mathcal{R}}$ *or the game* $\mathsf{G}$, *with probability* $1/p(t(n))$.

We make the following remarks:

- Requiring $f$ to be length preserving, which simplifies the notations in our proofs, is not a restriction since an arbitrary one-way function implies a length-preserving one via standard (black-box) techniques.
- The reduction $\mathsf{R}$ is black-box in the interactive argument $(\mathsf{P}, \mathsf{V})$, but not in the game $\mathsf{G}$.
- $\mathsf{R}$ only has to succeed given access to an inverter, $\mathsf{Inv}$, that inverts $f$ with non-negligible probability for *all* $n \in \mathbb{N}$. Namely, the definition captures reductions from i.o one-way functions.
- $\mathsf{R}$ receives $1^{t(n)}$ as an additional input, where $1/t(n)$ is the success probability of $\mathsf{Inv}$. Thus, the definition captures reductions that depend on this parameter.[17]
- $\mathsf{R}$ has to win one of the games, with probability $1/p(t(n))$. Namely, there should be an *a priori* polynomial relation between the inversion probability of $\mathsf{Inv}$ and the winning probability of $\mathsf{R}$. Such a guarantee, however, holds (or can be made to hold) in all reductions we could think of (recall that $\mathsf{R}$ gets $1^{t(n)}$ as an additional input).

### 3.2 Emulating Assumption-Dependent Reductions

In this section, we prove the main result of the paper: an emulation of assumption-dependent, fully black-box reductions from OWFs to interactive arguments.

[17] e.g., the hardcore predicate construction of [22].

**Theorem 5 (Emulating black-box reductions from OWFs to interactive arguments).** *Let* $(f, \mathsf{R})$ *be an assumption-dependent, fully black-box reduction from OWFs to non-laconic,*[18] *non-uniform,* $\ell$*-bit interactive arguments for an* NP*-relation* $\mathcal{R}$*, with respect to a game* $\mathsf{G}$*. Then there exists a non-uniform, poly-time pair of function* $g$ *and an oracle-aided randomized algorithm* $\widehat{R}$*, and a constant* $c > 0$*, such that for any non-uniform poly-time* $\mathsf{Inv}$ *that inverts* $g$ *with probability* $1/\text{poly}(n)$ *for all* $n \in \mathbb{N}$*, it holds that* $\widehat{R}^{\mathsf{Inv}}$ *wins the game* $\mathsf{G}$ *with probability at least* $c$*.*

*Moreover, the above holds even if the reduction only needs to work when the interactive argument oracle is perfect zero knowledge with a non-uniform simulator.*

That is, the interactive argument is redundant for the construction of (i.o) one-way functions: if there exists a reduction from one-way functions to *both* interactive arguments and a game $\mathsf{G}$, then there exists a reduction from i.o one-way functions to $\mathsf{G}$ alone.

*Remark 1 (Reductions to* $\text{P} \neq \text{NP}$*).* When applied to (reductions to) the game $\mathsf{G}^{\text{NP}}$, see Definition 13, Theorem 5 yields a reduction from OWFs to the assumption that $\text{NP} \not\subseteq \text{P/poly}$. Indeed, the coins of (and the amplified variant of) algorithm $\widehat{R}$ guaranteed by Theorem 5, can be fixed so that it wins $\mathsf{G}^{\text{NP}}$ on *all* inputs with probability one.

*Remark 2 (Reductions to zero-knowledge arguments).* We emphasize that Theorem 5 does *not* address fully black-box reductions from one-way functions to zero-knowledge arguments. In particular, the reduction $\widehat{R}$ from Definition 14 does *not* receive oracle access to the zero-knowledge simulator. Rather, the theorem applies to reductions that are only required to work when the argument $\Pi$ is (perfect) zero knowledge. In particular, this includes reductions that might attempt to exploit the fact that $\Pi$ is witness indistinguishable or witness hiding.

*Remark 3 (Reductions to non-interactive arguments).* Theorem 5 holds even if we allow the reduction to succeed *only* when given access to *non-interactive* arguments. This holds since in the proof, we only use such arguments.

*Remark 4 (Infinitely-often inverters).* If we modify Definition 14 to work against algorithms that invert the function $f$ (only) infinitely often, then Theorem 5 changes accordingly: holds even if we allow the inverter of $g$ to succeed infinitely often.

[18] Reductions to laconic interactive arguments are not only uninteresting (laconic arguments have only limited soundness), but they also exist: the reduction breaks the soundness of the argument by sending a uniform string.

### 3.3 Proof for Length-Preserving Reductions

In this section, we prove Theorem 5 for *length-preserving reductions*: reductions such that on input of length $n$, both $f$ and $\mathsf{R}$ query the interactive argument algorithms on statements of length $n$, and $\mathsf{R}$ queries the inverter of $f$ on inputs of length $n$. Let $(f, \mathsf{R})$ be a length-preserving, assumption-dependent, fully black-box reduction from OWFs to non-uniform $\ell$-bit interactive arguments for the NP-relation $\mathcal{R}$, with respect to a game $\mathsf{G}$, where $\ell(n) \in \omega(\log n)$ (recall the reduction is to non-laconic arguments). In the following, we fix the first input of $\mathsf{R}$, $1^{t(n)}$, to $1^8$ (i.e., $\mathsf{R}$ fixed to work against inverters with success probability at least 1/8), and omit it from the notation. Throughout, we assume that $f$ only makes well-formed, valid prover-queries, i.e., $(\phi, w) \in \mathcal{R}$ (by design, our prover returns $\perp$ on invalid queries). Let $p_f(n) \in \operatorname{poly}(n)$ be an upper bound on the total running time of $f$ and $\mathsf{R}$, on inputs of length $n$.

**3.3.1 The Interactive Argument.** We start by defining a non-interactive argument $\Pi$ to which the reduction will get oracle access. Towards this goal, we consider the following non-uniform, non-interactive argument, defined using an efficient $p_f(n)$-wise independent, function-family ensemble $\mathcal{H} = \{\mathcal{H}_n = \{h \colon \{0,1\}^n \to \{0,1\}^{\ell(n)}\}\}_{n\in\mathbb{N}}$.

**Algorithm 6** *[Hash-based argument $\widehat{\Pi} = (\widehat{\mathsf{P}}, \widehat{\mathsf{V}})$]*
*Parameter:* $h \in \mathcal{H}_n$.

$\widehat{\mathsf{P}}_h(\phi, w)$: *If* $(\phi, w) \in \mathcal{R}$, *return* $h(\phi)$; *otherwise return* $\perp$.
$\widehat{\mathsf{V}}_h(\phi, \pi)$: *If* $\pi = h(\phi)$, *return* 1; *otherwise return* 0.

That is, the prover simply applies the hash on the statement (if an appropriate witness is provided), and the verifier checks if the proof matches the hash of the statement. Algorithm 6 is not the argument on which we invoke $\mathsf{R}$, but will be used as an intermediate tool for characterizing the actual argument. In particular, we use the following "query function" $\mathsf{qry}$ that outputs the prover queries made by $f^{\widehat{\Pi}}$.

**Function 7** *[The query function $\mathsf{qry}$] On input $(h, x, i) \in \mathcal{H}_n \times \{0,1\}^n \times [p_f(n)]$, the function $\mathsf{qry}$ executes $f^{\widehat{\Pi}_h}(x)$ up to the $i^{\text{th}}$ prover-query $(\phi_i, w_i)$, and outputs $\phi_i$. If $f^{\widehat{\Pi}_h}(x)$ does not make $i$ prover queries, it outputs $\perp$.*

A key observation is that without loss of generality $\mathsf{qry}$ (defined for any value of $n$) is strongly invertible. Otherwise, there exists a black-box reduction from the inversion of $\mathsf{qry}$ to $\mathsf{G}$, and we are done.[19] Consequently, there exists a poly-time, non-uniform algorithm $\mathsf{stInv}$ that inverts $\mathsf{qry}$ with probability $1-\varepsilon(n)$ (over

[19] If a function $\mathsf{qry}$ is not strongly invertible, by Lemma 1 it can be amplified to a one-way function $g$ from which a security reduction can be defined to *any* game $\mathsf{G}$; any efficient inverter of $g$ breaks the hardness of $\mathsf{G}$ (since such inverter does not exist).

the uniform input distribution), for $\varepsilon(n) := 1/4p_f(n)$. We use $\mathsf{stInv}$ to construct the non-interactive argument $\Pi = (\mathsf{P}, \mathsf{V})$. The non-uniform prover and verifier are parameterized by two hash functions: $h^{\mathsf{C}}$, for "easy" instances, where the verifier checks for a witness, and $h^{\mathsf{T}}$, for "hard" instances, where the verifier must trust the proof.

**Algorithm 8** *[Prover $\mathsf{P}_{h^{\mathsf{C}},h^{\mathsf{T}}}$]*
*Parameters:* $h^{\mathsf{C}}, h^{\mathsf{T}} \in \mathcal{H}_n$.
*Input:* $(\phi, w) \in \{0,1\}^n \times \{0,1\}^*$
*Operation:*

1. *If* $(\phi, w) \notin \mathcal{R}$, *return* $\perp$.
2. *Let* $z \leftarrow \mathsf{stInv}(\phi)$.
3. *Return* $h^{\mathsf{C}}(\phi)$ *if* $\mathsf{qry}(z) = \phi$, *and* $h^{\mathsf{T}}(\phi)$ *otherwise.*

That is, the prover applies $h^{\mathsf{C}}$ on the statement if $\mathsf{stInv}$ succeeds in inverting it, and applies $h^{\mathsf{T}}$ otherwise.

**Algorithm 9** *[Verifier $\mathsf{V}_{h^{\mathsf{C}},h^{\mathsf{T}}}$]*
*Parameters:* $h^{\mathsf{C}}, h^{\mathsf{T}} \in \mathcal{H}_n$.
*Input:* $(\phi, \pi) \in \{0,1\}^n \times \{0,1\}^*$
*Operation:*

1. *If* $\pi = h^{\mathsf{T}}(\phi)$: *return* 1.
2. *If* $\pi = h^{\mathsf{C}}(\phi)$:
   (a) *Let* $z \leftarrow \mathsf{stInv}(\phi)$.
   (b) *If* $\mathsf{qry}(z) = \phi$, *return* 1.
3. *Return* 0.

That is, if the proof $\pi$ matches $h^{\mathsf{T}}(\phi)$, then the verifier accepts. If the proof matches $h^{\mathsf{C}}(\phi)$, the verifier runs $\mathsf{stInv}$, and if succeeds, which implies that $\phi \in \mathcal{L}_{\mathcal{R}}$, it accepts. For the non-uniform, non-interactive argument that is defined over *all* input lengths, we take $\Pi = \{(\mathsf{P}_{h_n^{\mathsf{C}},h_n^{\mathsf{T}}}, \mathsf{V}_{h_n^{\mathsf{C}},h_n^{\mathsf{T}}})\}_{(h_n^{\mathsf{C}},h_n^{\mathsf{T}})\in\mathcal{H}_n}$ (the choice of hash functions will be discussed later). For most parts, however, it will be sufficient to consider a single input length. Since $\mathsf{stInv}$ is deterministic, its executions by the prover and the verifier are identical. Hence, $\Pi$ has *perfect* completeness. Also note that $\Pi$ is a perfect zero-knowledge argument with a non-uniform simulator: on input $\phi$, the simulator acts according to $\mathsf{P}(\phi, \cdot)$ without the first step (i.e., not testing for $(\phi, w) \in \mathcal{R}$).

Towards presenting the (candidate one-way) function $g$ and the reduction $\widehat{R}$, we prove that the executions of $f^{\widehat{\Pi}}$ and $f^{\Pi}$ are close.

**Claim 1.** $\Pr_{(h^{\mathsf{C}},h^{\mathsf{T}},x)\xleftarrow{R}\mathcal{H}_n^2\times\{0,1\}^n}\left[f^{\widehat{\Pi}_{h^{\mathsf{C}}}}(x) \neq f^{\Pi_{h^{\mathsf{C}},h^{\mathsf{T}}}}(x)\right] \leq 1/2$ *for all* $n$ *with* $\ell(n) \geq 2 + \log 1/\varepsilon(n)$.

*Proof.* We prove the stronger statement that the *execution traces*—the input $x$ and the inputs/outputs of the oracle calls—of $f^{\Pi_{h^{\mathsf{C}},h^{\mathsf{T}}}}(x)$ and $f^{\widehat{\Pi}_{h^{\mathsf{C}}}}(x)$ are 1/2 close, for uniform $(x, h^{\mathsf{C}}, h^{\mathsf{T}})$. The proof is by coupling the two distributions.

**Algorithm 10** *[Coupling $f^{\Pi}$ and $f^{\widehat{\Pi}}$]*

1. *Sample* $(h^{\mathsf{C}}, h^{\mathsf{T}}) \xleftarrow{R} \mathcal{H}_n^2$ *and* $x \xleftarrow{R} \{0,1\}^n$.
2. *Let* $\mathsf{trace}^{\widehat{\Pi}}$ *and* $\mathsf{trace}^{\Pi}$ *denote the traces of the executions of* $f^{\widehat{\Pi}_{h^{\mathsf{C}}}}(x)$ *and* $f^{\Pi_{h^{\mathsf{C}},h^{\mathsf{T}}}}(x)$*, respectively.*
3. *Output* $(\mathsf{trace}^{\widehat{\Pi}}, \mathsf{trace}^{\Pi})$.

We prove the claim by showing that

$$\Pr\left[\mathsf{trace}^{\widehat{\Pi}} \neq \mathsf{trace}^{\Pi}\right] \leq 1/2 \tag{3}$$

Let $E_i$ be the event that $\mathsf{trace}^{\widehat{\Pi}}$ and $\mathsf{trace}^{\Pi}$ are identical up to the $i^{\text{th}}$ query. We show that $\Pr[\neg E_i \mid E_{i-1}] \leq 2\varepsilon(n)$, for every $i \in [p_f(n)]$, and since $E_0$ trivially holds, the proof of Equation (3) follows by a union bound. Assuming $E_{i-1}$ holds, the $i^{\text{th}}$ query generated by $f$ is the *same* in both executions. We bound the probability that the oracle responses on it differ (i.e., that $\neg E_i$ occurs), while separately handling prover and verifier queries. Since the reduction is length preserving, all queries are of the form $(\phi, \cdot) \in \{0,1\}^n \times \{0,1\}^*$.

**Prover query.** Let $(\phi, w)$ be a query to the prover. By our assumption on $f$, we have $(\phi, w) \in \mathcal{R}$. By definition, $\widehat{\mathsf{P}}_{h^{\mathsf{C}}}$ answers $h^{\mathsf{C}}(\phi)$. The response of $\mathsf{P}_{h^{\mathsf{C}},h^{\mathsf{T}}}$ depends on the output of $\mathsf{stInv}(\phi)$. Since $\phi$ is distributed as a uniform query of $f^{\widehat{\Pi}}$ conditioned on $E_{i-1}$, which by the induction assumption occurs with probability at least 1/2, it holds that $\mathsf{stInv}$ outputs a preimage $z$ with probability at least $1 - 2\varepsilon(n)$ (over the choice of $h^{\mathsf{C}}, x$). If this happens, then $\mathsf{P}$ also answers $h^{\mathsf{C}}(\phi)$.

**Verifier query.** Let $(\phi, \pi)$ be a query to the verifier. Assume $\pi$ was generated by a previous prover query. Since $E_{i-1}$ holds, we have $\pi = h^{\mathsf{C}}(\phi)$. Thus, $\mathsf{stInv}$ succeeds in inverting $\phi$, and both $\mathsf{V}_{h^{\mathsf{C}},h^{\mathsf{T}}}$ and $\widehat{\mathsf{V}}_{h^{\mathsf{C}}}$ accept.
Assume $\pi$ was not generated by a previous prover query. Since $\mathcal{H}$ is a $p_f$-wise independent family, $\widehat{\mathsf{V}}$ accepts with probability $2^{-\ell(n)}$, and $\mathsf{V}$ accepts with probability $\in [2^{-\ell(n)}, 2 \cdot 2^{-\ell(n)}]$. Hence, they answer the same value with probability at least $1 - 2^{1-\ell(n)}$, which is at least $1 - 2\varepsilon(n)$ for the considered $n$.

Combining the two cases, we deduce that $\Pr[\neg E_i \mid E_{i-1}] \leq 2\varepsilon(n)$, concluding the proof.

**3.3.2 The Function** $g$**.** The function $g$, whose security is reduced to the game $\mathsf{G}$, is defined using the function $g_{\mathsf{W}} \colon \mathcal{H}_n \times \{0,1\}^n \to \mathcal{H}_n \times \{0,1\}^n$, defined by:

$$g_{\mathsf{W}}(h, x) = (h, f^{\widehat{\Pi}_h}(x)). \tag{4}$$

Let $g$ and $\mathsf{R}_{\&}$ be the (efficient) non-uniform function and reduction guaranteed by Lemma 1, such that for any efficient non-uniform $\mathsf{A}$ that inverts $g$ with non-negligible probability, it holds that $\mathsf{R}_{\&}^{\mathsf{A}}$ inverts $g_{\mathsf{W}}$ with probability at least 3/4.

**3.3.3 The Reduction $\widehat{R}$.** The black-box reduction from the one-wayness of $g$ to the hardness of $\mathsf{G}$ is defined as follows.

---

**Algorithm 11** *[$\widehat{A}_h$]*
*Oracle:* $\mathsf{A}$.
*Parameter:* $h \in \mathcal{H}_n$.
*Input:* $y \in \{0,1\}^n$.
*Operation: Output* $\mathsf{R}_{\&}^{\mathsf{A}}(h, y)_2$, *i.e., the second output of* $\mathsf{R}_{\&}^{\mathsf{A}}$.

---

**Algorithm 12** *[Reduction $\widehat{R}$ from $g$ to $\mathsf{G}$ ]*
*Oracle:* $\mathsf{A}$.
*Input:* $1^n$.
*Operation:*

1. *Sample* $(h^{\mathsf{C}}, h^{\mathsf{T}}) \xleftarrow{R} \mathcal{H}_n^2$.
2. *Act in* $\mathsf{G}$ *according to* $\mathsf{R}^{\widehat{A}_{h^{\mathsf{C}}}, \Pi_{h^{\mathsf{C}}, h^{\mathsf{T}}}}(1^n)$.

---

We prove that $\widehat{R}$ wins $\mathsf{G}$ with constant probability. Let $p$ be the polynomial from Definition 14 with respect to $\mathsf{R}$.

**Claim 2.** *For any non-uniform poly-time* $\mathsf{A}$ *that inverts* $g$ *with probability* $1/\text{poly}$ *for all* $n \in \mathbb{N}$, *it holds that* $\widehat{R}^{\mathsf{A}}$ *wins* $\mathsf{G}$ *with probability* $1/9p(8)$.

*Proof.* Let $\mathsf{A}$ be a non-uniform poly-time algorithm that inverts $g$ with probability $1/\text{poly}$ for all $n \in \mathbb{N}$. By Lemma 1, $\mathsf{R}_{\&}^{\mathsf{A}}$ inverts $g_{\mathsf{w}}$ with probability at least $3/4$. Let $(g_{\mathsf{w}})_y(h, x) := g_{\mathsf{w}}(h, x)_2$, i.e., it outputs the second output of $g_{\mathsf{w}}$. By the definition of $\widehat{A}$,

$$\Pr_{(h^{\mathsf{C}},x) \xleftarrow{R} \mathcal{H}_n \times \{0,1\}^n; y \leftarrow (g_{\mathsf{w}})_y(h^{\mathsf{C}},x)} \left[ (g_{\mathsf{w}})_y(h^{\mathsf{C}}, \widehat{A}_{h^{\mathsf{C}}}(y)) = y \right] \geq 3/4.$$

Hence, by Claim 1

$$\Pr_{(h^{\mathsf{C}},h^{\mathsf{T}},x) \xleftarrow{R} \mathcal{H}_n^2 \times \{0,1\}^n; y \leftarrow f^{\Pi_{h^{\mathsf{C}},h^{\mathsf{T}}}}(x)} \left[ f^{\Pi_{h^{\mathsf{C}},h^{\mathsf{T}}}}(\widehat{A}_{h^{\mathsf{C}}}(y)) = y \right] \geq 1/4 \tag{5}$$

for all $n$ with $\ell(n) \geq 2 + \log 1/\varepsilon(n)$. Since we can modify $\widehat{A}$ to invert $g_{\mathsf{w}}$ with probability one on all small $n$, in the following we assume without loss of generality that Equation (5) holds for *all* $n \in \mathbb{N}$. Applying a Markov argument to Equation (5), we get that

$$\Pr_{d_n \leftarrow (h^{\mathsf{C}},h^{\mathsf{T}}) \xleftarrow{R} \mathcal{H}_n^2} \Bigg[ \underbrace{\Pr_{x \xleftarrow{R} \{0,1\}^n; y \leftarrow f^{\Pi_{d_n}}(x)} \left[ f^{\Pi_{d_n}}(\widehat{A}_{h^{\mathsf{C}}}(y)) = y \right] \geq 1/8}_{\delta(d_n)} \Bigg] \geq 1/8 \tag{6}$$

Let $(\mathsf{C}_{\mathsf{G}}, \mathcal{I})$ be the challenger and the family of sets of the game $\mathsf{G}$, respectively. For $n \in \mathbb{N}$ and $(h^{\mathsf{C}}, h^{\mathsf{T}}) \in \mathcal{H}_n^2$, let $\mathsf{C}_{h^{\mathsf{C}},h^{\mathsf{T}}}$ be the (possibly inefficient) algorithm that on common input $1^n$, acts according to $\mathsf{V}_{h^\mathsf{C},h^\mathsf{T}}$ and outputs 1 if $\mathsf{V}$ accepts a statement $x \in \{0,1\}^n \setminus \mathcal{L}_\mathcal{R}$ (i.e., the challenger of the game $G_{\mathsf{V},\mathcal{L}_\mathcal{R}}$ when defined only for input length $n$). We claim that for all $k \in \mathbb{N}$ and infinitely many $n \in \mathbb{N}$:

$$\Pr_{d_n \leftarrow (h^\mathsf{C},h^\mathsf{T}) \xleftarrow{\mathrm{R}} \mathcal{H}_n^2} \Big[ \underbrace{\Pr\Big[(\mathsf{R}^{\widehat{A}_{h^\mathsf{C}},\Pi_{d_n}}, \mathsf{C}_{d_n})(1^n) = 1 \vee (\mathsf{R}^{\widehat{A}_{h^\mathsf{C}},\Pi_{d_n}}, \mathsf{C}_\mathsf{G})(1^n, i_n^k) = 1\Big] \geq 1/p(8)}_{\rho(d_n)} \Big] \geq 1/8 \tag{7}$$

where the inner probability is over the randomness of $\mathsf{R}$. Indeed, assume Equation (7) does not hold. Hence, by Equation (6),

$$\Pr_{d_n}\left[\delta(d_n) \wedge \neg\rho(d_n)\right] > 0$$

for all but finitely many $n$. Hence, there exists $\{d_n \leftarrow (h_n^\mathsf{C}, h_n^\mathsf{T}) \in \mathcal{H}_n^2\}_{n\in\mathbb{N}}$ such that $\delta(d_n) = 1$ and $\rho(d_n) = 0$ for all but finitely many $n$. It follows that there exist a non-uniform interactive argument $\Pi$ that gets $\{d_n\}_{n\in\mathbb{N}}$ as a non-uniform advice, and a non-uniform algorithm $\widehat{A}$ that gets $\{h_n^\mathsf{C}\}_{n\in\mathbb{N}}$ as a non-uniform advice, such that the following holds:

- $\widehat{A}$ inverts $f^\Pi$ with probability at least $1/8$, for all $n$.
- $\mathsf{R}^{\widehat{A},\Pi}$ does *not* win $\mathsf{G}_{\mathsf{V},\mathcal{L}_\mathcal{R}}$ nor $\mathsf{G}$, with probability $1/p(8)$.

This, however, contradicts the definition of $\mathsf{R}$, and we conclude that Equation (7) holds.

We next claim that for any large enough $n \in \mathbb{N}$, and any $h^\mathsf{C} \in \mathcal{H}_n$, it holds that

$$\Pr_{h^\mathsf{T} \xleftarrow{\mathrm{R}} \mathcal{H}_n; d_n \leftarrow (h^\mathsf{C},h^\mathsf{T})} \left[(\mathsf{R}^{\widehat{A}_{h^\mathsf{C}},\Pi_{d_n}}, \mathsf{C}_{d_n})(1^n) = 1\right] \leq \mathrm{neg}(n) \tag{8}$$

Indeed, since $\mathsf{A}$ was fixed before $h^\mathsf{T}$ was sampled, and since $g$ is independent of $h^\mathsf{T}$, the calls to $\widehat{A}_{h^\mathsf{C}}$ reveal *no information* regarding $h^\mathsf{T}$. Since in addition $\mathsf{R}$ makes fewer than $p_f(n)$ calls to $\Pi_{h^\mathsf{C},h^\mathsf{T}}$, the probability it generates an accepting proof of the form $h^\mathsf{T}(\phi)$ for a statement $\phi$ of length $n$ that was not returned by $\mathsf{P}_{h^\mathsf{C},h^\mathsf{T}}$ is negligible, i.e., $2^{-\ell(n)}$. We also note that, by design, $\mathsf{V}_{h^\mathsf{C},h^\mathsf{T}}$ does not accept instances $x \notin \mathcal{L}_\mathcal{R}$ with a proof of the form $h^\mathsf{C}(x)$ (unless $h^\mathsf{C}(x) = h^\mathsf{T}(x)$, which occurs with negligible probability).

Combining Equations (7) and (8), we conclude that for all $k \in \mathbb{N}$ and infinitely many $n \in \mathbb{N}$:

$$\Pr_{d_n \leftarrow (h^\mathsf{C},h^\mathsf{T}) \xleftarrow{\mathrm{R}} \mathcal{H}_n^2} \left[(\mathsf{R}^{\widehat{A}_{h^\mathsf{C}},\Pi_{d_n}}, \mathsf{C}_\mathsf{G})(1^n, i_n^k) = 1\right] \geq 1/(8p(8)) - \mathrm{neg}(n).$$

Namely, $\widehat{R}^\mathsf{A}$ wins $\mathsf{G}$ with probability (at least) $1/(9p(8))$.

### 3.3.4 Putting it Together.

*Proof (Proving the length-preserving variant of Theorem* 5*).* The proof for length-preserving reductions follows directly from Claim 2.

### 3.4 Proof for Arbitrary Reductions

In this section, we prove Theorem 5 for arbitrary reductions. Let $(f, \mathsf{R})$ be an assumption-dependent, fully black-box reduction from OWFs to $\ell$-bit non-uniform interactive arguments for the NP-relation $\mathcal{R}$, with respect to a game $\mathsf{G}$, where $\ell(n) \in \omega(\log n)$. As in the length-preserving case, we fix the first input of $\mathsf{R}$, $1^{t(n)}$, to $1^8$, and omit it from the notation, and assume that $f$ only makes well-formed, valid prover-queries, i.e., $(\phi, w) \in \mathcal{R}$. In addition, we assume weak i.o non-uniform one-way functions do not exist.[20] Let $p_f(n) \in \text{poly}$ bound the running time of $f$ and $\mathsf{R}$, on inputs of length $n$. We assume without loss of generality that $p_f(n)$ is monotonically increasing, and thus the function $p_f^{-1}(n)$ is well defined.

#### 3.4.1 The Interactive Argument.

Let $\mathcal{H} = \{\mathcal{H}_n = \{h: \{0,1\}^n \rightarrow \{0,1\}^{\ell(n)}\}\}_{n\in\mathbb{N}}$ be an efficient $p_f(p_I(n))$-wise independent, function-family ensemble, where $p_I \in \text{poly}$ will be determined by the analysis. The non-interactive argument $\Pi = (\mathsf{P}, \mathsf{V})$, to which $f$ and $\mathsf{R}$ will get oracle access, is defined next, using the function $\mathsf{qry}$ and algorithm $\mathsf{stInv}$ to be defined afterwards.

**Algorithm 13** *[Prover $\mathsf{P}_{h^{\mathsf{C}},h^{\mathsf{T}}}$]*
*Parameters:* $h^{\mathsf{C}}, h^{\mathsf{T}} \in \mathcal{H}_n$.
*Input:* $(\phi, w) \in \{0,1\}^n \times \{0,1\}^*$.
*Operation:*

1. *If* $(\phi, w) \notin \mathcal{R}$, *return* $\perp$.
2. *For* $\lambda = \lceil p_f^{-1}(n) \rceil$ *to* $p_f(n)$*:*
   (a) *Let* $z \leftarrow \mathsf{stInv}(1^\lambda, \phi)$.
   (b) *If* $\mathsf{qry}(z) = \phi$, *return* $h^{\mathsf{C}}(\phi)$.
3. *Return* $h^{\mathsf{T}}(\phi)$.

**Algorithm 14** *[Verifier $\mathsf{V}_{h^{\mathsf{C}},h^{\mathsf{T}}}$]*
*Parameters:* $h^{\mathsf{C}}, h^{\mathsf{T}} \in \mathcal{H}_n$.
*Input:* $(\phi, \pi) \in \{0,1\}^n \times \{0,1\}^*$
*Operation:*

1. *If* $\pi = h^{\mathsf{T}}(\phi)$, *return* 1.
2. *If* $\pi = h^{\mathsf{C}}(\phi)$, *for* $\lambda = \lceil p_f^{-1}(n) \rceil$ *to* $p_f(n)$*:*
   (a) *Let* $z \leftarrow \mathsf{stInv}(1^\lambda, \phi)$.
   (b) *If* $\mathsf{qry}(z) = \phi$, *return* 1.
3. *Return* 0.

That is, the argument is similar to that of the length-preserving proof, but uses a more complicated query function $\mathsf{qry}$, defined next, and a strong

[20] In the length-preserving proof, we assumed that the query function $\mathsf{qry}$, defined by the reduction, is not one-way. The very same argument, however, applies for *any* efficient function: if a one-way function $g$ exists, then the trivial black-box reduction that does nothing is a black-box reduction from $g$ to $\mathsf{G}$.

inverter $\mathsf{stInv}$ of $\mathsf{qry}$. In addition, when it calls $\mathsf{stInv}$, it does so on *different* input lengths. This modification comes to handle a function $f$ that calls $\Pi$ on instances of length different than its input length. Recall that in the length-preserving proof we effectively prevented $f$ from accessing the hash function $h^{\mathsf{T}}$. Here, the above protocol only enables it to access $h^{\mathsf{T}}$ on short input, which suffices for retaining the soundness of the interactive argument against $\mathsf{R}$. For the non-uniform, non-interactive argument that is defined over *all* input lengths, we take $\Pi = \{(\mathsf{P}_{h_n^{\mathsf{C}},h_n^{\mathsf{T}}}, \mathsf{V}_{h_n^{\mathsf{C}},h_n^{\mathsf{T}}})\}_{(h_n^{\mathsf{C}},h_n^{\mathsf{T}})\in\mathcal{H}_n}$ (the choice of hash functions will be discussed later). As in the length-preserving proof, it is easy to see that $\Pi$ has perfect completeness, and is perfect zero knowledge.

*The query function* $\mathsf{qry}$. To define the query function $\mathsf{qry}$, we use the following notation: for $\mathbf{h} = (h_1, h_2, \ldots, h_n) \in \times_{j=1}^{n} \mathcal{H}_j = \mathcal{H}_1 \times \ldots \times \mathcal{H}_n$, $k \in [n]$ and $x \in \{0,1\}^k$, let $\mathbf{h}(x) := (\mathbf{h})_{|x|}(x)$.

**Function 15** *[Query function* $\mathsf{qry}$*]*
*Input:* $(i, x, \mathbf{h}^{\mathsf{C}}, \mathbf{h}^{\mathsf{T}}) \in [p_f(n)] \times \{0,1\}^n \times \times_{j=1}^{p_f(n)} \mathcal{H}_j \times \times_{j=1}^{\lceil p_I^{-1}(n)\rceil - 1} \mathcal{H}_j$.
*Operation:*

1. *Emulate $f(x)$ while answering its oracle queries as follows:*
   **Prover query** $(\phi, w)$:
   *(a) If* $(\phi, w) \notin \mathcal{R}$, *return* $\perp$.
   *(b) If* $|\phi| \geq p_I^{-1}(n)$, *return* $\mathbf{h}^{\mathsf{C}}(\phi)$. *Else, return* $\mathsf{P}_{(\mathbf{h}^{\mathsf{C}})_{|\phi|},(\mathbf{h}^{\mathsf{T}})_{|\phi|}}(\phi, w)$.
   **Verifier query** $(\phi, \pi)$:
   *If* $|\phi| \geq p_I^{-1}(n)$, *return* 1 *if and only if* $\pi = \mathbf{h}^{\mathsf{C}}(\phi)$.
   *Else, return* $\mathsf{V}_{(\mathbf{h}^{\mathsf{C}})_{|\phi|},(\mathbf{h}^{\mathsf{T}})_{|\phi|}}(\phi, \pi)$.
2. *If the execution reaches the* $i^{\text{th}}$ *prover query* $(\phi_i, w_i)$, *return* $\phi_i$. *Else, return* $\perp$.

That is, on "not too short statements", the query function only uses the hash function $\mathbf{h}^{\mathsf{C}}$ (i.e., as in the length-preserving proof). On short statements, it acts according to $\Pi$.

*The strong inverter* $\mathsf{stInv}$ *and the polynomial* $p_I$. We define the inversion algorithm $\mathsf{stInv}$, used above, and argue about the efficiency of the query function $\mathsf{qry}$ (and thus of $\Pi$). We also address here the polynomial $p_I$, used above to parameterize the construction.

Defining the efficient strong inverter $\mathsf{stInv}$ of the query function $\mathsf{qry}$ should be done with care since $\mathsf{qry}$ calls $\mathsf{stInv}$ (on shorter inputs). Yet, below we prove that such a strong inverter exists. Let $t(n) := p_f(n) + n + \sum_{j=1}^{p_f(n)} |h_j| + \sum_{j=1}^{\gamma(n)} |h_j|$, where for all $j$, $h_j \in \mathcal{H}_j$ and $\gamma(n) := \lceil p_I^{-1}(n)\rceil - 1$. Let $\mathbb{N}_q := \{t(n) : n \in \mathbb{N}\}$, i.e., all input lengths of $\mathsf{qry}$. Let $\varepsilon(m) := 1/p_f^3(m)$.

**Claim 3 (Existence of a strong inverter for** $\mathsf{qry}$**).** *There exists* $p_I \in \text{poly}$ *and a poly-time, non-uniform algorithm* $\mathsf{stInv}$ *such that*

$$\Pr_{z \xleftarrow{R} \{0,1\}^m} \left[\mathsf{stInv}(\mathsf{qry}(z)) \in \mathsf{qry}^{-1}(\mathsf{qry}(z))\right] \geq 1 - \varepsilon(m)$$

*for every* $m \in \mathbb{N}_q$.

Claim 3 immediately yields that $\mathsf{qry}$ is also poly-time non-uniform computable. To prove Claim 3, we use the following lemma, proved in ??, which gives good control on the inversion time of an efficient function.

**Lemma 2 (Universal inversion time for non-uniform functions).** *Assume that i.o non-uniform one-way functions do not exist. Then for every* $p_E \in \text{poly}$ *and* $\varepsilon(n) \geq 1/\text{poly}(n)$, *there exists* $p_I \in \text{poly}$ *such that the following holds: for* every *circuit* $f_n$ *over* $\{0,1\}^n$ *of size* $p_E(n)$, *there exists a* $p_I(n)$*-size circuit* $\mathsf{C}_n$ *such that* $\Pr_{x \xleftarrow{R} \{0,1\}^n}\left[\mathsf{C}_n(f_n(x)) \in f_n^{-1}(f_n(x))\right] \geq 1 - \varepsilon(n)$.

Namely, the size of a strong inverter of a $p_E(n)$-size $f$, is bounded by a (universal) polynomial in $p_E(n)$.

*Proof (Proof of Claim 3).* Let $p_I \in \text{poly}$ be the (smallest) polynomial guaranteed by Lemma 2 with respect to $p_E(m) := p_f^7(m)$ and $\varepsilon(m)$. We define $\mathsf{stInv}$ as a (poly-size) circuit family $\{\mathsf{stInv}_j\}_{j \in \mathbb{N}}$.[21] Conveniently, we also view the query function $\mathsf{qry}$ as a circuit family $\{\mathsf{qry}_m\}_{m \in \mathbb{N}_q}$.

We prove by induction on $m \in \mathbb{N}_q$, that $|\mathsf{qry}_m| \leq p_E(m)$, while defining the strong inverter $\mathsf{stInv}$ along the way. We assume that $\mathsf{qry}_m$ makes $p_f(t^{-1}(m))$ oracle queries, an over-counting that allows us to ignore the computation cost of the parts of $\mathsf{qry}_m$ that are not oracle queries. The base case is clear. Proving for $m \in \mathbb{N}_q$, the induction hypothesis yields that $|\mathsf{qry}_{m'}| \leq p_E(m')$ for all $m' \in \mathbb{N}_q$ with $m' < m$. For any such $m'$, let $\mathsf{C}_{m'}$ be the $p_I(m')$-size circuit guaranteed by Lemma 2, that inverts $\mathsf{qry}_{m'}$ on inputs of length $m'$. For $j \in \mathbb{N}$ with $t(j) < m$, let $\mathsf{stInv}_j(\phi) := \mathsf{C}_{t(j)}(\phi)$. We prove that

$$|\mathsf{qry}_m| \leq p_E(m) \tag{9}$$

To see the above, consider an execution of the algorithm $\mathsf{qry}$ on an input of length $m = t(n)$. The execution emulates $f(x)$ for $x \in \{0,1\}^n$, up to the $i^{\text{th}}$ oracle query, for $i \in [p_f(n)]$. In the following we bound the running time of each query $(\phi, \cdot)$. Let $k \leftarrow |\phi|$.

**Case** $k \geq p_I^{-1}(n)$**.** We assume without loss of generality that the polynomial that bounds the evaluation time of the hash functions $\mathcal{H}$ (see Section 2.2) is bounded by $p_f^2(p_I(n))$ (If this is not the case, we would consider larger $p_f \in \text{poly}$). Since $\mathsf{qry}$ computes $\mathbf{h}^{\mathsf{C}}(\phi)$ in this case, and since $k \leq p_f(n)$, the running time of this query is bounded by $p_f^2(p_I(p_f(n)))$.
Finally, since $t(n) > p_I(p_f(n))$ (recall that $t(n)$ also accounts for the description of $h \in \mathcal{H}_{p_f(n)}$), we conclude that $p_f^2(p_I(p_f(n))) \leq p_f^2(t(n)) = p_f^2(m)$.

**Case** $k < p_I^{-1}(n)$**.** On such queries, $\mathsf{qry}$ invokes $\Pi$ which in turn tries to invert $\phi$ using $\mathsf{stInv}(1^\lambda, \phi)$, for every $\lambda \in [\lceil p_f^{-1}(k) \rceil, p_f(k)]$. Since $m = t(n)$ and assuming without loss of generality that $p_I > p_f$, we deduce that for $k < p_I^{-1}(n)$

[21] Clearly, for such a family there exists a poly-time, non-uniform algorithm that computes it, as required by the claim.

it holds that $t(p_f(k)) < m$. Thus, we can apply the induction hypothesis to deduce that $\mathsf{qry}$ can be computed in time $p_E(t(p_f(k)))$. Hence, by Lemma 2, the computation size (and running time) of each inversion attempt is bounded by $p_I(t(p_f(k))) \leq t(p_f(n)) \leq p_f(m)$.[22] Finally, since $\Pi$ makes at most $p_f(k)$ inversion attempts, the total emulation time is bounded by $p_f(k) \cdot p_f(m) \leq p_f(m)^2 \leq p_f^2(m)$.[23]

Since $\mathsf{qry}$ makes at most $p_f(n)$ queries, its total running time is bounded by $p_f^3(m)$. Since we can assume without loss of generality that the size of the non-uniform advice of $f$ on input length $n$ (and thus of $\mathsf{qry}$ on input length $m$) is bounded by $p_f(n)$, and that the description of the algorithm $f$ is included in its non-uniform advice, we conclude that $\mathsf{qry}_m$ can be computed by a circuit of size $(p_f^3(m) + p_f(n))^2 < p_E(m)$.

Since the above also defines the circuit family $\{\mathsf{stInv}_j\}_{j\in\mathbb{N}}$ of size $p_I(t(j)) \in \mathrm{poly}(j)$, and proves that it inverts $\mathsf{qry}$ with probability $1 - \varepsilon(m)$ for all $m \in \mathbb{N}_q$, this concludes the proof.

**3.4.2 The Query Function of $f^\Pi$.** A key observation is that the above "query function" $\mathsf{qry}$ emulates well the (real) query function induced by $f^\Pi$—the queries $f^\Pi$ makes to the oracles in a random execution. (We later use this fact to deduce that an inverter for $\mathsf{qry}$ is also an inverter for the query function induced by $f^\Pi$.)

As in the length-preserving proof, we consider the function $f^\Pi_{\mathsf{trace}}$ that on input $x \in \{0,1\}^*$, outputs $x$ and all oracle queries/answers made by $f^\Pi(x)$. We compare it to the function $\mathsf{qry}_{\mathsf{trace}}$ that on input $(x, \mathbf{h}^{\mathsf{C}}, \mathbf{h}^{\mathsf{T}})$, outputs $x$ and the oracle queries/answers made by the emulated execution of $f$ in the execution of $\mathsf{qry}(p_f(|x|), x, \mathbf{h}^{\mathsf{C}}, \mathbf{h}^{\mathsf{T}})$. Specifically, we show that the output distributions of these transcript functions are statistically close.

**Claim 4 (Similarity between $f^\Pi_{\mathsf{trace}}$ and $\mathsf{qry}_{\mathsf{trace}}$).** *For every $n \in \mathbb{N}$: $\mathrm{SD}(f_{\mathsf{trace}}^{\Pi_{H^{\mathsf{C}},H^{\mathsf{T}}}}(X), \mathsf{qry}_{\mathsf{trace}}(X, H^{\mathsf{C}}, \widetilde{H^{\mathsf{T}}})) \leq p_f(n) \cdot 2^{-\ell(p_I^{-1}(n))}$, where $X \leftarrow U_n$, $(H^{\mathsf{C}}, H^{\mathsf{T}}) \xleftarrow{R} (\times_{j=1}^{p_f(n)} \mathcal{H}_j)^2$ and $\widetilde{H^{\mathsf{T}}} \leftarrow (H^{\mathsf{T}})_{\leq \lceil p_I^{-1}(n)\rceil - 1}$.*

*Proof.* We prove the claim by presenting a random process, parameterized by $n$, whose output distribution is identical to that of $\mathsf{qry}_{\mathsf{trace}}$, and statistically close to that of $f^\Pi_{\mathsf{trace}}$.

**Algorithm 16**

1. *Sample* $(x, \mathbf{h}^{\mathsf{C}}, \mathbf{h}^{\mathsf{T}}) \xleftarrow{R} \{0,1\}^n \times \left(\times_{j=1}^{\lceil p_I^{-1}(n)\rceil - 1} \mathcal{H}_j\right)^2$.
2. *Sample* $a_1, \ldots, a_{p_f(n)} \xleftarrow{R} \{0,1\}^{\ell(p_f(n))}$.
3. *Execute* $f(x)$ *while answering its* $i^{\text{th}}$ *oracle query* $(\phi, z)$ *as follows:*
**Short queries** $|\phi| \leq \lceil p_I^{-1}(n)\rceil - 1$**:** *Return according to* $\Pi_{(\mathbf{h}^{\mathsf{C}})_{|\phi|}, (\mathbf{h}^{\mathsf{T}})_{|\phi|}}$.

[22] While polynomial composition is not commutative for arbitrary polynomials, it does hold in our case since without loss of generality the leading coefficients of $t$ and $p_f$ are one.

[23] This holds since without loss of generality $p_f$ is of degree at least two.

**Long queries $|\phi| > \lceil p_I^{-1}(n) \rceil - 1$:**
**Prover query:** *Return* $(a_i)_{\leq \ell(|\phi|)}$.
**Verifier query:** *If* $z$ *was an answer to a previous prover query* $(\phi, \cdot)$, *accept. Otherwise, accept with probability* $2^{-\ell(|\phi|)}$.
4. *Output the transcript of the execution.*

The only difference between $\mathsf{qry}_{\mathsf{trace}}$ and $f^{\Pi}_{\mathsf{trace}}$ is the way long queries are answered; in $\mathsf{qry}_{\mathsf{trace}}$, it is (always) according to $\mathbf{h}^{\mathsf{C}}$. In $f^{\Pi}_{\mathsf{trace}}$, it is according to $\mathbf{h}^{\mathsf{C}}$ if the inversion succeeds, and according to $\mathbf{h}^{\mathsf{T}}$ otherwise. We separately analyze prover and verifier queries.

**Prover queries.** Since the number of queries made by $f$ (and thus by $\mathsf{qry}$) is smaller than the many-wise independence of the hash functions used for such long queries ($|\phi| > p_I^{-1}(n)$, hence $p_f(p_I(|\phi|)) > p_f(n)$), in both cases the hash functions' answers are uniform values, which is exactly what the prover replies in the above random process.

**Verifier queries.** In both cases the verifier accepts if the proof $\pi$ is consistent with the value that is generated by the prover. In the case where the verifier query was not generated by a prior prover query, in $\mathsf{qry}_{\mathsf{trace}}$ the verifier accepts only if the proof matches $\mathbf{h}^{\mathsf{C}}$, i.e., with probability $2^{-\ell(|\phi|)}$, as in the random process. In $f^{\Pi}_{\mathsf{trace}}$, the verifier accepts if the proof matches $\mathbf{h}^{\mathsf{T}}$, and might also accept if the proof matches $\mathbf{h}^{\mathsf{C}}$. The probability that the proof matches at least one of the hashes is at most $2 \cdot 2^{-\ell(|\phi|)}$. Since the number of queries is bounded by $p_f(n)$ and the length of the statement in such verifier queries is at least $p_I^{-1}(n)$, by a union bound, the statistical difference between the distributions is at most $p_f(n) \cdot 2^{-\ell(p_I^{-1}(n))}$.

**3.4.3 The Punctured Argument.** Towards defining the function $g$, whose one-wayness can be reduced to the game $\mathsf{G}$, we define the "punctured" variant $\Pi^{\mathsf{punct}}$ of $\Pi$ such that: (1) Inverting a function with oracle access to $\Pi^{\mathsf{punct}}$ is not useful for breaking the security of $\Pi$. (2) The execution of $f^{\Pi^{\mathsf{punct}}}$ is close to that of $f^{\Pi}$.[24] The above is achieved by removing the access to the hash function $h^{\mathsf{T}}$ on the relevant input lengths (i.e., we "punctured" $\Pi$). Let $\mathsf{tr}(n) := \lceil p_f^{-1}(n) \rceil - 1$.

**Algorithm 17** *[Prover* $\mathsf{P}^{\mathsf{punct}}_{\mathbf{h}^{\mathsf{C}},\mathbf{h}^{\mathsf{T}}}$*]*
*Parameters:* $\mathbf{h}^{\mathsf{C}} \in \times_{j=1}^{p_f(n)} \mathcal{H}_j$, $\mathbf{h}^{\mathsf{T}} \in \times_{j=1}^{\mathsf{tr}(n)} \mathcal{H}_j$.
*Input:* $(\phi, w) \in (\{0,1\}^*)^2$.
*Operation:*

1. *If* $(\phi, w) \notin \mathcal{R}$ *or* $|\phi| > p_f(n)$, *return* $\perp$.
2. *If* $|\phi| > \mathsf{tr}(n)$, *return* $\mathbf{h}^{\mathsf{C}}(\phi)$.
3. *Return* $\mathsf{P}_{(\mathbf{h}^{\mathsf{C}})_{|\phi|},(\mathbf{h}^{\mathsf{T}})_{|\phi|}}(\phi, w)$.

[24] In the length-preserving proof, the role of $\Pi^{\mathsf{punct}}$ was played by the hash-based argument $\widehat{\Pi}$.

**Algorithm 18** *[Verifier $\mathsf{V}^{\mathsf{punct}}_{\mathbf{h}^{\mathsf{C}},\mathbf{h}^{\mathsf{T}}}$]*

*Parameters:* $\mathbf{h}^{\mathsf{C}} \in \times_{j=1}^{p_f(n)} \mathcal{H}_j$, $\mathbf{h}^{\mathsf{T}} \in \times_{j=1}^{\mathsf{tr}(n)} \mathcal{H}_j$.
*Input:* $(\phi, \pi) \in (\{0,1\}^*)^2$.
*Operation:*

1. *If* $|\phi| > p_f(n)$, *return* 0.
2. *If* $|\phi| > \mathsf{tr}(n)$: *return* 1 *if* $\pi = \mathbf{h}^{\mathsf{C}}(\phi)$ *and* 0 *otherwise.*
3. *Return* $\mathsf{V}_{(\mathbf{h}^{\mathsf{C}})_{|\phi|},(\mathbf{h}^{\mathsf{T}})_{|\phi|}}(\phi, \pi)$.

That is, $\Pi^{\mathsf{punct}}$ operates similarly to $\Pi$, but the parties use *only* $\mathbf{h}^{\mathsf{C}}$ for long statements. We prove that the executions of $f^{\Pi}$ and $f^{\Pi^{\mathsf{punct}}}$ are similar (analogous to Claim 1 in the length-preserving proof).

For $\mathbf{h}^{\mathsf{C}}, \mathbf{h}^{\mathsf{T}} \in (\times_{j=1}^{n} \mathcal{H}_j)^2$, let $\Pi_{\mathbf{h}^{\mathsf{C}},\mathbf{h}^{\mathsf{T}}}$ be the argument that on input $(\phi, \cdot) \in \{0,1\}^k \times \{0,1\}^*$, for $k \le n$, acts according to $\Pi_{(\mathbf{h}^{\mathsf{C}})_k,(\mathbf{h}^{\mathsf{T}})_k}$.

**Claim 5 (Similarity between $f^{\Pi}$ and $f^{\Pi^{\mathsf{punct}}}$).**

$$\Pr_{(\mathbf{h}^{\mathsf{C}},\mathbf{h}^{\mathsf{T}},x) \xleftarrow{R} \left(\times_{j=1}^{p_f(n)} \mathcal{H}_j\right)^2 \times \{0,1\}^n} \left[ f^{\Pi_{\mathbf{h}^{\mathsf{C}},\mathbf{h}^{\mathsf{T}}}}(x) \neq f^{\Pi^{\mathsf{punct}}_{\mathbf{h}^{\mathsf{C}},(\mathbf{h}^{\mathsf{T}})_{\le \mathsf{tr}(n)}}}(x) \right] \le 1/2.$$

*for all* $n$ *with* $\ell(n) \ge 2 + \log(p_f^4(p_I(n)))$.

*Proof.* As in Claim 1, we prove the (stronger) statement that the execution traces of $f^{\Pi_{\mathbf{h}^{\mathsf{C}},\mathbf{h}^{\mathsf{T}}}}(x)$ and $f^{\Pi^{\mathsf{punct}}_{\mathbf{h}^{\mathsf{C}},(\mathbf{h}^{\mathsf{T}})_{\le \mathsf{tr}(n)}}}(x)$, for uniform $x$ and $\mathbf{h}^{\mathsf{C}}, \mathbf{h}^{\mathsf{T}}$, are 1/2 close. The proof is by coupling the two distributions.

**Algorithm 19** *[Coupling $f^{\Pi}$ and $f^{\Pi^{\mathsf{punct}}}$]*

1. *Sample* $(\mathbf{h}^{\mathsf{C}}, \mathbf{h}^{\mathsf{T}}, x) \xleftarrow{R} (\times_{j=1}^{p_f(n)} \mathcal{H}_j)^2 \times \{0,1\}^n$.
2. *Let* trace *and* $\mathsf{trace}^{\mathsf{punct}}$ *denote the traces of the executions of* $f^{\Pi_{\mathbf{h}^{\mathsf{C}},\mathbf{h}^{\mathsf{T}}}}(x)$ *and* $f^{\Pi^{\mathsf{punct}}_{\mathbf{h}^{\mathsf{C}},(\mathbf{h}^{\mathsf{T}})_{\le \mathsf{tr}(n)}}}(x)$, *respectively.*
3. *Return* $(\mathsf{trace}, \mathsf{trace}^{\mathsf{punct}})$.

Let $E_i$ be the event that trace and $\mathsf{trace}^{\mathsf{punct}}$ are identical up to the $i^{\text{th}}$ query. We show that for every $i \in [p_f(n)]$ it holds that $\Pr[\neg E_i \mid E_{i-1}] \le 3\varepsilon(n)$, and since $3\varepsilon(n) \cdot p_f(n) \le 1/2$, the proof follows by a union bound. Assume $E_{i-1}$ holds. Clearly, the $i^{\text{th}}$ query generated by $f$ is the same in both executions. We analyze the probability that the oracle responses differ (i.e., $\neg E_i$ occurs), separately handling prover and verifier queries.

**Prover query.** Let $(\phi, w)$ be a query to the prover. By our assumption on $f$, $(\phi, w) \in \mathcal{R}$. Note that if $|\phi| < \lceil p_f^{-1}(n) \rceil$, then the execution of $\mathsf{P}^{\mathsf{punct}}$ is identical to that of $\mathsf{P}$, and therefore their output is the same. Thus, it remains to handle the case $|\phi| \in \left[\lceil p_f^{-1}(n) \rceil, p_f(n)\right]$. On such a query, $\mathsf{P}^{\mathsf{punct}}$ returns $\mathbf{h}^{\mathsf{C}}(\phi)$, whereas the response of $\mathsf{P}$ depends on the success of $\mathsf{stInv}$. Specifically,

P calls $\mathsf{stInv}(1^\lambda, \phi)$ for all $j \in [\lceil p_f^{-1}(|\phi|)\rceil, p_f(|\phi|)]$, and if one of the calls succeeds, it also returns $\mathbf{h}^{\mathsf{C}}(\phi)$. Note that $\phi$ is a uniform query of $f^{\Pi}$, with respect to uniform choice of $(\mathbf{h}^{\mathsf{C}}, \mathbf{h}^{\mathsf{T}}, x)$, conditioned on $E_{i-1}$, and that by the induction assumption, $E_{i-1}$ occurs with probability at least 1/2. Also recall that by Claim 4, the output distribution of qry and the query distribution of $f^{\Pi}$ are $1 - \varepsilon(n)$ close, for the considered $n$ (with respect to uniform choice of $(\mathbf{h}^{\mathsf{C}}, \mathbf{h}^{\mathsf{T}}, x)$). Finally note that, $f^{\Pi}$, via the inversion attempts of $\Pi$, calls $\mathsf{stInv}_n(\phi)$. Thus, by Claim 3 the inverter stInv finds a preimage and P returns $\mathbf{h}^{\mathsf{C}}(\phi)$, with probability at least $1 - 2\varepsilon(t(n)) - \varepsilon(n) \geq 1 - 3\varepsilon(n)$.

**Verifier query.** Let $(\phi, \pi)$ be a query to the verifier. If $\pi$ was generated by a previous prover query, both V and $\mathsf{V}^{\mathsf{punct}}$ accept. So in the following, we assume $\pi$ was not generated previously in the execution. If $|\phi| < \lceil p_f^{-1}(n)\rceil$, the execution of $\mathsf{V}^{\mathsf{punct}}$ is *identical* to that of V, and therefore their output is identical. If $|\phi| \geq \lceil p_f^{-1}(n)\rceil$, since $\mathbf{h}^{\mathsf{C}}$ and $\mathbf{h}^{\mathsf{T}}$ are sampled from a $p_f(p_I(|\phi|))$-wise independent family for input size $|\phi|$, the probability that $\pi \in \{\mathbf{h}^{\mathsf{C}}(\phi), \mathbf{h}^{\mathsf{T}}(\phi)\}$ is $2 \cdot 2^{-\ell(|\phi|)} \leq 3\varepsilon(n)$.

Combining the two cases, we deduce that $\Pr[\neg E_i \mid E_{i-1}] \leq 3\varepsilon(n)$.

**3.4.4 The Function $g$.** We are now ready to define the function $g$, whose security is reduced to the game G. As in the length-preserving proof, we define $g$ to be the weak-to-strong amplification of the function $g_{\mathsf{w}} : \times_{j=1}^{p_f(n)} \mathcal{H}_j \times \times_{j=1}^{\mathsf{tr}(n)} \mathcal{H}_j \times \{0,1\}^n \to \times_{j=1}^{p_f(n)} \mathcal{H}_j \times \times_{j=1}^{\mathsf{tr}(n)} \mathcal{H}_j \times \{0,1\}^n$ defined by:

$$g_{\mathsf{w}}(\mathbf{h}^{\mathsf{C}}, \mathbf{h}^{\mathsf{T}}, x) = (\mathbf{h}^{\mathsf{C}}, \mathbf{h}^{\mathsf{T}}, f^{\Pi^{\mathsf{punct}}_{\mathbf{h}^{\mathsf{C}},\mathbf{h}^{\mathsf{T}}}}(x)) \tag{10}$$

Let $g$ and $\mathsf{R}_{\&}$ be the (efficient) function and reduction guaranteed by Lemma 1 such that for every PPT A that inverts $g$ with non-negligible probability, $\mathsf{R}_{\&}^{\mathsf{A}}$ inverts $g_{\mathsf{w}}$ with probability 3/4.

**3.4.5 The Reduction $\widehat{R}$.** We now define the reduction $\widehat{R}$ from the onewayness of $g$ to the security of G. We use the following wrapper algorithm.

**Algorithm 20** *[$\widehat{A}_{\mathbf{h}^{\mathsf{C}},\mathbf{h}^{\mathsf{T}}}$]*
*Parameter:* $(\mathbf{h}^{\mathsf{C}}, \mathbf{h}^{\mathsf{T}}) \in \{\mathcal{H}_j\}_{j=1}^{p_f(n)} \times \{\mathcal{H}_j\}_{j=1}^{\mathsf{tr}(n)}$.
*Oracle:* A.
*Input:* $y$.
*Operation: Return* $\mathsf{R}_{\&}^{\mathsf{A}}(\mathbf{h}^{\mathsf{C}}, \mathbf{h}^{\mathsf{T}}, y)_3$, *i.e., the third output of* $\mathsf{R}_{\&}^{\mathsf{A}}$.

**Algorithm 21** *[Reduction $\widehat{R}$ from $g$ to G ]*
*Oracle:* A.
*Input:* $1^n$.
*Operation:*

1. *Sample* $(\mathbf{h}^{\mathsf{C}}, \mathbf{h}^{\mathsf{T}}) \stackrel{R}{\leftarrow} \left(\times_{j=1}^{p_f^2(n)} \mathcal{H}_j\right)^2$.
2. *Play in* $\mathsf{G}$ *according to* $\mathsf{R}^{\widehat{A}_{\mathbf{h}^{\mathsf{C}},(\mathbf{h}^{\mathsf{T}})_{\leq n-1}}, \Pi_{\mathbf{h}^{\mathsf{C}},\mathbf{h}^{\mathsf{T}}}}(1^n)$.

Note that $\widehat{R}$ samples the hash functions up to $\mathcal{H}_{p_f^2(n)}$, since the reduction $\mathsf{R}$ on input of length $n$ might call the inverter of $f$ with input of length $p_f(n)$. In that inversion, the execution of $f$ might call the interactive argument on inputs of length $p_f(p_f(n))$. The following claim shows that $\widehat{R}$ is indeed a reduction from the one-wayness of $g$ to the game $\mathsf{G}$. Let $p$ be the polynomial from Definition 14 with respect to $\mathsf{R}$.

**Claim 6.** *For any non-uniform poly-time* $\mathsf{A}$ *that inverts* $g$ *with probability* $1/\text{poly}$ *for all* $n \in \mathbb{N}$*, it holds that* $\widehat{R}^{\mathsf{A}}$ *wins* $\mathsf{G}$ *with probability at least* $1/(9p(8))$.

*Proof.* See proof in [2].

### 3.4.6 Putting it Together.

*Proof (Proof of Theorem* 5*).* The proof follows directly from Claim 6.

**Acknowledgment.** We thank Noam Mazor for very insightful discussions.

## References

1. Attema, T., Cramer, R., Kohl, L.: A compressed sigma-protocol theory for lattices. In: Annual International Cryptology Conference (CRYPTO), pp. 549–579 (2021)
2. Baril, I., Haitner, I.: On the Complexity of Interactive Arguments. Technical Report, Cryptology ePrint Archive (2026)
3. Baum, C., Bootle, J., Cerulli, A., Del Pino, R., Groth, J., Lyubashevsky, V.: Sub-linear lattice-based zero-knowledge arguments for arithmetic circuits. In: Annual International Cryptology Conference (CRYPTO), pp. 669–699 (2018)
4. Ben-Sasson, E., Bentov, I., Horesh, Y., Riabzev, M.: Scalable, transparent, and post-quantum secure computational integrity. Technical Report, Cryptology ePrint Archive (2018)
5. Beullens, W., Seiler, G.: LaBRADOR: compact proofs for R1CS from Module-SIS. In: Annual International Cryptology Conference, pp. 518–548 (2023)
6. Bitansky, N., Kamath, C., Paneth, O., Rothblum, R.D., Vasudevan, P.N.: Batch proofs are statistically hiding. In: Annual ACM Symposium on Theory of Computing (STOC), STOC 2024. pp. 435–443 (2024)
7. Bitansky, N., Paneth, O.: ZAPs and non-interactive witness indistinguishability from indistinguishability obfuscation. In: Theory of Cryptography (TCC), pp. 401–427 (2015)
8. Bootle, J., Cerulli, A., Chaidos, P., Groth, J., Petit, C.: Efficient zero-knowledge arguments for arithmetic circuits in the discrete log setting. In: Annual International Conference on the Theory and Applications of Cryptographic Techniques (EUROCRYPT), pp. 327–357 (2016)
9. Bootle, J., Chiesa, A., Sotiraki, K.: Sumcheck arguments and their applications. In: Malkin, T., Peikert, C. (eds.) CRYPTO 2021. LNCS, vol. 12825, pp. 742–773. Springer, Cham (2021). https://doi.org/10.1007/978-3-030-84242-0_26

10. Bootle, J., Chiesa, A., Sotiraki, K.: Lattice-based succinct arguments for NP with polylogarithmic-time verification. In: Annual International Cryptology Conference (CRYPTO), pp. 227–251 (2023)
11. Bootle, J., Lyubashevsky, V., Nguyen, N.K., Seiler, G.: A non-PCP approach to succinct quantum-safe zero-knowledge. In: Micciancio, D., Ristenpart, T. (eds.) CRYPTO 2020. LNCS, vol. 12171, pp. 441–469. Springer, Cham (2020). https://doi.org/10.1007/978-3-030-56880-1_16
12. Bresson, E., Monnerat, J., Vergnaud, D.: Separation results on the "One-more" Computational problems. In: Topics in Cryptology —CT-RSA, pp. 71–87 (2008)
13. Bünz, B., Fisch, B., Szepieniec, A.: Transparent SNARKs from DARK compilers. In: Canteaut, A., Ishai, Y. (eds.) EUROCRYPT 2020. LNCS, vol. 12105, pp. 677–706. Springer, Cham (2020). https://doi.org/10.1007/978-3-030-45721-1_24
14. Lawrence Carter, J., Wegman, M.N.: New hash functions and their use in authentication and set equality. In: Journal of Computer and System Sciences, pp. 265–279 (1981)
15. Chen, L., Rothblum, R.D., Tell, R.: Fiat-Shamir in the plain model from derandomization (Or: Do efficient algorithms believe that NP = PSPACE?) In: Annual ACM Symposium on Theory of Computing (STOC), pp. 977–985 (2025)
16. Choudhuri, A.R., Jain, A., Jin, Z.: SNARGs for P from LWE. In: Annual Symposium on Foundations of Computer Science (FOCS), pp. 68–79 (2021)
17. Dwork, C., Naor, M.: Zaps and their applications. In: Annual Symposium on Foundations of Computer Science (FOCS), p. 283 (2000)
18. Feige, U., Lapidot, D., Shamir, A.: Multiple non-interactive zero knowledge proofs under general assumptions. In: SIAM Journal on Computing. Preliminary version in FOCS'90 (1999)
19. Gentry, C., Wichs, D.: Separating Succinct non-interactive arguments from all falsifiable assumptions. In: Annual ACM Symposium on Theory of Computing (STOC), pp. 99–108 (2011)
20. Gertner, Y., Kannan, S., Malkin, T., Reingold, O., Viswanathan, M.: The Relationship between public key encryption and oblivious transfer. In: Annual ACM Symposium on Theory of Computing (STOC) (2000)
21. Goldreich, O.: Foundations of Cryptography. Basic Tools. Cambridge University Press (2001)
22. Goldreich, O., Levin, L.A.: A hard-core predicate for all one-way functions. In: Annual ACM Symposium on Theory of Computing (STOC), pp. 25–32 (1989)
23. Goldreich, O., Micali, S., Wigderson, A.: Proofs that yield nothing but their validity and a methodology of cryptographic protocol design (Extended Abstract). In: Annual Symposium on Foundations of Computer Science (FOCS), pp. 174–187 (1986)
24. Goldreich, O., Micali, S., Wigderson, A.: Proofs that yield nothing but their validity or all languages in NP have zero-knowledge proof systems. J. ACM **38**(3), 690–728 (1991)
25. Goldreich, O., Vadhan, S., Wigderson, A.: On interactive proofs with a laconic prover. In: Automata, Languages and Programming, 24th International Colloquium (ICALP), pp. 334–345 (2001)
26. Goldwasser, S., Kalai, Y.T., Rothblum, G.N.: Delegating computation: interactive proofs for muggles. In: Annual ACM Symposium on Theory of Computing (STOC), pp. 113–122 (2008)
27. Groth, J.: On the size of pairing-based non-interactive arguments. In: Annual International Conference on the Theory and Applications of Cryptographic Techniques (EUROCRYPT), pp. 305–326 (2016)

28. Groth, J., Ostrovsky, R., Sahai, A.: Perfect non-interactive zero knowledge for NP. In: Annual International Conference on the Theory and Applications of Cryptographic Techniques (EUROCRYPT), pp. 339–358 (2006)
29. Haitner, I., Nukrai, D., Yogev, E.: Lower bound on SNARGs in the random oracle model. In: Annual International Cryptology Conference (CRYPTO), pp. 97–127 (2022)
30. Haitner, I., Rosen, A., Shaltiel, R.: On the (Im)possibility of arthur-merlin witness hiding protocols. In: Theory of Cryptography (TCC), pp. 220–237 (2009)
31. Hirahara, S., Nanashima, M.: One-way functions and zero knowledge. In: Annual ACM Symposium on Theory of Computing (STOC), pp. 1731–1738 (2024)
32. Impagliazzo, R., Luby, M.: One-way functions are essential for complexity based cryptography. In: Annual Symposium on Foundations of Computer Science (FOCS), pp. 230–235 (1989)
33. Impagliazzo, R., Rudich, S.: Limits on the provable consequences of one-way permutations. In: Annual ACM Symposium on Theory of Computing (STOC), pp. 44–61 (1989)
34. Kalai, Y., Paneth, O., Yang, L.: How to delegate computations publicly. In: Annual ACM Symposium on Theory of Computing (STOC), pp. 1115–1124 (2019)
35. Kilian, J.: A note on efficient zero-knowledge proofs and arguments. In: Annual ACM Symposium on Theory of Computing (STOC), pp. 723–732 (1992)
36. Komargodski, I., Naor, M., Yogev, E.: Collision resistant hashing for paranoids: dealing with multiple collisions. In: Nielsen, J.B., Rijmen, V. (eds.) EUROCRYPT 2018. LNCS, vol. 10821, pp. 162–194. Springer, Cham (2018). https://doi.org/10.1007/978-3-319-78375-8_6
37. Liu, Y., Mazor, N., Pass, R.: A note on zero-knowledge for –NP and one-way functions. Manuscript (2024)
38. Micali, S.: Computationally sound proofs. SIAM J. Comput. **30**(4), 1253–1298 (2000)
39. Naor, M.: Bit commitment using pseudorandomness. J. Cryptol. **4**(2), 151–158 (1991)
40. Naor, M.: On cryptographic assumptions and challenges. In: Annual International Cryptology Conference (CRYPTO) (2003)
41. Ostrovsky, R., Wigderson, A.: One-way functions are essential for non-trivial zero-knowledge. In: The Israel Symposium on Theory of Computing Systems, pp. 3–17 (1993)
42. Rothblum, R.D., Vasudevan, P.N.: Collision resistance from multi-collision resistance. J. Cryptol. **37**(2), 14 (2024)
43. Sahai, A., Waters, B.: How to use indistinguishability obfuscation: deniable encryption, and more. In: Annual ACM Symposium on Theory of Computing (STOC), pp. 475–484 (2014)
44. Setty, S.: Spartan: efficient and general-purpose zkSNARKs without trusted setup. In: Annual International Cryptology Conference, pp. 704–737 (2020)
45. Simon, D.: Finding collisions on a one-way street: can secure hash functions be based on general assumptions? In: Annual International Conference on the Theory and Applications of Cryptographic Techniques (EUROCRYPT), pp. 334–345 (1998)
46. Wee, H.: Finding pessiland. In: Theory of Cryptography (TCC), pp. 429–442 (2006)
47. Yao, A.C.: Theory and applications of trapdoor functions. In: Annual Symposium on Foundations of Computer Science (FOCS), pp. 80–91 (1982)

# Non-trivial Zero-Knowledge Implies One-Way Functions

Suvradip Chakraborty[1(✉)], James Hulett[2], Dakshita Khurana[2,3], and Kabir Tomer[2]

[1] Visa Research, Foster City, USA
suvchakr@visa.com
[2] UIUC, Champaign, USA
{jhulett2,dakshita,ktomer2}@illinois.edu
[3] NTT Research, Sunnyvale, USA

**Abstract.** A recent breakthrough [Hirahara and Nanashima, STOC'2024] established that if $\mathsf{NP} \not\subseteq \mathsf{ioP/poly}$, the existence of zero-knowledge (ZK) with negligible errors for $\mathsf{NP}$ implies the existence of one-way functions (OWFs). This work obtains a characterization of one-way functions from the worst-case complexity of zero-knowledge in the high-error regime.

Assuming $\mathsf{NP} \not\subseteq \mathsf{ioP/poly}$, we show that any *non-trivial, constant-round* public-coin ZK argument for $\mathsf{NP}$ implies the existence of OWFs, and therefore also (standard) four-message zero-knowledge arguments for $\mathsf{NP}$. Here, we call a ZK argument *non-trivial* if the sum of its completeness, soundness and zero-knowledge errors is bounded away from 1.

As a special case, we also prove that non-trivial non-interactive ZK (NIZK) arguments for $\mathsf{NP}$ imply the existence of OWFs. Using known amplification techniques, this also provides an unconditional transformation from weak to standard NIZK proofs for all meaningful error parameters. Prior work [Chakraborty, Hulett and Khurana, CRYPTO'2025] was limited to NIZKs with constant zero-knowledge error $\varepsilon_{\mathsf{zk}}$ and soundness error $\varepsilon_{\mathsf{s}}$ satisfying $\varepsilon_{\mathsf{zk}} + \sqrt{\varepsilon_{\mathsf{s}}} < 1$.

## 1 Introduction

Zero-knowledge proofs are a cornerstone of modern cryptography, allowing a prover to convince a verifier about the validity of an NP statement without leaking any information about the witness. A major research agenda, initiated by Ostrovsky and Wigderson [12,13], asks: what are the minimal cryptographic assumptions needed for zero-knowledge ($\mathsf{ZK}$) proof systems? Their celebrated results established that, assuming NP is hard on average, the existence of $\mathsf{ZK}$ proofs for NP implies the existence of one-way functions ($\mathsf{OWFs}$), a fundamental cryptographic primitive.

More recently, Hirahara and Nanashima [8] made a notable advance by proving that even the *worst-case* hardness of $\mathsf{NP}$ (specifically, $\mathsf{NP} \not\subseteq \mathsf{ioP/poly}$) suffices to construct one-way functions from zero-knowledge proofs for $\mathsf{NP}$. In fact, they


N. Heninger and M. Rosulek (Eds.): CRYPTO 2026, LNCS 16800, pp. 127–158, 2026.
https://doi.org/10.1007/978-3-032-35367-2_5

only require the existence of zero-knowledge proofs for a *specific* type of language outside ioP/poly, thereby opening up a new route for constructing one-way functions based solely on worst-case hardness.

**Non-trivial ZK and One-Way Functions.** What happens if we allow ZK proof systems with non-negligible and possibly large security errors? Unfortunately, techniques of [8,12,13] that link zero-knowledge to one-way functions are critically dependent on the assumption of small errors. As we will show, this is not merely an artifact of their analysis, but a fundamental limitation of their reductions. This state of affairs leaves open a basic gap in our understanding of the complexity of ZK.

Note that ZK proof systems with $\varepsilon_{\mathsf{c}} + \varepsilon_{\mathsf{s}} + \varepsilon_{\mathsf{zk}} \geq 1$ can be realized trivially[1], without any assumptions. Here $\varepsilon_{\mathsf{c}}, \varepsilon_{\mathsf{s}}$ and $\varepsilon_{\mathsf{zk}}$ denote the correctness, soundness and zero-knowledge errors of the proof system respectively. In this work, we will focus on *non-trivial* ZK proof systems with $\varepsilon_{\mathsf{c}} + \varepsilon_{\mathsf{s}} + \varepsilon_{\mathsf{zk}} < 1 - 1/p(|x|)$ for some polynomial $p(\cdot)$ in the input length $|x|$. We ask:

*Do non-trivial ZK proof systems imply the existence of OWFs?*

Non-trivial ZK proof systems may be a lot easier to construct than standard ZK: relaxing the negligible soundness or zero-knowledge error requirement can significantly lower the barriers to designing these protocols, potentially making them feasible even in settings where negligible-error notions are hard to build. But if we did manage to construct them, we would not know how to leverage them to build OWFs—leaving unresolved questions about whether such protocols could function as a stepping stone towards one-way functions, or if they are fundamentally weaker and cannot be used to construct basic cryptography.

*This Work.* Our main result is a complete characterization of the worst-case complexity of non-trivial constant round ZK.

**Theorem 1 (Informal).** *If* NP $\not\subseteq$ ioP/poly *and non-trivial public-coin, constant round (computational) ZK arguments for* NP *exist, then one-way functions exist.*

The above result requires the assumption that the underlying ZK argument is public-coin. We also obtain a result for private-coin protocols by showing that unless auxiliary-input one-way functions exist, we can convert any constant-round private-coin protocol into a public-coin one. Thus, non-trivial constant round ZK protocols yield auxiliary-input OWFs.

**Theorem 2 (Informal).** *If* NP $\not\subseteq$ ioP/poly *and non-trivial constant round (computational) ZK arguments for* NP *exist, then auxiliary-input one-way functions exist.*

[1] Observe that when $\varepsilon_{\mathsf{c}} + \varepsilon_{\mathsf{s}} + \varepsilon_{\mathsf{zk}} = 1$, one can have the CRS sample one of three protocols: have the verifier always reject, have the verifier always accept, or have the prover send the full witness in the clear and the verifier check it. If the CRS chooses the first with probability $\varepsilon_{\mathsf{c}}$, the second with probability $\varepsilon_{\mathsf{s}}$, and the third with probability $\varepsilon_{\mathsf{zk}}$, this trivial protocol will satisfy our requirements.

We also consider the special case of non-interactive zero-knowledge (NIZK) arguments for NP, where the prover sends a single proof string and both parties share a common reference string (CRS). We show that nontrivial NIZKs for NP, together with the assumption that NP $\not\subseteq$ ioP/poly, imply the existence of one-way functions.

**Theorem 3 (Informal).** *If* NP $\not\subseteq$ ioP/poly *and non-trivial (computational) NIZK arguments for* NP *exist, then one-way functions exist.*

This improves recent work [5] which obtained one-way functions from any NIZK with zero-knowledge error $\varepsilon_{\mathsf{zk}}$ and soundness error $\varepsilon_{\mathsf{s}}$ satisfying $\varepsilon_{\mathsf{zk}} + \varepsilon_{\mathsf{c}} + 2\sqrt{\varepsilon_{\mathsf{s}}} < 1 - \frac{1}{p(|x|)}$ for some polynomial $p(\cdot)$, or satisfying $\varepsilon_{\mathsf{zk}} + \sqrt{\varepsilon_{\mathsf{s}}} < 1$ in the case where $\varepsilon_{\mathsf{zk}}$ and $\varepsilon_{\mathsf{s}}$ are constants and $\varepsilon_{\mathsf{c}} = o(1)$. However, the regime where $\varepsilon_{\mathsf{zk}} + \varepsilon_{\mathsf{s}} < 1$ but $\varepsilon_{\mathsf{zk}} + \sqrt{\varepsilon_{\mathsf{s}}} \geq 1$ remained open until this work.

*Application: Amplifying* ZK. Arguably one of the most natural questions about non-trivial ZK proofs is whether they can be *amplified* to drive down their errors to negligible, and obtain "standard" ZK. For NIZKs, this question has been studied extensively recently, and such amplification has been shown to be possible under additional assumptions such as the existence of public-key encryption [7], and even just one-way functions [1,3].

Our theorem above can be viewed as eliminating the need to make any cryptographic assumptions when amplifying NIZK. In more detail, if NP is easy in the worst case then NIZKs for NP exist unconditionally, whereas if NP is hard in the worst case, then Informal Theorem 3 builds one-way functions from non-trivial NIZKs for NP. The resulting one-way functions can be used, together with weak NIZKs, to obtain standard NIZKs by relying on known amplification theorems in [1,3].

For technical reasons we will still need to make the extremely mild complexity-theoretic assumption that NP $\not\subseteq$ (ioP/poly) $\setminus$ BPP. In other words, if NP languages are efficiently decidable infinitely often with advice, then they are efficiently decidable on all input lengths. This is an extremely mild complexity assumption: it is implied by NP $\not\subseteq$ ioP/poly, which is already a mild worst case assumption.

**Corollary 1 (Informal).** *Suppose* NP $\not\subseteq$ (ioP/poly) $\setminus$ BPP. *Then non-trivial (computational) NIZK proofs imply standard NIZK proofs.*

Note that the corollary above applies only to NIZK proofs (with statistical soundness), since we currently do not have approaches to amplify arbitrary non-trivial NIZK arguments from assumptions weaker than public-key encryption.

A natural next question is whether similar amplification is possible for *interactive* ZK. Here, we note that one-way functions imply the existence of (private-coin) four-round ZK arguments [2], yielding the following informal Corollary.

**Corollary 2 (Informal).** *Suppose* NP $\not\subseteq$ (ioP/poly) $\setminus$ BPP. *Then non-trivial public-coin constant-round (computational) ZK arguments imply four-round (private-coin) ZK arguments.*

### 1.1 Concurrent Work

Concurrent to our work, [6] gave an alternative approach to building one-way functions from high-error zero-knowledge protocols. In the NIZK case, their results match ours exactly: assuming $\mathsf{NP} \not\subseteq \mathsf{ioP/poly}$, any non-trivial NIZK argument requires a one-way function. In the interactive case, their result is incomparable to ours: for a $k$-message public-coin protocol, they require the stronger guarantee that $\varepsilon_{\mathsf{c}} + \varepsilon_{\mathsf{s}} + (k-1)\varepsilon_{\mathsf{zk}} < 1 - \frac{1}{p(|x|)}$, but are able to work with an arbitrary (polynomial) $k$.[2]

## 2 Technical Overview

For simplicity throughout this overview, we will highlight our techniques assuming that the completeness error $\varepsilon_{\mathsf{c}} = 0$. Formally we work with the general case where $\varepsilon_{\mathsf{c}} \neq 0$, but this is a straightforward extension of the analysis described in this overview.

In the following two subsections, we recall techniques used in prior works [5,13] to show that zero-knowledge requires one-way functions, as well as barriers that prevent these techniques from working when $\varepsilon_{\mathsf{s}} + \varepsilon_{\mathsf{zk}} \approx 1$. These will build intuition towards our eventual approach. Readers that are already familiar with these works may skip ahead to our techniques described in Sect. 2.3.

We discuss prior ideas in the context of *non-interactive* zero-knowledge (NIZK), and then describe methods to close the gap in parameters in the non-interactive setting. However, we note that the more general interactive case requires the most significant new insights, discussed in Sect. 2.4.

### 2.1 Previous Techniques

[13] *Techniques.* The key tool used in [13] is Universal Extrapolation (UE): informally, UE lets us "reverse sample" the randomness that would generate a particular output of an efficient process. In more detail, given a polynomial-time sampler Samp and an output $y$ from its distribution, UE refers to the ability to efficiently and uniformly sample (up to small error) from the set of all inputs that Samp maps to $y$. UE is possible if and only if one-way functions do not exist [9].

Towards a contradiction, [13] assume the non-existence of one-way functions. Then using UE, they convert a NIZK $(\mathsf{Gen}, \mathsf{P}, \mathsf{V})$ and simulator Sim for a language $\mathcal{L}$ into an algorithm $\mathcal{A}$ that decides $\mathcal{L}$. In particular, $\mathcal{A}$ samples a *real* CRS from Gen, then uses UE to find a random string $r$ that would lead the *simulator* to output that same CRS. $\mathcal{A}$ then accepts if and only if V would accept the proof output by $\mathsf{Sim}(x; r)$.

[2] Note that we have rephrased this result slightly from how it appeared in [6] to be in terms of the number of *messages* instead of the number of *rounds* (i.e., pairs of messages). This is solely to avoid confusion, as in the rest of the paper we use the words message and round interchangeably.

To argue that $\mathcal{A}$ works, one has to show that it will accept $x \in \mathcal{L}$ with higher probability than it accepts $x \notin \mathcal{L}$. Consider each of these cases:

- If $x \notin \mathcal{L}$, $\mathcal{A}$ can only accept if it finds a proof *relative to a real CRS* that causes V to accept $x$. Soundness of the underlying NIZK will immediately tell us that this can happen with probability at most $\varepsilon_{\mathsf{s}}$.
- If $x \in \mathcal{L}$, note that by completeness V will accept a real CRS and proof with probability 1 and so by zero-knowledge will accept a simulated CRS and proof with probability at least $1 - \varepsilon_{\mathsf{zk}}$.
  Now consider an algorithm $\mathcal{B}$ that is *almost* identical to $\mathcal{A}$, except that it starts by sampling a CRS from Sim instead of from Gen. We note first that this is (up to the small statistical error of the UE) identically distributed to simply running V on a simulated CRS and proof, so by the above $\mathcal{B}$ accepts $x \in \mathcal{L}$ with probability at least $1 - \varepsilon_{\mathsf{zk}}$. But note that since the only difference between $\mathcal{A}$ and $\mathcal{B}$ is in the original sampling of the CRS, and so by zero-knowledge their outputs must be $\varepsilon_{\mathsf{zk}}$-close. Thus, $\mathcal{A}$ accepts $x \in \mathcal{L}$ with probability at least $1 - 2\varepsilon_{\mathsf{zk}}$.

Thus, $\mathcal{A}$ is a correct algorithm for $\mathcal{L}$ as long as $1 - 2\varepsilon_{\mathsf{zk}}$ is noticeably larger than $\varepsilon_{\mathsf{s}}$, which is equivalent to requiring that $\varepsilon_{\mathsf{s}} + 2\varepsilon_{\mathsf{zk}}$ is noticeably smaller than 1. Since one can implement $\mathcal{A}$ as long as one-way functions *don't* exist, this means that a NIZK for a hard language with $\varepsilon_{\mathsf{s}} + 2\varepsilon_{\mathsf{zk}} < 1$ *requires* the existence of a one-way function.

Note that in the analysis above, we first uses the zero-knowledge property to bound the difference between real and simulated proofs (costing one $\varepsilon_{\mathsf{zk}}$) and then again bound the difference between real and simulated crs (costing another $\varepsilon_{\mathsf{zk}}$). It is natural to wonder whether there may be a better way to analyze the same algorithm and show that $\mathcal{A}$ decides $\mathcal{L}$ whenever we have arbitrary *non-trivial NIZKs*, but in the following subsection (Sect. 2.2) we provide an explicit counterexample.

*Techniques in CHK* [5]. The improvement in [5] stems from the observation that one of the $\varepsilon_{\mathsf{zk}}$ errors occurs specifically when the analysis transitions the crs (and not the proof itself) from real to simulated. They then add a "CRS check" to the deciding algorithm $\mathcal{A}$ described above, which roughly predicts whether a CRS was sampled from the real or simulated distribution. This requires the use of Universal Approximation (UA), which intuitively allows one to approximate the probability of a given output coming from a given randomized process. Similar to the case of UE, [10] showed that UA is possible exactly when one-way functions don't exist[3].

In particular, [5] modifies the algorithm $\mathcal{A}$ above by adding a step that estimates the probability that the CRS it samples came from Gen or from Sim, and immediately rejects if the latter is at least $\frac{1}{\sqrt{\varepsilon_{\mathsf{s}}}}$ times larger than the former[4]. As

[3] [5] technically uses a stronger notion of UA than the one considered in [10], but for our purposes we will ignore this subtlety.

[4] In fact, [5] uses a slightly different algorithm in that they directly sample both the CRS and proof from Sim. However, the algorithm we describe here does appear as

in [13], one now has to show that the modified $\mathcal{A}$ accepts $x \in \mathcal{L}$ more often than $x \notin \mathcal{L}$.

- If $x \notin \mathcal{L}$, the above modification can only make $\mathcal{A}$ less likely to accept, so the acceptance probability is still upper-bounded by $\varepsilon_{\mathsf{s}}$.
- If $x \in \mathcal{L}$, all the hybrids considered above have to be modified to also include the CRS checking step. It is possible to show that a real CRS fails the check with probability at most $\sqrt{\varepsilon_{\mathsf{s}}}$ (ignoring a small error term from the UA), and thus a real CRS and proof will be accepted *and* pass the CRS check with probability at least $1 - \sqrt{\varepsilon_{\mathsf{s}}}$. Thus, by zero-knowledge a *simulated* CRS and proof must pass both checks with probability at least $1 - \sqrt{\varepsilon_{\mathsf{s}}} - \varepsilon_{\mathsf{zk}}$.
  The key step in the [5] analysis comes when considering $\mathcal{B}$, which as before is equivalent to $\mathcal{A}$ except that it starts with a simulated CRS. As in the prior analysis, this is identically distributed (up to the small statistical error of the UE) to sampling the CRS and proof from Sim directly, and so will accept $x \in \mathcal{L}$ with probability at least $1 - \sqrt{\varepsilon_{\mathsf{s}}} - \varepsilon_{\mathsf{zk}}$. However, instead of paying an *additive* $\varepsilon_{\mathsf{zk}}$ loss in acceptance probability between $\mathcal{B}$ and $\mathcal{A}$, [5] notes that one can instead pay a *multiplicative* $\sqrt{\varepsilon_{\mathsf{s}}}$ loss. Indeed, any CRS that is at most $\frac{1}{\sqrt{\varepsilon_{\mathsf{s}}}}$ times more likely to come from Sim as from Gen can "contribute" at most $\frac{1}{\sqrt{\varepsilon_{\mathsf{s}}}}$ times more the the acceptance probability of $\mathcal{B}$ as it does to $\mathcal{A}$; all other CRS are rejected by the checking step, and so "contribute" nothing in either algorithm. Thus, $\mathcal{A}$ accepts $x \in \mathcal{L}$ with probability at least $\sqrt{\varepsilon_{\mathsf{s}}}$ times the acceptance probability of $\mathcal{B}$, which gives a final bound of $\sqrt{\varepsilon_{\mathsf{s}}}\left(1 - \sqrt{\varepsilon_{\mathsf{s}}} - \varepsilon_{\mathsf{zk}}\right)$.

This means that $\mathcal{A}$ is a correct algorithm for $\mathcal{L}$ as long as $\sqrt{\varepsilon_{\mathsf{s}}}\left(1 - \sqrt{\varepsilon_{\mathsf{s}}} - \varepsilon_{\mathsf{zk}}\right)$ is noticeably larger than $\varepsilon_{\mathsf{s}}$; rearranging terms, this requires that $\varepsilon_{\mathsf{zk}} + 2\sqrt{\varepsilon_{\mathsf{s}}}$ is noticeably smaller than 1. As before, this says that a NIZK for a hard language with $\varepsilon_{\mathsf{zk}} + 2\sqrt{\varepsilon_{\mathsf{s}}} < 1$ must imply the existence of a one-way function.

### 2.2 Barriers to Improvement

We would ideally like a result that works for *any* non-trivial NIZK, meaning it should only need to assume that $\varepsilon_{\mathsf{s}} + \varepsilon_{\mathsf{zk}} < 1$. One might hope that a tighter analysis of the hybrids in [13] or [5] could achieve such a result, but this turns out to be impossible: there exists a (contrived) protocol with $\varepsilon_{\mathsf{s}} + \varepsilon_{\mathsf{zk}} < 1$ for which neither algorithm $\mathcal{A}$ described above give advantage in distinguishing $x \in \mathcal{L}$ from $x \notin \mathcal{L}$!

In particular, consider some language $\mathcal{L} \in \mathsf{P}$[5] and define a NIZK for $\mathcal{L}$ with errors $(\varepsilon_{\mathsf{s}}, \varepsilon_{\mathsf{zk}})$ as follows:

---

a hybrid in their analysis, and nothing in their techniques fundamentally changes if you treat that hybrid as the final algorithm for $\mathcal{L}$.

[5] Note that while this language is by definition easy, that doesn't matter for the purposes of our counterexample; we are simply trying to show that *the particular algorithm* $\mathcal{A}$ doesn't decide $\mathcal{L}$.

- Gen : Output

$$\mathsf{crs} = \begin{cases} 0 & \text{w.p. } 1 - \varepsilon_{\mathsf{zk}}, \\ 1 & \text{w.p. } \varepsilon_{\mathsf{zk}}. \end{cases}$$

- P(crs) outputs as proof a bit $\pi = \mathsf{crs}$.
- V decides $x$ on its own and if $x \in \mathcal{L}$, V outputs

$$\mathsf{V}(\mathsf{crs}, \pi, x) = \begin{cases} 1 & \text{if } \pi = \mathsf{crs}, \\ 0 & \text{if } \pi \neq \mathsf{crs}. \end{cases}$$

  If $x \notin \mathcal{L}$, V outputs

$$\mathsf{V}(\mathsf{crs}, \pi, x) = \begin{cases} 1 & \text{w.p. } \varepsilon_{\mathsf{s}}, \\ 0 & \text{w.p. } 1 - \varepsilon_{\mathsf{s}}. \end{cases}$$

- Sim($x$) outputs

$$(\mathsf{crs}, \pi) = \begin{cases} 00 & \text{w.p. } 1 - \varepsilon_{\mathsf{zk}}, \\ 01 & \text{w.p. } \varepsilon_{\mathsf{zk}}. \end{cases}$$

One can easily verify that the soundness error is exactly $\varepsilon_{\mathsf{s}}$ and the zero-knowledge error is exactly $\varepsilon_{\mathsf{zk}}$ by construction.

But now consider the behavior of the algorithm $\mathcal{A}$ from [13] if instantiated with this NIZK (assuming, for simplicity, that the UE has no errors):

- If $x \notin \mathcal{L}$, V will accept with probability $\varepsilon_{\mathsf{s}}$ regardless of what CRS and proof it is given, so $\mathcal{A}$ will accept with the same probability.
- If $x \in \mathcal{L}$, note that $\mathcal{A}$ can never sample the proof to be 1 if the CRS is 1, since Sim never outputs 11.[6] Thus, the only way for $\mathcal{A}$ to accept is if it samples the CRS as 0 (which happens with probability $1 - \varepsilon_{\mathsf{zk}}$ from Gen) and the proof as 0 (which happens with probability $(1 - \varepsilon_{\mathsf{zk}})$ from Sim conditioned on the CRS being 0). Thus, $\mathcal{A}$ will only accept $x \in \mathcal{L}$ with probability $(1 - \varepsilon_{\mathsf{zk}})^2$.

Thus, at a minimum, we need to assume that $(1-\varepsilon_{\mathsf{zk}})^2$ is noticeably larger than $\varepsilon_{\mathsf{s}}$ in order for the [13] algorithm to have any chance of working. This rules out the possibility of a better analysis of the same algorithm giving us the optimal result[7].

Additionally, the same counterexample also rules out the possibility of getting a tight result from the modified decision algorithm $\mathcal{A}$ in [5]. Indeed, if the

[6] Technically, Sim can never output a CRS of 1, and so the behavior of $\mathcal{A}$ if it samples 1 from Gen is undefined. Informally, we can say that if the distribution of Sim is undefined, $\mathcal{A}$ simply fails. Alternatively, we can fix this formally by having Sim output 10 with some tiny probability $\delta$, where we set $\delta$ to be small enough to not affect our analysis meaningfully.

[7] As an explicit example, the parameter setting of $\varepsilon_{\mathsf{zk}} = 0.5$ and $\varepsilon_{\mathsf{s}} = 0.25$ is non-trivial, but the [13] algorithm would accept $x$ with probability 0.25 regardless of if $x \in \mathcal{L}$ or not.

parameters are set such that the $\mathsf{CRS}$ check rejects when the $\mathsf{CRS}$ is 0, $\mathcal{A}$ will *never* accept $x \in \mathcal{L}$. If instead the $\mathsf{CRS}$ check accepts when the $\mathsf{CRS}$ is 0, then it accepts *every* $\mathsf{CRS}$[8], and thus (for this particular $\mathsf{NIZK}$) the algorithm from [5] is functionally equivalent to that from [13]!

### 2.3 Repetition to the Rescue

In order to improve on prior techniques, it will help to first understand *why* the above counterexample is bad for them. We note that the counterexample hinges on the fact that on $\mathsf{crs} = 0$ the simulator always has the *ability* to output a $\mathsf{Good}$ proof (i.e. 0), but still chooses to output a $\mathsf{Bad}$ proof (i.e. 1) some of the time. Here by $\mathsf{Good}$ we mean a proof that is statistically close to a real proof, and by $\mathsf{Bad}$ we mean a proof that is far from a real proof. This causes the distribution used by $\mathcal{A}$ to have $2\varepsilon_{\mathsf{zk}}$ error (once due to the distance between the real and simulated $\mathsf{CRS}$ and once due to the distance between the real and simulated proofs *conditioned on* a particular $\mathsf{CRS}$), while still keeping the real and simulated ($\mathsf{CRS}$, proof) distributions $\varepsilon_{\mathsf{zk}}$-close overall.

It turns out that this type of simulator behavior is the *only* reason prior techniques don't work with protocols where $\varepsilon_{\mathsf{s}} + \varepsilon_{\mathsf{zk}} \approx 1$. In particular, for every fixing of $x \in \mathcal{L}$, if every $\mathsf{CRS}$ was either $\mathsf{Good}$ (i.e., the simulator conditioned on this $\mathsf{CRS}$ *always* outputs an accepting proof for $x$) or $\mathsf{Bad}$ (i.e., the simulator conditioned on this $\mathsf{CRS}$ *never* outputs an accepting proof for $x$), then the algorithm $\mathcal{A}$ from [13] *will work* only assuming that $\varepsilon_{\mathsf{s}} + \varepsilon_{\mathsf{zk}} < 1$! This is because on any $\mathsf{Bad}$ $\mathsf{CRS}$ output by $\mathsf{Gen}$, the real prover is guaranteed to output an accepting proof whereas the simulator never does. This allows us to infer that $\mathsf{Gen}$ must output a $\mathsf{Good}$ $\mathsf{CRS}$ with probability at least $1 - \varepsilon_{\mathsf{zk}}$, and thus $\mathcal{A}$ will accept $x \in \mathcal{L}$ with the same probability.

Of course, we cannot in general assume that the simulator always works on certain CRSes and always fails on others. However, we can achieve a similar effect by sampling *many* simulated proofs for the same $\mathsf{CRS}$ and checking whether *at least one* accepts.[9] In particular, this allows us to consider a $\mathsf{CRS}$ to be $\mathsf{Good}$ as long as the simulator conditioned on this $\mathsf{CRS}$ outputs an accepting proof for $x$ with "not too small" probability, which means that our sampling will see *at least one* accepting proof with overwhelming probability. At the same time, we can still argue that we can't see a $\mathsf{BadCRS}$ too often, as the real prover will output an accepting proof for such a $\mathsf{CRS}$, whereas the simulator "almost never" will.

In more detail, we fix an appropriate polynomial $p(\cdot)$ and consider a modified algorithm $\mathcal{A}'$ that repeats the [13] algorithm $p(|x|)$ times (all with respect to the same $\mathsf{CRS}$, but reverse sampling fresh randomness each time) and accepts if *any* of the repetitions give an accepting proof.

[8] Note that $\mathsf{Sim}$ outputs the $\mathsf{CRS}$ as 1 with probability *smaller* than $\mathsf{Gen}$ does, so the $\mathsf{CRS}$ check can never reject this.

[9] We note that [14] use a similar idea, where they categorize the $\mathsf{crs}$ according to whether there *exists* an accepting proof relative to it. However, their analysis is limited to the negligible-error setting and doesn't seem to naturally generalize to the interactive setting.

- For $x \notin \mathcal{L}$, $\mathcal{A}'$ still needs to find an accepting proof relative to a real CRS in order to accept. Since repeatedly running the [13] algorithm is a valid strategy to break soundness of the NIZK, we have that the probability that even one of the proofs accept is at most $\varepsilon_{\mathsf{s}}$.
- For $x \in \mathcal{L}$, we call a CRS Good if Sim conditioned on outputting CRS gives an accepting proof for $x$ with probability $\geq \frac{|x|}{p(|x|)}$ and Bad otherwise. Very roughly, as long as $p(|x|)$ is large enough, we can as above argue that Gen can only output a Bad CRS with probability (approximately) $\varepsilon_{\mathsf{zk}}$, since doing so contributes directly to the zero-knowledge error of the NIZK[10]. And if Gen outputs a Good CRS, $\mathcal{A}'$ will find an accepting proof for $x$ with overwhelming probability. Thus, up to small errors, $\mathcal{A}'$ will accept $x \in \mathcal{L}$ with probability at least $1 - \varepsilon_{\mathsf{zk}}$.

As in prior analysis, we just need the probability that $\mathcal{A}'$ accepts $x \in \mathcal{L}$ to be noticeably larger than the probability it accepts $x \notin \mathcal{L}$. Rearranging terms, this only requires that $\varepsilon_{\mathsf{s}} + \varepsilon_{\mathsf{zk}}$ be noticeably smaller than 1—meaning we can work with *any* non-trivial NIZK!

We have swept some technical details under the rug, but the above ideas coarsely suffice to obtain OWFs from non-trivial NIZKs. In the following section, we discuss barriers and methods to extend these ideas to the interactive setting.

### 2.4 Generalizing to Interactive Zero Knowledge

As discussed in the introduction, our primary goal is to obtain an implication from non-trivial *honest-verifier* ZK to OWFs, since this gives us the strongest possible theorem statement. First, we note that techniques from [13] naturally extend to the interactive case, but get further from the desired result as the number of rounds increases: to get a one-way function from a $k$ round protocol, they require $\varepsilon_{\mathsf{s}} + k\varepsilon_{\mathsf{zk}} < 1$. Similarly, simple extensions of the [5] techniques require $(\varepsilon_{\mathsf{s}})^{1/k} + \varepsilon_{\mathsf{zk}} < 1$.

A natural goal is therefore to see if we can extend the techniques that gave us a tight result for NIZKs to the interactive setting, and more specifically, eliminate the dependence on $k$ in the above constraints.

In order to generalize our techniques to the interactive setting, it will help to take a slightly different view of our proof in the non-interactive case. We can treat our algorithm $\mathcal{A}$ as defining a malicious prover $\widetilde{\mathsf{P}}$, then simulating a run of $\widetilde{\mathsf{P}}$ and V to decide whether to accept $x$. In the analysis above, we treated $\widetilde{\mathsf{P}}$ as

[10] Specifically, note that Sim will almost never output a Bad CRS with an accepting proof, since by definition the probability Sim's proof is accepting conditioned on the CRS being bad is at most $\frac{1}{p(|x|)}$. Since we are assuming perfect completeness however, P will always output an accepting proof, even when the CRS from Gen is Bad. Thus, if Gen outputs a Bad CRS with probability much higher than $\varepsilon_{\mathsf{zk}}$, we can break zero-knowledge with a distinguisher that checks if the CRS is Bad but the proof is still accepting. Here, note that we can (probably approximately) estimate whether a CRS is Good or Bad *efficiently* by using UE to sample many possible simulated proofs relative to it, and checking what fraction of them are accepting.

using UE to sample many possible simulated proof strings, and outputting an accepting one if found. But note that we equally well could phrase $\widetilde{\mathsf{P}}$ as choosing whichever sampled proof string has the maximum probability of being accepted. Phrased this way, we can now begin to extend this idea to the interactive case.

*An Inefficient Prover.* We would like to define a malicious prover $\widetilde{\mathsf{P}}$ such that our algorithm $\mathcal{A}$ to decide $\mathcal{L}$ can simply simulate an interaction between $\widetilde{\mathsf{P}}$ and $\mathsf{V}$ on $x$ and output the result. Unlike the non-interactive case, $\widetilde{\mathsf{P}}$ can't immediately check if the message it is considering would lead to $\mathsf{V}$ accepting or rejecting, since this decision may depend on randomness sampled at a later point in the protocol. Thus, all we can hope for is to have $\widetilde{\mathsf{P}}$ choose the "best" message available to it, which means choosing the message that maximizes the probability that $\mathsf{V}$ accepts *if we continue to apply the prover strategy $\widetilde{P}$ in future rounds.* For now, we will assume that $\widetilde{P}$ can (inefficiently) find such messages, and we will later see how to make $\widetilde{P}$ efficient.

More formally, suppose for simplicity that we are starting from a protocol that satisfies statistical soundness and zero-knowledge. We can (recursively) define $\widetilde{\mathsf{P}}$ that, given $x$ and a partial transcript $\tau$, considers all possible next messages $m$ in the support of $\mathsf{Sim}$ and outputs whichever one maximizes the probability of $\mathsf{V}$ accepting $x$ if it interacts with $\widetilde{\mathsf{P}}$ starting from transcript $\tau \| m$. Here, defining this success probability based *only* on the transcript and not on $\mathsf{V}$'s internal state limits us to only working with public-coin protocols.

Let $\mathcal{A}(x)$ be the algorithm that runs $\widetilde{\mathsf{P}}$ and $\mathsf{V}$ on input $x$ and outputs $\mathsf{V}$'s decision bit; we can now argue that $\mathcal{A}$ correctly decides $\mathcal{L}$.

- If $x \notin \mathcal{L}$, statistical soundness tells us that no prover can convince $\mathsf{V}$ with probability greater than $\varepsilon_{\mathsf{s}}$, and so in particular $\widetilde{\mathsf{P}}$ cannot. Thus, $\mathcal{A}(x)$ will accept with probability at most $\varepsilon_{\mathsf{s}}$.
- If $x \in \mathcal{L}$, we can argue that $\widetilde{\mathsf{P}}$ performs "almost as well as" the honest prover $\mathsf{P}$. In particular, we note that since $\widetilde{\mathsf{P}}$ always chooses the best possible message in the support of $\mathsf{Sim}$, the only way for $\mathsf{P}$ to choose a better message is if it sends a message that $\mathsf{Sim}$ never would. But from statistical zero-knowledge, we know that this can happen with probability at most $\varepsilon_{\mathsf{zk}}$![11] Thus, the probability that $\widetilde{\mathsf{P}}$ convinces $\mathsf{V}$ is at least $(1 - \varepsilon_{\mathsf{zk}})$, which tells us that $\mathcal{A}$ accepts with probability at least $(1 - \varepsilon_{\mathsf{zk}})$.

As in the $\mathsf{NIZK}$ case, this immediately gives us an algorithm for $\mathcal{L}$ as long as $\varepsilon_{\mathsf{s}} + \varepsilon_{\mathsf{zk}}$ is noticeably smaller than 1.

*Making $\widetilde{\mathsf{P}}$ Efficient.* So far, we required $\widetilde{\mathsf{P}}$ to find the *best* possible next prover message in the support of $\mathsf{Sim}$, which may not be efficient to compute. This inefficiency meant that our eventual decision algorithm $\mathcal{A}$ is inefficient, which is a problem. To fix these issues, we need to modify how we define $\widetilde{\mathsf{P}}$ so that it

[11] Importantly, we are applying zero-knowledge *globally* to the entire transcript instead of on a message-by-message basis. This is the key reason why we avoid the $O(k)\varepsilon_{\mathsf{zk}}$ term in the analysis from [13].

has a polynomial run time, but still works well enough to argue that $\mathcal{A}(x)$ will accept with good probability when $x \in \mathcal{L}$.

Taking inspiration from the NIZK case, we can have $\widetilde{\mathsf{P}}$ use UE to sample many possible next messages from Sim, and simply choose the best message *among those it sampled.* While this won't guarantee that we get the best *possible* next message, it does guarantee that (with overwhelming probability) we get a message that is "one of the best". In particular, suppose we order all the messages in the support of Sim by the probability that $\widetilde{\mathsf{P}}$ will convince V if it chooses that message next. For any $\delta$, if we have $\widetilde{\mathsf{P}}$ sample $\frac{n}{\delta}$ many possible next messages, it will sample at least one in the top $\delta$ fraction of this order with overwhelming probability.

There is however one catch to this strategy that only arises in the interactive case: in order to choose the best message among those sampled, $\widetilde{\mathsf{P}}$ has to be able to compute the probability that each message will lead to it convincing V. Note though that as long as V is public coin (and so stateless), $\widetilde{\mathsf{P}}$ can get a very good estimate of this probability, as $\widetilde{\mathsf{P}}$ can simulate an interaction between itself and V "in its own head". A Chernoff bound says that $\widetilde{\mathsf{P}}$ only needs to run $\mathrm{poly}(n, \frac{1}{\delta})$ such simulations in order to (with overwhelming probability) estimate its success probability to within an additive $\delta$ factor for any $\delta$. Note, however, that since $\widetilde{\mathsf{P}}$ has to simulate itself a polynomial number of times on a transcript that is only one message longer, its run time will grow by a *multiplicative* factor of $\mathrm{poly}(n)$ for each round. This will give us a final run time of $\mathrm{poly}(n)^k$, which constrains us to only work with protocols where $k$ is a constant.

Putting this all together, we get an *efficient* $\widetilde{\mathsf{P}}$ that with overwhelming probability chooses a next message that has success probability at most $2\delta$ smaller than some message in the top $\delta$ fraction of messages in the support of Sim. We claim that as long as $\delta$ is set to a sufficiently small inverse polynomial, our prior analysis is robust enough to work with these weaker guarantees on $\widetilde{\mathsf{P}}$.

In more detail, note that all we have to change in the above analysis is the argument that P can't pick a "better" message than $\widetilde{\mathsf{P}}$ too commonly. Since our weaker guarantee on $\widetilde{\mathsf{P}}$ is that it picks a message (approximately) in the top $\delta$ fraction of possible messages from the support of Sim, we just have to bound the probability that P picks a message that is better than a $(1-\delta)$ fraction of the support of Sim.

By a union bound over each round, the probability that Sim ever outputs such a message is at most $\delta k$, so by (statistical) zero-knowledge, the probability that a real transcript contains such a message is at most $\varepsilon_{\mathsf{zk}} + \delta k$. By our guarantees on $\widetilde{\mathsf{P}}$, we know that it loses at most $2\delta$ success probability in each round compared to P conditioned on not picking such a "too good" message. Thus, since P will always convince V to accept $x \in \mathcal{L}$, we have that $\widetilde{\mathsf{P}}$ convinces V with probability at least $1 - \varepsilon_{\mathsf{zk}} - 3\delta k$.

Finally, in order for $\mathcal{A}$ to be correct, we will need $\varepsilon_{\mathsf{s}}$ to be noticeably smaller than $1 - \varepsilon_{\mathsf{zk}} - 3\delta k$. As long as $\varepsilon_{\mathsf{s}} + \varepsilon_{\mathsf{zk}}$ is noticeably smaller than 1, we can pick an appropriate inverse-polynomial $\delta$ that makes this happen.

**Working with Computational Zero-Knowledge.** Up until this point, we've been applying zero-knowledge with respect to a distinguisher $\mathcal{D}$ that *perfectly* answers questions about the support of $\mathsf{Sim}$—in particular, one that checks if a given prover message better than the bottom $(1-\delta)$ fraction of the support of $\mathsf{Sim}$. Here recall that a message $a$ is better than $b$ if the probability that $\widetilde{P}$ convinces $\mathsf{V}$ is higher if $\widetilde{P}$ chooses $a$ in its next round, compared with $b$.

If we want to work with protocols that only have computational zero-knowledge, we need to come up with an efficient distinguisher that still works well enough for our proof.

Our efficient distinguisher will try to *approximate* the fraction of messages from $\mathsf{Sim}$ that a given message is better than. To do this, it will sample a large number of possible next messages from the support of $\mathsf{Sim}$ and compare them to the given message. Formally, it will sample $\text{poly}(n, \frac{1}{\delta})$ such messages, and check if at most a $2\delta$ fraction of them are better than the given prover message. By a Chernoff bound, we have that if the given prover message is in fact better than a $(1-\delta)$ fraction of all possible messages in the support of $\mathsf{Sim}$, this check will pass with overwhelming probability.

As in the previous section, we note that while we may not be able to compute the *exact* success probability efficiently, the same estimation procedure can with overwhelming probability get us within an additive factor of $\delta$ for any inverse-polynomial $\delta$. Thus, except with negligible probability, we know that our distinguisher will say "real" if *any* prover message in its input transcript is at least $2\delta$ better than the bottom $(1-\delta)$ fraction of messages in the support of $\mathsf{Sim}$.

By a careful analysis, we can show that this efficient distinguisher still works for the analysis in the previous section. Indeed, there are only two points where we had to use properties of the distinguisher: first to argue that it rarely outputs "real" on a simulated transcript, and second to argue that $\widetilde{\mathsf{P}}$ does "almost as well" as $\mathsf{P}$ conditioned on the distinguisher saying "simulated".

- For the former case, we claim that the efficient distinguisher says "real" on a transcript from $\mathsf{Sim}$ with probability at most $2\delta k$. For any given round, we know that the prover message in the transcript was generated by $\mathsf{Sim}$, and hence comes from the same distribution as the messages the distinguisher samples. Thus, the probability that the message in the transcript is in the top $2\delta$ fraction of the sampled messages is just $2\delta$, regardless of what procedure we use to compare them.
- For the latter case, we note that the only change between this section and the last is that the efficient distinguisher may allow $\mathsf{P}$ to have messages that have up to $2\delta$ higher success probability than the bottom $(1-\delta)$ fraction of messages in the support of $\mathsf{Sim}$. Since in the last section we already allowed $\widetilde{\mathsf{P}}$ to output messages that have up to $2\delta$ *lower* probability than the top $\delta$ fraction of messages, we essentially are just doubling the error from there.

In both cases, we see that setting $\delta$ to be half as large as the setting of $\delta$ in the previous section suffices to make the same analysis go through.

**Working with Private Coins.** The above proof critically relies on the zero-knowledge protocol we start with being public-coin so that we can efficiently simulate V starting from an arbitrary transcript and thus estimate the probability of it accepting. However, we note that at least intuitively, we shouldn't have to make this assumption: if V is able to computationally hide information about its randomness in a private-coin protocol, intuitively the map from V's randomness to its messages is a one-way function.

We formalize this intuition in the full version of the paper, showing that either infinitely-often auxiliary-input uniform-secure OWFs exist or every constant-round private-coin protocol can be converted into an equivalent public-coin protocol.

We note that, unlike in the case of public-coin protocols, we obtain *auxiliary-input* one-way functions. This is because in our transformation, in order to achieve soundness the verifier has to resample its randomness such that it is consistent with the full transcript. Since the verifier does not have access to the malicious prover's code, there does not immediately seem to be a way to construct an efficient sampler such that UE on that sampler will allow us to do this. We get past this by allowing the sampler to take the transcript as auxiliary input, but this limits our result to achieving auxiliary-input one-way functions. Since this auxiliary input comes from the prover messages and not from the worst-case instance, switching to average-case hardness does not seem to improve the situation. Nonetheless, our results rule out information-theoretic constructions of (constant-round) non-trivial ZK even in the private-coin setting.

# 3 Preliminaries

We use the following notation:

- $[n]$ represents the set $\{1, 2, \ldots, n\}$ and $[n]_0$ represents the set $\{0, 1, \ldots, n\}$.
- We call a function $\mu$ negligible if it is smaller than any inverse polynomial, that is if for every polynomial $p$ there exists an $n_0 \in \mathbb{N}$ such that for all $n \geq n_0$, $\mu(n) < \frac{1}{p(n)}$. We let negl denote an unspecified negligible function.
- We call a function $\mu$ noticeable if it is asymptotically larger than some inverse polynomial, that is if there exists a polynomial $p$ and $n_0 \in \mathbb{N}$ such that for all $n \geq n_0$, $\mu(n) \geq \frac{1}{p(n)}$.
- $a <_n b$ represents that $a$ is noticeably less than $b$, that is that there exists a polynomial $p$ and $n_0 \in \mathbb{N}$ such that for all $n \geq n_0$, $a(n) < b(n) - \frac{1}{p(n)}$.

In this paper, our protocols will have (honest) participants that can be described as uniform Turing machines, whereas adversaries will (w.l.o.g.) be non-uniform Turing Machines, or equivalently, families of polynomial-sized circuits.

## 3.1 One-Way Functions

**Definition 1 (One-way Functions).** *Fix an alphabet $\Sigma$. We say that a family of functions $\{f_x\}_{x \in \Sigma^*}$ with $f_x : \{0,1\}^{m_i(|x|)} \to \{0,1\}^{m_o(|x|)}$ is one-way if*

- *[**Efficiency**] There exists a Turing machine $M$ and polynomial $p$ such that for all $x \in \Sigma^*$ and $r \in \{0,1\}^{m_i(|x|)}$, $M(x,r)$ outputs $f_x(r)$ in time at most $p(|x|)$*
- *[**One-Wayness**] For all non-uniform PPT machines $\mathcal{A}$, all polynomials $p$, and all sufficiently large $n$, there exists an $x \in \Sigma^n$ with*

$$\Pr[f_x(\mathcal{A}(x, f_x(r))) = f_x(r) | r \xleftarrow{\$} \{0,1\}^{m_i(|x|)}] \leq \frac{1}{p(n)}$$

**Definition 2 (Weak One-way Functions).** *Fix an alphabet $\Sigma$. We say that a family of functions $\{f_x\}_{x \in \Sigma^*}$ with $f_x : \{0,1\}^{m_i(|x|)} \to \{0,1\}^{m_o(|x|)}$ is weakly one-way if*

- *[**Efficiency**] There exists a Turing machine $M$ and polynomial $p$ such that for all $x \in \Sigma^*$ and $r \in \{0,1\}^{m_i(|x|)}$, $M(x,r)$ outputs $f_x(r)$ in time at most $p(|x|)$*
- *[**Weak One-Wayness**] For all non-uniform PPT machines $\mathcal{A}$ there exists a polynomial $p$ such that for sufficiently large $n$ there exists an $x \in \Sigma^n$ with*

$$\Pr[f_x(\mathcal{A}(x, f_x(r))) = f_x(r) | r \xleftarrow{\$} \{0,1\}^{m_i(|x|)}] \leq 1 - \frac{1}{p(n)}$$

*Remark 1.* A few remarks about these definitions are in order:

- The definition above can be used to define both (standard) one-way functions, and one-way functions with auxiliary input. If we take $\Sigma = \{0,1\}$, these definitions correspond to (weak) one-way functions with auxiliary inputs; if we take $\Sigma = \{1\}$, these definitions correspond to (weak) one-way functions with no auxiliary input. In this paper, if we refer to an "auxiliary input (weak) one-way function", we mean one with respect to $\Sigma = \{0,1\}$; if we don't otherwise specify $\Sigma$, we default to $\Sigma = \{1\}$. A similar remark applies to all our definitions that make reference to $\Sigma$.
- Since we require that $M$ is computable in time polynomial in $|x|$ (as opposed to in the size of its full input), we can assume WLOG that $m_i$ and $m_o$ are polynomially-bounded functions.

While weak one-way functions may at first seem much weaker than one-way functions, the two notions are existentially equivalent.

**Theorem 4** ([15]). *Fix an alphabet $\Sigma$. One-way functions exist with respect to $\Sigma$ if and only if weak one-way functions do.*

### 3.2 Universal Extrapolation

**Definition 3 (Sampler).** *Fix an alphabet $\Sigma$. We say that a probabilistic polynomial time machine $M$ is a sampler from $m_i$ input bits to $m_o$ output bits if for all $x \in \Sigma^*$, $M(x)$ uses at most $m_i(|x|)$ bits of randomness and for all $r \in \{0,1\}^{m_i(|x|)}$, $M(x;r) \in \{0,1\}^{m_o(|x|)}$.*

*Remark 2* Note that $m_i$ and $m_o$ can WLOG be bounded by the run time of $M$; since $M$ runs in time polynomial in $|x|$, we can freely assume that $m_i$ and $m_o$ are polynomially-bounded functions of $n$.

**Definition 4 (Infinitely-Often Universal Extrapolation).** *Fix an alphabet $\Sigma$. We say that Infinitely-Often Universal Extrapolation (io-UE) is possible if for every sampler $M$ from $m_i$ input bits to $m_o$ output bits and all polynomials $p$, there exists a non-uniform PPT machine $N$ such that for infinitely many $n$, the following two distributions are $\frac{1}{p(n)}$-close in statistical distance for every $x \in \Sigma^n$:*

1. *Sample $r \xleftarrow{\$} \{0,1\}^{m_i(n)}$ and output $r \| M(x;r)$*
2. *Sample $r \xleftarrow{\$} \{0,1\}^{m_i(n)}$ and output $N(x, M(x;r)) \| M(x;r)$*

**Theorem 5 ([9]).** *Fix an alphabet $\Sigma$. io-UE is possible with respect to $\Sigma$ if and only if one-way functions do* not *exist with respect to $\Sigma$.*

### 3.3 Zero-Knowledge

**Definition 5 ($(\varepsilon_c, \varepsilon_s, \varepsilon_{zk})$-ZK).** *An $(\varepsilon_c, \varepsilon_s, \varepsilon_{zk})$-ZK argument for an* NP *relation $\mathcal{R}$ is a pair of uniform PPT interactive algorithms* $(\mathsf{P}, \mathsf{V})$ *such that*

- ***Syntax***
  - $\mathsf{P}$ *is given input $(x, w)$ and* $\mathsf{V}$ *is given input $x$.*
  - $\mathsf{P}$ *and* $\mathsf{V}$ *interact over the course of $k$ rounds, creating a transcript $\tau$.*
  - *After the interaction,* $\mathsf{V}$ *outputs a single bit. We let $\langle \mathsf{P}(w), \mathsf{V}\rangle(x)$ denote this output.*
- ***Completeness:*** *For every $(x, w) \in \mathcal{R}$,*

$$\Pr[\langle \mathsf{P}(w), \mathsf{V}\rangle(x) = 1] \geq 1 - \varepsilon_c(|x|)$$

- ***Soundness:*** *For any* non-uniform *PPT algorithm $\widetilde{\mathsf{P}}$, we have that for $x \notin \mathcal{L}_\mathcal{R}$ such that $|x|$ is large enough,*

$$\Pr\left[\langle \widetilde{\mathsf{P}}, \mathsf{V}\rangle(x) = 1\right] \leq \varepsilon_s(|x|)$$

- ***Zero-Knowledge:*** *There exists a PPT simulator* Sim *such that for all non-uniform PPT distinguishers $\mathcal{D}$ and all $(x, w) \in \mathcal{R}$ with $|x|$ large enough,*

$$\left| \Pr[\mathcal{D}(r, \tau) = 1 \mid (r, \tau) \leftarrow \mathsf{Sim}(x)] - \Pr\left[\mathcal{D}(r, \tau) = 1 \,\middle|\, \begin{array}{c} r \xleftarrow{\$} \{0,1\}^m \\ \tau \leftarrow \langle \mathsf{P}(w), \mathsf{V}\rangle(x; r) \end{array}\right] \right| \leq \varepsilon_{zk}(|x|)$$

  *where we let $m$ be the number of random bits used by* $\mathsf{V}$ *and $\langle \mathsf{P}(w), \mathsf{V}\rangle(x; r)$ denote the transcript generated by* $\mathsf{P}$ *and* $\mathsf{V}$ *interacting, fixing* $\mathsf{V}$*'s random tape to $r$.*

*Remark 3.* We say a ZK argument for $\mathcal{L}$ is *public-coin* if the every message from V is simply a fresh random string. In particular, note that this implies without loss of generality that V does not maintain an internal state between rounds.

**Definition 6** (($\varepsilon_c, \varepsilon_s, \varepsilon_{zk}$)**-NIZK).** *An* $(\varepsilon_c, \varepsilon_s, \varepsilon_{zk})$*-NIZK for an* NP *relation* $\mathcal{R}$ *is a tuple of polynomial-time algorithms* $(\mathsf{Gen}, \mathsf{P}, \mathsf{V})$ *such that*

- ***Syntax***
  - $\mathsf{crs} \leftarrow \mathsf{Gen}(1^n)$*:* Gen *is a randomized algorithm that on input an instance size (in unary) outputs a common reference string.*
  - $\pi \leftarrow \mathsf{P}(\mathsf{crs}, x, w)$*:* P *is a randomized algorithm that on input a crs, instance, and witness for that instance outputs a proof.*
  - $b \leftarrow \mathsf{V}(\mathsf{crs}, x, \pi)$*:* V *is a* deterministic *algorithm that on input a crs, instance, and proof for that instance outputs a bit denoting acceptance or rejection.*
- ***Completeness:*** *For every* $(x, w) \in \mathcal{R}$*,*

$$\Pr\left[\mathsf{V}(\mathsf{crs}, x, \pi) = 1 \,\middle|\, \begin{array}{c} \mathsf{crs} \leftarrow \mathsf{Gen}(1^{|x|}) \\ \pi \leftarrow \mathsf{P}(\mathsf{crs}, x, w) \end{array}\right] \geq 1 - \varepsilon_c(|x|)$$

- ***Soundness:*** *For any* non-uniform *PPT algorithm* $\widetilde{\mathsf{P}}$*, we have that for* $x \notin \mathcal{L}_{\mathcal{R}}$ *such that* $|x|$ *is large enough,*

$$\Pr\left[\mathsf{V}(\mathsf{crs}, x, \tilde{\pi}) = 1 \,\middle|\, \begin{array}{c} \mathsf{crs} \leftarrow \mathsf{Gen}(1^{|x|}) \\ \tilde{\pi} \leftarrow \widetilde{\mathsf{P}}(\mathsf{crs}, x) \end{array}\right] \leq \varepsilon_s(|x|)$$

- ***Zero-Knowledge:*** *There exists a PPT simulator* Sim *such that for all non-uniform PPT distinguishers* $\mathcal{D}$ *and all* $(x, w) \in \mathcal{R}$ *with* $|x|$ *large enough,*

$$\left|\Pr\left[\mathcal{D}(\mathsf{crs}, \pi) = 1 \mid (\mathsf{crs}, \pi) \leftarrow \mathsf{Sim}(x)\right] - \Pr\left[\mathcal{D}(\mathsf{crs}, \pi) = 1 \,\middle|\, \begin{array}{c} \mathsf{crs} \leftarrow \mathsf{Gen}(1^{|x|}) \\ \pi \leftarrow \mathsf{P}(\mathsf{crs}, x, w) \end{array}\right]\right| \leq \varepsilon_{zk}(|x|)$$

*Remark 4.* We will often refer to a (non-interactive) zero-knowledge argument as being for the language defined by the relation $\mathcal{R}$, rather than for the relation itself.

*Remark 5.* We have defined soundness for NIZKs as being *computational* and *non-adaptive*. One can also consider *statistical* soundness, where our guarantee needs to hold even against inefficient $\widetilde{\mathsf{P}}$. Additionally, one can consider *adaptive* soundness, where the adversary is allowed to choose the instance after seeing the CRS. Formally, our soundness requirement would be replaced by

$$\Pr\left[\begin{array}{c} |x| = n \wedge x \notin \mathcal{L}_{\mathcal{R}} \\ \wedge\, \mathsf{V}(\mathsf{crs}, x, \tilde{\pi}) = 1 \end{array} \,\middle|\, \begin{array}{c} \mathsf{crs} \leftarrow \mathsf{Gen}(1^n) \\ (x, \tilde{\pi}) \leftarrow \tilde{\mathsf{P}}(\mathsf{crs}) \end{array}\right] \leq \varepsilon_s(n)$$

for sufficiently large $n$.

### 3.4 Complexity Classes

**Definition 7 (Infinitely-Often BPP).** *Let* ioBPP *be the class of languages* $\mathcal{L}$ *such that there exists a PPT algorithm* $\mathcal{A}$*, functions* $a, b : \mathbb{N} \to [0,1]$*, and a polynomial* $p$ *such that for infinitely many* $n$*,*

- *For all* $x \in \mathcal{L} \cap \{0,1\}^n$, $\Pr[\mathcal{A}(x) = 1] \geq a(n)$
- *For all* $x \in \{0,1\}^n - \mathcal{L}$, $\Pr[\mathcal{A}(x) = 1] \leq b(n)$
- $a(n) - b(n) \geq \frac{1}{p(n)}$

*We let* ioBPP/poly *be defined similarly, except that* $\mathcal{A}$ *is allowed to be non-uniform.*

**Definition 8 (Infinitely-Often P/poly).** *Let* ioP/poly *be the class of languages* $\mathcal{L}$ *such that there exists a non-uniform polynomial-time algorithm* $\mathcal{A}$ *such that for infinitely many* $n$*,*

- *For all* $x \in \mathcal{L} \cap \{0,1\}^n$, $\mathcal{A}(x) = 1$
- *For all* $x \in \{0,1\}^n - \mathcal{L}$, $\mathcal{A}(x) = 0$

*Remark 6.* The textbook proof that BPP ⊆ P/poly also says that ioBPP/poly ⊆ ioP/poly, so in particular ioBPP/poly = ioP/poly. Since ioP/poly is a more standard complexity class, we will state our results in terms of it, even when the algorithms we give are in fact probabilistic.

### 3.5 Chernoff Bounds

We will need a few different standard instantiations of Chernoff bounds for binomial random variables, as listed below.

**Theorem 6 (Chernoff Bounds).** *For every* $i \in [m]$*, let* $X_i$ *be an independent Bernoulli random variable that takes value* 1 *with probability* $p$*, and let* $X := \sum_i X_i$*. Then:*

1. *for any* $0 < \delta < 1$, $\Pr[X \geq (1+\delta)mp] \leq \exp\left(-\frac{\delta^2 mp}{3}\right)$.
2. *for any* $0 < \delta < 1$, $\Pr[X \leq (1-\delta)mp] \leq \exp\left(-\frac{\delta^2 mp}{2}\right)$.
3. *for any* $0 < \Delta$, $\Pr[|X - mp| \geq \Delta] \leq 2\exp\left(-\frac{\Delta^2}{m}\right)$.

### 3.6 Lemmas From [11]

In order to bridge the gap from auxiliary-input one-way functions to standard one-way functions, we recall the following definition and lemmas from [8] as presented in [11].

**Definition 9 (Infinitely-Often Average-Case BPP, [11] Definition 2.1).** *Let* $\mathcal{L}$ *be a language and* $\mathcal{D} = \{\mathcal{D}_n\}_{n\in\mathbb{N}}$ *be an efficiently sampleable distribution. We say* $(\mathcal{L}, \mathcal{D}) \in$ ioAvgBPP/poly *if there exists a non-uniform PPT* $\mathcal{A}$ *such that for infinitely many* $n \in \mathbb{N}$*:*

- *For all* $x \in \text{Supp}(\mathcal{D}_n)$*,* $\Pr[\mathcal{A}(x) \in \{\perp, \mathcal{L}(x)\}] \geq 0.9$
- $\Pr[\mathcal{A}(x) = \perp \mid x \xleftarrow{\$} \mathcal{D}_n] \leq 0.25$

**Lemma 1 ([11] Lemma 3.5).** *Suppose auxiliary-input one-way functions exist. Then there is a language* $\mathcal{L} \in \mathsf{NP}$ *and a polynomial* $m(\cdot)$ *such that* $(\mathcal{L}, \{U_{m(n)}\}_{n \in \mathbb{N}}) \notin \mathsf{ioAvgBPP/poly}$.

In order to fit the next lemma from [11] into our framework, it will help to introduce some new notation.

**Definition 10 (Decision-To-Inversion Reduction).** *Fix a language* $\mathcal{L}$*. A decision-to-inversion reduction for* $\mathcal{L}$ *is a PPT machine* $R^{(\cdot)}$*, a function family* $\{f_x\}_{x \in \{0,1\}^*}$*, and a polynomial* $p(\cdot)$ *such that for any non-uniform PPT* $\mathcal{A}$ *and sufficiently large*[12] $x$ *such that* $\mathcal{A}(x, \cdot)$ *inverts* $f_x$ *with probability at least* $\frac{1}{p(|x|)}$*,* $\Pr[R^{\mathcal{A}}(x) = \mathcal{L}(x)] \geq 1 - \frac{1}{p(|x|)}$.

**Lemma 2 (Implicit in proof of [11] Lemma 3.1).** *Let* $(\mathcal{L}, \mathcal{D}) \notin \mathsf{ioAvgBPP/poly}$*. If there exists a decision-to-inversion reduction for* $\mathcal{L}$ *with* $p(n) = \omega(1)$*, then one-way functions exist.*

## 4 OWF From Non-trivial NIZK

We begin with the simpler case of NIZKs.

**Theorem 7.** *Suppose there exists a language* $\mathcal{L} \notin \mathsf{ioP/poly}$ *such that* $\mathcal{L}$ *has an* $(\varepsilon_{\mathsf{c}}, \varepsilon_{\mathsf{s}}, \varepsilon_{\mathsf{zk}})$*-NIZK with* $\varepsilon_{\mathsf{c}} + \varepsilon_{\mathsf{s}} + \varepsilon_{\mathsf{zk}} <_n 1$*. Then there exists an auxiliary-input one-way function.*

*Proof.* Let $(\mathsf{Gen}, \mathsf{P}, \mathsf{V})$ be the $(\varepsilon_{\mathsf{c}}, \varepsilon_{\mathsf{s}}, \varepsilon_{\mathsf{zk}})$-NIZK for $\mathcal{L}$ guaranteed by the theorem statement, and $p(n)$ be a polynomial such that for sufficiently large $n$, $\varepsilon_{\mathsf{c}}(n) + \varepsilon_{\mathsf{s}}(n) + \varepsilon_{\mathsf{zk}}(n) < 1 - \frac{1}{p(n)}$.[13] Suppose for the sake of contradiction that auxiliary-input one-way functions don't exist. Define:

- $M$ as an auxiliary-input sampler where $M(x; r)$ computes $(\mathsf{crs}, \pi) \leftarrow \mathsf{Sim}(x; r)$ and outputs $\mathsf{crs}$.
- $N$ as the io-UE machine guaranteed by Theorem 5 with respect to sampler $M$ and polynomial $20p(n)$.
- $\Gamma$ as the (infinite) set of $n$ such that the guarantees of $N$ hold.

We now claim that Algorithm 1 decides $\mathcal{L}$ infinitely often, contradicting that $\mathcal{L} \notin \mathsf{ioP/poly}$.

To analyze this algorithm, we first consider what it does when $x \in \{0,1\}^n - \mathcal{L}$. In this case, $\mathcal{A}$ can only accept if it finds an accepting proof for $x$ relative to an honestly-generated CRS. Since $\mathcal{A}$ is efficient, soundness tells us that this happens with probability at most $\varepsilon_{\mathsf{s}}(n)$.

[12] Note here that we explicitly allow the notion of "sufficiently large" to depend on $\mathcal{A}$.
[13] In what follows, it will help to assume WLOG that $p(n) = \omega(n^2)$.

**Algorithm 1:** Algorithm $\mathcal{A}$ to decide $\mathcal{L}$

**Input:** $x \in \{0,1\}^n$
**Output:** Decision bit $b$, with $b = 1$ representing $x \in \mathcal{L}$

Compute $\mathsf{crs} \leftarrow \mathsf{Gen}(1^n)$
**for** $\_ \leftarrow 1$ **to** $20n \cdot p(n)$ **do**
    Compute $r' \leftarrow N(x, \mathsf{crs})$
    Compute $(\mathsf{crs}', \pi') \leftarrow \mathsf{Sim}(x; r')$
    **if** $\mathsf{V}(\mathsf{crs}, x, \pi') = 1$ **then**
        Output $b = 1$
    **end**
**end**
Output $b = 0$

Next, we consider what $\mathcal{A}$ does when $x \in \{0,1\}^n \cap \mathcal{L}$ for some $n \in \Gamma$. Let $p_{\mathsf{crs}}$ be the probability that a single iteration of the for loop in $\mathcal{A}$ accepts. We call $\mathsf{crs}$ "bad" if $p_{\mathsf{crs}} \leq \frac{1}{20p(n)}$, and "good" if $p_{\mathsf{crs}} \geq \frac{1}{10p(n)}$. The core of our analysis comes from the following claim:

**Claim 1.** *Suppose $x \in \{0,1\}^n \cap \mathcal{L}$ for some $n \in \Gamma$. Then* $\Pr[\mathsf{crs}$ *is bad* $\mid \mathsf{crs} \leftarrow \mathsf{Gen}(1^n)] \leq \varepsilon_{\mathsf{zk}}(n) + \varepsilon_{\mathsf{c}}(n) + \frac{1}{4p(n)}$.

**Algorithm 2:** Distinguisher $\mathcal{D}$

**Input:** $x \in \{0,1\}^n$, $(\mathsf{crs}, \pi)$
**Output:** Decision bit $b$, with $b = 0$ representing that $(\mathsf{crs}, \pi)$ was generated by $\mathsf{Sim}$

**for** $\_ \leftarrow 1$ **to** $20n \cdot p(n)$ **do**
    Compute $r' \leftarrow N(x, \mathsf{crs})$
    Compute $(\mathsf{crs}', \pi') \leftarrow \mathsf{Sim}(x; r')$
    Run $\mathsf{V}(\mathsf{crs}, x, \pi')$
**end**
Let count be the number of iterations where $\mathsf{V}$ accepted
**if** *count* $\leq 1.5n$ *and* $\mathsf{V}(x, \mathsf{crs}, \pi) = 1$ **then**
    Output $b = 1$
**else**
    Output $b = 0$
**end**

*Proof.* Consider the distinguisher $\mathcal{D}$ defined by Algorithm 2. We first claim that if $\mathcal{D}$ is given $(\mathsf{crs}, \pi)$ drawn from $\mathsf{Sim}(x)$, it will output 1 with probability at most $\frac{1}{5p(n)}$. First note that if we change $\pi$ to instead be the proof we get from using randomness $r' \leftarrow N(x, \mathsf{crs})$, our guarantees on $N$ tell us that this probability can change by at most $\frac{1}{20p(n)}$. Now there are two cases to consider: either $\mathsf{crs}$ is good, or it is not good.

In the case where $\mathsf{crs}$ is good, we note that each iteration of the for loop has $\mathsf{V}(\mathsf{crs}, x, \pi') = 1$ with probability at least $\frac{1}{10p(n)}$. Thus, bound 2 in Theorem 6 (with respect to $\delta = \frac{1}{4}$) tells us that the final value of count can be below $1.5n$ with probability at most $\exp(-n/16)$, which is at most $\frac{1}{20p(n)}$ for sufficiently large $n$.

In the case where $\mathsf{crs}$ is not good, we know that the probability that we get an accepting proof by computing $r' \leftarrow N(x, \mathsf{crs})$ and $(\mathsf{crs}', \pi') \leftarrow \mathsf{Sim}(x; r')$ is at most $\frac{1}{10p(n)}$. But note that this is exactly how our given proof is computed! Since $\mathcal{D}$ can only output 1 if $\mathsf{V}(x, \mathsf{crs}, \pi) = 1$, we have that when $\mathsf{crs}$ is not good this happens with probability at most $\frac{1}{10p(n)}$. Combining all of the above, we get that $\mathcal{D}$ outputs 1 on a simulated $(\mathsf{crs}, \pi)$ with probability at most $\frac{1}{5p(n)}$ as desired.

Now we turn to what $\mathcal{D}$ does when given $(\mathsf{crs}, \pi)$ generated by $\mathsf{Gen}$ and $\mathsf{P}$. We claim here that it will output 1 with probability at least $\Pr[\mathsf{crs} \text{ is bad} \mid \mathsf{crs} \leftarrow \mathsf{Gen}(1^n)] - \varepsilon_{\mathsf{c}}(n) - \frac{1}{20p(n)}$. Indeed, there are only two ways for $\mathcal{D}$ to output 0: either $\mathsf{V}(x, \mathsf{crs}, \pi)$ rejects, or the final value of count is at most $1.5n$. The former can happen with probability at most $\varepsilon_{\mathsf{c}}(n)$ by completeness. For the latter, if $\mathsf{crs}$ is bad, we know that each iteration of the for loop has $\mathsf{V}(\mathsf{crs}', x, \pi') = 1$ with probability at most $\frac{1}{20p(n)}$. Pessimistically assuming that this probability is *exactly* $\frac{1}{20p(n)}$, bound 1 of Theorem 6 (with respect to $\delta = \frac{1}{2}$) tells us that the final value of count can exceed $1.5n$ with probability at most $\exp(-n/12)$; for sufficiently large $n$, this can be bounded by $\frac{1}{20p(n)}$.

Putting this all together, we have that $\mathcal{D}$ distinguishes a real $(\mathsf{crs}, \pi)$ from a simulated one with advantage at least $\Pr[\mathsf{crs} \text{ is bad} \mid \mathsf{crs} \leftarrow \mathsf{Gen}(1^n)] - \varepsilon_{\mathsf{c}}(n) - \frac{1}{4p(n)}$. But by zero-knowledge, we know that this advantage can be at most $\varepsilon_{\mathsf{zk}}(n)$. Rearranging terms gives the desired claim.

We can now argue that $\mathcal{A}$ must accept $x \in \mathcal{L}$ with good probability. Suppose that $\mathsf{crs}$ is not bad. Then each iteration of the for loop must have $\mathsf{V}(\mathsf{crs}, x, \pi') = 1$ with probability at least $\frac{1}{20p(n)}$. Thus, the probability that *no* iteration of the for loop outputs 1 is at most $\left(1 - \frac{1}{20p(n)}\right)^{20n \cdot p(n)} \leq \exp(-n)$, which for sufficiently large $n$ is at most $\frac{1}{4p(n)}$. Thus, the probability that $\mathcal{A}$ accepts $x \in \{0,1\}^n \cap \mathcal{L}$ for $n \in \Gamma$ is at least the probability that $\mathsf{crs}$ is not bad minus $\frac{1}{4p(n)}$; plugging in Claim 1, this is at least $1 - \varepsilon_{\mathsf{zk}}(n) - \varepsilon_{\mathsf{c}}(n) - \frac{1}{2p(n)}$.

Finally, this all means that we can instantiate Definition 7 with respect to $a(n) = 1 - \varepsilon_{\mathsf{zk}}(n) - \varepsilon_{\mathsf{c}}(n) - \frac{1}{2p(n)}$ and $b(n) = \varepsilon_{\mathsf{s}}(n)$. The above shows that we satisfy the first two points of the definition for all $n \in \Gamma$. For sufficiently large $n$, we know that $\varepsilon_{\mathsf{c}}(n) + \varepsilon_{\mathsf{s}}(n) + \varepsilon_{\mathsf{zk}}(n) < 1 - \frac{1}{p(n)}$, so $a(n) - b(n) > \frac{1}{2p(n)}$, satisfying the third point. Thus, we have that $\mathcal{L} \in \mathsf{ioBPP/poly}$, so by Remark 6, $\mathcal{L} \in \mathsf{ioP/poly}$.

*Remark 7.* Theorem 7 can also be phrased in the following way: if $\mathcal{L}$ has an $(\varepsilon_{\mathsf{c}}, \varepsilon_{\mathsf{s}}, \varepsilon_{\mathsf{zk}})$-NIZK with $\varepsilon_{\mathsf{c}} + \varepsilon_{\mathsf{s}} + \varepsilon_{\mathsf{zk}} <_n 1$, then $\mathcal{L}$ has a decision-to-inversion reduction (Definition 10). Indeed, all we need to prove the correctness of Algorithm 1 is for $N$ to satisfy the io-UE guarantees on auxiliary input $x$. Additionally, we note that the proof of Theorem 5 constructs a candidate auxiliary-input one-way function $\{f_x\}_x$ and reduces inverting $f_x$ to satisfying io-UE guarantees on auxiliary input $x$. Putting these two together gives the desired reduction $R$.[14]

Given the above remark, the techniques from [8,11] immediately allow us to improve Theorem 7 from an *auxiliary-input* one-way function to a standard one-way function.

**Corollary 3.** *Suppose that every* $\mathcal{L} \in \mathsf{NP}$ *has an* $(\varepsilon_{\mathsf{c}}, \varepsilon_{\mathsf{s}}, \varepsilon_{\mathsf{zk}})$*-NIZK with* $\varepsilon_{\mathsf{c}} + \varepsilon_{\mathsf{s}} + \varepsilon_{\mathsf{zk}} <_n 1$ *and* $\mathsf{NP} \not\subseteq \mathsf{ioP/poly}$*. Then OWFs exist.*

*Proof.* Since $\mathsf{NP} \not\subseteq \mathsf{ioP/poly}$, we know there is a language $\mathcal{L} \in \mathsf{NP}$ (that thus has an appropriate NIZK) where $\mathcal{L} \notin \mathsf{ioP/poly}$. Theorem 7 thus tells us that there exists an auxiliary-input one-way function. We can then plug this into Lemma 1 to get a new language $\mathcal{L}' \in \mathsf{NP}$ and a polynomial $m(\cdot)$ such that $(\mathcal{L}', \{U_{m(n)}\}_{n\in\mathbb{N}}) \notin \mathsf{ioAvgBPP/poly}$. But since $\mathcal{L}' \in \mathsf{NP}$ (and thus has an appropriate NIZK), Remark 7 tells us that there is a decision-to-inversion reduction for $\mathcal{L}'$. Hence, Lemma 2 tells us that one-way functions exist.

## 5 OWF From Non-trivial Public-Coin ZK

We now turn to the more general case of interactive zero-knowledge.

**Theorem 8.** *Suppose there exists a language* $\mathcal{L} \notin \mathsf{ioP/poly}$ *such that* $\mathcal{L}$ *has a constant-round, public coin* $(\varepsilon_{\mathsf{c}}, \varepsilon_{\mathsf{s}}, \varepsilon_{\mathsf{zk}})$*-ZK argument with* $\varepsilon_{\mathsf{c}} + \varepsilon_{\mathsf{s}} + \varepsilon_{\mathsf{zk}} <_n 1$*. Then there exists an auxiliary-input one-way function.*

Before proving this theorem, it will help to define some tools that will assist us in the proof. In all of the sections below, let

- $(\mathsf{Gen}, \mathsf{P}, \mathsf{V})$ be the $(\varepsilon_{\mathsf{c}}, \varepsilon_{\mathsf{s}}, \varepsilon_{\mathsf{zk}})$-ZK argument for $\mathcal{L}$ guaranteed by the theorem statement with simulator $\mathsf{Sim}$,
- $k$ be the (constant) number of rounds of interaction in this argument,
- $p(n)$ be a polynomial such that for sufficiently large $n$, $\varepsilon_{\mathsf{c}}(n)+\varepsilon_{\mathsf{s}}(n)+\varepsilon_{\mathsf{zk}}(n) < 1 - \frac{1}{p(n)}$,
- $p_{\mathsf{Est}}(n)$ as the polynomial $256k^2 \cdot n \cdot p(n)^2$,
- $M$ as an auxiliary-input sampler where $M(x; r)$ interprets $r = r_1 \| r_2$ for $r_1 \in [k]$ and outputs the first $r_1 - 1$ rounds of the transcript generated by $\mathsf{Sim}(x; r_2)$,

[14] Technically, Algorithm 1 doesn't quite give a decision-to-inversion reduction as written, since we are only guaranteed a polynomial gap between the probability of accepting $x \in \mathcal{L}$ versus $x \notin \mathcal{L}$. However, standard BPP amplification can convert this into a reduction that outputs the correct answer with high probability.

- $N$ be the io-UE machine guaranteed (assuming auxiliary-input one-way functions don't exist) by Theorem 5 with respect to sampler $M$ and polynomial $8k^2 \cdot p(n)$, and
- $\Gamma$ as the (infinite) set of $n$ such that the guarantees of $N$ hold.

### 5.1 Prover $\widetilde{\mathsf{P}}$

We start by defining a malicious prover strategy $\widetilde{\mathsf{P}}$ for $(\mathsf{Gen}, \mathsf{P}, \mathsf{V})$. Intuitively, $\widetilde{\mathsf{P}}$ will, given the current partial transcript of interaction with $\mathsf{V}$, use $N$ to sample "many" possible next prover messages. In order to choose which to use, $\widetilde{\mathsf{P}}$ will estimate the probability of each leading to an accepting transcript if it continues to use this strategy in future rounds, and pick the one with the largest success probability. We formally define the behavior of $\widetilde{\mathsf{P}}$ in Algorithm 3; we've separated out the definition of the success probability estimation procedure $\mathsf{Est}$ as Algorithm 4, as this will see use elsewhere.

**Algorithm 3:** Malicious Prover $\widetilde{\mathsf{P}}$

**Input:** $x \in \{0,1\}^n$, partial transcript $\tau$ with $\mathsf{P}$ sending the next message
**Output:** $m$ as the next message to send

Let $i$ be the number of rounds already completed in $\tau$
**for** $\_ \leftarrow 1$ **to** $16k \cdot n \cdot p(n)$ **do**
  Compute $r' \leftarrow N(x, \tau)$
  Parse $r' = r'_1 \| r'_2$
  Compute $\tau'$ as the first $i+1$ messages of $\mathsf{Sim}(x; r'_2)$
  Compute $\mathsf{Est}(x, \tau')$
**end**
Let $\tau^*$ be the transcript with the highest value of $\mathsf{Est}(x, \tau')$ sampled above
Output $m^*$ as the $(i+1)$st message in $\tau^*$

**Algorithm 4:** Success Probability Estimator $\mathsf{Est}$

**Input:** $x \in \{0,1\}^n$, (possibly partial) transcript $\tau$
**Output:** Estimate of the probability that $\mathsf{V}$ will accept when interacting with $\widetilde{\mathsf{P}}$ starting on transcript $\tau$

**for** $\_ \leftarrow 1$ **to** $12 p_{\mathsf{Est}}(n)^4$ **do**
  Simulate[15] interaction between $\mathsf{V}$ and $\widetilde{\mathsf{P}}$ starting from partial transcript $\tau$
**end**
Output fraction of iterations where $\mathsf{V}$ accepted

[15] We note that this simulation is possible because $\mathsf{V}$ is public-coin, and thus has no internal state. In fact, this is the *only* reason we need to limit our proof to public-coin protocols.

*Remark 8.* We note that while the definitions of $\widetilde{\mathsf{P}}$ and $\mathsf{Est}$ refer to each other, $\widetilde{\mathsf{P}}$ always calls $\mathsf{Est}$ on a strictly longer transcript than it started with, so these definitions are not circular.

We now prove some useful properties of $\widetilde{\mathsf{P}}$ and $\mathsf{Est}$.

**Lemma 3.** *$\widetilde{\mathsf{P}}$ and $\mathsf{Est}$ run in polynomial time.*

**Lemma 4.** *On any input $\tau$, the output of $\mathsf{Est}$ is within an additive distance of $\frac{1}{p_{\mathsf{Est}}(n)}$ of the true acceptance probability with probability at least $1 - \frac{1}{p_{\mathsf{Est}}(n)}$.*

We defer the proofs of these lemmas to the full version of the paper. Before stating our next property, we need to introduce some notation.

**Definition 11.** *Fix a partial transcript $\tau$ where the prover is going next, and let $i$ be the number of messages in $\tau$. For any possible next prover message $m$, let $p_m$ be the probability that $\mathsf{V}$ would accept if it interacted with $\widetilde{\mathsf{P}}$ starting on the transcript $\tau \| m$. We define $q_{threshold}$ as the threshold such that $q_{threshold} \geq p_{m'}$ for at least $1 - \frac{1}{16k \cdot p(n)}$ fraction (by probability) of messages $m'$ sampled using $N$. More formally, let $q_{threshold}$ be the smallest value such that*

$$\Pr\left[ q_{threshold} \geq p_{m'} \;\middle|\; \begin{array}{c} r' = r'_1 \| r'_2 \leftarrow N(x, \tau) \\ \tau' \leftarrow \mathsf{Sim}(x; r'_2) \\ m' = \text{the } (i+1)\text{st message in } \tau' \end{array} \right] > 1 - \frac{1}{16k \cdot p(n)}$$

*We call $m$ $\mathsf{OK}$ if $p_m \geq q_{threshold} - \frac{2}{p_{\mathsf{Est}}(n)}$, $\mathsf{G}$ if $p_m \geq q_{threshold}$, and $\mathsf{VG}$ if $p_m \geq q_{threshold} + \frac{2}{p_{\mathsf{Est}}(n)}$.*

**Lemma 5.** *Let $\tau$ be any partial transcript where the prover sends the next message. If we run $\widetilde{\mathsf{P}}(x, \tau)$ to get a next prover message $m$, then $m$ is $\mathsf{OK}$ with probability at least $1 - \frac{1}{16k \cdot p(n)} - e^{-n}$.*

*Proof.* We note that $\widetilde{\mathsf{P}}$ makes $16k \cdot n \cdot p(n)$ calls to $\mathsf{Est}$. By Lemma 4 and a union bound, we know that the probability that any of these calls is more than $\frac{1}{p_{\mathsf{Est}}(n)}$ away from the true success probability is at most $\frac{16k \cdot n \cdot p(n)}{p_{\mathsf{Est}}(n)} = \frac{1}{16k \cdot p(n)}$.

But we now note that since each iteration of the for loop in $\widetilde{\mathsf{P}}$ samples from exactly the distribution of messages used in Definition 11, each iteration chooses a $\mathsf{G}$ message with probability at least $\frac{1}{16k \cdot p(n)}$. Thus, the probability that *no* iteration chooses a $\mathsf{G}$ message is at most $(1 - \frac{1}{16k \cdot p(n)})^{16k \cdot n \cdot p(n)} \leq e^{-n}$.

Now note that if neither of the above bad events happen, the message $m^*$ output by $\widetilde{\mathsf{P}}$ must be $\mathsf{OK}$.[16] Thus, we have that $\widetilde{\mathsf{P}}$ outputs an $\mathsf{OK}$ message with probability at least $1 - \frac{1}{16k \cdot p(n)} - e^{-n}$, as desired.

[16] In the worst case, we could underestimate the success probability of every $\mathsf{G}$ message we sampled by $\frac{1}{p_{\mathsf{Est}}(n)}$, and choose a different message due to overestimating its success probability by $\frac{1}{p_{\mathsf{Est}}(n)}$.

### 5.2 Distinguisher $\mathcal{D}$

We next define a distinguisher $\mathcal{D}$ that we will use in our proof. Intuitively, $\mathcal{D}$ will check each prover message to see if it is "much better" than "most" next messages that we would get by using $N$. In our proof, we will use the fact that this distinguisher can only have $\varepsilon_{\mathsf{zk}}(n)$ advantage in distinguishing a real from a simulated transcript in order to argue that our algorithm cannot lose too much success probability. We formally define $\mathcal{D}$ as Algorithm 5.

**Algorithm 5:** Distinguisher $\mathcal{D}$

**Input:** $x \in \{0,1\}^n$, (full) transcript $\tau$
**Output:** Decision bit $b$, with $b = 0$ representing that $\tau$ was generated by $\mathsf{Sim}$

**for** *each* P *round* $i$ **do**
  Let $\tau_i$ be the first $i$ rounds of $\tau$ and $\tau_{i-1}$ the first $i-1$ rounds
  Compute $\mathsf{Est}(x, \tau_i)$
  **for** $\_ \leftarrow 1$ **to** $8k \cdot n \cdot p(n)$ **do**
    Compute $r' \leftarrow N(x, \tau_{i-1})$
    Parse $r' = r'_1 \| r'_2$
    Compute $\tau'$ as $\tau_{i-1}$ concatenated with the $i$th message of $\mathsf{Sim}(x; r'_2)$
    Compute $\mathsf{Est}(x, \tau')$
  **end**
  Let count be the number of iterations where $\mathsf{Est}(x, \tau') \geq \mathsf{Est}(x, \tau_i)$
  **if** *count* $< n$ **then**
    Output $b = 1$
  **end**
**end**
Output $b = 0$

We now prove some useful properties of $\mathcal{D}$.

**Lemma 6.** *For large enough $n \in \Gamma$ and $x \in \{0,1\}^n$,* $\Pr[\mathcal{D}(x, \tau) = 1 \mid \tau \leftarrow \mathsf{Sim}(x)] \leq \frac{1}{4p(n)}$.

*Proof.* We first define a sequence of hybrids for how we generate $\tau$. For $i \in [k]_0$, let $\mathrm{Hyb}_i(x)$ be defined as in Algorithm 6. We note immediately that $\mathrm{Hyb}_k$ is identical to $\mathsf{Sim}$. Furthermore, the guarantees on $N$ tell us that $\mathrm{Hyb}_i(x)$ has statistical distance at most $\frac{1}{8k \cdot p(n)}$ from $\mathrm{Hyb}_{i+1}(x)$.[17] Thus, we have that $\mathsf{Sim}(x)$ has statistical distance at most $\frac{1}{8p(n)}$ from $\mathrm{Hyb}_0(x)$. To complete the proof, we now claim that $\Pr[\mathcal{D}(x, \tau) = 1 \mid \tau \leftarrow \mathrm{Hyb}_0(x)] \leq \frac{1}{8p(n)}$. Indeed, consider the iteration of $\mathcal{D}$ corresponding to prover round $i$. We note that because $\tau$ was sampled from $\mathrm{Hyb}_0$, $\tau_i$ is drawn from the same distribution as each $\tau'$ that

[17] Note that this loses a factor of $k$ compared to the overall guarantee on $N$ since we are specifically asking $N$ to work on a partial transcript with $i$ messages, where $M$ outputs such a transcript with probability $\frac{1}{k}$.

**Algorithm 6:** Hybrid Transcript Generation $\mathsf{Hyb}_i$

**Input:** $x \in \{0,1\}^n$
**Output:** (Full) transcript $\tau$
Let $\tau$ be the first $i$ rounds of $\mathsf{Sim}(x)$
**for** $j \leftarrow i+1$ **to** $k$ **do**
  Compute $r' \leftarrow N(x, \tau)$
  Parse $r' = r'_1 \| r'_2$
  Append the $j$th message in $\mathsf{Sim}(x; r'_2)$ to $\tau$
**end**
Output $\tau$

$\mathcal{D}$ samples in this iteration. Thus, if we order $\tau_i$ and each sampled $\tau'$ by their respective values of $\mathsf{Est}$ (breaking ties randomly), they will be in a random order. Since it is only possible for $\mathcal{D}$ to output 1 in this iteration if $\tau_i$ is in the top $n$ of this order, we have that the probability of this happening is at most $\frac{n}{8k \cdot n \cdot p(n)} = \frac{1}{8k \cdot p(n)}$. Taking a union bound over all prover rounds, we get our desired claim.

**Lemma 7.** *Let $\tau$ be a (full) transcript and $n = |x|$ sufficiently large. If any prover message in $\tau$ is VG (as in Definition 11, with respect to the partial transcript up to that message), $\mathcal{D}(x, \tau)$ will output $b = 1$ in the iteration corresponding to that round with probability at least $1 - \frac{1}{16k \cdot p(n)}$.*

*Proof.* Let $i$ be a prover round where the prover's message $m_i$ is VG. We first note that the corresponding iteration of $\mathcal{D}$ only makes $8k \cdot n \cdot p(n) + 1$ calls to $\mathsf{Est}$. Thus, by Lemma 4 and a union bound, we have that all values returned by $\mathsf{Est}$ are within a $\frac{1}{p_{\mathsf{Est}}(n)}$ additive distance of their corresponding correct values with probability at least $1 - \frac{8k \cdot n \cdot p(n)}{p_{\mathsf{Est}}(n)} = 1 - \frac{1}{32k \cdot p(n)} - \frac{1}{p_{\mathsf{Est}}(n)}$. For the remainder of the proof, we will assume this is the case.

Since every call to $\mathsf{Est}$ is within an additive $\frac{1}{p_{\mathsf{Est}}(n)}$ distance of the true acceptance probability, we have that for any $\tau'$ sampled in the iteration of $\mathcal{D}$ corresponding to round $i$, we can only have $\mathsf{Est}(x, \tau') \geq \mathsf{Est}(x, \tau_i)$ if $p_{m'} \geq p_{m_i} - \frac{2}{p_{\mathsf{Est}}(n)}$, where $m'$ is the $i$th message of $\tau'$. But since $m_i$ is VG, we know that this happens with probability at most $\frac{1}{16k \cdot p(n)}$ over the sampling of $\tau'$. Pessimistically assuming that this probability is exactly $\frac{1}{16k \cdot p(n)}$, bound 1 in Theorem 6 (with respect to $\delta = \frac{1}{2}$) will tell us that the final value of count can only exceed $\frac{3n}{4}$ with probability at most $\exp(-n/24)$; for sufficiently large $n$, this is at most $\frac{1}{p_{\mathsf{Est}}(n)}$. Since $\mathcal{D}$ will output 1 if count $< n$ (and so in particular if count $\leq \frac{3n}{4}$), this tells us that as long as no call to $\mathsf{Est}$ fails, $\mathcal{D}$ will output 1 with probability at least $1 - \frac{1}{p_{\mathsf{Est}}(n)}$.

Applying a union bound to the above two paragraphs, we get that overall $\mathcal{D}$ outputs 1 with probability at least $1 - \frac{1}{32k \cdot p(n)} - \frac{2}{p_{\mathsf{Est}}(n)} \geq 1 - \frac{1}{16k \cdot p(n)}$ as desired.

### 5.3 Algorithm $\mathcal{A}$

We can now describe our algorithm for deciding $\mathcal{L}$, as described in Algorithm 7.

**Algorithm 7:** Algorithm $\mathcal{A}$ for $\mathcal{L}$

**Input:** $x \in \{0,1\}^n$
**Output:** Decision bit $b$
Simulate an interaction between $\widetilde{\mathsf{P}}$ and $\mathsf{V}$ on input $x$
**if** $\mathsf{V}$ *accepts* **then**
  Output $b = 1$
**else**
  Output $b = 0$
**end**

**Lemma 8.** *For all* $x \in \{0,1\}^n - \mathcal{L}$, $\Pr[\mathcal{A}(x) = 1] \leq \varepsilon_{\mathsf{s}}(n)$.

*Proof.* By Lemma 3, we know that $\widetilde{\mathsf{P}}$ is an efficient prover strategy. Thus, soundness tells us that the probability that $\mathsf{V}$ accepts when interacting with $\widetilde{\mathsf{P}}$ on $x \notin \mathcal{L}$ is at most $\varepsilon_{\mathsf{s}}(|x|)$.

**Lemma 9.** *For all sufficiently large* $n \in \Gamma$ *and all* $x \in \{0,1\}^n \cap \mathcal{L}$, $\Pr[\mathcal{A}(x) = 1] \geq 1 - \varepsilon_{\mathsf{c}}(n) - \varepsilon_{\mathsf{zk}}(n) - \frac{1}{2p(n)}$.

*Proof.* Fix $n$ to be large enough that the guarantees of all the above lemmas hold, and $x$ as any element in $\{0,1\}^n \cap \mathcal{L}$. We define a sequence of hybrid experiments as follows. For each $i \in [k]_0$, let $\mathrm{Hyb}_i^1(x)$:

- Create a transcript $\tau$ by running the honest $\mathsf{P}$ and $\mathsf{V}$ on $x$ for the first $i$ rounds, and completing the remaining rounds by running $\widetilde{\mathsf{P}}$ and $\mathsf{V}$.[18]
- Run $\mathcal{D}(x, \tau)$. For every $j \in [k]_0$, let $R_j$ be the event that $\mathcal{D}$ outputs 1 in or before the iteration corresponding to round $j$.

To simplify notation in our proof, for each $i \in [k]$, we also define $\mathrm{Hyb}_i^2(x)$ as:

- Create a transcript $\tau$ by running the honest $\mathsf{P}$ and $\mathsf{V}$ on $x$ for the first $i$ rounds, and completing the remaining rounds by running $\widetilde{\mathsf{P}}$ and $\mathsf{V}$.
- Run $\mathcal{D}(x, \tau)$. For every $j \in [k]_0$, let $R_j$ be the event that $\mathcal{D}$ outputs 1 in or before the iteration corresponding to round $j$.
- Create a second transcript $\tau'$ by taking the first $i - 1$ rounds of $\tau$ and completing the remaining rounds by running $\widetilde{\mathsf{P}}$ and $\mathsf{V}$.

[18] As in our definition of $\widetilde{\mathsf{P}}$, this is possible because $\mathsf{V}$ is stateless.

Note that $\mathrm{Hyb}_0^1$ (ignoring $\mathcal{D}$) is exactly the same as $\mathcal{A}$, so our goal is to prove that V is unlikely to reject in that hybrid. On the other hand, $\mathrm{Hyb}_k^1$ involves generating an honest transcript, which we know can only be rejected with probability at most $\varepsilon_c(n)$. Thus, it suffices for us to show that as we move from $\mathrm{Hyb}_k^1$ to $\mathrm{Hyb}_0^1$[19] the probability that V rejects cannot increase by much. Specifically, we aim to prove

**Claim 2.** *Fix any* $i \in [k]$. *Then we have that*

$$\Pr_{\mathrm{Hyb}_{i-1}^1}[\mathsf{V}(x,\tau)=0 \wedge \overline{R_{i-1}}] \leq \Pr_{\mathrm{Hyb}_i^1}[\mathsf{V}(x,\tau)=0 \wedge \overline{R_i}] + \frac{1}{4k\cdot p(n)} + \Pr_{\mathrm{Hyb}_i^2}[\overline{R_{i-1}} \wedge R_i]$$

Indeed, by repeated application of the claim, we get that

$$\begin{aligned}\Pr[\mathcal{A}(x)=0] = \Pr_{\mathrm{Hyb}_0^1}[\mathsf{V}(x,\tau)=0] &= \Pr_{\mathrm{Hyb}_0^1}[\mathsf{V}(x,\tau)=0 \wedge \overline{R_0}]\\ &\leq \Pr_{\mathrm{Hyb}_k^1}[\mathsf{V}(x,\tau)=0 \wedge \overline{R_k}] + \frac{1}{4p(n)} + \sum_{i\in[k]}\Pr_{\mathrm{Hyb}_i^2}[\overline{R_{i-1}} \wedge R_i]\\ &\leq \Pr_{\mathrm{Hyb}_k^1}[\mathsf{V}(x,\tau)=0] + \frac{1}{4p(n)} + \sum_{i\in[k]}\Pr_{\mathrm{Hyb}_i^2}[\overline{R_{i-1}} \wedge R_i] \qquad (1)\end{aligned}$$

(For the second equality, we used the fact that $R_0$ is always false.) The first term is at most $\varepsilon_c(n)$ as noted above. For the last term, we note that the events $R_i$ and $R_{i-1}$ are defined over the first $i$ messages of $\tau$, which are sampled using the honest P and V. Thus, we have that $\Pr_{\mathrm{Hyb}_i^2}[\overline{R_{i-1}} \wedge R_i] = \Pr_{\mathrm{real}}[\overline{R_{i-1}} \wedge R_i]$, where real is the probability space where we sample the entire transcript $\tau$ from P and V, then run $\mathcal{D}(x,\tau)$. Since $R_{i-1} \subseteq R_i$ for all $i \in [k]$, the resulting sum telescopes; that is, $\sum_{i\in[k]}\Pr_{\mathrm{real}}[\overline{R_{i-1}} \wedge R_i] = \Pr_{\mathrm{real}}[\overline{R_0} \wedge R_k]$, which by the definition of $R_0$ and $R_k$ is just $\Pr_{\mathrm{real}}[\mathcal{D}(x,\tau)=1]$. Plugging this all back into (1), we get

$$\begin{aligned}\Pr[\mathcal{A}(x)=0] &\leq \varepsilon_c(n) + \Pr_{\mathrm{real}}[\mathcal{D}(x,\tau)=1] + \frac{1}{4p(n)}\\ &\leq \varepsilon_c(n) + \varepsilon_{zk}(n) + \Pr[\mathcal{D}(x,\tau)=1 \mid \tau \leftarrow \mathsf{Sim}(x)] + \frac{1}{4p(n)}\\ &\leq \varepsilon_c(n) + \varepsilon_{zk}(n) + \frac{1}{2p(n)}\end{aligned}$$

where the first inequality comes from zero-knowledge and the second comes from Lemma 6. All that now remains is to prove the claim. We do so by proving the following two claims.

**Claim 3.** *Fix any* $i \in [k]$. *Then we have that*

$$\Pr_{\mathrm{Hyb}_{i-1}^1}[\mathsf{V}(x,\tau)=0 \wedge \overline{R_{i-1}}] \leq \Pr_{\mathrm{Hyb}_i^2}[\mathsf{V}(x,\tau')=0 \wedge \overline{R_i}] + \Pr_{\mathrm{Hyb}_i^2}[\overline{R_{i-1}} \wedge R_i]$$

[19] The hybrids count down for ease of notation.

**Claim 4.** *Fix any $i \in [k]$. Then we have that*

$$\Pr_{\mathrm{Hyb}_i^2}[\mathsf{V}(x,\tau')=0 \wedge \overline{R_i}] \leq \Pr_{\mathrm{Hyb}_i^1}[\mathsf{V}(x,\tau)=0 \wedge \overline{R_i}] + \frac{1}{4k \cdot p(n)}$$

Note that Claim 2 trivially follows from Claim 3 and Claim 4.

*Proof (Proof of Claim 3).* We first note that

$$\Pr_{\mathrm{Hyb}_{i-1}^1}[\mathsf{V}(x,\tau)=0 \wedge \overline{R_{i-1}}] = \Pr_{\mathrm{Hyb}_i^2}[\mathsf{V}(x,\tau')=0 \wedge \overline{R_{i-1}}]$$

Indeed, in both cases we are checking if $\mathsf{V}$ accepts a transcript sampled by taking the first $i-1$ messages from $\mathsf{P}$ and $\mathsf{V}$ with the remainder from $\widetilde{\mathsf{P}}$ and $\mathsf{V}$, as well as if $\mathcal{D}$ outputs 1 within the first $i-1$ messages of that transcript. But now we can write

$$\begin{aligned}\Pr_{\mathrm{Hyb}_i^2}[\mathsf{V}(x,\tau')=0 \wedge \overline{R_{i-1}}] &= \Pr_{\mathrm{Hyb}_i^2}[\mathsf{V}(x,\tau')=0 \wedge \overline{R_i}] + \Pr_{\mathrm{Hyb}_i^2}[\mathsf{V}(x,\tau')=0 \wedge \overline{R_{i-1}} \wedge R_i] \\ &\leq \Pr_{\mathrm{Hyb}_i^2}[\mathsf{V}(x,\tau')=0 \wedge \overline{R_i}] + \Pr_{\mathrm{Hyb}_i^2}[\overline{R_{i-1}} \wedge R_i]\end{aligned}$$

which yields the desired claim.

*Proof (Proof of Claim 4).* First note that if $i$ is a verifier round, we have that

$$\Pr_{\mathrm{Hyb}_i^2}[\mathsf{V}(x,\tau')=0 \wedge \overline{R_i}] = \Pr_{\mathrm{Hyb}_i^1}[\mathsf{V}(x,\tau)=0 \wedge \overline{R_i}]$$

Indeed, the only place where these two hybrids could differ is at round $i$. But note that $\overline{R_i}$ is not affected by this difference, since $\mathcal{D}$ only looks at prover rounds. Additionally, $\tau$ and $\tau'$ are identically distributed (both use $\mathsf{V}$ to sample the $i$th message), so the event that $\mathsf{V}$ rejects is also unaffected. This means that the statement trivially holds when $i$ is a verifier round, so for the remainder of the proof we will assume that $i$ is a prover round.

Recalling the definitions of $\mathsf{OK}$ and $\mathsf{VG}$ from Definition 11, we have that

$$\begin{aligned}\Pr_{\mathrm{Hyb}_i^2}[\mathsf{V}(x,\tau')=0 \wedge \overline{R_i}] = &\quad \Pr_{\mathrm{Hyb}_i^2}[\mathsf{V}(x,\tau')=0 \wedge \overline{R_i} \wedge m_i \text{ is } \mathsf{VG}] \\ &+ \Pr_{\mathrm{Hyb}_i^2}[\mathsf{V}(x,\tau')=0 \wedge \overline{R_i} \wedge m_i \text{ is not } \mathsf{VG} \wedge m_i' \text{ is } \mathsf{OK}] \\ &+ \Pr_{\mathrm{Hyb}_i^2}[\mathsf{V}(x,\tau')=0 \wedge \overline{R_i} \wedge m_i \text{ is not } \mathsf{VG} \wedge m_i' \text{ is not } \mathsf{OK}] \\ \leq &\quad \Pr_{\mathrm{Hyb}_i^2}[\overline{R_i} \wedge m_i \text{ is } \mathsf{VG}] \\ &+ \Pr_{\mathrm{Hyb}_i^2}[\mathsf{V}(x,\tau')=0 \wedge \overline{R_i} \wedge m_i \text{ is not } \mathsf{VG} \wedge m_i' \text{ is } \mathsf{OK}] \\ &+ \Pr_{\mathrm{Hyb}_i^2}[m_i' \text{ is not } \mathsf{OK}]\end{aligned}$$

where $m_i$ is the $i$th message in $\tau$ and $m_i'$ is the $i$th message in $\tau'$. We note that the first term is at most $\frac{1}{16k \cdot p(n)}$ by Lemma 7; the third term is at most

$\frac{1}{16k \cdot p(n)} + e^{-n}$ by Lemma 5. For the second term, we note that since $m_i$ is not $\mathsf{VG}$ but $m_i'$ is $\mathsf{OK}$, the probability that $\mathsf{V}$ rejects $\tau'$ can be at most $\frac{4}{p_{\mathsf{Est}}(n)}$ higher than the probability that $\mathsf{V}$ rejects $\tau$. Thus, the second term can be bounded as

$$\begin{aligned}
&\Pr_{\mathrm{Hyb}_i^2}[\mathsf{V}(x,\tau') = 0 \wedge \overline{R_i} \wedge m_i \text{ is not } \mathsf{VG} \wedge m_i' \text{ is } \mathsf{OK}] \\
&\leq \Pr_{\mathrm{Hyb}_i^2}[\mathsf{V}(x,\tau) = 0 \wedge \overline{R_i} \wedge m_i \text{ is not } \mathsf{VG} \wedge m_i' \text{ is } \mathsf{OK}] + \frac{4}{p_{\mathsf{Est}}(n)} \\
&\leq \Pr_{\mathrm{Hyb}_i^2}[\mathsf{V}(x,\tau) = 0 \wedge \overline{R_i}] + \frac{4}{p_{\mathsf{Est}}(n)} = \Pr_{\mathrm{Hyb}_i^1}[\mathsf{V}(x,\tau) = 0 \wedge \overline{R_i}] + \frac{4}{p_{\mathsf{Est}}(n)}
\end{aligned}$$

where the equality comes from the fact that $\tau$ is sampled from the same distribution in the two hybrids. Plugging this all in, we get that

$$\Pr_{\mathrm{Hyb}_i^2}[\mathsf{V}(x,\tau') = 0 \wedge \overline{R_i}] \leq \Pr_{\mathrm{Hyb}_i^1}[\mathsf{V}(x,\tau) = 0 \wedge \overline{R_i}] + \frac{4}{p_{\mathsf{Est}}(n)} + \frac{1}{8k \cdot p(n)} + e^{-n}$$

Noting that $\frac{4}{p_{\mathsf{Est}}(n)} + \frac{1}{8k \cdot p(n)} + e^{-n} \leq \frac{1}{4k \cdot p(n)}$ for sufficiently large $n$, we get the desired claim.

### 5.4 Putting It All Together

*Proof (Proof of Theorem 8).* Suppose for the sake of contradiction that ai-OWFs don't exist, and hence $\Gamma$ is infinite. We then have that Algorithm 7 satisfies the requirements of Definition 7 with respect to $a(n) = 1 - \varepsilon_{\mathsf{c}}(n) - \varepsilon_{\mathsf{zk}}(n) - \frac{1}{2p(n)}$ and $b(n) = \varepsilon_{\mathsf{s}}(n)$. Indeed, Lemma 9 immediately tells us that we satisfy the first two points for infinitely many $n$. For the third point, we have that for sufficiently large $n$,

$$a(n) - b(n) = 1 - \varepsilon_{\mathsf{c}}(n) - \varepsilon_{\mathsf{zk}}(n) - \varepsilon_{\mathsf{s}}(n) - \frac{1}{2p(n)} \geq \frac{1}{2p(n)}$$

where the inequality comes from the definition of $p(n)$. Thus, we have that $\mathcal{L} \in \mathsf{ioBPP/poly}$, so by Remark 6, we have that $\mathcal{L} \in \mathsf{ioP/poly}$. This provides our contradiction.

*Remark 9.* Theorem 8 can also be phrased in the following way: if $\mathcal{L}$ has a constant-round, public-coin $(\varepsilon_{\mathsf{c}}, \varepsilon_{\mathsf{s}}, \varepsilon_{\mathsf{zk}})$-ZK argument with $\varepsilon_{\mathsf{c}} + \varepsilon_{\mathsf{s}} + \varepsilon_{\mathsf{zk}} <_n 1$, then $\mathcal{L}$ has a decision-to-inversion reduction (Definition 10). The reasoning for this is identical to that in Remark 7.

Given the above remark, the techniques from [8,11] immediately allow us to improve Theorem 8 from an *auxiliary-input* one-way function to a standard one-way function.

**Corollary 4.** *Suppose that every* $\mathcal{L} \in \mathsf{NP}$ *has a constant-round, public-coin* $(\varepsilon_{\mathsf{c}}, \varepsilon_{\mathsf{s}}, \varepsilon_{\mathsf{zk}})$*-ZK argument with* $\varepsilon_{\mathsf{c}} + \varepsilon_{\mathsf{s}} + \varepsilon_{\mathsf{zk}} <_n 1$ *and* $\mathsf{NP} \not\subseteq \mathsf{ioP/poly}$. *Then OWFs exist.*

The proof of this is essentially identical to that of Corollary 3.

# 6 Applications to Amplification

Similar to [5], we can plug the one-way function we get from a high-error zero-knowledge protocol into prior work in order to get (almost) unconditional amplification of these high-error protocols. Below, we separately consider the cases of non-interactive zero-knowledge and interactive zero-knowledge.

## 6.1 Non-interactive Zero-Knowledge

In the non-interactive case, a recent line of works [1,3,4,7] has explored what assumptions are needed in order to amplify (adaptively-sound) NIZKs with high errors to have negligible errors, with [1,3] only requiring one-way functions in certain cases. If we instantiate these results with the one-way function we get from Corollary 3, we get that we can amplify such NIZKs (almost) unconditionally. Formally, we recall the following theorem from [1], rephrased slightly to fit our terminology.

**Theorem 9** (**[1], Theorem 8.27**). *Suppose OWFs exist. Then if there exists an $(\varepsilon_{\mathsf{c}}, \varepsilon_{\mathsf{s}}, \varepsilon_{\mathsf{zk}})$-NIZK* proof *with adaptive and statistical soundness for a language $\mathcal{L}$ with (1) $\varepsilon_{\mathsf{c}}$ negligible and (2) $\varepsilon_{\mathsf{s}} + \varepsilon_{\mathsf{zk}} <_n 1$, then there is an $(\varepsilon'_{\mathsf{c}}, \varepsilon'_{\mathsf{s}}, \varepsilon'_{\mathsf{zk}})$-NIZK with adaptive and statistical soundness for $\mathcal{L}$ with negligible $\varepsilon'_{\mathsf{c}}$, $\varepsilon'_{\mathsf{s}}$, and $\varepsilon'_{\mathsf{zk}}$.*

Combining this with Corollary 3 immediately gives us the following result.

**Corollary 5.** *Suppose that $\mathsf{NP} \not\subseteq \mathsf{ioP/poly}$ or $\mathsf{NP} \subseteq \mathsf{BPP}$. Suppose further that all of $\mathsf{NP}$ has $(\varepsilon_{\mathsf{c}}, \varepsilon_{\mathsf{s}}, \varepsilon_{\mathsf{zk}})$-NIZKs with adaptive and statistical soundness where (1) $\varepsilon_{\mathsf{c}}$ is negligible and (2) $\varepsilon_{\mathsf{zk}} + \varepsilon_{\mathsf{s}} <_n 1$. Then all of $\mathsf{NP}$ has $(\varepsilon'_{\mathsf{c}}, \varepsilon'_{\mathsf{s}}, \varepsilon'_{\mathsf{zk}})$-NIZKs with adaptive and statistical soundness where $\varepsilon'_{\mathsf{c}}$, $\varepsilon'_{\mathsf{s}}$, and $\varepsilon'_{\mathsf{zk}}$ are all negligible.*

## 6.2 Interactive Zero-Knowledge

In the interactive case, a classic result of [2] shows that one-way functions alone suffice to construct a 4-round interactive zero-knowledge protocol with negligible errors. Similar to the non-interactive case, we can instantiate this result using the one-way function we get from Corollary 4 in order to (almost) unconditionally "amplify" (actually, just build from scratch) interactive zero-knowledge. Formally, we recall the following theorem from [2].

**Theorem 10** (**[2], Theorem 1.1**). *If OWFs exist, for any $\mathcal{L} \in \mathsf{NP}$, there exists a four-round $(\varepsilon_{\mathsf{c}}, \varepsilon_{\mathsf{s}}, \varepsilon_{\mathsf{zk}})$-ZK argument for $\mathcal{L}$ with $\varepsilon_{\mathsf{c}}$, $\varepsilon_{\mathsf{s}}$, and $\varepsilon_{\mathsf{zk}}$ all negligible.*

Combining this with Corollary 4 immediately gives us the following result.

**Corollary 6.** *Suppose that $\mathsf{NP} \not\subseteq \mathsf{ioP/poly}$ or $\mathsf{NP} \subseteq \mathsf{BPP}$. Suppose further that all of $\mathsf{NP}$ has a constant-round, public-coin $(\varepsilon_{\mathsf{c}}, \varepsilon_{\mathsf{s}}, \varepsilon_{\mathsf{zk}})$-ZK argument with $\varepsilon_{\mathsf{c}} + \varepsilon_{\mathsf{zk}} + \varepsilon_{\mathsf{s}} <_n 1$. Then all of $\mathsf{NP}$ has a 4-round $(\varepsilon'_{\mathsf{c}}, \varepsilon'_{\mathsf{s}}, \varepsilon'_{\mathsf{zk}})$-ZK argument with $\varepsilon'_{\mathsf{c}}$, $\varepsilon'_{\mathsf{s}}$, and $\varepsilon'_{\mathsf{zk}}$ all negligible.*

## References


1. Applebaum, B., Kachlon, E.: NIZK amplification via leakage-resilient secure computation. Cryptology ePrint Archive, Paper 2025/995 (2025). https://eprint.iacr.org/2025/995
2. Bellare, M., Jakobsson, M., Yung, M.: Round-optimal zero-knowledge arguments based on any one-way function. Cryptology ePrint Archive, Paper 1997/002 (1997). https://eprint.iacr.org/1997/002
3. Bitansky, N., Geier, N.: Amplification of non-interactive zero knowledge, revisited. In: Reyzin, L., Stebila, D. (eds.) Advances in Cryptology - CRYPTO 2024 - 44th Annual International Cryptology Conference, Santa Barbara, CA, USA, 18–22 August 2024, Proceedings, Part IX. Lecture Notes in Computer Science, vol. 14928, pp. 361–390. Springer (2024). https://doi.org/10.1007/978-3-031-68400-5_11
4. Bitansky, N., Kamath, C., Paneth, O., Rothblum, R.D., Vasudevan, P.N.: Batch proofs are statistically hiding. In: Mohar, B., Shinkar, I., O'Donnell, R. (eds.) Proceedings of the 56th Annual ACM Symposium on Theory of Computing, STOC 2024, Vancouver, BC, Canada, 24–28 June 2024, pp. 435–443. ACM (2024). https://doi.org/10.1145/3618260.3649775
5. Chakraborty, S., Hulett, J., Khurana, D.: On weak nizks, one-way functions and amplification. In: Annual International Cryptology Conference, pp. 580–610. Springer (2025)
6. Chatterjee, R., Li, Y., Vasudevan, P.N.: Weak zero-knowledge and one-way functions. Cryptology ePrint Archive, Paper 2026/299 (2026). https://eprint.iacr.org/2026/299
7. Goyal, V., Jain, A., Sahai, A.: Simultaneous amplification: the case of non-interactive zero-knowledge. In: Boldyreva, A., Micciancio, D. (eds.) CRYPTO 2019. LNCS, vol. 11693, pp. 608–637. Springer, Cham (2019). https://doi.org/10.1007/978-3-030-26951-7_21
8. Hirahara, S., Nanashima, M.: One-way functions and zero knowledge. In: Mohar, B., Shinkar, I., O'Donnell, R. (eds.) Proceedings of the 56th Annual ACM Symposium on Theory of Computing, STOC 2024, Vancouver, BC, Canada, 24–28 June 2024, pp. 1731–1738. ACM (2024). https://doi.org/10.1145/3618260.3649701
9. Impagliazzo, R., Levin, L.: No better ways to generate hard np instances than picking uniformly at random. In: Proceedings [1990] 31st Annual Symposium on Foundations of Computer Science, vol. 2, pp. 812–821. (1990). https://doi.org/10.1109/FSCS.1990.89604
10. Impagliazzo, R.: Pseudo-random generators for cryptography and for randomized algorithms. Ph.D. thesis, University of California, Berkeley (1992)
11. Liu, Y., Mazor, N., Pass, R.: A note on zero-knowledge for NP and one-way functions. Cryptology ePrint Archive, Paper 2024/800 (2024). https://eprint.iacr.org/2024/800
12. Ostrovsky, R.: One-way functions, hard on average problems, and statistical zero-knowledge proofs. In: Proceedings of the Sixth Annual Structure in Complexity Theory Conference, Chicago, Illinois, USA, 30 June–3 July 1991, pp. 133–138. IEEE Computer Society (1991). https://doi.org/10.1109/SCT.1991.160253
13. Ostrovsky, R., Wigderson, A.: One-way fuctions are essential for non-trivial zero-knowledge. In: Second Israel Symposium on Theory of Computing Systems, ISTCS 1993, Natanya, Israel, 7–9 June 1993, Proceedings, pp. 3–17. IEEE Computer Society (1993). https://doi.org/10.1109/ISTCS.1993.253489

14. Pass, R., Shelat, A.: Unconditional characterizations of non-interactive zero-knowledge. In: Shoup, V. (ed.) Advances in Cryptology – CRYPTO 2005. Springer, Heidelberg (2005)
15. Yao, A.C.: Theory and application of trapdoor functions. In: 23rd Annual Symposium on Foundations of Computer Science (SFCS 1982), pp. 80–91 (1982). https://doi.org/10.1109/SFCS.1982.45

# Lower Bounds on Black-Box Constructions of Pseudorandom Functions

Bar Alon[1(✉)], Itai Dinur[2,3], and Muthuramakrishnan Venkitasubramaniam[2]

[1] School of Electrical Engineering, Tel-Aviv University, Tel Aviv, Israel
alonbar08@gmail.com

[2] Department of Computer Science, Georgetown University, Washington, D.C., USA
dinuri@bgu.ac.il, mv783@georgetown.edu

[3] Department of Computer Science, Ben-Gurion University, Beersheba, Israel

**Abstract.** In their seminal work, Goldreich, Goldwasser, and Micali [CRYPTO 1984] constructed a pseudorandom function (PRF) using a black-box access to a pseudorandom generator (PRG). When combined with Levin's domain extension technique, the GGM construction invokes the PRG $\omega(\log n)$ times, where $n$ denotes the input length to the PRG. To this day, no black-box construction achieving fewer calls is known.

Recently, Beimel, Malkin, and Mazor [CRYPTO 2024] showed that for a certain family of constructions, which they termed *tree constructions*, the GGM construction is optimal. However, the basic challenge of whether a PRF can be built with just *one invocation* of the PRG still remains open.

In this work, we consider fully black-box constructions of PRFs from PRGs, where both the construction and the reduction are required to be black-box, and the number of interactions the reduction makes with the adversary is independent of the number of oracle calls the adversary makes to its underlying function within each interaction. Our main result shows that no such construction can have $o(n/\log n)$ and $o(\mathsf{in}/\log \mathsf{in})$ *non-adaptive* calls to the PRG, where $\mathsf{in}$ is the input length of the PRF. This impossibility holds even for weak PRFs with one-bit output, where the adversary is restricted to making i.i.d. uniformly random queries. In addition, we prove a lower bound for weak PRFs with sufficiently long outputs that holds even when the construction is allowed to make adaptive queries to the PRG.

## 1 Introduction

A pseudorandom function (PRF) family is a collection of functions that appear random to any efficient algorithm. PRFs are fundamental to cryptography, both in theory and in practice, and have found many applications in areas outside of cryptography, such as in complexity and learning theory.

The seminal work of Goldreich, Goldwasser, and Micali [9] (henceforth the GGM construction) shows that a PRF can be constructed from *any* pseudorandom generator – an efficient algorithm that on a random input, outputs a longer

B. Alon—Work was conducted while at Georgetown University.


N. Heninger and M. Rosulek (Eds.): CRYPTO 2026, LNCS 16800, pp. 159–189, 2026.
https://doi.org/10.1007/978-3-032-35367-2_6

string that appears random to any efficient algorithm. Specifically, they showed that given black-box access to a pseudorandom generator (PRG) $G : \{0,1\}^n \to \{0,1\}^{2n}$, one can construct a PRF $F = \left\{f_k : \{0,1\}^{\mathsf{in}(n)} \to \{0,1\}^n\right\}_{k \in \{0,1\}^n}$ for any polynomial $\mathsf{in}(n)$. The number of calls to $G$ in the GGM construction is $|x|$ for any input $x$. A variant of the GGM construction that relies on Levin's domain extension technique [12] improves the number of calls to $\omega(\log n)$.[1] However, a fundamental question has remained open since it was first discovered—is the construction optimal in the number of PRG invocations? More precisely, the following remains open:

> *What is the minimal number of invocations of a (length-doubling) PRG required to build a PRF?*

Recently, Beimel et al. [2] made progress in answering this question. For a limited class of constructions that they refer to as *tree constructions* and generalizes the GGM construction, they prove that the GGM construction is optimal. In fact, their result holds even when considering PRFs with one-bit output. However, the state of affairs for more general (i.e. not necessarily tree) constructions, still remains open. In fact, previous results do not rule out the possibility of building a PRF with a *single call* to the PRG.

### 1.1 Our Results

We take a step towards answering the above question. We show two results. Our first and main result considers the already challenging setting of designing PRFs via non-adaptive calls to the underlying PRG (i.e., the construction generates all of its queries to the PRG before sending them). We demonstrate a lower bound on the number of calls to the underlying PRG oracle required for a fully black-box construction of a PRF. The impossibility is for a class of black-box reductions, which we call *query-bounded* reductions, which we define below. For our second result, we provide a lower bound for PRFs with a long output, which additionally includes adaptive constructions.

*Lower Bounds for Black-Box Constructions with Non-adaptive Calls.* Our main result demonstrates the impossibility of building a PRF with input length $\mathsf{in}$ from a PRG with an arbitrary polynomial stretch, using $c$ *non-adaptive* calls, where $c = o(n/\log n)$ and $c = o(\mathsf{in}/\log \mathsf{in})$ via a fully black-box construction. We demonstrate this impossibility for a class of black-box reductions, which we call *query-bounded* reductions.

Roughly, a reduction is query-bounded if the number of interactions it makes with the adversary is upper-bounded by a polynomial that is independent of the adversary's query complexity (for all sufficiently successful adversaries). Recall that in the PRF setting, the adversary has access to a function oracle that it

[1] The final construction adds to the key a hash $h : \{0,1\}^{\mathsf{in}(n)} \to \{0,1\}^{\omega(\log n)}$ from pair-wise independent hash function family, and applies the GGM construction to $h(x)$.

may call a bounded number of times. We focus on reductions whose number of interactions with the adversary may depend on the adversary's success probability, but is independent of the number of oracle calls the adversary makes to the underlying function within each interaction. We believe this is a natural class of reductions and captures all reductions in the literature (see Sect. 2.1.3). In particular, it includes reductions whose number of interactions with the adversary decreases as the adversary's success probability increases. It is an intriguing question whether one could extend the lower bound to all black-box reductions.

**Theorem 1 (Informal, impossibility for fully black-box construction).** *There is no fully black-box construction of a PRF with input length* $\mathsf{in}$ *from a PRG using query-bounded reductions and* $c$ *non-adaptive calls, where* $c = o(n/\log n)$ *and* $c = o(\mathsf{in}/\log \mathsf{in})$*.*

The formal statement and proof of Theorem 1 appear in Sect. 4. A few notes are in place. First, our proof works even for *weak* PRFs, where the adversary can only make i.i.d. uniform queries to the oracle. Second, unlike our second result (see Theorem 2 below), Theorem 1 holds for PRFs with one-bit output. Finally, we argue that as a corollary of Theorem 1, there is no fully black-box construction of a PRF from a PRG using a query-bounded reduction and a *constant number* of non-adaptive calls, regardless of the input length of the PRF. Indeed, for $\mathsf{in} = O(\log n)$ PRFs can be constructed unconditionally by simply letting the key be the truth table of the function (in particular, there is no reduction). On the other hand, for $\mathsf{in} = \omega(\log n)$, Theorem 1 states that there is no fully black-box construction with a constant number of calls. Note that this resolves the question of the single call case for query-bounded reductions.

*A Lower-Bound for Black-Box Constructions with Long Outputs.* We show an additional lower bound for PRFs with long outputs. Unlike in Theorem 1, here the result holds for adaptive constructions and does not require assuming the reduction to be query-bounded.

**Theorem 2 (Informal, lower bounds for long output constructions).** *There is no fully black-box construction of a PRF with output length* $\mathsf{out}$ *from a PRG with stretch* $r$ *using at most* $\frac{\mathsf{out}}{\max(r,\omega(\log n))}$ *calls.*

Stated differently, if $r = O(\log n)$, then Theorem 2 states that there is no black-box construction using $o(\mathsf{out}/\log n)$ calls to the PRG. On the other hand, if $r = \omega(\log n)$, then there is no black-box construction using $o(\mathsf{out}/r)$ calls. Additionally, similarly to Theorem 1, the proof of Theorem 2 also applies to weak PRFs.

Let us compare Theorem 2 to the GGM construction (note that in the GGM construction, the output of the PRF is of length $n$, making it natural to compare to). The GGM construction (combined with Levin's trick) is an $n$-bit output PRF from an $n$-bit stretch PRG using $\omega(\log n)$ calls to the PRG. The PRG can be constructed from a 1-bit stretch PRG using $O(n/\log n)$ calls using the Goldreich-Levin hardcore function theorem [8]. Thus, the overall number of calls the PRF construction makes to a 1-bit stretch PRG is $\omega(n)$. By Theorem 2, the number of calls must be at least $n/\omega(\log n)$. This means that the GGM construction is optimal up to a factor of $\omega(\log n)$. The formal statement of Theorem 2 appears in Sect. 5.

### 1.2 Related Works

Separation of cryptographic primitives is a fundamental question in cryptography that qualitatively measures the relative hardness of different cryptographic primitives. The seminal work of Impagliazzo and Rudich [11] provided the first separations ruling out constructions of key exchange from one-way functions. The class of constructions ruled out in this work is referred to as a fully black-box construction (see [17] for a taxonomy on reductions) where the construction uses the underlying primitive as a black-box and the reduction is black-box.

Within the framework of black-box separations, the *meta-reduction* paradigm introduced in the work of Boneh and Venkatesan [4], considers designing a (possibly inefficient) attacker $\mathcal{A}$ that when invoked with the reduction breaks the challenge in the underlying security reduction, then emulating $\mathcal{A}$ in a manner that is efficient and does not affect the interaction of the reduction and the challenger (see also [5,6,10,15,16]). We follow the meta-reduction paradigm in this work (see [1] and references therein).

Miles and Viola [13,14] were the first to consider lower bounds on black-box constructions of PRFs from PRGs.[2] They ruled out single-call constructions where the output is one of the PRG's output bits. More recently, Beimel et al. [2] both generalized the result of [13,14], and proved a lower bound on the number of calls in tree constructions, which naturally generalize the GGM construction. Additionally, they showed a lower bound on the key length required for black-box constructions.

### 1.3 Organization

We give an overview of our techniques in Sect. 2. The preliminaries are given in Sect. 3. Then, in Sect. 4 we prove our main result, showing a lower bound for constructions with non-adaptive calls. Finally, in Sect. 5, we prove our lower bound for PRFs with long outputs.

## 2 Our Techniques

We now present our techniques. We start with showing the impossibility for non-adaptive black-box constructions.

[2] The paper considers the question of extending the stretch of a PRG; however, they noted in [14] that their result applies to constructing PRFs from PRGs as well.

## 2.1 Lower Bounds for Fully Black-Box Constructions

As a warm-up, we will rule out PRF constructions that make a single call to a PRG and then generalize this argument for multiple non-adaptive calls.

**2.1.1 Warm-Up: The Single Call Case** Since we assume the construction makes one call to the PRG, we may write it as

$$f_k^G(x) = P\left(x, k, G(S(x,k))\right),$$

for efficiently computable functions $S$ and $P$. In the following, let $\lambda$ denote the length of the keys, and let $r$ denote the stretch of $G$.

Standard black-box separation like the approaches in [2,13] construct an oracle $\mathcal{O}$ relative to which a PRG $G$ exists, and construct an oracle-aided algorithm $\mathcal{A}^{\mathcal{O}}$ that breaks the security of $F$ using a polynomial number of calls to $\mathcal{O}$. We argue that it may be impossible to use such an approach to rule out black-box constructions of PRF from a PRG. Consider the following PRF construction from an $r$-bit stretch PRG $G$:

$$f_{h,k}^G(x) = \langle G(h(x)), k\rangle$$

where the key is a pair $(h, k)$, where $h$ is sampled from a pairwise independent hash function family, $k \leftarrow \{0,1\}^{n+r}$, and $\langle\cdot,\cdot\rangle$ is the inner product computed modulo 2. If $G$ is instantiated via a random oracle, then, for any polynomial set of inputs $x_1, \ldots, x_m$, the set $\{h(x_1), \ldots, h(x_m)\}$ will all be distinct (except with negligible probability). This would imply that the entropy of each $G(x_i)$ is large enough (given the other outputs of $f$) and the inner product can extract a random bit, such that the $m$ bits are statistically close to a uniform sample from $\{0,1\}^m$. In fact, this argument works even if $G$ is only "mildly" random, e.g., $G$ applies a random function only to the first $\omega(\log n)$ bits. Since the proof of security of the PRF is information-theoretic and does not depend on the reduction, it may be impossible to rule out such constructions using random oracles and an adversary $\mathcal{A}^{\mathcal{O}}$ that calls $\mathcal{O}$ a polynomial number of times. Since the work of Gennaro and Trevisan [7], most black-box separations from a random oracle have pursued this approach.

We circumvent this challenge by relying on the meta-reduction paradigm. We first define an "ideal" adversary that breaks the PRF using an *exponential number* of queries to the PRG. We then construct an *inefficient* "real" adversary that can simulate the ideal adversary when given the queries made by the reduction to the PRG. The idea here is that such an adversary can be simulated together with the reduction. In other words, we construct an algorithm that breaks the security of the PRG by emulating the reduction with real adversary that together make only polynomial queries to the underlying PRG.

*A Naive Attempt.* Let us start with a naive construction for the real and ideal adversaries that *does not* work. Define the ideal adversary $\mathcal{A}_{\mathsf{ideal}}^{G,f}$ to query $G$ on all inputs, and query the PRF/random function $f$ on $m$ distinct inputs $x_1, \ldots, x_m$.

The adversary outputs 1, indicating PRF, if and only if it can find a key that is consistent with all the responses. Clearly, if $f$ is sampled from the PRF family, $\mathcal{A}_{\mathsf{ideal}}$ will always output 1. When $f$ is sampled from the random function family, we can show that it will output 1 with negligible probability, assuming $m$ is sufficiently large via an entropy argument. Since the key length is $\lambda$, if $m = \lambda + n$, then except with probability $2^{-n}$, there will not be a consistent key.

Now, consider the following "real adversary" that aims to emulate the ideal adversary. This adversary queries its oracle (whose answers are given by reduction) on $m$ inputs just like the ideal adversary, but along with the responses from the reduction, it also receives all queries made by the reduction to the PRG. The idea is that in order for the responses to be consistent with the PRF family, the reduction must have queried the PRG on all the points needed to emulate the PRF for some key $k$. Thus, using the query-answers provided to the real adversary, we let it (in exponential time) find the key $k$ without making any additional queries to the PRG itself. If it finds such a key, the adversary outputs 1 indicating PRF and outputs 0 otherwise.

This adversary seemingly emulates the ideal adversary. However, this is not the case. The reduction does not have to make all the queries to the PRG consistent with a particular key to compute the answers. In fact, in the GGM reduction, the adversary implants the challenge string as the output of a PRG call. This means that the above strategy for the real adversary fails, because the reduction may have computed some of the outputs using some key and querying $G$, but guessed the other outputs (without querying $G$). Therefore, the real adversary cannot find a consistent key, while the ideal adversary may find one.

Our first observation is that the reduction cannot guess too many of the outputs, while still being consistent with some key. Indeed, otherwise, the probability that it is consistent with some key becomes negligibly small. Thus, we can revise the strategy of the two adversaries to only look for a key that is consistent with, say, 0.8 fraction[3] of the inputs. Indeed, when using 0.8 as the threshold, if the ideal adversary interacts with a random function $f$, then for every key, on expectation, only 1/2 of the answers are consistent with the inputs. By a simple concentration bound, it will not find a key except with negligible probability.

Unfortunately, there is the issue of the reduction guessing too *few* of the outputs. Specifically, in the case where the reduction computed correctly only 0.7 fraction of the inputs, we do not know how to show that the ideal adversary will not find a *different* key that is consistent with 0.8 fraction of the inputs.

We introduce two ideas to solve this. Towards describing our ideas, we first introduce two *score functions* (one for each adversary). For the ideal adversary, the score function with respect to some key is simply the number of consistent input-output pairs. The real adversary estimates the score function of the ideal adversary by considering the probability that it will be consistent with the answers (instead of a binary value). Specifically, for every key $k$ the real score is computed as follows: for every $x$ that is one of the $m$ inputs (and $S(x, k)$ has not been queried by the reduction), compute the probability over a random $G'$ that

[3] The choice of 0.8 is arbitrary; any constant larger than 1/2 and smaller than 1 works.

is consistent with the reduction queries, that $f_k^{G'}(x)$ equals the value given to it by the reduction. This probability can be computed exactly by the real adversary. The final score of the real adversary for $k$ is the sum of these probabilities over all inputs. By linearity of expectation, it is equal to the expected score of the ideal adversary (for the same key). The final score of each of the real and ideal adversaries is its maximal score over all keys, and the answer (PRF/random function) is defined by comparing this score to some threshold.

However, choosing a fixed threshold could fail in case it falls between the real and ideal scores (which could happen even if the scores are very close). Therefore, the second idea is to choose a *random threshold* between 0.8 and 1. This helps to smoothen the difference and as long as the real and ideal scores are close enough.

However, there are still two issues with the above argument.

1. Although for every $k$, the score of the real adversary equals the expected score of the ideal adversary, the final outputs of the PRF on the $m$ inputs might be dependent. Hence, we cannot claim that the scores are close with high probability. For a key $k$, such dependencies occur if for two different inputs $x_i$ and $x_j$, $S(x_i, k) = S(x_j, k)$.
2. The second issue relates to the challenge $y^*$ held by the reduction. Recall that $y^*$ is either uniform over $\{0,1\}^{n+r}$, or equals to $G(s)$, where $s \leftarrow \{0,1\}^n$. In the latter case, if the reduction implant $y^*$ instead of $G(S(x_i, k))$ for some $i$, then this increases the ideal score by 1, but increases the real score only by a negligible amount. Otherwise, the challenge affects the scores the same, which may provide the reduction a way to distinguish between the two adversaries.

*Fixing the Issues.* To solve the problems, we aim to break the dependencies between the outputs of the PRF. This solves the first issue as it allows us to use Chernoff's inequality to argue that the two scores are close with high probability. It also solves the second one since if the outputs are independent, the challenge can only affect at most one output (keeping the scores close). Towards breaking the dependencies, we observe that for every key $k$, either there is a PRG query that appears for many inputs, or we can find a large set of inputs with distinct PRG seeds.

**Claim 3** (Informal). *For a positive integer parameter $p$ (to be chosen), one of the following must hold for every key $k$.*

1. *There exists a seed that appears at least $p$ times in $\{S(x_i, k) : i \in [m]\}$, or*
2. *There is a set $\mathcal{I} \subseteq [m]$ of at least $m/p$ inputs with distinct PRG seeds.*

*Proof.* Consider the graph $H = ([m], E)$, where $i, j$ is an edge if and only if $S(x_i, k) = S(x_j, k)$. If Item 1 does not hold, then the maximum degree in $H$ is at most $p - 1$. By greedily selecting the vertices, we conclude there is an independent set of size at least $m/p$. By definition, the PRG seeds associated with an independent set are distinct. □

Now, if for a key $k$ the second item holds, then our previous argument works when restricting to $\mathcal{I}$: Since we instantiate the PRG with a random oracle, this implies that the corresponding outputs are independent random variables (over the PRG random oracle). This independence allows us to use a concentration bound to argue that if $m/p$ is sufficiently large, then the real adversary can predict the output of the ideal adversary with good accuracy. As for the other keys, we argue that there is only a negligible fraction of them. Indeed, if for too many keys there is a seed $s$ that appears at least $p$ times then, intuitively, for a random key the entropy in the output for those $p$ inputs is bounded by $\lambda + n + r$. Thus, for a sufficiently large $p$, the PRF can be distinguished from random. As a result, we may allow both the real and ideal adversaries to *ignore* such keys.

With this, for any polynomial $u$, we can choose $m$ so that for every call made by the reduction to the adversary, the statistical gap between the real and ideal adversary's outputs is $1/u$-close. However, recall that the reduction can call the adversary polynomially many times, say $v$. If we want the argue that the statistical gap for all the combined outputs are close we need $v/u$ to be small. In other words $u$ should be chosen after $v$. Since $m$ depends on $u$, for our impossibility to hold, we need to assume that the number of calls made by the reduction $v$ is independent of $m$. We believe this is a reasonable restriction and discuss this further in Sect. 2.1.3.

**2.1.2 The General Case.** We now describe our ideas to generalize the single call case to $c$ non-adaptive calls, where $c = o(n/\log n)$ and $c = o(\mathsf{in}/\log \mathsf{in})$. Recall that to define the two adversaries, we define two score functions (one for each adversary) that aim to compute for how many inputs the reduction returned the correct output (with respect to some key). The two score functions are defined with respect to each key, via a procedure that depends only on the construction of the PRF (in particular, it is independent of the output of the PRG). This is important, since the score function does not require the real adversary to make any PRG queries.

As in the single call case, the goal of the functions is to find a large set of inputs that make disjoint PRG queries. At a high level, this is done by letting the score functions try to break the dependence between some PRF outputs by fixing PRG outputs on queries that are made by many PRF inputs. Specifically, the procedure works in iterations as we next describe.

In each iteration, the adversaries looks for a seed $s$ that appears for sufficiently many inputs (i.e., for many of the $x_i$'s, at least one of the seeds needed to compute $f_k^G(x_i)$ is $s$). For such seeds, the PRG will not contribute much entropy to the output of the PRF (taken over all inputs that query $s$). When we define the scores, we replace $G(s)$ with a fixed value that maximizes the score and is *independent* of $G$. In such a case, the construction is left with one less call to the PRG. This process continues until either no $s$ appear many times, or until the process finds $c$ such seeds. In the former case, we can apply (a generalization of) Claim 3 to argue that there is a large set of inputs with a mutually disjoint set of seeds, while in the latter case, we will later replace all calls to the PRG with fixed values.

In more detail, for every key $k$, the final output of the procedure is a list of $\ell(k) \leq c$ seeds $s_1, \ldots, s_{\ell(k)}$ and a list of nested sets of inputs $\mathcal{I}_1 \supseteq \ldots \supseteq \mathcal{I}_{\ell(k)}$. We require that each $s_t$ appears for sufficiently many inputs in $\mathcal{I}_t$. The score calculation is then done by replacing each $G(s_t)$ with a fixed value. If $\ell(k) = c$, then the scores are fixed and independent of $G$. Otherwise, there is a set $\mathcal{I} \subseteq \mathcal{I}_{\ell(k)}$ of inputs with mutually disjoint seeds. The score calculation is then done the same as in the single call case.

For the argument to work, we need to ensure that at every step, the set of inputs $\mathcal{I}_t$ that are being considered is sufficiently large. Specifically, if the procedure stops early, then Claim 3 implies the existence of a set of $\frac{|\mathcal{I}_t|}{(c-t)|\mathcal{I}_{t+1}|}$ inputs with mutually disjoint queries. For the concentration bound to work, this ratio needs to be sufficiently large (Specifically, it needs to be larger than some fixed polynomial that depends on the key length, the PRG stretch, and the reduction). If the procedure replaces every $G(s_t)$, we need $|\mathcal{I}_{\ell(k)}|$ to be sufficiently large as well to argue that the PRF can be distinguished from a random function. This implies that the number of inputs required is $m = (\text{poly}(n))^c \cdot c!$. For the adversaries to be well-defined, this value must be upper bounded by $2^{\mathsf{in}}$, which holds for all sufficiently large $n$'s by our assumption that $c = o(\mathsf{in}/\log \mathsf{in})$. Additionally, the total number of queries that $R$ makes to the PRG is $d \cdot m^\beta$, for some constant $\beta \in \mathbb{N}$ and where $d$ is the number of calls $R$ makes to the distinguishing adversary. Recall that $c = o(n/\log n)$, hence $d \cdot m^\beta \leq 2^{n/4}$ for all sufficiently large $n$'s. Since we instantiate the PRG with a random function, $2^{n/4}$ queries are insufficient to break its security (see Lemma 1 for the formal statement), resulting in a contradiction.

**2.1.3 Subtleties With Oracle Access to PRF Distinguishers.** The standard definition of a fully black-box reduction from PRF to PRG is as follows. Given access to an oracle-adversary $\mathcal{A}^{(\cdot)}$ that is able to distinguish the PRF from a random function, the reduction, a PPT oracle-aided algorithm $R$ is able to distinguish the output of $G(s)$, where $s \leftarrow \{0,1\}^n$, from a string uniformly sampled from $\{0,1\}^{|G(s)|}$.

Since we fixed $R$, its run-time is some fixed polynomial, say $T(n)$. The adversary $\mathcal{A}^f$ is allowed to query $f$ a polynomial $m$ number of inputs. When activated by the reduction, $\mathcal{A}$ expects $m(n)$ answers. These should be provided by $R$; however, $m$ is chosen by $\mathcal{A}$, which is fixed after $R$, hence $m$ cannot depend on $T$. In particular, if $m(n) > T(n)$, then $R$ has no time to answer $\mathcal{A}$'s queries.

For the model to make sense, we have to treat the $m$ inputs chosen by $\mathcal{A}$ as part of the reduction's input. However, now the reduction depends on $\mathcal{A}$. For example, after receiving the $m$ inputs from $\mathcal{A}$, the reduction can decide to call it $m$ more times. If we now replace $\mathcal{A}$ with another adversary that sends $m+1$ inputs, and apply $\mathcal{A}$ on the first $m$ answers (i.e., it ignores the last input and output), then $R$ calls it more times than with $\mathcal{A}$, thus the entire procedure changed, even though the adversary does the same. Such reductions are arguably not "black-box".

Recall that in our proof, we had to assume that the reduction cannot depend on the number of inputs given by the distinguishing oracle. This means that our proof does not hold for the standard notion of fully black-box constructions. Instead, we consider *query-bounded* reductions. These are reductions whose number of calls to the adversary is bounded by some polynomial $d(n)$ for all adversaries whose distinguishing advantage is sufficiently large. Specifically, for our proof, we assume that there exists a polynomial $d(n)$ such that for any adversary $\mathcal{A}$ whose distinguishing advantage is at least $\alpha(n) = 1-e^{-n}$, the reduction calls $\mathcal{A}$ at most $d(n)$ times. Note that any reduction whose number of calls to $\mathcal{A}$ *decreases* as a function of the distinguishing advantage of $\mathcal{A}$ is also query-bounded (perhaps with a different $\alpha(n)$). We argue that the class of query-bounded reductions is both natural and well-motivated. Indeed, all reductions previously considered in the literature, to the best of our knowledge, satisfy this property and thus fall within the class of query-bounded reductions. This includes, for example, the GGM construction [9], Goldreich and Levin [8] hardcore predicate construction, and Waters [18] construction of signature schemes. We refer the reader to Definition 4 for a formal definition of query-bounded reductions.

### 2.2 Lower Bounds for PRFs with Long Outputs

We now prove Theorem 2. To simplify this introduction, we will prove a simpler result that considers constructions with a single call to the PRG (see Sect. 5 for the proof of the general result). Although it is not as general, the proof highlights the key ideas of our techniques. Specifically, we show that if $\mathsf{out} - r = \omega(\log n)$, then there is no black-box construction of a PRF with output length $\mathsf{out}$ from a PRG with stretch $r$ using a single call to the PRG.

Let $\mathsf{in} = \mathsf{in}(n)$ and assume that $F = \{f_k^G : \{0,1\}^{\mathsf{in}} \rightarrow \{0,1\}^{\mathsf{out}}\}_{n\in\mathbb{N},k\in\{0,1\}^\lambda}$ is a PRF construction that calls $G : \{0,1\}^n \rightarrow \{0,1\}^{n+r}$ once. The main idea of the proof is to consider the entropy of sufficiently many applications of the function. That is, given access to a function $f$ (that is either truly random or sampled from $F$), we consider the total entropy of $m$ applications of $f$ on different inputs, where $m = m(n)$ is a sufficiently large polynomial. Observe that for a random function the entropy is maximized, i.e., it is $\mathsf{out} \cdot m$. However, we show how to construct a PRG $G$ such that the entropy of $m$ applications of $f_k^G$ is noticeably far from $\mathsf{out} \cdot m$. Intuitively, this is achieved by considering a PRG that is only applied to the first $\mathsf{out} - r - 1 = \omega(\log n)$ bits of the input. This ensures that the entropy in the output comes from the key $k$ and the $\mathsf{out} - 1$ (pseudo)random bits obtained from the stretch of $G$. Thus, the entropy will be at most $\lambda + m \cdot (\mathsf{out} - 1)$. Taking $m = \lambda + n$ results in a gap of $n$ from $\mathsf{out} \cdot m$, which we show is sufficient.

We note that the above argument works for all fully black-box reductions, and not just query-bounded ones, as was needed in Theorem 1.

# 3 Preliminaries

## 3.1 Notations

For $n, m \in \mathbb{N}$ we let $[n] = \{1, 2 \ldots n\}$ and let $\binom{[n]}{m} = \{\mathcal{S} \subseteq [n] : |\mathcal{S}| = m\}$. All logarithms are taken in base 2. For a set $\mathcal{S}$, we write $s \leftarrow \mathcal{S}$ to indicate that $s$ is selected uniformly at random from $\mathcal{S}$. Given a random variable (or a distribution) $X$, we write $x \leftarrow X$ to indicate that $x$ is selected according to $X$. PPT stands for probabilistic polynomial time. A function $\mu : \mathbb{N} \to [0,1]$ is called negligible, if for every positive polynomial $p(\cdot)$ and all sufficiently large $n$, $\mu(n) < 1/p(n)$. For $n, m \in \mathbb{N}$, we let $\mathcal{F}_{n,m} = \{f : \{0,1\}^n \to \{0,1\}^m\}$ denote the set of all functions from $\{0,1\}^n$ to $\{0,1\}^m$, and let $\mathcal{F}_n = \mathcal{F}_{n,1}$.

**Theorem 4 (Hoeffding's inequality).** *Let $X_1, \ldots, X_n \in \{0,1\}$ denote independent random variables such that $\Pr[X_i = 1] = p_i$ for all $i \in [n]$ for some $p_i \in (0,1)$. Let $p = \sum_{i=1}^{n} p_i$. Then for every $t > 0$,*

$$\Pr\left[\sum_{i=1}^{n} X_i \geq pn + t\right] \leq e^{-2t^2/n}$$

*and*

$$\Pr\left[\sum_{i=1}^{n} X_i \leq pn - t\right] \leq e^{-2t^2/n}.$$

## 3.2 Pseudorandom Generators

**Definition 1 (Pseudorandom generator (PRG)).** *An efficiently computable function $G$ is an $r(n)$-bit stretch PRG if for every $n \in \mathbb{N}$ and $s \in \{0,1\}^*$, $|G(s)| = |s| + r(|s|)$ and for every* PPT *algorithm $\mathcal{A}$, there exists a negligible function $\mu$ such that*

$$\left|\Pr_{s \leftarrow \{0,1\}^n}\left[\mathcal{A}(1^n, G(s)) = 1\right] - \Pr_{y \leftarrow \{0,1\}^{n+r(n)}}\left[\mathcal{A}(1^n, y) = 1\right]\right| \leq \mu(n).$$

The following lemma states that a random function is a PRG with overwhelming probability.

**Lemma 1.** *The following holds for every $r : \mathbb{N} \to \mathbb{N}$, and all sufficiently large $n \in \mathbb{N}$. Let $G : \{0,1\}^n \to \{0,1\}^{n+r(n)}$ be a function chosen uniformly at random and $C$ be a $2^{n/4}$-call oracle aided (possibly inefficient) algorithm. Then with probability at least $1 - 2^{-n/2}$,*

$$\left|\Pr_{s \leftarrow \{0,1\}^n}\left[C^G(G(s)) = 1\right] - \Pr_{y \leftarrow \{0,1\}^{n+r(n)}}\left[C^G(y) = 1\right]\right| \leq 2^{-n/4}.$$

*Proof.* By Markov's inequality, it suffices to show that

$$\mathrm{E}_{G \leftarrow \mathcal{F}_{n,n+r(n)}}\left[\left|\Pr_{s \leftarrow \{0,1\}^n}\left[C^G(G(s)) = 1\right] - \Pr_{y \leftarrow \{0,1\}^{n+r(n)}}\left[C^G(y) = 1\right]\right|\right] \leq 2^{-3n/4}.$$

This is done by lazy sampling [3]. Assume without loss of generality that $C$ makes only distinct queries to the oracle. Let $P_0 : \{0,1\}^n \to \{0,1\}^{n+r(n)}$ be the procedure defined as follows:

1. Sample $s \leftarrow \{0,1\}^n$ and $y \leftarrow \{0,1\}^{n+r(n)}$, independently.
2. On query $x \in \{0,1\}^n$, sample $y^* \leftarrow \{0,1\}^{n+r(n)}$.
3. If $s = x$, then set *bad* = true. Set $y = y^*$.
4. Return $y$.

Additionally, let $P_1 : \{0,1\}^n \to \{0,1\}^{n+r(n)}$ be the procedure defined as follows:

1. Sample $s \leftarrow \{0,1\}^n$ and $y \leftarrow \{0,1\}^{n+r(n)}$, independently.
2. On query $x \in \{0,1\}^n$, sample $y^* \leftarrow \{0,1\}^{n+r(n)}$.
3. If $s = x$, then set *bad* = true.
4. Return $y$.

First, note that

$$\mathrm{E}_{G\leftarrow\mathcal{F}_{n,n+r(n)}}\left[\Pr_{s\leftarrow\{0,1\}^n}\left[C^G(G(s))=1\right]\right] = \Pr_{y^*\leftarrow\{0,1\}^{n+r(n)}}\left[C^{P_0}(y^*)=1\right]$$

and that

$$\mathrm{E}_{G\leftarrow\mathcal{F}_{n,n+r(n)}}\left[\Pr_{y\leftarrow\{0,1\}^{n+r(n)}}\left[C^G(y)=1\right]\right] = \Pr_{y\leftarrow\{0,1\}^{n+r(n)}}\left[C^{P_1}(y)=1\right].$$

Therefore,

$$\begin{aligned}
&\mathrm{E}_{G\leftarrow\mathcal{F}_{n,n+r(n)}}\left[\left|\Pr_{s\leftarrow\{0,1\}^n}\left[C^G(G(s))=1\right] - \Pr_{y\leftarrow\{0,1\}^{n+r(n)}}\left[C^G(y)=1\right]\right|\right]\\
&\quad\le \left|\Pr_{y^*\leftarrow\{0,1\}^{n+r(n)}}\left[C^{P_0}(y^*)=1\right] - \Pr_{y\leftarrow\{0,1\}^{n+r(n)}}\left[C^{P_1}(y)=1\right]\right|
\end{aligned}$$

Now, observe that the procedures $P_0$ and $P_1$ are identical-until-*bad*, namely, they return identically distributed answers until *bad* occurs. Since $C$ can make $2^{n/4}$ queries, *bad* occurs with probability at most $2^{n/4-n} = 2^{-3n/4}$. Therefore,

$$\left|\Pr_{y^*\leftarrow\{0,1\}^{n+r(n)}}\left[C^{P_0}(y^*)=1\right] - \Pr_{y\leftarrow\{0,1\}^{n+r(n)}}\left[C^{P_1}(y)=1\right]\right| \le 2^{-3n/4}.$$

□

### 3.3 Black-Box Constructions of Pseudorandom Functions

We next define black-box constructions of a pseudorandom function (PRF) from PRGs.

**Definition 2 (Fully black-box PRF constructions).** *A* fully black-box construction *of a PRF from an $r(n)$-bit stretch PRG is a pair $(F, R)$ where*

$$F = \left\{f_k^{(\cdot)} : \{0,1\}^{\mathsf{in}(n)} \to \{0,1\}^{\mathsf{out}(n)}\right\}_{n\in\mathbb{N},k\in\{0,1\}^{\lambda(n)}}$$

*is an efficiently computable oracle-aided function family, and $R^{(\cdot),(\cdot)}$ is a* PPT *oracle-aided algorithm such that the following holds. There exists a polynomial $q : \mathbb{N} \to \mathbb{N}$ such that for every $G = \{G_n : \{0,1\}^n \to \{0,1\}^{n+r(n)}\}_{n\in\mathbb{N}}$ and every oracle-aided algorithm $\mathcal{A}^{(\cdot)}$ for which there exists a constant $c \in \mathbb{N}$ such that*

$$\left|\Pr_{k\leftarrow\{0,1\}^{\lambda(n)}}\left[\mathcal{A}^{f_k^G}(1^n)=1\right] - \Pr_{f\leftarrow\mathcal{F}_{\mathsf{in}(n),\mathsf{out}(n)}}\left[\mathcal{A}^f(1^n)=1\right]\right| \ge \frac{1}{n^c}$$

*for infinitely many n's,*

$$\left|\Pr_{s\leftarrow\{0,1\}^n}\left[R^{\mathcal{A},G}(1^n,G(s))=1\right]-\Pr_{y\leftarrow\{0,1\}^{n+r(n)}}\left[R^{\mathcal{A},G}(1^n,y)=1\right]\right|\geq\frac{1}{q(n^c)}$$

*for infinitely many n's.*

*(F, R) is fully black-box construction of a* weak PRF, *if the above holds for all algorithms $\mathcal{A}$ that query i.i.d. uniform queries to f.*

We next define the query complexity of a black-box construction.

**Definition 3 (c-call adaptive and non-adaptive constructions).** *Let* $\mathsf{in}(n)$, $\mathsf{out}(n)$, $r(n)$, *and* $\lambda(n)$ *be polynomials, and let*

$$F=\left\{f_k^{(\cdot)}:\{0,1\}^{\mathsf{in}(n)}\rightarrow\{0,1\}^{\mathsf{out}(n)}\right\}_{n\in\mathbb{N},k\in\{0,1\}^{\lambda(n)}}$$

*be a black-box PRF construction from an r(n)-bit stretch PRG. For a function* $c:\mathbb{N}\rightarrow\mathbb{N}$, *we say that F is a* $c(\cdot)$-call construction *if for every* $i\in[c(n)]$ *there exist* $S_i:\{0,1\}^{\mathsf{in}(n)}\times\{0,1\}^{\lambda(n)}\times(\{0,1\}^{n+r(n)})^{i-1}\rightarrow\{0,1\}^n$ *and* $P:\{0,1\}^{\mathsf{in}(n)}\times\{0,1\}^{\lambda(n)}\times(\{0,1\}^{n+r(n)})^{c(n)}\rightarrow\{0,1\}^{\mathsf{out}(n)}$ *such that*

$$f_k^G(x)=P\left(x,k,G\left(s_1\right),\ldots,G(s_c)\right)$$

*for all* $G:\{0,1\}^n\rightarrow\{0,1\}^{n+r(n)}$, *where* $s_i=S_i(x,k,G\left(s_1\right),\ldots,G(s_{i-1}))$ *for all* $i\in[c(n)]$. *We say that the construction is* non-adaptive *if every* $S_i$ *depends only on x and k.*

In our proof, we consider a restricted notion of black-box reductions that have access to a distinguisher with oracle access to a function. Roughly, this class captures reductions where the number of times it can query the adversary is bounded by a polynomial for all sufficiently good adversaries.

**Definition 4 (Query-bounded reductions).** *Let (F, R) be a fully black-box construction of a PRF from an r(n)-bit stretch PRG, where*

$$F=\left\{f_k^{(\cdot)}:\{0,1\}^{\mathsf{in}(n)}\rightarrow\{0,1\}^{\mathsf{out}(n)}\right\}_{n\in\mathbb{N},k\in\{0,1\}^{\lambda(n)}},$$

*let* $\varepsilon:\mathbb{N}\rightarrow[0,1]$, *and let* $d:\mathbb{N}\rightarrow\mathbb{N}$. *We say that* $R^{G,\mathcal{A}}$ *is* $(d,\varepsilon)$-query-bounded *if for every oracle-aided algorithm* $\mathcal{A}^{\cdot}$ *such that*

$$\left|\Pr_{k\leftarrow\{0,1\}^{\lambda(n)}}\left[\mathcal{A}^{f_k^G}(1^n)=1\right]-\Pr_{f\leftarrow\mathcal{F}_{\mathsf{in}(n),\mathsf{out}(n)}}\left[\mathcal{A}^f(1^n)=1\right]\right|\geq1-\varepsilon(n)$$

*for infinitely many n's,* $R^{G,\mathcal{A}}$ *calls* $\mathcal{A}$ *at most* $d(n)$ *times.*

Note that any reduction that is $(d,\varepsilon)$-query-bounded is also $(d,\varepsilon')$-query-bounded for any $\varepsilon'$ such that $\varepsilon'(n)\geq\varepsilon(n)$. Therefore, for our impossibility result, proving it for a *larger* $\varepsilon$ yields a stronger result.

# 4 Lower Bounds for Fully Black-Box Constructions of PRFs From PRGs

In this section, we prove our main result. We show that there is no fully black-box construction of PRF with input length in from a PRG with $c$ calls to the PRG and using a query-bounded reduction, where $c = o(n/\log n)$ and $c = o(\mathsf{in}/\log \mathsf{in})$.

We are now ready to state and prove our main result.

**Theorem 5.** *Fix polynomials $r : \mathbb{N} \to \mathbb{N}$ and $\mathsf{in} : \mathbb{N} \to \mathbb{N}$ such that $\mathsf{in}(n) = \omega(\log n)$. Then for every $c : \mathbb{N} \to \mathbb{N}$ such that $c(n) = o\left(n/\log n\right)$ and $c(n) = o\left(\mathsf{in}/\log \mathsf{in}\right)$, and for every polynomial $d : \mathbb{N} \to \mathbb{N}$, there is no $c(n)$-call non-adaptive fully black-box construction of a weak PRF with input length $\mathsf{in}(n)$ and a single-bit output from an $r(n)$-bit stretch PRG, with a $(d, e^{-n})$-query-bounded reduction.*

*Proof.* We first give an overview of the proof. Our proof has 4 major steps.

**Step 1:** We fix $m$ inputs $x_1, \ldots, x_m$ for a sufficiently large $m$. Then, for every key $k$, we identify a large subset of the inputs $\mathcal{I}_k$ based on repetitions in the seeds generated by the key and the inputs in $\mathcal{I}_k$. Specifically, we show that either there are $c$ seeds that are common to all inputs in $\mathcal{I}_k$, or there $t < c$ common seeds and the rest of the seeds are mutually disjoint. Importantly, this step is independent of the PRG, i.e., the set $\mathcal{I}_k$ is the same for every PRG. We formalize the properties of the set $\mathcal{I}_k$ and show its existence in Lemma 2.

**Step 2:** Next, we define an "ideal adversary" $\mathcal{A}_{\mathsf{ideal}}^{f,G}$ that breaks the PRF by inverting the PRG $G$. This adversary is not optimal. Instead of outputting 'PRF' when all input-output pairs (given by the oracle $f$) are consistent with respect to some key $k$, we define a score function based on the number of consistent input-output pairs in the set $\mathcal{I}_k$, and let $\mathcal{A}_{\mathsf{ideal}}^{f,G}$ output 'PRF' if and only if the score is larger then a random threshold sampled uniformly at random. We prove, nonetheless, that this ideal adversary breaks the PRF. This is formalized in Claim 8.

**Step 3:** We then define a "real adversary" whose goal is to simulate the ideal adversary without inverting the PRG. It is given the query-answer pairs generated by the reduction's interaction with the PRG. Roughly, the difference between the real adversary and the ideal adversary is in the definition of the score functions they compute. We show that the real adversary behaves close to the ideal adversary. We formally prove this in Lemma 3.

**Step 4:** Finally, we combine the previous steps to argue that the reduction can successfully break the PRG using the real adversary. Since the real adversary does not query the PRG, we conclude the existence of an algorithm for breaking the PRG using a sub-exponential number of queries. Thus, instantiating the PRG with a random function will contradict Lemma 1, concluding the proof.

Assume towards contradiction that the claim is false. That is, there exists polynomials $\mathsf{in} = \mathsf{in}(n)$, $\lambda = \lambda(n)$, and $r = r(n)$, there exists $c = c(n)$ such that $c = \frac{n}{w(n)\log n}$ and $c = \frac{\mathsf{in}}{w(n)\log \mathsf{in}}$ for some $w(n) = \omega(1)$, there exists a polynomial $d = d(n)$, and there exists a fully black-box construction $(F, R)$ such that $R$ is $(d, e^{-n})$-query-bounded. We write

$$F = \left\{ f_k^{(\cdot)} : \{0,1\}^{\mathsf{in}} \to \{0,1\} \right\}_{n\in\mathbb{N}, k\in\{0,1\}^{\lambda}}$$

where $f_k^{(\cdot)}$ is given by

$$f_k^G(x) = P\left(x, k, G(S_1(x,k)), G(S_2(x,k)), \ldots, G(S_c(x,k))\right),$$

for efficiently computable functions $S_1, S_2, \ldots, S_c : \{0,1\}^{\mathsf{in}} \times \{0,1\}^{\lambda} \to \{0,1\}^n$ and $P : \{0,1\}^{\mathsf{in}} \times \{0,1\}^{\lambda} \times (\{0,1\}^{n+r})^c \to \{0,1\}$.

The proof follows the meta-reduction paradigm. We first define an "ideal" adversary that breaks the PRF using an *exponential number* of queries to the PRG. We then construct an *inefficient* "real" adversary with *no* access to the PRG that is able to simulate the ideal adversary, when provided with the collection of query–answer pairs generated by the reduction's interaction with the PRG. We then conclude that there exists an algorithm that breaks the security of the PRG using fewer than $2^{n/4}$ queries, by running the reduction and using the real adversary.

For the argument to follow through, we have to ensure that the reduction cannot distinguish between the ideal and real adversaries. We are unable to show that the statistical distance between the responses of the adversaries is negligible. Instead, we show that the distance is $1/\operatorname{poly}(n)$, for some polynomial $\operatorname{poly}(n)$ that depends on both the number of calls $d$ made by the reduction to the adversary, and the number of queries $m(n)$ made by the adversary (to its oracle function). Thus, $\operatorname{poly}(n)$ must be sufficiently large, implying that $m(n)$ must be sufficiently large compared to $d$. Consequently, $d$ must be fixed prior to $m(n)$; otherwise, the argument would suffer from a circular dependence among $d$ and $m(n)$. This requirement is exactly the reason we assume the reduction to be query-bounded, as it ensures that $d$ is determined independently of the adversary. We note that if one could construct real and ideal adversaries whose response distributions have negligible statistical distance, our assumption would no longer be necessary.

We first introduce some notation. For every $t \in \{0, 1, \ldots, c\}$, let $m_t = m_t(n)$ be a parameter (not necessarily a polynomial) to be defined by the analysis below. Further, let $m = m_0$ and fix $m$ distinct inputs $x_1, \ldots, x_m \in \{0,1\}^{\mathsf{in}}$.[4]

*Step 1: Identifying frequent seeds.* In the first step of the proof, our goal is to identify for every key $k \in \{0,1\}^{\lambda}$ the set $\mathcal{I}_k$ of inputs with many common seeds. Towards defining $\mathcal{I}_k$, we use the following claim, which states that for every set

[4] Note that if we obtain a contradiction for all distinct inputs, then the same holds for random inputs (up to adding the birthday bound).

of $t < c$ seeds $\mathcal{S}$, if every PRG seed outside of $\mathcal{S}$ appears a few times among a subset $\mathcal{I}_0 \subseteq [m]$ of the inputs, then for a large fraction of these inputs, the only common seeds belong to $\mathcal{S}$.

**Claim 6.** *Fix a number $p \in [m]$ and a key $k \in \{0,1\}^\lambda$. Further fix a set of inputs $\mathcal{I}_0 \subseteq [m]$ and a set of seeds $\mathcal{S} \subseteq \{0,1\}^n$ of size $|\mathcal{S}| = t \in \{0, 1, \ldots, c-1\}$, such that for every $s \in \mathcal{S}$ and $i \in \mathcal{I}_0$ there exists $j \in [c]$ such that $s = S_j(x_i, k)$. Assume that there is no $s \in \{0,1\}^n \setminus \mathcal{S}$ and $\mathcal{I} \subseteq \mathcal{I}_0$ of size $p$ such that*

$$s \in \bigcap_{i \in \mathcal{I}} \{S_j(x_i, k) : j \in [c]\}.$$

*Then there exists a set $\mathcal{I}' \subseteq \mathcal{I}_0$ of size*

$$|\mathcal{I}'| \geq \frac{|\mathcal{I}_0|}{(c-t)(p-1)+1} \geq \frac{|\mathcal{I}_0|}{(c-t)p},$$

*such that the sets of PRG queries generated by them (outside of $\mathcal{S}$) are mutually disjoint, i.e.,*

$$S_j(x_i, k) \notin \{S_{j'}(x_{i'}, k) : j' \in [c], i' \in \mathcal{I}' \setminus \{i\}\} \setminus \mathcal{S},$$

*for every $i \in \mathcal{I}'$ and $j \in [c]$.*

*Proof.* Consider the graph $H = (\mathcal{I}_0, E)$ where $\{i, i'\} \in E$ for $i \neq i'$ if and only if $x_i$ and $x_{i'}$ share a common PRG query outside of $\mathcal{S}$, i.e.,

$$(\{S_j(x_i, k) : j \in [c]\} \setminus \mathcal{S}) \cap (\{S_j(x_{i'}, k) : j \in [c]\} \setminus \mathcal{S}) \neq \emptyset.$$

Observe that the set $\mathcal{I}'$ we aim to show exists, corresponds to an independent set in $H$. By assumption, every PRG query $s \in \{0,1\}^n \setminus \mathcal{S}$ appears at most $p-1$ among the set of all seeds in $\{S_j(x_i, k) : i \in \mathcal{I}_0, j \in [c]\}$. Thus, for every vertex $i \in \mathcal{I}_0$, every $j \in [c]$ such that $S_j(x_i, k) \notin \mathcal{S}$ contributes 1 to the degree of $i$. Since by assumption there are exactly $t$ indexes $j \in [c]$ such that $S_j(x_i, k) \in \mathcal{S}$, the degree of each vertex in $H$ is at most $(c-t)(p-1)$. Therefore, by greedily picking vertices for an independent set and removing their neighbors, we conclude that there exists an independent set of vertices of size at least $|\mathcal{I}_0|/((c-t)(p-1)+1)$. □

Recall that to construct the two adversaries, we define two *score functions* (one for each adversary) that aim to compute for how many inputs the reduction returned the correct output (with respect to some key). The two score functions are defined with respect to each key, via a procedure that depends only on the construction of the PRF (in particular, it is independent of the output of the PRG). This is important, since the score function does not require the real adversary to make any PRG queries.

At a high level, the procedure works in iterations, where in each iteration it looks for a seed $s$ that appears for sufficiently many inputs (i.e., for many of the $x_i$'s, at least one of the seeds needed to compute $f_k^G(x_i)$ is $s$). The process continues until either no $s$ appear many times, or until the process finds $c$ such seeds. In the former case, we can apply Claim 6 to argue there is a large set of inputs with mutually disjoint set of seeds, while in the latter case, we will later replace all calls to the PRG with fixed values. The following lemma summarizes this.

**Lemma 2.** *For every key $k \in \{0,1\}^\lambda$, there exists a number $\ell(k) \in \{0,1,\ldots,c\}$, there exist $\ell(k)$ distinct seeds $\mathbf{s}_k = (s_{k,1},\ldots,s_{k,\ell(k)}) \in (\{0,1\}^n)^{\ell(k)}$, and there exists a set $\mathcal{I}_k \subseteq [m]$ such that the following holds.*

1. *If $\ell(k) = c$, then $|\mathcal{I}_k| = m_c$ and $s_{k,t} \in \bigcap_{i\in\mathcal{I}_k}\{S_j(x_i,k) : j \in [c]\}$ for every $t \in [c]$.*
2. *Otherwise, if $\ell(k) < c$, then $|\mathcal{I}_k| = \frac{m_{\ell(k)}}{(c-\ell(k)+1)m_{\ell(k)+1}}$,*

$$S_j(x_i,k) \notin \{S_{j'}(x_{i'},k) : j' \in [c], i' \in \mathcal{I}_k \setminus \{i\}\},$$

*for every $i \in \mathcal{I}_k$ and $j \in [c]$, and there exists a set $\mathcal{I} \subseteq [m]$ of size $|\mathcal{I}| = m_{\ell(k)}$ such that $\mathcal{I}_k \subseteq \mathcal{I}$ and $s_{k,t} \in \bigcap_{i\in\mathcal{I}}\{S_j(x_i,k) : j \in [c]\}$ for every $t \in [\ell(k)]$.*

*Proof.* The proof follows from greedily looking for the next seed $s_{k,t}$ and the (sufficiently large) set of inputs generating it, until we found $c$ such seeds, or it does not exist and we can apply Claim 6. Formally, the lemma follows from considering the following procedure:

1. Let $\mathcal{I}_{k,0} = [m]$ and $t = 1$.
2. While $t \le c$ do the following:
   - If there exists a seed $s \in \{0,1\}^n \setminus \{s_{k,1},\ldots,s_{k,t-1}\}$ and $\mathcal{I} \subseteq \mathcal{I}_{k,t-1}$ of size $|\mathcal{I}| = m_t$ such that $s \in \bigcap_{i\in\mathcal{I}}\{S_j(x_i,k) : j \in [c]\}$, then let $s_{k,t}$ and $\mathcal{I}_{k,t}$ denote the lexicographically smallest such seed $s$ and set $\mathcal{I}$, and increment $t$ by 1.
   - Otherwise, by Claim 6, there exists a set of inputs $\mathcal{I} \subseteq \mathcal{I}_{k,t-1}$ of size

$$|\mathcal{I}| = \frac{|\mathcal{I}_{k,t-1}|}{(c-t)\cdot m_t} = \frac{m_{t-1}}{(c-t)\cdot m_t}$$

   such that

$$S_j(x_i,k) \notin \{S_{j'}(x_{i'},k) : j' \in [c], i' \in \mathcal{I} \setminus \{i\}\},$$

   for every $i \in \mathcal{I}$ and $j \in [c]$. Let $\ell(k) = t-1$, and let $\mathcal{I}_k$ denote lexicographically smallest such set $\mathcal{I}$, and halt.
3. Let $\ell(k) = c$ and $\mathcal{I}_k = \mathcal{I}_{k,c}$.

□

It will be convenient to consider the value $\nu = \min_k |\mathcal{I}_k|$.

*Step 2: Defining the ideal adversary.* We next define the first score function, which we call the *ideal score function.* It depends on the entire PRG oracle and will only be used by the ideal adversary. Given a key and a sequence of possible outputs $\mathbf{z} \in (\{0,1\})^m$,[5] the score is defined by using Lemma 2 to find the seeds that appear many times. It then replaces the output of $G$ on those seeds with fixed values, and returns the number of inputs in $\mathcal{I}_k$ that are consistent with $\mathbf{z}$.

In what follows, for every pair of sequences $\mathbf{s} = (s_1, \ldots, s_t) \in (\{0,1\}^n)^t$ and $\mathbf{y} = (y_1, \ldots, y_t) \in (\{0,1\}^{n+r})^t$, define

$$F_{\mathbf{s},\mathbf{y}} = \left\{ f_{k,\mathbf{s},\mathbf{y}}^{(\cdot)} : \{0,1\}^{\mathsf{in}} \to \{0,1\} \right\}_{n \in \mathbb{N}, k \in \{0,1\}^\lambda},$$

where $f_{k,\mathbf{s},\mathbf{y}}^{(\cdot)}$ is the same as $f_k^{(\cdot)}$, except that for oracle queries in $\mathbf{s}$, the oracle answer for the seed $s_i$ is replaced with $y_i$, for every $i \in [t]$.

**Definition 5 (Ideal score function).** *For every key $k \in \{0,1\}^\lambda$, every sequence of possible outputs $\mathbf{z} = (z_1, \ldots, z_m)$, and every function $G : \{0,1\}^n \to \{0,1\}^{n+r}$, define the ideal score of $k$ to be*

$$\mathsf{is}_k^G(\mathbf{z}) = \max_{\mathbf{y} \in (\{0,1\}^{n+r})^{\ell(k)}} \left( \left| \left\{ i \in \mathcal{I}_k : f_{k,\mathbf{s}_k,\mathbf{y}}^G(x_i) = z_i \right\} \right| \right).$$

Observe that if $\ell(k) = c$, then $\mathsf{is}_k^G(\mathbf{z})$ is independent of $G$.

Next, we define the "ideal" adversary $\mathcal{A}_{\mathsf{ideal}}^{f,G}$ for the PRF. This adversary queries the PRG on *exponentially many* inputs. We will then show that the reduction can simulate this adversary efficiently, resulting in an efficient distinguisher for the PRG. Roughly, $\mathcal{A}_{\mathsf{ideal}}^{f,G}$ works as follows. First, it queries the oracle $f$ on $x_1, \ldots, x_m$. The adversary outputs PRF if and only if there is a key whose ideal score is at least $\alpha \cdot |\mathcal{I}_k|$, where $\alpha \in [0.8, 1]$ *is sampled uniformly at random.*

**Algorithm 7** ($\mathcal{A}_{\mathsf{ideal}}$.)
*Input: The security parameter* $1^n$.
*Oracle access: A function* $f : \{0,1\}^{\mathsf{in}} \to \{0,1\}$ *and a PRG* $G : \{0,1\}^n \to \{0,1\}^{n+r}$.

1. *Query* $G$ *on every input in* $\{0,1\}^n$.
2. *Query* $f$ *on* $x_1, \ldots, x_m$. *Let* $\mathbf{z} = (z_1, \ldots, z_m)$ *denote the respective answers.*
3. *Sample* $\alpha \in [0.8, 1]$ *uniformly at random.*
4. *Output 1 if and only if there exists* $k \in \{0,1\}^\lambda$ *such that* $\mathsf{is}_k^G(\mathbf{z}) \geq \alpha \cdot |\mathcal{I}_k|$.

We first show that $\mathcal{A}_{\mathsf{ideal}}^{f,G}$ indeed distinguishes the PRF from a random function.

**Claim 8.** *For all* $G : \{0,1\}^n \to \{0,1\}^{n+r}$,

$$\left| \Pr_{k \leftarrow \{0,1\}^\lambda} \left[ \mathcal{A}_{\mathsf{ideal}}^{f_k^G, G}(1^n) = 1 \right] - \Pr_{f \leftarrow \mathcal{F}_{\mathsf{in}}} \left[ \mathcal{A}_{\mathsf{ideal}}^{f,G}(1^n) = 1 \right] \right| \geq 1 - e^{\lambda + c(n+r) - \nu/10}.$$

[5] The score also implicitly depends on the inputs $x_1, \ldots, x_m$ we fixed earlier.

*Proof.* We first show that $\mathcal{A}_{\text{ideal}}^{f_k^G,G}(1^n)$ always outputs 1. Indeed, observe that

$$\mathsf{is}_k^G(\mathbf{z}) = \max_{\mathbf{y}\in(\{0,1\}^{n+r})^{\ell(k)}} \left(\left|\{i \in \mathcal{I}_k : f_{k,\mathbf{s}_k,\mathbf{y}}^G(x_i) = f_k^G(x_i)\}\right|\right).$$

Then taking $y_i = G(s_{k,i})$ for every $i \in [\ell(k)]$ results in $\mathsf{is}_k^G(\mathbf{z}) = |\mathcal{I}_k|$.

To conclude the proof, we next show that for a random function $f$, $\mathcal{A}_{\text{ideal}}^{f,G}(1^n)$ outputs 1 with negligible probability. For every key $k \in \{0,1\}^\lambda$, every $\mathbf{y} \in (\{0,1\}^{n+r})^{\ell(k)}$, and every $i \in \mathcal{I}_k$, define the random variable $X_{k,\mathbf{y},i}$ to be the indicator for the event $f_{k,\mathbf{s}_k,\mathbf{y}}^G(x_i) = f(x_i)$. Then

$$\mathsf{is}_k^G(\mathbf{z}) = \max_{\mathbf{y}\in(\{0,1\}^{n+r})^{\ell(k)}} \left(\sum_{i\in\mathcal{I}_k} X_{k,\mathbf{y},i}\right).$$

Since $f$ is a random function, these indicators are independent and have expectation $1/2$. Therefore, for every $k \in \{0,1\}^\lambda$ and every $\mathbf{y} \in (\{0,1\}^{n+r})^{\ell(k)}$, Hoeffding's inequality (see Theorem 4) implies that

$$\begin{aligned}\Pr_{f\leftarrow\mathcal{F}_{\text{in}}}\left[\sum_{i\in\mathcal{I}_k} X_{k,\mathbf{y},i} > 0.8\cdot|\mathcal{I}_k|\right] &\le e^{-2\cdot(0.8-0.5)^2\cdot|\mathcal{I}_k|}\\ &\le e^{-|\mathcal{I}_k|/10}.\end{aligned}$$

Therefore, by the union bound,

$$\begin{aligned}&\Pr_{f\leftarrow\mathcal{F}_{\text{in}}}\left[\mathcal{A}_{\text{ideal}}^{f,G}(1^n) = 1\right]\\ &\le \Pr_{f\leftarrow\mathcal{F}_{\text{in}}}\left[\exists k \in \{0,1\}^\lambda : \mathsf{is}_k^G(f(x_1),\ldots,f(x_m)) \ge 0.8\cdot|\mathcal{I}_k|\right]\\ &= \Pr_{f\leftarrow\mathcal{F}_{\text{in}}}\left[\exists k \in \{0,1\}^\lambda\ \exists \mathbf{y} \in (\{0,1\}^{n+r})^{\ell(k)} : \sum_{i\in\mathcal{I}_k} X_{k,\mathbf{y},i} \ge 0.8\cdot|\mathcal{I}_k|\right]\\ &\le 2^{\lambda+c(n+r)}\cdot e^{-\nu/10}\\ &\le e^{\lambda+c(n+r)-\nu/10}.\end{aligned}$$

□

Recall that for every $k \in \{0,1\}^\lambda$, $|\mathcal{I}_k| = m_c$ or $|\mathcal{I}_k| = \frac{m_{t-1}}{(c-t+1)m_t}$ for some $t \in [c]$. Since $\nu \ge |\mathcal{I}_k|$ for every $k \in \lambda$, taking $m_c \ge 10(\lambda + c(n+r) + n)$ and $m_{t-1} \ge (c-t+1)m_t \cdot 10(\lambda + c(n+r) + n)$ for all $t \in [c]$, results in the ideal adversary's advantage begin at least $1 - e^{-n}$.

*Step 3: Defining the real adversary.* We now define the *real score*, which will be used by the real adversary. It is defined with respect to a set of query-answer pairs $\mathcal{G}$ instead of a PRG. The set $\mathcal{G}$ will later be instantiated with respect to the queries the reduction made to the PRG. Similarly to the ideal score, the computation of the real score also starts by replacing calls to $G$ on seeds that appear many times with fixed inputs. The only difference is the end of the recursive process. There are two cases: either every call to $G$ was replaced, or the inputs in $\mathcal{I}_k$ have mutually disjoint seeds. In the former case, the real score is identical to the ideal score. In the latter case, the score is defined as follows. Every input $x_i$ for which every remaining seed (i.e., for which the output of $G$ was not fixed) belongs to the set $\mathcal{G}$ can be computed using $G$. Such inputs contribute the same value as in the ideal score. For other inputs, the real score estimates its contribution to the ideal score by computing the probability over the PRG that the answer is correct. Since this is the case where all remaining seeds are mutually disjoint, the outputs corresponding to these inputs are independent random variables, and we can estimate their contribution to the score with high precision (see Lemma 3 below).

In the following, for a set of PRG query-answer pairs $\mathcal{G} = \{(s_1^{\mathcal{G}}, y_1^{\mathcal{G}}), \ldots, (s_q^{\mathcal{G}}, y_q^{\mathcal{G}})\} \subseteq \{0,1\}^n \times \{0,1\}^{n+r}$ we let $\mathbf{s}^{\mathcal{G}}$ denote the sequence of queries in $\mathcal{G}$ that *do not appear in* $\mathbf{s}_k$, and let $\mathbf{y}^{\mathcal{G}}$ denote the corresponding sequence of outputs. The reason not to include the queries in $\mathbf{s}_k$ is that any query $s$ made by the reduction is unknown to the ideal adversary, which maximizes its score over all possible values of $G(s)$. Thus, the real adversary does the same, obtaining consistency between the two scores.

**Definition 6 (Real score function).** *For every key $k \in \{0,1\}^\lambda$, every sequence of possible outputs $\mathbf{z} = (z_1, \ldots, z_m)$, and every set of PRG query-answer pairs $\mathcal{G} = \{(s_1^{\mathcal{G}}, y_1^{\mathcal{G}}), \ldots, (s_q^{\mathcal{G}}, y_q^{\mathcal{G}})\} \in \{0,1\}^n \times \{0,1\}^{n+r}$, define $\mathsf{rs}_k^{\mathcal{G}}(\mathbf{z})$ as follows.*

- *If $\ell(k) = c$, then let*

$$\mathsf{rs}_k^{\mathcal{G}}(\mathbf{z}) = \max_{\mathbf{y} \in (\{0,1\}^{n+r})^c} \left(\left|\{i \in \mathcal{I}_k : P(x_i, k, y_1', \ldots, y_c') = z_i\}\right|\right),$$

*where for every $j \in [c]$, $y_j' = y_{j'}$ for the unique $j' \in [c]$ such that $S_j(x_i, k) = s_{k,j'}$.*
- *If $\ell(k) < c$, then let*

$$\mathsf{rs}_k^{\mathcal{G}}(\mathbf{z}) = \max_{\mathbf{y} \in (\{0,1\}^{n+r})^{\ell(k)}} \left(\sum_{i \in \mathcal{I}_k} \Pr_{G' \leftarrow \mathcal{F}_{n,n+r}} \left[f^{G'}_{k,(\mathbf{s}_k \| \mathbf{s}^{\mathcal{G}}),(\mathbf{y} \| \mathbf{y}^{\mathcal{G}})}(x_i) = z_i\right]\right).$$

Similarly to the ideal score, if $\ell(k) = c$ then $\mathsf{rs}_k^{\mathcal{G}}(\mathbf{z})$ is independent of $\mathcal{G}$. In particular, in such a case, $\mathsf{rs}_k^{\mathcal{G}}(\mathbf{z}) = \mathsf{is}_k^{G}(\mathbf{z})$.

Since every ideal adversary we consider has advantage at least $1 - e^{-n}$, it follows that there exists a constant $\gamma \in \mathbb{N}$ such that for any $G \in \mathcal{F}_{n,n+r}$,

$$\left|\Pr_{s \leftarrow \{0,1\}^n}\left[R^{\mathcal{A}_{\mathsf{ideal}},G}(1^n, G(s)) = 1\right] - \Pr_{y \leftarrow \{0,1\}^{n+r}}\left[R^{\mathcal{A}_{\mathsf{ideal}},G}(1^n, y) = 1\right]\right| \geq \frac{1}{n^\gamma} \quad (1)$$

for infinitely many $n$'s. To obtain a contradiction, we construct an algorithm $\widetilde{R}^{(\cdot)}$ that successfully breaks a *randomly chosen* PRG with noticeable probability, using at most $2^{n/4}$ queries to $G$ and *without* having access to $\mathcal{A}_{\mathsf{ideal}}$. Specifically, we define $\widetilde{R}$ such that

$$\Pr_{G \leftarrow \mathcal{F}_{n,n+r}}\left[\mathrm{Adv}\left(\widetilde{R}^G\right) \leq \frac{1}{3n^{\gamma}}\right] \leq \frac{3}{4}, \tag{2}$$

for infinitely many $n$'s, where

$$\mathrm{Adv}\left(\widetilde{R}^G\right) := \left|\Pr_{s \leftarrow \{0,1\}^n}\left[\widetilde{R}^G(1^n, G(s)) = 1\right] - \Pr_{y \leftarrow \{0,1\}^{n+r}}\left[\widetilde{R}^G(1^n, y) = 1\right]\right|,$$

is the advantage of $\widetilde{R}^G$. for infinitely many $n$'s. Note that Eq. (2) contradicts Lemma 1.

Before defining $\widetilde{R}$, we first introduce an adversary $\mathcal{A}_{\mathsf{real}}$ that, intuitively, efficiently emulates $\mathcal{A}_{\mathsf{ideal}}$ using the set of queries to $G$ used so far by the reduction. Roughly, $\mathcal{A}_{\mathsf{real}}$ works similarly to $\mathcal{A}_{\mathsf{ideal}}$, but uses $\mathsf{rs}$ instead of $\mathsf{is}$. We then show by letting $\widetilde{R}$ run $R$, and replacing each call to $\mathcal{A}_{\mathsf{ideal}}$ with running $\mathcal{A}_{\mathsf{real}}$ using the set of query-answer pairs of the PRG used so far, the answers of the two distinguishing oracles are close in statistical distance.

**Algorithm 9** ($\mathcal{A}_{\mathsf{real}}$)
*Input: The security parameter* $1^n$, *a sequence* $\mathbf{z} \in \{0,1\}^m$, *and a set of query-answer pairs* $\mathcal{G} \subseteq \{0,1\}^n \times \{0,1\}^{n+r}$.

1. *Sample* $\alpha \in [0.8, 1]$ *uniformly at random.*
2. *Output 1 if and only if there exists* $k \in \{0,1\}^{\lambda}$ *such that* $\mathsf{rs}_k^{\mathcal{G}}(\mathbf{z}) \geq \alpha \cdot |\mathcal{I}_k|$.

We are now ready to define $\widetilde{R}$. The algorithm simply runs $R$, replacing all calls to $\mathcal{A}_{\mathsf{ideal}}$ by running $\mathcal{A}_{\mathsf{real}}$.

**Algorithm 10** ($\widetilde{R}$)
*Input: The security parameter* $1^n$ *and a challenge* $y^* \in \{0,1\}^{n+r}$.
*Oracle access: A PRG* $G : \{0,1\}^n \rightarrow \{0,1\}^{n+r}$.

1. *Simulate* $R^{\mathcal{A},G}$ *as follows.*
   - *Whenever* $R$ *calls* $G$, *query* $G$ *with the same input.*
   - *Whenever* $R$ *calls* $\mathcal{A}_{\mathsf{ideal}}$, *send it* $x_1, \ldots, x_m$ *(if* $R$ *queries* $G$ *during this call then query it as well). Let* $\mathbf{z} = (z_1, \ldots, z_m) \in \{0,1\}^m$ *denote the respective answers of* $R$. *Call* $\mathcal{A}_{\mathsf{real}}(1^n, \mathbf{z}, \mathcal{G})$, *where* $\mathcal{G}$ *is the current set of query-answer pairs with respect to* $G$, *and send to* $R$ *the same answer.*
2. *Output whatever* $R$ *outputs.*

We next show that $\widetilde{R}$ and $R$ output the same value with high probability. We do so by showing that the statistical distance between the states of $R$ and $\widetilde{R}$ after every call to the adversary is small. Towards proving this, we first show that for every possible sequence of responses $\mathbf{z}$ made by the reduction, the two scores computed by the real and ideal adversaries at any given call are somewhat close except with a negligible probability, where the probability is taken over $G$ and $y^*$ (the randomness of the reduction is fixed). In the following, for a set $\mathcal{G} \subseteq \{0,1\}^n \times \{0,1\}^{n+r}$ we let $\mathcal{F}^{\mathcal{G}}_{n,n+r}$ denote the set of all functions that are consistent with $\mathcal{G}$.

**Lemma 3.** *Consider a call made by the reduction to the distinguishing oracle, and fix the query-answer pairs $\mathcal{G} \subseteq \{0,1\}^n \times \{0,1\}^{n+r}$ made so far by the reduction. Let $Y$ denote the distribution over $\{0,1\}^{n+r}$ for the challenge given to the reduction (i.e., it is either uniform over $\{0,1\}^{n+r}$ or is $G(S)$ for $S$ uniform over $\{0,1\}^n$), and let $\mathbf{z} \in (\{0,1\})^m$ denote the reduction's answers to the distinguishing oracle on inputs $x_1, \ldots, x_m$. Then for every $\delta \geq 2/\nu$,*

$$\Pr_{G \leftarrow \mathcal{F}^{\mathcal{G}}_{n,n+r}, y^* \leftarrow Y}\left[\exists k \in \{0,1\}^\lambda : \left|\mathsf{is}^G_k(\mathbf{z}) - \mathsf{rs}^{\mathcal{G}}_k(\mathbf{z})\right| \geq \delta \cdot |\mathcal{I}_k|\right] \leq e^{\lambda - \frac{\delta^2}{2} \cdot \nu}. \quad (3)$$

*Proof.* By the union bound, it suffices to show that

$$\Pr_{G \leftarrow \mathcal{F}^{\mathcal{G}}_{n,n+r}, y^* \leftarrow Y}\left[\left|\mathsf{is}^G_k(\mathbf{z}) - \mathsf{rs}^{\mathcal{G}}_k(\mathbf{z})\right| \geq \delta \cdot |\mathcal{I}_k|\right] \leq e^{-\frac{\delta^2}{2} \cdot \nu} \quad (4)$$

for every key $k \in \{0,1\}^\lambda$.

As noted before, if $\ell(k) = c$, then the two scores are identical and the difference is 0. In the remainder of the proof, we assume that $\ell(k) < c$.

For every $\mathbf{y} \in (\{0,1\}^{n+r})^{\ell(k)}$, let

$$\mathsf{is}^G_k(\mathbf{z}, \mathbf{y}) = \left|\left\{i \in \mathcal{I}_k : f^G_{k,\mathbf{s}_k,\mathbf{y}}(x_i) = z_i\right\}\right|$$

and let

$$\mathsf{rs}^{\mathcal{G}}_k(\mathbf{z}, \mathbf{y}) = \sum_{i \in \mathcal{I}_k} \Pr_{G' \leftarrow \mathcal{F}_{n,n+r}}\left[f^{G'}_{k,(\mathbf{s}_k||\mathbf{s}^{\mathcal{G}}),(\mathbf{y}||\mathbf{y}^{\mathcal{G}})}(x_i) = z_i\right],$$

where $\mathbf{s}^{\mathcal{G}}$ is the sequence of seeds in $\mathcal{G}$ that do not appear in $\mathbf{s}_k$, and $\mathbf{y}^{\mathcal{G}}$ is the sequence of corresponding outputs.

We show that for any sequence $\mathbf{y} \in (\{0,1\}^{n+r})^{\ell(k)}$,

$$\Pr_{G \leftarrow \mathcal{F}^{\mathcal{G}}_{n,n+r}, y^* \leftarrow Y}\left[\left|\mathsf{is}^G_k(\mathbf{z}, \mathbf{y}) - \mathsf{rs}^{\mathcal{G}}_k(\mathbf{z}, \mathbf{y})\right| \geq \delta \cdot |\mathcal{I}_k|\right] \leq e^{-\frac{\delta^2}{2} \cdot \nu}. \quad (5)$$

In particular, this holds for the $\mathbf{y}$ that maximizes the scores, which implies Eq. (4). Note that the string $\mathbf{y}$ that maximizes the scores for the real and ideal adversaries could be different, but Eq. (5) implies Eq. (4) nevertheless.

Fixing $k$ and $\mathbf{y} \in (\{0,1\}^{n+r})^{\ell(k)}$, we simplify notation by writing $\mathsf{is}$ and $\mathsf{rs}$ for the ideal and real scores, respectively. We next show that

$$\mathsf{rs} \leq \mathrm{E}_{G \leftarrow \mathcal{F}^{\mathcal{G}}_{n,n+r}, y^* \leftarrow Y}\left[\mathsf{is}\right] \leq \mathsf{rs} + 1. \quad (6)$$

By linearity of expectation, it follows that the contribution of every $i \in \mathcal{I}_k$ to $\mathrm{E}_G[\mathsf{is}]$ is

$$\Pr_{G \leftarrow \mathcal{F}^{\mathcal{G}}_{n,n+r}, y^* \leftarrow Y}\left[f^G_{k,\mathbf{s}_k,\mathbf{y}}(x_i) = z_i\right]$$

(where $z_i$ may depend on $y^*$ and $G$).

If $Y$ is the uniform distribution over $\{0,1\}^{n+r}$, then

$$\Pr_{G \leftarrow \mathcal{F}^{\mathcal{G}}_{n,n+r}, y^* \leftarrow Y}\left[f^G_{k,\mathbf{s}_k,\mathbf{y}}(x_i) = z_i\right] = \Pr_{G' \leftarrow \mathcal{F}^{\mathcal{G}}_{n,n+r}, y^* \leftarrow Y}\left[f^{G'}_{k,(\mathbf{s}_k||\mathbf{s}^{\mathcal{G}}),(\mathbf{y}||\mathbf{y}^{\mathcal{G}})}(x_i) = z_i\right]$$

for every $i \in \mathcal{I}_k$, hence $\mathrm{E}_{G,y^*}[\mathsf{is}] = \mathsf{rs}$. Otherwise, if the distribution of $Y$ is $G(S)$ where $S$ is uniform over $\{0,1\}^n$, then every $i \in \mathcal{I}_k$ such that $z_i = P(x_i, k, \mathbf{y}')$, where $Y$ appears in $\mathbf{y}'$, contributes 1 to $\mathrm{E}_{G,y^*}[\mathsf{is}]$. Since the sets $\{S_j(x_i,k) : j \in [c]\}$ are pairwise disjoint, there is at most 1 such $i$. On the other hand, for the real score, each $i$ contributes a value between 0 and 1, thus $\mathrm{E}_{G,y^*}[\mathsf{is}] \leq \mathsf{rs} + 1$.

For every $i \in \mathcal{I}_k$ let $X_i$ denote the indicator for the event $f^G_{k,\mathbf{s}_k,\mathbf{y}}(x_i) = z_i$ (over sampling $G \leftarrow \mathcal{F}^{\mathcal{G}}_{n,n+r}$ and $y^* \leftarrow Y$). Then $\mathsf{is} = \sum_{i \in \mathcal{I}_k} X_i$. These random variables are independent since the sets $\{S_j(x_i,k) : j \in [c]\}$ are pairwise disjoint. Since $\delta \geq 2/\nu \geq 2/|\mathcal{I}_k|$, by Hoeffding's inequality, it follows that

$$\begin{aligned}
&\Pr_{G \leftarrow \mathcal{F}^{\mathcal{G}}_{n,n+r}, y^* \leftarrow Y}\left[|\mathsf{is} - \mathsf{rs}| \geq \delta \cdot |\mathcal{I}_k|\right] \\
&\leq \Pr_{G \leftarrow \mathcal{F}^{\mathcal{G}}_{n,n+r}, y^* \leftarrow Y}\left[|\mathsf{is} - \mathrm{E}[\mathsf{is}]| \geq \delta \cdot |\mathcal{I}_k| - 1\right] \\
&\leq \Pr_{G \leftarrow \mathcal{F}^{\mathcal{G}}_{n,n+r}, y^* \leftarrow Y}\left[|\mathsf{is} - \mathrm{E}[\mathsf{is}]| \geq \frac{\delta}{2} \cdot |\mathcal{I}_k|\right] \\
&\leq e^{-\frac{2\left(\frac{\delta}{2}\cdot|\mathcal{I}_k|\right)^2}{|\mathcal{I}_k|}} \\
&= e^{-\frac{\delta^2}{2}\cdot|\mathcal{I}_k|}.
\end{aligned}$$

□

We now show that for any call by the reduction to the distinguishing oracle, the statistical distance (taken over $G$ and the challenge $y^*$) between the answers of $\mathcal{A}_{\mathsf{ideal}}$ and $\mathcal{A}_{\mathsf{real}}$ is small.

**Lemma 4.** *Fix a call to the distinguishing oracle. Let $\mathcal{G} \subseteq \{0,1\}^n \times \{0,1\}^{n+r}$ denote the set of query-answer pairs made by $R$ to $G$, let $Y$ denote the distribution over the challenge, and let $\mathbf{z} = (z_1, \ldots, z_m) \in \{0,1\}^m$ denote the answers of $R$ when receiving inputs $x_1, \ldots, x_m$ from the distinguishing oracle. Finally, for every $G \in \mathcal{F}^{\mathcal{G}}_{n,n+r}$ and $y^* \in \{0,1\}^{n+r}$ let $\mathsf{ip}^{G,y^*}$ denote the probability that $\mathcal{A}_{\mathsf{ideal}}(1^n)$ outputs 1 when given $\mathbf{z}$ as the oracle answers, and let $\mathsf{rp}^{\mathcal{G},y^*}$ denote the probability that $\mathcal{A}_{\mathsf{real}}(1^n, \mathbf{z}, \mathcal{G})$ outputs 1. Then, for every $\delta \geq 2/\nu$*

$$\mathrm{SD}_{G \leftarrow \mathcal{F}^{\mathcal{G}}_{n,n+r}, y^* \leftarrow Y}\left(\mathsf{ip}^{G,y^*}, \mathsf{rp}^{\mathcal{G},y^*}\right) \leq e^{\lambda - \frac{\delta^2}{2}\cdot\nu} + 5\delta.$$

*Proof.* For every $G \in \mathcal{F}^{\mathcal{G}}_{n,n+r}$ and every $y^* \in \{0,1\}^{n+r}$ let

$$\mu^{G,y^*} = \max_{k \in \{0,1\}^\lambda} \frac{\left|\mathsf{is}^G_k(\mathbf{z}) - \mathsf{rs}^{\mathcal{G}}_k(\mathbf{z})\right|}{|\mathcal{I}_k|}.$$

Additionally, for every $\alpha \in [0.8, 1]$ let

$$\mathsf{ip}^{G,y^*}(\alpha) = \begin{cases} 1 & \text{if } \exists k \in \{0,1\}^\lambda : \mathsf{is}_k^G(\mathbf{z}) \geq \alpha|\mathcal{I}_k| \\ 0 & \text{otherwise,} \end{cases}$$

and let

$$\mathsf{rp}^{\mathcal{G},y^*}(\alpha) = \begin{cases} 1 & \text{if } \exists k \in \{0,1\}^\lambda : \mathsf{rs}_k^{\mathcal{G}}(\mathbf{z}) \geq \alpha|\mathcal{I}_k| \\ 0 & \text{otherwise.} \end{cases}$$

Then by Jensen's inequality,

$$\left|\mathrm{E}_{\alpha\leftarrow[0.8,1]}\left[\mathsf{ip}^{G,y^*}(\alpha) - \mathsf{rp}^{\mathcal{G},y^*}(\alpha)\right]\right| \leq \mathrm{E}_{\alpha\leftarrow[0.8,1]}\left[\left|\mathsf{ip}^{G,y^*}(\alpha) - \mathsf{rp}^{\mathcal{G},y^*}(\alpha)\right|\right].$$

Note that any $\alpha$ contributes to the expectation on the right-hand side if and only if $\alpha$ is between $\mathsf{is}_k^G(\mathbf{z})/|\mathcal{I}_k|$ and $\mathsf{rs}_{k'}^{\mathcal{G}}(\mathbf{z})/|\mathcal{I}_{k',\ell'(k')}|$ for (possibly distinct) $k, k' \in \{0,1\}^\lambda$. Observe that this distance is at most $\mu^{G,y^*}$ (i.e., the distance with respect to the same key). Therefore,

$$\begin{aligned}
&\mathrm{E}_{\alpha\leftarrow[0.8,1]}\left[\left|\mathsf{ip}^{G,y^*}(\alpha) - \mathsf{rp}^{\mathcal{G},y^*}(\alpha)\right|\right] \\
&\quad\leq \mathrm{Pr}_{\alpha\leftarrow[0.8,1]}\left[\exists k \in \{0,1\}^\lambda : \min\left\{\mathsf{is}_k^G(\mathbf{z}), \mathsf{rs}_k^{\mathcal{G}}(\mathbf{z})\right\} \leq \alpha \cdot |\mathcal{I}_k| \leq \max\left\{\mathsf{is}_k^G(\mathbf{z}), \mathsf{rs}_k^{\mathcal{G}}(\mathbf{z})\right\}\right] \\
&\quad\leq \frac{\mu^{G,y^*}}{1-0.8} \\
&\quad= 5\mu^{G,y^*}.
\end{aligned}$$

Hence, by Lemma 3,

$$\begin{aligned}
&\mathrm{Pr}_{G\leftarrow\mathcal{F}^{\mathcal{G}}_{n,n+r}, y^*\leftarrow Y}\left[\left|\mathrm{E}_\alpha\left[\mathsf{ip}^{G,y^*}(\alpha) - \mathsf{rp}^{\mathcal{G},y^*}(\alpha)\right]\right| \geq 5\delta\right] \\
&\quad\leq \mathrm{Pr}_{G\leftarrow\mathcal{F}^{\mathcal{G}}_{n,n+r}, y^*\leftarrow Y}\left[\exists k \in \{0,1\}^\lambda : \left|\mathsf{is}_k^G(\mathbf{z}) - \mathsf{rs}_k^{\mathcal{G}}(\mathbf{z})\right| \geq \delta \cdot |\mathcal{I}_k|\right] \\
&\quad\leq e^{\lambda - \frac{\delta^2}{2}\cdot\nu}.
\end{aligned}$$

Therefore, the statistical distance is bounded by

$$\begin{aligned}
&\mathrm{SD}_{G\leftarrow\mathcal{F}^{\mathcal{G}}_{n,n+r}, y^*\leftarrow Y}\left(\mathsf{ip}^{Gy^*}, \mathsf{rp}^{\mathcal{G},y^*}\right) \\
&\quad\leq \mathrm{E}_{G\leftarrow\mathcal{F}^{\mathcal{G}}_{n,n+r}, y^*\leftarrow Y}\left[\left|\mathsf{ip}^{G,y^*} - \mathsf{rp}^{\mathcal{G},y^*}\right|\right] \\
&\quad= \mathrm{E}_{G\leftarrow\mathcal{F}^{\mathcal{G}}_{n,n+r}, y^*\leftarrow Y}\left[\left|\mathrm{E}_\alpha\left[\mathsf{ip}^{G,y^*}(\alpha) - \mathsf{rp}^{\mathcal{G},y^*}(\alpha)\right]\right|\right] \\
&\quad\leq \mathrm{Pr}_{G\leftarrow\mathcal{F}_{n,n+r}, y^*\leftarrow Y}\left[\left|\mathrm{E}_\alpha\left[\mathsf{ip}^{G,y^*}(\alpha) - \mathsf{rp}^{\mathcal{G},y^*}(\alpha)\right]\right| \geq 5\delta\right] + 5\delta \\
&\quad\leq e^{\lambda - \frac{\delta^2}{2}\cdot\nu} + 5\delta.
\end{aligned}$$

□

For every $t \in \{0, 1, \ldots, d\}$, let $\mathsf{st}_t$ and $\widetilde{\mathsf{st}}_t$ denote the states of $R$ and $\widetilde{R}$, respectively, after the $t^{\text{th}}$ call to the distinguishing oracle, where the state consists of, the challenge $y^*$, the (current) query-answer pairs $\mathcal{G}$ made to the PRG, and the $t$ answers of the distinguishing oracle.[6] Then by Lemma 4 and the triangle inequality, for every $t \in [d]$, after the $t^{\text{th}}$ call to the distinguishing oracle,

$$\mathrm{SD}\left(\mathsf{st}_t, \widetilde{\mathsf{st}}_t\right) \leq \mathrm{SD}\left(\mathsf{st}_{t-1}, \widetilde{\mathsf{st}}_{t-1}\right) + e^{\lambda - \frac{\delta^2}{2}\cdot\nu} + 5\delta \leq t \cdot e^{\lambda - \frac{\delta^2}{2}\cdot\nu} + 5t\delta,$$

where the statistical distances are taken over $G \leftarrow \mathcal{F}^{\mathcal{G}}_{n,n+r}$, $y^* \leftarrow Y$ where $Y$ is the distribution of the challenge, and over the reductions' randomness. Thus,

$$\Pr\left[\widetilde{R}^G(y^*) \neq R^{\mathcal{A}_{\mathsf{ideal}}, G}(y^*)\right] \leq d \cdot e^{\lambda - \frac{\delta^2}{2}\cdot\nu} + 5d\delta, \tag{7}$$

where the probability is taken over $G \leftarrow \mathcal{F}^{\mathcal{G}}_{n,n+r}$, $y^* \leftarrow Y$ where $Y$ is the distribution of the challenge, and over the reductions' randomness.

*Step 4: Putting it all together.* Our goal is to upper-bound

$$\Delta := \Pr_{G \leftarrow \mathcal{F}_{n,n+r}}\left[\begin{array}{l}\left|\Pr_{s \leftarrow \{0,1\}^n}\left[\widetilde{R}^G(1^n, G(s)) = 1\right]\right. \\ \qquad \left. - \Pr_{y \leftarrow \{0,1\}^{n+r}}\left[\widetilde{R}^G(1^n, y) = 1\right]\right| \leq \dfrac{1}{3n^\gamma}\end{array}\right]$$

Towards bounding $\Delta$, we first upper-bound the expected difference between the answers of $R$ and $\widetilde{R}$ (where the expectation is taken over $G$). To alleviate notations, throughout the rest of the proof we remove $\mathcal{A}_{\mathsf{ideal}}$ from the notations and write $R^G$ instead. Additionally, all probabilities are taken over the reductions' randomness and we ignore this for brevity.

**Claim 11.** *Let $Y$ denote the distribution over the challenge. Then for all sufficiently large $n$'s,*

$$\mathrm{E}_{G \leftarrow \mathcal{F}_{n,n+r}}\left[\left|\Pr_{y^* \leftarrow Y}\left[\widetilde{R}^G(y^*) = 1\right] - \Pr_{y^* \leftarrow Y}\left[R^G(y^*) = 1\right]\right|\right] \leq d \cdot e^{\lambda - \frac{\delta^2}{2}\cdot\nu} + 5d\delta.$$

*Proof.* For every $G \in \mathcal{F}_{n,n+r}$, observe that

$$\Pr_{y^* \leftarrow Y}\left[\widetilde{R}^G(y^*) = 1\right] \leq \Pr_{y^* \leftarrow Y}\left[R^G(y^*) = 1\right] + \Pr_{y^* \leftarrow Y}\left[\widetilde{R}^G(y^*) \neq R^G(y^*)\right]$$

and that

$$\Pr_{y^* \leftarrow Y}\left[\widetilde{R}^G(y^*) = 1\right] \geq \Pr_{y^* \leftarrow Y}\left[\widetilde{R}^G(y^*) = R^G(y^*)\right] \cdot \Pr_{y^* \leftarrow Y}\left[R^G(y^*) = 1\right].$$

Let $\widetilde{\mathcal{F}}$ denote the set of all functions in $\mathcal{F}_{n,n+r}$ such that

$$\Pr_{y^* \leftarrow Y}\left[\widetilde{R}^G(y^*) = 1\right] \geq \Pr_{y^* \leftarrow Y}\left[R^G(y^*) = 1\right].$$

[6] Formally, it should also depend on the randomness. Since all our claims hold for every randomness, we ignore it for simplicity.

Then

$$\begin{aligned}
&\mathrm{E}_{G\leftarrow\mathcal{F}_{n,n+r}}\left[\left|\Pr_{y^*\leftarrow Y}\left[\widetilde{R}^G(y^*)=1\right]-\Pr_{y^*\leftarrow Y}\left[R^G(y^*)=1\right]\right|\right]\\
&\quad\le\frac{1}{2^{2^n(n+r)}}\cdot\sum_{G\in\widetilde{\mathcal{F}}}\left(\Pr_{y^*\leftarrow Y}\left[\widetilde{R}^G(y^*)=1\right]-\Pr_{y^*\leftarrow Y}\left[R^G(y^*)=1\right]\right)\\
&\qquad+\frac{1}{2^{2^n(n+r)}}\cdot\sum_{G\in\mathcal{F}_{n,n+r}\setminus\widetilde{\mathcal{F}}}\left(\Pr_{y^*\leftarrow Y}\left[R^G(y^*)=1\right]-\Pr_{y^*\leftarrow Y}\left[\widetilde{R}^G(y^*)=1\right]\right)\\
&\quad\le\frac{1}{2^{2^n(n+r)}}\cdot\sum_{G\in\widetilde{\mathcal{F}}}\Pr_{y^*\leftarrow Y}\left[\widetilde{R}^G(y^*)\neq R^G(y^*)\right]\\
&\qquad+\frac{1}{2^{2^n(n+r)}}\cdot\sum_{G\in\mathcal{F}_{n,n+r}\setminus\widetilde{\mathcal{F}}}\Pr_{y^*\leftarrow Y}\left[R^G(y^*)=1\right]\cdot\Pr_{y^*\leftarrow Y}\left[\widetilde{R}^G(y^*)\neq R^G(y^*)\right]\\
&\quad\le\mathrm{E}_{G\leftarrow\mathcal{F}_{n,n+r}}\left[\Pr_{y^*\leftarrow Y}\left[\widetilde{R}^G(y^*)\neq R^G(y^*)\right]\right]\\
&\quad\le d\cdot e^{\lambda-\frac{\delta^2}{2}\cdot\nu}+5d\delta,
\end{aligned}$$

where the last inequality follows from Eq. (7). □

Now, observe that

$$\begin{aligned}
\Delta\le&\Pr_{G\leftarrow\mathcal{F}_{n,n+r}}\left[\begin{array}{r}\left|\Pr_{s\leftarrow\{0,1\}^n}\left[R^G(1^n,G(s))=1\right]\right.\\ \left.-\Pr_{y\leftarrow\{0,1\}^{n+r}}\left[R^G(1^n,y)=1\right]\right|<\dfrac{1}{n^\gamma}\end{array}\right]\\
&+\Pr_{G\leftarrow\mathcal{F}_{n,n+r}}\left[\begin{array}{r}\left|\Pr_{s\leftarrow\{0,1\}^n}\left[R^G(1^n,G(s))=1\right]\right.\\ \left.-\Pr_{s\leftarrow\{0,1\}^n}\left[\widetilde{R}^G(1^n,G(s))=1\right]\right|>\dfrac{1}{3n^\gamma}\end{array}\right]\\
&+\Pr_{G\leftarrow\mathcal{F}_{n,n+r}}\left[\begin{array}{r}\left|\Pr_{y\leftarrow\{0,1\}^{n+r}}\left[R^G(1^n,y)=1\right]\right.\\ \left.-\Pr_{y\leftarrow\{0,1\}^{n+r}}\left[\widetilde{R}^G(1^n,y)=1\right]\right|>\dfrac{1}{3n^\gamma}\end{array}\right].
\end{aligned}$$

Note that by Eq. (1), the first term is 0 for infinitely many $n$'s. As for the other two terms, by Markov's inequality and Claim 11, it follows that both terms are upper-bounded by

$$3n^\gamma\cdot\left(d\cdot e^{\lambda-\frac{\delta^2}{2}\cdot\nu}+5d\delta\right).$$

We conclude that

$$\Delta\le 6n^\gamma\cdot\left(d\cdot e^{\lambda-\frac{\delta^2}{2}\cdot\nu}+5d\delta\right)$$

for infinitely many $n$'s.

We next choose the parameters such that $\Delta\le 3/4$ for infinitely many $n$'s. Specifically, we choose $\delta$ and $\nu$ (which we later translate to choosing $m_t$ for every $t\in[c]$). Let $\delta=1/48dn^\gamma\sqrt[4]{\nu}$ and let $\nu=2(\lambda+n)\cdot d^2n^{2\gamma}$. Then $\delta\ge 2/\nu$ and $\nu\ge 2(\lambda+n)/\delta^2$ if $\nu$ is sufficiently large. In this case, $e^{\lambda-\frac{\delta^2}{2}\cdot\nu}\le e^{-n}$. Since $\nu$ is a polynomial of $n$, $\nu \leq 2de^n$ for all sufficiently large $n$'s. Therefore $\delta \geq 2/\nu \geq e^{-n}/d$, hence $e^{-n} \leq d\delta$. Thus, for such choices of $\nu$, $\Delta \leq 36dn^\gamma \cdot \delta \leq 3/4$.

Now, recall that $\nu = \min_{k \in \{0,1\}^\lambda} |\mathcal{I}_k|$, and that for every $k \in \{0,1\}^\lambda$, either $|\mathcal{I}_k| = m_c$ or $|\mathcal{I}_k| = \frac{m_{t-1}}{(c-t)m_t}$ for some $t \in [c]$. Further recall that for $\mathcal{A}_{\mathsf{ideal}}$ to be have $1 - e^{-n}$ advantage, we took $m_c \geq 10(\lambda + c(n+r) + n)$ and $m_{t-1} \geq (c-t+1)m_t \cdot 10(\lambda + c(n+r) + n)$ for all $t \in [c]$. Therefore, we let[7]

$$m_c = 10(\lambda + c(n+r) + n) + 2(\lambda + n) \cdot d^2 n^{2\gamma}$$

and

$$m_{t-1} = (c-t+1)\left(10(\lambda + c(n+r) + n) + 2(\lambda + n) \cdot d^2 n^{2\gamma}\right) \cdot m_t$$

for every $t \in [c]$. As a result, the adversaries query the function on $m = m_0 \leq n^{\alpha c} \cdot c!$ inputs, for some constant $\alpha \in \mathbb{N}$.[8]. Since there are $2^{\mathsf{in}}$ possible inputs, for the adversaries to be well-defined, it must be the case where $n^{\alpha c} \cdot c! \leq 2^{\mathsf{in}}$. Indeed, since $c = \frac{\mathsf{in}}{w(n) \cdot \log \mathsf{in}}$ for some $w(n) = \omega(1)$,

$$n^{\alpha c} \cdot c! \leq n^{\alpha c} \cdot c^c = 2^{\alpha c \log n + c \log c} \leq 2^{\alpha \frac{\mathsf{in}}{w(n) \log \mathsf{in}} \log n + \frac{\mathsf{in}}{w(n) \log \mathsf{in}} \log \mathsf{in}} \leq 2^{\mathsf{in}},$$

for all sufficiently large $n$'s, where the last inequality is due to the fact that $\mathsf{in} = \mathrm{poly}(n)$, hence $\log n = O(\log \mathsf{in})$.

Finally, in order to contradict Lemma 1, we show that the total number of queries $\widetilde{R}$ makes to $G$ is at most $2^{n/4}$. Indeed, in each of the $d$ calls to the distinguishing oracle, the number of calls to $G$ that the reduction makes is at most

$$\mathrm{poly}(m) \leq n^{\beta c} \cdot (c!)^\beta \leq n^{\beta c} \cdot c^{\beta c} = 2^{\beta c \log n + \beta c \log c}$$

for some constant $\beta \in \mathbb{N}$. Recall that $c = \frac{n}{w(n) \cdot \log n}$, where $w(n) = \omega(1)$. Therefore, the total number of calls that $R$ makes is at most

$$d \cdot 2^{\beta c \log n + \beta c \log c} = d \cdot 2^{\frac{\beta n}{w(n)} + \frac{\beta n}{w(n) \log n} \log \frac{n}{w(n) \log n}} \leq d \cdot 2^{\frac{2\beta n}{w(n)}} \leq 2^{n/4},$$

for sufficiently large $n$'s.

*Remark 1 (On the definition of black-box reduction).* In the definition we considered, the advantage of the reduction $R$ is a polynomial of the advantage of the distinguishing oracle $\mathcal{A}$. This in particular allowed us to conclude the existence of $\gamma \in \mathbb{N}$ for which Eq. (1) holds. In the definition for black box constructions of PRF from Beimel et al. [2], it is only required that if $\mathcal{A}$ succeeds with noticeable probability, then so does $R$. Under this definition, Eq. (1) does not necessarily hold, since the advantage of $R$ might decrease as a function of the advantage of $\mathcal{A}$.

---

[7] The bound on $m_c$ can be improved to $10(\lambda + c(n+r) + n)$. This is because the other term comes from considering $k$'s such that $\ell(k) < c$ (recall that if $\ell(k) = c$ then both scores are identical).

[8] $\alpha$ depends on the degree of the polynomials $\lambda$, $r$, $d$, and $\gamma$.

Nevertheless, to the best of our knowledge, all black-box reductions studied in the literature satisfy the stronger requirement. Moreover, our proof continues to hold under the weaker assumption that the advantage of $R$ is bounded below for all distinguishing oracles with a sufficiently large advantage.

## 5 Lower Bounds for Black-Box Constructions of a PRF With a Long Output

In this section, we show our lower bounds for fully black-box constructions of PRF with a long output from a PRG, with adaptive calls. We will use the following result, stating the existence of a PRG with respect to some oracle $f$.

**Lemma 5** ([2, Lemma 3.5]). *For every oracle $f = \{f_n : \{0,1\}^n \to \{0,1\}^n\}_{n\in\mathbb{N}}$ and $w, r : \mathbb{N} \to \mathbb{N}$ such that $n+r(n) = 2^{o(w(n))}$, there exists a (possibly inefficient) function $G = \{G_n : \{0,1\}^{w(n)} \to \{0,1\}^{n+r(n)}\}_{n\in\mathbb{N}}$ such that the following holds. For every* PPT *oracle-aided algorithm $A$, there exists a negligible function $\mu$ such that*

$$\left|\Pr_{s\leftarrow\{0,1\}^{w(n)}}\left[A^{f,G}\left(1^n, G\left(1^n, s\right)\right) = 1\right] - \Pr_{y\leftarrow\{0,1\}^{n+r(n)}}\left[A^{f,G}\left(1^n, y\right) = 1\right]\right| \le \mu(n).$$

In what follows, we refer to the function $G$ as the PRG with respect to the oracle $f$. We are now ready to state and prove our lower bound on the number of calls to the PRG required to construct a PRF with a long output. Throughout the section we fix the input length $\mathsf{in} = \mathsf{in}(n)$, the output length $\mathsf{out} = \mathsf{out}(n)$, the key length $\lambda = \lambda(n)$, and the PRG stretch $r = r(n)$.

**Theorem 7.** *For every $c(n) = \frac{\mathsf{out}}{r+\omega(\log n)}$, there is no $c(n)$-call fully black-box construction of a weak PRF with output length* $\mathsf{out}$ *from an $r$-bit stretch PRG.*

*Proof.* Fix $w = w(n) = \omega(\log n)$ and let $c = c(n) = \mathsf{out}/(r+w)$. Assume towards contradiction that there exists a $c$-call fully black-box construction $(F, R)$ from an $r$-bit stretch PRG, where

$$F = \left\{f_k^{(\cdot)} : \{0,1\}^{\mathsf{in}} \to \{0,1\}^{\mathsf{out}}\right\}_{n\in\mathbb{N}, k\in\{0,1\}^\lambda}.$$

That is, for every $i \in [c]$ there exist $S_i : \{0,1\}^{\mathsf{in}} \times \{0,1\}^\lambda \times (\{0,1\}^{(n+r)})^{i-1} \to \{0,1\}^n$, and there exists $P : \{0,1\}^m \times \{0,1\}^\lambda \times (\{0,1\}^{n+r})^c \to \{0,1\}^{\mathsf{out}}$ such that

$$f_k^G(x) = P\left(x, k, G\left(s_1\right), \ldots, G(s_c)\right)$$

for all $G : \{0,1\}^n \to \{0,1\}^{n+r}$, where $s_i = S_i(x, k, G\left(s_1\right), \ldots, G(s_{i-1}))$ for all $i \in [c]$.

To obtain a contradiction, we consider a PRG that is applied only to the first $w$ bits of the seed. This, intuitively, implies that the entropy of the output of the PRF over $m$ inputs is provided only by the key (which has $\lambda$ entropy) and $m \cdot (w + r) \cdot c$ additional bits from all applications of the $r$-bit stretch PRG. On the other hand, for a random function, the amount of entropy is $m \cdot \mathsf{out}$. Taking $m = (n+\lambda)/c$ results in a large gap between the two cases.

In the following, for a string $s = (s_1, \ldots, s_n) \in \{0,1\}^n$ and $i \in [n]$ we let $s_{<i} = (s_1, \ldots, s_{i-1})$ and let $s_{\geq i} = (s_i, \ldots, s_n)$. We use $||$ to denote the concatenation of strings.

We first define a distinguisher $\mathcal{A}^{(\cdot)}$ for the PRF.

**Algorithm 13** ($\mathcal{A}$)
*Input: The security parameter* $1^n$.
*Oracle access: A function* $f : \{0,1\}^{\mathsf{in}} \to \{0,1\}^{\mathsf{out}}$.

1. *Let* $m = m(n) = (n+\lambda)/c$ *and let* $x_1, \ldots, x_m \in \{0,1\}^{\mathsf{in}}$ *denote the lexicographically first* $m$ *inputs.*
2. *Query* $f$ *on* $x_1, \ldots, x_m$*, and let* $z_1, \ldots, z_m \in \{0,1\}^{\mathsf{out}}$ *denote the respective answers.*
3. *Output 1 if and only if there exists* $k \in \{0,1\}^\lambda$ *and* $(y_{i,j})_{i\in[m],j\in[c]} \in (\{0,1\}^{w+r-1})^{m\cdot c}$ *such that*
$$P\left(x_i, k, (y_{i,1}||s_{i,1}), \ldots, (y_{i,c}||s_{i,c})\right) = z_i$$
*for all* $i \in [m]$*, where*
$$s_{i,j} = S_j\left(x_i, k, (y_{i,1}||s_{i,1}), \ldots, (y_{i,j-1}||s_{i,j-1})\right)_{\geq \frac{\mathsf{out}}{c} - r}$$
*For all* $i \in [m]$ *and* $j \in [c]$.

[12] Note that if we obtain a contradiction for all distinct inputs, then the same holds for random inputs (up to adding the birthday bound).

We next define a PRG for which $\mathcal{A}$ breaks the security of $F$. Since $w = \omega(\log n)$ and $r$ is a polynomial, it follows that $n + r = 2^{o(w-1)}$. Thus, by Lemma 5 there exists a PRG $G' : \{0,1\}^{w-1} \to \{0,1\}^{w+r-1}$ with respect to the oracle $\mathcal{A}$, that cannot be broken with non-negligible probability. Consider the PRG $G : \{0,1\}^n \to \{0,1\}^{n+r}$ defined as
$$G(s) = G'\left(s_{<w}\right)||s_{\geq w}.$$

Observe that $\mathcal{A}^{f_k^G}$ always outputs 1. To reach a contradiction, we next show that for a random function $f$, this probability is at most $2^{-n}$. Indeed, by the union bound,

$$\begin{aligned}
&\Pr_{f\leftarrow\mathcal{F}_{\mathsf{in}}}\left[\mathcal{A}^f(1^n) = 1\right] \\
&= \Pr_{f\leftarrow\mathcal{F}_{\mathsf{in}}}\left[\begin{array}{c}\exists k \in \{0,1\}^\lambda \; \exists \left(y_{i,j}\right)_{i\in[m],j\in[c]} \in \left(\{0,1\}^{w+r-1}\right)^{m\cdot c} \; \forall i \in [m] : \\ P\left(x_i, k, (y_{i,j}||s_{i,j})_{j=1}^c\right) = f(x_i)\end{array}\right] \\
&\leq 2^{\lambda + m\cdot c\cdot(w+r-1)} \cdot \Pr_{f\leftarrow\mathcal{F}_{\mathsf{in}}}\left[\forall i \in [m] : P\left(x_i, k, (y_{i,j}||s_{i,j})_{j=1}^c\right) = f(x_i)\right] \\
&= \frac{2^{\lambda + m\cdot\mathsf{out} - m\cdot c}}{2^{m\cdot\mathsf{out}}} \\
&= 2^{-n}.
\end{aligned}$$

Since $(F, R)$ is assumed to be a fully black-box PRF construction, it follows that $R^{\mathcal{A},G}$ breaks $G$. However, this implies the existence of a PPT algorithm $\widetilde{R}^{\mathcal{A},G'}$ breaking $G'$, contradicting Lemma 5. □

## References


1. Baecher, P., Brzuska, C., Fischlin, M.: Notions of black-box reductions, revisited. In: Sako, K., Sarkar, P. (eds.) ASIACRYPT 2013. LNCS, vol. 8269, pp. 296–315. Springer, Heidelberg (2013). https://doi.org/10.1007/978-3-642-42033-7_16
2. Beimel, A., Malkin, T., Mazor, N.: Structural lower bounds on black-box constructions of pseudorandom functions. In: Reyzin, L., Stebila, D. (eds.) Advances in Cryptology - CRYPTO 2024, Part V. Lecture Notes in Computer Science, vol. 14924, pp. 459–488. Springer (2024)
3. Bellare, M., Rogaway, P.: The security of triple encryption and a framework for code-based game-playing proofs. In: Vaudenay, S. (ed.) EUROCRYPT 2006. LNCS, vol. 4004, pp. 409–426. Springer, Heidelberg (2006). https://doi.org/10.1007/11761679_25
4. Boneh, D., Venkatesan, R.: Breaking RSA may not be equivalent to factoring. In: Nyberg, K. (ed.) EUROCRYPT 1998. LNCS, vol. 1403, pp. 59–71. Springer, Heidelberg (1998). https://doi.org/10.1007/BFb0054117
5. Bresson, E., Monnerat, J., Vergnaud, D.: Separation results on the "one-more" computational problems. In: Malkin, T. (ed.) CT-RSA 2008. LNCS, vol. 4964, pp. 71–87. Springer, Heidelberg (2008). https://doi.org/10.1007/978-3-540-79263-5_5
6. Fischlin, M., Schröder, D.: On the impossibility of three-move blind signature schemes. In: Gilbert, H. (ed.) EUROCRYPT 2010. LNCS, vol. 6110, pp. 197–215. Springer, Heidelberg (2010). https://doi.org/10.1007/978-3-642-13190-5_10
7. Gennaro, R., Trevisan, L.: Lower bounds on the efficiency of generic cryptographic constructions. In: 41st Annual Symposium on Foundations of Computer Science, FOCS 2000, Redondo Beach, California, USA, 12–14 November 2000, pp. 305–313. IEEE Computer Society (2000)
8. Goldreich, O., Levin, L.A.: A hard-core predicate for all one-way functions. In: Johnson, D.S. (ed.) Proceedings of the 21st Annual ACM Symposium on Theory of Computing, 14–17 May 1989, Seattle, Washington, USA, pp. 25–32. ACM (1989)
9. Goldreich, O., Goldwasser, S., Micali, S.: How to construct random functions. J. ACM (JACM) **33**(4), 792–807 (1986)
10. Haitner, I., Rosen, A., Shaltiel, R.: On the (im)possibility of arthur-merlin witness hiding protocols. In: Reingold, O. (ed.) TCC 2009. LNCS, vol. 5444, pp. 220–237. Springer, Heidelberg (2009). https://doi.org/10.1007/978-3-642-00457-5_14
11. Impagliazzo, R., Rudich, S.: Limits on the provable consequences of one-way permutations. In: Johnson, D.S. (ed.) Proceedings of the 21st Annual ACM Symposium on Theory of Computing, 14–17 May 1989, Seattle, Washington, USA, pp. 44–61. ACM (1989)
12. Levin, L.A.: One-way functions and pseudorandom generators. In: Proceedings of the Seventeenth Annual ACM Symposium on Theory of Computing, pp. 363–365 (1985)
13. Miles, E., Viola, E.: On the complexity of non-adaptively increasing the stretch of pseudorandom generators. In: Ishai, Y. (ed.) TCC 2011. LNCS, vol. 6597, pp. 522–539. Springer, Heidelberg (2011). https://doi.org/10.1007/978-3-642-19571-6_31

14. Miles, E., Viola, E.: On the complexity of constructing pseudorandom functions (especially when they don't exist). J. Cryptol. **28**(3), 509–532 (2015)
15. Pass, R.: Limits of provable security from standard assumptions. In: Fortnow, L., Vadhan, S.P. (eds.) Proceedings of the 43rd ACM Symposium on Theory of Computing, STOC 2011, San Jose, CA, USA, 6–8 June 2011, pp. 109–118. ACM (2011)
16. Pass, R.: Unprovable security of perfect NIZK and non-interactive non-malleable commitments. In: Sahai, A. (ed.) TCC 2013. LNCS, vol. 7785, pp. 334–354. Springer, Heidelberg (2013). https://doi.org/10.1007/978-3-642-36594-2_19
17. Reingold, O., Trevisan, L., Vadhan, S.: Notions of reducibility between cryptographic primitives. In: Naor, M. (ed.) TCC 2004. LNCS, vol. 2951, pp. 1–20. Springer, Heidelberg (2004). https://doi.org/10.1007/978-3-540-24638-1_1
18. Waters, B.: Efficient identity-based encryption without random oracles. In: Cramer, R. (ed.) EUROCRYPT 2005. LNCS, vol. 3494, pp. 114–127. Springer, Heidelberg (2005). https://doi.org/10.1007/11426639_7

# Unique SNARGs with Adaptive Security: Constructions and Black-Box Separations

Cody Freitag[1,2(✉)] and Daniel Wichs[1,3]

[1] Northeastern University, Boston, USA
codyrfreitag@gmail.com, wichs@ccs.neu.edu
[2] The Hebrew University of Jerusalem, Jerusalem, Israel
[3] NTT Research, Sunnyvale, USA

**Abstract.** Succinct non-interactive arguments (SNARGs) for NP allow an efficient prover to convince a verifier that an NP statement is true with a proof that is much shorter than the original NP witness. Gentry and Wichs (STOC '11) showed that adaptive soundness of such SNARGs cannot be proven via a black-box reduction from any falsifiable assumption. However, recent works by Waters, Wu and Zhandry (STOC '24, CRYPTO '24, CRYPTO '25) circumvent this negative result by relying on subexponential hardness assumptions and having a long common reference string (CRS) that is longer than the statement size.

In this work, we study *unique* SNARGs where each statement has at most one accepting proof. The above constructions of adaptively sound SNARGs are *not* unique and crucially rely on the existence of multiple valid proofs in their security analysis. We explore to what extent this is inherent as follows:

- On the negative side, we give a strengthened Gentry-Wichs style black-box separation for the case of perfectly complete and unique SNARGs for NP with adaptive security. Our black-box separation extends *even* to reductions that rely on subexponentially hard falsifiable assumptions *and* to SNARGs that have an arbitrarily long CRS.
- On the positive side, we construct perfectly unique and adaptively secure SNARGs for NP with a long CRS based on subexponentially hard one-way functions and indistinguishability obfuscation. We do so by relaxing *perfect completeness* and allowing for a negligible completeness error.

## 1 Introduction

**SNARGs.** A succinct non-interactive argument (SNARG) for NP gives a way for an efficient prover to convince a verifier that an NP statement $x$ is true with a proof $\pi$ that is much shorter than the original NP witness $w$ or the statement $x$. More formally, a SNARG must satisfy *completeness* and *soundness*: an honest


N. Heninger and M. Rosulek (Eds.): CRYPTO 2026, LNCS 16800, pp. 190–217, 2026.
https://doi.org/10.1007/978-3-032-35367-2_7

prover should give convincing proofs for true statements, yet a (computationally-bounded) cheating prover should not be able to generate convincing proofs for false statements.

While SNARGs for NP are known to exist in the random oracle model [40,44], such proofs cannot exist in the plain model under the widely believed complexity assumption that $\mathsf{NP} \not\subseteq \mathsf{BPTIME}(2^{o(n)})$ [4,57].[1] For this reason, we consider SNARGs in the *common reference string* (CRS) model that are defined relative to a (potentially structured) random public value. A long line of work has studied the minimal assumptions needed to construct SNARGs in the CRS model for various sub-classes of NP (see, e.g., [11,16,19,25,27,32–34,37,38,52–56]).

**The GW Barrier.** The work of Gentry and Wichs [25] provides a fundamental barrier for SNARGs for NP by showing that (under mild hardness assumptions) it is impossible to construct SNARGs for all of NP where adaptive soundness is proven via a black-box reduction from any falsifiable assumption. Following [46], an assumption is *falsifiable* if it can be formulated as an interactive game between an efficient challenger and adversary. In modern cryptography, falsifiable assumptions are greatly preferred since the resulting security reductions give rise to natural "win-win" arguments (breaking a cryptographic system falsifies the underlying assumption, which often resolves a long-standing open mathematical problem). All "standard" cryptographic assumptions such as DDH or LWE are falsifiable. Of course, one could simply assume that a given SNARG for a particular NP language is sound, but this is inherently *not* falsifiable since it requires the challenger to efficiently test that an NP statement is false.

**Overcoming the Barrier.** There are major caveats to the "Gentry-Wichs" (GW) barrier, which offer a path for overcoming it:

1. It only applies to adaptively sound SNARGs, where a cheating prover can choose which false statement to prove adaptively after seeing the CRS.
2. It only applies to either:
   (a) SNARGs from polynomial hardness assumptions (even with a long CRS), or
   (b) SNARGs with a short CRS (even from sub-exponential hardness assumptions).

And indeed, prior works were able to exploit the above caveats to overcome the barrier. Firstly, Sahai and Waters [52] showed how to construct *selectively secure* SNARGs for NP from indistinguishability obfuscation (iO) and one-way functions (OWF). Following the breakthrough works of Jain, Lin, and Sahai [29, 30] that construct iO from sub-exponentially secure falsifiable assumptions, the Sahai-Waters SNARG can be proven secure via a black-box reduction from a sub-exponentially hard falsifiable assumption.

More recently, a series of works [54–56] showed how to construct *adaptively secure* SNARGs for NP from sub-exponentially secure iO and OWF. These

[1] At least with respect to the standard notion of non-uniform security that reduces to the statistical setting.

results are not subject to the GW barrier since they rely on sub-exponential hardness assumptions *and* have a long CRS that exceeds the statement size.

**Uniqueness.** Interestingly, there is a downside of the above adaptively secure constructions. The original selectively secure SNARG of Sahai and Waters can achieve a strong *uniqueness* property, where for every true statement $x$ *there exists* a single unique accepting proof $\pi$.[2] Aside from being a natural property, uniqueness also has interesting applications (e.g.,) for constructing constant-round concurrent zero-knowledge protocols [21,22]. Unfortunately, in the adaptively secure constructions of [54–56], each statement has at least two accepting proofs. Furthermore, this appears to be critical to the proof of security in those works, which follows a general "two-challenge" approach that seems at odds with uniqueness. In this work, we ask if relaxing uniqueness is necessary:

*Can we construct* unique *SNARGs for NP with*
*adaptive security from falsifiable assumptions,*
*even based on sub-exponential hardness or with a long CRS?*

### 1.1 Our Results

We provide both positive and negative results to answer the above question. First, we give a negative result for SNARGs that satisfy perfect completeness.

**Theorem 1.1 (Informal; see Theorem** 3.1**).** *Assume sub-exponentially secure one-way functions exist. Then, for any candidate SNARG for NP with perfect completeness and uniqueness, security cannot be proven via a black-box reduction from any falsifiable assumption. This holds even for SNARGs with long CRS or assuming sub-exponential security for the underlying assumption.*

To the best of our knowledge, the above result is the first black-box separation result for a natural class of SNARGs for NP that applies to sub-exponential hardness assumptions and constructions with a long CRS. The result covers SNARGs where the proof size is $(|x|+|w|)^{o(1)} \cdot \mathsf{poly}(\lambda)$ for security parameter $\lambda$. If we assume PRGs with stronger exact security, the result can also cover SNARGs with proof size $(|x| + |w|)^{1-\varepsilon} \cdot \mathsf{poly}(\lambda)$ for any constant $\varepsilon > 0$. The result also extends beyond perfect uniqueness to cover SNARGs with even "weak statistical uniqueness" where, for every true statement $x$ there is at least some inverse polynomial probability over an honestly generated CRS that $x$ has a unique valid proof. It also extends beyond perfect completeness to cover SNARGs with

[2] We note that our notion of uniqueness is statistical and requires that there do not exist multiple valid proofs. This is in contrast to the notion of unambiguous SNARGs of [14], which only require that it should be hard to find multiple valid proofs. Achieving unique selectively secure SNARGs can be done easily by using injective OWFs in the original construction of [52], or via a slight modification based on arbitrary OWFs; see Sect. 1.3.2.

"super-strong statistical completeness" where for every true statement $x$ and witness $w$ the probability over an honestly generated CRS that the honestly generated proof $\pi$ fails to verify is at most $2^{-|\pi|}$.

We complement the negative result above with a positive result by relaxing perfect completeness. At a very high level, we show how to implement the "two-challenge" approach of [54] with just *one challenge*, though at the cost of introducing a completeness error. Concretely, for any statement $x$, our prover will fail to find a proof with negligible probability $2^{-\lambda}$ over the choice of the CRS. The SNARG has perfect uniqueness, where for every honesty generated CRS and every true statement $x$ there is at most a single accepting proof. Similar to all other prior positive results, our SNARG has a long CRS that grows with the statement and witness length and our reduction relies on sub-exponential hardness assumptions.

**Theorem 1.2 (Informal; see Theorem** 4.1**).** *Assuming sub-exponentially secure iO and OWF, there exist adaptively secure perfectly unique SNARGs for NP. The SNARGs have a long CRS and a negligible completeness error. In particular, this holds assuming sub-exponential security of the falsifiable assumptions shown to imply iO in [29, 30].*

To the best of our knowledge, our construction is the first unique SNARG even for P with adaptive security from falsifiable assumptions. We note that the recent work of [23] gives a construction of unique SNARGs with adaptive security for NP languages that can be efficiently verified with a trapdoor. However, as the verifier in their construction scales with the trapdoor verification time, it is not succinct for the class P. We also note that unique SNARGs for NP (plus OWFs) are known to imply witness encryption [13], and therefore the reliance on some strong falsifiable assumptions in the above theorem is necessary.

### 1.2 Related Work

**Black-Box Separations for Cryptographic Primitives.** In this work, we consider separations ruling out constructions with black-box security reductions that may make non-black-box use of the underlying primitives. This is in contrast to ruling out "fully" black-box constructions that assume black-box use of the underlying primitive à la the seminal work of Impagliazzo and Rudich [28] (see [51] for a taxonomy on black-box separations).

Along these lines, there have been many works ruling out various cryptographic primitives with black-box reductions from various cryptographic assumptions (see, e.g., [1–3,6,12,15,20,25,41,45,47–50]). Most relevant to this work, [25,49] rule out types of adaptively secure non-interactive arguments from efficiently falsifiable assumptions (under relatively mild additional assumptions). Specifically, [25] focuses on succinctness whereas [49] focuses on zero-knowledge. As in our work, these black-box separations follow from the general "meta-reduction" paradigm introduced by [8].

**Computationally Unique SNARGs.** In this work, we focus on SNARGs with statistical uniqueness, where there *exists* at most one accepting proof for each statement. This notion can be relaxed to computational uniqueness—also known as *unambiguity*—where it is only computationally hard to find two distinct accepting proofs for any statement. Unambiguous SNARGs have been constructed for various deterministic computations from a variety of assumptions (see, e.g., [5,14,17,18,24,31,35,42]) most notably for their applications to constructing hard-on-average instances in PPAD. We emphasize that the adaptively secure SNARGs for NP of [54–56] based on [52] lose perfect uniqueness though are still computationally unique.

**Designated-Verifier SNARGs.** In this work, we focus on SNARGs that are publicly verifiable given the CRS value. This is in contrast to the designated verifier setting, or *delegation schemes* as introduced by [36,37], where the setup phase also specifies an additional secret verification key. The recent work of [43] shows how to make the Sahai-Waters SNARG [52] adaptively secure in the designated verifier setting while preserving uniqueness based on sub-exponentially secure iO and OWF. This highlights that the negative results in this work for uniqueness crucially rely on the public verification property of SNARGs.

### 1.3 Technical Overview

We consider SNARGs for NP in the CRS model. For both our positive and negative results, we allow SNARGs with a long CRS that can depend polynomially on the statement and witness size. A SNARG for an NP language $L$ consists of three algorithms $\Pi = (\mathsf{Setup}, \mathsf{Prove}, \mathsf{Ver})$. The setup algorithm outputs the common reference string $\mathsf{crs} \leftarrow \mathsf{Setup}(1^\lambda, 1^m)$ indexed by the security parameter $\lambda$ and input-length $m$. On input a statement $x$ with a valid witness $w$ of combined length at most $m$, the SNARG prover computes the proof $\pi = \mathsf{Prove}(\mathsf{crs}, x, w)$. The verifier accepts if $\mathsf{Ver}(\mathsf{crs}, x, \pi) = 1$. Completeness ensures that the verifier accepts honestly generated proofs with overwhelming probability, and perfect completeness ensures that this holds with probability 1. Adaptive soundness ensures that for any polynomial-time adversary who is given $\mathsf{crs}$ and adaptively chooses a false statement $x$ along with a proof $\pi$, the probability that $\mathsf{Ver}(\mathsf{crs}, x, \pi) = 1$ is negligible.

#### 1.3.1 A Black-Box Separation for Unique SNARGs with Perfect Completeness

**Overview of GW.** We first recall the GW [25] black-box separation result for general SNARGs. Following the "meta-reduction" paradigm, the main component of that work is a simulatable attacker against any SNARG. This is a carefully crafted inefficient attacker $P^\star$ that breaks the adaptive security of the SNARG, so on input a CRS it generates a false statement $x$ and a valid proof $\pi$ for $x$. At the same time, there is an efficient simulator $P^\star_{\mathsf{sim}}$ such that no efficient algorithm can distinguish the output of $P^\star$ from $P^\star_{\mathsf{sim}}$. The simulator $P^\star_{\mathsf{sim}}$ outputs true statements $x$ and proofs $\pi$, and therefore does not break the security of the SNARG. Constructing a simulatable attacker is the main technical challenge in GW and relies on a fundamental *leakage lemma* with deep connections across cryptography and complexity theory.

A simulatable attacker rules out black-box reductions from falsifiable assumptions. Intuitively, this is because simulatable attackers are *useless* from the point of view of any reduction: anything a reduction can do using this attacker, it could also have done on its own by running the efficient simulator. In more detail, suppose there is a black-box reduction $R$ such that $R^{P^\star}$ breaks some underlying assumption with non-negligible advantage. Then $R^{P^\star_{\mathsf{sim}}}$ must also necessarily break the assumption by the indistinguishability of $P^\star$ and $P^\star_{\mathsf{sim}}$. However, since $P^\star_{\mathsf{sim}}$ is efficient, $R^{P^\star_{\mathsf{sim}}}$ is an efficient attack on the assumption, meaning that the assumption was false to begin with!

There is an important subtlety in the above argument. The attacker $P^\star$ and the simulator $P^\star_{\mathsf{sim}}$ are only indistinguishable by polynomial time distinguishers, or at best distinguishers of size $2^{o(|x|)}$. However, they are easily distinguishable by distinguishers of size $2^{|x|}$ who can recognize whether the statements $x$ are true or false.[3] Therefore, the above argument only covers polynomial reductions breaking polynomial security assumptions, but it does not cover subexponential reductions that break subexponential security assumptions. And indeed, the prior works of [52,54–56] exactly make use of such reductions to prove the security of SNARGs from subexponential assumptions.

**Strengthening GW for Unique SNARGs.** We strengthen the GW black-box separation result for *unique SNARGs with perfect completeness*, showing that we cannot have a black-box reduction even from subexponentially secure falsifiable assumptions. More generally, we consider $c$-exponential security assumptions for arbitrary constant $c > 0$, which stipulate that attackers running in time $\mathsf{poly}(2^{\lambda^c}) = 2^{O(\lambda^c)}$ have advantage $\mathsf{negl}(2^{\lambda^c}) = 2^{-\omega(\lambda^c)}$.

Our main technical tool for proving the above is to define a new simulatable attacker for these types of SNARGs. As in GW, the simulatable attacker consists of an inefficient attacker $P^\star$ that breaks SNARG security and a polynomial-time simulator $P^\star_{\mathsf{sim}}$ such that the two are indistinguishable. The main new feature of our simulatable attacker $P^\star$ is that it is *semi-efficient*. In particular, it runs in time $2^{O(p(\lambda))}$ for some polynomial $p(\lambda)$, and ensures that distinguishers of size $2^{p(\lambda)}$ cannot distinguish it from $P^\star_{\mathsf{sim}}$ with advantage better than $2^{-p(\lambda)}$. In other words, the attacker's run-time is *polynomial* in the size (and inverse-advantage) of the distinguishers it protects against. This is contrast to GW where $P^\star$ had size $2^{|\mathsf{crs}|}$, but was easy to distinguish from the simulator by distinguishers of

[3] For simplicity we focus on run-time, but the above also applies to the inverse advantage of the reduction and the assumption.

size $2^{|x|}$; when $|\mathsf{crs}| = \omega(|x|)$ then the attacker's size is super-polynomially larger than the size of the distinguishers it protects against.[4]

The existence of a semi-efficient simulatable attacker rules out black-box reductions even from subexponential falsifiable assumptions. Intuitively, black-box access to a semi-efficient simulatable attacker is useless for reductions that run in less than $2^{p(\lambda)}$ time, since they cannot distinguish it from an efficient simulator, but it is also useless for reductions that run in more than $2^{p(\lambda)}$ time since they can simply run the attack themselves. In more detail, suppose we have some reduction $R$ based on the $c$-exponential security of a falsifiable assumption. This means that, for some $T(\lambda) = 2^{O(\lambda^c)}$ the reduction $R$ runs in time $T(\lambda)$ and $R^{P^\star}$ has advantage $1/T(\lambda)$ in breaking the assumption (for infinitely many $\lambda$). We can consider two cases. If $2T^2(\lambda) \leq 2^{p(\lambda)}$ then we can replace $P^\star$ by the polynomial-time $P^\star_{\mathsf{sim}}$ and rely on indistinguishability to argue that $R^{P^\star_{\mathsf{sim}}}$, which runs in time $T(\lambda) = 2^{O(\lambda^c)}$ and makes at most $T(\lambda)$ calls to the oracle, has advantage at least $1/T(\lambda) - T(\lambda)/2^{p(\lambda)} \geq 1/(2T(\lambda)) = 2^{-O(\lambda^c)}$ in breaking the assumption (for infinitely many $\lambda$), meaning that the assumption is not $c$-exponentially secure to begin with. This part mirrors GW. On the other hand if $2T^2(\lambda) > 2^{p(\lambda)}$ then we can rely on the semi-efficiency of $P^\star$ to argue that the total run time of $R^{P^\star}$ is at most $T(\lambda) \cdot 2^{O(p(\lambda))} = \mathsf{poly}(T(\lambda)) = 2^{O(\lambda^c)}$ and therefore this directly gives an attack on the $c$-exponential security of the assumption. In either case, the existence of a black-box reduction implies that the assumption is false to being with!

To summarize, black-box access to such a semi-efficient simulatable attacker is "useless" for reductions that run in *too little* time to distinguish it from an efficient simulator, and also for reductions that run in *too much* time so as to able to run the attacker themselves. For the GW simulatable attacker there was a large gap between these two extremes, and in that gap the simulatable attacker was useful and allowed a meaningful reduction to go through. In the special case of unique SNARGs with perfect completeness, we show how to close the gap ensuring that our semi-efficient simulatable attacker is "useless" for all reductions no matter their running time.

**A Semi-efficient Simulatable Attack on Unique SNARGs.** We now describe our semi-efficient simulatable attacker against unique SNARGs with perfect completeness. The simulatable attacker of GW relied on the leakage lemma, which made it inefficient. It did so to carefully sample the correct distribution of proofs for false statements that would be indistinguishable from honestly generated proofs for true statements. In the case of unique SNARGs

[4] For those familiar with GW, the attacker $P^\star$ there relies on the leakage lemma to sample some distribution, and semi-efficient variants of the leakage lemma exist. However, it needs to sample a different distribution for each choice of the $\mathsf{crs}$ and the mapping from $\mathsf{crs}$ to the appropriate distribution is not efficient; the only known strategy is to simply write down the appropriate distribution for each possible choice of the $\mathsf{crs}$, making the total size of the attacker exponential in the size of $\mathsf{crs}$. The run-time of $P^\star$ was irrelevant for GW.

with perfect completeness, we show how to avoid the leakage lemma entirely and give a much simpler simulatable attacker.

Let $\Pi = (\mathsf{Setup}, \mathsf{Prove}, \mathsf{Ver})$ be any candidate SNARG for NP that has perfect completeness and uniqueness. As in GW, we consider a language $L$ with a subexponentially hard subset membership problem. For concreteness, let $G\colon \{0,1\}^n \to \{0,1\}^{2n}$ be a subexponentially secure pseudorandom generator (PRG) and consider the language of PRG images: $L = \{x : \exists w, G(w) = x\}$. For a sufficiently large seed length $n = \mathsf{poly}(\lambda)$, there is some polynomial $p$ such that for witnesses $w \in \{0,1\}^n$ and statements $x = G(w)$ the SNARG proofs have length $|\pi| \leq p(\lambda)$ and the underlying PRG has $2^{p(\lambda)}$-security, meaning that distinguishers with run-time $\mathsf{poly}(2^{p(\lambda)})$ have advantage $\mathsf{negl}(2^{p(\lambda)})$.

As an initial incomplete attempt, our semi-efficient attacker $P^\star$ is easy to describe; it samples a random false statement and does a brute-force search to find a unique accepting proof. Specifically, on input crs, it does the following:

- $P^\star(\mathsf{crs})$ samples $x^\star \leftarrow \{0,1\}^{2n}$ and checks if there is a unique proof $\pi^\star$ such that $\mathsf{Ver}(\mathsf{crs}, x^\star, \pi^\star) = 1$. If so it outputs $(x^\star, \pi^\star)$ and else it outputs $\perp$.

Note that $x^\star$ is unlikely to be in the image of $G$, so $x^\star$ will be false with overwhelming probability. It is easy to see that $P^\star$ runs in time $2^{O(p(\lambda))}$. It remains to show that (1) $P^\star$ breaks soundness and (2) $P^\star$ can be efficiently simulated.

For (1), we crucially leverage the fact that $P^\star$ runs in time $\mathsf{poly}(2^{p(\lambda)})$, which is notably *less time than needed to break the PRG*. Therefore, if a random true statement $x = G(w)$ has a unique accepting proof, then a random false statement $x^\star \leftarrow \{0,1\}^{2n}$ will have a unique accepting proof too with overwhelming probability—otherwise the PRG would not be $2^{p(\lambda)}$ secure.

For (2), we consider a simple simulation strategy that chooses a random true statement and gives an honestly generated proof:

- $P^\star_{\mathsf{sim}}(\mathsf{crs})$ samples $w \leftarrow \{0,1\}^n$, $x := G(w)$ and outputs $(x, \pi)$ where $\pi = \mathsf{Prove}(\mathsf{crs}, x, w)$.

Note that $P^\star_{\mathsf{sim}}$ runs in time $\mathsf{poly}(\lambda, n)$ since the SNARG prover is efficient. For any crs where perfect completeness and uniqueness hold we have:

$$\{(x^\star, \pi^\star) \leftarrow P^\star(\mathsf{crs})\} \approx \{(x, \pi) \leftarrow P^\star_{\mathsf{sim}}(\mathsf{crs})\},$$

where distinguishers running in time $2^{p(\lambda)}$ will have distinguishing advantage $2^{-p(\lambda)}$. The proof follows in two steps: first we replace a random $x^\star \leftarrow \{0,1\}^{2n}$ by a random $x = G(w)$ for $w \leftarrow \{0,1\}^n$ while still generating $\pi^\star$ using brute force. Indistinguishability follows from PRG security. We then replace the brute force $\pi^\star$ by an honesty generated proof, and by perfect completeness/uniqueness we ensure that the two are the same.

Unfortunately, there is a issue with the above strategy, and it does not quite work as is. Perfect completeness/uniqueness are only defined with respect to honestly generated CRS, but the CRS that is given to $P^\star$ can be chosen arbitrarily by the reduction (potentially from outside of the support of honestly generated ones) and there is no guarantee that completeness/uniqueness should hold for it. To handle this, we can have $P^\star$ first do a *completeness/uniqueness check* on the given $\mathsf{crs}$: it samples $2^{p(\lambda)}$ random true statements and checks that the honestly generated proof for them is the unique proof that verifies. If so it proceeds as before, and if not it simply acts as $P^\star_{\mathsf{sim}}$ above. This then ensures that, if the check passes, then for an honestly generated true statement $x$ we can replace the brute-force proof $\pi^\star$ with an honestly generated proof $\pi$ and the two are likely to be the same with all but $2^{-p(\lambda)}$ probability. Our full construction is somewhat more complex to also handle the case of weak uniqueness, and we defer to Sect. 3 for the full details.

**Reductions that Do Not Preserve the Security Parameter.** In our discussion of both GW and our result so far, we only considered restricted reductions $R$ that, when given security parameter $\lambda$, only call their oracle on the same value $\lambda$. We call such reduction "security parameter preserving". For security parameter preserving reductions, GW didn't need any restriction on the CRS size. Therefore, for such reductions, the main difference is that GW's result only applied to polynomial security assumptions, while our result applies even to subexponential security assumptions.

But general reductions may not be security parameter preserving and may call their oracle on different values of $\lambda' \neq \lambda$. Even if we have a simulatable attacker $(P^\star, P^\star_{\mathsf{sim}})$, a reduction running in time $\mathsf{poly}(\lambda)$ that calls its oracle on a sufficiently small values of $\lambda' \ll \lambda$ will be able to distinguish between $P^\star$ and $P^\star_{\mathsf{sim}}$. Therefore, for general reductions, we need to be more careful when arguing that simulatable attackers are useless. To handle this case, GW crucially imposed an additional requirement that the CRS also needs to be as short as the proof size. They showed that in this case there is some sharp threshold such that, if $\lambda'$ is below that threshold then the output of $P^\star$ can be generated efficiently and if $\lambda'$ is above the threshold then the output is indistinguishable from $P^\star_{\mathsf{sim}}$. In either case, the output of $P^\star$ can be efficiently simulated and so oracle access to $P^\star$ is useless.

Using our semi-efficient simulatable attacker, we can instantiate a similar strategy without requiring a short CRS.[5] In particular, suppose there is a general reduction $R$ based on the $c$-subexponential security of a falsifiable assumption. This means that, for some $T(\lambda) = 2^{O(\lambda^c)}$ the reduction $R$ runs in time $T(\lambda)$ and $R^{P^\star}(1^\lambda)$ has advantage $1/T(\lambda)$ in breaking the assumption (for infinitely many $\lambda$). The reduction may call its oracle on different values of $\lambda' \neq \lambda$. Consider an algorithm $R^\star$ (without oracles) that runs $R$ and for each oracle call that $R$ makes with security parameter $\lambda'$: if $2T^2(\lambda) \leq 2^{p(\lambda')}$ then $R^\star$ responds using $P^\star_{\mathsf{sim}}$ and else it responds by running $P^\star$ itself. The run-time of $R^\star$ is $\mathsf{poly}(T(\lambda)) = 2^{O(\lambda^c)}$ and its advantage in breaking the assumption is at least $T(\lambda)/2 \geq 2^{-O(\lambda^c)}$ by essentially the same analysis as before. This means that $R^\star$ gives an attack on the $c$-subexponential security of the assumption, so the assumption was false to begin with!

[5] GW essentially relied on the fact that their simulatable attacker is semi-efficient when the CRS is short to get their result, while our simulatable attacker is semi-efficient even if the CRS is long.

*Remark: On Subexponential Hardness Assumptions via Complexity-Leveraging.* We note that once we allow for general reductions, any subexponential security assumption can be rewritten as an equivalent polynomial security assumption. This is because, for any constant $c > 0$, assuming that every $2^{O(\lambda^c)}$-size attacker has advantage $2^{-\omega(\lambda^c)}$ in some game with a challenger defined by $C(1^\lambda)$ is the same as assuming that every polynomial attacker has negligible advantage in a "rescaled game" with challenger $\hat{C}(1^\lambda)$ who runs $C(1^{\hat{\lambda}})$ for $\hat{\lambda} = \log^{1/c} \lambda$; this holds since $\mathsf{poly}(\lambda) \equiv 2^{O(\hat{\lambda}^c)}$ and $\mathsf{negl}(\lambda) \equiv 2^{-\omega(\hat{\lambda}^c)}$. However, showing the black-box equivalence of these assumptions relies on a general non-security parameter preserving reduction! Therefore, the black-box separation of GW for SNARGs with a short CRS, which worked for general reductions from polynomial security assumptions, already (implicitly) also covers subexponential security assumptions due to the above equivalence.

**Fine-Grained Exponential Security.** We note that our negative result rules out black-box reductions from any subexponential falsifiable assumptions, or more concretely, from any $c$-exponential assumption for any constant $c > 0$. However, it still leaves open the possibility of a black-box reduction from the fine-grained exact security of a falsifiable assumption. For example, it may be possible to get a proof by assuming that some assumption is secure against $2^\lambda$ time attackers, even though it is not secure against $2^{2\lambda}$ attackers. This is because we showed that a reduction from a $2^{O(\lambda^c)}$-security assumption implies a $2^{O(\lambda^c)}$ attack, but the constant hidden in the $O(\cdot)$ may be larger in the second term than the first. Exploiting or closing this loophole is a fascinating open problem for future work.

### 1.3.2 Constructing Unique SNARGs with Imperfect Completeness

**Overview of the Sahai-Waters SNARG.** We first recall the construction of Sahai and Waters [52], which is unique but only proven to be selectively secure.[6] Let $L$ be an NP language with corresponding NP relation $R$. Their construction relies on an iO scheme $\mathsf{Obf}$ and a puncturable PRF $F$. The $\mathsf{Setup}$ algorithm generates two obfuscated programs for the CRS: one to generate proofs and the other to verify proofs. The proof generation algorithm $\mathsf{GenProof}$ has a hard-coded random PRF key $k$, takes as input $(x, w)$, checks that $w$ is a good witness for $x$, and if so, outputs a "signature" of the form $F(k, x)$, else $\bot$. The proof verification algorithm $\mathsf{VerProof}$ takes $(x, \pi)$ as input and verifies the "signature" by checking if $\pi = F(k, x)$. The CRS then consists of obfuscated versions of these programs $\mathsf{Obf}(\mathsf{GenProof}[k])$ and $\mathsf{Obf}(\mathsf{VerProof}[k])$, and the SNARG prover and verifier simply run the respective obfuscated programs. We summarize the $\mathsf{GenProof}$ and $\mathsf{VerProof}$ programs for the Sahai-Waters construction below.

[6] Technically, we describe a slight simplification of their original protocol, which can be proven secure based on the new techniques of [55].

| GenProof$[k](x, w)$: | VerProof$[k](x, \pi)$: |
| --- | --- |
| – If $(x, w) \notin R$, output $\bot$.<br>– Output $F(k, x)$. | – Output 1 iff $\pi = F(k, x)$. |

It is clear by construction that this results in perfectly unique SNARGs; every (true or false) statement has exactly one proof $\pi = F(k, x)$ that verifies. Furthermore, it is a SNARG where the CRS depends on (and grows polynomially with) a specific input-length for $(x, w) \in R$.

In terms of security, this construction is only *selectively* rather than adaptively secure. In the selective security game, the adversarial prover $P^{\star}$ must declare the false statement $x$ that it will find an accepting proof for before seeing the CRS. Security is then shown via the following sequence of hybrid experiments:

- We first switch the PRF key $k$ in the CRS by a "punctured" key $k^{(x)}$ and set $F(k, x)$ to be a random value $x^{\star}$ in VerProof. Indistinguishability follows from iO and the punctured security of $F$ and relies on the fact that GenProof never queries $F(k, x)$ for false statements $x \notin L$.[7]
- We next replace the check in VerProof that $\pi = x^{\star}$ with the check that $f(\pi) = f(x^{\star})$ for any injective OWF $f$. Indistinguishability follows from iO security since $f$ is injective.[8]

Security then follows via a simple reduction to the one-wayness of $f$. Specifically, the reduction can embed the one-way function challenge $y^{\star} = f(x^{\star})$ into the CRS so any accepting proof $\pi$ produced by $P^{\star}$ for $x$ is a valid pre-image of $y^{\star}$ by construction.

**Our Construction.** Our construction is a very simple modification of the Sahai-Waters SNARG above. The only difference is that we use a "selector" PRF with key $k_{\mathsf{sel}}$ to determine whether or not the GenProof program gives out an honest proof for each statement $x$.

In more detail, for valid statements $x$, the GenProof algorithm computes a $\lambda$-bit selector PRF output $F(k_{\mathsf{sel}}, x) \in \{0,1\}^{\lambda}$. If the output is equal to a random string $z \leftarrow \{0,1\}^{\lambda}$, the GenProof algorithm aborts and outputs $\bot$. Otherwise, it gives out a proof $F(k, x)$ just as in the Sahai-Waters construction. The VerProof program is identical to the Sahai-Waters SNARG in that it just outputs 1 iff $\pi = F(k, x)$. The CRS then consists of the obfuscated programs

[7] Recall that punctured PRF security guarantees that the punctured key preserves functionality for all $x' \neq x$ so $F(k, x') = F(k^{(x)}, x')$, but $F(k, x)$ remains pseudorandom even given $k^{(x)}$.

[8] We recall that [7] show that an injective OWF $f$ can be constructed from iO and any plain OWF. Waters and Wu [55] show that it suffices to use an injective OWF $f$ with an inefficient sampler, which can be built from OWF alone.

$\mathsf{Obf}(\mathsf{GenProof}[k, k_{\mathsf{sel}}, z])$ and $\mathsf{Obf}(\mathsf{VerProof}[k])$, and the prover and verifier simply run their associated programs. We summarize the GenProof and VerProof programs for our construction below.

$\mathsf{GenProof}[k, k_{\mathsf{sel}}, z](x, w)$:

- If $(x, w) \notin R$, output $\bot$.
- If $F(k_{\mathsf{sel}}, x) = z$, output $\bot$.
- Output $F(k, x)$.

$\mathsf{VerProof}[k](x, \pi)$:

- Output 1 iff $\pi = F(k, x)$.

It's clear by inspection that our SNARG construction is unique as the verification program is identical to Sahai-Waters. However, we have lost perfect completeness since there is a $2^{-\lambda}$ chance that $F(k_{\mathsf{sel}}, x) = z$ for a random $z \leftarrow \{0,1\}^{\lambda}$, at which point the honest prover cannot find $F(k, x)$.

We next argue adaptive security using a very similar argument as in the work of Waters and Wu [55]. Suppose there is an adversarial prover $P^\star$ that, on input a honestly sampled CRS, breaks adaptive soundness and outputs a false statement $x$ and accepting proof $\pi$ with noticeable probability. We show how to embed an injective one-way function challenge $y^\star = f(x^\star)$ into the CRS as follows:

- First, we argue that the success probability of $P^\star$ is essentially independent of the value $F(k_{\mathsf{sel}}, x)$. As such, the probability that $P^\star$ succeeds on statements $x$ such that $F(k_{\mathsf{sel}}, x) = z$ is
$$\Pr[P^\star \text{ wins} \wedge F(k_{\mathsf{sel}}, x) = z] \approx \frac{1}{2^\lambda} \cdot \Pr[P^\star \text{ wins}].$$
At a high level, this holds for each false statement $x \notin L$ since the value $F(k_{\mathsf{sel}}, x)$ is indistinguishable from random as GenProof never queries $F(k_{\mathsf{sel}}, x)$ on false $x$. To argue this holds for all false statements $x$, we use $O(2^{|x|})$-many hybrids relying on subexponential iO and puncturable PRF security.
- Next, we embed a single injective OWF challenge $y^\star = f(x^\star)$ into the VerProof program in the "off-path" case, resulting in the following program:

$\mathsf{VerProof}^\star[k, k_{\mathsf{sel}}, z](x, \pi)$:

- If $F(k_{\mathsf{sel}}, x) = z$, output 1 iff $y^\star = f(\pi \oplus F(k, x))$.
- Otherwise, output 1 iff $\pi = F(k, x)$.

At a high level, this change is indistinguishable to $P^\star$ since GenProof reveals nothing about $F(k, x)$ for any statement $x$ where $F(k_{\mathsf{sel}}, x) = z$. Following [55], we rely on the fact that for any $x^\star$
$$\pi = F(k, x) \text{ iff } x^\star = x^\star \oplus F(k, x) \oplus \pi.$$

At the same time, it holds that

$$x^\star \oplus F(k,x) \approx F(k,x)$$

since both sides are indistinguishable from random. Then by injectivity of $f$, it follows that

$$x^\star = F(k,x) \oplus \pi \text{ iff } y^\star = f(F(k,x) \oplus \pi).$$

Notably, indistinguishably switching to the program $\mathsf{VerProof}^\star$ only relies on $O(2^{|x|})$-many hybrids based on iO and puncturable PRF security, and never invokes the injective OWF security.

Finally, security follows via a reduction to the one-wayness of $f$. Namely, if $P^\star$ wins and outputs $(x, \pi)$ such that $F(k_{\mathsf{sel}}, x) = z$ and $f(\pi \oplus F(k,x)) = y^\star$, then $x^\star = \pi \oplus F(k,x)$ is a valid pre-image of $y^\star$. Compared to [55], our reduction succeeds with roughly $2^{-\lambda}$ times the probability that $P^\star$ wins. As a result, we need to rely on subexponential security of the injective OWF $f$. Importantly for this step, we only have to increase the domain and range of $f$ to be polynomial in $\lambda$ instead of $|x|$, ensuring our resulting SNARG maintains succinctness.

## 2 Preliminaries

We let $\mathbb{N} = \{1, 2, 3, \ldots\}$ denote the set of natural numbers, and for any $n \in \mathbb{N}$, we write $[n]$ to denote the set $[n] = \{1, \ldots, n\}$. For integers $a, b \in \mathbb{Z}$ with $a \leq b$, we write $[a, b]$ to denote the set $\{a, a+1, \ldots, b\}$. For a string $s \in \{0,1\}^*$, we let $|s|$ denote the length of $s$.

We say that a function $p \colon \mathbb{N} \to \mathbb{N}$ is in the set $\mathsf{poly}(n)$ and is *polynomially-bounded* if there exists a constant $c$ and an index $i \in \mathbb{N}$ such that $p(n) \leq n^c$ for all $n \geq i$. We say that a function $\epsilon \colon \mathbb{N} \to \mathbb{R}$ is in the set $\mathsf{negl}(n)$ and is *negligible* if for every constant $c > 0$ there exists $i \in \mathbb{N}$ such that $\epsilon(n) \leq n^{-c}$ for all $n \geq i$.

A uniform algorithm $A$ is one with a constant description size, and a non-uniform algorithm $A$ consists of a sequence of algorithms $\{A_\lambda\}_{\lambda \in \mathbb{N}}$. We assume for simplicity that $A_\lambda$ always receives $1^\lambda$ as its first input and may write $A(\cdot)$ instead of $A_\lambda(\cdot)$ when the index $\lambda$ is clear from context. We use PPT to denote the acronym *probabilistic, polynomial time.* A non-uniform PPT algorithm is one where the description size of $A_\lambda$ as a function of $\lambda$ is in $\mathsf{poly}(\lambda)$. When referring to an algorithm implemented as a circuit $C$, we let $|C|$ denote the size of the circuit. For two circuits $C, C'$, we write $C \equiv C'$ to denote that they are functionally equivalent, so for all inputs $x$, it holds that $C(x) = C'(x)$.

For a distribution $D$, we write $x \leftarrow D$ to denote the process of sampling a value $x$ from the distribution $D$. For a set $S$, we use $x \leftarrow S$ to denote the process of sampling a value $x$ from the uniform distribution over $S$. We use $x = A(\cdot)$ to denote the output of a deterministic algorithm and $x \leftarrow A(\cdot)$ to denote the output of a randomized algorithm. We write $x := y$ to denote the assignment of value $y$ to $x$. For a distribution $D$, we define $\mathrm{Supp}(D)$ to denote the support of the distribution $D$. We write $U_n$ to denote the uniform distribution over $\{0,1\}^n$.

We say that a language $L$ over $\{0,1\}^*$ is in the class NP if there exists a polynomial-time verifiable witness relation $R$ such that $x \in L$ if and only if there exists a witness $w \in \{0,1\}^{\mathsf{poly}(|x|)}$ such that $(x, w) \in R$. For simplicity in this work, we identify an NP language $L$ by its corresponding witness relation $R$, although we note that such a language $L$ may have many valid witness relations.

## 2.1 Succinct Non-interactive Arguments

Succinct non-interactive arguments (SNARGs) for an NP witness relation $R$ are non-interactive and computationally sound proofs in the CRS model, where the proofs are significantly shorter than the corresponding NP witnesses. Following the notion from [52,54], we also consider SNARGs where the CRS may depend on a specific input-length $m$ for the relation $R$. We first define the more standard notion perfect completeness and adaptive soundness, and discuss imperfect completeness and uniqueness below.

**Definition 2.1 (SNARGs for NP).** *Let $L$ be an NP language with witness relation $R$. We say that a tuple $\Pi$ = $(\mathsf{Gen}, \mathsf{Prove}, \mathsf{Ver})$ is a* succinct non-interactive argument (SNARG) for $R$ *if it has the following syntax and efficiency:*

- $\mathsf{crs} \leftarrow \mathsf{Gen}(1^\lambda, 1^m)$*: A randomized polynomial-time algorithm that on input the security parameter $1^\lambda$ and input length $1^m$ in unary outputs a common reference string* $\mathsf{crs}$. *We assume for simplicity that* $\mathsf{crs}$ *contains $1^\lambda$.*
- $\pi = \mathsf{Prove}(\mathsf{crs}, x, w)$*: A deterministic polynomial-time algorithm that on input the common reference string* $\mathsf{crs}$, *an input $x$, and a witness $w$, outputs a proof $\pi$.*
- $b = \mathsf{Ver}(\mathsf{crs}, x, \pi)$*: A deterministic polynomial-time algorithm that on input the common reference string* $\mathsf{crs}$, *an input $x$, and a proof $\pi$, outputs a bit $b$ indicating whether to accept or reject.*

*We require that $\Pi = (\mathsf{Gen}, \mathsf{Prove}, \mathsf{Ver})$ satisfy the following properties:*

- ***(Perfect) Completeness:*** *For all $\lambda, m \in \mathbb{N}$ and $(x, w) \in R \cap \{0,1\}^m$, it holds that*

$$\Pr\left[\begin{matrix}\mathsf{crs} \leftarrow \mathsf{Gen}(1^\lambda, 1^m) \\ \pi = \mathsf{Prove}(\mathsf{crs}, x, w)\end{matrix} : \mathsf{Ver}(\mathsf{crs}, x, \pi) = 1\right] = 1.$$

- ***(Adaptive) Soundness:*** *For all non-uniform PPT attackers $A$ and polynomials $m$, there exists a negligible function $\epsilon$ such that for all $\lambda \in \mathbb{N}$, it holds that*

$$\Pr\left[\begin{matrix}\mathsf{crs} \leftarrow \mathsf{Gen}(1^\lambda, 1^{m(\lambda)}) \\ (x, \pi) \leftarrow A(\mathsf{crs})\end{matrix} : \begin{matrix}\mathsf{Ver}(\mathsf{crs}, x, \pi) = 1 \\ \wedge\, x \notin L\end{matrix}\right] \leq \epsilon(\lambda).$$

- ***Succinct Proofs:*** *There exists a function $p(\lambda, m) \in \mathsf{poly}(\lambda) \cdot m^{o(1)}$ such that for all $\lambda, m \in \mathbb{N}$, $(x, w) \in R \cap \{0,1\}^m$, $\mathsf{crs} \in \mathrm{Supp}\left(\mathsf{Gen}(1^\lambda, 1^m)\right)$, $\pi =$ $\mathsf{Prove}(\mathsf{crs}, x, w)$, it holds that*

$$|\pi| \leq p(\lambda, m).$$

In this work, we consider relaxing the notion of completeness to allow for some error, formalized below.

**Definition 2.2 (Completeness Error).** *Let $\delta\colon \mathbb{N} \to [0,1]$. We say that a SNARG $\Pi$ = $(\mathsf{Gen}, \mathsf{Prove}, \mathsf{Ver})$ for a language $L$ with witness relation $R$ has $\delta$-completeness error if for all $\lambda, m \in \mathbb{N}$ and $(x, w) \in R \cap \{0,1\}^m$, it holds that*

$$\Pr\left[\begin{matrix}\mathsf{crs} \leftarrow \mathsf{Gen}(1^\lambda, 1^m) \\ \pi = \mathsf{Prove}(\mathsf{crs}, x, w)\end{matrix} : \mathsf{Ver}(\mathsf{crs}, x, \pi) = 1\right] \geq 1 - \delta(\lambda).$$

We also consider a notion of (statistical) uniqueness, which says that any statement $x$ has at most one accepting proof. We formalize this below.

**Definition 2.3 (Uniqueness).** *Let $\alpha\colon \mathbb{N} \to [0,1]$. We say that a SNARG $\Pi$ = $(\mathsf{Gen}, \mathsf{Prove}, \mathsf{Ver})$ for a language $L$ with witness relation $R$ has $\alpha$-uniqueness if for all $\lambda, m \in \mathbb{N}$ and $(x, w) \in R \cap \{0,1\}^m$, it holds that*

$$\Pr\left[\mathsf{crs} \leftarrow \mathsf{Gen}(1^\lambda, 1^m) : \exists \pi \neq \pi' \text{ s.t. } \begin{matrix}\mathsf{Ver}(\mathsf{crs}, x, \pi) = 1 \wedge \\ \mathsf{Ver}(\mathsf{crs}, x, \pi') = 1\end{matrix}\right] \leq 1 - \alpha(\lambda).$$

## 2.2 Falsifiable Cryptographic Assumptions

Falsifiable cryptographic assumptions are modeled via security games between interactive algorithm. To model communication between two interactive algorithms, we assume each algorithm has a specified part of its memory for messages to and from another algorithm. When one algorithm temporarily halts with a message to another algorithm, we assume that this message is copied as an input for the other algorithm. Interaction proceeds until one algorithm halts communication and produces an overall output for the interaction.

Let $C$ and $A$ be two interactive algorithms representing the "challenger" and "attacker", respectively. We denote by $b \leftarrow \langle C, A\rangle(1^\lambda)$ the random variable representing the output $b \in \{0,1\}$ of $C$ when interacting with $A$ on common input $1^\lambda$, when the random tape of each algorithm is uniformly and independently chosen. When $b = 1$, we say that the attacker "wins" in the interaction.

In contrast to [25], we define subexponential time falsifiable cryptographic assumptions by default.

**Definition 2.4 (Subexponential Time Falsifiable Cryptographic Assumptions).** *Let $c > 0$. Let $C$ be an interactive probabilistic $2^{O(\lambda^c)}$-time algorithm and $\alpha \geq 0$ a constant. We say that the pair $(C, \alpha)$ is a* $c$-subexponential time falsifiable cryptographic assumption *if for every non-uniform $2^{O(\lambda^c)}$-time interactive algorithm $A$, there exists a negligible function $\epsilon$ such that for all $\lambda \in \mathbb{N}$, it holds that*

$$\Pr\left[b \leftarrow \langle C, A\rangle(1^\lambda) : b = 1\right] \leq \alpha + \epsilon(2^{\lambda^c}).$$

### 2.3 Black-Box Reductions

We define a notion of black-box reductions in line with [25]. For concreteness, we focus specifically on reductions showing the soundness of some SNARG based on a subexponential time falsifiable cryptographic assumption.

**Definition 2.5 (SNARG Adversaries).** *Let $\Pi = (\mathsf{Gen}, \mathsf{Prove}, \mathsf{Ver})$ be a SNARG. We say that an (possibly inefficient) algorithm $A$ is a $\Pi$-adversary if there exist polynomials $m, q$ such that for infinitely many $\lambda \in \mathbb{N}$, it holds that*

$$\Pr\left[\begin{matrix}\mathsf{crs} \leftarrow \mathsf{Gen}(1^\lambda, 1^{m(\lambda)}) \\ (x, \pi) \leftarrow A(\mathsf{crs})\end{matrix} : \begin{matrix}\mathsf{Ver}(\mathsf{crs}, x, \pi) = 1 \\ \wedge\, x \notin L\end{matrix}\right] > 1/q(\lambda).$$

**Definition 2.6 (Black-Box Reductions).** *Let $\Pi$ be a SNARG and $(C, \alpha)$ be a c-subexponential time falsifiable cryptographic assumption for $c > 0$. A probabilistic $2^{O(\lambda^c)}$-time oracle machine $R^{(\cdot)}$ is an* $c$-subexponential time black-box reduction from the soundness of $\Pi$ to $(C, \alpha)$ *if for every $\Pi$-adversary $A$, there exists a polynomial $q'$ such that for infinitely many $\lambda \in \mathbb{N}$, it holds that*

$$\Pr\left[b \leftarrow \langle C, R^A\rangle(1^\lambda) : b = 1\right] > \alpha + 1/q'(2^{\lambda^c}).$$

### 2.4 Efficiently Samplable Hard Subset Membership Problems

We define a new notion of hard subset membership problems, slightly modifying the corresponding notion from [25]. The definition from [25] stipulates that there are two indistinguishable sequences of distributions $\mathcal{L} = \{\mathcal{L}_\lambda\}_{\lambda \in \mathbb{N}}$ and $\bar{\mathcal{L}} = \{\bar{\mathcal{L}}_\lambda\}_{\lambda \in \mathbb{N}}$, where $\mathcal{L}$ is over true statements $x$ in a language $L$ and $\bar{\mathcal{L}}$ is over false statements $\bar{x}$ from $\bar{L} = \{0,1\}^* \setminus L$. They require that $\mathcal{L}_\lambda$ is samplable by an efficient algorithm $\mathsf{Sam}(1^\lambda)$ that additionally outputs valid witnesses $w$.

In our new notion formalized below, we syntactically replace $\bar{\mathcal{L}}$ with a different sequence of distributions $\mathcal{L}^\star$, which differs from $\bar{\mathcal{L}}$ in two key ways: (1) we require that $\mathcal{L}^\star$ is efficiently samplable, yet (2) we only require $\mathcal{L}^\star$ to output false statements up to some negligible error probability. We note that all candidate instantiations from [25] satisfy our new notion with slight modifications. For example, for a subexponentially secure PRG $G$, we can define $\mathcal{L}_\lambda$ to be the distribution over random PRG images $G(U_\lambda)$ and $\mathcal{L}^\star_\lambda$ to be the uniform distribution over the co-domain of $G$ on inputs of length $\lambda$. It is clear that $\mathcal{L}^\star_\lambda$ is efficiently samplable and yields enough false statements for any sufficiently length-expanding function $G$.

**Definition 2.7 (Efficiently Samplable Hard Subset Membership Problems).** *Let $L$ be an NP language with relation $R$ and $c > 0$. We say that a tuple $(\mathcal{L}, \mathcal{L}^\star, \mathsf{Sam})$ is an* efficiently samplable $c$-subexponentially hard subset membership problem for $L$ *if the following hold:*

- ***Efficient Sampling:*** *$\mathcal{L} = \{\mathcal{L}_\lambda\}_{\lambda \in \mathbb{N}}$, $\mathcal{L}^\star = \{\mathcal{L}^\star_\lambda\}_{\lambda \in \mathbb{N}}$, and $\{\mathsf{Sam}(1^\lambda)\}_{\lambda \in \mathbb{N}}$ are efficiently samplable sequences of distributions.*

- ***Correctness of $\mathcal{L}$ and*** Sam*: For all $\lambda \in \mathbb{N}$, it holds that*

$$\{x \leftarrow \mathcal{L}_\lambda\} \equiv \{x : (x, w) \leftarrow \mathsf{Sam}(1^\lambda)\},$$

*and for any $(x, w) \in \text{Supp}(\mathsf{Sam}(1^\lambda))$, it holds that $(x, w) \in R$.*
- ***Correctness of $\mathcal{L}^\star$:** There exists a negligible function $\epsilon$ such that for all $\lambda \in \mathbb{N}$, it holds that*

$$\Pr[x \leftarrow \mathcal{L}^\star_\lambda : x \notin L] > 1 - \epsilon(\lambda).$$

- ***Hardness:** For any non-uniform probabilistic $2^{O(\lambda^c)}$-size algorithm $D$, there exists a negligible function $\epsilon$ such that for all $\lambda \in \mathbb{N}$, it holds that*

$$|\Pr[x \leftarrow \mathcal{L}_\lambda : D(x) = 1] - \Pr[x^\star \leftarrow \mathcal{L}^\star_\lambda : D(x^\star) = 1]| \leq \epsilon(2^{\lambda^c}).$$

*We say that $(\mathcal{L}, \mathcal{L}^\star, \mathsf{Sam})$ has input-length $m(\lambda)$ if it holds for any $(x, w) \in \text{Supp}((\mathsf{Sam}(1^\lambda))$ that $(|x| + |w|) \leq m(\lambda)$.*

## 3 Black-Box Separation for Unique SNARGs

In this section, we prove our lower bound separating unique SNARGs for NP from any falsifiable assumption, assuming the existence of an efficiently samplable subexponentially hard subset membership problem as per Definition 2.7.

**Theorem 3.1 (Black-Box Separation).** *Let $L$ be an NP language with relation $R$ and an efficiently samplable subset membership problem $(\mathcal{L}, \mathcal{L}^\star, \mathsf{Sam})$ with input-length $m(\lambda)$. Let $\Pi = (\mathsf{Gen}, \mathsf{Prove}, \mathsf{Ver})$ be a SNARG for $R$ with proof length $p(\lambda)$ on inputs of length $m(\lambda)$. Let $c > 0$ such that $p(\lambda) \in O(\lambda^c)$ and $q_{\mathsf{uniq}}$ be any polynomial. Assuming $(\mathcal{L}, \mathcal{L}^\star, \mathsf{Sam})$ is $c$-subexponentially hard and $\Pi$ has $2^{-p(\lambda)}$-completeness error and $1/q_{\mathsf{uniq}}(\lambda)$-uniqueness, then for any $d$-subexponential time falsifiable cryptographic assumption $(C, \alpha)$ for constant $d > 0$, one of the following must hold:*

- *The assumption $(C, \alpha)$ is false.*
- *There is no $d$-subexponential time black-box reduction from the soundness of $\Pi$ to $(C, \alpha)$.*

To prove the theorem, we first construct a basic adversary $P^\star$ in Lemma 3.2 below against the soundness of $\Pi$ that is a *semi-efficient simulatable* attacker, meaning that it can be efficiently simulated for essentially any algorithm that can't already compute $P^\star$. We then finish the proof of the theorem by showing that this immediately gives a way to efficiently simulate any reduction to a falsifiable assumption that only makes black-box use of $P^\star$.

**Lemma 3.2 (Simulatable Attacker).** *For the same values of $p$ and $c$ from Theorem 3.1, there exists an algorithm $P^\star$, called a semi-efficient simulatable $\Pi$-adversary, such that the following hold:*

- ***Efficiency:*** *For any* crs *corresponding to security parameter* $1^\lambda$, $P^\star(\mathsf{crs})$ *runs in time* $2^{2\cdot p(\lambda)} \cdot \mathsf{poly}(\lambda)$.
- ***Correctness:*** $P^\star$ *is a valid* $\Pi$*-adversary for adaptive soundness.*
- ***Simulation:*** *There exists an efficient simulator* $P^\star_{\mathsf{sim}}$ *such that for any non-uniform* $2^{O(\lambda^c)}$*-size distinguisher* $D$ *and input* crs *corresponding to sufficiently large security parameter* $\lambda \in \mathbb{N}$, *it holds that*

$$|\Pr[D(P^\star(\mathsf{crs})) = 1] - \Pr[D(P^\star_{\mathsf{sim}}(\mathsf{crs})) = 1]| \leq 2^{-p(\lambda)}.$$

For space, we defer the proof of the lemma to the full version.

*Proof (Proof of Theorem* 3.1*).* Suppose there exists a probabilistic $2^{O(\lambda^d)}$-time black-box reduction $R^{(\cdot)}$ from the soundness of $\Pi$ to $(C, \alpha)$. It suffices to prove that the $d$-subexponential time assumption $(C, \alpha)$ must be false.

Let $P^\star$ be the semi-efficient simulatable $\Pi$-adversary guaranteed to exist by Lemma 3.2. Since $R$ is a valid reduction and $P^\star$ a valid $\Pi$-adversary for input length $m(\lambda)$, there exists a polynomial $q'$ such that for infinitely many $\lambda \in \mathbb{N}$, it holds that

$$\Pr\left[1 = \langle C, R^{P^\star}\rangle(1^\lambda)\right] > \alpha + 1/q'(2^{\lambda^d}).$$

For simplicity of notation, let $t(\lambda)$ be the combined running time of $C$ and $R$ in the interaction $\langle C, R^{(\cdot)}\rangle(1^\lambda)$ and $\delta(\lambda) = 1/q'(2^{\lambda^d})$, and note that $t(\lambda), 1/\delta(\lambda) \in 2^{O(\lambda^d)}$. We construct an attacker $A$ that depends on $t$ and $\delta$ and breaks the assumption $(C, \alpha)$.

$A(1^\lambda)$ emulates the oracle algorithm $R^{(\cdot)}(1^\lambda)$ in the interaction $\langle C, R^{(\cdot)}\rangle(1^\lambda)$ and responds to oracle queries to $P^\star$ on input crs corresponding to security paramcter $1^n$ as follows:

- If $2^{p(n)} \leq 2t(\lambda)/\delta(\lambda)$, respond with $P^\star(\mathsf{crs})$.
- Otherwise, when $2^{p(n)} > 2t(\lambda)/\delta(\lambda)$, respond with $P^\star_{\mathsf{sim}}(\mathsf{crs})$.

In terms of running time, observe that $A(1^\lambda)$ runs in time $t(\lambda)$ plus the time to respond to each of at most $t(\lambda)$ queries. We show that responding to each query always takes time at most $2^{O(\lambda^d)}$ by analyzing each case separately:

- When $2^{p(n)} \leq 2t(\lambda)/\delta(\lambda)$, it follows from the efficiency of $P^\star$ that directly computing $P^\star(\mathsf{crs})$ takes time $2^{2p(n)} \cdot \mathsf{poly}(n)$. However, observe that $2^{2p(n)} \leq (2t(\lambda)/\delta(\lambda))^2 \in 2^{O(\lambda^d)}$, and $n \leq t(\lambda) \in 2^{O(\lambda^d)}$ since crs contains $1^n$ in unary and is computed by $R$. Thus, the time to respond to queries in this case is at most $2^{O(\lambda^d)}$.
- Whenever $2^{p(n)} > 2t(\lambda)/\delta(\lambda)$, it takes time $\mathsf{poly}(n)$ to respond to the query by the efficiency of $P^\star_{\mathsf{sim}}$. As discussed above, $n \leq t(\lambda) \in 2^{O(\lambda^d)}$, so it follows that responding to such queries also takes time at most $2^{O(\lambda^d)}$.

Thus, the overall running time of $A(1^\lambda)$ is in $2^{O(\lambda^d)}$, so $A$ is has the required efficiency to violate the assumption $(C, \alpha)$.

We next argue correctness of the attacker $A$ via a sequence of hybrid experiments. Specifically, for each $\lambda \in \mathbb{N}$ and $i \in [0, t(\lambda)]$, we define a hybrid experiment $H_i$ as follows:

- $H_i(1^\lambda)$ emulates $\langle C, R^{(\cdot)} \rangle(1^\lambda)$ and answers the first $t(\lambda) - i$ queries by $R$ using $P^\star$ and the last $i$ queries using the strategy of $A$.

Note that by construction it holds that $H_0(1^\lambda)$ corresponds to the interaction $\langle C, R^{P^\star} \rangle(1^\lambda)$ and $H_{t(\lambda)}(1^\lambda)$ corresponds to $\langle C, A \rangle(1^\lambda)$. It follows by assumption that, for infinitely many $\lambda \in \mathbb{N}$,

$$\Pr\left[H_0(1^\lambda) = 1\right] > \alpha + \delta(\lambda).$$

In the following claim, we argue that, for sufficiently large $\lambda \in \mathbb{N}$, it holds that each pair of hybrids outputs 1 with similar probability.

**Claim 3.3.** Let $\lambda \in \mathbb{N}$ be sufficiently large, then for each $i \in [t(\lambda)]$, it holds that

$$\left|\Pr\left[H_{i-1}(1^\lambda) = 1\right] - \Pr\left[H_i(1^\lambda) = 1\right]\right| \le \delta(\lambda)/(2t(\lambda)).$$

*Proof.* The experiments $H_{i-1}$ and $H_i$ are identically distributed except potentially for the response that $R$ receives to its $(t(\lambda) - i + 1)$th query. As such, consider fixing the randomness and transcript in the experiment up until this query, and let $\mathsf{crs}$ be the subsequent query. The next query response is always generated as $P^\star(\mathsf{crs})$ in $H_{i-1}$ but may be generated as $P^\star_{\mathsf{sim}}(\mathsf{crs})$ in $H_i$ when $2^{p(n)} > 2t(\lambda)/\delta(\lambda)$. When $2^{p(n)} \le 2t(\lambda)/\delta(\lambda)$, the experiments are identically distributed since $H_i$ also receives $P^\star(\mathsf{crs})$ as a response.

Let $D$ be an algorithm that hardcodes any such transcript and randomness, receives as input the response to the next query, and then continues the emulation of $H_i(1^\lambda)$ until it outputs a bit. It follows by construction that

$$\begin{aligned}&\left|\Pr\left[H_{i-1}(1^\lambda) = 1\right] - \Pr\left[H_i(1^\lambda) = 1\right]\right| \\ &\le \left|\Pr\left[D(P^\star(\mathsf{crs})) = 1\right] - \Pr\left[D(P^\star_{\mathsf{sim}}(\mathsf{crs})) = 1\right]\right|,\end{aligned}$$

where $\mathsf{crs}$ corresponds to a security parameter $n$ such that $2^{p(n)} > 2t(\lambda)/\delta(\lambda)$. Note, however, that $D$ runs in time $2^{O(\lambda^d)} \in 2^{O(p(n))}$ as all remaining queries are answered using the strategy of $A$. By Lemma 3.2, it then holds, for sufficiently large $n \in \mathbb{N}$, that

$$\left|\Pr\left[D(P^\star(\mathsf{crs})) = 1\right] - \Pr\left[D(P^\star_{\mathsf{sim}}(\mathsf{crs})) = 1\right]\right| \le 2^{-p(n)} \le \delta(\lambda)/(2t(\lambda)).$$

The claim follows for sufficiently large $\lambda \in \mathbb{N}$ that ensure that $n$ is large enough given $2^{p(n)} > 2t(\lambda)/\delta(\lambda)$.

Given Claim 3.3, it follows for infinitely many $\lambda \in \mathbb{N}$ that

$$\begin{aligned}\Pr\left[1 = \langle C, A\rangle(1^\lambda)\right] &= \Pr\left[H_{t(\lambda)}(1^\lambda) = 1\right] \\ &\geq \Pr\left[H_0(1^\lambda) = 1\right] \\ &\quad - \sum_{i=1}^{t(\lambda)} \left|\Pr\left[H_{i-1}(1^\lambda) = 1\right] - \Pr\left[H_i(1^\lambda) = 1\right]\right| \\ &> \alpha + \delta(\lambda) - t(\lambda) \cdot \delta(\lambda)/(2t(\lambda)) \\ &\geq \alpha + \delta(\lambda)/2.\end{aligned}$$

As $2/\delta(\lambda) \in 2^{O(\lambda^d)}$, it follows that $A$ violates the $d$-subexponential time assumption $(C, \alpha)$, as required.

# 4 Constructing Unique SNARGs with Adaptive Security

In this section, we show how to circumvent the lower bound of Sect. 3 by relaxing completeness, resulting in the following theorem.

**Theorem 4.1 (Adaptively Secure Unique SNARG).** *Let $L$ be any NP language with witness relation $R$. Assuming the existence of sub-exponentially secure iO for circuits and OWFs, there exists a SNARG for $R$ that on security parameter $\lambda$ and inputs of length $m$ has CRS length* $\mathsf{poly}(\lambda + m)$, *proof length* $\mathsf{poly}(\lambda)$, *1-uniqueness, and $2^{-\lambda}$-completeness error.*

To prove the theorem, we first define the necessary ingredients in Sect. 4.1, then give the construction in Sect. 4.2, and prove the necessary properties in Sect. 4.3.

## 4.1 Ingredients

Our construction relies on injective OWFs with inefficient samplers, puncturable PRFs, and iO for circuits, all of which are implied by only iO and OWF as required for Theorem 4.1.

For simplicity in this section, we adopt the notion of $c$-subexponential security from [55], but we note that it is implied by the notion of $c'$-subexponential security from Definition 2.4 for any $c' > c$. As such, these assumptions are also ruled out by our black-box separation from Theorem 3.1.

**Injective One-Way Functions with Inefficient Samplers.** An (injective) OWF is an efficiently computable (injective) function that is hard to invert for a uniform input. As in [55], we consider a modified notion that allows for inefficient sampling, captured by the following definition.

**Definition 4.2 (Injective One-Way Functions with Inefficient Samplers).** *Let $c > 0$ be a constant. We say that a pair of algorithms* $(\mathsf{GenChal}, \mathsf{VerChal})$ *is a* $c$-subexponentially secure injective one-way function with an inefficient sampler *with the following syntax and efficiency:*

- $(y, x) \leftarrow \mathsf{GenChal}(1^\lambda)$: *A randomized (potentially inefficient) algorithm that on input the security parameter* $1^\lambda$ *outputs a challenge* $y \in \{0,1\}^{\mathsf{poly}(\lambda)}$ *with corresponding solution* $x \in \{0,1\}^{\mathsf{poly}(\lambda)}$.
- $b = \mathsf{VerChal}(y, x)$: *A deterministic polynomial-time algorithm that on input a challenge* $y$ *with potential solution* $x$ *outputs a bit* $b$.

*We require that* $(\mathsf{GenChal}, \mathsf{VerChal})$ *satisfy the following properties:*

- ***Correctness:*** *For all* $\lambda \in \mathbb{N}$, *it holds that*

$$\Pr\left[(y, x) \leftarrow \mathsf{GenChal}(1^\lambda) : \mathsf{VerChal}(y, x) = 1\right] = 1.$$

- ***Injectivity:*** *For all* $\lambda \in \mathbb{N}$, $(y, x) \in \mathrm{Supp}\left(\mathsf{GenChal}(1^\lambda)\right)$, *and* $x' \neq x$, *it holds that*

$$\mathsf{VerChal}(y, x') = 0.$$

- ***One-wayness:*** *For all non-uniform PPT attackers* $A$, *there exists* $\lambda_A \in \mathbb{N}$ *such that for all* $\lambda \geq \lambda_A$, *it holds that*

$$\Pr\left[\begin{matrix}(y, x) \leftarrow \mathsf{GenChal}(1^\lambda) \\ x' \leftarrow A(1^\lambda, y)\end{matrix} : \mathsf{VerChal}(y, x') = 1\right] \leq 2^{-\lambda^c}.$$

Waters and Wu [55] show how to construct injective OWFs with inefficient samplers from plain OWFs. Furthermore, their construction is sub-exponentially secure if the underlying OWF is.

**Theorem 4.3** ([55]). *Assuming the existence of subexponentially secure OWFs, there exist subexponentially secure injective OWFs with inefficient samplers*

We note that the construction of standard injective OWFs from [7] based on iO and OWF does not suffice for our construction since their construction only achieves statistical rather than perfect injectivity. Adapting their construction to get perfect injectivity requires inefficient sampling for the same reason as in [55].

**Puncturable Pseudorandom Functions.** A PRF is an efficient keyed function that is indistinguishable from a random function without access to the key. A *puncturable* PRF allows a key to be punctured at a specific input $x^\star$ such that the function is pseudorandom at $x^\star$ even given the punctured key.

**Definition 4.4 (Puncturable PRFs).** *Let* $c > 0$ *be a constant. We say that a tuple of algorithms* $(\mathsf{KeyGen}, \mathsf{Eval}, \mathsf{Puncture})$ *is a* $c$-subexponentially secure puncturable pseudorandom function *with the following syntax and efficiency:*

- $k \leftarrow \mathsf{KeyGen}(1^\lambda, 1^{\ell_{\mathsf{in}}}, 1^{\ell_{\mathsf{out}}})$: *A randomized polynomial-time algorithm that takes as input a security parameter* $1^\lambda$, *input length* $1^{\ell_{\mathsf{in}}}$, *and output length* $1^{\ell_{\mathsf{out}}}$, *and outputs a key* $k$. *We assume that the key* $k$ *implicitly specifies* $\ell_{\mathsf{in}}$ *and* $\ell_{\mathsf{out}}$.
- $k^{(x^\star)} = \mathsf{Puncture}(k, x^\star)$: *A deterministic polynomial-time algorithm that takes as input a key* $k$ *and an input* $x^\star \in \{0,1\}^{\ell_{\mathsf{in}}}$ *and outputs a punctured key* $k^{(x^\star)}$ *for the same input and output length.*

- $y = \mathsf{Eval}(k, x)$: *A deterministic polynomial-time algorithm that takes as input a key $k$ and an input $x \in \{0,1\}^{\ell_{\mathsf{in}}}$ and outputs a value $y \in \{0,1\}^{\ell_{\mathsf{out}}}$.*

*We require that* (KeyGen, Eval, Puncture) *satisfy the following properties:*

- ***Functionality-Preserving:*** *For all $\lambda, \ell_{\mathsf{in}}, \ell_{\mathsf{out}} \in \mathbb{N}$, punctured inputs $x^\star \in \{0,1\}^{\ell_{\mathsf{in}}}$, and other inputs $x \in \{0,1\}^{\ell_{\mathsf{in}}}$ such that $x \neq x^\star$, it holds that*

$$\Pr\left[\begin{array}{l} k \leftarrow \mathsf{KeyGen}(1^\lambda, 1^{\ell_{\mathsf{in}}}, 1^{\ell_{\mathsf{out}}}) \\ k^{(x^\star)} = \mathsf{Puncture}(k, x^\star) \end{array} : \mathsf{Eval}(k, x) = \mathsf{Eval}(k^{(x^\star)},\ x)\right] = 1.$$

- ***Punctured Pseudorandomness:*** *For all stateful non-uniform PPT attackers $A$, there exists $\lambda_A \in \mathbb{N}$ such that for all $\lambda \geq \lambda_A$, it holds that*

$$\Pr\left[\begin{array}{l} (1^{\ell_{\mathsf{in}}}, 1^{\ell_{\mathsf{out}}}, x^\star) \leftarrow A(1^\lambda) \\ k \leftarrow \mathsf{KeyGen}(1^\lambda, 1^{\ell_{\mathsf{in}}}, 1^{\ell_{\mathsf{out}}}) \\ k^{(x^\star)} = \mathsf{Puncture}(k, x^\star) \\ b \leftarrow \{0,1\} \\ y_0 = \mathsf{Eval}(k, x^\star) \\ y_1 \leftarrow \{0,1\}^{\ell_{\mathsf{out}}} \\ b' \leftarrow A(k^{(x^\star)}, y_b) \end{array} : b' = b\right] \leq 1/2 + 2^{-\lambda^c}.$$

*We say that the puncturable PRF is simply subexponentially secure if there exists a constant $c > 0$ such that it is $c$-subexponentially secure.*

The standard GGM PRF construction [26] from OWFs can be adapted to give a puncturable PRF as observed by [9,10,39,52].

**Theorem 4.5** ([26,52]). *Assuming the existence of sub-exponentially secure one-way functions, there exist sub-exponentially secure puncturable PRFs.*

**Indistinguishability Obfuscation.** An indistinguishability obfuscator (iO) for circuits is an efficient algorithm that produces an obfuscated circuit $C'$ of some circuit $C$, which is indistinguishable from any obfuscation of another functionally equivalent circuit of the same size as $C$.

**Definition 4.6 (Indistinguishability Obfuscation).** *Let $c > 0$ be a constant. We say that an algorithm* Obf *is a* $c$-subexponentially secure indistinguishability obfuscator (iO) for circuits *if it has the following syntax and efficiency:*

- $C' \leftarrow \mathsf{Obf}(1^\lambda, 1^s, C)$: *A randomized polynomial-time algorithm that takes as input a security parameter $1^\lambda$, circuit size $1^s$, and circuit $C$, and outputs a new circuit $C'$.*

*We require that* Obf *satisfies the following properties:*

- ***Correctness:*** *For all $\lambda, s \in \mathbb{N}$ and circuits $C$ of size at most $s$, it holds that*

$$\Pr\left[C' \leftarrow \mathsf{Obf}(1^\lambda, 1^s, C) : C' \equiv C\right] = 1.$$

- ***Indistinguishability:*** *For all stateful non-uniform PPT attackers $A$, there exists $\lambda_A \in \mathbb{N}$ such that for all $\lambda \geq \lambda_A$, it holds that*

$$\Pr\left[\begin{array}{l} b \leftarrow \{0,1\} \\ (1^s, C_0, C_1) \leftarrow A(1^\lambda) \\ C' \leftarrow \mathsf{Obf}(1^\lambda, 1^s, C_b) \\ b' \leftarrow A(C') \end{array} : \begin{array}{c} |C_0| = |C_1| \leq s \\ \wedge\, C_0 \equiv C_1 \\ \wedge\, b' = b \end{array}\right] \leq 2^{-\lambda^c}.$$

*We say that* Obf *is simply subexponentially secure if there exists a constant $c > 0$ such that it is c-subexponentially secure.*

Jain, Lin, and Sahai [29,30] show how to construct iO for circuits from the following falsifiable subexponential assumptions. We defer to [30] for precise definitions and parameter ranges for these assumptions.

**Theorem 4.7** ([30]). *Assuming subexponential security of the LPN and DLIN assumptions and the existence of subexponentially secure boolean PRGs in $NC^0$, there exist a subexponentially secure iO for circuits.*

## 4.2 Construction

Let $L$ be the NP language with witness relation $R$ corresponding to input-length $|x| = n$ and $|(x, w)| = m$. Our construction relies on the following ingredients:

- Let Obf be an iO for circuits with $c_{\mathsf{obf}}$-subexponential security for some constant $c_{\mathsf{obf}} > 0$. Let $\lambda_{\mathsf{obf}} = (2\lambda + n)^{1/c_{\mathsf{obf}}}$ be the iO security parameter.
- Let (KeyGen, Puncture, Eval) be a puncturable PRF with $c_{\mathsf{prf}}$-subexponential security for constant $c_{\mathsf{prf}} > 0$. Let $\lambda_{\mathsf{prf}} = (2\lambda + n)^{1/c_{\mathsf{prf}}}$ be the PRF security parameter.
- Let (GenChal, VerChal) be an injective OWF with an inefficient sampler that has input length $\ell(\lambda) \in \mathsf{poly}(\lambda)$ with $c_{\mathsf{owf}}$-subexponential security for constant $c_{\mathsf{owf}} > 0$. Let $\lambda_{\mathsf{owf}} = (2\lambda)^{1/c_{\mathsf{owf}}}$.

Our construction $\Pi = (\mathsf{Gen}, \mathsf{Prove}, \mathsf{Ver})$ closely follows the blueprint of [55]. The setup algorithm Gen outputs two obfuscated circuits GenProof′ and VerProof′. At a high level, the honest prover computes GenProof on input $(x, w)$ to get a PRF signature on $x$, and VerProof simply checks the signature is valid. More concretely, GenProof only outputs a signature for $x$ if $(x, w) \in R$ *and* a different "selector" PRF on $x$ doesn't hit a random hardcoded value $z \in \{0,1\}^\lambda$. Otherwise, the program aborts and outputs $\perp$ (meaning the honest prover won't find a proof for $x$). We formalize this below.

$\mathsf{Gen}(1^\lambda, 1^m)$:

1. Sample PRF keys $k_{\mathsf{sel}} \leftarrow \mathsf{KeyGen}(1^{\lambda_{\mathsf{prf}}}, 1^n, 1^\lambda)$ and $k \leftarrow \mathsf{KeyGen}(1^{\lambda_{\mathsf{prf}}}, 1^n, 1^{\ell(\lambda_{\mathsf{owf}})})$.

2. Sample a random value $z \leftarrow \{0,1\}^{\lambda}$.
3. Define the program $\mathsf{GenProof}[k, k_{\mathsf{sel}}, z](x, w)$ as follows:
   - If $(x, w) \notin R$, output $\perp$.
   - If $\mathsf{Eval}(k_{\mathsf{sel}}, x) = z$, output $\perp$.
   - Otherwise, output $\mathsf{Eval}(k, x)$.
4. Define the program $\mathsf{VerProof}[k](x, \pi)$ as follows:
   - Output 1 iff $\mathsf{Eval}(k, x) = \pi$.
5. Let $s \in \mathsf{poly}(\lambda + m)$ denote the maximum size of the programs $\mathsf{GenProof}$ and $\mathsf{VerProof}$ in the hybrids from the security analysis below.
6. Compute the obfuscated circuits $\mathsf{GenProof}' \leftarrow \mathsf{Obf}(1^{\lambda_{\mathsf{obf}}}, 1^s, \mathsf{GenProof}[k, k_{\mathsf{sel}}, z])$ and $\mathsf{VerProof}' \leftarrow \mathsf{Obf}(1^{\lambda_{\mathsf{obf}}}, 1^s, \mathsf{VerProof}[k])$.
7. Output $(\mathsf{GenProof}', \mathsf{VerProof}')$.

$\mathsf{Prove}(\mathsf{crs}, x, w)$: Parse $\mathsf{crs} = (\mathsf{GenProof}', \mathsf{VerProof}')$ and output $\pi = \mathsf{GenProof}'(x, w)$.

$\mathsf{Ver}(\mathsf{crs}, x, \pi)$: Parse $\mathsf{crs} = (\mathsf{GenProof}', \mathsf{VerProof}')$ and output $\mathsf{VerProof}'(x, \pi)$.

### 4.3 Analysis

It remains to argue that the construction above satisfies the required efficiency, uniqueness, completeness, and soundness properties for Theorem 4.1. We prove these properties in the following lemmas.

**Lemma 4.8 (Efficiency).** *The algorithms* $\mathsf{Gen}$, $\mathsf{Prove}$, *and* $\mathsf{Ver}$ *run in polynomial-time and for any* $\lambda, m \in \mathbb{N}$, $(x, w) \in R \cap \{0,1\}^m$, *and* $\mathsf{crs} \in \mathrm{Supp}\left(\mathsf{Gen}(1^{\lambda}, 1^m)\right)$, *it holds that* $|\mathsf{crs}| \in \mathsf{poly}(\lambda + m)$ *and* $|\pi| \in \mathsf{poly}(\lambda)$.

*Proof* Efficiency of $\mathsf{Gen}$ follows from the efficiency of the relation $R$, $\mathsf{KeyGen}$, $\mathsf{Eval}$, and $\mathsf{Obf}$, and the bounds on $\lambda_{\mathsf{obf}}$, $\lambda_{\mathsf{prf}}$, and $s$. Furthermore, $s$ is polynomially bounded also due to the efficiency of $\mathsf{Puncture}$ and $\mathsf{VerChal}$ (see Lemma 4.11). This immediately implies the existence of a polynomial $q$ such that $|\mathsf{crs}|$, $|\mathsf{GenProof}'|$, $|\mathsf{VerProof}'| \leq q(\lambda + m) \in \mathsf{poly}(\lambda + m)$, which also gives the required efficiency for $\mathsf{Prove}$ and $\mathsf{Ver}$.

For succinctness, we note that for any $\lambda, m \in \mathbb{N}$, statement $(x, w) \in R \cap \{0,1\}^m$, and $\mathsf{crs} \in \mathrm{Supp}\left(\mathsf{Gen}(1^{\lambda}, 1^m)\right)$, the honest proof $\pi = \mathsf{Prove}(\mathsf{crs}, x, w)$ is either $\perp$ or equal to $\mathsf{Eval}(k, x)$ where $k \in \mathrm{Supp}\left(\mathsf{KeyGen}(\cdot, \cdot, 1^{\ell(\lambda_{\mathsf{owf}})})\right)$. It follows that $|\pi| \leq \ell(\lambda_{\mathsf{owf}}) = \ell((2\lambda)^{1/c_{\mathsf{owf}}}) \in \mathsf{poly}(\lambda)$ by the syntax of $\mathsf{KeyGen}$ and $\mathsf{Eval}$ and since $\ell$ is polynomially bounded.

**Lemma 4.9 (Uniqueness).** *For all* $\lambda, m \in \mathbb{N}$, $\mathsf{crs} \in \mathrm{Supp}\left(\mathsf{Gen}(1^{\lambda}, 1^m)\right)$, *and statement $x$ corresponding to inputs of $R$ of length $m$, it holds that*

$$|\{\pi : \mathsf{Ver}(\mathsf{crs}, x, \pi) = 1\}| = 1.$$

*Proof* We observe that $\mathsf{VerProof}[k](x,\pi)$ only outputs 1 for the unique value $\pi = \mathsf{Eval}(k,x)$ by construction. It follows that the same holds for $\mathsf{VerProof}'$ by the correctness of $\mathsf{Obf}$, so this also holds for $\mathsf{Ver}$ since $\mathsf{Ver}(\mathsf{crs},x,\pi)$ simply outputs $\mathsf{VerProof}'(x,\pi)$. We note that this holds for false statements as well as true statements.

**Lemma 4.10 (Completeness).** *For all $\lambda, m \in \mathbb{N}$ and $(x,w) \in R \cap \{0,1\}^m$, it holds that*

$$\Pr\left[\begin{matrix}\mathsf{crs} \leftarrow \mathsf{Gen}(1^\lambda, 1^m) \\ \pi = \mathsf{Prove}(\mathsf{crs}, x, w)\end{matrix} : \mathsf{Ver}(\mathsf{crs}, x, \pi) \neq 1\right] = 2^{-\lambda}.$$

*Proof* Let $\pi = \mathsf{Prove}(\mathsf{crs},x,\pi)$ in the experiment above. By correctness of $\mathsf{Obf}$, it follows that $\pi$ is computed according to $\mathsf{GenProof}[k, k_{\mathsf{sel}}, z](x,w)$ for a random value $z \leftarrow \{0,1\}^\lambda$. For any fixed key $k_{\mathsf{sel}}$ and input $x$, it holds that $\mathsf{Eval}(k_{\mathsf{sel}},x) = z'$ for some value $z' \in \{0,1\}^\lambda$, so the probability that $z' = z$ is exactly $2^{-\lambda}$ since $z$ and $z'$ are independent. This implies that $\pi = \perp$ with probability $2^{-\lambda}$ and is equal to $\mathsf{Eval}(k,x)$ otherwise. By construction of $\mathsf{VerProof}$ and correctness of $\mathsf{Obf}$, it holds that $\mathsf{Ver}(\mathsf{crs},x,\pi) = \mathsf{VerProof}'(x,\pi) = 1$ iff $\mathsf{Eval}(k,x) = \pi$. It follows that $\mathsf{Ver}(\mathsf{crs},x,\pi) \neq 1$ with probability exactly $2^{-\lambda}$, as required.

**Lemma 4.11 (Adaptive Soundness).** *The construction $\Pi = (\mathsf{Gen}, \mathsf{Prove}, \mathsf{Ver})$ satisfy adaptive soundness.*

The proof of soundness follows essentially the same structure as in [54,55]. The main difference is we lose a factor of $2^{-\lambda}$ in the advantage by checking that the adversary outputs a statement $x$ such that $\mathsf{Eval}(k_{\mathsf{sel}},x) = z$. The rest of the hybrids and reductions are essentially identical, so we defer the proof details to the full version.

**Acknowledgments.** Cody Freitag is supported in part by a Khoury College Distinguished Postdoctoral Fellowship and the European Union (ERC, SCALE, 101162665). Views and opinions expressed are however those of the author(s) only and do not necessarily reflect those of the European Union or the European Research Council. Neither the European Union nor the granting authority can be held responsible for them. Daniel Wichs is supported by NSF grants CNS-2349972 and CNS-2055510.

## References

1. Alagic, G., Dachman-Soled, D., Shingane, M., Struck, P.: Quantum black-box separations: succinct non-interactive arguments from falsifiable assumptions. IACR Cryptol. ePrint Arch. 1763 (2024)
2. Baldimtsi, F., Lysyanskaya, A.: On the security of one-witness blind signature schemes. In: Sako, K., Sarkar, P. (eds.) ASIACRYPT 2013. LNCS, vol. 8270, pp. 82–99. Springer, Heidelberg (2013). https://doi.org/10.1007/978-3-642-42045-0_5
3. Ball, M., Dachman-Soled, D.: Uniform black-box separations via non-malleable extractors. In: CRYPTO (1). Lecture Notes in Computer Science, vol. 16000, pp. 585–616. Springer (2025)

4. Barak, B., Pass, R.: On the possibility of one-message weak zero-knowledge. In: Naor, M. (ed.) TCC 2004. LNCS, vol. 2951, pp. 121–132. Springer, Heidelberg (2004). https://doi.org/10.1007/978-3-540-24638-1_7
5. Bitansky, N., et al.: PPAD is as hard as LWE and iterated squaring. In: TCC (2022)
6. Bitansky, N., et al.: Why "Fiat-Shamir for proofs" lacks a proof. In: Sahai, A. (ed.) TCC 2013. LNCS, vol. 7785, pp. 182–201. Springer, Heidelberg (2013). https://doi.org/10.1007/978-3-642-36594-2_11
7. Bitansky, N., Paneth, O., Wichs, D.: Perfect structure on the edge of chaos. In: Kushilevitz, E., Malkin, T. (eds.) TCC 2016. LNCS, vol. 9562, pp. 474–502. Springer, Heidelberg (2016). https://doi.org/10.1007/978-3-662-49096-9_20
8. Boneh, D., Venkatesan, R.: Breaking RSA may not be equivalent to factoring. In: Nyberg, K. (ed.) EUROCRYPT 1998. LNCS, vol. 1403, pp. 59–71. Springer, Heidelberg (1998). https://doi.org/10.1007/BFb0054117
9. Boneh, D., Waters, B.: Constrained pseudorandom functions and their applications. In: Sako, K., Sarkar, P. (eds.) ASIACRYPT 2013. LNCS, vol. 8270, pp. 280–300. Springer, Heidelberg (2013). https://doi.org/10.1007/978-3-642-42045-0_15
10. Boyle, E., Goldwasser, S., Ivan, I.: Functional signatures and pseudorandom functions. In: Krawczyk, H. (ed.) PKC 2014. LNCS, vol. 8383, pp. 501–519. Springer, Heidelberg (2014). https://doi.org/10.1007/978-3-642-54631-0_29
11. Brakerski, Z., Brodsky, M.F., Kalai, Y.T., Lombardi, A., Paneth, O.: Snargs for monotone policy batch NP. In: CRYPTO (2). Lecture Notes in Computer Science, vol. 14082, pp. 252–283. Springer (2023)
12. Campanelli, M., Ganesh, C., Khoshakhlagh, H., Siim, J.: Impossibilities in succinct arguments: black-box extraction and more. In: AFRICACRYPT. Lecture Notes in Computer Science, vol. 14064, pp. 465–489. Springer (2023)
13. Chakraborty, S., Prabhakaran, M., Wichs, D.: Witness maps and applications. In: Kiayias, A., Kohlweiss, M., Wallden, P., Zikas, V. (eds.) PKC 2020. LNCS, vol. 12110, pp. 220–246. Springer, Cham (2020). https://doi.org/10.1007/978-3-030-45374-9_8
14. Chen, L., Freitag, C., Jin, Z., Wichs, D.: Unambiguous snargs for P from LWE with applications to PPAD hardness. In: Koucký, M., Bansal, N. (eds.) Proceedings of the 57th Annual ACM Symposium on Theory of Computing, STOC 2025, Prague, Czechia, 23–27 June 2025, pp. 941–951. ACM (2025). https://doi.org/10.1145/3717823.3718159
15. Chen, L., Jin, Z.: On the impossibility of SNARGs with short CRS (or: revisiting gentry-wichs barrier in the non-adaptive setting). In: FOCS (2025)
16. Choudhuri, A.R., Garg, S., Jain, A., Jin, Z., Zhang, J.: Correlation intractability and snargs from sub-exponential DDH. In: CRYPTO (4). Lecture Notes in Computer Science, vol. 14084, pp. 635–668. Springer (2023)
17. Choudhuri, A.R., Hubáček, P., Kamath, C., Pietrzak, K., Rosen, A., Rothblum, G.N.: Finding a Nash equilibrium is no easier than breaking Fiat-Shamir. In: 51st ACM SIGACT Symposium on Theory of Computing, STOC, pp. 1103–1114 (2019)
18. Choudhuri, A.R., Hubáček, P., Kamath, C., Pietrzak, K., Rosen, A., Rothblum, G.N.: PPAD-hardness via iterated squaring modulo a composite. IACR Cryptology ePrint Archive **2019**, 667 (2019)
19. Choudhuri, A.R., Jain, A., Jin, Z.: SNARGs for P from LWE. In: 62nd IEEE Annual Symposium on Foundations of Computer Science, FOCS, pp. 68–79 (2021)
20. Chung, K., Lin, H., Mahmoody, M., Pass, R.: On the power of nonuniformity in proofs of security. In: ITCS, pp. 389–400. ACM (2013)

21. Chung, K., Lin, H., Pass, R.: Constant-round concurrent zero knowledge from P-certificates. In: 54th Annual IEEE Symposium on Foundations of Computer Science, FOCS, pp. 50–59 (2013)
22. Chung, K.-M., Lin, H., Pass, R.: Constant-round concurrent zero-knowledge from indistinguishability obfuscation. In: Gennaro, R., Robshaw, M. (eds.) CRYPTO 2015. LNCS, vol. 9215, pp. 287–307. Springer, Heidelberg (2015). https://doi.org/10.1007/978-3-662-47989-6_14
23. Datta, P., Jain, A., Jin, Z., Korb, A., Mathialagan, S., Sahai, A.: Incrementally verifiable computation for NP from standard assumptions. In: CRYPTO (7). Lecture Notes in Computer Science, pp. 611–642. Springer (2025)
24. Ephraim, N., Freitag, C., Komargodski, I., Pass, R.: Continuous verifiable delay functions. In: Canteaut, A., Ishai, Y. (eds.) EUROCRYPT 2020. LNCS, vol. 12107, pp. 125–154. Springer, Cham (2020). https://doi.org/10.1007/978-3-030-45727-3_5
25. Gentry, C., Wichs, D.: Separating succinct non-interactive arguments from all falsifiable assumptions. In: STOC, pp. 99–108. ACM (2011)
26. Goldreich, O., Goldwasser, S., Micali, S.: How to construct random functions (extended abstract). In: FOCS, pp. 464–479. IEEE Computer Society (1984)
27. Hulett, J., Jawale, R., Khurana, D., Srinivasan, A.: Snargs for P from subexponential DDH and QR. In: EUROCRYPT (2). Lecture Notes in Computer Science, vol. 13276, pp. 520–549. Springer (2022)
28. Impagliazzo, R., Rudich, S.: Limits on the provable consequences of one-way permutations. In: CRYPTO. Lecture Notes in Computer Science, vol. 403, pp. 8–26. Springer (1988)
29. Jain, A., Lin, H., Sahai, A.: Indistinguishability obfuscation from well-founded assumptions. In: STOC, pp. 60–73. ACM (2021)
30. Jain, A., Lin, H., Sahai, A.: Indistinguishability obfuscation from LPN over $\mathbb{F}\_p$, dlin, and PRGs in $NC^0$. In: EUROCRYPT (1). Lecture Notes in Computer Science, vol. 13275, pp. 670–699. Springer (2022)
31. Jawale, R., Kalai, Y.T., Khurana, D., Zhang, R.Y.: Snargs for bounded depth computations and PPAD hardness from sub-exponential LWE. In: STOC 2021: 53rd Annual ACM SIGACT Symposium on Theory of Computing, STOC, pp. 708–721 (2021)
32. Jin, Z., Kalai, Y., Lombardi, A., Vaikuntanathan, V.: Snargs under LWE via propositional proofs. In: STOC, pp. 1750–1757. ACM (2024)
33. Jin, Z., Kalai, Y.T., Lombardi, A., Mathialagan, S.: Universal snargs for NP from proofs of correctness. In: STOC, pp. 933–943. ACM (2025)
34. Kalai, Y.T., Paneth, O., Yang, L.: How to delegate computations publicly. In: STOC, pp. 1115–1124. ACM (2019)
35. Kalai, Y.T., Paneth, O., Yang, L.: Delegation with updatable unambiguous proofs and PPAD-hardness. In: Micciancio, D., Ristenpart, T. (eds.) CRYPTO 2020. LNCS, vol. 12172, pp. 652–673. Springer, Cham (2020). https://doi.org/10.1007/978-3-030-56877-1_23
36. Kalai, Y.T., Raz, R., Rothblum, R.D.: Delegation for bounded space. In: STOC, pp. 565–574. ACM (2013)
37. Kalai, Y.T., Raz, R., Rothblum, R.D.: How to delegate computations: the power of no-signaling proofs. In: STOC, pp. 485–494. ACM (2014)
38. Kalai, Y.T., Vaikuntanathan, V., Zhang, R.Y.: Somewhere statistical soundness, post-quantum security, and SNARGs. In: Nissim, K., Waters, B. (eds.) TCC 2021. LNCS, vol. 13042, pp. 330–368. Springer, Cham (2021). https://doi.org/10.1007/978-3-030-90459-3_12

39. Kiayias, A., Papadopoulos, S., Triandopoulos, N., Zacharias, T.: Delegatable pseudorandom functions and applications. In: CCS, pp. 669–684. ACM (2013)
40. Kilian, J.: A note on efficient zero-knowledge proofs and arguments (extended abstract). In: Proceedings of the 24th Annual ACM Symposium on Theory of Computing, STOC, pp. 723–732 (1992)
41. Kiyoshima, S.: Black-box impossibilities of obtaining 2-round weak ZK and strong WI from polynomial hardness. In: Nissim, K., Waters, B. (eds.) TCC 2021. LNCS, vol. 13042, pp. 369–400. Springer, Cham (2021). https://doi.org/10.1007/978-3-030-90459-3_13
42. Lombardi, A., Vaikuntanathan, V.: Fiat-Shamir for repeated squaring with applications to ppad-hardness and VDFs. In: Advances in Cryptology - CRYPTO, pp. 632–651 (2020)
43. Mathialagan, S., Peters, S., Vaikuntanathan, V.: Adaptively sound zero-knowledge snarks for UP. In: CRYPTO (10). Lecture Notes in Computer Science, pp. 38–71. Springer (2024)
44. Micali, S.: CS proofs (extended abstracts). In: 35th Annual Symposium on Foundations of Computer Science, FOCS, pp. 436–453 (1994)
45. Moran, T., Wichs, D.: Incompressible encodings. In: Micciancio, D., Ristenpart, T. (eds.) CRYPTO 2020. LNCS, vol. 12170, pp. 494–523. Springer, Cham (2020). https://doi.org/10.1007/978-3-030-56784-2_17
46. Naor, M.: On cryptographic assumptions and challenges. In: Advances in Cryptology - CRYPTO, pp. 96–109 (2003)
47. Pass, R.: Parallel repetition of zero-knowledge proofs and the possibility of basing cryptography on np-hardness. In: CCC, pp. 96–110. IEEE Computer Society (2006)
48. Pass, R.: Limits of provable security from standard assumptions. In: STOC, pp. 109–118. ACM (2011)
49. Pass, R.: Unprovable security of perfect NIZK and non-interactive non-malleable commitments. In: Sahai, A. (ed.) TCC 2013. LNCS, vol. 7785, pp. 334–354. Springer, Heidelberg (2013). https://doi.org/10.1007/978-3-642-36594-2_19
50. Pass, R., Tseng, W.-L.D., Venkitasubramaniam, M.: Towards non-black-box lower bounds in cryptography. In: Ishai, Y. (ed.) TCC 2011. LNCS, vol. 6597, pp. 579–596. Springer, Heidelberg (2011). https://doi.org/10.1007/978-3-642-19571-6_35
51. Reingold, O., Trevisan, L., Vadhan, S.: Notions of reducibility between cryptographic primitives. In: Naor, M. (ed.) TCC 2004. LNCS, vol. 2951, pp. 1–20. Springer, Heidelberg (2004). https://doi.org/10.1007/978-3-540-24638-1_1
52. Sahai, A., Waters, B.: How to use indistinguishability obfuscation: deniable encryption, and more. In: STOC, pp. 475–484. ACM (2014)
53. Waters, B., Wu, D.J.: Batch arguments for np and more from standard bilinear group assumptions. In: CRYPTO (2). Lecture Notes in Computer Science, vol. 13508, pp. 433–463. Springer (2022)
54. Waters, B., Wu, D.J.: Adaptively-sound succinct arguments for NP from indistinguishability obfuscation. In: STOC, pp. 387–398. ACM (2024)
55. Waters, B., Wu, D.J.: A pure indistinguishability obfuscation approach to adaptively-sound snargs for NP. In: CRYPTO (2025)
56. Waters, B., Zhandry, M.: Adaptive security in snargs via io and lossy functions. In: CRYPTO (10). Lecture Notes in Computer Science, vol. 14929, pp. 72–104. Springer (2024)
57. Wee, H.: On round-efficient argument systems. In: Caires, L., Italiano, G.F., Monteiro, L., Palamidessi, C., Yung, M. (eds.) ICALP 2005. LNCS, vol. 3580, pp. 140–152. Springer, Heidelberg (2005). https://doi.org/10.1007/11523468_12

# Bulletproofs are Optimal: Lower Bounds for Vector Commitments from Fiat-Shamir in Pairing-Free Groups

Marian Dietz(✉) and Emanuele Giunta

Department of Computer Science ETH Zurich, Zurich, Switzerland
{marian.dietz,emanuele.giunta}@inf.ethz.ch

**Abstract.** Vector Commitments allow parties to commit to an (ordered) vector and to later succinctly open it at any desired position. In plain (i.e., known order and pairing-free) prime-order groups, all state-of-the-art constructions rely on the combination of a generalized Pedersen commitment and an inner product argument. This includes the celebrated constructions of Bootle et al. (EUROCRYPT 2016) and Bünz et al. (S&P 2018), and subsequent improvements. All of these achieve proofs consisting of $\Theta(\log n)$ group elements, and further provide useful properties including malleability, subvector opening and transparent setup. However, breaking the $O(\log n)$ barrier in the plain discrete logarithm setting has proven to be a hard problem. This is in stark contrast with other settings, e.g. from pairing-friendly groups or groups of unknown order, where constructions with constant-size commitment and openings have been known for over a decade.

In this work we investigate whether this limitation is inherent to constructions based on prime-order groups. Specifically we prove new lower bounds for any accumulator (a weaker object than vector commitments, thus making our result more general), with interactive public-coin membership proof in Maurer's Generic Group Model. An implication of our result is that in such setting at least one of the following must occur: (i) the commitment has super-constant size; (ii) the opening proof contains $\Omega(\log n)$ group elements; (iii) the opening proof has length $n^{1-o(1)}$.

Our bound further extends to primitives that directly imply accumulators/VCs including polynomial/functional commitments and inner product arguments.

## 1 Introduction

Vector Commitments (VC) [CF13] are a cryptographic primitive allowing a sender to commit to an ordered list of $n$ messages, and only later opening to a specific entry of this vector in a publicly verifiable way. Along with *correctness*, the key properties VCs are required to satisfy are *position binding* and *succinctness*. The first mandates that opening a commitment in a given position to two different values is infeasible, while the latter requires commitment and openings to be short, i.e., to depend only poly-logarithmically on $n$.


N. Heninger and M. Rosulek (Eds.): CRYPTO 2026, LNCS 16800, pp. 218–249, 2026.
https://doi.org/10.1007/978-3-032-35367-2_8

Over the years, Vector Commitments have found applications in many concrete settings and in the realizations of more structured primitives. Among them, zero-knowledge sets [MRK03, LY10, CF13], proof of retrievability [JK07], space [DFKP15] and sequential work [MMV13], stateless blockchain [CPZ18, BBF19, GRWZ20] and succinct arguments, e.g. [Kil92].

The first realization of VC dates back to Merkle trees [Mer88], where however opening proofs have size $\Theta(\log n)$. VCs with constant (in $n$) commitment and opening size were later realized from a variety of public-key settings including pairing groups [LY10, KZG10, CF13] and groups of unknown order [CF13]. These also provide additional functionalities, including homomorphism/malleability, subset opening, and functional opening [LRY16] (with the most prominent example being that of polynomial commitments).

**VC from Pairing-Free Prime-Order Groups.** Despite the existence of constant size group-theoretic constructions, realizing VC from plain prime-order groups has remained an elusive problem. To this day, two classes of constructions achieve $\Theta(\log n)$ opening proof size, while keeping commitment size $O(1)$ in $n$:

On the one hand, Merkle trees based on Pedersen hash provides $\Theta(\log n)$ opening length and verification time. However, due to the non-algebraic usage of the group, these constructions offer no homomorphic properties or efficient subvector opening.

On the other hand, in the Random Oracle Model, a generalized version of Pedersen commitments can be combined with an inner product argument (IPA) of knowledge to yield a VC. Specifically, given a commitment $C = m_1 G_1 + \ldots + m_n G_n$ to a vector $(m_1, \ldots, m_n)$, opening to $m_i$ can be done by proving knowledge of scalars $m_1, \ldots m_{i-1}, m_{i+1}, \ldots, m_n$ such that $C - m_i G_i = \sum_{j \neq i} m_j G_j$. This approach further allows opening to any linear function of the committed vector, and may offer succinct subset openings depending on the underlying IPA.

**Inner Products Arguments.** The opening size of VC in this second family is directly linked to the efficiency of the underling IPA. The first construction of an IPA with logarithmic proof length has been proposed in [BCC+16], where $4 \log n$ group elements and $2 \log n$ field elements, along with a constant number of extra terms, are needed per proof. [BBB+18] later reduced the proof length to $2 \log n$ group elements and $O(1)$ field elements. Subsequently, [AC20] revisited their construction within the compressed sigma-protocol framework, while [CHJ+22, EKRN24] provided concrete constant improvements, especially in the applications of IPA to range proofs. Given the current state of the art, we therefore identify the following open question:

*Do there exist Vector Commitments from pairing-free prime-order groups based on Fiat-Shamir that (i) use the group algebraically (up to the usage of Fiat-Shamir) and (ii) have $O(1)$ commitment and $o(\log n)$ opening length?*

We find this problem to be of significant interest both in practice, given the scale at which vector commitments and IPA (for range proofs an more) are deployed, and in theory. Indeed, as the $\log n$ limitation in currently known constructions appears to stem from the reliance on recursive folding argument, any positive answer would likely require new techniques.

### 1.1 Our Results

In this we answer the above question *negatively* in many cases of interest. We do so by providing lower bounds for set accumulators [BdM94] with public-coin interactive membership proofs making black-box usage of a prime-order group. These are weaker objects than (public-coin, interactive) VCs in that they allow committing to an *unordered* set $S$, and thus only support membership proofs, as opposed to positional opening.

Specifically, when accumulating a set $S$ of size $n$, if the accumulator has $\rho$ rounds, digest length $|\mathsf{cm}|$, membership proof length $|w|$ and each round $i$ requires $\mu_i$ many group elements to be sent from the prover, then asymptotically our bound implies that

$$|\mathsf{cm}| \cdot |w| \cdot 2^{\left(\sum_{i=1}^{\rho-1} \mu_i\right)} = \Omega(n).$$

In particular, this shows that one of the following conditions must be met:

- the digest does not have constant size in $n$;
- the total number of group elements[1] per proof is $\sum_{i=1}^{\rho-1} \mu_i = \Omega(\log n)$; or
- the proof bit-length is $|w| = \Omega(n^{\epsilon})$ for any constant $\epsilon > 0$.

Furthermore, our results naturally extend to any primitive which directly yields an accumulator, such as vector commitments and inner product arguments.

We formally prove our result assuming the accumulator to be in Maurer's Generic Group Model (GGM) [Mau05], and that security holds in the GGM against computationally unbounded adversaries. These assumptions are necessary to avoid schemes that ignore the given prime-order group entirely, or whose security would otherwise reduce to assumptions that are not group-theoretic. In line with similar group-based impossibility results (see e.g. [DHH+21, CFGG22, DKT26]), our barrier can be bypassed in the following ways:

- making non-black-box use of the group, which in our case includes explicitly relying on the group element's bit representations;
- assuming additional structure about the group, such as pairings or unknown order; or
- reducing security to hardness assumptions that do not hold statistically in the GGM.

[1] even excluding those sent in the last round.

### 1.2 Technical Overview

**Impossibility of Signatures in the GGM.** Our starting point are the negative results for signatures and vector commitments in the GGM (without interaction) from [DHH+21, CFGG22]. Both results, in line with other lower bounds in the area [DKT26], essentially rely on the following facts that hold in Maurer's GGM.

1. Equality queries made by a procedure $\mathcal{M}$ in the GGM are equivalent to testing whether a given vector of scalars $\mathbf{x} \in \mathbb{F}_q^n$ is orthogonal to the vector of group elements $\mathfrak{a} \in \mathbb{G}^n$ passed to $\mathcal{M}$ as input.
2. For any procedure $\mathcal{M}$ in the GGM on input $(\mathfrak{a}, x) \in \mathbb{G}^n \times \{0,1\}^m$ we can extract the space of linear relations on $\mathfrak{a}$ that $\mathcal{M}$ found in its execution by looking at its query history. A linear relation is a vector $\mathbf{x} \in \mathbb{F}_q^n$ for which $\mathbf{x}^\top \cdot \mathfrak{a} = \mathfrak{o}$ holds.
3. For any procedure $\mathcal{M}$ in the GGM, we can *simulate* its execution by replacing group elements $\mathbf{a} \in \mathbb{G}^n$ with a space of linear relations $L \subseteq \mathbb{F}_q^n$ that $\mathbf{a}$ satisfies. Specifically, when $\mathcal{M}$ asks whether $\mathbf{x}^\top \mathfrak{a} = \mathfrak{o}$ is true, a simulator replies positively iff $\mathbf{x} \in L$. The simulation itself does not cost any group operations.
4. For any procedure $\mathcal{M}$ and input $(\mathfrak{a}, x) \in \mathbb{G}^n \times \{0,1\}^m$ with $\mathfrak{a}$ satisfying all relations in $L$, either $\mathcal{M}$ finds a new relation on $\mathfrak{a}$ (i.e., it finds some $\mathbf{x} \notin L$ with $\mathbf{x}^\top \cdot \mathfrak{a} = \mathfrak{o}$), or it returns the same output as when simulated with $L$ and input $x$.

Given the above observations, assume there exists a signature scheme with statistical security in the GGM, i.e., against an unbounded adversary that makes at most a polynomial number of group operations. Then one considers the following EUF-CMA adversary[2] $\mathcal{A}$, which for each message $m$ either is able to produce a forgery for $m$, or it will find a new linear relation on the verification key's group elements after querying a signature for $m$. Since there are at most polynomially many linearly independent relations $\mathcal{A}$ can find, the adversary is guaranteed to find a forgery after sufficiently many iterations.

In order to make this argument about impossibility of signatures in the GGM more precise, let us fix some notation. W.l.o.g., the verification key is of the form $\mathsf{vk} = (\mathfrak{c}, t_0) \in \mathbb{G}^{\mu_0} \times \{0,1\}^{\eta_0}$, and signatures are of the form $\sigma = (\mathfrak{a}, t_1) \in \mathbb{G}^{\mu_1} \times \{0,1\}^{\eta_1}$. Given $\mathsf{vk}$, $\mathcal{A}$ maintains a set of all linear relations $L_0 \subseteq \mathbb{F}_q^{\mu_0}$ on $\mathfrak{c}$ found so far. For each message $m$ then $\mathcal{A}$ proceeds as follows:

- First, for all strings $t_1$ and all spaces of linear relations $L_1 \subseteq \mathbb{F}_q^{\mu_0} \times \mathbb{F}_q^{\mu_1}$ consistent with $L_0$,[3] $\mathcal{A}$ simulates the verifier as described above with $L_1$ and input $t_0||t_1$. Note there may be an exponential number of such $L_1$'s and $t_1$'s, but since simulation requires no actual group operation, this does not affect the efficiency of $\mathcal{A}$ in the GGM.

[2] Technically, the adversaries in [DHH+21, CFGG22] follow somewhat different strategies, but we opt for the following formulation to better present our techniques.

[3] By consistent here we mean that the relations in $L_1$ involving only verification key elements are the same as those in $L_0$. Formally, $L_0 \times \{0^{\mu_1}\} = L_1 \cap \mathbb{F}_q^{\mu_0} \times \{0^{\mu_1}\}$.

If no pair $(L_1, t_1)$ such that the simulated verifier accepts is found, $\mathcal{A}$ gives up and requests a signature $\sigma = (\mathfrak{a}, t_1)$ for $m$. In this case the space of all relations the verifier finds when validating $\sigma$ must contain a new relation on $\mathfrak{c}$ (or else an accepting pair $(L_1, t_1)$ would have been found).

- Conversely, if an accepting $(L_1, t_1)$ is found, $\mathcal{A}$ samples a uniformly random $\mathfrak{a} \in \mathbb{G}^{\mu_1}$, conditioned on $\mathfrak{c}||\mathfrak{a}$ satisfying all relations in $L_1$. This can be done with polynomially many group operations given only $\mathfrak{c}$ and $L_1$. Next, $\mathcal{A}$ checks whether $\sigma = (\mathfrak{a}, t_1)$ is a valid signature. If so, then $\mathcal{A}$ successfully found a forgery $\sigma$ for $m$. Otherwise, the verifier must have found a new relation $\mathbf{x}$ on $\mathfrak{c}||\mathfrak{a}$ not in $L_1$. Finally, due to $\mathbf{x}$ and $\mathfrak{a}$ being independent, with high probability $\mathbf{x}$ is of the form $\mathbf{x}_0||0^{\mu_0}$, i.e., we found a new relation $\mathbf{x}_0 \notin L_0$ on $\mathfrak{c}$.

For showing that non-interactive VC is impossible in the GGM, the argument in [CFGG22] is closely related. The idea there is to compile a given VC into an artificial signature with large enough message space, where the verification key corresponds to the VC public parameters and commitment to a vector $\mathbf{m} \in \{0,1\}^n$, while signatures for a message $i \in \{1, \ldots, n\}$ correspond to the opening in position $i$.

**Issues in the Interactive Settings.** Although the above strategy works well against non-interactive signatures and VCs, the interactive setting is significantly more challenging. Indeed, since public-coin "interactive signatures" based on the GGM exist, we cannot hope to rely on a generic VC-to-signature compiler as in [CFGG22].

Concretely, the issue is that when reducing to the signature's security, our adversary is only allowed to query signatures on a given message, with no control over the random challenges.

**Our Approach Through a Compression Argument.** To circumvent the issue above, we refine the strategy in [CFGG22] through a compression argument. Introduced implicitly in [GT00], a compression argument is an information-theoretical technique where, assuming towards contradiction the existence of a particularly efficient instantiation of a given primitive, one can define a computationally unbounded encoder-decoder pair $(\mathcal{E}, \mathcal{D})$ capable of transmitting a message $\mathbf{m}$ with less that $\mathrm{H}_\infty(\mathbf{m})$ bits. This applies more generally to $(\mathcal{E}, \mathcal{D})$ which can share the same random tape (of arbitrary length), and are allowed to interact during their execution.

Applying this to our setting, assuming existence of an efficient set accumulator[4], we will construct an interactive encoder-decoder pair $(\mathcal{E}, \mathcal{D})$ such that: $\mathcal{E}$ encodes a message $\mathbf{m}$ by first converting it into a set $S = \{(i, m_i) : i \in [n]\}$, computing a commitment $\mathsf{cm}$ to $S$, and sending $\mathsf{cm}$ to $\mathcal{D}$. Then, for all $i \in [n]$, $\mathcal{D}$

[4] Recall we will prove our bound for set accumulator, as opposed to Vector Commitments, for the sake of generality.

will attempt to either (1) extract $m_i$ through a $\mathsf{Forge}$ procedure, without talking to $\mathcal{E}$, or (2) query $\mathcal{E}$ for $m_i$ and afterwards extract a linear relation on the group elements in $\mathsf{pp}$ and in $\mathsf{cm}$ through an $\mathsf{Extract}$ procedure (which requests some costly information from $\mathcal{E}$).

Importantly, the amount of communication inside $\mathsf{Extract}$ must be small enough so that $\mathbf{m}$ is actually being *compressed*. We discuss these two procedure separately.

**Extract Procedure.** The key idea for our extract procedure is to mirror a special-soundness extractor strategy by collecting a tree of transcripts. Specifically, to fix notation, say that $\mathfrak{p}||\mathfrak{c} \in \mathbb{G}^{\mu_0}$ are the group elements in the public parameters $\mathsf{pp}$ and digest $\mathsf{cm}$ respectively, while an opening transcript (for proving $(i, m_i) \in S$) consists of $w_1, c_1, \ldots, w_\rho, c_\rho$ with $w_i = (\mathfrak{a}_i, t_i) \in \mathbb{G}^{\mu_i} \times \{0,1\}^{\eta_i}$ being the $i$-th message sent from the prover to the verifier, and $c_i \leftarrow^{\$} \mathcal{C}_i$ being $i$-th challenge chosen by the verifier after receiving $w_i$.

Given an accepting transcript with group elements $\mathfrak{p}||\mathfrak{c}, \mathfrak{a}_1, \ldots, \mathfrak{a}_{\rho-1}, \mathfrak{a}_\rho$, $\mathsf{Extract}$ maintains a sequence of consistent[5] spaces $L_0, \ldots, L_{\rho-1}$ where $L_i$ contains all relations found so far on $\mathfrak{p}||\mathfrak{c}||\mathfrak{a}_1|| \ldots ||\mathfrak{a}_i$. Then, it performs essentially the same attack as in [DHH+21], treating $(\mathsf{pp}, \mathsf{cm}, w_1, \ldots, w_{\rho-1})$ as the verification key, the challenge space $\mathcal{C}_{\rho-1}$ as the message space, and $w_\rho$ as the signature. If successful, $\mathsf{Extract}$ finds a new relation among group elements $\mathfrak{p}||\mathfrak{c}||\mathfrak{a}_1|| \ldots ||\mathfrak{a}_j$ for some $j < \rho$. Thus, $\mathsf{Extract}$ updates its space $L_j$ with the new relation, and proceeds with requesting a new transcript with freshly sampled challenges $c'_{j+1}, \ldots, c'_\rho$.

Informally, we show that if all of its intermediate attempts succeed, then $\mathsf{Extract}$ finds a new relation among $\mathfrak{p}||\mathfrak{c}$ (i.e., a relation solely among those group elements from $\mathsf{pp}$ and $\mathsf{cm}$) using at most $\prod_{i=1}^{\rho-1}(\mu_i + 1)$ transcripts, where $\mu_i$ is the number of group elements in $w_i = (\mathfrak{a}_i, t_i)$.

**To Extract or Not to Extract?** In light of our compression argument, $\mathsf{Extract}$ as described above is very expensive. Not only does $\mathcal{D}$ have to request $m_i$ from $\mathcal{E}$, but it must also rely on $\mathcal{E}$ transmitting $\prod_{i=1}^{\rho-1}(\mu_i + 1)$ transcripts. Therefore it is crucial to devise a criteria to determine when extractions are performed in such a way that

1. when $\mathsf{Extract}$ is executed, the probability for it to find a new linear relation must be very high;
2. when $\mathsf{Forge}$ instead of $\mathsf{Extract}$ is executed, there is a very high probability for correctly predicting $m_i$ (or, alternatively, to find a new linear relation on $\mathfrak{p}||\mathfrak{c}$ through other means) without communicating with $\mathcal{E}$.

Identifying such criteria is among our main technical contributions. Specifically, we do so via an information theoretical game: Fix $L_0 \subseteq \mathbb{F}_q^{\mu_0}$ (where $\mu_0$

[5] As before, we say $L_i \subseteq \mathbb{F}_q^{n_i}$ is consistent with $L_{i+1} \subseteq \mathbb{F}_q^{n_{i+1}}$ if $L_i \times \{0^{n_{i+1}-n_i}\} = L_{i+1} \cap (\mathbb{F}_q^{n_i} \times \{0^{n_{i+1}-n_i}\})$ for $n_i \leq n_{i+1}$.

is the number of group elements in $\mathfrak{p}||\mathfrak{c}$), the bit-string $t_0$ that comprises both the bit-string contained in $\mathsf{pp}$ and that contained in $\mathsf{cm}$, and $s = (i, m_i)$. In each round $i \in [\rho]$ of this game, the first player sends $(L_i, t_i)$ and the second one replies with a challenge $c_i$. The game ends after $\rho$ rounds and we say that the first player wins if all the spaces $L_0, \dots L_\rho$ are consistent and if the accumulator's verifier would accept when simulated with $L_\rho$.

Having defined this game, we let $\mathcal{D}$ perform an extraction on $i$ only when the winning probability $p$ of this game is very low for both $s = (i, 0)$ and $s = (i, 1)$. In the main body, we prove that the first of the two criteria is now satisfied.

Note that while estimating the winning probability of the above game requires exponential time, it does not involve any group operation or communication with the encoder, and therefore does not affect our information-theoretical argument.

**Forge Procedure.** To conclude, we must equip $\mathcal{D}$ with a procedure $\mathsf{Forge}$ to extract $m_i$ when the winning probability for $(L_0, t_0), (i, b)$ for some $b \in \{0, 1\}$ is greater than $p$. Note that in this case there exists an optimal strategy $(\bar{L}_i, \bar{t}_i)$ for the first player, where $\bar{L}_i, \bar{t}_i$ are functions of the previous challenges $c_1, \dots, c_{i-1}$.

Given this strategy, $\mathsf{Forge}$ can use it to simulate an attack against the accumulator's security as follows. For each step $j$ in the interactive protocol, given $c_1, \dots, c_{j-1}$ it computes the next optimal $\bar{L}_j, \bar{t}_j$ and samples $\mathfrak{a}_j$ uniformly conditioned on $\mathfrak{p}||\mathfrak{c}||\mathfrak{a}_1|| \dots ||\mathfrak{a}_j$ satisfying all relations in $\bar{L}_j$ and stores the proof message $w_i = (\mathfrak{a}_i, t_i)$. With probability $p$, it will eventually end with a transcript containing group elements $\mathfrak{p}, \mathfrak{c}, \mathfrak{a}_1, \dots, \mathfrak{a}_\rho$ satisfying all relations in $\bar{L}_\rho$, and the accumulator's verifier accepting when simulated on this transcript, set element $(i, b)$ and relations $L_\rho$. At this point one of two cases may occur.

- The verifier accepts the transcript $w_1, c_1, \dots w_\rho, c_\rho$, which confirms that $m_i = b$ is indeed true. (Otherwise, note that we have constructed a successful attack against the accumulator!)
- The verifier rejects the transcript. Then we show that the verifier must have found a new relation on $\mathfrak{p}||\mathfrak{c}$ with high probability.

**Ignoring Public Parameters.** Finally, we note that the number of $\mathsf{Extract}$'s executed by our decoder is upper bounded by the number of linear relations it finds on $\mathfrak{p}||\mathfrak{c}$. While the digest $\mathsf{cm}$ (and hence also $\mathfrak{c}$) is expected to be short if the accumulator is succinct, the same may not be true for the public parameters $\mathfrak{p}$. To ensure we only run $\mathsf{Extract}$ at most as many times as group elements in $\mathsf{cm}$, we add an initial exploration step to the decoder, where it simulates its interaction with the encoder on a randomly sampled message $\mathbf{m}'$, each time storing relations the execution found only pertaining $\mathfrak{p}$.

Calling $\vartheta_0$ the number of group elements in $\mathfrak{p} \in \mathbb{G}^{\vartheta_0}$, then a new relation on $\mathfrak{p}$ can be found at most $\vartheta_0$ times. Hence, the idea is to run $i \cdot \vartheta_0$ simulated executions in the exploration step, where $i \leftarrow^{\$} [C \cdot \vartheta_0]$. Doing so ensures that there is a $\leq 1/C$ probability of finding a new relation on $\mathfrak{p}$ during the real execution between $\mathcal{E}$ and $\mathcal{D}$, where $C$ can be an arbitrarily large polynomial.

### 1.3 Related Works

*Lower Bounds in the Generic Group Model.* The study of the limitations of cryptographic primitives in generic models of computation is a rich and active area of research. Negative results have been provided in the pairing-free known order setting for Identity Based Encryption in both Maurer's GGM [PRV12,SGS21] and Shoup's GGM [Zha22] model; order revealing encryption [ZZ18]; Verifiable Delay Functions [RSS20]; digital signatures [DHH+21]; non-interactive zero-knowledge proofs [Giu23]; round-optimal blind-signatures in the GGM+ROM model [DKT26], and for Registration Based Encryption in Shoup's GGM [HMQS23]. Generic model of computations have also been used in black-box separations for other primitives, e.g. in [GM24] for separating sequential function from one-way functions.

[SGS20] provides a lower bound on the time-complexity of batch verification in generic groups possibly of unknown order. Their bound for batch of size 1 implies $\Omega(\lambda/\log\lambda)$ operations are needed in general, with no direct implication for membership proof length.

Most directly related to our work are the results from [CFGG22], where it is shown that for any (non-interactive) vector commitment in Maurer's GGM, when committing to a vector of $n$ elements, then $|\mathsf{cm}| \cdot |w| = \Omega(n)$ (with $|\mathsf{cm}|$ denoting the commitment's bit length and $|w|$ the opening's bit length). We remark that our main result, applied to the special case of a 1-round accumulator/VC, directly implies $|\mathsf{cm}| \cdot |w| = \Omega(n)$, and therefore our result subsumes that of [CFGG22].

We further remark that our approach of establishing lower bounds of a primitive, *restricted to the case where it is derived using a Fiat-Shamir transform*, has already previously appeared in [BGZ23], where lower bounds for identification protocols and signatures from generic *group actions* are provided.

*Lower Bounds for Vector Commitments.* (Vector) commitments and accumulators, even beyond the scope of algebraic construction based on the GGM, have been extensively studied in terms of inherent efficiency limitations. [AIIO12] has shown how structure preserving commitments do not shrink, which does not apply in our case as we explicitly restrict the universe to bit strings only. A recently very active line of research studied lower bounds for the update frequency in dynamic accumulators/vector commitments in various regimes [CH10,BCD+17,CB23,BCCK25,AAAG25,Qi25]. The focus in all these works is on the efficiency of update operations, which is an orthogonal to our problem, namely bounding the membership proof length. Moreover, we stress that our bound is proven assuming only static accumulators for the sake of generality.

## 2 Preliminaries

### 2.1 Notation

Given a set $X$, we write $X^*$ to denote $\cup_{n\in\mathbb{N}} X^n$. Given sets $X_1, \ldots, X_n$, an element $\mathbf{x} \in \prod_{j=1}^{n} X_j$ is written in bold font, and we use $x_1, \ldots, x_n$

to denote its elements. Given $\mathbf{x} \in \prod_{j=1}^{n} X_j$ and $\mathbf{x}' \in \prod_{j=1}^{n} X'_j$, we write $\mathbf{x}\|\mathbf{x}' = (x_1, \ldots, x_n, x'_1, \ldots, x'_n)$ to denote their concatenation. We use $\pi_i : \prod_{j=1}^{n} X_j \to \prod_{j=1}^{i} X_j$ to denote the projection over the first $i$ components, i.e., $\pi_i(\mathbf{x}) = (x_1, \ldots, x_i)$. Similarly, $\pi_{-i}$ denotes the projection over the last $i$ components, i.e., $\pi_{-i}(\mathbf{x}) = (x_{n-i+1}, \ldots, x_n)$.

We use $(x == y)$ to denote the indicator function of "$x = y$", i.e., it is 1 if $x = y$ and 0 otherwise. Similarly, we use $(x \in S)$ to denote the indicator function of "$x \in S$", i.e., it is 1 if $x \in S$ and 0 otherwise.

In pseudocode, we use "$\leftarrow$" for deterministic assignment or for assignment of a value computed by a (probabilistic) machine, and we use "$\leftarrow^{\$}$" for sampling a uniformly random element from a given set. Running a machine $\mathcal{M}$ on input $x$ with randomness $r$ is denoted by $\mathcal{M}(x; r)$. Writing only $\mathcal{M}(x)$ means that the random tape $r$ is chosen uniformly at random.

**Groups.** In this work we only consider prime-order groups. We always write the group operation *additively*, and its elements are always written in mathfrak font (e.g. $\mathfrak{g}$). When a group $\mathbb{G}$ of order $q$ is clear from context, we denote its neutral element by $\mathfrak{o}$. Given $r \in \mathbb{N}$, we define $r \cdot \mathfrak{g}$ as the $r$-fold sum of $\mathfrak{g}$ with itself. Note that $\mathbb{G}^n$ forms an $\mathbb{F}_q$-vector space for any $n \in \mathbb{N}$.

**Vector Spaces.** Given any vector space $V$, we write $W \leq V$ to denote that $W$ is a subspace of $V$. $\mathsf{Sub}(V) := \{W : W \leq V\}$ denotes the lattice of subspaces of $V$. Given vectors $\mathbf{v}_1, \ldots, \mathbf{v}_n$, we write $\mathsf{span}(\mathbf{v}_1, \ldots, \mathbf{v}_n) \leq V$ to denote the linear span of those vectors. If $V = \mathbb{F}_q^n$ is clear from context, we use $\mathbf{e}_1, \ldots, \mathbf{e}_n$ to denote the canonical basis vectors.

We define $\pi_m^* : \mathsf{Sub}(\mathbb{F}_q^n) \to \mathsf{Sub}(\mathbb{F}_q^m)$ as the slice map $\pi_m^*(V) = \pi_m(V \cap \mathbb{F}_q^m \times \{0^{n-m}\})$, i.e., $\pi_m^*(V)$ is the vector space consisting of all vectors in $V$ for which the last $n - m$ coordinates are zero, with their last $n - m$ coordinates removed.

Given vector space $V \leq \mathbb{F}_q^n$ and a group $\mathbb{G}$ of prime order $q$, we define the annihilator $\mathrm{Ann}_{\mathbb{G}}(V) = \{\mathfrak{a} \in \mathbb{G}^n \mid \forall \mathbf{v} \in V, \mathbf{v} \cdot \mathfrak{a} = \mathfrak{o}\}$, where $\cdot$ denotes the inner product. Note that $\mathrm{Ann}_{\mathbb{G}}(V)$ is a subspace of $\mathbb{G}^n$.

## 2.2 Compression Arguments

Compression arguments, introduced implicitly in [GT00], is a proof strategy particularly effective to show efficiency lower bounds for a targeted primitive. Assuming toward contradiction that a very efficient instantiations exists, one uses it then to realize a *computationally unbounded* encoder-decoder pair: the encoder receives a random messages and attempt to compress it. The decoder instead attempts to recover the given message. Contradiction is reached if the input message can be compressed beyond its entropy. We will eventually phrase our result in a more general setting, where $\mathcal{E}, \mathcal{D}$ are further allowed to communicate and share common random coins (independent from the input message). This relaxation does not technically yield a stronger proof technique, but greatly simplifies the exposition. Below we provide a formal definition for an encoder-decoder pair, and the core information-theoretically lemma we will base our main result on.

**Definition 1.** *Let* $(\mathcal{E}, \mathcal{D})$ *be a pair of deterministic machines* $\mathcal{E}, \mathcal{D}$ *with input space* $Z_{\mathcal{E}} \times Q \subseteq \{0,1\}^* \times \{0,1\}^*$ *and* $Z_{\mathcal{D}} \subseteq \{0,1\}^*$*, respectively, s.t.* $\mathcal{D}$ *additionally has access to some oracle with input set* $Q$*. Then, if for any* $(z_1, z_2) \in Z_{\mathcal{E}} \times Z_{\mathcal{D}}$ *the execution* $\mathcal{D}^{\mathcal{E}(z_1,\cdot)}(z_2)$ *terminates,* $(\mathcal{E}, \mathcal{D})$ *is called an encoder-decoder pair.*

*Furthermore, we denote by* $\chi_{\mathcal{E},\mathcal{D}}(z_1, z_2)$ *the total number of queries made by* $\mathcal{D}$ *when running* $\mathcal{D}^{\mathcal{E}(z_1,\cdot)}(z_2)$*. If* $y_i$ *is the* $i$*-th query made by* $\mathcal{D}^{\mathcal{E}(z_1,\cdot)}(z_2)$ *and* $x_i = \mathcal{E}(z_1, y_i)$ *the corresponding response, then we define* $\mathsf{len}_{\mathcal{E},\mathcal{D}}(z_1, z_2) = \sum_{i=1}^{\chi} |x_i|$*, i.e., the total length of all responses provided by the encoder* $\mathcal{E}$*.*

To capture the shared randomness setting, it is meaningful to consider $Z_{\mathcal{E}} = M \times R$, with $M$ message space and $R$ random coins set, and $Z_{\mathcal{D}} = R$. If for a random $(m, r)$, the decoder guesses $m$ only given $r$ and access to $\mathcal{E}((m, r), \cdot)$, then the incoming communication form $\mathcal{E}$ should match the min-entropy of $m$. A proof of the following Lemma appears in the full version of this paper.

**Lemma 1.** *Let* $(\mathcal{E}, \mathcal{D})$ *be an encoder-decoder pair with input spaces* $M \times R$ *and* $R$*, respectively. For* $(m, r)$ *uniformly sampled and* $E$ *an event*[6] *such that* $E$ *implies* $\mathcal{D}^{\mathcal{E}((m,r),\cdot)}(r) = m$*, then*

$$\log |M| \leq 1 + \max_{(m,r)\in E} \mathsf{len}_{\mathcal{E},\mathcal{D}}((m, r), r) - \log \Pr[E]$$

## 2.3 Generic and Type-Safe Algorithms

In order to model black-box usage of the underlying group, we rely on Maurer's GGM [Mau05]. Here, group elements are treated as syntactically different objects than bit strings, and the only operations allowed are additions and equality tests. In [Mau05] this is captured by equipping generic algorithms with two stateful oracles performing those operations, without providing any representation for the group elements involved. [Zha22, §3.3] instead proposed the notion of *Type-Safe* circuits, where an explicit representation for group elements is provided, but computation on them only happens via addition or equality gates.

Compromising between these two approaches, we will adopt the same approach as [DKT26]: we distinguish between a *generic* algorithm (that has oracle access to group operations) and a *type-safe* algorithm, which is essentially a generic algorithm instantiated with a specific group (hence, the type-safe algorithm does not require a group operation oracle anymore).

**Definition 2.** *A generic (or GGM) algorithm is a probabilistic oracle machine* $\mathcal{M}$ *with access to two oracles* $\mathsf{add}$ *and* $\mathsf{eq}$*, input in* $\mathbb{N} \times \mathbb{N} \times \{0,1\}^*$ *and output in* $\mathbb{N}^* \times \{0,1\}^*$*. We further say* $\mathcal{M}$ *is:*

6 Formally, given that the probability space is defined over $M \times R$ with the normalized counting measure, $E$ is a subset of $M \times R$ and $(m_0, r_0) \in E$ iff $\Pr[E \mid (m, r) = (m_0, r_0)] = 1$.

- *$\chi$-queries if $\mathcal{M}^{\mathsf{add},\mathsf{eq}}(q, n, x)$ performs at most $\chi(q, n, x)$ queries;*
- *query-efficient if it is $\chi$-queries with $\chi(q, n, x)$ being a polynomial in $\log q$, $n$, and $|x|$;*
- *bits-output if its output is in $\{0, 1\}^*$.*

**Definition 3.** *Let $\mathcal{M}$ be a GGM algorithm, and let $\mathbb{G}$ of prime order $q$. Given $(\mathfrak{a}, x) \in \mathbb{G}^* \times \{0,1\}^*$ and random coins $r \in \{0,1\}^*$, the* execution *of $\mathcal{M}$ is defined as $\mathsf{Exec}_{\mathcal{M}}(q, \mathfrak{a}, x; r)$, as detailed in Fig. 1.*

$\mathsf{Exec}_{\mathcal{M}}(q, \mathfrak{a}, x; r)$: // $\mathfrak{a} = (\mathfrak{a}_1, \ldots, \mathfrak{a}_n) \in \mathbb{G}^n$

Run $\mathcal{M}^{\mathsf{add},\mathsf{eq}}(q, n, x; r)$
**When** $\mathcal{M}$ queries $\mathsf{add}(i, j)$:
  **If** $i, j \in \{1, \ldots, n\}$:
    $\mathfrak{a}_{n+1} \leftarrow \mathfrak{a}_i + \mathfrak{a}_j$, $n \leftarrow n + 1$
**When** $\mathcal{M}$ queries $\mathsf{eq}(i, j)$:
  **If** $i, j \in \{1, \ldots, n\}$:
    **Reply** $(\mathfrak{a}_i == \mathfrak{a}_j)$
  **Else**: **Reply** $\bot$
**When** $\mathcal{M}$ returns $(i_1, \ldots, i_m, y)$:
  **If** $i_j \in \{1, \ldots, n\}$ $\forall j \in \{1, \ldots, m\}$:
    **Return** $(\mathfrak{a}_{i_1}, \ldots, \mathfrak{a}_{i_m}, y)$
  **Else**: **Return** $\bot$

**Fig. 1.** Execution of a GGM algorithm $\mathcal{M}$ using a group $\mathbb{G}$ of prime order $q$.

**Definition 4.** *A probabilistic machine $\mathcal{T}$ is type-safe w.r.t. some group $\mathbb{G}$ of prime order $q$ if there exists a GGM-algorithm $\langle \mathcal{T} \rangle$ such that for every input $(\mathfrak{a}, x) \in \mathbb{G}^* \times \{0,1\}^*$ and random coins $r \in \{0,1\}^*$, it holds that:*

$$\mathcal{T}(q, \mathfrak{a}, x; r) = \mathsf{Exec}_{\langle \mathcal{T} \rangle}(q, \mathfrak{a}, x; r).$$

*We further say $\mathcal{T}$ is respectively $\chi$-query, query-efficient, or bits-output, whenever there exists a choice of $\langle \mathcal{T} \rangle$ for which $\langle \mathcal{T} \rangle$ is $\chi$-query, query-efficient, or bits-output.*[7]

For proving lower bounds, it will be important to execute a GGM algorithm $\mathcal{M}$ using different "modes" that allow either simulating it (for free) or learning the relations that its execution implies about the input $\mathfrak{a}$:

[7] Note that the bits-output property is independent of the choice of $\langle \mathcal{T} \rangle$, while the other two properties are not.

**Definition 5.** *Let $\mathcal{M}$ be a GGM algorithm, and let $\mathbb{G}$ be a group of prime order $q$. Given input $(\mathfrak{a}, x) \in \mathbb{G}^n \times \{0,1\}^*$ and random coins $r \in \{0,1\}^*$, the* implied vector space of relations $\mathsf{Rel}_{\mathcal{M}}(q, \mathfrak{a}, x; r)$ *(which is a subset of $\mathbb{F}_q^n$) is defined on the right-hand side of Fig. 2.*

*If $\mathcal{M}$ further is bits-output, then given a vector space $R \leq \mathbb{F}_q^n$, bitstring $x \in \{0,1\}^*$ and random coins $r \in \{0,1\}^*$, the* simulation of $\mathcal{M}$ according to $R$ *is defined as $\mathsf{Sim}_{\mathcal{M}}(q, R, x; r)$, as detailed on the left-hand side of Fig. 2.*

| $\mathsf{Sim}_{\mathcal{M}}(q, R, x; r)$: // $R \leq \mathbb{F}_q^n$ | $\mathsf{Rel}_{\mathcal{M}}(q, \mathfrak{a}, x; r)$: // $\mathfrak{a} \in \mathbb{G}^n$ |
|---|---|
| $\mathbf{v}_i \leftarrow \mathbf{e}_i \in \mathbb{F}_q^n$ for $i \in \{1, \ldots, n\}$ | $\mathbf{v}_i \leftarrow \mathbf{e}_i \in \mathbb{F}_q^n$ for $i \in \{1, \ldots n\}$ |
| | $R \leftarrow \{0^n\}$ |
| Run $\mathcal{M}^{\mathsf{add},\mathsf{eq}}(q, n, x; r)$ | Run $\mathcal{M}^{\mathsf{add},\mathsf{eq}}(q, n, x; r)$ |
| **When** $\mathcal{M}$ queries $\mathsf{add}(i, j)$: | **When** $\mathcal{M}$ queries $\mathsf{add}(i, j)$: |
|   **If** $i, j \in \{1, \ldots, n\}$: |   **If** $i, j \in \{1, \ldots, n\}$: |
|     $\mathbf{v}_{n+1} \leftarrow \mathbf{v}_i + \mathbf{v}_j$, $n \leftarrow n + 1$ |     $\mathbf{v}_{n+1} \leftarrow \mathbf{v}_i + \mathbf{v}_j$, $n \leftarrow n + 1$ |
| **When** $\mathcal{M}$ queries $\mathsf{eq}(i, j)$: | **When** $\mathcal{M}$ queries $\mathsf{eq}(i, j)$: |
|   **If** $i, j \in \{1, \ldots, n\}$: |   **If** $i, j \in \{1, \ldots, n\}$: |
|     **Reply** $(\mathbf{v}_i - \mathbf{v}_j \in R)$ |     **Reply** $(\mathbf{v}_i^T \cdot \mathfrak{a} == \mathbf{v}_j^T \cdot \mathfrak{a})$ |
| |     **If** $\mathbf{v}_i^T \cdot \mathfrak{a} = \mathbf{v}_j^T \cdot \mathfrak{a}$: |
| |       $R \leftarrow R + \mathsf{span}(\mathbf{v}_i - \mathbf{v}_j)$ |
|   **Else**: **Reply** $\bot$ |   **Else**: **Reply** $\bot$ |
| **When** $\mathcal{M}$ returns $y \in \{0,1\}^*$: | **When** $\mathcal{M}$ halts: |
|   **Return** $y$ |   **Return** $R$ |

**Fig. 2.** Simulation of a GGM algorithm $\mathcal{M}$ according to a vector space $R \leq \mathbb{F}_q^n$ (left) and the vector space of relations implied by running a GGM algorithm $\mathcal{M}$ (right).

We now state a variety of properties referring to the notions defined above. Many of them have been used in implicit form in previous works [DHH+21, CFGG22, DKT26]. We give full proofs for all of these lemmas in the full version.

**Lemma 2.** *Consider any GGM algorithm $\mathcal{M}$, a group $\mathbb{G}$ of prime order $q$, and any input $(\mathfrak{a}, x) \in \mathbb{G}^* \times \{0,1\}^*$. Then, denoting*

$$R \leftarrow \mathsf{Rel}_{\mathcal{M}}(q, \mathfrak{a}, x; r) ,$$

*we have that $\mathfrak{a} \in \mathrm{Ann}_{\mathbb{G}}(R)$.*

*Proof.* By construction, the output $R$ of $\mathsf{Rel}$ is $R = \mathsf{span}(\mathbf{w}_1, \ldots, \mathbf{w}_k)$ for some vectors $\mathbf{w}_i$ with $\mathbf{w}^T \cdot \mathfrak{a} = \mathfrak{o}$. Hence, by linearity, $\mathfrak{a} \in \mathrm{Ann}_{\mathbb{G}}(R)$. □

**Lemma 3.** *Consider any bits-output GGM algorithm $\mathcal{M}$, a group $\mathbb{G}$ of prime order $q$, any input $(\mathfrak{a}, x) \in \mathbb{G}^n \times \{0,1\}^*$, random tape $r \in \{0,1\}^*$ and vector space $R \leq \mathbb{F}_q^n$, and denote*

$$y = \mathsf{Exec}_{\mathcal{M}}(q, \mathfrak{a}, x; r), \quad R' \leftarrow \mathsf{Rel}_{\mathcal{M}}(q, \mathfrak{a}, x; r), \quad y' \leftarrow \mathsf{Sim}_{\mathcal{M}}(q, R, x; r).$$

*Whenever both $R' \subseteq R$ and $\mathfrak{a} \in \mathrm{Ann}_{\mathbb{G}}(R)$ hold, then $y = y'$. In particular, $R' = R$ implies $y = y'$.*

**Lemma 4.** *Fix any $\chi$-queries bits-output GGM algorithm $\mathcal{M}$, a group $\mathbb{G}$ of prime order $q$, a vector space $R \leq \mathbb{F}_q^{n+m}$ (with $n, m \in \mathbb{N}$), group elements $\mathfrak{a} \in \mathrm{Ann}_{\mathbb{G}}(\pi_n^*(R))$, and strings $x, r \in \{0,1\}^*$ let $\mathfrak{b}$ be uniformly distributed over $\{\mathfrak{b} \in \mathbb{G}^m \mid (\mathfrak{a}||\mathfrak{b}) \in \mathrm{Ann}_{\mathbb{G}}(R)\}$. Then, calling $y = \mathsf{Exec}_{\mathcal{M}}(q, \mathfrak{a}||\mathfrak{b}, x; r)$, $R' = \mathsf{Rel}_{\mathcal{M}}(q, \mathfrak{a}||\mathfrak{b}, x; r)$ and $y' = \mathsf{Sim}_{\mathcal{M}}(q, R, x; r)$, we get*

$$\Pr\left[y = y' \ \vee \ \pi_n^*(R + R') \nsubseteq \pi_n^*(R)\right] \geq 1 - \frac{\chi(q, n+m, x)}{q}.$$

**Lemma 5.** *Given any group $\mathbb{G}$ of prime order $q$, vector spaces $R_i \leq \mathbb{F}_q^{n+\sum_{j=1}^{i} m_j}$ for $i \in \{0, \ldots, \ell\}$ (with $n, m_1, \ldots, m_\ell \in \mathbb{N}$) such that $\pi^*_{n+\sum_{j=1}^{i-1} m_j}(R_i) = R_{i-1}$ for all $i \in \{1, \ldots, \ell\}$, as well as group elements $\mathfrak{b}_0 \in \mathrm{Ann}_{\mathbb{G}}(R_0)$, the following two distributions are identical:*

- *For $i$ from 1 to $\ell$, sample $\mathfrak{b}_i$ uniformly conditioned on $(\mathfrak{b}_0|| \ldots ||\mathfrak{b}_{i-1}||\mathfrak{b}_i) \in \mathrm{Ann}_{\mathbb{G}}(R_i)$. Then output $(\mathfrak{b}_0|| \ldots ||\mathfrak{b}_\ell)$.*
- *Sample $(\mathfrak{b}_1|| \ldots ||\mathfrak{b}_\ell)$ uniformly conditioned on $(\mathfrak{b}_0|| \ldots ||\mathfrak{b}_\ell) \in \mathrm{Ann}_{\mathbb{G}}(R_\ell)$, and output $(\mathfrak{b}_0|| \ldots ||\mathfrak{b}_\ell)$.*

**Lemma 6.** *For any group $\mathbb{G}$ of prime order $q$ with generator $\mathfrak{g}$, there exists a $O(n \cdot m \cdot \log q)$-queries type-safe probabilistic machine $\mathcal{T}$, s.t. given input $(\mathfrak{g}||\mathfrak{a}, (n, m, R)) \in \mathbb{G}^{n+1} \times \{0,1\}^{*}$[8] (with a vector space $R \leq \mathbb{F}_q^{n+m}$ s.t. $\mathfrak{a} \in \mathrm{Ann}_{\mathbb{G}}(\pi_n^*(R))$), the output distribution is identical to the uniform distribution over $\{\mathfrak{b} \in \mathbb{G}^m \mid (\mathfrak{a}||\mathfrak{b}) \in \mathrm{Ann}_{\mathbb{G}}(R)\}$.*

## 2.4 Interactive Type-Safe Accumulators

In the following we adapt the definition of cryptographic accumulators from [FN02,BCY20]. Specifically, as we are interested in black-box construction based entirely on the hardness of a prime-order group, we restrict all primitives to be type-safe, and require security only to hold against query-efficient adversaries, but otherwise unbounded.[9] Moreover, since our goal is to capture only constructions based on Fiat-Shamir [FS87], we allow membership proofs to be interactive but also require them to be public-coin.

[8] We abuse notation to denote with $(n, m, R)$ an arbitrarily chosen encoding in $\{0,1\}^*$ of the triple $(n, m, R) \in \mathbb{N} \times \mathbb{N} \times \mathsf{Sub}(\mathbb{F}_q^{n+m})$.

[9] In fact, our lower bound would even hold if only A.Ver is type-safe, but for the sake of simplicity we put the same restriction on all algorithms.

**Definition 6.** *A type-safe $\rho(\lambda, n)$-rounds public-coin interactive accumulator* $\mathsf{A}$ *consists of a group $\mathbb{G} = \mathbb{G}(\lambda)$ whose prime order $q = q(\lambda)$ fulfills $q = 2^{\Theta(\lambda)}$, a generator $\mathfrak{g} \in \mathbb{G}$, polynomially bounded functions $\rho, \vartheta_0, \vartheta_1, \zeta_0, \zeta_1$, $(\mu_i, \eta_i, \ell_i)_{i\in\mathbb{N}\setminus\{0\}}$ in $\lambda, n$, and a tuple of query-efficient type-safe algorithms* $(\mathsf{A.Gen}, \mathsf{A.Acc}, \mathsf{A.Wit}, \mathsf{A.Ver})$ *as follows:*

- $\mathsf{A.Gen}(\mathfrak{g}, 1^\lambda, 1^n) \xrightarrow{\$} \mathsf{pp}$ *where* $\mathsf{pp} = (\mathfrak{p}, \tau_0) \in \mathbb{G}^{\vartheta_0} \times \{0,1\}^{\zeta_0}$ *returns the accumulator's public parameters;*[10]
- $\mathsf{A.Acc}(\mathsf{pp}, S) \xrightarrow{\$} (\mathsf{cm}, \mathsf{aux})$ *where* $\mathsf{cm} = (\mathfrak{c}, \tau_1) \in \mathbb{G}^{\vartheta_1} \times \{0,1\}^{\zeta_1}$ *is the digest of a set $S \subseteq \{0,1\}^\lambda$;*
- $\mathsf{A.Wit}(\mathsf{pp}, \mathsf{aux}, s, c_1, \ldots, c_{i-1}) \xrightarrow{\$} w_i$, *for $i \in [\rho]$ with challenges $c_j \in \{0,1\}^{\ell_j}$ (for $j \in \{1, \ldots, i-1\}$) outputs the i-th message $w_i = (\mathfrak{a}_i, t_i) \in \mathbb{G}^{\mu_i} \times \{0,1\}^{\eta_i}$ in the interactive proof of membership of $s$ in* $\mathsf{cm}$*;*
- $\mathsf{A.Ver}(\mathsf{pp}, \mathsf{cm}, s, \mathsf{tr}) \rightarrow 1/0$ *deterministically checks whether the transcript* $\mathsf{tr} = (w_1, c_1, \ldots, w_\rho, c_\rho)$ *is a valid proof for the membership of $s$ in the set accumulated by* $\mathsf{cm}$.

*We use $\chi = \chi(\lambda, n)$ to denote a bound on the query-efficiency of* $\langle\mathsf{A.Ver}\rangle$.[11]

*Remark 1.* Note that, despite the formal definition above requiring $\mathsf{A.Ver}$ to be deterministic, this model still captures randomized verification procedures: observe that the $\rho$-th challenge $c_\rho$ remains *unanswered* by the prover, and hence we may identify $c_\rho$ with the random tape that a randomized verification procedure would have. Our lower bound does not depend at all on $\ell_\rho$, and hence the restriction to let $\mathsf{A.Ver}$ be deterministic is without loss of generality.

*Remark 2.* Strictly speaking, the (somewhat structured) input/output spaces of the accumulator's algorithms do not match the requirements of Definition 4, which only supports spaces of the form $\mathbb{G}^* \times \{0,1\}^*$. However, since all length functions $\rho, \vartheta_0, \vartheta_1, (\mu_i, \nu_i, \ell_i)_{i\in\mathbb{N}}$ are fixed, we will abuse notation when writing

$$\mathsf{A.Ver}(\mathfrak{p}||\mathfrak{c}||\mathfrak{a}_1||\ldots||\mathfrak{a}_\rho, (\tau_0, \tau_1, t_1, \ldots, t_\rho, c_1, \ldots, c_\rho))$$

to mean $\mathsf{A.Ver}((\mathfrak{p}, \tau_0), (\mathfrak{c}, \tau_1), \mathsf{tr})$, where $\mathsf{tr} = ((\mathfrak{a}_1, t_1), c_1, \ldots, (\mathfrak{a}_\rho, t_\rho), c_\rho)$. Doing so will allow us to apply $\mathsf{Exec}$, $\mathsf{Sim}$, and $\mathsf{Rel}$ to the modified $\mathsf{A.Ver}$ interface.

**Definition 7 (Correctness).** *An accumulator* $\mathsf{A}$ *as per Definition 6 is $\varepsilon = \varepsilon(\lambda, n)$-correct if for any $\lambda, n \in \mathbb{N}$, any set $S \subseteq \{0,1\}^\lambda$ of size $|S| \leq n$ and any element $s \in S$,*

$$\Pr[\mathsf{A.Ver}(\mathsf{pp}, \mathsf{cm}, s, \mathsf{tr}) = 0] \leq \varepsilon(\lambda, n) ,$$

*taken over* $\mathsf{pp} \xleftarrow{\$} \mathsf{A.Gen}(\mathfrak{g}, 1^\lambda, 1^n)$, *digest* $(\mathsf{cm}, \mathsf{aux}) \xleftarrow{\$} \mathsf{A.Acc}(\mathsf{pp}, S)$, *challenges $c_i \xleftarrow{\$} \{0,1\}^{\ell_i}$ and witnesses $w_i \leftarrow$* $\mathsf{A.Wit}(\mathsf{pp}, \mathsf{aux}, s, c_1, \ldots, c_{i-1}; r_{\mathsf{wit}})$ *for some common random tape $r_{\mathsf{wit}} \xleftarrow{\$} \{0,1\}^*$, and where we define* $\mathsf{tr} = (w_1, c_1, \ldots, w_\rho, c_\rho)$.

---

[10] Note that we need to pass the generator $\mathfrak{g}$ to $\mathsf{A.Gen}$ since a type-safe algorithm cannot create group elements on its own if it doesn't have any as input.

[11] Note that $\chi$ is a polynomial in $\lambda, n$ due to $\mathsf{A.Ver}$'s input being polynomial in $\lambda, n$.

**Definition 8 (Collision Freeness).** *An accumulator* $\mathsf{A}$ *as per Definition 6 is collision-free if for any query-efficient type-safe adversary* $\mathcal{A}$ *and polynomially bounded function* $n = n(\lambda)$*, there exists a negligible* $\varepsilon$ *such that for all* $\lambda \in \mathbb{N}$*:*

$$\mathsf{Adv}^{\mathsf{coll\text{-}free}}_{\mathsf{A},\mathcal{A}}(\lambda, n) := \Pr\left[\mathsf{Exp}^{\mathsf{coll\text{-}free}}_{\mathsf{A},\mathcal{A}}(\lambda, n) = 1\right] \leq \varepsilon(\lambda) ,$$

*where the experiment* $\mathsf{Exp}^{\mathsf{coll\text{-}free}}_{\mathsf{A},\mathcal{A}}(\lambda, n)$ *is defined in Fig. 3.*

$\mathsf{Exp}^{\mathsf{coll\text{-}free}}_{\mathsf{A},\mathcal{A}}(\lambda, n)$:

$\mathsf{pp} \leftarrow^{\$} \mathsf{A.Gen}(\mathfrak{g}, 1^\lambda, 1^n)$
$S \leftarrow^{\$} \mathcal{A}(1^\lambda, 1^n, \mathsf{pp})$
$(\mathsf{cm}, \mathsf{aux}) \leftarrow^{\$} \mathsf{A.Acc}(\mathsf{pp}, S)$
$s \leftarrow^{\$} \mathcal{A}(1^\lambda, 1^n, \mathsf{pp}, \mathsf{cm}, \mathsf{aux})$
For $i \in [\rho]$:
  **Wait** for $\mathcal{A}$ to send $w_i \in \mathbb{G}^{\mu_i} \times \{0,1\}^{\eta_i}$
  Sample $c_i \leftarrow^{\$} \{0,1\}^{\ell_i}$ and **reply** to $\mathcal{A}$ with $c_i$
$\mathsf{tr} \leftarrow (w_1, c_1, \ldots, w_\rho, c_\rho)$
$b \leftarrow \mathsf{A.Ver}(\mathsf{pp}, \mathsf{cm}, s, \mathsf{tr})$
**Return** $b \wedge (s \notin S)$

**Fig. 3.** Collision-freeness experiment (see Definition 8).

*Remark 3.* In the definition of collision-freeness above, we are again slightly abusing notation by having an *interactive* adversary $\mathcal{A}$, something that is not immediately captured by our definition of type-safe algorithms. However, we can easily transform any such interactive adversary into a non-interactive one by letting it halt each time it sends a message, and then re-executing it with the entire history of messages (as well as the same random coins) once a response is sent to the adversary. "Query-efficient" now means that each execution of $\mathcal{A}$ is query-efficient (in terms of the length of all messages received so far combined).

*Remark 4.* For any $\mathsf{A}$ accumulator as per Definition 6, whenever objects $\mathsf{pp} \in \mathrm{Supp}(\mathsf{A.Gen}(\mathfrak{g}, 1^\lambda, 1^n))$, and $(\mathsf{cm}, \mathsf{aux}) \in \mathrm{Supp}(\mathsf{A.Acc}(\mathsf{pp}, \cdot))$ are fixed, we will write $\mathfrak{p}$, $\mathfrak{c}$, $\tau_1$, and $\tau_2$ to implicitly mean the values $(\mathfrak{p}, \tau_0) = \mathsf{pp}$ and $(\mathfrak{c}, \tau_1) = \mathsf{cm}$. We further implicitly define $t_0 = \tau_0 || \tau_1$.

## 3 Internal Procedures

In this section we define subroutines $\mathsf{Forge}$ and $\mathsf{Extract}$ as required by our main result. To this end, we first describe an information-theoretical game in Sect. 3.1 and then use this to construct $\mathsf{Extract}$ in Sect. 3.2 and $\mathsf{Forge}$ in Sect. 3.3.

### 3.1 Information Theoretical Game

We now define an information-theoretical game that is at the heart of our compression argument. Informally, given a fixed element $s \in \{0,1\}^\lambda$ (as per Definition 6), the first player impersonates the prover $\mathsf{A.Wit}$, sending at each round the next witness message, while the second player acts as the honest verifier, replying with uniformly sampled challenges. Intuitively, the first player should win whenever it successfully convinces the second player of the membership $s \in S$.

However, we need the winning probability to be measurable in a *query-efficient* way. Hence, we replace the group elements $\mathfrak{a}_i$ in witness $w_i$ with an "approximation", i.e., a vector space of linear relations $L_i$ satisfied by $\mathfrak{p}||\mathfrak{c}||\mathfrak{a}_1||\dots||\mathfrak{a}_i$. In order to win the game, (1) *simulated* verification $\mathsf{Sim}_{\mathsf{A.Ver}}$ must succeed, and (2) each $L_i$ must be consistent with the previous $L_{i-1}$ (since, later on, we will need to be able to actually run the "real" accumulator security game where the witnesses $w_i$ must be producible according to $L_i$ if it is consistent to $L_{i-1}$).

**Definition 9 (Terminal Game History).** *Let $\lambda, n \in \mathbb{N}$ and $\mathsf{A}$ be an accumulator as per Definition 6. We define $\mathcal{Z}^{(\mathsf{A},\lambda,n)}$ as the set of all "terminal game history" tuples $((L_0,t_0), s, (L_1,t_1), c_1, \dots, (L_\rho,t_\rho), c_\rho)$ which, denoting $\mu_0 = \vartheta_0+\vartheta_1$, $\eta_0 = \zeta_0 + \zeta_1$ and $\bar{\mu}_i := \mu_0 + \dots + \mu_i$, fulfill*

$$t_i \in \{0,1\}^{\eta_i}, \quad s \in \{0,1\}^\lambda, \quad c_i \in \{0,1\}^{\ell_i}, \quad L_i \leq \mathbb{F}_q^{\bar{\mu}_i}$$

*Given some terminal game history $h \in \mathcal{Z}^{(\mathsf{A},\lambda,n)}$, we define its output as*

$$\mathsf{out}(h) := \mathsf{Sim}_{\langle \mathsf{A.Ver} \rangle}(q, L_\rho, (t_0, s, t_1, c_1, \dots, t_\rho, c_\rho)).$$

**Definition 10 (Game History).** *Let $\lambda, n \in \mathbb{N}$ and $\mathsf{A}$ be an accumulator as per Definition 6. We define $\mathcal{H}^{(\mathsf{A},\lambda,n)} = \{\pi_i(h) | h \in \mathcal{Z}^{(\mathsf{A},\lambda,n)},\ i \in \mathbb{N}\}$ as the set of game histories associated to $\mathsf{A}$. Moreover, we define*

- *$\mathcal{H}_i^{(\mathsf{A},\lambda,n)} = \{\pi_i(h) | h \in \mathcal{Z}^{(\mathsf{A},\lambda,n)}\}$ the set of game histories of $i$ rounds*
- *$\mathcal{H}_{\geq i}^{(\mathsf{A},\lambda,n)} = \cup_{j \geq i} \mathcal{H}_j^{(\mathsf{A},\lambda,n)}$ the set of games histories of $i$ or more rounds.*

*Remark 5.* When clear from context we may omit $(\mathsf{A}, \lambda, n)$ and simply denote $\mathcal{Z} = \mathcal{Z}^{(\mathsf{A},\lambda,n)}$ and $\mathcal{H} = \mathcal{H}^{(\mathsf{A},\lambda,n)}$.

**Definition 11 (Winning State and Winning Probability).** *Given $\mathsf{A}$ as in Definition 6, $\lambda, n \in \mathbb{N}$ we define the winning condition on terminal game histories as $\omega : \mathcal{Z} \to \{0,1\}$ such that $\omega(h) = 1$ iff*

$$\mathsf{out}(h) = 1 \quad \wedge \quad \bigwedge_{i=0}^{\rho-1} (L_i = \pi^*_{\bar{\mu}_i}(L_{i+1}))$$

*We also extend $\omega$ to arbitrary game histories as $\omega : \mathcal{H}_{\geq 2} \to [0,1]$ so that for $i \in \{1, \dots, \rho\}$ when:*

- *$h \in \mathcal{H}_{2i}$, then $\omega(h) = \max\{\omega(h||(L_i,t_i)) : h||(L_i,t_i) \in \mathcal{H}_{2i+1}\}$;*

– $h \in \mathcal{H}_{2i+1}$, *then* $\omega(h) = \frac{1}{2^{\ell_i}} \cdot \sum_{c_i \in \{0,1\}^{\ell_i}} \omega(h||c_i)$.

The following lemma, stating that for any $L_0, t_0, s$ there exists a way for the adversary to win with probability $\omega((L_0, t_0), s)$, follows immediately from how we defined the winning probability $\omega$ on game histories:

**Lemma 7 (Optimal Strategy).** *Given* $\mathsf{A}$ *as per Definition 6,* $\lambda, n \in \mathbb{N}$, *for any* $L_0 \leq \mathbb{F}_q^{\mu_0}$, $t_0 \in \{0,1\}^n$, $s \in \{0,1\}^\lambda$ *there exist functions* $(\bar{L}_i, \bar{t}_i)_{i=1}^{\rho}$,

$$\bar{L}_i : \prod_{j=1}^{i-1} \{0,1\}^{\ell_j} \to \mathsf{Sub}(\mathbb{F}_q^{\bar{\mu}_i}), \qquad \bar{t}_i : \prod_{j=1}^{i-1} \{0,1\}^{\ell_j} \to \{0,1\}^{\eta_i},$$

*s.t. sampling* $\mathbf{c} \xleftarrow{\$} \prod_{j=1}^{\rho-1} \{0,1\}^{\ell_j}$, *setting* $L_i = \bar{L}_i(c_1, \ldots, c_{i-1})$, $t_i = \bar{t}_i(c_1, \ldots, c_{i-1})$, *and* $h = ((L_0, t_0), s, (L_1, t_1), c_1, \ldots, (L_\rho, t_\rho), c_\rho)$ *then*

$$\Pr[\omega(h) = 1] = \omega(((L_0, t_0), s)).$$

The following lemma states that it is impossible to win with probability larger than $\omega((L_0, t_0), s)$. It follows immediately from basic probability theory:

**Lemma 8.** *Fix* $\mathsf{A}$ *as per Definition 6,* $\lambda, n \in \mathbb{N}$, *and* $L_0 \leq \mathbb{F}_q^{\mu_0}$, $t_0 \in \{0,1\}^n$, $s \in \{0,1\}^\lambda$. *For every stateful unbounded probabilistic machine* $\mathcal{A}$ *that, for each* $i \in [\rho]$, *outputs* $(L_i, t_i)$ *and receives a uniformly random* $c_i \xleftarrow{\$} \{0,1\}^{\ell_i}$, *we have*

$$\Pr[\omega(h) = 1] \leq \omega(((L_0, t_0), s)),$$

*where* $h = ((L_0, t_0), s, (L_1, t_1), c_1, \ldots, (L_\rho, t_\rho), c_\rho)$.

### 3.2 Extraction Subroutine

We present the full Extract subroutine in Fig. 4. It is intended to be called as $\mathsf{Extract}^{\mathcal{W},\mathcal{C}}(1, \mathsf{pp}, \mathsf{cm}, s, L_0)$ for some $s \in \{0,1\}^\lambda$ and $L_0 \leq \mathbb{F}_q^{\mu_0}$ such that $\mathfrak{p}||\mathfrak{c} \in \mathrm{Ann}_{\mathbb{G}}(L_0)$. As we will show in Lemma 10, as long as the winning probability $\omega((L_0, t_0), s)$ is indeed sufficiently low, then there is a high chance that Extract returns a strictly larger vector space $L_0' \supsetneq L_0$ of linear constraints satisfied by $\mathfrak{p}||\mathfrak{c}$.

**Lemma 9.** *Fix any* $\mathsf{A}$ *as per Definition 6,* $\lambda, n \in \mathbb{N}$, $S \subseteq \{0,1\}^\lambda$, *as well as* $\mathsf{pp} \in \mathrm{Supp}(\mathsf{A.Gen}(\mathfrak{g}, 1^\lambda, 1^n))$, $(\mathsf{cm}, \mathsf{aux}) \in \mathrm{Supp}(\mathsf{A.Acc}(\mathsf{pp}, S))$, $L_0 \leq \mathbb{F}_q^{\mu_0}$ *such that* $\mathfrak{p}||\mathfrak{c} \in \mathrm{Ann}_{\mathbb{G}}(L_0)$, *and (potentially randomized) oracles* $\mathcal{W}$ *and* $\mathcal{C}$.

*Then, for any* $L_0' \in \mathrm{Supp}(\mathsf{Extract}^{\mathcal{W},\mathcal{C}}(1, \mathsf{pp}, \mathsf{cm}, s, L_0))$, *we have* $L_0 \subseteq L_0'$ *and* $\mathfrak{p}||\mathfrak{c} \in \mathrm{Ann}_{\mathbb{G}}(L_0')$.

Lemma 9 follows easily by construction; a full proof appears in the full version of this paper.

$\mathsf{Extract}^{\mathcal{W},\mathcal{C}}(i, \mathsf{pp}, \mathsf{cm}, s, L_{i-1}, (w_1, c_1, j_1), \ldots, (w_{i-1}, c_{i-1}, j_{i-1}))$ :

1 : $/\!/\ i \in \{1, \ldots, \rho\},\ L_{i-1} \in \mathsf{Sub}(\mathbb{F}_q^{\bar{\mu}_{i-1}})$
2 : **If** $i = \rho + 1$:
3 :     Parse $\mathsf{pp} = (\mathfrak{p}, \tau_0)$ and $\mathsf{cm} = (\mathfrak{c}, \tau_1)$, set $t_0 = \tau_0 || \tau_1$
4 :     Parse $w_i = (\mathfrak{a}_i, t_i)$ for all $i \in \{1, \ldots, \rho\}$
5 :     **Return** $\mathsf{Rel}_{\langle \mathsf{A.Ver} \rangle}(q, \mathfrak{p}||\mathfrak{c}||\mathfrak{a}_1|| \ldots ||\mathfrak{a}_\rho, (t_0, s, t_1, c_1, \ldots, t_\rho, c_\rho))$
6 : **Else**:
7 :     $w_i \leftarrow \mathcal{W}(s, c_1, \ldots, c_{i-1})$, parse $w_i = (\mathfrak{a}_i, t_i)$
8 :     $L_i \leftarrow L_{i-1} \times \{0^{\mu_i}\}$ $/\!/ \in \mathsf{Sub}(\mathbb{F}_q^{\bar{\mu}_i})$
9 :     **For** each $j_i \in \{0, \ldots, \mu_i\}$:
10 :         $c_i \leftarrow \mathcal{C}(i, j_1, \ldots, j_i, L_i, t_i)$
11 :         $L_i \leftarrow L_i + \mathsf{Extract}^{\mathcal{W},\mathcal{C}}(i+1, \mathsf{pp}, \mathsf{cm}, s, L_i, (w_1, c_1, j_1), \ldots, (w_i, c_i, j_i))$
12 :     **Return** $\pi^*_{\bar{\mu}_{i-1}}(L_i)$

$\mathcal{W}_{\mathsf{real}}^{[\mathsf{pp}, \mathsf{aux}, r_{\mathsf{wit}}]}(s, c_1, \ldots, c_i)$ :

1 : **Return** $\mathsf{A.Wit}(\mathsf{pp}, \mathsf{aux}, s, c_1, \ldots, c_i; r_{\mathsf{wit}})$

$\mathcal{C}_{\mathsf{rand}}^{\mathsf{Extract}}(i, j_1, \ldots, j_i, L_i, t_i)$

1 : **Return** $c_i \leftarrow^{\$} \{0,1\}^{\ell_i}$

**Fig. 4.** Extractor subroutine, for any fixed accumulator $\mathsf{A}$ and $\lambda, n \in \mathbb{N}$. It expects oracles $\mathcal{W}$ for generating the proofs $w_i$, and $\mathcal{C}$ for sampling challenges $c_i$. We normally consider $\mathcal{W} = \mathcal{W}_{\mathsf{real}}^{[\mathsf{pp}, \mathsf{aux}, r_{\mathsf{wit}}]}$, but later (Section 4.1) we will use $\mathcal{W}$ to inject proofs generated in a different way. Similarly, we normally consider $\mathcal{C} = \mathcal{C}_{\mathsf{rand}}^{\mathsf{Extract}}$, but in the proof of Lemma 10 we will replace it with challenges generated from a different source (which is why $\mathcal{C}$ takes as input the values $j_1, \ldots, j_i, L_i, t_i$ ignored by $\mathcal{C}_{\mathsf{rand}}^{\mathsf{Extract}}$).

**Lemma 10.** *Fix any $\varepsilon$-correct $\mathsf{A}$ as per Definition 6, $\lambda \in \mathbb{N}$, $n = n(\lambda)$ polynomially bounded, $S \subseteq \{0,1\}^\lambda$, and some $p \in [0,1]$.*

*Then, denoting $\mathcal{C} := \mathcal{C}_{\mathsf{rand}}^{\mathsf{Extract}}$, we have*

$$\Pr\left[\begin{matrix}\omega((L_0, t_0), s) \leq p \ \wedge \\ \mathsf{Extract}^{\mathcal{W},\mathcal{C}}(1, \mathsf{pp}, \mathsf{cm}, s, L_0) = L_0\end{matrix}\right] \leq \left(\prod\nolimits_{i=1}^{\rho} (\mu_i + 1)\right) \cdot (n \cdot \varepsilon + \ p) \ , \quad (1)$$

*where this probability is taken over $\mathsf{pp} \leftarrow^{\$} \mathsf{A.Gen}(\mathfrak{g}, 1^\lambda, 1^n)$, the execution of $(\mathsf{cm}, \mathsf{aux}) \leftarrow^{\$} \mathsf{A.Acc}(\mathsf{pp}, S)$, an arbitrarily distributed random variable $L_0 \leq \mathbb{F}_q^{\mu_0}$ that fulfills $\mathfrak{p}||\mathfrak{c} \in \mathrm{Ann}_{\mathbb{G}}(L_0)$, an arbitrarily distributed random variable $s \in S$, and the choice of the random tape $r_{\mathsf{wit}}$ for which we define $\mathcal{W} := \mathcal{W}_{\mathsf{real}}^{[\mathsf{pp}, \mathsf{aux}, r_{\mathsf{wit}}]}$.*

*Proof.* We label points in the execution of $\mathsf{Extract}^{\mathcal{W},\mathcal{C}}(1, \mathsf{pp}, \mathsf{cm}, s, L_0)$ using tuples $(j_1, \ldots, j_k) \in \mathbb{Z}_{\mu_1+1} \times \ldots \times \mathbb{Z}_{\mu_{k-1}+1} \times \mathbb{Z}_{\mu_k+2}$, where $1 \leq k \leq \rho$ is the current depth of the recursion. Such a tuple $\mathbf{j} = (j_1, \ldots, j_k)$ identifies the following state:

- For $i < k$, $\mathsf{Extract}^{\mathcal{W},\mathcal{C}}(i, \mathsf{pp}, \mathsf{cm}, s, L_{i-1}, \ldots)$ is currently inside iteration $j_i$ of its for-loop in line 11 *in the process of calling* $\mathsf{Extract}^{\mathcal{W},\mathcal{C}}(i + 1, \mathsf{pp}, \mathsf{cm}, s, L_i, \ldots)$.

- For $i = k$, $\mathsf{Extract}^{\mathcal{W},\mathcal{C}}(k, \mathsf{pp}, \mathsf{cm}, s, L_{k-1}, \dots)$ is currently inside iteration $j_k$ of its for-loop in line 11 *about to call* $\mathsf{Extract}^{\mathcal{W},\mathcal{C}}(i+1, \mathsf{pp}, \mathsf{cm}, s, L_i, \dots)$, or if $j_k = \mu_k + 1$ then it is in line 12 about to return to its caller.

Note that the call stack corresponding to a tuple $\mathbf{j} = (j_1, \dots, j_k)$ defines vector spaces $L_0, \dots, L_k$ (while $L_k$ does not currently belong to the input of any $\mathsf{Extract}$, it is still is defined as a variable in the scope of $\mathsf{Extract}(k, \dots)$), which we denote by $L_1^{(\mathbf{j})}, \dots, L_k^{(\mathbf{j})}$. Furthermore, whenever $j_k \le \mu_k$, the call stack also defines witnesses $w_1, \dots, w_k$ and challenges $c_1, \dots, c_k$, which we denote by $w_1^{(\mathbf{j})}, \dots, w_k^{(\mathbf{j})}$ and $c_1^{(\mathbf{j})}, \dots, c_k^{(\mathbf{j})}$ with $w_i^{(\mathbf{j})} = (\mathbf{a}_i^{(\mathbf{j})}, t_i^{(\mathbf{j})})$.

If $k = \rho$, then we additionally define write $\mathbf{u}^{(\mathbf{j})} = \mathbf{p}||\mathbf{c}||\mathbf{a}_1^{(\mathbf{j})}|| \dots ||\mathbf{a}_\rho^{(\mathbf{j})}$ to mean the concatenation of all group elements in the transcript. Note that by Lemma 2 we always have $\mathbf{u}^{(\mathbf{j})} \in \mathrm{Ann}_{\mathbb{G}}(L_\rho^{(\mathbf{j})})$.

We call a tuple $\mathbf{j}$ that is in $\mathbb{Z}_{\mu_1+1} \times \dots \times \mathbb{Z}_{\mu_\rho+1}$ *terminating*, as it corresponds to an execution path that defines an entire transcript consisting of $c_i^{(\mathbf{j})}$ and $w_i^{(\mathbf{j})}$ defined for all $i \in \{1, \dots, \rho\}$. For a terminating tuple $\mathbf{j}$, we define the following two bad events:

- $\mathsf{bad}_1(\mathbf{j})$ : $\mathsf{Exec}_{\langle \mathsf{A.Ver} \rangle}(q, \mathbf{u}^{(\mathbf{j})}, (t_0, s, t_1, c_1, \dots, t_\rho, c_\rho)) = 0$.
- $\mathsf{bad}_2(\mathbf{j})$ : $\omega(((L_0, t_0), s)) \le p$ and $\mathsf{Sim}_{\langle \mathsf{A.Ver} \rangle}(q, L_\rho^{(\mathbf{j})}, (t_0, s, t_1, c_1, \dots, t_\rho, c_\rho)) = 1$ and $L_{i-1}^{(\mathbf{j})} = \pi^*_{\bar{\mu}_{i-1}}(L_i^{(\mathbf{j})})$ for $1 \le i \le \rho$.

We will start by showing, for all terminating tuples $\mathbf{j}$: $\Pr[\mathsf{bad}_1(\mathbf{j})] \le n \cdot \varepsilon(\lambda, n)$ and $\Pr[\mathsf{bad}_2(\mathbf{j})] \le p$.

First, by $\varepsilon$-correctness of $\mathsf{A}$, for any fixed set element $s_0 \in S$, we have $\Pr[\mathsf{bad}_1(\mathbf{j}) \wedge s = s_0] \le \varepsilon(\lambda, n)$, because $\mathsf{bad}_1(\mathbf{j})$ implies that the real execution of $\mathsf{A.Ver}$ (for fixed $S$ and $s = s_0$, using uniformly random challenges $c_i^{(\mathbf{j})}$ for $c \in [\rho]$) resulted in the verifier returning 0. The additional clause "$s = s_0$" does not increase this probability. Therefore, we obtain

$$\Pr[\mathsf{bad}_1(\mathbf{j})] = \sum_{s_0 \in S} \Pr[\mathsf{bad}_1(\mathbf{j}) \wedge s = s_0] \le \sum_{s_0 \in S} \varepsilon(\lambda, n) = n \cdot \varepsilon(\lambda, n) .$$

Second, using the following oracle $\mathcal{C}^{(\mathbf{j})}$, the algorithm $\mathsf{Extract}^{\mathcal{W}_{\mathsf{real}}^{[\mathsf{pp},\mathsf{aux},r_{\mathsf{wit}}]},\mathcal{C}^{(\mathbf{j})}}(1, \mathsf{pp}, \mathsf{cm}, s, L_0)$, is a player against the information-theoretical game from Sect. 3.1 (as per Lemma 8).

$\mathcal{C}^{(\mathbf{j})}(i, j'_1, \dots, j'_i, L_i, t_i)$ :

```
If (j'_1, ..., j'_i) = (j_1, ..., j_i):
    Send (L_i, t_i) to the challenger and receive c_i
    Return c_i
Else:
    Return c_i <-$ {0,1}^{ℓ_i}
```

Let us briefly assume that all the random variables (such as $\mathsf{pp}, \mathsf{cm}, \mathsf{aux}, L_0, s, r_{\mathsf{wit}}$, and the random strings generated within $\mathcal{C}^{(\mathbf{j})}$) are fixed. Then, there are two cases: Either $\omega(((L_0, t_0), s)) > p$ or $\omega(((L_0, t_0), s)) \leq p$. In the former case, we always have $\mathsf{bad}_2(\mathbf{j})$ false by definition, and therefore $\Pr[\mathsf{bad}_2(\mathbf{j})] = 0 \leq p$. In the latter case, we have

$$\mathsf{bad}_2(\mathbf{j}) \iff \omega((L_0, t_0), s, (L_1^{(\mathbf{j})}, t_1^{(\mathbf{j})}), c_1^{(\mathbf{j})}, \ldots, (L_\rho^{(\mathbf{j})}, t_\rho^{(\mathbf{j})}), c_\rho^{(\mathbf{j})}) = 1 .$$

Hence, the probability $\Pr[\mathsf{bad}_2(\mathbf{j})]$ (taken over the information-theoretical game challenger) is exactly the probability that $\mathsf{Extract}^{\mathcal{W}, \mathcal{C}^{(\mathbf{j})}}(1, \mathsf{pp}, \mathsf{cm}, s, L_0)$ wins the information-theoretical game from Lemma 8 on starting point $((L_0, t_0), s)$, which means that $\Pr[\mathsf{bad}_2(\mathbf{j})] \leq \omega(((L_0, t_0), s)) \leq p$. Combining both cases, even when considering the full random process described in the lemma statement, we have $\Pr[\mathsf{bad}_2(\mathbf{j})] \leq p$ for any fixed terminating tuple $\mathbf{j}$.

For any tuple $\mathbf{j} = (j_1, \ldots, j_k)$, we define $d_i^{(\mathbf{j})} := \dim(L_i^{(\mathbf{j})}) - \dim(L_{i-1}^{(\mathbf{j})})$ for $i \in \{1, \ldots, k\}$ as the number of additional relations that have been learned at level $i$ compared to level $i-1$.

We now prove the following invariant by induction over all tuples $\mathbf{j} = (j_1, \ldots, j_k)$ in lexicographic order, under the assumption that none of the bad events occur for any terminating tuple:

(1) either $d_i^{(\mathbf{j})} \geq j_i$ for every $1 \leq i \leq k$; or
(2) there exists an index $i^* \in \{1, \ldots, k\}$ such that $d_i^{(\mathbf{j})} \geq j_i$ for every $1 \leq i < i^*$ and $L_{i^*-1}^{(\mathbf{j})} \subsetneq \pi^*_{\bar{\mu}_{i^*-1}}(L_{i^*}^{(\mathbf{j})})$.

We distinguish the following cases:

$\mathbf{j} = (0)$ (base case). Invariant (1) clearly holds for $\mathbf{j} = (0)$ due to $j_1 = 0$.

$\mathbf{j} = (j_1, \ldots, j_k)$ for $1 \leq k < \rho$. The new state will be $\mathbf{j}' = (j_1, \ldots, j_k, 0)$. Clearly any invariant that holds for $(j_1, \ldots, j_k)$ transfers over to $(j_1, \ldots, j_k, 0)$.

$\mathbf{j} = (j_1, \ldots, j_{k-1}, \mu_k + 1)$ for $2 \leq k \leq \rho$. Then, $\mathbf{j}' := (j_1, \ldots, j_{k-1} + 1)$ will be the new state. First note that invariant (1) on $\mathbf{j}$ would also imply invariant (2) on $\mathbf{j}$: due to $d_k^{(\mathbf{j})} \geq j_k = \mu_k + 1$ we have $L_{k-1}^{(\mathbf{j})} \subsetneq \pi^*_{\bar{\mu}_{k-1}}(L_k^{(\mathbf{j})})$ (otherwise, since there exist at least $\mu_k + 1$ linearly independent vectors $\mathbf{v}_1, \ldots, \mathbf{v}_{\mu_k+1} \notin L_{k-1}^{(\mathbf{j})}$ with $L_{k-1}^{(\mathbf{j})} + \mathsf{span}(\mathbf{v}_1, \ldots, \mathbf{v}_{\mu_k+1}) \subseteq L_k^{(\mathbf{j})}$, we would have $\mathsf{span}(\mathbf{v}_1, \ldots, \mathbf{v}_{\mu_k+1}) \cap \mathbb{F}_q^{\bar{\mu}_{k-1}} = \{0\}$, contradicting the fact that all vectors have dimension $\bar{\mu}_k = \bar{\mu}_{k-1} + \mu_k$).

Hence, we may assume that invariant (2) holds on $\mathbf{j}$, and we show that the same invariant also holds in $\mathbf{j}'$. If invariant (2) holds on $\mathbf{j}$ for some index $i^* < k$, then this immediately also applies to $\mathbf{j}'$. Suppose invariant (2) holds in $\mathbf{j}$ for $i^* = k$. Then, we will have

$$L_{k-1}^{(\mathbf{j}')} = \pi^*_{\bar{\mu}_{k-1}}(L_k^{(\mathbf{j})}) + L_{k-1}^{(\mathbf{j})} \not\subseteq L_{k-1}^{(\mathbf{j})} ,$$

i.e., we get the strict inequality $d_{k-1}^{(\mathbf{j}')} > d_{k-1}^{(\mathbf{j})}$, which together with $d_i^{(\mathbf{j}')} = d_i^{(\mathbf{j})} \geq j_i$ (for all $i < k-1$) implies that invariant (1) holds in the new state.

$\mathbf{j} = (j_1, \ldots, j_\rho)$ for $j_\rho \leq \mu_\rho$, i.e., $\mathbf{j}$ is terminal. Then, $\mathbf{j}' := (j_1, \ldots, j_{\rho-1}, j_\rho + 1)$ will be the new state. By definition of $\overline{\mathsf{bad}_1(\mathbf{j})}$ and $\overline{\mathsf{bad}_2(\mathbf{j})}$, there are two cases: either we have $L_{i-1}^{(\mathbf{j})} \neq \pi^*_{\bar{\mu}_{i-1}}(L_i^{(\mathbf{j})})$ for some $1 \leq i \leq \rho$, i.e., invariant (2) holds for $\mathbf{j}'$; or both of the following two conditions hold:

$$\mathsf{Exec}_{\langle \mathsf{A.Ver} \rangle}(q, \mathbf{u}^{(j)}, (t_0, s, t_1, c_1, \ldots, t_\rho, c_\rho)) = 1$$

$$\mathsf{Sim}_{\langle \mathsf{A.Ver} \rangle}(q, L_\rho^{(\mathbf{j})}, (t_0, s, t_1, c_1, \ldots, t_\rho, c_\rho)) = 0$$

In this case, because the real and the simulated outputs differ, Lemma 3 combined with the fact that $\mathbf{u}^{(\mathbf{j})} \in \mathrm{Ann}_{\mathbb{G}}(L_\rho^{(\mathbf{j})})$ implies $R \not\subseteq L_\rho^{(\mathbf{j})}$, where

$$R := \mathsf{Rel}_{\langle \mathsf{A.Ver} \rangle}(q, \mathbf{u}^{(j)}, (t_0, s, t_1, c_1, \ldots, t_\rho, c_\rho))$$

is the set of relations learned during the real execution. Then, because $R$ is exactly what is being computed by $\mathsf{Extract}(\rho + 1, \ldots)$, we have $L_\rho^{(\mathbf{j}')} = L_\rho^{(\mathbf{j})} + R \supsetneq L_\rho^{(\mathbf{j})}$, i.e., $d_\rho^{(\mathbf{j}')} > d_\rho^{(\mathbf{j})}$. Hence, if invariant (1) holds for $\mathbf{j}$, it also holds for $\mathbf{j}'$ (and invariant (2) on $\mathbf{j}$ would immediately transfer over to $\mathbf{j}'$ regardless).

To summarize, we know that (unless a bad event occurs), the invariant holds for the largest tuple $\mathbf{j} = (\mu_1 + 1)$. As before, invariant (1) would imply invariant (2) in this case due to $d_1^{(\mathbf{j})} \geq \mu_1 + 1$ implying $L_0 \subsetneq \pi^*_{\bar{\mu}_0}(L_1^{(\mathbf{j})})$. With invariant (2) on the final state $\mathbf{j} = (\mu_1 + 1)$, the event in (1) indeed holds because the final output of $\mathsf{Extract}$ ($\pi^*_{\bar{\mu}_0}(L_1^{(\mathbf{j})})$) is not a subset of $L_0$.

Therefore, taking a union bound of $\overline{\mathsf{bad}_1(\mathbf{j})}$ and $\overline{\mathsf{bad}_2(\mathbf{j})}$ over all possible terminating tuples (of which there are exactly $\prod_{i=1}^{\rho}(\mu_i + 1)$ many) concludes the proof. □

### 3.3 Forge Subroutine

We present the full $\mathsf{Forge}$ subroutine in Fig. 5. It is intended to be called as $\mathsf{Forge}^{\mathcal{C}}(L_0, \mathsf{pp}, \mathsf{cm}, s, \kappa)$ for some $s \in \{0,1\}^\lambda$ and $L_0 \leq \mathbb{F}_q^{\mu_0}$ such that $\mathbf{p}||\mathbf{c} \in \mathrm{Ann}_{\mathbb{G}}(L_0)$. It runs $\kappa$ attempts of forging a proof of membership of $s$. In Lemma 11 we show that as long as the winning probability $\omega((L_0, t_0), s)$ is sufficiently high, then forge will indeed succeed with high probability (or, alternatively, it will find a new relation on $L_0$). This is due to the collision-freeness of $\mathsf{A}$. The proof of the following lemma will be presented in the full version of this paper.

**Lemma 11.** *Let* $\mathsf{A}$ *be as per Definition 6,* $\lambda \in \mathbb{N}$, $n \in \mathbb{N}$, $S \subseteq \{0,1\}^\lambda$, $s \in \{0,1\}^\lambda$ *(not necessarily* $s \in S$*),* $\kappa \in \mathbb{N}$, $\mathsf{pp} \in \mathrm{Supp}(\mathsf{A.Gen}(\mathfrak{g}, 1^\lambda, 1^n))$, $(\mathsf{cm}, \mathsf{aux}) \in \mathrm{Supp}(\mathsf{A.Acc}(\mathsf{pp}, S))$, *and* $L_0 \leq \mathbb{F}_q^{\mu_0}$ *such that* $\mathbf{p}||\mathbf{c} \in \mathrm{Ann}_{\mathbb{G}}(L_0)$.

*Then, denoting* $\mathcal{C} := \mathcal{C}_{\mathsf{rand}}^{\mathsf{Forge}}$, *and letting* $\chi$ *denote a bound on the query-efficiency of* $\langle \mathsf{A.Ver} \rangle$, *we have*

$$\Pr\left[\mathsf{Forge}^{\mathcal{C}}(L_0, \mathsf{pp}, \mathsf{cm}, s, \kappa) = \bot\right] \leq \left(1 - \omega((L_0, t_0), s) + \frac{\chi}{q}\right)^\kappa .$$

$\mathsf{Forge}^{\mathcal{C}}(L_0, \mathsf{pp}, \mathsf{cm}, s, \kappa)$ : // $L_0 \leq \mathbb{F}_q^{\mu_0}$, $s \in \{0,1\}^\lambda$, $\kappa \in \mathbb{N}$

Parse $\mathsf{pp} = (q, \mathfrak{p}, \tau_0)$ and $\mathsf{cm} = (\mathfrak{c}, \tau_1)$
Set $\mathfrak{u}_0 = \mathfrak{p}||\mathfrak{c} \in \mathbb{G}^{\mu_0}$ and $t_0 = \tau_0||\tau_1$
Compute $\bar{t}_i, \bar{L}_i$ optimal strategies for $((L_0, t_0), s)$ // See Lemma 7
**For** $k \in \{1, \dots, \kappa\}$:
  $\mathfrak{u}_0^{(k)} \leftarrow \mathfrak{u}_0$
  **For** $i \in \{1, \dots, \rho\}$:
    $t_i^{(k)} \leftarrow \bar{t}_i(c_1, \dots, c_{i-1})$
    $L_i^{(k)} \leftarrow \bar{L}_i(c_1, \dots, c_{i-1})$
    $\mathfrak{a}_i^{(k)} \leftarrow^{\$} \mathbb{G}^{\mu_i}$ such that $\mathfrak{u}_{i-1}^{(k)}||\mathfrak{a}_i^{(k)} \in \mathrm{Ann}_{\mathbb{G}}(L_i^{(k)})$ // use Lemma 6
    $\mathfrak{u}_i^{(k)} \leftarrow \mathfrak{u}_{i-1}^{(k)}||\mathfrak{a}_i^{(k)}$
    Set $w_i^{(k)} = (\mathfrak{a}_i^{(k)}, t_i^{(k)})$ and query $c_i^{(k)} \leftarrow \mathcal{C}(s, k, i, w_i^{(k)})$
  $b^{(k)} \leftarrow \mathsf{A.Ver}(\mathsf{pp}, \mathsf{cm}, s, (w_1^{(k)}, c_1^{(k)}, \dots, w_\rho^{(k)}, c_\rho^{(k)}))$
  $R^{(k)} \leftarrow \mathsf{Rel}_{\langle \mathsf{A.Ver} \rangle}(q, \mathfrak{u}^{(k)}, (t_0, s, t_1^{(k)}, c_1^{(k)}, \dots, t_\rho^{(k)}, c_\rho^{(k)}))$
// After all iterations, check for any successful proof or new relation
**For** $k \in \{1, \dots, \kappa\}$ :
  **If** $b^{(k)} = 1$: **Return accept** // w.h.p. $s$ is in the accumulated set
  **If** $\pi_{\mu_0}^*(L_\rho^{(k)} + R^{(k)}) \nsubseteq L_0$: **Return** $L_0 + \pi_{\mu_0}^*(L_\rho^{(k)} + R^{(k)})$
**Return** $\perp$

$\mathcal{C}_{\mathsf{rand}}^{\mathsf{Forge}}(s, k, i, w_i^{(k)})$

**Return** $c_i \leftarrow^{\$} \{0,1\}^{\ell_i}$

**Fig. 5.** The Forge subroutine, for any fixed accumulator $\mathsf{A}$ and $\lambda, n \in \mathbb{N}$. $L_0$ is a set of initially known relations among the group elements of $\mathsf{pp}, \mathsf{cm}$, and $\kappa \in \mathbb{N}$ denotes the number of forging attempts before giving up. Note that $\mathsf{Forge}$ takes an oracle $\mathcal{C}$ for generating the challenges $c_i$. We are normally interested in the case $\mathcal{C} = \mathcal{C}_{\mathsf{rand}}^{\mathsf{Forge}}$ that always returns random challenges, but in our final reduction to collision-freeness (see proof of Theorem 1) we will need to inject challenges from a different source.

*Furthermore,* $\mathrm{Supp}(\mathsf{Forge}^{\mathcal{C}}(L_0, \mathsf{pp}, \mathsf{cm}, s, \kappa)) \subseteq \{\perp, \mathtt{accept}\} \cup \mathsf{Sub}(\mathbb{F}_q^{\mu_0})$*, and any potential vector space output* $L_0' \in \mathrm{Supp}(\mathsf{Forge}^{\mathcal{C}}(L_0, \mathsf{pp}, \mathsf{cm}, s, \kappa))$ *fulfills* $L_0 \subsetneq L_0'$ *and* $\mathfrak{p}||\mathfrak{c} \in \mathrm{Ann}_{\mathbb{G}}(L_0')$.

## 4 Witness Length Bound

Before proving our main result, we first fix some notation and parameters that we will throughout the section. Let $\mathsf{A}$ be an accumulator as per Definition 6, and let $\lambda, n \in \mathbb{N}$ be fixed s.t. $\lambda \geq 1 + \log_2 n$.

- Given a message vector $\mathbf{m} \in \{0,1\}^n$, we define $S_{\mathbf{m}} := \{(i, m_i) : i \in [n]\} \subseteq [n] \times \{0,1\}$. Furthermore, due to $\lambda \geq 1 + \log_2 n$, we can treat $S_{\mathbf{m}}$ as a size-$n$ subset of $\{0,1\}^\lambda$ (i.e., $S_{\mathbf{m}}$ may be used as an input to $\mathsf{A.Acc}$).
- Let $\gamma_{\mathsf{pp}}$, $\gamma_{\mathsf{cm}}$, and $\gamma_{\mathsf{wit}}$ be upper bounds on the number of random coins used by $\mathsf{A.Gen}$, $\mathsf{A.Acc}$, and $\mathsf{A.Wit}$ respectively.
- For random tape $r_{\mathsf{pp}} \in \{0,1\}^{\gamma_{\mathsf{pp}}}$, we implicitly define $\mathsf{pp} \leftarrow \mathsf{A.Gen}(\mathfrak{g}, 1^\lambda, 1^n; r_{\mathsf{pp}})$, and given random tape $r_{\mathsf{cm}} \in \{0,1\}^{\gamma_{\mathsf{cm}}}$ as well as message $\mathbf{m}$, we implicitly define $(\mathsf{cm}, \mathsf{aux}) \leftarrow \mathsf{A.Acc}(\mathsf{pp}, S_{\mathbf{m}}; r_{\mathsf{cm}})$. Then, $\mathfrak{p}$, $\mathfrak{c}$, and $t_0$ are also defined by Remark 4.
- We denote the bitlength of a commitment $\mathsf{cm}$ and a proof (consisting of witnesses $w_1, \ldots, w_\rho$) as

$$\xi_{\mathsf{cm}} := \eta_0 + \log q \vartheta_1, \qquad \xi_{\mathsf{wit}} := \sum_{i=1}^{\rho} \eta_i + \log q \sum_{i=1}^{\rho} \mu_i,$$

respectively.
- We define $p$ and $\kappa$ (as needed by the extract and forge subroutines, respectively) as follows:

$$p := \frac{1}{12n \prod_{i=1}^{\rho}(\mu_i + 1)} - n\varepsilon, \qquad \kappa := \left\lceil \frac{2\ln(12n)}{p} \right\rceil.$$

### 4.1 Basic Decoding Strategy

In Fig. 6, we define the "basic" encoder-decoder pair $(\mathcal{E}_0, \mathcal{D}_0)$. Note that, by themselves, they are not used for a compression argument yet. Instead, we will use them as subroutines inside $(\mathcal{E}, \mathcal{D})$ (defined in Sect. 4.2), where $\mathcal{D}_0$ will first be repeated a large number of times (using a self-simulated encoder $\mathcal{E}_0$) in order to find relations about the group elements $\mathfrak{p}$ from $\mathsf{pp}$, before then running $\mathcal{D}_0$ one final time to decode the message $\mathbf{m}$ without finding new relations about $\mathfrak{p}$.

First, the following lemma captures some basic facts about $(\mathcal{D}_0, \mathcal{E}_0)$, which we prove in the full version of this paper.

**Lemma 12.** *Given* $\mathsf{A}$ *as per Definition 6,* $\lambda, n \in \mathbb{N}$ *with* $\lambda \geq 1 + \log_2 n$, $\mathbf{m} \in \{0,1\}^n$, $\mathsf{pp} \in \mathrm{Supp}(\mathsf{A.Gen}(\mathfrak{g}, 1^\lambda, 1^n))$, $(\mathsf{cm}, \mathsf{aux}) \in \mathrm{Supp}(\mathsf{A.Acc}(\mathsf{pp}, S_{\mathbf{m}}))$, $r_{\mathsf{wit}} \in \{0,1\}^{\gamma_{\mathsf{wit}}}$*, and an oracle* $\mathcal{C}$*, the following holds:*

1. *When running* $\mathcal{D}_0^{\mathcal{C}, \mathcal{E}_0(\mathbf{m}, \mathsf{pp}, \mathsf{cm}, \mathsf{aux}, r_{\mathsf{wit}}, \cdot)}(L_0, \mathsf{pp})$ *for some vector space* $L_0 \leq \mathbb{F}_q^{\mu_0}$ *with* $\mathfrak{p} \| \mathfrak{c} \in \mathrm{Ann}_{\mathbb{G}}(L_0)$*, then* $L_0^{(i)} \subseteq L_0^{(i+1)}$ *and* $\mathfrak{p} \| \mathfrak{c} \in \mathrm{Ann}_{\mathbb{G}}(L_0^{(i+1)})$ *for all* $i \in \{1, \ldots, n'\}$*, where* $n'$ *is the number of executed iterations of the For loop in Line 3 that did not abort by returning* $\perp$.
2. *If* $\mathcal{C}$ *is deterministic,* $r_0$ *is some fixed randomness, and the output of the basic decoder* $\mathcal{D}_0^{\mathcal{C}, \mathcal{E}_0(\mathbf{m}, \mathsf{pp}, \mathsf{cm}, \mathsf{aux}, r_{\mathsf{wit}}, \cdot)}(L_0, \mathsf{pp}; r_0)$ *is* $(\bar{\mathbf{m}}, L_0') \neq \perp$*, then*

$$\begin{aligned} &\mathsf{len}_{\mathcal{E}_0, \mathcal{D}_0^{\mathcal{C}}}((\mathbf{m}, \mathsf{pp}, \mathsf{cm}, \mathsf{aux}, r_{\mathsf{wit}}), (L_0, \mathsf{pp}; r_0)) \\ &\leq \xi_{\mathsf{cm}} + (\dim(L_0') - \dim(L_0)) \cdot \left(1 + \xi_{\mathsf{wit}} \cdot \prod_{i=1}^{\rho-1} (\mu_i + 1)\right). \end{aligned}$$

$\mathcal{D}_0^{\mathcal{C},\mathcal{E}^*}(L_0, \mathsf{pp})$ : // Basic decoder taking hint $L_0 \leq \mathbb{F}_q^{\mu_0}$

---

Parse $\mathsf{pp} = (\mathfrak{p}, \tau_0)$ and set $L_0^{(1)} = L_0$<br>
**Send** $\mathtt{init}$ and wait for $\mathsf{cm} = (\mathfrak{c}, \tau_1)$; Set $t_0 = \tau_0 || \tau_1$<br>
**For** $i \in [n]$:<br>
  $B^{(i)} \leftarrow \{b \in \{0,1\} : \omega((L_0^{(i)}, t_0), (i, b)) \geq p\}$<br>
  **If** $B^{(i)} \neq \varnothing$: // Given high winning probability, guess $m_i$<br>
    Choose $b^{(i)} \leftarrow \min(B^{(i)})$<br>
    $\mathsf{res}^{(i)} \leftarrow \mathsf{Forge}^{\mathcal{C}}(L_0^{(i-1)}, \mathsf{pp}, \mathsf{cm}, (i, b^{(i)}), \kappa)$<br>
    **If** $\mathsf{res}^{(i)} = \bot$: **Return** $\bot$<br>
    **Elif** $\mathsf{res}^{(i)} = \mathtt{accept}$: Store $\bar{m}_i \leftarrow b^{(i)}$; Set $L_0^{(i+1)} \leftarrow L_0^{(i)}$<br>
    **Else**: // Forge did not validate $b^{(i)}$ but found a new relation<br>
      $L_0^{(i+1)} \leftarrow \mathsf{res}^{(i)}$<br>
      $\bar{m}_i \leftarrow \mathcal{E}^*(\mathtt{bit}, i)$<br>
  **Else**: // Given low winning probability, extract new relations<br>
    $\bar{m}_i \leftarrow \mathcal{E}^*(\mathtt{bit}, i)$; Set $s \leftarrow (i, \bar{m}_i)$<br>
    $L_0^{(i+1)} \leftarrow \mathsf{Extract}^{\mathcal{W}, \mathcal{C}_{\mathsf{rand}}^{\mathsf{Extract}}}(1, \mathsf{pp}, \mathsf{cm}, s, L_0^{(i)})$ // oracle $\mathcal{W}$ defined as follows:<br>
    **When** it queries $\mathcal{W}(s, c_1, \ldots, c_k)$: **Reply** $w \leftarrow \mathcal{E}^*(\mathtt{wit}, s, c_1, \ldots, c_k)$<br>
    **If** $L_0^{(i+1)} \subseteq L_0^{(i)}$: **Return** $\bot$<br>
**Return** $((\bar{m}_1, \ldots, \bar{m}_n), L_0^{(n+1)})$

$\mathcal{E}_0(\mathbf{m}, \mathsf{pp}, \mathsf{cm}, \mathsf{aux}, r_{\mathsf{wit}}, x)$ : // Basic encoder

---

**If** $x = \mathtt{init}$: **Return** $\mathsf{cm}$<br>
**If** $x = (\mathtt{bit}, i)$: **Return** $m_i$<br>
**If** $x = (\mathtt{wit}, s, c_1, \ldots, c_k)$: **Return** $\mathsf{A.Wit}(\mathsf{pp}, \mathsf{aux}, s, (c_1, \ldots, c_k); r_{\mathsf{wit}})$

**Fig. 6.** Basic decoder, for any fixed accumulator $\mathsf{A}$ and $\lambda, n \in \mathbb{N}$ with $\lambda \geq 1 + \log_2 n$. Parameters $p$ and $\kappa$ are defined at the beginning of Section 4. The decoder makes queries to the it's encoder oracle $\mathcal{E}^*$, which by default (i.e., using $\mathcal{E}_0$) just replies using some predefined information $\mathbf{m}$, $\mathsf{pp}$, $\mathsf{cm}$, $\mathsf{aux}$, and $r_{\mathsf{wit}}$.

Next, the following lemma (showing that $\mathcal{D}_0$ is unlikely to abort) essentially follows from our results on Extract and Forge. Its proof appears in the full version of this paper.

**Lemma 13.** *Let* $\mathsf{A}$ *be as per Definition 6,* $\lambda, n \in \mathbb{N}$ *with* $\lambda \geq 1 + \log_2 n$*, and* $\mathbf{m} \leftarrow^{\$} \{0,1\}^n$*. If* $\chi/q \leq p/2$ *then*

$$\Pr\left[\mathcal{D}_0^{\mathcal{C}_{\mathsf{rand}}^{\mathsf{Forge}}, \mathcal{E}_0(\mathbf{m}, \mathsf{pp}, \mathsf{cm}, \mathsf{aux}, r_{\mathsf{wit}}, \cdot)}(L_0, \mathsf{pp}) = \bot\right] \leq \frac{1}{6}$$

*where the probability is taken over* $\mathsf{pp} \leftarrow^{\$} \mathsf{A.Gen}(\mathfrak{g}, 1^\lambda, 1^n)$*,* $(\mathsf{cm}, \mathsf{aux}) \leftarrow^{\$} \mathsf{A.Acc}(\mathsf{pp}, S_{\mathbf{m}})$*,* $r_{\mathsf{wit}} \leftarrow^{\$} \{0,1\}^{\gamma_{\mathsf{wit}}}$*, an arbitrarily distributed random variable*

*$L_0 \in \mathsf{Sub}(\mathbb{F}_q^{\mu_0})$ for which $\mathfrak{p}||\mathfrak{c} \in \mathrm{Ann}_{\mathbb{G}}(L_0)$ is fulfilled, and the randomness used both inside $\mathcal{D}_0$ and inside $C_{\mathsf{rand}}^{\mathsf{Forge}}$.*

### 4.2 Full Compression Argument

We define the full encoder-decoder pair $(\mathcal{E}, \mathcal{D})$ in Fig. 7.

The decoder $\mathcal{D}$ uses another helper decoder $\overline{\mathcal{D}}$ (also defined in Fig. 7), which requires an oracle $\mathcal{C}$ for supplying challenges to the Forge subroutine inside the final invocation of $\mathcal{D}_0$ (see Line 11 of $\overline{\mathcal{D}}$). The purpose of $\overline{\mathcal{D}}$ is to later allow a reduction to collision-freeness, in which only $\overline{\mathcal{D}}$ but not $\mathcal{D}$ will be required.

In the following, and in Fig. 7, we use the following additional notation:

- $\gamma_{\mathcal{C}}$ denotes an upper bound on the number of random coins used by an oracle $C_{\mathsf{rand}}^{\mathsf{Forge}}$ when it is passed as the oracle $\mathcal{C}$ supplied to an execution of $\mathcal{D}_0$ (i.e., $\gamma_{\mathcal{C}}$ must be large enough to provide challenges to $n$ invocations of Forge).
- $\gamma_{\overline{\mathcal{D}}}$ denotes an upper bound on the number of random coins used by $\overline{\mathcal{D}}$ (which includes up to $6\vartheta_0$ random messages $\mathbf{m}^{(i)}$, random tapes $r_{\mathsf{wit}}^{(i)}$, and random coins used within up to $6\vartheta_0$ invocations of $\mathcal{D}_0$ as well as their oracles $C_{\mathsf{rand}}^{\mathsf{Forge}}$)
- $\gamma := \gamma_{\mathsf{pp}} + r_{\mathsf{cm}} + r_{\mathsf{wit}} + \gamma_{\mathcal{C}} + \gamma_{\overline{\mathcal{D}}}$ denotes an upper bound on the entire randomness used by $\mathcal{D}$ and $\mathcal{E}$

Inside $\mathcal{E}$ and $\mathcal{D}$, we make the randomness $r$ explicit in the definition of $\mathcal{E}$ and $\mathcal{D}$ so that they become deterministic machines, allowing us to then apply a compression argument. Hence, the randomness $r$ is composed of $r = r_{\mathsf{pp}}||r_{\mathsf{cm}}||r_{\mathsf{wit}}||r_{\mathcal{C}}||\bar{r}$, with $r_{\mathsf{pp}} \in \{0,1\}^{\gamma_{\mathsf{pp}}}$, $r_{\mathsf{cm}} \in \{0,1\}^{\gamma_{\mathsf{cm}}}$, $r_{\mathsf{wit}} \in \{0,1\}^{\gamma_{\mathsf{wit}}}$, $r_{\mathcal{C}} \in \{0,1\}^{\gamma_{\mathcal{C}}}$, $\bar{r} \in \{0,1\}^{\gamma_{\overline{\mathcal{D}}}}$.

We again start with some basic facts about $\mathcal{D}$ and $\mathcal{E}$, which we prove in the full version of this paper.

**Lemma 14.** *Given $\mathsf{A}$ as per Definition 6, $\lambda, n \in \mathbb{N}$ with $\lambda \geq 1 + \log_2 n$, $\mathbf{m} \in \{0,1\}^n$, and randomness $r \in \{0,1\}^{\gamma}$, the following holds:*

- *When running $\mathcal{D}^{\mathcal{E}(\mathbf{m},r,\cdot)}(r)$, then $P^{(i)} \subseteq P^{(i+1)}$ (for $i \in [i^* - 1]$) and $\mathfrak{p} \in \mathrm{Ann}_{\mathbb{G}}(P^{(i)})$ (for $i \in [i^*]$), where $i^*$ and $P^{(i)}$ refer to the variables inside $\overline{\mathcal{D}}$.*
- *If $\mathcal{D}^{\mathcal{E}(\mathbf{m},r,\cdot)}(r) = \mathbf{m}$, then*

$$\mathsf{len}_{\mathcal{E},\mathcal{D}}((\mathbf{m}, r), r) \leq \xi_{\mathsf{cm}} + \vartheta_0 \cdot \left(1 + \xi_{\mathsf{wit}} \cdot \prod\nolimits_{i=1}^{\rho-1} (\mu_i + 1)\right)$$

Next, we show that $\mathcal{D}$ is unlikely to abort, which follows (1) from Lemma 13, and (2) from the fact that, with high probability, no new relations about $\mathfrak{p}$ are found in the final $\mathcal{D}_0$-call due to the preceding exploration phase that is executed for a random number of iterations. The proof of the following lemma will be presented in the full version of this paper.

**Lemma 15.** *Given $\mathsf{A}$ as per Definition 6 and $\lambda, n \in \mathbb{N}$ with $\lambda \geq 1 + \log_2 n$. If $\chi/q \leq p/2$ then*

$$\Pr\left[\mathcal{D}^{\mathcal{E}(\mathbf{m},r,\cdot)}(r) = \bot\right] \leq \frac{1}{3},$$

*with probability taken over message $\mathbf{m} \xleftarrow{\$} \{0,1\}^n$ and randomness $r \xleftarrow{\$} \{0,1\}^{\gamma}$.*

$\overline{\mathcal{D}}^{\mathcal{C},\mathcal{E}^*}(\mathsf{pp})$ : // Full decoder helper, taking an additional Forge challenge oracle $\mathcal{C}$

$P^{(1)} \leftarrow \{0^{\vartheta_0}\}$<br>
// 1. Exploration Phase<br>
Sample $i^* \leftarrow^{\$} [6\vartheta_0]$<br>
**For** $i \in \{1, \ldots, i^*-1\}$:<br>
    Sample $\mathbf{m}^{(i)} \leftarrow^{\$} \{0,1\}^n$ and $r_{\mathsf{wit}}^{(i)} \leftarrow^{\$} \{0,1\}^{\gamma_{\mathsf{wit}}}$<br>
    $(\mathsf{cm}^{(i)}, \mathsf{aux}^{(i)}) \leftarrow \mathsf{A.Acc}(\mathsf{pp}, S_{\mathbf{m}^{(i)}})$<br>
    $\mathsf{res} \leftarrow \mathcal{D}_0^{\mathcal{C}^{\mathsf{Forge}}_{\mathsf{rand}}, \mathcal{E}_0(\mathbf{m}^{(i)}, \mathsf{pp}, \mathsf{cm}^{(i)}, \mathsf{aux}^{(i)}, r_{\mathsf{wit}}^{(i)}, \cdot)}(P^{(i)} \times \{0^{\vartheta_1}\}, \mathsf{pp})$<br>
    **If** $\mathsf{res} = \bot$: Set $P^{(i+1)} = P^{(i)}$<br>
    **Elif** $\mathsf{res} = (\bar{\mathbf{m}}^{(i)}, L^{(i)})$: Set $P^{(i+1)} \leftarrow \pi^*_{\vartheta_0}(L^{(i)})$<br>
// 2. Interactive Decoding Phase<br>
$\mathsf{res} \leftarrow \mathcal{D}_0^{\mathcal{C},\mathcal{E}^*}(P^{(i^*)} \times \{0^{\vartheta_1}\}, \mathsf{pp})$ // i.e. with the real encoder $\mathcal{E}^*$<br>
**If** $\mathsf{res} = \bot$: **Return** $\bot$<br>
**Elif** $\mathsf{res} = (\bar{\mathbf{m}}, L^{(i^*)})$:<br>
    **If** $\pi^*_{\vartheta_0}(L^{(i^*)}) \not\subseteq P^{(i^*)}$: **Return** $\bot$<br>
    **Else**: **Return** $\bar{\mathbf{m}}$

$\mathcal{D}^{\mathcal{E}^*}(r)$ // Full decoder

Parse $r = r_{\mathsf{pp}} || r_{\mathsf{cm}} || r_{\mathsf{wit}} || r_{\mathcal{C}} || \bar{r}$<br>
Set $\mathsf{pp} \leftarrow \mathsf{A.Gen}(\mathfrak{g}, 1^\lambda, 1^n; r_{\mathsf{pp}})$<br>
**Return** $\overline{\mathcal{D}}^{\mathcal{C}^{\mathsf{Forge}}_{\mathsf{rand}}(\cdot; r_{\mathcal{C}}), \mathcal{E}^*}(\mathsf{pp}; \bar{r})$

$\mathcal{E}(\mathbf{m}, r, x)$: // Full encoder

Parse $r = r_{\mathsf{pp}} || r_{\mathsf{cm}} || r_{\mathsf{wit}} || r_{\mathcal{C}} || \bar{r}$<br>
Set $\mathsf{pp} \leftarrow \mathsf{A.Gen}(\mathfrak{g}, 1^\lambda, 1^n; r_{\mathsf{pp}})$<br>
Set $(\mathsf{cm}, \mathsf{aux}) \leftarrow \mathsf{A.Acc}(\mathsf{pp}, S_{\mathbf{m}}; r_{\mathsf{cm}})$<br>
**Return** $\mathcal{E}_0(\mathbf{m}, \mathsf{pp}, \mathsf{cm}, \mathsf{aux}, r_{\mathsf{wit}}, x)$

**Fig. 7.** Full encoder-decoder pair $(\mathcal{E}, \mathcal{D})$, for any fixed accumulator $\mathsf{A}$ and $\lambda, n \in \mathbb{N}$ with $\lambda \geq 1 + \log_2 n$. The random tape $r \in \{0,1\}^\gamma$ given to $\mathcal{E}$ and $\mathcal{D}$ is split into $r_{\mathsf{pp}} \in \{0,1\}^{\gamma_{\mathsf{pp}}}$, $r_{\mathsf{cm}} \in \{0,1\}^{\gamma_{\mathsf{cm}}}$, $r_{\mathsf{wit}} \in \{0,1\}^{\gamma_{\mathsf{wit}}}$, $r_{\mathcal{C}} \in \{0,1\}^{\gamma_{\mathcal{C}}}$, and $\bar{r} \in \{0,1\}^{\gamma_{\overline{\mathcal{D}}}}$.

### 4.3 Lower Bound

Now we are ready to present our main result.

**Theorem 1.** *Let* $\mathsf{A}$ *be an accumulator as per Definition 6, and* $n = n(\lambda) \geq 1$ *a polynomially bounded function. Then, asymptotically in* $\lambda \in \mathbb{N}$,[12] *it holds that*

$$2 + \xi_{\mathsf{cm}} + \vartheta_1 + \vartheta_1 \cdot \xi_{\mathsf{wit}} \cdot \prod_{i=1}^{\rho-1} (\mu_i + 1) \;\geq\; n$$

*Proof.* Towards contradiction assume the asymptotic bound above does not hold, i.e. that it is false for infinitely many $\lambda \in \Lambda_0 \subseteq \mathbb{N}$. Observe this implies that $\prod_{i=1}^{\rho-1}(\mu_i + 1) < n$ for all $\lambda \in \Lambda_0$ (because of $\vartheta_1 \geq 0$; and if we had $\xi_{\mathsf{wit}} = 0$ then $\mu_i = 0$ for every $i$, i.e., the product would be equal to $1 \leq n$).

[12] Formally, there exists some $\lambda_0$ s.t. this inequality holds for all $\lambda \geq \lambda_0$.

$\mathcal{A}(1^\lambda, 1^n, \mathsf{pp})$ :

**If** $\prod_{i=1}^{\rho-1}(\mu_i + 1) > n$: **Return** $\bot$ // Do nothing when $\lambda \notin \Lambda_0$
Sample $j_0 \leftarrow^{\$} [n], k_0 \leftarrow^{\$} [\kappa]$ // Guess s.t. $\bar{m}_{j_0} \neq m_{j_0}$ and Forge wins the $k_0$-th attempt.
Sample $\mathbf{m} \leftarrow^{\$} \{0,1\}$, $r_{\mathsf{wit}} \leftarrow^{\$} \{0,1\}^{\gamma_{\mathsf{wit}}}$
**Send** $S_{\mathbf{m}}$ to the challenger and wait for $\mathsf{cm}, \mathsf{aux}$
**Send** $(j_0, 1 - m_{j_0})$ // element not in $S$ we prove membership of
$\overline{\mathcal{D}}^{\mathcal{C}, \mathcal{E}_0(\mathbf{m}, \mathsf{pp}, \mathsf{cm}, \mathsf{aux}, r_{\mathsf{wit}}, \cdot)}(\mathsf{pp})$ // oracle $\mathcal{C}$ defined as follows:
**When** it queries $\mathcal{C}(s, k, i, w_i^{(k)})$:
  Parse $s = (j, b)$
  **If** $(j, k) \neq (j_0, k_0)$: **Reply** $c_i \leftarrow^{\$} \{0,1\}^{\ell_i}$
  **Else**: **Send** $w_i^{(k)}$ to the challenger, wait for $c_i$; **Reply** $c_i$

**Fig. 8.** Adversary against the collision-freeness of A against query-efficient type-safe attacks, for any fixed accumulator A and $\lambda, n \in \mathbb{N}$ with $\lambda \geq 1 + \log_2 n$. The parameter $\kappa$ is the defined at the beginning of Section 4.

In particular, given our definition of $p$, we have $p \geq (12n^2(\mu_\rho + 1))^{-1} - n\varepsilon$ for all $\lambda \in \Lambda_0$ as well as $\kappa = \lceil 2\ln(12n)/p \rceil \leq 1 + 2/n(\mu_\rho + 1)$. Since $\mu_\rho$ is bounded by polynomials in $\lambda$ (otherwise the Theorem would be trivial), this means that both $1/p$ and $\kappa$ are bounded by polynomials in $\lambda$ for all $\lambda \in \Lambda_0$.

We further refine $\lambda$ as follows. Since both $\varepsilon(\lambda, n(\lambda))$ and $\chi/q$ are negligible in $\lambda$ (due to correctness of A and due to A.Ver being query-efficient, respectively), and because $q$ is exponential in $\lambda$, we can find a $\lambda_1$ such that $\lambda \geq \lambda_1$ implies

$$\frac{1}{24n^2(\mu_\rho + 1)} \geq \frac{n\varepsilon}{2} + \frac{\chi}{q} \quad \text{and} \quad \lambda \geq 1 + \log_2 n \,. \tag{2}$$

Let us denote $\Lambda_1 = \Lambda_0 \cap \{\lambda \in \mathbb{N} : \lambda \geq \lambda_1\}$, which is still infinite. Then, combining this with the bound on $p$ from above, we have $p/2 \geq \chi/q$ for all $\lambda \in \Lambda_1$.

Next, consider the interactive compression argument $(\mathcal{E}, \mathcal{D})$ from Fig. 7 with message space $\{0,1\}^\lambda$, and common random coins $\{0,1\}^\gamma$. With $\mathbf{m}, r$ uniformly sampled, let $E$ be the event $\mathcal{D}^{\mathcal{E}(\mathbf{m}, r, \cdot)}(r) = \mathbf{m}$. Then, Lemma 14 implies that for all $\lambda \in \mathbb{N}$ and each choice of $\mathbf{m}, r$ for which $E$ holds, we have

$$\mathsf{len}_{\mathcal{E},\mathcal{D}}((\mathbf{m}, r), r) \;\leq\; \xi_{\mathsf{cm}} + \vartheta_0 \left(1 + \xi_{\mathsf{wit}} \cdot \prod_{i=1}^{\rho-1} (\mu_i + 1)\right).$$

Next we need to bound $\Pr[E]$. For $\lambda \in \Lambda_1$ we can apply Lemma 15, meaning that $\Pr\left[\mathcal{D}^{\mathcal{E}(\mathbf{m}, r, \cdot)}(r) = \bot\right] \leq 1/3$. To further bound the probability that $\mathcal{D}$ outputs an incorrect $\bar{\mathbf{m}} \neq \mathbf{m}$ without aborting, we will reduce to the collision-freeness of A against query-bounded TS-machines. A full description of the reduction is given in Fig. 8.

Observe that in both the collision-freeness experiment $\mathsf{Exp}^{\mathsf{coll\text{-}free}}_{\mathsf{A}, \mathcal{A}, q}(\lambda, n)$ and in the execution of $\mathcal{D}^{\mathcal{E}(\mathbf{m}, r, \cdot)}(r)$ (for a uniform choice of $\mathbf{m}, r$), exactly one call to $\overline{\mathcal{D}}$ is made. Let $\bar{\mathbf{m}}$ denote $\overline{\mathcal{D}}$'s return value, and let Abort be the event that $\bar{\mathbf{m}} = \bot$.

The two executions of $\overline{\mathcal{D}}$ have identical behavior in their respective experiments: (1) $\overline{\mathcal{D}}$'s input $\mathsf{pp}$ is generated honestly by $\mathsf{A.Gen}$ in both cases, (2) the encoder oracles $\mathcal{E}_0(\mathbf{m}, \mathsf{pp}, \mathsf{cm}, \mathsf{aux}, r_{\mathsf{wit}}, \cdot)$ and $\mathcal{E}(\mathbf{m}, r, \cdot)$ have identical behavior (both utilize a uniformly random message $\mathbf{m}$ and $r_{\mathsf{wit}}$, and both utilize $(\mathsf{cm}, \mathsf{aux})$ generated by $\mathsf{A.Acc}(\mathsf{pp}, S_{\mathbf{m}})$), and (3) the oracles $\mathcal{C}$ and $\mathcal{C}_{\mathsf{rand}}^{\mathsf{Forge}}$ have identical behavior (both always reply with uniformly random challenges; note that in case of $\mathcal{C}$ as defined in Line 7 of $\mathcal{A}$ this is due to the definition of the collision-freeness experiment).

Denoting by $\mathsf{tr}_{j',k'} = (t_1^{(k')}, c_1^{(k)}, \ldots, t_\rho^{(k')}, c_\rho^{(k')})$ the transcript computed in Line 12 of $\mathsf{Forge}$'s $k'$-th execution when it is queried on $s = (j', b_{j'})$, we now have (where, by the discussion above it doesn't matter whether the probability space is the collision-freeness experiment or the execution of $\mathcal{D}^{\mathcal{E}(\mathbf{m},r)}(r)$):

$$
\begin{aligned}
&\Pr\left[\neg\mathsf{Abort} \wedge \bar{\mathbf{m}} \neq \mathbf{m}\right] \\
&\leq \sum\nolimits_{j'=1}^{n} \Pr\left[\neg\mathsf{Abort} \wedge \bar{m}_{j'} \neq m_{j'}\right] \\
&\leq \sum\nolimits_{j'=1}^{n} \Pr\begin{bmatrix} B_{j'} \neq \varnothing \wedge b_{j'} \neq m_{j'} \wedge \\ (\vee_{k'=1}^{\kappa} \mathsf{A.Ver}(\mathsf{pp}, \mathsf{cm}, (j', b_{j'}), \mathsf{tr}_{j',k'}) = 1) \end{bmatrix} && (3) \\
&\leq \sum\nolimits_{j'=1}^{n} \sum\nolimits_{k'=1}^{\kappa} \Pr\begin{bmatrix} B_{j'} \neq \varnothing \wedge b_{j'} \neq m_{j'} \wedge \\ \mathsf{A.Ver}(\mathsf{pp}, \mathsf{cm}, (j', b_{j'}), \mathsf{tr}_{j',k'}) = 1 \end{bmatrix} \\
&\leq \sum\nolimits_{j'=1}^{n} \sum\nolimits_{k'=1}^{\kappa} \Pr\left[\mathsf{A.Ver}(\mathsf{pp}, \mathsf{cm}, (j', 1 - m_{j'}), \mathsf{tr}_{j',k'}) = 1\right] && (4) \\
&= \sum\nolimits_{j'=1}^{n} \sum\nolimits_{k'=1}^{\kappa} \Pr\begin{bmatrix} \mathsf{A.Ver}(\mathsf{pp}, \mathsf{cm}, (j', 1 - m_{j'}), \mathsf{tr}_{j',k'}) = 1 \wedge \\ j_0 = j' \wedge k_0 = k' \end{bmatrix} \cdot n\kappa && (5) \\
&= \sum\nolimits_{j'=1}^{n} \sum\nolimits_{k'=1}^{\kappa} \Pr\left[\mathsf{Exp}_{\mathsf{A},\mathcal{A},q}^{\mathsf{coll\text{-}free}}(\lambda, n) = 1 \wedge j_0 = j' \wedge k_0 = k'\right] \cdot n\kappa && (6) \\
&= \mathsf{Adv}_{\mathsf{A},\mathcal{A}}^{\mathsf{coll\text{-}free}}(\lambda, n) \cdot n\kappa.
\end{aligned}
$$

(3) holds because whenever $\neg\mathsf{Abort}$ then $\bar{m}_{j'} \neq m_{j'}$ implies that $B_{j'} \neq \varnothing$, since otherwise $\mathcal{D}_0$ sets $\bar{m}_{j'} \leftarrow (\mathtt{bit}, j')$ in Line 14, which is always equal to $m_{j'}$. For the same reason it implies $\mathsf{Forge}$ must have returned $\mathtt{accept}$ on the set element $(j, \min(B_{j'})) = (j, b_{j'})$ and therefore $b_{j'} = \bar{m}_{j'} \neq m_{j'}$. (4) holds as $B_{j'} \neq \varnothing$ implies $b_{j'} \in \{0,1\}$ and $b_{j'} \neq m_{j'} \in \{0,1\}$ implies $b_{j'} = 1 - m_{j'}$. (5) holds since $j_0, k_0$, as sampled by $\mathcal{A}$, are statistically independent from any randomness visible to $\overline{\mathcal{D}}$ (in fact, we could modify $\mathsf{Exp}_{\mathsf{A},\mathcal{A},q}^{\mathsf{coll\text{-}free}}(\lambda, n)$ so that $j_0, k_0$ are only sampled at the very end of the experiment). Finally, (6) holds since the transcript $\mathsf{tr}_{j_0,k_0}$ is exactly the transcript that is checked by the collision-freeness challenger for validity.

To conclude we remark that $\mathcal{A}$ is query-efficient (i.e., the number of group operations is polynomial): since $n$ and $\kappa$ are both polynomial in $\lambda$ as shown before, the only computationally inefficient step is Line 3 of $\mathsf{Forge}$ where the optimal strategy is computed. However, doing so requires no group operations. By collision-freeness the advantage of $\mathcal{A}$ is smaller than a negligible function $\varepsilon'(\lambda)$. Thus for all $\lambda \in \Lambda_1$, $\Pr\left[\bar{\mathbf{m}} \neq \mathbf{m} \wedge \neg\mathsf{Abort}\right] \leq \kappa n \varepsilon'(\lambda)$, and there exists a $\lambda_2$ s.t. this term is $\leq 1/6$ for all $\lambda \in \Lambda_2$ where $\Lambda_2 := \Lambda_1 \cap \{\lambda \in \mathbb{N} : \lambda \geq \lambda_2\}$.

We therefore get a bound on $\Pr[E]$ for $\lambda \in \Lambda_2$ as follows:

$$\Pr[E] \leq \Pr\left[\mathcal{D}^{\mathcal{E}(\mathbf{m},r,\cdot)} = \bot\right] + \Pr\left[\mathcal{D}^{\mathcal{E}(\mathbf{m},r,\cdot)} \neq \bot \wedge \bar{\mathbf{m}} \neq \mathbf{m}\right] \leq \frac{1}{3} + \frac{1}{6} = \frac{1}{2}.$$

In conclusion, by Lemma 1 we have shown that for infinitely many $\lambda \in \Lambda_2$

$$\begin{aligned} n &\leq 1 + \left(\xi_{\mathsf{cm}} + \vartheta_1 \cdot \left(1 + \xi_{\mathsf{wit}} \prod_{i=1}^{\rho-1} (\mu_i + 1)\right)\right) - \log \Pr[E] \\ &\leq 2 + \xi_{\mathsf{cm}} + \vartheta_1 \cdot \left(1 + \xi_{\mathsf{wit}} \prod_{i=1}^{\rho-1} (\mu_i + 1)\right) \end{aligned}$$

which contradicts our initial hypothesis. □

**Corollary 1.** *Let* $\mathsf{A}$ *be an accumulator as per Definition 6, and* $n = n(\lambda) \geq 1$ *a polynomially bounded function. Let* $\mu = \sum_{i=1}^{\rho-1} \mu_i$ *be the number of group elements per proof (except those sent in the last round). Then, asymptotically in* $\lambda \in \mathbb{N}$*, it holds that*

$$2 + \xi_{\mathsf{cm}} + \vartheta_1 + \vartheta_1 \cdot \xi_{\mathsf{wit}} \cdot 2^{\mu} \geq n\ ,$$

*and in particular also* $\xi_{\mathsf{cm}} \cdot \xi_{\mathsf{wit}} \cdot 2^{\mu} = \Omega(n)$*. If further* $\rho \geq 2$ *then also*

$$\xi_{\mathsf{cm}} \cdot \xi_{\mathsf{wit}} \cdot \mu^{\rho-1} = \Omega(n)\ .$$

## References


AAAG25. Abusalah, H., Anthoine, G., Avitabile, G., Giunta, E.: Lower bounding update frequency in short accumulators and vector commitments. Cryptology ePrint Archive, Report 2025/1558 (2025)

AC20. Attema, T., Cramer, R.: Compressed $\Sigma$-protocol theory and practical application to plug & play secure algorithmics. In: Micciancio, D., Ristenpart, T. (eds.) CRYPTO 2020. Part III, volume 12172 of LNCS, pp. 513–543. Springer, Cham (2020). https://doi.org/10.1007/978-3-030-56877-1_18

AHO12. Abe, M., Haralambiev, K., Ohkubo, M.: Group to group commitments do not shrink. In: Pointcheval, D., Johansson, T. (eds.) EUROCRYPT 2012. LNCS, vol. 7237, pp. 301–317. Springer, Berlin, Heidelberg (2012)

BBB+18. Bünz, B., Bootle, J., Boneh, D., Poelstra, A., Wuille, P., Maxwell, G.: Bulletproofs: Short proofs for confidential transactions and more. In: 2018 IEEE Symposium on Security and Privacy, pp. 315–334. IEEE Computer Society Press (2018)

BBF19. Boneh, D., Bünz, B., Fisch, B.: Batching techniques for accumulators with applications to IOPs and stateless blockchains. In: Boldyreva, A., Micciancio, D. (eds.) CRYPTO 2019. Part I, volume 11692 of LNCS, pp. 561–586. Springer, Cham (2019)

BCC+16. Bootle, J., Cerulli, A., Chaidos, P., Groth, J., Petit, C.: Efficient zero-knowledge arguments for arithmetic circuits in the discrete log setting. In: Fischlin, M., Coron, J.-S. (eds.) EUROCRYPT 2016. Part II, volume 9666 of LNCS, pp. 327–357. Springer, Berlin, Heidelberg (2016)

BCCK25. Bonneau, J., Chen, J., Christ, M., Karantaidou, I.: Merkle Mountain Ranges are Optimal: On Witness Update Frequency for Cryptographic Accumulators. In: Tauman Kalai, Y., Kamara, S.F. (eds) Advances in Cryptology – CRYPTO 2025. CRYPTO 2025. Lecture Notes in Computer Science, vol. 16001. Springer, Cham (2025). https://doi.org/10.1007/978-3-032-01878-6_6

BCD+17. Baldimtsi, F., et al.: Accumulators with applications to anonymity-preserving revocation. In: 2017 IEEE European Symposium on Security and Privacy, pp. 301–315. IEEE Computer Society Press (2017)

BCY20. Baldimtsi, F., Canetti, R., Yakoubov, S.: Universally composable accumulators. In: Jarecki, S. (ed.) CT-RSA 2020. LNCS, vol. 12006, pp. 638–666. Springer, Cham (2020)

BdM94. Josh Cohen Benaloh and Michael de Mare: One-way accumulators: A decentralized alternative to digital sinatures (extended abstract). In: Helleseth, T. (ed.) EUROCRYPT'93. LNCS, vol. 765, pp. 274–285. Springer, Berlin, Heidelberg (1994)

BGZ23. Boneh, D., Guan, J., Zhandry, M.: A lower bound on the length of signatures based on group actions and generic isogenies. In: Hazay, C., Stam, M. (eds.) EUROCRYPT 2023. Part V, volume 14008 of LNCS, pp. 507–531. Springer, Cham (2023)

CB23. Christ, M., Bonneau, J.: Limits on revocable proof systems, with implications for stateless blockchains. In: Baldimtsi, F., Cachin, C. (eds.) FC 2023. Part II, volume 13951 of LNCS, pp. 54–71. Springer, Cham (2023)

CF13. Catalano, D., Fiore, D.: Vector Commitments and Their Applications. In: Kurosawa, K., Hanaoka, G. (eds.) PKC 2013. LNCS, vol. 7778, pp. 55–72. Springer, Heidelberg (2013). https://doi.org/10.1007/978-3-642-36362-7_5

CFGG22. Catalano, D., Fiore, D., Gennaro, R., Giunta, E.: On the impossibility of algebraic vector commitments in pairing-free groups. In: Kiltz, E., Vaikuntanathan, V. (eds.) TCC 2022. Part II, volume 13748 of LNCS, pp. 274–299. Springer, Cham (2022)

CH10. Camacho, P., Hevia, A.: On the Impossibility of Batch Update for Cryptographic Accumulators. In: Abdalla, M., Barreto, P.S.L.M. (eds.) LATINCRYPT 2010. LNCS, vol. 6212, pp. 178–188. Springer, Heidelberg (2010). https://doi.org/10.1007/978-3-642-14712-8_11

CHJ+22. Chung, H., Han, K., Ju, C., Kim, M., Seo, J.H.: Bulletproofs+: Shorter proofs for a privacy-enhanced distributed ledger. IEEE Access **10**, 42081–42096 (2022)

CPZ18. Chepurnoy, A., Papamanthou, C., Zhang, Y.: Edrax: A cryptocurrency with stateless transaction validation. Cryptology ePrint Archive, Report 2018/968 (2018)

DFKP15. Dziembowski, S., Faust, S., Kolmogorov, V., Pietrzak, K.: Proofs of Space. In: Gennaro, R., Robshaw, M. (eds.) CRYPTO 2015. LNCS, vol. 9216, pp. 585–605. Springer, Heidelberg (2015). https://doi.org/10.1007/978-3-662-48000-7_29

DHH+21. Döttling, N., Hartmann, D., Hofheinz, D., Kiltz, E., Schäge, S., Ursu, B.: On the impossibility of purely algebraic signatures. In: Nissim, K., Waters, B. (eds.) TCC 2021. Part III, volume 13044 of LNCS, pp. 317–349. Springer, Cham (2021)

DKT26. Dietz, M., Kastner, J., Tessaro, S.: On the impossibility of round-optimal pairing-free blind signatures in the ROM. Cryptology ePrint Archive, Paper 2026/090 (2026)

EKRN24. Eagen, L., Kanjalkar, S., Ruffing, T., Nick, J.: Bulletproofs++: Next generation confidential transactions via reciprocal set membership arguments. In: Joye, M., Leander, G. (eds.) EUROCRYPT 2024. Part V, volume 14655 of LNCS, pp. 249–279. Springer, Cham (2024)

FN02. Fazio, N., Nicolosi, A.: Cryptographic accumulators: Definitions, constructions and applications. Paper written for course at New York University: www.cs.nyu.edu/nicolosi/papers/accumulators.pdf (2002)

FS87. Fiat, A., Shamir, A.: How to prove yourself: Practical solutions to identification and signature problems. In: Odlyzko, A.M. (ed.) CRYPTO'86. LNCS, vol. 263, pp. 186–194. Springer, Berlin, Heidelberg (1987)

Giu23. Giunta, E.: On the impossibility of algebraic NIZK in pairing-free groups. In: Handschuh, H., Lysyanskaya, A. (eds.) CRYPTO 2023. Part IV, volume 14084 of LNCS, pp. 702–730. Springer, Cham (2023)

GM24. Guan, J., Montgomery, H.: On sequential functions and fine-grained cryptography. In: Reyzin, L., Stebila, D. (eds.) CRYPTO 2024. Part V, volume 14924 of LNCS, pp. 393–428. Springer, Cham (2024)

GRWZ20. Gorbunov, S., Reyzin, L., Wee, H., Zhang, Z.: Pointproofs: Aggregating proofs for multiple vector commitments. In: Ligatti, J., Ou, X., Katz, J., Vigna, G., (eds.) ACM CCS 2020, pp. 2007–2023. ACM Press (2020)

GT00. Gennaro, R., Trevisan, L.: Lower bounds on the efficiency of generic cryptographic constructions. In: 41st FOCS, pp. 305–313. IEEE Computer Society Press (2000)

HMQS23. Hajiabadi, M., Mahmoody, M., Qi, W., Sarfaraz, S.: Lower Bounds on Assumptions Behind Registration-Based Encryption. In: Rothblum, G., Wee, H. (eds.) Theory of Cryptography. TCC 2023. Lecture Notes in Computer Science, vol. 14370. Springer, Cham (2023). https://doi.org/10.1007/978-3-031-48618-0_11

JK07. Juels, A., Kaliski, B.S., Jr.: Pors: proofs of retrievability for large files. In: Ning, P., di Vimercati, S.C., Syverson, P.F., (eds.) ACM CCS 2007, pp. 584–597. ACM Press (2007)

Kil92. Kilian, J.: A note on efficient zero-knowledge proofs and arguments (extended abstract). In: 24th ACM STOC, pp. 723–732. ACM Press (1992)

KZG10. Kate, A., Zaverucha, G.M., Goldberg, I.: Constant-size commitments to polynomials and their applications. In: Abe, M. (ed.) ASIACRYPT 2010. LNCS, vol. 6477, pp. 177–194. Springer, Berlin, Heidelberg (2010)

LRY16. Libert, B., Ramanna, S.C., Yung, M.: Functional commitment schemes: From polynomial commitments to pairing-based accumulators from simple assumptions. In: Chatzigiannakis, I., Mitzenmacher, M., Rabani, Y., Sangiorgi, D. (eds.) ICALP 2016, volume 55 of LIPIcs, pp. 30:1–30:14. Schloss Dagstuhl (2016)

LY10. Libert, B., Yung, M.: Concise mercurial vector commitments and independent zero-knowledge sets with short proofs. In: Micciancio, D. (ed.) TCC 2010. LNCS, vol. 5978, pp. 499–517. Springer, Berlin, Heidelberg (2010)

Mau05. Ueli, M.: Maurer. Abstract models of computation in cryptography (invited paper). In: Smart, N.P. (ed.) 10th IMA International Conference on Cryptography and Coding. LNCS, vol. 3796, pp. 1–12. Springer, Berlin, Heidelberg (2005)

Mer88. Ralph, C.: Merkle. A digital signature based on a conventional encryption function. In: Pomerance, C. (ed.) CRYPTO'87. LNCS, vol. 293, pp. 369–378. Springer, Berlin, Heidelberg (1988)

MMV13. Mahmoody, M., Moran, T., Vadhan, S.P.: Publicly verifiable proofs of sequential work. In: Kleinberg, R.D., (ed.) ITCS 2013, pp. 373–388. ACM (2013)

MRK03. Micali, S., Rabin, M.O., Kilian, J.: Zero-knowledge sets. In: 44th FOCS, pp. 80–91. IEEE Computer Society Press (2003)

PRV12. Papakonstantinou, P.A., Rackoff, C.W., Vahlis, Y.: How powerful are the DDH hard groups? Cryptology ePrint Archive, Report 2012/653 (2012)

Qi25. Qi, W.: Tight lower bound on witness update frequency in additive positive accumulators. Cryptology ePrint Archive, Report 2025/1378 (2025)

RSS20. Rotem, L., Segev, G., Shahaf, I.: Generic-group delay functions require hidden-order groups. In: Canteaut, A., Ishai, Y. (eds.) EUROCRYPT 2020. Part III, volume 12107 of LNCS, pp. 155–180. Springer, Cham (2020)

SGS20. Schul-Ganz, G., Segev, G.: Accumulators in (and beyond) generic groups: Non-trivial batch verification requires interaction. In: Pass, R., Pietrzak, K. (eds.) TCC 2020. Part II, volume 12551 of LNCS, pp. 77–107. Springer, Cham (2020)

SGS21. Schul-Ganz, G., Segev, G.: Generic-group identity-based encryption: A tight impossibility result. In: Tessaro, S., (ed.) ITC 2021, vol. 199 LIPIcs, pp. 26:1–26:23. Schloss Dagstuhl (2021)

Zha22. Zhandry, M.: To label, or not to label (in generic groups). In: Dodis, Y., Shrimpton, T. (eds.) CRYPTO 2022. Part III, volume 13509 of LNCS, pp. 66–96. Springer, Cham (2022)

ZZ18. Zhandry, M., Zhang, C.: Impossibility of order-revealing encryption in idealized models. In: Beimel, A., Dziembowski, S. (eds.) TCC 2018. Part II, volume 11240 of LNCS, pp. 129–158. Springer, Cham (2018)

# Achieving Shannon Capacity for Computationally Bounded Errors

George Lu[1(✉)], Jad Silbak[2], and Daniel Wichs[3,4]

[1] University of Texas at Austin, Austin, TX, USA
gclu@cs.utexas.edu
[2] Massachusetts Institute of Technology, Cambridge, MA, USA
[3] Northeastern University, Boston, MA, USA
[4] NTT Research, Sunnyvale, CA, USA

**Abstract.** We study error correction in a computationally bounded world, where errors are introduced by an arbitrary polynomial-time adversarial channel. Recent works construct *seeded* codes in this model, where the encoding and decoding procedure share a public random seed. They achieve significantly better tradeoffs between rate and error tolerance than what is possible information theoretically for unique decoding, essentially matching the parameters of the best known efficiently list-decodable codes. Over the binary alphabet, however, this is still well short of the optimal *Shannon capacity* with rate $R \approx 1 - H_2(p)$ for a $p < 1/4$ fraction of errors. Even heuristic constructions meeting this target were not previously known. We make progress towards this goal.

- **Secret-Key Codes.** We first study *secret-key* codes, where the encoder and decoder share a secret key hidden from the adversarial channel. Lipton (STACS '94) constructed *one-time secure* secret-key codes achieving Shannon capacity in this setting, but it was unknown whether one can get CPA (resp. CCA) security where the adversary may query an encoding oracle (resp. also a decoding oracle). We construct CCA-secure secret-key codes achieving Shannon capacity via *pseudorandom codes (PRCs)*.
- **Seeded Codes (Heuristic).** We can heuristically upgrade the resulting secret-key codes to seeded codes by publishing an obfuscation of the encoding/decoding procedures with a hard-coded secret key as a seed. Security holds in the ideal obfuscation model.
- **Public-key Codes.** We also consider *public-key* codes, where the decoder has a secret key and the encoder has the corresponding public key. We construct such CPA-secure public-key codes achieving Shannon capacity with unique decoding for $p < 1/4$ errors, and list decoding all the way to $p < 1/2$ errors, assuming PRCs and the subexponential security of standard crypto assumptions (e.g., LWE or DDH or QR or DCR). We also show how to get CCA security in the random oracle model.

Our secret-key and public-key codes meeting Shannon capacity are also simultaneously pseudorandom codes.


N. Heninger and M. Rosulek (Eds.): CRYPTO 2026, LNCS 16800, pp. 250–281, 2026.
https://doi.org/10.1007/978-3-032-35367-2_9

# 1 Introduction

*Coding Theory.* The theory of error correction originates in the seminal works of Shannon [Sha48] and Hamming [Ham50]. In its most basic form, a sender encodes a message $m \in \{0,1\}^k$ into a codeword $c = \mathsf{Enc}(m) \in \{0,1\}^n$ and transmits $c$ over a noisy channel that may corrupt some of the $n$ transmitted bits. A receiver observes a possibly corrupted value $c' \in \{0,1\}^n$ and runs a decoding procedure $\mathsf{Dec}(c')$ that should uniquely recover the original message $m$.[1] Shannon's work considered *random errors* (i.e., the binary symmetric channel (BSC)), where the channel flips each codeword bit with some probability $p$, while Hamming considered *worst-case/adversarial* errors, where the channel can flip an arbitrary subset of $pn$ codeword bits. The main parameters of interest are the *rate* of the code, which is defined as $R = k/n$ and measures how much data can be packed into the codeword, and the *relative error tolerance* $p$ of the code, which measures the fraction of errors that the code can correct. There is an inherent tension between these parameters; higher error tolerance $p$ typically requires more redundancy and hence smaller rate $R$. The goal is to achieve optimal tradeoffs between them.

*Information-Theoretic Bounds.* In Shannon's model, the optimal tradeoffs between rate and error-tolerance are well understood. It is possible to correct random errors for any error probability $p < 1/2$ with rate $R \approx 1 - H_2(p)$, where $H_2(p) := p \log_2 \frac{1}{p} + (1-p)\log_2 \frac{1}{1-p}$ is the binary entropy function.[2] We refer to the above rate as the *Shannon capacity*. Moreover, we have efficient constructions that achieve Shannon capacity and are guaranteed to recover the original message with overwhelming probability.

In Hamming's model, the optimal tradeoffs are still not fully understood, despite decades of study. It is known that unique error correction is only possible for $p < 1/4$ fraction of errors. The best achievable rate *existentially* (i.e., derived via the probabilistic method without an efficient construction) is given by the Gilbert-Varshamov (GV) bound $R \approx 1 - H_2(2p)$. In other words, this only allows us to correct half as many errors compared to Shannon's model for any given rate. It is widely conjectured that this is asymptotically optimal, but we do not actually know how to prove this. Moreover, we also do not know how to achieve the GV bound efficiently, and the best known efficient constructions for the Hamming model only achieve the somewhat worse *Zyablov bound* [Zya71].

In the Hamming model, we can also consider a relaxation of unique decoding called *list-decoding*, where the decoding algorithm only needs to output a polynomial-size list of messages that includes the original message. Existentially, it is known that list-decoding is achievable for $p < 1/2$ fraction of errors with a rate matching Shannon capacity $R \approx 1 - H_2(p)$, which is optimal. However,

---

[1] One can also consider coding over larger alphabets, but in this work we focus on the binary alphabet.

[2] Throughout the introduction, we use $\approx$ to hide additive constants that we can set arbitrarily close to 0.

the best known efficiently list-decodable codes only achieve the somewhat worse *Blokh-Zyablov (BZ) bound* [BZ76].

While the formulations of the Zyablov and BZ bounds are complicated, we give numeric examples in Table 1.

*Computationally Bounded Errors.* Following the usual paradigm in cryptography, it is natural to assume that the channel is adversarial but *computationally bounded*, meaning that the error pattern it introduces must be computable in polynomial time. This model lies between Shannon's model of random errors and Hamming's model of (computationally unbounded) worst-case errors. While, for all intents and purposes, it is as good as Hamming's model in a computationally bounded world, it may allow for parameters that match those of Shannon's much weaker model. Indeed, a long line of works shows that one can achieve improved parameters in this model over Hamming's. For the corresponding codes, there must exist error patterns that the code fails to correct, but no efficient adversary is able to find them. In order to achieve this, we also need to relax the coding syntax, where the encoding/decoding algorithms are public deterministic procedures – otherwise a non-uniform efficient adversary can always just hard-code a worst-case error pattern for which error correction fails. Several such relaxations were considered in prior works, and are surveyed below.

*Secret-Key Codes.* Lipton [Lip94] introduced a model where the encoder $\mathsf{Enc}_{\mathsf{sk}}$ and decoder $\mathsf{Dec}_{\mathsf{sk}}$ share a secret key $\mathsf{sk}$ hidden from the channel. In this setting, it is possible to achieve Shannon capacity $R \approx 1 - H_2(p)$ for any $p < 1/2$ via a simple construction. In fact, this can be even accomplished information-theoretically against computationally unbounded adversaries with a sufficiently large shared key, and computational security is only needed to shrink the key size. A major limitation of this result is that it only provides *one-time security*, analogously to one-time pad encryption, and security does not hold if an adversary can observe multiple codewords generated using the same key. Ideally, we would also like to achieve *chosen-plaintext attack (CPA)* (resp. *chosen-codeword attack (CCA)*) security, where the adversary additionally gets access to the encoding oracle $\mathsf{Enc}_{\mathsf{sk}}$ (resp. also the decoding oracle $\mathsf{Dec}_{\mathsf{sk}}$), analogously to CPA/CCA secure symmetric-key encryption. For CPA security, it is easy to see that one cannot uniquely correct $p > 1/4$ fraction of errors with rate $R > 0$.[3] But even for $p < 1/4$, Lipton's result does not readily extend to provide CPA security.

*Public-Key Decoding.* Micali, Peikert, Sudan, and Wilson [MPSW10] proposed a public-key analogue, where the encoder $\mathsf{Enc}_{\mathsf{sk}}$ holds a secret key $\mathsf{sk}$ while the decoder (and the channel) get a corresponding public key $\mathsf{pk}$. Assuming just digital signatures (one-way functions), for any error tolerance $p < 1/2$ they construct a uniquely decodable code with a rate $R$ that matches that of *best*

[3] If an adversary observes two random codewords, their relative Hamming distance is likely to be $< 1/2$. The adversary can therefore choose a mid-point that is of relative distance $< 1/4$ from each one, and decoding will fail to uniquely output at least one of the two starting messages.

*known efficiently list-decodable code* with error tolerance $p$. In particular, the rate of these codes meets the BZ bound. While they consider a setting where the adversary has access to the encoding oracle, their result only holds if the encoder is stateful and the adversary only gets access to the encoding oracle before seeing the challenge codeword but not after. If we remove these restrictions, then the maximal achievable tolerance becomes $p < 1/4$.[4]

*Seeded Codes.* Grossman, Holmgren, and Yogev [GHY20] proposed *seeded codes*, where the encoder $\mathsf{Enc}_s$ and decoder $\mathsf{Dec}_s$ only share a random *public seed* $s$ that is also known to the adversarial channel. They construct such codes achieving the BZ bound for any $p < 1/4$ in the random oracle model. Subsequent works of Lu, Silbak and Wichs [SW25b, SW25a, LSW25] study seeded codes in the standard model, and the state of the art [LSW25] achieves the BZ bound for $p < 1/4$ under standard cryptographic assumptions such as DDH or LWE or QR or DCR.

*Additional Models.* The work of [SW25b] also considers *randomized codes* without any shared seed, where the encoding algorithm uses fresh local randomness on each invocation. However, they only construct these for large alphabets and it remains open to get constructions over a binary alphabet. The works of [GS16, SS21a, SS22, SS24b] consider a setting where the complexity of the code can exceed that of the adversarial channel. For example the work of [SS24b] shows that for $p < 1/4$ and any polynomial $n^c$, there is a randomized code with polynomial complexity $n^d > n^c$ that achieves Shannon capacity $R \approx 1 - H_2(p)$ for channels running in time $n^c$. In contrast, in this work we focus on the standard cryptographic setting where the codes must run in some fixed polynomial time, and can protect against arbitrary polynomial time channels, including ones whose run-time vastly exceeds that of the code.

*Summary of the Remaining Gaps.* To summarize, existing results demonstrate that codes for computationally bounded errors can circumvent classical information-theoretic barriers. Under standard cryptographic assumptions, prior work constructed seeded codes in this setting with unique decoding, where the rate matches that of the best known efficiently list-decodable codes, for error tolerance $p < 1/4$. Unfortunately, the rate of the currently best known efficiently list-decodable codes only achieves the BZ bound, which is significantly worse than the optimal goal of reaching Shannon capacity. While one may hope that future improvements in list-decodable codes will allow us to efficiently reach Shannon capacity, this would require breaking through a long-standing barrier in coding theory. Without such a breakthrough, prior binary codes for computationally bounded channels are stuck at the BZ bound, even if we consider relaxations of seeded codes, such as public-key codes or symmetric-key codes with CPA security. Reaching Shannon capacity for any such codes was previously unknown even heuristically.

[4] It appears likely, although not entirely trivial, that the result of [MPSW10] can be extended to achieve the BZ bound for $p < 1/4$ without the above restrictions.

## 1.1 Our Results

In this work, we make progress towards constructing codes for computationally bounded errors and achieving Shannon capacity.

*Secret-Key Codes.* We first consider *secret-key* codes $(\mathsf{Enc}_{\mathsf{sk}}, \mathsf{Dec}_{\mathsf{sk}})$, where the encoder and decoder share a secret key hidden from the adversarial channel. Previously, Lipton [Lip94] gave a simple construction with *one-time security* achieving Shannon capacity, but it was unknown whether one can get CPA (resp. CCA) security where the adversary may also query an encoding oracle (resp. also a decoding oracle). We construct CCA-secure secret-key codes that meet Shannon capacity for $p < 1/4$. We do so via the use of *pseudorandom codes (PRCs)* [CG24,GM24,GG25,AAC+25,CGG+26], which were originally introduced in a seemingly completely unrelated context of watermarking large language models. A PRC is a secret-key encoding scheme that is simultaneously: (i) pseudorandom, in that any polynomial number of codeword are computationally indistinguishable from uniform, and (ii) error-correcting or robust in that decoding succeeds even when errors are introduced. We rely on pseudorandom codes that can tolerate any $p < 1/4$ rate of errors (but can have arbitrarily poor rate). Such PRCs are known assuming $2^{O(\sqrt{n})}$-hardness of the *learning parity with noise (LPN)* assumption [CG24], or the *permuted codes assumption* [CGG+26].

*Seeded Codes.* We observe that CCA-secure secret-key codes can be converted into seeded codes by obfuscating the encoding/decoding procedures (with a hard-coded secret key) and publishing the obfuscated programs as the seed. Security trivially holds in the *ideal obfuscation model*, where we replace the obfuscated programs by black-box oracles. The work of [JLLW23] showed that one can instantiate ideal obfuscation in a variant of the random oracle model called the *pseudorandom oracle (PRO) model*, assuming indistinguishability obfuscation, and therefore we also get such codes in the PRO model. Overall, this provides strong heuristic evidence that we can securely instantiate our construction. In particular, it gives the first heuristic candidate for seeded codes achieving Shannon capacity for any $p < 1/4$.

*Public-Key Codes.* We next consider *public-key* codes $(\mathsf{Enc}_{\mathsf{pk}}, \mathsf{Dec}_{\mathsf{sk}})$, where the decoder has a secret key $\mathsf{sk}$ and the encoder has the corresponding public key $\mathsf{pk}$.[5] This notion lies in between symmetric-key codes and seeded codes. We first show how to construct such *list-decodable* CPA-secure public-key codes that achieve Shannon capacity for any $p < 1/2$ fraction of errors. We do so via public-key PRCs, which can in turn be constructed assuming $2^{O(\sqrt{n})}$-hardness of the *learning parity with noise (LPN)* assumption [CG24]. We then convert the above list-decodable codes into *uniquely-decodable* CPA-secure public-key codes that achieve Shannon capacity for any $p < 1/4$ fraction of errors via

[5] This is the reverse of the *public-key decoder* codes of [MPSW10] where the encoder had a secret key and the decoder had the corresponding public key.

the use of correlation-intractable (CI) hashing, relying on the paradigm of [SW25a, LSW25]. The needed CI hash functions can be instantiated from the subexponential security of standard crypto assumptions such as DDH or LWE or QR or DCR. Finally we show to make the corresponding list-decodable or uniquely-decodable codes CCA secure in the random oracle model.

*Pseudorandomness.* While this was not our main goal, we also show that our constructions of CPA/CCA secret-key and public-key codes achieving Shannon capacity are also simultaneously *pseudorandom codes* themselves. In particular, the codewords in these constructions look pseudorandom even to an adversary with the corresponding encoding/decoding oracles. Therefore we get corresponding pseudorandom codes that achieve Shannon capacity.

*Discussion of Parameters.* In Table 1 we give some numeric examples of the best known rates achievable in different error models. Note that, for information-theoretic unique decoding for worst-case errors, the rate $R$ goes to 0 as error tolerance $p$ approaches .25 from below, and this is inherent. Interestingly, for computationally bounded errors, both prior works and our results in rows 4 and 5 achieve some positive rate $R$ as $p$ approaches .25 from below (in our case $R \approx .188$), but then the rate drops to 0 at $p > .25$, meaning that the graph is not continuous at $p = .25$. (This was already observed in prior works.) To see the dramatic differences in parameters between the different models, consider a high-error regime where we want to correct a 20% fraction of errors. The best prior efficient information-theoretic codes had rate $R < .001$, meaning that the codeword had to be $> 1,000\times$ larger than the message! The best prior codes for computationally bounded errors had rate $R = .073$ meaning that the codeword had to be $> 13\times$ larger than the message. Our results achieve $R = .278$ meaning that the codeword only has to be $< 3.6\times$ larger than the message.

## 2 Technical Overview

*One-Time Secure Secret-Key Codes.* We start by recalling the one-time secure secret-key codes of Lipton [Lip94]. The construction is very simple. The encoder and decoder share a random secret key consisting of a permutation $\pi : [n] \rightarrow [n]$ and an $n$-bit one-time pad. The encoder first encodes the data with an optimal code for *random errors*, which can correct from a random subset of $pn$ flips with overwhelming probability. This is a small variant of the binary symmetric channel considered by Shannon, and we have efficiently computable codes for this setting with optimal rate $R \approx 1 - H_2(p)$ for $p < 1/2$. Let $\hat{c} \in \{0,1\}^n$ be the resulting codeword. The encoder then permutes the bits of the codeword with the permutation $\pi$ and applies a one-time pad, resulting in the final codeword $c \in \{0,1\}^n$. Intuitively, the one-time pad completely hides the permutation, which then translates worst-case adversarial errors on $c$ into random errors on $\hat{c}$.

Unfortunately, the above construction is completely insecure under a CPA attack where the adversary can observe many codewords of chosen messages.

**Table 1.** Best known rates $R$ for unique decoding for different error models (rows) and error-tolerance $p$ (columns). *(1) is the Shannon bound* $R = 1 - H_2(p)$*, (2) is the GV bound* $R = 1 - H_2(2p)$*, (3) is the Zyablov bound for distance* $2p$*, (4) is the Blokh-Zyablov bound, and (5) is the Shannon bound. For rows 2-5, the rate drops to* 0 *for* $p > 0.25$*. Prior works for Row (4) include* [MPSW10, GHY20, SW25b, SW25a, LSW25]. *Rows 1 and 5 are known to be optimal for the given model.*

| **Model** | $p = 0.05$ | $p = 0.10$ | $p = 0.15$ | $p = 0.20$ |
|---|---|---|---|---|
| (1) Random | 0.713 | 0.531 | 0.390 | 0.278 |
| (2) Worst-Case – (Existential) | 0.531 | 0.278 | 0.118 | 0.029 |
| (3) Worst-Case – (Efficient) | 0.141 | 0.041 | 0.009 | $< 0.001$ |
| (4) Comp. Bounded: Prior Work | 0.415 | 0.233 | 0.132 | 0.073 |
| (5) Comp. Bounded: Our Result | 0.713 | 0.531 | 0.390 | 0.278 |

Eventually it can learn the one-time pad and entire permutation $\pi$ (e.g., an encoding of the all 0 message reveals the pad, and encodings of the $n$ unit vectors then fully reveal the permutation). One may be tempted to apply the usual trick of converting a one-time secure scheme into a many-time secure scheme by using a pseudorandom function (PRF) whose key is shared by the encoder and decoder. The encoder would choose a fresh random nonce $r$ each time and then use $PRF(r)$ to derive a fresh one-time pad for the one-time scheme. This would work if the decoder could reliably get $r$, but how can we securely transmit it in the face of errors, and prevent the adversary from removing it by strategically focusing its errors?

*CPA-Secure Secret-Key Codes.* To get around the above issues, our construction relies on a powerful recent cryptographic primitive called *pseudorandom codes (PRCs)* [CG24, GM24, GG25, AAC+25, CGG+26], originally introduced in the seemingly unrelated context of watermarking LLM outputs. A PRC is a symmetric-key or public-key encoding with two properties: (1) *robustness*: it can correctly decode from up to a $p$-fraction of adversarial errors, (2) *pseudorandomness*: no polynomial-time adversary can distinguish between the encoding of a chosen message and a uniformly random and independent string. We can consider CPA or CCA secure PRCs depending on whether the adversary has access to the encoding or also decoding oracles. The work of [CG24] constructed public-key PRCs under the sub-exponential LPN assumption, and the work of [GG25] did so under various "planted structure" assumptions. One downside is that these constructions can be broken in quasi-polynomial time. The recent work of [CGG+26] gave an alternate construction of symmetric-key PRCs with plausibly sub-exponential security under a "permuted codes" assumption, studied previously in the context of doubly efficient private information retrieval. We will rely on symmetric-key CPA-secure PRCs that can tolerate up to $p < 1/4$ errors, but we will only use them to encode small messages and hence will not care about the *rate* of the PRC.

Using such a PRC, we can construct a CPA-secure secret-key code that achieves Shannon capacity for up to a $p$ fraction of computationally bounded errors. The encoder and decoder share the secret key of a PRC along with a random permutation $\pi$. On each invocation, the encoder chooses a fresh random seed $s$ for a pseudorandom generator (PRG) $G$ that it expands into a long one-time pad $y = G(s)$. It encodes the seed $s$ with a PRC resulting in a small codeword $c_{PRC}$. As in Lipton's construction, it encodes the message with an optimal code for *random errors* that meets Shannon capacity yielding a codeword $c_{RE}$. Finally it permutes the bits of the tuple $(c_{PRC}, c_{RE} \oplus y)$ via the permutation $\pi$ to yield the final codeword $c$. The decoder gets some erroneous codeword $c'$, undoes the permutation to recover $(c'_{PRC}, z')$, decodes $c'_{PRC}$ to recover $s'$ and the corresponding $y' = G(s')$, $c'_{RE} = z' \oplus y'$, and finally decodes $c'_{RE}$ to recover the message.

The security analysis relies on the fact that, by the pseudorandomness of the PRC and the PRG security, CPA queries to the overall code generate responses that look uniformly random even given the permutation $\pi$. Therefore, the error pattern chosen by the adversary for the challenge codeword $c$ is computationally independent of $\pi$. This ensures that, when decoding $c$, we can guarantee:

- Since the overall errors are randomly scattered by the permutation $\pi$, the relative distance between $c'_{PRC}$ and $c_{PRC}$ is $\approx p$ and therefore the robustness of the PRC ensures that $c'_{PRC}$ correctly decodes to $s$.
- The error pattern on the codeword $c'_{RE} = z' \oplus G(s)$ is randomly permuted by $\pi$, and therefore the codeword correctly decodes to the original message by error-correction for random errors.

Furthermore the above construction preserves pseudorandomness and therefore yields CPA-secure secret-key PRCs that achieve Shannon capacity. We note that the above construction is similar to a transformation of [AAC+25] to amplify the rate of a PRC. However, the goal there is to achieve a rate that matches information-theoretic codes for worst-case errors, while here we match information-theoretic codes for random errors! In particular, we make use of the fact that the adversary cannot control the implicit error pattern on the underlying codeword $c_{RE}$ since it is scrambled by an unknown permutation $\pi$, and therefore resilience to random errors suffices.

*CCA-Secure Secret-Key Codes.* The above achieves CPA security. The recent work of [AAC+25] shows how to generically upgrade CPA-secure secret-key PRCs to CCA-secure ones while preserving the rate and error tolerance. Therefore, we can generically apply their transformation to achieve CCA-secure secret-key codes (and, in fact, PRCs) that achieve Shannon capacity for any $p < 1/4$ errors.

*Seeded Codes.* As mentioned earlier, CCA-secure secret key codes can trivially be converted into seeded codes by obfuscating the encoding and decoding procedures (with the hard-coded secret key) using ideal obfuscation and publishing the obfuscated program as the seed. Ideal obfuscation can then be instantiated heuristically using an indistinguishability obfuscator. Overall, this gives the first heuristic construction of seeded codes that achieve Shannon capacity for any $p < 1/4$ errors.

*Public-Key Codes.* As an intermediate primitive between symmetric-key and seeded codes, we also consider public-key codes, where the decoder has a secret key $\mathsf{sk}$ and the encoder has a corresponding public key $\mathsf{pk}$. We construct these from public-key PRCs while avoiding the use of ideal obfuscation that was needed for seeded codes. Let us first consider CPA security.

Our previous construction template, even if we were to instantiate it with public-key PRCs, would only yield a secret-key code since the encoder and decoder need to share a secret permutation $\pi$. Can we avoid this shared secret? We can think of $\pi$ as performing two distinct jobs: (1) firstly, it randomly permutes the errors on $c_{RE}$, translating worst-case errors to random errors, (2) secondly, it hides the positions that contain $c_{PRC}$, preventing the adversary from concentrating its errors there. We can perform the first job without a shared secret, by simply deriving the permutation to apply on $c_{RE}$ from the PRG seed $s$ encoded in the PRC. But we cannot do this for the second job since, without knowing where $c_{PRC}$ is first, we cannot hope to decode it. At the same time, we cannot put $c_{PRC}$ in any fixed location since then the adversary could concentrate its errors there.

Our solution is for the encoder to create many random PRC codewords, all encoding the same PRG seed $s$, and sprinkle these whole PRC codewords into random chunks of our overall codeword. This approach of hiding a small but crucial piece of information inside a much larger codeword via pseudorandom-looking encodings already appears in the work of Guruswami and Smith [GS16], and was further used in several follow-up works [SS21a,KSS19,SS21b,SS22, SS24a]. Our construction is inspired by this line of work.[6]

More concretely, we first encode the message with an optimal code for random errors that meets Shannon capacity yielding a codeword $c_{RE}$. We choose a PRG seed $s$ and expand it to derive $(\pi, y) = G(s)$ consisting of a permutation $\pi$ and a pad $s$. Let $\hat{c}_{RE} := \pi(c_{RE} \oplus y)$ denote the padded and permuted bits (abusing notation). We then create $t$ fresh PRC encodings of $s$, where $t$ can be small (e.g., security parameter). If each PRC codeword is of some small size $m$, we think of the $n$-bit codeword $\hat{c}_{RE}$ as consisting of $n/m$ chunks of $m$ bits each. We

[6] While the high-level paradigm is inspired by Guruswami and Smith [GS16] and subsequent follow-up works, our setting is different. In the Guruswami–Smith setting, the adversary is computationally weaker than the encoding and decoding procedures, so such hiding can be achieved without a secret key. In our setting, by contrast, the adversary is computationally stronger than the encoding and decoding procedures, which is why we rely on the cryptographic notion of pseudorandom codes. This distinction leads to different challenges in both the construction and the analysis.

choose a random subset of $t$ of these chunks at random and replace them with the corresponding PRC codewords while keeping the remaining chunks intact to derive our final codeword $c$. The decoder tries to decode each chunk one by one via the PRC decoding algorithm. If it succeeds to recover some $(\pi', y')$, it uses it to recover a candidate $c'_{RE}$, which it finally decodes via the code for random errors to recover the message. Overall, the decoding procedure may output a list of up to $n/m$ messages, one per chunk.

As a first step, we argue that this gives us a good *list-decodable code*, meaning that the correct message is likely to be in the list. We rely on the pseudorandomness of the PRC (and the PRG) to argue that the adversary does not learn anything about the permutation $\pi$ or the locations of the $t$ chosen chunks in the challenge codeword. Therefore, for any adversarial choice of $pn$ errors:

- With overwhelming probability at least one of the $t$ chosen chunks gets hit with at most $\approx pm$ errors and therefore decodes correctly.
- For that chunk, the corresponding candidate $c'_{RE}$ is hit with errors randomly permuted by $\pi$ and therefore decodes to the original message with overwhelming probability by error-correction for random errors.[7]

This gives us CPA-secure list-decoding for $p < 1/4$ errors achieving Shannon capacity, which is already interesting. However, in this range we would like to get unique decoding.

To get uniqueness, we need to ensure that there is only one valid candidate in the list. We rely on the techniques of [SW25a,LSW25], which show how to convert certain list-decodable codes into uniquely decodable codes using a form of correlation-intractable (CI) hashing, which can in turn be instantiated under standard crypto assumptions. The high level idea is to encode $(x, h(x))$ where $h$ is an appropriate CI hash function, and show that the adversary cannot find $x \neq x'$ where the encodings of $(x, h(x))$ and $(x', h(x'))$ are sufficiently close to possibly show up in the same list. Unfortunately, we cannot use that result as a black box. It operates in the setting where the underlying list-decodable code is a traditional deterministic linear code with some additional mild properties. However, our Shannon-rate list-decodable code is both randomized and non-linear. Nevertheless, we manage to show how to make this approach work, by going under the hood of the proof in [LSW25]. In particular, we show how to use the techniques of [LSW25] to achieve a stronger and more general form of correlation intractability that suffices for our application.

Lastly, we follow the work of [AAC+25] to convert CPA-secure public-key PRCs into CCA-secure ones in the Random Oracle model while preserving the rate and error-tolerance. It turns out that in the random oracle model, we can also achieve uniqueness more easily, allowing us to avoid the reliance on CI hashing.

*Public-Key List-Decodable Codes for $p < 1/2$.* In the above construction, we first construct CPA-secure list-decoding achieving Shannon capacity for any $p < 1/4$

[7] This includes the adversarial errors, as well as the small number of additional errors created when we replace some chunks of $\hat{c}_{RE}$ with PRC codewords.

errors. Ideally, if we only want list-decoding, we could go all the way to any $p < 1/2$. The restriction to $p < 1/4$ came from the underlying (low-rate) PRCs, which can only be robust to $p < 1/4$ errors. But we observe that the construction works just as well if we relax PRC robustness to only require list-decodability rather than unique decodability. So if we plug in (low-rate) PRCs that are list-decodable for any $p < 1/2$ errors then our overall construction achieves list-decoding at Shannon capacity for any $p < 1/2$ as well. We also show how to upgrade the resulting CPA-secure list-decodable codes to CCA-secure ones in the random oracle model via the same transformation as for unique decoding.

*Public-Key PRCs with High Error Tolerance.* The last missing component in the above public-key constructions (for both unique and list decoding) is a PRC that is list-decodable with high error-tolerance – at least up to $p < 1/4$ to get our optimal unique decoding result, and ideally all the way to $p < 1/2$ to also get our optimal list decoding result. For this part, we do not care about the *rate* of the PRCs, and the codeword can be polynomially larger than the message. We rely on the transformations above, which only use such PRCs to encode small messages, to reach Shannon capacity. Prior work [AAC+25] achieved unique decoding for any $p < 1/4$ in the secret-key setting, but in the public-key setting they only achieved this for much lower values of $p < 1/32$, and they did not consider list-decoding. We show how to get such list-decodable public-key PRCs up to the optimal $p < 1/2$ errors.

The previous works of [CG24, AAC+25] construct public-key *zero-bit PRCs* that have robustness for up to $p < 1/2$ errors. In a zero-bit PRC the encoding procedure does not take any message, and the decoding procedure only needs to detect whether the received value is close to a codeword or not. These satisfy *pseudorandomness*, where codewords look uniformly random even given the public key, and *robustness*, ensuring that an adversary given a public-key and a random codeword cannot induce a $p$ fraction of errors that cause decoding to fail to detect. They also satisfy a *soundness* (non-triviality) property, which says that most arbitrary strings are not detected as codewords – for any string $c$ chosen a-priori, decoding only detects with negligible probability over the random choice of the public/secret keys.

Our first step is to upgrade from a zero-bit PRC with error tolerance $p < 1/2$ to a list-decodable PRC with the same error tolerance $p$, but only for a polynomial-size message space (i.e., messages of logarithmic bit length). If the messages are values in $[q]$ for some polynomial $q$, then we choose $q$ independent public/secret key pairs for a zero-bit PRC. To encode the message $i \in [q]$ we sample a codeword using the $i$'th public-key. The decoder tries decoding with all $q$ secret keys and outputs the list of values $i \in [q]$ for which decoding detects. Robustness of the underlying zero-bit PRC ensures that the correct message is in the list. We use soundness to argue that the list size $\ell$ cannot be too large, and is much smaller than the full message space $[q]$. This is because the probability of any string being detected by a specific subset of $\ell$ codes is $\varepsilon^{\ell}$ for a negligible soundness error $\varepsilon$ and then we can do a union bound over all such sets and all strings to argue that no string can be in more than $\ell$ lists.

Our next step is to upgrade from a list-decodable PRC with error tolerance $p$ for a polynomial-size message space $q$ into one for arbitrary exponential-size message space (i.e., arbitrary polynomial bit-length messages). We do so by relying on *list-recoverable codes* over a polynomial alphabet $[q]$. Such codes can decode by being given small input-lists of size $\ell \ll q$ for each alphabet symbol of the codeword, and are guaranteed to recover a polynomial-size output-list that contains the correct message as long as sufficiently large fraction (e.g., any constant fraction) of the input-lists contain the correct codeword symbol. We first encode the message with a list-recoverable code and then encode each codeword symbol in $[q]$ with the previously constructed PRC. If the overall error rate is some constant $p < 1/2$ then a constant fraction of small PRC codewords will have error-rate bounded by some constant $p' < 1/2$ and PRC decoding will ensure that the correct codeword symbol appears in the corresponding lists, allowing the decoding of the list-recoverable code to succeed.

## Papers Organization

In Sect. 3 we give general notations and formally define secret-key and public-key codes as well as CPA and CCA security. In Sect. 4 we state and prove our result for secret-key codes. In Sect. 6 we show how to construct list-decodable codes from zero-bit codes. Due to space limitation, we defer the results on public-key CPA and CCA codes to the full version of this paper.

## 3 Preliminaries

*Notation.* We use $\Delta(x_0, x_1)$ to refer to the Hamming distance between $x_0 \in \{0,1\}^n$ and $x_1 \in \{0,1\}^n$ and $\delta(x_0, x_1) = \Delta(x_0, x_1)/n$ to be the relative hamming distance. We omit the second argument ($\Delta(x), \delta(x)$) to refer to the hamming *weight* of a single string (i.e. hamming distance to $0^n$). For a permutation $\pi : [n] \rightarrow [n]$ and a string $x = (x_1, \dots x_n) \in \{0,1\}^n$, we abuse notation and let $\pi(x)$ denote a permutation on the bits of $(x_{\pi(1)}, \dots, x_{\pi(n)})$. For a set $S$, let $x \leftarrow S$ denote that $x$ was drawn uniformly from $S$.

### 3.1 Standard Error-Correcting Codes

**Definition 3.1 (Standard Error-Correcting Codes).** *A standard error-correcting code on message space* $\{0,1\}^k$ *and codeword space* $\{0,1\}^n$ *is a set of deterministic algorithms* ($\mathsf{Enc}, \mathsf{Dec}$) *with the following syntax:*

- $\mathsf{Enc}(x) \rightarrow c$*: On input message* $x \in \{0,1\}^k$*, the encoding algorithm outputs codeword* $c$*.*
- $\mathsf{Dec}(c') \rightarrow x$*: On input string* $c' \in \{0,1\}^n$*, the decoding algorithm outputs a message* $x$ *(or* $\perp$*).*

- **Distance:** *We define the distance of a code as the minimum relative hamming distance between two codewords*

$$\min_{x \neq x' \in \{0,1\}^k} \delta(\mathsf{Enc}(x), \mathsf{Enc}(x')).$$

- **Rate:** *We measure the rate $R$ of the code as the ratio $\frac{k}{n}$.*

### 3.1.1 List-Decodable and List-Recoverable Codes

**Definition 3.2 (List-Decodable Codes** [Eli57, Woz58]**).** *For parameters $p \in [0, 1/2), L \in \mathbb{N}$, we say a code $\Pi_{\mathsf{code}}$ with message space $\{0,1\}^k$ and codeword space $\{0,1\}^n$ is $(p, L)$ list-decodable if there exists additional algorithm* ListDec*:*

- $\mathsf{ListDec}(c') \to T$ *On input string $c' \in \{0,1\}^n$, the list decoding algorithm outputs a list $T$ of messages which satisfy the following properties:*
  - *The size of the output list $|T| \leq L$.*
  - *For any message $m$, if there exists codeword $c \in \{0,1\}^n$ such that $\delta(c', c) \leq p$, then $m \in T$.*

Observe that unique decoding is the special case of list decoding with list size $L = 1$, in which there exists at most one codeword within relative distance $p$ of any received word.

**Definition 3.3 (List-Recoverable Codes** [GI01, GS98]**).** *For parameters $\alpha \in [0, 1], \ell, L \in \mathbb{N}$, we say a code $\Pi_{\mathsf{code}} = (\mathsf{Enc}, \mathsf{ListRec})$, such that $\mathsf{Enc} : \{0,1\}^k \to [q]^n$ is $(\alpha, \ell, L)$ list-recoverable if the algorithm* ListRec *satisfies the following:*

- $\mathsf{ListRec}(S_1, \cdots, S_n) \to T$: *On input sets $S_i \subseteq [q]$ such that $|S_i| \leq \ell$ for each index $i \in [n]$, the list recovery algorithm outputs a list $T$ of messages which satisfy the following properties:*
  - *The size of the output list $|T| \leq L$.*
  - *The list $T$ contains all messages $m \in \{0,1\}^k$, such that $\Pr_{i \leftarrow [n]}[\mathsf{Enc}(m)_i \in S_i] \geq \alpha$.*

We note that list-recoverable codes are a strict generalization of list-decodable codes (which correspond to the special case of $\ell = 1$).

### 3.1.2 Codes for Permuted Errors

In our constructions we require codes that recover from binary symmetric noise (BSC), that approach the Shannon capacity $R(p) = 1 - H(p)$. In fact, we require a slightly stronger property in which the decoding recovers from permuted errors (not just random and independent errors). We will use the following theorem taken from [SS22] that was used in previous results. On a high level, the code below is constructed using standard code concatenation where the outer code is a linear code with distance $\varepsilon$ and rate $1 - \varepsilon$, and the inner code is a BSC code found in brute force search. The main observation is that random independent noise and randomly permuted fixed noise string are locally statistically close, which implies that the small inner codewords recover from permuted errors.

**Theorem 3.4 (Codes for permuted errors,** [Smi07,GS16,SS21a,KSS19, SS22]**).** *Let $R(p) = 1 - H(p)$. For every constant $0 \le p < \frac{1}{2}$, and every sufficiently small constant $\varepsilon > 0$, there exists functions $\mathsf{Enc}_{\mathsf{BSC}} : \{0,1\}^{k=(R(p)-\varepsilon)\cdot n} \rightarrow \{0,1\}^n$, $\mathsf{Dec}_{\mathsf{BSC}} : \{0,1\}^n \rightarrow \{0,1\}^k$ such that:*

- *For every $m \in \{0,1\}^k$, and error pattern $e \in \{0,1\}^n$, such that $\delta(e) < p$, let $\pi : [n] \rightarrow [n]$ be a random and independent permutation,*

$$\Pr[\mathsf{Dec}_{\mathsf{BSC}}(\mathsf{Enc}_{\mathsf{BSC}}(m) + \pi(e)) = m] > 1 - 2^{-\Omega(n^{0.1})}$$

  *where the probability is taken over the random choice of $\pi$ from the set of all possible permutations.*
- $(\mathsf{Enc}_{\mathsf{BSC}}, \mathsf{Dec}_{\mathsf{BSC}})$ *are explicit.*
- $(\mathsf{Enc}_{\mathsf{BSC}}, \mathsf{Dec}_{\mathsf{BSC}})$ *has "monotone decoding" meaning that for every $m \in \{0,1\}^k$ and every $e, e' \in \{0,1\}^n$ such that for every $i \in [n]$, $e_i \le e'_i$,*

$$\mathsf{Dec}_{\mathsf{BSC}}(\mathsf{Enc}_{\mathsf{BSC}}(m) \oplus e') = m \Rightarrow \mathsf{Dec}_{\mathsf{BSC}}(\mathsf{Enc}_{\mathsf{BSC}}(m) \oplus e) = m.$$

## 3.2 Secret-Key and Public-Key Codes, with CPA and CCA Security

We begin by formalizing the notion of secret-key codes with CPA security, which will serve as the basic primitive in our constructions.

We use slightly different definitions and formulations than those in [AAC+25]. In particular, the notion of robustness defined in [AAC+25], termed *adaptive robustness*, implies our CPA notion of robustness defined below. In the secret-key setting these two notions are equivalent. However, this equivalence does not extend to the public-key setting (we elaborate on this after defining public-key codes).

**Definition 3.5 (CPA Secret Key Codes).** *A secret key (computational) code $\Pi_{\mathsf{code}}$ on message space $\{0,1\}^k$ and codeword space $\{0,1\}^n$ for $n = n(\lambda)$ is a set of efficient algorithms* $(\mathsf{Setup}, \mathsf{Enc}, \mathsf{Dec})$ *with the following syntax:*

- $\mathsf{Setup}(1^\lambda) \rightarrow \mathsf{sk}$*: On input security parameter $\lambda$, the setup algorithm outputs a secret key* $\mathsf{sk}$.
- $\mathsf{Enc}(\mathsf{sk}, x) \rightarrow c$*: On input secret key* $\mathsf{sk}$ *and message $x \in \{0,1\}^k$, the encoding algorithm samples a codeword $c$.*
- $\mathsf{Dec}(\mathsf{sk}, c') \rightarrow x$*: On input secret key* $\mathsf{sk}$ *and string $c' \in \{0,1\}^n$, the decoding algorithm outputs a message $x$.*

*The rate of the code is defined to be $R = k/n$. If the scheme can only encode a singular message (i.e. $k = 0$), then we call it a* **zero-bit** *code,*[8] *and similarly, if it can encode one bit of information (i.e. $k = 1$), then we call it a* **one-bit** *code. We consider the following properties for $\Pi_{\mathsf{code}}$:*

[8] To avoid trivial constructions, zero-bit codes must additionally satisfy a soundness property (see Sect. 6).

- **CPA $p$-Robustness:** *For a security parameter $\lambda \in \mathbb{N}$, the CPA $p$-robustness* $\mathsf{ExptAR}(\mathcal{A}, \lambda)$ *for some $p = p(\lambda)$ between an efficient adversary $\mathcal{A}$ and challenger is as follows:*
  1. *On input security parameter $1^\lambda$, the challenger samples* $\mathsf{sk} \leftarrow \mathsf{Setup}(1^\lambda)$. *The challenger prepares encoding oracle* $\mathcal{O}_E = \mathsf{Enc}(\mathsf{sk}, \cdot)$ *for the adversary.*
  2. *The adversary $\mathcal{A}^{\mathcal{O}_E}$ submits a challenge $x \in \{0,1\}^k$. The challenger samples* $c \leftarrow \mathsf{Enc}(\mathsf{sk}, x)$ *and sends $c$ to $\mathcal{A}^{\mathcal{O}_E}$.*
  3. *The adversary $\mathcal{A}^{\mathcal{O}_E}$ submits a string $c'$. The output of the experiment is 1 iff $\delta(c', c) \leq p$ and* $\mathsf{Dec}(\mathsf{sk}, c') \neq x$ *(and 0 otherwise).*

  *We say a code $\Pi_{\mathsf{PRC}}$ is CPA $p$-robust if for all efficient adversaries $\mathcal{A}$, there exists* $\mathsf{negl}(\cdot)$ *such that for all $\lambda \in \mathbb{N}$*

$$\Pr[\mathsf{ExptAR}(\mathcal{A}, \lambda)] = \mathsf{negl}(\lambda).$$

- **CPA Pseudorandomness:** *For a security parameter $\lambda \in \mathbb{N}$, the pseudorandomness experiment* $\mathsf{ExptPR}^{(b)}(\mathcal{A}, \lambda)$ *between an efficient adversary $\mathcal{A}$ and challenger is as follows:*
  1. *On input security parameter $1^\lambda$, the challenger samples* $\mathsf{sk} \leftarrow \mathsf{Setup}(1^\lambda)$. *The challenger prepares encoding oracle* $\mathcal{O}_E = \mathsf{Enc}(\mathsf{sk}, \cdot)$ *for the adversary.*
  2. *The adversary $\mathcal{A}^{\mathcal{O}_E}$ submits a challenge $x \in \{0,1\}^k$. If $b = 0$, the challenger samples* $c \leftarrow \mathsf{Enc}(\mathsf{sk}, x)$. *If $b = 1$, the challenger samples $c \leftarrow \{0,1\}^n$. In either case, the challenger sends $c$ to $\mathcal{A}^{\mathcal{O}_E}$.*
  3. *The adversary $\mathcal{A}^{\mathcal{O}_E}$ submits a guess bit $b'$, which is the output of the experiment.*

  *We say a code $\Pi_{\mathsf{code}}$ is pseudorandom if for all efficient adversaries $\mathcal{A}$, there exists* $\mathsf{negl}(\cdot)$ *such that for all $\lambda \in \mathbb{N}$*

$$\left|\Pr[\mathsf{ExptPR}^{(0)}(\mathcal{A}, \lambda)] - \Pr[\mathsf{ExptPR}^{(1)}(\mathcal{A}, \lambda)]\right| = \mathsf{negl}(\lambda).$$

*Public Key Codes and CPA p-Simulatable Decoding.*

**Definition 3.6 (Public Key Codes).** *For (computational) codes in the public key setting, we adjust the syntax and security of the secret key codes as follows:*

- *The setup algorithm* $\mathsf{Setup}(1^\lambda)$ *outputs a public key* $\mathsf{pk}$ *in addition to* $\mathsf{sk}$.
- *The encoding algorithm* $\mathsf{Enc}$ *takes in* $\mathsf{pk}$ *instead of* $\mathsf{sk}$.
- *In step* (1) *of both the pseudorandomness and robustness games, the adversary additionally receives public key* $\mathsf{pk}$ *(rather than access to an encoding oracle).*

Beyond the 'standard' definition of public key computational codes (with pseudorandomness and robustness) considered above, we also consider the following property. This will be needed to achieve CCA security in the public key setting. Informally, this property allows for an efficient simulator without access to the decoding key the ability to simulate decoding errors. We defer the formal definition of this property to the full version of this paper.

*Codes with CCA Security*

**Definition 3.7 (Chosen Codeword Attack (CCA) Security).** *For both public and secret key codes, we also consider a stronger notion of CCA security - in other words security relative to a p-decoding oracle*[9]. *This modifies the security games as follows:*

- *In Step* (1) *of the robustness game, the challenger additionally prepares decoding oracle* $\mathcal{O}_D = \mathsf{Dec}(\mathsf{sk}, \cdot)$. *which the adversary has access to for the remainder of the experiment.*
- *In Step* (1) *of the pseudorandomness game, the challenger once again prepares decoding oracle* $\mathcal{O}_D = \mathsf{Dec}(\mathsf{sk}, \cdot)$ *for the adversary, which the adversary has access to until it submits a challenge in Step* (2). *This is then replaced with a punctured decoding oracle*

$$\mathcal{O}_{D^*}(c') = \begin{cases} x & \text{if } \delta(c,c') \leq p \\ \mathsf{Dec}(\mathsf{sk}, c') & \text{otherwise} \end{cases}$$

*which the adversary has access to for the remainder of the experiment.*

*Secret-Key/Public-Key CPA/CCA List-Decodable Codes*

**Definition 3.8 (List-Decodable Computational Codes).** *Analogous to the traditional notion of list-decodable codes, we consider a relaxation of (both public and secret key) codes to the list decoding setting (enabling a larger decoding/robustness radius). This modifies the syntax and security of Definition 3.5 and Definition 3.7 as follows:*

- *There exists efficient algorithm* $\mathsf{ListDec}(\mathsf{sk}, c') \to T$, *which outputs a list* $T$ *of messages.*
- *In the CPA p-robustness game, the output of the experiment is* 1 *iff* $\delta(c', c) \leq p$ *and* $x \notin \mathsf{ListDec}(\mathsf{sk}, c')$.
- *In the CPA p-simulatable decoding game, when* $b = 0$, *the challenger outputs* 1 *iff* $x \in \mathsf{ListDec}(\mathsf{sk}, c')$ *and* 0 *otherwise.*
- *When considering CCA security Definition 3.7, the decoding oracle and punctured decoding oracle are replaced with their list-decoding variants:*

$$\mathcal{O}_D = \mathsf{ListDec}(\mathsf{sk}, \cdot) \quad , \quad \mathcal{O}_{D^*} = \begin{cases} \mathsf{ListDec}(\mathsf{sk}, c') \cup \{x\} & \text{if } \delta(c,c') \leq p \\ \mathsf{ListDec}(\mathsf{sk}, c') & \text{otherwise} \end{cases}$$

*For both CPA security and CCA security, we say that the code is* $(p, L)$*-robust if in addition the robustness definition above it holds that size of the list is at most* $L$.

[9] While syntactically this constant $p$ could differ from the $p$ in $p$-robustness, for our purposes we will only consider cases where these are equal.

### 3.2.1 Known Results for Pseudorandom Codes

We make use of the following prior constructions of pseudorandom codes.

**Theorem 3.9 (Public-key CPA zero-bit codes, [AAC+25]).** *Assuming* learning parity with noise (LPN) *with some constant noise rate is hard for all adversaries running in time* $2^{O(\sqrt{n})}$*:*

- *For every constant* $0 \leq p < 1/2$ *there exists a public-key CPA zero-bit code that is pseudorandom and p-robust.*
- *For every constant* $0 \leq p < 1/4$ *there exists a public-key CPA one-bit code that is pseudorandom and p-robust.*

*Moreover, both codes satisfy p-simulatable decoding.*

We note that the prior result of [AAC+25] does not state the simulatable decoding property explicitly, but their notion of adaptive-robustness implies it.

**Theorem 3.10 (Secret-key CPA zero-bit codes, [CGG+26]).** *Assuming the* "permuted codes" assumption [BHMW21,BW21,CGG+26] *the following holds:*

- *For every constant* $0 \leq p < 1/2$ *there exists a secret-key CPA zero-bit code that is pseudorandom and p-robust.*
- *For every constant* $0 \leq p < 1/4$ *there exists a secret-key CPA one-bit code that is pseudorandom and p-robust.*

The "permuted codes" assumption in its full generality says that some security property holds for any linear code with sufficiently large dual distance. To get the above, we need it to hold for some codes that are efficiently list-decodable for $p < 1/2$ errors or efficiently uniquely decodable for $p < 1/4$ errors respectively.

*Upgrading the Message Domain Size for Secret-Key CPA Codes.* The following result from [AAC+25] showed how to increase the domain size of the code, and preserve robustness. Here, we leave the rate unspecified and allow it to be arbitrarily poor, as long as the codeword length is polynomial size.

**Theorem 3.11 (From one-bit codes to many-bit codes, [AAC+25]).** *Let* $0 < p, \varepsilon$ *be constants such that* $p + \varepsilon < 1/4$ *and let* $\lambda \in \mathbb{N}$ *be the security parameter. Given a secret-key one-bit CPA code* $\Pi$ *that is pseudorandom and* $(p+\varepsilon)$*-robust. Then there exists a CPA code* $\Pi' = (\mathsf{Enc}, \mathsf{Dec})$ *that is pseudorandom and p-robust such that* $\Pi'.\mathsf{Enc} : \{0,1\}^\lambda \to \{0,1\}^{m(\lambda)}$ *for* $m \in \mathsf{poly}$.

*Upgrading CPA Secure Codes to CCA Secure Codes.* We will make use of the following theorem from [AAC+25] that showed how to upgrade a secret key CPA pseudorandom code into a secret key CCA pseudorandom code, we will make use of this transformation.

**Theorem 3.12 (From secret key CPA codes to CCA codes, [AAC+25]).** *Given a secret-key CPA code* $\Pi$ *that is pseudorandom and p-robust with rate R. Then for any constant* $0 < \varepsilon$*, there exists a secret-key CCA code* $\Pi'$ *that is pseudorandom and p-robust with rate* $R' = R - \varepsilon$.

## 4 Shannon-Rate Secret Key Codes

In this section we show a simple transformation that takes a one-bit CPA secret-key pseudorandom code with $p < 1/4$-robustness, and an arbitrarily poor rate, and outputs a CCA secret-key code for arbitrary length messages with $p$-robustness and the optimal Shannon rate $1 - H(p) - \varepsilon$.

**Theorem 4.1.** *Let $p, \varepsilon > 0$ be constants such that $p < 1/4$. Suppose there exists a* one-bit *secret-key CPA code that is pseudorandom and $(p + \varepsilon)$-robust. Then there exists a secret-key CCA code that is pseudorandom and p-robust for arbitrary length messges with rate $R = 1 - H(p) - \varepsilon$.*

Secret-key one-bit CPA pseudorandom codes with constant robustness can be obtained from several known constructions. In particular, such codes are known to exist assuming sub-exponential *learning parity with noise (LPN)* assumption [CG24, AAC+25], or a *permuted codes assumption* (for a code with error tolerance $p$) introduced in [CGG+26]. Applying Theorem 4.1 to any such construction immediately yields secret-key CCA-secure pseudorandom codes that are $p$-robust and achieve rate $1 - H(p) - \varepsilon$, matching the Shannon capacity up to an arbitrarily small loss.

*Construction.* The proof for the above theorem is given below. Note that by Theorem 3.12 any CPA secure pseudorandom code can be generically transformed into a CCA secure pseudorandom code with essentially the same rate. Thus, in the following construction we start by presenting a CPA secure code with a rate that matches the Shannon bound.

**Construction 4.2.** Let $\lambda \in \mathbb{N}$ be a security parameter and let $0 < p, \alpha$ be constants such that $p + \alpha < 1/4$, and let $m, n \in \mathsf{poly}(\lambda)$. We now describe the ingredients:

- Let $\Pi_{\mathsf{PRC}} = (\mathsf{Setup}, \mathsf{Enc}, \mathsf{Dec})$ be a $(p + \alpha)$-robust secret key pseudorandom code from $\{0,1\}^\lambda$ to $\{0,1\}^m$.
- Let $\Pi_{\mathsf{BSC}} = (\mathsf{Enc}, \mathsf{Dec})$ be a code from $\{0,1\}^k$ to $\{0,1\}^n$ that decodes from permuted errors of relative weight $p + \alpha$ (see Theorem 3.4).
- Let $\mathsf{PRG}$ be a pseudorandom generator with seed length $\lambda$ and output in $\{0,1\}^n$.

We now describe the new code $\Pi = (\mathsf{Setup}, \mathsf{Enc}, \mathsf{Dec})$:

- $\mathsf{Setup}(1^\lambda) \to \mathsf{sk}$: On input security parameter $\lambda$, the setup algorithm simply runs $\mathsf{sk}_{\mathsf{PRC}} \leftarrow \Pi_{\mathsf{PRC}}.\mathsf{Setup}(1^\lambda)$ and samples two random permutations $\pi : [n+m] \to [n+m]$, and $\pi_d : [n] \to [n]$ and outputs $\mathsf{sk} = (\mathsf{sk}_{\mathsf{PRC}}, \pi, \pi_d)$.
- $\mathsf{Enc}(\mathsf{sk}, x) \to c$: On input secret key $\mathsf{sk} = (\mathsf{sk}_{\mathsf{PRC}}, \pi, \pi_d)$ and message $x \in \{0,1\}^k$, the encoding algorithms computes the following:
  - Sample PRG seed $s \leftarrow \{0,1\}^\lambda$, and compute $w = \mathsf{PRG}(s)$.
  - Compute $c_{\mathsf{PRC}} \leftarrow \Pi_{\mathsf{PRC}}.\mathsf{Enc}(s)$.
  - Compute encoding of the message $c_{\mathsf{BSC}} = \Pi_{\mathsf{BSC}}.\mathsf{Enc}(x)$.

  - Set $z = (w \oplus c_{\mathsf{BSC}})$, and $y = (v :- \pi_d(z), c_{\mathsf{PRC}})$.
  - Output $c = \pi(y)$.
- $\mathsf{Dec}(\mathsf{sk}, c') \to x'$: On input secret key $\mathsf{sk} = (\mathsf{sk}_{\mathsf{PRC}}, \pi, \pi_d)$ and possibly noisy codeword $c'$, the decoding algorithm computes the following:
  - Unpermute: $y' = \pi^{-1}(c')$, parse $y' = (v', c'_{\mathsf{PRC}})$ and compute $z' = \pi_d^{-1}(v')$.
  - Compute $s' = \Pi_{\mathsf{PRC}}.\mathsf{Dec}(c'_{\mathsf{PRC}})$.
  - Compute $w' = \mathsf{PRG}(s')$ and $c'_{\mathsf{BSC}} = w' \oplus z'$.
  - Output $x' = \Pi_{\mathsf{BSC}}.\mathsf{Dec}(c'_{\mathsf{BSC}})$.

The following is our technical lemma that argues the correctness of the above construction.

**Lemma 4.3 (Robustness, pseudorandomness and rate for the construction).** *Let $0 < p, \alpha$ be constants with $p + \alpha < 1/4$. Assume the ingredients in Construction 4.2. Then the code $\Pi$ defined in Construction 4.2 is a CPA pseudorandom and $p$-robust with rate $R = k/(n+m)$.*

The proof for Lemma 4.3 is given in Sect. 4.1, but first we prove Theorem 4.1.

*Proof (Theorem 4.1).* For constants $0 < p, \varepsilon$ such that $p < 1/4$. By assumption we are given a one-bit CPA secret-key pseudorandom code. For any constant $\varepsilon' < \varepsilon$ applying Theorem 3.11, we obtain a secret-key CPA pseudorandom code $\Pi_{\mathsf{PRC}}$ from $\lambda$ bits to $m(\lambda)$ bits that is $(p + \varepsilon')$-robust.

Let $0 < \alpha \leq \varepsilon'$ be a sufficiently small constant such that

$$1 - H(p+\alpha) - \alpha \geq 1 - H(p) - \varepsilon/2.$$

Note that since $\alpha < \varepsilon'$, $\Pi_{\mathsf{PRC}}$ is also $(p+\alpha)$-robust. Let $\Pi_{\mathsf{BSC}}$ be the code guaranteed in Theorem 3.4 from $k$ bits to $n$ bits with rate $1 - H(p+\alpha) - \alpha$, and let $k$ and $n$ to be sufficiently large such that $m < n \cdot (\varepsilon/3)$. Let $\Pi$ be the code defined in Construction 4.2 using ingredient $\Pi_{\mathsf{PRC}}$, $\Pi_{\mathsf{BSC}}$ and a pseudorandom generator $\mathsf{PRG}$ (which is implied by one way functions and hence $\Pi_{\mathsf{PRC}}$). By Lemma 4.3 it follows that the code $\Pi$ is CPA $p$-robust and pseudorandom with rate

$$R = \tfrac{k}{n+m} \geq \tfrac{k}{n \cdot (1+\varepsilon/3)} \geq \tfrac{k}{n} \cdot (1 - \varepsilon/3)$$
$$\geq (1 - H(p) - \varepsilon/2) \cdot (1 - \varepsilon/3) \geq 1 - H(p) - \varepsilon \cdot 5/6$$

Finally, by Theorem 3.12 it follows that there exists a code $\Pi'$ that is CCA $p$-robust and pseudorandom with rate $1 - H(p) - \varepsilon$ as desired.

## 4.1 Proof of Lemma 4.3

We make use of the following notation. In Construction 4.2, the secret key is $\mathsf{sk} = (\mathsf{sk}_{\mathsf{PRC}}, \pi, \pi_d)$ where $\pi_d$ and $\pi$ are independent uniformly random permutations, where $\pi_d$ is a permutation on $[n]$ and $\pi$ is permutation on $[N]$ where $N := n + m$ is the codeword size of $\Pi$.

**Rate.** It follows immediately by construction that the code has rate $R = k/N = k/(n+m)$ as desired.

**The Code is Pseudorandom.** We now prove the pseudorandom property of the code. In fact, we prove something mildly stronger which we will make use of when we prove the robustness property. For a security parameter $\lambda \in \mathbb{N}$ and an efficient adversary $\mathcal{A}$, we define the follows experiment:

$\mathsf{StrongExptPR}^{(b)}(\mathcal{A}, \lambda)$

1. On input security parameter $1^\lambda$, the challenger samples $\mathsf{sk} = (\mathsf{sk}_{\mathsf{PRC}}, \pi, \pi_d) \leftarrow \mathsf{Setup}(1^\lambda)$. The challenger prepares encoding oracle $\mathcal{O}_E = \Pi.\mathsf{Enc}(\mathsf{sk}, \cdot)$ for the adversary.
2. The adversary $\mathcal{A}^{\mathcal{O}_E}$ submits a challenge $x \in \{0,1\}^k$. If $b = 0$, the challenger samples $c \leftarrow \Pi.\mathsf{Enc}(\mathsf{sk}, x)$. If $b = 1$, the challenger samples $c \leftarrow \{0,1\}^n$. In either case, the challenger sends $c$ with $\pi$ and $\pi_d$ to $\mathcal{A}^{\mathcal{O}_E}$.
3. The adversary $\mathcal{A}^{\mathcal{O}_E}$ submits a guess bit $b'$, which is the output of the experiment.

We prove that

**Claim 1.** $\left|\Pr[\mathsf{StrongExptPR}^{(0)}(\mathcal{A}, \lambda)] - \Pr[\mathsf{StrongExptPR}^{(1)}(\mathcal{A}, \lambda)]\right| \leq \mathsf{negl}(\lambda)$

Note that this implies the pseudorandom property since

$$\begin{aligned} &\left|\Pr[\mathsf{ExptPR}^{(0)}(\mathcal{A}, \lambda)] - \Pr[\mathsf{ExptPR}^{(1)}(\mathcal{A}, \lambda)]\right| \\ \leq &\left|\Pr[\mathsf{StrongExptPR}^{(0)}(\mathcal{A}, \lambda)] - \Pr[\mathsf{StrongExptPR}^{(1)}(\mathcal{A}, \lambda)]\right|. \end{aligned}$$

where $\mathsf{ExptPR}^{(b)}(\mathcal{A}, \lambda)$ is the standard pseudorandom experiment defined in Definition 3.5. That is, StrongExptPR implies that the pseudorandom property should hold even when the adversary is given access to $\pi$ and $\pi_d$ as an input.

*Proof (Claim 1).* Consider the following simple hybrid

$H_0$: Same as $\mathsf{StrongExptPR}^{(0)}(\mathcal{A}, \lambda)$, except replace $c_{\mathsf{PRC}} = \Pi_{\mathsf{PRC}}.\mathsf{Enc}(s)$ by a truly uniform string $u \leftarrow \{0,1\}^m$ in every encoding query. By (a straightforward hybrid over) pseudorandomness of $\Pi_{\mathsf{PRC}}$, and since $\mathsf{PRG}(s)$ is efficiently computable given $s$,

$$\left|\Pr[\mathsf{StrongExptPR}^{(0)}(\mathcal{A}, \lambda)] - \Pr[H_0]\right| \leq \mathsf{negl}(\lambda).$$

$H_1$: Same as $H_0$, except replace $\mathsf{PRG}(s)$ by a truly uniform $w \leftarrow \{0,1\}^n$ and note that this means that $H_1$ is identical to $\mathsf{StrongExptPR}^{(1)}(\mathcal{A}, \lambda)$. By the security of the PRG,

$$\left|\Pr[H_0] - \Pr[H_1]\right| \leq \mathsf{negl}(\lambda).$$

The above implies that

$$\left|\Pr[\mathsf{StrongExptPR}^{(0)}(\mathcal{A},\lambda)] - \Pr[\mathsf{StrongExptPR}^{(1)}(\mathcal{A},\lambda)]\right| = \mathsf{negl}(\lambda),$$

which concludes the proof.

**The Code is $p$-Robust.**
For fixed security parameter $\lambda \in \mathbb{N}$ and efficient adversary $\mathcal{A}$ let $\mathsf{ExptAR} := \mathsf{ExptAR}(\mathcal{A},\lambda)$ denote the robustness experiment as defined in Definition 3.5. That is,

$\mathsf{ExptAR}$

1. On input security parameter $1^\lambda$, the challenger samples $\mathsf{sk} \leftarrow \mathsf{Setup}(1^\lambda)$. The challenger prepares encoding oracle $\mathcal{O}_E = \mathsf{Enc}(\mathsf{sk},\cdot)$ for the adversary.
2. The adversary $\mathcal{A}^{\mathcal{O}_E}$ submits a challenge $x \in \{0,1\}^k$. The challenger samples $c \leftarrow \mathsf{Enc}(\mathsf{sk},x)$ and sends $c$ to $\mathcal{A}^{\mathcal{O}_E}$.
3. The adversary $\mathcal{A}^{\mathcal{O}_E}$ submits a string $c'$. The output of the experiment is 1 iff $\delta(c',c) \le p$ and $\mathsf{Dec}(\mathsf{sk},c') \ne x$ (and 0 otherwise).

We now define an alternative decoding experiment that depends only on the error pattern induced and the permutations.

*Alternative Decoding Predicate.* For a message $x$, permutations $\pi, \pi_d$, and an error pattern $e$, define $f(x,\pi,\pi_d,e) = 1$ if and only if the following conditions hold for $e^\pi := \pi^{-1}(e) = (e_d, e_c) \in \{0,1\}^n \times \{0,1\}^m$ :

$$\delta(e_d) \le p+\alpha \text{ and } \delta(e_c) \le p+\alpha \text{ and } \Pi_{\mathsf{BSC}}.\mathsf{Dec}\left(\Pi_{\mathsf{BSC}}.\mathsf{Enc}(x) \oplus \pi_d^{-1}(e_d)\right) = x.$$

Otherwise, define $f(x,\pi,\pi_d,e) = 0$.

We now define a new decoding experiment $\mathsf{Exp}^f$ that uses the predicate $f$. Specifically,

$\mathsf{Exp}^f$:

1. On input security parameter $1^\lambda$, the challenger samples $\mathsf{sk} = (\mathsf{sk}_{\mathsf{PRC}}, \pi, \pi_d) \leftarrow \mathsf{Setup}(1^\lambda)$. The challenger prepares encoding oracle $\mathcal{O}_E = \mathsf{Enc}(\mathsf{sk},\cdot)$ for the adversary.
2. The adversary $\mathcal{A}^{\mathcal{O}_E}$ submits a challenge $x \in \{0,1\}^k$. The challenger samples $c \leftarrow \mathsf{Enc}(\mathsf{sk},x)$ and sends $c$ to $\mathcal{A}^{\mathcal{O}_E}$.
3. The adversary $\mathcal{A}^{\mathcal{O}_E}$ submits a string $c'$. The output of the experiment is 1 iff $\delta(c',c) \le p$ and
$$f(x,\pi,\pi_d, e := c \oplus c') \ne 1.$$

Finally, consider the experiment $\mathsf{Exp}^{f,ps}$: Define identically to $Exp^f$, but where the oracle $\mathcal{O}_E$ returns random strings (instead of codewords) and the challenge $c$ is uniformly sampled. That is,

$\mathsf{Exp}^{f,ps}$:

1. On input security parameter $1^\lambda$, the challenger samples $\mathsf{sk} = (\mathsf{sk}_{\mathsf{PRC}}, \pi, \pi_d) \leftarrow \mathsf{Setup}(1^\lambda)$. The challenger prepares encoding oracle $\mathcal{O}_E$ that when called returns uniform random strings of size $N$.
2. The adversary $\mathcal{A}^{\mathcal{O}_E}$ submits a challenge $x \in \{0,1\}^k$. The challenger samples $c \leftarrow \{0,1\}^N$ and sends $c$ to $\mathcal{A}^{\mathcal{O}_E}$.
3. The adversary $\mathcal{A}^{\mathcal{O}_E}$ submits a string $c'$. The output of the experiment is 1 iff $\delta(c', c) \leq p$ and

$$f(x, \pi, \pi_d, e := c \oplus c') \neq 1.$$

The proof for robustness is immediate from the following claims:

**Claim 2.** $\Pr[\mathsf{Exp}^f] \geq \Pr[\mathsf{ExptAR}] - \mathsf{negl}(\lambda)$.

**Claim 3.** $\left|\Pr[\mathsf{Exp}^f] - \Pr[\mathsf{Exp}^{f,ps}]\right| \leq \mathsf{negl}(\lambda)$.

**Claim 4.** $\Pr[\mathsf{Exp}^{f,ps}] \leq \mathsf{negl}(\lambda)$.

Putting together Claims 2 to 4 we conclude that $\Pr[\mathsf{ExptAR}] = \mathsf{negl}$ as desired. Thus it suffices to prove Claims 2 to 4 which we do below.

*Proof (Claim 2).* The experiments $\mathsf{ExptAR}$ and $\mathsf{Exp}^f$ are identical except for the final predicate. In both experiments, the challenger samples $x$, computes $c \leftarrow \mathsf{Enc}(\mathsf{sk}, x)$, the adversary outputs $c'$, and we define the induced error pattern

$$e := c \oplus c'.$$

Conditioned on the event $\delta(c', c) \leq p$, we have $\mathsf{ExptAR} = 1$ iff $\mathsf{Dec}(\mathsf{sk}, c') \neq x$, whereas $\mathsf{Exp}^f = 1$ iff $f(x, \pi, \pi_d, e) \neq 1$. Hence it suffices to show that

$$f(x, \pi, \pi_d, e) = 1 \quad \Longrightarrow \quad \mathsf{Dec}(\mathsf{sk}, c') = x$$

except with negligible probability.

Assume $f(x, \pi, \pi_d, e) = 1$. By definition of $f$, letting $e^\pi := \pi^{-1}(e) = (e_d, e_c)$ we have $\delta(e_c) < p + \alpha$, $\delta(e_d) < p + \alpha$ and

$$\Pi_{\mathsf{BSC}}.\mathsf{Dec}\big(\Pi_{\mathsf{BSC}}.\mathsf{Enc}(x) \oplus \pi_d^{-1}(e_d)\big) = x.$$

Now consider $\mathsf{Dec}(\mathsf{sk}, c')$. The decoder first unpermutes

$$\pi^{-1}(c') = \pi^{-1}(c \oplus e) = \pi^{-1}(c) \oplus e^\pi.$$

Writing $\pi^{-1}(c) = y = (v, c_{\mathsf{PRC}})$, the PRC component is corrupted by $e_c$, and when after inverting $\pi_d$, that is $z = \pi_d^{-1}(v)$, the data component is corrupted with $\pi_d^{-1}(e_d)$. By the $(p+\alpha)$-robustness of $\Pi_{\mathsf{PRC}}$ and the fact that $\delta(e_c) < p+\alpha$, the decoder recovers the correct PRG seed $s$ except with negligible probability, and therefore reconstructs the correct mask $w = \mathsf{PRG}(s)$. Removing the mask yields the codeword $\Pi_{\mathsf{BSC}}.\mathsf{Enc}(x)$ whose corruption is precisely $\pi_d^{-1}(e_d)$, and so by the assumption that $f(x, \pi, \pi_d, e) = 1$ the final decoding outputs $x$. This proves the claim.

*Proof (Claim 3).* The claim follows directly from the strong pseudorandomness property established in Claim 1. In particular, the pseudorandomness guarantee holds even when the adversary is given the permutations $\pi$ and $\pi_d$. Moreover, by a simple hybrid argument we can assume that all calls made to the oracle $\mathcal{A}^{\mathcal{O}_E}$ in the experiment $\mathsf{StrongExptPR}^{(1)}(\mathcal{A}, \lambda)$ return a random string.

Observe that in both experiments $\mathsf{Exp}^f$ and $\mathsf{Exp}^{f,ps}$ the winning condition is identical, namely $f(x, \pi, \pi_d, e) \neq 1$, where $e = c \oplus c'$. Moreover, this predicate depends only on $(x, \pi, \pi_d, e)$ (and does not require the knowledge of the PRC seed).

Therefore, by the strong pseudorandomness property, the joint distributions of $(x, \pi, \pi_d, e)$ in the two experiments are computationally indistinguishable, and hence

$$\left| \Pr[\mathsf{Exp}^f = 1] - \Pr[\mathsf{Exp}^{f,ps} = 1] \right| \leq \mathsf{negl}(\lambda),$$

which proves the claim.

*Proof (Proof of Claim 4).* Fix any PPT adversary $\mathcal{A}$ and consider the experiment $\mathsf{Exp}^{f,ps}$. Let $c \in \{0,1\}^N$ be the (uniform) challenge string and let $c'$ be the adversary's output. Define the induced error vector

$$e := c \oplus c'.$$

Notice that in the experiment $\mathsf{Exp}^{f,ps}$ the permutations $\pi$ and $\pi_d$ are random and independent from $e$ and $c$. Let $e^\pi := \pi^{-1}(e) = (e_d, e_c)$, and recall that $\mathsf{Exp}^{f,ps} = 1$ iff $\mathsf{wt}(e) \leq pN$ and $f(x, \pi, \pi_d, e) \neq 1$.

Let $T \subseteq [N]$ denote the (hidden) set of positions that correspond, under $\pi^{-1}$, to the PRC block, so $|T| = m$. Since $c$ is uniform and independent of $\pi$, the adversary's (possibly randomized) choice of $E$ as a function of $c$ is independent of the random subset $T$. Therefore $\mathbb{E}[\mathsf{wt}(e_c)] \leq p \cdot |T| \leq pm$, and by standard tail bound for hypergeometric sampling (e.g., Hoeffding),

$$\Pr\left[\mathsf{wt}(e_c) > (p + \alpha)m\right] \leq 2^{-\Omega(\alpha^2 m)}.$$

and similarly, $\Pr\left[\mathsf{wt}(e_d) > (p+\alpha)n\right] \leq 2^{-\Omega(\alpha^2 n)}$. Define the good splitting event

$$\mathsf{GoodSplit} := \left\{\mathsf{wt}(e_c) \leq (p + \alpha)m \ \wedge \ \mathsf{wt}(e_d) \leq (p + \alpha)n\right\}.$$

By a union bound, $\Pr[\neg\mathsf{GoodSplit}] = \mathsf{negl}(\lambda)$ (here we implicitly assume that $m, n$ are $\Omega(\lambda)$). By the properties of the code $\Pi_{\mathsf{BSC}}$ (see, Theorem 3.4), it holds if $\mathsf{wt}(e_d) \leq (p + \alpha) \cdot n$,

$$\Pr[\Pi_{\mathsf{BSC}}.\mathsf{Dec}(\Pi_{\mathsf{BSC}}.\mathsf{Enc}(x) \oplus \pi_d^{-1}(e_d)) = x \wedge \mathsf{GoodSplit}] \geq 1 - \mathsf{negl}(\lambda).$$

Since $f(x, \pi, \pi_d, e) = 1$ iff $\{\Pi_{\mathsf{BSC}}.\mathsf{Dec}(\Pi_{\mathsf{BSC}}.\mathsf{Enc}(x) \oplus \pi_d^{-1}(e_d)) = x \wedge \mathsf{GoodSplit}\}$, it follows that $\Pr[\mathsf{Exp}^{f,ps} = 1] = \mathsf{negl}(\lambda)$, which proves the claim.

## 5 Heuristic Seeded Codes via Ideal Obfuscation

We observe that the CCA-secure secret-key codes from the previous section can be transformed into seeded codes by obfuscating the encoding and decoding procedures and publishing the resulting obfuscated programs as the seed. In more detail, we can first make our CCA-secure secret key codes deterministic by using a pseudorandom function (PRF) of the message as the encoding randomness. The resulting code no longer satisfies the definition of pseudorandomness (which inherently requires a randomized code), but it is easy to see that it maintains robustness. We then take the resulting deterministic encoding and decoding procedures with a hard-coded secret key, obfuscate them, and publish the obfuscated programs as the seed. In the ideal obfuscation model, the adversary only gets black-box access to the obfuscated program, which is the same as oracle access to the encoding and decoding procedures. Therefore, the CCA security of the secret key codes ensures the security of the seeded code in the ideal obfuscation model.

**Theorem 5.1.** *Let $p, \varepsilon > 0$ be constants such that $p < 1/4$. Suppose there exists a* one-bit *secret-key CPA code that is pseudorandom and $(p+\varepsilon)$-robust. Then, in the idea obfuscation model, there exists a seeded code that is $p$-robust for arbitrary length messages with rate $R = 1 - H(p) - \varepsilon$.*

While ideal obfuscation does not exist, constructions in the ideal obfuscation model give heuristic evidence that security holds when the idea obfuscation is replaced with indistinguishability obfuscation, analogously to random oracle constructions giving heuristic evidence of security when replaced with a real-world hash functions. In fact, this analogy was formalized in the work of [JLLW23], which showed that one can instantiate ideal obfuscation in a variant of the random oracle model called the *pseudorandom oracle model* (PRO), assuming indistinguishability obfuscation. Combining the above, we get a construction of seeded codes that achieve Shannon capacity in the PRO model assuming secret-key PRCs and indistinguishability obfuscation. Overall, this yields the first heuristic candidate for seeded codes achieving Shannon capacity for $p < 1/4$.

## 6 List Decodable Pseudorandom Codes with Optimal Robustness

In this section we present a transformation from zero-bit pseudorandom codes to list-decodable codes with large message spaces and optimal robustness. In the list-decoding setting, our constructions tolerate error rates throughout the full range $0 \leq p < \frac{1}{2}$. This construction works for both secret-key and public-key PRCs, but we mainly focus on the latter.

*Zero-Bit Pseudorandom Codes and Soundness.* Our construction here will also make use of zero-bit pseudorandom codes, which, in addition to satisfying, the previous notions of pseudorandomness and $p$-robustness, will also need to satisfy *soundness*.

- **Soundness:** For a security parameter $\lambda \in \mathbb{N}$, a computational code $\Pi_{\mathsf{PRC}} = (\mathsf{Setup}, \mathsf{Enc}, \mathsf{Dec})$ is *sound* if for all fixed bit-strings $c' \in \{0,1\}^n$:

$$\Pr[\mathsf{Dec}(\mathsf{sk}, c) = \bot \mid (\mathsf{pk}, \mathsf{sk}) \leftarrow \mathsf{Setup}(1^\lambda)] = 1 - \mathsf{negl}(\lambda),$$

where the probability is taken over the randomness of $\lambda$.

Soundness for secret-key codes is defined analogously. As noted in [CG24], this condition is needed in the zero-bit case to ensure a meaningful primitive (otherwise, a trivial 'pseudorandom code' could be constructed by considering all strings in $\{0,1\}^n$ as codewords). As such, all constructions of (zero-bit) pseudorandom codes satisfy soundness.

We now state our result for list-decodable codes with $(p, L)$-robustness for $0 \leq p < 1/2$. To the best of our knowledge the notion of list-decoding for pseudorandom codes was not formalized and explored prior to this work. The results below are stated for public-key codes, but the construction and proof also hold for the secret-key codes.

**Theorem 6.1 (List-decodable pseudorandom: From zero-bit to large message domain).** *Let $p \geq 0, \varepsilon > 0$ be constants such that $p + \varepsilon < \frac{1}{2}$. Suppose there exists a public-key [resp., secret-key] CPA zero-bit pseudorandom code that is $(p + \varepsilon)$-robust and sound. Then there exists polynomials $n(\lambda)$ and $L(\lambda)$ and an explicit public-key [resp., secret-key] CPA list-decodable code $\Pi = (\mathsf{Enc}, \mathsf{Dec}_{\mathsf{ListDec}})$ with $\mathsf{Enc} : \{0,1\}^\lambda \to \{0,1\}^{n(\lambda)}$, such that $\Pi$ is pseudorandom and $(p, L(\lambda))$-robust. Moreover, if the zero-bit code has $(p + \varepsilon)$-simulatable decoding then $\Pi$ also has $p$-simulatable decoding.*

Note that the result of [AAC+25] for zero-bit codes stated in Theorem 3.9 satisfy the simulatable decoding property, and suffice to instantiate this theorem from LPN in the public (or secret) key setting, and the result of [CGG+26] suffices to instantiate this theorem in the secret key setting from permuted codes.

The proof for Theorem 6.1 is given in section Sect. 6.3.

## 6.1 Polynomial Message Space List-Decodable Pseudorandom Codes

We begin by showing how to obtain list-decodable pseudorandom codes for any polynomial-size message space, assuming the existence of a zero-bit pseudorandom code. The construction is conceptually simple: we associate each possible message with an independent instance of the underlying zero-bit code and decode by collecting all indices whose corresponding code accepts. The main technical challenge is to argue that the resulting list size remains polynomial in the security parameter and, crucially, independent of the message space size. The following lemma formalizes this guarantee.

**Lemma 6.2.** *Let $p < \frac{1}{2}$ be an arbitrary constant and let $\lambda \in \mathbb{N}$ be a security parameter. Suppose there exists a public-key [resp., secret-key] CPA zero-bit* *pseudorandom code which is sound and p-robust. Then there exists a polynomial $L(\lambda)$ such that, for any polynomial $q(\lambda)$, there is a public-key [resp., secret-key] CPA list-decodable code $\Pi$ with message space $[q]$ that is pseudorandom and $(p, L(\lambda))$-robust. Importantly, note that $L$ is a fixed function of the security parameter and independent of $q$. Moreover, if the zero-bit code has p-simulatable decoding then $\Pi$ also has p-simulatable decoding.*

*Proof (Lemma* 6.2*).* We make use of the following construction:

**Construction 6.3.** Take the message space $q$ to be an arbitrary polynomial in $\lambda$.

- Let $\Pi_{\mathsf{PRC}} = (\mathsf{Setup}, \mathsf{Enc}, \mathsf{Dec})$ be a zero-bit public-key pseudorandom code with codeword space $\{0,1\}^m$.

Our construction proceeds as follows:

- $\mathsf{Setup}(1^\lambda) \to (\mathsf{pk}, \mathsf{sk})$: On input security parameter $\lambda$, the setup algorithm samples an independent key pair $(\mathsf{pk}^{(i)}, \mathsf{sk}^{(i)}) \leftarrow \mathsf{Setup}(1^\lambda)$ for each $i \in [q]$. It returns $\mathsf{pk} = \{\mathsf{pk}^{(i)}\}_{i\in[q]}, \mathsf{sk} = \{\mathsf{sk}^{(i)}\}_{i\in[q]}$.
- $\mathsf{Enc}(\mathsf{pk}, x) \to c$: On input public key $\mathsf{pk} = \{\mathsf{pk}^{(i)}\}_{i\in[q]}$, message $x \in [q]$, the encoding algorithm samples and returns codeword $c \leftarrow \mathsf{Enc}(\mathsf{pk}^{(x)}, 1)$.
- $\mathsf{ListDec}(\mathsf{sk}, c') \to L$ : On input secret key $\mathsf{sk} = \{\mathsf{sk}^{(i)}\}_{i\in[q]}$ and string $c' \in \{0,1\}^m$, the decoding algorithm computes and outputs set

$$L = \{i \in [q] \mid \mathsf{Dec}(\mathsf{sk}^{(i)}, c') = 1\}.$$

Since codewords of Construction 6.3 are simply codewords of the underlying $\Pi_{\mathsf{PRC}}$, pseudorandomness of this construction follows immediately from pseudorandomness of $\Pi_{\mathsf{PRC}}$. Similarly, $p$-robustness follows from $p$-robustness of $\Pi_{\mathsf{PRC}}$ (recall in the list-decoding robustness game Definition 3.8, it suffices for the codeword $x$ to be contained in the output list $L$, which corresponds exactly to a noisy codeword of the selected zero-bit code decoding to 1). In the same vein, we can satisfy simulated decoding Construction 6.3 by defining simulator $\mathsf{Sim}(\mathsf{pk}, x, r, c)$ to simply invoke the underlying simulator $\Pi_{\mathsf{PRC}}.\mathsf{Sim}(\mathsf{pk}^{(x)}, 1, r, c)$. Thus, to complete Lemma 6.2, it remains to argue a bound on the list size of Construction 6.3.

**Claim 5.** With overwhelming probability (over the randomness of $\mathsf{Setup}$), the list $L$ output by $\mathsf{ListDec}$ is of size $< m$ on all strings $\in \{0,1\}^m$.

*Proof.* Fix an arbitrary string $c^* \in \{0,1\}^m$. Recall that by soundness of $\Pi_{\mathsf{PRC}}$, the probability $\mathsf{Dec}(\mathsf{sk}, c^*) = 1$ is negligible over the randomness of sampling $\mathsf{sk}$ in $\mathsf{Setup}$. Let $f = f(\lambda)$ refer to this negligible function. Thus, in our scheme for any fixed subset $T \subset [q]$ of $m$ keys, the probability all of $\{\mathsf{sk}^{(i)}\}_{i\in T}$ decode $c^*$ to 1 can be bounded by $f^m$, as the keys are sampled independently.

We can now union bound over all $2^m$ strings $c^*$ and all $\binom{q}{m} \leq q^m$ size $m$ subsets of $[q]$ to conclude that the probability there exists *any* string $c^*$ and size $m$ subset of keys $\{\mathsf{sk}^{(i)}\}_{i \in T}$ which decode $c^*$ to 1 can be bounded by $f^m \cdot q^m \cdot 2^m = (2 \cdot q \cdot f)^m$. Since $q$ is polynomially bounded while $f$ is negligible, $2 \cdot q \cdot f$ is negligible as well.

Notice that $m$ is simply a parameter $\Pi_{\mathsf{PRC}}$, which is instantiated independently of $q$, and so this is sufficient to complete the proof of our lemma.

## 6.2 From Polynomial Message Space to Exponential Message Space

We now extend the previous construction to support an exponential-size message space by combining pseudorandom list-decodable codes with standard list-recoverable codes via concatenation. The main idea is to encode the message using a list-recoverable outer code and then protect each outer symbol using an independent instance of the underlying pseudorandom code. The resulting scheme preserves pseudorandomness while tolerating error rates up to $p < \frac{1}{2}$. Crucially, this transformation preserves the list size up to a polynomial factor, so the final list size remains of the same order as that of the underlying pseudorandom code.

**Construction 6.4.** Let $0 < p, \varepsilon$ be constants such that $0 \leq p + \varepsilon < 1/2$. Ingredients:

- Let $q \in \mathsf{poly}$ and let $\Pi_{\mathsf{PRC}} = (\mathsf{Setup}, \mathsf{Enc}, \mathsf{ListDec})$ be a $(p+\varepsilon, \ell_{\mathsf{PRC}})$-robust list-decodable pseudorandom code on message space $[q(\lambda)]$ where $\lambda$ is the security parameter.
- Let $n, k \in \mathsf{poly}$, and let $\Pi_{\mathsf{LRC}} = (\mathsf{Enc}, \mathsf{Dec})$ be an $(\varepsilon, \ell, L)$-list-recoverable code such that $\mathsf{Enc} : \{0,1\}^{k(\lambda)} \to [q(\lambda)]^{n(\lambda)}$, and $\ell = \ell_{\mathsf{PRC}}$.

Our construction proceeds as follows:

- $\mathsf{Setup}(1^\lambda) \to (\mathsf{pk}, \mathsf{sk})$: On input security parameter $\lambda$, the setup algorithm simply runs the $(\mathsf{pk}_{\mathsf{PRC}}, \mathsf{sk}_{\mathsf{PRC}}) \leftarrow \Pi_{\mathsf{PRC}}.\mathsf{Setup}(1^\lambda)$ and outputs $\mathsf{pk} = \mathsf{pk}_{\mathsf{PRC}}$, $\mathsf{sk} = \mathsf{sk}_{\mathsf{PRC}}$.
- $\mathsf{Enc}(\mathsf{pk}, x) \to c$: On input public key $\mathsf{pk} = \mathsf{pk}_{\mathsf{PRC}}$ and input $x$, the encoding algorithm computes the following:
  - Compute $a_1, \ldots a_n \leftarrow \Pi_{\mathsf{LRC}}.\mathsf{Enc}(x)$.
  - For each $i \in [n]$, compute $c_i \leftarrow \Pi_{\mathsf{PRC}}.\mathsf{Enc}(\mathsf{pk}, a_i)$.
  - Output $c = c_1, \ldots c_n$.
- $\mathsf{ListDec}(\mathsf{sk}, c) \to T$: On input secret key $\mathsf{sk} = \mathsf{sk}_{\mathsf{PRC}}$ and codeword $c$, the (list) decoding algorithm computes the following:
  - Parse $c = c_1, \ldots c_n$.
  - For each $i \in [n]$, recover a set $S_i \leftarrow \Pi_{\mathsf{PRC}}.\mathsf{ListDec}(\mathsf{sk}_{\mathsf{PRC}}, c_i)$.
  - Compute list $T' \leftarrow \Pi_{\mathsf{LRC}}.\mathsf{Dec}(S_1, \cdots, S_n)$.
  - For each $x \in T'$:
    * Recompute $a_1, \ldots a_n \leftarrow \Pi_{\mathsf{LRC}}.\mathsf{Enc}(x)$.

  * For each $i \in [n]$, check if $a_i \in S_i$.
  * Let $\varepsilon'$ be the total fraction of indices for which this is true. If $\varepsilon' \geq \varepsilon$, add $x$ to $T$.
- Output $T$.

**Theorem 6.5.** *Let $\Pi_{\mathsf{PRC}}$ be a public-key [resp., secret-key] CPA pseudorandom list-decodable code that is $(p+\varepsilon, \ell_{\mathsf{PRC}})$-robust and let $\Pi_{\mathsf{LRC}}$ be a $(\varepsilon, \ell := \ell_{\mathsf{PRC}}, L)$-list-recoverable (standard) code that satisfy the conditions in Construction 6.4. Then the code $\Pi = (\mathsf{Enc}, \mathsf{Dec})$ is a public-key [resp., secret-key] CPA list-decodable code that is pseudorandom and $(p, L)$-robust. Moreover, if the $\Pi_{\mathsf{PRC}}$ has $(p+\varepsilon)$-simulatable decoding then $\Pi$ also has $p$-simulatable decoding.*

*Proof (Theorem* 6.5*).* Let $\lambda \in \mathbb{N}$ be the security parameter for the code $\Pi_{\mathsf{PRC}}$.

**Pseudorandomness:** Note that by construction the pseudorandomness of the code follows directly from a simple hybrid argument, since the codeword is simply the concatenation of $n$ pseudorandom codewords computed with independent randomness, and $n$ is polynomial in $\lambda$.

**List-Decoding $p$-Robust:** For a security parameter $\lambda \in \mathbb{N}$, recall the $p$-robustness experiment $\mathsf{ExptAR}(\mathcal{A}, \lambda)$ (see Definition 3.5). Let $x \in \{0,1\}^k$ denote the challenge chosen by the adversary and let $c$ denote the response and recall that $(a_1, \cdots, a_n) = \Pi_{\mathsf{LRC}}.\mathsf{Enc}(x)$ and $c = (c_1, \cdots, c_n)$ where for every $i \in [n]$, $c_i \leftarrow \Pi_{\mathsf{PRC}}.\mathsf{Enc}(\mathsf{pk}, a_i)$, and let $c'$ denote the final noisy codeword sent by the $\mathcal{A}$.

Recall that we can assume that $\delta(c, c') \leq p$. For every $i \in [n]$, define the adversary $\mathcal{A}_i$ to be the adversary that acts like $\mathcal{A}$ restricted to the $i$ block. That is for $i \in [n]$, $\mathcal{A}_i$ receives as input $\mathsf{pk}$, internally runs $\mathcal{A}(\mathsf{pk})$ to get $x$ and sends $a_i = \mathsf{Enc}_{\mathsf{LRC}}(x)_i$ to the challenger and receives $c_i$, it internally constructs the codewords for the remaining indices and sends $c = (c_1, \cdots, c_i, \cdots, c_n)$ to $\mathcal{A}$ and receives the noisy codeword $c' = (c'_1, \ldots, c'_n)$, and outputs the $i$-th block $c'_i$. Let

$$p_i := \delta(c_i, c'_i) \in [0,1] \qquad \text{so that} \qquad \delta(c, c') = \frac{1}{n}\sum_{i=1}^{n} p_i \leq p.$$

Define the set of *bad* indices $B := \{\, i \in [n] : p_i > p + \varepsilon \,\}$. By Markov's inequality, we have

$$\frac{|B|}{n} = \Pr_{i \leftarrow [n]}[p_i > p + \varepsilon] \leq \frac{\mathbb{E}_{i \leftarrow [n]}[p_i]}{p+\varepsilon} \leq \frac{p}{p+\varepsilon} \leq 1 - \varepsilon.$$

In particular, for at least $\varepsilon \cdot n$ indices $i$, we have $p_i \leq p + \varepsilon$. For each $i \in [n]$, let $S_i \leftarrow \Pi_{\mathsf{PRC}}.\mathsf{Dec}(\mathsf{sk}_{\mathsf{PRC}}, c'_i)$ be the list output by the inner decoder. By $(p+\varepsilon)$-robustness of $\Pi_{\mathsf{PRC}}$, for every $i \notin B$ we have $a_i \in S_i$ except with negligible probability. Therefore, except with negligible probability, the sequence of lists $(S_1, \ldots, S_n)$ contains the correct outer codeword symbols $(a_1, \ldots, a_n)$ in at least $\varepsilon$ fraction of positions. Applying the $(\varepsilon, \ell, L)$-list-recovery guarantee of $\Pi_{\mathsf{LRC}}$, we conclude that $x$ is contained in the final output list $T \leftarrow \mathsf{ListRec}(S_1, \ldots, S_n)$, as required.

**$p$-Simulatable Decoding:** Consider the following decoding simulator:

- $\mathsf{Sim}(\mathsf{pk}, x, r, c)$: On input public key $\mathsf{pk} = \mathsf{pk}_{\mathsf{PRC}}$, message $x \in \{0,1\}^k$, randomness $r = (r_1, \dots r_n)$, and codeword $c = (c_1, \dots, c_n)$, the decoding simulator:
  - Compute $(a_1, \dots, a_n) \leftarrow \Pi_{\mathsf{LRC}}.\mathsf{Enc}(x)$.
  - For each $i \in [n]$, check if $\Pi_{\mathsf{PRC}}.\mathsf{Sim}(\mathsf{pk}_{\mathsf{PRC}}, a_i, r_i, c_i) = 1$. Let $\varepsilon'$ be the total fraction of indices for which this is true.
  - If $\varepsilon' \geq \varepsilon$, output 1, otherwise output 0.

For a security parameter $\lambda \in \mathbb{N}$, recall the $p$-simulatable decoding experiment $\mathsf{ExptDS}^{(b)}$. First, note that in the real decoding algorithm, the adversary computes set $S_i$ via $\Pi_{\mathsf{PRC}}.\mathsf{ListDec}$. By $p$-simulatable decoding of $\Pi_{\mathsf{PRC}}$, checking $a_i \in S_i$ on the challenge codeword $c_i$ is computationally indistinguishable from querying $\Pi_{\mathsf{PRC}}.\mathsf{Sim}(a_i, r_i, c_i)$ when given randomness $r_i$. Now, since both $\mathsf{ListDec}$ and $\mathsf{Sim}$ only add messages whose $\mathsf{LRC}$ codewords agree on at least $\varepsilon$ fraction of indices, by the correctness of $\Pi_{\mathsf{LRC}}$, $\mathsf{ListDec}$ and $\mathsf{Sim}$ will both correctly recover $x$.

### 6.3 Proof of Theorem 6.1

To prove Theorem 6.1, we instantiate the domain extension framework of Theorem 6.5 using Reed–Solomon codes as the outer list-recoverable code and the list-decodable pseudorandom codes from Lemma 6.2 as the inner component. This immediately yields the desired list-decodable construction with polynomial list size.

We rely on the following list-recovery result for Reed–Solomon codes due to Sudan [Sud97] and Guruswami–Sudan [GS99].

**Theorem 6.6 (Reed–Solomon list recovery,** [Sud97,GS99]**).** *Let $q$ be a prime power and let $n \leq q$. There is an explicit code $\Pi_{\mathsf{code}} = (\mathsf{Enc}, \mathsf{ListRec})$ over alphabet $[q]$ (namely a Reed–Solomon code) with $\mathsf{Enc} : \mathbb{F}_q^k \to \mathbb{F}_q^n$ such that for every $\ell \geq 1$ and every $\varepsilon > 0$, the code is $(\alpha, \ell, L)$-list-recoverable for*

$$\alpha \geq \sqrt{\frac{(k-1)\ell}{n}} + \varepsilon, \text{ and } L \leq \mathsf{poly}\left(k, \ell, \frac{1}{\varepsilon}\right),$$

*and there is a (deterministic) list-recovery algorithm running in $\mathsf{poly}(n, q, \ell, \frac{1}{\varepsilon})$ time.*

*Proof (Theorem 6.1).* Let $\lambda \in \mathbb{N}$ be the security parameter, and let $\Pi_{\mathsf{PRC}} = (\mathsf{Enc}, \mathsf{ListDec})$ the zero-bit pseudorandom $(p+\varepsilon)$-robust list-decodable code guaranteed by the assumption. Let $L_{\mathsf{PRC}}$ be the polynomial guaranteed by Lemma 6.2, and choose $q(\lambda) \geq (L_{\mathsf{PRC}}(\lambda) \cdot \lambda)^4$ such that $\Pi_{\mathsf{PRC}}.\mathsf{Enc} : [q] \to \{0,1\}^m$ and $q$ is a prime. Let $\Pi_{\mathsf{LRC}}$ be a list-recoverable code guaranteed by Theorem 6.6 such that $\Pi_{\mathsf{LRC}}.\mathsf{Enc} : \{0,1\}^\lambda \to [q(\lambda)]^{q(\lambda)}$. Note that for a constant $\varepsilon' < \varepsilon/2$ by Theorem 6.6 the code is $(\alpha, \ell_{\mathsf{PRC}}, L)$-list-recoverable for

$$\alpha := \sqrt{\frac{(\lambda-1)\ell_{\mathsf{PRC}}(\lambda)}{q(\lambda)}} + \varepsilon/2 \leq \frac{1}{\lambda} + \varepsilon/2 \leq \varepsilon$$

and $L \in \mathsf{poly}(\lambda)$. Thus, $\Pi_{\mathsf{PRC}}$ and $\Pi_{\mathsf{LRC}}$ satisfy the conditions in Theorem 6.5 since $\alpha \leq \varepsilon$, thus for a security parameter $\lambda \in \mathbb{N}$, there exists a code $\Pi$ from $\lambda$ bits to $n(\lambda)$ bits that is pseudorandom and $p$-robust list-decodable with list-size $L(\lambda)$ where $L, n \in \mathsf{poly}$ and satisfies simulatable decoding. This concludes the proof.

**Acknowledgements.** The third author's research was supported by NSF grants CNS-2349972 and CNS-2055510. Research supported in part by a grant from the UC Noyce Initiative to the Simons Institute for the Theory of Computing. Part of this work was conducted while the authors were visiting the Simons Institute for the Theory of Computing.

## References

[AAC+25] Alrabiah, O., Ananth, P., Christ, M., Dodis, Y., Gunn, S.: Ideal pseudorandom codes. In: Proceedings of the 57th Annual ACM Symposium on Theory of Computing, pp. 1638–1647 (2025)

[BHMW21] Boyle, E., Holmgren, J., Ma, F., Weiss, M.: On the security of doubly efficient PIR. IACR Cryptol. ePrint Arch. 1113 (2021)

[BW21] Blackwell, K., Wootters, M.: A note on the permuted puzzles toy conjecture. CoRR, abs/2108.07885 (2021)

[BZ76] Blokh, E.L., Zyablov, V.V.: Generalized concatenated codes. Svyaz', Moscow (1976)

[CG24] Christ, M., Gunn, S.: Pseudorandom error-correcting codes. In: Reyzin, L., Stebila, D. (eds.) CRYPTO 2024, Part VI. LNCS, vol. 14925, pp. 325–347. Springer, Cham (2024)

[CGG+26] Christ, M., Golowich, N., Gunn, S., Moitra, A., Wichs, D.: Improved pseudorandom codes from permuted puzzles (2026)

[Eli57] Elias, P.: List decoding for noisy channels (1957)

[GG25] Ghentiyala, S., Guruswami, V.: New constructions of pseudorandom codes. In: Ene, A., Chattopadhyay, E. (eds.) Approximation, Randomization, and Combinatorial Optimization. Algorithms and Techniques, APPROX/RANDOM 2025, Berkeley, CA, USA, 11–13 August 2025. LIPIcs, vol. 353, pp. 54:1–54:22. Schloss Dagstuhl - Leibniz-Zentrum für Informatik (2025)

[GHY20] Grossman, O., Holmgren, J., Yogev, E.: Transparent error correcting in a computationally bounded world. In: Pass, R., Pietrzak, K. (eds.) TCC 2020. LNCS, vol. 12552, pp. 530–549. Springer, Cham (2020). https://doi.org/10.1007/978-3-030-64381-2_19

[GI01] Guruswami, V., Indyk, P.: Expander-based constructions of efficiently decodable codes. In: 42nd FOCS, pp. 658–667, Las Vegas, NV, USA, 14–17 October 2001. IEEE Computer Society Press (2001)

[GM24] Golowich, N., Moitra, A.: Edit distance robust watermarks via indexing pseudorandom codes. In: Globersons, A., et al. (eds.) Advances in Neural Information Processing Systems 38: Annual Conference on Neural Information Processing Systems 2024, NeurIPS 2024, Vancouver, BC, Canada, 10–15 December 2024 (2024)

[GS98] Guruswami, V., Sudan, M.: Improved decoding of Reed-Solomon and algebraic-geometric codes. In: 39th FOCS, pp. 28–39, Palo Alto, CA, USA, 8–11 November 1998. IEEE Computer Society Press (1998)
[GS99] Guruswami, V., Sudan, M.: Improved decoding of reed-solomon and algebraic-geometry codes. IEEE Trans. Inf. Theory **45**(6), 1757–1767 (1999)
[GS16] Guruswami, V., Smith, A.: Optimal rate code constructions for computationally simple channels. J. ACM (JACM) **63**(4), 35 (2016)
[Ham50] Hamming, R.W.: Error detecting and error correcting codes. Bell Syst. Tech. J. **29**(2), 147–160 (1950)
[JLLW23] Jain, A., Lin, H., Luo, J., Wichs, D.: The pseudorandom oracle model and ideal obfuscation. In: Handschuh, H., Lysyanskaya, A. (eds.) CRYPTO 2023, Part IV. LNCS, vol. 14084, pp. 233–262. Springer, Cham (2023)
[KSS19] Kopparty, S., Shaltiel, R., Silbak, J.: Quasilinear time list-decodable codes for space bounded channels. To appear in the 60th Annual Symposium on Foundations of Computer Science (FOCS) (2019)
[Lip94] Lipton, R.J.: A new approach to information theory. In: Enjalbert, P., Mayr, E.W., Wagner, K.W. (eds.) STACS 1994. LNCS, vol. 775, pp. 699–708. Springer, Heidelberg (1994). https://doi.org/10.1007/3-540-57785-8_183
[LSW25] Lu, G., Silbak, J., Wichs, D.: Binary codes for computationally bounded errors under standard crypto assumptions. In: FOCS (2025)
[MPSW10] Micali, S., Peikert, C., Sudan, M., Wilson, D.A.: Optimal error correction for computationally bounded noise. IEEE Trans. Inf. Theory **56**(11), 5673–5680 (2010)
[Sha48] Shannon, C.E.: A mathematical theory of communication. Bell Syst. Tech. J. **27**(4), 623–656 (1948)
[Smi07] Smith, A.D.: Scrambling adversarial errors using few random bits, optimal information reconciliation, and better private codes. In: Proceedings of the Eighteenth Annual ACM-SIAM Symposium on Discrete Algorithms, SODA, pp. 395–404 (2007)
[SS21a] Shaltiel, R., Silbak, J.: Explicit list-decodable codes with optimal rate for computationally bounded channels. Comput. Complex. **30**(1), 3 (2021)
[SS21b] Shaltiel, R., Silbak, J.: Explicit uniquely decodable codes for space bounded channels that achieve list-decoding capacity. In: STOC 2021: 53rd Annual ACM SIGACT Symposium on Theory of Computing, pp. 1516–1526 (2021)
[SS22] Shaltiel, R., Silbak, J.: Error correcting codes that achieve BSC capacity against channels that are poly-size circuits. In: 63rd IEEE Annual Symposium on Foundations of Computer Science, FOCS, pp. 13–23 (2022)
[SS24a] Shaltiel, R., Silbak, J.: Explicit codes for poly-size circuits and functions that are hard to sample on low entropy distributions. In: Electronic Colloquium on Computational Complexity (ECCC) (2024)
[SS24b] Shaltiel, R., Silbak, J.: Explicit codes for poly-size circuits and functions that are hard to sample on low entropy distributions. In: Mohar, B., Shinkar, I., O'Donnell, R. (eds.) 56th ACM STOC, pp. 2028–2038, Vancouver, BC, Canada, 24–28 June 2024. ACM Press (2024)
[Sud97] Sudan, M.: Decoding of Reed Solomon codes beyond the error-correction bound. J. Complex. **13** (1997)

[SW25a] Silbak, J., Wichs, D.: Binary codes for error detection and correction in a computationally bounded world. In: Fehr, S., Fouque, P.-A. (eds.) Advances in Cryptology - EUROCRYPT 2025, Part I. LNCS, vol. 15601, pp. 186–211. Springer (2025)

[SW25b] Silbak, J., Wichs, D.: Detecting and correcting computationally bounded errors: a simple construction under minimal assumptions. In: Meka, R. (ed.) 16th Innovations in Theoretical Computer Science Conference, ITCS 2025, Columbia University, New York, NY, USA, 7–10 January 2025. LIPIcs, vol. 325, pp. 88:1–88:23. Schloss Dagstuhl - Leibniz-Zentrum für Informatik (2025)

[Woz58] Wozencraft, J.M.: List decoding (1958)

[Zya71] Zyablov, V.V.: An estimate of the complexity of constructing binary linear cascade codes. Problemy Peredachi Informatsii **7**(1), 5–13 (1971). In Russian. Also cited as "On Estimation of Complexity of Construction of Binary Linear Concatenated Codes." English translation: *Problems of Information Transmission*, 7(1):3–10, 1971

# Chosen Ciphertext Secure Pseudorandom Codes in the Standard Model

Nico Döttling[1], Antoine Joux[1], Venkata Koppula[2], Mahesh Sreekumar Rajasree[1], and Hendrik Waldner[1(✉)]

[1] CISPA Helmholtz Center for Information Security, Saarbrücken, Germany
{doettling,joux,hendrik.waldner}@cispa.de
[2] Indian Institute of Technology Delhi, New Delhi, India
kvenkata@iitd.ac.in

**Abstract.** Pseudorandom codes (PRCs), recently proposed by Christ and Gunn (CRYPTO'24), are encryption schemes that have pseudorandom ciphertexts and a decryption algorithm which is resilient against a bounded number of Hamming errors. This notion provides a significant strengthening over standard PKE and has exciting applications in, e.g., watermarking LLMs. The recent work of Alrabiah et al. (STOC'25) initiated the study of CCA-secure public-key PRCs, where the adversary is additionally given access to a decoding oracle. In terms of realizations, they provide one that can be proven secure in the random oracle model. Constructing CCA-secure public-key PRCs in the standard model remained an open problem.

In this work, we resolve this problem and provide the first construction of CCA-secure public-key PRCs in the standard model. Our construction achieves a constant rate and can decode from a constant fraction of adversarial errors. In fact, our construction is a general blueprint that can be instantiated from a broad range of standard cryptographic assumptions. As an additional contribution, we construct a strong adaptively robust public-key pseudorandom code with conjectured sub-exponential security based on a new family of assumptions we call Noisy McEliece. In a nutshell, these assumptions mask a scrambled generator matrix from an efficiently decodable inner-code family with sparse Bernoulli noise; this additional error is meant to obscure the algebraic structure targeted by known attacks and thereby permits candidate instantiations from broader classes of codes.

## 1 Introduction

### 1.1 Pseudorandom Codes

Error-correcting codes and pseudorandomness are two of the most fundamental notions in theoretical computer science and cryptography. Error-correcting codes enable reliable communication over noisy channels, while pseudorandom generators (PRGs) are indispensable for derandomization and cryptographic security. While error-correction requires redundancy and hence structure, pseudorandomness makes any structure undetectable.


N. Heninger and M. Rosulek (Eds.): CRYPTO 2026, LNCS 16800, pp. 282–313, 2026.
https://doi.org/10.1007/978-3-032-35367-2_10

The notion of pseudorandom codes (PRCs), recently proposed by Christ and Gunn [13], connects these seemingly contradictory notions. In a nutshell, a PRC is a family of keyed error-correcting codes whose codewords are computationally indistinguishable from uniformly random ones to an outside observer. But, a legitimate receiver who is in possession of the secret key can efficiently decode the codeword even in the presence of a large fraction of Hamming errors. While pseudorandom codes were originally motivated by the problem of watermarking large language models (LLMs), they have emerged as an exciting cryptographic notion in their own right.

However, constructing pseudorandom codes has turned out to be a highly non-trivial task. Current constructions [4,12,13,30,32] are based on hardness assumptions relating to coding theory, and there is evidence that even constructing just the weakest private-key notions cannot be achieved from *generic* hardness assumptions [23,28]. In particular, [28] argues that even the most powerful tools available in cryptography such as (indistinguishability) obfuscation do not help when attempting to construct pseudorandom codes with generic recipes.

### 1.2 Adaptive Robustness and CCA Security

*Adaptive Robustness:* Early PRC constructions addressed errors introduced obliviously by a memoryless channel. Subsequent works [4,14] argued that, in realistic settings, robustness must be defined against *adaptive* adversaries that have access to an encoding oracle (or to the public key in the public-key setting). Such an adversary must output a message $m$, randomness $r$, and a $c$ such that encoding $m$ with randomness $r$ yields a codeword close to $c$, yet decoding $c$ produces a different message. In this work, we rely on this stronger notion of robustness.

*CCA Security:* The standard security notion for pseudorandom codes [13] mirrors the basic *chosen plaintext* security notion (CPA) for encryption schemes with pseudorandom ciphertexts: the adversary is given access to an oracle $\mathcal{O}_{Enc}$ that produces strings $c_i$ (as well as potentially the PRC public key) and must decide whether the strings produced by the oracle are well-formed codes of the PRC or just uniformly random strings. Several real-world attacks [33,42] exploit access to both the encoding and decoding oracles in order to remove/counterfeit watermarks. Alrabiah et al. [4] introduced stronger security notions in the private key and public key setting, where the adversary also has access to the decoding oracle. In the private key setting, they introduced the notion of *ideal pseudorandom codes* for pseudorandom codes. In this notion, the adversary is additionally given access to a *decoding* oracle $\mathcal{O}_{Dec}$ which provides the adversary access to the decoding algorithm. Implementing this oracle for the case that $\mathcal{O}_{Enc}$ actually implements the encoding algorithm is easy. However, if $\mathcal{O}_{Enc}$ produces uniformly random strings, a more refined argument is required. Specifically, in this case $\mathcal{O}_{Enc}$ and $\mathcal{O}_{Dec}$ must share a joint state, and $\mathcal{O}_{Dec}$ needs to handle strings produced by $\mathcal{O}_{Enc}$ differently from codewords produced by the adversary.

In the public key setting, which is the focus of this work, [4] proposed a simple *chosen ciphertext* security notion (CCA) and provided a construction in the random oracle model [6]. Specifically, in this security notion the adversary is given the public key, as well as access to a decoding oracle $\mathcal{O}_{Dec}$ which implements the decoding algorithm. At some point, the adversary asks for a challenge and is either given a well-formed codeword, or a uniformly random string. As in the standard CCA experiment, access to the decoding oracle is now restricted. While, at this point in the CCA experiment for public key encryption, the decryption oracle accepts every query *except* the challenge ciphertext, this formulation is insufficient for pseudorandom codes. Specifically, the adversary can always introduce a small amount of errors to the challenge and obtain a different string. Hence, in the PRC-setting the post-challenge decoding oracle must be restricted in a more stringent way. Roughly speaking, the post-challenge decoding oracle now summarily rejects any input within (say) the decoding-radius of the challenge.

### 1.3 Constructing CCA-Secure Pseudorandom Codes

However, in light of mounting impossibility results for PRCs [23,28], and given the growing body of random oracle uninstantiability results [5,10,31,36,41, 48]the very existence of the notion of CCA-secure PRC rests on uncertain grounds. This naturally raises the following question:

*Can CCA-secure pseudorandom codes be realized in the standard model under standard assumptions?*

### 1.4 Our Results

In this work, we present the first construction of public-key pseudorandom codes that achieves indistinguishability against chosen-ciphertext attacks in the standard model. We also present a new candidate construction of an adaptively robust PRC.

**New Candidates for Robust PRCs.** Existing constructions of robust public-key PRCs need to assume sub-exponential hardness of LPN [4], while only providing quasi-polynomial security. Furthermore, constructions attaining sub-exponential security are known only in the secret-key setting [12]. As an additional contribution, we propose a new family of assumptions which we call *Noisy McEliece* assumptions. Recall that the decisional McEliece assumption [38] conjectures that the generator matrices of *scrambled Goppa codes* are pseudorandom. Specifically, if $\mathbf{G} \in \mathbb{F}_2^{m \times n}$ is the generator matrix of a binary Goppa code, $\mathbf{\Pi} \in S_m$ is a random permutation matrix, and $\mathbf{T} \in \mathsf{GL}_n(\mathbb{F}_2)$ is a random invertible matrix, then we set $\mathbf{A} = \mathbf{\Pi} \cdot \mathbf{G} \cdot \mathbf{T}$. Under the decisional McEliece assumption this matrix $\mathbf{A}$ is pseudorandom. Notoriously, virtually all attempts to replace binary Goppa codes in this construction with other efficiently decodable linear codes have led to insecure constructions [1,11,15,19,29,44,47]. These attacks show that the choice of the code family is central. In our Noisy McEliece assumptions, one fixes a specified code family and masks the scrambled generator matrix by Bernoulli noise, that is, we consider matrices of the form $\mathbf{A} = \mathbf{\Pi} \cdot \mathbf{G} \cdot \mathbf{T} + \mathbf{E}$, where $\mathbf{E} \leftarrow \mathsf{Ber}_\rho^{m \times n}$ is chosen from a $\rho = O(1/\sqrt{n})$-noise Bernoulli distribution. The hope is that the noise disrupts the exact algebraic invariants exploited by existing attacks, but this depends on the chosen code family. In Sect. 4 we discuss candidate code families, insecure regimes, and the need for further cryptanalysis, and provide a construction of an adaptively robust pseudorandom code with conjectured sub-exponential security from this assumption.

**Public-Key Pseudorandom Codes with CCA Security.** In Sect. 5, we describe a generic transformation for constructing an IND-CCA-secure PRC scheme using a primitive called *hinting pseudorandom generator (HPRG)* [35].

**Theorem 1 (Informal).** *Assuming the existence of an IND-CPA-secure PRC scheme with adaptive robustness, and a secure hinting PRG, there exists an IND-CCA-secure PRC scheme.*

*Instantiations.* Since every PRC is a PKE scheme, the required building blocks can be instantiated using several well-studied hardness assumptions:

- **Adaptively Robust PRC:** Under sub-exponential Learning Parity with noise (exLPN) [4], or our noisy McEliece assumption.
- **Hinting PRGs:** Constructions are known from Learning with Errors (LWE) [35] Computational DiffieHellman (CDH) [35], Decisional DiffieHellman (DDH) [2].

These instantiations yield the following corollary.

**Corollary 1.** *Assuming the hardness of $\mathcal{X}$ and $\mathcal{Y}$, where $\mathcal{X} \in \{\mathsf{LWE}, \mathsf{DDH}, \mathsf{CDH}\}$ and $\mathcal{Y} \in \{\text{noisy McEliece}, \mathsf{exLPN}\}$, there exists an IND-CCA-secure PRC scheme.*

*Remark 1 (Instantiating our results).* The above construction relies on a specialized form of hinting PRG, which we refer to as an *entropic hinting PRG*. This is essentially a hinting PRG that remains secure even when its seed is not sampled uniformly at random, but instead drawn from a distribution with sufficiently high entropy. Notably, most of the known constructions of hinting PRGs employ the *leftover hash lemma* in their security analysis, thereby ensuring the entropic property. For further details, see Sect. 3.2.

One exception to the above is the Linear Hidden Shift (LHS)-based construction of [2]. In the proof of this construction, the pseudorandomness of the output is directly argued by relying on the LHS assumption. While this is out of scope of our current work, we believe that the same proof strategy as in [2] gives rise to entropic hinting PRGs, if one is willing to rely on a high entropy version of the LHS assumption. If such an assumption is plausible, we would obtain an additional instantiation of the result above.

### 1.5 Related Works

Christ and Gunn [13] introduced the notion of PRCs and gave constructions in both, the secret-key and public-key settings. The subsequent work [4] strengthened the security model by allowing the adversary to have access to the decoding algorithm, introducing the corresponding CCA notion. More recently, [12] constructed secret-key PRCs that, for the first time, simultaneously achieve plausible subexponential pseudorandomness security, robustness to worst-case edit errors over a binary alphabet, and resilience even against computationally unbounded adversaries equipped with the decoding key. Achieving this combination of properties requires overcoming several barriers, as prior constructions neither attained subexponential security nor provided strong resilience guarantees. Zero-bit PRCs[1] were constructed in [32] under the assumption of local weak pseudorandom functions, which in turn follow from the hardness of learning $\log(n)$-juntas over the uniform distribution on $\{0,1\}^n$. Additional constructions of pseudorandom codes were explored in [30]. In particular, they construct public-key PRCs based on the planted hyperloop assumption [9] and pseudorandom generators, and also obtain statistically secure PRCs against space-bounded adversaries. On the contrary, two independent works [23,28] establish strong impossibility results for black-box constructions of pseudorandom codes from a broad class of strong cryptographic primitives including virtual black-box obfuscation.

In addition to the recent results in the area of pseudorandom codes, we also present an overview of IND-CPA to IND-CCA transformations. This overview is given in the full version.

As already mentioned in Sect. 1.4, in this work, we rely on the hinting PRG framework of Koppula-Waters [35]. We leave it as an interesting open problem if any of the other mentioned CCA transformations can also be applied to handle efficient error correction and obtain IND-CCA secure PRCs.

## 2 Technical Overview

In this section, we give a high-level overview of our construction. We begin by recalling the Koppula-Waters (KW) [35] construction of an IND-CCA-2 scheme.

### 2.1 The KW Construction

The KW construction gave a template for upgrading any IND-CPA PKE scheme to a CCA secure one, using a special kind of pseudorandom generators called *hinting PRGs.* A hinting PRG is a deterministic function $\mathsf{HPRG} : \{0,1\}^\lambda \rightarrow \{0,1\}^{\ell+\lambda^2}$ (where $\ell$ is polynomial in $\lambda$) with the following security property: for any PPT adversary, the following distribution looks uniform:

- sample seed $s \leftarrow \{0,1\}^\lambda$ and compute $\mathsf{HPRG}(s) = (r_0, r_1, \ldots, r_\lambda)$. Here $r_0 \in \{0,1\}^\ell$ and each $r_i \in \{0,1\}^\lambda$.

[1] A zero-bit PRC can encode only a single message $\mathsf{msg} = 0$.

- For each $i$, set $y_{i,s_i} = r_i$, and sample $y_{i,\overline{s_i}} \leftarrow \{0,1\}^\lambda$.
- Output $\left(r_0, (y_{i,b})_{i,b}\right)$.

Additionally, the KW construction uses *perfectly binding tag-based equivocal bit commitments.* In a tag-based commitment scheme, we have a setup algorithm that outputs the public parameters. The commitment algorithm $\mathsf{Com}$ takes as input the public parameters, the message bit and the tag, and produces a commitment string. For perfect binding, we require that for any public parameters $\mathsf{pp}$, any $\mathsf{tag}$, there does not exist randomness $v_0, v_1$ such that $\mathsf{Com}(\mathsf{pp}, 0, \mathsf{tag}; v_0) = \mathsf{Com}(\mathsf{pp}, 1, \mathsf{tag}; v_1)$. The equivocal property states that it is possible to generate 'fake' public parameters $\mathsf{pp}^*$ together with randomness $v_0^*, v_1^*$ for a challenge $\mathsf{tag}^*$ such that $\mathsf{pp}^*$ is computationally indistinguishable from the regular public parameters, but $\mathsf{Com}(\mathsf{pp}^*, 0, \mathsf{tag}^*; v_0^*) = \mathsf{Com}(\mathsf{pp}^*, 1, \mathsf{tag}^*; v_1^*)$. Almost perfectly binding tag-based equivocal bit commitment schemes can be constructed using any (regular) PRG [35,39].

The KW transformation also requires the underlying PKE scheme to satisfy the following two properties:

- *almost perfect correctness* - for almost all public keys $\mathsf{pk}$, for all messages $m$ and randomness $r$, $\mathsf{Dec}(\mathsf{sk}, \mathsf{Enc}(\mathsf{pk}, m; r)) = m$; and
- *decryption using randomness* - ciphertexts can be decrypted given the encryption randomness.

Both these properties can be achieved for free. Dwork, Naor and Reingold [22] showed that any $\mathsf{IND\text{-}CPA}$ PKE scheme can be transformed into another PKE scheme that satisfies almost perfect correctness. Likewise, any PKE scheme can be modified to also support decryption using randomness [35]. Now, we describe the setup, encryption and decryption algorithms of the KW scheme:

**Key Generation.** The setup algorithm generates key pairs $(\mathsf{pk}_{i,b}, \mathsf{sk}_{i,b})$ for all $i \in [\lambda]$, $b \in \{0,1\}$, where $\lambda$ is the seed length of $\mathsf{HPRG}$. The public key is the collection $\left(\mathsf{pk}_{i,b}\right)_{i,b}$, while the secret key consists of $(\mathsf{sk}_{i,0})_i$.[2]

**Encryption.** To encrypt a message $m$, the sender samples a random seed $s \in \{0,1\}^\lambda$ and computes $(r_0, r_1, \ldots, r_\lambda) = \mathsf{HPRG}(s)$. Next, it samples a one-time signing/verification key $(\mathsf{ds.sk}, \mathsf{ds.vk})$ and randomness $(v_i)_i$ for the commitment scheme. The ciphertext consists of two parts:

- The payload $c = m \oplus r_0$.
- For each $i \in [\lambda]$, it computes a commitment to the bit $s_i$ with tag $\mathsf{ds.vk}$ and randomness $v_i$ (that is, $\mathsf{com}_i \leftarrow \mathsf{Com}(s_i, \mathsf{ds.vk}; v_i)$). Then, it sets

$$c_{i,s_i} = \mathsf{Enc}\left(\mathsf{pk}_{i,s_i}, 1\|v_i; \tilde{r}_i\right), \qquad c_{i,\overline{s_i}} \leftarrow \mathsf{Enc}\left(\mathsf{pk}_{i,\overline{s_i}}, 0^\lambda\right)$$

Finally, the encryption algorithm signs $\mathsf{ds}.x = \left(c, (c_{i,b}, \mathsf{com}_i)_{i,b}\right)$ using $\mathsf{ds.sk}$, resulting in the signature $\mathsf{ds}.\sigma$. The full ciphertext is $(\mathsf{ds.vk}, \mathsf{ds}.x, \mathsf{ds}.\sigma)$.

[2] Note that only the $\mathsf{sk}_{i,0}$ secret keys are included, the remaining are discarded.

**Decryption.** First, the decryption algorithm verifies the signature using the verification key $\mathsf{ds.vk}$. If the signature verifies, the decryption algorithm recovers a candidate seed $s$, performs consistency checks using $s$, and finally recovers the message from the payload. More formally,

1. *Recovering the seed.* For each $i$, it uses $\mathsf{sk}_{i,0}$ to decrypt $c_{i,0}$. If the result is of the form $1\|v_i$ and $v_i$ is a valid opening of $\mathsf{com}_i$ to 0 (with respect to tag $\mathsf{ds.vk}$), it sets $s_i = 0$. Otherwise, it sets $s_i = 1$. This yields a candidate seed $s$.
2. *Verification and message recovery.* Using $s$, it recomputes $(r_0, (r_i)_i) = \mathsf{HPRG}(s)$. For each $i \in [\lambda]$,
   - it checks that decrypting $c_{i,s_i}$ with randomness $r_i$[3] yields a message of the form $1\|w_i$, and that $w_i$ is a valid opening of $\mathsf{com}_i$ for bit $s_i$ (with respect to $\mathsf{ds.vk}$)
   - it checks that re-encrypting $1\|w_i$ using randomness $r_i$ yields $c_{i,s_i}$.

   If all checks pass, it outputs $m = c \oplus r_0$; otherwise, it outputs $\perp$.

The KW scheme, like many other CCA secure encryption schemes, uses the *secret hiding principle* [26], where we have multiple secret keys for the same public key. In the security proof, we switch from using one secret key to another. This is a key technical step in the security proof of KW. Note that in the above described construction, for any $\mathfrak{p} \in \{0,1\}^n$, we could have used the secret keys $(\mathsf{sk}_{i,\mathfrak{p}_i})_i$ for decryption, and correctness would still hold. KW showed that even for maliciously crafted ciphertexts, decryption of $\mathsf{ct}$ using $(\mathsf{sk}_{i,0})_i$ is equal to the decryption of $\mathsf{ct}$ using $(\mathsf{sk}_{i,\mathfrak{p}_i})_i$. Below, we briefly discuss why this property holds (assuming almost-perfect correctness of PKE and almost-perfect binding of the commitment scheme).

Let $\mathsf{Dec}^\dagger$ denote the decryption using $(\mathsf{sk}_{i,\mathfrak{p}_i})_{i\in[\lambda]}$. Fix any ciphertext $\mathsf{ct}$, and let $s$ (resp. $s^\dagger$) denote the candidate seed found in the first step of $\mathsf{Dec}$ (resp. $\mathsf{Dec}^\dagger$). Clearly, $s \neq s^\dagger$, otherwise both decryption routines produce the same output. Suppose $s_i = 0$ and $s_i^\dagger = 1$, and suppose $\mathsf{Dec}$ does not output $\perp$. First, note that since $s_i \neq s_i^\dagger$, $\mathfrak{p}_i$ must be 1. Next, since $\mathsf{Dec}$ does not output $\perp$, it follows that $\mathsf{ct}_{i,0}$ is an encryption of $1\|w_i$, and $w_i$ is a valid opening for certifying that $\mathsf{com}_i$ is a commitment to bit 0. Finally, let us see why $\mathsf{Dec}^\dagger$ set $s_i^\dagger = 1$ : it decrypted $\mathsf{ct}_{i,1}$ and obtained $1\|w_i^\dagger$ such that $w_i^\dagger$ is a valid decommitment of $\mathsf{com}_i$ for bit 1. But this is a contradiction since we assumed perfect binding for the commitment scheme. The other case (where $s_i = 1$ and $s_i^\dagger = 0$) relies on the perfect correctness of PKE and is handled similarly.

## 2.2 IND-CCA PRC with Low Error Rate

In this section, we present our first CCA-PRC construction. This construction is adaptively $\alpha$-robust, where $\alpha = \Theta(1/\lambda)$. In the next section, we discuss how to achieve constant rate robustness.

[3] Here, we use the decryption-using-randomness property of the base PKE scheme.

***Making KW ciphertexts pseudorandom:*** Note that the ciphertexts in the KW encryption scheme are neither pseudorandom, nor error tolerant. We first discuss how to make the ciphertexts pseudorandom. There are three obstacles:

1. *PKE ciphertexts.* The ciphertext components $c_{i,b}$ may not be pseudorandom. This can be fixed by requiring the underlying PKE scheme to have pseudorandom ciphertexts.
2. *Commitments.* The commitments used in the construction may also fail to be pseudorandom. This can be addressed by employing a commitment scheme with pseudorandom commitments. For instance, Naor's commitment scheme (based solely on the existence of a PRG) suffices.
3. *Verification key.* The most crucial issue is that the verification key $\mathsf{vk}$, together with a valid signature, is never pseudorandom, since the verification algorithm itself acts as a distinguisher. However, Lamport's signature scheme provides signatures that are indistinguishable from random strings in the absence of $\mathsf{vk}$. To hide $\mathsf{vk}$, we can embed it inside one of the PKE encryptions, e.g., in both $c_{1,0}$ and $c_{1,1}$. Including it in both components is necessary for the security proof.

We note that CCA-secure schemes with pseudorandom ciphertexts have already been constructed in prior works.

***Adding Robustness:*** A first attempt is to replace the CPA-PKE ciphertexts in the previous construction with CPA-PRC ciphertexts. Since each of the ciphertexts are individually pseudorandom, and the payload is also pseudorandom, one can hope that this directly results in an $\mathsf{IND\text{-}CCA}$-secure PRC scheme. Unfortunately, this natural attempt is not compatible with the KW proof strategy. In particular, the decryptor must be able to detect if the PRC ciphertexts contain too much noise (otherwise the adversary can create ciphertexts which can detect the set of secret keys being used for decryption), and this is not possible if the decryptor recovers only half the randomness used for the PRC encoding.

We address this issue by using a two-layered approach—first encrypting the commitment openings using a PKE scheme, and then encrypting the resulting ciphertexts and commitments using a CPA-PRC scheme. The key generation algorithm samples $2n$ public/secret key pairs for the PKE scheme $\left(\mathsf{pke.pk}_{i,b}, \mathsf{pke.sk}_{i,b}\right)_{i,b}$. It also samples $2n$ PRC encoding/decoding keys $\left(\mathsf{prc.pk}_{i,b}, \mathsf{prc.sk}_{i,b}\right)$, and the public parameters $\mathsf{com.pp}$ for the commitment scheme,[4] and the public parameters $\mathsf{hprg.pp}$ for the hinting PRG scheme. We also sample a number $\zeta$ uniformly at random (from a sufficiently large field $\mathbb{F}$). The public and secret key for our CCA-PRC scheme are as follows:

$$\mathsf{PK} = \left(\zeta, \mathsf{com.pp}, \mathsf{hprg.pp}, \left(\mathsf{pke.pk}_{i,b}, \mathsf{prc.pk}_{i,b}\right)_{i,b}\right), \quad \mathsf{SK} = \left(\mathsf{pke.sk}_{i,b}, \mathsf{prc.sk}_{i,b}\right)_{i,b}.$$

**Encryption.** The encryption algorithm samples a HPRG seed $s$ and signing/verification keys $(\mathsf{ds.sk}, \mathsf{ds.vk})$. It computes $(r_0, r_1, \ldots, r_\lambda) = \mathsf{HPRG}(s)$ and

[4] In our construction, we also require an additional property from the commitment scheme - the commitment to bit 0 should not depend upon the tag.

parses $r_0 = (r_{00}, r_{01})$, where both $r_{00}, r_{01}$ are $\lambda$ bits long. Next, it samples commitment openings $(v_i)_i$, computes $\mathsf{com}_i = \mathsf{Com}(\mathsf{com.pp}, s_i, \mathsf{ds.vk}; v_i)$, and follows the KW template for computing the PKE ciphertexts. For each $i$, it sets

$$\mathsf{pke.ct}_{i,s_i} = \mathsf{PKE.Enc}\left(\mathsf{pke.pk}_{i,s_i}, 1\|v_i\|\mathsf{ds.vk}; r_i\right)$$
$$\mathsf{pke.ct}_{i,\overline{s_i}} \leftarrow \mathsf{PKE.Enc}\left(\mathsf{pke.pk}_{i,\overline{s_i}}, 0^{2\lambda+1}\right)$$

Next, it samples randomness $(z_{i,b})_{i,b}$ and computes PRC encodings of each ciphertext and commitment. That is, for each $i, b$, it sets

$$c_{i,b} = \mathsf{PRC.Encode}\left(\mathsf{prc.pk}_{i,b}, (\mathsf{pke.ct}_{i,b}, \mathsf{com}_i); z_{i,b}\right).$$

It then computes the payload $c$, which contains an encoding of the message $m$, randomness $(z_{i,b})_{i,b}$ used for PRC encoding, the commitments and the PKE ciphertexts. The payload is

$$c = \mathsf{PRG}(r_{00}) + \zeta \cdot \mathsf{ECC.Encode}\left(m, (z_{i,b}, \mathsf{pke.ct}_{i,b}, \mathsf{com}_i)_{i,b}\right).$$

Here, $\mathsf{PRG}$ is a regular pseudorandom generator (with sufficient stretch) and the output of the PRG is a number in a large field $\mathbb{F}$, and $\mathsf{ECC}$ is a regular error correcting code (over the binary alphabet). The output of the ECC will be interpreted as a number in $\mathbb{F}$. Looking ahead, we will argue that with overwhelming probability over the choice of $\zeta$, once the payload is fixed, the underlying components $\left(m, (z_{i,b}, \mathsf{pke.ct}_{i,b}, \mathsf{com}_i)_{i,b}\right)$ are fixed.

Finally, the encryption algorithm computes a signature on the payload and PRC codewords. It computes $\mathsf{ds.}\sigma = \mathsf{Sign}\left(\mathsf{ds.sk}, \left(c, (c_{i,b})_{i,b}\right)\right)$, and a masked version $\sigma = \mathsf{PRG}(r_{01}) \oplus \mathsf{ECC.Encode}(\mathsf{ds.}\sigma)$. The final ciphertext is $(c, (c_{i,b})_{i,b}, \sigma)$.

*Information Rate of our PRC Scheme:* Our PRC scheme preserves the information rate of the underlying error correcting code. Suppose $\mathsf{ECC}$ maps $t$ bit messages to $k_{\mathsf{ecc}} \cdot t$ bits for some $k_{\mathsf{ecc}} > 1$, and let $\ell_{\mathsf{msg}}$ denote the length of the message being encoded by our PRC scheme. The payload size is $k_{\mathsf{ecc}} \cdot (\ell_{\mathsf{msg}} + \mathsf{poly}(\lambda))$, since each CPA-PKE ciphertext encrypts $O(\lambda)$ bit strings, and the commitments are also $\mathsf{poly}(\lambda)$ bits long. The CPA-PRC codewords encode $\mathsf{poly}(\lambda)$ bit strings, and therefore have size $\mathsf{poly}(\lambda)$. Finally, the signature is only $O(\lambda)$ bits long. Putting everything together, the ciphertext size is dominated by $k_{\mathsf{ecc}} \cdot \ell_{\mathsf{msg}}$ (for long messages).

**Decryption.** The decryption algorithm uses the secret keys corresponding to the $0^n$ path (i.e., $(\mathsf{prc.sk}_{i,0}, \mathsf{pke.sk}_{i,0})_i$), and proceeds as follows:

- *Recovering a candidate seed.*
  1. First, it decrypts each $c_{i,0}$ using $\mathsf{prc.sk}_{i,0}$, recovering $\left(\underline{\mathsf{pke.ct}_{i,0}}, \underline{\mathsf{com}_i}\right)$. If any of the decryptions fail, it is set to a default value (but do not abort the decryption).

2. Next, for each $i$, it decrypts $\mathsf{pke.ct}_{i,0}$. If the decrypted message is of the form $1\|\underline{\mathsf{op}_i}\|\underline{\mathsf{ds.vk}_i}$ and $\underline{\mathsf{com}_i} = \mathsf{Com}\left(0, \underline{\mathsf{ds.vk}_i}; \underline{\mathsf{op}_i}\right)$, then it guesses that $t_i = 0$, else it guesses $t_i = 1$. Again, decryption does not abort if the decryption of $\mathsf{pke.ct}_{i,0}$ fails, it simply guesses $t_i = 1$.

- *Checking noise in the ciphertext components*
  1. Having obtained a candidate seed $t$, the decryption algorithm computes $(r_{00}, r_{01}, r_1, \ldots, r_\lambda) = \mathsf{HPRG}(t)$.
  2. It then recovers the (error-free) message, the randomness used for the PRC encodings, the commitments, and PKE ciphertexts from the payload. It computes $\left(\mathsf{msg}, (z_{i,b}, \mathsf{pke.ct}_{i,b}, \mathsf{com}_i)_i\right) = \mathsf{ECC.Decode}\left(\zeta^{-1}\left(\mathsf{PRG}\left(r_{00}\right) \oplus c\right)\right)$.
  3. Similarly, it recovers the error-free digital signature from $\sigma$—$\mathsf{ds}.\sigma = \mathsf{ECC.Decode}\left(\mathsf{PRG}\left(r_{01}\right) \oplus \sigma\right)$.
  4. It re-encrypts each PRC ciphertext using the error-free PKE ciphertexts and commitments, and the randomness obtained from the payload. For each $i, b$, it computes $c'_{i,b} = \mathsf{PRC.Encode}(\mathsf{prc.pk}_{i,b}, (\mathsf{pke.ct}_{i,b}, \mathsf{com}_i); z_{i,b})$ and checks that $\Delta\left(c_{i,b}, c'_{i,b}\right)$ is small (which ensures that the amount of noise in each PRC codeword is bounded).
  5. Similarly, it checks that the noise in $c$ and $\sigma$ is bounded. It then computes $c' = \mathsf{PRG}\left(r_{00}\right) \oplus \left(\mathsf{msg}, (z_{i,b}, \mathsf{pke.ct}_{i,b}, \mathsf{com}_i)_{i,b}\right)$, $\sigma' = \mathsf{PRG}\left(r_{01}\right) \oplus \mathsf{ds}.\sigma$, and checks that $\Delta\left(c, c'\right)$ and $\Delta\left(\sigma, \sigma'\right)$ are small.
- *Comparing the commitments and PKE ciphertexts recovered via decryption, with the commitments and PKE ciphertexts recovered from the payload.*
  1. For each $i$ such that $t_i$ is set to 0, we recovered a PKE ciphertext and commitment from $c_{i,0}$. The decryption algorithm checks that these are consistent with the PKE ciphertexts and commitments in the payload. If $t_i = 0$, we check that $\mathsf{pke.ct}_{i,0} = \mathsf{pke.ct}_{i,0}$ and $\mathsf{com}_i = \underline{\mathsf{com}_i}$.
- *Performing the KW checks*
  1. For each $i$, it decrypts $\mathsf{pke.ct}_{i,t_i}$ using the randomness $r_i$, recovers $1\|v_i\|\mathsf{ds.vk}_i$, checks that $v_i$ is a valid opening of $\mathsf{com}_i$ for the bit $s_i$ (w.r.t. $\mathsf{ds.vk}_i$), and that re-encryption of $1\|v_i\|\mathsf{ds.vk}_i$ with randomness $r_i$ gives $\mathsf{pke.ct}_{i,s_i}$. If any of these checks fail, it outputs $\perp$.
- *Checking the digital signature*: Finally, the decryption algorithm checks that all the verification keys $\mathsf{ds.vk}_i$ are equal, and that the signature $\mathsf{ds}.\sigma$ (obtained from $\sigma$) on $\left(c', \left(c'_{i,b}\right)_{i,b}\right)$ is valid (with respect to the common verification key).

**Security of Our Construction.** At a high level, our proof follows the KW proof structure. Let $t^*$ denote the seed, and $\mathsf{ds.vk}^*$ the verification key used in the challenge ciphertext. First, using the security of the signature scheme, we can argue that for all decryption queries not close to the challenge ciphertext, if the verification key extracted from the ciphertext is equal to $\mathsf{ds.vk}^*$, then such decryption queries can be rejected. Next, we switch the commitment scheme's public parameters to make them equivocal at $\mathsf{ds.vk}^*$, this follows from the security of the commitment scheme. After this, we decrypt using the secret keys $\left(\mathsf{prc.sk}_{i,t_i^*}, \mathsf{pke.sk}_{i,t_i^*}\right)_i$. Using the perfect correctness of the PKE scheme, the perfect binding of the commitment scheme and adaptive robustness of the base PRC scheme, we argue that this switch in the decryption oracle goes unnoticed by the adversary. This indistinguishability proof is one of the key technical challenges in our proof, and we discuss this separately in the next paragraph. Assuming the decryption switch works, we then switch the PKE ciphertexts in the challenge ciphertext that are not on the $t^*$ path. Instead of encrypting $\mathbf{0}$, we encrypt a commitment opening for bit $\overline{t_i^*}$ wrt $\mathsf{ds.vk}^*$ (recall, since our commitments are equivocal for tag $\mathsf{ds.vk}^*$, we can produce openings for both 0 and 1). This switch follows from the CPA security of the PKE scheme since the corresponding secret keys are not used in the decryption oracle. We now switch back the decryption oracle to use $\left(\mathsf{prc.sk}_{i,0}, \mathsf{pke.sk}_{i,0}\right)_i$. At this point, note that the HPRG seed is only used to compute the randomness $(r_{00}, r_{01}, r_1, \ldots, r_\lambda)$. We can now use the HPRG security to switch all these to uniformly random, and then use the regular PRG security to make the payload $c$ and signature component $\sigma$ uniformly random. Next, we use the PRC security to replace the PRC ciphertexts $c_{i,1}$ with uniformly random strings (note that the corresponding PRC secret keys are not needed for decryption, and we already switched the payload $c$ to a uniformly random string). At this point, the only components that are not uniformly random are the PRC ciphertexts $c_{i,0}$. We now switch the decryption oracle again, using the secret keys $\left(\mathsf{prc.sk}_{i,1}, \mathsf{pke.sk}_{i,1}\right)_i$. Now, we can finally replace the codewords $\left(c_{i,0}\right)_i$ with uniformly random strings. Therefore, all that remains is to show that if an adversary can distinguish between various modes of decryption, then this adversary can break adaptive robustness of the base PRC.

*Switching the Decryption Oracle.* Let $\mathsf{Dec}$ denote the regular decryption, and $\mathsf{Dec}^\dagger$ denote the decryption along path $\mathfrak{p}$. We want to argue that no p.p.t. adversary can produce a ciphertext $\mathsf{ct} = \left(c, \left(c_{i,b}\right)_{i,b}, \sigma\right)$ such that the outputs of $\mathsf{Dec}$ and $\mathsf{Dec}^\dagger$ on $\mathsf{ct}$ are different (and this argument does not rely on the hiding of $\mathfrak{p}$). We will prove the following statements:

1. Suppose $\mathsf{Dec}$ finds a candidate seed $t$, and finally produces a non-$\perp$ message, then $\mathsf{Dec}^\dagger$ must also produce the same candidate $t$.[5]
2. If $\mathsf{Dec}$ and $\mathsf{Dec}^\dagger$ find the same candidate seed $t$, then they must produce the same output.

Let us consider the first statement. Suppose, on the contrary, $\mathsf{Dec}$ uses a candidate seed $t$ and produces a non-$\perp$ output, and $\mathsf{Dec}^\dagger$ produces a different candidate seed $t^\dagger$ such that $t_i \neq t_i^\dagger$. As in the KW decryption switching proof, we will consider two sub-cases: $t_i = 0$ and $t_i^\dagger = 1$ and $t_i = 1$ and $t_i^\dagger = 0$.

[5] We observe that the following is also true, i.e., suppose $\mathsf{Dec}^\dagger$ finds a candidate seed $t$, and finally produces a non-$\perp$ message, then $\mathsf{Dec}$ must also produce the same candidate $t$.

- $t_i = 0$ and $t_i^\dagger = 1$: For the first sub-case, we will arrive at a contradiction by relying on the perfect binding of the commitments and the adaptive robustness. First, note that if $t_i \neq t_i^\dagger$, then $\mathfrak{p}_i$ must be equal to 1 (otherwise the strings $t$ and $t^\dagger$ cannot differ at the $i^{th}$ index. Next, from the structure of our payload, it follows that with all but negligible probability over the choice of $\zeta$, there exists at most one $r_{00}$, $\mathsf{ds}.x = \left(\mathsf{msg}, (z_{i,b}, \mathsf{pke.ct}_{i,b}, \mathsf{com}_i)_i\right)$ such that $c = \mathsf{PRG}(r_{00}) + \zeta \cdot \mathsf{ECC}(\mathsf{ds}.x)$.
  Let $\left(\underline{\mathsf{pke.ct}_{i,0}}, \underline{\mathsf{com}_i}\right)$ be the ciphertext and commitment recovered from $c_{i,0}$. Since $t_i = 0$ and $\mathsf{Dec}$ does not output $\perp$, we get that
  - $\underline{\mathsf{com}_i} = \mathsf{com}_i$, $\underline{\mathsf{pke.ct}_{i,0}} = \mathsf{pke.ct}_{i,0}$
  - decryption of $\underline{\mathsf{pke.ct}_{i,0}}$ produces $1 \| v_i \| \mathsf{ds.vk}_i$ such that $v_i$ is an opening of $\mathsf{com}_i$ for bit 0
  - $\Delta\left(c_{i,0}, c'_{i,0}\right)$ and $\Delta\left(c_{i,1}, c'_{i,1}\right)$ are bounded

  Next, we use the fact that $t_i^\dagger$ is set to 1. This means that $c_{i,1}$ decrypts to some $\left(\underline{\mathsf{pke.ct}_{i,1}}^\dagger, \underline{\mathsf{com}}_{i,1}^\dagger\right)$ and $\underline{\mathsf{com}}_i^\dagger$ is a commitment to 1 (with respect to some $\mathsf{ds.vk}^\dagger$). Now, if $\underline{\mathsf{com}}_i^\dagger = \mathsf{com}_i$, then we break the perfect binding property of the commitment scheme. This is because $\mathsf{com}_i = \underline{\mathsf{com}_i}$ is a commitment to the bit 0 (and commitments to the bit 0 do not depend on the tag), and also a commitment to the bit 1 wrt $\mathsf{ds.vk}^\dagger$ if $\underline{\mathsf{com}}_i^\dagger = \mathsf{com}_i$. On the other hand, if $\underline{\mathsf{com}}_i^\dagger \neq \mathsf{com}_i$, then we break the adaptive robustness of the base PRC scheme. This is because $c_{i,1}$ decrypts to $\left(\ldots, \underline{\mathsf{com}}_{i,1}^\dagger\right)$, and $c'_{i,1}$ (which is a PRC encryption of $(\mathsf{pke.ct}_{i,1}, \mathsf{com}_i)$ with randomness $z_{i,1}$) is close to $c_{i,1}$.
- $t_i = 1, t_i^\dagger = 0$: For the second sub-case, we will show a contradiction by relying on the perfect correctness of the PKE and the adaptive robustness of the PRC.

Next, let us consider the second case. If both $\mathsf{Dec}$ and $\mathsf{Dec}^\dagger$ recover the same candidate seed $t$ and $\mathsf{Dec}$ outputs non-$\perp$, then $\mathsf{Dec}^\dagger$ must also output the same non-$\perp$ message. This again follows from the fact that $c$ is binding to $(\mathsf{msg}, (z_{i,b}, \mathsf{pke.ct}_{i,b}, \mathsf{com}_i)_i)$, and since both recover the same guess $t$, both modes of decryption would output $\mathsf{msg}$.

## 2.3 Improving the Error Rate of Our CCA-PRC Construction

One limitation of the previous construction is that it cannot handle errors at a constant fraction of the positions, as this would mean that some of the PRC ciphertexts can be completely lost. To achieve better error tolerance, the decryption algorithm must be able to recover the hinting PRG seed $s$ even if some PRC components are corrupted. A natural fix is to use an error-correcting code: rather than feeding $s$ directly into the hinting PRG, we encode it as $t = \mathsf{ECC.Encode}(s)$ and evaluate the HPRG on $t$. This way, even if several PRC ciphertexts are corrupted, the decryption algorithm can still reconstruct $s$ and proceed with decryption. This gives us a PRC with constant rate adaptive robustness, assuming the base PRC and ECC have constant rate robustness.

**Security Proof.** One nuance that arises is with respect to the security of hinting PRGs. Existing hinting PRG constructions prove security when the seed is sampled uniformly at random. However, it is easy to check that the proofs of security for standard hinting PRG constructions rely only on min-entropy of the input. Since ECC is a deterministic encoding, the entropy of $t$ is identical to that of $s$. Hence, this modification is sound.

The security proof for the constant rate construction follows the same proof steps as the low-rate construction. The only step that requires some attention is the oracle switching step. To address this, we give a *lifting lemma* (in the full version). This lemma essentially shows that if an adversary produces a ciphertext ct such that it can distinguish between Dec and $\mathsf{Dec}^\dagger$, then there exists an index $i$ such that $\mathfrak{p}_i = 1$, $\tilde{t}_i$ (the noisy candidate seed recovered by Dec) is not equal to the corresponding bit $\widetilde{t_i^\dagger}$ recovered by $\mathsf{Dec}^\dagger$, and both $c_{i,0}$ and $c_{i,1}$ have bounded noise. Note that this is all that we required for the oracle switching proof for the low-rate scheme.

## 3 Preliminaries

**Notations:** Let PPT denote probabilistic polynomial-time. We denote the set of all positive integers up to $n$ as $[n] := \{1, \ldots, n\}$. For any set $S$, we denote $\mathcal{P}(S)$ as the power set of $S$. We denote vectors/binary strings using bold font. For any two binary strings $\mathbf{x}, \mathbf{y}$, we use the notation $\mathbf{x} \| \mathbf{y}$ to denote $\mathbf{x}$ concatenated with $\mathbf{y}$. Here, $x_i$ denotes the $i^{th}$ bit of $\mathbf{x}$. For any $\mathbf{x} \in \mathbb{F}^n$, we denote $\mathsf{Ham}(\mathbf{x})$ as the Hamming weight of $\mathbf{x}$, i.e., the number of non-zero entries in $\mathbf{x}$. And, $\mathsf{Ham}(\mathbf{x}, \mathbf{y})$ denotes the Hamming distance between the binary strings $\mathbf{x}$ and $\mathbf{y}$, i.e., the number of indices where $\mathbf{x}$ and $\mathbf{y}$ differ. We also write $\Delta(\mathbf{x}, \mathbf{y})$ for Hamming distance. We denote $\mathcal{B}_\delta(\mathbf{x}, \mathbb{F}^n)$ as the set $\{\mathbf{x}' \in \mathbb{F}^n \mid \mathsf{Ham}(\mathbf{x}, \mathbf{x}') \leq \delta \cdot n\}$, i.e., the set of all strings with Hamming distance of $r$ from $\mathbf{x}$. Furthermore, we define $\mathcal{B}_\delta(\mathbb{F}^n) := \mathcal{B}_\delta(\mathbf{0}, \mathbb{F}^n)$. We denote by $\mathsf{Ber}_\rho^{m \times n}$ the distribution over $m \times n$ matrices defined as follows: each entry is sampled independently, taking a value uniformly at random from $\mathbb{F} \setminus \{0\}$ with probability $\rho$, and 0 otherwise. For any finite set $S$, $x \leftarrow S$ denotes a uniformly random element $x$ from the set $S$. Similarly, for any distribution $\mathcal{D}$, $x \leftarrow \mathcal{D}$ denotes an element $x$ drawn from the distribution $\mathcal{D}$.

### 3.1 Public-Key Pseudorandom Codes

A public-key PRC with $\kappa$-correctness $\alpha$-robustness is described by three algorithms $(\mathsf{Setup}, \mathsf{Encode}, \mathsf{Decode})$, satisfying the following criteria:

**Syntax:** There exist functions $s, p, \ell_{\mathsf{cw}}, \ell_{\mathsf{msg}}, r, \ell_{\mathsf{Enc}}, r'' : \mathbb{N} \to \mathbb{N}$ such that for all $\lambda \in \mathbb{N}$, $\mathsf{Setup} : 1^\lambda \times \{0,1\}^{r''(\lambda)} \to \{0,1\}^{p(\lambda)} \times \{0,1\}^{s(\lambda)}$, $\mathsf{Encode} : \{0,1\}^{p(\lambda)} \times \{0,1\}^{\ell_{\mathsf{msg}}(\lambda)} \times \{0,1\}^{\ell_{\mathsf{Enc}}(\lambda)} \to \{0,1\}^{\ell_{\mathsf{cw}}(\lambda)}$, and $\mathsf{Decode} : \{0,1\}^{s(\lambda)} \times \{0,1\}^{\ell_{\mathsf{cw}}(\lambda)} \times \{0,1\}^{r(\lambda)} \to \{0,1\}^{\ell_{\mathsf{msg}}(\lambda)} \cup \perp$.

**Error correction, or robustness:** For any $\lambda \in \mathbb{N}$, message $\mathsf{msg} \in \{0,1\}^{\ell_{\mathsf{msg}}(\lambda)}$,

$$\Pr\left[\mathsf{Decode}(\mathsf{sk}, \mathbf{c}+\mathbf{e}) \neq \mathsf{msg} \;\middle|\; \begin{array}{r} (\mathsf{pk},\mathsf{sk}) \leftarrow \mathsf{Setup}(1^\lambda) \\ \mathbf{c} \leftarrow \mathsf{Encode}(\mathsf{pk},\mathsf{msg}) \\ \mathbf{e} \leftarrow \mathcal{B}_\alpha^{\ell_{\mathsf{cw}}} \end{array}\right] \leq \kappa(\lambda).$$

where the probability is over the randomness of Setup, Encode and error $e$.
Pseudorandomness: For any polynomial-time adversary $\mathcal{A}$,

$$\Pr_{(\mathsf{pk},\mathsf{sk})\leftarrow\mathsf{Setup}(1^\lambda)}\left[\mathcal{A}^{\mathsf{O}_{\mathsf{pk}}(\cdot)}(1^\lambda,\mathsf{pk}) = 1\right] - \Pr_{\substack{(\mathsf{pk},\mathsf{sk})\leftarrow\mathsf{Setup}(1^\lambda)\\ U}}\left[\mathcal{A}^{U(1^\lambda,\cdot)}(1^\lambda,\mathsf{pk}) = 1\right] \leq \mathrm{negl}(\lambda),$$

where $\mathsf{O}_{\mathsf{pk}}$ on any (even previously queried) input msg samples a random $r \in \{0,1\}^{\ell_{\mathsf{Enc}}(\lambda)}$ and outputs $\mathsf{Encode}(\mathsf{pk},\mathsf{msg};r)$ and $U$ denotes an oracle that on any (even previously queried) input returns a fresh uniform string in $\{0,1\}^{\ell_{\mathsf{cw}}}$.

**CCA-Security:** For any stateful polynomial time adversary $\mathcal{A}$, we require the following to hold:

$$\Pr\left[b' = b \;\middle|\; \begin{array}{r} (\mathsf{pk},\mathsf{sk}) \leftarrow \mathsf{Setup}(1^\lambda) \\ m \leftarrow \mathcal{A}^{\mathsf{Decode}(\mathsf{sk},\cdot)}(\mathsf{pk}) \\ b \leftarrow \{0,1\} \\ \text{if } b=0: \mathsf{ct} \leftarrow \mathsf{Encode}(\mathsf{pk},m) \\ \text{if } b=1: \mathsf{ct} \leftarrow \{0,1\}^{\ell_{\mathsf{cw}}(\lambda)} \\ b' \leftarrow \mathcal{A}^{\mathcal{O}(\cdot)}(\mathsf{ct}) \end{array}\right] \leq \frac{1}{2} + \mathsf{negl}(\lambda).$$

where

$$\mathcal{O}(\mathsf{ct}') = \begin{cases} \mathsf{Decode}(\mathsf{sk},\mathsf{ct}') & \text{if } \forall \mathbf{e}: \mathsf{ct}' \oplus \mathbf{e} \neq \mathsf{ct}, \text{ where } \mathsf{Ham}(\mathbf{e}) \leq \alpha\ell_{\mathsf{cw}}(\lambda) \\ \perp & \text{otherwise}. \end{cases}$$

where $\ell_{\mathsf{cw}}(\lambda)$ is the length of the ciphertext and $\alpha$ is the robustness of the PRC.

The information rate of a PRC is the ratio between $\ell_{\mathsf{cw}}$ and $\ell_{\mathsf{msg}}$.

**Definition 1 (Soundness).** *A public-key PRC with codeword space $\mathcal{Y}_\lambda$ is sound if* $\Pr\left[\mathsf{Decode}(\mathsf{sk},\mathbf{u}) \neq \perp \mid (\mathsf{pk},\mathsf{sk}) \leftarrow \mathsf{Setup}(1^\lambda),\ \mathbf{u} \leftarrow \mathcal{Y}_\lambda\right] \leq \mathsf{negl}(\lambda)$. *For the binary syntax above,* $\mathcal{Y}_\lambda = \{0,1\}^{\ell_{\mathsf{cw}}(\lambda)}$.

**Definition 2 (Adaptive Robustness).** *A stronger notion of robustness called adaptive robustness is defined via the following game parameterized by a constant* $\alpha \in (0,1/2)$.

1. *The challenger samples* $(\mathsf{pk},\mathsf{sk}) \leftarrow \mathsf{Setup}(1^\lambda)$ *and sends* pk *to the adversary.*

2. *The adversary sends* $(m, r, x)$ *to the challenger.*
3. *The challenger computes* $c = \mathsf{Encode}(\mathsf{pk}, m; r)$ *and* $m' \leftarrow \mathsf{Decode}(\mathsf{sk}, x)$. *If* $\mathsf{Ham}(c, x) \leq \alpha n$ *and* $m \neq m'$, *then output the adversary wins. Otherwise, it loses.*

*We say that a public-key pseudorandom code PRC is adaptively* $\alpha$*-robust if, for any PPT adversary* $\mathcal{A}$, *there exists a negligible function* $\mathsf{negl}(\cdot)$ *such that for all* $\lambda \in \mathbb{N}$, $\Pr[\mathcal{A}$ *wins in the above game*$] \leq \mathsf{negl}(\lambda)$.

**Theorem 2** ([4]). *Assuming* $2^{O(\sqrt{\lambda})}$ *hardness of* $\mathsf{LPN}$, *there exists an adaptively robust public key PRC with error rate* $\delta/8$ *for any* $\delta \in (0, 1/4)$.

If, in addition, the adversary is given the secret key $\mathsf{sk}$ in the first step of the above game, then the notion is referred to as *strong adaptive robustness* [12].

### 3.2 Hinting Pseudorandom Generator

A hinting PRG ($\mathsf{HPRG}$) is a pair of algorithms $(\mathsf{Setup}, \mathsf{Eval})$ such that:

$\mathsf{Setup}(1^\lambda, 1^\ell)$ : The generation algorithm is a randomized algorithm that takes as input a unary representation of the security parameter $\lambda$, a length parameter $\ell$ and outputs a public parameter $\mathsf{pp}$ and input length $n = n(\lambda, \ell)$.

$\mathsf{Eval}(\mathsf{pp}, s, i)$ : The evaluation algorithm is a deterministic algorithm that takes as input a public parameter $\mathsf{pp}$, a seed $s \in \{0,1\}^n$ and an index $i \in \{0\} \cup [n]$ and outputs a bit string $y \in \{0,1\}^\ell$.

*Security:* A hinting PRG scheme $(\mathsf{Setup}, \mathsf{Eval})$ is said to be secure if for any $\mathsf{PPT}$ adversary $\mathcal{A}$, polynomial $\ell(\cdot)$ there exists a negligible function $\mathsf{negl}(\cdot)$ such that for all $\lambda \in \mathbb{N}$, the following holds:

$$\Pr\left[1 \leftarrow \mathcal{A}\left(\mathsf{pp}, y_0^\beta, \left\{y_{i,b}^\beta\right\}\right) \;\middle|\; \begin{array}{r} (\mathsf{pp}, n) \leftarrow \mathsf{Setup}(1^\lambda, 1^\ell), s \leftarrow \{0,1\}^n, \\ \beta \leftarrow \{0,1\}, y_0^0 \leftarrow \{0,1\}^\ell, y_0^1 = \mathsf{Eval}(\mathsf{pp}, s, 0), \\ y_{i,b}^0 \leftarrow \{0,1\}^\ell \,\forall i \in [n], b \in \{0,1\}, \\ y_{i,s_i}^1 = \mathsf{Eval}(\mathsf{pp}, s, i), y_{i,\overline{s_i}}^1 \leftarrow \{0,1\}^\ell \,\forall i \in [n] \end{array}\right] \leq \frac{1}{2} + \mathsf{negl}(\lambda)$$

**Theorem 3** ([2,35]). *Assuming hardness of* $\mathcal{X}$ *where* $\mathcal{X} \in \{\mathsf{LWE}, \mathsf{CDH}, \mathsf{DDH}, \mathsf{LHS}\}$, *there exist secure hinting PRGs.*

We additionally require a security notion that we refer to as entropic security.

*Entropic Security:* A hinting PRG scheme (Setup, Eval) is said to be $k$-entropic secure if for any PPT adversary $\mathcal{A}$, polynomial $\ell(\cdot)$ there exists a negligible function $\mathsf{negl}(\cdot)$ such that for all $\lambda \in \mathbb{N}$, for all distributions $\mathcal{D}$ over $\{0,1\}^n$ such that $\mathcal{H}_\infty(\mathcal{D}) \geq k$ the following holds:

$$\Pr\left[1 \leftarrow \mathcal{A}\left(\mathsf{pp}, y_0^\beta, \left\{y_{i,b}^\beta\right\}\right) \middle| \begin{array}{r} (pp, n) \leftarrow \mathsf{Setup}(1^\lambda, 1^\ell), s \leftarrow \mathcal{D}, \\ \beta \leftarrow \{0,1\}, y_0^0 \leftarrow \{0,1\}^\ell, y_0^1 = \mathsf{Eval}(\mathsf{pp}, s, 0), \\ y_{i,b}^0 \leftarrow \{0,1\}^\ell \forall i \in [n], b \in \{0,1\}, \\ y_{i,s_i}^1 = \mathsf{Eval}(\mathsf{pp}, s, i), y_{i,\overline{s_i}}^1 \leftarrow \{0,1\}^\ell \forall i \in [n] \end{array}\right] \leq \frac{1}{2} + \mathsf{negl}(\lambda)$$

*Remark 2 (On the instantiation of Entropic HPRGs).* Both the CDH and LWE based constructions of hinting PRGs given by Koppula and Waters [35] remain secure even when the seed is not uniform but only has sufficiently high min-entropy. The only point in their analysis where the uniformity of the seed $s$ is invoked is in a hybrid that applies a randomness-extraction style argument. In the CDH instantiation, this hybrid replaces $h = \prod_{k=1}^{n} g_{i,s_i}$ with a uniformly random group element $h$, and statistical closeness is justified using the Leftover Hash Lemma (see the full version). Likewise, in the LWE construction, the analogous hybrid replaces $a = \sum_{k=1}^{n} a_{i,s_i}$ with a uniform vector $a$.

This argument remains valid verbatim when the seed $s$ is sampled from any distribution $s$ of sufficiently large min-entropy. Specifically, if $H_\infty(s) \geq m + 2\log(1/\varepsilon)$, where $m$ is the number of bits that must be statistically close to uniform in the hybrid, then the Leftover Hash Lemma guarantees that the corresponding hybrid remains indistinguishable up to error $\varepsilon$. Consequently, by ensuring that the seed distribution provides this entropy margin, every hybrid in the Koppula-Waters proof continues to hold unchanged. Since both the CDH and LWE based instantiations in [35] implement the same extractor-like structure required for this step, their constructions immediately yield an *entropic* hinting PRG.

In the DDH-based construction of the hinting PRG by Alamati and Patranabis [2], the only place where the uniformity of the seed $s$ is required is in establishing the pseudorandomness property of the generator. Somewhat surprisingly, their proof of the *hinting* security itself does not rely on any stronger guarantee about the distribution of $s$, such as full uniformity. In particular, they invoke an application of the Leftover Hash Lemma to argue that $([M], [Ms]) \approx_c ([M], [u])$, where $u$ is uniformly distributed. Consequently, if the uniform seed is replaced by any distribution $D$ with sufficiently high min-entropy so that the above extraction step continues to hold, the pseudorandomness property remains valid. With the parameters adjusted to satisfy this entropy requirement, their construction therefore yields an *entropic hinting PRG*.

Looking ahead, in our construction we will use an error-correction code applied on a randomly sampled $k$-bit string as our distribution $\mathcal{D}$. Given the correctness of the decoder of the error-correcting code, we will obtain as an output a string of length $n$ which has at least min-entropy $k$. This fulfills the entropy requirement in the above definition.

## 4 Candidate Robust PRC from Noisy-McEliece Type Assumptions

In this section, we propose a new family of hardness assumptions which give rise to adaptively robust pseudorandom codes. Recall the decisional McEliece assumption: let $\mathbf{G} \in \mathbb{F}_2^{m \times n}$ be a generator matrix of a binary Goppa code, let $\mathbf{\Pi} \leftarrow S_m$[6] be a uniformly random permutation on $m$ elements, and let $\mathbf{T} \leftarrow \mathsf{GL}_n(\mathbb{F}_2)$ be a uniformly random invertible matrix in $\mathbb{F}_2^{n \times n}$. The decisional McEliece assumption [21,38] then posits that the matrix

$$\mathbf{A} = \mathbf{\Pi} \cdot \mathbf{G} \cdot \mathbf{T}$$

is pseudorandom. Binary Goppa codes can only decode from a sublinear number of Hamming errors, specifically $O(n/\log(n))$ Hamming errors. Hence a tremendous research effort has been devoted to finding alternatives for binary Goppa codes in this construction. Notoriously, though, virtually all attempts to replace the binary Goppa code with other families of efficiently decodable linear codes have turned out to be insecure [1,7,8,11,15–19,24,25,29,34,37,40,44,47]. Furthermore, even the classical McEliece scheme was recently targeted by an algebraic distinguishing attack [43]. A fundamental reason for the presence of such algebraic attacks is that the generator matrix $\mathbf{A}$ shares many algebraic invariants with the generator $\mathbf{G}$.

We observe that all currently known algebraic attacks against McEliece-type assumptions fail if we only provide the matrix $\mathbf{A}$ masked by a suitable amount of Bernoulli noise. Indeed, the problem of solving algebraic systems of equations is mostly considered in the presence of exact equations. Hence, we propose the following general assumptions.

**Assumption 1 (McEliece with Noise).** *Let $\mathbb{F}$ be a finite field, let $m = m(\lambda)$, $k = k(\lambda)$, $n = n(\lambda)$ with $m \geq k \geq 2n > 0$ and $\ell = \ell(\lambda)$ be integers that are polynomial in $\lambda$, and let $\rho = \rho(\lambda) = O(1/\sqrt{n})$ and $\epsilon \in [0,1]$ be a constant. Further let $(\mathsf{C}_\kappa)_{\kappa \in K}$, where $\mathsf{C}_\kappa \subseteq \mathbb{F}^m$, be a family of linear codes of length $m$ and dimension $k$ specified by a set $K = K(\lambda)$. For each $\kappa \in K$, let $\mathbf{G}_\kappa \in \mathbb{F}^{m \times k}$ be a generator matrix for $\mathsf{C}_\kappa$. Let $\mathbf{\Pi} \leftarrow S_m$, $\kappa \leftarrow K$, let $\mathbf{T} \leftarrow (\mathbb{F}^{k \times 2n})_{full}$ be a uniformly random full-column-rank matrix, and let $\mathbf{E} \leftarrow \mathsf{Ber}_\rho^{m \times 2n}$. Let*

$$\mathbf{A} = \mathbf{\Pi} \cdot \mathbf{G}_\kappa \cdot \mathbf{T} + \mathbf{E}.$$

[6] We denote the symmetric group on $\{1, \dots, m\}$ by $S_m$.

*Now parse* $\mathbf{A} = (\mathbf{A}_1 \| \mathbf{A}_2)$ *where* $\mathbf{A}_1, \mathbf{A}_2 \in \mathbb{F}^{m \times n}$. *Further let* $\mathbf{s}_1, \ldots, \mathbf{s}_\ell \leftarrow \mathcal{B}_\rho(\mathbb{F}^n)$ *and* $\mathbf{e}_1, \ldots, \mathbf{e}_\ell \leftarrow \mathcal{B}_\epsilon(\mathbb{F}^m)$. *Then we conjecture that*

$$(\mathbf{A}, \mathbf{A}_1\mathbf{s}_1 + \mathbf{e}_1, \ldots, \mathbf{A}_1\mathbf{s}_\ell + \mathbf{e}_\ell) \approx_c (\mathbf{A}, \mathbf{u}_1, \ldots, \mathbf{u}_\ell),$$

*where the* $\mathbf{u}_1, \ldots, \mathbf{u}_\ell \leftarrow \mathbb{F}^m$ *are chosen uniformly at random. That is, we conjecture that the* $\mathbf{A}_1\mathbf{s}_1 + \mathbf{e}_1, \ldots, \mathbf{A}_1\mathbf{s}_\ell + \mathbf{e}_\ell$ *are pseudorandom given* $\mathbf{A}$.

We remark that if a matrix $\mathbf{T}$ has $t$ columns and $k \geq t + \lambda$, then a uniformly random matrix $\mathbf{T} \leftarrow \mathbb{F}^{k \times t}$ has full column rank except with negligible probability. In this case, we can drop the requirement that $\mathbf{T}$ be sampled conditioned on full column rank.

The choice of the code family $(\mathsf{C}_\kappa)_\kappa$ is part of the security assumption: the assumptions below should be read for explicitly specified, efficiently decodable families, not as consequences of generic coding-theoretic parameters. In particular, high dual distance is only a necessary sanity check against simple distinguishers, not a hardness guarantee. With this caveat, and for families that do not have an unusually small dual distance, we can, from a cryptanalytic perspective, make the following somewhat stronger assumption, which, similar to the decisional McEliece assumption, requires that the matrix $\mathbf{A} = \mathbf{\Pi} \cdot \mathbf{G}_\kappa \cdot \mathbf{T} + \mathbf{E}$ itself is pseudorandom.

**Assumption 2 (Strong McEliece with Noise).** *Let* $\mathbb{F}$ *be a finite field, let* $m = m(\lambda)$, $k = k(\lambda)$, $n = n(\lambda)$ *with* $m \geq k \geq n > 0$ *be integers that are polynomial in* $\lambda$, *and let* $\rho = \rho(\lambda) = O(1/\sqrt{n})$. *Further let* $(\mathsf{C}_\kappa)_{\kappa \in K}$, *where* $\mathsf{C}_\kappa \subseteq \mathbb{F}^m$, *be a family of linear codes of length* $m$ *and dimension* $k$ *specified by a set* $K = K(\lambda)$. *For each* $\kappa \in K$, *let* $\mathbf{G}_\kappa \in \mathbb{F}^{m \times k}$ *be a generator matrix for* $\mathsf{C}_\kappa$. *Let* $\mathbf{\Pi} \leftarrow S_m$, $\kappa \leftarrow K$, *let* $\mathbf{T} \leftarrow (\mathbb{F}^{k \times n})_{full}$ *be a uniformly random full-column-rank matrix, and let* $\mathbf{E} \leftarrow \mathsf{Ber}_\rho^{m \times n}$. *Then we conjecture that the matrix*

$$\mathbf{A} = \mathbf{\Pi} \cdot \mathbf{G}_\kappa \cdot \mathbf{T} + \mathbf{E}$$

*is pseudorandom in* $\mathbb{F}^{m \times n}$. *That is, for any PPT distinguisher* $\mathcal{D}$ *it holds that* $|\Pr[\mathcal{D}(\mathbf{\Pi} \cdot \mathbf{G}_\kappa \cdot \mathbf{T} + \mathbf{E}) = 1] - \Pr[\mathcal{D}(\mathbf{U}) = 1]| < \mathsf{negl}(\lambda)$, *where* $\mathbf{U} \leftarrow \mathbb{F}^{m \times n}$ *is uniformly random.*

We do not present the strong McEliece with Noise assumption as a new route to ordinary public-key encryption. In our use of this assumption, it is combined with the standard $1/\sqrt{n}$-noise LPN assumption to obtain the McEliece with Noise assumption above, and LPN is already known to imply public-key encryption [3].

*Candidate Code Families and Limitations.* We view the noisy McEliece assumptions as candidate assumption families rather than as fully cryptanalyzed concrete proposals. A plausible instantiation should use a code family with efficient decoding, good relative distance, sufficiently large dual distance, and no known algebraic structure that remains exploitable after coordinate permutation and the addition of noise. Our main candidate is obtained by taking suitable algebraic-geometric codes over $\mathbb{F}_{16}$, for example from the Garcia–Stichtenoth tower, and expanding them to binary codes. Over $\mathbb{F}_{16}$, this tower has genus-to-length ratio tending to 1/3; by the standard AG-code bounds, choosing a divisor of relative degree 3/4 yields asymptotically good families with rate $R \geq 3/4 - 1/3 = 5/12$, relative distance $\delta \geq 1/4$, dual-distance bound $\delta^{\perp} \geq 3/4 - 2/3 = 1/12$, and efficient unique decoding from half the designed distance, i.e., a 1/8 fraction of errors [27,46]. After binary expansion these constants degrade by at most a constant factor.

Concretely, for an $\mathbb{F}_{16}$-linear code C one can write each symbol as a vector in $\mathbb{F}_2^4$, optionally composing the embedding in each coordinate with a public random invertible $\mathbb{F}_2$-linear map. The McEliece permutation is then applied bit-wise rather than symbol-wise. This is intended to obscure the extension-field structure used by Schur-product and square-code attacks against algebraic-code variants of McEliece [15,16]. A second natural cryptanalytic target is given by the binary Raw Reed–Solomon codes of [45]. These codes have very strong distance properties and polynomially large dual distance, and they share the same high-level rationale of viewing an algebraic code over an extension field as a binary code. However, because they remain Reed–Solomon-derived, they are close to regimes where square-code and Schur-product distinguishers are especially relevant. We therefore regard Raw Reed–Solomon codes as an important target for further cryptanalysis rather than as our primary proposed instantiation. More generally, further work is needed to analyze whether noisy permuted binary expansions resist adaptations of known algebraic attacks, including the attacks and parameter regimes discussed in [12].

One basic necessary condition is that the dual code of $\mathsf{C}_\kappa$ does not contain non-zero vectors of very low Hamming weight. In particular, if there are vectors of constant Hamming weight in the dual, then a simple polynomial-time distinguisher exists. To avoid this basic vulnerability, we require the codes used in any proposed instantiation to have high dual distance, following [12], who impose a similar condition to guarantee the absence of low-weight parity constraints and to rule out low-degree statistical or algebraic distinguishers in their assumptions. For completeness, we briefly describe the attack that arises when this condition is not enforced.

Assume that the dual distance $\bar{d}$ of the code generated by $\mathbf{G}_\kappa$ is very small (e.g. constant). Let $\mathbf{H}$ be a parity check matrix for this code, i.e., it holds that $\mathbf{H} \cdot \mathbf{G}_\kappa = 0$. Then there is a vector $\mathbf{t}$ in the row-span of $\mathbf{H}$ with Hamming weight $\bar{d}$. The attacker does not know $\mathbf{H}$ or $\mathbf{t}$, but can enumerate all public-coordinate vectors $\mathbf{h} \in \mathbb{F}^m$ of Hamming weight $c = \bar{d}$. Since $\mathbf{\Pi}$ is a permutation, this enumeration includes $\mathbf{h} = \mathbf{t} \cdot \mathbf{\Pi}^{-1}$ and takes time $m^c$ for constant $c$. For this vector, the attacker calculates: $\mathbf{h} \cdot \mathbf{A} = \mathbf{h} \cdot (\mathbf{\Pi} \cdot \mathbf{G}_\kappa \cdot \mathbf{T} + \mathbf{E}) = \underbrace{\mathbf{t} \cdot \mathbf{G}_\kappa \cdot \mathbf{T}}_{=0} + \underbrace{\mathbf{t} \cdot \mathbf{\Pi}^{-1} \cdot \mathbf{E}}_{=:\mathbf{h}'}$.

Indeed, if $\mathsf{Ham}(\mathbf{t}) = c$, then each coordinate of $\mathbf{t} \cdot \mathbf{\Pi}^{-1}\mathbf{E}$ is nonzero with probability at most $c\rho$, and hence the resulting vector has sublinear weight with overwhelming probability when $c$ is constant and $\rho = O(1/\sqrt{n})$. By contrast, for a random matrix and any non-zero choice of $\mathbf{h}$, the output of this procedure has high weight with overwhelming probability. Therefore, the attacker easily distinguishes between the two cases.

We can also show that the strong McEliece with Noise assumption implies the McEliece with Noise assumption under the additional standard $1/\sqrt{n}$-noise LPN assumption.

**Lemma 1.** *Assume that the strong McEliece with Noise assumption and the $1/\sqrt{n}$-noise LPN assumption hold. Then the McEliece with Noise assumption holds.*

*Proof (Sketch).* The proof is a simple hybrid argument. First, we use the strong McEliece with Noise assumption to replace the matrix $\mathbf{A}$ with a uniformly random matrix. Then, in the following hybrids, we successively replace the values $\mathbf{A}_1\mathbf{s}_i + \mathbf{e}_i$ by uniformly random $\mathbf{u}_i$, with $\mathbf{A} := (\mathbf{A}_1 \| \mathbf{A}_2)$.

For the latter step we use a standard consequence of low-noise LPN. Starting from LPN with a uniform secret and Bernoulli noise of rate $\rho = O(1/\sqrt{n})$, one first puts the sample matrix in systematic form and applies the corresponding parity-check transformation. This eliminates the original secret and yields an LPN instance in which both the new secret and the new error are distributed according to $\mathsf{Ber}_\rho$. Since our assumption uses a constant error rate $\epsilon$ and $\rho = o(1)$, we can add an independent smoothing error to the right-hand side, chosen so that the sum of the low-noise error and the smoothing error is distributed as $\mathsf{Ber}_\epsilon$; this operation is oblivious and preserves indistinguishability. Finally, the leakage lemma of [20, Lemma 6] allows us to reveal the Hamming weights of the new secret and of the smoothed error, losing only a polynomial factor. Conditioning on these weights gives the fixed-weight, and hence Hamming-ball, distributions used here. The cited lemma is stated over $\mathbb{F}_2$, but the argument is linear-algebraic and extends directly to any fixed finite field.

*Construction.* We will now show that the noisy McEliece assumption for a suitable family of codes $(\mathsf{C}_\kappa)_\kappa$, together with the standard $1/\sqrt{n}$-noise LPN assumption, gives rise to adaptively robust pseudorandom codes. Importantly, this PRC construction enjoys essentially the same robustness properties as $\mathsf{C}_\kappa$.

Now fix a family of codes $(\mathsf{C}_\kappa)_\kappa$ which can efficiently decode from an $\alpha$ fraction of errors. Fix constants $\epsilon, \delta > 0$. Let $m = O(n)$ and $\rho$ be such that $4\rho^2 \cdot n + \epsilon + \delta \leq \alpha$ (e.g. $\rho = \sqrt{(\alpha - \epsilon - \delta)/(4n)} = O(1/\sqrt{n})$). For soundness, we additionally require $2n + H_q(\alpha)m \leq m - \omega(\log_q \lambda)$, where $q = |\mathbb{F}|$ and $H_q$ denotes the $q$-ary entropy function. The pseudorandom code $\mathsf{PRC} = (\mathsf{Setup}, \mathsf{Encode}, \mathsf{Decode})$ is given as follows.

- $\mathsf{Setup}(1^\lambda)$: Choose $\mathbf{\Pi} \leftarrow S_m$, $\kappa \leftarrow K$ and $\mathbf{T} \leftarrow (\mathbb{F}^{k \times 2n})_{\mathrm{full}}$ uniformly at random, and sample $\mathbf{E} \leftarrow \mathsf{Ber}_\rho^{m \times 2n}$. Set $\mathbf{A} = \mathbf{\Pi}\mathbf{G}_\kappa\mathbf{T} + \mathbf{E}$. Output $\mathsf{pk} = \mathbf{A}$ and $\mathsf{sk} = (\mathbf{\Pi}, \kappa, \mathbf{T})$.
- $\mathsf{Encode}(\mathsf{pk} = \mathbf{A}, \mathsf{msg} \in \mathcal{B}_\rho(\mathbb{F}^n))$: Sample $\mathbf{s} \leftarrow \mathcal{B}_\rho(\mathbb{F}^n)$ uniformly at random, set $\mathbf{x} = (\mathsf{s}, \mathsf{msg}) \in \mathcal{B}_\rho(\mathbb{F}^{2n})$ and sample $\mathbf{e} \leftarrow \mathcal{B}_\epsilon(\mathbb{F}^m)$. Compute and output $\mathbf{c} = \mathbf{A} \cdot \mathbf{x} + \mathbf{e}$.

- $\mathsf{Decode}(\mathsf{sk} = (\mathbf{\Pi}, \kappa, \mathbf{T}), \tilde{\mathbf{c}})$: Compute $\mathbf{c}' = \mathbf{\Pi}^{-1}\tilde{\mathbf{c}}$ and then $\mathbf{y} = \mathsf{C}_\kappa.\mathsf{Decode}(\mathbf{c}')$. If this outputs $\perp$, output $\perp$. If $\mathsf{Ham}(\mathbf{c}' - \mathbf{G}_\kappa \mathbf{y}) > \alpha m$, output $\perp$. Otherwise, compute the unique $\mathbf{x}$ such that $\mathbf{T} \cdot \mathbf{x} = \mathbf{y}$, parse $\mathbf{x} = (\mathbf{s}, \mathsf{msg})$ and check if $\mathbf{s} \in \mathcal{B}_\rho(\mathbb{F}^n)$ and $\mathsf{msg} \in \mathcal{B}_\rho(\mathbb{F}^n)$. If any of these steps fail, output $\perp$; otherwise, output $\mathsf{msg}$.

We note that in the above construction, we require the message $\mathsf{msg}$ to be sparse. To encode a dense message $\mathsf{msg}' \in \mathbb{F}^\ell$, given $\rho$, we choose $n$ such that $|\mathbb{F}^\ell| \leq |\mathcal{B}_\rho(\mathbb{F}^n)|$.

*Pseudorandomness.* The pseudorandomness property of PRC follows immediately from (in fact, is equivalent to) the noisy McEliece assumption.

**Lemma 2** *The code* PRC *has pseudorandom codewords, given that the noisy McEliece assumption holds.*

*Soundness.* We first record that the construction satisfies the usual soundness property: a uniformly random word is rejected except with negligible probability.

**Lemma 3** *Assume that $2n + H_q(\alpha)m \leq m - \omega(\log_q \lambda)$, where $q = |\mathbb{F}|$ and $H_q$ is the $q$-ary entropy function. Then* PRC *is sound.*

*Proof* Fix any secret key $\mathsf{sk} = (\mathbf{\Pi}, \kappa, \mathbf{T})$. Since $\mathbf{G}_\kappa$ has rank $k$ and $\mathbf{T}$ has full column rank, the effective code

$$\mathsf{C}_{\kappa,\mathbf{T}} = \{\mathbf{\Pi}\mathbf{G}_\kappa\mathbf{T}\mathbf{x} : \mathbf{x} \in \mathbb{F}^{2n}\}$$

has size $q^{2n}$. By the explicit distance check in $\mathsf{Decode}$, if a word $\mathbf{u} \in \mathbb{F}^m$ is accepted, then $\mathbf{u}$ lies in an $\alpha m$-Hamming ball around some codeword in $\mathsf{C}_{\kappa,\mathbf{T}}$. Hence

$$\begin{aligned}\Pr_{\mathbf{u} \leftarrow \mathbb{F}^m}[\mathsf{Decode}(\mathsf{sk}, \mathbf{u}) \neq \perp] \leq & \frac{|\mathsf{C}_{\kappa,\mathbf{T}}| \cdot |\mathcal{B}_\alpha(\mathbb{F}^m)|}{q^m} \\ \leq & q^{2n + H_q(\alpha)m - m} \leq q^{-\omega(\log_q \lambda)} = \mathsf{negl}(\lambda).\end{aligned}$$

The bound is uniform over the choice of $\mathsf{sk}$, and therefore also holds over the randomness of $\mathsf{Setup}$.

*Adaptive Robustness.* We will now argue adaptive robustness of PRC. We will use the following simple facts about Bernoulli distributed matrices in the proof. For a matrix $\mathbf{M} = (\mathbf{m}_1, \ldots, \mathbf{m}_N) \in \mathbb{F}^{m \times N}$, we define the induced matrix weight $\mathsf{Ham}(\mathbf{M})$ via $\mathsf{Ham}(\mathbf{M}) = \max_{i \in [N]} \mathsf{Ham}(\mathbf{m}_i)$. This matrix weight is sub-multiplicative, that is, it holds for every $\mathbf{x} \in \mathbb{F}^N$ that $\mathsf{Ham}(\mathbf{M} \cdot \mathbf{x}) \leq \mathsf{Ham}(\mathbf{M}) \cdot \mathsf{Ham}(\mathbf{x})$. If $\mathbf{E} \leftarrow \mathsf{Ber}_\rho^{m \times N}$, then a simple Chernoff bound and a union bound imply that $\mathsf{Ham}(\mathbf{E}) \leq 2\rho m$ except with probability $N \cdot e^{-\frac{1}{3}\rho m}$, which is negligible for our parameter choices.

**Lemma 4** *Assume that* $\mathsf{C}_\kappa$ *can efficiently uniquely decode from up to an* $\alpha < 1/4$ *fraction of Hamming errors and that* $4\rho^2 n + \epsilon + \delta \leq \alpha$*. Then* PRC *is a strong adaptively robust PRC against a* $\delta$*-fraction of adversarial errors, except with negligible probability over the choice of the public key* $\mathbf{A}$.

*Proof* As discussed above, it follows by a Chernoff bound and a union bound that $\mathsf{Ham}(\mathbf{E}) \leq 2\rho m$, except with negligible probability $2n \cdot e^{-\frac{1}{3}\rho m}$. Hence, fix a public key $\mathsf{pk} = \mathbf{A}$ where $\mathbf{A} = \mathbf{\Pi} \cdot \mathbf{G}_\kappa \cdot \mathbf{T} + \mathbf{E}$, such that $\mathsf{Ham}(\mathbf{E}) \leq 2\rho m$. Consider a codeword $\mathbf{c} = \mathbf{Ax} + \mathbf{e} = \mathbf{\Pi G}_\kappa \mathbf{Tx} + \mathbf{Ex} + \mathbf{e}$. It holds that

$$\mathsf{Ham}(\mathbf{Ex}+\mathbf{e}) \leq \mathsf{Ham}(\mathbf{E})\cdot\mathsf{Ham}(\mathbf{x})+\mathsf{Ham}(\mathbf{e}) \leq 2\rho\cdot m\cdot 2\rho\cdot n+\epsilon\cdot m = (4\rho^2 n+\epsilon)m.$$

As we require $4\rho^2 n + \epsilon \leq \alpha - \delta$, it follows that PRC is adaptively robust against errors of weight at most $\delta \cdot m$: fix any adversarial error $\mathbf{e}^*$ with Hamming weight at most $\delta \cdot m$. Then

$$\hat{\mathbf{c}} = \mathbf{c} + \mathbf{e}^* = \mathbf{\Pi G}_\kappa \mathbf{Tx} + \mathbf{Ex} + \mathbf{e} + \mathbf{e}^* = \mathbf{\Pi G}_\kappa \mathbf{Tx} + \mathbf{d},$$

where we set $\mathbf{d} = \mathbf{Ex}+\mathbf{e}+\mathbf{e}^*$. As $\mathsf{Ham}(\mathbf{Ex}+\mathbf{e}) \leq (\alpha-\delta)m$ and $\mathsf{Ham}(\mathbf{e}^*) \leq \delta m$, it follows by the triangle inequality that $\mathsf{Ham}(\mathbf{d}) \leq \alpha m$. Hence $\mathbf{c}' = \mathbf{\Pi}^{-1}(\hat{\mathbf{c}}) = \mathbf{G}_\kappa \mathbf{Tx} + \mathbf{\Pi}^{-1}\mathbf{d}$. Thus we get that $\mathbf{c}'$ has distance at most $\alpha m$ from $\mathsf{C}_\kappa$ as $\mathsf{Ham}(\mathbf{\Pi}^{-1}\mathbf{d}) = \mathsf{Ham}(\mathbf{d}) \leq \alpha m$. Hence $\mathsf{C}_\kappa.\mathsf{Decode}$ will uniquely recover $\mathbf{Tx}$. Since $\mathbf{T}$ has full column rank, the final linear solve recovers $\mathbf{x}$ and therefore $\mathsf{msg}$. □

## 5 CCA Secure Pseudorandom Codes

In this section, we present our CCA PRC transformation. In general, constructing PRCs becomes easier when the underlying field is large [23]. As in prior work, we focus exclusively on the binary case for clarity of presentation. Nevertheless, we expect that our transformation extends naturally to arbitrary finite fields, provided that the underlying primitives are replaced by their corresponding counterparts over such fields, for example by relying on the noisy McEliece assumption (Sect. 4) defined over general finite fields.

Our construction requires the following primitives:

- $\mathsf{DS} = (\mathsf{DS.Setup}, \mathsf{DS.Sign}, \mathsf{DS.Verify})$: a one-time strong unforgeable signature scheme with message space $\{0,1\}^*$, verification key space $\{0,1\}^{\ell_{\mathsf{vk}}}$ and signature space $\{0,1\}^\lambda$
- $\mathsf{Com} = (\mathsf{Com.Setup}, \mathsf{Com.Commit}, \mathsf{Com.Open}, \mathsf{Com.Equiv})$: a statistically binding equivocal tag-based set-commitment scheme with pseudorandom commitments, with tag space $\{0,1\}^{\ell_{\mathsf{vk}}}$, commitment space $\{0,1\}^{\ell_{\mathrm{com}}}$ and opening space $\{0,1\}^{\ell_{\mathrm{op}}}$.
- $\mathsf{PKE} = (\mathsf{PKE.Setup}, \mathsf{PKE.Enc}, \mathsf{PKE.Dec})$: an almost perfect-correctness IND-CPA secure PKE with message space $\{0,1\}^{\ell_{\mathrm{op}}+\ell_{\mathsf{vk}}+1}$ and randomness $\{0,1\}^\lambda$. The ciphertext size is $\ell_{\mathrm{pke.ct}}$.
- $\mathsf{ECC} = (\mathsf{ECC.Setup}, \mathsf{ECC.Encode}, \mathsf{ECC.Decode})$: a $\gamma$-robust error-correcting code over alphabet $\{0,1\}$, with message-rate $c_{\mathrm{ecc}}$ (that is, for binary strings of length $k$, it produces codewords of length $c_{\mathrm{ecc}} \cdot k$)

- HPRG = (HPRG.Setup, HPRG.Eval): a hinting pseudorandom generator that takes $n = c_{\text{ecc}} \cdot \lambda$ bits as input, and outputs $n+2$ blocks where each block of the output has $\lambda$ bits
- PRF = (PRF.Setup, PRF.Eval): a pseudorandom function with key space, input and output space $\{0,1\}^\lambda$.
- PRG: a (regular) pseudorandom generator that maps $\lambda$ bits to $\ell_{\text{PRG}}$ bits, where $\ell_{\text{PRG}} = 2c_{\text{ecc}} \cdot (\ell_{\mathsf{msg}} + \lambda + 2n \cdot \ell_{\text{pke.ct}} + n \cdot (\ell_{\text{com}})) + 3\lambda$. We will interpret the output as a number in $\mathbb{F}_{2^{\ell_{\text{PRG}}}}$.
- PRC = (PRC.Setup, PRC.Encode, PRC.Decode): an $\alpha$ adaptively-robust CPA secure public-key pseudorandom code with message space $\{0,1\}^{\ell_{\text{pke.ct}} + \ell_{\text{com}}}$, randomness $\{0,1\}^\lambda$. The codeword length is $\ell_{\mathsf{cw}} = \ell_{\text{PRG}}/(2 \cdot n)$.[7]

$\mathsf{Setup}(1^\lambda)$: The setup algorithm performs the following steps:

1. Sample $\mathsf{ecc.pp} \leftarrow \mathsf{ECC.Setup}(1^\gamma)$ and $\mathsf{hprg.pp} \leftarrow \mathsf{HPRG.Setup}(1^\lambda)$.
2. Sample $2n$ different PKE and PRC keys, i.e., $(\mathsf{pke.pk}_{i,b}, \mathsf{pke.sk}_{i,b}) \leftarrow \mathsf{PKE.Setup}(1^\lambda)$ and $(\mathsf{prc.pk}_{i,b}, \mathsf{prc.sk}_{i,b}) \leftarrow \mathsf{PRC.Setup}(1^\lambda)$ for all $b \in \{0,1\}, i \in [n]$.
3. Sample $\mathsf{com.pp} \leftarrow \mathsf{Com.Setup}\left(1^\lambda, 1^n\right)$.
4. Sample $B_{\mathsf{pl}} \leftarrow \{0,1\}^{\ell_{\text{PRG}}}$.
5. Output the public key $\mathsf{pk} = (\mathsf{ecc.pp}, \mathsf{hprg.pp}, B_{\mathsf{pl}}, \mathsf{com.pp}, (\mathsf{pke.pk}_{i,b}, \mathsf{prc.pk}_{i,b})_{i \in [n], b \in \{0,1\}})$ and the secret key $\mathsf{sk} = (\mathsf{pke.sk}_{i,0}, \mathsf{prc.sk}_{i,0})_{i \in [n]}$.

$\mathsf{Enc}(\mathsf{pk}, m)$: Parse the public key $\mathsf{pk} = (\mathsf{ecc.pp}, \mathsf{hprg.pp}, B_{\mathsf{pl}}, \mathsf{com.pp}, (\mathsf{pke.pk}_{i,b}, \mathsf{prc.pk}_{i,b})_{i \in [n], b \in \{0,1\}})$.

1. Sampling the various random strings needed for encryption:
   (a) Sample $s \leftarrow \{0,1\}^\lambda$, set $t = \mathsf{ECC.Encode}(\mathsf{ecc.pp}, s)$.
   (b) Sample $(\mathsf{ds.vk}, \mathsf{ds.sk}) \leftarrow \mathsf{DS.Setup}(1^\lambda)$.
   (c) Sample $\mathsf{K} \leftarrow \mathsf{PRF.Setup}(1^\lambda)$.
   (d) For each $i \in [n]$, choose $\tilde{r}_i \leftarrow \{0,1\}^\lambda$.
   (e) Let $(r_{00}, r_{01}, r_1, \ldots, r_n) = \mathsf{HPRG.Eval}(\mathsf{hprg.pp}, t)$.
2. Compute the PKE ciphertexts and the commitments.
   First compute $(\mathsf{com}_i, \mathsf{op}_i)_i \leftarrow \mathsf{Commit}(\mathsf{com.pp}, t, \mathsf{ds.vk})$ (here, $\mathsf{ds.vk}$ is the tag used for the commitment). For each $i \in [n]$,

$$\mathsf{pke.ct}_{i,t_i} := \mathsf{PKE.Enc}\left(\mathsf{pke.pk}_{i,t_i}, 1 \| \mathsf{op}_i \| \mathsf{ds.vk}; r_i\right)$$
$$\mathsf{pke.ct}_{i,1-t_i} := \mathsf{PKE.Enc}\left(\mathsf{pke.pk}_{i,1-t_i}, 0^{\ell_{\text{op}} + \ell_{\mathsf{vk}} + 1}; \tilde{r}_i\right)$$

3. Compute the PRC ciphertexts and the header.
   (a) For each $i \in [n]$ and $b \in \{0,1\}$, $c_{i,b} := \mathsf{PRC.Enc}(\mathsf{prc.pk}_{i,b}, (\mathsf{pke.ct}_{i,b}, \mathsf{com}_i); \mathsf{PRF}(\mathsf{K}, (i,b))))$.
   (b) Set $c := \mathsf{PRG}(r_{00}) + \mathsf{ECC.Encode}(m, \mathsf{K}, (\mathsf{pke.ct}_{i,b}, {,_i})_{i,b}) \cdot B_{\mathsf{pl}}$.
4. Computing the digital signature:
   (a) Let $\mathsf{ds}.x = \left(c, (c_{i,0}, c_{i,1})_{i \in [n]}\right)$. Compute $\mathsf{ds}.\sigma \leftarrow \mathsf{DS.Sign}(\mathsf{ds.sk}, \mathsf{ds}.x)$. Pad the signature so that the length is $\ell_{\text{PRG}}$.

[7] If needed, the message is padded so that the PRC codeword length is $\ell_{\text{PRG}}/2n$.

(b) Compute $\sigma = \mathsf{PRG}(r_{01}) \oplus \mathsf{ECC.Encode}(\mathsf{ecc.pp}, \mathsf{ds}.\sigma)$.
5. Output $\mathsf{ct} = (\mathsf{ds}.x, \sigma)$.

Note that the final ciphertext consists of three parts, each of length $\ell_{\mathrm{PRG}}$: $c$, $(c_{i,b})_{i,b}$ and $\sigma$.

$\mathsf{Dec}(\mathsf{sk}, \mathsf{ct})$: Parse the secret key $\mathsf{sk} := (\mathsf{pke.sk}_{i,0}, \mathsf{prc.sk}_{i,0})_{i\in[n]}$ and the ciphertext $\mathsf{ct} = (\mathsf{ds}.x, \sigma)$ where $\mathsf{ds}.x = \left(c, \{c_{i,0}, c_{i,1}\}_{i\in[n]}\right)$:

1. Compute $t = \mathsf{PRC.Find}\left(\mathsf{sk}, (c_{i,0})_i\right)$ (Fig. 1).
2. Compute $\left(\mathsf{msg}, \mathsf{K}, c', \left(c'_{i,b}, \mathsf{pke.ct}_{i,b}, \mathsf{com}_i\right)_{i,b}, \mathsf{ds}.\sigma\right) \leftarrow \mathsf{PRC.CheckNoise}$ $\left(c, (c_{i,b})_{i,b}, \sigma, t, (\mathsf{prc.sk}_{i,0})_i\right)$ (Fig. 2).
3. Let $\mathsf{ds}.x' = \left(c', \left(c'_{i,b}\right)_{i,b}\right)$. Compute $\mathsf{ds.vk} \leftarrow \mathsf{PRC.CheckPKE}(t, (\mathsf{pke.ct}_{i,t_i}, \mathsf{com}_i)_i)$ (Fig. 3).
4. If $\mathsf{DS.Verify}(\mathsf{ds.vk}, \mathsf{ds}.x', \mathsf{ds}.\sigma) = 1$, output $\mathsf{msg}$, else output $\perp$.

**PRC.Find**

**Inputs:**

Secret Key $\mathsf{sk} = (\mathsf{pke.sk}_{i,0}, \mathsf{prc.sk}_{i,0})_{i\in[n]}$
PRC ciphertexts $(c_{i,0})_{i\in[n]}$

**Output:** $t$

1. For each $i \in [n]$, do the following:
   (a) Let $(\mathsf{pke.ct}_{i,0}, \mathsf{com}_i) = \mathsf{PRC.Decode}(\mathsf{prc.sk}_{i,0}, c_{i,0})$
   (b) Let $m_i = \mathsf{PKE.Dec}(\mathsf{pke.sk}_{i,0}, \mathsf{pke.ct}_{i,0})$.
   (c) If $m_i = 1 \,\|\, \mathsf{op}_i \,\|\, \mathsf{ds.vk}_i$ and $\mathsf{Open}(\mathsf{com.pp}, 0, \mathsf{com}_i, \mathsf{op}_i, \mathsf{ds.vk}_i) = \top$, set $\tilde{t_i} = 0$. Else set $\tilde{t_i} = 1$.
2. Compute $s = \mathsf{ECC.Decode}\left(\mathsf{ecc.pp}, \tilde{t}\right)$ and $t = \mathsf{ECC.Encode}(\mathsf{ecc.pp}, s)$.
3. Output $t$.

**Fig. 1.** Routine PRC.Find.

*Information Rate:* Suppose that ECC encodes $t$-bit messages into codewords of length $k_{\mathrm{ecc}} \cdot t$ for some constant $k_{\mathrm{ecc}} > 1$, and let $\ell_{\mathsf{msg}}$ denote the message length in our PRC scheme. Since both $|\mathsf{op}_i|$ and $|\mathsf{ds.vk}|$ are polynomial in the security parameter, it follows that $|\mathsf{pke.ct}_{i,t_i}| = \mathsf{poly}(\lambda)$. Likewise, because $|\mathsf{com}_i| = \mathsf{poly}(\lambda)$, we have $|c_{i,b}| = \mathsf{poly}(\lambda)$. As $n = \mathsf{poly}(\lambda)$, this further implies that $|\{c_{i,b}\}| = \mathsf{poly}(\lambda)$. Since, $|\mathsf{K}| = \mathsf{poly}(\lambda)$, total payload size is therefore $|c| = k_{\mathrm{ecc}} \cdot (\ell_{\mathsf{msg}} + \mathsf{poly}(\lambda))$, while the signature contributes $O(\lambda)$ additional bits.

**PRC.CheckNoise**

**Inputs:**

$c, (c_{i,b})_{i,b}, \sigma$ (the ciphertext)
$t$ (output by $\mathsf{Find}$)
$(\mathsf{prc.sk}_{i,0})_i$

**Output:** $\left(\mathsf{msg}, \mathsf{K}, c', \left(c'_{i,b}, \mathsf{pke.ct}_{i,b}, \mathsf{com}_i\right)_{i,b}, \mathsf{ds}.\sigma\right)$

1. Computing noise-free version of ciphertext:
   (a) Compute $(r_{00}, r_{01}, r_1, \ldots, r_n) = \mathsf{HPRG.Eval}(\mathsf{hprg.pp}, t)$.
   (b) Compute $\left(\mathsf{msg}, \mathsf{K}, (\mathsf{pke.ct}_{i,b}, \mathsf{com}_i)_{i,b}\right) = \mathsf{ECC.Decode}(\mathsf{ecc.pp}, \left((c - \mathsf{PRG}(r_{00})) \cdot B_{\mathsf{pl}}^{-1}\right))$.
   (c) Compute $\mathsf{ds}.\sigma = \mathsf{ECC.Decode}(\mathsf{ecc.pp}, (\mathsf{PRG}(r_{01}) \oplus \sigma))$.
   (d) Compute $c' = \mathsf{PRG}(r_{00}) + \mathsf{ECC.Encode}(\mathsf{ecc.pp}, ((\mathsf{msg}, \mathsf{K}, (\mathsf{pke.ct}_{i,b}, \mathsf{com}_i)_{i,b}))) \cdot B_{\mathsf{pl}}$.
   (e) For each $i, b$, compute $c'_{i,b} = \mathsf{PRC.Encode}(\mathsf{prc.pk}_{i,b}, \{\mathsf{pke.ct}_{i,b}, \mathsf{com}_i\}_{i,b}; \mathsf{PRF.Eval}(\mathsf{K}, (i, b)))$.
   (f) Compute $\sigma' = \mathsf{PRG}(r_{01}) \oplus \mathsf{ECC.Encode}(\mathsf{ecc.pp}, \mathsf{ds}.\sigma)$.
2. Checking noise is within bounds:
   (a) If $\Delta\left(\left(c, (c_{i,b})_{i,b}, \sigma\right), \left(c', (c'_{i,b})_{i,b}, \sigma'\right)\right) > \delta\ell_{\mathsf{ct}}$, output $\perp$.
3. Checking the commitments and ciphertexts in $c$ are consistent with the commitments and ciphertexts used in $\mathsf{Find}$.
   (a) For each $i \in [n]$, compute $\left(\underline{\mathsf{pke.ct}_{i,0}}, \underline{\mathsf{com}_i}\right) = \mathsf{PRC.Decode}(\mathsf{prc.sk}_{i,0}, c_{i,0})$.
   (b) For each $i \in [n]$ s.t. $\Delta(c_{i,b}, c'_{i,b}) \leq \alpha\ell_{\mathsf{cw}}$ for both $b \in \{0,1\}$, check $\mathsf{com}_i = \underline{\mathsf{com}_i}$ and $\mathsf{pke.ct}_{i,0} = \underline{\mathsf{pke.ct}_{i,0}}$. If any checks fail, output $\perp$.
4. Output $\left(\mathsf{msg}, \mathsf{K}, c', \left(c'_{i,b}, \mathsf{pke.ct}_{i,b}, \mathsf{com}_i\right)_{i,b}, \mathsf{ds}.\sigma\right)$.

**Fig. 2.** Routine PRC.CheckNoise.

Consequently, the information rate of the scheme is $\frac{\ell_{\mathsf{msg}}}{k_{\mathrm{ecc}} \cdot (\ell_{\mathsf{msg}} + \mathsf{poly}(\lambda)) + \mathsf{poly}(\lambda)} = \left(k_{\mathrm{ecc}} + \frac{k_{\mathrm{ecc}} \cdot \mathsf{poly}(\lambda)}{\ell_{\mathsf{msg}}} + \frac{\mathsf{poly}(\lambda)}{\ell_{\mathsf{msg}}}\right)^{-1}$. In particular, as $\ell_{\mathsf{msg}}$ grows large, the information rate approaches $k_{\mathrm{ecc}}^{-1}$.

**Theorem 4 (Adaptive Robustness).** *Assuming* PRC *is $\alpha$-robust,* ECC *is $\gamma$-robust, then the above scheme is $\frac{\alpha \cdot \gamma}{6}$- adaptively robust.*

*Proof* Let $\ell_c := |c|, \ell_{\mathsf{cw}} = |c_{i,b}|, \ell_\sigma = |\sigma|$, we have $|\ell_c| = |\ell_\sigma| = 2n \cdot \ell_{\mathsf{cw}}$, and $\ell_{\mathsf{ct}} := \ell_c + 2n \cdot \ell_{\mathsf{cw}} + \ell_\sigma$. Let $\delta = \alpha\gamma/6$. We then need to argue, to prove adaptive corruptness, that an adversary cannot output a tuple $(m, r, x)$ where $\mathsf{Ham}(\mathsf{Enc}(\mathsf{pk}, m; r), x) \leq \delta\ell_{\mathsf{ct}}$ while $m \neq \mathsf{Dec}(\mathsf{sk}, x)$ with non-negligible probability. To prove this, we argue something stronger,

**PRC.CheckPKE**

**Inputs:**

$\left(\mathsf{pke.pk}_{i,b}\right)_{i,b}$ (part of public key)
$t$ (produced by Find).
$(\mathsf{pke.ct}_{i,t_i}, \mathsf{com}_i)_{i,b}$ (commitments and ciphertexts produced by CheckNoise)

**Output:** ds.vk

1. Compute $(r_{00}, r_{01}, r_1, \ldots, r_n) = \mathsf{HPRG.Eval}(\mathsf{hprg.pp}, t)$.
2. For each $i \in [n]$, do the following:
   (a) If $t_i = 0$, compute $m_i = \mathsf{PKE.Recover}(\mathsf{pke.pk}_{i,0}, \mathsf{pke.ct}_{i,0}, r_i)$. Perform the following checks. If any of the checks fail, output $\bot$.
      i. $m_i = 1\|\mathsf{op}_i\|\mathsf{ds.vk}_i$ and $\mathsf{Open}\left(\mathsf{com.pp}, 0, \mathsf{com}_i, \mathsf{op}_i, \mathsf{ds.vk}_i\right) = \top$.
      ii. $\mathsf{pke.ct}_{i,0} = \mathsf{PKE.Enc}(\mathsf{pke.pk}_{i,0}, m_i; r_i)$.
   (b) If $t_i = 1$, compute $m_i = \mathsf{PKE.Recover}(\mathsf{pke.pk}_{i,1}, \mathsf{pke.ct}_{i,1}, r_i)$. Perform the following checks. If any of the checks fail, output $\bot$.
      i. $m_i = 1\|\mathsf{op}_i\|\mathsf{ds.vk}_i$ and $\mathsf{Open}\left(\mathsf{com.pp}, 1, \mathsf{com}_i, \mathsf{op}_i, \mathsf{ds.vk}_i\right) = \top$.
      ii. $\mathsf{pke.ct}_{i,1} = \mathsf{PKE.Enc}(\mathsf{pke.pk}_{i,1}, m_i; r_i)$.
3. If $\mathsf{ds.vk}_i = \mathsf{ds.vk}$ for all $i \in [n]$, output ds.vk. Else output $\bot$.

**Fig. 3.** Routine PRC.CheckPKE.

we consider an adversary that submits a message-randomness pair $(m, r)$ as well as three error vectors $\mathbf{e}_1 \in \{0,1\}^{\ell_c}, \mathbf{e}_2 \in \{0,1\}^{2n\ell_{\mathsf{cw}}}, \mathbf{e}_3 \in \{0,1\}^{\ell_\sigma}$ with $\mathsf{Ham}(\mathbf{e}_i) \leq \delta\ell_{\mathsf{ct}}$ for all $i \in [3]$. Now, we say that such an adversary wins the game if it holds that $\mathsf{Dec}\left(\mathsf{sk}, \left(c, (c_{i,b})_{i\in[n],b\in\{0,1\}}, \sigma\right)\right) \neq \mathsf{Dec}\left(\mathsf{sk}, \left(c \oplus \mathbf{e}_1, (c_{i,b})_{i\in[n],b\in\{0,1\}} \oplus \mathbf{e}_2, \sigma \oplus \mathbf{e}_3\right)\right)$ with $\mathsf{ct} = \left(c, (c_{i,b})_{i,b}, \sigma\right) = \mathsf{Enc}(\mathsf{pk}, m; r)$. We can directly see that such a game achieves stronger security than the adaptive robustness game since the adaptive robustness adversary is only allowed to submit a single vector $\mathbf{e} \in \{0,1\}^{\ell_c + 2n\ell_{\mathsf{cw}} + \ell_\sigma}$ with $\mathsf{Ham}(\mathbf{e}) \leq \delta\ell_{\mathsf{ct}}$. Let $c' := c \oplus \mathbf{e}_1$, $c'_{i,b} := c_{i,b} \oplus \mathbf{e}_2$, $\sigma' := \sigma \oplus \mathbf{e}_3$, and let $\mathsf{ct}' = \left(c', \left(c'_{i,b}\right)_{i,b}, \sigma'\right)$.

To prove the above equality, it suffices to show that the procedures Find and CheckNoise output the same for the ciphertexts ct and ct′. Now, we are walking through the different steps of the two procedures to bound these probabilities.

*Claim.* $\mathsf{Find}(\mathsf{sk}, \mathsf{ct}) = \mathsf{Find}(\mathsf{sk}, \mathsf{ct}')$.

*Proof.* First, note that if $t$ is the HPRG seed used to encrypt $m$, then Step 1 of $\mathsf{Find}(\mathsf{sk}, \mathsf{ct})$ computes $\tilde{t} = t$, and as a result, $\mathsf{Find}(\mathsf{sk}, \mathsf{ct})$ outputs $t$. This follows from the perfect correctness of the PKE and commitment schemes. We will now argue that if $\mathsf{Ham}(\mathbf{e}_2) \leq \delta \cdot \ell_{\mathsf{ct}}$, then Step 1 of $\mathsf{Find}(\mathsf{sk}, \mathsf{ct}')$ produces a $\tilde{t}'$ such that $\Delta\left(\tilde{t}', t\right) \leq \gamma \cdot n$, assuming $\alpha$-adaptive robustness of the base PRC scheme.

Parse $\mathbf{e}_2 = (\mathbf{e}_{2,i,b})_{i\in[n],b\in\{0,1\}}$, and let $\mathcal{I} = \{i : \mathsf{Ham}(\mathbf{e}_{2,i,b}) \leq \alpha \cdot \ell_{\mathsf{cw}}$ for both $b \in \{0,1\}\}$. Since $\delta = \alpha \cdot \gamma/6$, it follows that $|\mathcal{I}| \geq (1-\gamma)\cdot n$.[8] Using the adaptive robustness of the base PRC scheme (and the perfect correctness of the PKE scheme and the commitment scheme), we get that $\tilde{t}_i' = t_i$ for all $i \in \mathcal{I}$. In particular, if $c_{i,b}$ is the PRC encoding of $(\mathsf{pke.ct}_{i,b}, \mathsf{com}_i)$ with randomness $z_{i,b}$ and $\mathsf{Dec}(\mathsf{prc.sk}_{i,b}, (c_{i,b} \oplus \mathbf{e}_{2,i,b})) \neq (\mathsf{pke.ct}_{i,b}, \mathsf{com}_i)$, then the reduction algorithm can break $\alpha$-adaptive robustness of the base PRC scheme by sending $(\mathsf{pke.ct}_{i,b}, \mathsf{com}_i)$ as the message, $z_{i,b}$ as the randomness and $(c_{i,b} \oplus \mathbf{e}_{2,i,b})$ as the codeword.

It remains to analyze the behavior of $\mathsf{CheckNoise}$ on the inputs $\mathsf{ct}$ and $\mathsf{ct}'$ where both procedures take as an input the same $t$ (which follows from the above analysis of $\mathsf{Find}$). Given that both procedures take as an input the same $t$, it follows that step 1 (a) will also output the same values. Next, we rely on the robustness of ECC. In more detail, since $\delta\ell_{\mathsf{ct}} \leq \gamma\ell_c = \gamma\ell_\sigma$, for the steps 1. (b) and (c), it must hold that $\mathsf{ECC.Decode}\left(\mathsf{ecc.pp}, \left(c - \mathsf{PRG}(r_{00}) \cdot B_{\mathsf{pl}}^{-1}\right)\right) = \mathsf{ECC.Decode}\left(\mathsf{ecc.pp}, \left((c \oplus \mathbf{e}_1) - \mathsf{PRG}(r_{00}) \cdot B_{\mathsf{pl}}^{-1}\right)\right)$ and $\mathsf{ECC.Decode}(\mathsf{ecc.pp}, (\mathsf{PRG}(r_{01}) \oplus \sigma) = \mathsf{ECC.Decode}(\mathsf{ecc.pp}, (\mathsf{PRG}(r_{01}) \oplus \sigma \oplus \mathbf{e}_3))$.

If the above holds, then the steps 1 (d)-(f) directly have the same output as well. The bounds in step 2. are all satisfied due to our restriction $\mathsf{Ham}(\mathbf{e}_i) \leq \delta\ell_{\mathsf{ct}}$. To argue that step 3 yields the same output, we can, again, rely on the adaptive robustness as it has been done in the beginning of the proof. In more detail, the decoding output computed in step 3 (a) is the same as the decoding that is computed as the 1. step of $\mathsf{Find}$. Only violating adaptive robustness would lead to a failing check in the step 3 (b), given the above analysis involving the error-correcting codes.

**Theorem 5.** *Assuming that* PKE *is an* IND-CPA *secure PKE scheme with almost perfect-correctness,* PRC *is an $\alpha$ adaptively robust* IND-CPA *secure PRC scheme,* ECC *is a $\gamma$-robust error-correcting code,* Com *is a commitment scheme satisfies statistical binding, equivocality, pseudorandomness of commitments and independence of tag for* 0*-commitments,* HPRG *is a secure hinting PRG,* PRG *is a secure PRG,* PRF *is a secure PRF and* DS *is a secure signature scheme. Then the above construction is a* IND-CCA *secure PRC scheme.*

*Proof.* Our proof proceeds via a sequence of hybrids. First, we will describe all hybrids, and then show that the hybrids are computationally indistinguishable.

**Hybrid $\mathcal{H}_0$:** The corresponds to the original security game with a few modifications. The main change is in the introduction of an initialization phase in which all the input-independent steps of the scheme are executed before encryption or decryption queries are asked. The full description is given in the full version.

[8] If $|\mathcal{I}| < (1-\gamma)\cdot n$, then there exist at least $\gamma \cdot n$ indices $i$ where either $\mathsf{Ham}(\mathbf{e}_{2,i,0}) > \alpha \cdot \ell_{\mathsf{cw}}$ or $\mathsf{Ham}(\mathbf{e}_{2,i,1}) > \alpha \cdot \ell_{\mathsf{cw}}$. Therefore, $\mathsf{Ham}(\mathbf{e}) > \gamma \cdot n \cdot (\alpha \cdot \ell_{\mathsf{cw}})$. But this is a contradiction, since we assumed $\mathsf{Ham}(\mathbf{e}) \leq \delta \cdot \ell_{\mathsf{ct}}$, $\delta = \alpha \cdot \gamma/6$ and $\ell_{\mathsf{ct}} = 6n \cdot \ell_{\mathsf{cw}}$.

**Hybrid $\mathcal{H}_1$**: This hybrid proceeds as the previous one, with the only difference that the decryption oracle rejects queries where the underlying verification key $\mathsf{ds.vk}$ is equal to the verification key $\mathsf{ds.vk}^*$ used in the challenge encryption query. The indistinguishability of this and the previous hybrid can be argued using the unforgeability of the signature scheme $\mathsf{DS}$ by showing that the probability of an adversary submitting such a query is negligible. The details on this are given in the full version.

**Hybrid $\mathcal{H}_2$**: In this hybrid, during the initialization phase, the commitment scheme is in equivocal mode, i.e., $\left(\mathsf{com.pp}, \left(\mathsf{com}_i^*, \mathsf{op}_{i,0}^*, \mathsf{op}_{i,1}^*\right)_i\right) \leftarrow \mathsf{Equiv}(1^\lambda, 1^n, \mathsf{ds.vk}^*)$ and $\mathsf{op}_i^* := \mathsf{op}_{i,t_i^*}^*$. The indistinguishability of this and the previous hybrid can be argued using the equivocality of $\mathsf{Com}$. The details on this are given in the full version.

**Hybrid $\mathcal{H}_3$**: In this hybrid, the decryption queries are handled using the procedures $\mathsf{PRC.Find}^\dagger$ (see the full version) and $\mathsf{PRC.CheckNoise}^\dagger$ (see the full version) on path $t^*$, instead of $\mathsf{PRC.Find}$ and $\mathsf{PRC.CheckNoise}$. To argue the indistinguishability between this and the previous hybrid, we rely on the perfect correctness of $\mathsf{PKE}$ and $\mathsf{ECC}$, and the adaptive robustness of $\mathsf{PRC}$. This transition is quite delicate, and we prove it in detail in the full version.

**Hybrid $\mathcal{H}_4$**: In this hybrid, the ciphertexts $\mathsf{pke.ct}_{i,\overline{t_i^*}}^*$ are generated as $\mathsf{PKE.Enc}(\mathsf{pke}_{i,\overline{t_i^*}}, 1\|\mathsf{op}_{i,\overline{t_i^*}}\|\mathsf{ds.vk}^*; r_i^*)$ for all $i \in [n]$. The indistinguishability of this and the previous hybrid can be argued using the IND-CPA security of $\mathsf{PKE}$. The details on this are given in the full version.

**Hybrid $\mathcal{H}_5$**: In this hybrid, the procedure $\mathsf{PRC.Find}$ instead of $\mathsf{PRC.Find}^\dagger$ is executed in the pre- and post-challenge phases. The transition from the previous hybrid to this hybrid proceeds analogously to the transition from $\mathcal{H}_2$ to $\mathcal{H}_3$, therefore, we refer to the full version for more details.

**Hybrid $\mathcal{H}_6$**: In this hybrid, the values $\tilde{r}_i^*, c^*$ and $\sigma^*$ are chosen uniformly at random for all $i \in [n]$. The indistinguishability of this and the previous hybrid can be argued using the security of the hinting PRG $\mathsf{HPRG}$ and the standard PRG $\mathsf{PRG}$. The details on this are given in the full version.

**Hybrid $\mathcal{H}_7$**: In this hybrid, the ciphertexts $c_{i,b}^*$ for all $i \in [n], b \in \{0,1\}$ are generated as $c_{i,b}^* := \mathsf{PRC.Enc}(\mathsf{prc.pk}_{i,b}, (\mathsf{pke.ct}_{i,b}^*, \mathsf{com}_i^*); u_{i,b})$ where $u_{i,b}$ are sampled uniformly at random. The indistinguishability of this and the previous hybrid can be argued using the pseudorandomness of $\mathsf{PRF}$. The details on this are given in the full version.

**Hybrid $\mathcal{H}_8$**: In this hybrid, the challenger chooses $c_{i,1}^*$ uniformly at random for all $i \in [n]$. The indistinguishability of this and the previous hybrid can be argued using the pseudorandomness of $\mathsf{PRC}$. The details on this are given in the full version.

**Hybrid $\mathcal{H}_9$**: In this hybrid, the challenger uses $\mathsf{PRC.Find}^\dagger$ on path $\overline{1}$ instead of $\mathsf{PRC.Find}$ in the pre-challenge and post-challenge phases. The transition from the previous hybrid to this hybrid proceeds analogously to the transition from $\mathcal{H}_2$ to $\mathcal{H}_3$, therefore, we refer to the full version for more details.

**Hybrid $\mathcal{H}_{10}$**: In this hybrid, the challenger chooses $c_{i,0}^*$ uniformly at random for all $i \in [n]$. The transition from the previous hybrid to this hybrid proceeds analogously to the transition from $\mathcal{H}_7$ to $\mathcal{H}_8$, relying on the pseudorandomness of PRC. We refer to the full version for more details.

**Hybrid** $\mathcal{H}_{11}$: In this hybrid, the challenger uses PRC.Find instead of $\mathsf{PRC.Find}^{\dagger}$ in the pre-challenge and post-challenge phases. The transition from the previous hybrid to this hybrid proceeds analogously to the transition from $\mathcal{H}_2$ to $\mathcal{H}_3$, therefore, we refer to the full version for more details.

**Hybrid** $\mathcal{H}_{12}$: In this hybrid, during the initialization phase, the setup of the commitment scheme is changed back to the standard setup, i.e., $\mathsf{com.pp} \leftarrow \mathsf{Com.Setup}(1^{\lambda}, 1^{n})$. The transition from the previous hybrid to this hybrid proceeds analogously to the transition from $\mathcal{H}_1$ to $\mathcal{H}_2$, relying on the equivocality of Com. We refer to the full version for more details.

**Hybrid** $\mathcal{H}_{13}$: In this hybrid, during the decryption queries, the challenger does not reject queries when $\mathsf{ds.vk} = \mathsf{ds.vk}^*$. The transition from the previous hybrid to this hybrid proceeds analogously to the transition from $\mathcal{H}_0$ to $\mathcal{H}_1$, relying on the unforgeability of DS. We refer to the full version for more details. Observe that hybrid $\mathcal{H}_{13}$ corresponds to the original security game, in which the challenger outputs a truly random string during the challenge phase.

Combining the below lemmas, using the triangle inequality, we conclude that for every PPT adversary $\mathcal{A}$, there exists a negligible function $\mathsf{negl}(\cdot)$ such that for all $\lambda \in \mathbb{N}$, $\left|\Pr[\mathcal{H}_0(\lambda, \mathcal{A}) = 1] - \Pr[\mathcal{H}_{12}(\lambda, \mathcal{A}) = 1]\right| \leq \mathsf{negl}(\lambda)$, where $\mathcal{H}_i(\lambda, \mathcal{A})$ denotes the output of $\mathcal{A}$ in hybrid $\mathcal{H}_i$. The proofs for the transitions of the different hybrids can be found in the full version.

**Acknowledgements.** We thank the anonymous Crypto 2026 reviewers for their helpful feedback, and in particular one reviewer for suggesting Raw Reed–Solomon codes as a useful cryptanalytic target for noisy McEliece-type assumptions. Nico Döttling and Mahesh Sreekumar Rajasree: Funded by the European Union (ERC, LACONIC, 101041207). Views and opinions expressed are however those of the author(s) only and do not necessarily reflect those of the European Union or the European Research Council. Neither the European Union nor the granting authority can be held responsible for them. Neither the European Union nor the granting authority can be held responsible for them.This work has been partly done while the third author was at IIT Delhi Abu Dhabi and the CISPA Helmholtz Center for Information Security.

## References

1. Classic McEliece (2026). https://classic.mceliece.org/papers.html. Accessed 12 Feb 2026
2. Alamati, N., Patranabis, S.: Cryptographic primitives with hinting property. In: Agrawal, S., Lin, D. (eds.) ASIACRYPT 2022, Part I. LNCS, vol. 13791, pp. 33–62. Springer, Cham (2022). https://doi.org/10.1007/978-3-031-22963-3_2
3. Alekhnovich, M.: More on average case vs approximation complexity. In: 44th Annual Symposium on Foundations of Computer Science. pp. 298–307. IEEE Computer Society Press, Cambridge (2003). https://doi.org/10.1109/SFCS.2003.1238204

4. Alrabiah, O., Ananth, P., Christ, M., Dodis, Y., Gunn, S.: Ideal pseudorandom codes. In: Proceedings of the 57th Annual ACM Symposium on Theory of Computing, STOC 2025, pp. 1638–1647. Association for Computing Machinery, New York (2025). https://doi.org/10.1145/3717823.3718309
5. Bellare, M., Boldyreva, A., Palacio, A.: An uninstantiable random-oracle-model scheme for a hybrid-encryption problem. In: Cachin, C., Camenisch, J.L. (eds.) EUROCRYPT 2004. LNCS, vol. 3027, pp. 171–188. Springer, Heidelberg (2004). https://doi.org/10.1007/978-3-540-24676-3_11
6. Bellare, M., Rogaway, P.: Random oracles are practical: a paradigm for designing efficient protocols. In: Denning, D.E., Pyle, R., Ganesan, R., Sandhu, R.S., Ashby, V. (eds.) ACM CCS 93: 1st Conference on Computer and Communications Security, pp. 62–73. ACM Press, Fairfax (1993). https://doi.org/10.1145/168588.168596
7. Bernstein, D.J., Chou, T.: CryptAttackTester: high-assurance attack analysis. In: Reyzin, L., Stebila, D. (eds.) CRYPTO 2024, Part VI. LNCS, vol. 14925, pp. 141–182. Springer, Cham (2024). https://doi.org/10.1007/978-3-031-68391-6_5
8. Bernstein, D.J., Lange, T., Peters, C.: Attacking and defending the McEliece cryptosystem. In: Buchmann, J., Ding, J. (eds.) PQCrypto 2008. LNCS, vol. 5299, pp. 31–46. Springer, Heidelberg (2008). https://doi.org/10.1007/978-3-540-88403-3_3
9. Bogdanov, A., Kothari, P.K., Rosen, A.: Public-key encryption, local pseudorandom generators, and the low-degree method. In: Rothblum, G., Wee, H. (eds.) TCC 2023. LNCS, vol. 14369, pp. 268–285. Springer, Cham (2023). https://doi.org/10.1007/978-3-031-48615-9_10
10. Branco, P., Döttling, N., Dujmovic, J.: Rate-1 incompressible encryption from standard assumptions. In: Kiltz, E., Vaikuntanathan, V. (eds.) TCC 2022, Part II. LNCS, vol. 13748, pp. 33–69. Springer, Cham (2022). https://doi.org/10.1007/978-3-031-22365-5_2
11. Canteaut, A., Chabaud, F.: A new algorithm for finding minimum-weight words in a linear code: application to McEliece's cryptosystem and to narrow-sense BCH codes of length 511. IEEE Trans. Inf. Theory **44**(1), 367–378 (1998)
12. Christ, M., Golowich, N., Gunn, S., Moitra, A., Wichs, D.: Improved pseudorandom codes from permuted puzzles. Cryptology ePrint Archive, Paper 2025/2222 (2025). https://eprint.iacr.org/2025/2222. To appear in STOC 2026
13. Christ, M., Gunn, S.: Pseudorandom error-correcting codes. In: Reyzin, L., Stebila, D. (eds.) CRYPTO 2024, Part VI. LNCS, vol. 14925, pp. 325–347. Springer, Cham (2024). https://doi.org/10.1007/978-3-031-68391-6_10
14. Cohen, A., Hoover, A., Schoenbach, G.: Watermarking language models for many adaptive users. In: Blanton, M., Enck, W., Nita-Rotaru, C. (eds.) IEEE Symposium on Security and Privacy, SP 2025, San Francisco, CA, USA, 12–15 May 2025, pp. 2583–2601. IEEE (2025). https://doi.org/10.1109/SP61157.2025.00084
15. Couvreur, A., Gaborit, P., Gauthier-Umaña, V., Otmani, A., Tillich, J.P.: Distinguisher-based attacks on public-key cryptosystems using Reed-Solomon codes. Des. Codes Crypt. **73**(2), 641–666 (2014)
16. Couvreur, A., Márquez-Corbella, I., Pellikaan, R.: Cryptanalysis of McEliece cryptosystem based on algebraic geometry codes and their subcodes. IEEE Trans. Inf. Theory **63**(8), 5404–5418 (2017)
17. Couvreur, A., Mora, R., Tillich, J.P.: A new approach based on quadratic forms to attack the McEliece cryptosystem. In: Guo, J., Steinfeld, R. (eds.) ASIACRYPT 2023. LNCS, vol. 14441, pp. 3–38. Springer, Cham (2023). https://doi.org/10.1007/978-981-99-8730-6_1
18. Couvreur, A., Otmani, A., Tillich, J.P.: Polynomial time attack on wild McEliece over quadratic extensions. IEEE Trans. Inf. Theory **63**(1), 404–427 (2016)

19. Couvreur, A., Otmani, A., Tillich, J.-P., Gauthier–Umaña, V.: A polynomial-time attack on the BBCRS scheme. In: Katz, J. (ed.) PKC 2015. LNCS, vol. 9020, pp. 175–193. Springer, Heidelberg (2015). https://doi.org/10.1007/978-3-662-46447-2_8
20. Döttling, N.: Low noise LPN: KDM secure public key encryption and sample amplification. In: Katz, J. (ed.) PKC 2015. LNCS, vol. 9020, pp. 604–626. Springer, Heidelberg (2015). https://doi.org/10.1007/978-3-662-46447-2_27
21. Döttling, N., Dowsley, R., Müller-Quade, J., Nascimento, A.C.A.: A CCA2 secure variant of the McEliece cryptosystem. IEEE Trans. Inf. Theory **58**(10), 6672–6680 (2012)
22. Dwork, C., Naor, M., Reingold, O.: Immunizing encryption schemes from decryption errors. In: Cachin, C., Camenisch, J.L. (eds.) EUROCRYPT 2004. LNCS, vol. 3027, pp. 342–360. Springer, Heidelberg (2004). https://doi.org/10.1007/978-3-540-24676-3_21
23. Döttling, N., Müller, A., Rajasree, M.S.: Separating pseudorandom codes from local oracles. Cryptology ePrint Archive, Paper 2025/1020 (2025). https://eprint.iacr.org/2025/1020
24. Faugere, J.C., Otmani, A., Perret, L., De Portzamparc, F., Tillich, J.P.: Structural cryptanalysis of McEliece schemes with compact keys. Des. Codes Crypt. **79**(1), 87–112 (2016)
25. Faugère, J.-C., Otmani, A., Perret, L., Tillich, J.-P.: Algebraic cryptanalysis of McEliece variants with compact keys. In: Gilbert, H. (ed.) EUROCRYPT 2010. LNCS, vol. 6110, pp. 279–298. Springer, Heidelberg (2010). https://doi.org/10.1007/978-3-642-13190-5_14
26. Feige, U., Shamir, A.: Witness indistinguishable and witness hiding protocols. In: 22nd Annual ACM Symposium on Theory of Computing, pp. 416–426. ACM Press, Baltimore (1990). https://doi.org/10.1145/100216.100272
27. Garcia, A., Stichtenoth, H.: A tower of Artin-Schreier extensions of function fields attaining the Drinfeld-Vladut bound. Invent. Math. **121**(1), 211–222 (1995). https://doi.org/10.1007/BF01884295
28. Garg, S., Gunn, S., Wang, M.: Black-box crypto is useless for pseudorandom codes. Cryptology ePrint Archive, Paper 2025/1021 (2025). https://eprint.iacr.org/2025/1021
29. Gauthier, V., Otmani, A., Tillich, J.P.: A distinguisher-based attack on a variant of McEliece's cryptosystem based on Reed-Solomon codes. arXiv preprint arXiv:1204.6459 (2012)
30. Ghentiyala, S., Guruswami, V.: New constructions of pseudorandom codes. arXiv preprint arXiv:2409.07580 (2024)
31. Goldwasser, S., Kalai, Y.T.: On the (in)security of the Fiat-Shamir paradigm. In: 44th Annual Symposium on Foundations of Computer Science, pp. 102–115. IEEE Computer Society Press, Cambridge (2003). https://doi.org/10.1109/SFCS.2003.1238185
32. Golowich, N., Moitra, A.: Edit distance robust watermarks for language models. arXiv preprint arXiv:2406.02633 (2024)
33. Jovanovic, N., Staab, R., Vechev, M.T.: Watermark stealing in large language models. In: Salakhutdinov, R., Kolter, Z., Heller, K.A., Weller, A., Oliver, N., Scarlett, J., Berkenkamp, F. (eds.) Forty-first International Conference on Machine Learning, ICML 2024, Vienna, Austria, 21–27 July 2024. Proceedings of Machine Learning Research, vol. 235, pp. 22570–22593. PMLR/OpenReview.net (2024). https://proceedings.mlr.press/v235/jovanovic24a.html

34. Kirshanova, E., May, A.: Breaking Goppa-based McEliece with hints. Inf. Comput. **293**, 105045 (2023)
35. Koppula, V., Waters, B.: Realizing chosen ciphertext security generically in attribute-based encryption and predicate encryption. In: Boldyreva, A., Micciancio, D. (eds.) CRYPTO 2019. LNCS, vol. 11693, pp. 671–700. Springer, Cham (2019). https://doi.org/10.1007/978-3-030-26951-7_23
36. Leurent, G., Nguyen, P.Q.: How risky is the random-oracle model? In: Halevi, S. (ed.) CRYPTO 2009. LNCS, vol. 5677, pp. 445–464. Springer, Heidelberg (2009). https://doi.org/10.1007/978-3-642-03356-8_26
37. Loidreau, P., Sendrier, N.: Weak keys in the McEliece public-key cryptosystem. IEEE Trans. Inf. Theory **47**(3), 1207–1211 (2002)
38. McEliece, R.J.: A public-key cryptosystem based on algebraic. Coding Thv **4244**(1978), 114–116 (1978)
39. Naor, M.: Bit commitment using pseudo-randomness. In: Brassard, G. (ed.) CRYPTO 1989. LNCS, vol. 435, pp. 128–136. Springer, New York (1990). https://doi.org/10.1007/0-387-34805-0_13
40. Niederreiter, H.: Knapsack-type cryptosystems and algebraic coding theory. Prob. Contr. Inform. Theory **15**(2), 157–166 (1986)
41. Nielsen, J.B.: Separating random oracle proofs from complexity theoretic proofs: the non-committing encryption case. In: Yung, M. (ed.) CRYPTO 2002. LNCS, vol. 2442, pp. 111–126. Springer, Heidelberg (2002). https://doi.org/10.1007/3-540-45708-9_8
42. Pang, Q., Hu, S., Zheng, W., Smith, V.: No free lunch in LLM watermarking: trade-offs in watermarking design choices (2024). https://arxiv.org/abs/2402.16187
43. Randriambololona, H.: The syzygy distinguisher. In: Fehr, S., Fouque, P. (eds.) EUROCRYPT 2025, Part VI. LNCS, vol. 15606, pp. 324–354. Springer, Cham (2025). https://doi.org/10.1007/978-3-031-91095-1_12
44. Sidelnikov, V.M., Shestakov, S.O.: On insecurity of cryptosystems based on generalized Reed-Solomon codes (1992)
45. Silbak, J., Kopparty, S., Shaltiel, R.: Quasilinear time list-decodable codes for space bounded channels. In: Zuckerman, D. (ed.) 60th Annual Symposium on Foundations of Computer Science, pp. 302–333. IEEE Computer Society Press, Baltimore (2019). https://doi.org/10.1109/FOCS.2019.00028
46. Stichtenoth, H.: Algebraic Function Fields and Codes. Graduate Texts in Mathematics, 2 edn., vol. 254. Springer, Cham (2009). https://doi.org/10.1007/978-3-540-76878-4
47. van Tilburg, J.: Security-analysis of a class of cryptosystems based on linear error-correcting codes (1994)
48. Zhandry, M.: Augmented random oracles. In: Dodis, Y., Shrimpton, T. (eds.) CRYPTO 2022, Part III. LNCS, vol. 13509, pp. 35–65. Springer, Cham (2022). https://doi.org/10.1007/978-3-031-15982-4_2

# Obfuscation and Functional Encryption

# How to Use Polynomially-Hard iO: Turing Machine Obfuscation and More


Jesko Dujmovic[1], Yao-Ching Hsieh[2(✉)], Abhishek Jain[3,4], and Willy Quach[5]

[1] Northeastern University, Boston, USA
[2] University of Washington, Seattle, USA
ychsieh@cs.washington.edu
[3] NTT Research, Sunnyvale, USA
[4] Johns Hopkins University, Baltimore, USA
[5] CISPA, Saarbrücken, Germany



**Abstract.** We revisit the notion of PViO [Jain-Jin, FOCS'22] – an indistinguishability obfuscation (iO) scheme for Turing machines with unbounded input length that guarantees security for pairs of machines whose equivalence can be proven in Cook's Theory PV.

Known constructions of PViO require subexponentially-hard iO for circuits. We give the first construction based on *polynomially*-hard iO and other standard assumptions. We further show how to replace iO with EFiO – an efficiently falsifiable variant, thus obtaining a construction based on efficiently falsifiable assumptions.

Central to our result is a new twist to the celebrated punctured programming technique [Sahai-Waters, STOC'14], where one can program an obfuscated probabilistic function on its entire input domain in *one shot* instead of an input-by-input manner. Our key ingredient is the notion of function secret sharing [Boyle-Gilboa-Ishai, EUROCRYPT'15]. We further show the versatility of our technique by removing the use of complexity-leveraging in two applications of iO: unleveled fully homomorphic encryption, and adaptively-sound succinct non-interactive arguments for "trapdoor" languages.


## 1 Introduction

Indistinguishability obfuscation (iO) [8,27] guarantees that the obfuscations of any two functionally equivalent programs are computationally indistinguishable. Following a long line of work, iO was recently realized from well-studied assumptions [32,33,50]. Furthermore, a parallel line of work over the last decade has established iO as a seeming panacea that can enable most cryptographic applications.

A common limitation of all existing constructions of iO for general-purpose computations is that they employ a security reduction that incurs a loss exponential in the input length of the program. This means that they can only handle programs with an a priori bounded input length and require assumptions that



N. Heninger and M. Rosulek (Eds.): CRYPTO 2026, LNCS 16800, pp. 317–349, 2026.
https://doi.org/10.1007/978-3-032-35367-2_11

are $2^{|x|}$-hard for programs of maximum input length $|x|$. As a consequence, the size of the obfuscated program grows with $|x|$.

Prior works [28,34,40] have observed that this limitation might be inherent. Intuitively, since the iO security guarantee only holds for functionally equivalent programs, the security reduction must be able to decide whether the (adversarially chosen) programs are equivalent. A natural way to check equivalence is by iterating over all inputs to the programs one by one. This brute-force strategy (employed in prior works) results in a $2^{|x|}$ security loss.

**iO via Mathematical Proofs of Equivalence.** Jain and Jin [34] presented an approach to overcome this barrier by leveraging mathematical proofs of equivalence. They consider the following relaxed notion of security that we refer to as PViO: obfuscations of two programs are computationally indistinguishable if the programs are functionally equivalent, and, moreover, their equivalence can be proven in a proof system called Theory PV [22]. Intuitively, since a PV proof of equivalence is an efficient witness to attest to the equivalence of two programs, the notion of PViO is not subject to the aforementioned barriers. Although not all functionally equivalent programs admit such proofs of equivalence, recent work has demonstrated that many applications of iO can be obtained from PViO when used in combination with cryptographic primitives whose basic properties (such as correctness) can be proven in PV [4,34,35,42].[1]

Jain and Jin presented a construction of PViO for Turing machines with *unbounded* input length. Their key insight is that a PV proof of equivalence can be used to devise an efficient security reduction that incurs only a polynomial loss in the input length. Unfortunately, their construction still relies on *sub-exponential* hardness assumptions. Specifically, they construct PViO assuming the sub-exponential hardness of iO for circuits and of learning with errors (LWE), where the sub-exponential function depends (only) on the security parameter of the scheme.

This raises the following question:

*Can we build PViO from polynomial hardness assumptions?*

## 1.1 Our Results (I)

Our main result is a positive resolution to this question. We present a construction of PViO for Turing machines of unbounded input length relying only on the *polynomial hardness* of iO for circuits of fixed polynomial size, of LWE and of time-lock puzzles [51]. We further show how to weaken the requirement on iO to

[1] This is analogous to how iO can often be combined with other cryptographic primitives to handle programs that are not functionally equivalent [53].

achieve a stronger result based only on efficiently falsifiable assumptions [45].[2] We expand upon our results in the following.

**Theorem 1.1 ((Informal)) PViO from Polynomial Hardness).** *There exists a PViO scheme for all Turing machines under the polynomial hardness of the following assumptions:*

- *iO for circuits of size at most* $p(\lambda)$*, where* $p(\cdot)$ *is a fixed polynomial and* $\lambda$ *is the security parameter.*
- *Learning with errors (with sub-exponential modulus-to-noise ratio), and time-lock puzzles.*

Time-lock puzzles are known from various assumptions such as the polynomial hardness of repeated squaring [51], or iO and non-parallelizing languages [10], or non-parallelizing languages, ring LWE and decomposed LWE [2].

**One-Shot Programming.** Central to our approach is a new twist on the celebrated punctured programming technique of [53] that is widely used in the iO literature. Recall that the standard iO security guarantee only holds for deterministic circuits. However, when building new applications from iO, we often need to obfuscate probabilistic circuits. The standard approach to achieve this goal is to obfuscate a deterministic circuit that generates randomness using a pseudorandom function (PRF). To argue security, we modify the program *input-by-input* using the punctured programming technique. This, however, incurs a security loss proportional to the input domain size, thus necessitating the use of sub-exponential hardness assumptions. This is in fact one of the key reasons behind the use of sub-exponential hardness assumptions in [34].

To avoid this security loss, we devise a *one-shot programming* technique wherein we change the functionality of the obfuscated program on the entire domain at once. Our key ingredient is the notion of *function secret sharing* (FSS) [16] satisfying a strong form of correctness[3]. In a nutshell, FSS allows two parties, given respective function shares, to locally derive additive shares of any desired output of the function. Moreover, FSS can be built from the *polynomial hardness* of LWE. We believe that this technique is of broader interest, since many applications of iO in the literature require an input-by-input puncturing argument. To support this view, we present two additional applications of our technique; see Sect. 1.2.

**A Stronger Result from Efficiently Falsifiable Assumptions.** Theorem 1.1 relies on iO for circuits of size polynomial in the security parameter. This

[2] We say that a hardness assumption is *efficiently falsifiable* if the challenger in the security experiment runs in polynomial time, and can decide in polynomial time whether an adversary wins. For iO, the latter requirement amounts to checking whether two circuits are functionally equivalent.

[3] FSS evaluation for a large enough class of computations is known to be a PRF [16].

assumption, however, is not efficiently falsifiable [45], for the reasons discussed earlier. We show how to weaken this requirement to obtain a stronger result based on efficiently falsifiable assumptions.

To formally state our result, we first recall the notion of EFiO, a relaxation of iO for circuits introduced in [34]. Informally, a circuit obfuscation scheme is said to achieve EFiO security if it guarantees indistinguishability for any pair of circuits whose equivalence can be proven in the extended Frege propositional proof system [23]. Intuitively, EFiO can be viewed as a circuit analogue of PViO which is defined for Turing machines. Cook's propositional translation theorem [22,23] shows that a proof of equivalence of a pair of circuit families in theory PV can be translated into proofs of circuit equivalence on each input length in the extended Frege system.

Unlike standard iO for circuits, EFiO is an efficiently falsifiable assumption thanks to the propositional proof of equivalence. We show that it suffices to use EFiO instead of iO in Theorem 1.1. Thus, we obtain PViO from efficiently falsifiable assumptions.

**Theorem 1.2 ((Informal) PViO from Efficiently Falsifiable Assumptions).** *There exists a PViO scheme for all Turing machines under the same assumptions as Theorem 1.1, except that we replace iO with EFiO.*

To achieve this result, we rely on a careful use of cryptographic tools that admit proofs of their key properties (such as perfect correctness) in the extended Frege system, and which can be instantiated from LWE. As it turns out, no known construction of FSS – a key component in our scheme – admits such a proof. At a high-level, this is because all known constructions only achieve correctness with overwhelming probability. To this end, we propose a new method to transform a function secret sharing with approximate correctness – here in the sense that additive reconstruction of the FSS is only up to a bounded additive error – into one that achieves *perfect* correctness. The key ingredient in this transformation is the notion of correlation-intractable (CI) hashing [20]. Approximately correct FSS [7,26,48] as well as CI hashing [19,49] are known from the polynomial hardness of LWE. We believe that this technique is of independent interest and is likely to be relevant for future work on PViO.

## 1.2 Our Results (II)

We propose our one-shot programming technique, based on function secret sharing, as a versatile proof technique of independent interest. We provide evidence by showing how to use this technique for the following applications of iO.

**Fully Homomorphic Encryption.** First, we show a construction of fully homomorphic encryption (FHE) relying on polynomial hardness assumptions.

**Theorem 1.3 ((Informal) FHE from Polynomial Hardness).** *There exists an (unleveled) fully homomorphic encryption scheme under the polynomial hardness of the following assumptions:*

- $\mathsf{iO}$ *for circuits (of size at most $p(\lambda)$, where $p(\cdot)$ is a fixed polynomial and $\lambda$ is the security parameter).*
- *Function secret sharing, time-lock puzzles, and Decisional Diffie-Hellman.*

Previously, iO-based constructions were only known under either the sub-exponential security of $\mathsf{iO}$ and of other additional assumptions [21], or under the polynomial security of $\mathsf{iO}$ and the *exponential* hardness of DDH [3]. Both these works used an input-by-input argument; in contrast, we use our one-shot programming technique. Our construction additionally relies on a special-purpose encryption scheme, which can be instantiated from DDH.

Here again, by carefully instantiating our cryptographic tools, we show that it suffices to use EFiO instead of iO in Theorem 1.3.

**Theorem 1.4 ((Informal) FHE from Efficiently Falsifiable Assumptions).** *There exists an unleveled FHE scheme under the following assumptions:*

- *EFiO.*
- *Function secret sharing, time-lock puzzles, Decisional Diffie-Hellman.*
- *Correlation intractable hashing for the FSS-correctness-error relation (LWE with superpolynomial modulus-to-noise ratio).*

**Adaptively-sound SNARGs for Trapdoor Languages.** Our second application is to succinct non-interactive arguments (SNARGs) – a non-interactive, computationally-sound proof system in the common reference string model with proofs shorter than the statement and witness size. We present a construction of *adaptively-sound* SNARGs for trapdoor languages based on *polynomial hardness assumptions.* Trapdoor languages [18,25] are a subclass of NP where there exists a (hard to compute) trapdoor to efficiently decide the language.

Our construction is a simple variant of the Sahai-Waters [53] SNARG for NP based on iO and pseudorandom functions (PRFs). Their original construction only achieves non-adaptive soundness. We prove that it, in fact, satisfies adaptive soundness for trapdoor languages when the PRF is instantiated with FSS.

**Theorem 1.5 (Informal).** *The Sahai-Waters construction is an adaptively sound SNARG for trapdoor languages when the PRF is instantiated with an FSS evaluation.*

Previously, such a result was only known from *sub-exponential* hardness of iO and of one-way functions [55–57].

**Our One-Shot Programming Technique via Function Secret Sharing.** Finally, we briefly discuss our core one-shot programming technique. In a nutshell, we use FSS to change the functionality of the obfuscated program on every input. Thus, we rely on FSS *with perfect correctness* (over the randomness of the function shares), and this functionality change needs to be supported by the FSS, which depends on the exact application. In whole generality, one could rely on such FSS for all (bounded-depth) circuits, which can be instantiated from LWE (with sub-exponential modulus-to-noise ratio).

However, given a specific application, one can hope to weaken the expressivity required from the FSS. For example, in our application to FHE, the one-shot programming roughly corresponds to decryption of a special-purpose encryption scheme. Appropriately instantiating the latter allows us to rely on FSS for $\mathsf{NC}^1$ instead, thus enabling our technique to be instantiated from the decisional composite residuosity (DCR) assumption [47,52].

**Future Directions.** We leave the following fascinating research directions for future work.

- (EFiO from Standard Assumptions.) Our work shows that PViO can be built from (weaker) *polynomial hardness assumptions* (Theorems 1.1and 1.2). Our construction relies on EFiO for small circuits, which is an efficiently-falsifiable assumption. It remains open, however, to construct EFiO from the polynomial hardness of standard assumptions, for instance the ones known to imply general-purpose iO [32,33,50].
- (Probabilistic iO from Polynomial Assumptions.) Our one-shot programming technique opens the possibility of recovering applications of so-called *probabilistic iO* (piO) [21], from polynomial hardness assumptions. In this work, we achieve this in the specific case of FHE Theorems (1.3 and 1.4). Our current techniques require algebraic structure from the probabilistic program. Extending our techniques to handle more general probabilistic programs is an exciting avenue of future research.

# 2 Technical Overview

We give here a broad overview of our results and techniques. The first part of this overview is dedicated to improving the construction of PViO from [34]:

- We start by providing a summary of the relevant parts of [34] in Sect. 2.1.
- Next, we present our one-shot programming technique in Sect. 2.2. Readers interested in our techniques independently of PViO may jump directly to this section.
- Finally, we present our improved construction of PViO in Sect. 2.3.

In the second part of this overview, we present more applications of our techniques, notably to fully homomorphic encryption, in Sect. 2.4.

**FSS vs Shiftable PRFs.** As discussed earlier, a key ingredient underlying our techniques is the notion of function secret sharing (FSS). For convenience of presentation, throughout this overview, we describe our technical ideas through the lens of *shiftable PRFs* [41,48], which can be viewed as a strengthening of FSS. We emphasize, however, that FSS suffices for our final claims; see Sect. 2.5.

## 2.1 Background on iO via Propositional Proofs of Equivalence

As discussed in the introduction, Jain and Jin [34] introduced the notion of PViO, a relaxation of iO for Turing machines that guarantees security for pairs of programs with short proofs of equivalence in theory PV. Their construction relies on *inefficiently falsifiable* assumptions, both in the form of relying on sub-exponential hardness assumptions, and relying on general-purpose iO for circuits. Addressing these drawbacks will be the focus of the present section, Sects. 2.2, and Sect. 2.3.

We start with an overview of the construction JJ22 construction [34], in order to highlight the sources of the drawbacks. Looking ahead, we will mostly improve on their proof techniques, and only lightly modify their construction.

**The JJ22Template.** The construction of JJ22 goes in two steps. First, it introduces a new template to build iO for *circuits*. Then, the latter is upgraded to an obfuscation for Turing machines. We start with the first step, which captures most of the technical challenges we need to overcome; we address the second in Sect. 2.3.

At a high level, the core of the first step is to obfuscate circuits *gate-by-gate*, meaning that the obfuscated circuit consists of a collection of obfuscated gates. Independent of the use of obfuscation, it is crucial for security that (1) the contents of the original internal wires are kept private, and (2) the internal wires between obfuscated gates are authenticated, in order to prevent mix-and-match attacks that attempt to feed as input to an obfuscated gate an unrelated circuit wire, say coming from a non-adjacent obfuscated gate or an execution of the program on a different input. Thus, JJ22 compiles every gate $g$ from the original circuit into a circuit $C_g$, with input and output being encryptions of the original internal wires, along with authentications of these ciphertexts with respect to both the wire location and the execution at hand. These gates are then obfuscated using a general-purpose iO for circuits.

Their main idea is that if the size of these authentications is short, then so are the resulting circuits $C_g$ and thus the obfuscated circuit $\{\mathsf{iO}(C_g)\}$. However, the authentication part must be of size at least $\omega(\log(\lambda))$ for security (otherwise it could be broken by brute force). Thus, in JJ22, *the input size of these obfuscated gates grows with the security parameter.*

The security proof of JJ22 proceeds as follows. Assume for notational convenience that these obfuscated gates $\mathsf{iO}(C_g)$ have input size $\lambda$. The proof switches the behavior of an obfuscated gate using a standard puncturing technique, which goes through one hybrid per possible input to $\mathsf{iO}(C_g)$. This translates to the use of $2^\lambda$-secure iO for circuits and puncturable PRFs.

Summing up so far, there are two sources behind the efficient unfalsifiability of assumptions used in the JJ22 construction (for circuits):

1. The puncturing technique, which is iterated over all possible $2^\lambda$ inputs to the obfuscated gates $\mathsf{iO}(C_g)$, which incurs a large security loss;

2. The use of general-purpose iO for circuits with $\lambda$-bit inputs, in order to obfuscate $C_g$, which is not efficiently falsifiable in general.

## 2.2 One-Shot Programming via Shiftable PRFs

We first tackle issue (1). We provide a tighter security proof while keeping the construction for circuits nearly syntactically identical to the one of JJ22. To demonstrate our main technical tool for tighter reductions, we look at toy versions of encryption and authentication functionalities. Looking ahead, we introduce our new technique from the perspective of *shiftable PRFs.* We refer to Sect. 2.5 for how to make this technique rely on the weaker notion of function secret sharing instead.

**Obfuscating Encryption.** In order to introduce and illustrate our main technical idea, we first look at obfuscating a circuit implementing encryption. Suppose we wish to obfuscate the following circuit:

Circuit $\mathsf{Enc}_P$

Hard-coded: A PRF key $K$, a program $P: \{0,1\}^n \to \{0,1\}$.
On input $x \in \{0,1\}^n$, output $\mathsf{PRF}_K(x) + P(x)$.

In words, on input $x$, $\mathsf{Enc}_P$ computes a message $P(x)$, for an arbitrary hard-coded, private program $P$, and encrypts it under a symmetric encryption key $K$. Intuitively, in the JJ22 construction, one can think of $x$ as an authenticated encryption of an input wire under key (say) $K'$, and $P(x)$ computing (given the key $K'$) the next unencrypted output wire. Our goal is to prove that obfuscating $\mathsf{Enc}_P$ using iO hides $P$.

This is typically done using the celebrated puncturing technique of [53]. Namely, obfuscating $\mathsf{Enc}_P$ using an iO scheme and instantiating the PRF in $\mathsf{Enc}_P$ by a puncturable PRF, the standard proof that, for all (efficient) programs $P, P'$, the obfuscated programs $\mathsf{iO}(\mathsf{Enc}_P)$ and $\mathsf{iO}(\mathsf{Enc}_{P'})$ are indistinguishable, goes as follows. For any fixed input $x^*$, one can puncture the PRF on $x^*$ (by puncturable PRF security) and hard-code, on input $x^*$, a fresh random output $r^*$ instead (by iO security). Doing so allows one to undetectably switch, for any input $x^*$, from outputting $\mathsf{PRF}_K(x^*)+P(x^*)$ to outputting $r^*$, and then to $\mathsf{PRF}_K(x^*)+P'(x^*)$. Iterating this argument over all possible input $x^*$ shows the claimed indistinguishability.

**A Tighter Proof using Shiftable PRFs.** The central bottleneck in the proof above is that puncturable PRFs only allow changing the output on a single input $x^*$ at a time, which in turn induces a $2^{|x|}$ security loss overall.

Our idea to avoid this loss is very natural: we would like to rely instead on a PRF which allows us to undetectably modify exponentially many outputs at once. Observe that $\mathsf{Enc}_P$ implements a "shifted PRF evaluation". From this perspective, in terms of security, we would like the ability to undetectably switch the "shift" from $P(x)$ to another program $P'(x)$, using only polynomial hardness.

This very object, that we call a shiftable PRF, turns out to have been previously studied! (In the literature, this was called a shift-hiding shiftable function [41,48].) In a nutshell, shiftable PRFs are a structured form of constraint-hiding constrained PRFs. In a shiftable PRF, one can generate a master PRF key $K$ that can be used to compute $x \mapsto \mathsf{PRF}_K(x)$. Moreover, one can generate so-called shifted keys $K_P$ with respect to shifts $P$, where $P : \{0,1\}^n \rightarrow \{0,1\}$ is an efficient program, which instead allow computing $x \mapsto \mathsf{PRF}_K(x) + P(x)$. The main security property of shiftable PRFs is that they are *shift-hiding*, that is, that a shifted key hides its underlying shift.

Importantly, shiftable PRFs for efficient shifts are known to exist assuming the *polynomial hardness* of LWE [48].[4] Another interpretation of the previous proof is that shiftable PRFs can be built from sub-exponentially secure iO and sub-exponentially secure one-way functions [41].

We now adapt the previous security proof that $\mathsf{iO}(\mathsf{Enc}_P)$ and $\mathsf{iO}(\mathsf{Enc}_{P'})$ are indistinguishable,[5] relying instead on shift-hiding PRFs:

- We first switch the obfuscated program $\mathsf{iO}(\mathsf{Enc}_P)$ to one that uses a shifted key $K_\mathbf{0}$ associated with the all-zero shift instead. This has the same functionality as the original program and is therefore indistinguishable from the original $\mathsf{iO}(\mathsf{Enc}_P)$ by iO security.
- We then switch the shift from computing the all-0 function to computing $-P + P'$; this change is undetectable by the shift-hiding property of the shiftable PRF. Note that the output of the obfuscated program on an input $x$ is now $(\mathsf{PRF}_K(x) - P(x) + P'(x)) + P(x)$.
- We now compute the output using the master key as $\mathsf{PRF}_K(x) + P'(x)$, which is undetectable by iO security. This proves the indistinguishability of $\mathsf{iO}(\mathsf{Enc}_P)$ and $\mathsf{iO}(\mathsf{Enc}_{P'})$.

Crucially, we only used a constant number of hybrids, and in particular did not go through an "input-by-input" proof strategy. Instead we modified the behavior of $\mathsf{iO}(\mathsf{Enc}_P)$ on *all* $2^n$ *inputs*, using a single invocation of the shift-hiding property.

Overall, this allows us to argue that when the PRF is instantiated by a shiftable PRF, $\mathsf{iO}(\mathsf{Enc}_P)$ and $\mathsf{iO}(\mathsf{Enc}_{P'})$ are indistinguishable assuming only the polynomial hardness of iO and polynomial security of the shiftable PRF.

---

[4] We discuss in Sect. 2.5 how to generalize this proof technique to obtain more instantiations by relying instead on (polynomially-secure) function secret-sharing.

[5] The savvy reader might observe that in order to implement the functionality of $\mathsf{Enc}_P$ while preserving privacy of $P$, using a shiftable PRF on its own is sufficient, without the use of obfuscation. We present the obfuscated variant to keep the parallel to the puncturing technique. For our final construction, keeping the obfuscation does not cause additional assumptions; we require obfuscation for the authentication anyway.

**Obfuscating Authentication, and the Hidden Sparse Trigger Technique.** Next, we turn to the case of authentication. On a technical level, we provide further evidence that shiftable PRFs are highly synergistic with iO, and in particular with the so-called "hidden sparse trigger" technique [53].

Consider the following circuit to obfuscate. Here, the circuit has a PRF key $K$ and an efficient program $P$ hard-coded.

Circuit $V_P$

Hard-coded: A PRF key $K$, a program $P : \{0,1\}^n \rightarrow \{0,1\}$.
On input $(x, y)$, output 1 if $P(x) = 1$ and $\mathsf{PRF}_K(x) = y$, and 0 otherwise.

In words, taking the convention that 1 means accepting, and denoting by $\mathbf{1}$ the "always accepting" predicate, $V_{\mathbf{1}}$ corresponds to a standard verification procedure for a signature. That is, it only checks whether $\mathsf{PRF}_K(x) = y$. On the other hand, $V_P$ corresponds to a "constrained" verification procedure that only verifies signatures on "good" inputs $x$, i.e., if $P(x) = 1$. Our goal is to argue that $\mathsf{iO}(V_{\mathbf{1}})$ and $\mathsf{iO}(V_P)$ are indistinguishable, namely, that obfuscated "constrained verification keys" hide their underlying constraint $P$.

Intuitively, in the JJ22 construction, one can roughly think of $x$ as being an authenticated encryption of an input wire, and $P(x)$ verifying the authenticity of $x$ using secret information. At a high level, the security property above allows one to *fully disable unauthorized inputs* from the obfuscated compiled gate $\mathsf{iO}(C_g)$, which is crucial to later rely on iO security; otherwise, there would be no guarantee of functional equivalence over unauthorized inputs, including ones that the adversary might use in a mix-and-match attack.

The standard proof of security for the above goes as follows. Start with $\mathsf{iO}(V_{\mathbf{1}})$. Fix any input $x^*$ such that $P(x^*) = 0$. The first step is to use the puncturing technique: now, on any input of the form $(x^*, y)$, output 1 if $y = r^*$ for a uniformly random hard-coded value $r^*$. We now disable inputs $(x^*, y)$ using the hidden sparse trigger technique, as follows. We modify the check to output 1 on input $(x^*, y)$ iff $G(y) = G(r^*)$ where $G$ is an injective PRG; this is undetectable by iO security. Now, instead of checking $G(y) = G(r^*)$, we check $G(y) = s$ for a uniformly random $s$; this follows by PRG security. At this point, if $G$ is sufficiently expanding, then the probability that there exists any $y$ such that $G(y) = s$ is negligible over the random choice of $s$ alone. Therefore one can now output 0 on every input of the form $(x^*, \cdot)$ instead, by relying on iO security. The proof that $\mathsf{iO}(V_{\mathbf{1}})$ and $\mathsf{iO}(V_P)$ are indistinguishable follows by iterating the argument over all $x^*$ such that $P(x^*) = 0$.[6]

As before, this iteration over all possible bad inputs $x^*$ induces in general an exponential loss in the input size. The key source of this loss is that the combination of puncturable PRFs and hidden sparse trigger technique allows us to disable only a single bad input at a time.

---

[6] As mentioned in Footnote 5, for authentication we require the obfuscation. Here, if the adversary learned the output of the PRF—shifted or not—any security would break down.

We show that via a careful use of shiftable PRFs, we can *disable all the bad inputs in one shot*, thus obtaining a tighter security proof in this setting as well. We modify the previous proof as follows:

- We first switch the obfuscated program $\mathsf{iO}(V_1)$ to one that uses a shifted key $K_0$ for the all 0 shift. Doing so is indistinguishable by $\mathsf{iO}$ security.
- We change the shifted key, from one computing the all 0 shift to one computing $x \mapsto (P(x) - 1) \cdot R$ for a fixed, uniformly random $R$. In other words, the original PRF output is now shifted by $-R$ iff $P(x) = 0$. This is undetectable by the shift-hiding property of the PRF. The output of the obfuscated program on input $(x, y)$ is now 1 iff $\mathsf{PRF}_K(x) - (1 - P(x)) \cdot R = y$.
- We change how the check is computed. The obfuscated program now uses the unshifted, master PRF key $K$, and outputs 1 iff $G(\mathsf{PRF}_K(x) - y) = G((1 - P(x)) \cdot R)$, where $G$ is an injective PRG. This is undetectable by $\mathsf{iO}$ security.
- We now switch the check whenever $P(x) = 0$ to instead output 1 iff $G(\mathsf{PRF}_K(x) - y) = s$ for a uniformly random $s$ hard-coded in the obfuscated program; this follows by $\mathsf{PRG}$ security with seed $R$ and $\mathsf{iO}$.
- The obfuscated program now always outputs 0 whenever $P(x) = 0$. This is indistinguishable by $\mathsf{iO}$ whenever $s$ is not in the range of the $\mathsf{PRG}$ $G$, which holds with overwhelming probability over the random choice of $s$, as long as $G$ is expanding enough. This program now corresponds to $V_P$, which finishes the proof.

Here again, relying on shift-hiding allowed us to change the behavior of the PRF on exponentially many inputs at once. An important additional mechanism that we use here is that, by carefully correlating the shift over all the different inputs, we managed to disable exponentially many outputs of the obfuscated circuit by arguing that a *single* random value $s$ hard-coded in the program is outside of the range of the PRG.

In typical applications however, the indistinguishability statement above would not suffice, as adversaries would also have access to valid signatures. Thankfully, the proof above naturally extends when additionally giving out an associated constrained signing program, which provides signatures for any authorized inputs with respect to $P$, computed by the following circuit:

**Circuit $E_P$**

<u>Hard-coded:</u> A PRF key $K$, a program $P : \{0,1\}^n \to \{0,1\}$.
On input $x$, output $y = \mathsf{PRF}_K(x)$ if $P(x) = 1$ and $\perp$ otherwise.

Namely, one can show that $\mathsf{iO}(V_1)$ and $\mathsf{iO}(V_P)$ are indistinguishable even given $\mathsf{iO}(E_P)$. The proof is almost identical, the only differences being that (1) in the first step, all PRF keys get shifted, and (2) in the third step, we additionally rely on $\mathsf{iO}$ to switch back the shifted key used in $\mathsf{iO}(E_P)$ to the master PRF key (which is needed to argue that, at that point, the only information the adversary has on $R$ is $G(R)$).

Overall, we abstract this construction as a constrained signature satisfying constraint-hiding for a rich class of predicates $P$, assuming the polynomial hardness of $\mathsf{iO}$, of a shiftable PRF, and of an injective PRG. We refer to Sect. 4 for more details.

## 2.3 Wrapping Up the Construction of PViO

We describe here our improved construction of $\mathsf{PViO}$ from polynomial hardness assumptions, and further, how to rely only on efficiently falsifiable assumptions.

**EFiO from Polynomial Hardness.** Armed with our new technical tools, we now return to the JJ22 template for circuits. We use shiftable PRFs instead of puncturable PRFs to instantiate the authenticated encryption components of the compiled gates $C_g$. Then, a direct combination of the techniques above and the original proof of JJ22 yields a construction of $\mathsf{iO}$ for circuits with efficient proofs of equivalence, namely $\mathsf{EFiO}$, assuming the polynomial hardness of $\mathsf{iO}$, of shiftable PRFs, and of other building blocks implied by the polynomial hardness of LWE. This improves on JJ22, which instead relied on sub-exponentially secure $\mathsf{iO}$, sub-exponentially secure one-way functions, and the same other building blocks. As a side note, we stress that both results only require $\mathsf{iO}$ for circuits with small input size $\mathsf{poly}(\lambda)$ for a fixed $\mathsf{poly}$ (the polynomial depending on the other building blocks), independent of the actual input size of the original circuit (up to polylogarithmic factors). We refer to Sect. 5.1 for more details.

**PViO from Polynomial Hardness via Time-Lock Puzzles.** Next, we give a brief sketch on how to extend the above construction to Turing machines. Intuitively, in JJ22, this is done by (implicitly) releasing super-polynomially many circuit obfuscations, one per possible input size. Evaluation is performed by obtaining, given an input, the circuit obfuscation corresponding to that input size (using the construction of $\mathsf{EFiO}$ above), and evaluating this obfuscated circuit. However, given two Turing Machines, security is argued by showing that *every pair* of circuit obfuscations, one pair per input size, are indistinguishable. This in turn results in JJ22 relying on super-polynomially secure $\mathsf{EFiO}$, and thus on super-polynomial hardness.

We observe that one can substantially reduce this loss using time-lock puzzles: instead of releasing the (implicit representations of) circuit obfuscations in the clear, we encrypt them using time-lock puzzles. In more detail, we encrypt (the implicit descriptions of) all the obfuscated circuits corresponding to input sizes up to $2^i$ in a single time-lock puzzle with time bound $T_i = 2^i$. This is done up to an input size bound $N = 2^\lambda$. Evaluation on input $x$ naturally proceeds by first decrypting the circuit obfuscations supporting the input from the time-lock puzzle, which has time bound $T_{\lceil \log |x| \rceil} \leq 2|x|$ and is efficiently solvable for polynomial-size inputs, and then evaluating the resulting $\mathsf{EFiO}$.

In the security proof, we can argue that for any adversary running in time $T$, the obfuscated circuits corresponding to input size larger than $T$ are hidden by the time-lock puzzles. Only $\lambda$ invocations of time-lock puzzle security are necessary for this proof step. Now, all but at most $\approx T$ obfuscated circuits are hidden from the adversary. We argue indistinguishability using $\approx T$ invocations of $\mathsf{EFiO}$ security. Since $T$ is a polynomial, these steps only introduce a polynomial security loss.

Putting everything together, we obtain overall a construction of $\mathsf{PViO}$ (for Turing machines) assuming the polynomial hardness of $\mathsf{iO}$ (for small circuits), of LWE, and of time-lock puzzles. We refer to the full version for more details.

**Tackling the Non-falsifiability of $\mathsf{iO}$ via Propositional Proofs, Again.** So far, we spent most of this overview discussing how to resolve Issue (1), namely the loss of security induced by the puncturing arguments, along with the extension to Turing machines discussed above.

We now discuss Issue (2). Note that our construction of PViO discussed above relies on general-purpose $\mathsf{iO}$ for circuits of input size $\mathsf{poly}(\lambda)$, which is not an efficiently falsifiable assumption. We show how to replace $\mathsf{iO}$ with $\mathsf{EFiO}$ – still for circuits with small input size $\mathsf{poly}(\lambda)$ – whose security is efficiently falsifiable. To achieve this goal, it is necessary to ensure that we require iO security only for pairs of circuits that admit EF proofs of equivalence. In our context, for circuits hardcoding randomized elements (e.g., a ciphertext), we require a proof of equivalence for every possible randomness for these hardcoded elements.

To this end, we build upon observations from prior work [36,44] that show how to formalize basic properties of many crypto systems in EF proof system. A key challenge in our setting, however, is that the building blocks used in our one-shot programming technique are not known to admit EF proofs of their key properties. We focus on shiftable PRFs in this overview and defer discussion on other primitives to the full version.

In our one-shot programming technique, it is crucial that the shifted evaluation is correct on *every input*: otherwise the resulting circuits wouldn't be functionally equivalent. Such a strong correctness property is typically proven through a *counting argument*, which shows that "most" of the random setups provide correctness. Such a guarantee is insufficient for applying EFiO, where we need a proof for every fixed "valid setup". To tackle the issue, we provide a new construction of a shiftable PRF with a propositional proof of *perfect correctness* for shifted evaluation. Our construction relies on the notion of (somewhere statistically) *correlation-intractable* (CI) hash functions [19,20,49]. Such schemes support hash keys $\mathsf{hk}_C$ hiding some relation $C$, with the guarantee that for all inputs $x$, $\mathsf{H}(\mathsf{hk}, x) \neq C(x)$.

Our starting point is a form of *approximately correct* shiftable PRF from [48], where instead of requiring the shifted evaluation to be exactly correct on most randomness, it only requires the evaluation output to be correct *up to some small additive error*, but on *all* randomness. As pointed out in [48], one can cast this form of approximate correctness to standard correctness via rounding, at the cost of introducing a possible rounding error whenever the evaluation is close to the rounding boundary.

We observe that one can avoid such rounding errors with the aid of somewhere statistically CI hash functions. In particular, we shift the evaluation by the CI hash value before rounding. In this case, rounding errors only occur for "bad" hash values that are close to the PRF evaluation modulo the rounding modulus. With appropriate parameters, the bad hash value can be uniquely computed for every input given the master PRF key. Therefore, if the hash is set up to be *statistically CI* in the actual construction over the above "bad" relation, no input will lead to rounding errors, resulting in a perfectly correct scheme. Even though the CI hash key depends on the master PRF key, security of the PRF is preserved as CI hash keys computationally hide their underlying statistical correlation. Finally, both this form of approximate correctness of the shiftable PRF from [48] and the statistical CI of the CI hash from [49] are provable in $\mathsf{PV}$: they both boil down to the correctness of lattice homomorphic evaluations, and many recent works have shown how to give $\mathsf{PV}$ proofs of correctness for (different variants of) such homomorphism [36,44].

## 2.4 More Applications of Shiftable PRFs and iO

We now shift gears, and depart from our previous goal of building $\mathsf{iO}$ for circuits or Turing machines with propositional proofs of equivalence. Rather, we propose shiftable PRFs as a powerful and possibly general tool to obtain tighter versions of several known applications of $\mathsf{iO}$, typically in settings where known security proofs are loose due to an input-by-input argument.

**Additional Application 1: Fully Homomorphic Encryption.** We first turn to *fully homomorphic encryption* (FHE). It is currently known that FHE can be built from sub-exponentially secure $\mathsf{iO}$, one-way functions, and (perfectly) rerandomizable encryption [21], which famously gives a possible alternative route to FHE that does not rely on lattices. We show how to make their security proof rely on polynomial assumptions, using shiftable PRFs as a core ingredient.

**The CLTV15 Construction for Leveled FHE.** To illustrate our techniques, we first focus on the setting of *leveled* FHE. As we will heavily build on the template of CLTV15, we start with a quick overview of their construction.

For clarity of the exposition, let us focus on building a homomorphic encryption supporting a *single homomorphic* NAND, starting with an $\mathsf{iO}$ scheme, a PRF, and a public-key encryption scheme with properties to be determined later. The homomorphic encryption scheme uses two pairs of public-secret key pairs, $(\mathsf{pk}_0, \mathsf{sk}_0), (\mathsf{pk}_1, \mathsf{sk}_1)$. The evaluation key for our homomorphic encryption consists of an obfuscation of the following circuit:

Circuit $C_{\mathsf{ReEnc}}$

Hard-coded: $\mathsf{pk}_1, \mathsf{sk}_0$, and a PRF key $K$
On input $x = (\mathsf{ct}^0 \| \mathsf{ct}^1)$, compute $b_x = NAND(\mathsf{Dec}_{\mathsf{sk}_0}(\mathsf{ct}^0), \mathsf{Dec}_{\mathsf{sk}_0}(\mathsf{ct}^1))$, and output:

$$\mathsf{ct} = \mathsf{Enc}(\mathsf{pk}_1, b_x \, ; \, \mathsf{PRF}_K(x)).$$

In words, $C_{\mathsf{ReEnc}}$ parses its input as two ciphertexts under $\mathsf{pk}_0$, decrypts them using its hard-coded key $\mathsf{sk}_0$, and computes a NAND of the resulting plaintexts, resulting in a bit $b_x$. It then outputs an encryption of $b_x$ under $\mathsf{pk}_1$, using randomness derived by applying a PRF to its input. The secret key for the scheme is $\mathsf{sk}_1$, the public key $\mathsf{pk}_0$, and encryption consists of encrypting under $\mathsf{pk}_0$. Homomorphic evaluation proceeds by evaluating an obfuscation of $C_{\mathsf{ReEnc}}$ on the input ciphertexts.

The crux of the security proof is to argue that semantic security holds even given the obfuscated circuit $\mathsf{iO}(C_{\mathsf{ReEnc}})$. To do so, it is sufficient to argue that $\mathsf{iO}(C_{\mathsf{ReEnc}})$ is indistinguishable (given $\mathsf{pk}_0$) from a circuit that does not have $\mathsf{sk}_0$ hard-coded: security would then follow by semantic security under $\mathsf{pk}_0$. Suppose now that the encryption scheme with keys $(\mathsf{pk}_1, \mathsf{sk}_1)$ has a *perfectly lossy* mode, that is, public keys can be indistinguishably set up to a special mode, which we will denote $\overline{\mathsf{pk}}_1$, under which encryptions *perfectly hide the underlying message.* The security proof of CLTV15 then goes as follows:

- First switch the public key $\mathsf{pk}_1$ to a perfectly lossy key $\overline{\mathsf{pk}}_1$;
- Fix any input $x^* = (\mathsf{ct}^{0^*} \| \mathsf{ct}^{1^*})$ to $C_{\mathsf{ReEnc}}$.
  - Puncture the PRF $K$ on $x^* = (\mathsf{ct}^{0^*} \| \mathsf{ct}^{1^*})$, and modify the circuit $C_{\mathsf{ReEnc}}$, on input $(\mathsf{ct}^{0^*} \| \mathsf{ct}^{1^*})$, to output instead a hard-coded ciphertext: $\mathsf{Enc}\left(\overline{\mathsf{pk}}_1, b_x \, ; \, r^*\right)$, where $r^*$ is uniformly random and $b_x$ is computed as before using $\mathsf{sk}_0$. This is indistinguishable assuming puncturable PRF security and iO.
  - By perfect lossiness, the distributions

    $$\mathsf{Enc}\left(\overline{\mathsf{pk}}_1, b_x \, ; \, r^*\right), \quad \mathsf{Enc}\left(\mathsf{pk}_1, 0 \, ; \, r^*\right)$$

    are identical over the randomness of $r^*$. So hard-coding a sample for the right distribution instead of the left distribution yields identical distributions. Now the output on $x^*$ does not depend on $\mathsf{sk}_0$.
- After iterating the argument over all possible inputs $x^* = (\mathsf{ct}_0^*, \mathsf{ct}_1^*)$, the resulting circuit to be obfuscated does not depend on $\mathsf{sk}_0$ anymore, as it no longer decrypts its inputs and always outputs encryptions of zeroes. This finishes the proof.

As in the case of the security proof from JJ22, the proof above uses an input-by-input argument, each invoking iO and puncturable PRF security, which results in the overall security relying on the sub-exponential security of both iO and puncturable PRF. Again, the technical culprit is the inability for puncturable PRFs to change the behavior of the underlying circuit on more than one input at once.

**A Tighter Proof from Shiftable PRFs and Algebraically Rerandomizable Encryption.** We naturally turn to shiftable PRFs to attempt to improve the proof above. Doing so allows us to controllably switch, for all inputs $x$, the randomness used in the lossy encryption, from using $F_K(x)$ to using $F_K(x)+P(x)$ for an efficient function $P$, thus outputting $\mathsf{Enc}\left(\overline{\mathsf{pk}}_1, b_x\, ;\, \mathsf{PRF}_K(x) + P(x)\right)$. At this stage, we would like to rely on iO to switch this ciphertext to an encryption of the form $\mathsf{Enc}\left(\overline{\mathsf{pk}}_1, 0\, ;\, \mathsf{PRF}_K(x) + P'(x)\right)$. It would thus suffice to find efficient functions $P$ and $P'$ such that the two quantities above are equal for all $x$:

$$\mathsf{Enc}\left(\overline{\mathsf{pk}}_1, b_x\, ;\, \mathsf{PRF}_K(x) + P(x)\right) \stackrel{?}{=} \mathsf{Enc}\left(\overline{\mathsf{pk}}_1, 0\, ;\, \mathsf{PRF}_K(x) + P'(x)\right). \quad (1)$$

However, while the two encryptions are identically distributed when using uniformly random $r^*$, meaning that the equality holds for *some* functions $P, P'$, it is not clear at all that such functions should be efficiently computable in general.

Instead, we rely on a special-purpose perfectly lossy encryption to argue that such efficient functions $P, P'$ exist. In order to build such perfectly lossy encryption, we take inspiration from the instantiation in CLTV15, who build such a standard perfectly lossy encryption starting from a perfectly rerandomizable encryption as follows:[7]

- The public key of the perfectly lossy encryption consists of two rerandomizable ciphertexts, one of message 0, $\mathsf{Rerand.ct}_0$, and one of 1, $\mathsf{Rerand.ct}_1$;
- Encryption of a bit $b$ proceeds by rerandomizing the ciphertext $\mathsf{Rerand.ct}_b$. We will denote this by $\mathsf{Rerandomize}(\mathsf{Rerand.ct}_b)$.
- In lossy mode, both ciphertexts $\mathsf{Rerand.ct}_b$ are instead encryptions of 0.

Lossy public keys are indeed indistinguishable from standard public keys by semantic security of the rerandomizable encryption, and perfect rerandomizability translates to perfect lossiness of the construction.

We observe that in this construction, structure on the rerandomization procedure translates to structure on the resulting lossy encryption. Suppose that the rerandomization procedure works by *shifting* the underlying ciphertext randomness by the randomness of the rerandomization procedure: writing $\mathsf{Rerand.ct} = \mathsf{Rerand.Enc}(b; r)$, this means:

$$\mathsf{Rerandomize}(\mathsf{Rerand.ct}; r') = \mathsf{Rerand.Enc}(b; r + r'). \quad (2)$$

We call rerandomizable encryption schemes satisfying Eq. 2 *algebraically rerandomizable*, and observe that they can be built assuming the (polynomial hardness of) DDH: ElGamal satisfies such a property. Using such a rerandomizable encryption to build a perfectly lossy encryption à la CLTV15, and writing the lossy public key as

$$\overline{\mathsf{pk}}_1 = \left(\mathsf{Rerand.ct}_0 = \mathsf{Rerand.Enc}(0; r_0), \mathsf{Rerand.ct}_1 = \mathsf{Rerand.Enc}(0; r_1)\right),$$

[7] A perfectly rerandomizable encryption is an encryption scheme, such that any ciphertext can be rerandomized into a perfectly distributed encryption of the same message.

Equation 1 then becomes:

$$\mathsf{Rerand.Enc}(\mathsf{pk}_1, 0\,;\, r_{b_x} + \mathsf{PRF}_K(x) + P(x)) \stackrel{?}{=} \mathsf{Rerand.Enc}(\mathsf{pk}_1, 0\,;\, r_0 + \mathsf{PRF}_K(x) + P'(x)).$$

We can now define $P$ as follows: given $\mathsf{sk}_0$ and $r_0, r_1$ hard-coded, on input $x$, compute $b_x$ using $\mathsf{sk}_0$ and output $r_0 - r_{b_x}$, while $P'$ is defined as the 0 function. This makes Eq. 1 hold for all $x$, which in turn makes the security proof go through assuming only the polynomial hardness of iO, of shiftable PRFs, and of an algebraically rerandomizable encryption (namely, one satisfying Eq. 2).

**Unleveled FHE via Time-Lock-Puzzles, Again.** In the full version, we show how to extend this construction to obtain unleveled FHE, additionally assuming (polynomially secure) time-lock puzzles. The construction and proof are very similar to the extension of EFiO to PViO: we implicitly release super-polynomially many circuits $C_{\mathsf{ReEnc}}$, for a super-polynomially long chain of keys $(\mathsf{pk}_0, \mathsf{sk}_0), \cdots, (\mathsf{pk}_{2^\lambda}, \mathsf{sk}_{2^\lambda})$. We then similarly encrypt appropriate intervals of the chain using time-lock puzzles.

**Application 2: Adaptively Sound SNARGs for Trapdoor Languages.** We briefly discuss our second application related to SNARGs. We say that a family of languages in NP is *trapdoored* if one can sample a language along with an efficient trapdoor program that decides it. We show that the SNARG construction of Sahai-Waters [53] is, without any modification, adaptively sound if the underlying language is trapdoored and if the underlying PRF is a shiftable PRF. Moreover, adaptive soundness only relies on the polynomial security of iO and of the shiftable PRF.

The construction actually follows directly from our construction of constraint-hiding constrained signature, sketched in Sect. 2.2: the SNARG prover runs an obfuscation of the circuit $E_P$, where $P$ authorizes $(x, w)$ only if $w$ is a valid witness for $x$. The verification algorithm corresponds to an obfuscation of the circuit $V_1$ for the all-accepting constraint (which only verifies the signature, by only taking $x$ as input). Observe that this almost exactly corresponds to the construction of [53] instantiated with a shiftable PRF, up to the fact that their construction adds an additional layer of one-way function to verify signatures. We show that the construction is adaptively sound even without this additional layer (but remains sound with it).[8]

The proof of adaptive soundness goes as follows: given a trapdoor decider for the language at hand, we switch how $P$ is computed, relying on the trapdoor instead; this is indistinguishable by iO security. Now, constraint hiding of the signature states that the view of the adversary is indistinguishable from one where no valid proof for unauthorized statements exists, namely ones that are not in the language, and adaptive soundness follows.[9]

---

[8] This is essentially because we use injective PRGs *in the proof* to implement a similar check.

[9] We previously only showed how to build constraint-hiding constrained signatures from the polynomial hardness of iO, of shiftable PRFs, and of *injective PRGs*. We

## 2.5 Relaxing Shiftable PRFs to Function Secret Sharing

Last, we observe that the main techniques we presented in this overview do not actually need the full power of shiftable PRFs, and that function secret sharing (FSS) [16] suffices. We first recall the notion of FSS.

In a two-party FSS with additive reconstruction, Alice and Bob are respectively given function shares $\mathsf{sh}_{A,f}, \mathsf{sh}_{B,f}$ with respect to some function $f$. Given these shares, and any input $x$, they can respectively compute some output $y_A(x), y_B(x)$ locally, such that $y_B(x) - y_A(x) = f(x)$.[10] Security of FSS states that the share $\mathsf{sh}_{A,f}$ (resp. $\mathsf{sh}_{B,f}$) hides the function $f$.

The notion of FSS is very similar to shiftable PRFs: interpreting the master key of a shiftable PRF and a shifted key as two respective shares directly gives an FSS. Conversely, shiftable PRFs is a strengthening of FSS: the master key of a shiftable PRF is generated independently of the shift $f$, which is not always possible in FSS.

We observe here that this strong latter property is superfluous for our one-shot programming technique, as long as the "master key" hides the shift, which exactly corresponds to FSS. We illustrate this with the same circuit $\mathsf{Enc}_P$ used in Sect. 2.2: we prove that $\mathsf{iO}(\mathsf{Enc}_P)$ and $\mathsf{iO}(\mathsf{Enc}_{P'})$ are indistinguishable, where PRF evaluation is replaced by local evaluation of an FSS supporting sufficiently expressive computations. We highlight the differences in red:

Circuit $\mathsf{Enc}_P$

Hard-coded: An FSS share $\mathsf{sh}_{A,0}$ for Alice, a program $P : \{0,1\}^n \to \{0,1\}$.
On input $x \in \{0,1\}^n$, output $y_A(x) + P(x)$.

- We first switch the obfuscated program $\mathsf{iO}(\mathsf{Enc}_P)$ to one that uses the Bob share $\mathsf{sh}_{B,0}$ (and the local evaluation for Bob) instead. This has the same functionality as the original program by correctness of the FSS, and is therefore indistinguishable from the original $\mathsf{iO}(\mathsf{Enc}_P)$ by iO security.
- We then switch the function in Bob's share from computing the all-0 function to computing $-P + P'$; this change is undetectable by security of the FSS. So now, the obfuscated program uses the share $\mathsf{sh}_{B,-P+P'}$. The output of the obfuscated program on an input $x$ is now $y_B(x) + P(x) = (y_A(x) - P(x) + P'(x)) + P(x)$.
- We now compute the output using the Alice share $\mathsf{sh}_{A,-P+P'}$, and computing $y_A(x) + P'(x)$ instead, which is undetectable by iO security.

show in the full version that injective PRGs follow from the polynomial hardness of iO and of one-way functions, and we thus do not require any additional assumptions here.

[10] We use subtractive reconstruction for convenience of exposition and analogy to shiftable PRFs here, but everything readily extends to standard additive reconstruction by introducing appropriate signs.

– (New Hybrid) We switch back the Alice share from using $\mathsf{sh}_{A,-P+P'}$ to $\mathsf{sh}_{A,0}$. This follows by security of the FSS, and finishes the proof of indistinguishability of $\mathsf{iO}(\mathsf{Enc}_P)$ and $\mathsf{iO}(\mathsf{Enc}_{P'})$.

One can readily adapt the argument above to all our uses of shiftable PRFs discussed previously. Alternatively, another interpretation of the proof above is that one can build shiftable PRFs from the *polynomial security* of iO and of FSS (for a related class of functions). In any case, this allows us to weaken the assumptions in our theorem statements, from relying on shiftable PRFs to relying on FSS.

We stress that, in order to instantiate our one-shot programming technique, we crucially rely on both (1) additive reconstruction of the FSS (over some group) and (2) correctness on *all* inputs. We do not know how to leverage FSS without these specific properties. Still, in applications where the shift can be computed in $\mathsf{NC}^1$, this allows us to instantiate our one-shot programming technique, assuming the polynomial hardness of DCR [47,52], or of DDH over class groups [1].

Our use of FSS is perhaps not so surprising in hindsight. Above, we improved the punctured programming technique of [53] relying on punctured PRFs, by developing a one-shot programming technique relying on shiftable PRFs. Both notions of PRFs are examples of *constrained PRFs* [14,17,38]: punctured PRFs are constrained PRFs for (the negation of) point function constraints, and shiftable PRFs are a strong form of *constraint-hiding* constrained PRFs. Meanwhile, FSS and constrained PRFs were previously observed to be related [24] – constrained PRFs can roughly be thought as a "staged" version of FSS. Similarly, shiftable PRFs are a strengthening of FSS, where one of the shares, namely the master PRF key, does not depend on the function to be computed. One critical difference is that, in our context, shiftable PRFs and FSS are *constraint/function hiding*, whereas previous work on staged FSS heavily leverage that the shared function is public. Still, we find it intriguing that FSS can technically replace shiftable PRFs in the context of $\mathsf{iO}$.

**On the Necessary Assumptions for Our One-Shot Technique.** One interpretation of our work is that we obtain significantly tighter reductions in the context of $\mathsf{iO}$, by leveraging additional structure out of the underlying PRF. Intuitively, this requires the use of "algebraically structured" assumptions, as illustrated by our instantiations of FSS and shiftable PRFs from (the polynomial hardness of) LWE or DCR.

Curiously, it is also unlikely that such FSS and shiftable PRFs *formally require* structure: as noted in Sect. 2.2 and by [41], they can be built under the *sub-exponential* hardness of $\mathsf{iO}$ and of one-way functions, via a standard puncturing argument. While this latter construction is mostly uninteresting for the main purposes of this paper (our objective being constructions from polynomial hardness assumptions), it is quite insightful in terms of complexity of the primitives. Indeed, because this construction is black-box in the sense of Asharov-Segev [6], FSS and shiftable PRFs consequently do not imply in a black-box manner either collision resistant hashing [6], nor hardness of the complexity class $\mathsf{SZK}$ [9]. On the other hand, most concrete "structured" assumptions, such as LWE or DCR, imply either (and most often both).

We stress again that our one-shot programming technique currently relies both on a strong form of correctness ensuring correct evaluation on *all possible inputs*, and on additive reconstruction. We leave the construction of such an FSS from DDH (say over a subgroup of $\mathbb{Z}_q^*$ or elliptic curves) as an open problem.

### 2.6 Related Work

While iO is now famous for enabling constructions of almost all known cryptographic primitives, many constructions rely on sub-exponential assumptions (e.g. [11,12,15,21,26,43,54,56]).

Consequently, a parallel line of work explored the possibility of relaxing the use of (sub-exponential) iO to *functional encryption* (FE), for which constructions from efficiently falsifiable assumptions are now known [32,33,50]. These works typically leveraged that, in some applications, iO was only used to obfuscate specific, structured computations [29–31]. This line of work culminated in the works [37,40], which show how to build a relaxed form of iO from FE, where iO security only holds whenever the circuits share some specific common structure.[11] However, this common structure is very specific and tied to the technical transformation from FE to iO [5,13]. In contrast, we believe our one-shot programming technique opens the way to reduce this sub-exponential dependence for *unstructured programs*, such as deterministic encryption of an arbitrary function of the input, or constrained signatures for arbitrary constraints, as discussed in Sect. 2.2.

The work of [3] also focused on weakening this required sub-exponential hardness, by relying on extremely lossy functions (ELFs) [58] (and polynomially secure iO). However, it is currently unknown whether ELFs can be instantiated without *exponential* assumptions – currently, the only known construction of ELFs relies on the exponential hardness of DDH.

Prior and concurrent works, e.g. [39,46], also attempted to remove this reliance on sub-exponential security by using constrained PRFs, a relaxation of shiftable PRFs. In our setting, shiftable PRFs offer significantly more expressive control over the programming, which we crucially use in all our applications.

## 3 Preliminaries

In this section, we briefly recall the definitions of necessary building blocks for our main results.

[11] In a nutshell, this structure corresponds to natural decision tree representations of the two circuits having large overlaps. This is notably the case whenever the circuits behave *identically* conditioned on small prefixes of the input.

## 3.1 Shiftable PRF

In this section, we revisit the notion of shiftable PRF, originally introduced in [48] under the name *Shift-hiding Shiftable Function.* To align with its role as an iO-friendly pseudorandom source in our applications, we adopt the term *Shiftable PRF* in this work.

**Definition 3.1 (Shiftable PRF).** *A shiftable PRF for a function class* $\mathcal{F} = \{F_\lambda\}$ *with input space* $\{0,1\}^{n(\lambda)}$ *and output space* $R^{m(\lambda)}$ *for some ring* $R$ *consists of the following algorithms:*

- $\mathsf{Setup}(1^\lambda) \to (\mathsf{pp}, k)$ *takes as input the security parameter and outputs the public parameter* $\mathsf{pp}$ *and the master key* $k$.
- $\mathsf{Eval}(\mathsf{pp}, k, x \in \{0,1\}^n) \to y \in R^m$ *takes as input the public parameter* $\mathsf{pp}$, *the master key* $k$ *and an input* $x$, *outputs PRF evaluation* $y$.
- $\mathsf{Shift}(\mathsf{pp}, k, f \in F_\lambda) \to k_f$ *takes as input the public parameter* $\mathsf{pp}$, *the master key* $k$ *and a function* $f\colon \{0,1\}^n \to R^m$ *from the function class* $F_\lambda$, *outputs shifted key* $k_f$.
- $\mathsf{EvalShifted}(\mathsf{pp}, k_f, x \in \{0,1\}^n) \to y \in R^m$ *takes as input the public parameter* $\mathsf{pp}$, *the shifted key* $k_f$ *and an input* $x$, *outputs PRF evaluation* $y$.

*We require the shiftable PRF to satisfy the following properties:*

- **Everywhere Correctness:** *There exists a negligible function* $\mathsf{negl}$ *such that for every* $\lambda \in \mathbb{N}$ *and every function* $f \in F_\lambda$, *it holds that*

$$\Pr\left[\forall x \in \{0,1\}^n,\ \mathsf{EvalShifted}(\mathsf{pp}, k_f, x) = \mathsf{Eval}(\mathsf{pp}, k, x) + f(x)\right] \geq 1 - \mathsf{negl}(\lambda),$$

*where the probability is taken over the randomness of* $(\mathsf{pp}, k) \leftarrow \mathsf{Setup}(1^\lambda)$ *and* $k_f \leftarrow \mathsf{Shift}(\mathsf{pp}, k, f)$. *We say that the shiftable PRF scheme is perfectly correct if the above holds with probability 1.*
- **Shift Hiding:** *For every efficient adversary* $\mathcal{A}$, *there exists a negligible function* $\mathsf{negl}$ *such that for every* $\lambda \in \mathbb{N}$ *and any two functions* $f_1, f_2 \in F_\lambda$, *it holds that*

$$\left|\Pr\left[\mathcal{A}(1^\lambda, \mathsf{pp}, k_{f_1}) = 1\right] - \Pr\left[\mathcal{A}(1^\lambda, \mathsf{pp}, k_{f_2}) = 1\right]\right| \leq \mathsf{negl}(\lambda),$$

*where the probabilities are taken over the randomness of* $(\mathsf{pp}, k) \leftarrow \mathsf{Setup}(1^\lambda)$ *and* $k_{f_i} \leftarrow \mathsf{Shift}(\mathsf{pp}, k, f_i)$ *for* $i = 1, 2$.

**Theorem 3.2** *([48]). Assuming polynomially hard LWE (with sub-exponential modulus-to-noise ratio), there exists an everywhere correct shiftable PRF for all bounded-size circuits.*

## 3.2 EFiO and PViO

In this section, we recall the definition of EFiO and PViO from [34], which are iO with security restricted to circuit pairs with $\mathcal{EF}$ proof of equivalence/TM pairs with PV proof of equivalence.

**Definition 3.3 ($\Delta$ -Equivalent Circuits).** *Two families of circuits $\{C^0_\lambda\}$ and $\{C^1_\lambda\}$ are said to be $\Delta$-equivalent with subcircuit size $s(\lambda) = O(\log \lambda)$ if there exists some polynomial $\ell(\lambda)$ such that for any $\lambda \in \mathbb{N}$, there exist circuits $\{C_1, C_2, \ldots, C_{\ell(\lambda)}\}$ such that*

- *$C_1 = C^0_\lambda$ and $C_{\ell(\lambda)} = C^1_\lambda$.*
- *For any $i \in [\ell(\lambda) - 1]$, $C_i$ and $C_{i+1}$ have the same circuit topology. Furthermore, there exists a subcircuit $S$ consisting of at most $s(\lambda)$ gates such that*
  - *For every gate outside of $S$, the corresponding gates in $C_i$ and $C_{i+1}$ are identical.*
  - *The subcircuits of $C_i$ and $C_{i+1}$ induced by $S$ are functionally equivalent.*

*We say that the two families are $\delta$-equivalent if they are $\Delta$-equivalent with $\ell(\lambda) = 2$.*

**Lemma 3.4** *($\mathcal{EF}$ Proofs of Equivalence imply $\Delta$-Equivalence [34]). Two circuit families $\{C^0_\lambda\}$ and $\{C^1_\lambda\}$ with a polynomial-size $\mathcal{EF}$ proof of equivalence are $\Delta$-equivalent up to padding.*

For Turing machines, we recall the circuit representation of Turing machines and define $\Delta$-equivalence above them.

**Lemma 3.5 (Circuit representation of Turing machines).** *For any Turing machine $M$ that runs in polynomial time $T(\cdot)$ and any length $n$, one can efficiently construct a circuit $M_n$ of size $T(n) \cdot \mathsf{poly}(\log T(n))$ that simulates $M$ on inputs of length $n$. Furthermore, there exists an efficient algorithm that, given as input a length bound $N$, outputs a circuit $[M]_N(\cdot,\cdot)$ of size $\mathsf{poly}(\log T(N), |M|)$, which takes as input an input length $n \in [N]$ and a gate index $g \in [|M_n|]$, and outputs the gate description $(\mathsf{in}_g, \mathsf{out}_g, f_g)$ of gate $g$ in the circuit $M_n$. Here, $\mathsf{in}_g/\mathsf{out}_g$ are the lists of input/output wires of gate $g$, and $f_g$ is the function $\{0,1\}^{|\mathsf{in}_g|} \to \{0,1\}^{|\mathsf{out}_g|}$ computed by gate $g$.*

**Definition 3.6** *($\Delta$ -Equivalent Turing Machines). Two Turing machines $M_0$ and $M_1$ that run in time $T(\cdot)$ are said to be $\Delta$-equivalent with subcircuit size $s(n) = O(\log n)$ if there exists a function $\ell = \mathsf{poly}(n, \log N)$ and a bound $D(N) = \mathsf{poly}(\log N)$ such that for any input length bound $N$ and any $n \leq N$, there exists a sequence of circuits $\{C'_1, C'_2, \ldots, C'_{\ell(n,N)}\}$ such that*

- *$C'_1$ and $C'_{\ell(n,N)}$ are functionally equivalent to $[M_0]_N(n,\cdot)$ and $[M_1]_N(n,\cdot)$ respectively, and each circuit $C'_i$ has size at most $D(N)$.*
- *For any $i \in [\ell(n,N)-1]$, let $C_i$ and $C_{i+1}$ be the circuit described by the succinct description $C'_i$ and $C'_{i+1}$ respectively. Then $C_i$ and $C_{i+1}$ are $\delta$-equivalent with subcircuit size $s(n)$.*

**Lemma 3.7** *($\mathsf{PV}$ Proofs of Equivalence imply $\Delta$-Equivalence [34]) Two Turing machines $M_0$ and $M_1$ with a $\mathsf{PV}$ proof of equivalence are $\Delta$-equivalent.*

**Definition 3.8 (PViO and EFiO).** *An EFiO scheme is an iO scheme for circuits where the security is only required to hold for pairs of circuit families with $\mathcal{EF}$ proof of equivalence. A PViO scheme is an iO scheme for Turing machines where the security is only required to hold for pairs of Turing machines with $\mathsf{PV}$ proof of equivalence.*

### 3.3 Time-Lock Puzzles

**Definition 3.9 (Time-Lock Puzzles).** *A time-lock puzzle scheme with message length $m = m(\lambda)$ consists of the following two efficient algorithms:*

- $\mathsf{Gen}(1^\lambda, T, x \in \{0,1\}^m) \to Z$ *takes as input the security parameter, a time parameter $T$, and a message $x$, and outputs a puzzle $Z$.*
- $\mathsf{Solve}(1^\lambda, 1^T, Z) \to x \in \{0,1\}^m$ *takes as input the security parameter, a time parameter $T$ encoded in unary, and a puzzle $Z$, and outputs the solution $x$.*

*A time-lock puzzle scheme satisfies the following properties:*

- **Efficiency**: *For every $\lambda \in \mathbb{N}$, and every time parameter $T$,* $\mathsf{Gen}(1^\lambda, T, \cdot)$ *runs in time* $\mathsf{poly}(\lambda, \log T)$ *and* $\mathsf{Solve}(1^\lambda, 1^T, \cdot)$ *runs in time* $T \cdot \mathsf{poly}(\lambda)$.
- **Correctness**: *For every $\lambda \in \mathbb{N}$, every time parameter $T$, every message $x \in \{0,1\}^m$, and every $Z \leftarrow \mathsf{Gen}(1^\lambda, T, x)$, it holds that* $\mathsf{Solve}(1^\lambda, 1^T, Z) = x$.
- **Security**: *The puzzle* $(\mathsf{Gen}, \mathsf{Solve})$ *is a time-lock puzzle with gap $\epsilon < 1$ if there exists a polynomial $t_{\mathsf{min}}(\cdot)$, such that for every time parameter $2^\lambda \geq T(\lambda) \geq t_{\mathsf{min}}(\lambda)$, every polynomial $p$, and every adversary $\mathcal{A}$ running in time at most* $\min(p(\lambda), T^\epsilon(\lambda))$, *there exists a negligible function* $\mathsf{negl}(\cdot)$ *so that for every $\lambda \in \mathbb{N}$ and any two messages $x_0, x_1 \in \{0,1\}^{m(\lambda)}$, it holds that*

$$\left|\Pr[\mathcal{A}(1^\lambda, Z_0) = 1] - \Pr[\mathcal{A}(1^\lambda, Z_1) = 1]\right| \leq \mathsf{negl}(\lambda),$$

*where* $Z_b \leftarrow \mathsf{Gen}(1^\lambda, T(\lambda), x_b)$ *for* $b \in \{0,1\}$.

**Remark 3.1 (Time-lock Puzzles with Large Time Parameter).** Note that the security definition we provide in Definition 3.9 is slightly stronger than the ones in prior works [10,43,51]. Prior definitions argue security for ciphertexts $Z \leftarrow \mathsf{Gen}(1^\lambda, T, x)$ for some polynomial-size time parameter $T$. However, for our purpose of handling adversaries with unbounded-size input, we require *polynomial hardness* for ciphertexts with *superpolynomial time parameters.*

We note that our strengthened formulation is still a polynomially falsifiable security definition. Furthermore, for natural sequentially hard functions such as repeated squaring [51], or repeated application of unstructured hash functions, the polynomial hardness of efficiently computing sub-exponentially long sequences seems to be a natural and believable assumption.

In fact, when $T$ is superpolynomial but the adversary's runtime is only polynomial, the security assumptions of these time-lock puzzles become intuitively weaker, because the computational gap between $\mathsf{Solve}$ and the adversary is then superpolynomial. We therefore believe that our strengthened formulation is reasonable.

# 4 Deterministic Constrained Signatures

In this section, we define a notion of *deterministic constrained signature* scheme, which is a crucial building block for applications of iO from polynomial assumptions.

**Definition 4.1** *A deterministic constrained signature scheme is defined with message space* $\{0,1\}^{\ell(\lambda)}$ *and constraint space* $\mathcal{F} = \{F_\lambda\}$ *consisting of functions* $f : \{0,1\}^{\ell(\lambda)} \to \{0,1\}$. *Without loss of generality, we assume the all-accepting function is in* $\mathcal{F}_\lambda$.

*The signature scheme consists of the following PPT algorithms:*

- $\mathsf{Setup}(1^\lambda) \to \mathsf{msk}$ *takes as input the security parameter* $\lambda$, *and outputs a master signing key* $\mathsf{msk}$.
- $\mathsf{Constrain}(\mathsf{msk}, f) \to (\mathsf{vk}_f, \mathsf{sk}_f)$ *takes as input the master secret key* $\mathsf{msk}$ *and a constraint function* $f \in \mathcal{F}_\lambda$, *and outputs a constrained key pair* $(\mathsf{vk}_f, \mathsf{sk}_f)$.
- $\mathsf{Sign}(\mathsf{sk}_f, x) \to \sigma$ *takes as input the constrained signing key* $\mathsf{sk}_f$ *and a message* $x \in \{0,1\}^\ell$, *and outputs a signature* $\sigma$.
- $\mathsf{Ver}(\mathsf{vk}_f, x, \sigma^*) \to \{0,1\}$ *takes as input a constrained verification key* $\mathsf{vk}_f$, *a message* $x \in \{0,1\}^\ell$ *and a signature* $\sigma^*$, *outputs 1 if the signature is valid and 0 otherwise.*

*The deterministic constrained signature scheme should satisfy the following properties:*

- **Correctness:** *For any* $\lambda \in \mathbb{N}$, *any* $f \in \mathcal{F}_\lambda$, *any* $x \in \{0,1\}^{\ell(\lambda)}$ *such that* $f(x) = 1$, *any* $\mathsf{msk} \leftarrow \mathsf{Setup}(1^\lambda)$, *and any* $(\mathsf{vk}_f, \mathsf{sk}_f) \leftarrow \mathsf{Constrain}(\mathsf{msk}, f)$, *it holds that* $\mathsf{Ver}(\mathsf{vk}_f, x, \mathsf{Sign}(\mathsf{sk}_f, x)) = 1$.
- **Deterministic Signing:** *For any* $\lambda \in \mathbb{N}$, *any* $f_0, f_1 \in \mathcal{F}_\lambda$, *any* $x \in \{0,1\}^{\ell(\lambda)}$ *such that* $f_0(x) = f_1(x) = 1$, *any* $\mathsf{msk} \leftarrow \mathsf{Setup}(1^\lambda)$, *and any* $(\mathsf{vk}_{f_b}, \mathsf{sk}_{f_b}) \leftarrow \mathsf{Constrain}(\mathsf{msk}, f_b)$, *it holds that* $\mathsf{Sign}(\mathsf{sk}_{f_0}, x) = \mathsf{Sign}(\mathsf{sk}_{f_1}, x)$.
- **Statistical Soundness:** *There exists a negligible function* $\mathsf{negl}$ *such that for any* $\lambda \in \mathbb{N}$ *and any* $f \in \mathcal{F}_\lambda$, *it holds that* $\Pr[\forall x \in f^{-1}(0),\ \mathsf{Ver}(\mathsf{vk}_f, x, \cdot) = \mathsf{Null}] \geq 1 - \mathsf{negl}(\lambda)$, *where* $f^{-1}(0)$ *denotes the set* $\{x \in \{0,1\}^\ell \mid f(x) = 0\}$, *and the probability is taken over the randomness of* Setup *and* Constrain *computing* $\mathsf{vk}_f$. *We say that the signature scheme is* perfectly sound *if the above probability is 1.*
- **Constraint hiding:** *For any* $\lambda \in \mathbb{N}$, *any function* $f \in \mathcal{F}_\lambda$, *it holds that* $(\mathsf{vk}_f, \mathsf{sk}_f) \approx (\mathsf{vk}_{\mathbf{1}}, \mathsf{sk}_f)$ *where the keys are sampled under consistent master secret key* $\mathsf{msk}$, *and* $\mathbf{1}$ *is the all-one function.*

## 4.1 Construction

In this section, we show how to construct a deterministic constrained signature scheme from polynomially-secure shiftable PRF and indistinguishability obfuscation.

**Construction 4.1** *Let* $\mathsf{iO}$ *be an indistinguishability obfuscation scheme, and let* $\mathsf{sPRF} = (\mathsf{Setup}, \mathsf{Eval}, \mathsf{Shift}, \mathsf{EvalShifted})$ *be a shiftable PRF scheme for all bounded-size circuits with input space* $\{0,1\}^{\ell(\lambda)}$ *and output space* $R^{m(\lambda)}$ *for a ring* $R$. *We construct a deterministic constrained signature scheme with message space* $\{0,1\}^{\ell(\lambda)}$ *and signature space* $R^{m(\lambda)}$ *as follows:*

- $\mathsf{Setup}(1^\lambda)$: *Run* $(\mathsf{pp}, k) \leftarrow \mathsf{sPRF.Setup}(1^\lambda)$, *output* $\mathsf{msk} = (\mathsf{pp}, k)$.
- $\mathsf{Constrain}(\mathsf{msk}, f)$: *Parse* $\mathsf{msk} = (\mathsf{pp}, k)$, *and define the following two circuits:*

| |
|---|
| $E_{\mathsf{pp},k,f}(x \in \{0,1\}^\ell)$: *If* $f(x) = 0$, *output* $\bot$. *Else, output* $\mathsf{sPRF.Eval}(\mathsf{pp}, k, x)$. |

| |
|---|
| $V_{\mathsf{pp},k,f}(x \in \{0,1\}^\ell, y \in R^m)$: *If* $f(x) = 1$ *and* $\mathsf{sPRF.Eval}(\mathsf{pp}, k, x) = y$, *output 1. Else, output 0.* |

*Output* $\mathsf{vk}_f = \mathsf{iO}(V_{\mathsf{pp},k,f})$ *and* $\mathsf{sk}_f = \mathsf{iO}(E_{\mathsf{pp},k,f})$.
- $\mathsf{Sign}(\mathsf{sk}_f, x)$: *Parse* $\mathsf{sk}_f = \widetilde{E}_{\mathsf{pp},k,f}$ *as an obfuscated program. Output* $\sigma = \widetilde{E}_{\mathsf{pp},k,f}(x)$.
- $\mathsf{Ver}(\mathsf{vk}_f, x, \sigma^*)$: *Parse* $\mathsf{vk}_f = \widetilde{V}_{\mathsf{pp},k,f}$ *as an obfuscated program. Output* $\widetilde{V}_{\mathsf{pp},k,f}(x, \sigma^*)$.

It is straightforward from the construction that, if the obfuscation scheme is perfectly correct, then the deterministic constrained signature scheme is perfectly correct, perfectly sound, and has deterministic signing. We state the following theorem for the constraint hiding property. We refer the reader to the full version for the proof.

**Theorem 4.2.** *If* $\mathsf{iO}$ *is a polynomially secure indistinguishability obfuscation scheme,* $\mathsf{sPRF}$ *is a polynomially-secure shiftable PRF scheme for all bounded-size circuits with input space* $\{0,1\}^{\ell(\lambda)}$ *and output space* $R^{m(\lambda)}$, *and if there exists a polynomially secure injective PRG* $\mathsf{PRG}$ *with input space* $R^{m(\lambda)}$ *and output space* $\{0,1\}^{m'(\lambda)}$ *with* $\lambda$ *bit stretch (i.e.,* $m'(\lambda) - |R|m(\lambda) \geq \lambda$*), then Construction 4.1 is a constraint hiding deterministic constrained signature scheme.*

# 5 PViO from iO for Small Circuits

## 5.1 Construction of EFiO

In this section, we show how to construct EFiO (Definition3.8) for polynomial-size circuits from (fixed-size) polynomial assumptions. Following the observation from JJ22 [34] (restated in Lemma 3.4), it suffices to construct a $\Delta$iO scheme for circuits with sub-circuit size $s(\lambda) = O(\log \lambda)$.

Our construction largely follows the blueprint of JJ22. At a high level, they construct $\Delta$iO by providing an obfuscation for each gate of the original circuit. To hide the intermediate computation, which is essential for iO security, the input and output to each gate should be encrypted and authenticated. The JJ22 construction of gate obfuscation takes as input encryptions of input wires, along with MAC tags of these ciphertexts, and outputs a ciphertext of output wires along with MAC tags only if the inputs are valid. The encryptions and MACs are all instantiated with puncturable PRFs, resulting in the need of $2^\lambda$ hybrids when arguing security using $\mathsf{iO}$.

**Construction 5.1.** *Consider the following building blocks:*

- *A fully homomorphic encryption scheme* $\mathsf{FHE} = (\mathsf{KeyGen}, \mathsf{Enc}, \mathsf{Dec}, \mathsf{Eval})$.
- *A somewhere extractable hash with prefix consistency proof scheme* $\mathsf{SEH} = (\mathsf{Gen}, \mathsf{TGen}, \mathsf{Hash}, \mathsf{Open}, \mathsf{Ver}, \mathsf{Ext}, \mathsf{ProveCons}, \mathsf{VerCons})$.
- *A shiftable PRF scheme* $\mathsf{sPRF} = (\mathsf{Setup}, \mathsf{Eval}, \mathsf{Shift}, \mathsf{EvalShifted})$ *with output over a ring $R$ (Definition 3.1).*
- *A deterministic constrained signature scheme* $\mathsf{Sig} = (\mathsf{Setup}, \mathsf{Constrain}, \mathsf{Sign}, \mathsf{Ver})$ *(Definition 4.1).*
- *An indistinguishability obfuscation scheme* $\mathsf{iO}$ *secure for circuits of size at most $p(\lambda)$, where $p$ will be instantiated later.*

*The obfuscation for subcircuit size $s(\lambda) = O(\log \lambda)$ (where the size is counted as the number of wires in the subcircuit) is defined by the following procedure.*
$\underline{\Delta\mathsf{iO}(1^\lambda, C)}$:

- *Sample FHE key pair* $(\mathsf{pk}, \mathsf{sk}) \leftarrow \mathsf{FHE.KeyGen}(1^\lambda)$.
- *For each wire $i$ of the circuit, sample shiftable PRF keys* $(\mathsf{pp}_i, k_i) \leftarrow \mathsf{sPRF.Setup}(1^\lambda)$ *and the master constrained signature key* $\mathsf{msk}_i \leftarrow \mathsf{Sig.Setup}(1^\lambda)$. *Compute the constrained key pair* $(\mathsf{vk}_i, \mathsf{sk}_i) \leftarrow \mathsf{Sig.Constrain}(\mathsf{msk}_i, \mathbf{1})$, *where* $\mathbf{1}$ *denotes the all-one function.*
- *Define the block size $B$ as the ciphertext length of FHE when encrypting $s(\lambda)$-bit messages, plus the encoding length of one PRF output. Compute* $\mathsf{hk} \leftarrow \mathsf{SEH.Gen}(1^\lambda, 1^{|C|\cdot B}, 1^{s(\lambda)\cdot B})$.
- *Let $|\mathsf{td}|$ denote the size of the SEH trapdoor generated by* $\mathsf{TGen}(1^\lambda, 1^{|C|\cdot B}, 1^{s(\lambda)\cdot B}, \cdot)$, *and $|\mathsf{sPRF}|$ denote the size of shiftable PRF master output* $(\mathsf{pp}, k) \leftarrow \mathsf{sPRF.Setup}(1^\lambda)$. *Compute the dummy ciphertexts* $\mathsf{ct}_{\mathsf{FHE}} \leftarrow \mathsf{FHE.Enc}(\mathsf{pk}, 0^{|\mathsf{td}|+|\mathsf{sPRF}|\cdot s(\lambda)})$.
- *For each gate $g$ of the circuit $C$ with description* $\langle g \rangle = (\mathsf{in}, \mathsf{out}, f_{\mathsf{out}})$, *compute the obfuscated gate* $\widetilde{\mathsf{Gate}}_g = \mathsf{iO}(1^\lambda, \mathsf{Gate}_{[\langle g \rangle, \mathsf{hk}, \{(\mathsf{pp}_i, k_i), \mathsf{vk}_i\}_{i \in \mathsf{in}}, \{(\mathsf{pp}_o, k_o), \mathsf{sk}_o\}_{o \in \mathsf{out}}, \mathsf{pk}, \mathsf{ct}_{\mathsf{FHE}}]})$ *where the circuit* $\mathsf{Gate}$ *is defined below in Fig. 1.*
- *Output the final obfuscated circuit $\widetilde{C}$ described as follows.*
  - *The circuit has hardcoded: the hash key* $\mathsf{hk}$, *shiftable PRF keys* $(\mathsf{pp}_i, k_i)$ *and constrained signature keys* $\mathsf{sk}_i$ *for each input wire $i$ of the circuit, shiftable PRF keys* $(\mathsf{pp}_o, k_o)$ *for each output wire $o$ of the circuit, and all the obfuscated gates* $\{\widetilde{\mathsf{Gate}}_g\}$.
  - *Evaluate the circuit by the wire index as follows:*
    * *Maintain the string* $m_i = \{(\mathsf{ct}_j, h_j)\}_{j<i}$, *which denotes the concatenation of all previous wire ciphertexts and compressed hashes* $(\mathsf{ct}_j, h_j)$, *padded with zero blocks to length $|C| \cdot B$, as follows:*
    * *Compute* $H_i \leftarrow \mathsf{SEH.Hash}(\mathsf{hk}, m_i)$. *Compute the compressed hash* $h_i = \mathsf{FHE.Eval}(\mathsf{pk}, \mathsf{Ext\&Dec}(\mathsf{hk}, H_i, \cdot), \mathsf{ct}_{\mathsf{FHE}})$ *as in the circuit* $\mathsf{Gate}$, *and where the function* $\mathsf{Ext\&Dec}$ *is defined in Fig. 2.*

  - * *If $i$ is an input wire of the original circuit $C$, compute the ciphertext* $\mathsf{ct}_i = x_i + \mathsf{Eval}(\mathsf{pp}_i, k_i, h_i)$ *and the signature* $\sigma_i \leftarrow \mathsf{Sign}(\mathsf{sk}_i, (\mathsf{ct}_i, h_i))$.
  - * *If $i$ is an output wire of some gate $g$, then for every input wire $j$ of $g$, compute the opening* $\rho_j \leftarrow \mathsf{SEH.Open}(\mathsf{hk}, m_i, [(j-1)B, jB-1])$, *i.e. the opening for the $j$-th block of $m_i$, and the prefix consistency proof* $\pi_j \leftarrow \mathsf{SEH.ProveCons}(\mathsf{hk}, m_i, m_j, (j-1)B)$, *i.e., the proof that the non-zero parts of $m_j$ are consistent with the prefix of $m_i$. Run the obfuscated gate* $\widetilde{\mathsf{Gate}}_g(H_i, i, \{H_j, \mathsf{ct}_j, \rho_j, \pi_j, \sigma_j\}_{j\in\mathsf{in}})$ *to obtain* $(\mathsf{ct}_i, \sigma_i)$.
- *Finally, for each output wire $o$ of the circuit, decrypt the wire ciphertext* $\mathsf{ct}_o$ *by* $x_o = \mathsf{ct}_o - \mathsf{Eval}(\mathsf{pp}_o, k_o, h_o)$ *and output the wire values* $\{x_o\}$.

The correctness of the above construction follows directly from the correctness of the underlying primitives. Therefore, it suffices to prove the security against $\Delta$-equivalent circuits. Similar to the proof in [34], we start by the following core theorem regarding $\delta$-equivalent circuits.

**Theorem 5.1 ($\delta$-security of Construction** *5.1***).** *Let $\{C^0_\lambda\}$ and $\{C^1_\lambda\}$ be two ensembles of topologically identical circuits, where every $C^0_\lambda$ and $C^1_\lambda$ differ only on a sub-circuit $S_\lambda$ of size at most $s(\lambda) = O(\log \lambda)$. We suppress the subscript $\lambda$ in the notation for simplicity. Let $S.\mathsf{in}$ and $S.\mathsf{out}$ denote the input and output wires of the sub-circuit $S$. Then, under polynomial security of iO, of FHE, of SEH with prefix consistency proof, of shiftable PRF, and of constrained signature, the distribution $\mathcal{D}_0, \mathcal{D}_1$ defined as follows are (polynomially) indistinguishable:*

$$\mathcal{D}_b \,:\, (\mathsf{pk}, \mathsf{ct}_{\mathsf{FHE}}, \mathsf{hk}, \{(\mathsf{pp}_i, k_i), \mathsf{sk}_i\}_{i\in S.\mathsf{in}}, \{(\mathsf{pp}_o, k_o), \mathsf{vk}_o\}_{o\in S.\mathsf{out}}, \{\widetilde{\mathsf{Gate}}^b_g\}_{g\in S}),$$

*where the elements* $(\mathsf{pk}, \mathsf{ct}_{\mathsf{FHE}}, \mathsf{hk}, \{(\mathsf{pp}_i, k_i), \mathsf{sk}_i\}_{i\in S.\mathsf{in}}, \{(\mathsf{pp}_o, k_o), \mathsf{vk}_o\}_{o\in S.\mathsf{out}})$ *are generated as in the obfuscation procedure of Construction 5.1 (which has identical distribution when obfuscating $C^0$ or $C^1$), and each obfuscated gate*

$$\widetilde{\mathsf{Gate}}^b_g = \mathsf{iO}(1^\lambda, \mathsf{Gate}_{[\langle g^b\rangle, \mathsf{hk}, \{(\mathsf{pp}_i, k_i), \mathsf{vk}_i\}_{i\in\mathsf{in}}, \{(\mathsf{pp}_o, k_o), \mathsf{sk}_o\}_{o\in\mathsf{out}}, \mathsf{pk}, \mathsf{ct}_{\mathsf{FHE}}]}),$$

*is the gate obfuscation of gate $g$ (with description $\langle g^b\rangle$ in circuit $C^b$) computed as in Construction 5.1 when obfuscating circuit $C^b$.*

We refer the reader to the full version for the proof.

Note that the distribution of $\Delta\mathsf{iO}(1^\lambda, C^b)$ can be perfectly simulated given $\mathcal{D}_b$, as every element in $\mathcal{D}_b$ does not depend on the rest of the components of the $\Delta\mathsf{iO}$ computation. Therefore, Theorem 5.1 directly implies the indistinguishability of $\Delta\mathsf{iO}(1^\lambda, C^0)$ and $\Delta\mathsf{iO}(1^\lambda, C^1)$. Following a direct hybrid argument of $\ell(\lambda)$ steps of subcircuit replacements, we immediately conclude that Construction 5.1 is a secure $\Delta\mathsf{iO}$ scheme for circuits.

Combining Theorem 5.1 with the fact that all circuits with $\mathcal{EF}$ proof of equivalence are Lemma 3.4), we immediately conclude the main theorem of this section.

$\mathsf{Gate}_{[\langle g\rangle,\mathsf{hk},\{(\mathsf{pp}_i,k_i),\mathsf{vk}_i\}_{i\in\mathsf{in}},\{(\mathsf{pp}_o,k_o),\mathsf{sk}_o\}_{o\in\mathsf{out}},\mathsf{pk},\mathsf{ct}_{\mathsf{FHE}}]}(H_o, o, \{H_i, \mathsf{ct}_i, \rho_i, \pi_i, \sigma_i\}_{i\in\mathsf{in}})$

**Hardcoded values:**

- *The description* $\langle g\rangle$ *of the gate* $g$ *with input wire set* in *and output wire set* out, *along with the computed function* $f_{\mathsf{out}} = \{f_o : \{0,1\}^{|\mathsf{in}|} \to \{0,1\}\}$ *for each output wire* $o \in \mathsf{out}$.
- *Hash key* hk *for SEH.*
- *For each input wire* $i \in \mathsf{in}$, *a shiftable PRF setup* $(\mathsf{pp}_i, k_i)$ *and a constrained signature verification key* $\mathsf{vk}_i$; *for each output wire* $o \in \mathsf{out}$, *a shiftable PRF setup* $(\mathsf{pp}_o, k_o)$ *and a constrained signature signing key* $\mathsf{sk}_o$.
- *FHE public key* pk *and FHE ciphertexts* $\mathsf{ct}_{\mathsf{FHE}}$ *of* $|\mathsf{td}| + |\mathsf{sPRF}| \cdot s(\lambda)$ *bits.*

**Inputs:**

- *The index* $o$ *of the output wire to be computed, and the hash value* $H_o$ *which is supposed to be the SEH hash of* $\{(\mathsf{ct}_j, h_j)\}_{j<o}$.
- *For each input wire* $i \in \mathsf{in}$, *the following values:*
  - *SEH hash value* $H_i$ *which is supposed to be the SEH hash of* $\{(\mathsf{ct}_j, h_j)\}_{j<i}$.
  - *Ciphertext* $\mathsf{ct}_i$ *supposed to be* $x_i + \mathsf{Eval}(\mathsf{pp}_i, k_i, h_i)$ *where* $x_i$ *is the input wire value.*
  - *Opening* $\rho_i$ *for* $H_o$ *at block* $i$. *For honest input* $H_o$, $\rho_i$ *should open to* $(\mathsf{ct}_i, h_i)$ *where* $h_i$ *is a compressed hash computed from* $H_i$.
  - *Prefix consistency proof* $\pi_i$ *showing that* $H_i$ *is consistent with* $H_o$ *for the first* $i-1$ *blocks.*
  - *Signature* $\sigma_i$ *of message* $(\mathsf{ct}_i, h_i)$ *under signing key* $\mathsf{sk}_i$.

**Evaluation Procedure:**

1. *Compute the compressed hash* $h_o$, *which is an FHE ciphertext obtained by homomorphically evaluating the function* $\mathsf{Ext\&Dec}(\mathsf{hk}, H_o, \cdot)$ *on the hardcoded ciphertext* $\mathsf{ct}_{\mathsf{FHE}}$:
$$h_o \leftarrow \mathsf{FHE.Eval}(\mathsf{pk}, \mathsf{Ext\&Dec}(\mathsf{hk}, H_o, \cdot), \mathsf{ct}_{\mathsf{FHE}}),$$
*where the function* Ext&Dec *is defined in Figure 2. For each* $i \in \mathsf{in}$, *similarly compute*
$$h_i \leftarrow \mathsf{FHE.Eval}(\mathsf{pk}, \mathsf{Ext\&Dec}(\mathsf{hk}, H_i, \cdot), \mathsf{ct}_{\mathsf{FHE}}).$$
2. *If* $o \notin \mathsf{out}$, *output* $\perp$. *Otherwise, for each input wire* $i \in \mathsf{in}$, *run the following checks and output* $\perp$ *if any of them fails:*
   - *Run* $\mathsf{SEH.Ver}(\mathsf{hk}, H_o, [(i-1)B : iB-1], (\mathsf{ct}_i, h_i), \rho_i)$ *to verify the opening* $\rho_i$, *which certifies that the hash* $H_o$ *opens to* $(\mathsf{ct}_i, h_i)$ *on the specified block interval. Here we abuse the notation to denote opening verification on block intervals.*
   - *Run* $\mathsf{SEH.VerCons}(\mathsf{hk}, H_i, H_o, (i-1)B, \pi_i)$ *to verify the prefix consistency proof* $\pi_i$ *for the first* $(i-1)B$ *blocks, which certifies that* $H_i$ *is consistent with* $H_o$ *up to the first* $(i-1)B$ *bits /* $(i-1)$ *blocks.*
   - *Run* $\mathsf{Sig.Ver}(\mathsf{vk}_i, (\mathsf{ct}_i, h_i), \sigma_i)$ *to verify the signature* $\sigma_i$ *on message* $(\mathsf{ct}_i, h_i)$ *under verification key* $\mathsf{vk}_i$.
3. *Decrypt each input wire value* $x_i = \mathsf{ct}_i - \mathsf{Eval}(\mathsf{pp}_i, k_i, h_i)$ *for each* $i \in \mathsf{in}$. *If* $x_i \notin \{0,1\}$, *output* $\perp$. *Otherwise, compute the output wire value* $x_o = f_o(\{x_i\}_{i\in\mathsf{in}})$.
4. *Compute the output ciphertext* $\mathsf{ct}_o = x_o + \mathsf{Eval}(\mathsf{pp}_o, k_o, h_o)$ *and compute the signature* $\sigma_o \leftarrow \mathsf{Sign}(\mathsf{sk}_o, (\mathsf{ct}_o, h_o))$. *Here* $x_o \in \{0,1\}$ *is treated as an element in the ring* $R$.
5. *Output* $(\mathsf{ct}_o, \sigma_o)$.

**Fig. 1.** Definition of the Gate circuit

**Theorem 5.2** (EFiO **for Circuits**). *There exists a fixed polynomial* $p$ *such that, assuming polynomial security of iO for* $p(\lambda)$*-size circuits, of one-way functions, of FHE, and of shiftable PRF for bounded-size circuits, for all polynomials* $S(\lambda)$,

$\underline{\mathsf{Ext\&Dec}(\mathsf{hk}, H, (\mathsf{td}, \{(\mathsf{pp}_i, k_i)\}_{i \in S.\mathsf{in}}))}$

1. *Extract* $\{(\mathsf{ct}_i, h_i)\}_{i \in S.\mathsf{in}} \leftarrow \mathsf{Ext}(\mathsf{hk}, \mathsf{td}, H)$.
2. *Decrypt each ciphertext by* $x_i = \mathsf{ct}_i - \mathsf{Eval}(\mathsf{pp}_i, k_i, h_i)$ *for each* $i \in S.\mathsf{in}$. *If* $x_i \notin \{0, 1\}$, *set* $x_i = 0$.
3. *Output a length* $s(\lambda)$ *bit string* $\{x_i\}_{i \in S.\mathsf{in}}$.

**Fig. 2.** Definition of the Extract-and-Decrypt function Ext&Dec

$\ell(\lambda)$, *Theorem 5.1 with subcircuit size* $s = O(\log S + \log \ell)$ *is an* EFiO *for all circuits of size at most* $S(\lambda)$ *with* $\mathcal{EF}$ *proof of equivalence of length at most* $\ell(\lambda)$.

## 5.2 Construction for PViO

We can further build PViO for Turing machines from the EFiO for circuits following the blueprint of [34] and [42]. To avoid the need of subexponential assumptions in existing constructions, we rely on time-lock puzzles, as described in 2.3. Due to the page limit, we refer the reader to the full version for the full construction and proof, and provide here only the final theorem statement.

**Theorem 5.3.** *Assuming the polynomial security of iO for circuits, of puncturable PRF, of FHE, of SEH with proof of prefix consistency, of shiftable PRFs, and of time-lock puzzles, there exists a PViO for Turing machines.*

*In particular, assuming the polynomial security of* iO, *of LWE with subexponential modulus-to-noise ratio, and of time-lock puzzles, there exists a PViO for Turing machines.*

**Acknowledgements.** We thank George Lu for discussions on injective PRGs.

A. Jain was supported in part by NSF CAREER 1942789, Johns Hopkins University Catalyst award, JP Morgan Faculty Award and research gifts from Ethereum Foundation, Stellar Development Foundation, and Cisco.

Part of this work was done while the authors were visiting the Simons Institute for the Theory of Computing, UC Berkeley.

# References

1. Abram, D., Damgård, I., Orlandi, C., Scholl, P.: An algebraic framework for silent preprocessing with trustless setup and active security. In: Dodis, Y., Shrimpton, T. (eds.) CRYPTO 2022, Part IV. LNCS, vol. 13510, pp. 421–452. Springer, Cham (2022). https://doi.org/10.1007/978-3-031-15985-5_15
2. Abram, D., Malavolta, G., Roy, L.: Key-homomorphic computations for RAM: fully succinct randomised encodings and more. In: Kalai, Y.T., Kamara, S.F. (eds.) CRYPTO 2025, Part III. LNCS, vol. 16002, pp. 236–268. Springer, Cham (2025). https://doi.org/10.1007/978-3-032-01881-6_8

3. Agrikola, T., Couteau, G., Hofheinz, D.: The usefulness of sparsifiable inputs: how to avoid subexponential iO. In: Kiayias, A., Kohlweiss, M., Wallden, P., Zikas, V. (eds.) PKC 2020, Part I. LNCS, vol. 12110, pp. 187–219. Springer, Cham (2020). https://doi.org/10.1007/978-3-030-45374-9_7
4. Alwen, J., Brzuska, C., Govinden, J., Harasser, P., Tessaro, S.: Succinct PPRFs via memory-tight reductions. In: Kalai, Y.T., Kamara, S.F. (eds.) CRYPTO 2025, Part V. LNCS, vol. 16004, pp. 628–662. Springer, Cham (2025). https://doi.org/10.1007/978-3-032-01901-1_20
5. Ananth, P., Jain, A.: Indistinguishability obfuscation from compact functional encryption. In: Gennaro, R., Robshaw, M.J.B. (eds.) CRYPTO 2015, Part I. LNCS, vol. 9215, pp. 308–326. Springer, Heidelberg (2015). https://doi.org/10.1007/978-3-662-47989-6_15
6. Asharov, G., Segev, G.: Limits on the power of indistinguishability obfuscation and functional encryption. In: Guruswami, V. (ed.) 56th FOCS, pp. 191–209. IEEE Computer Society Press (2015). https://doi.org/10.1109/FOCS.2015.21
7. Attema, T., Capitão, P., Kohl, L.: On homomorphic secret sharing from polynomial-modulus LWE. In: Boldyreva, A., Kolesnikov, V. (eds.) PKC 2023, Part II. LNCS, vol. 13941, pp. 3–32. Springer, Cham (2023). https://doi.org/10.1007/978-3-031-31371-4_1
8. Barak, B., et al.: On the (im)possibility of obfuscating programs. In: Kilian, J. (ed.) CRYPTO 2001. LNCS, vol. 2139, pp. 1–18. Springer, Heidelberg (2001). https://doi.org/10.1007/3-540-44647-8_1
9. Bitansky, N., Degwekar, A., Vaikuntanathan, V.: Structure vs. hardness through the obfuscation lens. In: Katz, J., Shacham, H. (eds.) CRYPTO 2017, Part I. LNCS, vol. 10401, pp. 696–723. Springer, Cham (2017). https://doi.org/10.1007/978-3-319-63688-7_23
10. Bitansky, N., Goldwasser, S., Jain, A., Paneth, O., Vaikuntanathan, V., Waters, B.: Time-lock puzzles from randomized encodings. In: Sudan, M. (ed.) ITCS 2016, pp. 345–356. ACM (2016). https://doi.org/10.1145/2840728.2840745
11. Bitansky, N., Paneth, O., Rosen, A.: On the cryptographic hardness of finding a Nash equilibrium. In: Guruswami, V. (ed.) 56th FOCS, pp. 1480–1498. IEEE Computer Society Press (2015). https://doi.org/10.1109/FOCS.2015.94
12. Bitansky, N., Paneth, O., Wichs, D.: Perfect structure on the edge of chaos - trapdoor permutations from indistinguishability obfuscation. In: Kushilevitz, E., Malkin, T. (eds.) TCC 2016-A, Part I. LNCS, vol. 9562, pp. 474–502. Springer, Heidelberg (2016). https://doi.org/10.1007/978-3-662-49096-9_20
13. Bitansky, N., Vaikuntanathan, V.: Indistinguishability obfuscation from functional encryption. In: Guruswami, V. (ed.) 56th FOCS, pp. 171–190. IEEE Computer Society Press (2015). https://doi.org/10.1109/FOCS.2015.20
14. Boneh, D., Waters, B.: Constrained pseudorandom functions and their applications. In: Sako, K., Sarkar, P. (eds.) ASIACRYPT 2013, Part II. LNCS, vol. 8270, pp. 280–300. Springer, Heidelberg (2013). https://doi.org/10.1007/978-3-642-42045-0_15
15. Boneh, D., Zhandry, M.: Multiparty key exchange, efficient traitor tracing, and more from indistinguishability obfuscation. In: Garay, J.A., Gennaro, R. (eds.) CRYPTO 2014, Part I. LNCS, vol. 8616, pp. 480–499. Springer, Heidelberg (2014). https://doi.org/10.1007/978-3-662-44371-2_27
16. Boyle, E., Gilboa, N., Ishai, Y.: Function secret sharing. In: Oswald, E., Fischlin, M. (eds.) EUROCRYPT 2015, Part II. LNCS, vol. 9057, pp. 337–367. Springer, Heidelberg (2015). https://doi.org/10.1007/978-3-662-46803-6_12

17. Boyle, E., Goldwasser, S., Ivan, I.: Functional signatures and pseudorandom functions. In: Krawczyk, H. (ed.) PKC 2014. LNCS, vol. 8383, pp. 501–519. Springer, Heidelberg (2014). https://doi.org/10.1007/978-3-642-54631-0_29
18. Campanelli, M., Ganesh, C., Khoshakhlagh, H., Siim, J.: Impossibilities in succinct arguments: black-box extraction and more. In: El Mrabet, N., De Feo, L., Duquesne, S. (eds.) AFRICACRYPT 23. LNCS, vol. 14064, pp. 465–489. Springer, Cham (2023). https://doi.org/10.1007/978-3-031-37679-5_20
19. Canetti, R., et al.: Fiat-Shamir: from practice to theory. In: Charikar, M., Cohen, E. (eds.) 51st ACM STOC, pp. 1082–1090. ACM Press (2019). https://doi.org/10.1145/3313276.3316380
20. Canetti, R., Goldreich, O., Halevi, S.: The random oracle methodology, revisited (preliminary version). In: 30th ACM STOC, pp. 209–218. ACM Press (1998). https://doi.org/10.1145/276698.276741
21. Canetti, R., Lin, H., Tessaro, S., Vaikuntanathan, V.: Obfuscation of probabilistic circuits and applications. In: Dodis, Y., Nielsen, J.B. (eds.) TCC 2015, Part II. LNCS, vol. 9015, pp. 468–497. Springer, Berlin, Heidelberg (2015). https://doi.org/10.1007/978-3-662-46497-7_19
22. Cook, S.A.: Feasibly constructive proofs and the propositional calculus (preliminary version). In: STOC 1975, pp. 83–97 (1975). https://doi.org/10.1145/800116.803756
23. Cook, S.A., Reckhow, R.A.: The relative efficiency of propositional proof systems. J. Symb. Log. **44**(1), 36–50 (1979). https://doi.org/10.2307/2273702
24. Couteau, G., Meyer, P., Passelègue, A., Riahinia, M.: Constrained pseudorandom functions from homomorphic secret sharing. In: Hazay, C., Stam, M. (eds.) EUROCRYPT 2023, Part III. LNCS, vol. 14006, pp. 194–224. Springer, Cham (2023). https://doi.org/10.1007/978-3-031-30620-4_7
25. Datta, P., Jain, A., Jin, Z., Korb, A., Mathialagan, S., Sahai, A.: Incrementally verifiable computation for NP from standard assumptions. In: Kalai, Y.T., Kamara, S.F. (eds.) CRYPTO 2025, Part VII. LNCS, vol. 16006, pp. 611–642. Springer, Cham (2025). https://doi.org/10.1007/978-3-032-01907-3_20
26. Dodis, Y., Halevi, S., Rothblum, R.D., Wichs, D.: Spooky encryption and its applications. In: Robshaw, M., Katz, J. (eds.) CRYPTO 2016, Part III. LNCS, vol. 9816, pp. 93–122. Springer, Heidelberg (2016). https://doi.org/10.1007/978-3-662-53015-3_4
27. Garg, S., Gentry, C., Halevi, S., Raykova, M., Sahai, A., Waters, B.: Candidate indistinguishability obfuscation and functional encryption for all circuits. In: 54th FOCS, pp. 40–49. IEEE Computer Society Press (2013). https://doi.org/10.1109/FOCS.2013.13
28. Garg, S., Gentry, C., Sahai, A., Waters, B.: Witness encryption and its applications. In: Boneh, D., Roughgarden, T., Feigenbaum, J. (eds.) 45th ACM STOC, pp. 467–476. ACM Press (2013). https://doi.org/10.1145/2488608.2488667
29. Garg, S., Pandey, O., Srinivasan, A.: Revisiting the cryptographic hardness of finding a nash equilibrium. In: Robshaw, M., Katz, J. (eds.) CRYPTO 2016, Part II. LNCS, vol. 9815, pp. 579–604. Springer, Berlin, Heidelberg (2016). https://doi.org/10.1007/978-3-662-53008-5_20
30. Garg, S., Pandey, O., Srinivasan, A., Zhandry, M.: Breaking the sub-exponential barrier in obfustopia. In: Coron, J.S., Nielsen, J.B. (eds.) EUROCRYPT 2017, Part III. LNCS, vol. 10212, pp. 156–181. Springer, Cham (2017). https://doi.org/10.1007/978-3-319-56617-7_6

31. Garg, S., Srinivasan, A.: Single-key to multi-key functional encryption with polynomial loss. In: Hirt, M., Smith, A.D. (eds.) TCC 2016-B, Part II. LNCS, vol. 9986, pp. 419–442. Springer, Berlin, Heidelberg (2016). https://doi.org/10.1007/978-3-662-53644-5_16
32. Jain, A., Lin, H., Sahai, A.: Indistinguishability obfuscation from well-founded assumptions. In: Khuller, S., Williams, V.V. (eds.) 53rd ACM STOC, pp. 60–73. ACM Press (2021). https://doi.org/10.1145/3406325.3451093
33. Jain, A., Lin, H., Sahai, A.: Indistinguishability obfuscation from LPN over $\mathbb{F}_p$, DLIN, and PRGs in $NC^0$. In: Dunkelman, O., Dziembowski, S. (eds.) EUROCRYPT 2022, Part I. LNCS, vol. 13275, pp. 670–699. Springer, Cham (2022). https://doi.org/10.1007/978-3-031-06944-4_23
34. Jain, A., Jin, Z.: Indistinguishability obfuscation via mathematical proofs of equivalence. In: 63rd FOCS, pp. 1023–1034. IEEE Computer Society Press (2022). https://doi.org/10.1109/FOCS54457.2022.00100
35. Jain, A., Jin, Z.J., Mathialagan, S., Paneth, O.: On succinct obfuscation via propositional proofs. In: FOCS (2025)
36. Jin, Z., Kalai, Y.T., Lombardi, A., Mathialagan, S.: Universal SNARGs for NP from proofs of correctness. In: Koucký, M., Bansal, N. (eds.) 57th ACM STOC, pp. 933–943. ACM Press (2025). https://doi.org/10.1145/3717823.3718104
37. Kang, Y., Lin, C., Malkin, T., Raykova, M.: Obfuscation from polynomial hardness: beyond decomposable obfuscation. In: Catalano, D., De Prisco, R. (eds.) SCN 2018. LNCS, vol. 11035, pp. 407–424. Springer, Cham (2018). https://doi.org/10.1007/978-3-319-98113-0_22
38. Kiayias, A., Papadopoulos, S., Triandopoulos, N., Zacharias, T.: Delegatable pseudorandom functions and applications. In: Sadeghi, A.R., Gligor, V.D., Yung, M. (eds.) ACM CCS 2013, pp. 669–684. ACM Press (2013). https://doi.org/10.1145/2508859.2516668
39. Koppula, V., Waters, B., Zhandry, M.: Adaptive multiparty NIKE. In: Kiltz, E., Vaikuntanathan, V. (eds.) TCC 2022, Part II. LNCS, vol. 13748, pp. 244–273. Springer, Cham (2022). https://doi.org/10.1007/978-3-031-22365-5_9
40. Liu, Q., Zhandry, M.: Decomposable obfuscation: a framework for building applications of obfuscation from polynomial hardness. In: Kalai, Y., Reyzin, L. (eds.) TCC 2017, Part I. LNCS, vol. 10677, pp. 138–169. Springer, Cham (2017). https://doi.org/10.1007/978-3-319-70500-2_6
41. Lombardi, A., Vaikuntanathan, V.: Correlation-intractable hash functions via shift-hiding. In: Braverman, M. (ed.) ITCS 2022, vol. 215, pp. 102:1–102:16. LIPIcs (2022).https://doi.org/10.4230/LIPIcs.ITCS.2022.102
42. Ma, Y., Dai, C., Shi, E.: Quasi-linear indistinguishability obfuscation via mathematical proofs of equivalence and applications. In: Fehr, S., Fouque, P.A. (eds.) EUROCRYPT 2025, Part III. LNCS, vol. 15603, pp. 157–186. Springer, Cham (2025). https://doi.org/10.1007/978-3-031-91131-6_6
43. Malavolta, G., Thyagarajan, S.A.K.: Homomorphic time-lock puzzles and applications. In: Boldyreva, A., Micciancio, D. (eds.) CRYPTO 2019, Part I. LNCS, vol. 11692, pp. 620–649. Springer, Cham (2019). https://doi.org/10.1007/978-3-030-26948-7_22
44. Mathialagan, S.: Succinct cryptography via propositional proofs. Thesis, Massachusetts Institute of Technology (2025). https://dspace.mit.edu/handle/1721.1/164048
45. Naor, M.: On cryptographic assumptions and challenges (invited talk). In: Boneh, D. (ed.) CRYPTO 2003. LNCS, vol. 2729, pp. 96–109. Springer, Heidelberg (2003). https://doi.org/10.1007/978-3-540-45146-4_6

46. Nassar, S., Waters, B.: Adaptive NIKE for unbounded parties. Cryptology ePrint Archive (2026)
47. Orlandi, C., Scholl, P., Yakoubov, S.: The rise of paillier: homomorphic secret sharing and public-key silent OT. In: Canteaut, A., Standaert, F.X. (eds.) EUROCRYPT 2021, Part I. LNCS, vol. 12696, pp. 678–708. Springer, Cham (2021). https://doi.org/10.1007/978-3-030-77870-5_24
48. Peikert, C., Shiehian, S.: Privately constraining and programming PRFs, the LWE way. In: Abdalla, M., Dahab, R. (eds.) PKC 2018, Part II. LNCS, vol. 10770, pp. 675–701. Springer, Cham (2018). https://doi.org/10.1007/978-3-319-76581-5_23
49. Peikert, C., Shiehian, S.: Noninteractive zero knowledge for NP from (plain) learning with errors. In: Boldyreva, A., Micciancio, D. (eds.) CRYPTO 2019, Part I. LNCS, vol. 11692, pp. 89–114. Springer, Cham (2019). https://doi.org/10.1007/978-3-030-26948-7_4
50. Ragavan, S., Vafa, N., Vaikuntanathan, V.: Indistinguishability obfuscation from bilinear maps and LPN variants. In: Boyle, E., Mahmoody, M. (eds.) TCC 2024, Part IV. LNCS, vol. 15367, pp. 3–36. Springer, Cham (2024). https://doi.org/10.1007/978-3-031-78023-3_1
51. Rivest, R.L., Shamir, A., Wagner, D.A.: Time-lock puzzles and timed-release crypto (1996)
52. Roy, L., Singh, J.: Large message homomorphic secret sharing from DCR and applications. In: Malkin, T., Peikert, C. (eds.) CRYPTO 2021, Part III. LNCS, vol. 12827, pp. 687–717. Springer, Cham (2021). https://doi.org/10.1007/978-3-030-84252-9_23
53. Sahai, A., Waters, B.: How to use indistinguishability obfuscation: deniable encryption, and more. In: Shmoys, D.B. (ed.) 46th ACM STOC, pp. 475–484. ACM Press (2014). https://doi.org/10.1145/2591796.2591825
54. Srinivasan, S., Loss, J., Malavolta, G., Nayak, K., Papamanthou, C., Thyagarajan, S.A.K.: Transparent batchable time-lock puzzles and applications to byzantine consensus. In: Boldyreva, A., Kolesnikov, V. (eds.) PKC 2023, Part I. LNCS, vol. 13940, pp. 554–584. Springer, Cham (2023). https://doi.org/10.1007/978-3-031-31368-4_20
55. Waters, B., Wu, D.J.: Adaptively-sound succinct arguments for NP from indistinguishability obfuscation. In: Mohar, B., Shinkar, I., O'Donnell, R. (eds.) 56th ACM STOC, pp. 387–398. ACM Press (2024). https://doi.org/10.1145/3618260.3649671
56. Waters, B., Wu, D.J.: A pure indistinguishability obfuscation approach to adaptively-sound SNARGs for NP. In: Kalai, Y.T., Kamara, S.F. (eds.) CRYPTO 2025, Part VII. LNCS, vol. 16006, pp. 292–326. Springer, Cham (2025). https://doi.org/10.1007/978-3-032-01907-3_10
57. Waters, B., Zhandry, M.: Adaptive security in SNARGs via iO and lossy functions. In: Reyzin, L., Stebila, D. (eds.) CRYPTO 2024, Part X. LNCS, vol. 14929, pp. 72–104. Springer, Cham (2024). https://doi.org/10.1007/978-3-031-68403-6_3
58. Zhandry, M.: The magic of ELFs. In: Robshaw, M., Katz, J. (eds.) CRYPTO 2016, Part I. LNCS, vol. 9814, pp. 479–508. Springer, Heidelberg (2016). https://doi.org/10.1007/978-3-662-53018-4_18

# Adaptive NIKE for Unbounded Parties

Shafik Nassar[1(✉)] and Brent Waters[1,2]

[1] University of Texas at Austin, Austin, TX, USA
shafik@cs.utexas.edu
[2] NTT Research, Sunnyvale, CA, USA

**Abstract.** This paper presents the first construction of adaptively secure non-interactive key exchange (NIKE) for an unbounded number of parties in the standard model. While prior unbounded protocols were restricted to static security or required random oracles, this work achieves adaptive security in the standard model. The proposed scheme supports an unbounded number of honest and malicious users, as well as unbounded party sizes, while tolerating a bounded number of dynamic user corruptions. The construction is based on sub-exponential indistinguishability obfuscation and sub-exponential fully-homomorphic encryption. A key technical contribution is a new application of what we call a function-extractable hash function. This is a variant of a function binding hash function that enables resilient extraction of properties from maliciously hashed digests.

As an additional contribution, we present a compiler in the random oracle model that upgrades any (unbounded) NIKE that does not support dynamic user corruptions at all into a fully adaptive (unbounded) NIKE that supports an unbounded number of dynamic corruptions. This compiler is completely generic, does not introduce any additional assumptions, and does not rely on sub-exponential hardness.

## 1 Introduction

Non-interactive key exchange (NIKE) is a fundamental cryptographic primitive that allows two or more parties to agree on a shared secret key without any interaction, beyond a public key that each party posts once-and-for-all on a repository, which can be reused across different invocations of the protocol. The concept was first introduced by Diffie and Hellman in their seminal work [DH76], in which they presented a protocol for the two-party case, and their protocol constitutes the backbone of secure communication today. Extending the Diffie-Hellman NIKE beyond two parties remained open for decades, until Joux [Jou00] gave a solution for three parties based on bilinear maps. With the prevalence of chat groups and conference calls in the current communication ecosystem, getting a NIKE protocol in the *multiparty* setting is of great interest. But even going beyond three seemed very difficult, and was a "major open problem" according to Boneh and Silverberg [BS02], who demonstrated how Joux's construction can be extended to the multiparty setting, assuming the existence of multilinear maps. A decade later, multilinear maps candidates were proposed [GGH13a, CLT13, GGH15] alongside their


N. Heninger and M. Rosulek (Eds.): CRYPTO 2026, LNCS 16800, pp. 350–381, 2026.
https://doi.org/10.1007/978-3-032-35367-2_12

corresponding multiparty NIKE constructions. However, multilinear maps have fallen out of favor in the cryptographic community due to "zeroizing" attacks [GGH13a, CHL+15, HJ16, CLLT16] which, among other things, completely broke NIKE constructions based on multilinear maps.

*Multiparty NIKE from iO.* The landscape of multiparty NIKE changed dramatically with the emergence of indistinguishability obfuscation (iO) [BGI+01, GGH+13b] and the punctured programming paradigm [SW14]. While initial iO candidates were based on multilinear maps [GGH+13b], a long line of works concluded with constructions of iO from "well-founded" assumptions [JLS21, JLS22, RVV25]. Boneh and Zhandry [BZ14] gave the first multiparty NIKE construction from iO and one-way functions (OWFs), which roughly works as follows: the secret key sk for each user is a seed for some pseudorandom generator (PRG) $G$, and the corresponding public key is $\mathsf{pk} = G(\mathsf{sk})$. A trusted setup samples a key $K$ of a punctured pseudorandom function (PPRF) $F$, and obfuscates the following program $P$: on input a set of public keys $U = \{\mathsf{pk}_i\}_{i \in [n]}$ and a secret key sk, the program $P(U, \mathsf{sk})$ outputs $F(K, U)$ if there exists some $\mathsf{pk} \in U$ such that $G(\mathsf{sk}) = \mathsf{pk}$, and outputs $\perp$ otherwise. It is easy to see that the Boneh-Zhandry construction is inherently limited to only bounded parties, since the program circuit size grows with its input size, which in this case constitutes the full description of the parties.

Ananth et al. [ABG+13] showed how to generalize the Boneh-Zhandry [BZ14] construction to the *unbounded* setting by hashing the public keys using a hash with succinct local openings (e.g., a Merkle hash [Mer89]). This strategy works with a Merkle hash only if we assume *differing-inputs obfuscation* [ABG+13, BCP14], a strong notion with serious implausibility results [BSW16, GGHW17]. Subsequently, Khurana, Rao and Sahai [KRS15] demonstrated that the unbounded NIKE framework [ABG+13] can work with iO by replacing the Merkle hash with a somewhere-statistically binding hash (SSB) [HW15]. Additionally, Alwen et al. [ABG+25] found another way to construct NIKE for unbounded parties using iO for Turing machines with unbounded inputs [JJ22] and succinct PPRFs.

*Adaptive Security.* The main drawback of prior unbounded NIKE constructions [KRS15, ABG+25] from iO is that they only achieve static security[1], where the adversary commits to the set of users it wants to attack ahead of time. Khurana et al. [KRS15] concluded by saying "it would be interesting to design protocols that tolerate more active attacks by adversaries, for an unbounded number of parties". Indeed, achieving adaptive security appears to be of paramount importance in the context of multiparty NIKE, since users dynamically join the system and the target set of the adversary and whom it will deploy resources to compromise may realistically change depending on information it learns from prior key compromises.

[1] We point out that even by relying on differing inputs obfuscation, Ananth et al. [ABG+13] only prove static security.

The relationship between selective and adaptive security for multiparty NIKE is subtle. When the party bound $n$ is constant, we could simply guess the target set of the adversary in order to upgrade static security to adaptive security. Since an efficient adversary can at most register a polynomial number of users $q$, we only incur an $O(q^n)$ loss, a polynomial. When the party bound $n$ is polynomial, we incur an exponential loss, which can still be mitigated by relying on sub-exponential assumptions and using complexity leveraging. However, the situation is completely different in the unbounded setting, since $q^n$ would be an unbounded exponential, meaning that even complexity leveraging cannot help.

*State-of-the-Art.* Achieving adaptive security for unbounded NIKE remained elusive, even in the *random oracle model* (ROM). Namely, Hofheinz et al. [HJK+16] introduced universal samplers and showed how they can be used to construct adaptive NIKE, and they constructed universal samplers in the ROM from sub-exponentially secure iO. However, their construction only supports bounded parties. We point out a couple of additional works that get adaptive security without random oracles nor sub-exponential assumptions, but also only work in the bounded multiparty setting:

- Rao [Rao14] proposed a new primitive she called obliviously-patchable puncturable pseudorandom functions, and constructed adaptive multiparty NIKE from that primitive in conjunction with iO. However, the security of this new primitive is itself an interactive assumption that does not seem any easier to construct than adaptive multiparty NIKE.
- The work of Koppula, Waters and Zhandry et al. [KWZ22] constructs adaptive bounded multiparty NIKE from polynomially-secure iO and standard polynomially-secure group-based assumptions. Their techniques do not seem to easily transfer to the unbounded-party setting, even if we allow sub-exponential security.

As such, there are currently no known constructions of adaptive unbounded-party NIKE in the standard model or the ROM, even if we allow sub-exponential assumptions.

## 1.1 Our Results

**Adaptive Unbounded NIKE in the Standard Model**

In this work, we construct the *first* adaptively secure unbounded-party NIKE in the standard model, without a random oracle nor a trusted setup. Our construction relies on sub-exponential iO and sub-exponential fully-homomorphic encryption (FHE), and supports unbounded party size, unbounded honest users and unbounded malicious users. In addition to adaptively choosing the target set, our model allows the adversary to *dynamically corrupt* honest users of its choosing. Our construction supports a bounded number of dynamic corruptions, in the sense that our parameters grow polynomially with the number of dynamic corruptions. Formally, our main theorem is stated below:

**Theorem 1.1.** *Assume there exists sub-exponentially secure indistinguishability obfuscation and sub-exponentially secure fully-homomorphic encryption. Then there exists an adaptively secure NIKE where the number of honest users, the number of malicious users and the party size are all unbounded. The only bound is on the number of* dynamically corrupted *users.*

Our main construction, which we present in Sect. 5, in fact utilizes a trusted setup, but Koppula et al. [KWZ22] show how to generically compile any NIKE with a trusted setup into a trustless NIKE by additionally assuming iO, which we assume in our construction anyway.

Along the way of getting our main construction, we extend the notion of function-binding hash which was introduced by Freitag, Waters and Wu [FWW23] to function-*extractable* hash, which gives an interesting new technique of using such hash functions with iO.

**Unbounded Dynamic Corruptions in the ROM**

As an additional contribution, we present a compiler in the ROM that upgrades any adaptive NIKE (for unbounded parties) to support *unbounded* dynamic corruptions:

**Theorem 1.2.** *Assume there exists an adaptively secure NIKE for unbounded parties, that does not support dynamic corruptions. Then there exists an adaptively secure NIKE for unbounded parties in the random oracle that supports unbounded dynamic corruptions.*

We emphasize that Theorem 1.2 is generic, and does not assume any additional cryptographic primitives, does not use complexity leveraging, and does not require super-polynomial security. Therefore, it could be of independent interest and can be potentially useful for NIKE constructions that do not rely on iO. As a corollary, we get the first adaptive NIKE in the ROM with unbounded party size and unbounded dynamic corruptions.[2]

Essentially, our work offers the following tradeoff for adaptively secure NIKE for unbounded parties: either support bounded dynamic corruptions in the standard model, or unbounded dynamic corruptions in the ROM. Supporting unbounded dynamic corruptions in the standard model without guessing the challenge set remains an interesting open question, even in the case of *bounded* multiparty NIKE [KWZ22].

---

[2] The sub-exponential security in Theorem 1.1 is only required for supporting dynamic corruptions and constructing constrained PRFs. See Theorem 5.2 for more details. Theorem 1.2 does not need the underlying NIKE to support dynamic corruptions. Constrained PRFs can be constructed from sub-exponentially secure iO and OWFs in the standard model, which is why we did not need to explicitly state it in Theorem 1.1. However, there are constructions of constrained PRFs from polynomially secure iO and LWE [DKN+20]. As such, it is possible to base the ROM NIKE construction on *polynomial* security of the underlying primitives.

## 1.2 Technical Overview

In this section, we give an overview of our main construction. We will construct a *succinct* multiparty NIKE, meaning that the length of the public parameters is essentially independent of the number of parties that the scheme supports, which suffices to get unbounded-party NIKE. Our main construction will initially have two caveats:

1. The construction utilizes a trusted setup. However, the trusted setup can be removed in multiple ways, as we discuss at the end of this section.
2. The construction will not support dynamic corruptions: this means that the challenger-generated keys cannot be corrupted by the adversary[3], but the adversary can still adaptively choose the challenge set. In the full version [NW26], we prove that we can generically upgrade any such NIKE to support a bounded number of dynamic corruptions.

**Prior Work: Blueprint For Static Security**

Our construction follows the approach of Ananth et al. [ABG+13] and Khurana et al. [KRS15], but with crucial differences that we highlight later. We start with a brief overview of the iO [KRS15] construction. The ingredients they use are:

1. An indistinguishability obfuscator $i\mathcal{O}$.
2. A length-doubling pseudorandom generator $G : \{0,1\}^\lambda \to \{0,1\}^{2\lambda}$.
3. A puncturable pseudorandom function (PPRF) $F$. Recall that a PPRF is a pseudorandom function equipped with a puncturing algorithm that takes a key $K$ and a string $x^*$, and outputs a punctured key $K\{x^*\}$. The punctured key behaves identically to $K$ on all $x \neq x^*$, and moreover the security guarantees that $F(K, x^*)$ remains pseudorandom even given $K\{x^*\}$.
4. A somewhere-statistically binding (SSB) hash [HW15]. We recall that an SSB is a succinct hash with succinct local openings, which can be verified using a $\mathsf{Verify}$ algorithm, but the hash key can be sampled in binding mode on a specific index $i \in [n]$. Such a hash key *statistically* guarantees that any digest can only be opened to one value on index $i$. Additionally, a binding key is computationally indistinguishable from a (standard) key.

Let $n$ be a bound on the party size. The NIKE setup algorithm samples a hash key $\mathsf{hk}$ and a PPRF key $K$, and obfuscates the following program:

Denote the obfuscated program by $P$. The CRS consists of $P$ and $\mathsf{hk}$. To publish a public key, a user samples a secret key $\mathsf{sk} \xleftarrow{R} \{0,1\}^\lambda$ and publishes $\mathsf{pk} = G(\mathsf{sk})$. To generate a shared key for an ordered tuple of public keys $U = (\mathsf{pk}_1, \ldots, \mathsf{pk}_t)$, the user must hold the secret key $\mathsf{sk}_j$ for some $\mathsf{pk}_j$ in the tuple. Then, that user can hash $(\mathsf{dig}, \pi_1, \ldots, \pi_t) = \mathsf{Hash}(\mathsf{hk}, U)$ (we assume that the

[3] This setting is close to the notion of semi-static security [BZ14], where the adversary a priori declares a set of users which cannot be corrupted, and the challenge has to be a subset of that set.

**Constants:** A PPRF key $K$, and a SSB hash key $\mathsf{hk}$.
**Inputs:** A digest $\mathsf{dig}$, an index $j \in [n]$, a public key $\mathsf{pk}_j$, a secret $\mathsf{sk}_j$, and an opening $\pi_j$.

1. If $\mathsf{Verify}(\mathsf{hk}, \mathsf{dig}, j, \mathsf{pk}_j, \pi_j) = 0$, outputs $\perp$.
2. If $G(\mathsf{sk}_j) \neq \mathsf{pk}_j$, outputs $\perp$.
3. Outputs $F(K, \mathsf{dig})$.

**Fig. 1.** Program $\mathsf{crsProg}[K, \mathsf{hk}]$.

hashing algorithm outputs the local openings in addition to the digest), and output $P(\mathsf{dig}, j, \mathsf{pk}_j, \mathsf{sk}_j, \pi_j)$ as the shared key.

In the NIKE security game without dynamic corruptions, the adversary can make the following queries:

- **Honest user registration:** the challenger increments a counter $i$, samples $\mathsf{sk}_i \xleftarrow{R} \{0,1\}^\lambda$. and sends $\mathsf{pk}_i = G(\mathsf{sk}_i)$ to the adversary.
- **Malicious user registration:** the adversary sends a (potentially malicious) public key $\mathsf{pk}$, the challenger increments the same counter $i$, and sets $\mathsf{pk}_i = \mathsf{pk}$.
- **Evaluation:** the adversary sends a set of indices $\mathcal{I} \subseteq [2^\lambda]$ and an index $j^* \in \mathcal{I}$ such that $\mathcal{I}$ consists of indices that all have associated public keys, and $j^*$ specifically was generated by the challenger (i.e., the challenger knows its corresponding secret key). The challenger would typically use the secret key $\mathsf{sk}_{j^*}$ to generate the shared key, but since the challenger knows the PPRF key $K$, it can compute the shared key directly as follows: hashes $\mathsf{dig}^* = \mathsf{Hash}(\mathsf{hk}, U)$ where $U = (\mathsf{pk}_i)_{i \in \mathcal{I}}$ and outputs $F(K, \mathsf{dig}^*)$ as the shared key.

At any point, the adversary can make a challenge query $\mathcal{I}^* \subseteq [2^\lambda]$, to which the challenger responds with either the shared key $y_0 = F(K, U^*)$ or a random string $y_1$ in the codomain of the PPRF. The adversary is called admissible if $\mathcal{I}^*$ consists of challenger-generated users only, and it was never sent as an evaluation query before. Finally, the adversary breaks the NIKE security if it can guess whether it got $y_0$ or $y_1$.

*Static Security.* In the static security game, the adversary has to commit to the challenge set $\mathcal{I}^*$ ahead of time. This makes the proof strategy straightforward: we want to get to a hybrid where the PPRF key $K$ is punctured on the digest $\mathsf{dig}^*$ of the challenge set. To do so, we first use the PRG security in order to change all public keys of users in $\mathcal{I}^*$ to truly random strings in the codomain of the PRG. This is possible because the adversary never gets to see the corresponding secret keys[4], and the challenger does not need any secret key in order to answer **evaluation** queries.

[4] Even if we allow corruption queries, an admissible adversary cannot corrupt a user in the challenge set.

Now, we can define a sequence of hybrids, where the obfuscated program refuses to evaluate $F(K, \mathsf{dig}^*)$ for a subset of (hash) indices. Specifically, in $\mathsf{Hyb}_k$, the CRS program is changed as follows (Fig. 2):

**Constants:** A constrained PRF key $K$, a SSB hash key $\mathsf{hk}$, a digest $\mathsf{dig}^*$, an index $k$.
**Inputs:** A digest $\mathsf{dig}$, an index $j \in [n]$, a public key $\mathsf{pk}_j$, a secret $\mathsf{sk}_j$, and an opening $\pi_j$.

1. If $\mathsf{Verify}(\mathsf{hk}, \mathsf{dig}, j, \mathsf{pk}_j, \pi_j) = 0$, outputs $\bot$.
2. If $G(\mathsf{sk}_j) \neq \mathsf{pk}_j$, outputs $\bot$.
3. If $\mathsf{dig} = \mathsf{dig}^*$ and $j \leq k$, outputs $\bot$.
4. Outputs $F(K, \mathsf{dig})$.

**Fig. 2.** Program $\mathsf{crsProg}[K, \mathsf{hk}, \mathsf{dig}^*, k]$

It is easy to see that by iO security, $\mathsf{Hyb}_0$ is computationally indistinguishable from the real security game and $\mathsf{Hyb}_n$ is computationally indistinguishable from a game where we use a PPRF key that is punctured on $\mathsf{dig}^*$ (since the $k$ then covers all possible indices). Therefore, the problem now only reduces to proving that $\mathsf{Hyb}_k$ and $\mathsf{Hyb}_{k+1}$ are computationally indistinguishable for all $k \in [0, n-1]$. This is done as follows: make the SSB key $\mathsf{hk}$ binding on index $k+1$, which goes unnoticed by SSB mode indistinguishability. Using SSB binding security, the digest $\mathsf{dig}^*$ can be only opened to the one (truly random) public key $\mathsf{pk}_{k+1}$ that was sampled by the challenger. Since the PRG is length doubling, this public key lies outside of the image of $G$ with overwhelming probability, therefore there does not exist any string $\mathsf{sk}$ such that $G(\mathsf{sk}) = \mathsf{pk}_{k+1}$, therefore the program would output $\bot$ anyway, so we can just advance $k$ to $k+1$. We then change $\mathsf{hk}$ back to non-binding, which gets us to $\mathsf{Hyb}_{k+1}$.

### This Work: Getting Adaptive Security

*Constraining Over Puncturing.* In the adaptive security game, the adversary reveals the challenger query much later than the setup in which the PRF key is sampled. Puncturing the PRF key at a single point is inherently "static", and requires the challenger to know the digest, and hence the challenge set, in advance. To overcome this problem, we use the notion of *constrained PRFs* (CPRF) [BW13,KPTZ13,BGI14]: a constrained PRF with a input length $\ell_{\mathsf{in}}$ is just like a PRF, but is additionally equipped with a constraining algorithm that inputs a key $K$ and a predicate $C : \{0,1\}^{\ell_{\mathsf{in}}} \to \{0,1\}$, and outputs a constrained key $K^{(C)}$. Correctness states that this key can be used to evaluate $F(K, x)$ for all $x$ satisfying $C(x) = 1$. Security requires that $F(K, x)$ remains pseudorandom for any $x$ satisfying $C(x) = 0$. Our NIKE construction uses the same program from Fig. 1, but replaces the PPRF with a CPRF. In the security proof, if we reach an experiment where the CPRF key is constrained on *all* digests that are computed from challenger-generated keys exclusively, then we would be done: any admissible challenge set consists of challenger-generated keys exclusively, therefore the CPRF security implies that the shared key, computed as the evaluation of the CPRF on the corresponding digest, is pseudorandom if the adversary is only given the constrained key. We remark that Boneh and Zhandry [BZ14] use a CPRF to prove that their bounded NIKE construction is "semi-statically" secure, but their CPRF key has to grow at least with the size of the challenge set.

*Labeling Keys.* For constraining to make sense, we need a way to distinguish challenger-generated public keys from whatever malicious or honest public keys the adversary can produce. Here, we borrow an idea from Koppula et al. [KWZ22], and use *pseudorandom deterministic encryption* (PDE)[5]: a PDE is a secret key encryption scheme $(\mathsf{Gen}, \mathsf{Enc}, \mathsf{Dec})$ in which the encryption algorithm is deterministic. Security requires that without the secret key, ciphertexts look pseudorandom. Strong correctness requires that under any encryption key $\mathsf{ek}$, every ciphertext $\mathsf{ct}$ decrypts to a message $i$ if and only if $i$ encrypts to $\mathsf{ct}$. This means that "invalid" ciphertexts decrypt to some special symbol $\perp$. This primitive can be built from PRFs [KPW17]. Now the first two steps in our hybrid argument consist of switching the challenger-generated keys to truly random (using PRG security), and then to pseudorandom deterministic encryptions: the public key of the $i^{\text{th}}$ challenger-generated user is simply the encryption of its index $i$, that is $\mathsf{pk}_i = \mathsf{Enc}(\mathsf{ek}, i)$, where $\mathsf{ek}$ is the encryption key. We refer to such keys as *labeled keys*. Since the key $\mathsf{ek}$ does not appear anywhere in the view of the adversary, the second step can be reduced to the PDE security. Given the PDE key $\mathsf{ek}$, we can check whether a public key $\mathsf{pk}$ is labeled simply by checking whether $\mathsf{pk}$ is a valid ciphertext

*Everything, Everywhere, all at Once.* We now have a way to identify a challenger-generated key. However, the problem now is that the obfuscated program only gets access to a hash of the public keys: the SSB hash (respectively, somewhere-*extractable* hash) allows statistical binding (respectively extraction) only on one location, whereas our goal is to decide whether *every* key in the hashed set is labeled. Indeed, if we have a succinct hash function with an extraction trapdoor that extracts whether all keys are labeled, then we can constrain our CPRF key to not work on any digest that only includes labeled keys. The idea is that if the PRG is sufficiently expanding (say, length-tripling), then all labeled keys are outside of the image of the PRG with overwhelming probability[6], therefore

[5] In [KWZ22], they actually use a stronger notion of *puncturable PDE*. By structuring our hybrids correctly, we do not need any puncturing.

[6] To make this argument go through, the labeled keys have to be PDE ciphertexts XORed with a random pad, but we ignore this point in the overview.

constraining the CPRF key does not really change the functionality of the obfuscated program, which allows us to appeal to iO security. For this idea to work with iO, we need a *resilient function extraction* security: for any digest, even one that is *maliciously* generated, if the trapdoor decides that all keys are labeled then it is statistically impossible to open *any* index to an unlabeled key.

Recently, many hash functions with "global" guarantees have been introduced and constructed from various assumptions [FWW23,BBK+23,NWW24, NWW25]. Unfortunately, none of the previous hash functions suffice for our use case out-of-the-box. Brakerski et al. [BBK+23] and Nassar et al. [NWW24, NWW25] construct hash functions that allow extracting some global properties, however, their constructions only support bit-fixing/zero-fixing predicates which are not expressive enough for our application. The function-binding hash (FBH) of Freitag et al. [FWW23] supports conjunction/disjunction of block functions, which is exactly the function family that we need in our context, and moreover, can be constructed from fully-homomorphic encryption. While FBH [FWW23] is not equipped with an extraction algorithm, we observe that we can easily add such an algorithm to the Freitag et al. [FWW23] construction. But the FBH definition does not guarantee anything about maliciously-generated digests, therefore the crucial question is whether this construction actually supports resilient function extraction. In the full version [NW26], we prove that this is indeed the case. We refer to hash functions with this property as *function-extractable hash* functions (FEH), and give the definition in Sect. 3. We believe that FEH can find additional applications, be it in conjunction with iO or not, similar to how somewhere-*extractable* hash was a useful and meaningful extension of SSB hash.

This concludes the overview of our main NIKE construction. The full construction and security proofs can be found in Sect. 5.

*Security Against Dynamic Corruptions.* Dynamic corruptions throw a wrench in our previous analysis, since we cannot just make all challenger-generated keys labeled: if the adversary corrupts an honest user with public key $\mathsf{pk}$, the challenger should be able to produce a secret key $\mathsf{sk}$ such that $\mathsf{pk} = G(\mathsf{sk})$. However, our analysis relies on the fact that such a secret does not exist! The solution is for the challenger to guess the indices of the corrupted users ahead of time, and sample those keys normally, i.e., not labeled. If the guess is correct, then the challenger will be able to answer the corruption queries, and at the same time, an admissible challenge set should not include any of the corrupted users, which means that we can use the CPRF security as before to argue that the challenge shared key is pseudorandom. Recall that an efficient adversary can register less than $2^\lambda$ honest users (for sufficiently large $\lambda$), therefore if we bound the number of dynamic corruptions by $c \in \mathbb{N}$, then the guess comes with a $2^{c\lambda}$ loss, which we can afford if we assume sub-exponential hardness. In fact, this transformation is generic and can turn any sub-exponentially secure adaptive NIKE *without* dynamic corruptions into an adaptive NIKE *with* bounded dynamic corruptions. The transformation is formally presented and proved in the full version [NW26].

*Removing the Trusted Setup.* Removing the trusted setup can be done generically (assuming iO) using a transformation introduced by Koppula et al. [KWZ22, Section 3]. In the full version [NW26], we also present a direct construction without a trusted setup.

**Unbounded Dynamic Corruptions in the Random Oracle.** As an independent contribution, we present a compiler that takes any adaptive NIKE in the plain model, and upgrades it to support unbounded dynamic corruptions in the random oracle model (ROM). This gives a new avenue to achieving full adaptive security in the ROM. Notably, our compiler is completely generic, and does not introduce new assumptions or require super-polynomial hardness. This means that it can potentially be useful for future NIKE constructions that do not rely on iO.

Our transformation is similar in spirit to the two-key simulation technique of Gentry and Waters [GW09], which is used to achieve adaptively secure broadcast encryption in the standard model. However, the NIKE application causes the techniques to depart: we will use $2\lambda$ keys instead of 2, and we will additionally rely on a random oracle.

The transformation is simple: given a plain model NIKE $\Pi_{\mathsf{NIKE}}$, the key publishing algorithm of the new ROM NIKE samples $2\lambda$ key pairs which we denote by $(\mathsf{sk}_{i,b}, \mathsf{pk}_{i,b})_{i\in[\lambda],b\in\{0,1\}}$. The public key consists of all $2\lambda$ sub-public keys $\mathsf{pk} = (\mathsf{pk}_{i,b})_{i\in[\lambda],b\in\{0,1\}}$. The secret consists of half the sub-secret keys: the algorithm samples a uniform selecting string $s = s_1 \cdots s_\lambda \xleftarrow{R} \{0,1\}^\lambda$, and the secret key is $\mathsf{sk} = s, (\mathsf{sk}_{i,s_i})_{i\in[\lambda]}$. The publishing algorithm does not use the random oracle.

Given a hash function $\mathcal{H}$ modeled as a random oracle, the key generation algorithm takes a set of public keys $U = \{\mathsf{pk}^{(1)}, \cdots, \mathsf{pk}^{(n)}\}$ and a corresponding secret key $\mathsf{sk}^{(j)} = s^{(j)}, (\mathsf{sk}^{(j)}_{i,s_i})_{i\in[\lambda]}$ for the $j^{\text{th}}$ public key. The algorithm queries the random oracle on $U$ to decide which sub-keys are used. That is, let $R = \mathcal{H}(U)$ and parse $R = R^{(1)} \| \cdots \| R^{(n)}$. For each $k \in [n]$, the sub-public keys determined by the selection string $R^{(k)}$ are the ones participating in the key evaluation. That is, denote the set $V^{(k)} = \left\{\mathsf{pk}^{(k)}_{1,R^{(k)}_1}, \cdots, \mathsf{pk}^{(k)}_{n,R^{(k)}_n}\right\}$ and let $V$ be the union of all $V^{(k)}$. Then the key generation algorithm invoke the underlying NIKE on the set $V$. Of course, this only succeeds if $R^{(j)}$ and $s^{(j)}$ happen to agree on at least one index: if such an index $i'$ exists, then the evaluating user can use $\mathsf{sk}^{(j)}_{i',s_{i'}}$ as the secret key for the underlying NIKE key generation invocation. Luckily, this happens with probability $1 - 2^{-\lambda}$, leaving us with a negligible correctness error.

The security reduction to the underlying NIKE works as follows: whenever the adversary registers an honest user, the reduction samples the selection string uniformly, and samples the corresponding sub-keys itself, whereas the others are registered as honest users in the underlying NIKE. This allows the reduction to answer all key evaluation queries even without going through the underlying NIKE challenger (with all but negligible probability). The key challenge is that we want the challenge set to consist exclusively of challenger-generated sub-keys. To do so, the reduction guesses the index of the random oracle query corresponding to the challenge set, and programs that query to be answered with the negation of the corresponding selections strings. On one hand, if the guess is correct then this translates the high level challenge query to a valid low-level challenge query (since the non-selection sub-keys are generated by the underlying adversary). On the other hand, this allows the reduction to answer all evaluation queries (with overwhelming probability), by the same logic that gives us the negligible correctness error. When proving this formally, there are some subtleties we need to take care of, like: how does the reduction program the random oracle on the challenge set to depend on the selection strings, even though the selection strings determine how other key evaluation queries are answered? We go through a careful hybrid argument to prove that this is indeed possible. The construction and formal proofs can be found in The full version [NW26].

## 2 Preliminaries

For any positive integer $n \in \mathbb{N}$, we denote $[n] := \{1, \ldots, n\}$. The security parameter will be denoted by $\lambda$. For a binary string $x \in \{0,1\}^*$, we denote the length of $x$ by $|x|$. A function $\varepsilon(\lambda)$ is called negligible if for every positive constant $c$, we have $\varepsilon(\lambda) = o(\lambda^{-c})$. A function $f(\lambda)$ is polynomial if there exists a positive constant $c$ such that $f(c) = O(\lambda^c)$. We denote this by writing $f(\lambda) = \mathsf{poly}(\lambda)$. For any set $S$, when we write $x \xleftarrow{R} S$ we mean that $x$ is sampled uniformly from $S$. Given two Boolean circuits $C_0, C_1 : \{0,1\}^n \to \{0,1\}^m$, we say that $C_0$ and $C_1$ are functionally equivalent if $C_0(x) = C_1(x)$ for all $x \in \{0,1\}^n$.

**Definition 2.1 (Indistinguishability Obfuscation[BGI+12, GGH+13b]).** *Let $\mathcal{C} = \{\mathcal{C}_\lambda\}_{\lambda \in \mathbb{N}}$ be a family of polynomial-size circuits. An indistinguishability obfuscator $i\mathcal{O}$ for $\mathcal{C}$ is an efficient algorithm that takes as input the security parameter $\lambda$, a circuit $C \in \mathcal{C}_\lambda$ and outputs a circuit $C'$. An $i\mathcal{O}$ scheme should satisfy the following properties:*

- **Functionality-preserving:** *For all security parameters $\lambda \in \mathbb{N}$, all $C \in \mathcal{C}_\lambda$, and all inputs $x$, we have that $C'(x) = C(x)$ where $C' \leftarrow i\mathcal{O}(1^\lambda, C)$.*
- **Security:** *We say that $i\mathcal{O}$ is $\varepsilon$-secure if for all polynomial time adversaries $\mathcal{A}$ there exists $\Lambda \in \mathbb{N}$ and a negligible function $\mathsf{negl}(\lambda)$ such that for all $\lambda \geq \Lambda$ and all functionally equivalent $C_0, C_1 \in \mathcal{C}_\lambda$*

$$\left| \Pr[\mathcal{A}(\mathsf{st}, i\mathcal{O}(1^\lambda, C_0)) = 1] - \Pr[\mathcal{A}(\mathsf{st}, i\mathcal{O}(1^\lambda, C_1)) = 1] \right| \leq \varepsilon(\lambda) \cdot \mathsf{negl}(\lambda),$$

*We say that $i\mathcal{O}$ is polynomially secure if $\varepsilon(\lambda) = 1$.*

**Definition 2.2 (Pseudorandom Generator).** *Let $\ell_{\mathsf{in}}(\lambda)$ and $\ell_{\mathsf{out}}(\lambda)$ be any polynomials such that $\ell_{\mathsf{in}}(\lambda) < \ell_{\mathsf{out}}(\lambda)$. A pseudorandom generator (PRG) on domain $\mathcal{X} = \left\{\{0,1\}^{\ell_{\mathsf{in}}(\lambda)}\right\}_{\lambda \in \mathbb{N}}$ and range $\mathcal{Y} = \left\{\{0,1\}^{\ell_{\mathsf{out}}(\lambda)}\right\}_{\lambda \in \mathbb{N}}$ is a deterministic polynomial time algorithm $G : \mathcal{X} \to \mathcal{Y}$. We say that $G$ is a $\varepsilon$-secure PRG if for* *any efficient adversary $\mathcal{A}$ there exists a $\Lambda \in \mathbb{N}$ and a negligible function* $\mathsf{negl}(\lambda)$ *such that for all $\lambda > \Lambda$ the following holds:*

$$\left| \Pr\left[\mathcal{A}(1^\lambda, G(s)) = 1 : s \xleftarrow{\text{R}} \{0,1\}^{\ell_{\mathsf{in}}(\lambda)}\right] - \Pr\left[\mathcal{A}(1^\lambda, x) = 1 : x \xleftarrow{\text{R}} \{0,1\}^{\ell_{\mathsf{out}}(\lambda)}\right] \right| \leq \varepsilon(\lambda) \cdot \mathsf{negl}(\lambda).$$

*We say that $G$ is polynomially secure if $\varepsilon(\lambda) = 1$.*

*By a simple hybrid argument, we can extend the definition to support any number of PRG samples. Specifically, if $G$ is an $\varepsilon$-secure PRG then for any $k \in \mathbb{N}$ and any efficient adversary $\mathcal{A}$ there exists a $\Lambda \in \mathbb{N}$ such that for all $\lambda > \Lambda$ the following holds:*

$$\left|\Pr\left[\mathcal{A}(1^\lambda, G(s_1), \ldots, G(s_k)) = 1\right] - \Pr\left[\mathcal{A}(1^\lambda, x_1, \ldots, x_k) = 1\right]\right| \leq k \cdot \varepsilon(\lambda) \cdot \mathsf{negl}(\lambda),$$

*where $s_i \xleftarrow{\text{R}} \{0,1\}^{\ell_{\mathsf{in}}(\lambda)}$ and $x_i \xleftarrow{\text{R}} \{0,1\}^{\ell_{\mathsf{out}}(\lambda)}$ for all $i \in [k]$.*

The following definition of a *constrained pseudorandom function* is adapted from [BZ14] and is a generalization of *puncturable PRFs* [BW13,KPTZ13,BGI14]. In our application, it suffices to give only a single constrained key to the adversary. A more general definition where the adversary requests multiple constrained keys has also been considered.

**Definition 2.3 (Constrained Pseudorandom Function**[BW13,KPTZ13, BGI14]**).** *A constrained pseudorandom function for a circuit class $\mathcal{C} = \{\mathcal{C}_\lambda\}_{\lambda \in \mathbb{N}}$ is a tuple of efficient algorithms $\Pi_{\mathsf{CPRF}} = (\mathsf{Setup}, \mathsf{Eval}, \mathsf{Constrain})$ with the following syntax:*

- $\mathsf{Setup}(1^\lambda, 1^{\ell_{\mathsf{in}}}, 1^{\ell_{\mathsf{out}}}) \to K$: *On input a security parameter $\lambda$, an input length $\ell_{\mathsf{in}}$, and an output length $\ell_{\mathsf{out}}$, the key generation algorithm outputs an evaluation key $K$.*
- $\mathsf{Eval}(K, x) \to y$: *On input an evaluation key $K$ and a string $x \in \{0,1\}^{\ell_{\mathsf{in}}}$, outputs a string $y \in \{0,1\}^{\ell_{\mathsf{out}}}$.*
- $\mathsf{Constrain}(K, C) \to K^{(C)}$: *On input a key $K$, and a binary circuit $C : \{0,1\}^{\ell_{\mathsf{in}}} \to \{0,1\}$ in the class $\mathcal{C}_\lambda$, outputs a constrained evaluation key $K^{(C)}$.*

*A constrained pseudorandom function should satisfy the following properties:*

- ***Constrained correctness:*** *For any $\lambda, \ell_{\mathsf{in}}, \ell_{\mathsf{out}} \in \mathbb{N}$, any Boolean circuit $C : \{0,1\}^{\ell_{\mathsf{in}}} \to \{0,1\}$ in $\mathcal{C}_\lambda$, any $K$ in the support of* $\mathsf{Setup}(1^\lambda, 1^{\ell_{\mathsf{in}}}, 1^{\ell_{\mathsf{out}}})$*, and any $K^{(C)}$ in the support of* $\mathsf{Constrain}(K, C)$*, we have*

$$\mathsf{Eval}(K^{(C)}, x) = \begin{cases} \mathsf{Eval}(K, x) & C(x) = 1 \\ \bot & C(x) = 0 \end{cases}$$

- ***Selective constrained pseudorandomness:*** *For any adversary $\mathcal{A}$, define the constrained security game with the parameter $b$ as follows:*

1. *On input a security parameter* $1^\lambda$, *the adversary* $\mathcal{A}$ *chooses an input length* $1^{\ell_{\mathsf{in}}}$, *an output length* $1^{\ell_{\mathsf{out}}}$, *and a binary circuit* $C : \{0,1\}^{\ell_{\mathsf{in}}} \to \{0,1\}$, *and sends* $(1^{\ell_{\mathsf{in}}}, 1^{\ell_{\mathsf{out}}}, C)$ *to the challenger.*
2. *The challenger samples a key* $K \leftarrow \mathsf{Setup}(1^\lambda, 1^{\ell_{\mathsf{in}}}, 1^{\ell_{\mathsf{out}}})$ *and a constrained key* $K^{(C)} \leftarrow \mathsf{Constrain}(K, C)$, *and sends* $K^{(C)}$ *to* $\mathcal{A}$.
3. *The adversary can make evaluation queries* $x$, *and the challenger responds with* $\mathsf{Eval}(K, x)$.
4. *The adversary submits a challenge* $x^*$ *satisfying the two following requirements:*
   - $x^*$ *was not queried before.*
   - $C(x^*) = 0$, *meaning that the constrained key* $K^{(C)}$ *cannot evaluate* $x^*$.

   *The challenger computes* $y_0 = \mathsf{Eval}(K, x^*)$, *samples* $y_1 \xleftarrow{\text{R}} \{0,1\}^{\ell_{\mathsf{out}}}$ *and sends* $y_b$ *to* $\mathcal{A}$.
5. *The adversary outputs a guess* $b'$, *which is the output of the experiment.*

*We say that #1 satisfies* $\varepsilon$*-#2 if for every efficient adversary* $\mathcal{A}$ *there exists a* $\Lambda \in \mathbb{N}$ *and a negligible function* $\mathsf{negl}(\lambda)$ *such that for all* $\lambda \geq \Lambda$ *it holds that*

$$|\Pr[b' = 1 : b = 0] - \Pr[b' = 1 : b = 1]| \leq \varepsilon(\lambda) \cdot \mathsf{negl}(\lambda).$$

*If* $\varepsilon(\lambda) = 1$, *then* $\Pi_{\mathsf{CPRF}}$ *satisfies punctured pseudorandomness.*

Next, we describe the notion of a *pseudorandom deterministic encryption* (PDE), which can be constructed from pseudorandom functions. We note that a stronger *puncturable* version of PDE due to [KPW17] (which can be constructed from puncturable PRFs) was used in [KWZ22] to construct adaptively secure NIKE for bounded parties. For our construction, the unpunctured notion suffices.

**Definition 2.4 (Pseudorandom Deterministic Encryption).** *A pseudorandom deterministic encryption (PDE) with message space* $\{0,1\}^\lambda$ *and ciphertexts of length* $\ell := \ell(\lambda)$ *is a tuple of efficient algorithms* $\Pi_{\mathsf{PDE}} = (\mathsf{Gen}, \mathsf{Enc}, \mathsf{Dec})$ *with the following syntax:*

- $\mathsf{Gen}(1^\lambda) \to \mathsf{ek}$: *On input a security parameter* $\lambda$, *the setup algorithm outputs a key* $\mathsf{ek}$.
- $\mathsf{Enc}(\mathsf{ek}, m) \to \mathsf{ct}$: *On input a key* $\mathsf{ek}$ *and a message* $m \in \{0,1\}^\lambda$, *the encryption algorithm outputs a ciphertext* $\mathsf{ct} \in \{0,1\}^\ell$. *This algorithm is deterministic.*
- $\mathsf{Dec}(\mathsf{ek}, \mathsf{ct}) \to m$: *On input a key* $\mathsf{ek}$ *and a ciphertext* $\mathsf{ct} \in \{0,1\}^\ell$, *outputs a message* $m \in \{0,1\}^\lambda$ *or* $\perp$.

*In addition,* $\Pi_{\mathsf{PDE}}$ *must satisfy the following properties:*

- ***Strong Correctness:*** *For all* $\lambda \in \mathbb{N}$, *all keys in the support of* $\mathsf{Gen}(1^\lambda)$, *all* $m \in \{0,1\}^\lambda$ *and all ciphertexts* $\mathsf{ct} \in \{0,1\}^\ell$:

$$\mathsf{Dec}(\mathsf{ek}, \mathsf{ct}) = m \Leftrightarrow \mathsf{Enc}(\mathsf{ek}, m) = \mathsf{ct}$$

– ***Ciphertext pseudorandomness:*** *We define the following security game which is parameterized by a bit* $b$*:*
  1. *The challenger samples the key* $\mathsf{ek} \leftarrow \mathsf{Gen}(1^\lambda)$.
  2. *The adversary can make* unique *encryption queries. For each query* $m$*, the challenger responds with* $\mathsf{ct}$ *which is computed as follows:*
     - *If* $b = 0$*, the challenger samples* $\mathsf{ct} \xleftarrow{R} \{0,1\}^\ell$.
     - *If* $b = 1$*, the challenger sets* $\mathsf{ct} = \mathsf{Enc}(\mathsf{ek}, m)$.
  3. *The adversary outputs a guess* $b' \in \{0,1\}$ *which is the output of the experiment.*

  *We say that* $\Pi_{\mathsf{CPRF}}$ *satisfies* $\varepsilon$*-constrained pseudorandomness if for every efficient adversary* $\mathcal{A}$ *there exists a* $\Lambda \in \mathbb{N}$ *and a negligible function* $\mathsf{negl}(\lambda)$ *such that for all* $\lambda \geq \Lambda$ *it holds that*

$$|\Pr[b' = 1 : b = 0] - \Pr[b' = 1 : b = 1]| \leq \varepsilon(\lambda) \cdot \mathsf{negl}(\lambda).$$

  *If* $\varepsilon(\lambda) = 1$*, then* $\Pi_{\mathsf{PDE}}$ *satisfies polynomial ciphertext pseudorandomness.*

## 3 Function-Extractable Hash

In this section, we strengthen the definition of *function-binding hash* [FWW23]. Roughly speaking, a function-binding hash (FBH) is a hash with succinct local openings, where the hash key can bind on a specific function $f$. Statistical function binding guarantees the following statistical property: if the honestly-generated digest of some string $x$ (with respect to the binding key) can be opened on position $i$ to value $\bar{x}_i$, then there must exist an extension $\bar{x}$ of the value $\bar{x}_i$ such that $f(x) = f(\bar{x})$. We emphasize that this statistical property is required to hold only for honestly-generated digests.

We extend the definition to function-*extractable* hash (FEH) by first adding an extraction algorithm that allows for extracting the value $f(x)$ from the digest on $x$. Next, we require that for *any* digest, if we extract the value $y$ and open position $i$ to $\bar{x}_i$, then there must exist an extension $\bar{x}$ such that $f(\bar{x}) = y$. This time, we emphasize that the property should hold even for maliciously-generated digests. We call this property *resilient function extraction.*

**Definition 31. (Function-Extractable Hash).** *Let* $s(\cdot)$ *and* $\ell_{\mathsf{out}}(\cdot)$ *be two polynomials. Let* $\mathcal{X} = \{\mathcal{X}_\lambda\}_{\lambda \in \mathbb{N}}$ *be an input domain and* $\mathcal{Y} = \{\mathcal{Y}_\lambda\}_{\lambda \in \mathbb{N}}$ *be an output codomain where each* $y \in \mathcal{Y}_\lambda$ *can be represented using* $\ell_{\mathsf{out}}(\lambda)$ *bits, and let* $\mathcal{F} = \{\mathcal{F}_\lambda\}_\lambda$ *be a class of functions, where* $\mathcal{F}_\lambda$ *is a collection of functions* $f : \mathcal{X}_\lambda^* \to \mathcal{Y}_\lambda$ *each implementable by a circuit of size* $s(\lambda) \cdot \mathsf{poly}(n)$ *where* $n$ *is the number of input blocks to* $f$*. A* function-extractable hash *(FEH) for* $\mathcal{F}$ *is a tuple of polynomial time algorithms* $\mathsf{FEH} = (\mathsf{Setup}, \mathsf{Hash}, \mathsf{Open}, \mathsf{Verify}, \mathsf{Extract})$ *with the following syntax:*

– $\mathsf{Setup}(1^\lambda, n) \to \mathsf{hk}$*: On input a security parameter* $\lambda$*, a number of blocks* $n$ *(in binary), outputs a hash key* $\mathsf{hk}$*. We implicitly assume that* $\mathsf{hk}$ *includes* $\lambda$ *and* $n$*.*

- $\mathsf{SetupBinding}(1^\lambda, n, f) \rightarrow (\mathsf{hk}, \mathsf{td})$: *On input a security parameter* $\lambda$, *a number of blocks* $n$ *(in binary), a function* $f \in \mathcal{F}_\lambda$, *outputs a hash key* $\mathsf{hk}$ *and a secret trapdoor* $\mathsf{td}$.
- $\mathsf{Hash}(\mathsf{hk}, x) \rightarrow (\mathsf{dig}, \pi_1, \ldots, \pi_n)$: *On input a hash key* $\mathsf{hk}$ *and a string* $x \in \mathcal{X}_\lambda^n$, *the hash algorithm outputs a digest* $\mathsf{dig}$ *and* $n$ *openings* $\pi_1, \ldots, \pi_n$. *This algorithm is deterministic.*
- $\mathsf{Verify}(\mathsf{hk}, \mathsf{dig}, i, \sigma, \pi) \rightarrow b$: *On input a hash key* $\mathsf{hk}$, *a digest* $\mathsf{dig}$, *an index* $i \in [n]$, *a symbol* $\sigma \in \mathcal{X}_\lambda$, *and an opening* $\pi$, *the verification algorithm outputs a bit* $b \in \{0, 1\}$. *The verification algorithm is deterministic.*
- $\mathsf{Extract}(\mathsf{td}, \mathsf{dig}) \rightarrow y$: *On input a trapdoor* $\mathsf{td}$ *and a digest* $\mathsf{dig}$, *the extraction algorithm outputs a* $y \in \mathcal{Y}_\lambda$. *This algorithm is deterministic.*

*We require that* $\Pi_{\mathsf{FEH}}$ *satisfies the following properties:*

- ***Efficiency:*** *For all parameters* $\lambda, n \in \mathbb{N}$, *all* $\mathsf{hk}$ *in the support of* $\mathsf{Setup}(1^\lambda, n)$, *all inputs* $x \in \mathcal{X}_\lambda^n$:
  - **Efficient setup:** $\mathsf{Setup}(1^\lambda, n)$ *runs in time at most* $\mathsf{poly}(\lambda, \log n)$. *Note that this implies* $\mathsf{hk}$ *has size at most* $\mathsf{poly}(\lambda, \log n)$.
  - **Succinct digest:** *The digest* $\mathsf{dig}$ *output by* $\mathsf{Hash}(\mathsf{hk}, x)$ *has size at most* $\mathsf{poly}(\lambda, \log n)$.
  - **Succinct openings:** *Each opening* $\pi_i$ *output by* $\mathsf{Hash}(\mathsf{hk}, x)$ *has size at most* $\mathsf{poly}(\lambda, \log n)$.
  - **Efficient verification:** *Since we have the size bounds* $|\mathsf{hk}|, |\mathsf{dig}|$ *and* $|\pi|$, *and* $\mathsf{Verify}$ *is a polynomial time algorithm, then we get that it runs in time* $\mathsf{poly}(\lambda, \log n)$.
- **Correctness:** *For all* $\lambda, n \in \mathbb{N}$, *every* $x = x_1 \cdots x_n \in \mathcal{X}^n$, *and every* $i \in [n]$:

$$\Pr\left[\mathsf{Verify}(\mathsf{hk}, \mathsf{dig}, i, x_i, \pi_i) = 1 : \begin{array}{r}\mathsf{hk} \leftarrow \mathsf{Setup}(1^\lambda, n) \\ (\mathsf{dig}, \pi_1, \ldots, \pi_n) = \mathsf{Hash}(\mathsf{hk}, x)\end{array}\right] = 1.$$

- **Extraction correctness:** *For all* $\lambda, n \in \mathbb{N}$, *every* $x = x_1 \cdots x_n \in \mathcal{X}_\lambda^n$, *and every* $f \in \mathcal{F}_\lambda$:

$$\Pr\left[f(x) = \mathsf{Extract}(\mathsf{td}, \mathsf{dig}) : \begin{array}{r}(\mathsf{hk}, \mathsf{td}) \leftarrow \mathsf{SetupBinding}(1^\lambda, n, f) \\ (\mathsf{dig}, \pi_1, \ldots, \pi_n) \leftarrow \mathsf{Hash}(\mathsf{hk}, x)\end{array}\right] = 1.$$

*We additionally require the following security properties:*

- ***Mode indistinguishability:*** *For a bit* $b \in \{0, 1\}$ *and an adversary* $\mathcal{A}$, *we define the mode indistinguishability game* $\mathsf{ExptMI}_{\mathcal{A}}(\lambda, b)$ *as follows:*
  1. *On input* $1^\lambda$, *the adversary* $\mathcal{A}$ *sends* $n \in \mathbb{N}$ *and* $f \in \mathcal{F}_\lambda$ *to the challenger.*
  2. *The challenger samples the hash keys* $\mathsf{hk}_0 \leftarrow \mathsf{Setup}(1^\lambda, n)$ *and* $(\mathsf{hk}_1, \mathsf{td}) \leftarrow \mathsf{SetupBinding}(1^\lambda, n, f)$. *The challenger gives* $\mathsf{hk}_b$ *to* $\mathcal{A}$.
  3. *Algorithm* $\mathcal{A}$ *outputs a bit* $b'$ *which is the output of the experiment.*

  *We say that #1 satisfies* $\varepsilon$*-#2 if for every efficient adversary* $\mathcal{A}$ *there exists a* $\Lambda \in \mathbb{N}$ *and a negligible function* $\mathsf{negl}(\lambda)$ *such that for all* $\lambda \geq \Lambda$ *it holds that*

$$|\Pr[b' = 1 : b = 0] - \Pr[b' = 1 : b = 1]| \leq \varepsilon(\lambda) \cdot \mathsf{negl}(\lambda).$$

  *If* $\varepsilon(\lambda) = 1$, *then #1 satisfies polynomial #2.*

– ***Resilient function extraction:*** *We say that* $\Pi_{\mathsf{FEH}}$ *satisfies resilient function extraction if for all* $\lambda, n \in \mathbb{N}$, *all functions* $f \in \mathcal{F}_\lambda$, *and all* $(\mathsf{hk}, \mathsf{td})$ *in the support of* $\mathsf{SetupBinding}(1^\lambda, n, f)$, *as well as any (potentially adversarially computed) digest* $\mathsf{dig}$, *index* $i \in [n]$, *block* $\sigma$ *and opening* $\pi$, *the following holds:*

$$\mathsf{Verify}(\mathsf{hk}, \mathsf{dig}, i, \sigma, \pi) = 1 \Rightarrow \exists x \in \mathcal{X}_\lambda^n \text{ , } x_i = \sigma \wedge f(x) = \mathsf{Extract}(\mathsf{td}, \mathsf{dig})$$

*Function-extraction and Collision-resistance.* In our specific use case, it will be helpful to assume that $\Pi_{\mathsf{FEH}}$ is also collision-resistant. We formally define what it means for a function-extractable hash to be collision-resistant:

**Definition 3.2.** *Let* $\Pi_{\mathsf{FEH}} = (\mathsf{Setup}, \mathsf{Hash}, \mathsf{Open}, \mathsf{Verify}, \mathsf{Extract})$ *be a function-extractable hash. We say that* $\Pi_{\mathsf{FEH}}$ *is* $\varepsilon$*-collision-resistant if* $(\mathsf{Setup}, \mathsf{Hash})$ *is an* $\varepsilon$*-collision-resistant hash.*

As it turns out, we can generically compose any function-extractable hash with a collision-resistant hash, by simply appending the CRH digest to the FEH digest, in order to get a function-extractable hash that is collision-resistant.

**Proposition 3.3.** *Assume there exists an* $\varepsilon_{\mathsf{CRH}}$*-secure collision-resistant hash and an* $\varepsilon_{\mathsf{FEH}}$*-secure function-extractable hash. Then there exists an* $\varepsilon_{\mathsf{FEH}}$*-secure function-extractable hash that is* $\varepsilon_{\mathsf{CRH}}$*-collision-resistant.*

For completeness, we give a proof of Proposition 3.3 in the full version [NW26].

## 3.1 Function-Extractable Hash for Conjunction of Block Functions

In this work, we require function-extractable hash for conjunction of block functions[7]. We start by defining this class of functions:

**Definition 3.4 (Conjunction of Block Functions).** *Let* $\mathcal{X} = \{\mathcal{X}_\lambda\}_{\lambda \in \mathbb{N}}$ *be an input domain. We say a function* $f_g : \mathcal{X}^* \to \{0, 1\}$ *is a conjunction of block functions if we can express it as*

$$f_g(x_1, \ldots, x_n) = \bigwedge_{i \in [n]} g(x_i),$$

*where the function* $g : \mathcal{X} \to \{0, 1\}$ *is a predicate over the alphabet* $\mathcal{X}$. *We say that* $\mathcal{F} = \{\mathcal{F}_\lambda\}_\lambda$ *is the class of conjunction of block functions over the alphabet* $\mathcal{X}_\lambda$ *with size* $s(\lambda)$ *and depth* $d(\lambda)$ *if* $\mathcal{F}_\lambda$ *contains all conjunction of block functions* $f_g$ *such that* $g$ *can be computed using a circuit of size* $s(\lambda)$ *and depth* $d(\lambda)$.

[7] The construction can be easily extended to disjunction of block functions as well.

*Function-extractable Hash from Homomorphic Encryption.* It turns out that the construction of function-binding hash of [FWW23] from *leveled homomorphic encryption* naturally extends to function-extractable hash. The digest in the [FWW23] construction consists of an encryption of the function evaluated on the hashed string. We can simply extract the evaluation if we decrypt the digest. Resilient function extraction can be proved using the decryption correctness of the encryption and a simple inductive argument. Formally:

**Theorem 3.5.** *Assume there exists a leveled homomorphic encryption scheme. Then there exists a function-extractable hash for conjunction of block functions.*

In the full version [NW26], we recall the construction of [FWW23] and provide the proof that it is a function-extractable hash.

## 4 Multiparty Non-interactive Key Exchange

We begin by defining succinct multiparty non-interactive key exchange (NIKE) with a trusted setup. A trustless NIKE can be thought of as a NIKE in which the CRS is an empty string. We require the NIKE to allow an unbounded number of users to publish their public keys (up to $2^\lambda$). We will require that the sizes of the CRS, key pairs and the shared key are all succinct in the set size that the NIKE supports, i.e., if the NIKE supports shared key evaluations of up to $n$ users at a time, then the parameters should grow with $\mathsf{polylog}(n)$. Finally, we allow the NIKE setup to take in a bound $c$ on the number of dynamic honest user corruptions it can support, and allow the parameters to grow polynomially with $c$.

**Definition 4.1 (Succinct Multiparty Non-interactive Key Exchange).** *A succinct multiparty non-interactive key exchange scheme (NIKE) is a tuple of polynomial time algorithms* $(\mathsf{Setup}, \mathsf{Publish}, \mathsf{KeyGen})$ *with the following syntax:*

- $\mathsf{Setup}(1^\lambda, 1^c, n) \to \mathsf{crs}$*: On input a security parameter* $\lambda$*, a bound on the set size* $n$ *(in binary), and a bound on the number of corruptions* $c$*, the setup algorithm outputs common reference string* $\mathsf{crs}$.
- $\mathsf{Publish}(1^\lambda, 1^c) \to (\mathsf{pk}, \mathsf{sk})$*: On input a security parameter, the key publishing algorithm outputs a key pair* $(\mathsf{pk}, \mathsf{sk})$.
- $\mathsf{KeyGen}(\mathsf{crs}, \mathsf{sk}, U) \to \mathsf{sh}$*: On input* $\mathsf{crs}$*, a secret key* $\mathsf{sk}$ *and a set (without repetitions) of public keys* $U$ *of size at most* $n$*, the key generation algorithm outputs a shared key* $\mathsf{sh}$*. This algorithm is deterministic and can run in time* $\mathsf{poly}(\lambda, c, n)$ *even if* $|U|$ *is much smaller than* $n$.

*A NIKE scheme is called* ***trustless*** *if there is no* $\mathsf{Setup}$ *algorithm, and* $\mathsf{KeyGen}$ *does not take a common reference string.*

*The algorithms must satisfy the following properties:*

- ***Perfect correctness:*** *For all* $\lambda, n, c \in \mathbb{N}$*, all* $t \in [n]$*, any* $\mathsf{crs}$ *in the support of* $\mathsf{Setup}(1^\lambda, 1^c, n)$*, any* $j, j' \in [t]$*, any two honest key pairs* $(\mathsf{pk}_j, \mathsf{sk}_j)$ *and*

$(\mathsf{pk}_{j'}, \mathsf{sk}_{j'})$ *in the support of* $\mathsf{Publish}(1^\lambda, 1^c)$, *and any (not necessarily honest) set of keys* $\{\mathsf{pk}_i\}_{i \in [t] \setminus \{j,j'\}}$, *it holds that*

$$\mathsf{KeyGen}(\mathsf{crs}, \mathsf{sk}_j, U) = \mathsf{KeyGen}(\mathsf{crs}, \mathsf{sk}_{j'}, U)$$

*where* $U = \{\mathsf{pk}_1, \ldots, \mathsf{pk}_t\}$.[8]

- ***Succinctness:*** *For all* $\lambda, c, n \in \mathbb{N}$, *all* crs *in the support of* $\mathsf{Setup}(1^\lambda, 1^c, n)$ *and all* $(\mathsf{pk}, \mathsf{sk})$ *in the support of* $\mathsf{Publish}(1^\lambda, 1^c)$, *the following holds:*
  - ***CRS succinctness:*** $|\mathsf{crs}| = \mathsf{poly}(\lambda, c, \log n)$.
  - ***Key pair succinctness:*** $|\mathsf{pk}| + |\mathsf{sk}| = \mathsf{poly}(\lambda, c, \log n)$. *By our syntax, this follows immediately since* Publish *is an efficient algorithm that only gets* $1^\lambda$ *and* $1^c$ *as input.*
  - ***Shared key succinctness:*** *for any honestly-generated key pairs* $(\mathsf{pk}_1, \mathsf{sk}_1), \ldots, (\mathsf{pk}_n, \mathsf{sk}_n)$ *and any index* $i \in [n]$, *the shared key* $\mathsf{sh} = \mathsf{KeyGen}(\mathsf{crs}, \mathsf{sk}_i, \{\mathsf{pk}_1, \ldots, \mathsf{pk}_n\})$ *has size at most* $\mathsf{poly}(\lambda, c, \log n)$.

Next, we define two notions of security: adaptive security with dynamic corruptions, and adaptive security with static corruptions. In both notions, the adversary is allowed to adaptively pick its challenge; the difference is whether the adversary can dynamically corrupt honest users or not.

**Definition 4.2 (Adaptive Security with Dynamic Corruptions).** *Let* $\Pi_{\mathsf{NIKE}}$ *be a succinct NIKE scheme. For any adversary* $\mathcal{A}$, *we define the following security experiment parameterized by a bit* $b \in \{0, 1\}$:

1. *On input* $1^\lambda$, *adversary* $\mathcal{A}$ *sends* $1^c, n$ *to the challenger. The challenger initializes two empty tables* $T_{\mathsf{users}}$ *and* $T_{\mathsf{evals}}$ *and a counter* $i \leftarrow 0$, *and sends* $\mathsf{crs} \leftarrow \mathsf{Setup}(1^\lambda, 1^c, n)$ *to* $\mathcal{A}$.
2. $\mathcal{A}$ *can make the following queries:*
   - ***Honest user registration:*** *The challenger increments* $i \leftarrow i + 1$, *runs* $(\mathsf{pk}, \mathsf{sk}) \leftarrow \mathsf{Publish}(1^\lambda, 1^c)$, *adds the entry* $(i, \mathsf{pk}, \mathsf{sk}, \mathsf{uncorrupted})$ *to the table* $T_{\mathsf{users}}$, *and sends* pk *to* $\mathcal{A}$.
   - ***Malicious user registration:*** *The adversary sends a public key* pk *If there is* no *entry in* $T_{\mathsf{users}}$ *with the same public key, the challenger increments* $i \leftarrow i + 1$, *and adds the entry* $(i, \mathsf{pk}, \perp, \mathsf{corrupted})$ *to the table* $T_{\mathsf{users}}$. *Otherwise, we say that the adversary is not admissible, and the experiment outputs a random bit* $b' \xleftarrow{R} \{0, 1\}$.
   - ***Evaluation:*** *The adversary sends a set of indices* $\mathcal{I} \subseteq [2^\lambda]$ *without repetitions and an index* $j^* \in \mathcal{I}$. *For each* $j \in \mathcal{I}$, *the adversary looks for an entry* $(j, \mathsf{pk}_j, \perp, \cdot)$ *in* $T_{\mathsf{users}}$. *For* $j^*$, *the challenger looks for an entry with a secret key* $(j^*, \mathsf{pk}_{j^*}, \mathsf{sk}_{j^*}, \cdot)$ *If any entry is not found or* $\mathsf{sk}_{j^*} = \perp$, *then we say that the adversary is not admissible, and the experiment outputs a random bit* $b' \xleftarrow{R} \{0, 1\}$. *The challenger then computes the set*

[8] We can think of perfect correctness as a strong notion of *adversarial correctness*, where two honest players in a set *always* agree on the shared key, even if the other players in the set are chosen maliciously. We remark that our plain model constructions - as well as many others - satisfy this strong and natural notion.

$U = \{\mathsf{pk}_j\}_{j\in\mathcal{I}}$ *and responds with* $\mathsf{KeyGen}(\mathsf{crs}, \mathsf{sk}_{j^*}, U)$. *Additionally, the challenger adds* $\mathcal{I}$ *to the table* $T_{\mathsf{evals}}$.

- ***Honest user corruption:*** *The adversary sends an index* $i'$. *The challenger looks in* $T_{\mathsf{users}}$ *for an entry* $(i', \mathsf{pk}, \mathsf{sk}, \mathsf{uncorrupted})$, *updates the entry to* $(i', \mathsf{pk}, \mathsf{sk}, \mathsf{corrupted})$ *and sends* $\mathsf{sk}$ *to* $\mathcal{A}$. *If the entry is not found, then we say that the adversary is not admissible, and the experiment outputs a random bit* $b' \xleftarrow{R} \{0,1\}$.

*The adversary is allowed to make up to c* ***honest user corruption*** *queries.*

3. *At any point, the adversary sends the challenge set (without repetitions)* $\mathcal{I}^*$, *such that for each* $j \in \mathcal{I}^*$ *there exists an entry* $(j, \mathsf{pk}_j, \mathsf{sk}_j, \mathsf{uncorrupted})$ *in* $T_{\mathsf{users}}$. *The challenger then computes the set* $U^* = \{\mathsf{pk}_j\}_{j\in\mathcal{I}^*}$ *and sends* $y_b$, *where* $y_0 = \mathsf{KeyGen}(\mathsf{crs}, \mathsf{sk}_{\mathsf{idx}_1}, U^*)$ *(where* $\mathsf{idx}_1$ *is the first index in* $\mathcal{I}^*$*) and* $y_1$ *is uniform over the range of* $\mathsf{KeyGen}$. *If* $\mathcal{I}^*$ *is in the table* $T_{\mathsf{evals}}$, *or there exists* $j \in \mathcal{I}^*$ *such that* $(j, \mathsf{pk}_j, \mathsf{sk}_j, \mathsf{uncorrupted})$ *is not in* $T_{\mathsf{users}}$, *then we say that the adversary is not admissible, and the experiment outputs a random bit* $b' \xleftarrow{R} \{0,1\}$.
4. *The adversary outputs a bit* $b' \in \{0,1\}$, *which is the output of the experiment.*

*We say that #1 satisfies #2 if for every efficient adversary* $\mathcal{A}$ *there exists a negligible function* $\mathsf{negl}(\lambda)$ *such that*

$$|\Pr[b' = 1 : b = 0] - \Pr[b' = 1 : b = 1]| = \mathsf{negl}(\lambda).$$

**Definition 4.3 (Adaptive Security with Static Corruptions).** *Let* $\Pi_{\mathsf{NIKE}}$ *be a succinct NIKE scheme. The adaptive security game with static corruptions is identical to the adaptive security game with dynamic corruptions, except that the adversary sets* $c = 0$, *namely, no* ***honest user corruption*** *queries are allowed*[9]. *We say that #1 satisfies* $\varepsilon$*-#2 if for every efficient adversary* $\mathcal{A}$ *there exists a* $\Lambda \in \mathbb{N}$ *and a negligible function* $\mathsf{negl}(\lambda)$ *such that for all* $\lambda \geq \Lambda$ *it holds that*

$$|\Pr[b' = 1 : b = 0] - \Pr[b' = 1 : b = 1]| \leq \varepsilon(\lambda) \cdot \mathsf{negl}(\lambda).$$

*If* $\varepsilon(\lambda) = 1$, *then #1 satisfies polynomial #2.*

*Remark 4.4.* We note that Koppula et al. [KWZ22, Section 3] proved that adaptive security *without* **malicious user registration** queries and **evaluation** queries can be generically lifted to support such queries, assuming iO. As we will see, our scheme readily supports such queries so we elect to keep them as part of the definition.

*Static corruptions to adaptive corruptions.* It turns out that using complexity leveraging, we can prove that if a (succinct) NIKE scheme is sub-exponentially adaptively secure against static corruptions, then it is also adaptively secure against dynamic corruptions. Formally:

---

[9] We call this security against static corruptions because it is equivalent to a game where the adversary a priori commits to the set of honest users that it wants to corrupt.

**Theorem 4.5 (Security Against Dynamic Corruptions).** *Let $\delta \in (0,1)$ and $\Pi_{\mathsf{NIKE}}$ be a (succinct) NIKE scheme that is $2^{-\lambda^\delta}$-adaptively secure against* static *corruptions, where $\lambda$ is the security parameter and $n$ is a bound the set size, and where the CRS, shared key and key pair all have size polynomial in $\lambda, \log n$. Then for any $c \in \mathbb{N}$, there exists a (succinct) NIKE scheme that is adaptively secure against $c$ dynamic corruptions with polynomial hardness, where the CRS, shared key and key pair all have size polynomial in $\lambda, c, \log n$.*

We provide the proof in the full version [NW26].

*Succinctness to Unboundedness.* We argue that the succinctness notion we require in Definition 4.1 implies a NIKE for unbounded parties (up to $2^\lambda$ parties). The idea is simple: given a NIKE $\Pi_{\mathsf{NIKE}} = (\mathsf{Setup}, \mathsf{Publish}, \mathsf{KeyGen})$ satisfying Definition 4.1 and a bound on the number of corruptions $c \in \mathbb{N}$, we run $\lambda$ instances of $\Pi_{\mathsf{NIKE}}$:

- In the setup, we sample $\mathsf{crs}_i \leftarrow \mathsf{Setup}(1^\lambda, 1^c, 2^i)$ for each $i \in [\lambda]$, then set $\mathsf{crs} = (\mathsf{crs}_1, \ldots, \mathsf{crs}_\lambda)$. This procedure runs in time $\mathsf{poly}(\lambda, c)$.
- To publish a key pair, it suffices to sample $(\mathsf{pk}, \mathsf{sk}) \leftarrow \mathsf{Publish}(1^\lambda, 1^c)$, since the publishing algorithm is independent of $n$. This procedure runs in time $\mathsf{poly}(\lambda, c)$.
- To generate a shared key for a set $U$ of size $n \in (2^{i-1}, 2^i]$ with the secret key $\mathsf{sk}$, we use $\mathsf{crs}_i$ and compute $\mathsf{sh} = \mathsf{KeyGen}(\mathsf{crs}_i, \mathsf{sk}, U)$.

Therefore in this work, we focus on constructing succinct NIKE.

## 5 Constructing Adaptive NIKE with Static Corruptions

In this section, we present our construction of adaptively secure NIKE against static corruptions. Since no adaptive corruptions are allowed, we omit the parameter $c$ from the input to Setup.

**Construction 5.1 (NIKE Construction).** Our construction uses the following ingredients:

- An indistinguishability obfuscator $i\mathcal{O}$ for the class of circuits that implement the algorithm in Fig. 3 as per Definition 2.1.
- A length tripling PRG $G : \{0,1\}^\lambda \rightarrow \{0,1\}^{3\lambda}$ as per Definition 2.2.
- A pseudorandom deterministic encryption scheme $\Pi_{\mathsf{PDE}} = (\mathsf{Gen}, \mathsf{Enc}, \mathsf{Dec})$ as per Definition 2.4 with ciphertexts of length $3\lambda$. Assume that the decryption algorithm $\mathsf{PDE.Dec}$ can be implemented by a circuit of size $s(\lambda)$ and depth $d(\lambda)$. This ingredient only appears in the security analysis, not in the construction itself.
- A function-extractable hash $\Pi_{\mathsf{FEH}} = (\mathsf{Setup}, \mathsf{Hash}, \mathsf{Open}, \mathsf{Verify}, \mathsf{Extract})$ as per Definition 31 over the domain $\mathcal{X}_\lambda = \{0,1\}^{3\lambda}$. We assume that $\Pi_{\mathsf{FEH}}$ supports conjunction of block functions of size $s(\lambda)$ and depth $d(\lambda)$. Denote the digest length by $\ell_{\mathsf{FEH}} := \ell_{\mathsf{FEH}}(\lambda, n)$. And let $\mathcal{C}_\lambda = \{\mathsf{FEH.Extract}(\mathsf{td}, \cdot)\}_{\mathsf{td}}$ be the class of circuits that implements the extraction algorithm.

- A constrained PRF scheme $\Pi_{\mathsf{CPRF}} = (\mathsf{Setup}, \mathsf{Eval}, \mathsf{Constrain})$ as per Definition 2.3 for a class of circuits $\mathcal{C}_\lambda$ that can implements the extraction algorithm of the function-extractable hash.

Throughout this construction, we assume that any set (without repetitions) $U$ is represented by the *lexicographically ordered* tuple $(\mathsf{pk}_1, \ldots, \mathsf{pk}_t)$, where $U = \{\mathsf{pk}_1, \ldots, \mathsf{pk}_t\}$. The algorithms are defined as follows:

- $\mathsf{Setup}(1^\lambda, n)$:
  1. Samples a PRF key $K \leftarrow \mathsf{CPRF.Setup}(1^\lambda, 1^{\ell_{\mathsf{FEH}}}, 1^\lambda)$.
  2. Samples a FEH key $\mathsf{hk} \leftarrow \mathsf{FEH.Setup}(1^\lambda, n)$.
  3. Samples $P \leftarrow i\mathcal{O}(\mathtt{crsProg}[K, \mathtt{hk}])$ where $\mathtt{crsProg}$ is described in Fig. 3.
  4. Outputs $\mathsf{crs} = (\mathsf{hk}, P)$.

**Constants:** A constrained PRF key $K$ (which could be a master key or a constrained key), and a FEH hash key $\mathsf{hk}$.
**Inputs:** A digest $\mathsf{dig}$, an index $j \in [n]$, a public key $\mathsf{pk}_j$, a secret $\mathsf{sk}_j$, and an opening $\pi_j$.

1. If $\mathsf{FEH.Verify}(\mathsf{hk}, \mathsf{dig}, j, \mathsf{pk}_j, \pi_j) = 0$, outputs $\perp$.
2. If $G(\mathsf{sk}_j) \neq \mathsf{pk}_j$, outputs $\perp$.
3. Outputs $\mathsf{CPRF.Eval}(K, \mathsf{dig})$.

**Fig. 3.** Program $\mathsf{crsProg}[K, \mathsf{hk}]$

- $\mathsf{Publish}(1^\lambda)$: samples a uniform $\mathsf{sk} \xleftarrow{R} \{0,1\}^\lambda$, sets $\mathsf{pk} = G(\mathsf{sk})$, and outputs $(\mathsf{pk}, \mathsf{sk})$.
- $\mathsf{KeyGen}(\mathsf{crs}, \mathsf{sk}, U)$:
  1. Parses $\mathsf{crs} = (\mathsf{hk}, P)$.
  2. Parses $U = (\mathsf{pk}_1, \ldots, \mathsf{pk}_t)$, where $t = |U|$.
  3. Looks for $j \in [t]$ such that $\mathsf{pk}_j = G(\mathsf{sk})$. If no such $j$ exists, outputs $\perp$.
  4. Pads the string $\widetilde{U} = U \circ \mathbf{0}^{n-t}$, where $\mathbf{0} = 0^{3\lambda}$.
  5. Hashes $(\mathsf{dig}, \pi_1, \ldots, \pi_n) = \mathsf{FEH.Hash}(\mathsf{hk}, \widetilde{U})$.
  6. Outputs $P(\mathsf{dig}, j, \mathsf{pk}_j, \mathsf{sk}, \pi_j)$.

*Perfect Correctness.* Observe that for any honestly generated key pair $\mathsf{pk}, \mathsf{sk}$ that is output by $\mathsf{Publish}$, the check $G(\mathsf{sk}) = \mathsf{pk}$ follows. In addition, the program $\mathsf{crsProg}[K, \mathsf{hk}]$ from Fig. 3 outputs the same string $\mathsf{sh}$ on any $\mathsf{dig}$, as long as it is given a valid opening $\pi_j$ to some key $\mathsf{pk}_j$ in position $j$, as well as the secret key $\mathsf{sk}_j$ corresponding to $\mathsf{pk}_j$. Therefore for any set $U$ and any two parties $\mathsf{pk}_j, \mathsf{pk}_{j'} \in U$ with the corresponding secret keys $\mathsf{sk}_j, \mathsf{sk}_{j'}$, by the perfect correctness of $\Pi_{\mathsf{FEH}}$ and the functionality preserving of $i\mathcal{O}$, we have $\mathsf{KeyGen}(\mathsf{crs}, \mathsf{sk}_j, U) = \mathsf{KeyGen}(\mathsf{crs}, \mathsf{sk}_{'j}, U)$ and perfect completeness of $\Pi_{\mathsf{NIKE}}$ follows.

*Succinctness.* Key pair succinctness follows trivially since $\mathsf{Publish}$ is an efficient algorithm that just samples $\mathsf{sk} \xleftarrow{R} \{0,1\}^\lambda$ and outputs $\mathsf{pk} = G(\mathsf{sk}), \mathsf{sk}$. Shared key succinctness also follows immediately by the functionality preserving of $i\mathcal{O}$. Namely, the shared key is computed by an obfuscation of the program $\mathsf{crsProg}[K, \mathsf{hk}]$ from Fig. 3, which just outputs the evaluation of the CPRF, and the output length of the CPRF is set to be $\lambda$. Finally, the CRS consists of the hash key $\mathsf{hk}$ and the obfuscated program $P$. The hash key $\mathsf{hk}$ has length $\mathsf{poly}(\lambda, \log n)$ by the succinctness of $\Pi_{\mathsf{FEH}}$. The program $\mathsf{crsProg}$ has the following complexity:

1. The first step of verifying the opening of FEH can be implemented by in time $\mathsf{poly}(\lambda, \log n)$ by the succinctness of $\Pi_{\mathsf{FEH}}$.
2. The second step consists of evaluating a length tripling PRG on a seed of length $\lambda$, therefore can be implemented in time $\mathsf{poly}(\lambda)$.
3. The final step can be computed in time $\mathsf{poly}(\lambda, \ell_{\mathsf{FEH}})$ which is $\mathsf{poly}(\lambda, \log n)$ by the succinctness of $\Pi_{\mathsf{FEH}}$. Note that this step might use the constrained key of $\Pi_{\mathsf{CPRF}}$, but this key has size $\mathsf{poly}(\lambda, \ell_{\mathsf{FEH}})$ which is $\mathsf{poly}(\lambda, \log n)$.

In total, $\mathsf{crsProg}$ can be implemented by a circuit of size $\mathsf{poly}(\lambda, \log n)$. Since this is the class of circuits that $i\mathcal{O}$ needs to support, then the obfuscated program $P$ has size $\mathsf{poly}(\lambda, \log n)$. In total, the CRS is also succinct.

### 5.1 Security Analysis

In this section, we prove that Construction 5.1 is adaptively secure against static corruptions. We prove the following theorem:

**Theorem 5.2.** *Assume that $i\mathcal{O}$ is an $\varepsilon$-secure indistinguishability obfuscator, $G$ is an $\varepsilon$-secure PRG, $\Pi_{\mathsf{CPRF}}$ satisfies $\varepsilon$-constrained pseudorandomness, $\Pi_{\mathsf{PDE}}$ satisfies $\varepsilon$-ciphertext pseudorandomness, and $\Pi_{\mathsf{FEH}}$ satisfies $\varepsilon$-collision-resistance, $\varepsilon$-mode indistinguishability, and resilient function extraction. Then Construction 5.1 satisfies $\varepsilon$-adaptive security against static corruptions.*

Let $\mathcal{A}$ be an adversary for the adaptive security with static corruptions game. Throughout this section, we assume that $\mathcal{A}$ is admissible. We define the following sequence of hybrids starting with the real security game $\mathsf{Real}^b$.

- $\mathsf{Real}^b$: This is the real security game with parameter $b$.
  1. **Setup Phase:**
     (a) On input $1^\lambda$, the adversary $\mathcal{A}$ sends $n$ to the challenger.
     (b) The challenger initializes two empty tables $T_{\mathsf{users}} \leftarrow \varnothing$ and $T_{\mathsf{evals}} \leftarrow \varnothing$, and a counter $i \leftarrow 0$.
     (c) Samples a PRF key $K \leftarrow \mathsf{CPRF.Setup}(1^\lambda, 1^{\ell_{\mathsf{FEH}}}, 1^\lambda)$.
     (d) Samples a FEH key $\mathsf{hk} \leftarrow \mathsf{FEH.Setup}(1^\lambda, n)$.
     (e) Samples $P \leftarrow i\mathcal{O}(\mathtt{crsProg}[K, \mathtt{hk}])$ where $\mathtt{crsProg}$ is described in Fig. 3.
     (f) The challenger sends $\mathsf{crs} = (\mathsf{hk}, P)$ to $\mathcal{A}$.

2. **Query Phase:** $\mathcal{A}$ can adaptively make the following queries.
   - **Honest user registration:**
     (a) The challenger increments $i \leftarrow i + 1$.
     (b) The challenger samples a uniform $\mathsf{sk} \xleftarrow{R} \{0,1\}^\lambda$ and sets $\mathsf{pk} = G(\mathsf{sk})$.
     (c) The challenger adds the entry $(i, \mathsf{pk}, \mathsf{sk}, \mathsf{uncorrupted})$ to the table $T_{\mathsf{users}}$.
     (d) The challenger sends $\mathsf{pk}$ to $\mathcal{A}$.
   - **Malicious user registration:**
     (a) The adversary sends a public key $\mathsf{pk}$.
     (b) The challenger increments $i \leftarrow i + 1$.
     (c) The challenger adds the entry $(i, \mathsf{pk}, \perp, \mathsf{corrupted})$ to the table $T_{\mathsf{users}}$.
   - **Evaluation:**
     (a) The adversary sends a set of indices $\mathcal{I}$ and a specific index $j^* \in \mathcal{I}$.
     (b) The challenger retrieves $(j, \mathsf{pk}_j, \cdot, \cdot)$ for all $j \in \mathcal{I}$.
     (c) The challenger forms the ordered set $U = (\mathsf{pk}_j)_{j \in \mathcal{I}}$, extends it to $\widetilde{U}$ by padding with zeros, hashes $(\mathsf{dig}, \cdot) = \mathsf{FEH.Hash}(\mathsf{hk}, \widetilde{U})$ and sends $\mathsf{CPRF.Eval}(K, \mathsf{dig})$ to $\mathcal{A}$.[10]
     (d) Additionally, the challenger adds $U$ to the table $T_{\mathsf{evals}}$.
3. **Challenge Phase:**
   (a) At any point, $\mathcal{A}$ sends the challenge set of indices $\mathcal{I}^*$.
   (b) The challenger computes the ordered set $U^* = (\mathsf{pk}_j)_{j \in \mathcal{I}^*}$.
   (c) The challenger computes the challenge value $y_b$.
   - If $b = 0$, the challenger extends $U^*$ to $\widetilde{U}$ by padding with zeros, and then hashes $(\mathsf{dig}^*, \cdot) = \mathsf{FEH.Hash}(\mathsf{hk}, U)$ and sets $y_0 = \mathsf{CPRF.Eval}(K, \mathsf{dig}^*)$.
   - If $b = 1$, the challenger samples a uniformly random key $y_1 \xleftarrow{R} \{0,1\}^\lambda$.

   (d) The challenger sends $y_b$ to $\mathcal{A}$.
4. **Output Phase:**
   (a) $\mathcal{A}$ is allowed to continue making queries as in the **Query Phase**.
   (b) $\mathcal{A}$ outputs a bit $b' \in \{0,1\}$, which is the output of the experiment.

– $\mathsf{Hyb}_1^b$: This is the same as $\mathsf{Real}^b$, except that the experiment aborts and outputs a random bit if the hash of the challenge set is equal to the hash of any set in $T_{\mathsf{evals}}$. Specifically:
  - **Query Phase:** for each **Evaluation** query $\mathcal{I}$, the challenger adds to the table $T_{\mathsf{evals}}$ the entry $(\mathcal{I}, \mathsf{dig})$.

[10] We justify applying the PRF directly on $\mathsf{dig}$ instead of feeding everything to $\mathsf{crsProg}$ by the functionality-preserving of $i\mathcal{O}$ and the fact that the key pair $(\mathsf{pk}_{j^*}, \mathsf{sk}_{j^*})$ and the digest were computed honestly. As we will see later on, this is a crucial modification since it allows the challenger to answer queries even when the challenger-generated keys are not computed according to the specification of $\mathsf{Publish}(1^\lambda)$.

- **Challenge Phase:** The challenger always computes $\mathsf{dig}^*$. If there exists an entry $(\cdot, \mathsf{dig}^*)$ in $T_{\mathsf{evals}}$, the experiment aborts and outputs a random bit $b' \xleftarrow{R} \{0,1\}$.

– $\mathsf{Hyb}_2^b$: This is the same as $\mathsf{Hyb}_1^b$, except that the challenger responds to **honest user registration** with random public keys instead of the output of $G$. Specifically, the challenger makes the following changes:
  - **Query Phase:** The challenger modifies how it responds to **honest user registration** queries as follows:
    1. The challenger increments $i \leftarrow i + 1$.
    2. The challenger samples $\mathsf{pk}_i \xleftarrow{R} \{0,1\}^{3\lambda}$.
    3. The challenger adds the entry $(i, \mathsf{pk}, \perp, \mathsf{uncorrupted})$ to the table $T$.
    4. The challenger sends $\mathsf{pk}$ to $\mathcal{A}$.

– $\mathsf{Hyb}_3^b$: This is the same as $\mathsf{Hyb}_2^b$, except that the challenger responds to **honest user registration** with what we call *labeled public keys*. Specifically, the challenger makes the following changes:
  - **Setup Phase:** The challenger additionally samples a PDE key $\mathsf{ek} \leftarrow \mathsf{PDE.Gen}(1^\lambda)$ and a uniform string $\mathsf{pad} \xleftarrow{R} \{0,1\}^{3\lambda}$.
  - **Query Phase:** The challenger modifies how it responds to **honest user registration** queries as follows:
    1. The challenger sets $\mathsf{pk}_i = \mathsf{PDE.Enc}(\mathsf{ek}, i) \oplus \mathsf{pad}$.

– $\mathsf{Hyb}_4^b$: This is the same as $\mathsf{Hyb}_3^b$, except that the FEH hash key is binding on the function that checks whether all the hashed keys are labeled. Specifically, the challenger makes the following changes:
  - **Setup Phase:** The challenger samples the FEH hash key as $(\mathsf{hk}, \mathsf{td}) \leftarrow \mathsf{FEH.SetupBinding}(1^\lambda, n, f_g)$, where $f_g(x_1, \ldots, x_n) = \bigwedge_{i\in[n]} g(x_i)$ and

$$g(x) = \begin{cases} 1 & \mathsf{PDE.Dec}(\mathsf{ek}, x \oplus \mathsf{pad}) \neq \perp \\ 0 & \text{otherwise} \end{cases}$$

– $\mathsf{Hyb}_5^b$: This is the same as $\mathsf{Hyb}_4^b$, except that the PRF key is constrained so that it does *not* evaluate FEH digests that extract to 1, i.e., when all the hashed keys are labeled. Specifically, the challenger makes the following changes:
  - **Setup Phase:** The challenger computes $K' = \mathsf{CPRF.Constrain}(K, C)$ where

$$C(\mathsf{dig}) = \neg\mathsf{FEH.Extract}(\mathsf{td}, \mathsf{dig})$$

**Lemma 5.3.** *Assume that* $\Pi_{\mathsf{FEH}}$ *is* $\varepsilon$*-collision-resistant as per Definition 3.2. Then for any efficient* $\mathcal{A}$ *and any* $b \in \{0,1\}$ *there exists* $\Lambda \in \mathbb{N}$ *and a negligible function* $\mathsf{negl}(\lambda)$ *such that for all* $\lambda \geq \Lambda$ *it holds that*

$$\left|\Pr[\mathsf{Real}^b(\mathcal{A}) = 1] - \Pr[\mathsf{Hyb}_1^b(\mathcal{A}) = 1]\right| \leq \varepsilon(\lambda) \cdot \mathsf{negl}(\lambda)$$

Due to space constraints, we defer the proof to the supplemental material.

**Lemma 5.4.** *Assume that $G$ is an $\varepsilon$-secure PRG. Then for any efficient $\mathcal{A}$ that makes $q(\lambda)$* ***honest user registration*** *queries and any $b \in \{0,1\}$ there exists $\Lambda \in \mathbb{N}$ and a negligible function $\mathsf{negl}(\lambda)$ such that for all $\lambda \geq \Lambda$ it holds that*

$$\left|\Pr[\mathsf{Hyb}_1^b(\mathcal{A}) = 1] - \Pr[\mathsf{Hyb}_2^b(\mathcal{A}) = 1]\right| \leq \varepsilon(\lambda) \cdot \mathsf{negl}(\lambda)$$

Due to space constraints, we differ the proof to the supplemental material.

**Lemma 5.5.** *Assume that $\Pi_{\mathsf{PDE}}$ satisfies $\varepsilon$-ciphertext pseudorandomness. Then for any efficient $\mathcal{A}$ and any $b \in \{0,1\}$ there exists $\Lambda \in \mathbb{N}$ and a negligible function $\mathsf{negl}(\lambda)$ such that for all $\lambda \geq \Lambda$ it holds that*

$$\left|\Pr[\mathsf{Hyb}_2^b(\mathcal{A}) = 1] - \Pr[\mathsf{Hyb}_3^b(\mathcal{A}) = 1]\right| \leq \varepsilon(\lambda) \cdot \mathsf{negl}(\lambda)$$

Due to space constraints, we differ the proof to the supplemental material.

**Lemma 5.6.** *Assume that $\Pi_{\mathsf{FEH}}$ satisfies $\varepsilon$-mode indistinguishability. Then for any efficient $\mathcal{A}$ and any $b \in \{0,1\}$ there exists $\Lambda \in \mathbb{N}$ and a negligible function $\mathsf{negl}(\lambda)$ such that for all $\lambda \geq \Lambda$ it holds that*

$$\left|\Pr[\mathsf{Hyb}_3^b(\mathcal{A}) = 1] - \Pr[\mathsf{Hyb}_4^b(\mathcal{A}) = 1]\right| \leq \varepsilon(\lambda) \cdot \mathsf{negl}(\lambda)$$

Due to space constraints, we differ the proof to the supplemental material.

**Lemma 5.7.** *Assume that $i\mathcal{O}$ is an $\varepsilon$-secure indistinguishability obfuscator, $\Pi_{\mathsf{FEH}}$ satisfies resilient function extraction, $\Pi_{\mathsf{CPRF}}$ satisfies constrained correctness, and $\Pi_{\mathsf{PDE}}$ satisfies strong correctness. Then for any efficient $\mathcal{A}$ and any $b \in \{0,1\}$ there exists $\Lambda \in \mathbb{N}$ and a negligible function $\mathsf{negl}(\lambda)$ such that for all $\lambda \geq \Lambda$ it holds that*

$$\left|\Pr[\mathsf{Hyb}_4^b(\mathcal{A}) = 1] - \Pr[\mathsf{Hyb}_5^b(\mathcal{A}) = 1]\right| \leq \varepsilon(\lambda) \cdot \mathsf{negl}(\lambda)$$

*Proof.* Let $\mathcal{A}$ be an adversary for the adaptive security with static corruptions. We construct an adversary $\mathcal{B}$ for the security game of $i\mathcal{O}$ as follows:

1. Algorithm $\mathcal{A}$ sends $n$ to $\mathcal{B}$.
2. Algorithm $\mathcal{B}$ initializes tables $T_{\mathsf{users}}, T_{\mathsf{evals}}$ and counter $i \leftarrow 0$, and samples $K, \mathsf{hk}, \mathsf{td}, \mathsf{ek}, \mathsf{pad}$ as in the setup of $\mathsf{Hyb}_4^b$ and $\mathsf{Hyb}_5^b$.
3. Algorithm $\mathcal{B}$ additionally computes $K' = \mathsf{CPRF.Constrain}(K, C)$, where the circuit is define as $C(\mathsf{dig}) = \neg\mathsf{FEH.Extract}(\mathsf{td}, \mathsf{dig})$.
4. Algorithm $\mathcal{B}$ sends a challenge to the $i\mathcal{O}$ challenger consisting of two circuits $C_0, C_1$ which compute the programs $\mathsf{crsProg}[K, \mathsf{hk}]$ and $\mathsf{crsProg}[K', \mathsf{hk}]$, respectively. Note that both circuits are in the class that supported by $i\mathcal{O}$ since they are instantiations of the algorithms from Fig. 3.
5. The challenger responds with an obfuscated program $P$.
6. Algorithm $\mathcal{B}$ sends $\mathsf{crs} = (\mathsf{hk}, P)$ to $\mathcal{A}$.

7. Algorithm $\mathcal{B}$ answers all queries as well as the challenge exactly as specified in the descriptions of $\mathsf{Hyb}_4^b$ and $\mathsf{Hyb}_5^b$. Note that the query-answering logic is identical in both hybrids. Similar to before, we crucially rely on the fact that **honest user corruption** queries are not allowed.
8. When $\mathcal{A}$ outputs its guess $b'$, algorithm $\mathcal{B}$ forwards $b'$ as its own output to the $i\mathcal{O}$ challenger.

If $\mathcal{A}$ is efficient, then so is $\mathcal{B}$. Clearly, if $P$ is an obfuscation of $C_0$ then $\mathcal{B}$ perfectly simulates $\mathsf{Hyb}_4^b(\mathcal{A})$, and if $P$ is an obfuscation of $C_1$ then $\mathcal{B}$ perfectly simulates $\mathsf{Hyb}_5^b(\mathcal{A})$. For $\mathcal{B}$ to be a valid adversary for the indistinguishability obfuscation game, $C_0$ and $C_1$ have to be equivalent. If $C_0$ and $C_1$ are *not* functionally equivalent with probability at most $\delta(\lambda)$, then the advantage of $\mathcal{B}$ against $i\mathcal{O}$ is:

$$\left|\Pr[\mathsf{Hyb}_4^b(\mathcal{A}) = 1] - \Pr[\mathsf{Hyb}_5^b(\mathcal{A}) = 1]\right| - \delta(\lambda)$$

All that remains is to prove that $C_0, C_1$ are functionally equivalent with probability $\varepsilon(\lambda) \cdot \mathsf{negl}(\lambda)$ and the claim would follow by the $\varepsilon$-security of $i\mathcal{O}$. We start by proving the following statistical claim:

**Claim 5.8.** *Let* $\mathsf{A}$ *be the following event over the reduction:*

$$\exists\, \mathsf{dig}, j, \pi, s \ s.t.\ \mathsf{FEH.Extract}(\mathsf{td}, \mathsf{dig}) = 1 \ \wedge\ \mathsf{FEH.Verify}(\mathsf{hk}, \mathsf{dig}, j, G(s), \pi) = 1.$$

*If* $\Pi_{\mathsf{FEH}}$ *satisfies resilient function extraction and* $\Pi_{\mathsf{PDE}}$ *satisfies strong correctness then:*

$$\Pr\left[\mathsf{A} : \mathsf{pad} \xleftarrow{R} \{0,1\}^{3\lambda}\right] = 2^{-\lambda}.$$

*Proof.* Fix $\lambda, n \in \mathbb{N}$. Fix $\mathsf{ek}$ in the support of $\mathsf{PDE.Gen}(1^\lambda)$ and $(\mathsf{hk}, \mathsf{td})$ in the support of $\mathsf{FEH.SetupBinding}(1^\lambda, n, f_g)$. We start by observing that for each $x \in \{0,1\}^{3\lambda}$, we have

$$\Pr\left[\exists s \in \{0,1\}^\lambda \text{ such that } G(s) \oplus \mathsf{pad} = x : \mathsf{pad} \xleftarrow{R} \{0,1\}^{3\lambda}\right] \le 2^{-2\lambda}$$

just by a union bound over all possible values of $s$. By taking a union bound over all $i \in \{0,1\}^\lambda$, we get

$$\Pr\left[\exists s, i \in \{0,1\}^\lambda \text{ s.t. } G(s) \oplus \mathsf{pad} = \mathsf{PDE.Enc}(\mathsf{ek}, i) : \mathsf{pad} \xleftarrow{R} \{0,1\}^{3\lambda}\right] \le 2^{-\lambda}$$

By the strong correctness of $\Pi_{\mathsf{PDE}}$ and the fact that the message space of $\Pi_{\mathsf{PDE}}$ is $\{0,1\}^\lambda$, the event we bounded is equivalent to the event

$$\mathsf{B} \equiv (\exists s \in \{0,1\}^\lambda \text{ such that } \mathsf{PDE.Dec}(\mathsf{ek}, G(s) \oplus \mathsf{pad}) \ne \bot).$$

Therefore, we can write $\Pr\left[\mathsf{B} : \mathsf{pad} \xleftarrow{R} \{0,1\}^{3\lambda}\right] \le 2^{-\lambda}$. Recall the definition of $g$ used for the function $f_g$ in $\mathsf{SetupBinding}$: $g(x) = 1$ if and only if $\mathsf{PDE.Dec}(\mathsf{ek}, x \oplus$

$\mathsf{pad}) \neq \bot$. Thus, the event $\neg\mathsf{B}$ is equivalent to saying that for all $s \in \{0,1\}^\lambda$, $g(G(s)) = 0$. We can bound the probability of $\mathsf{A}$ by conditioning on $\mathsf{B}$:

$$\Pr[\mathsf{A}] = \Pr[\mathsf{A} \wedge \mathsf{B}] + \Pr[\mathsf{A} \wedge \neg\mathsf{B}] \leq \Pr[\mathsf{B}] + \Pr[\mathsf{A} \mid \neg\mathsf{B}]$$

Now we bound $\Pr[\mathsf{A} \mid \neg\mathsf{B}]$. Assume $\neg\mathsf{B}$ holds. By the resilient function extraction of $\Pi_{\mathsf{FEH}}$, there do not exist $\mathsf{dig}, j, \pi, s$ such that $\mathsf{FEH.Extract}(\mathsf{td}, \mathsf{dig}) = 1$ and $\mathsf{FEH.Verify}(\mathsf{hk}, \mathsf{dig}, j, G(s), \pi) = 1$ since $\neg\mathsf{B}$ implies $g(G(s)) = 0$ for all $s$. Therefore $\Pr[\mathsf{A} \mid \neg\mathsf{B}] = 0$, and in total: $\Pr[\mathsf{A}] \leq 2^{-\lambda}$ and the claim follows.

By the constrained correctness of $\Pi_{\mathsf{CPRF}}$ and the choice of the constrain $C$, the key $K'$ can be evaluated on all $\mathsf{dig}$ such that $\mathsf{FEH.Extract}(\mathsf{td}, \mathsf{dig}) = 0$. Claim 5.8 implies that with probability $\varepsilon(\lambda) \cdot \mathsf{negl}(\lambda)$, for every $\mathsf{dig}, j, \pi, \mathsf{sk}, \mathsf{pk}$ such that $\mathsf{Verify}(\mathsf{hk}, \mathsf{dig}, j, \mathsf{pk}, \pi) = 1$ and $G(\mathsf{sk}) = \mathsf{pk}$ we have that $\mathsf{FEH.Extract}(\mathsf{td}, \mathsf{dig}) = 0$. Thus, the circuits $C_0$ and $C_1$ are functionally equivalent except with probability $\varepsilon(\lambda) \cdot \mathsf{negl}(\lambda)$ and the claim follows.

**Lemma 5.9.** *Assume that $\Pi_{\mathsf{CPRF}}$ satisfies $\varepsilon$-constrained pseudorandomness. Then for any efficient $\mathcal{A}$ there exists $\Lambda \in \mathbb{N}$ such that for all $\lambda \geq \Lambda$ and a negligible function $\mathsf{negl}(\lambda)$ it holds that*

$$\left|\Pr[\mathsf{Hyb}_5^0(\mathcal{A}) = 1] - \Pr[\mathsf{Hyb}_5^1(\mathcal{A}) = 1]\right| \leq \varepsilon(\lambda) \cdot \mathsf{negl}(\lambda)$$

*Proof.* Let $\mathcal{A}$ be an adversary distinguishing between $\mathsf{Hyb}_5^0$ and $\mathsf{Hyb}_5^1$. The idea is that if the experiment does not abort, then $\mathcal{A}$ can distinguish between a truly random string and the constrained PRF on a fresh value $\mathsf{dig}^*$ (which it has not queried before). We construct an adversary $\mathcal{B}$ for the constrained pseudorandomness game of $\Pi_{\mathsf{CPRF}}$ as follows:

1. Algorithm $\mathcal{A}$ sends $n$ to $\mathcal{B}$.
2. Algorithm $\mathcal{B}$ samples $\mathsf{ek}$, $\mathsf{pad}$, and $(\mathsf{hk}, \mathsf{td})$. Next, algorithm $\mathcal{B}$ defines the constraint circuit $C(\mathsf{dig}) = \mathsf{FEH.Extract}(\mathsf{td}, \mathsf{dig})$, and sends the circuit $C$ as well as $1^{\ell_{\mathsf{in}}} = 1^{\ell_{\mathsf{FEH}}}$ and $1^{\ell_{\mathsf{out}}} = 1^\lambda$ to the $\Pi_{\mathsf{CPRF}}$ challenger.
3. The $\Pi_{\mathsf{CPRF}}$ challenger responds with $K' = \mathsf{CPRF.Constrain}(K, C)$. Algorithm $\mathcal{B}$ samples $P \leftarrow i\mathcal{O}(\mathtt{crsProg}[K, \mathtt{hk}])$ where $\mathtt{crsProg}$ is described in Fig. 3. and sends $\mathsf{crs} = (\mathsf{hk}, P)$ to $\mathcal{A}$.
4. Algorithm $\mathcal{B}$ answers **honest user registration** and **malicious user registration** exactly as specified in the descriptions of $\mathsf{Hyb}_5^b$. Note that the query-answering logic is identical in both hybrids.
5. Whenever $\mathcal{A}$ makes an **evaluation** query $\mathcal{I}$, algorithm $\mathcal{B}$ computes $\mathsf{dig}$ exactly like the challenger does in $\mathsf{Hyb}_5^b$, and sends $\mathsf{dig}$ as a query to the $\Pi_{\mathsf{CPRF}}$ challenger, who in turn responds with $\mathsf{sh} = \mathsf{CPRF.Eval}(K, \mathsf{dig})$. Algorithm $\mathcal{B}$ forwards $\mathsf{sh}$ to $\mathcal{A}$.
6. When $\mathcal{A}$ makes its challenge query $\mathcal{I}$, algorithm $\mathcal{B}$ computes $\mathsf{dig}^*$ exactly like the challenger does in $\mathsf{Hyb}_5^b$. If $\mathsf{dig}^*$ is equal to some $\mathsf{dig}_i$ that was produced a prior **evaluation** query, then $\mathcal{B}$ aborts the experiment and outputs a random $b' \xleftarrow{R} \{0,1\}$. Otherwise, $\mathcal{B}$ sends $\mathsf{dig}^*$ as a challenge. The $\Pi_{\mathsf{CPRF}}$ challenger responds with $y_b$ which $\mathcal{B}$ forwards to $\mathcal{A}$.

7. When $\mathcal{A}$ outputs its guess $b'$, algorithm $\mathcal{B}$ forwards $b'$ as its own output to the $\Pi_{\mathsf{FEH}}$ challenger.

If $\mathcal{A}$ is efficient then so $\mathcal{B}$. If $b = 0$, then $y_0 = \mathsf{CPRF.Eval}(K, \mathsf{dig}^*)$ and therefore $\mathcal{B}$ perfectly simulates $\mathsf{Hyb}_5^0(\mathcal{A})$. If $b = 1$, then $y_1 \xleftarrow{R} \{0,1\}^\lambda$ and therefore $\mathcal{B}$ perfectly simulates $\mathsf{Hyb}_5^1(\mathcal{A})$. Define the following event

$$E \equiv \left(\exists(\widetilde{U}_i, \mathsf{dig}_i) \in T_{\mathsf{evals}} \text{ s.t. } \mathsf{dig}^* = \mathsf{dig}_i\right).$$

Note that until $\mathcal{A}$ submits the challenge query, its view in the two experiments is identical, therefore $\Pr[E]$ is a well-define probability that is identical in both experiments. Moreover, given the event $E$, we know that both experiments output 1 with probability exactly 1/2, therefore:

$$\Pr[E] \cdot \left|\Pr[\mathsf{Hyb}_5^0(\mathcal{A}) = 1|E] - \Pr[\mathsf{Hyb}_5^1(\mathcal{A}) = 1|E]\right| = \Pr[E] \cdot \left|\frac{1}{2} - \frac{1}{2}\right| = 0.$$

Therefore the advantage of $\mathcal{A}$ in distinguishing the two experiments is at most:

$$\left|\Pr[\mathsf{Hyb}_5^0(\mathcal{A}) = 1|\neg E] - \Pr[\mathsf{Hyb}_5^1(\mathcal{A}) = 1|\neg E]\right|.$$

Similarly, this is exactly the advantage of $\mathcal{B}$ in breaking the constrained pseudorandomness of $\Pi_{\mathsf{CPRF}}$.

Assuming $\neg E$, the algorithm $\mathcal{B}$ submits a legal challenge query to the $\Pi_{\mathsf{CPRF}}$ challenger, therefore by the $\varepsilon$-constrained pseudorandomness of $\Pi_{\mathsf{CPRF}}$ we conclude that there exists $\Lambda \in \mathbb{N}$ and a negligible function $\mathsf{negl}(\lambda)$ such that for all $\lambda \geq \Lambda$ it holds that

$$\left|\Pr[\mathsf{Hyb}_5^0(\mathcal{A}) = 1|\neg E] - \Pr[\mathsf{Hyb}_5^1(\mathcal{A}) = 1|\neg E]\right| \leq \varepsilon(\lambda) \cdot \mathsf{negl}(\lambda)$$

and the claim follows.

*Proof of Theorem* 5.2. Let $\mathcal{A}$ be an adversary for the adaptive security with static corruptions game against Construction 5.1. By Lemma 5.3 and 5.7, there exists a $\Lambda_1 \in \mathbb{N}$ and a negligible function $\mathsf{negl}_1(\lambda)$ such that for all $\lambda \geq \Lambda_1$ and all $b \in \{0,1\}$ it holds that

$$\left|\Pr[\mathsf{Real}^b(\mathcal{A}) = 1] - \Pr[\mathsf{Hyb}_5^b(\mathcal{A}) = 1]\right| \leq \varepsilon(\lambda) \cdot \mathsf{negl}_1(\lambda)$$

By Lemma 5.9, there exists a $\Lambda_2 \in \mathbb{N}$ and a negligible function $\mathsf{negl}_2(\lambda)$ such that for all $\lambda \geq \Lambda_2$ it hods that

$$\left|\Pr[\mathsf{Hyb}_5^0(\mathcal{A}) = 1] - \Pr[\mathsf{Hyb}_5^1(\mathcal{A}) = 1]\right| \leq \varepsilon(\lambda) \cdot \mathsf{negl}_2(\lambda)$$

In total, there exists a negligible function $\mathsf{negl}(\lambda)$ such that for any $\lambda \geq \Lambda = \max\{\Lambda_1, \Lambda_2\}$, we have

$$\left|\Pr[\mathsf{Real}^0(\mathcal{A}) = 1] - \Pr[\mathsf{Real}^1(\mathcal{A}) = 1]\right| \leq \varepsilon(\lambda) \cdot \mathsf{negl}(\lambda)$$

Therefore Construction 5.1 satisfies $\varepsilon$-adaptive security against static corruptions. □

As a corollary, we get that if all of the underlying ingredients are sub-exponentially secure, then Construction 5.1 is also sub-exponentially secure. Formally:

**Corollary 5.10.** *Let $\delta \in (0,1)$. Assume that $i\mathcal{O}$ is a $2^{-\lambda^\delta}$-secure indistinguishability obfuscator, $G$ is an $2^{-\lambda^\delta}$-secure PRG, $\Pi_{\mathsf{CPRF}}$ satisfies $2^{-\lambda^\delta}$-constrained pseudorandomness, $\Pi_{\mathsf{PDE}}$ satisfies $2^{-\lambda^\delta}$-ciphertext pseudorandomness, and $\Pi_{\mathsf{FEH}}$ satisfies $2^{-\lambda^\delta}$-collision-resistance, $2^{-\lambda^\delta}$-mode indistinguishability, and resilient function extraction. Then Construction 5.1 satisfies $2^{-\lambda^\delta}$-adaptive security against static corruptions.*

Finally, we can get our main result by combining Corollary 5.10 with Theorem 4.5, as well as the facts that constrained pseudorandom functions can be constructed from one-way functions and indistinguishability obfuscation, function-extractable hash with collision-resistance can be constructed from leveled homomorphic encryption, and pseudorandom deterministic encryption and pseudorandom generators can be constructed from one-way functions:

**Corollary 5.11.** *Let $\delta \in (0,1)$. Assume there exists a $2^{-\lambda^\delta}$-secure indistinguishability obfuscator, a $2^{-\lambda^\delta}$-secure one-way function, and leveled homomorphic encryption satisfying $2^{-\lambda^\delta}$-IND-CPA security. Then for any $c \in \mathbb{N}$, there exists a succinct NIKE scheme that is adaptively secure against $c$ adaptive corruptions with polynomial hardness, where the CRS, shared key and key pair all have size polynomial in $\lambda, \log n, c$, where $n$ is a bound on the set size.*

*Getting rid of the CRS Generically.* One downside of Construction 5.1 is the fact that it requires a trusted setup to generate the common reference string. Boneh and Zhandry [BZ14] give a generic approach for removing the CRS, but this approach fails in the presence of **malicious user registration** queries. Koppula et al. [KWZ22] give a generic compiler (assuming iO) for lifting adaptive NIKE to the trustless setting. Their compiler proceeds in three steps:

1. The first step uses a non-interactive zero-knowledge proof to achieve what they call "adversarial correctness".
2. The second step applies a Boneh-Zhandry-style approach to remove the CRS at the expense of no longer supporting **malicious user registration** and **evaluation** queries. This step uses iO and preserves adversarial correctness.
3. The final step reintroduces those queries using a clever application of error-correcting codes. This step makes no additional assumptions, but relies on adversarial correctness.

Importantly, and as noted in [KWZ22], this compiler preserves the support for unbounded parties, therefore we can apply it to Construction 5.1 to get rid of the CRS and get a trustless adaptive NIKE for unbounded parties.

*Direct Construction without a CRS.* In addition, our ideas can be used to get a direct construction in the trustless setting. This construction replaces the PRG in Construction 5.1 with *puncturable signatures* [GVW19], and does not need to go through the compiler of [KWZ22]. We give this construction and prove its security in the full version [NW26].

**Acknowledgments.** Shafik Nassar would like to thank George Lu for useful discussions. Brent Waters is supported by NSF CNS-2318701 and a Simons Investigator award.

## References

ABG+13. Ananth, P., Boneh, D., Garg, S., Sahai, A., Zhandry, M.: Differing-inputs obfuscation and applications. Cryptology ePrint Archive (2013)

ABG+25. Alwen, J., Brzuska, C., Govinden, J., Harasser, P., Tessaro, S.: Succinct PPRFS via memory-tight reductions. In: Annual International Cryptology Conference, pp. 628–662. Springer (2025)

BBK+23. Brakerski, Z., Farber Brodsky, M., Tauman Kalai, Y., Lombardi, A., Paneth, O.: SNARGs for monotone policy batch NP. In: CRYPTO, pp. 252–283 (2023)

BCP14. Boyle, E., Chung, K.-M., Pass, R.: On extractability obfuscation. In: Theory of Cryptography Conference, pp. 52–73. Springer (2014)

BGI+01. Barak, B., et al.: On the (im)possibility of obfuscating programs. In: CRYPTO (2001)

BGI+12. Barak, B., et al.: On the (im)possibility of obfuscating programs. J. ACM **59**(2) (2012)

BGI14. Boyle, E., Goldwasser, S., Ivan, I.: Functional signatures and pseudorandom functions. In: International Workshop on Public Key Cryptography, pp. 501–519. Springer (2014)

BS02. Boneh, D., Silverberg, A.: Applications of multilinear forms to cryptography. Cryptology ePrint Archive (2002)

BSW16. Bellare, M., Stepanovs, I., Waters, B.: New negative results on differing-inputs obfuscation. In: Annual International Conference on the Theory and Applications of Cryptographic Techniques, pp. 792–821. Springer (2016)

BW13. Boneh, D., Waters, B.: Constrained pseudorandom functions and their applications. In: Sako, K., Sarkar, P. (eds.) ASIACRYPT 2013. LNCS, vol. 8270, pp. 280–300. Springer, Heidelberg (2013). https://doi.org/10.1007/978-3-642-42045-015

BZ14. Boneh, D., Zhandry, M.: Multiparty key exchange, efficient traitor tracing, and more from indistinguishability obfuscation. In: CRYPTO (2014)

CHL+15. Hee Cheon, J., Han, K., Lee, C., Ryu, H., Stehlé, D.: Cryptanalysis of the multilinear map over the integers. In: Annual International Conference on the Theory and Applications of Cryptographic Techniques, pp. 3–12. Springer (2015)

CLLT16. Coron, J.S., Sung Lee, M., Lepoint, T., Tibouchi, M.: Cryptanalysis of ggh15 multilinear maps. In: Annual International Cryptology Conference, pp. 607–628. Springer (2016)

CLT13. Coron, J.S., Lepoint, T., Tibouchi, M.: Practical multilinear maps over the integers. In: Annual Cryptology Conference, pp. 476–493. Springer (2013)

DH76. Diffie, W., Hellman, M.E.: New directions in cryptography. IEEE Trans. Inf. Theory **22**(6) (1976)

DKN+20. Davidson, A., Katsumata, S., Nishimaki, R., Yamada, S., Yamakawa, T.: Adaptively secure constrained pseudorandom functions in the standard model. In: Annual International Cryptology Conference, pp. 559–589. Springer (2020)

FWW23. Freitag, C., Waters, B., Wu, D.J.: How to use (plain) witness encryption: registered ABE, flexible broadcast, and more. In: CRYPTO (2023)

GGH13a. Garg, S., Gentry, C., Halevi, S.: Candidate multilinear maps from ideal lattices. In: Annual International Conference on The Theory And Applications of Cryptographic Techniques, pp. 1–17. Springer (2013)

GGH+13b. Garg, S., Gentry, C., Halevi, S., Raykova, M., Sahai, A., Waters, B.: Candidate indistinguishability obfuscation and functional encryption for all circuits. In: FOCS (2013)

GGH15. Gentry, C., Gorbunov, S., Halevi, S.: Graph-induced multilinear maps from lattices. In: Theory of Cryptography Conference, pp. 498–527. Springer (2015)

GGHW17. Garg, S., Gentry, C., Halevi, S., Wichs, D.: On the implausibility of differing-inputs obfuscation and extractable witness encryption with auxiliary input. Algorithmica **79**(4), 1353–1373 (2017)

GVW19. Goyal, R., Vusirikala, S., Waters, B.: Collusion resistant broadcast and trace from positional witness encryption. In: IACR International Workshop on Public Key Cryptography, pp. 3–33. Springer (2019)

GW09. Gentry, C., Waters, B.: Adaptive security in broadcast encryption systems (with short ciphertexts). In: Annual International Conference on the Theory and Applications of Cryptographic Techniques, pp. 171–188. Springer (2009)

HJ16. Hu, Y., Jia, H.: Cryptanalysis of GGH map. In: Annual International Conference on the Theory and Applications of Cryptographic Techniques, pp. 537–565. Springer (2016)

HJK+16. Hofheinz, D., Jager, T., Khurana, D., Sahai, A., Waters, B., Zhandry, M.: How to generate and use universal samplers. In: International Conference on the Theory and Application of Cryptology and Information Security, pp. 715–744. Springer (2016)

HW15. Hubácek, P., Wichs, D.: On the communication complexity of secure function evaluation with long output. In: ITCS (2015)

JJ22. Jain, A., Jin, Z.: Indistinguishability obfuscation via mathematical proofs of equivalence. In: 2022 IEEE 63rd Annual Symposium on Foundations of Computer Science (FOCS), pp. 1023–1034. IEEE (2022)

JLS21. Jain, A., Lin, H., Sahai, A.: Indistinguishability obfuscation from well-founded assumptions. In: STOC (2021)

JLS22. Jain, A., Lin, H., Sahai, A.: Indistinguishability obfuscation from LPN over $\mathbb{F}\_p$, DLIN, and PRGs in $NC^0$. In: EUROCRYPT (2022)

Jou00. Joux, A.: A one round protocol for tripartite diffie-hellman. In: International Algorithmic Number Theory Symposium, pp. 385–393. Springer (2000)

KPTZ13. Kiayias, A., Papadopoulos, S., Triandopoulos, N., Zacharias, T.: Delegatable pseudorandom functions and applications. In: Proceedings of the 2013 ACM SIGSAC Conference on Computer & Communications Security, pp. 669–684 (2013)

KPW17. Koppula, V., Poelstra, A., Waters, B.: Universal samplers with fast verification. In: IACR International Workshop on Public Key Cryptography, pp. 525–554. Springer (2017)

KRS15. Khurana, D., Rao, V., Sahai, A.: Multi-party key exchange for unbounded parties from indistinguishability obfuscation. In: International Conference on the Theory and Application of Cryptology and Information Security, pp. 52–75. Springer (2015)

KWZ22. Koppula, V., Waters, B., Zhandry, M.: Adaptive multiparty nike. In: Theory of Cryptography Conference, pp. 244–273. Springer (2022)

Mer89. Merkle, R.C.: A certified digital signature. In: CRYPTO (1989)

NW26. Nassar, S., Waters, B.: Adaptive nike for unbounded parties. Cryptology ePrint Archive(2026)

NWW24. Nassar, S., Waters, B., Wu, D.J.: Monotone policy BARGs from BARGs and additively homomorphic encryption. In: Theory of Cryptography Conference, pp. 399–430. Springer (2024)

NWW25. Nassar, S., Waters, B., Wu, D.J.: Monotone-policy BARGs and more from BARGs and quadratic residuosity. In: IACR International Conference on Public-Key Cryptography, pp. 283–313. Springer (2025)

Rao14. Rao, V.: Adaptive multiparty non-interactive key exchange without setup in the standard model. Cryptology ePrint Archive, (2014)

RVV25. Ragavan, S., Vafa, N., Vaikuntanathan, V.: Indistinguishability obfuscation from bilinear maps and LPN variants. In: Theory of Cryptography Conference, pp. 3–36. Springer (2025)

SW14. Sahai, A., Waters, B.: How to use indistinguishability obfuscation: deniable encryption, and more. In: STOC (2014)

# Pairing-Based Registered ABE for Boolean Formulas with a Linear-Size CRS

Roy Stracovsky[1(✉)], Brent Waters[2,3], and David J. Wu[2]

[1] Georgia Institute of Technology, Atlanta, GA, USA
[2] UT Austin, Austin, TX, USA
[3] NTT Research, Sunnyvale, CA, USA

**Abstract.** Registered attribute-based encryption (ABE) is a generalization of ABE that replaces the central trusted key-issuer with an untrusted key curator. In registered (ciphertext-policy) ABE, users generate their own public keys and there is a transparent aggregation process that takes the public keys of the users together with their attributes and aggregates them into a short master public key that functions as the public key for a standard ABE scheme.

A sequence of works has focused on improving the efficiency and expressivity of pairing-based registered ABE. Today, all constructions of pairing-based registered ABE rely on a structured common reference string (CRS) whose size scales with the total number of users in the system $N$. While the first pairing-based constructions needed a CRS of size $O(N^2)$, a recent line of work has shown how to reduce it to $N^{1+o(1)}$ in the case of general policies (albeit with extremely large constant factors), and to $O(N)$ if we restrict the policy family to conjunctions and DNFs (earlier schemes could support general monotone Boolean formulas) and if we analyze security in the generic group model (earlier schemes could be proven secure in the plain model).

In this work, we give the first pairing-based registered ABE scheme with a linear-size CRS that supports general policies (i.e., monotone span programs which include monotone Boolean formulas as well as threshold policies). We can show static security based on a $q$-type assumption in the plain model and adaptive security if we instead work in the random oracle model. Our scheme is also the first pairing-based construction where users can be identified by arbitrary strings (e.g., identities) rather than by integers from a polynomial-size range. This directly enables registered ABE with *stateless* key-generation. Namely, users in our system can sample their key independently of the current state of the system. Previous approaches require users either to first retrieve the current state of the system before they could generate their key or to generate multiple public keys to avoid collisions.

## 1 Introduction

Registration-based cryptography [GHMR18] is a paradigm for building advanced cryptographic notions without having to rely on any central trusted authority. In this work, we focus on ciphertext-policy attribute-based encryption


N. Heninger and M. Rosulek (Eds.): CRYPTO 2026, LNCS 16800, pp. 382–413, 2026.
https://doi.org/10.1007/978-3-032-35367-2_13

(ABE) [SW05, GPSW06] where each secret key is associated with an attribute $x$ and each ciphertext is associated with an access policy $P$. Decryption is possible whenever the attribute satisfies the policy (e.g., when $P(x) = 1$). Traditionally, in an ABE scheme, a trusted authority is responsible for generating and issuing the decryption keys. If the authority is compromised, then the security of every user in the system is also compromised. Registered ABE [HLWW23] provides one solution to this problem. In registered ABE, users independently generate their own public/secret key-pair and then "register" the public key with a "key curator." The key curator can then aggregate the individual public keys along with their respective access policies to obtain a succinct master public key $\mathsf{mpk}$. Importantly, this aggregation process is deterministic and transparent (i.e., does not depend on any secrets). The aggregated master public key $\mathsf{mpk}$ then functions as the master public key for a standard ABE scheme; namely, anyone can encrypt a message with respect to a policy such that only registered users with attributes that satisfy the policy can decrypt. Registered ABE allows us to combine the fine-grained decryption capabilities of attribute-based encryption with the trustless model of classic public-key encryption where users retain full control of their key material.

*Our Focus: Pairing-based Registered ABE.* In the last few years, many works have studied registered ABE from a broad range of cryptographic assumptions, including pairing-based assumptions [HLWW23, ZZGQ23, AT24, GLWW24, GHK+25] and lattice-based assumptions [CHW25, WW25, ZZC+25, YZGC25, PST25], as well as constructions from general-purpose primitives such as witness encryption [FWW23] or indistinguishability obfuscation [HLWW23]. In this work, we focus on pairing-based constructions. The main advantage of the pairing-based approaches is that they are concretely efficient. The concrete efficiency of pairing-based registered ABE schemes is comparable to that of pairing-based centralized ABE schemes, which have been successfully implemented [AC17, RW22] and even deployed [Ver23]. A number of recent works have also implemented and used similar pairing-based primitives like registration-based encryption [GKMR23], distributed broadcast encryption [GLWW23], and threshold encryption with silent setup [GKPW24] to construct privacy-preserving systems with minimal trust assumptions. This is in contrast to lattice-based schemes, which all rely on the homomorphic evaluation procedures from [BGG+14] that, to our knowledge, have not been successfully implemented. Constructions based on tools like witness encryption or indistinguishability obfuscation are even less practical than lattice-based ABE. Moreover, schemes based on these general-purpose tools can only be instantiated assuming a combination of multiple cryptographic assumptions or by relying on new non-standard assumptions. This is also the case for the lattice-based constructions where security relies on either new assumptions like succinct LWE (*and* the random oracle model) or non-falsifiable assumptions like evasive LWE. An appealing property of pairing-based schemes is that we can prove security from simple assumptions in the plain model.

*The CRS Size in Pairing-based Registered ABE Schemes.* All existing pairing-based registered ABE schemes rely on a structured common reference string (CRS) whose size grows with the maximum number of users $N$ in the system. The first constructions of pairing-based registered ABE [HLWW23, ZZGQ23, AT24] required a CRS whose size scales *quadratically* with $N$. This makes these schemes suitable only for a small number of users. Subsequently, the work of [GLWW24] showed how to reduce the CRS size to be *nearly linear* in the number of users (i.e., $N^{1+o(1)}$) using combinatorial techniques. However, the authors note that the asymptotic improvement only translates to an efficiency improvement for extremely large values of $N$, and for practical parameters of interest, the size of the CRS in their approach scales with $N^{\log_2 3} \approx N^{1.6}$. The main open problem in this line of research is to build a registered ABE scheme with a linear-size CRS. The recent work of [GHK+25] gives a partial answer to this problem by constructing a pairing-based registered ABE scheme with a linear-size CRS. However, their construction comes at the expense of expressivity: the scheme can only support conjunction policies (and more generally, DNF policies via concatenation). In contrast, all of the aforementioned works on registered ABE support monotone span programs (or more), which in particular includes the class of monotone Boolean formulas and threshold policies. In addition, the security of the construction in [GHK+25] critically relies on the generic group model, whereas earlier pairing-based schemes were shown secure in the plain model.

*This Work.* Our main contribution in this work is the first pairing-based registered ABE scheme with a linear-size CRS that supports all monotone span programs. We prove static security of our scheme under a $q$-type assumption in the plain model (which holds unconditionally in the generic bilinear group model of [Sho97, BBG05]) and adaptive security in the random oracle model. We provide a comparison of our scheme to previous schemes in Table 1.

*An Additional Feature: Registered ABE with Large Index Space.* An appealing property of our registered ABE scheme is that it natively supports a large index space. In more detail, in all pairing-based registered ABE schemes, when a user generates their public key, they also associate it with an index $i \in [N]$ where $N$ is the bound on the number of users. Correctness only holds if every user in the system associates a different index with their public key. Thus, when a user joins the system, they need to first choose an index $i \in [N]$ that is not already taken. In practice, this means that users would interact with a key curator to agree on an index $i$ and then generate their key for the particular index. Alternatively, a user could generate public keys for multiple distinct indices and have the key curator associate a distinct index with each user [GLWW23]. The first approach requires interaction while the second increases the size of each user's public key. Our construction in this work natively supports a "large" index space where the index associated with a key can be an *arbitrary* string (or "identity"). We retain the restriction that every user in the system has a distinct index. However, since the indices can be drawn from an exponential-size universe, individual users can simply pick a random index when generating their key, and with overwhelming

**Table 1.** Comparison with previous registered ABE schemes. Here, crs denotes the common reference string, pk denotes an individual user's public key, mpk denotes the master public key, and ct denotes the ciphertext. We consider a system with $N$ users, an attribute universe $\mathcal{U}$, and a policy $\mathcal{P}$. We write MSP to denote monotone span programs (which includes monotone Boolean formulas and threshold policies), ABP to denote arithmetic branching programs (which generalize MSPs), NM-MSP to denote non-monotone span programs, and DNF to denote formulas in disjunctive normal form ("an OR of ANDs"). We write $i\mathcal{O}$ to denote indistinguishability obfuscation, OWF to denote one-way functions, and ROM to denote the random oracle model. For the pairing-based schemes, we indicate whether they are based on static assumptions or $q$-type assumptions over composite-order or prime-order groups, or if they rely on the generic bilinear group model. We write $p(\cdot)$ to denote a fixed polynomial and suppress all polynomials in the security parameter and all polylogarithmic terms. For each scheme, we also indicate whether it can be shown to be adaptively secure ("AD") under the stated assumption and whether it supports a large index space ("LI") where user keys can be associated with an arbitrary bitstring (rather than an index from a polynomial-size range).

| **Scheme** | $\lvert\mathsf{crs}\rvert$ | $\lvert\mathsf{pk}\rvert$ | $\lvert\mathsf{mpk}\rvert$ | $\lvert\mathsf{ct}\rvert$ | Policy | Assumption | AD | LI |
|---|---|---|---|---|---|---|---|---|
| [HLWW23] | 1 | 1 | 1 | $p(\lvert\mathcal{P}\rvert)$ | circuits | $i\mathcal{O}$ + OWF | ✓ | ✓ |
| [FWW23] | $p(s)$ | 1 | $p(s)$ | $p(s)$ | size-$s$ circuits | witness encryption + LWE | ✗ | ✓ |
| [CHW25]* | $N^2 \cdot p(d)$ | $N \cdot p(d)$ | $p(d)$ | $p(d, \lvert\mathsf{a}\rvert)$ | depth-$d$ circuits | succinct LWE + ROM | ✗ | ✗ |
| [WW25]* | $p(d)$ | $p(d)$ | $p(d)$ | $p(d)$ | depth-$d$ circuits | succinct LWE + ROM | ✗ | ✓ |
| [ZZC+25]* | $p(d)$ | $p(d)$ | $p(d)$ | $p(d, \lvert\mathsf{a}\rvert)$ | depth-$d$ circuits | evasive LWE | ✗ | ✓ |
| [YZGC25]* | $N \cdot p(d)$ | $p(d)$ | $p(d)$ | $p(d, \lvert\mathsf{a}\rvert)$ | depth-$d$ circuits | evasive LWE | ✗ | ✗ |
| [PST25] | 1 | 1 | 1 | 1 | circuits | evasive LWE | ✗ | ✓ |
| [HLWW23] | $\lvert\mathcal{U}\rvert \cdot N^2$ | $N$ | $\lvert\mathcal{U}\rvert$ | $\lvert\mathcal{P}\rvert$ | MSP | composite order (static) | ✓ | ✗ |
| [ZZGQ23] | $\lvert\mathcal{U}\rvert \cdot N^2$ | $N$ | $\lvert\mathcal{U}\rvert$ | $\lvert\mathcal{P}\rvert$ | ABP | prime order (static) | ✓ | ✗ |
| [GLWW24] | $N^{1+o(1)}$ | $N$ | $\lvert\mathcal{U}\rvert$ | $\lvert\mathcal{P}\rvert$ | MSP | prime order ($q$-type) | ✗ | ✗ |
| [AT24]† | $N^2$ | $N$ | $\lvert\mathsf{a}\rvert^2$ | $\lvert\mathsf{a}\rvert \cdot \lvert\mathcal{P}\rvert$ | NM-MSP | prime order (static) | ✓ | ✗ |
| [GHK+25] | $N$ | $N$ | $\lvert\mathcal{U}\rvert$ | $\lvert\mathcal{P}\rvert$ | DNF formulas | generic group model | ✓ | ✗ |
| [RT26]† | $N^{1+o(1)}$ | $N$ | $\lvert\mathsf{a}\rvert^2$ | $\lvert\mathcal{P}\rvert$ | NM-MSP | generic group model + ROM | ✓ | ✗ |
| **Corollary** 4.8 | $N$ | $N$ | $\lvert\mathcal{U}\rvert$ | $\lvert\mathcal{P}\rvert$ | MSP | prime order ($q$-type) | ✗ | ✓ |
| **Corollary** 4.9‡ | $N \cdot p(K)$ | $N \cdot p(K)$ | $\lvert\mathcal{U}\rvert \cdot p(K)$ | $p(K)$ | MSP | prime order ($q$-type) + ROM | ✓ | ✗ |

∗ These schemes are *key-policy* schemes and we write $\lvert\mathsf{a}\rvert$ to denote the length of the attribute in the ciphertext.

† For these schemes, we write $\lvert\mathsf{a}\rvert$ to denote the maximum number of attributes associated with a single user in the system.

‡ This scheme assumes an a priori bound on the size $K$ of a policy and relies on subexponential hardness of the underlying assumption.

probability over the choice of the random index, no two users will share the same index. This way, we obtain a scheme where users can sample their keys completely independently of all other users. In particular, this immediately gives a registered ABE scheme with "stateless key generation"—namely, a scheme where users can generate their key independently of the current state of the system.

## 1.1 Technical Overview

Like nearly all constructions of registered ABE, we focus on constructing a simpler primitive called a *slotted* registered ABE scheme, which was formally introduced in the work of [HLWW23]. We start by recalling the general syntax:

- **Common reference string:** The CRS for a slotted registered ABE scheme defines an a priori fixed number of users $N$ (also called "slots").
- **Key generation:** When a user joins the system, they use the CRS to sample a public/private key-pair $(\mathsf{pk}_i, \mathsf{sk}_i)$ associated with a specific slot index $i \in [N]$.
- **Aggregation:** Given a collection of exactly $N$ public keys $\mathsf{pk}_1, \ldots, \mathsf{pk}_N$, where $\mathsf{pk}_i$ is a public key for slot $i$, along with their respective sets of attributes $S_1, \ldots, S_N$, the aggregation algorithm outputs a succinct master public key $\mathsf{mpk}$ together with a *public* decryption hint $\mathsf{hsk}_i$ for each user $i \in [N]$. We refer to $\mathsf{hsk}_i$ as the "helper decryption key" for user $i$. Importantly, in registered ABE, the aggregation process is deterministic and requires no secrets. Everyone can compute and verify the output of the aggregation algorithm.
- **Encryption:** Using the master public key $\mathsf{mpk}$, anyone can encrypt a message $\mu$ with respect to a policy $P$, just like in a standard ciphertext-policy ABE scheme.
- **Decryption:** Any user $i \in [N]$ associated with attributes $S_i$ that satisfy the policy $P$ can use their secret key $\mathsf{sk}_i$ together with their public decryption hint $\mathsf{hsk}_i$ to recover the message $\mu$.

The main difference between slotted registered ABE and the standard notion of registered ABE is the lack of support for dynamic registration. In the slotted setting, *all* of the public keys and attribute sets must be provided together in order to generate the master public key. The standard notion of registered ABE allows users to join the system one at a time, and each time a user joins, the master public key and helper decryption keys are updated to reflect the current set of registered users. The abstraction of a slotted registered ABE scheme is simpler to work with since we only need to support one-shot aggregation as opposed to dynamic aggregation. The work of [HLWW23] shows how to lift the slotted scheme into the standard setting (with dynamic registration) with only logarithmic overhead. For this reason, we focus on the simpler setting of slotted registered ABE throughout this overview (and for much of the technical sections).

*Starting point: a Variant of the* [HLWW23] *Registered ABE Scheme.* Next, we start with the general template from [HLWW23] for constructing a slotted registered ABE scheme. The cross-term cancellation structure introduced in that work is the cryptographic core of many pairing-based registered ABE schemes [ZZGQ23, GLWW24, AT24, RT26]. Specifically, we describe a slimmed-down variant of the prime-order scheme from [GLWW24, Construction B.3], which can be viewed as a prime-order analog of [HLWW23]. For compatibility with our subsequent exposition, we describe the scheme over an asymmetric pairing group (as opposed to a symmetric pairing group).

Let $(\mathbb{G}_1, \mathbb{G}_2, \mathbb{G}_T, p, g_1, g_2, e)$ be an asymmetric pairing group where $\mathbb{G}_1, \mathbb{G}_2, \mathbb{G}_T$ are groups of prime order $p$, $g_1$ is a generator of $\mathbb{G}_1$, $g_2$ is a generator of $\mathbb{G}_2$, and $e: \mathbb{G}_1 \times \mathbb{G}_2 \to \mathbb{G}_T$ is an efficiently computable non-degenerate bilinear map. We write group elements using implicit notation [EHK+13]. In particular, for a vector $\mathbf{v} \in \mathbb{Z}_p^n$, we write $[\mathbf{v}]_1, [\mathbf{v}]_2, [\mathbf{v}]_T$ to denote $g_1^{\mathbf{v}}$, $g_2^{\mathbf{v}}$, and $e(g_1, g_2)^{\mathbf{v}}$, respectively, where exponentiation is defined component-wise. The slotted registered ABE scheme now works as follows:

- **Common reference string:** Let $N$ be the number of slots. Sample $\alpha, y \xleftarrow{R} \mathbb{Z}_p$. For each slot $i \in [N]$, sample exponents $t_i, u_i \xleftarrow{R} \mathbb{Z}_p$. The CRS consists of the following set of terms (which we highlight in green):
  - the encryption components $[\alpha]_T$ and $[y]_1$,
  - the slot components $([t_i]_2, [u_i]_1, [\alpha + yt_i]_2)$ for all $i \in [N]$, and
  - the cross terms $[t_i u_j]_1$ for all $i \neq j$.
- **Key generation:** To generate a key for slot $i$, the user samples $r_i \xleftarrow{R} \mathbb{Z}_p$ and sets their public key to be $\mathsf{pk}_i = [r_i]_1$ and the secret key to be $\mathsf{sk}_i = r_i$. In addition, they also include the cross terms $[t_j r_i]_2 = r_i [t_j]_2$ for all $j \neq i$ as part of their public key. The cross terms are used to construct the decryption hints.
- **Aggregation:** The aggregation algorithm takes public keys $\mathsf{pk}_1, \ldots, \mathsf{pk}_N$ where $\mathsf{pk}_i = ([r_i]_1, \{[t_j r_i]_2\}_{j \neq i})$ and the attributes $S_1, \ldots, S_N$ and computes the aggregated master public key and the helper decryption key as follows (which we highlight in blue):
  - **Attribute-independent public key:** Compute $[\hat{r}]_1 = \sum_{i \in [N]} [r_i]_1$. In addition, for each $i \in [N]$, compute the cross terms $[\hat{v}_i]_2 = \sum_{j \neq i} [t_i r_j]_2$.
  - **Attribute-specific public key:** For each attribute $a$, let $[\hat{u}_a]_1 = \sum_{i \in [N]: a \notin S_i} [u_i]_1$. In addition, for each $i \in [N]$, compute the cross terms $[\hat{w}_{a,i}]_1 = \sum_{j \neq i: a \notin S_j} [t_i u_j]_1$.

  Let $\mathcal{U} = \bigcup_{i \in [N]} S_i$ be the set of attributes associated with the users. The aggregated master public key is $\mathsf{mpk} = ([\hat{r}]_1, \{[\hat{u}_a]_1\}_{a \in \mathcal{U}})$. The helper decryption key $\mathsf{hsk}_i$ for user $i$ contains the slot components associated with slot $i$ from the CRS as well as the cross terms:

  $$\mathsf{hsk}_i = ([t_i]_2, [\alpha + yt_i]_2, [\hat{v}_i]_2, \{[\hat{w}_{a,i}]_1\}_{a \in \mathcal{U}}).$$

- **Encryption:** Let $P$ be a policy over a set of attributes $A = (a_1, \ldots, a_K) \subseteq \mathcal{U}$. We assume that $P$ has a linear secret sharing scheme over $\mathbb{Z}_p$ where each attribute is associated with a single share, which is an element of $\mathbb{Z}_p$.[1] To encrypt a message $[\mu]_T$ (i.e., we take the message to be an element of the target group $\mathbb{G}_T$) with respect to the policy $P$, the encrypter proceeds as follows:

[1] This restriction is for ease of exposition. Our actual construction (Construction 4.1) does not have this restriction.

  - Sample the encryption randomness $s \xleftarrow{\text{R}} \mathbb{Z}_p$ and $s_1, s_2 \xleftarrow{\text{R}} \mathbb{Z}_p$ such that $s_1 + s_2 = s$.[2]
  - Secret share $s_2$ according to the policy $P$ over $\mathbb{Z}_p$. Let $s_{2,1}, \ldots, s_{2,K} \in \mathbb{Z}_p$ be the shares of $s_2$ associated with the attributes $a_1, \ldots, a_K$ respectively. Recall that for ease of exposition, we are assuming that $P$ has a linear secret sharing scheme where each attribute is associated with a single share (i.e., a single element of $\mathbb{Z}_p$).
  - Compute the attribute-independent component $s_1[y]_1 - s[\hat{r}]_1 = [s_1 y - s\hat{r}]_1$. For each attribute $a_k \in A$, sample a blinding term $s'_k \xleftarrow{\text{R}} \mathbb{Z}_p$ and compute the attribute-specific component

$$\left(s_{2,k}[y]_1 - s'_k[\hat{u}_{a_k}]_1 \,, [s'_k]_2\right) = \left([s_{2,k}y - s'_k\hat{u}_{a_k}]_1 \,,\ [s'_k]_2\right).$$

  - The ciphertext then consists of the following group elements (which we highlight in purple):

$$\mathsf{ct} = \left([s\alpha]_\mathsf{T} + [\mu]_\mathsf{T}, [s]_1, [s_1 y - s\hat{r}]_1, \{[s_{2,k}y - s'_k\hat{u}_{a_k}]_1, [s'_k]_2\}_{k\in[K]}\right).$$

- **Decryption:** Suppose a user $i \in [N]$ has a set of attributes $S_i \subseteq \mathcal{U}$ that satisfies the policy $P$. The user's goal is to compute the blinding factor $[s\alpha]_\mathsf{T}$. To do so, the user proceeds as follows:
  - **Slot check:** First, the user uses their secret key $r_i$ together with the helper decryption components $[t_i]_2$ and $[\hat{v}_i]_2$ to compute

$$\begin{aligned}&[s_1 y - s\hat{r}]_1 \cdot [t_i]_2 + [s]_1 \cdot [\hat{v}_i]_2 + r_i \cdot [s]_1 \cdot [t_i]_2 \\ &\qquad = [s_1 y t_i - \textstyle\sum_{j\in[N]} s t_i r_j + \sum_{j\neq i} s t_i r_j + s t_i r_i]_\mathsf{T} \\ &\qquad = [s_1 y t_i]_\mathsf{T}.\end{aligned}$$

  - **Attribute check:** For each attribute $a_k$ that the user possesses, they use the slot component $[t_i]_2$ and the cross term $[\hat{w}_{a_k,i}]_1$ from their helper decryption key to compute

$$\begin{aligned}&[s_{2,k}y - s'_k\hat{u}_{a_k}]_1 \cdot [t_i]_2 + [\hat{w}_{a_k,i}]_1 \cdot [s'_k]_2 \\ &\qquad = [s_{2,k} y t_i - \textstyle\sum_{j\in[N]:a_k\notin S_j} s'_k t_i u_j + \sum_{j\neq i:a_k\notin S_j} s'_k t_i u_j]_\mathsf{T} \\ &\qquad = [s_{2,k} y t_i]_\mathsf{T}.\end{aligned}$$

    Note that this equality relies on the fact that $a_k \in S_i$, which means

$$\{j \in [N] : a_k \notin S_j\} = \{j \in [N] \setminus \{i\} : a_k \notin S_j\}.$$

[2] The schemes from [HLWW23, GLWW24] secret share the element $[y]_1$ from the CRS instead of the encryption randomness $s$. However, since the exponents $s$ and $y$ play similar roles in the ciphertext, we can interchange them. The variant we describe here is more amenable to our strategy for obtaining a scheme with a linear-size CRS.

Since $s_{2,1}, \ldots, s_{2,K}$ is a linear secret sharing of $s_2$, we can view each $[s_{2,k} y t_i]_T$ as a share of $[s_2 y t_i]_T$. If $S_i$ satisfies the policy, then the user can take a linear combination of these shares to reconstruct $[s_2 y t_i]_T$.

Since $s_1 + s_2 = s$, the user can now compute $[s_1 y t_i]_T + [s_2 y t_i]_T = [s y t_i]_T$. Finally, the user computes

$$[s]_1 \cdot [\alpha + y t_i]_2 - [s y t_i]_T = [s\alpha]_T,$$

which is sufficient to recover the message $[\mu]_T$ from $[s\alpha]_T + [\mu]_T$.

*Reducing the CRS Size.* The CRS size in the above scheme is quadratic due to the presence of the cross terms $[t_i u_j]_1$ for all $i \neq j$. These cross terms are needed to compute the attribute-specific component $\hat{w}_{a_k,i}$ of each user's helper decryption key. As shown above, the key relationship needed for decryption is that whenever $a_k \in S_i$, it holds that

$$[s'_k \hat{u}_{a_k}]_1 \cdot [t_i]_2 = \left[\textstyle\sum_{j \in [N]: a_k \notin S_j} s'_k t_i u_j\right]_T = [\hat{w}_{a_k,i}]_1 \cdot [s'_k]_2. \tag{1.1}$$

The work of [GLWW24] shows how to compress the CRS by choosing the exponents $t_i$ and $u_i$ in a *structured* way so that the set of cross terms $[t_i u_j]_1$ have a succinct description. Specifically, they take $t_i$ and $u_i$ to be powers. To illustrate, suppose $t_i = \tau^i$ and $u_i = \beta\tau^i$, where $\tau, \beta \xleftarrow{R} \mathbb{Z}_p$. In this way, the cross terms $t_i u_j$ can be written as $t_i u_j = \beta\tau^{i+j}$, which can be described compactly using just $2N$ group elements $[\beta\tau]_1, \ldots, [\beta\tau^{2N}]_1$. The savings come from the fact that multiple distinct pairs of $(i, j)$ can now share the *same* cross term. This seemingly already yields a scheme with a linear-size CRS (since there are now only $2N$ cross terms in the CRS).

The problem with this approach is that if the CRS contains $[\beta\tau]_1, \ldots, [\beta\tau^{2N}]_1$, it is simultaneously giving out the non-cross-terms $[t_i u_i]_1 = [\beta\tau^{2i}]_1$. This compromises security of the above construction since it would allow a user who does *not* have an attribute $a_k$ to nonetheless compute the term $[s'_k \hat{u}_{a_k} t_i]_T$ in Eq. 1.1. To preserve security, the work of [GLWW24] chooses $t_i, u_i$ so that the cross-terms have a compact description without simultaneously giving out the non-cross-terms. They achieve this by taking the powers from a "progression-free set" [ET36] instead of the integers $\{1, \ldots, N\}$. This leads to a scheme where the size of the CRS is $N^{1+o(1)}$, though the asymptotic improvement is only meaningful for very large values of $N$ (cf. [GGK25, Table 8]). For typical values of $N$, the size of the CRS would scale with $N^{\log_2 3} \approx N^{1.6}$.

*Using the Polynomial Basis.* In this work, we show that working in the Lagrange interpolation basis rather than the power basis from [GLWW24] enables a construction with a linear-size CRS. This idea of using the Lagrange interpolation basis for aggregation[3] has been used in a number of previous settings, includ-

[3] Specifically, we can view registered ABE as needing to devise a mechanism to *aggregate* user public keys into a short master public key (and then support encryption with respect to the aggregated key).

ing distributed threshold encryption [DP08], identity-based broadcast encryption [DPP07,Del07], polynomial commitments [KZG10], locally verifiable signatures [GV20], and batch arguments for NP [CEW25]. Our goal is still to design a mechanism such that the decrypter can satisfy a relation analogous to the attribute check shown in Eq. 1.1 whenever they have the attribute $a_k$. Conversely, they should not be able to combine components from the public parameters and their helper decryption key to satisfy the relation if they do not have the attribute. We now describe our approach to implement this:

- Let $Z(X) = \prod_{i \in [N]}(X - i)$ be the polynomial that vanishes on the indices $[N]$. All polynomials are defined over $\mathbb{Z}_p$ where $p$ is prime (i.e., $\mathbb{Z}_p$ is a field).
- For each $i \in [N]$, we define

$$L_i(X) = \prod_{j \in [N] \setminus \{i\}} (X - j) = \frac{Z(X)}{X - i} \tag{1.2}$$

  to be the basis polynomial that vanishes on the indices $[N] \setminus \{i\}$ and is nonzero at index $i$. Note that we do *not* normalize $L_i(X)$ to have value 1 at index $i$.
- In the scheme, we set the slot exponents to be $t_i = L_i(\tau)$ where $\tau \xleftarrow{R} \mathbb{Z}_p$. If we consider a parallel to pairing-based identity-based broadcast encryption schemes [DPP07,Del07], the slot exponents in our scheme share the same structure as the secret keys in the broadcast encryption schemes, but scaled up by the vanishing polynomial $Z(X)$. The scaling will be helpful for deriving the analogous attribute check from Eq. 1.1.
- Next, we modify how we compute the attribute-specific public keys at aggregation time. Let $S_1, \ldots, S_N$ be the attributes associated with the $N$ users. Specifically, for each attribute $a$, we define the polynomial

$$F_a(X) := \prod_{j \in [N] : a \notin S_j} (X - j). \tag{1.3}$$

  This is the polynomial whose roots correspond to the indices of users that do *not* possess the attribute. We take the attribute-specific public key to be $[\hat{u}_a]_2 = [F_a(\tau)]_2$.
- Observe now that for all indices $i \in [N]$ and all attributes $a$, the polynomial $F_a(X)$ divides $L_i(X)$ if and only if $a \in S_i$. Moreover, when $a \in S_i$, the quotient polynomial $F_{a,i}(X) := L_i(X)/F_a(X)$ has degree at most $N - 1$.
- We can now write down a similar relation for the attribute check from Eq. 1.1:

$$[s'_k]_1 \cdot [t_i]_2 = [s'_k L_i(\tau)]_\mathsf{T} = [s'_k F_{a_k}(\tau) F_{a_k,i}(\tau)]_\mathsf{T} = [F_{a_k,i}(\tau)]_1 \cdot [s'_k \hat{u}_{a_k}]_2.$$

  In particular, for each attribute $a$ and each user $i \in [N]$, we now define their attribute-specific helper decryption key $[\hat{w}_{a,i}]_1$ to be $\hat{w}_{a,i} = F_{a,i}(\tau)$. Since each $F_{a,i}$ is a polynomial of degree at most $N-1$, it suffices to publish encodings of the powers of $\tau$ in the CRS. That is, the CRS includes $[\tau]_1, [\tau^2]_1, \ldots, [\tau^{N-1}]_1$, and the aggregator can use these terms to construct the helper decryption terms $[\hat{w}_{a,i}]_1 = [F_{a,i}(\tau)]_1$ for all attributes $a$ and indices $i \in [N]$.

Putting all the pieces together, we now arrive at our new registered ABE scheme with a linear-size CRS:

- **Common reference string:** Let $N$ be the number of slots and sample $\alpha, \tau, y \xleftarrow{R} \mathbb{Z}_p$. The CRS now includes the following components:
  - the powers of $\tau$ used for key-generation and aggregation $[\boldsymbol{\tau}]_1$ and $[\boldsymbol{\tau}]_2$ where $\boldsymbol{\tau} = (\tau, \tau^2, \ldots, \tau^{N-1})$,
  - the encryption components $[\alpha]_T$ and $[y]_1$, and
  - the slot components $[y]_2, [y\tau]_2, \ldots, [y\tau^{N-2}]_2, [\alpha + y\tau^{N-1}]_2$.

  By construction, this consists of exactly $3N$ group elements.
- **Key-generation:** To generate a key for slot $i \in [N]$, the user samples $r_i \xleftarrow{R} \mathbb{Z}_p$. The public key consists of $[r_i]_1$ together with the cross terms $[r_i(\tau - i)]_2, [r_i\tau(\tau - i)]_2, \ldots, [r_i\tau^{N-2}(\tau - i)]_2$, which the user can compute from $[\boldsymbol{\tau}]_2$ published in the CRS. The secret key is $\mathsf{sk}_i = r_i$.
- **Aggregation:** Given public keys $\mathsf{pk}_1, \ldots, \mathsf{pk}_N$ with

$$\mathsf{pk}_i = ([r_i]_1, [r_i(\tau - i)]_2, [r_i\tau(\tau - i)]_2, \ldots, [r_i\tau^{N-2}(\tau - i)]_2),$$

  as well as their respective attribute sets $S_1, \ldots, S_N$, we compute the aggregated master public key and helper decryption components as follows:
  - **Pre-computed decryption components:** For each $i \in [N]$, compute $[t_i]_2 = [L_i(\tau)]_2$ and $[\alpha + yt_i]_2 = [\alpha + yL_i(\tau)]_2$, where $L_i$ is the polynomial from Eq. 1.2. These can be computed from $[\boldsymbol{\tau}]_2$ and the slot components $[y]_2, [y\tau]_2, \ldots, [y\tau^{N-2}]_2, [\alpha + y\tau^{N-1}]_2$ published in the CRS.
  - **Attribute-independent public key:** Compute $[\hat{r}]_1 = \sum_{i \in [N]} [r_i]_1$ as before. Then, for each $i \in [N]$, compute the cross terms $[\hat{v}_i]_2 = \sum_{j \neq i} [r_j L_i(\tau)]_2 = \sum_{j \neq i} [t_i r_j]_2$. Note that $[r_j L_i(\tau)]_2$ can be computed using the $[r_j(\tau - j)]_2, [r_j\tau(\tau - j)]_2, \ldots, [r_j\tau^{N-2}(\tau - j)]_2$ components from $\mathsf{pk}_j$. Here, we use the property that for all $j \neq i$, the polynomial $(X - j)$ is a factor of $L_i(X)$.
  - **Attribute-specific public key:** Let $\mathcal{U} = \bigcup_{i \in [N]} S_i$ be the set of attributes associated with the users. For each attribute $a \subset \mathcal{U}$, define the attribute-specific public key to be $[\hat{u}_a]_2 = [F_a(\tau)]_2$, where $F_a$ is the polynomial from Eq. 1.3. In addition, for each $i \in [N]$, compute the attribute-specific helper decryption key $[\hat{w}_{a,i}]_1 = [F_{a,i}(\tau)]_1$, where $F_{a,i}(\tau) = L_i(\tau)/F_a(\tau)$. As argued above, these terms can all be computed from $[\boldsymbol{\tau}]_1$ and $[\boldsymbol{\tau}]_2$ published in the CRS.

  The aggregated master public key is $\mathsf{mpk} = ([\hat{r}]_1, \{[\hat{u}_a]_2\}_{a \in \mathcal{U}})$. The helper decryption key $\mathsf{hsk}_i$ for user $i$ consists of the pre-computed decryption components and the cross terms: $\mathsf{hsk}_i = ([t_i]_2, [\alpha + yt_i]_2, [\hat{v}_i]_2, \{[\hat{w}_{a,i}]_1\}_{a \in \mathcal{U}})$.
- **Encryption:** Let $P$ be a policy over attributes $(a_1, \ldots, a_K)$ and as before, suppose $P$ has a linear secret sharing scheme over $\mathbb{Z}_p$. To encrypt a message $[\mu]_T$, the encrypter proceeds as follows:
  - Sample $s \xleftarrow{R} \mathbb{Z}_p$ and $s_1, s_2 \xleftarrow{R} \mathbb{Z}_p$ such that $s = s_1 + s_2$.
  - Secret share $s_2$ according to the policy $P$. Let $s_{2,1}, \ldots, s_{2,K} \in \mathbb{Z}_p$ be the shares associated with $a_1, \ldots, a_K$.

• The ciphertext is then

$$\mathsf{ct} = \big([s\alpha]_\mathsf{T} + [\mu]_\mathsf{T}, [s]_1, [s_1 y - s\hat{r}]_1, \{[s_{2,k} y - s'_k]_1, [s'_k \hat{u}_{a_k}]_2\}_{k \in [K]}\big),$$

where again, the encrypter samples $s'_k \xleftarrow{\mathrm{R}} \mathbb{Z}_p$ for all $k \in [K]$.

– **Decryption:** Decryption proceeds similarly to before. Suppose a user $i \in [N]$ has a set of attributes $S_i$ that satisfies the policy $P$. The user proceeds as follows:
  • **Slot check:** This is the same as before. Namely, the user uses their secret key $r_i$ together with the helper decryption components $[t_i]_2$ and $[\hat{v}_i]_2$ to compute

$$\begin{aligned}[s_1 y - s\hat{r}]_1 \cdot [t_i]_2 + [s]_1 \cdot [\hat{v}_i]_2 + r_i \cdot [s]_1 \cdot [t_i]_2 \\ &= [s_1 y t_i - \textstyle\sum_{j \in [N]} s r_j t_i + \sum_{j \neq i} s r_j t_i + s r_i t_i]_\mathsf{T} \\ &= [s_1 y t_i]_\mathsf{T},\end{aligned}$$

where we have used the fact that $\hat{r} = \sum_{j \in [N]} r_j$ and $\hat{v}_i = \sum_{j \neq i} r_j t_i$.

  • **Attribute check:** For each attribute $a_k$ that the user possesses, they use the cross term $[\hat{w}_{a_k,i}]_1$ and the slot component $[t_i]_2$ from their helper decryption key $\mathsf{hsk}_i$ to compute

$$\begin{aligned}[s_{2,k} y - s'_k]_1 \cdot [t_i]_2 + [\hat{w}_{a_k,i}]_1 \cdot [s'_k \hat{u}_{a_k}]_2 \\ &= [s_{2,k} y t_i - s'_k t_i + s'_k F_{a_k,i}(\tau) \cdot F_{a_k}(\tau)]_\mathsf{T} \\ &= [s_{2,k} y t_i]_\mathsf{T},\end{aligned}$$

where the final equality uses the fact that $F_{a_k,i}(\tau) \cdot F_{a_k}(\tau) = L_i(\tau) = t_i$ whenever $a_k \in S_i$. Once again, the decrypter recovers a share of $[s_2 y t_i]_\mathsf{T}$. If the decrypter has a set of attributes that satisfy the policy $P$, then they can interpolate to fully obtain $[s_2 y t_i]_\mathsf{T}$.

The rest of the decryption process proceeds exactly as before. The decrypter computes $[syt_i]_\mathsf{T} = [s_1 y t_i]_\mathsf{T} + [s_2 y t_i]_\mathsf{T}$ and $[s\alpha]_\mathsf{T} = [s]_1 \cdot [\alpha + y t_i]_2 - [syt_i]_\mathsf{T}$. This can then be used to recover the message from $[s\alpha]_\mathsf{T} + [\mu]_\mathsf{T}$.

We provide the formal description in Construction 4.1.

*Security Under a q-type Assumption.* We prove that our scheme satisfies security under a $q$-type assumption. Here, we sketch our proof strategy against an adversary that is not allowed to make any corruption queries in the security game (i.e., request the secret key for an honest user). For ease of exposition in the overview, we will also assume here that the adversary declares the slots associated with corrupted users at the beginning of the security game (though this relaxation is not required in our actual analysis). Even with this restriction, the adversary can still adaptively choose the public keys for the corrupted users and the attribute set for all users *after* seeing the scheme parameters. Similar to [GLWW24], we rely on a partitioning proof strategy. To carry out this proof strategy, we rely on a $q$-type assumption that captures the polynomial structure we embed. The inverse structure used in this assumption can be viewed as a strengthening of the strong Diffie-Hellman assumption previously used to analyze the soundness of the polynomial commitment scheme of [KZG10]. We state the assumption below:

- The assumption is parameterized by an integer $N$.
- Sample $\gamma \xleftarrow{R} \mathbb{Z}_p$ and $\tau \xleftarrow{R} \mathbb{Z}_p \setminus [N]$. Let $\beta = \sum_{i \in [N]} \frac{1}{\tau - i} \in \mathbb{Z}_p$.
- Given

$$\mathsf{params} = \begin{pmatrix} [\tau]_1, \ldots, [\tau^{N-1}]_1, [\tau]_2, \ldots, [\tau^{N-1}]_2, \\ [\beta]_1, [\frac{\gamma}{\tau-1}]_1, \ldots, [\frac{\gamma}{\tau-N}]_1, \\ [\gamma]_2, [\gamma\tau]_2, \ldots, [\gamma\tau^{N-2}]_2, [\gamma\beta]_2, [\gamma\beta\tau]_2, \ldots, [\gamma\beta\tau^{N-2}]_2 \end{pmatrix},$$

the goal is to distinguish the group element $[\gamma\beta^2\tau^{N-1}]_\mathsf{T}$ from a random element of $\mathbb{G}_\mathsf{T}$.

We show that this assumption holds unconditionally in the generic bilinear group model in the full version of this paper [SWW26]. We now provide a sketch of the partitioning argument underlying our security analysis. In the sketch, we focus on the core cancellations needed to simulate all of the components arising in the security analysis. We omit the additional randomization needed to generate the correct distribution. The cancellations illustrate the main idea underlying our reduction strategy while the additional randomization needed to obtain the right distribution is standard. We refer to the proof of Theorem 4.6 for the formal proof (with proper re-randomization).

- **Setup:** Let $N$ be the number of users. We consider an instance of the assumption with parameter $N$. For ease of exposition, recall that we also assume that the adversary declares the indices of the corrupted users $\mathcal{C} \subseteq [N]$. Let $\mathcal{H} = [N] \setminus \mathcal{C}$ be the indices of the honest users.
- **Simulating the CRS:** First, the reduction needs to simulate the components of the CRS from the components given in the assumption.
  - The reduction sets $[\boldsymbol{\tau}]_1$ and $[\boldsymbol{\tau}]_2$ using the corresponding terms from the assumption.
  - Next, the reduction implicitly defines $y = \gamma\beta$. This allows the reduction to simulate the slot components $[y]_2, [y\tau]_2, \ldots, [y\tau^{N-2}]_2$ using the corresponding terms from the assumption. Since $\beta = \sum_{i \in [N]} \frac{1}{\tau - i}$, the reduction can also simulate $[y]_1 = [\gamma\beta]_1 = \sum_{i \in [N]} [\frac{\gamma}{\tau - i}]_1$.
  - Finally, the reduction implicitly sets $\alpha = -y\tau^{N-1} = -\gamma\beta\tau^{N-1}$. Then it can compute $[\alpha]_\mathsf{T} = [-\tau^{N-1}]_1 \cdot [\gamma\beta]_2$. Observe now that we have the cancellation $\alpha + y\tau^{N-1} = 0$, which allows the reduction to simulate the CRS component $[\alpha + y\tau^{N-1}]_2$ even though $[\gamma\beta\tau^{N-1}]_2$ is not (and cannot be) given out in the assumption.
- **Key-generation queries:** For the honest users $i \in \mathcal{H}$, the reduction will implicitly set the user's secret key to be $r_i = \frac{\gamma}{\tau - i}$. In this case, the reduction can simulate the public key $[r_i]_1 = [\frac{\gamma}{\tau - i}]_1$ using the term from the assumption. For the cross terms $[r_i(\tau - i)\tau^j]_2$ for $j = 0, 1, \ldots, N-2$ in the public key,

we can rely on the cancellation $r_i(\tau - i) = \frac{\gamma}{\tau - i} \cdot (\tau - i) = \gamma$. Thus, the cross terms can be simulated using $[\gamma]_2, \ldots, [\gamma\tau^{N-2}]_2$.

- **Challenge ciphertext:** For each corrupted user $i \in \mathcal{C}$, the adversary needs to specify the public key $[r_i]_1$. To simplify the analysis, we work in the registered-key model [RY07] where we additionally require the adversary to provide the associated secret key $r_i \in \mathbb{Z}_p$ when registering. A scheme with security in the registered-key model can be generically lifted to a scheme in the standard definition simply by having each user include a non-interactive zero-knowledge proof of knowledge of the secret key at registration time; we refer to [LWW25] for a formal proof of this statement.

Let $P$ be the challenge policy and $[\mu]_T$ be the challenge message. When simulating the challenge ciphertext, the reduction will implicitly set $s_1 = \sum_{i \in \mathcal{H}} \frac{1}{\tau - i}$ and $s_2 = \sum_{i \in \mathcal{C}} \frac{1}{\tau - i}$. Recall from the construction that $s_1$ is the randomness associated with the slot check while $s_2$ is the randomness associated with the attribute check. For the honest users $i \in \mathcal{H}$, the adversary does not know the associated secret key $r_i$ whereas for the corrupted users $i \in \mathcal{C}$, their set of attributes $S_i$ does not satisfy the challenge policy $P$. We now describe how the reduction simulates the components of the challenge ciphertext for this choice of $s_1$ and $s_2$:

- Since $\mathcal{H}$ and $\mathcal{C}$ form a partition of $[N]$ and $s = s_1 + s_2$, this means $[s]_1 = \sum_{i \in [N]} [\frac{1}{\tau - i}]_1 = [\beta]_1$, which the reduction has from the assumption.
- Next, for the attribute-independent component, we use the fact that for $i \in \mathcal{H}$, the reduction implicitly set $r_i = \frac{\gamma}{\tau - i}$. Since $y = \gamma\beta$, we have

$$s_1 y = \gamma\beta \sum_{i \in \mathcal{H}} \frac{1}{\tau - i} = \beta \sum_{i \in \mathcal{H}} r_i = s \sum_{i \in \mathcal{H}} r_i.$$

In this case,

$$s_1 y - s\hat{r} = s \sum_{i \in \mathcal{H}} r_i - s \left( \sum_{i \in \mathcal{H}} r_i + \sum_{i \in \mathcal{C}} r_i \right) = -s \sum_{i \in \mathcal{C}} r_i.$$

Since the reduction knows $r_i \in \mathbb{Z}_p$ for all $i \in \mathcal{C}$ (recall we are working in the registered-key model), it can simulate the attribute-independent ciphertext component as $[s_1 y - s\hat{r}]_1 = -\sum_{i \in \mathcal{C}} r_i [s]_1 = -\sum_{i \in \mathcal{C}} r_i [\beta]_1$.
- For the attribute-specific components, we first have that

$$\hat{u}_{a_k} = F_{a_k}(\tau) = \prod_{i \in [N] : a_k \notin S_i} (\tau - i).$$

Now, by the (information-theoretic) security of the secret sharing scheme, for every corrupted index $i \in \mathcal{C}$, there exists a secret share $(\tilde{s}_{i,1}, \ldots, \tilde{s}_{i,K})$ of 1 with respect to the policy $P$ where $\tilde{s}_{i,k} = 0$ whenever $a_k \in S_i$. This is because $S_i$ does not satisfy the policy so the subset of shares where

$a_k \in S_i$ must be consistent with *every* possible secret. The reduction now implicitly sets the shares of $(s_{2,1}, \ldots, s_{2,K})$ to be

$$s_{2,k} = \sum_{i \in C} \frac{\tilde{s}_{i,k}}{\tau - i}.$$

Since each $(\tilde{s}_{i,1}, \ldots, \tilde{s}_{i,K})$ is a secret share of 1, we can appeal to linearity of the secret sharing scheme to conclude that $(s_{2,1}, \ldots, s_{2,K})$ is a valid secret sharing of $\sum_{i \in C} \frac{1}{\tau - i} = s_2$, as required. Finally, to complete the proof, the reduction sets $s'_k = \gamma\beta \sum_{i \in C : a_k \notin S_i} \frac{\tilde{s}_{i,k}}{\tau - i}$. Since $\tilde{s}_{i,k} = 0$ whenever $a_k \in S_i$ (and $y = \gamma\beta$), this means

$$s'_k = \gamma\beta \sum_{i \in C : a_k \notin S_i} \frac{\tilde{s}_{i,k}}{\tau - i} = \gamma\beta \sum_{i \in C} \frac{\tilde{s}_{i,k}}{\tau - i} = s_{2,k} y,$$

which now yields our desired cancellation: $s_{2,k} y - s'_k = 0$. This allows the reduction to simulate $[s_{2,k} y - s'_k]_1$. For the remaining attribute-specific component, we have

$$s'_k \hat{u}_{a_k} = \gamma\beta \sum_{i \in C : a_k \notin S_i} \frac{\tilde{s}_{i,k}}{\tau - i} \cdot \prod_{j \in [N] : a_k \notin S_j} (\tau - j) = \gamma\beta \sum_{i \in C : a_k \notin S_i} \tilde{s}_{i,k} \cdot f_{i,k}(\tau),$$

where each $f_{i,k}$ is a polynomial of degree at most $N - 2$. This is because $\hat{u}_{a_k}$ has degree at most $N - 1$ since the aggregation algorithm constructs $\hat{u}_{a_k}$ only if there is at least one index $i \in [N]$ such that $a_k \in S_i$. Thus, the reduction can use the components $\{[\gamma\beta\tau^j]_2\}_{j \in [0, N-2]}$ to simulate $[s'_k \hat{u}_{a_k}]_2$.
- Let $[z]_T$ be the challenge element. The reduction sets the encryption of $[\mu]_T$ to be $[\mu]_T - [z]_T$. Observe that if $z = \gamma\beta^2\tau^{N-1}$, then for the above choice of variables ($s = \beta$ and $\alpha = -\gamma\beta\tau^{N-1}$), this means $\mu - z = \mu + s\alpha$, and the ciphertext is distributed exactly as in the real scheme. Conversely if $z \xleftarrow{R} \mathbb{Z}_p$, then the ciphertext perfectly hides the message.

The above sketch illustrates how to use the components from the assumption to simulate the corresponding components in the scheme. We refer to the proof of Theorem 4.6 for the formal description (that properly re-randomizes the CRS, public keys, and ciphertexts).

*Adaptive Security in the Random Oracle Model.* Technically, our reduction strategy described above proves a slightly stronger notion of security: adaptive security where the adversary cannot make any corruption queries (i.e., ask to see the secret keys for a user with an honestly-generated key). Previously, the work of [FWW23] described a generic transformation that takes any registered ABE scheme that is secure in a model without corruptions and transforms it into a scheme that is adaptively secure in the random oracle model. Strictly speaking, the [FWW23] transformation only yields a scheme that is selectively secure in the policy. When the size of the policy is *a priori* bounded, we can use standard complexity leveraging to obtain a scheme that is adaptively secure (see Corollary 4.9). Taken together, our work also yields the first pairing-based adaptively secure registered ABE scheme with a linear-size CRS that supports monotone Boolean formulas.

*Extending to a Large Index Space and its Benefits.* In the scheme described above, each user's public key is associated with a slot index $i \in [N]$. However, there is no restriction that the indices have to be drawn from the set $\{1, \ldots, N\}$. Indeed, each user could have chosen an *arbitrary* index $i \in \mathbb{Z}_p$, and as long as every user picks a distinct index, aggregation is successful. If $I \subseteq \mathbb{Z}_p$ represents the set of identities associated with the different users, then we would modify the above aggregation algorithm to set $Z(X) = \prod_{i \in I}(X - i)$ as the polynomial that vanishes on the users' indices. The user polynomial $L_i(X)$ from Eq. 1.2 and the attribute polynomial $F_a(X)$ from Eq. 1.3 would be defined analogously with respect to $I$ instead. Namely, $L_i(X) = \prod_{j \in I \setminus \{i\}}(X - j)$ and $F_a(X) = \prod_{j \in I : a \notin S_j}(X - j)$. Essentially, the basic version described above corresponds to the special case where $I = [N]$. When proving security (for a specific set of identities $I$), we consider a modified version of the assumption where $\beta = \sum_{i \in I} \frac{1}{\tau - i}$ and the assumption gives out $\left[\frac{\gamma}{\tau - i_1}\right]_1, \ldots, \left[\frac{\gamma}{\tau - i_N}\right]_1$ where $i_1, \ldots, i_N \in I$ are the elements of $I$. We state the formal version in Assumption 4.4. Since the index set $I$ is hardcoded into the assumption, we only prove security against adversaries that commit to the index set in advance. For this reason, our scheme for a large index space (Corollary 4.8) does not satisfy full adaptive security.

As noted earlier, the advantage of a slotted registered ABE scheme with a large index space is that users do not have to coordinate when generating their public key. They can simply pick a random slot index $i \xleftarrow{\text{R}} \mathbb{Z}_p$ and generate keys with respect to index $i$. With overwhelming probability, their chosen indices will be distinct from those chosen by other users. In previous schemes with a smaller index space, if users chose random indices, there would be a good chance that their choices would collide and their keys could not be aggregated together. One way around this is to have some coordination with the key curator when generating keys to avoid such collisions. However, this has limitations. For example, a user might want to generate a single public key and have it be used across multiple registered ABE systems run by different key curators. To get around this coordination, prior works like that of [GLWW23] developed a transformation where a public key would consist of multiple public keys for different random indices in the base system. At aggregation time, the key curator would run a matching algorithm to associate each user with a distinct index (from the ones they made available) so that none collide. This incurs a logarithmic blowup in key sizes and has the added complexity of needing to implement the matching algorithm. In contrast, if the scheme supports a large index space, users can simply choose a random index and know with very high probability that there will be no collisions.

For completeness, we show in the full version of this paper [SWW26] that the same powers-of-two-style transformation from [GHMR18, HLWW23] suffices to lift a slotted registered ABE scheme with large indices to a standard registered

ABE scheme (that supports dynamic registration). The transformed scheme automatically supports stateless key-generation as described above. We note that our transformation from the statically secure scheme to the adaptively secure one only applies in the setting with a small index space. Achieving adaptive security with a large index space (while retaining our other efficiency properties) is an interesting challenge.

## 1.2 Additional Related Work

*Registration-based Cryptography.* The goal of registration-based cryptography is to enable expressive encryption capabilities without needing to rely on any central authority. This paradigm has been successfully integrated into a multitude of settings, including notions like registration-based encryption (i.e., registered identity-based encryption) [GHMR18, GHM+19, GV20, CES21, GKMR23, DKL+23, FKdP23], registered ABE (see Table 1), registered functional encryption [FFM+23, DPY24, PST25], distributed broadcast encryption [WQZD10, BZ14, KMW23, FWW23, GKPW24, CW24, CHW25, WW25, AMR26, GY26b, GY26a], threshold encryption with silent setup [GKPW24, GHK+25, WW26, GWWW26], and distributed monotone-policy encryption [ADM+24, DJWW25, CW26, AGY26].

*Cross-term Cancellation and Polynomials.* The cross-term cancellation technique underlying pairing-based registered ABE schemes (e.g., [HLWW23]) has facilitated many other pairing-based cryptographic primitives, including vector commitments [CF13], batch arguments [WW22, GLWW24, CEW25], and aggregate signatures [HWW25]. Because of the need to publish cross terms, many of these constructions (e.g., [CF13, WW22, HLWW23, HWW25]) require a quadratic-size CRS. A common theme in many of these settings is that subsequent constructions show that by encoding things as polynomials it is possible to avoid needing to publish quadratically-many cross terms. This idea of working in the Lagrange polynomial basis to enable more efficient aggregation has been used in a variety of settings, including distributed threshold encryption [DP08], identity-based broadcast encryption [DPP07, Del07], polynomial commitments [KZG10], locally-verifiable signatures [GV22], and batch arguments for NP [CEW25]. We expect these ideas to provide a general template for reducing the CRS size in other cryptographic schemes that currently rely on a cross-term cancellation technique (which is the case for many pairing-based registration-based cryptographic schemes).

*Comparison with* [GHK+25]. The work of [GHK+25] proposes a modular framework for building registration-based encryption schemes by designing special-purpose witness encryption schemes for specific relations. Notably, their work provides the first registered ABE scheme with a linear-size CRS that supports the class of conjunctions (and by concatenation, the class of DNF policies). To obtain the registered ABE scheme for conjunctions, they rely on a special-purpose witness encryption for a set membership policy, and they show how to express a conjunction policy as a set membership policy. Since it is unclear how to encode more complex policies like a monotone Boolean formula as a set membership policy, we cannot directly apply their framework to obtain registered ABE for policies beyond conjunctions (and DNFs). Moreover, the security analysis in their framework critically relies on extractable witness encryption, which in turn necessitates the use of the generic group model. In this work, we show how to directly obtain an algebraic construction of registered ABE that can support general policies (i.e., monotone span programs) and whose security can be based on a $q$-type assumption in the plain model.

## 2 Preliminaries

Throughout this work, we write $\lambda$ to denote the security parameter. For integers $m, n \in \mathbb{Z}$ with $m \leq n$, we write $[m, n] := \{m, \ldots, n\}$ and, provided $n \in \mathbb{N}$, $[n] := [1, n]$. For a modulus $p \in \mathbb{N}$, we write $\mathbb{Z}_p$ to denote the ring of integers modulo $p$. We let $\{0,1\}^k$ denote bit-strings of length $k$ and assume they can be implicitly interpreted as elements of $\{0, 1, \ldots, 2^k - 1\}$. For a set $S$, we write $\{x_i\}_{i \in S}$ to denote the set of *pairs* $\{(i, x_i) : i \in S\}$. In particular, $\{x_i\}_{i \in S}$ specifies both the set $S$ and the association between each index $i \in S$ and the corresponding element $x_i$. We call $\{x_i\}_{i \in S}$ a sequence if either $S = [n]$ for some $n \in \mathbb{N}$ or $S = \mathbb{N}$. When $S$ is a finite set, we write $x \xleftarrow{\text{R}} S$ to denote a uniform random sample from $S$. When $\mathcal{D}$ is a distribution (or a probabilistic algorithm), we write $x \leftarrow \mathcal{D}$ to denote a random draw from $\mathcal{D}$. For a polynomial $F(X)$ of degree at most $N$ over $\mathbb{Z}_p$, we define its coefficient vector $\mathbf{f} = (f_1, f_2, \ldots, f_{N+1}) \in \mathbb{Z}_p^{N+1}$ such that $F(X) = \sum_{i \in [N+1]} f_i X^{i-1}$.

We use boldface lowercase letters (e.g., $\mathbf{u}, \mathbf{v}$) to denote vectors and boldface uppercase letters (e.g., $\mathbf{A}, \mathbf{B}$) to denote matrices. We use non-boldface letters to denote their components; namely, we write $\mathbf{u} = (u_1, \ldots, u_n)$. We write $\mathsf{poly}(\lambda)$ to denote a function that is upper bounded by a fixed polynomial in $\lambda$ and $\mathsf{negl}(\lambda)$ to denote a function that is $o(\lambda^{-c})$ for all constants $c \in \mathbb{N}$. We say an algorithm is efficient if it runs in probabilistic polynomial time in the length of its input. We say two (ensembles of) distributions $\mathcal{D}_0 = \{\mathcal{D}_{0,\lambda}\}_{\lambda \in \mathbb{N}}$ and $\mathcal{D}_1 = \{\mathcal{D}_{1,\lambda}\}_{\lambda \in \mathbb{N}}$ are computationally indistinguishable if, for all efficient adversaries $\mathcal{A}$, there exists a negligible function $\mathsf{negl}(\cdot)$ such that for all $\lambda \in \mathbb{N}$,

$$|\Pr[\mathcal{A}(1^\lambda, x) = 1 : x \leftarrow \mathcal{D}_{0,\lambda}] - \Pr[\mathcal{A}(1^\lambda, x) = 1 : x \leftarrow \mathcal{D}_{1,\lambda}]| = \mathsf{negl}(\lambda).$$

In the full version of this paper [SWW26], we review some additional preliminaries on prime-order pairing groups and linear secret sharing schemes.

## 3 Registered Attribute-Based Encryption

Following [HLWW23], we focus on a simpler notion of *slotted* registered ABE, where each user in the system is assigned a *slot index* used for key generation, and the key curator runs an *aggregation* algorithm that takes all users' slot indices, public keys, and attributes and outputs a master public key. This can be compiled into a standard registered ABE scheme that supports dynamic registration [HLWW23]. For completeness, we include the usual definition of registered ABE in the full version of this paper [SWW26]. There, we also show how to adapt the transformation of [HLWW23] from slotted registered ABE to standard registered ABE in the large-index setting. As we show there, the ability to support large indices immediately implies support for stateless key generation, in which users can sample their public key without knowledge of the current state of the system.

### 3.1 Slotted Registered Attribute-Based Encryption

We recall the syntax and definitions for slotted registered ABE. Our definition is adapted from the corresponding definition in [HLWW23], but generalized to support an arbitrary index space (e.g., an index space of exponential size). Specifically, in a slotted registered ABE scheme, each public key is associated with an index $\mathsf{id} \in \mathcal{I}$ from an index space $\mathcal{I}$, and we only support aggregation of public keys associated with distinct indices. In [HLWW23], the index space was fixed to the integers $\mathcal{I} = \{1, \ldots, N\}$, where $N$ is the total number of users in the system. This means that users must either coordinate to generate their keys with respect to distinct indices, or alternatively, users have to generate keys for multiple indices so that there is a way to associate each user with a unique index. In this work, we consider a more general setting where the index space can have exponential size, and we support aggregating any collection of $N$ public keys as long as each one is still associated with a distinct index. Observe that in this setting, each of the $N = \mathsf{poly}(\lambda)$ users can generate their key with respect to a *random* index, and with overwhelming probability, all of the keys will have a distinct index. Supporting a large index space is thus useful for enabling stateless key generation, in which users can generate their keys independently of all other users in the system. We now give the formal definition:

**Definition 3.1 (Slotted Registered ABE).** *Let $\mathcal{U} = \{\mathcal{U}_\lambda\}_{\lambda \in \mathbb{N}}$ be an attribute universe and $\mathcal{P} = \{\mathcal{P}_\lambda\}_{\lambda \in \mathbb{N}}$ be a set of policies over $\mathcal{U}$. Let $\mathcal{I} = \{\mathcal{I}_\lambda\}_{\lambda \in \mathbb{N}}$ be an index space. A slotted registered ABE scheme with attribute universe $\mathcal{U}$, policy space $\mathcal{P}$, and index space $\mathcal{I}$ is a tuple of algorithms $\Pi_{\mathsf{sRABE}} = (\mathsf{Setup}, \mathsf{KeyGen}, \mathsf{IsValid}, \mathsf{Aggregate}, \mathsf{Encrypt}, \mathsf{Decrypt})$ with the following properties:*

- $\mathsf{Setup}(1^\lambda, 1^N) \to \mathsf{crs}$: *On input the security parameter $\lambda$ and a number of slots $N$, the setup algorithm outputs a common reference string $\mathsf{crs}$. We assume that $\mathsf{crs}$ implicitly contains the security parameter $1^\lambda$ and a description of the message space $\mathcal{M}_\lambda$ associated with the scheme.*
- $\mathsf{KeyGen}(\mathsf{crs}, \mathsf{id}) \to (\mathsf{pk}_{\mathsf{id}}, \mathsf{sk}_{\mathsf{id}})$: *On input the common reference string $\mathsf{crs}$ and an index $\mathsf{id} \in \mathcal{I}_\lambda$, the key-generation algorithm outputs a public key $\mathsf{pk}_{\mathsf{id}}$ and a secret decryption key $\mathsf{sk}_{\mathsf{id}}$ for index $\mathsf{id}$.*
- $\mathsf{IsValid}(\mathsf{crs}, \mathsf{id}, \mathsf{pk}_{\mathsf{id}}) \to b$: *On input the common reference string $\mathsf{crs}$, an index $\mathsf{id} \in \mathcal{I}_\lambda$, and a public key $\mathsf{pk}_{\mathsf{id}}$, the key-validation algorithm outputs a bit $b \in$*

$\{0,1\}$ *indicating whether or not* $\mathsf{pk}_{\mathsf{id}}$ *is valid. This algorithm is deterministic. In certain instances, this algorithm may be omitted.*

- $\mathsf{Aggregate}(\mathsf{crs}, \{(\mathsf{pk}_{\mathsf{id}}, S_{\mathsf{id}})\}_{\mathsf{id} \in I}) \to (\mathsf{mpk}, \{\mathsf{hsk}_{\mathsf{id}}\}_{\mathsf{id} \in I})$*: On input the common reference string* $\mathsf{crs}$ *and a collection of public keys and associated attributes* $\{(\mathsf{pk}_{\mathsf{id}}, S_{\mathsf{id}})\}_{\mathsf{id} \in I}$ *where* $|I| = N$*, the aggregation algorithm outputs the master public key* $\mathsf{mpk}$ *and a collection of helper decryption keys* $\{\mathsf{hsk}_{\mathsf{id}}\}_{\mathsf{id} \in I}$*. This algorithm is deterministic. We assume that the master public key* $\mathsf{mpk}$ *and the helper decryption keys* $\mathsf{hsk}_{\mathsf{id}}$ *implicitly contain (from* $\mathsf{crs}$*) the security parameter* $1^\lambda$ *and a description of the message space* $\mathcal{M}_\lambda$ *associated with the scheme.*
- $\mathsf{Encrypt}(\mathsf{mpk}, P, \mu) \to \mathsf{ct}$*: On input the master public key* $\mathsf{mpk}$*, an access policy* $P \in \mathcal{P}_\lambda$*, and a message* $\mu \in \mathcal{M}_\lambda$*, the encryption algorithm outputs a ciphertext* $\mathsf{ct}$.
- $\mathsf{Decrypt}(\mathsf{sk}_{\mathsf{id}}, \mathsf{hsk}_{\mathsf{id}}, \mathsf{ct}) \to \mu$*: On input a secret key* $\mathsf{sk}_{\mathsf{id}}$*, a helper decryption key* $\mathsf{hsk}_{\mathsf{id}}$*, and a ciphertext* $\mathsf{ct}$*, the decryption algorithm outputs either a message* $\mu \in \mathcal{M}_\lambda$ *or a special symbol* $\mu = \perp$ *to indicate decryption failure.*

**Definition 3.2 (Completeness).** *Let* $\Pi_{\mathsf{sRABE}} = (\mathsf{Setup}, \mathsf{KeyGen}, \mathsf{IsValid}, \mathsf{Aggregate}, \mathsf{Encrypt}, \mathsf{Decrypt})$ *be a slotted registered ABE scheme with index space* $\mathcal{I} = \{\mathcal{I}_\lambda\}_{\lambda \in \mathbb{N}}$*. We say it is* complete *if, for all parameters* $\lambda, N \in \mathbb{N}$*, all* $\mathsf{crs}$ *in the support of* $\mathsf{Setup}(1^\lambda, 1^N)$*, and all indices* $\mathsf{id} \in \mathcal{I}_\lambda$*, the following holds:*

$$\Pr\left[\mathsf{IsValid}(\mathsf{crs}, \mathsf{id}, \mathsf{pk}_{\mathsf{id}}) = 1 : (\mathsf{pk}_{\mathsf{id}}, \mathsf{sk}_{\mathsf{id}}) \leftarrow \mathsf{KeyGen}(\mathsf{crs}, \mathsf{id})\right] = 1.$$

**Definition 3.3 (Correctness).** *Let* $\Pi_{\mathsf{sRABE}} = (\mathsf{Setup}, \mathsf{KeyGen}, \mathsf{IsValid}, \mathsf{Aggregate}, \mathsf{Encrypt}, \mathsf{Decrypt})$ *be a slotted registered ABE scheme with index space* $\mathcal{I} = \{\mathcal{I}_\lambda\}_{\lambda \in \mathbb{N}}$*. We say it is* correct *if, for all parameters* $\lambda, N \in \mathbb{N}$*, all but a negligible fraction of* $\mathsf{crs}$ *in the support of* $\mathsf{Setup}(1^\lambda, 1^N)$*, all index sets* $I \subseteq \mathcal{I}_\lambda$ *where* $|I| = N$*, all indices* $\mathsf{id} \in I$*,* $(\mathsf{pk}_{\mathsf{id}}, \mathsf{sk}_{\mathsf{id}}) \leftarrow \mathsf{KeyGen}(\mathsf{crs}, \mathsf{id})$*, all collections of public keys* $\{\mathsf{pk}_{\mathsf{id}'} : \mathsf{IsValid}(\mathsf{crs}, \mathsf{id}', \mathsf{pk}_{\mathsf{id}'}) = 1\}_{\mathsf{id}' \in I \setminus \{\mathsf{id}\}}$*, all messages* $\mu \in \mathcal{M}_\lambda$ *where* $\mathcal{M}_\lambda$ *is the message space associated with* $\mathsf{crs}$*, all attribute sets* $\{S_{\mathsf{id}'}\}_{\mathsf{id}' \in I}$ *with each* $S_{\mathsf{id}'} \subseteq \mathcal{U}_\lambda$*, and all policies* $P \in \mathcal{P}_\lambda$ *such that* $S_{\mathsf{id}}$ *satisfies* $P$*, the following holds:*

$$\Pr\left[\mathsf{Decrypt}(\mathsf{sk}_{\mathsf{id}}, \mathsf{hsk}_{\mathsf{id}}, \mathsf{ct}) = \mu\right] = 1,$$

*where*

$$\begin{aligned}(\mathsf{mpk}, \{\mathsf{hsk}_{\mathsf{id}'}\}_{\mathsf{id}' \in I}) &\leftarrow \mathsf{Aggregate}(\mathsf{crs}, \{(\mathsf{pk}_{\mathsf{id}'}, S_{\mathsf{id}'})\}_{\mathsf{id}' \in I}) \\ \mathsf{ct} &\leftarrow \mathsf{Encrypt}(\mathsf{mpk}, P, \mu).\end{aligned}$$

**Definition 3.4 (Compactness).** *Let* $\Pi_{\mathsf{sRABE}} = (\mathsf{Setup}, \mathsf{KeyGen}, \mathsf{IsValid}, \mathsf{Aggregate}, \mathsf{Encrypt}, \mathsf{Decrypt})$ *be a slotted registered ABE scheme. We say it is* compact *if there exists a universal polynomial* $\mathsf{poly}(\cdot,\cdot,\cdot)$ *such that the master public key* $\mathsf{mpk}$ *and each helper decryption key* $\mathsf{hsk}$ *output by* $\mathsf{Aggregate}$ *are* $\mathsf{poly}(\lambda, |A|, \log N)$ *size, where* $A$ *is the union of all attribute sets input to aggregation.*

**Definition 3.5 (Adaptive Security).** *Let* $\Pi_{\mathsf{sRABE}} = (\mathsf{Setup}, \mathsf{KeyGen}, \mathsf{IsValid}, \mathsf{Aggregate}, \mathsf{Encrypt}, \mathsf{Decrypt})$ *be a slotted registered ABE scheme with attribute universe* $\mathcal{U} = \{\mathcal{U}_\lambda\}_{\lambda \in \mathbb{N}}$*, policy space* $\mathcal{P} = \{\mathcal{P}_\lambda\}_{\lambda \in \mathbb{N}}$*, and index space* $\mathcal{I} = \{\mathcal{I}_\lambda\}_{\lambda \in \mathbb{N}}$*. The adaptive security game between an adversary* $\mathcal{A}$ *and a challenger is parameterized by a positive integer-valued polynomial* $N = N(\lambda)$*, a bit* $b \in \{0,1\}$*, and a security parameter* $\lambda$*; it consists of the following phases:*

- **Setup phase:** *The challenger samples* $\mathsf{crs} \leftarrow \mathsf{Setup}(1^\lambda, 1^N)$*, which it provides to the adversary* $\mathcal{A}$*. It additionally initializes a counter* $\mathsf{ctr} = 0$*, an empty set* $\mathcal{C}$ *to keep track of corrupted users, and an empty dictionary* $\mathsf{D}$ *to keep track of key-generation queries.*
- **Query phase:** *During the query phase, the adversary* $\mathcal{A}$ *can make the following queries:*
  - **Key-generation query:** *In a key-generation query, the adversary specifies an index* $\mathsf{id} \in \mathcal{I}_\lambda$*. In response, the challenger generates* $(\mathsf{pk}_{\mathsf{id}}, \mathsf{sk}_{\mathsf{id}}) \leftarrow \mathsf{KeyGen}(\mathsf{crs}, \mathsf{id})$ *and provides* $\mathsf{pk}_{\mathsf{id}}$ *to* $\mathcal{A}$*. It also increments the counter* $\mathsf{ctr} = \mathsf{ctr} + 1$ *and adds the mapping* $\mathsf{D}[\mathsf{ctr}] = (\mathsf{id}, \mathsf{pk}_{\mathsf{id}}, \mathsf{sk}_{\mathsf{id}})$ *to the dictionary.*
  - **Corruption query:** *In a corruption query, the adversary specifies a counter value* $c \in [\mathsf{ctr}]$*. In response, the challenger looks up the tuple* $(\mathsf{id}, \mathsf{pk}_{\mathsf{id}}, \mathsf{sk}_{\mathsf{id}}) = \mathsf{D}[c]$ *and gives* $\mathsf{sk}_{\mathsf{id}}$ *to the adversary.*
- **Challenge phase:** *For each* $i \in [N]$*, the adversary* $\mathcal{A}$ *specifies a tuple* $(c_i, \mathsf{id}_i^*, S_i^*, \mathsf{pk}_i^*)$ *where either* $c_i \in [\mathsf{ctr}]$ *to reference a challenger-generated key or* $c_i = \perp$ *to reference a key outside this set. The adversary additionally submits a challenge policy* $P^* \subset \mathcal{P}_\lambda$ *and messages* $\mu_0^*, \mu_1^* \in \mathcal{M}_\lambda$ *where* $\mathcal{M}_\lambda$ *is the message space associated with* $\mathsf{crs}$*. First, the challenger defines* $I = \{\mathsf{id}_i^* : i \in [N]\}$*. If* $|I| \neq N$ *(i.e., the adversary specified two public keys for the same slot index), the challenger halts with output* 0*. Next, for each* $i \in [N]$*, the challenger proceeds as follows:*
  - *If* $c_i \in [\mathsf{ctr}]$*, the challenger retrieves* $(\mathsf{id}_i, \mathsf{pk}_i, \mathsf{sk}_i) \leftarrow \mathsf{D}[c_i]$*. If* $\mathsf{id}_i \neq \mathsf{id}_i^*$*, the challenger halts with output* 0*. Otherwise, the challenger sets* $\mathsf{pk}_{\mathsf{id}_i} = \mathsf{pk}_i$ *and* $S_{\mathsf{id}_i} = S_i^*$*. If the adversary previously issued a corruption query on counter* $c_i$*, then the challenger adds the index* $\mathsf{id}_i$ *to* $\mathcal{C}$*.*
  - *If* $c_i = \perp$*, then the challenger sets* $\mathsf{id}_i = \mathsf{id}_i^*$*,* $\mathsf{pk}_{\mathsf{id}_i} = \mathsf{pk}_i^*$*, and* $S_{\mathsf{id}_i} = S_i^*$*. It then adds* $\mathsf{id}_i$ *to* $\mathcal{C}$*.*

  *For each index* $\mathsf{id} \in I$*, the challenger also checks that* $\mathsf{IsValid}(\mathsf{crs}, \mathsf{id}, \mathsf{pk}_{\mathsf{id}}) = 1$ *and halts with output* 0 *if any check fails. If all checks pass, the challenger computes* $(\mathsf{mpk}, \{\mathsf{hsk}_{\mathsf{id}}\}_{\mathsf{id} \in I}) \leftarrow \mathsf{Aggregate}(\mathsf{crs}, \{(\mathsf{pk}_{\mathsf{id}}, S_{\mathsf{id}})\}_{\mathsf{id} \in I})$ *and a challenge ciphertext* $\mathsf{ct} \leftarrow \mathsf{Encrypt}(\mathsf{mpk}, P^*, \mu_b^*)$*. The challenger provides* $\mathsf{ct}$ *to* $\mathcal{A}$*.*
- **Output phase:** *At the end of the experiment, the adversary* $\mathcal{A}$ *outputs a bit* $b^*$*, which is the output of the game.*

*We say an adversary* $\mathcal{A}$ *is admissible for the adaptive security game if, for all* $\mathsf{id} \in \mathcal{C}$*, the set* $S_{\mathsf{id}}$ *does not satisfy* $P^*$ *(i.e., the attributes associated with corrupted indices do not satisfy the challenge policy). Next, we define the adversary's advantage in the adaptive security game with parameter* $N$ *to be*

$$\mathsf{Adv}_{\mathcal{A},N}(\lambda) := |\Pr[b^* = 1 : b = 0] - \Pr[b^* = 1 : b = 1]|.$$

*Finally, we say that* $\Pi_{\mathsf{sRABE}}$ *is adaptively secure if there exists a negligible function* $\mathsf{negl}(\cdot)$ *such that for all efficient admissible adversaries* $\mathcal{A}$ *and all positive integer-valued polynomials* $N = N(\lambda)$*, there exists a positive polynomial* $\mathsf{poly}(\cdot)$ *such that for all* $\lambda \in \mathbb{N}$*,*

$$\mathsf{Adv}_{\mathcal{A},N}(\lambda) \leq \mathsf{poly}(\lambda) \cdot \mathsf{negl}(\lambda). \tag{3.1}$$

**Definition 3.6 (Relaxed Notions of Security).** *Let* $\Pi_{\mathsf{sRABE}}$ *be a slotted registered ABE scheme with policy space* $\mathcal{P} = \{\mathcal{P}_\lambda\}_{\lambda \in \mathbb{N}}$ *and index space* $\mathcal{I} = \{\mathcal{I}_\lambda\}_{\lambda \in \mathbb{N}}$*. We will also consider the following relaxed variants of adaptive security:*

- **Index-set-selective security:** *For a positive integer-valued polynomial* $N = N(\lambda)$*, a collection of index sets* $I = \{I_\lambda\}_{\lambda \in \mathbb{N}}$ *where each* $I_\lambda \subseteq \mathcal{I}_\lambda$ *and* $|I_\lambda| = N(\lambda)$*, a bit* $b \in \{0,1\}$*, and a security parameter* $\lambda$*, we define the index-set-selective security game exactly as the adaptive security game in Definition 3.5, except we impose the following additional restrictions on the adversary* $\mathcal{A}$*:*
  - *The adversary can only make key-generation queries on indices* $\mathsf{id} \in I_\lambda$*.*
  - *In the challenge phase, the adversary can only specify tuples* $(c_i, \mathsf{id}_i^*, S_i^*, \mathsf{pk}_i^*)$ *where* $\mathsf{id}_i^* \in I_\lambda$*.*

  *In other words, the set of indices is fixed to be* $I_\lambda$ *in the index-set-selective security game. Then, we say that* $\Pi_{\mathsf{sRABE}}$ *satisfies index-set-selective security if there exists a negligible function* $\mathsf{negl}(\cdot)$ *such that for all polynomials* $N = N(\lambda)$*, all collections of index sets* $I = \{I_\lambda\}_{\lambda \in \mathbb{N}}$ *where* $|I_\lambda| = N(\lambda)$*, and all efficient admissible adversaries* $\mathcal{A}$*, there exists a positive polynomial* $\mathsf{poly}(\cdot)$ *such that for all* $\lambda \in \mathbb{N}$*,*

  $$\mathsf{Adv}_{\mathcal{A},N,I}(\lambda) := |\Pr[b^* = 1 : b = 0] - \Pr[b^* = 1 : b = 1]| \leq \mathsf{poly}(\lambda) \cdot \mathsf{negl}(\lambda)$$

  *in the index-set-selective security game with parameters* $(N, I)$*.*
- **Policy-selective security:** *We define the policy-selective security game to be the adaptive security game from Definition 3.5, except we require that the adversary* $\mathcal{A}$ *declare the challenge policy* $P^* \in \mathcal{P}_\lambda$ *at the beginning of the security game (before the setup phase). We say* $\Pi_{\mathsf{sRABE}}$ *satisfies policy-selective security if Eq. 3.1 holds for all efficient admissible adversaries* $\mathcal{A}$ *and all polynomials* $N = N(\lambda)$ *in the policy-selective security game.*
- **Adaptive security without corruptions:** *We define the adaptive security without corruptions game to be the adaptive security game except we do not allow the adversary to make any corruption queries during the query phase. We then say* $\Pi_{\mathsf{sRABE}}$ *satisfies adaptive security without corruptions if Eq. 3.1 holds for all efficient admissible adversaries* $\mathcal{A}$ *and all polynomials* $N = N(\lambda)$ *in the adaptive security without corruptions game.*

*Combinations of these relaxations are defined in the natural way. For instance, in analyzing a scheme that satisfies index-set-selective security without corruptions, we fix the index set* $I = \{I_\lambda\}_{\lambda \in \mathbb{N}}$ *in the security game and disallow the adversary from making any corruption queries.*

**Definition 3.7 (Large Index Space).** *Let* $\Pi_{\mathsf{sRABE}}$ *be a slotted registered ABE scheme with index space* $\mathcal{I} = \{\mathcal{I}_\lambda\}_{\lambda \in \mathbb{N}}$. *We say that* $\Pi_{\mathsf{sRABE}}$ *has a* large index space *if* $1/|\mathcal{I}_\lambda| = \mathsf{negl}(\lambda)$.

*Remark 3.8* (Amplifying Security). We now describe two known techniques for amplifying the security of a (slotted) registered ABE scheme:

- **Security without corruptions to security with corruptions.** The work of [FWW23] describes a generic transformation that compiles a slotted registered ABE scheme with policy-selective security *without* corruptions into a slotted registered ABE scheme with policy-selective security that supports corruptions in the random oracle model. The transformation of [FWW23] only incurs constant overhead in the scheme parameters.
- **Policy-selective security to adaptive security.** If the policy size is *a priori* bounded, and we additionally have a policy-selective slotted registered ABE scheme with sub-exponential security, then using standard complexity leveraging (where the reduction guesses the adversary's policy at the beginning of the security game), we can obtain an adaptively secure slotted registered ABE scheme. Complexity leveraging will scale up all of the scheme parameters by a $\mathsf{poly}(K)$ factor, where $K$ is the bound on the policy size.

By composing the two transformations, we can generically lift a slotted registered ABE scheme that is secure without corruptions into an adaptively secure slotted registered ABE scheme in the random oracle model. Note that we cannot directly apply complexity leveraging to go from a scheme without corruptions into a scheme with corruptions; this is because the naïve complexity leveraging strategy of guessing the indices of the corrupted users would incur a $2^N$ loss in the security reduction, where $N$ is the number of users. As a result, complexity leveraging would incur a $\mathsf{poly}(N)$ overhead in the scheme parameters, and the resulting scheme no longer satisfies the efficiency requirements of slotted registered ABE. For this reason, we need both transformations to lift a scheme that has security without corruptions into one that is adaptively secure.

*Registered-key Model.* To simplify the exposition, we analyze correctness and security of our construction in the *registered-key model* [RY07], which assumes that all of the public keys appearing in the correctness and security games are in the support of the key-generation algorithm. It is straightforward to compile a scheme with correctness and security in the registered-key model into a scheme that satisfies the full correctness and security requirements in Definitions 3.3 and 3.5 by having the user include a (simulation-sound) non-interactive zero-knowledge (NIZK) proof of knowledge of the associated secret key. Aggregation would only proceed if all of the public keys come with an accepting NIZK proof. The work of [LWW25] provides a formal proof of this transformation in the setting of multi-authority registered ABE. Specializing their analysis to a single authority yields a proof for standard registered ABE (in the registered-key model). We note that previous registered ABE schemes [HLWW23, ZZGQ23, GLWW24] essentially incorporated an algebraic

NIZK proof of knowledge as part of the scheme itself; we believe a similar mechanism could be integrated into our scheme as well to avoid reliance on the registered-key model. For ease of exposition, we elide this extra complication and instead focus on the core ideas that enable a registered ABE scheme with a linear-size CRS. We now give the correctness and security definitions in the registered-key model:

**Definition 3.9 (Correctness in the Registered-Key Model).** *We say a slotted registered ABE scheme $\Pi_{\mathsf{sRABE}}$ satisfies correctness in the registered-key model if, in the correctness definition (Definition 3.3), we replace the quantification over collections of public keys* $\{\mathsf{pk}_{\mathsf{id}'} : \mathsf{IsValid}(\mathsf{crs}, \mathsf{id}', \mathsf{pk}_{\mathsf{id}'}) = 1\}_{\mathsf{id}' \in \mathcal{I} \setminus \{\mathsf{id}\}}$ *with quantification over collections* $\{\mathsf{pk}_{\mathsf{id}'} : \mathsf{pk}_{\mathsf{id}'}$ *is in the support of* $\mathsf{KeyGen}(\mathsf{crs}, \mathsf{id}')\}_{\mathsf{id}' \in \mathcal{I} \setminus \{\mathsf{id}\}}$.

**Definition 3.10 (Adaptive Security in the Registered-Key Model).** *We say a slotted registered ABE scheme $\Pi_{\mathsf{sRABE}}$ satisfies adaptive security in the registered-key model if, in the adaptive security definition (Definitions 3.5), during the challenge phase, for every $i \in [N]$ for which the adversary's tuple $(c_i, \mathsf{id}_i^*, S_i^*, \mathsf{pk}_i^*)$ has $c_i = \perp$, the adversary must additionally specify the secret key $\mathsf{sk}_i^*$ and the randomness $r_i^*$ such that $(\mathsf{pk}_i^*, \mathsf{sk}_i^*) = \mathsf{KeyGen}(\mathsf{crs}, \mathsf{id}_i^*; r_i^*)$. Since all of the public keys in this experiment are in the support of the honest key-generation algorithm, the challenger no longer runs the* IsValid *predicate in the adaptive security game. We define the relaxed variants from Definitions 3.6 in the registered-key model in an analogous manner.*

*Remark 3.11 (Removing the* IsValid *Algorithm in the Registered-Key Model).* When we work in the registered-key model, we will drop the IsValid algorithm from the description of the slotted registered ABE scheme. This is because, per Definitions 3.9 and 3.10, we only need to consider correctness and security in the setting where all public keys are in the support of KeyGen, and thus are always valid.

## 4 Slotted Registered ABE with Linear-Size CRS

In this section, we show how to use asymmetric prime-order pairing groups to construct a slotted registered ABE scheme with a linear-size CRS in the registered-key model. Our scheme supports a large index space (i.e., $\{0,1\}^\lambda$) and any policy that can be described by a linear secret sharing scheme. We refer to Sect. 1.1 for an overview of our construction.

**Construction 4.1 (Slotted Registered ABE).** Let $\lambda$ be a security parameter. Let GroupGen be a prime-order asymmetric pairing-group generator that outputs groups of order $p = p(\lambda)$. Let $\mathcal{U} = \{\mathcal{U}_\lambda\}_{\lambda \in \mathbb{N}}$ be an attribute universe and let $\mathcal{P} = \{\mathcal{P}_\lambda\}_{\lambda \in \mathbb{N}}$ be an ensemble where each $\mathcal{P}_\lambda$ is a collection of policies that can be described by a linear secret sharing scheme for $\mathcal{U}$ over $\mathbb{Z}_p$. We construct a slotted registered ABE scheme $\Pi_{\mathsf{sRABE}} = (\mathsf{Setup}, \mathsf{KeyGen}, \mathsf{Aggregate}, \mathsf{Encrypt}, \mathsf{Decrypt})$ with attribute universe $\mathcal{U}$, policy space $\mathcal{P}$, and index space $\mathcal{I} = \{\{0,1\}^\lambda\}_{\lambda \in \mathbb{N}}$ in the registered-key model as follows:

- $\mathsf{Setup}(1^\lambda, 1^N)$: On input the security parameter $\lambda$ and number of slots $N$, the setup algorithm proceeds as follows:
  - Sample a prime-order pairing group $\mathcal{G} = (\mathbb{G}_1, \mathbb{G}_2, \mathbb{G}_T, p, g_1, g_2, e) \leftarrow \mathsf{GroupGen}(1^\lambda)$ as well as random generators $\hat{g}_1 \xleftarrow{R} \mathbb{G}_1 \setminus \{g_1^0\}$ and $\hat{g}_2 \xleftarrow{R} \mathbb{G}_2 \setminus \{g_2^0\}$. Define $[1]_1 := \hat{g}_1$ and $[1]_2 := \hat{g}_2$.
  - Sample random exponents $\alpha, \tau, y \xleftarrow{R} \mathbb{Z}_p$.
  - Let $\boldsymbol{\tau} = (1, \tau, \tau^2, \ldots, \tau^{N-1}) \in \mathbb{Z}_p^N$ and $\mathbf{y} = (y, y\tau, y\tau^2, \ldots, y\tau^{N-2}, \alpha + y\tau^{N-1}) \in \mathbb{Z}_p^N$.

  Output the common reference string $\mathsf{crs} = (\mathcal{G}, [\alpha]_T, [\boldsymbol{\tau}]_1, [\boldsymbol{\tau}]_2, [y]_1, [\mathbf{y}]_2)$. The message space is $\mathcal{M}_\lambda := \mathbb{G}_T$.
- $\mathsf{KeyGen}(\mathsf{crs}, \mathsf{id})$: On input the common reference string $\mathsf{crs}$ where $\mathsf{crs} = (\mathcal{G}, [\alpha]_T, [\boldsymbol{\tau}]_1, [\boldsymbol{\tau}]_2, [y]_1, [\mathbf{y}]_2)$ and an index $\mathsf{id} \in \{0,1\}^\lambda$, the key-generation algorithm first samples a random exponent $r_{\mathsf{id}} \xleftarrow{R} \mathbb{Z}_p$. Interpret $\mathsf{id}$ as an integer in $[0, 2^\lambda - 1]$ and parse $[\boldsymbol{\tau}]_2 = ([1]_2, [\tau]_2, [\tau^2]_2, \ldots, [\tau^{N-1}]_2)$. The algorithm computes

$$\begin{aligned}[\mathbf{r}'_{\mathsf{id}}]_2 &= \left(r_{\mathsf{id}}([\tau]_2 - \mathsf{id}[1]_2), r_{\mathsf{id}}([\tau^2]_2 - \mathsf{id}[\tau]_2), \ldots, r_{\mathsf{id}}([\tau^{N-1}]_2 - \mathsf{id}[\tau^{N-2}]_2)\right) \\ &= \left([r_{\mathsf{id}}(\tau - \mathsf{id})]_2, [r_{\mathsf{id}}(\tau - \mathsf{id})\tau]_2, \ldots, [r_{\mathsf{id}}(\tau - \mathsf{id})\tau^{N-2}]_2\right).\end{aligned}$$

  Finally, it outputs the public key $\mathsf{pk}_{\mathsf{id}} = ([r_{\mathsf{id}}]_1, [\mathbf{r}'_{\mathsf{id}}]_2)$ and the secret key $\mathsf{sk}_{\mathsf{id}} = r_{\mathsf{id}}$.
- $\mathsf{Aggregate}(\mathsf{crs}, \{(\mathsf{pk}_{\mathsf{id}}, S_{\mathsf{id}})\}_{\mathsf{id} \in I})$: On input the common reference string $\mathsf{crs} = (\mathcal{G}, [\alpha]_T, [\boldsymbol{\tau}]_1, [\boldsymbol{\tau}]_2, [y]_1, [\mathbf{y}]_2)$ and a collection of public keys $\mathsf{pk}_{\mathsf{id}} = ([r_{\mathsf{id}}]_1, [\mathbf{r}'_{\mathsf{id}}]_2)$ and associated attributes $S_{\mathsf{id}} \subseteq \mathcal{U}_\lambda$ for indices $\mathsf{id} \in I$ (where $|I| = N$), the aggregation algorithm proceeds as follows:
  - Compute the attribute-independent public key $[\hat{r}]_1 = \sum_{\mathsf{id} \in I} [r_{\mathsf{id}}]_1$.
  - Next, let $A = \bigcup_{\mathsf{id} \in I} S_{\mathsf{id}}$. For each attribute $a \in A$, define the polynomial

$$F_a(X) := \prod_{\mathsf{id} \in I : a \notin S_{\mathsf{id}}} (X - \mathsf{id}).$$

    By construction, $F_a$ is a polynomial of degree at most $N-1$ because $a$ must be in at least one $S_{\mathsf{id}}$. Let $\mathbf{f}_a \in \mathbb{Z}_p^N$ be its associated coefficient vector. Then, compute the attribute-specific public key

$$[\hat{u}_a]_2 = \mathbf{f}_a^{\mathsf{T}}[\boldsymbol{\tau}]_2 = [F_a(\tau)]_2.$$

  - Define the master public key to be $\mathsf{mpk} = (\mathcal{G}, [\alpha]_T, [y]_1, [\hat{r}]_1, \{[\hat{u}_a]_2\}_{a \in A})$.

  Next, to compute the helper decryption keys, the aggregation algorithm proceeds as follows:
  - Define the vanishing polynomial $Z_I(X) = \prod_{\mathsf{id} \in I}(X - \mathsf{id})$ associated with $I$.
  - For each $\mathsf{id} \in I$, define $L_{\mathsf{id}}(X) := Z_I(X)/(X - \mathsf{id}) = \prod_{\mathsf{id}' \in I \setminus \{\mathsf{id}\}}(X - \mathsf{id}')$. By construction, $L_{\mathsf{id}}$ is a monic polynomial of degree at most $N-1$. Let $\boldsymbol{\ell}_{\mathsf{id}} \in \mathbb{Z}_p^N$ be its associated coefficient vector.

- For each distinct $\mathsf{id}, \mathsf{id}' \in I$, define $L_{\mathsf{id},\mathsf{id}'}(X) := L_{\mathsf{id}}(X)/(X - \mathsf{id}') = \prod_{\mathsf{id}'' \in I \setminus \{\mathsf{id},\mathsf{id}'\}}(X - \mathsf{id}'')$. By construction, $L_{\mathsf{id},\mathsf{id}'}$ is a polynomial of degree at most $N-2$. Let $\boldsymbol{\ell}_{\mathsf{id},\mathsf{id}'} \in \mathbb{Z}_p^{N-1}$ be its associated coefficient vector.
- For each $\mathsf{id} \in I$, compute the attribute-independent decryption components

$$\begin{aligned}
[\hat{v}_{\mathsf{id},1}]_2 &= \boldsymbol{\ell}_{\mathsf{id}}^{\mathsf{T}}[\boldsymbol{\tau}]_2 = [L_{\mathsf{id}}(\tau)]_2, \\
[\hat{v}_{\mathsf{id},2}]_2 &= \boldsymbol{\ell}_{\mathsf{id}}^{\mathsf{T}}[\mathbf{y}]_2 = [\alpha + y \cdot L_{\mathsf{id}}(\tau)]_2, \\
[\hat{v}_{\mathsf{id},3}]_2 &= \sum_{\mathsf{id}' \in I \setminus \{\mathsf{id}\}} \boldsymbol{\ell}_{\mathsf{id},\mathsf{id}'}^{\mathsf{T}}[\mathbf{r}'_{\mathsf{id}'}]_2 = \sum_{\mathsf{id}' \in I \setminus \{\mathsf{id}\}} [r_{\mathsf{id}'}(\tau - \mathsf{id}') \cdot L_{\mathsf{id},\mathsf{id}'}(\tau)]_2 \\
&= \sum_{\mathsf{id}' \in I \setminus \{\mathsf{id}\}} [r_{\mathsf{id}'} \cdot L_{\mathsf{id}}(\tau)]_2.
\end{aligned}$$

- For each attribute $a \in S_{\mathsf{id}}$, define the polynomial $F_{a,\mathsf{id}}(X) := L_{\mathsf{id}}(X)/F_a(X) = \prod_{\mathsf{id}' \in I \setminus \{\mathsf{id}\} : a \in S_{\mathsf{id}'}}(X - \mathsf{id}')$. By construction, $F_{a,\mathsf{id}}$ has degree at most $N-1$. Let $\mathbf{f}_{a,\mathsf{id}} \in \mathbb{Z}_p^N$ be its associated coefficient vector. Define the attribute-specific decryption component

$$[\hat{w}_{a,\mathsf{id}}]_1 = \mathbf{f}_{a,\mathsf{id}}^{\mathsf{T}}[\boldsymbol{\tau}]_1 = [F_{a,\mathsf{id}}(\tau)]_1.$$

- For each index $\mathsf{id} \in I$, let the helper decryption key be

$$\mathsf{hsk}_{\mathsf{id}} = (\mathcal{G}, [\hat{v}_{\mathsf{id},1}]_2, [\hat{v}_{\mathsf{id},2}]_2, [\hat{v}_{\mathsf{id},3}]_2, \{[\hat{w}_{a,\mathsf{id}}]_1\}_{a \in S_{\mathsf{id}}}).$$

Output the master public key $\mathsf{mpk}$ and the helper decryption key $\mathsf{hsk}_{\mathsf{id}}$ for each $\mathsf{id} \in I$.

– $\mathsf{Encrypt}(\mathsf{mpk}, (\mathbf{M}, \rho), [\mu]_{\mathsf{T}})$: On input the master public key

$$\mathsf{mpk} = (\mathcal{G}, [\alpha]_{\mathsf{T}}, [y]_1, [\hat{r}]_1, \{[\hat{u}_a]_2\}_{a \in A}),$$

a policy $(\mathbf{M}, \rho)$ where $\mathbf{M} \in \mathbb{Z}_p^{\ell \times n}$ and $\rho \colon [\ell] \to A$ is a row-labeling function, and a message $[\mu]_{\mathsf{T}} \in \mathbb{G}_{\mathsf{T}}$, the encryption algorithm starts by sampling $s_1, s_2 \xleftarrow{\text{R}} \mathbb{Z}_p$ and sets $s = s_1 + s_2$. Then, it constructs the ciphertext components as follows:

- **Message-embedding components:** Let $[c_1]_{\mathsf{T}} = s[\alpha]_{\mathsf{T}} + [\mu]_{\mathsf{T}}$ and $[c_2]_1 = [s]_1$.
- **Index-specific component:** Let $[c_3]_1 = s_1[y]_1 - s[\hat{r}]_1$.
- **Attribute-specific components:** Sample $v_2, \ldots, v_n \xleftarrow{\text{R}} \mathbb{Z}_p$ and define $\mathbf{v} = (1, v_2, \ldots, v_n)^{\mathsf{T}}$. For each $k \in [\ell]$, sample $s'_k \xleftarrow{\text{R}} \mathbb{Z}_p$. Let $[c_{4,k}]_1 = (s_2 \mathbf{m}_k^{\mathsf{T}} \mathbf{v})[y]_1 - [s'_k]_1$ and $[c_{5,k}]_2 = s'_k[\hat{u}_{\rho(k)}]_2$ where $\mathbf{m}_k^{\mathsf{T}}$ is the $k^{\text{th}}$ row of $\mathbf{M}$.

Finally, output the ciphertext as follows:

$$\mathsf{ct} = ((\mathbf{M}, \rho), [c_1]_{\mathsf{T}}, [c_2]_1, [c_3]_1, \{([c_{4,k}]_1, [c_{5,k}]_2)\}_{k \in [\ell]}). \tag{4.1}$$

– $\mathsf{Decrypt}(\mathsf{sk}_{\mathsf{id}}, \mathsf{hsk}_{\mathsf{id}}, \mathsf{ct})$: On input a secret key $\mathsf{sk}_{\mathsf{id}} = r_{\mathsf{id}}$, a helper decryption key $\mathsf{hsk}_{\mathsf{id}}$, and a ciphertext $\mathsf{ct}$ where

$$\mathsf{hsk}_{\mathsf{id}} = (\mathcal{G}, [\hat{v}_{\mathsf{id},1}]_2, [\hat{v}_{\mathsf{id},2}]_2, [\hat{v}_{\mathsf{id},3}]_2, \{[\hat{w}_{a,\mathsf{id}}]_1\}_{a \in S_{\mathsf{id}}}), \text{ and}$$
$$\mathsf{ct} = ((\mathbf{M}, \rho), [c_1]_\mathsf{T}, [c_2]_1, [c_3]_1, \{([c_{4,k}]_1, [c_{5,k}]_2)\}_{k \in [\ell]}),$$

the decryption algorithm proceeds as follows:

- If the user's set of attributes $S_{\mathsf{id}}$ is not authorized by $(\mathbf{M}, \rho)$, output $\perp$.
- Otherwise, let $J = \{k \in [\ell] : \rho(k) \in S_{\mathsf{id}}\}$ be the indices of the rows of $\mathbf{M}$ associated with the attributes in the user's attribute set $S_{\mathsf{id}}$. Write $J = \{k_1, \ldots, k_{|J|}\}$.
- Now, let $\mathbf{M}_J$ be the matrix formed by taking the subset of rows in $\mathbf{M}$ indexed by $J$. Since $S_{\mathsf{id}}$ is authorized, there exists a vector $\boldsymbol{\omega}_{S_{\mathsf{id}}} = (\omega_{S_{\mathsf{id}},1}, \ldots, \omega_{S_{\mathsf{id}},|J|}) \in \mathbb{Z}_p^{|J|}$ such that $\boldsymbol{\omega}_{S_{\mathsf{id}}}^{\mathsf{T}} \mathbf{M}_J = \mathbf{e}_1^{\mathsf{T}}$.
- Compute the following values:

$$[d_{\mathsf{id}}]_\mathsf{T} = (r_{\mathsf{id}}[c_2]_1 + [c_3]_1) \cdot [\hat{v}_{\mathsf{id},1}]_2 + [c_2]_1 \cdot [\hat{v}_{\mathsf{id},3}]_2,$$
$$[d_{\mathsf{attrib}}]_\mathsf{T} = \sum_{j \in [|J|]} \omega_{S_{\mathsf{id}},j} \cdot ([c_{4,k_j}]_1 \cdot [\hat{v}_{\mathsf{id},1}]_2 + [\hat{w}_{\rho(k_j),\mathsf{id}}]_1 \cdot [c_{5,k_j}]_2).$$

- Finally, compute and output

$$[\mu]_\mathsf{T} = [c_1]_\mathsf{T} - [c_2]_1 \cdot [\hat{v}_{\mathsf{id},2}]_2 + [d_{\mathsf{id}}]_\mathsf{T} + [d_{\mathsf{attrib}}]_\mathsf{T}. \quad (4.2)$$

*Correctness and Compactness.* We now state the correctness and compactness theorems for Construction 4.1, but defer their formal proofs to the full version of this paper [SWW26].

**Theorem 4.2 (Correctness).** *Construction 4.1 is correct in the registered-key model.*

**Theorem 4.3 (Compactness).** *Construction 4.1 is compact.*

## 4.1 Security Analysis

We prove that our slotted scheme achieves index-set-selective security without corruptions in the registered-key model from the following assumption. In the full version of this paper [SWW26], we show this assumption holds unconditionally in the generic bilinear group model [Sho97,BBG05].

**Assumption 4.4 (Main Assumption).** Let $\mathsf{GroupGen}$ be an asymmetric prime-order pairing-group generator. For a security parameter $\lambda$, a positive integer-valued polynomial $N = N(\lambda)$, a set sequence $S = \{S_\lambda\}_{\lambda \in \mathbb{N}}$ where $S_\lambda \subseteq \{0, 1, \ldots, 2^\lambda - 1\}$ and $|S_\lambda| = N(\lambda)$, and a bit $b \in \{0, 1\}$, we define the distribution $\mathcal{D}_{\lambda,N,S,b}$ as follows:

- Sample $\mathcal{G} = (\mathbb{G}_1, \mathbb{G}_2, \mathbb{G}_T, p, g_1, g_2, e) \leftarrow \mathsf{GroupGen}(1^\lambda)$.
- Sample random generators $\hat{g}_1 \xleftarrow{R} \mathbb{G}_1 \setminus \{g_1^0\}$ and $\hat{g}_2 \xleftarrow{R} \mathbb{G}_2 \setminus \{g_2^0\}$. Define $[1]_1 := \hat{g}_1$ and $[1]_2 := \hat{g}_2$.
- Sample $\gamma \xleftarrow{R} \mathbb{Z}_p$ and $\tau \xleftarrow{R} \mathbb{Z}_p \setminus S_\lambda$. Let $\beta = \sum_{i \in [N]} \frac{1}{\tau - s_i} \in \mathbb{Z}_p$ where $S_\lambda = \{s_1, \ldots, s_N\}$, and define

$$\mathsf{params} = \begin{pmatrix} [1]_1, [\tau]_1, \ldots, [\tau^{N-1}]_1, [1]_2, [\tau]_2, \ldots, [\tau^{N-1}]_2, \\ [\beta]_1, [\frac{\gamma}{\tau - s_1}]_1, \ldots, [\frac{\gamma}{\tau - s_N}]_1, \\ [\gamma]_2, [\gamma\tau]_2, \ldots, [\gamma\tau^{N-2}]_2, [\gamma\beta]_2, [\gamma\beta\tau]_2, \ldots, [\gamma\beta\tau^{N-2}]_2 \end{pmatrix}.$$

- If $b = 0$, let $T = [\gamma\beta^2\tau^{N-1}]_T$, and if $b = 1$, let $T \xleftarrow{R} \mathbb{G}_T$. Output $(\mathcal{G}, \mathsf{params}, T)$.

We say Assumption 4.4 holds with respect to $\mathsf{GroupGen}$, a positive integer-valued function $N = N(\lambda)$, and a set sequence $S$ if the distributions $\mathcal{D}_0 = \{\mathcal{D}_{\lambda,N,S,0}\}_{\lambda \in \mathbb{N}}$ and $\mathcal{D}_1 = \{\mathcal{D}_{\lambda,N,S,1}\}_{\lambda \in \mathbb{N}}$ are computationally indistinguishable. We further say that Assumption 4.4 holds with respect to $\mathsf{GroupGen}$ if there exists a negligible function $\mathsf{negl}(\cdot)$ such that for all efficient adversaries $\mathcal{A}$, all polynomials $N = N(\lambda)$, and all set sequences $S = \{S_\lambda\}_{\lambda \in \mathbb{N}}$ where $S_\lambda \subseteq \{0, 1, \ldots, 2^\lambda - 1\}$ and $|S_\lambda| = N(\lambda)$, there exists a polynomial $\mathsf{poly}(\lambda) \geq 1$ such that for all $\lambda \in \mathbb{N}$,

$$\begin{aligned} |\Pr[\mathcal{A}(1^\lambda, \mathsf{params}) = 1 : \mathsf{params} \leftarrow \mathcal{D}_{\lambda,N,S,0}] - \\ \Pr[\mathcal{A}(1^\lambda, \mathsf{params}) = 1 : \mathsf{params} \leftarrow \mathcal{D}_{\lambda,N,S,1}]| \leq \mathsf{poly}(\lambda) \cdot \mathsf{negl}(\lambda). \end{aligned}$$

*Remark 4.5 (Structure of Assumption* 4.4). Before stating the security analysis, we first discuss the structure of Assumption 4.4. In particular, we note that the assumption does *not* hold if we set $\gamma = 1$. This is because, for all $i \in [N]$, we can write

$$\frac{\tau}{\tau - s_i} = \frac{\tau - s_i}{\tau - s_i} + \frac{s_i}{\tau - s_i} = 1 + \frac{s_i}{\tau - s_i}.$$

Since the elements $s_i$ are fixed (and known to the adversary), the adversary can now compute (when $\gamma = 1$)

$$\sum_{i \in [N]} [1]_1 + s_i \cdot \left[\frac{1}{\tau - s_i}\right]_1 = \sum_{i \in [N]} \left[\frac{\tau}{\tau - s_i}\right]_1 = [\beta\tau]_1.$$

Now, the adversary can pair $[\tau\beta]_1$ with $[\beta\tau^{N-2}]_2$ and obtain $[\beta^2\tau^{N-1}]_T$, which completely breaks the assumption (when $\gamma = 1$). If we introduce the randomizing exponent $\gamma$, then the above procedure would allow the adversary to compute $[\gamma\beta\tau]_1$.[4] However, since the other $\mathbb{G}_2$ components either lack $\beta$ or also include $\gamma$, the adversary cannot simply pair this element with another term

[4] Strictly speaking, computing this term would also require giving out $[\gamma]_1$, which the assumption does not do. However, even if the assumption gave out $[\gamma]_1$, the attack would not apply.

in the assumption to reach the challenge $[\gamma\beta^2\tau^{N-1}]_T$. Essentially, the extra $\gamma$ term is introduced to prevent this attack. As we show in the full version of this paper [SWW26], adding $\gamma$ is sufficient to prove the assumption holds unconditionally in the generic bilinear group model [Sho97, BBG05].

**Theorem 4.6 (Index-Set-Selective Security without Corruptions).** *Suppose Assumption 4.4 holds with respect to* GroupGen. *Then Construction 4.1 is index-set-selectively secure without corruptions in the registered-key model.*

*Proof* Due to space constraints, we defer the security proof to the full version of this paper [SWW26].

**Corollary 4.7 (Slotted Registered ABE from Pairings).** *Let $\lambda$ be a security parameter and* GroupGen *be an asymmetric prime-order pairing-group generator that outputs groups of order $p = p(\lambda)$. Suppose Assumption 4.4 holds with respect to* GroupGen. *Let $\mathcal{U} = \{\mathcal{U}_\lambda\}_{\lambda\in\mathbb{N}}$ be any attribute universe and let $\mathcal{P} = \{\mathcal{P}_\lambda\}_{\lambda\in\mathbb{N}}$ be a set of policies that can be described by a linear secret sharing scheme with attribute universe $\mathcal{U}$ over $\mathbb{Z}_p$. Then there exists a slotted registered ABE scheme with attribute universe $\mathcal{U}$, policy space $\mathcal{P}$, and index space $\mathcal{I} = \{\{0,1\}^\lambda\}_{\lambda\in\mathbb{N}}$. The scheme is index-set-selectively secure without corruptions in the registered-key model. To support $N$ users, the scheme has the following efficiency properties:*

- *The common reference string* crs *contains $N+1$ elements in $\mathbb{G}_1$, $2N$ elements in $\mathbb{G}_2$, and 1 element in $\mathbb{G}_T$.*
  *Each user public key* $\mathsf{pk}_{\mathsf{id}}$ *contains 1 element in $\mathbb{G}_1$ and $N-1$ elements in $\mathbb{G}_2$.*
- *The master public key* mpk *contains 2 elements in $\mathbb{G}_1$, $|A|$ elements in $\mathbb{G}_2$, and 1 element in $\mathbb{G}_T$. Here, $A$ denotes the union of all users' sets of attributes.*
- *Each helper decryption key* $\mathsf{hsk}_{\mathsf{id}}$ *contains $|S_{\mathsf{id}}|$ elements in $\mathbb{G}_1$ and 3 elements in $\mathbb{G}_2$. Here, $S_{\mathsf{id}}$ is the attribute set of the user with index* id.
- *A ciphertext* ct *contains $|P|+2$ elements in $\mathbb{G}_1$, $|P|$ elements in $\mathbb{G}_2$, and 1 element in $\mathbb{G}_T$, where $P$ is the policy.*

*Lifting to Standard Registered ABE.* As discussed in Sect. 3.1, we can lift Corollary 4.7 from the registered-key model to the plain model using a (simulation-sound) NIZK proof of knowledge (cf. [LWW25, Appendix A]). Then, we can apply the powers-of-two transformation from [HLWW23] to obtain a full-fledged registered ABE scheme in the plain model (that supports dynamic registration). Technically, the transformation from [HLWW23] only considers a fixed-size index space; for completeness, we show in the full version of this paper [SWW26] that the transformation still applies when we consider a large index space. Taken together, we obtain the following corollary:

**Corollary 4.8 (Statically-Secure Registered ABE from Pairings).** *Let $\lambda$ be a security parameter and* GroupGen *be an asymmetric prime-order pairing-group generator that outputs groups of order $p = p(\lambda)$. Suppose Assumption 4.4* *holds with respect to* $\mathsf{GroupGen}$. *Let* $\mathcal{U} = \{\mathcal{U}_\lambda\}_{\lambda \in \mathbb{N}}$ *be any attribute universe and let* $\mathcal{P} = \{\mathcal{P}_\lambda\}_{\lambda \in \mathbb{N}}$ *be a set of policies that can be described by a linear secret sharing scheme with attribute universe* $\mathcal{U}$ *over* $\mathbb{Z}_p$. *Then there exists a registered ABE scheme with attribute universe* $\mathcal{U}$, *policy space* $\mathcal{P}$, *and index space* $\mathcal{I} = \{\{0,1\}^\lambda\}_{\lambda \in \mathbb{N}}$. *The scheme satisfies static security (i.e., where the adversary has to declare the index set upfront and is not allowed to corrupt any users). To support up to* $N$ *users, the scheme has the following efficiency properties:*

- *The size of the common reference string* $\mathsf{crs}$ *is* $N \cdot \mathsf{poly}(\lambda, \log N)$.
- *The size of each user public key* $\mathsf{pk}_{\mathsf{id}}$ *is* $N \cdot \mathsf{poly}(\lambda, \log N)$.
- *The size of the master public key* $\mathsf{mpk}$ *is* $|A| \cdot \mathsf{poly}(\lambda, \log N)$ *where* $A$ *is the attribute set for all aggregated users.*
- *The size of each helper decryption key* $\mathsf{hsk}_{\mathsf{id}}$ *is* $|S_{\mathsf{id}}| \cdot \mathsf{poly}(\lambda, \log N)$ *where* $S_{\mathsf{id}}$ *is the attribute set for the user with index* $\mathsf{id}$.
- *The size of a ciphertext* $\mathsf{ct}$ *is* $|P| \cdot \mathsf{poly}(\lambda, \log N)$ *where* $P$ *is the policy.*

*Adaptive Security in the Random Oracle Model.* We can also consider Construction 4.1 in the setting where we fix the index space to be $\mathcal{I} = \{\mathcal{I}_\lambda\}_{\lambda \in \mathbb{N}}$ where $\mathcal{I}_\lambda = \{1, \ldots, N(\lambda)\}$. This coincides with the setting considered in previous pairing-based registered ABE schemes [HLWW23, ZZGQ23, GLWW23, AT24, LWW25, GHK+25]. Since the index set is completely fixed in this case, Corollary 4.7 gives a slotted registered ABE scheme with index space $\mathcal{I}$ that is *adaptively secure without corruptions* in the registered-key model. We can now appeal to the transformations in Remark 3.8 to obtain an *adaptively secure* registered ABE for the same attribute universe and policy family in the random oracle model. We summarize this instantiation below:

**Corollary 4.9 (Adaptively-Secure Registered ABE from Pairings in the Random Oracle Model).** *Let* $\lambda$ *be a security parameter and* $\mathsf{GroupGen}$ *be an asymmetric prime-order pairing-group generator that outputs groups of order* $p = p(\lambda)$. *Suppose Assumption 4.4 holds with respect to* $\mathsf{GroupGen}$ *with sub-exponential security.*[5] *Let* $\mathcal{U} = \{\mathcal{U}_\lambda\}_{\lambda \in \mathbb{N}}$ *be any attribute universe and let* $\mathcal{P} = \{\mathcal{P}_\lambda\}_{\lambda \in \mathbb{N}}$ *be a set of policies where each policy is of size at most* $|\mathcal{P}|$ *and can be described by a linear secret sharing scheme with attribute universe* $\mathcal{U}$ *over* $\mathbb{Z}_p$. *Then there exists an adaptively secure registered ABE scheme with attribute universe* $\mathcal{U}$, *policy space* $\mathcal{P}$, *and index set* $\mathcal{I} = \{[N(\lambda)]\}_{\lambda \in \mathbb{N}}$ *in the random oracle model. To support up to* $N$ *users, the scheme has the following efficiency properties:*

- *The size of the common reference string* $\mathsf{crs}$ *is* $N \cdot \mathsf{poly}(\lambda, |\mathcal{P}|, \log N)$.
- *The size of each user's public key* $\mathsf{pk}_{\mathsf{id}}$ *is* $N \cdot \mathsf{poly}(\lambda, |\mathcal{P}|, \log N)$.
- *The size of the master public key* $\mathsf{mpk}$ *is* $|A| \cdot \mathsf{poly}(\lambda, |\mathcal{P}|, \log N)$ *where* $A$ *is the attribute set for all aggregated users.*

[5] Namely, there is a constant $\delta > 0$ such that for all efficient adversaries $\mathcal{A}$, there exists a negligible function $\mathsf{negl}(\cdot)$ such that the distinguishing advantage of $\mathcal{A}$ is at most $2^{-\lambda^\delta}$.

– *The size of each helper decryption key* $\mathsf{hsk}_{\mathsf{id}}$ *is* $|S_{\mathsf{id}}| \cdot \mathsf{poly}(\lambda, |\mathcal{P}|, \log N)$ *where* $S_{\mathsf{id}}$ *is the attribute set for the user with index* $\mathsf{id}$.
– *The size of a ciphertext* $\mathsf{ct}$ *is* $\mathsf{poly}(\lambda, |\mathcal{P}|, \log N)$.

**Acknowledgments.** We thank Shota Yamada for helpful discussions and pointers to related work. Brent Waters is supported by NSF CNS-2318701 and a Simons Investigator Award. David J. Wu is supported by NSF CNS-2140975, CNS-2318701, a Sloan Fellowship, a Microsoft Research Faculty Fellowship, a Google Research Scholar Award, an Amazon Research Award, and a gift from the Stellar Development Foundation.

## References

AC17. Agrawal, S., Chase, M.: FAME: fast attribute-based message encryption. In: ACM CCS (2017)
ADM+24. Avitabile, G., Döttling, N., Magri, B., Sakkas, C., Wohnig, S.: Signature-based witness encryption with compact ciphertext. In: ASIACRYPT (2024)
AGY26. Afshar, A., Goyal, R., Yadugiri, S.: Distributed monotone-policy encryption with silent setup from lattices. IACR Cryptol. ePrint Arch. (2026)
AMR26. Abram, D., Malavolta, G., Roy, L.: How to authenticate a non-deterministic computation: shift-hiding functions, compressed LWE sampling, broadcast encryption, and obfuscation. IACR Cryptol. ePrint Arch (2026)
AT24. Attrapadung, N., Tomida, J.: A modular approach to registered ABE for unbounded predicates. In: CRYPTO (2024)
BBG05. Boneh, D., Boyen, X., Goh, E.-J.: Hierarchical identity based encryption with constant size ciphertext. In: EUROCRYPT (2005)
BGG+14. Boneh, D., et al.: Fully key-homomorphic encryption, arithmetic circuit ABE and compact garbled circuits. In: EUROCRYPT (2014)
BZ14. Boneh, D., Zhandry, M.: Multiparty key exchange, efficient traitor tracing, and more from indistinguishability obfuscation. In: CRYPTO (2014)
CES21. Cong, K., Eldefrawy, K., Smart, N.P.: Optimizing registration based encryption. In: Cryptography and Coding (2021)
CEW25. Chen, B., Elias, N., Wu, D.J.: Pairing-based batch arguments for NP with a linear-size CRS. In: ASIACRYPT (2025)
CF13. Catalano, D., Fiore, D.: Vector commitments and their applications. In: PKC (2013)
CHW25. Champion, J., Hsieh, Y.-C., Wu, D.J.: Registered ABE and adaptively-secure broadcast encryption from succinct LWE. In: CRYPTO (2025)
CW24. Champion, J., Wu, D.J.: Distributed broadcast encryption from lattices. In: TCC (2024)
CW26. Champion, J., Wu, D.J.: Distributed monotone-policy encryption for DNFs from lattices. In: EUROCRYPT (2026)
Del07. Delerablée, C.: Identity-based broadcast encryption with constant size ciphertexts and private keys. In: ASIACRYPT (2007)
DJWW25. Devadas, L., Jain, A., Waters, B., Wu, D.J.: Succinct witness encryption for batch languages and applications. In: ASIACRYPT (2025)
DKL+23. Döttling, N., Kolonelos, D., Lai, R.W.F., Lin, C., Malavolta, G., Rahimi, A.: efficient laconic cryptography from learning with errors. In: EUROCRYPT (2023)

DP08. Delerablée, C., Pointcheval, D.: Dynamic threshold public-key encryption. In: CRYPTO (2008)

DPP07. Delerablée, C., Paillier, P., Pointcheval, D.: Fully collusion secure dynamic broadcast encryption with constant-size ciphertexts or decryption keys. In: Pairing-Based Cryptography (2007)

DPY24. Datta, P., Pal, T., Yamada, S.: Registered FE beyond predicates: (attribute-based) linear functions and more. In: ASIACRYPT (2024)

EHK+13. Escala, A., Herold, G., Kiltz, E., Ràfols, C., Villar, J..: An algebraic framework for Diffie-Hellman assumptions. In: CRYPTO (2013)

ET36. Erdös, P., Turán, P.: On some sequences of integers. J. London Math. Soc. **1**(4) (1936)

FFM+23. Francati, D., Friolo, D., Maitra, M., Malavolta, G., Rahimi, A., Venturi, D.: Registered (inner-product) functional encryption. In: ASIACRYPT (2023)

FKdP23. Fiore, D., Kolonelos, D., de Perthuis, P.: Cuckoo commitments: registration-based encryption and key-value map commitments for large spaces. In: ASIACRYPT (2023)

FWW23. Freitag, C., Waters, B., Wu, D.J.: How to use (plain) witness encryption: registered ABE, flexible broadcast, and more. In: CRYPTO (2023)

GGK25. Gasarch, W., Glenn, J., Kruskal, C.: Finding large sets without arithmetic progressions of length three: an empirical view and survey ii. arXiv preprint arXiv:2501.01634 (2025)

GHK+25. Garg, S., Hajiabadi, M., Kolonelos, D., Kothapalli, A., Policharla, G.-V.: A framework for witness encryption from linearly verifiable SNARKs and applications. In: CRYPTO (2025)

GHM+19. Garg, S., Hajiabadi, M., Mahmoody, M., Rahimi, A., Sekar, S.: Registration-based encryption from standard assumptions. In: PKC (2019)

GHMR18. Garg, S., Hajiabadi, M., Mahmoody, M., Rahimi, A.: Registration-based encryption: removing private-key generator from IBE. In: TCC (2018)

GKMR23. Glaeser, N., Kolonelos, D., Malavolta, G., Rahimi, A.: Efficient registration-based encryption. In: ACM CCS (2023)

GKPW24. Garg, S., Kolonelos, D., Policharla, G.-V., Wang, M.: Threshold encryption with silent setup. In: CRYPTO (2024)

GLWW23. Garg, R., Lu, G., Waters, B., Wu, D.J.: Realizing flexible broadcast encryption: How to broadcast to a public-key directory. In: ACM CCS (2023)

GLWW24. Garg, R., Lu, G., Waters, B., Wu, D.J.: Reducing the CRS size in registered ABE systems. In: CRYPTO (2024)

GPSW06. Goyal, V., Pandey, O., Sahai, A., Waters, B.: Attribute-based encryption for fine-grained access control of encrypted data. In: ACM CCS (2006)

GV20. Goyal, R., Vusirikala, S.: Verifiable registration-based encryption. In: CRYPTO (2020)

GV22. Goyal, R., Vaikuntanathan, V.: Locally verifiable signature and key aggregation. In: CRYPTO (2022)

GWWW26. Gong, J., Waters, B., Wee, H., Wu, D.J.: Threshold batched identity-based encryption from pairings in the plain model. In: EUROCRYPT (2026)

GY26a. Goyal, R., Yadugiri, S.: Adaptively-secure flexible and identity-based broadcast encryption from decomposed LWE. IACR Cryptol. ePrint Arch. (2026)

GY26b. Goyal, R., Yadugiri, S.: Equivocal broadcast encryption: adaptively-secure optimal distributed broadcast encryption from lattices. In: CRYPTO (2026)

HLWW23. Hohenberger, S., Lu, G., Waters, B., Wu, D.J.: Registered attribute-based encryption. In: EUROCRYPT (2023)

HWW25. Hohenberger, S., Waters, B., Wu, D.J.: Pairing-based aggregate signatures without random oracles. In: ASIACRYPT (2025)

KMW23. Kolonelos, D., Malavolta, G., Wee, H.: Distributed broadcast encryption from bilinear groups. In: ASIACRYPT (2023)

KZG10. Kate, A., Zaverucha, G.M., Goldberg, I.: Constant-size commitments to polynomials and their applications. In: ASIACRYPT (2010)

LWW25. Lu, G., Waters, B., Wu, D.J.: Multi-authority registered attribute-based encryption. In: EUROCRYPT (2025)

PST25. Pal, T., Schädlich, R., Tairi, E.: Registered functional encryption for pseudorandom functionalities from lattices: registered ABE for unbounded depth circuits and turing machines, and more. IACR Cryptol. ePrint Arch (2025)

RT26. Rouselakis, Y., Tomida, J.: Towards practical registered ABE: more efficient, non-monotone, and CCA-secure. IACR Cryptol. ePrint Arch. (2026)

RW22. Riepel, D., Wee, H.: FABEO: fast attribute-based encryption with optimal security. In: ACM CCS (2022)

RY07. Ristenpart, T., Yilek, S.: The power of proofs-of-possession: securing multiparty signatures against rogue-key attacks. In: EUROCRYPT,(2007)

Sho97. Shoup, V.: Lower bounds for discrete logarithms and related problems. In: EUROCRYPT (1997)

SW05. Sahai, A., Waters, B.: Fuzzy identity-based encryption. In: EUROCRYPT (2005)

SWW26. Stracovsky, R., Waters, B., Wu, D.J.: Pairing-based registered ABE for boolean formulas with a linear-size CRS (2026). https://eprint.iacr.org/2026/1062.pdf

Ver23. Verma, T.: Inside Geo Key Manager v2: re-imagining access control for distributed systems. The CloudFlare Blog (2023). https://blog.cloudflare.com/inside-geo-key-manager-v2/

WQZD10. Wu, Q., Qin, B., Zhang, L., Domingo-Ferrer, J.: Ad hoc broadcast encryption. In: ACM CCS (2010)

WW22. Waters, B., Wu, D.J.: Batch arguments for NP and more from standard bilinear group assumptions. In: CRYPTO (2022)

WW25. Wee, H., Wu, D.J.: Unbounded distributed broadcast encryption and registered ABE from succinct LWE. In: CRYPTO (2025)

WW26. Waters, B., Wu, D.J.: Silent threshold cryptography from pairings: expressive policies in the plain model. In: EUROCRYPT (2026)

YZGC25. Yang, X., Zhang, Y., Gao, Y., Chen, J.: Registered ABE for circuits from evasive lattice assumptions. IACR Cryptol. ePrint Arch (2025)

ZZC+25. Zhu, Z., Zhang, K., Chen, Z., Gong, J., Qian, H.: Black-box registered ABE from lattices. IACR Cryptol. ePrint Arch (2025)

ZZGQ23. Zhu, Z., Zhang, K., Gong, J., Qian, J.: Registered ABE via predicate encodings. In: ASIACRYPT (2023)

# Equivocal Broadcast Encryption: Adaptively-Secure Optimal Distributed Broadcast Encryption from Lattices

Rishab Goyal(✉) and Saikumar Yadugiri

University of Wisconsin-Madison, Madison, WI 53706, USA
{rishab,saikumar}@cs.wisc.edu

**Abstract.** We present the first Distributed Broadcast Encryption (DBE) scheme from falsifiable lattice assumptions that achieves adaptive security with optimal parameters (short public/secret keys and ciphertexts). Our construction enjoys transparent setup and offers flexible instantiation: we achieve a succinct CRS in the Random Oracle Model, or a long CRS in the standard model. Previously, no lattice-based DBE simultaneously achieved adaptivity and optimal parameters in either setting.

To achieve this, we introduce a new methodology for proving adaptive security: *Equivocal Encryption Systems.* This framework operates in two indistinguishable modes: a 'real' mode utilizing standard algorithms, and a 'fake' mode where keys and ciphertexts are jointly sampled with auxiliary trapdoors, enabling the dynamic equivocation of ciphertexts to arbitrary challenge values. While our approach is technically distinct from the celebrated Dual System Encryption (Waters, CRYPTO'09), we believe it could serve as a similarly powerful paradigm for realizing adaptive security across a broad class of lattice-based encryption systems.

## 1 Introduction

Broadcast Encryption (BE) [12] is a fundamental primitive that allows a sender to securely transmit data to a dynamically chosen subset of users. While traditional BE relies on a central authority, Distributed Broadcast Encryption (DBE) [7,41] eliminates this single point of failure and trust, allowing users to generate their own keys and join the system permissionlessly. As post-quantum security becomes imperative, constructing efficient DBE from lattice assumptions has become a central goal in cryptography.

**The State of the Art: The "Selectivity" Barrier.** Recent breakthroughs have brought lattice-based DBE closer to reality. Under the hardness of a new falsifiable lattice assumption ($\ell$-succinct/decomposed-LWE) [1,38], a line of recent works [1,9,10,40] have successfully constructed DBE schemes[1] with varying efficiency profiles. However, these constructions face a fundamental dichotomy:

[1] [1] constructed a registered ABE scheme [16,22,26] with *very selective* security which generically yields a selectively secure DBE scheme [13].


N. Heninger and M. Rosulek (Eds.): CRYPTO 2026, LNCS 16800, pp. 414–445, 2026.
https://doi.org/10.1007/978-3-032-35367-2_14

**Efficiency without Adaptivity:** The most recent work by Wee and Wu [40] achieves fully optimal parameters—where public keys, secret keys, and ciphertexts are all small—but is limited to *selective security*. The adversary must declare the target set before seeing the public parameters, a restriction that is often unrealistic in dynamic distributed systems.

**Adaptivity with Inefficiency:** Conversely, the only available DBE scheme that achieves adaptive security, due to the recent work of Champion-Hsieh-Wu [9], incurs a significant overhead. For $N$ users, they require prohibitively large public keys ($|\mathsf{pk}| \propto N$) and large public parameters ($|\mathsf{crs}| \propto N^2$), and rely on the Random Oracle Model (ROM) [4] to achieve even these tradeoffs. Moreover, their scheme does not achieve "transparent setup" which goes against the main motivation of decentralization in DBE.

Essentially, if we want a post-quantum DBE with adaptive security, then the only existing approach, by Champion-Hsieh-Wu [9], comes with large public keys, large CRS *and* relies on ROM.

**The Complexity Leveraging Bottleneck.** In many cryptographic settings, one can generically lift selective security to adaptive security via complexity leveraging. While this standard approach works for identity-based or attribute-based encryption, it incurs an exponential loss in the reduction's advantage. Due to this exponential loss, complexity leveraging is insufficient in the context of (distributed) broadcast encryption. The reason is, in DBE, the reduction loss scales exponentially with the number of users $N$, requiring parameters to grow by at least a factor of $N$. DBE with such parameters trivially follows from vanilla public-key encryption, and not useful for applications.

**The Problem.** In light of the current state-of-the-art, designing a DBE scheme that is (simultaneously) *adaptively secure and fully-succinct* (optimal parameters) from falsifiable assumptions remains a fascinating open problem. Going one step further, the problem of designing an adaptively-secure post-quantum DBE in the plain model (without ROs) is also completely open.

## 1.1 Our Contributions

**Our Techniques: A New Methodology to Realize Adaptive Security.** We introduce a new methodology, that we call *'Equivocal Encryption System'*, to bridge the gap between selective and adaptive security in DBE and related encryption systems.

In an Equivocal Encryption System, one can set up the system in two modes – 'real' mode and 'fake' mode. In the real mode, the secret keys and ciphertexts are generated using the actual system's key generation and encryption procedure. While in the fake mode, the secret keys and ciphertexts are jointly sampled along with auxiliary trapdoor information with one very special feature. By using the auxiliary trapdoor, ciphertexts sampled in the fake mode can be "equivocated" dynamically to any challenge value later. The special property of an Equivocal Encryption System is that an adversary cannot distinguish a 'real' ciphertext from an 'equivocated' ciphertext, while a 'fake' ciphertext (before equivocation) still provides a meaningful notion of semantic security.

Equivocal Encryption Systems opens up a new way to prove adaptive security in DBE. While Dual System Encryption [37] relies on the algebraic indistinguishability of 'semi-functional' keys and ciphertexts which reside in hidden subspaces and functionally fail against specific ciphertexts, Equivocal Encryption operates via a trapdoor-governed fake mode. Instead of managing the orthogonality of semi-functional components, our framework generates 'empty' ciphertexts that allow the reduction to adaptively equivocate (or program) them to explain any choice of the adversary's challenge. Although our methodology is technically distinct from the celebrated Dual System Encryption, we believe it offers a similarly powerful template for realizing adaptive security across a broad class of lattice-based encryption systems.

**Our Results.** Using our methodology, we resolve the aforementioned open problems in DBE. We present the first DBE scheme that achieves adaptive security and fully optimal parameters, while proving security under a falsifiable assumption. Our schemes are plausibly post-quantum secure, and rely on the same lattice assumptions as prior state-of-the-art, requiring no new hardness assumptions. We summarize our results along two axes below:

1. Fully-Optimal in ROM: We construct an adaptively-secure DBE scheme in the Random Oracle Model where all parameters—ciphertext size, user secret/public keys, and global public parameters—are optimal (polylogarithmic in the number of users, $N$). This is the *first* lattice-based scheme to achieve full succinctness and adaptive security simultaneously.
2. Standard Model with Long CRS: We also construct an adaptively-secure DBE scheme in the standard model. In this construction, user secret/public keys and ciphertexts remain fully-succinct, while only the global public parameters (i.e., CRS) grows with $N$. This is the *first* adaptively-secure DBE in the standard model from any falsifiable lattice assumption.

**Programmable Pseudorandom Set Sampler.** Our standard model DBE construction crucially relies on a new tool that we call Programmable Pseudorandom Set Samplers (PPS). PPS captures the essential ability to adaptively program a subset of sampled values while keeping the remaining values pseudorandom. We provide two instantiations of PPS. One based on standard LWE [35] and another on a new falsifiable LWE assumption, demonstrating the flexibility of this tool for constructing adaptively secure systems. These constructions may be of independent interest, especially in the context of removing random oracles.

All our DBE schemes enjoy *transparent setup*, and are thus in line with the main motivation of decentralization behind DBE. We summarize our results and compare them with the state of the art in Table 1.

**Table 1.** Comparison of our results with prior works on Distributed Broadcast Encryption. $|\mathsf{crs}|$, $|\mathsf{pk}|$, $|\mathsf{sk}|$, and $|\mathsf{ct}|$ denotes the sizes of the common random string, user public keys, user secret keys, and ciphertext sizes respectively for $N$ users. The values reported in these columns hide $\mathsf{poly}(\lambda, \log N)$ terms. For instance, if $|\mathsf{crs}|$ is reported as $X$, it signifies $|\mathsf{crs}| = X\mathsf{poly}(\lambda, \log N)$. **TP**, **PQ**, **AD**, and **No RO** denote transparent setup, post-quantumness, adaptive security, and absence of random oracles in the scheme respectively. Technically, [23] constructed a standard broadcast encryption but the techniques used can be adapted to DBE.

| Reference | Assumption | $\|\mathsf{crs}\|$ | $\|\mathsf{pk}\|$ | $\|\mathsf{sk}\|$ | $\|\mathsf{ct}\|$ | TP | PQ | AD | No RO |
|---|---|---|---|---|---|---|---|---|---|
| [7] | $i\mathcal{O}$ + OWF | – | 1 | 1 | 1 | ✓ | – | ✓ | ✓ |
| [23] | Positional WE | 1 | 1 | 1 | 1 | ✓ | – | ✓ | ✓ |
| [13] | WE + LWE | 1 | 1 | 1 | 1 | ✓ | – | ✓ | ✓ |
| [41] | Bilinear Diffie-Hellman Exponent | $N$ | $N^2$ | $N$ | 1 | ✓ | ✗ | ✗ | ✓ |
| [31] | Bilinear Diffie-Hellman Exponent | $N$ | $N$ | 1 | 1 | ✗ | ✗ | ✓ | ✓ |
| [17] | Generic Bilinear Group | $N$ | $N$ | 1 | 1 | ✗ | ✗ | ✗ | ✓ |
| [10] | succinct LWE | $N^2$ | $N$ | 1 | 1 | ✗ | ✓ | ✗ | ✓ |
| [9] | succinct LWE | $N^2$ | $N$ | 1 | 1 | ✗ | ✓ | ✓ | ✗ |
| [1] | decomposed LWE | $N$ | 1 | 1 | 1 | ✓ | ✓ | ✗ | ✓ |
| [40] | decomposed LWE | 1 | 1 | 1 | 1 | ✓ | ✓ | ✗ | ✓ |
| Corollary 1 | decomposed LWE | 1 | 1 | 1 | 1 | ✓ | ✓ | ✓ | ✗ |
| Corollary 2 | decomposed LWE + 1-key LWE | $N$ | 1 | 1 | 1 | ✓ | ✓ | ✓ | ✓ |
| Corollary 3 | decomposed LWE | $N^2$ | 1 | 1 | 1 | ✓ | ✓ | ✓ | ✓ |

## 2 Technical Overview

A Distributed Broadcast Encryption (DBE) [7,41] scheme is a generalization of Broadcast Encryption [12] in which each user can generate their own public-secret key pair. Encryption uses public keys for a subset $S \subseteq [N]$ of users to encrypt a message $\mu$ to generate a compact ciphertext $\mathsf{ct}$ such that any one of these users can decrypt $\mathsf{ct}$.

**DBE Security.** We start by recalling various security notions commonly studied in the DBE literature. The most general and powerful security notion is that of (full) adaptive security, described as follows:

**Setup Phase.** Attacker $\mathcal{A}$ sends the number of users $1^N$. Generate $\mathsf{crs} \leftarrow \mathsf{GSetup}(1^\lambda, 1^N)$ and send it to $\mathcal{A}$. Also initiate set $\mathcal{I} \leftarrow \emptyset$.

**Query Phase.** $\mathcal{A}$ can now make two types of queries.

**Key Generation.** $\mathcal{A}$ sends $i \in [N]$ and receives $\mathsf{pk}_i$ where $(\mathsf{pk}_i, \mathsf{sk}_i) \leftarrow \mathsf{KGen}(i)$. Add $i$ to $\mathcal{I}$.

**Key Corruption.** $\mathcal{A}$ sends $i \in \mathcal{I}$ and receives $\mathsf{sk}_i$. Remove $i$ from $\mathcal{I}$.

**Challenge Phase.** $\mathcal{A}$ submits a challenge set $S^* \subseteq \mathcal{I}$, to which the challenger responds with $\mathsf{ct} \leftarrow \mathsf{Enc}(\{\mathsf{pk}_i\}_{i \in S^*}, \mu)$ for a random $\mu \leftarrow \{0,1\}$.

A DBE scheme is said to be adaptively secure if there doesn't exist any poly-time attacker $\mathcal{A}$ that can correctly predict $\mu$ with non-negligible advantage in the above game. Due to the technical difficulty in proving adaptive security directly for any DBE scheme, many works typically prove security under one of two alternate security notions – *semi-static and selective security.*

In a semi-static security game, $\mathcal{A}$ submits an 'honest' set $S' \subseteq [N]$ at the beginning and receives only the public keys corresponding to $S'$. That is, $\mathcal{A}$ chooses $S'$, and receives $\{\mathsf{pk}_i\}_{i \in S'}$ along with $\mathsf{crs}$. During the challenge phase, $\mathcal{A}$ can *adaptively* select any subset $S^*$ as the challenge set as long as $S^* \subseteq S'$. Basically, unlike the (full) adaptive game, $\mathcal{A}$ can not corrupt any secret keys within $S'$, but it still can choose challenge set adaptively.

In a selective security game, the adversary is maximally constrained as it must submit the challenge set $S^*$ during setup phase and it receives $(\mathsf{crs}, \{\mathsf{pk}_i\}_{i \in S^*}, \mathsf{ct})$ in one shot. In short, unlike adaptive and semi-static games, adversary must choose everything at the beginning, and is not permitted to make any adaptive choices.

**Semi-static is as Good as Adaptive.** Starting with the beautiful work of Gentry and Waters [20], prior works [20,28,31] have shown that a semi-statically secure DBE can be generically boosted into an adaptively secure DBE. Despite these generic compilers, most prior works have only been successful in proving selective security for DBE, highlighting the large gap between selective and semi-static security.

**The Matrix Programming Barrier:** *Why is it difficult to prove semi-static security from lattices?* Proving that lattice-based DBE is semi-static/adaptively secure is difficult for the same fundamental reason the seminal BGG+ paradigm [5] is restricted to selective security. Both face the same underlying barrier in their security reductions. Let us elaborate. In the BGG+ paradigm for designing attribute-based encryption, a reduction algorithm needs to program the LWE matrix $\mathbf{A}$ as $\mathbf{A} := \mathbf{BR} - \mathbf{x}^\top \otimes \mathbf{G}$, where $\mathbf{x}$ is the attribute string and $\mathbf{G}$ is a gadget matrix. This is essential for two reasons: (a) this lets the reduction answer key queries for any unsatisfying predicate, and (b) the challenge ciphertext can be simulated given an LWE challenge.

Prior lattice-based DBE schemes [1,10,40] directly builds on the BGG+ paradigm, thus also inherit the same 'matrix programming' barrier. In particular, in all these schemes, they need to program the global LWE matrix $\mathbf{A}$ as $\mathbf{A} := \mathbf{BR} - \mathsf{Com}(S^*)$, where $\mathsf{Com}(S^*)$ is a structured *succinct* commitment of the challenge set $S^*$. Since in, both, semi-static and adaptive security games, the adversary can adaptively choose $S^*$ after receiving the public keys and global parameters, thus one cannot design a reduction algorithm that can correctly simulate the challenge ciphertext from an LWE challenge. Essentially, the reduction must program the matrix $\mathbf{A}$ to encode $\mathsf{Com}(S^*)$; thus, prior works could only prove selective security.

### 2.1 Equivocal Encryption: A New Methodology to Prove Adaptive Security

As discussed in the introduction, one of our key technical contributions is the introduction of a new methodology that we call the *Equivocal Encryption System.*

The central goal of our methodology is to get around the aforementioned 'Matrix Programming Barrier' in lattices.

At a very high level, our intuition is to establish a 'fake' mode in our encryption system such that, while we are in the fake mode, we can sample a fake ciphertext (say an encryption of dummy challenge set in the case of DBE) such that a fake ciphertext can later be *equivocated to a 'real-looking' ciphertext for any adaptively selected challenge* (i.e., an adaptive set $S^*$ in the case of DBE). The advantage of defining a 'fake' mode is that we can bypass the *Matrix Programming Barrier* as the LWE matrices can be programmed w.r.t. a dummy challenge, and this dummy challenge can be selectively fixed (before the adversary even begins). Thus, our insight is to use the fake mode while proving security to ensure we do not need to embed $S^*$ into the global parameters and/or public keys, yet we can design a reduction algorithm that can simulate a challenge ciphertext given an LWE challenge. In short, we bypass the matrix programming issue by using the power of "indistinguishable" ciphertext equivocation.

Although we explain our intuition in the context of DBE, our methodology is far more general and could be useful in many other areas of lattice-based cryptography to prove adaptive security. Next, we explain our methodology in more detail while focussing primarily on DBE.

**Defining Equivocal Distributed Broadcast Encryption (EqDBE).** To demonstrate our equivocal encryption framework for DBE, we define a strengthening of DBE, Equivocal DBE (EqDBE). An EqDBE scheme consists of $(\mathsf{GSetup}, \mathsf{KGen}, \mathsf{Enc}, \mathsf{Dec})$ whose functionality is similar to a DBE scheme. In addition, in an EqDBE scheme there are two new algorithms $\mathsf{FakeSetup}, \mathsf{Equivocate}$. The $\mathsf{FakeSetup}$ algorithm uses the set $S' \subseteq [N], \mu \in \{0,1\}$ to generate a fake crs, $\widetilde{\mathsf{crs}}$, fake public keys $\{\widetilde{\mathsf{pk}_i}\}_{i \in S'}$, and more importantly a "fake ciphertext" $\widetilde{\mathsf{ct}}$. It also outputs $\mathsf{aux}$ which can be used to equivocate $\widetilde{\mathsf{ct}}$ during the challenge phase. The equivocation algorithm simply uses this $\mathsf{aux}$ and $S^*$ to generate ciphertext $\mathsf{ct}$ for any $S^* \subseteq S'$. EqDBE's $(\mathsf{GSetup}, \mathsf{KGen}, \mathsf{Enc}, \mathsf{Dec})$ algorithms satisfy correctness and compactness conditions like any DBE scheme. In addition, EqDBE also satisfies the following properties:

**Mode Indistinguishability.** The distribution of $(\mathsf{crs}, \{\mathsf{pk}_i\}_{i \in S'}, \mathsf{ct})$ generated via $(\mathsf{GSetup}, \mathsf{KGen}, \mathsf{Enc})$ algorithms (respectively) is indistinguishable from $(\widetilde{\mathsf{crs}}, \{\widetilde{\mathsf{pk}_i}\}_{i \in S'}, \mathsf{ct}_{\mathsf{eq}})$ generated using $(\mathsf{FakeSetup}, \mathsf{Equivocate})$ algorithms. Here the equivocated ciphertext $\mathsf{ct}_{\mathsf{eq}}$ is generated by taking the fake ciphertext $\widetilde{\mathsf{ct}}$ (generated by $\mathsf{FakeSetup}$), and equivocating to the adaptively chosen $S^*$ supplied by the attacker $\mathcal{A}$.

**Selective Security for Fake Setup.** For any selectively declared set $S'$, the distribution of $(\widetilde{\mathsf{crs}}, \{\widetilde{\mathsf{pk}_i}\}_{i \in S'}, \widetilde{\mathsf{ct}}, \mathsf{aux}) \leftarrow \mathsf{FakeSetup}(S', \mu)$ should hide $\mu$ from any poly-time attacker $\mathcal{A}$. Crucially, we want $\mu$ to be hidden even when $\mathcal{A}$ receives the auxiliary trapdoor $\mathsf{aux}$ that can be used to equivocate $\widetilde{\mathsf{ct}}$ arbitrarily.

We show that an EqDBE scheme is tremendously useful in constructing a semi-statically secure DBE. Let us explain.

**Semi-static DBE from EqDBE.** To construct a DBE scheme from EqDBE, we simply use the $(\mathsf{GSetup}, \mathsf{KGen}, \mathsf{Enc}, \mathsf{Dec})$ algorithms of the EqDBE scheme as is. As these algorithms satisfy correctness and compactness properties, so will the resulting DBE scheme. EqDBE's FakeSetup and Equivocate algorithms are only used in the security proof as we explain below:

(1) Start with the semi-static security game described earlier.
(2) Next, instead of using $\mathsf{GSetup}, \mathsf{KGen}, \mathsf{Enc}$, use $\mathsf{FakeSetup}, \mathsf{Equivocate}$ algorithms to sample the challenge ciphertext. Note that a semi-static attacker declares $S'$ at the beginning, thus we could run FakeSetup w.r.t. $S'$.

We use *mode indistinguishability* to argue indistinguishability of (1)-(2), and then rely on *selective security for fake setup* to show that no polytime attacker can win with non-negligible probability in (2). Coupling this with known generic compilers [20,28,31], we obtain an adaptively secure DBE scheme. More details are provided in Sect. 4.

Taking a step back, the central advantage in using EqDBE is that it breaks the difficulty of proving semi-static security into two tractable pieces – mode indistinguishability and selective security. Since the seminal BGG+ paradigm is typically sufficient to prove selective security, thus our intuition is that all we need to do is come up with an approach to equivocate ciphertexts and prove mode indistinguishability. Once we achieve this, then an adaptively secure DBE scheme should follow naturally by applying our methodology.

## 2.2 Equivocal DBE in Random Oracle Model

Our construction of EqDBE uses the matrix commitment scheme introduced in [39]. We provide a brief description here. A reader familiar with this scheme can safely skip the next paragraph.

**Matrix Commitments.** Let $(n, m, q, \chi, \sigma)$ be Learning with Errors (LWE) [35] parameters and $\mathsf{com.pp} := (\mathbf{W}, \mathbf{D}, \mathbf{B})$ be from the decomposed LWE assumption [1]. Then, there exist three *deterministic* algorithms $(\mathsf{Com}, \mathsf{Verify}, \mathsf{Open})$ which take com.pp implicitly such that $\forall\ N \in \mathbb{N}$, any matrix $\mathbf{M} \in \mathbb{Z}_q^{n\times N}$,

$$\mathbf{C}\mathbf{V}_N = \mathbf{M} - \mathbf{B}\mathbf{Z}$$

where $\mathbf{C} = \mathsf{Com}(\mathbf{M}), \mathbf{V}_N = \mathsf{Verify}(1^N), \mathbf{Z} = \mathsf{Open}(\mathbf{M}), \mathbf{C} \in \mathbb{Z}_q^{n\times m}, \mathbf{V}_N \in \mathbb{Z}_q^{m\times N}, \mathbf{Z} \in \mathbb{Z}_q^{m\times N}$. Moreover, $\mathbf{V}_N, \mathbf{Z}$ have bounded norms independent of $N$. Full definition is provided in Sect. 3.1. Decomposed LWE assumption[2] [1] conjectures that given $(\mathbf{W}, \mathbf{D}, \mathbf{B})^3$, $\{\mathbf{s}^\top \mathbf{B} + \mathsf{err}\} \approx_c \{\mathbf{c}^\top\}$ where $\mathbf{s} \leftarrow \mathbb{Z}_q^n, \mathbf{c} \leftarrow \mathbb{Z}_q^m$. By err we mean bounded norm discrete gaussian noise. The exact structure of

[2] $\ell$-decomposed LWE is implied by $\ell$-succinct LWE [38] as shown in [1].

[3] We are imprecise in our description about the size of $\mathbf{B}$. Throughout overview, we assume $\mathbf{B} \in \mathbb{Z}_q^{n\times m}$ but it's column length is much larger (Assumption 1). Nevertheless, our design can be adapted as we demonstrate in main body.

$(\mathbf{W}, \mathbf{D}, \mathbf{B})$ is not relevant to the discussion. We refer the reader to Assumption 1 for full definition.

**Starting Point: A Simplified View of Selective DBE from [40].** We describe a *selectively-secure* DBE scheme from the decomposed LWE assumption inspired by [40] (WW from henceforth). Our presentation slightly deviates the original WW selective DBE. We find that our selective DBE offers a much better starting point in understanding our EqDBE constructions. In this selective DBE scheme for $N$ users,

$$\mathsf{crs} = (\mathsf{com.pp} := (\mathbf{W}, \mathbf{D}, \mathbf{B}), \mathbf{A}, \mathbf{p}, N), \text{ where } \mathbf{A} \leftarrow \mathbb{Z}_q^{n \times m}, \mathbf{p} \leftarrow \mathbb{Z}_q^n$$
$$(\mathsf{pk}_i, \mathsf{sk}_i) = (\mathbf{t}_i, \mathbf{r}_i), \text{ such that } \mathbf{t}_i := \mathbf{B}\mathbf{r}_i + \mathbf{p} - \mathbf{A}\mathbf{v}_i, \mathbf{r}_i \leftarrow \{\pm 1\}^m$$

where $\mathbf{v}_i$ is $i$-th column of $\mathbf{V}_N = \mathsf{Verify}(1^N)$ from matrix commitments. The $\mathsf{Enc}$ algorithm uses public keys $\{\mathbf{t}_i\}_{i \in S}$ to construct a matrix $\mathbf{M} = [\mathbf{m}_1 \mid \ldots \mid \mathbf{m}_N] \in \mathbb{Z}_q^{n \times N}$ whose $j$-th column $\mathbf{m}_j$ is

$$\mathbf{m}_j = \begin{cases} \mathbf{t}_j & \text{if } j \in S \\ \mathbf{0} & \text{otherwise} \end{cases} \tag{1}$$

Then, $\mathsf{Enc}$ computes $\mathbf{C} = \mathsf{Com}(\mathbf{M})$, samples $\mathbf{s} \leftarrow \mathbb{Z}_q^n$, and outputs

$$\mathsf{ct} := (\mathbf{c}_1^\top, \mathbf{c}_2^\top, c_3) := (\mathbf{s}^\top \mathbf{B} + \mathsf{err}, \mathbf{s}^\top (\mathbf{A} + \mathbf{C}) + \mathsf{err}, \mathbf{s}^\top \mathbf{p} + \mathsf{err} + \lfloor q/2 \rfloor \mu)$$

In order to decrypt given $\mathbf{r}_j$ for $j$-th user, $\mathsf{Dec}$ computes $\mathbf{V}_N = \mathsf{Verify}(1^N)$ and also $\mathbf{M}$ using the public keys $\{\mathbf{t}_i\}_{i \in S}$ (by Eq. (1)). Using $\mathbf{M}$, $\mathsf{Dec}$ can compute $\mathbf{Z} = \mathsf{Open}(\mathbf{M})$. Then, $\mathsf{Dec}$ computes the expanded vector $\mathbf{c}_{exp}^\top = \mathbf{c}_2^\top \mathbf{V}_N + \mathbf{c}_1^\top \mathbf{Z} \approx \mathbf{s}^\top (\mathbf{A}\mathbf{V}_N + \mathbf{M}) \in \mathbb{Z}_q^{1 \times N}$. Note that the $j$-th element of $\mathbf{c}_{exp}^\top$ is roughly $\mathbf{s}^\top(\mathbf{t}_j + \mathbf{A}\mathbf{v}_j) = \mathbf{s}^\top(\mathbf{B}\mathbf{r}_j + \mathbf{p})$ if $j \in S$. Thus, using $\mathbf{r}_j$ and $\mathbf{c}_1^\top$, $\mathsf{Dec}$ roughly computes $\mathbf{s}^\top \mathbf{p}$ which can be used to retrieve $\mu$ with high probability.

**Selective Security of this DBE.** We provide a sketch of the selective security proof below.

(1) This is the selective security game where poly-time attacker $\mathcal{A}$ selectively submits the challenge set $S^* \subseteq [N]$. It receives $(\mathsf{crs}, \{\mathbf{t}_i\}_{i \in S^*}, \mathsf{ct})$ generated as above for any $\mu$.
(2) Using leftover hash lemma, we sample $\mathbf{t}_i \leftarrow \mathbb{Z}_q^n$ for each $i \in S^*$.
(3) Once again, using leftover hash lemma, we set $\mathbf{A}$ and $\mathbf{p}$ in $\mathsf{crs}$ as $\mathbf{B}\mathbf{R}_\mathbf{A} - \mathsf{Com}(\mathbf{M}^*)$ and $\mathbf{B}\mathbf{r}_\mathbf{p}$ respectively. Here, $\mathbf{M}^*$ is the matrix constructed using Eq. (1) for set $S^*$. This lets us set $\mathsf{ct}$ as $(\mathbf{c}_1^\top, \mathbf{c}_2^\top \approx \mathbf{c}_1^\top \mathbf{R}_\mathbf{A}, c_3 \approx \mathbf{c}_1^\top \mathbf{r}_\mathbf{p} + \lfloor q/2 \rfloor \mu)$.
(4) Now, using decomposed LWE security we can change $\mathbf{c}_1^\top$ to a random string, which then would mean $c_3$ loses all information about $\mu$.

Note that in step (3), we program $\mathsf{crs}$ with information about $\mathbf{M}^*$ and thus inherit the matrix programming barrier as explained above. If we consider the semi-static security game, where $\mathcal{A}$ adaptively chooses challenge set $S^*$, it is unclear if we can set $\mathbf{c}_2^\top$ using $\mathbf{c}_1^\top$ like in step (3).

**Equivocating DBE Ciphertexts.** To construct an EqDBE scheme, we should be able to take a $\mathsf{ct}'$ for the set $S'$ and explain it for any set $S^* \subseteq S'$ under the same $\mathsf{crs}$. To do so, we add random masks to the ciphertext which will allow us to equivocate $\mathsf{ct}'$ for $S^*$. We expand on this below.

In our EqDBE scheme, $\mathsf{crs}, (\mathsf{pk}_i, \mathsf{sk}_i)$ for any $i \in [N]$ remain unchanged from the selective DBE scheme described above. $\mathsf{Enc}$ on the other hand, now generates $\mathbf{M} = [\mathbf{m}_1 \mid \ldots \mid \mathbf{m}_N] \in \mathbb{Z}_q^{n \times N}$ as

$$\mathbf{m}_j = \begin{cases} \mathbf{t}_j + \boxed{\mathbf{B}\mathbf{x}_j} & \text{if } j \in S \\ \boxed{\mathbf{d}_j} & \text{otherwise} \end{cases} \tag{2}$$

where $\mathbf{x}_j \leftarrow \{\pm 1\}^m$ and $\mathbf{d}_j \leftarrow \mathbb{Z}_q^n$. $\mathsf{Enc}$ now computes $\mathbf{C} = \mathsf{Com}(\mathbf{M})$, samples $\mathbf{s} \leftarrow \mathbb{Z}_q^n$, and outputs

$$\mathsf{ct} := \left(\mathbf{s}^\top \mathbf{B} + \mathsf{err}, \mathbf{s}^\top (\mathbf{A} + \mathbf{C}) + \mathsf{err}, \mathbf{s}^\top \mathbf{p} + \mathsf{err} + \lfloor q/2 \rfloor \mu, \boxed{\{\mathbf{x}_j\}_{j \in S}}, \boxed{\{\mathbf{d}_j\}_{j \notin S}}\right)$$

Here, $\boxed{X}$ represents the random masks we add to the ciphertext. This process helps in transforming the matrix commitment scheme to be lossy/imperfectly binding while still preserving all the properties provided by this scheme. In order to decrypt given $\mathbf{r}_j$ for $j$-th user, $\mathsf{Dec}$ can still compute $\mathbf{c}_{exp}^\top = \mathbf{c}_2^\top \mathbf{V}_N + \mathbf{c}_1^\top \mathbf{Z} \approx \mathbf{s}^\top(\mathbf{A}\mathbf{V}_N + \mathbf{M})$. The $j$-th element of $\mathbf{c}_{exp}^\top$ is $\mathbf{s}^\top(\mathbf{t}_j + \mathbf{A}\mathbf{v}_j + \mathbf{B}\mathbf{x}_j) = \mathbf{s}^\top(\mathbf{B}(\mathbf{r}_j + \mathbf{x}_j) + \mathbf{p})$ if $j \in S$. Thus, using $\mathbf{x}_j, \mathbf{c}_1^\top, \mathbf{r}_j$, user can compute $\mu$. We point out that it is essential to give out the random masks $\boxed{\{\mathbf{x}_j\}_{j \in S}}$ and $\boxed{\{\mathbf{d}_j\}_{j \notin S}}$ as part of $\mathsf{ct}$. Only then $\mathsf{Dec}$ can compute $\mathbf{M}$ fully and $\mathbf{Z} = \mathsf{Open}(\mathbf{M})$. $\mathsf{Dec}$ also needs $\mathbf{x}_j$ to properly compute $\mu$.

**Fake Setup and Equivocation.** The $\mathsf{FakeSetup}$ algorithm uses $S' \subseteq [N], \mu \in \{0,1\}$ to sample public keys $\mathbf{t}_i \leftarrow \mathbb{Z}_q^n$ for each $i \in S'$. It also samples $\{\mathbf{x}'_j\}_{j \in S'}, \{\mathbf{d}'_j\}_{j \notin S'}$ and computes matrix $\mathbf{M}'$ (for set $S'$ using Eq. (2)). It then sets $\mathbf{A} = \mathbf{A}' - \mathsf{Com}(\mathbf{M}')$ after sampling random $\mathbf{A}'$ and $\mathbf{p}$. $\widetilde{\mathsf{ct}}$ is set as $(\mathbf{s}^\top \mathbf{B} + \mathsf{err}, \mathbf{s}^\top(\mathbf{A} + \mathbf{C}') + \mathsf{err}, \mathbf{s}^\top \mathbf{p} + \mathsf{err} + \lfloor q/2 \rfloor \mu)$ after sampling $\mathbf{s} \leftarrow \mathbb{Z}_q^n$. $\mathsf{aux}$ information contains $(S', \{\mathbf{x}_j\}_{j \in S'}, \{\mathbf{d}_j\}_{j \notin S'}, \widetilde{\mathsf{ct}})$ among other things.

The $\mathsf{Equivocate}$ algorithm given a set $S^* \subseteq S'$, sets $\mathbf{x}_j^*$ and $\mathbf{d}_j^*$ as follows:

$$\mathbf{x}_j^* = \mathbf{x}'_j \text{ for } j \in S^* \text{ and } \mathbf{d}_j^* = \begin{cases} \mathbf{d}'_j & \text{if } j \notin S' \\ \mathbf{t}_j + \mathbf{B}\mathbf{x}'_j & \text{if } j \in S' \backslash S^* \end{cases}$$

It then outputs $\mathsf{ct} := \left(\widetilde{\mathsf{ct}}, \boxed{\{\mathbf{x}_j^*\}_{j \in S^*}}, \boxed{\{\mathbf{d}_j^*\}_{j \notin S^*}}\right)$.

Crucially, observe that matrix $\mathbf{M}^* = [\mathbf{m}_1^* \mid \ldots \mid \mathbf{m}_N^*]$ computed according to Eq. (2) for the set $S^* \subseteq S'$ using the random masks $\{\mathbf{x}_j^*\}_j, \{\mathbf{d}_j^*\}_j$ given out by $\mathsf{Equivocate}$, and $\mathbf{M}' = [\mathbf{m}'_1 \mid \ldots \mid \mathbf{m}'_N]$ computed according to Eq. (2) for $S'$ using $\{\mathbf{x}'_j\}_j, \{\mathbf{d}'_j\}_j$ sampled by $\mathsf{FakeSetup}$ are exactly the same. The only difference in these matrices is for $j$-th columns when $j \in S' \backslash S^*$. In these columns, $\mathbf{m}'_j$ is $\mathbf{t}_j + \mathbf{B}\mathbf{x}'_j$ and $\mathbf{m}_j^* = \mathbf{d}_j^* = \mathbf{t}_j + \mathbf{B}\mathbf{x}'_j$. Thus, they are both identical.

**Security Analysis.** We prove that the above construction satisfies mode indistinguishability and selective security for fake setup properties. For simplicity assume that $N = 3, S' = \{1, 2\}$, $S^* = \{1\}$.

**Mode Indistinguishability.** We provide a sketch of the proof below.

(1) This is the semi-static game where we generate $(\mathsf{crs}, \mathsf{pk}_1, \mathsf{pk}_2, \mathsf{ct})$ using $\mathsf{GSetup}, \mathsf{KGen}, \mathsf{Enc}$ described above for any $\mu \in \{0, 1\}$.
(2) Using leftover hash lemma, we sample $\mathsf{pk}_1 = \mathbf{t}_1 \leftarrow \mathbb{Z}_q^n$ and $\mathsf{pk}_2 = \mathbf{t}_2 \leftarrow \mathbb{Z}_q^n$.
(3) Now, we will sample $\mathbf{x}_1', \mathbf{x}_2' \leftarrow \{\pm 1\}^m, \mathbf{d}_3' \leftarrow \mathbb{Z}_q^n$, compute $\mathbf{M}' = [\mathbf{t}_1 + \mathbf{B}\mathbf{x}_1' \mid \mathbf{t}_2 + \mathbf{B}\mathbf{x}_2' \mid \mathbf{d}_3']$ and $\mathbf{C}' = \mathsf{Com}(\mathbf{M}')$. We still compute $\mathsf{ct}$ similar to $\mathsf{Enc}$, i.e., by sampling fresh $\mathbf{x}_1^* \leftarrow \{\pm 1\}^m, \mathbf{d}_2^*, \mathbf{d}_3^* \leftarrow \mathbb{Z}_q^n$.
Till now, the view of $\mathcal{A}$ only changed a little. Moreover, $\mathbf{x}_1', \mathbf{x}_2', \mathbf{d}_3'$ do not appear anywhere in $\mathsf{crs}$, $\{\mathbf{t}_1, \mathbf{t}_2\}$, or $\mathsf{ct}$.
(4) Using leftover hash lemma, we switch $\mathbf{d}_2^* := \mathbf{t}_2 + \mathbf{B}\mathbf{x}_2'$ $(2 \in S' \backslash S^*)$. Moreover, we will also set $\mathbf{x}_1^* := \mathbf{x}_1', \mathbf{d}_3^* := \mathbf{d}_3'$ as they are from the same distribution.
(5) This is the semi-static game where we generate $(\mathsf{crs}, \mathsf{pk}_1, \mathsf{pk}_2, \mathsf{ct})$ using the $\mathsf{FakeSetup}, \mathsf{Equivocate}$ algorithms described above for any $\mu \in \{0, 1\}$.

Steps (4)–(5) are simply semantic changes. Thus, mode indistinguishability holds statistically.

**Selective Security for Fake Setup.** Note that $\widetilde{\mathsf{ct}}$ is a ciphertext for $S'$ distributed similarly to the ciphertext in our selectively secure DBE scheme. The auxiliary information $\mathsf{aux} := (S', \mathbf{x}_1, \mathbf{x}_2, \mathbf{d}_3, \widetilde{\mathsf{ct}})$ does not reveal much information about a $\widetilde{\mathsf{ct}}$ for $S'$ and can only be used to recreate $\mathbf{M}'$ or equivocation. Thus, selective security for fake setup holds by a similar argument to that of our selectively secure DBE scheme.

**Final Step: Using ROM to Make Ciphertext Compact.** Unfortunately, the ciphertext $\mathsf{ct}$ in our scheme is no longer compact and grows with $N$. This is because we have $N$ random masks $(\{\mathbf{x}_j\}_{j \in S}, \{\mathbf{d}_j\}_{j \notin S})$ which we have to provide for correctness. Our idea is to use a random function to make $\mathsf{ct}$ compact. More specifically, we consider two hash functions $\mathcal{H}_1 : \{0, 1\}^\lambda \times [N] \to \{\pm 1\}^m$ and $\mathcal{H}_2 : \{0, 1\}^\lambda \times [N] \to \mathbb{Z}_q^n$ which will be part of the $\mathsf{crs}$. During encryption, we sample two handles $\mathsf{sd}_1, \mathsf{sd}_2 \leftarrow \{0, 1\}^\lambda$ and compute $\mathbf{x}_j = \mathcal{H}_1(\mathsf{sd}_1, j)$ for $j \in S$ and $\mathbf{d}_j = \mathcal{H}_2(\mathsf{sd}_2, j)$ for $j \notin S$ and send $\mathsf{sd}_1, \mathsf{sd}_2$ along with $\mathsf{ct}$. This way $\mathsf{Dec}$ can recreate $\mathbf{M}$ efficiently. We show that by viewing these hash functions as random oracles [4], we can prove mode indistinguishability readily. As handles $\mathsf{sd}_1, \mathsf{sd}_2$ are short and their size is independent of $N$, this yields a fully compact ciphertext. This concludes the description of our EqDBE scheme in the random oracle model. Full construction is provided in Sect. 5.

### 2.3 Equivocal DBE in Standard Model

Our next goal is to remove random oracles from previous construction and attain adaptively secure DBE scheme in the standard model. To the best of our knowledge, there does not exist an adaptively secure DBE scheme from lattices without random oracles.

Our observation is that we need random oracles in the previous EqDBE construction to sample the random masks in such a way that they can be "adaptively" programmed during the challenge phase. In a bit more detail, we highlight two important properties that random oracles $\mathcal{H}_1, \mathcal{H}_2$ present in $\mathsf{crs}$ of previous EqDBE construction yield.

1. **Compactness.** The $\mathsf{crs}$ remains short and allows to compute $N$ random masks given the handles $\mathsf{sd}_1, \mathsf{sd}_2 \in \{0,1\}^\lambda$. Moreover, given $\mathsf{sd}_1, \mathsf{sd}_2 \in \{0,1\}^\lambda$, we can sample any $N$ random masks deterministically.
2. **Adaptive Correlation Hiding.** For $j \in S' \backslash S^*$, the random mask sampled during $\mathsf{FakeSetup}$, $\mathbf{x}'_j$ and the random mask revealed by $\mathsf{Equivocate}$ $\mathbf{d}^*_j = \mathbf{t}_j + \mathbf{B}\mathbf{x}'_j$ are correlated. Random oracles allow us to hide this correlation by adaptively, during equivocation, program $\mathcal{H}_1(\mathsf{sd}_1, j), \mathcal{H}_2(\mathsf{sd}_2, j)$ with $\mathbf{x}^*_j, \mathbf{d}^*_j$ respectively where $\mathbf{x}^*_j$ is completely independent of $\mathbf{x}'_j$.

We remark that achieving property 2 in standard model requires great care. This is because while working in the standard model, $\mathsf{crs}$ sampled by $\mathsf{FakeSetup}$ is computed without the knowledge of $S^*$. Still, this $\mathsf{crs}$ should reveal either $\mathbf{x}'_j$ or $\mathbf{t}_j + \mathbf{B}\mathbf{x}'_j$ (only one of these) based on whether ($j \in S^*$?) all while keeping the handles short. To address these challenges in the standard model, we introduce a new tool called, *Programmable Pseudorandom Set Sampler* (PPS). This tool may be of independent interest in the context of removing (programmable) random oracles. We provide definition of PPS below.

**Programmable Pseudorandom Set Sampler.** A PPS scheme for message space $\mathcal{M}$ consists of 6 main algorithms ($\mathsf{PPGen}, \mathsf{MSKGen}, \mathsf{KGen}, \mathsf{pkEnc}, \mathsf{skEnc}, \mathsf{Dec}$). $\mathsf{PPGen}$ takes $1^N$ as input and generates $\mathsf{crs}$ that the rest of the algorithms use implicitly. $\mathsf{MSKGen}$ generates a master secret key $\mathsf{msk}$. $\mathsf{KGen}$ uses a $\mathsf{msk}$ and a set $S \subseteq [N]$ to compute a short secret key $\mathsf{sk}_S$. The $\mathsf{skEnc}$ algorithm uses a $\mathsf{msk}$, and index $i \in [N]$, message $\mu \in \mathcal{M}$ to generate ciphertext $\mathsf{ct}$. The $\mathsf{pkEnc}$ algorithm simply uses index $i$ to generate a garbage ciphertext $\mathsf{ct}$. $\mathsf{Decode}$ algorithm uses $(i, \mathsf{ct}, S, \mathsf{sk}_S)$ to output message $\mu' \in \mathcal{M} \cup \{\perp\}$. A PPS scheme needs to satisfy the following properties.

**Correctness.** We say PPS is correct if $i \in S \implies \mu = \mathsf{Decode}(i, \mathsf{ct}, S, \mathsf{sk}_S)$, where $\mathsf{sk}_S \leftarrow \mathsf{KGen}(\mathsf{msk}, S)$, $\mathsf{ct} \leftarrow \mathsf{skEnc}(\mathsf{msk}, i, \mu)$.

**Compactness.** $|\mathsf{sk}_S| = \mathsf{poly}(\lambda, \log N)$.

**Payload Hiding.** For any $i, \mu$ (even adversarially chosen), $\mathsf{ct} \leftarrow \mathsf{skEnc}(\mathsf{msk}, i, \mu)$ and $\mathsf{ct} \leftarrow \mathsf{pkEnc}(i)$ should be indistinguishable to an attacker $\mathcal{A}$ that adaptively queries for a single $\mathsf{sk}_{S^*}$ for $S^*$ such that $i \notin S^*$. This property should hold even if $\mathcal{A}$ sees multiple $\mathsf{skEnc}$ ciphertexts for indices in set $P$ such that $i \notin P$.

**Mode Indistinguishability.** For any $i$, $\mathsf{ct} \leftarrow \mathsf{skEnc}(\mathsf{msk}, i, \mu)$ and $\mathsf{ct} \leftarrow \mathsf{pkEnc}(i)$ should be indistinguishable to an attacker $\mathcal{A}$ that adaptively queries for a single $\mathsf{sk}_{S^*}$ for $S^*$ such that $i \in S^*$. More importantly, $\mu$ is *chosen ran-*

*domly by the challenger*[4]. This property should hold even if $\mathcal{A}$ sees multiple $\mathsf{skEnc}$ ciphertexts for indices in set $P$ such that $i \notin P$.

Full definition of a PPS scheme is provided in Sect. 6.

**EqDBE in Standard Model via PPS.** At a very high level, the idea is to simply replace hash functions $\mathcal{H}_1$, $\mathcal{H}_2$ with two instantiation of PPS, one for message space $\{\pm 1\}^m$ and other for $\mathbb{Z}_q^n$. $\mathsf{crs}$ will now contain $2N$ PPS ciphertexts, $N$ from each instantiation. The handles $\mathsf{sd}_1, \mathsf{sd}_2$ we sample during $\mathsf{Enc}$ will be replaced with secret keys of PPS. We substitute $\mathcal{H}(\mathsf{sd}, i)$ evaluation with PPS $\mathsf{Decode}$.

Compact secret keys of PPS allow us to achieve short ciphertexts while still allowing to reveal $N$ random masks (property 1). Although it isn't immediately clear how PPS helps us adaptively reveal at most one of $\mathbf{x}'_j, \mathbf{t}_j + \mathbf{B}\mathbf{x}'_j$ for $j \in S' \backslash S^*$, we show that by a careful combination of payload hiding and mode indistinguishability, this feature can be achieved. We provide our construction of EqDBE in standard model using PPS below.

$\mathsf{GSetup}$: Along with $\mathsf{com.pp}, \mathbf{A} \leftarrow \mathbb{Z}_q^{n\times m}, \mathbf{p} \leftarrow \mathbb{Z}_q^n$, we sample two PPS instantiations $\mathsf{PPS}^{(1)}$, $\mathsf{PPS}^{(2)}$. We then sample $\{\mathsf{ct}_i^{(1)} \leftarrow \mathsf{PPS}^{(1)}.\mathsf{pkEnc}(i)\}_{i\in[N]}$ and $\{\mathsf{ct}_i^{(2)} \leftarrow \mathsf{PPS}^{(2)}.\mathsf{pkEnc}(i)\}_{i\in[N]}$. $\mathsf{crs} := (\mathsf{com.pp}, \mathbf{A}, \mathbf{p}, \{\mathsf{ct}_i^{(1)}\}_{i\in[N]}, \{\mathsf{ct}_i^{(2)}\}_{i\in[N]})$

$\mathsf{Enc}$: Sample $\mathsf{msk}^{(1)} \leftarrow \mathsf{PPS}^{(1)}.\mathsf{MSKGen}, \mathsf{msk}^{(2)} \leftarrow \mathsf{PPS}^{(2)}.\mathsf{MSKGen}$. Further, $\mathsf{sk}_S \leftarrow \mathsf{PPS}^{(1)}.\mathsf{KGen}(\mathsf{msk}^{(1)}, S)$ and $\mathsf{sk}_{\overline{S}} \leftarrow \mathsf{PPS}^{(2)}.\mathsf{KGen}(\mathsf{msk}^{(2)}, [N]\backslash S)$. For each $j \in [N]$, if $j \in S$, compute $\mathbf{x}_j = \mathsf{PPS}^{(1)}.\mathsf{Decode}(j, \mathsf{ct}_j^{(1)}, S, \mathsf{sk}_S)$ and if $j \notin S$, $\mathbf{d}_j = \mathsf{PPS}^{(2)}.\mathsf{Decode}(j, \mathsf{ct}_j^{(2)}, [N]\backslash S, \mathsf{sk}_{\overline{S}})$. Then compute matrix $\mathbf{M} = [\mathbf{m}_1 \mid \ldots \mid \mathbf{m}_N] \in \mathbb{Z}_q^{n\times N}$ using these random masks according to Eq. (2) and $\mathbf{C} = \mathsf{Com}(\mathbf{M})$. Sample $\mathbf{s} \leftarrow \mathbb{Z}_q^n$, output $\mathsf{ct} := (\mathbf{s}^\top\mathbf{B} + \mathsf{err}, \mathbf{s}^\top(\mathbf{A} + \mathbf{C}) + \mathsf{err}, \mathbf{s}^\top\mathbf{p} + \mathsf{err} + \lfloor q/2 \rfloor \mu, \mathsf{sk}_S, \mathsf{sk}_{\overline{S}})$.

$\mathsf{KGen}$ remains unchanged from Sect. 2.2. For $\mathsf{Dec}$, we can use $\mathsf{sk}_S, \mathsf{sk}_{\overline{S}}$ which are provided as part of EqDBE ciphertext and $\mathsf{crs}$ to reconstruct matrix $\mathbf{M}$ via PPS $\mathsf{Decode}$ algorithm. From there we proceed similarly to EqDBE from Sect. 2.2. Compactness holds because PPS secret keys are independent of $N$. We will now describe $\mathsf{FakeSetup}$ and $\mathsf{Equivocate}$ algorithms.

$\mathsf{FakeSetup}$ : We leverage the correctness of PPS and program $\{\mathbf{x}'_j\}_{j\in S'}$ and $\{\mathbf{d}'_j\}_{j\notin S'}$ using PPS $\mathsf{skEnc}$ algorithm as follows. Sample $\widetilde{\mathsf{pk}}_i = \mathbf{t}_i \leftarrow \mathbb{Z}_q^n$ for each $i \in S'$. Sample $\mathsf{msk}^{(1)} \leftarrow \mathsf{PPS}^{(1)}.\mathsf{MSKGen}, \mathsf{msk}^{(2)} \leftarrow \mathsf{PPS}^{(2)}.\mathsf{MSKGen}$. Sample random masks $\mathbf{x}'_j \leftarrow \{\pm 1\}^m$ if $j \in S'$ and $\mathbf{d}'_j \leftarrow \mathbb{Z}_q^n$ if $j \notin S'$. Compute $\mathbf{M}'$ for set $S'$ according to Eq. (2) with these random masks. Compute $\mathbf{C}' = \mathsf{Com}(\mathbf{M}')$ and $\mathbf{A} = \mathbf{A}' - \mathbf{C}'$ where $\mathbf{A}' \leftarrow \mathbb{Z}_q^{n\times m}$. Also, $\mathbf{p} \leftarrow \mathbb{Z}_q^n$. Sample

[4] Indeed if $\mathcal{A}$ can choose $\mu$, it can trivially break this property by using $\mathsf{Decode}$ algorithm as $\mathsf{pkEnc}$ doesn't use $\mu$.

$\mathsf{ct}_j^{(1)}, \mathsf{ct}_j^{(2)}$ for $j \in [N]$ as follows

$$\mathsf{ct}_j^{(1)} \leftarrow \begin{cases} \mathsf{PPS}^{(1)}.\mathsf{skEnc}(j, \mathbf{x}_j) & \text{if } j \in S' \\ \mathsf{PPS}^{(1)}.\mathsf{pkEnc}(j) & \text{if } j \notin S' \end{cases} \text{ and } \mathsf{ct}_j^{(2)} \leftarrow \begin{cases} \mathsf{PPS}^{(2)}.\mathsf{skEnc}(j, \mathbf{t}_j + \mathbf{B}\mathbf{x}_j) & \text{if } j \in S' \\ \mathsf{PPS}^{(2)}.\mathsf{skEnc}(j, \mathbf{d}'_j) & \text{if } j \notin S' \end{cases}$$

Sample $\mathbf{s} \leftarrow \mathbb{Z}_q^n$ and compute $\widetilde{\mathsf{ct}} := (\mathbf{s}^\top \mathbf{B} + \mathsf{err}, \mathbf{s}^\top(\mathbf{A} + \mathbf{C}') + \mathsf{err}, \mathbf{s}^\top \mathbf{p} + \mathsf{err} + \lfloor q/2 \rfloor \mu)$. Set $\mathsf{aux} := (S', \mathsf{msk}^{(1)}, \mathsf{msk}^{(2)}, \widetilde{\mathsf{ct}})$ among other things. Output $\left(\widetilde{\mathsf{crs}} := \left(\mathsf{com.pp}, \mathbf{A}, \mathbf{p}, \{\mathsf{ct}_i^{(1)}\}_{i \in [N]}, \{\mathsf{ct}_i^{(2)}\}_{i \in [N]}\right), \{\widetilde{\mathsf{pk}_i}\}_{i \in S'}, \widetilde{\mathsf{ct}}, \mathsf{aux}\right)$

Equivocate: Given $S^* \subseteq S'$, sample $\mathsf{sk}_{S^*} \leftarrow \mathsf{PPS}^{(1)}.\mathsf{KGen}(\mathsf{msk}^{(1)}, S^*), \mathsf{sk}_{\overline{S^*}} \leftarrow \mathsf{PPS}^{(2)}.\mathsf{KGen}(\mathsf{msk}^{(2)}, [N] \backslash S^*)$ using $\mathsf{msk}^{(1)}, \mathsf{msk}^{(2)}$ that are present in aux. Output $\mathsf{ct} := (\widetilde{\mathsf{ct}}, \mathsf{sk}_{S^*}, \mathsf{sk}_{\overline{S^*}})$.

Observe that using $\mathsf{sk}_{S^*}, \mathsf{sk}_{\overline{S^*}}$ from EqDBE ciphertext and $\{\mathsf{ct}_j^{(1)}\}_{j \in [N]}, \{\mathsf{ct}_j^{(2)}\}_{j \in [N]}$ present in crs, by correctness of $\mathsf{PPS}^{(1)}, \mathsf{PPS}^{(2)}$ one can only learn the values of $\mathbf{M}'$. Take $\{\mathsf{ct}_j^{(1)}\}_{j \in [N]}$ and $\mathsf{sk}_{S^*}$, using these only if $j \in S^*$, $\mathsf{PPS}^{(1)}.\mathsf{Decode}$ reveals $\mathbf{x}'_j$. Similarly, using $\{\mathsf{ct}_j^{(2)}\}_{j \in [N]}$ and $\mathsf{sk}_{\overline{S^*}}$, only if $j \notin S^*$, we can learn $\mathbf{d}'_j$ if $j \notin S'$ and $\mathbf{t}_j + \mathbf{B}\mathbf{x}'_j$ if $j \in S' \backslash S^*$. These are the exact same values that $\mathbf{M}'$ uses in its columns. Thus, $\mathbf{M}'$ computed for set $S'$ and $\mathbf{M}^*$ computed for set $S^*$ according to Eq. (2) are exactly the same. For illustrative purposes, we provide this for the simple case of $N = 3, S' = \{1, 2\}, S^* = \{1\}$ in Fig. 1.

| $i = 1$ | $i = 2$ | $i = 3$ | |
|---|---|---|---|
| $\mathsf{skEnc}(1, \mathbf{x}'_1)$ | $\mathsf{skEnc}(2, \mathbf{x}'_2)$ | $\mathsf{pkEnc}(3)$ | $\leftarrow \mathsf{PPS}^{(1)}$ |
| $\mathsf{skEnc}(1, \mathbf{t}_1 + \mathbf{B}\mathbf{x}'_1)$ | $\mathsf{skEnc}(2, \mathbf{t}_2 + \mathbf{B}\mathbf{x}'_2)$ | $\mathsf{skEnc}(3, \mathbf{d}'_3)$ | $\leftarrow \mathsf{PPS}^{(2)}$ |

| | |
|---|---|
| $\mathsf{sk}_{S^*}$ | $\mathsf{sk}_{\overline{S^*}}$ |

**Fig. 1.** Structure of crs and values that can be learned from crs and secret keys yielded by FakeSetup, Equivocate algorithms. $x$ means that there is either no value programmed in this slot or with the secret keys present, this value cannot be learned. $x$ can be decoded using $\mathsf{sk}_{S^*}$ and $x$ can be decoded using $\mathsf{sk}_{\overline{S^*}}$ respectively. (Color figure online)

**Security Analysis.** We prove that the above construction satisfies mode indistinguishability and selective security for fake setup properties.

**Selective Security for Fake Setup.** Note that only useful part of aux is $\mathsf{msk}^{(1)}$, $\mathsf{msk}^{(2)}$ of PPS instantiations. Using these an adversary can either recreate $\mathbf{M}'$ from crs or equivocate. Thus, selective security is almost identical to Sect. 2.2 but in the standard model with PPS.

**Mode Indistinguishability.** This is tricky. Firstly, we can set $\mathbf{t}_i \leftarrow \mathbb{Z}_q^n$ for each $i \in S'$ by leftover hash lemma. Then for each $i \notin S'$, we can set

$\mathsf{ct}_i^{(2)} \leftarrow \mathsf{PPS}^{(2)}.\mathsf{skEnc}(i, \mathbf{d}'_i)$ for randomly sampled $\mathbf{d}'_i \leftarrow \mathbb{Z}_q^n$ using mode indistinguishability property of $\mathsf{PPS}^{(2)}$.

Next, we would like to program for each $i \in S'$, $\mathsf{ct}_i^{(1)}, \mathsf{ct}_i^{(2)}$ such that they decode to $\mathbf{x}'_i, \mathbf{t}_i + \mathbf{B}\mathbf{x}'_i$. We do this via a hybrid argument, iterating through each user $i \in S'$. The main hurdle is that the correct programming strategy for user $i$ depends on the bit $b_i := (i \in S^*)$, which is unknown during $\mathsf{crs}$ generation. If we guess full set $S^*$ we suffer exponential loss. To bypass this, we utilize the 'Piecewise Guessing Framework' [14,15,25,27,29,30,32]. In the $i$-th hybrid transition, we only need to correctly guess the single bit $b_i$. This localized guessing strategy keeps the security loss minimal.

In a nutshell, here is the proof strategy: for each $i \in S'$, we will guess one bit of information corresponding to $(i \in S^*)$. If yes: firstly, we will use the mode indistinguishability property of $\mathsf{PPS}^{(1)}$ to change $\mathsf{ct}_i^{(1)} \leftarrow \mathsf{PPS}^{(1)}.\mathsf{skEnc}(i, \mathbf{x}'_i)$ and then use the payload hiding property of $\mathsf{PPS}^{(2)}$ to change $\mathsf{ct}_i^{(2)} \leftarrow \mathsf{PPS}^{(2)}.\mathsf{skEnc}(i, \mathbf{t}_i + \mathbf{B}\mathbf{x}'_i)$. If no: then we first use the mode indistinguishability property of $\mathsf{PPS}^{(2)}$ to change $\mathsf{ct}_i^{(2)} \leftarrow \mathsf{PPS}^{(2)}.\mathsf{skEnc}(\mathsf{msk}^{(2)}, i, \mathbf{d}'_i)$ for uniformly random $\mathbf{d}'_i \leftarrow \mathbb{Z}_q^n$. At this point, $\mathbf{x}'_i$ is not appearing anywhere in the view of the attacker. Thus, we can use leftover hash lemma to switch $\mathbf{d}'_i$ to be $\mathbf{t}_i + \mathbf{B}\mathbf{x}'_i$. Then, we will use payload hiding property of $\mathsf{PPS}^{(1)}$ to change $\mathsf{ct}_i^{(1)} \leftarrow \mathsf{PPS}^{(1)}.\mathsf{skEnc}(i, \mathbf{x}'_i)$.

Crucially, observe that in both yes and no cases, we arrive at the same hybrid where both $\mathsf{ct}_i^{(1)}$ and $\mathsf{ct}_i^{(2)}$ are sampled using $\mathsf{skEnc}$. Thus, by the piecewise guessing strategy from [29,32], the difference between the hybrids where $\mathsf{ct}_i^{(1)}, \mathsf{ct}_i^{(2)}$ are sampled using $\mathsf{pkEnc}$ and the one where they are sampled using $\mathsf{skEnc}$ is at most $2\max\{\epsilon_{yes}, \epsilon_{no}\}$ where $\epsilon_{yes}$ and $\epsilon_{no}$ are the advantages of an attacker in distinguishing the yes and no strands of hybrids respectively. Similar techniques were used in the context of registered attribute-based encryption in [26,42]. An illustrative flow of hybrids in mode indistinguishability proof can be found in Fig. 2 below.

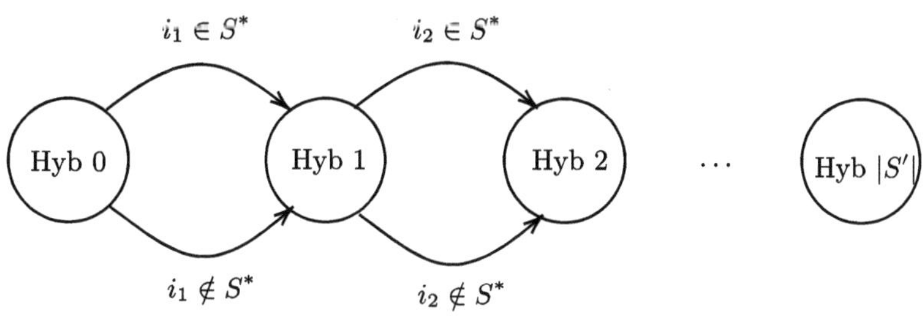


**Fig. 2.** Flow of hybrids and piecewise guessing framework description

This way, using the piecewise guessing strategy, after $|S'|$-many hybrids, we can set the $\mathsf{crs}$ to be exactly as we do in $\mathsf{FakeSetup}$. The rest of the changes are just semantic and mode indistinguishability property of the design holds.

**On the Size of** $\mathsf{crs}$**.** Interestingly, $\mathsf{crs}$ in our EqDBE in standard model construction grows with $\Omega(N)$ due to presence of $2N$ PPS ciphertexts ($N$ per each instantiation). If our $\mathsf{crs}$ doesn't grow with $N$, sampling and programming $N$ random masks in the $\mathsf{crs}$ with short handles $\mathsf{sk}_S, \mathsf{sk}_{\overline{S}}$ might incur certain incompressibility barriers similar to non-committing encryption [34]. We leave it as an interesting open problem to either prove a barrier to reducing the $\mathsf{crs}$ size or to construct an adaptively secure DBE with short $\mathsf{crs}$ in standard model.

This concludes the description of our EqDBE scheme in standard model construction from decomposed LWE and PPS. Full construction is provided in Sect. 7.

### 2.4 Programmable Pseudorandom Set Sampler Constructions

We now provide two constructions of PPS scheme with varying efficiencies. The first is from standard LWE and the second is from a new falsifiable assumption that we call 1-key LWE. Full definition of PPS is provided in Sect. 6. A sanitized version is provided in Sect. 2.3.

**PPS from LWE.** Our construction for message space $\mathcal{M} = \mathbb{Z}_2$ is as follows:

$\mathsf{PPGen}$ : Sample a matrix $\mathbf{A} \leftarrow \mathbb{Z}_q^{n \times m}$. Output $\mathsf{crs} := (N, \mathbf{A})$ along with other LWE parameters.

$\mathsf{MSKGen}$ : For each $i \in [N]$ sample $\mathbf{s}_{i,0}, \mathbf{s}_{i,1} \leftarrow \mathbb{Z}_q^n$. Output $\mathsf{msk} := (\mathbf{s}_{i,b})_{i \in [N], b \in \{0,1\}}$.

$\mathsf{KGen}(S)$ : Let $\mathbf{r} = (r_1, \ldots, r_N) \in \{0,1\}^N$ denote the characteristic vector of $S$, i.e., $r_i = 1$ if and only $i \in S$. Output $\mathsf{sk}_S := \sum_{i \in [N]} \mathbf{s}_{i,r_i} \in \mathbb{Z}_q^n$.

$\mathsf{skEnc}(i, \mu)$ : Sample $\mathbf{x} \leftarrow \{\pm 1\}^m$ and set $\mathbf{c}_0 := \mathbf{A}\mathbf{x}$. Also sample $\{z_j\}_{j \in [N]}$ such that $\sum_{j \in [N]} z_j = 0$. For each $j \in [N], b \in \{0,1\}$,

$$c_{j,b} = \begin{cases} (\mathbf{s}_{j,b}^\top \mathbf{A} + \mathsf{err})\mathbf{x} + z_j & \text{if } j \neq i \\ (\mathbf{s}_{i,1}^\top \mathbf{A} + \mathsf{err})\mathbf{x} + z_i + t & \text{if } j = i, b = 1 \end{cases} \quad \text{and } c_{i,0} \leftarrow \mathbb{Z}_q$$

Output $\mathsf{ct}_i := (\mathbf{c}_0, (c_{j,b})_{j \in [N], b \in \{0,1\}}, \lceil t \rfloor_2 + \mu) \in \mathbb{Z}_q^n \times \mathbb{Z}_q^{2N} \times \mathbb{Z}_2$.

$\mathsf{pkEnc}(i)$ : Sample $\mathsf{ct}_i \leftarrow \mathbb{Z}_q^n \times \mathbb{Z}_q^{2N} \times \mathbb{Z}_2$.

$\mathsf{Decode}(i, \mathsf{ct}, S, \mathsf{sk}_S)$ : Parse $\mathsf{ct}$ as $(\mathbf{c}_0, (c_{j,b})_{j \in [N], b \in \{0,1\}}, c_T)$. If $i \notin S$, output $\perp$. Otherwise, using characteristic vector $(r_1, \ldots, r_N)$ for $S$ do the following. Compute $c' = \left(\sum_{j \in [N]} c_{j,r_j}\right) - \mathsf{sk}_S^\top \mathbf{c}_0$. Then, output $c_T - \lceil c' \rfloor_2$.

Note that compactness is immediate as $\mathsf{sk}_S \in \mathbb{Z}_q^n$ which is independent of number of users $N$. Correctness is argued as follows: as $c_{j,r_j} = (\mathbf{s}_{j,r_j}^\top \mathbf{A} + \mathsf{err})\mathbf{x} + z_j + \delta_{ji} t$[5], if $i \in S, r_i = 1$, then $c_{i,1}$ contains $t$. So, $\sum_{j \in [N]} c_{j,r_j} = \left(\sum_{j \in [N]} \mathbf{s}_{j,r_j}^\top \mathbf{A} + \mathsf{err}\right) \mathbf{x} + t$ as $\sum_{j \in [N]} z_j = 0$. Hence, $c' \approx t$ and thus $c_T - \lceil c' \rfloor_2 \approx \mu$.

**Security Analysis.** We prove that above design for PPS satisfies payload hiding and mode indistinguishability. Essentially we show that for an index $i \in [N]$,

[5] $\delta_{ji}$ denotes the Kronecker delta function. That is, $\delta_{ji} = 1$ if and only if $j = i$.

$\mathsf{skEnc}(i, \mu)$ is indistinguishable from a random string of $\mathbb{Z}_q$, $\mathbb{Z}_2$ elements even when an attacker $\mathcal{A}$ is given a secret key $\mathsf{sk}_S$ for $i \in S$ and $i \notin S$.

**Payload Hiding.** In this game, attacker queries an encryption for $(i, \mu) \in [N] \times \mathbb{Z}_2$ and later adaptively queries for a secret key for $S$ such that $i \notin S$. Note that as $i \notin S$, $\mathbf{s}_{i,1}$ is not used anywhere in the game. Particularly, $\mathsf{skEnc}$ queries for other indices $k \neq i$ can be constructed given $\mathbf{s}_{i,1}^\top \mathbf{A} + \mathsf{err}$ as opposed to $\mathbf{s}_{i,1}$. Thus, we can use LWE and leftover hash lemma to switch $c_{i,1}$ in the challenge ciphertext to a uniformly random element in $\mathbb{Z}_q$. As a consequence, both $z_i$ and $t$ are hidden from $\mathcal{A}$'s view. Hence, we can set $c_T$ in the challenge ciphertext for index $i$ to be a uniformly random element of $\mathbb{Z}_2$ and also compute $\{z_j\}_{j \neq i}$ as uniformly random elements from $\mathbb{Z}_q$.

Next, we define $N$ hybrids, where in each Hybrid $j$, we would like to set $c_{\leq j,0}$ and $c_{\leq j,1}$ as random elements in $\mathbb{Z}_q$. However, there is an issue with this. Both $c_{j,0}$ and $c_{j,1}$ share a common random element $z_j$. To resolve this, let us guess if $j \in S$ for the single key query $S$. If yes: we can use LWE security and leftover hash lemma to set $c_{j,0}$ to be a uniformly random element in $\mathbb{Z}_q$ as $\mathbf{s}_{j,0}$ is revealed as part of key query (we can use $\mathbf{s}_{j,0}^\top \mathbf{A} + \mathsf{err}$ to construct other $\mathsf{skEnc}$ ciphertexts). Now, $z_j$ only appears in $c_{j,1}$ and is a uniformly random element form $\mathbb{Z}_q$. This allows us to set $c_{j,1}$ as a uniformly random element and move to the next hybrid. If no: we proceed in a flipped manner, now $\mathbf{s}_{j,1}$ is not used anywhere which lets us set $c_{j,1}$ as a random element using LWE security and leftover hash lemma. Then as $z_j$ only appears in $c_{j,0}$, we can set this as a random element as well. As both paths result in the same hybrid, we can use the piecewise guess framework [29,32] (similar to proof of EqDBE from PPS) to argue that $\mathsf{skEnc}(i, \mu)$ is indistinguishable from a uniformly random string. Thus, payload hiding holds.

**Mode Indistinguishability.** In this game, attacker queries an encryption for $i \in [N]$ and later adaptively queries for a secret key for $S$ such that $i \notin S$. More importantly $\mu \leftarrow \mathbb{Z}_2$ is chosen by the challenger. Thus, we can readily set $c_T$ to be a random element from $\mathbb{Z}_2$ in the challenge ciphertext. As a consequence, $t$ only appears in $c_{i,1}$ of the challenge ciphertext and thus, $c_{i,1}$ can be sampled as a random element in $\mathbb{Z}_q$. Now, we can do the same piecewise guessing argument that we did in payload hiding analysis and set the entire challenge ciphertext to be a random string of $\mathbb{Z}_q$ and $\mathbb{Z}_2$ elements.

We remark that it is important to set $c_{i,0}$ in $\mathsf{skEnc}(i, \mu)$ to be a random element in the construction. For instance, if we set $c_{i,0}$ as a structured element akin to $(\mathbf{s}_{i,0}^\top \mathbf{A} + \mathsf{err})\mathbf{x} + z_i$, then we cannot argue security. Specifically, $\mathcal{A}$ in possession of $\mathsf{sk}_S$ for $i \notin S$ can compute $\sum_{j \neq i} c_{j,r_j} + c_{i,0} - \mathsf{sk}_S^\top \mathbf{c}_0$ which will be a low norm element in $\mathbb{Z}_q$ and thus distinguishable from a uniformly random element. This concludes the description of our PPS construction from LWE.

**PPS from 1-key LWE.** Note that the definition of our PPS scheme is very much close to a private-key ABE scheme [24,36] with pseudorandom ciphertexts and compact secret keys. The celebrated work of Boneh et al. [5] does provide the same. So, it looks straight-forward to use [5] to construct a PPS scheme.

Using this insight, we give a construction of PPS for message space $\mathbb{Z}_2$. One benefit is that $|\mathsf{ct}|$ in this scheme is virtually independent of $N$.

$\mathsf{PPGen}$ : Simply output LWE parameters.
$\mathsf{MSKGen}$ : Sample $\mathbf{A} \in \mathbb{Z}_q^{n\times m}$ with a trapdoor $\mathbf{T_A}$, $\mathbf{B} \leftarrow \mathbb{Z}_q^{n\times\lceil\log N\rceil m}, \mathbf{d} \leftarrow \mathbb{Z}_q^n$.
$\mathsf{KGen}(S)$ : Let mem-$S$ denote the membership verification circuit for $S$, i.e., mem-$S(i) = 0$ if and only if $i \in S$[6]. Sample $\mathbf{r}_S \leftarrow [\mathbf{A} \mid \mathbf{B}_S]^{-1}(\mathbf{d})$ where $\mathbf{B}_S = \mathsf{EvalF}(\mathbf{B}, \text{mem-}S)$. Output $\mathsf{sk}_S := (\mathbf{r}_S, \mathbf{B}) \in \mathbb{Z}_q^{2m} \times \mathbb{Z}_q^{n\times\lceil\log N\rceil m}$.
$\mathsf{skEnc}(i,\mu)$ : Sample $\mathbf{s} \leftarrow \mathbb{Z}_q^n$. Output $\mathsf{ct}_i := (\mathbf{s}^\top\mathbf{A} + \mathsf{err}, \mathbf{s}^\top(\mathbf{B} + \mathbf{i}^\top \otimes \mathbf{G}) + \mathsf{err}, \lceil \mathbf{s}^\top\mathbf{d}\rfloor_2 + \mu)$ where $\mathbf{i} \in \{0,1\}^{\lceil\log N\rceil}$ is the bit-vector representation of $i$ and $\mathbf{G}$ is the gadget matrix [33].
$\mathsf{pkEnc}(i)$ : Sample $\mathsf{ct}_i \leftarrow \mathbb{Z}_q^{1\times(1+\lceil\log N\rceil)m} \times \mathbb{Z}_2$.
$\mathsf{Decode}(i, \mathsf{ct}, S, \mathsf{sk}_S)$ : Parse $\mathsf{ct}$ as $(\mathbf{c}_1^\top, \mathbf{c}_2^\top, c_T)$. If $i \notin S$, output $\perp$. Otherwise, compute $c' = [\mathbf{c}_1^\top \mid \mathbf{c}_2^\top\mathbf{H}_{S,\mathbf{i}}]\mathbf{r}_S$ where $\mathbf{H}_{S,\mathbf{i}} = \mathsf{EvalFX}(\mathbf{B}, \text{mem-}S, \mathbf{i})$. Then, output $c_T - \lceil c'\rfloor_2$.

Here, $\mathsf{EvalF}, \mathsf{EvalFX}$ are the lattice matrix homomorphic computation functions [5,19]. Compactness is immediate as $\mathsf{sk}_S$ only grows with $\log N$. Correctness follows as $\mathbf{c}_2^\top\mathbf{H}_{S,\mathbf{i}} \approx \mathbf{s}^\top(\mathbf{B} + \mathbf{i}^\top \otimes \mathbf{G})\mathbf{H}_{S,\mathbf{i}} = \mathbf{s}^\top\mathbf{B}_S$. Thus, $c' \approx \mathbf{s}^\top\mathbf{d} \implies c_T - \lceil c'\rfloor_2 \approx \mu$. In fact, we can also argue payload hiding readily. If $i \notin S$, the challenge ciphertext can be set to a random string by hardness of LWE and leftover hash lemma similar to the selective security argument of [5]. All that is left is to argue mode indistinguishability. Before that, we describe our falsifiable lattice-based assumption that we call '1-key LWE'.

**1-key LWE.** We describe this assumption using the following game:

1. $\mathcal{A}$ sends $i \in [N]$. Challenger samples $\mathbf{B} \leftarrow \mathbb{Z}_q^{n\times\lceil\log N\rceil m}, \mathbf{d} \leftarrow \mathbb{Z}_q^n$, $\mathbf{A}$ sampled with trapdoor $\mathbf{T_A}$, and samples a bit $\beta \leftarrow \{0,1\}$.
   If $\beta = 0$, challenger sets $\mathbf{c}_1^\top := \mathbf{s}^\top\mathbf{A} + \mathsf{err}, \mathbf{c}_2^\top := \mathbf{s}^\top(\mathbf{B} + \mathbf{i}^\top \otimes \mathbf{G}) + \mathsf{err}$ for $\mathbf{s} \leftarrow \mathbb{Z}_q^n$. Otherwise, if $\beta = 1$, challenger samples $\mathbf{c}_1 \leftarrow \mathbb{Z}_q^m, \mathbf{c}_2 \leftarrow \mathbb{Z}_q^{\lceil\log N\rceil m}$.
   Challenger sends $(\mathbf{A}, \mathbf{B}, \mathbf{d}, \mathbf{c}_1^\top, \mathbf{c}_2^\top)$ to $\mathcal{A}$.
2. $\mathcal{A}$ sends $S \subseteq [N]$ and receives $\mathbf{r}_S \in \mathbb{Z}_q^{2m}$ such that $[\mathbf{A}|\mathbf{B}_S]\mathbf{r}_S = \mathbf{d}$. $\mathcal{A}$ declares its guess $\beta'$.

We say the assumption holds if $|\Pr[\beta' = \beta] - 1/2| \leq \mathsf{negl}(\lambda)$. Clearly, this is a falsifiable assumption. Also, observe that if $i \notin S$, this assumption follows from LWE. Intuitively, hardness of this assumption holds as the most an attacker can do is take the vectors $\mathbf{s}^\top\mathbf{A} + \mathsf{err}, \mathbf{s}^\top(\mathbf{B} + \mathbf{i}^\top \otimes \mathbf{G}) + \mathsf{err}, \mathbf{r}_S$ and get a new LWE sample for $\mathbf{d}$[7]. This does not reveal too much information about the prior vectors as this new LWE sample itself is pseudorandom. We provide a more detailed preliminary cryptanalysis of this assumption in full version.

[6] Following the convention for lattices, 0 denotes accept.
[7] If challenger also provides $c_3 = \mathbf{s}^\top\mathbf{d} + \mathsf{err}$, $\mathcal{A}$ can trivially win. It is important that this is not provided.

**Mode Indistinguishability from 1-key LWE.** We need to show that $\mathsf{skEnc}(i, \mu)$ is a pseudorandom string even if $\mathcal{A}$ *adaptively* queries a secret key for set $S$ such that $i \in S$ and $\mu \leftarrow \mathbb{Z}_2$ sampled by challenger. $\mathsf{skEnc}(i, \mu)$ has the form $(\mathbf{s}^\top \mathbf{A} + \mathsf{err}, \mathbf{s}^\top(\mathbf{B} + \mathbf{i}^\top \otimes \mathbf{G}) + \mathsf{err}, \lceil \mathbf{s}^\top \mathbf{d} \rfloor_2 + \mu)$. Thus, we can use the hardness 1-key LWE assumption to set the first two components as uniformly random strings. Any $\mathsf{skEnc}$ queries for indices $k \neq i$ can be constructed using $\mathbf{A}, \mathbf{B}, \mathbf{d}$ provided by the 1-key LWE challenger. Then, as $\mu \leftarrow \mathbb{Z}_2$ is unknown to the $\mathcal{A}$, we can also set the third component as a uniformly random element from $\mathbb{Z}_2$.

**Mode Indistinguishability from LWE?** We remark that mode indistinguishability of above design might not be possible from standard LWE. If $\mathcal{A}$ *selectively* declares set $S$, then we can sample $\mathbf{r}_S$ from appropriate gaussian distribution and set $\mathbf{d} = [\mathbf{A} \mid \mathbf{B}_S]\mathbf{r}_S$. Even in this case, $\mathbf{d}$ is close to random by pre-image distribution properties of lattice trapdoors [2,8,18,33]. However, if $\mathcal{A}$ adaptively declares $S$ such that $i \in S$, without a trapdoor for $\mathbf{A}$, it doesn't seem possible to sample $\mathbf{r}_S$ such that $[\mathbf{A} \mid \mathbf{B}_S]\mathbf{r}_S = \mathbf{d}$ for any $S$. Thus, we rely on 1-key LWE assumption for mode indistinguishability. We leave it as an interesting open problem to prove mode indistinguishability of above design from standard LWE. This concludes the description of our PPS constructions. Full constructions of PPS from LWE is in Sect. 8 and PPS from 1-key LWE is provided in full version.

**Related Work for PPS.** At a high level, our PPS abstraction can be viewed as a one-key, secret-key analogue to batched Identity-Based Encryption [6,11]. However, the core distinguishing feature of PPS is its mode indistinguishability property, which ensures that a ciphertext remains pseudorandom even to an evaluator holding an accepting secret key as long as the encrypted message is sampled randomly. In this regard, mode indistinguishability conceptually mirrors the pseudorandomness guarantees of projective PRGs [3,28]. Our PPS primitive fundamentally diverges from projective PRGs due to its requirement of simultaneously achieving both mode indistinguishability and payload hiding.

Syntactically, our PPS framework also shares similarities with the mixed FE scheme introduced in [21]. Despite these parallels, the underlying requirements are different. Rather than demanding the full expressiveness of FE, PPS is much closer in scope to a mixed attribute-based encryption scheme for inner product predicates. This targeted functionality allows us to instantiate PPS efficiently from standard LWE.

**Further Extensions.** We conclude with a few extensions possible for our equivocal framework in the context of DBE. One can alternatively define a strongly-secure EqDBE scheme which readily yields an adaptively secure DBE. This way we can skip the $2\times$ ciphertext blowup incurred by the semi-static to adaptively secure transformations of [20,28,31]. Alternatively, we can also consider the following. Our EqDBE scheme can equivocate at most one ciphertext. One can define an EqDBE scheme with a $\mathsf{FakeSetup}$ algorithm that can produce a fake ciphertext for two disjoint sets and size of the fake ciphertext is less than two ciphertexts of regular EqDBE combined. This way we can equivocate two subsets and rely on the two-key transformation of [20,31] to construct an adaptively secure DBE scheme with even shorter ciphertexts.

## 3 Preliminaries

We provide the statement of $\ell$-decomposed LWE assumption below.

**Assumption 1** ([1], adapted from [39,40]). *Let $(n, m, q, \chi)$ be LWE parameters. Then, the $(\ell, \sigma)$-decomposed LWE assumption states that*

$$\{(\mathbf{W}, \mathbf{D}, \mathbf{B}, \mathbf{s}^\top \mathbf{B} + \mathbf{e}^\top)\} \approx_c \{(\mathbf{W}, \mathbf{D}, \mathbf{B}, \mathbf{c}^\top)\}$$

*where $\mathbf{W} \leftarrow \mathbb{Z}_q^{n \times \ell m}, \mathbf{D} \leftarrow \mathcal{D}_{\mathbb{Z},\sigma}^{m \times \ell m}, \mathbf{s} \leftarrow \mathbb{Z}_q^n, \mathbf{e} \leftarrow \mathcal{D}_{\mathbb{Z},\chi}^{\ell^2 m}, \mathbf{c} \leftarrow \mathbb{Z}_q^{\ell^2 m}$ and $\mathbf{B} = \mathbf{W}(\mathbf{I}_\ell \otimes \mathbf{D}) + \mathsf{vec}(\mathbf{I}_\ell)^\top \otimes \mathbf{G} \in \mathbb{Z}_q^{n \times \ell^2 m}$. When $\sigma = \mathsf{poly}(\lambda, \ell, m)$ we simply call this as $\ell$-decomposed LWE assumption.*

### 3.1 Matrix Commitment Scheme

We provide the definition of a matrix commitment scheme ($\mathsf{MCOM}$) from decomposed LWE adapted from [39, Appendix C].

**Syntax.** An $\mathsf{MCOM}$ scheme consists of the following polynomial time algorithms.

$\mathsf{Setup}(1^n, 1^m, q, \sigma) \rightarrow (\mathbf{W}, \mathbf{D}, \mathbf{B})$. The randomized *public-coin* setup algorithm takes as input LWE parameters $(n, m, q, \sigma)$ where $\sigma = \mathsf{poly}(\lambda, m)$ and outputs $\mathbf{W} \leftarrow \mathbb{Z}_q^{n \times 2m^3}, \mathbf{D} \leftarrow \mathcal{D}_{\mathbb{Z},\sigma}^{m \times 2m^3}$, and $\mathbf{B} = \mathbf{W}(\mathbf{I}_{2m^2} \otimes \mathbf{D}) + \mathsf{vec}(\mathbf{I}_{2m^2})^\top \otimes \mathbf{G}$. The following algorithms take $(\mathbf{W}, \mathbf{D}, \mathbf{B})$ implicitly.

$\mathsf{Com}(\mathbf{M}) \rightarrow \mathbf{C}$. The deterministic commitment algorithm takes as input matrix $\mathbf{M} \in \mathbb{Z}_q^{n \times N}$ and outputs commitment matrix $\mathbf{C} \in \mathbb{Z}_q^{n \times m}$.

$\mathsf{Verify}(1^N) \rightarrow \mathbf{V}_N$. The deterministic verification algorithm takes as input column length $N$ and outputs verification matrix $\mathbf{V}_N \in \mathbb{Z}_q^{m \times N}$.

$\mathsf{Open}(\mathbf{M}) \rightarrow \mathbf{Z}$. The deterministic opening algorithm takes as input matrix $\mathbf{M} \in \mathbb{Z}_q^{n \times N}$ and outputs opening matrix $\mathbf{Z} \in \mathbb{Z}_q^{4m^5 \times N}$.

**Definition 1** ($\mathsf{MCOM}$). *A* $\mathsf{MCOM}$ *scheme* $(\mathsf{Setup}, \mathsf{Com}, \mathsf{Verify}, \mathsf{Open})$ *satisfies the following properties.*

**Correctness.** *For any $n, q \in \mathbb{N}, m = \Omega(n \log q), \sigma = \mathsf{poly}(n, m), N = \mathsf{poly}(\lambda)$, any $(\mathbf{W}, \mathbf{D}, \mathbf{B}) \leftarrow \mathsf{Setup}(1^n, 1^m, q, \sigma)$, any matrix $\mathbf{M} \in \mathbb{Z}_q^{n \times N}$, $\mathbf{C}\mathbf{V}_N = \mathbf{M} - \mathbf{B}\mathbf{Z}$ where $\mathbf{C} = \mathsf{Com}(\mathbf{M}), \mathbf{V}_N = \mathsf{Verify}(1^N), \mathbf{Z} = \mathsf{Open}(\mathbf{M})$.*

**Compactness.** *For any $n, q \in \mathbb{N}, m = \Omega(n \log q), \sigma = \mathsf{poly}(n, m), N = \mathsf{poly}(\lambda)$, any $(\mathbf{W}, \mathbf{D}, \mathbf{B}) \leftarrow \mathsf{Setup}(1^n, 1^m, q, \sigma)$, any matrix $\mathbf{M} \in \mathbb{Z}_q^{n \times N}$, $\|\mathbf{V}_N\| \leq O(\|\mathbf{D}\| \, m^4 \log q)$ and $\|\mathbf{Z}\| \leq O(\|\mathbf{D}\| \, m^7 \log q \log N)$ where $\mathbf{V}_N = \mathsf{Verify}(1^N)$ and $\mathbf{Z} = \mathsf{Open}(\mathbf{M})$.*

### 3.2 Distributed Broadcast Encryption

**Syntax.** A distributed broadcast encryption scheme (DBE) consists of the following polynomial-time algorithms.

$\mathsf{GSetup}(1^\lambda, 1^N) \to \mathsf{crs}$. The possibly randomized global setup algorithm takes as input number of users $N$ and outputs common reference string $\mathsf{crs}$. The following algorithms take $\mathsf{crs}$ implicitly.

$\mathsf{KGen}(i) \to (\mathsf{pk}_i, \mathsf{sk}_i)$. The randomized key generation algorithm takes as input index $i \in [N]$ and outputs public-secret key pair $(\mathsf{pk}_i, \mathsf{sk}_i)$.

$\mathsf{Enc}(\{\mathsf{pk}_i\}_{i \in S}, \mu) \to \mathsf{ct}$. The randomized encryption algorithm takes as input public keys for users in set $S$, message $\mu \in \{0,1\}$, and outputs a ciphertext $\mathsf{ct}$.

$\mathsf{Dec}(\{\mathsf{pk}_i\}_{i \in S}, (j, \mathsf{sk}_j), \mathsf{ct}) \to \mu'$ The deterministic decryption algorithm takes as input public keys for users in set $S$, secret key for user $j$, $\mathsf{sk}_j$, ciphertext $\mathsf{ct}$, and outputs $\mu' \in \{0,1\} \cup \{\perp\}$.

**Definition 2.** *A* DBE *scheme* $(\mathsf{GSetup}, \mathsf{KGen}, \mathsf{Enc}, \mathsf{Dec})$ *is said to be a DBE scheme if it satisfies the following properties.*

**Correctness.** *For any $\lambda \in \mathbb{N}$, positive polynomial $N \in \mathbb{N}$, $S \subseteq [N]$, $j \in S, \mu \in \{0,1\}$,*

$$\Pr\left[\mu = \mathsf{Dec}(\{\mathsf{pk}_i\}_{i \in S}, (j, \mathsf{sk}_j), \mathsf{ct}) \;:\; \begin{array}{c} \mathsf{crs} \leftarrow \mathsf{GSetup}(1^\lambda, 1^N), \\ \forall\, i \in S, (\mathsf{pk}_i, \mathsf{sk}_i) \leftarrow \mathsf{KGen}(i), \\ \mathsf{ct} \leftarrow \mathsf{Enc}(\{\mathsf{pk}_i\}_{i \in S}, \mu) \end{array}\right] = 1$$

**Compactness.** *There exists three polynomials* $\mathsf{poly}_{\mathsf{pk}}(\cdot,\cdot), \mathsf{poly}_{\mathsf{sk}}(\cdot,\cdot), \mathsf{poly}_{\mathsf{ct}}(\cdot,\cdot)$ *such that for any $\lambda, N \in \mathbb{N}, S \subseteq [N], \forall\, i \in [N]$,* $|\mathsf{pk}_i| = \mathsf{poly}_{\mathsf{pk}}(\lambda, \log N)$, $|\mathsf{sk}_i| = \mathsf{poly}_{\mathsf{sk}}(\lambda, \log N)$, $|\mathsf{ct}| = \mathsf{poly}_{\mathsf{ct}}(\lambda, \log N)$.

**Adaptive Security.** *For any admissible* PPT *adversary $\mathcal{A}$, there exists a negligible function such that $\forall\ \lambda \in \mathbb{N}$,*

$$\left|\Pr\left[b \leftarrow \mathcal{A}(\mathsf{ct}) \;:\; \begin{array}{l} 1^N \leftarrow \mathcal{A}(1^\lambda), \\ \mathsf{crs} \leftarrow \mathsf{GSetup}(1^\lambda, 1^N), \\ S \leftarrow \mathcal{A}^{\mathcal{O}(\cdot)}(\mathsf{crs}), \\ b \leftarrow \{0,1\}, \mathsf{ct} \leftarrow \mathsf{Enc}(\{\mathsf{pk}_i\}_{i \in S}, b) \end{array}\right] - \frac{1}{2}\right| \le \mathsf{negl}(\lambda)$$

*where $\mathcal{O}$ is a stateful oracle that responds to the following queries.*

$(\mathsf{KGen}, i)$. *$\mathcal{A}$ sends index $i \in [N]$. $\mathcal{O}$ checks if $i$ was already queried for* $\mathsf{KGen}$. *If so, it returns $\perp$. Otherwise, $\mathcal{O}$ performs* $(\mathsf{pk}_i, \mathsf{sk}_i) \leftarrow \mathsf{KGen}(i)$ *and sends* $\mathsf{pk}_i$ *to $\mathcal{A}$.*

$(\mathsf{Corr}, i)$ *$\mathcal{A}$ sends index $i$. $\mathcal{O}$ checks if $i$ was already queried for* $\mathsf{KGen}$. *If so, it responds to $\mathcal{A}$ with* $\mathsf{sk}_i$. *Otherwise, it outputs $\perp$.*

*A stateful* PPT *machine $\mathcal{A}$ is said to be admissible if $S \subseteq [N]$ and $\forall\ i^* \in S$, $\mathcal{A}$ made* $(\mathsf{KGen}, i^*)$ *query but not* $(\mathsf{Corr}, i^*)$ *query.*

**Definition 3 (Semi-Static Security).** *A* DBE *scheme* (GSetup, KGen, Enc, Dec) *is said to be semi-statically secure if satisfies correctness and compactness of Definition 2 and the weaker semi-static security defined as follows: $\mathcal{A}$ can no longer corrupt any users and $\mathcal{A}$ selectively, before receiving* crs *specifies a set $S' \subseteq [N]$ and receives $\{\mathsf{pk}_i\}_{i \in S'}$ along with* crs. *After that, $\mathcal{A}$ sends a set $S^* \subseteq S'$. $\mathcal{A}$ wins the game if it can guess $b \leftarrow \{0,1\}$ encrypted using $\{\mathsf{pk}_i\}_{i \in S^*}$.*

**Theorem 2** ([20,31])**.** *Assuming the existence of a semi-statically secure DBE scheme, there exists an adaptively-secure DBE scheme in the random oracle model.*

**Theorem 3** ([28])**.** *Assuming the existence of a semi-statically secure DBE scheme and hardness of* LWE *with subexponential modulus-to-noise ratio, there exists an adaptively-secure DBE scheme in the standard model.*

## 4 Equivocal DBE: A New Methodology for Adaptive Security

In this section, we introduce our notion of equivocal DBE scheme (EqDBE) and show that this generically implies semi-statically secure DBE. In turn this yields an adaptively secure DBE in the random oracle model [20,31] with optimal parameters or in the standard model in conjunction with the hardness of LWE assumption [28].

**Syntax.** An EqDBE consists of the following polynomial-time algorithms.

GSetup, KGen, Enc, Dec. These algorithms are defined similar to a DBE scheme (Sect. 3.2).

$\mathsf{FakeSetup}(1^\lambda, 1^N, S', \mu) \rightarrow (\widetilde{\mathsf{crs}}, \{\widetilde{\mathsf{pk}}_i\}_{i \in S'}, \widetilde{\mathsf{ct}}, \mathsf{aux})$. The randomized fake setup algorithm takes as input number of users $N$, set $S' \subseteq [N]$, message $\mu \in \{0,1\}$, outputs fake CRS, $\widetilde{\mathsf{crs}}$, fake public keys for all users in $i \in S'$, $\{\widetilde{\mathsf{pk}}_i\}_{i \in S'}$, fake ciphertext $\widetilde{\mathsf{ct}}$, and auxiliary information aux.

$\mathsf{Equivocate}(\mathsf{aux}, S^*) \rightarrow \mathsf{ct}$. The possibly randomized ciphertext equivocation algorithm takes as input auxiliary information aux, set $S^* \subseteq S'$, and outputs ciphertext ct.

**Definition 4.**
*An* EqDBE *scheme* (GSetup, KGen, Enc, Dec, FakeSetup, Equivocate) *should satisfy the following properties.*

**Correctness and Compactness.** *These are defined for* (GSetup, KGen, Enc, Dec)*, exactly as correctness and compactness for a DBE scheme (Definition 2).*

*Mode Indistinguishability. For any* PPT *admissible adversary* $\mathcal{A}$, *there exists a negligible function* $\mathsf{negl}(\cdot)$ *such that* $\forall\ \lambda \in N$,

$$\left| \Pr\left[ b \leftarrow \mathcal{A}(\mathsf{ct}^{(b)}) \ : \begin{array}{l} b \leftarrow \{0,1\}, (1^N, S', \mu) \leftarrow \mathcal{A}(1^\lambda), \\ \mathit{if}\ b = 0, \mathsf{crs}^{(0)} \leftarrow \mathsf{GSetup}(1^\lambda, 1^N), \\ \forall\ i \in S', \{\mathsf{pk}_i^{(0)}, \mathsf{sk}_i^{(0)}\} \leftarrow \mathsf{KGen}(i), \\ \mathit{if}\ b = 1, (\mathsf{crs}^{(1)}, \{\mathsf{pk}_i^{(1)}\}_{i \in S'}, \widetilde{\mathsf{ct}}, \mathsf{aux}) \leftarrow \\ \mathsf{FakeSetup}(1^\lambda, 1^N, S', \mu) \\ S^* \leftarrow \mathcal{A}(\mathsf{crs}^{(b)}, \{\mathsf{pk}_i^{(b)}\}_{i \in S'}), \\ \mathit{if}\ b = 0, \mathsf{ct}^{(0)} \leftarrow \mathsf{Enc}(\{\mathsf{pk}_i^{(0)}\}_{i \in S^*}, \mu), \\ \mathit{if}\ b = 1, \mathsf{ct}^{(1)} \leftarrow \mathsf{Equivocate}(\mathsf{aux}, S^*) \end{array} \right] - \frac{1}{2} \right| \leq \mathsf{negl}(\lambda)$$

*A stateful* PPT *machine* $\mathcal{A}$ *is said to be admissible if* $S^* \subseteq S' \subseteq [N]$.

**Selective Security for Fake Setup.** *For any* PPT *adversary* $\mathcal{A}$, *there exists a negligible function* $\mathsf{negl}(\cdot)$ *such that* $\forall\ \lambda \in \mathbb{N}$,

$$\left| \Pr\left[ \begin{array}{l} b \leftarrow \\ \mathcal{A}(\widetilde{\mathsf{crs}}, \{\widetilde{\mathsf{pk}_i}\}_{i \in S'}, \\ \widetilde{\mathsf{ct}}, \mathsf{aux}) \end{array} : \begin{array}{l} (1^N, S') \leftarrow \mathcal{A}(1^\lambda), b \leftarrow \{0,1\}, \\ (\widetilde{\mathsf{crs}}, \{\widetilde{\mathsf{pk}_i}\}_{i \in S'}, \widetilde{\mathsf{ct}}, \mathsf{aux}) \leftarrow \\ \mathsf{FakeSetup}(1^\lambda, 1^N, S', b) \end{array} \right] - \frac{1}{2} \right| \leq \mathsf{negl}(\lambda)$$

### 4.1 Semi-statically Secure DBE from Equivocal DBE

**Construction 4.** *We provide the construction of a DBE scheme that is semi-statically secure (Definition 3) from EqDBE (Definition 4) as follows.*

$\mathsf{GSetup}(1^\lambda, 1^N)$ : *Sample* $\mathsf{dbe.crs} \leftarrow \mathsf{EqDBE.GSetup}(1^\lambda, 1^N)$. *Output* $\mathsf{crs} := \mathsf{dbe.crs}$.

$\mathsf{KGen}(i)$ : *Sample* $(\mathsf{dbe.pk}, \mathsf{dbe.sk}) \leftarrow \mathsf{EqDBE.KGen}(i)$. *Output* $(\mathsf{pk}, \mathsf{sk}) := (\mathsf{dbe.pk}, \mathsf{dbe.sk})$.

$\mathsf{Enc}(\{\mathsf{pk}_i\}_{i \in S}, \mu)$ : *Parse* $\mathsf{pk}_i$ *as* $\mathsf{dbe.pk}_i$ *for each* $i \in S$ *and sample* $\mathsf{dbe.ct} \leftarrow \mathsf{EqDBE.Enc}(\{\mathsf{dbe.pk}_i\}_{i \in S}, \mu)$. *Output* $\mathsf{ct} := \mathsf{dbe.ct}$.

$\mathsf{Dec}(\{\mathsf{pk}_i\}_{i \in S}, (j, \mathsf{sk}_j), \mathsf{ct})$ : *Parse* $\mathsf{pk}_i$ *as* $\mathsf{dbe.pk}_i$ *for each* $i \in S$, $\mathsf{sk}_j$ *as* $\mathsf{dbe.sk}_j$, *and* $\mathsf{ct}$ *as* $\mathsf{dbe.ct}$. *Output* $\mu' = \mathsf{EqDBE.Dec}(\{\mathsf{dbe.pk}\}_{i \in S}, (j, \mathsf{dbe.sk}_j), \mathsf{dbe.ct})$.

**Correctness and Compactness.** This follows from correctness and compactness of EqDBE.

**Theorem 5.** *If* EqDBE *is an equivocal DBE scheme (Definition 4), then Construction 4 is a semi-statically secure DBE scheme (Definition 3).*

*Proof.* Full proof is provided in full version. □

## 5 Equivocal DBE in Random Oracle Model

**Parameters.** We describe the LWE parameters that our construction uses for $N = N(\lambda)$ users. Let $n = \mathsf{poly}(\lambda), m = \Omega(n \log q), \chi = \mathsf{poly}(\lambda), \sigma = \mathsf{poly}(\lambda, m), q > O(\sigma\chi m^{13} \log q \log N)$.

**Construction 6.** *We provide the construction of an EqDBE scheme assuming the hardness of* $2m^2$*-decomposed LWE in the random oracle model. We will use the matrix commitment scheme* MCOM *from Sect. 3.1.*

$\mathsf{GSetup}(1^\lambda, 1^N)$ : *Sample* $\mathbf{W}, \mathbf{D}, \mathbf{B} \leftarrow \mathsf{MCOM.Setup}(1^n, 1^m, q, \sigma)$. *Sample* $\mathbf{A} \leftarrow \mathbb{Z}_q^{n\times m}, \mathbf{p} \leftarrow \mathbb{Z}_q^n$. *Sample hash functions* $\mathcal{H}_1 : \{0,1\}^\lambda \times [N] \rightarrow \{\pm 1\}^{4m^5}$ *and* $\mathcal{H}_2 : \{0,1\}^\lambda \times [N] \rightarrow \mathbb{Z}_q^n$. *Output* $\mathsf{crs} := (N, \mathbf{W}, \mathbf{D}, \mathbf{B}, \mathbf{A}, \mathbf{p}, \mathcal{H}_1, \mathcal{H}_2)$.

$\mathsf{KGen}(i)$ : *Compute* $\mathbf{V}_N = \mathsf{MCOM.Verify}(1^N)$. *Let* $\mathbf{v}_i$ *denote the* $i$*-th column of* $\mathbf{V}_N$. *Sample* $\mathbf{r} \leftarrow \{\pm 1\}^{4m^5}$. *Compute* $\mathbf{t}_i = \mathbf{Br} + \mathbf{p} - \mathbf{A}\mathbf{v}_i \in \mathbb{Z}_q^n$. *Output* $\mathsf{pk}_i := (i, \mathbf{t})$ *and* $\mathsf{sk}_i := \mathbf{r}$.

$\mathsf{Enc}(\{\mathsf{pk}_i\}_{i\in S}, \mu)$ : *Parse* $\mathsf{pk}_i$ *as* $(i, \mathbf{t}_i)$ *for each* $i \in S$.

1. *Sample* $\mathsf{sd}_1, \mathsf{sd}_2 \leftarrow \{0,1\}^\lambda$.
2. *For each* $j \in [N]$, *if* $j \in S$, *let* $\mathbf{x}_j = \mathcal{H}_1(\mathsf{sd}_1, j)$ *and if* $j \notin S$, $\mathbf{d}_j = \mathcal{H}_2(\mathsf{sd}_2, j)$.
3. *Construct an* $n \times N$ *matrix* $\mathbf{M}$ *where the* $j$*-th column* $\mathbf{m}_j$ *is as follows*

$$\mathbf{m}_j = \begin{cases} \mathbf{t}_j + \mathbf{B}\mathbf{x}_j & \text{if } j \in S \\ \mathbf{d}_j & \text{if } j \notin S \end{cases}$$

4. *Compute* $\mathbf{C} = \mathsf{MCOM.Com}(\mathbf{M})$.
5. *Sample* $\mathbf{s} \leftarrow \mathbb{Z}_q^n, \mathbf{e} \leftarrow \mathcal{D}_{\mathbb{Z},\chi}^{4m^5}, \mathbf{R}_\mathbf{A} \leftarrow \{\pm 1\}^{4m^5 \times m}, \mathbf{r}_\mathbf{p} \leftarrow \{\pm 1\}^{4m^5}$.
6. *Compute* $\mathbf{c}_1^\top = \mathbf{s}^\top\mathbf{B} + \mathbf{e}^\top, \mathbf{c}_2^\top = \mathbf{s}^\top(\mathbf{A} + \mathbf{C}) + \mathbf{e}^\top\mathbf{R}_\mathbf{A}, c_3 = \mathbf{s}^\top\mathbf{p} + \mathbf{e}^\top\mathbf{r}_\mathbf{p} + \lfloor q/2 \rfloor\mu$.

*Output* $\mathsf{ct} := (\mathbf{c}_1^\top, \mathbf{c}_2^\top, c_3, \mathsf{sd}_1, \mathsf{sd}_2) \in \mathbb{Z}_q^{1\times(4m^5+m+1)} \times \{0,1\}^{2\lambda}$.

$\mathsf{Dec}(\{\mathsf{pk}_i\}_{i\in S}, (j, \mathsf{sk}_j), \mathsf{ct})$ : *Parse* $\mathsf{pk}_i$ *as* $(i, \mathbf{t}_i)$ *for each* $i \in S$, $\mathsf{sk}_j$ *as* $\mathbf{r}_j$, *and* $\mathsf{ct}$ *as* $(\mathbf{c}_1^\top, \mathbf{c}_2^\top, c_3, \mathsf{sd}_1, \mathsf{sd}_2)$. *If* $j \notin S$, *output* $\perp$. *Otherwise,*

1. *For each* $k \in [N]$, *if* $k \in S$, *let* $\mathbf{x}_k = \mathcal{H}_1(\mathsf{sd}_1, k)$ *and if* $k \notin S$, $\mathbf{d}_k = \mathcal{H}_2(\mathsf{sd}_2, k)$.
2. *Compute matrix* $\mathbf{M}$ *like in* $\mathsf{Enc}$. *Compute* $\mathbf{V}_N = \mathsf{MCOM.Verify}(1^N), \mathbf{Z} = \mathsf{MCOM.Open}(\mathbf{M})$.
3. *Compute* $\mathbf{c}_{exp}^\top = \mathbf{c}_2^\top\mathbf{V}_N + \mathbf{c}_1^\top\mathbf{Z} \in \mathbb{Z}_q^{1\times N}$. *Let* $c_j$ *denote the* $j$*-th element of* $\mathbf{c}_{exp}^\top$.
4. *Compute* $y = c_3 - c_j + \mathbf{c}_1^\top(\mathbf{x}_j + \mathbf{r}_j) \in \mathbb{Z}_q$.

*Output* $0$ *if* $-q/4 < y < q/4$ *and* $1$ *otherwise.*

**Comparison to Prior Works.** Before proceeding further, we want to highlight major differences of our constructions and prior works on DBE from decomposed

LWE. Like in [9,10,40][8], our $\mathsf{KGen}$ algorithm is also an Ajtai commitment to $\mathbf{p}-\mathbf{A}\mathbf{v}_i$. However, the major difference is in our $\mathsf{Enc}$ and $\mathsf{Dec}$ algorithms. Specifically, in Items 1 and 2 of $\mathsf{Enc}$ algorithm, we commit a matrix $\mathbf{M} \in \mathbb{Z}_q^{n\times N}$ that is not sparse and contains entries from random oracles $\mathcal{H}_1, \mathcal{H}_2$. While this makes our DBE scheme bounded / non-flexible, we achieve adaptive security (via semi-static security in ROM). It is an interesting problem to design adaptively secure unbounded DBE [40].

**Correctness and Compactness.** Full analysis is provided in full version.

### 5.1 Fake Setup and Equivocation

Now, we describe our $\mathsf{FakeSetup}$ and $\mathsf{Equivocate}$ algorithms. These algorithms are defined with respect to a programmable random oracle. $\mathsf{FakeSetup}$ provides handles $\mathcal{H}_1, \mathcal{H}_2$. However, they are treated as a single programmable oracle $\mathsf{H}$ (by augmenting the input with an additional slot $\iota \in \{1,2\}$) by $\mathsf{Equivocate}$.

$\mathsf{FakeSetup}(1^\lambda, 1^N, S', \mu)$ : Perform the following steps.

1. For each $i \in S' \subseteq [N]$, sample $\mathbf{t}_i \leftarrow \mathbb{Z}_q^n$. Set $\widetilde{\mathsf{pk}_i} := (i, \mathbf{t}_i)$ for each $i \in S'$.
2. Sample $(\mathbf{W}, \mathbf{D}, \mathbf{B}) \leftarrow \mathsf{MCOM.Setup}(1^n, 1^m, q, \sigma)$.
3. Sample $\mathbf{X}' \leftarrow \{\pm 1\}^{4m^5 \times N}, \mathbf{D}' \leftarrow \mathbb{Z}_q^{n\times N}$. Let $\mathbf{x}'_j$ and $\mathbf{d}'_j$ denote the $j$-th column of $\mathbf{X}'$ and $\mathbf{D}'$ respectively.
4. Compute matrix $\mathbf{M}' \in \mathbb{Z}_q^{n\times N}$ where the $j$-th column $\mathbf{m}'_j = \mathbf{t}_j + \mathbf{B}\mathbf{x}'_j$ if $j \in S'$. Otherwise $\mathbf{m}'_j = \mathbf{d}'_j$. Compute $\mathbf{C}' = \mathsf{MCOM.Com}(\mathbf{M}')$. Sample $\mathbf{A}' \leftarrow \mathbb{Z}_q^{n\times m}$ and set $\mathbf{A} = \mathbf{A}' - \mathbf{C}'$.
5. Sample $\mathbf{p} \leftarrow \mathbb{Z}_q^n$. Set $\mathsf{crs} := (N, \mathbf{W}, \mathbf{D}, \mathbf{B}, \mathbf{A}, \mathbf{p}, \mathcal{H}_1, \mathcal{H}_2)$ where $\mathcal{H}_1 : \{0,1\}^\lambda \times [N] \rightarrow \{\pm 1\}^{4m^5}$ and $\mathcal{H}_2 : \{0,1\}^\lambda \times [N] \rightarrow \mathbb{Z}_q^n$ are handles to random oracles.
6. Sample $\mathbf{s} \leftarrow \mathbb{Z}_q^n, \mathbf{e} \leftarrow \mathcal{D}_{\mathbb{Z},\chi}^{4m^5}, \mathbf{R}_\mathbf{A} \leftarrow \{+1\}^{4m^5\times m}, \mathbf{r}_\mathbf{p} \leftarrow \{\pm 1\}^{4m^5}$. Compute $\mathbf{c}_1^\top = \mathbf{s}^\top\mathbf{B} + \mathbf{e}^\top, \mathbf{c}_2^\top = \mathbf{s}^\top\mathbf{A}' + \mathbf{e}^\top\mathbf{R}_\mathbf{A}, c_3 = \mathbf{s}^\top\mathbf{p} + \mathbf{e}^\top\mathbf{r}_\mathbf{p} + \lfloor q/2 \rfloor \mu$. Set $\widetilde{\mathsf{ct}} := (\mathbf{c}_1^\top, \mathbf{c}_2^\top, c_3)$.
7. Set $\mathsf{aux} := (\widetilde{\mathsf{crs}}, \{\widetilde{\mathsf{pk}_i}\}_{i\in S'}, \widetilde{\mathsf{ct}}, \mathbf{X}', \mathbf{D}', S')$.

Output $(\widetilde{\mathsf{crs}}, \{\widetilde{\mathsf{pk}_i}\}_{i\in S'}, \widetilde{\mathsf{ct}}, \mathsf{aux})$.

$\mathsf{Equivocate}^{\mathsf{H}(\cdot)}(\mathsf{aux}, S^*)$ : Parse $\mathsf{aux}$ as $(\widetilde{\mathsf{crs}}, \{\widetilde{\mathsf{pk}_i}\}_{i\in S'}, \widetilde{\mathsf{ct}}, \mathbf{X}', \mathbf{D}', S')$.

1. Sample $\mathsf{sd}_1, \mathsf{sd}_2 \leftarrow \{0,1\}^\lambda$. Given access to a programmable oracle $\mathsf{H}$, if $\mathsf{H}$ contains entries for $(\mathsf{sd}_1, i, 1)$ or $(\mathsf{sd}_2, j, 2)$ for any $i, j \in [N]$, output $\mu$. Otherwise, proceed as follows.
2. For each $j \in [N]$, if $j \in S^*$, set $\mathsf{H}[(\mathsf{sd}_1, j, 1)] = \mathbf{x}'_j$. If $j \notin S'$, set $\mathsf{H}[(\mathsf{sd}_2, j, 2)] = \mathbf{d}'_j$. Otherwise, if $j \in S' \backslash S^*$, set $\mathsf{H}[(\mathsf{sd}_1, j, 1)] = \mathbf{x}^*_j$ and $\mathsf{H}[(\mathsf{sd}_2, j, 2)] = \mathbf{t}_j + \mathbf{B}\mathbf{x}'_j$ where $\mathbf{x}^*_j \leftarrow \{\pm 1\}^{4m^5}$.
3. Parse $\widetilde{\mathsf{ct}}$ as $(\mathbf{c}_1^\top, \mathbf{c}_2^\top, c_3)$. Set $\mathsf{ct} := (\mathbf{c}_1^\top, \mathbf{c}_2^\top, c'_3, \mathsf{sd}_1, \mathsf{sd}_2)$.

Output $\mathsf{ct}$.

[8] Although security of these constructions rely on $\ell$-succinct LWE [38], they could be modified to work with $\ell$-decomposed LWE [1] as shown in [40].

### 5.2 Security Analysis

**Theorem 7 (Mode Indistinguishability).** *Construction 6 satisfies mode indistinguishability property against any admissible* PPT *adversary* $\mathcal{A}$.

*Proof.* Full proof is provided in full version. □

**Theorem 8 (Selective Security for Fake Setup).** *If* $2m^2$*-decomposed LWE assumption (Assumption 1) holds, then Construction 6 satisfies selective security for fake setup property.*

*Proof.* Full proof is provided in full version. □

**Corollary 1.** *Assuming the hardness of* $2m^2$*-decomposed LWE with polynomial modulus-to-noise ratio, there exists an adaptively secure DBE scheme with optimal parameters in the random oracle model.*

## 6 Programmable Pseudorandom Set Sampler

In this section, we introduce a new tool that we call Programmable Pseudorandom Set Sampler (PPS). We use this tool to replace the random oracles from our EqDBE construction.

**Syntax.** A programmable pseudorandom set sampler (PPS) scheme for message space $\mathcal{M}$ consists of the following polynomial time algorithms.

$\mathsf{PPGen}(1^\lambda, 1^N) \rightarrow \mathsf{pp}$. The randomized public parameter generation algorithm takes as input security parameter $\lambda$, number of users $N$, and outputs public parameters $\mathsf{pp}$. The following algorithms takes $\mathsf{pp}$ implicitly.

$\mathsf{MSKGen} \rightarrow \mathsf{msk}$ The randomized master secret key generation algorithm takes as input public parameters $\mathsf{pp}$ and outputs master secret key $\mathsf{msk}$.

$\mathsf{pkEnc}(i) \rightarrow \mathsf{ct}$. The randomized *public-key* encryption algorithm takes as input index $i \in [N]$ and outputs ciphertext $\mathsf{ct}$.

$\mathsf{KGen}(\mathsf{msk}, S) \rightarrow \mathsf{sk}_S$. The possibly randomized secret key generation algorithm takes as input master secret key $\mathsf{msk}$, set $S \subseteq [N]$, and outputs secret key $\mathsf{sk}_S$.

$\mathsf{Decode}(i, \mathsf{ct}, S, \mathsf{sk}_S) \rightarrow \mu'$. The deterministic decoding algorithm takes as input a ciphertext $\mathsf{ct}$, secret key $\mathsf{sk}_S$ for set $S$, and outputs $\mu' \in \mathcal{M} \cup \{\perp\}$.

$\mathsf{skEnc}(\mathsf{msk}, \{i \rightarrow \mu_i\}_{i \in P}) \rightarrow (\mathsf{ct}_i)_{i \in P}$. The randomized *secret-key* encryption algorithm takes as input master secret key $\mathsf{msk}$, a programming dictionary which contains $\{i \rightarrow \mu_i\}_{i \in P}$ for a set of indices $P \subseteq [N]$ such that $\mu_i \in \mathcal{M}$, and outputs ciphertexts $(\mathsf{ct}_i)_{i \in P}$.

**Definition 5 (PPS).** *A* PPS *scheme* ($\mathsf{PPGen}, \mathsf{MSKGen}, \mathsf{pkEnc}, \mathsf{KGen}, \mathsf{Decode}, \mathsf{skEnc}$) *is said to be a programmable pseudorandom set sampler scheme (PPS) if it satisfies the following properties.*

**Correctness.** *For any* $\lambda \in \mathbb{N}$, *positive polynomials* $N = N(\lambda)$, *sets* $S, P \subseteq [N], i \in P \cap S$, *for any* $\mu_j \in \mathcal{M}$ *for every* $j \in P$,

$$\Pr\left[\begin{array}{l}\mu_i = \\ \mathsf{Decode}(i, \mathsf{ct}_i, S, \mathsf{sk}_S)\end{array} : \begin{array}{l}\mathsf{pp} \leftarrow \mathsf{PPGen}(1^\lambda, 1^N), \\ \mathsf{msk} \leftarrow \mathsf{MSKGen}(\mathsf{pp}), \\ (\mathsf{ct}_j)_{j \in P} \leftarrow \mathsf{skEnc}(\mathsf{msk}, \{j \to \mu_j\}_{j \in P}), \\ \mathsf{sk}_S \leftarrow \mathsf{KGen}(\mathsf{msk}, S)\end{array}\right] = 1$$

**Compactness.** *There exists a polynomial* $\mathsf{poly}(\cdot, \cdot)$ *such that* $\forall\ \lambda, N \in \mathbb{N}$, $S \subseteq [N]$, $|\mathsf{sk}_S| = \mathsf{poly}(\lambda, \log N)$.

**Mode Indistinguishability, Payload Hiding.** *Mode indistinguishability implies* $\mathsf{skEnc}(\mathsf{msk}, \{i \to \mu\}) \approx_c \mathsf{pkEnc}(i)$ *for random* $\mu$ *and adaptive choice of* $\mathsf{sk}_S$ *such that* $i \in S$. *Payload hiding is the dual where* $\mathsf{skEnc}(\mathsf{msk}, \{i \to \mu\}) \approx_c \mathsf{pkEnc}(i)$ *for* any $\mu$ *and adaptive choice of* $\mathsf{sk}_S$ *such that* $i \notin S$. *Both definitions hold even if* $\mathcal{A}$ *sees additional* $\mathsf{ct}_j$ *from* $\mathsf{skEnc}$ *with* $j \neq i$. *We provide full definition in full version.*

## 7 Equivocal DBE in Standard Model from Programmable Pseudorandom Set Sampler

**Construction 9.** *We provide the construction of* $\mathsf{EqDBE}$ *in standard model assuming the hardness of* $2m^2$*-decomposed LWE (Assumption 1). We will use the matrix commitment scheme* $\mathsf{MCOM}$ *(Sect. 3.1) and Programmable Pseudorandom Set Samplers (Definition 5)* $\mathsf{PPS}^{(1)}, \mathsf{PPS}^{(2)}$, *for message space* $\{\pm 1\}^{4m^5}$ *and* $\mathbb{Z}_q^n$ *respectively.*

$\mathsf{GSetup}(1^\lambda, 1^N)$ : *Sample* $(\mathbf{W}, \mathbf{D}, \mathbf{B}) \leftarrow \mathsf{MCOM.Setup}(1^n, 1^m, q, \sigma)$. *Sample* $\mathbf{A} \leftarrow \mathbb{Z}_q^{n \times m}, \mathbf{p} \leftarrow \mathbb{Z}_q^n$. *Sample* $\mathsf{samp.pp}^{(1)} \leftarrow \mathsf{PPS.PPGen}(1^\lambda, 1^N)$, $\mathsf{samp.pp}^{(2)} \leftarrow \mathsf{PPS.PPGen}(1^\lambda, 1^N)$.

1. *For each* $i \in [N]$, *sample* $\mathsf{samp.ct}_i^{(1)} \leftarrow \mathsf{PPS.pkEnc}(\mathsf{samp.pp}^{(1)}, i)$.
2. *For each* $i \in [N]$, *sample* $\mathsf{samp.ct}_i^{(2)} \leftarrow \mathsf{PPS.pkEnc}(\mathsf{samp.pp}^{(2)}, i)$.

*Output* $\mathsf{crs} := (N, \mathsf{samp.pp}^{(1)}, \mathsf{samp.pp}^{(2)}, \mathbf{W}, \mathbf{D}, \mathbf{B}, \mathbf{A}, \mathbf{p}, (\mathsf{samp.ct}_i^{(1)})_{i \in [N]}, (\mathsf{samp.ct}_i^{(2)})_{i \in [N]})$.

$\mathsf{KGen}(i)$ : *This is same as* $\mathsf{KGen}(i)$ *from Construction 6.*

$\mathsf{Enc}(\{\mathsf{pk}_i\}_{i \in S}, \mu)$ : *Parse* $\mathsf{pk}_i$ *as* $(i, \mathbf{t}_i)$ *for each* $i \in S$.

1. *Sample* $\mathsf{samp.msk}^{(1)} \leftarrow \mathsf{PPS.MSKGen}(\mathsf{samp.pp}^{(1)})$, $\mathsf{samp.msk}^{(2)} \leftarrow \mathsf{PPS.MSKGen}(\mathsf{samp.pp}^{(2)})$. *Then sample* $\mathsf{samp.sk}_S \leftarrow \mathsf{PPS.KGen}(\mathsf{samp.msk}^{(1)}, S)$ *and* $\mathsf{samp.sk}_{\overline{S}} \leftarrow \mathsf{KGen}(\mathsf{samp.msk}^{(2)}, [N] \backslash S)$.
2. *For each* $j \in [N]$, *if* $j \in S$, *let* $\mathbf{x}_j = \mathsf{PPS.Decode}(j, \mathsf{samp.ct}_j^{(1)}, S, \mathsf{samp.sk}_S)$ *and if* $j \notin S$, $\mathbf{d}_j = \mathsf{PPS.Decode}(j, \mathsf{samp.ct}_j^{(2)}, [N] \backslash S, \mathsf{samp.sk}_{\overline{S}})$.

3–6. *Perform steps 2–5 from Construction 6.*

*Output* $\mathsf{ct} := (\mathbf{c}_1^\top, \mathbf{c}_2^\top, c_3, \mathsf{samp.sk}_S, \mathsf{samp.sk}_{\overline{S}})$.

$\mathsf{Dec}(\{\mathsf{pk}_i\}_{i \in S}, (j, \mathsf{sk}_j), \mathsf{ct})$ : *Parse* $\mathsf{pk}_i$ *as* $(i, \mathbf{t}_i)$ *for each* $i \in S$, $\mathsf{sk}_j$ *as* $\mathbf{r}_j$, *and* $\mathsf{ct}$ *as* $(\mathbf{c}_1^\top, \mathbf{c}_2^\top, c_3, \mathsf{samp.sk}_S, \mathsf{samp.sk}_{\overline{S}})$. *If* $j \notin S$, *output* $\perp$. *Otherwise,*

1. *For each* $k \in [N]$, *if* $k \in S$, *let* $\mathbf{x}_k = \mathsf{PPS.Decode}(k, \mathsf{samp.ct}_k^{(1)}, S, \mathsf{samp.sk}_S)$ *and if* $k \notin S$, $\mathbf{d}_k = \mathsf{PPS.Decode}(k, \mathsf{samp.ct}_k^{(2)}, [N] \backslash S, \mathsf{samp.sk}_{\overline{S}})$.

2–4. *Perform steps 2-4 from Construction 6.*
*Output* 0 *if* $-q/4 < y < q/4$ *and* 1 *otherwise.*

**Correctness and Compactness.** Full analysis is provided in full version.

### 7.1 Fake Setup and Equivocation

$\mathsf{FakeSetup}(1^\lambda, 1^N, S', \mu)$ : Sample $\mathsf{samp.pp}^{(1)} \leftarrow \mathsf{PPS.PPGen}(1^\lambda, 1^N)$, $\mathsf{samp.pp}^{(2)} \leftarrow \mathsf{PPS.PPGen}(1^\lambda, 1^N)$, and perform the following steps.

1. For each $i \in S' \subseteq [N]$, sample $\mathbf{t}_i \leftarrow \mathbb{Z}_q^n$. Set $\widetilde{\mathsf{pk}}_i := \mathbf{t}_i$ for each $i \in S'$.
2. Sample $(\mathbf{W}, \mathbf{D}, \mathbf{B}) \leftarrow \mathsf{MCOM.Setup}(1^n, 1^m, q, \sigma)$.
3. Sample $\mathbf{X}' \leftarrow \{0,1\}^{4m^5 \times N}, \mathbf{D}' \leftarrow \mathbb{Z}_q^{n \times N}$. Let $\mathbf{x}'_j$ and $\mathbf{d}'_j$ denote the $j$-th column of $\mathbf{X}'$ and $\mathbf{D}'$ respectively.
4. Compute matrix $\mathbf{M}' \in \mathbb{Z}_q^{n \times N}$ where the $j$-th column $\mathbf{m}'_j = \mathbf{t}_j + \mathbf{B}\mathbf{x}'_j$ if $j \in S'$. Otherwise $\mathbf{m}'_j = \mathbf{d}'_j$. Compute $\mathbf{C}' = \mathsf{MCOM.Com}(\mathbf{M}')$. Sample $\mathbf{A}' \leftarrow \mathbb{Z}_q^{n \times m}$ and set $\mathbf{A} = \mathbf{A}' - \mathbf{C}'$.
5. Sample $\mathbf{p} \leftarrow \mathbb{Z}_q^n$.
6. Sample $\mathsf{samp.msk}^{(1)} \leftarrow \mathsf{PPS.MSKGen}(\mathsf{samp.pp}^{(1)}), \mathsf{samp.msk}^{(2)} \leftarrow \mathsf{PPS.MSKGen}(\mathsf{samp.pp}^{(2)})$.
7. Set $T^{(1)} = \{j \rightarrow \mathbf{x}'_j\}_{j \in S'}$. Also, set $T^{(2)} = \{j \rightarrow \mathbf{t}_j + \mathbf{B}\mathbf{x}'_j\}_{j \in S'} \cup \{j \rightarrow \mathbf{d}'_j\}_{j \notin S'}$. For each $j \notin S'$, sample $\widetilde{\mathsf{samp.ct}}_j^{(1)} \leftarrow \mathsf{PPS.pkEnc}(\mathsf{samp.pp}^{(1)}, i)$.
8. Sample $(\widetilde{\mathsf{samp.ct}}^{(1)})_{j \in S'} \leftarrow \mathsf{PPS.skEnc}(\mathsf{samp.msk}^{(1)}, T^{(1)})$ and $(\widetilde{\mathsf{samp.ct}}^{(2)})_{j \in [N]} \leftarrow \mathsf{PPS.skEnc}(\mathsf{samp.msk}^{(2)}, T^{(2)})$.
9. Set $\mathsf{crs} := (N, \mathsf{samp.pp}^{(1)}, \mathsf{samp.pp}^{(2)}, \mathbf{W}, \mathbf{D}, \mathbf{B}, \mathbf{A}, \mathbf{p}, (\widetilde{\mathsf{samp.ct}}_i^{(1)})_{i \in [N]}, (\widetilde{\mathsf{samp.ct}}_i^{(2)})_{i \in [N]})$.
10. Sample $\mathbf{s} \leftarrow \mathbb{Z}_q^n, \mathbf{e} \leftarrow \mathcal{D}_{\mathbb{Z},\chi}^{4m^5}, \mathbf{R_A} \leftarrow \{\pm 1\}^{4m^5 \times m}, \mathbf{r_p} \leftarrow \{\pm 1\}^{4m^5}$. Compute $\mathbf{c}_1^\top = \mathbf{s}^\top \mathbf{B} + \mathbf{e}^\top, \mathbf{c}_2^\top = \mathbf{s}^\top \mathbf{A}' + \mathbf{e}^\top \mathbf{R_A}, c_3 = \mathbf{s}^\top \mathbf{p} + \mathbf{e}^\top \mathbf{r_p} + \lfloor q/2 \rfloor \mu$. Set $\widetilde{\mathsf{ct}} := (\mathbf{c}_1^\top, \mathbf{c}_2^\top, c_3)$. Set $\mathsf{aux} := (S', \mathsf{samp.msk}^{(1)}, \mathsf{samp.msk}^{(2)}, \widetilde{\mathsf{ct}})$.

Output $(\widetilde{\mathsf{crs}}, \{\widetilde{\mathsf{pk}}_i\}_{i \in S'}, \widetilde{\mathsf{ct}}, \mathsf{aux})$.

$\mathsf{Equivocate}(\mathsf{aux}, S^*)$ : Parse $\mathsf{aux}$ as $(S', \mathsf{samp.msk}^{(1)}, \mathsf{samp.msk}^{(2)})$.

1. Sample $\mathsf{samp.sk}_{S^*} \leftarrow \mathsf{PPS.KGen}(\mathsf{samp.msk}^{(1)}, S^*)$ and $\mathsf{samp.sk}_{\overline{S^*}} \leftarrow \mathsf{PPS.KGen}(\mathsf{samp.msk}^{(2)}, [N] \backslash S^*)$
2. Parse $\widetilde{\mathsf{ct}}$ as $(\mathbf{c}_1^\top, \mathbf{c}_2^\top, c_3)$. Set $\mathsf{ct} := (\mathbf{c}_1^\top, \mathbf{c}_2^\top, c_3, \mathsf{samp.sk}_{S^*}, \mathsf{samp.sk}_{\overline{S^*}})$.

Output ct.

### 7.2 Security Analysis

**Theorem 10 (Mode Indistinguishability).** *If* PPS *satisfies mode indistinguishability and payload hiding properties (Definition 5), then Construction 9 satisfies mode indistinguishability.*

*Proof.* Full description of hybrids and proof is provided in full version. □

**Theorem 11 (Selective Security for Fake Setup).** *If $2m^2$-decomposed LWE assumption (Assumption 1) holds, then Construction 9 satisfies selective security for fake setup property.*

*Proof.* Full proof is provided in full version. □

## 8 Programmable Pseudorandom Set Sampler from LWE

**Parameters.** Let $n = \mathsf{poly}(\lambda), m > (n+1+2N)\log q + \lambda, \chi = \mathsf{poly}(\lambda), B \geq Nm^{3/2}\chi, q > B\lambda^{\omega(1)}$.

**Construction 12.** *We provide the construction of a* PPS *scheme (Definition 5) for message space $\mathcal{M} = \mathbb{Z}_2$ from the LWE assumption below.*

$\mathsf{PPGen}(1^\lambda, 1^N)$ : *Sample* $\mathbf{A} \leftarrow \mathbb{Z}_q^{n\times m}$ *Output* $\mathsf{pp} := (n, m, q, \chi, B, \mathbf{A}, N)$.

$\mathsf{MSKGen}$ : *Sample* $\mathbf{s}_{i,b} \leftarrow \mathbb{Z}_q^n, \mathbf{e}_{i,b} \leftarrow \mathcal{D}_{\mathbb{Z},\chi}^m$ *for each* $i \in [N], b \in \{0,1\}$. *Compute* $\mathbf{b}_{i,b}^\top = \mathbf{s}_{i,b}^\top\mathbf{A} + \mathbf{e}_{i,b}^\top$. *Output* $\mathsf{msk} := (\mathbf{s}_{i,b}, \mathbf{b}_{i,b})_{i\in[N],b\in\{0,1\}}$.

$\mathsf{KGen}(\mathsf{msk}, S)$ : *Let* $\mathbf{r} \in \{0,1\}^N$ *denote the characteristic vector of set* $S \subseteq [N]$. *That is* $\mathbf{r} = (r_1, \ldots, r_N)$ *such that* $r_i = 1$ *if and only if* $i \in S$. *Output* $\mathsf{sk}_S := \sum_{j\in[N]} \mathbf{s}_{j,r_j} \in \mathbb{Z}_q^n$.

$\mathsf{skEnc}(\mathsf{msk}, \{j \to \mu_j\}_{j\in P})$ : *Given* $P \subseteq [N], \forall\, j \in P, \mu_j \in \mathbb{Z}_2$, *parse* $\mathsf{msk}$ *as* $(\mathbf{s}_{i,b}, \mathbf{b}_{i,b})_{i\in[N],b\in\{0,1\}}$. *For each* $j \in P$, *perform the following steps.*

1. *Sample* $\mathbf{x}_j \leftarrow \{\pm 1\}^m$, *set* $\mathbf{c}_{j,0} = \mathbf{A}\mathbf{x}_j$.
2. *Sample for each* $k \in [N]$, *random* $z_{j,k} \in \mathbb{Z}_q$ *such that* $\sum_{k\in[N]} z_{j,k} = 0$.
3. *Sample* $t_j \leftarrow \mathbb{Z}_q$ *subject to the constraint that* $t_j \notin [-\lfloor q/4\rfloor - B, -\lfloor q/4\rfloor + B] \cup [\lfloor q/4\rfloor - B, \lfloor q/4\rfloor + B]$. *As* $q > \lambda^{\omega(1)}B$, *the set of valid* $t_j$ *is non-empty.*
4. *Set* $c_{j,j,1} = \mathbf{b}_{j,1}^\top\mathbf{x}_j + z_{j,j} + t_j$ *and sample* $c_{j,j,0} \leftarrow \mathbb{Z}_q$.
5. *For* $k \in [N], k \neq j$ *for each* $b \in \{0,1\}$, *set* $c_{j,k,b} := \mathbf{b}_{k,b}^\top\mathbf{x}_j + z_{j,k}$.
6. *Set* $c_{j,T} = \lceil t_j \rfloor_2 + \mu_j$
7. *Set* $\mathsf{ct}_j := (\mathbf{c}_{j,0}, (c_{j,k,b})_{k,b}, c_{j,T}) \in \mathbb{Z}_q^n \times \mathbb{Z}_q^{2N} \times \mathbb{Z}_2$.

*Output* $(\mathsf{ct}_j)_{j\in P}$.

$\mathsf{pkEnc}(i)$ : *Output* $\mathsf{ct} \leftarrow \mathbb{Z}_q^n \times \mathbb{Z}_q^{2N} \times \mathbb{Z}_2$.

$\mathsf{Decode}(i, \mathsf{ct}, S, \mathsf{sk}_S)$ : *Parse* $\mathsf{ct}$ *as* $(\mathbf{c}_0, (c_{j,b})_{j\in[N],b\in\{0,1\}}, c_T)$. *Let* $\mathbf{r} = (r_1, \ldots, r_N)$ *denote the characteristic vector of* $S$ *similar to* $\mathsf{KGen}$. *If* $i \notin S$, *abort and output* $\perp$. *Otherwise, compute* $c' = \sum_{j\in[N]} c_{j,r_j} - (\mathsf{sk}_S)^\top\mathbf{c}_0$. *Output* $\mu' = c_T - \lceil c' \rfloor_2$.

**Correctness and Compactness.** Full analysis is provided in full version.

### 8.1 Security Analysis

**Theorem 13.** *Assuming the hardness of* LWE, *Construction 12 satisfies mode indistinguishability and payload hiding.*

*Proof.* Full proof is provided in full version. □

**Corollary 2.** *Assuming the hardness of* $2m^2$*-decomposed LWE and* 1*-key LWE, there exists an adaptively secure DBE scheme for* $N$ *users in the standard model. Moreover, the public-key, secret-key and ciphertext sizes are independent of* $N$ *and* crs *size grows proportional to* $N$*.*

**Corollary 3.** *Assuming the hardness of* $2m^2$*-decomposed LWE, there exists an adaptively secure DBE scheme for* $N$ *users in the standard model. Moreover, the public-key, secret-key and ciphertext sizes are independent of* $N$ *and* crs *size grows proportional to* $N^2$*.*

**Acknowledgments.** We would like to thank the anonymous reviewers of Crypto 2026 conference for their useful comments about the editorial quality and pointers towards related works on our PPS tool.

## References

1. Abram, D., Malavolta, G., Roy, L.: Key-homomorphic computations for RAM: fully succinct randomised encodings and more. In: Kalai, Y.T., Kamara, S.F. (eds.) Advances in Cryptology – CRYPTO 2025, Part III. Lecture Notes in Computer Science, vol. 16002, pp. 236–268. Springer, Cham (2025). https://doi.org/10.1007/978-3-032-01881-6_8
2. Agrawal, S., Boneh, D., Boyen, X.: Efficient lattice (H)IBE in the standard model. In: Gilbert, H. (ed.) EUROCRYPT 2010. LNCS, vol. 6110, pp. 553–572. Springer, Heidelberg (2010). https://doi.org/10.1007/978-3-642-13190-5_28
3. Applebaum, B., Beimel, A., Ishai, Y., Kushilevitz, E., Liu, T., Vaikuntanathan, V.: Succinct computational secret sharing. In: Saha, B., Servedio, R.A. (eds.) 55th Annual ACM Symposium on Theory of Computing, pp. 1553–1566. ACM Press, Orlando, FL, USA (2023). https://doi.org/10.1145/3564246.3585127
4. Bellare, M., Rogaway, P.: Random oracles are practical: a paradigm for designing efficient protocols. In: Denning, D.E., Pyle, R., Ganesan, R., Sandhu, R.S., Ashby, V. (eds.) ACM CCS 93: 1st Conference on Computer and Communications Security, pp. 62–73. ACM Press, Fairfax, Virginia, USA (1993). https://doi.org/10.1145/168588.168596
5. Boneh, D., et al.: Fully key-homomorphic encryption, arithmetic circuit ABE and compact garbled circuits. In: Nguyen, P.Q., Oswald, E. (eds.) EUROCRYPT 2014. LNCS, vol. 8441, pp. 533–556. Springer, Heidelberg (2014). https://doi.org/10.1007/978-3-642-55220-5_30
6. Boneh, D., Laufer, E., Tas, E.N.: Threshold batch identity-based encryption without epochs. Cryptology ePrint Archive, Paper 2025/1254 (2025). https://eprint.iacr.org/2025/1254

7. Boneh, D., Zhandry, M.: Multiparty key exchange, efficient traitor tracing, and more from indistinguishability obfuscation. In: Garay, J.A., Gennaro, R. (eds.) CRYPTO 2014. LNCS, vol. 8616, pp. 480–499. Springer, Heidelberg (2014). https://doi.org/10.1007/978-3-662-44371-2_27
8. Cash, D., Hofheinz, D., Kiltz, E., Peikert, C.: Bonsai trees, or how to delegate a lattice basis. In: Gilbert, H. (ed.) EUROCRYPT 2010. LNCS, vol. 6110, pp. 523–552. Springer, Heidelberg (2010). https://doi.org/10.1007/978-3-642-13190-5_27
9. Champion, J., Hsieh, Y.C., Wu, D.J.: Registered ABE and adaptively-secure broadcast encryption from succinct LWE. In: Kalai, Y.T., Kamara, S.F. (eds.) Advances in Cryptology – CRYPTO 2025, Part III. LNCS, vol. 16002, pp. 3–34. Springer, Cham (2025). https://doi.org/10.1007/978-3-032-01881-6_1
10. Champion, J., Wu, D.J.: Distributed broadcast encryption from lattices. In: Boyle, E., Mahmoody, M. (eds.) TCC 2024: 22nd Theory of Cryptography Conference, Part III. Lecture Notes in Computer Science, vol. 15366, pp. 156–189. Springer, Cham (2024). https://doi.org/10.1007/978-3-031-78020-2_6
11. Choudhuri, A.R., Garg, S., Piet, J., Policharla, G.V.: Mempool privacy via batched threshold encryption: attacks and defenses. In: Balzarotti, D., Xu, W. (eds.) USENIX Security 2024: 33rd USENIX Security Symposium. USENIX Association, Philadelphia, PA, USA (2024). https://www.usenix.org/conference/usenixsecurity24/presentation/choudhuri
12. Fiat, A., Naor, M.: Broadcast encryption. In: Stinson, D.R. (ed.) CRYPTO 1993. LNCS, vol. 773, pp. 480–491. Springer, Heidelberg (1994). https://doi.org/10.1007/3-540-48329-2_40
13. Freitag, C., Waters, B., Wu, D.J.: How to use (plain) witness encryption: registered ABE, flexible broadcast, and more. In: Handschuh, H., Lysyanskaya, A. (eds.) Advances in Cryptology – CRYPTO 2023, Part IV. LNCS, vol. 14084, pp. 498–531. Springer, Cham (2023). https://doi.org/10.1007/978-3-031-38551-3_16
14. Fuchsbauer, G., Jafargholi, Z., Pietrzak, K.: A quasipolynomial reduction for generalized selective decryption on trees. In: Gennaro, R., Robshaw, M. (eds.) CRYPTO 2015. LNCS, vol. 9215, pp. 601–620. Springer, Heidelberg (2015). https://doi.org/10.1007/978-3-662-47989-6_29
15. Fuchsbauer, G., Konstantinov, M., Pietrzak, K., Rao, V.: Adaptive security of constrained PRFs. In: Sarkar, P., Iwata, T. (eds.) ASIACRYPT 2014. LNCS, vol. 8874, pp. 82–101. Springer, Heidelberg (2014). https://doi.org/10.1007/978-3-662-45608-8_5
16. Garg, S., Hajiabadi, M., Mahmoody, M., Rahimi, A.: Registration-based encryption: removing private-key generator from IBE. In: Beimel, A., Dziembowski, S. (eds.) TCC 2018. LNCS, vol. 11239, pp. 689–718. Springer, Cham (2018). https://doi.org/10.1007/978-3-030-03807-6_25
17. Garg, S., Kolonelos, D., Policharla, G.V., Wang, M.: Threshold encryption with silent setup. In: Reyzin, L., Stebila, D. (eds.) Advances in Cryptology – CRYPTO 2024, Part VII. LNCS, vol. 14926, pp. 352–386. Springer, Cham (2024). https://doi.org/10.1007/978-3-031-68394-7_12
18. Gentry, C., Peikert, C., Vaikuntanathan, V.: Trapdoors for hard lattices and new cryptographic constructions. In: Ladner, R.E., Dwork, C. (eds.) 40th Annual ACM Symposium on Theory of Computing, pp. 197–206. ACM Press, Victoria, BC, Canada (2008). https://doi.org/10.1145/1374376.1374407
19. Gentry, C., Sahai, A., Waters, B.: Homomorphic encryption from learning with errors: conceptually-simpler, asymptotically-faster, attribute-based. In: Canetti, R., Garay, J.A. (eds.) CRYPTO 2013. LNCS, vol. 8042, pp. 75–92. Springer, Heidelberg (2013). https://doi.org/10.1007/978-3-642-40041-4_5

20. Gentry, C., Waters, B.: Adaptive security in broadcast encryption systems (with short ciphertexts). In: Joux, A. (ed.) EUROCRYPT 2009. LNCS, vol. 5479, pp. 171–188. Springer, Heidelberg (2009). https://doi.org/10.1007/978-3-642-01001-9_10
21. Goyal, R., Koppula, V., Waters, B.: Collusion resistant traitor tracing from learning with errors. In: Diakonikolas, I., Kempe, D., Henzinger, M. (eds.) 50th Annual ACM Symposium on Theory of Computing, pp. 660–670. ACM Press, Los Angeles (2018). https://doi.org/10.1145/3188745.3188844
22. Goyal, R., Vusirikala, S.: Verifiable registration-based encryption. In: Micciancio, D., Ristenpart, T. (eds.) CRYPTO 2020. LNCS, vol. 12170, pp. 621–651. Springer, Cham (2020). https://doi.org/10.1007/978-3-030-56784-2_21
23. Goyal, R., Vusirikala, S., Waters, B.: Collusion resistant broadcast and trace from positional witness encryption. In: Lin, D., Sako, K. (eds.) PKC 2019. LNCS, vol. 11443, pp. 3–33. Springer, Cham (2019). https://doi.org/10.1007/978-3-030-17259-6_1
24. Goyal, V., Pandey, O., Sahai, A., Waters, B.: Attribute-based encryption for fine-grained access control of encrypted data. In: Juels, A., Wright, R.N., De Capitani di Vimercati, S. (eds.) ACM CCS 2006: 13th Conference on Computer and Communications Security, pp. 89–98. ACM Press, Alexandria (2006). https://doi.org/10.1145/1180405.1180418. available as Cryptology ePrint Archive Report 2006/309
25. Hemenway, B., Jafargholi, Z., Ostrovsky, R., Scafuro, A., Wichs, D.: Adaptively secure garbled circuits from one-way functions. In: Robshaw, M., Katz, J. (eds.) CRYPTO 2016. LNCS, vol. 9816, pp. 149–178. Springer, Heidelberg (2016). https://doi.org/10.1007/978-3-662-53015-3_6
26. Hohenberger, S., Lu, G., Waters, B., Wu, D.J.: Registered attribute-based encryption. In: Hazay, C., Stam, M. (eds.) Advances in Cryptology – EUROCRYPT 2023, Part III. LNCS, vol. 14006, pp. 511–542. Springer, Cham (2023). https://doi.org/10.1007/978-3-031-30620-4_17
27. Hohenberger, S., Waters, B.: Short and stateless signatures from the RSA assumption. In: Halevi, S. (ed.) CRYPTO 2009. LNCS, vol. 5677, pp. 654–670. Springer, Heidelberg (2009). https://doi.org/10.1007/978-3-642-03356-8_38
28. Hsieh, Y.C., Waters, B., Wu, D.J.: A generic approach to adaptively-secure broadcast encryption in the plain model. In: Fehr, S., Fouque, P.A. (eds.) Advances in Cryptology – EUROCRYPT 2025, Part III. LNCS, vol. 15603, pp. 336–365. Springer, Cham (2025). https://doi.org/10.1007/978-3-031-91131-6_12
29. Jafargholi, Z., Kamath, C., Klein, K., Komargodski, I., Pietrzak, K., Wichs, D.: Be adaptive, avoid overcommitting. In: Katz, J., Shacham, H. (eds.) CRYPTO 2017. LNCS, vol. 10401, pp. 133–163. Springer, Cham (2017). https://doi.org/10.1007/978-3-319-63688-7_5
30. Jafargholi, Z., Wichs, D.: Adaptive security of Yao's garbled circuits. In: Hirt, M., Smith, A. (eds.) TCC 2016. LNCS, vol. 9985, pp. 433–458. Springer, Heidelberg (2016). https://doi.org/10.1007/978-3-662-53641-4_17
31. Kolonelos, D., Malavolta, G., Wee, H.: Distributed broadcast encryption from bilinear groups. In: Guo, J., Steinfeld, R. (eds.) Advances in Cryptology – ASIACRYPT 2023, Part V. Lecture Notes in Computer Science, vol. 14442, pp. 407–441. Springer, Singapore (2023). https://doi.org/10.1007/978-981-99-8733-7_13
32. Kowalczyk, L., Wee, H.: Compact adaptively secure ABE for $NC^1$ from $k$-Lin. J. Cryptol. **33**(3), 954–1002 (2019). https://doi.org/10.1007/s00145-019-09335-x
33. Micciancio, D., Peikert, C.: Trapdoors for lattices: simpler, tighter, faster, smaller. In: Pointcheval, D., Johansson, T. (eds.) EUROCRYPT 2012. LNCS, vol. 7237, pp.

700–718. Springer, Heidelberg (2012). https://doi.org/10.1007/978-3-642-29011-4_41
34. Nielsen, J.B.: Separating random oracle proofs from complexity theoretic proofs: the non-committing encryption case. In: Yung, M. (ed.) CRYPTO 2002. LNCS, vol. 2442, pp. 111–126. Springer, Heidelberg (2002). https://doi.org/10.1007/3-540-45708-9_8
35. Regev, O.: On lattices, learning with errors, random linear codes, and cryptography. In: Gabow, H.N., Fagin, R. (eds.) 37th Annual ACM Symposium on Theory of Computing, pp. 84–93. ACM Press, Baltimore (2005). https://doi.org/10.1145/1060590.1060603
36. Sahai, A., Waters, B.: Fuzzy identity-based encryption. In: Cramer, R. (ed.) EUROCRYPT 2005. LNCS, vol. 3494, pp. 457–473. Springer, Heidelberg (2005). https://doi.org/10.1007/11426639_27
37. Waters, B.: Dual system encryption: realizing fully secure IBE and HIBE under simple assumptions. In: Halevi, S. (ed.) CRYPTO 2009. LNCS, vol. 5677, pp. 619–636. Springer, Heidelberg (2009). https://doi.org/10.1007/978-3-642-03356-8_36
38. Wee, H.: Circuit ABE with poly(depth, $\lambda$)-sized ciphertexts and keys from lattices. In: Reyzin, L., Stebila, D. (eds.) Advances in Cryptology – CRYPTO 2024, Part III. LNCS, vol. 14922, pp. 178–209. Springer, Cham (2024). https://doi.org/10.1007/978-3-031-68382-4_6
39. Wee, H.: Almost optimal KP and CP-ABE for circuits from succinct LWE. In: Fehr, S., Fouque, P.A. (eds.) Advances in Cryptology – EUROCRYPT 2025, Part III. LNCS, vol. 15603, pp. 34–62. Springer, Cham (2025). https://doi.org/10.1007/978-3-031-91131-6_2
40. Wee, H., Wu, D.J.: Unbounded distributed broadcast encryption and registered ABE from succinct LWE. In: Kalai, Y.T., Kamara, S.F. (eds.) Advances in Cryptology – CRYPTO 2025, Part III. LNCS, vol. 16002, pp. 204–235. Springer, Cham (2025). https://doi.org/10.1007/978-3-032-01881-6_7
41. Wu, Q., Qin, B., Zhang, L., Domingo-Ferrer, J.: Ad hoc broadcast encryption (poster presentation). In: Al-Shaer, E., Keromytis, A.D., Shmatikov, V. (eds.) ACM CCS 2010: 17th Conference on Computer and Communications Security, pp. 741–743. ACM Press, Chicago (2010). https://doi.org/10.1145/1866307.1866416
42. Zhu, Z., Zhang, K., Gong, J., Qian, H.: Registered ABE via predicate encodings. In: Guo, J., Steinfeld, R. (eds.) Advances in Cryptology – ASIACRYPT 2023, Part V. LNCS, vol. 14442, pp. 66–97. Springer, Singapore (2023). https://doi.org/10.1007/978-981-99-8733-7_3

# Advanced Cryptography from Lattice Isomorphism—New Constructions of IBE and FHE

Huck Bennett[1], Zhengnan Lai[2], and Noah Stephens-Davidowitz[2(✉)]

[1] University of Colorado, Boulder, USA
[2] Cornell University, Ithaca, USA
noahsd@gmail.com

**Abstract.** We show how to translate some of the more advanced techniques used in LWE-based cryptography to the setting of lattice-isomorphism-based cryptography, which was recently introduced by Ducas and van Woerden [Eurocrypt, 2022]. In particular, we show constructions of two powerful cryptographic primitives, identity-based encryption (IBE) and leveled fully homomorphic encryption (FHE). We then prove their security under the assumption that a suitable version of the Lattice Isomorphism Problem is hard.

Our constructions use quite general and modular techniques, and we expect them to have other applications. Specifically, we show that the now-ubiquitous techniques introduced by Gentry, Peikert, and Vaikuntanathan [STOC, 2008] to build IBE and Gentry, Sahai, and Waters [Crypto, 2013] to build FHE can be made to work in our setting using any sufficiently "nice" lattice.

**Keywords:** Lattice isomorphism · Identity-based encryption · Fully homomorphic encryption

## 1 Introduction

A lattice $\mathcal{L} \subset \mathbb{R}^n$ is the set of all integer linear combinations of $n$ linearly independent basis vectors $\boldsymbol{B} = (\boldsymbol{b}_1, \ldots, \boldsymbol{b}_n) \in \mathbb{R}^{n \times n}$, i.e.,

$$\mathcal{L} := \mathcal{L}(\boldsymbol{B}) = \{z_1 \boldsymbol{b}_1 + \cdots + z_n \boldsymbol{b}_n \ : \ z_1, \ldots, z_n \in \mathbb{Z}\} .$$

Lattices play an extremely important role in cryptography. Indeed, lattice-based cryptography is nearing widespread deployment. In particular, because of their apparent security against quantum adversaries, lattice-based constructions were recently standardized by NIST [53,54] as the preferred way to implement both public-key encryption [10] (more formally, key encapsulation) and digital signatures [11,34].

Perhaps even more excitingly, lattices can also be used to construct much more powerful cryptographic primitives like fully homomorphic encryption


N. Heninger and M. Rosulek (Eds.): CRYPTO 2026, LNCS 16800, pp. 446–476, 2026.
https://doi.org/10.1007/978-3-032-35367-2_15

(FHE) [9,22–24,31,35,37], identity-based encryption (IBE) [3,4,26,36], fully homomorphic signatures [19,40], attribute-based encryption (ABE) [20,39,59], functional encryption [1,5,6,38,61], and many more. (See [56] for a survey.) All of these schemes are secure under the assumption that certain computational problems associated with the geometry of a lattice—like the problem of estimating the length of the shortest non-zero vector in a lattice—are hard (in many instances, even in the worst case [7,55,57]).

In fact, essentially all of these schemes have their security based on variants of a *single* computational hardness assumption, known as the Learning With Errors (LWE) assumption [57]. (To the authors' knowledge, the only exceptions in the many schemes referenced above are [19,35] and [34], which are respectively based on an ad-hoc assumption and on NTRU [42].) Evidently, LWE is a remarkably useful and versatile tool. So, it is natural to ask whether there are also other ways of using lattices to build cryptography.

Recently, Ducas and van Woerden [33] and Bennett, Ganju, Peetathawatchai, and Stephens-Davidowitz [16] proposed a different way to do lattice-based cryptography based on the *Lattice Isomorphism Problem* (LIP). At the heart of the constructions in [16,33], there is a fixed underlying "nice" lattice $\mathcal{L}_{\mathsf{nice}}$ like $\mathbb{Z}^n$ or the Barnes-Wall lattice that is known to all.[1] $\mathcal{L}_{\mathsf{nice}}$ is "nice" in the sense that some computational problem—like the problem of determining whether a given point $\boldsymbol{c} \in \mathbb{R}^n$ is close or far from the lattice—is easy when restricted to $\mathcal{L}_{\mathsf{nice}}$ but hard for typical lattices $\mathcal{L}$.

To generate the public and secret keys for these cryptosystems, one can imagine sampling an orthogonal transformation $\boldsymbol{O} \in \mathcal{O}_n(\mathbb{R})$ and taking the secret key to be the corresponding transformation $\boldsymbol{B}_{\mathsf{sk}} := \boldsymbol{O}\boldsymbol{B}_{\mathsf{nice}}$ of some fixed, known "nice" basis $\boldsymbol{B}_{\mathsf{nice}}$ of $\mathcal{L}_{\mathsf{nice}}$. The public key can be thought of as a "bad" $\boldsymbol{B}_{\mathsf{pk}}$ basis of $\boldsymbol{O}\mathcal{L}_{\mathsf{nice}} = \mathcal{L}(\boldsymbol{B}_{\mathsf{sk}})$.[2] This is useful because bases are certainly not unique. For example, one could take $\boldsymbol{B}_{\mathsf{nice}} := \boldsymbol{I}_2$ to be the nice basis of $\mathcal{L}_{\mathsf{nice}} = \mathbb{Z}^2$, and $\boldsymbol{B}_{\mathsf{pk}} := \boldsymbol{O}\boldsymbol{B}_{\mathsf{bad}}$ where

$$\boldsymbol{B}_{\mathsf{bad}} := \begin{pmatrix} 12345 & 1234 \\ 2471 & 247 \end{pmatrix} .$$

(Interestingly, this paradigm of "nice bases and bad bases" is often used as a simple way to give some intuition for how lattice-based cryptography works—e.g., in a talk to a general computer science audience. However, most LWE-based constructions do not actually follow this paradigm in any real sense.)

[1] Ducas and van Woerden considered general "nice" lattices $\mathcal{L}_{\mathsf{nice}}$, which they referred to as "remarkable." Bennett, Ganju, Peetathawatchai, and Stephens-Davidowitz restricted their attention to $\mathcal{L}_{\mathsf{nice}} = \mathbb{Z}^n$.

[2] In both [16,33], one does not directly work with bases $\boldsymbol{B}$ of an orthogonal transformation $\boldsymbol{O}\mathcal{L}_{\mathsf{nice}}$ of the nice lattice. Instead, it is far more mathematically elegant to work with the associated quadratic forms $\boldsymbol{Q} := \boldsymbol{B}^\top \boldsymbol{B}$. In the sequel, we also work with quadratic forms. But, in the introduction, we work with bases of lattices because we find them to be more intuitive. See the full version of the present work [17] for more discussion.

To prove security, we assume that it is hard to distinguish a "bad" basis $\boldsymbol{B}_{\mathsf{pk}}$ of $\mathcal{L} = \boldsymbol{O}\mathcal{L}_{\mathsf{nice}}$ from a basis $\boldsymbol{B}'_{\mathsf{pk}}$ of an orthogonal transformation $\boldsymbol{O}'$ of some *other* lattice $\mathcal{L}'$, and we carefully choose $\mathcal{L}'$ so that breaking our cryptographic scheme is simply information-theoretically impossible when $\mathcal{L}_{\mathsf{nice}}$ is replaced by $\mathcal{L}'$. E.g., for an encryption scheme, we choose $\mathcal{L}'$ so that the resulting distribution of ciphertexts $\boldsymbol{c}'_0$ and $\boldsymbol{c}'_1$ encrypting 0 and 1 respectively are statistically close, and we immediately see that the scheme is secure as long as it is hard to determine whether the input basis is a basis for an orthogonal transformation of $\mathcal{L}_{\mathsf{nice}}$ or of $\mathcal{L}'$.[3]

Using this approach, Ducas and van Woerden [33] proposed a public-key encryption scheme (formally, a KEM), a signature scheme, and a zero-knowledge proof of knowledge and showed security under the assumption that it is hard to distinguish a basis of (an orthogonal transformation of) a sufficiently "nice" lattice from a very different lattice. Bennett, Ganju, Peetathawatchai, and Stephens-Davidowitz [16] proposed a different public-key encryption scheme using "good and bad bases" of $\mathbb{Z}^n$ and similarly showed its security under the assumption that it is hard to distinguish a basis of (an orthogonal transformation of) $\mathbb{Z}^n$ from a basis of a lattice with "very different geometry than $\mathbb{Z}^n$." Both works showed worst-case to average-case reductions, effectively showing a way to sample the public key basis $\boldsymbol{B}_{\mathsf{pk}}$ so that the average-case problem of distinguishing $\boldsymbol{B}_{\mathsf{pk}}$ from $\boldsymbol{B}'_{\mathsf{pk}}$ is provably as hard as the worst-case problem of distinguishing *any* basis of any orthogonal transformation of $\mathcal{L}_{\mathsf{nice}}$ from any basis of any orthogonal transformation of $\mathcal{L}'$.

This is now called *lattice-isomorphism-based* cryptography. To see where the name comes from, first note that two lattices $\mathcal{L}_0, \mathcal{L}_1$ are said to be *isomorphic* if $\mathcal{L}_0 = \boldsymbol{O}\mathcal{L}_1$ for some orthogonal linear transformation $\boldsymbol{O} \in \mathsf{O}_n(\mathbb{R})$. The problem of determining whether two bases generate isomorphic lattices is naturally known as the *Lattice Isomorphism Problem (*LIP*)*. Thus, the name "lattice-isomorphism-based cryptography."[4]

In the few years since [16,33], there has been quite a remarkable amount of excitement around LIP and lattice-isomorphism-based cryptography. In particular, there has been a flurry of work studying LIP itself and related problems [8,12–15,18,28–30,41,44,47,48,51,52,58,60] and another flurry of work building additional lattice-isomorphism-based cryptography [2,25,27,43,45,46],

[3] One could imagine simply directly assuming that the underlying computational problem of breaking the scheme is hard, rather than factoring through $\mathcal{L}'$. E.g., for an encryption scheme, one might directly assume that $\boldsymbol{c}_0$ and $\boldsymbol{c}_1$ are computationally indistinguishable. But, it seems more sound to base security on a less contrived assumption.

[4] Really, this is cryptography based on a particular promise problem variant of LIP in which in the YES case $\boldsymbol{B}$ generates an orthogonal transformation of some fixed very special $\mathcal{L}_{\mathsf{nice}}$ and in the NO case $\boldsymbol{B}$ generates an orthogonal transformation of some other fixed lattice $\mathcal{L}'$ that "has very different geometry from $\mathcal{L}_{\mathsf{nice}}$." See the full version [17] for more discussion.

including a signature scheme that has been proposed for standardization [21,32]. Indeed, there seems to be quite a large design space to explore here.[5]

Of course, lattice-isomorphism-based cryptography is still nowhere near as mature as traditional lattice-based cryptography based on LWE, and it is so far unclear how such constructions compare to traditional lattice-based constructions.

A natural next step in the development of lattice-isomorphism-based cryptography is to ask whether there are constructions of more advanced cryptographic primitives in this framework. In other words, can we use the ideas above to build the powerful cryptographic primitives—like FHE, IBE, ABE, and Functional Encryption—that we already know how to build from LWE? Such schemes are inherently interesting, and they might lead to better security, improved efficiency, or even constructions of novel cryptographic primitives.

Perhaps the most natural advanced cryptographic primitive to try to build first in this context is FHE, which is a very important cryptographic primitive that now has many different lattice-based constructions but no non-lattice-based constructions. Indeed, just recently, Branco, Malavolta, and Maradni [25] and Leporati, Rovida, and van Woerden [46] proposed constructions of variants of lattice-isomorphism-based FHE. Specifically, [25] constructed an encryption scheme capable of homomorphically evaluating branching programs.[6] [46] outlined two whole frameworks for building FHE schemes that capture many known constructions, and which they say can likely be instantiated from suitable versions of lattice isomorphism. But, they do not formally prove security and correctness of the resulting lattice-isomorphism-based scheme. ([46] were more interested in their frameworks than in particular instantiations. They do prove security formally for non-lattice-isomorphism-based instantiations of their framework, and they give an informal argument for security of their lattice-isomorphism-based instantiations.)

### 1.1 Our Results

We continue the study of constructions of advanced lattice-isomorphism-based cryptographic primitives. In particular, we demonstrate that some of the core techniques used to build advanced primitives from LWE can be modified to construct such primitives from lattice isomorphism as well.

Our concrete contributions are constructions of two advanced cryptographic primitives—IBE and leveled FHE. As we will discuss, our constructions closely

[5] In the original work of [33], they observed that constructions of truly "remarkable" lattices could potentially yield better security and efficiency or even novel functionalities. That particular direction is still largely unexplored, and it is still quite exciting.

[6] [25] says that the generic technique of bootstrapping can be used to make this scheme work for arbitrary circuits, therefore achieving true FHE. This seems plausible, but the details are not worked out in [25]. See Sect. 6.6 for a brief discussion of the subtleties involved in applying bootstrapping in this context.

parallel two celebrated constructions from traditional lattice-based cryptography, the Gentry, Peikert, and Vaikuntanathan IBE scheme [36], and the Gentry, Sahai, and Waters FHE scheme [37].

*Identity-Based Encryption.* First, we show (in Sects. 3 and 4) the first construction of lattice-isomorphism-based identity-based encryption (IBE). Recall that IBE is a variant of public-key encryption in which "Alice and Bob's public keys are simply their names." More specifically, in an IBE scheme, a trusted authority can use a master secret key $\mathsf{msk}$ to generate a secret key $\mathsf{sk}_{\mathsf{id}}$ corresponding to any identity $\mathsf{id} \in \{0,1\}^*$, e.g., the names "Alice" and "Bob" (in ASCII, say). Anyone can then use a master public key $\mathsf{mpk}$ together with the associated $\mathsf{id}$ to encrypt a message $\mu$ so that it can be decrypted using just $\mathsf{sk}_{\mathsf{id}}$. (I.e., $\mathsf{Dec}(\mathsf{sk}_{\text{Alice}}, \mathsf{Enc}(\mathsf{mpk}, \text{"Alice"}, \mu)) = \mu$.) Security requires that it is difficult for an adversary to distinguish an encryption under some identity $\mathsf{id}$ of 0 from an encryption under $\mathsf{id}$ of 1, even if the adversary can request many secret keys for many identities $\mathsf{id}' \neq \mathsf{id}$.

We construct an IBE scheme in the style of the celebrated LWE-based IBE scheme of Gentry, Peikert, and Vaikuntanathan [36]. We then prove the security of our scheme assuming the hardness of a suitable version of LIP (in the random oracle model), which appears to be incomparable to the version of LWE used in [36].

The scheme itself is quite simple and follows the paradigm of "good and bad bases" described above. In particular, $\mathsf{mpk}$ is (effectively) a bad basis $\boldsymbol{B}_{\mathsf{mpk}}$ for an orthogonal transformation of some "nice" lattice $\mathcal{L}_{\mathsf{nice}}$ and the master secret key $\mathsf{msk}$ is effectively a good basis of the same lattice. Given an identity $\mathsf{id}$, the trusted authority uses its good basis to find a (suitably sampled) dual lattice vector $\boldsymbol{w}$ that is close to $\boldsymbol{t} := \mathcal{H}(\mathsf{id})$ (where $\mathcal{H}$ is a random oracle with an appropriate range) and sets $\mathsf{sk}_{\mathsf{id}} := \boldsymbol{w}$.

An encryption of a bit $\mu \in \{0,1\}$ then has the form $(\boldsymbol{c} := \boldsymbol{y} + \boldsymbol{e}, d := \langle \boldsymbol{y}, \boldsymbol{t}\rangle + \mu/2 \bmod 1)$, where $\boldsymbol{y}$ is a lattice vector and $\boldsymbol{e} \in \mathbb{R}^n$ is "short". Since $\boldsymbol{y}$ is a lattice vector and $\boldsymbol{w}$ is a dual lattice vector, their inner product is an integer. Therefore, when reducing modulo 1, we can ignore the inner product of $\boldsymbol{w}$ and $\boldsymbol{y}$ to see that

$$\langle \boldsymbol{c}, \boldsymbol{t} - \boldsymbol{w}\rangle = \langle \boldsymbol{e}, \boldsymbol{t} - \boldsymbol{w}\rangle + \langle \boldsymbol{y}, \boldsymbol{t}\rangle = \langle \boldsymbol{e}, \boldsymbol{t} - \boldsymbol{w}\rangle + d - \mu/2 \bmod 1 \; .$$

One can then decrypt by computing $\langle \boldsymbol{c}, \boldsymbol{t} - \boldsymbol{w}\rangle - d$ and checking whether the result is close to an integer. As long as $\langle \boldsymbol{e}, \boldsymbol{t} - \boldsymbol{w}\rangle$ is much smaller than 1, this will work. And, since we have chosen $\boldsymbol{e}$ to be short and $\boldsymbol{w}$ to be close to $\boldsymbol{t}$, we can choose our parameters so that this inner product will in fact be small.

For security, we assume that the lattice $\mathcal{L} = \boldsymbol{O}\mathcal{L}_{\mathsf{nice}}$ generated by $\boldsymbol{B}_{\mathsf{mpk}}$ is indistinguishable from some other lattice $\mathcal{L}'$ whose geometry is such that the element $d$ is nearly uniformly random modulo one, even conditioned on $\boldsymbol{c}$. (One must also argue that security holds even against an adversary with access to many secret keys $\mathsf{sk}_{\mathsf{id}}$, but we ignore this here. In Sect. 4, we prove full security.) At a technical level, we show (using a slightly modified version of an argument from [33]) that it suffices if $\mathcal{L}'$ contains a sufficiently dense sublattice (specifically, a sublattice of sufficiently large rank that has small smoothing parameter).

This scheme will be familiar to anyone who is well-versed in the GPV IBE construction. Indeed, we view our construction (including the details that we have glossed over here for simplicity, but which are included in Sects. 3 and 4) as showing that the celebrated techniques of [36] work in the setting of LIP.

In more detail, like in [36], one can view our IBE scheme as a sort of "merger of a signature scheme and a compatible public-key encryption scheme." (Note that this provides the intuition for our scheme, but we do not attempt to make this "merger" formal.) In [36], they introduce the GPV signature scheme and the dual Regev public-key encryption scheme and show that the secret key of the encryption scheme is essentially a signature of a random string that is included in the public key. They then construct an IBE scheme by taking $\mathsf{msk}$ and $\mathsf{mpk}$ to be the corresponding keys of the signature and set $\mathsf{sk}_{\mathsf{id}}$ to be a signature of a hash of $\mathsf{id}$ (with the hash function modeled as a random oracle).

Our construction also has this form. In particular, the signature scheme underlying our construction (which we do not describe explicitly) is precisely the elegant signature scheme from [33]. We present in Sect. 3 a public-key encryption scheme, which is a simple variant of the encryption scheme in [33]. This variant of [33]'s scheme is naturally designed to have the property that the secret key can be viewed as a signature of a random string. At a technical level, our scheme differs from [33] in that we replace the strong extractor used by [33] with a simple inner product. We show directly using Fourier-analytic techniques that the inner product is sufficient without changing domains. See Theorem 1. (The authors of [25] do something similar, but they use an inner product over a smaller domain because they treat the inner product as a generic extractor. We view Theorem 1 as an additional important contribution of the present work, though it is rather technical.)

Our presentation is quite modular in the sense that correctness of our IBE scheme follows more-or-less immediately from correctness of the much simpler public-key encryption scheme that we present in Sect. 3. Security of our IBE scheme follows from a simulation argument (similar to the proof of security of the signature in [33], which itself follows [36]) together with the security of the public-key encryption scheme.

*Fully Homomorphic Encryption.* Second, we show (in Sects. 5 and 6) a construction of lattice-isomorphism-based fully homomorphic encryption (FHE). More formally, we obtain a leveled FHE scheme, which is a scheme that allows for homomorphic evaluation of circuits up to a certain depth. We can specifically handle circuits up to any depth that is bounded by some polynomial in the security parameter, matching state-of-the-art constructions from LWE.[7]

Here, we closely follow the elegant LWE-based construction of (leveled) FHE due to Gentry, Sahai, and Waters [37]. At a high level, our scheme works by

[7] All known true FHE constructions require additional circular security assumptions, which might also work in our setting. See Sect. 6.6 for more discussion.

replacing the Regev public-key encryption scheme on which the GSW FHE scheme is based with a suitable, general variant of the public-key encryption scheme from [16]. We present this public-key encryption scheme in Sect. 5, and then show how to make it fully homomorphic in Sect. 6.

We include detailed discussion of the design decisions behind our public-key encryption scheme and FHE scheme at the start of Sect. 5. Here, we simply note that our FHE scheme makes heavy use of Micciancio and Peikert's celebrated *gadget matrix* $\boldsymbol{G}$ [50] (see Eq. (1)). The gadget matrix is a key tool in [37] specifically, but it is also used in *many* beautiful lattice-based cryptographic constructions, and we show how to make it work in the context of lattice isomorphism.

We show how to make gadget-based techniques work relatively painlessly, although we do encounter a subtlety that requires care to get around. The specific subtlety is rather technical and discussed in Sect. 5, but it amounts to the question of whether $\boldsymbol{s}^\top \boldsymbol{G} \bmod q$ is "large or small," where $\boldsymbol{s}$ is the secret key. If this vector is small, then all valid ciphertexts will decrypt to 0, and the scheme will certainly not be correct. In LWE-based constructions, it is trivial to see that $\boldsymbol{s}^\top \boldsymbol{G} \bmod q$ is large,[8] but there seems to be no guarantee that this remains true here.[9] We solve this by replacing $\boldsymbol{G}$ with $\boldsymbol{H} := (\boldsymbol{h}, \boldsymbol{G})$ where $\boldsymbol{h}$ is chosen so that $\langle \boldsymbol{s}, \boldsymbol{h} \rangle \bmod q$ is large. However, if we chose $\boldsymbol{h}$ in such a way that this depended on the secret key $\boldsymbol{s}$, this could break security (and certainly we would not be able to prove security). So, we instead choose $\boldsymbol{h}$ randomly from a suitable set and show that with high probability this inner product will be large. (To make this work with high probability, we actually take our secret key to be a whole matrix $\boldsymbol{S}$ rather than a single vector $\boldsymbol{s}$. See Sect. 5 for a detailed discussion.)

We briefly compare the security assumption that we need for our LIP-based FHE scheme to the assumptions needed by LWE-based schemes. We prove that our FHE scheme is secure assuming the hardness of distinguishing orthogonal linear transformations of lattices $\mathcal{L}_{\mathsf{nice}}$ and $\mathcal{L}'$ satisfying certain properties. For the concrete choices of $\mathcal{L}_{\mathsf{nice}}$ and $\mathcal{L}'$ that we discuss in Sect. 6.5, this in turn requires the hardness of $\gamma$-GapSVP with $\gamma = n^{L+\Theta(1)}$, where $L$ is the depth of the circuit to be homomorphically evaluated and $\gamma$-GapSVP is the problem of approximating the length of the shortest non-zero vector in a lattice to within a factor of $\gamma$.

Using simple constructions, one can prove security of LWE-based FHE assuming the hardness of $\gamma$-GapSVP for a similar factor $\gamma = n^{L+\Theta(1)}$. E.g., one can prove security of the GSW FHE scheme [37] assuming the hardness of LWE with certain parameters, and one can then apply Regev's worst-case to average-case reduction for LWE to $\gamma$-GapSVP with $\gamma = n^{L+\Theta(1)}$ to LWE with these

[8] Here, we are parameterizing the scheme so that the last coordinate of $\boldsymbol{s}$ is always 1, in which case this fact is guaranteed by the fact that the last column of the gadget matrix is $(q/2)\boldsymbol{e}_n$. This parameterization is often not made explicit.

[9] In their informal construction of FHE from LIP (which they present as just one part of a more general framework), [46] quite reasonably simply assume that $\boldsymbol{s}^\top \boldsymbol{G} \bmod q$ is large. In their notation, this amounts to the assumption that $\langle \boldsymbol{d}_1, \boldsymbol{s} \rangle = 1 \bmod p$.

parameters. However, [24] showed how to use sophisticated techniques to reduce this approximation factor to $\gamma = n^{\Theta(1)}$, independent of $L$—a weaker assumption than the one that we require (for $L$ larger than some small constant). So, if one compares our scheme to similarly simple LWE-based constructions of FHE, one finds that the corresponding security assumptions are incomparable (or at least not known to be comparable). If one compares to the state of the art, one sees that our assumption is stronger than the relevant version of LWE. (This was originally observed by [25].) We leave it as an open problem to make ideas like those in [24] work in our setting in order to achieve security under a weaker hardness assumption. This is closely related to the discussion of bootstrapping in Sect. 6.6. See the full version [17] for more discussion.

*Generality and Modularity.* In our presentation, we endeavor to be general. In particular, we try to use quite natural and quite weak properties of the lattice $\mathcal{L}_{\mathsf{nice}}$ in order to prove correctness of our schemes, and we try to use similarly weak and natural properties of the lattice $\mathcal{L}'$ in order to prove security. We then plug in simple but careful choices of $\mathcal{L}_{\mathsf{nice}}$ and $\mathcal{L}'$ that were originally proposed by Ducas and van Woerden [33]. In particular, in both schemes, we take $\mathcal{L}_{\mathsf{nice}} = a\mathbb{Z}^{n/2} \oplus b\mathbb{Z}^{n/2}$ and $\mathcal{L}' = a'\mathbb{Z}^{n/2} \oplus b'\mathbb{Z}^{n/2}$ for appropriate $a$, $b$, $a'$, and $b'$. But, we work to avoid using any unnecessary properties of these lattices—such as the fact that decoding is easy. We note that this modularity allows for drop-in replacement of other "nice" lattices, and we view this as a strength of our work and, more generally, of lattice-isomorphism-based cryptography. It is an interesting open question to find new interesting examples of "nice" families of lattices that are suitable for our constructions (and other similar constructions).

## 1.2 Related Work

As we noted above, our IBE scheme is really an adaptation to the LIP setting of the beautiful LWE-based IBE scheme of Gentry, Peikert, and Vaikuntanathan [36]. Analogously, our FHE scheme is an adaptation of the elegant LWE-based FHE scheme of Gentry, Sahai, and Waters [37]. Furthermore, many of the specific "lattice-isomorphism-based" methods that we use to construct our schemes are heavily inspired by the ideas in Ducas and van Woerden [33] and in Bennett, Ganju, Peetathawatchai, and Stephens-Davidowitz [16]. Indeed, our IBE scheme is heavily inspired by both the signature and the public-key encryption scheme in [33]—and can be viewed as a "merger" of the two, as we described above. Similarly, the public-key encryption scheme that we present in Sect. 5 (which we then use in Sect. 6 to build FHE) is a variant of the public-key encryption scheme in [16].

The other works that are most closely related to ours are the two other works that consider lattice-isomorphism-based FHE. Indeed, Branco, Malavolta, and Maradni built a lattice-isomorphism-based encryption scheme that can homomorphically evaluate branching programs [25], while we build an encryption scheme that can handle the much larger class of polynomial-depth circuits.[10] The construction of [25] is quite a bit different than ours. They actually start out with an encryption scheme that is quite similar to the one that we present in Sect. 3, which we use in our IBE construction. However, they use Micciancio's "ground up" approach to convert this scheme into a homomorphic scheme [49], whereas we start with our scheme from Sect. 5 and make it homomorphic using the very different approach from [37].

Leporati, Rovida, and van Woerden also considered building lattice-based FHE from assumptions "beyond LWE" [46]. They suggested two frameworks for building (leveled) FHE, one generalizing [22], and the other generalizing [37]. When they instantiate the [37]-based framework using LIP, they naturally obtain a construction that looks quite similar to our own [37]-based scheme. In particular, they similarly use the gadget matrix $\boldsymbol{G}$. However, they are more interested in their general framework, so their construction is heuristic and not proven. In contrast, we are certainly not nearly as general, but we provide a full proof of correctness and security.

## 2 Preliminaries

We typically use bold capital letters for matrices, like $\boldsymbol{X} \in \mathbb{Z}^{n \times m}$, and lower-case bold letters for vectors, like $\boldsymbol{x} \in \mathbb{R}^n$. All vectors are column vectors except where otherwise noted. For a positive integer $q$, we write $\mathbb{T}_q := \{0, 1/q, \ldots, (q-1)/q\}$, which we think of as an additive group modulo 1.

We use $\mathcal{S}_n^{>0}(\mathbb{R})$ and $\mathcal{S}_n^{>0}(\mathbb{Z})$ to denote the set of $n \times n$ symmetric positive definite matrices over the reals and the integers, respectively.

Due to space constraints, we defer some basic mathematical preliminaries to the full version of the present work [17]. Here, we simply emphasize a technical theorem that will be crucial for the security of our IBE scheme. See [17] for the relevant definitions and for the proof.

**Theorem 1.** *For any quadratic form $\boldsymbol{Q} \in \mathcal{S}_n^{>0}(\mathbb{Z})$, integer $1 \le k \le n$, a prime modulus $q \ge 2$, parameter $s \ge 2q^{1/k} \cdot \eta_\varepsilon^{(k)}(\boldsymbol{Q})$ for some $\varepsilon \in (0, 1/2)$, and shift vector $\boldsymbol{c} \in \mathbb{R}^n$, let $\boldsymbol{z} \sim D_{\boldsymbol{Q},s,\boldsymbol{c}}$ and $\boldsymbol{t} \sim \mathbb{Z}_q^n$. Then, the distribution $(\boldsymbol{t}, \langle \boldsymbol{z}, \boldsymbol{t} \rangle \bmod q)$ is within statistical distance at most $2\varepsilon + 2^{3-k/2}$ of the uniform distribution over $\mathbb{Z}_q^n \times \mathbb{Z}_q$.*

## 3 A Public-Key Encryption Scheme that We Will Use to Build IBE

We first describe a public-key encryption scheme that we will use to build IBE. Our scheme has as parameters a quadratic form $\boldsymbol{Q} \in \mathcal{S}_n^{>0}(\mathbb{Z})$, a parameter

[10] [25] claim that generic bootstrapping-based techniques can be used to convert this to a fully homomorphic public-key encryption scheme, but they do not prove correctness or security of the resulting scheme. We briefly discuss some of the subtleties that arise in this context in Sect. 6.6.

$s := s(n) \geq \sqrt{\log n}\|\boldsymbol{Q}\|$ (which controls the size of $\boldsymbol{P}$), a noise parameter $r := r(n) \geq \sqrt{n \log n} \cdot s/q$, a prime discretization parameter $q := q(n) \geq 10$, and a distance bound $\rho := \rho(n) > 0$.

We require that $\boldsymbol{Q}$ is such that there is some efficient algorithm that outputs $\boldsymbol{t}' \sim \mathbb{T}_q^n$ together with $\boldsymbol{y}' \in \mathbb{Z}^n$ such that $\|\boldsymbol{y}' - \boldsymbol{t}'\|_{\boldsymbol{Q}^{-1}} \leq \rho$.[11] We write $h := (q+1)/(2q) \in \mathbb{T}_q$.

- $\mathsf{Gen}(1^n)$: Sample $\boldsymbol{U} \leftarrow \mathcal{D}_s(\boldsymbol{Q}) \in \mathrm{GL}_n(\mathbb{Z})$, and compute $\boldsymbol{P} := \boldsymbol{U}^\top \boldsymbol{Q} \boldsymbol{U}$. Sample $(\boldsymbol{t}', \boldsymbol{y}') \in \mathbb{T}_q^n \times \mathbb{Z}^n$ such that $\|\boldsymbol{t}' - \boldsymbol{y}'\|_{\boldsymbol{Q}^{-1}} \leq \rho$ as above and set $\boldsymbol{t} := \boldsymbol{U}^\top \boldsymbol{t}' \bmod 1$ and $\boldsymbol{y} := \boldsymbol{U}^\top \boldsymbol{y}'$ (so that $\|\boldsymbol{t} - \boldsymbol{y}\|_{\boldsymbol{P}^{-1}} = \|\boldsymbol{t}' - \boldsymbol{y}'\|_{\boldsymbol{Q}^{-1}} \leq \rho$). Output $\mathsf{sk} := \boldsymbol{y}$ and $\mathsf{pk} := (\boldsymbol{P}, \boldsymbol{t})$.
- $\mathsf{Enc}(\mathsf{pk}, \mu \in \{0,1\})$: Sample $\boldsymbol{e} \sim D_{\boldsymbol{P}, rq}/q \in \mathbb{Z}^n/q$ using the algorithm described in [33]. (See the full version of the present work [17] for the specific properties that we need.) Compute $\boldsymbol{c} := \boldsymbol{e} \bmod 1 \in \mathbb{T}_q^n$ and $d := \langle \boldsymbol{e} - \boldsymbol{c}, \boldsymbol{t} \rangle + \mu h \bmod 1 \in \mathbb{T}_q$. Output $(\boldsymbol{c}, d)$.
- $\mathsf{Dec}(\mathsf{sk}, (\boldsymbol{c}, d))$: Compute $d + \langle \boldsymbol{c}, \boldsymbol{t} - \boldsymbol{y} \rangle \bmod 1$. Output 1 if the result is in the interval $[1/4, 3/4]$, and 0 otherwise.

This scheme is effectively a lattice-isomorphism variant of the dual-Regev encryption scheme introduced in [36]. It is also quite similar to the simplest encryption scheme presented in [25], and to the key-encapsulation mechanism proposed in [33]. The main difference from [33] is that we avoid using a generic extractor like in [33]. Instead, we show directly (using Theorem 1) that $\langle \boldsymbol{e} - \boldsymbol{c}, \boldsymbol{t} \rangle \bmod 1$ is pseudorandom, even conditioned on $\boldsymbol{t} \neq \boldsymbol{0}$ and $\boldsymbol{c}$. ( [25] also use a linear extractor, but they must switch moduli to make their proof work.)

To understand roughly why this scheme is correct, notice that because $\boldsymbol{e} - \boldsymbol{c} \in \mathbb{Z}^n$ and $\boldsymbol{y} \in \mathbb{Z}^n$, we have that

$$d = \langle \boldsymbol{e} - \boldsymbol{c}, \boldsymbol{t} \rangle + \mu h = \langle \boldsymbol{e} - \boldsymbol{c}, \boldsymbol{t} - \boldsymbol{y} \rangle + \mu h \bmod 1 .$$

Therefore,

$$d + \langle \boldsymbol{c}, \boldsymbol{t} - \boldsymbol{y} \rangle = \mu h + \langle \boldsymbol{e}, \boldsymbol{t} - \boldsymbol{y} \rangle \bmod 1 .$$

Since $\|\boldsymbol{t} - \boldsymbol{y}\|_{\boldsymbol{P}^{-1}}$ is small and $\|\boldsymbol{e}\|_{\boldsymbol{P}}$ is small, we expect $\langle \boldsymbol{e}, \boldsymbol{t} - \boldsymbol{y} \rangle$ to be small (this holds by the Cauchy-Schwarz inequality, although we use a more sophisticated argument below), and therefore that $d + \langle \boldsymbol{c}, \boldsymbol{t} - \boldsymbol{y} \rangle \approx \mu h \approx \mu/2 \bmod 1$. We prove this formally in Theorem 2.

[11] In Sect. 4, the algorithm effectively directly samples $\boldsymbol{t}' \sim \mathbb{Z}_q^n$ uniformly at random and then it samples $\boldsymbol{y}' \sim D_{\boldsymbol{Q}^{-1}, \rho/\sqrt{n}, \boldsymbol{t}'}$. But, in many similar schemes, a short $\boldsymbol{x}' \in \mathbb{Z}^n/q$ is sampled first and then $\boldsymbol{t}'$ is simply set to $\boldsymbol{x}' \bmod 1$ and $\boldsymbol{y}' = \boldsymbol{t}' - \boldsymbol{x}'$. We leave this unspecified here, since in this section, we are agnostic to how $\boldsymbol{y}'$ and $\boldsymbol{t}'$ are generated. (Of course, $\rho$ must be at least the covering radius in order for this to be plausibly possible.) Indeed, security of our scheme in Sect. 4 will crucially rely on the fact that there is this alternative way to sample $\boldsymbol{t}'$ and $\boldsymbol{y}'$, effectively sampling $\boldsymbol{t}' - \boldsymbol{y}'$ first and then setting $\boldsymbol{t}' := \boldsymbol{t}' - \boldsymbol{y}' \bmod 1$. (A similar dynamic occurs in [36].) Of course, we could simply ask that the distribution of $\boldsymbol{t}'$ is statistically close to uniform, but in our applications we will have true uniformity.

On the other hand, imagine that $\boldsymbol{P}$ is indistinguishable from some $\boldsymbol{P}'$ that has the following property. If we were to sample $\boldsymbol{e} \sim D_{\boldsymbol{P}',rq}/q$ (rather than from $D_{\boldsymbol{P},rq}/q$), then even conditioned on $\boldsymbol{c} = \boldsymbol{e} \bmod 1$, the vector $\boldsymbol{e} - \boldsymbol{c}$ still has high entropy. Then, one might roughly hope that the ciphertext $(\boldsymbol{c}, \langle \boldsymbol{e} - \boldsymbol{c}, \boldsymbol{t}\rangle + \mu h \bmod 1)$ information-theoretically hides the plaintext $\mu$. This is effectively how we will prove security in Theorem 3, using the machinery on smooth sublattices that we develop in the full version [17].

### 3.1 Correctness

**Theorem 2.** *Let $\boldsymbol{Q} \in \mathcal{S}_n^{>0}(\mathbb{Z})$, $r := r(n) \geq \sqrt{n \log n} \cdot s/q$ and $\rho := \rho(n) > 0$ be as in the encryption scheme above. Then, for any $\mu \in \{0, 1\}$,*

$$\Pr_{\substack{(\mathsf{sk},\mathsf{pk})\leftarrow\mathsf{Gen}(1^n)\\ (\boldsymbol{c},d)\leftarrow\mathsf{Enc}(\mathsf{pk},\mu)}}[\mathsf{Dec}(\mathsf{sk}, (\boldsymbol{c}, d)) \neq \mu] \leq 2\exp(-\pi/(25r^2\rho^2)) .$$

*In particular, the encryption scheme is correct (i.e., has negligible chance of decryption failure) if $r\rho < o(1/\sqrt{\log n})$.*

*Proof.* We have

$$\begin{aligned} d + \langle \boldsymbol{c}, \boldsymbol{t} - \boldsymbol{y}\rangle &= \mu h + \langle \boldsymbol{e} - \boldsymbol{c}, \boldsymbol{t}\rangle + \langle \boldsymbol{c}, \boldsymbol{t} - \boldsymbol{y}\rangle \\ &= \mu h + \langle \boldsymbol{e} - \boldsymbol{c}, \boldsymbol{t} - \boldsymbol{y}\rangle + \langle \boldsymbol{c}, \boldsymbol{t} - \boldsymbol{y}\rangle \\ &= \mu h + \langle \boldsymbol{e}, \boldsymbol{t} - \boldsymbol{y}\rangle \bmod 1 , \end{aligned}$$

where the second equality uses the fact that $\langle \boldsymbol{e} - \boldsymbol{c}, \boldsymbol{y}\rangle = 0 \bmod 1$, as we discussed above.

Recall that we have $\|\boldsymbol{y}' - \boldsymbol{t}'\|_{\boldsymbol{Q}^{-1}} \leq \rho$ by assumption, which implies that $\|\boldsymbol{y} - \boldsymbol{t}\|_{\boldsymbol{P}^{-1}} \leq \rho$. Since $\boldsymbol{e} \sim D_{\boldsymbol{P},rq}/q$, it follows immediately from the subgaussianity of the discrete Gaussian (see the full version [17]) that $|\langle \boldsymbol{e}, \boldsymbol{t} - \boldsymbol{y}\rangle| < 1/5$ except with probability at most $2\exp(-\pi/(25r^2\rho^2))$, and the result follows. □

### 3.2 Security

We now show the semantic security of this scheme. In fact, we show the slightly stronger fact that the ciphertexts are pseudorandom. We note that a very similar argument appeared in [33]; the main difference is that we use Theorem 1 in order to avoid using an extractor like in [33].

**Theorem 3.** *Suppose that there exists some $\boldsymbol{Q}' \in \mathcal{S}_n^{>0}(\mathbb{Z})$ such that for the parameters $\boldsymbol{Q} \in \mathcal{S}_n^{>0}(\mathbb{Z})$, $s := s(n) \geq \sqrt{\log(n)\|\boldsymbol{Q}\|}$, $r := r(n) \geq \sqrt{n \log n} \cdot s/q$ and $q := q(n) \geq 10$ in the encryption scheme above, $\mathcal{D}_s$-acLIP$^{\boldsymbol{Q},\boldsymbol{Q}'}$ is hard and*

$$r \geq 2q^{1/k} \cdot \eta_\varepsilon^{(k)}(\boldsymbol{Q}')$$

*for some $\varepsilon < \mathrm{negl}(n)$ and $k > \omega(\log(n))$. Then the joint distribution $(\boldsymbol{t}, \langle \boldsymbol{e} - \boldsymbol{c}, \boldsymbol{t}\rangle \bmod 1)$ is computationally indistinguishable from $(\boldsymbol{t}, u) \sim \mathbb{T}_q^n \times \mathbb{T}_q$, even conditioned on $\boldsymbol{c}$. In particular, the encryption scheme above is semantically secure.*

*Proof.* Consider $\mathbf{Game}_1$ and $\mathbf{Game}_2$, where $\mathbf{Game}_1$ is the security game with respect to the original encryption scheme, and $\mathbf{Game}_2$ is almost identical but with public key drawn with respect to $\boldsymbol{Q}'$. By assumption, the two games are computationally indistinguishable. Now we argue that any adversary wins $\mathbf{Game}_2$ with negligible advantage.

Because $\boldsymbol{U} \in \mathrm{GL}_n(\mathbb{Z})$ has $\det(\boldsymbol{U}) = \pm 1$ it is invertible mod $q$, and therefore the map $\boldsymbol{s} \mapsto \boldsymbol{U}^\top \boldsymbol{s} \bmod 1$ is a bijection on $\mathbb{T}_q^n$. Because we assume that $\boldsymbol{t}' \sim \mathbb{T}_q^n$ is uniformly random and $\boldsymbol{t} := \boldsymbol{U}^\top \boldsymbol{t}' \bmod 1$, we therefore have that $\boldsymbol{t}$ is also uniformly random in $\mathbb{T}_q^n$. Furthermore, conditioned on a fixed vector $\boldsymbol{c}$, the distribution of $\boldsymbol{e} - \boldsymbol{c}$ is precisely $D_{\boldsymbol{P}',r,-\boldsymbol{c}}$, where $\boldsymbol{P}' := \boldsymbol{U}^\top \boldsymbol{Q}' \boldsymbol{U}$. Using the fact that $\eta_\varepsilon^{(k)}(\boldsymbol{P}') = \eta_\varepsilon^{(k)}(\boldsymbol{Q}')$ and the assumption that $r \geq 2q^{1/k} \cdot \eta_\varepsilon^{(k)}(\boldsymbol{Q}')$, we therefore have that $(\boldsymbol{t}, \langle \boldsymbol{e} - \boldsymbol{c}, \boldsymbol{t}\rangle \bmod 1)$ is within statistical distance $2\varepsilon + 2^{3-k/2} < \mathrm{negl}(n)$ of uniformly random $(\boldsymbol{t}, u) \sim \mathbb{T}_q^n \times \mathbb{T}_q$ by Theorem 1 (applied with values scaled by a factor of $q$). □

## 4 Identity-Based Encryption

The scheme has the same parameters as the simpler scheme from Sect. 3. In particular, let $\boldsymbol{Q} \in \mathcal{S}_n^{>0}(\mathbb{Z})$ be a quadratic form, $s := s(n) \geq \sqrt{\|\boldsymbol{Q}\| \log n}$ a parameter that controls the size of $\boldsymbol{P}$, $r := r(n) \geq s\sqrt{n \log n}/q$ a noise parameter, $q := q(n) \geq 10$ a prime discretization parameter, and $\rho := \rho(n) > 0$ a distance bound.

In addition, we now also require that $\rho > \omega\big(\sqrt{\|\boldsymbol{Q}^{-1}\| \cdot n \log n}\big)$. Furthermore, let $\mathcal{H} : \{0,1\}^* \to \mathbb{T}_q^n$ be a hash function modeled as a random oracle. We again write $h := (q+1)/(2q) \in \mathbb{T}_q$.

- $\mathsf{Setup}(1^n)$: Sample $\boldsymbol{U} \leftarrow \mathcal{D}_s(\boldsymbol{Q}) \in \mathrm{GL}_n(\mathbb{Z})$, and compute $\boldsymbol{P} := \boldsymbol{U}^\top \boldsymbol{Q} \boldsymbol{U}$. Output $(\mathsf{mpk}, \mathsf{msk}) = (\boldsymbol{P}, \boldsymbol{U})$.
- $\mathsf{KeyGen}(\mathsf{msk}, \mathsf{id})$: Compute $\boldsymbol{t} := \mathcal{H}(\mathsf{id}) \in \mathbb{T}_q^n$. Sample $\boldsymbol{y}' \sim D_{\boldsymbol{Q}^{-1},\rho/\sqrt{n},\boldsymbol{U}^{-\top}\boldsymbol{t}}$ (using the algorithm from [36]). Compute $\boldsymbol{y} := \boldsymbol{U}^\top \boldsymbol{y}'$, and output $\mathsf{sk}_{\mathsf{id}} := \boldsymbol{y} \in \mathbb{Z}^n$.
- $\mathsf{Enc}(\mathsf{mpk}, \mathsf{id}, \mu \in \{0,1\})$: Compute $\boldsymbol{t} = \mathcal{H}(\mathsf{id})$. Sample $\boldsymbol{e} \sim D_{\boldsymbol{P},rq}/q$ using the algorithm described in [33].[12] Compute $\boldsymbol{c} := \boldsymbol{e} \bmod 1 \in \mathbb{T}_q^n$ and $d := \langle \boldsymbol{e} - \boldsymbol{c}, \boldsymbol{t}\rangle + \mu h \bmod 1 \in \mathbb{T}_q$. Output $(\boldsymbol{c}, d)$.
- $\mathsf{Dec}(\mathsf{sk}_{\mathsf{id}}, (\boldsymbol{c}, d))$: Compute $d + \langle \boldsymbol{c}, \boldsymbol{t} - \boldsymbol{y}\rangle \bmod 1$. Output 1 if the result is in $[1/4, 3/4]$, or 0 otherwise.

Notice that our new requirement that $\rho > \omega\big(\sqrt{\|\boldsymbol{Q}^{-1}\| n \log n}\big)$ guarantees that we can run the algorithm in [36] to sample $\boldsymbol{y}' \sim D_{\boldsymbol{Q}^{-1},\rho/\sqrt{n},\boldsymbol{U}^{-\top}\boldsymbol{t}}$. (See the full version [17].)

More interestingly, notice that this scheme is closely related to the simpler public-key encryption scheme from Sect. 3. Indeed, one more-or-less recovers the scheme from Sect. 3 if one simply ignores the identity $\mathsf{id}$ and instead replaces

[12] See the full version of the present work [17] for the specific properties that we need.

$\boldsymbol{t} := \mathcal{H}(\mathsf{id})$ with a uniformly random element $\boldsymbol{t} \sim \mathbb{T}_q^n$ that is included with the public key. In particular, we have that with high probability $\|\boldsymbol{y}' - \boldsymbol{t}'\|_{\boldsymbol{Q}^{-1}} < \rho$ where letting $\boldsymbol{t}' := \boldsymbol{U}^{-\top}\boldsymbol{t}$, so with high probability $\boldsymbol{y}$ and $(\boldsymbol{P}, \boldsymbol{t})$ satisfy the same relationship as the secret key and public key in Sect. 3. (See the full version [17].) This is quite similar to the relationship between the GPV IBE scheme and the dual-Regev encryption scheme in [36].

### 4.1 Correctness

**Theorem 4.** *Let* $\boldsymbol{Q} \in \mathcal{S}_n^{>0}(\mathbb{Z})$, $r := r(n) \geq \sqrt{n \log n} \cdot s/q$ *and* $\rho := \rho(n) > \omega(\sqrt{\|\boldsymbol{Q}^{-1}\| n \log n})$ *be as in the encryption scheme above. Then, for any* $\mu \in \{0, 1\}$,

$$\Pr_{\substack{(\mathsf{msk},\mathsf{mpk}) \leftarrow \mathsf{Setup}(1^n) \\ \mathsf{sk}_{\mathsf{id}} \leftarrow \mathsf{KeyGen}(\mathsf{msk},\mathsf{id})}} \left[\mathsf{Dec}(\mathsf{sk}_{\mathsf{id}}, \mathsf{Enc}(\mathsf{mpk}, \mathsf{id}, \mu)) \neq \mu\right] \leq 2\exp(-\pi/(25r^2\rho^2)) + 2^{-n}.$$

*In particular, the encryption scheme is correct, provided that* $r\rho < o(1/\sqrt{\log n})$.

*Proof.* Let $\boldsymbol{t}' := \boldsymbol{U}^{-\top}\boldsymbol{t}$ and notice that since $\boldsymbol{t}$ is a uniformly random element of $\mathbb{T}_q$, $\boldsymbol{t}' \bmod 1$ is also a uniformly random element of $\mathbb{T}_q$ (since $\det(\boldsymbol{U}) = \pm 1$ and therefore $\boldsymbol{U}$ is invertible modulo $q$). By an appropriate tail bound on the discrete Gaussian, we have that $\|\boldsymbol{y}' - \boldsymbol{t}'\|_{\boldsymbol{Q}^{-1}} < \rho$ where $\boldsymbol{t}' := \boldsymbol{U}^{-\top}\boldsymbol{t}$ except with probability at most $2^{-n}$. (See the full version [17].) Conditioned on this event, we see that we are in the setting of Theorem 2, which tells us that the failure probability is at most $2\exp(-\pi/(25r^2\rho^2))$. The result then follows from the union bound. □

### 4.2 Full Security

The following theorem is proven in the full version of the present work [17].

**Theorem 5.** *Suppose that there exists some* $\boldsymbol{Q}' \in \mathcal{S}_n^{>0}(\mathbb{Z})$ *such that for the parameters* $\boldsymbol{Q} \in \mathcal{S}_n^{>0}(\mathbb{Z})$, $s := s(n) \geq \sqrt{\log(n)\|\boldsymbol{Q}\|}$, $r := r(n) \geq \sqrt{n \log n} \cdot s/q$, *prime* $q := q(n) \geq 2^{n/2}$, *and* $\rho := \rho(n) > \omega(\sqrt{\|\boldsymbol{Q}^{-1}\| n \log n})$ *in the encryption scheme above,* $\mathcal{D}_s$*-acLIP*$^{\boldsymbol{Q},\boldsymbol{Q}'}$ *is hard and*

$$r \geq 2q^{1/k} \cdot \eta_\varepsilon^{(k)}(\boldsymbol{Q}')$$

*for some* $\varepsilon < \mathrm{negl}(n)$ *and* $k > \omega(\log(n))$. *Then the IBE scheme is fully secure.*

### 4.3 Putting Everything Together

The following theorem follows immediately from combining Theorems 4 and 5.

**Theorem 6.** *Suppose that the parameters in the IBE scheme satisfy that* $s := s(n) \geq \sqrt{\log n}\|\boldsymbol{Q}\|$, $r := r(n) \geq \sqrt{n \log n} s/q$, $q = q(n) \geq 2^{n/2}$, $\rho = \rho(n) > \omega(\sqrt{\|\boldsymbol{Q}^{-1}\|} \cdot n \log n)$, *and* $r\rho < o(1/\sqrt{\log n})$. *And, suppose that there exists some* $\boldsymbol{Q}' \in \mathcal{S}_n^{>0}(\mathbb{Z})$ *such that* $\mathcal{D}_s$-acLIP$^{\boldsymbol{Q},\boldsymbol{Q}'}$ *is hard and* $r \geq 2q^{1/k} \cdot \eta_\varepsilon^{(k)}(\boldsymbol{Q}')$ *for some* $\varepsilon < \text{negl}(n)$ *and* $k > \omega(\log n)$.

*Then,* (Setup, KeyGen, Enc, Dec) *is a correct and fully secure identity-based encryption scheme.*

### 4.4 Instantiating Our IBE Scheme with Specific Quadratic Forms and Parameters

Thus far, we have described our IBE scheme abstractly in terms of an arbitrary quadratic form $\boldsymbol{Q} \in \mathcal{S}_n^{>0}(\mathbb{Z})$ and a rather large number of parameters with a number of relations between them (as in Theorem 6), and we proved security assuming the existence of some other quadratic form $\boldsymbol{Q}' \in \mathcal{S}_n^{>0}(\mathbb{Z})$ with sufficiently small $\eta^{(k)}$ for which $\mathcal{D}_s$-acLIP$^{\boldsymbol{Q},\boldsymbol{Q}'}$ is hard.

It remains to show that we can pick parameters and $\boldsymbol{Q}$ and $\boldsymbol{Q}'$ satisfying these constraints, and for which $\mathcal{D}_s$-acLIP$^{\boldsymbol{Q},\boldsymbol{Q}'}$ is plausibly hard.

To that end, we use the simple and elegant forms suggested by [33] in a similar context. Specifically, we take

$$\boldsymbol{Q} = \begin{pmatrix} g\boldsymbol{I}_{n/2} & 0 \\ 0 & (g+1)\boldsymbol{I}_{n/2} \end{pmatrix},$$

where $g := g(n)$ is a positive integer to be chosen later. (We have assumed that $n$ is even for simplicity.) And, we take[13]

$$\boldsymbol{Q}' = \begin{pmatrix} g(g+1)\boldsymbol{I}_{n/2} & 0 \\ 0 & \boldsymbol{I}_{n/2} \end{pmatrix}.$$

Notice that $\boldsymbol{Q}$ is not very different from a rescaling of the identity matrix, while $\boldsymbol{Q}'$ is quite unbalanced. Formally, this is captured by the fact that $\eta_\varepsilon^{(n/2)}(\boldsymbol{Q}') - \eta_\varepsilon(\boldsymbol{I}_{n/2}) = \sqrt{\log(n/\varepsilon)/\pi} + o(1)$, while $\eta_\varepsilon^{(n/2)}(\boldsymbol{Q}) = \eta_\varepsilon^{(n/2)}(g\boldsymbol{I}_{n/2}) = g\eta_\varepsilon^{(n/2)}(\boldsymbol{Q}')$, which is quite a bit larger.

[13] These quadratic forms $\boldsymbol{Q}, \boldsymbol{Q}'$ are carefully chosen to have the same *genus*. For example, if we instead made the seemingly very similar choice $\boldsymbol{P} = g\boldsymbol{I}_n$ and $\boldsymbol{P}' = g^2\boldsymbol{I}_{n/2} \oplus \boldsymbol{I}_{n/2}$ instead of $\boldsymbol{Q}$ and $\boldsymbol{Q}'$, one might expect the scheme to behave similarly. Unfortunately, this is not the case, as $\mathcal{D}_s$-acLIP$^{\boldsymbol{P},\boldsymbol{P}'}$ is trivial to solve. Indeed, notice that for these two forms, any $\boldsymbol{S} \equiv \boldsymbol{P}$ must have all entries divisible by $g$, while any $\boldsymbol{S} \equiv \boldsymbol{P}'$ must have at least some entries not divisible by $g$. This phenomenon might worry the reader, as perhaps a similar attack could be used to solve $\mathcal{D}_s$-acLIP$^{\boldsymbol{Q},\boldsymbol{Q}'}$. But, this phenomenon is actually well understood in terms of the genus of a quadratic form. Roughly speaking, the genus captures any "arithmetic" invariant (like divisibility of all entries by $g$) of the quadratic form, and [33] carefully chose $\boldsymbol{Q}$ and $\boldsymbol{Q}'$ so that they have the same genus and therefore "cannot be distinguished arithmetically." See [33] for more discussion.

Now we discuss how to set the parameters $r$, $s$, $q$, $\rho$, and $g$. First, for security, we need $r \geq 2q^{2/n} \cdot \eta_\varepsilon^{(n/2)}(\boldsymbol{Q}')$ for some negligible $\varepsilon$. (This is used in the security argument when we argue that if $\boldsymbol{Q}$ is replaced by $\boldsymbol{Q}'$, then the resulting ciphertext is statistically close to random.) Therefore, from the above, we see that it suffices to take any $r > \omega(q^{2/n}\sqrt{\log n})$. We take $r = \log n$ for simplicity (since we do not care much about polylogarithmic factors, and since we will eventually take $q \leq 2^{O(n)}$). For correctness, we need that $r\rho < o(1/\sqrt{\log n})$, and we can therefore take any $\rho < o(1/\log^{3/2} n)$. So, we take $\rho = 1/\log^2 n$ for simplicity.

To set $g$, recall that we need that $\|\boldsymbol{Q}^{-1}\| < o(\rho^2/(n \log n)) = o(1/(n \log^5 n))$. (This is needed for security, as we discuss in the full version [17].) So, noting that $\|\boldsymbol{Q}^{-1}\| = 1/g$, we see that it suffices to take, say,

$$g = n \log^6 \text{ n} .$$

It remains to set $s$ and $q$, and here we have two natural choices. We need $s \geq \sqrt{\log(n)\|\boldsymbol{Q}\|} = \sqrt{\log(n)(g+1)} = \sqrt{\log(n)(n\log^6 n + 1)}$ (in order for $\mathcal{D}_s$ to work). So, we could simply take, say, $s = 2\sqrt{n}\log^{7/2}(n)$. We then anyway need $q \geq 2^{n/2}$ to be a prime for security, so we can simply take $q$ to be some prime between, say, $2^{n/2}$ and $2^{n/2+1}$. The only remaining requirement is that $q \geq s\sqrt{n \log n}/r$, which is needed so that the sampling in the encryption algorithm can be done efficiently, which is trivially satisfied here (for sufficiently large $n$). (See the full version for the details [17].) Then, we obtain security under the assumption that $\mathcal{D}_s$-acLIP$^{\boldsymbol{Q},\boldsymbol{Q}'}$ is hard.

But, we might wish to invoke the worst-case hardness in [33]. In order to do that, we need $s \geq 2^{n/2} \cdot \sqrt{g(g+1)}$, so we can take, say, $s = 2^{n/2+1}g = 2^{n/2+1}n\log^6 n$. And, to satisfy the inequality that $q \geq s\sqrt{n \log n}/r = 2^{n/2+1}n^{3/2}\log^{5.5} n$. So, we must take $q$ to be very slightly larger. This choice of parameters is slightly less efficient, mostly because the larger choice of $s$ means that $\|\boldsymbol{P}\| \approx \text{poly}(n)s$ will be larger, leading to a larger public key and slower operations involving $\boldsymbol{P}$. In exchange for this penalty in efficiency, we can invoke the worst-case to average-case reduction in [33]. And, we obtain security under the assumption that wcLIP$^{\boldsymbol{Q},\boldsymbol{Q}'}$ is hard. (See the full version [17].)

All of the above parameter choices are quite similar to what one obtains for the IBE scheme in [36] that our IBE scheme is based on. In particular, the best known attacks on LIP$^{\boldsymbol{Q},\boldsymbol{Q}'}$ (either the worst-case version or the average-case version) use essentially the same algorithms as the best known attacks on [36], with nearly identical parameters. Specifically, the best known attacks on LIP$^{\boldsymbol{Q},\boldsymbol{Q}'}$ work via reduction to the problem of approximating the length of a shortest non-zero vector in a lattice up to a factor of $\sqrt{g}$. (And the best known attacks on [36] are essentially the same.) For any polynomial approximation factor, our best known algorithms for this problem run in time $2^{\Theta(n)}$, and this is widely believed to be optimal. See [33, Section 7] for more discussion (including discussion that one might heuristically expect to solve LIP$^{\boldsymbol{Q},\boldsymbol{Q}'}$ using a slightly faster (but still $2^{\Theta(n)}$-time) algorithm that in the worst case only approximates the length of the shortest non-zero lattice vector up to the slightly larger factor $\sqrt{ng}$).

## 5 A Public-Key Encryption Scheme that We Will Use to Build FHE

In this section, we present a simple public-key encryption scheme that is very similar to the scheme presented in [16]. But, our new version has the advantage that we can modify it to make it fully homomorphic, which we do in Sect. 6.

Recall that the high-level idea behind the scheme in [16] is as follows. There is some fixed, "nice" quadratic form $\boldsymbol{Q} \in \mathcal{S}_n^{>0}(\mathbb{Z})$. Indeed, in [16], $\boldsymbol{Q}$ is simply the identity matrix, which is certainly a "nice" quadratic form. More generally, we will assume that $\boldsymbol{Q}$ is such that there exist some known linearly independent vectors $\boldsymbol{Z} := (\boldsymbol{z}_1, \ldots \boldsymbol{z}_k) \in \mathbb{Z}^{n \times k}$ such that $\|\boldsymbol{z}_i\|_{\boldsymbol{Q}^{-1}}^2 = \boldsymbol{z}_i^\top \boldsymbol{Q}^{-1} \boldsymbol{z}_i$ is rather small—notice that the norm is with respect to $\boldsymbol{Q}^{-1}$ and not $\boldsymbol{Q}$. (In terms of lattices, these are the coordinates of short linearly independent vectors in the *dual* basis.) Of course, if $\boldsymbol{Q}$ is the identity matrix, then one should naturally takes the $\boldsymbol{Z}$ to be the identity matrix as well. [16] therefore did not describe the matrix $\boldsymbol{Z}$ explicitly. (More generally, our discussion below is really of our modified scheme, which is more general and does not require $\boldsymbol{Q}$ to be the identity matrix.)

The key-generation algorithm samples a unimodular transformation $\boldsymbol{U} \in \mathrm{GL}_n(\mathbb{Z})$ (sampled appropriately), sets the public key to be the quadratic form $\boldsymbol{P} := \boldsymbol{U}^T \boldsymbol{Q} \boldsymbol{U}$, and the secret key is $\boldsymbol{S} := (\boldsymbol{s}_1, \ldots, \boldsymbol{s}_k) := \boldsymbol{U}^T \boldsymbol{Z} \in \mathbb{Z}^{n \times k}$. So, $\boldsymbol{P}$ is a quadratic form that is equivalent to $\boldsymbol{Q}$, and notice that the $\boldsymbol{s}_i \in \mathbb{Z}^n$ have the property that

$$\|\boldsymbol{s}_i\|_{\boldsymbol{P}^{-1}}^2 - (\boldsymbol{U}^\top \boldsymbol{z}_i)^\top \boldsymbol{U}^{-1} \boldsymbol{Q}^{-1} \boldsymbol{U}^{-\top} \boldsymbol{U}^\top \boldsymbol{z}_i = \|\boldsymbol{z}_i\|_{\boldsymbol{Q}^{-1}}^2$$

is small.

The idea here is that $\boldsymbol{S}$ can be used to roughly determine whether for a given vector $\boldsymbol{t} \in \mathbb{R}^n$, $\mathrm{dist}_{\boldsymbol{P}}(\boldsymbol{t}, \mathbb{Z}^n)$ is large or small. In particular, notice that if $\boldsymbol{y} \in \mathbb{Z}^n$ such that $\|\boldsymbol{t} - \boldsymbol{y}\|_{\boldsymbol{P}}$ is small, then

$$\langle \boldsymbol{t}, \boldsymbol{s}_i \rangle = \langle \boldsymbol{t} - \boldsymbol{y}, \boldsymbol{s}_i \rangle \bmod 1 .$$

And, by the Cauchy-Schwarz inequality, we have that

$$|\langle \boldsymbol{t} - \boldsymbol{y}, \boldsymbol{s}_i \rangle| \leq \|\boldsymbol{t} - \boldsymbol{y}\|_{\boldsymbol{P}} \|\boldsymbol{s}_i\|_{\boldsymbol{P}^{-1}} = \|\boldsymbol{t} - \boldsymbol{y}\|_{\boldsymbol{P}} \|\boldsymbol{z}_i\|_{\boldsymbol{Q}^{-1}} ,$$

where the terms on the right-hand side are small by assumption. So, we have that if $\mathrm{dist}_{\boldsymbol{P}}(\boldsymbol{t}, \mathbb{Z}^n) \ll 1/\|\boldsymbol{s}_i\|_{\boldsymbol{P}^{-1}}$ then $\langle \boldsymbol{t}, \boldsymbol{s}_i \rangle$ will be close to an integer (i.e., small modulo 1).

With this, we can describe our decryption procedure (admittedly before we have explained how to encrypt). We do not wish to work with real numbers modulo 1, so we instead work with $\mathbb{Z}_q$ where $q$ is some discretization parameter. ([16] does not bother with this discretization. But, for us, it will matter when we build FHE. We could work with $\mathbb{T}_q$ instead of $\mathbb{Z}_q$ as we did in Sects. 3 and 4, but this choice yields significantly nicer notation.) Ciphertexts will be $\boldsymbol{c} \in \mathbb{Z}_q^n$, and to decrypt, we compute

$$d := \|\boldsymbol{S}^\top \boldsymbol{c} \bmod q\|^2 = \sum_{i=1}^{k} (\langle \boldsymbol{c}, \boldsymbol{s}_i \rangle \bmod q)^2 ,$$

where we represent values modulo $q$ according to their representatives in the range $[-q/2, q/2)$. If $d$ is smaller than some threshold, we output 0. Otherwise, we output 1. In the case when $\boldsymbol{Q}$ is the identity matrix considered in [16], this sum is precisely equal to $\mathrm{dist}_{\boldsymbol{P}}(\boldsymbol{c}, q\mathbb{Z}^n)^2$. Here, we think of this sum as a sort of proxy for this distance. (Indeed, in [16] they can simply assume that such distances can be computed directly, which is true when $\boldsymbol{Q} = \boldsymbol{I}_n$. They therefore do not explicitly use matrices $\boldsymbol{Z}$ and $\boldsymbol{S}$. We are careful to be more general.)

We next describe how to encrypt a bit $\mu \in \{0, 1\}$ into a ciphertext $\boldsymbol{c}_\mu$ under the public key $\boldsymbol{P}$. Naturally, we want our ciphertexts to have the property that encryptions $\boldsymbol{c}_0 \in \mathbb{Z}_q^n$ of 0 should have small inner product with all of the $\boldsymbol{s}_i$. And, we have already seen that it suffices to take $\boldsymbol{c}_0$ such that $\mathrm{dist}(\boldsymbol{c}_0, q\mathbb{Z}^n)$ is small. To that end, we sample $\boldsymbol{x} \in \mathbb{Z}^n$ (from an appropriate distribution—namely, a discrete Gaussian with variance proportional to $\boldsymbol{P}$) so that $\|\boldsymbol{x}\|_{\boldsymbol{P}} \ll q/\|\boldsymbol{s}_i\|_{\boldsymbol{P}^{-1}}$ and then set $\boldsymbol{c}_0 := \boldsymbol{x} \bmod q$. The analysis above immediately tells us that $\boldsymbol{c}_0$ will decrypt to 0.

To encrypt $\mu = 1$ under the public key $\boldsymbol{P}$, one can simply sample a ciphertext $\boldsymbol{c}_1 \in \mathbb{Z}_q^n$ that is uniformly random as is done in [16]. However, we will need a bit more structure for our eventual FHE scheme, so we instead set $\boldsymbol{c}_1 := \boldsymbol{x} + \boldsymbol{h} \bmod q$ where $\boldsymbol{x}$ is sampled as above (from a discrete Gaussian) and $\boldsymbol{h} \in \mathbb{Z}_q^n$ is an additional element included in the public key with the property that $\|\boldsymbol{S}^\top \boldsymbol{h} \bmod q\|^2$ is large.

This way of doing things yields a pleasant symmetry, as now our ciphertext $\boldsymbol{c}_\mu$ has the form

$$\boldsymbol{c}_\mu = \boldsymbol{x} + \mu \boldsymbol{h} \bmod \mathrm{q} .$$

Of course, readers who have seen Regev's encryption scheme [57] (or its many variants) will recognize this as being remarkably similar, which is certainly not a coincidence. From our perspective, it is crucial for our ciphertexts to have this form (specifically, to have this form with some $\boldsymbol{h}$ that is fixed by the public key) in order to make our scheme compatible with the gadget-matrix-based techniques that we will use in Sect. 6 to build FHE.

However, there is one subtlety left to worry about. Where does $\boldsymbol{h} \in \mathbb{Z}_q^n$ come from?[14] It would be relatively natural to choose some fixed $\boldsymbol{h}' \in \mathbb{Z}_q^n$ such that $\|\boldsymbol{Z}^\top \boldsymbol{h}' \bmod q\|^2$ is large and to set $\boldsymbol{h} := \boldsymbol{U}^{-1}\boldsymbol{h}'$. (E.g., if $\boldsymbol{Z} = \boldsymbol{I}_n$ is simply the identity, then it is natural to set $\boldsymbol{h}' = (q/2, \ldots, q/2)^\top$.) But, it is not clear how to prove that the scheme remains secure if we include such an $\boldsymbol{h}$ in the public key,

[14] In Regev's encryption scheme, $\boldsymbol{h}$ is effectively $(q/2)\boldsymbol{e}_{n+1}$, though the scheme is typically not written in this way.

since such an $\boldsymbol{h}$ depends on the secret value $\boldsymbol{U}$. Instead, we simply set $\boldsymbol{h} \sim \mathbb{Z}_q^n$ to be uniformly random, which of course leaks nothing about $\boldsymbol{U}$. We then observe that as long as the $\boldsymbol{s}_i$ are linearly independent modulo $q$ (which is equivalent to the $\boldsymbol{z}_i$ being linearly independent modulo $q$), it is easy to see that the inner products $\langle \boldsymbol{s}_i, \boldsymbol{h} \rangle \bmod q \in \mathbb{Z}_q$ are uniformly random and independent. Therefore,

$$\|\boldsymbol{S}^\top \boldsymbol{h} \bmod q\|^2 = \sum_{i=1}^{k} (\langle \boldsymbol{s}_i, \boldsymbol{h} \rangle \bmod q)^2$$

will be the sum of $k$ independent random variables, so it will be highly concentrated around its rather large mean (which when $q$ is even is precisely equal to $k(q^2+2)/12$).

Notice that, in order to achieve this concentration, we need $k$ to be reasonably large. (In fact, $k > \omega(\log n)$ is sufficient for negligible error.) This in particular is why we do not simply take $k = 1$. (One can view Regev encryption as a variant of this scheme in which $k = 1$ but in which the public key is sampled in a very different way that allows one to take $\boldsymbol{h} = (q/2)\boldsymbol{e}_{n+1}$.)

### 5.1 The Scheme

Our public-key encryption scheme comes with public parameters consisting of a quadratic form $\boldsymbol{Q} \in \mathcal{S}_n^{>0}(\mathbb{Z})$, a parameter $s := s(n) \geq \sqrt{\log(n)\|\boldsymbol{Q}\|}$ (which roughly controls the size of $\boldsymbol{P}$), a noise parameter $r := r(n) \geq \sqrt{n \log ns}/q$, and a discretization parameter $q := q(n) \geq 10$.

We also require that there exist known vectors $\boldsymbol{Z} := (\boldsymbol{z}_1, \ldots, \boldsymbol{z}_k) \in \mathbb{Z}^{n \times k}$ that are linearly independent modulo $q$ and such that $\|\boldsymbol{z}_i\|_{\boldsymbol{Q}^{-1}}$ is small.

- $\mathsf{Gen}(1^n)$: Sample $\boldsymbol{U} \leftarrow \mathcal{D}_s(\boldsymbol{Q}) \in \mathrm{GL}_n(\mathbb{Z})$, and compute $\boldsymbol{P} = \boldsymbol{U}^\top \boldsymbol{Q} \boldsymbol{U}$ using the algorithm described in [33].[15] Sample $\boldsymbol{h} \sim \mathbb{Z}_q^n$. Set $\mathsf{sk} := \boldsymbol{S} := \boldsymbol{U}^\top \boldsymbol{Z} \in \mathbb{Z}^{n \times k}$ and $\mathsf{pk} := (\boldsymbol{P}, \boldsymbol{h})$.
- $\mathsf{Enc}(\mathsf{pk}, \mu \in \{0,1\})$: Sample $\boldsymbol{x} \sim D_{\boldsymbol{P},rq}$ using the algorithm described in [33]. Output $\boldsymbol{c} := \boldsymbol{x} + \mu \boldsymbol{h} \bmod q \in \mathbb{Z}_q^n$.
- $\mathsf{Dec}(\mathsf{sk}, \boldsymbol{c})$: Compute
$$d := \|\boldsymbol{S}^\top \boldsymbol{c} \bmod q\|^2 ,$$
where we represent elements modulo $q$ in the interval $[-q/2, q/2)$. Output 0 if $d < kq^2/100$ and 1 otherwise.

Notice in particular that the condition that $s \geq \sqrt{\log(n)\|\boldsymbol{Q}\|}$ is needed for the key-generation algorithm to run $\mathcal{D}_s$, while the fact that $qr \geq s\sqrt{n \log n}$ implies that the algorithm from [33] used by the encryption algorithm correctly generates a sample $\boldsymbol{x} \sim D_{\boldsymbol{P},rq}$ in polynomial time. (See the full version [17].)

---

[15] See the full version of the present work [17] for the specific properties that we need.

### 5.2 Correctness

**Theorem 7.** *Suppose that the parameters* $\boldsymbol{Q} \in S_n^{>0}(\mathbb{Z})$, $r := r(n) \geq \sqrt{n \log n} \cdot s/q$, *an integer* $q = q(n) \geq 10$, *and* $\boldsymbol{Z} := (\boldsymbol{z}_1, \ldots, \boldsymbol{z}_k) \in \mathbb{Z}^{n \times k}$ *in the encryption scheme above satisfy*

$$r \leq \frac{1}{10\sqrt{n d_z}} ,$$

*where* $d_z := \frac{1}{k} \cdot \sum_{i=1}^k \|\boldsymbol{z}_i\|_{\boldsymbol{Q}^{-1}}^2$.

*Then, the above scheme is correct, in the sense that for any* $\mu \in \{0, 1\}$,

$$\Pr_{(\mathsf{sk},\mathsf{pk}) \leftarrow \mathsf{Gen}(1^n)} [\mathsf{Dec}(\mathsf{sk}, \mathsf{Enc}(\mathsf{pk}, \mu)) = \mu] \geq 1 - 2^{-k} - 2^{-n} .$$

*More generally, with probability at least* $1 - 2^{-k}$ *over the choice of* $\boldsymbol{h} \sim \mathbb{Z}_q^n$, *we have*

$$\mathsf{Dec}(\mathsf{sk}, \boldsymbol{x} + \mu \boldsymbol{h} \bmod q) = \mu$$

*for* any $\boldsymbol{x} \in \mathbb{Z}^n$ *with* $\|\boldsymbol{x}\|_{\boldsymbol{P}} < \frac{q}{10\sqrt{d_z}}$.

*Proof.* It suffices to prove the "more generally" statement. The correctness of the encryption algorithm then follows from a suitable tail bound on the discrete Gaussian, as is shown in the full version.

To prove the "more generally", let

$$d := \|\boldsymbol{S}^\top \boldsymbol{c} \bmod q\|^2 = \sum_{i=1}^k (\langle \boldsymbol{s}_i, \boldsymbol{x} \rangle + \mu \langle \boldsymbol{s}_i, \boldsymbol{h} \rangle \bmod q)^2 ,$$

as in the decryption algorithm. Let

$$d' := \|\boldsymbol{S}^\top \boldsymbol{x}\|^2 = \sum_{i=1}^k \langle \boldsymbol{s}_i, \boldsymbol{x} \rangle^2 .$$

It follows from the Cauchy-Schwarz inequality that

$$d' \leq \|\boldsymbol{x}\|_{\boldsymbol{P}}^2 \sum_{i=1}^k \|\boldsymbol{s}_i\|_{\boldsymbol{P}^{-1}}^2 < \frac{kq^2}{100} ,$$

where we have used the fact that $\sum_{i=1}^k \|\boldsymbol{s}_i\|_{\boldsymbol{P}^{-1}}^2 = \sum_{i=1}^k \|\boldsymbol{z}_i\|_{\boldsymbol{Q}^{-1}}^2 = k d_z$. This immediately implies that the decryption algorithm outputs 0 when $\mu = 0$, as needed.

When $\mu = 1$, we need to also consider

$$d_{\boldsymbol{h}} := \|\boldsymbol{S}^\top \boldsymbol{h} \bmod q\|^2 = \sum_{i=1}^k (\langle \boldsymbol{s}_i, \boldsymbol{h} \rangle \bmod q)^2 .$$

Indeed, we have from triangle inequality that

$$\sqrt{d} \geq \sqrt{d_{\boldsymbol{h}}} - \sqrt{d'} \geq \sqrt{d_{\boldsymbol{h}}} - \sqrt{k} q/10 .$$

So, it suffices to prove that $d_{\boldsymbol{h}} \geq kq^2/25$ with high probability over $\boldsymbol{h} \sim \mathbb{Z}_q^n$.

To that end, notice that because $\boldsymbol{z}_1, \ldots, \boldsymbol{z}_k$ are linearly independent modulo $q$ and $\boldsymbol{U} \in \mathrm{GL}_n(\mathbb{Z})$ has determinant $\pm 1$, $\boldsymbol{s}_1 := \boldsymbol{U}^\top \boldsymbol{z}_1, \ldots, \boldsymbol{s}_k := \boldsymbol{U}^\top \boldsymbol{z}_k$ are also linearly independent modulo $q$. It follows that the random variables $\langle \boldsymbol{s}_i, \boldsymbol{h} \rangle \in \mathbb{Z}_q$ are uniformly random and independent. So, we can write $d_{\boldsymbol{h}} = \sum_{i=1}^k \chi_i^2$ where $\chi_i \sim [-q/2, q/2)$ are independent and uniform. A simple computation then shows that $\mathbb{E}[d_{\boldsymbol{h}}] = k(q^2+2)/12$ if $q$ is even and $\mathbb{E}[d_{\boldsymbol{h}}] = k(q^2-1)/12 > kq^2/15$ if $q$ is odd. Either way, by the Chernoff-Hoeffding bound, we have that $d_{\boldsymbol{h}} > kq^2/25$ except with probability at most $2^{-k}$, as needed. □

### 5.3 Security

**Theorem 8.** *Suppose that there exists some $\boldsymbol{Q}' \in \mathcal{S}_n^{>0}(\mathbb{Z})$ such that for the parameters $\boldsymbol{Q} \in \mathcal{S}_n^{>0}(\mathbb{Z})$, $s := s(n) \geq \sqrt{\log(n)\|\boldsymbol{Q}\|}$, and $r := r(n) \geq \sqrt{n \log n} \cdot s/q$ in the encryption scheme above, we have that $\mathcal{D}_s$-acLIP$^{\boldsymbol{Q},\boldsymbol{Q}'}$ is hard and $r \geq \eta_\varepsilon(\boldsymbol{Q}')$ for some $\varepsilon < \mathrm{negl}(n)$. Then, the ciphertext $\boldsymbol{c} \in \mathbb{Z}_q^n$ produced by the encryption algorithm is computationally indistinguishable from uniformly random $\boldsymbol{u} \sim \mathbb{Z}_q^n$.*

*Proof.* Consider **Game**$_1$ and **Game**$_2$, where in **Game**$_1$ the goal is to distinguish $\boldsymbol{c} = \boldsymbol{x} + \mu\boldsymbol{h} \bmod q$ for $\boldsymbol{x} \sim D_{\boldsymbol{P},rq}$ from a uniformly random element $\boldsymbol{u} \sim \mathbb{Z}_q^n$. **Game**$_2$ is the same as **Game**$_1$, but with $\boldsymbol{U}$ drawn from $\mathcal{D}_s(\boldsymbol{Q}')$ instead of $\mathcal{D}_s(\boldsymbol{Q})$ and the public key set to $\boldsymbol{P}' := \boldsymbol{U}^\top \boldsymbol{Q}' \boldsymbol{U}$ instead of $\boldsymbol{P} := \boldsymbol{U}^\top \boldsymbol{Q} \boldsymbol{U}$. By the hardness of $\mathcal{D}_s$-acLIP$^{\boldsymbol{Q},\boldsymbol{Q}'}$, the advantage of any efficient adversary in **Game**$_1$ is at most negligibly larger than his advantage in **Game**$_2$. Now we argue that *any* adversary (even computationally unbounded adversaries) in **Game**$_2$ is at most $2\varepsilon$.

Indeed, since $\boldsymbol{x} \sim D_{\boldsymbol{P}',rq}$ and $r \geq \eta_\varepsilon(\boldsymbol{Q}') = \eta_\varepsilon(\boldsymbol{P}')$ by assumption, we have that $\boldsymbol{x} \bmod q$ is within statistical distance $2\varepsilon < \mathrm{negl}(n)$ of uniformly random by a suitable smoothing parameter argument, as we show in the full version [17]. The result follows. □

## 6 Fully Homomorphic Encryption

We next present our FHE scheme.

### 6.1 The Encryption Scheme

Our FHE scheme uses the same set of parameters $\boldsymbol{Q} \in \mathcal{S}_n^{>0}(\mathbb{Z}), s := s(n) \geq \sqrt{\log(n)\|\boldsymbol{Q}\|}, r := r(n) \geq \sqrt{n \log n} s/q$, and $q := q(n) \geq 10$ from Sect. 5, as well as the set of known vectors $\boldsymbol{Z} := (\boldsymbol{z}_1, \ldots, \boldsymbol{z}_k) \in \mathbb{Z}^{n \times k}$ such that $\|\boldsymbol{z}_i\|_{\boldsymbol{Q}^{-1}}$ is small.

We will assume for simplicity that $q$ is a power of 2. Let $m = n \log_2 q + 1$. As in [37,50], we define the gadget *row* vector $\boldsymbol{g} := (1, 2, 4, \ldots, q/2) \in \mathbb{Z}_q^{\log_2 q}$, and the gadget matrix $\boldsymbol{G}$ to be

$$\boldsymbol{G} := \boldsymbol{I}_n \otimes \boldsymbol{g} = \begin{pmatrix} \boldsymbol{g} & \boldsymbol{0} & \cdots & \boldsymbol{0} & \boldsymbol{0} \\ \boldsymbol{0} & \boldsymbol{g} & \cdots & \boldsymbol{0} & \boldsymbol{0} \\ \vdots & \vdots & \ddots & \vdots & \vdots \\ \boldsymbol{0} & \boldsymbol{0} & \cdots & \boldsymbol{g} & \boldsymbol{0} \\ \boldsymbol{0} & \boldsymbol{0} & \cdots & \boldsymbol{0} & \boldsymbol{g} \end{pmatrix} \in \mathbb{Z}_q^{n\times(m-1)} . \tag{1}$$

Then, our encryption scheme is as follows.

- $\mathsf{Gen}(1^n)$: Sample $\boldsymbol{U} \leftarrow \mathcal{D}_s(\boldsymbol{Q}) \in \mathrm{GL}_n(\mathbb{Z})$, and compute $\boldsymbol{P} = \boldsymbol{U}^\top \boldsymbol{Q} \boldsymbol{U}$. Sample $\boldsymbol{h} \sim \mathbb{Z}_q^n$. Set $\mathsf{sk} := \boldsymbol{S} := \boldsymbol{U}^\top \boldsymbol{Z} \in \mathbb{Z}^{n\times k}$ and $\mathsf{pk} := (\boldsymbol{P}, \boldsymbol{h})$.
- $\mathsf{Enc}(\mathsf{pk}, \mu \in \{0,1\})$: Sample $\boldsymbol{X} \leftarrow D^m_{\boldsymbol{P},rq}$. Output $\boldsymbol{C} := \boldsymbol{X} + \mu\boldsymbol{H} \bmod q$, where
$$\boldsymbol{H} := (\boldsymbol{h}, \boldsymbol{G}) \in \mathbb{Z}_q^{n\times m} .$$
- $\mathsf{Dec}(\mathsf{sk}, \boldsymbol{C})$: Compute
$$d := \|\boldsymbol{S}^\top \boldsymbol{C}_1 \bmod q\|^2 ,$$
where $\boldsymbol{C}_1$ is the first column of $\boldsymbol{C}$ and we represent elements modulo $q$ in the interval $[-q/2, q/2)$. Output 0 if $d < kq^2/100$ and 1 otherwise.

Notice that this scheme is very similar to the scheme in Sect. 5 except that our ciphertext $\boldsymbol{C} \in \mathbb{Z}_q^{n\times m}$ is an entire matrix

$$\boldsymbol{C} = \boldsymbol{X} + \mu\boldsymbol{H} \bmod \mathrm{q} ,$$

where $\boldsymbol{X} \sim D^m_{\boldsymbol{P},rq}$ instead of just a single column vector $\boldsymbol{c} = \boldsymbol{x} + \mu\boldsymbol{h} \bmod q$ (where $\boldsymbol{x} \sim D_{\boldsymbol{P},rq}$). Indeed, the first column $\boldsymbol{C}_1$ of $\boldsymbol{C}$ is precisely the same as the ciphertext $\boldsymbol{c}$ generated by the scheme in Sect. 5. The remaining columns can be viewed as independent encryptions of 0 plus a term that depends on $\mu$ (specifically, plus $\mu\boldsymbol{G}$). As we will see, this means that Theorem 8 more-or-less immediately implies the security of the above scheme. It also immediately implies that the above scheme is correct as a public-key encryption scheme, but we do not bother to show this, since we will prove the much stronger fact that there exists an $\mathsf{Eval}$ algorithm making the scheme fully homomorphic.

(The relationship between the two encryption schemes as we describe it above is nearly identical to the relationship between Regev's encryption scheme [57] and the GSW fully homomorphic encryption scheme [37]. Of course, this is not a coincidence, as we designed our scheme to mimic [37].)

### 6.2 Security

**Theorem 9.** *Suppose that there exists some $\boldsymbol{Q}' \in \mathcal{S}_n^{>0}(\mathbb{Z})$ such that for the parameters $\boldsymbol{Q} \in \mathcal{S}_n^{>0}(\mathbb{Z})$, $s := s(n) \geq \sqrt{\log(n)}\|\boldsymbol{Q}\|$ and $r := r(n) \geq \sqrt{n \log n} \cdot s/q$ in the encryption scheme above, $\mathcal{D}_s$-acLIP$^{\boldsymbol{Q},\boldsymbol{Q}'}$ is hard and $r \geq \eta_\varepsilon(\boldsymbol{Q}')$ for some $\varepsilon < \mathrm{negl}(n)$. Then, the ciphertext $\boldsymbol{C} \in \mathbb{Z}_q^{n\times m}$ produced by the encryption algorithm is computationally indistinguishable from uniformly random $\boldsymbol{U} \sim \mathbb{Z}_q^{n\times m}$. In particular, the scheme is secure.*

*Proof.* Notice that each column $\boldsymbol{C}_i = \boldsymbol{X}_i + \mu \boldsymbol{H}_i \bmod q$ of the ciphertext is sampled independently, and that these columns can be written as $\boldsymbol{C}_i = \boldsymbol{c}_i + \mu \boldsymbol{H}_i \bmod q$, where $\boldsymbol{c}_i$ is distributed identically to an encryption of 0 produced by the scheme from Sect. 5. By Theorem 8, $\boldsymbol{c}_i$ is computationally indistinguishable from a random $\boldsymbol{u} \sim \mathbb{Z}_q^n$. Thus, by a hybrid argument, the whole ciphertext $\boldsymbol{C}$ is computationally indistinguishable from uniformly random $\boldsymbol{U} \sim \mathbb{Z}_q^{n \times m}$. □

### 6.3 The Eval Function and Homomorphic Operations

Suppose that we wish to homomorphically evaluate a $(\oplus, \times)$-circuit $f : \{0,1\}^\ell \to \{0,1\}$ on input bits $\mu_1, \ldots, \mu_\ell \in \{0,1\}$. Notice that Theorem 7 immediately implies that our decryption algorithm will output $\mu$ whenever its input has the form $\boldsymbol{C} = \boldsymbol{X} + \mu \boldsymbol{H} \bmod q$ for $\boldsymbol{X}$ that is sufficiently small (in the $\boldsymbol{P}$ norm). So, it suffices to show how to convert ciphertexts $\boldsymbol{C}_1, \ldots, \boldsymbol{C}_\ell$ of the form $\boldsymbol{C}_i = \boldsymbol{X}_i + \mu_i \boldsymbol{H} \bmod q$ into a ciphertext $\boldsymbol{C}_f = \boldsymbol{X}_f + \mu_f \boldsymbol{H} \bmod q$ of this form, where $\mu_f = f(\mu_1, \ldots, \mu_\ell)$.

Before defining how to perform homomorphic operations on ciphertexts, we define the (right) inverse map $I_{\boldsymbol{H}} : \mathbb{Z}_q^{n \times m} \to \{0,1\}^{m \times m}$ of $\boldsymbol{H}$ as

$$I_{\boldsymbol{H}}(\boldsymbol{C}) = \begin{pmatrix} \boldsymbol{0} & \boldsymbol{0} & \cdots & \boldsymbol{0} \\ \mathrm{BitDecomp}(C_{1,1}) & \mathrm{BitDecomp}(C_{1,2}) & \cdots & \mathrm{BitDecomp}(C_{1,m}) \\ \vdots & \vdots & \ddots & \vdots \\ \mathrm{BitDecomp}(C_{n,1}) & \mathrm{BitDecomp}(C_{n,2}) & \cdots & \mathrm{BitDecomp}(C_{n,m}) \end{pmatrix} \in \{0,1\}^{m \times m},$$

where for $a \in \mathbb{Z}_q$, $a = \sum_{i=1}^{\log_2 q} x_i 2^{i-1}$ for bits $x_1, \ldots, x_{\log_2 q} \in \{0,1\}$ the bit decomposition function $\mathrm{BitDecomp} : \mathbb{Z}_q \to \{0,1\}^{\log_2 q}$ is defined as

$$\mathrm{BitDecomp}(a) = \mathrm{BitDecomp}\left(\sum_{i=1}^{\log_2 q} x_i 2^{i-1}\right) = (x_1, x_2, \ldots, x_{\log_2 q})^\top \in \{0,1\}^{\log_2 q}.$$

Notice that $I_{\boldsymbol{H}}(\boldsymbol{C})$ is a matrix with small entries (in fact $\{0,1\}$ entries), and it is actually an inverse of $\boldsymbol{H}$ in the sense that

$$\boldsymbol{H} I_{\boldsymbol{H}}(\boldsymbol{C}) = \boldsymbol{C}.$$

(In particular, we have that $\boldsymbol{g} \cdot \mathrm{BitDecomp}(c) = c$ for any $c \in \mathbb{Z}_q$.) This is exactly the same as the standard inverse map used with the gadget matrix $\boldsymbol{G}$ in, e.g., [37], except that our gadget matrix $\boldsymbol{H}$ has an extra column $\boldsymbol{h}$ prepended to it, and therefore $I_{\boldsymbol{H}}(\boldsymbol{C})$ has an extra row of zeros prepended to it.[16]

Now, assume we have two ciphertexts

$$\boldsymbol{C}_1 = \boldsymbol{X}_1 + \mu_1 \boldsymbol{H} \bmod q, \qquad \boldsymbol{C}_2 = \boldsymbol{X}_2 + \mu_2 \boldsymbol{H} \bmod q,$$

[16] There is different notation for maps of this form. Most recent works use the notation $\boldsymbol{H}^{-1}(\boldsymbol{C})$—or, rather, they write $\boldsymbol{G}^{-1}$ for the analogous map for $\boldsymbol{G}$. We prefer the notation $I_{\boldsymbol{H}}$ because we do not wish to suggest that $I_{\boldsymbol{H}}$ is a linear map. [37] called their analogous map Flatten. These are all more-or-less the same thing.

where $\boldsymbol{X}_1$ and $\boldsymbol{X}_2$ are in some sense "short." We would like to compute

$$\boldsymbol{C}_{\oplus} = \boldsymbol{X}_{\oplus} + (\mu_1 \oplus \mu_2)\boldsymbol{H} \bmod q\ , \qquad \boldsymbol{C}_{\times} = \boldsymbol{X}_{\times} + (\mu_1\mu_2)\boldsymbol{H} \bmod q\ ,$$

where $\boldsymbol{X}_{\oplus}$ and $\boldsymbol{X}_{\times}$ are also short. To that end, we define

$$\boldsymbol{C}_{\times} := \boldsymbol{C}_1 \cdot I_{\boldsymbol{H}}(\boldsymbol{C}_2) \bmod q\ ,$$

and

$$\boldsymbol{C}_{\oplus} := \boldsymbol{C}_1 + \boldsymbol{C}_2 - 2\boldsymbol{C}_{\times} \bmod q\ ,$$

which correspond to homomorphic evaluation of a $\times$ gate and a $\oplus$ gate, respectively. We will prove this carefully soon, but notice that by applying the identity $\boldsymbol{H}I_{\boldsymbol{H}}(\boldsymbol{C}) = \boldsymbol{C}$ and recalling that $I_{\boldsymbol{H}}(\boldsymbol{C})$ has small entries, $\boldsymbol{C}_{\oplus}$ and $\boldsymbol{C}_{\times}$ do in fact have the desired form. Indeed, applying this identity yields

$$\boldsymbol{C}_1 \cdot \boldsymbol{I}_{\boldsymbol{H}}(\boldsymbol{C}_2) = (\boldsymbol{X}_1 + \mu_1\boldsymbol{H}) \cdot \boldsymbol{I}_{\boldsymbol{H}}(\boldsymbol{C}_2) = \boldsymbol{X}_1\boldsymbol{I}_{\boldsymbol{H}}(\boldsymbol{C}_2) + \mu_1\boldsymbol{C}_2 = \boldsymbol{X}_1\boldsymbol{I}_{\boldsymbol{H}}(\boldsymbol{C}_2) + \mu_1\boldsymbol{X}_2 + \mu_1\mu_2\boldsymbol{H} \bmod q$$

which has the desired form with $\boldsymbol{X}_{\times} := \boldsymbol{X}_1\boldsymbol{I}_{\boldsymbol{H}}(\boldsymbol{C}_2) + \mu_1\boldsymbol{X}_2$. And, $\boldsymbol{C}_{\oplus}$ works out similarly after applying the similar identity $\mu_1 \oplus \mu_2 = \mu_1 + \mu_2 - 2\mu_1\mu_2$. (Again, all of this is very closely analogous to [37].)

Iterating the above construction yields the following definition and the Eval function for our scheme.

**Definition 1.** *For a $(\oplus, \times)$-circuit $f : \{0,1\}^\ell \to \{0,1\}$ of depth $L = L(n) \geq 0$ and ciphertexts $\boldsymbol{C}_1, \ldots, \boldsymbol{C}_\ell \in \mathbb{Z}_q^{n\times m}$, we define $\boldsymbol{C}_f \in \mathbb{Z}_q^{n\times m}$ recursively as follows.*

1. *If $f(\mu_1, \ldots, \mu_\ell) = \mu_i$ for some $i \in [\ell]$ (i.e., if $L = 0$), $\boldsymbol{C}_f := \boldsymbol{C}_i$.*
2. *If $f(\mu_1, \ldots, \mu_\ell) = f_1(\mu_1, \ldots, \mu_\ell) \times f_2(\mu_1, \ldots, \mu_\ell)$ for some $(\oplus, \times)$-circuits $f_1$ and $f_2$ of depth at most $L - 1$, then $\boldsymbol{C}_f := \boldsymbol{C}_{f_1} \cdot I_{\boldsymbol{H}}(\boldsymbol{C}_{f_2}) \bmod q$.*
3. *If $f(\mu_1, \ldots, \mu_\ell) = f_1(\mu_1, \ldots, \mu_\ell) \oplus f_2(\mu_1, \ldots, \mu_\ell)$ for some $(\oplus, \times)$-circuits $f_1$ and $f_2$ of depth at most $L-1$, then $\boldsymbol{C}_f := \boldsymbol{C}_{f_1} + \boldsymbol{C}_{f_2} - 2\boldsymbol{C}_{f_1} \cdot I_{\boldsymbol{H}}(\boldsymbol{C}_{f_2}) \bmod q$.*

*Then, we define the evaluation algorithm as* $\mathsf{Eval}(\mathsf{pk}, f, \boldsymbol{C}_1, \ldots, \boldsymbol{C}_\ell) := \boldsymbol{C}_f$.

We next prove correctness of our fully homomorphic encryption scheme, which requires showing that $\mathsf{Eval}(\mathsf{pk}, f, \boldsymbol{C}_1, \ldots, \boldsymbol{C}_\ell)$ outputs a ciphertext $\boldsymbol{C}_f = \boldsymbol{X}_f + \mu_f\boldsymbol{H}$ where $\|(\boldsymbol{X}_f)_i\|_P$ is relatively small for each of the columns of $(\boldsymbol{X}_f)_i$ of $\boldsymbol{X}_f$.

**Theorem 10.** *For a $(\oplus, \times)$-circuit $f : \{0,1\}^\ell \to \{0,1\}$ of depth $L$, if for all $1 \leq i \leq \ell$, $\boldsymbol{C}_i \leftarrow \mathsf{Enc}(pk, \mu_i)$, then $\boldsymbol{C}_f = \boldsymbol{X}_f + \mu_f\boldsymbol{H} \bmod q$, where $\boldsymbol{X}_f \in \mathbb{Z}^{n\times m}$ has columns $(\boldsymbol{X}_f)_i$ satisfying*

$$\|(\boldsymbol{X}_f)_i\|_P \leq (2m+2)^L\sqrt{n}rq$$

*with probability at least $1 - \ell m 2^{-n}$, where $\mu := f(\mu_1, \ldots, \mu_\ell)$.*

*In particular, so long as the parameter* $r := r(n) \geq \sqrt{n \log n} \cdot s/q$ *in the encryption scheme is taken so that*

$$r \leq \frac{1}{10\sqrt{nd_z}(2m+2)^L},$$

*where* $d_z := \frac{1}{k}\sum_{i=1}^{k} \|\boldsymbol{z}_i\|^2_{\boldsymbol{Q}^{-1}}$, *we have*

$$\Pr[\mathsf{Dec}(\mathsf{sk}, \mathsf{Eval}(\mathsf{pk}, f, \boldsymbol{C}_1, \ldots, \boldsymbol{C}_\ell)) = f(\mu_1, \ldots, \mu_\ell)] \geq 1 - 2^{-n} - 2^{-k}.$$

*In other words, our scheme is a level L fully homomorphic encryption scheme for such parameters, provided that* $k > \omega(\log n)$.

*Proof.* First, let $\boldsymbol{C}_i := \boldsymbol{X}_i + \mu_i \boldsymbol{H} \bmod q$ where $\boldsymbol{X}_i \sim D^m_{\boldsymbol{P},rq}$ as in our encryption scheme. By a suitable tail bound for the discrete Gaussian (see [17]) and the union bound, we have that for each $i$ and $j$, the $j$th column $(\boldsymbol{X}_i)_j$ of $\boldsymbol{X}_i$ has $\|(\boldsymbol{X}_i)_j\|_{\boldsymbol{P}} < \sqrt{n}rq$ except with probability at most $\ell m 2^{-n}$.

Assuming that this holds, we prove the result by induction on the depth $L$ of $f$. In the base case, if $f$ has depth 0, then $\boldsymbol{X} = \boldsymbol{X}_i$ for some $i$, and we are done.

Otherwise, the circuit has depth $L \geq 1$, and there are two cases to consider, depending on whether $f = f_1 \times f_2$ or $f = f_1 \oplus f_2$ for circuits $f_1$ and $f_2$ with depth at most $L - 1$.

In the first case, $f = f_1 \times f_2$ and $\boldsymbol{C}_f = \boldsymbol{C}_{f_1} I_{\boldsymbol{H}}(\boldsymbol{C}_{f_2})$. By induction, we can write $\boldsymbol{C}_{f_i} = \boldsymbol{X}_{f_i} + \mu_{f_i}\boldsymbol{H} \bmod q$ for $i \in \{1,2\}$, where $\|(\boldsymbol{X}_{f_i})_j\|_{\boldsymbol{P}} \leq (2m+2)^{L-1}\sqrt{n}rq$. Using the identity $\boldsymbol{H} I_{\boldsymbol{H}}(\boldsymbol{C}) = \boldsymbol{C}$, we see that

$$\begin{aligned}
\boldsymbol{C}_f &= (\boldsymbol{X}_{f_1} + \mu_{f_1}\boldsymbol{H}) I_{\boldsymbol{H}}(\boldsymbol{C}_{f_2}) \bmod q \\
&= \boldsymbol{X}_{f_1} I_{\boldsymbol{H}}(\boldsymbol{C}_{f_2}) + \mu_{f_1}\boldsymbol{X}_{f_2} + \mu_{f_1}\mu_{f_2}\boldsymbol{H} \bmod q \\
&= \boldsymbol{X}_f + \mu_f \boldsymbol{H} \bmod q\ ,
\end{aligned}$$

where $\boldsymbol{X}_f := \boldsymbol{X}_{f_1} I_{\boldsymbol{H}}(\boldsymbol{C}_{f_2}) + \mu_{f_1}\boldsymbol{X}_{f_2}$ and $\mu_f := \mu_{f_1}\mu_{f_2}$.

Since $I_{\boldsymbol{H}}(\boldsymbol{C}_{f_2}) \in \{0,1\}^{m \times m}$ it follows from the induction hypothesis that for $i = 1, \ldots, n$, the $i$th column of $\boldsymbol{X}_{f_1} I_{\boldsymbol{H}}(\boldsymbol{C}_{f_2})$ satisfies

$$\|(\boldsymbol{X}_{f_1} I_{\boldsymbol{H}}(\boldsymbol{C}_{f_2}))_i\|_{\boldsymbol{P}} \leq \sum_{j=1}^{m} \|(\boldsymbol{X}_{f_1})_j\|_{\boldsymbol{P}} \leq m(2m+2)^{L-1}\sqrt{n}\ \mathrm{rq}\ .$$

Furthermore, $\|\mu_{f_1}\boldsymbol{X}_{f_2}\|_{\boldsymbol{P}} \leq (2m+2)^{L-1}\sqrt{n}rq$ by the induction hypothesis, and so by triangle inequality we have $\|(\boldsymbol{X}_f)_i\|_{\boldsymbol{P}} \leq (2m+2)^L\sqrt{n}rq$, as needed.

The second case where $f = f_1 \oplus f_2$ is very similar. In that case, we have

$$\begin{aligned}
\boldsymbol{C}_f &= \boldsymbol{C}_{f_1} + \boldsymbol{C}_{f_2} - 2\boldsymbol{C}_{f_1} I_{\boldsymbol{H}}(\boldsymbol{C}_{f_2}) \bmod q \\
&= (\boldsymbol{X}_{f_1} + \mu_{f_1}\boldsymbol{H}) + (\boldsymbol{X}_{f_2} + \mu_{f_2}\boldsymbol{H}) - 2(\boldsymbol{X}_{f_1} + \mu_{f_1}\boldsymbol{H}) I_{\boldsymbol{H}}(\boldsymbol{C}_{f_2}) \bmod q \\
&= \boldsymbol{X}_{f_1} - 2\boldsymbol{X}_{f_1} I_{\boldsymbol{H}}(\boldsymbol{C}_{f_2}) + \boldsymbol{X}_{f_2} - 2\mu_{f_1}\boldsymbol{X}_{f_2} + (\mu_{f_1} + \mu_{f_2} - 2\mu_{f_1}\mu_{f_2})\boldsymbol{H} \bmod q \\
&= \boldsymbol{X}_{f_1} - 2\boldsymbol{X}_{f_1} I_{\boldsymbol{H}}(\boldsymbol{C}_{f_2}) + (1 - 2\mu_{f_1})\boldsymbol{X}_{f_2} + (\mu_{f_1} \oplus \mu_{f_2})\boldsymbol{H} \bmod q \\
&= \boldsymbol{X}_f + \mu_f \boldsymbol{H} \bmod q\ ,
\end{aligned}$$

where $\boldsymbol{X}_f := \boldsymbol{X}_{f_1} - 2\boldsymbol{X}_{f_1} I_{\boldsymbol{H}}(\boldsymbol{C}_{f_2}) + (1-2\mu_{f_1})\boldsymbol{X}_{f_2}$ and $\mu_f := \mu_{f_1} \oplus \mu_{f_2}$. It again follows from the induction hypothesis and triangle inequality that $\|(\boldsymbol{X}_f)_i\|_{\boldsymbol{P}} \leq (2m+2)^L \sqrt{n} r q$, as needed.

Finally, since,

$$\|(\boldsymbol{X}_f)_1\|_{\boldsymbol{P}}^2 \leq \frac{q^2}{100 d_z},$$

correctness follows by Theorem 7. □

*Remark 1.* We note that our scheme inherits from [37] a peculiar asymmetry in noise growth. In particular, when one homomorphically computes a ciphertext $\boldsymbol{C}_f := \boldsymbol{X}_f + \mu_f \boldsymbol{H} \bmod q$ from two ciphertexts $\boldsymbol{C}_{f_1} := \boldsymbol{X}_{f_1} + \mu_{f_1}\boldsymbol{H} \bmod q$ and $\boldsymbol{C}_{f_2} := \boldsymbol{X}_{f_2} + \mu_{f_2}\boldsymbol{H} \bmod q$, the resulting "noise" $\boldsymbol{X}_f$ satisfies $\|\boldsymbol{X}_f\|_{\boldsymbol{P}} \leq (2m+1)\|\boldsymbol{X}_{f_1}\|_{\boldsymbol{P}} + \|\boldsymbol{X}_{f_2}\|_{\boldsymbol{P}}$. In the above, we simply bound this by $(2m+2)\max_i \|\boldsymbol{X}_{f_i}\|_{\boldsymbol{P}}$. But, notice that we can potentially design our circuit $f$ so that we know that $\|\boldsymbol{X}_{f_1}\|_{\boldsymbol{P}}$ is quite a bit smaller than $\|\boldsymbol{X}_{f_2}\|_{\boldsymbol{P}}$, in which case this bound is quite loose. This can allow us to evaluate much deeper circuits. For example, we can homomorphically evaluate the XOR of $\ell$ ciphertexts while only increasing the noise by a factor of $\ell(2m+1)+1$, while naively applying our theorem would suggest that the noise should increase by a factor of $(2m+2)^{\log \ell}$ (using a balanced circuit).

In the case of [37], this is sometimes quite useful. Specifically, this is useful for *bootstrapping* (which we discuss in Sect. 6.6) when one is specifically interested in minimizing the noise growth in the decryption circuit. This was used in [9, 24,31] to homomorphically evaluate the decryption circuit of (variants of) GSW encryption with noise growth bounded by a polynomial in $n$, even though it has depth $\mathrm{poly}(\log n)$. See Sect. 6.6 for discussion of bootstrapping in this context.

### 6.4 Putting Everything Together

By combining the security and correctness results in Theorems 9 and 10, we obtain the following result.

**Theorem 11.** *Suppose that the parameters* $\boldsymbol{Q} \in S_n^{>0}(\mathbb{Z})$, $s := s(n) \geq \sqrt{\log(n)\|\boldsymbol{Q}\|}$, $r := r(n) \geq \sqrt{n \log n}s/q$, *and* $q := q(n) \geq 20$ *a power of two, and* $\boldsymbol{Z} := (\boldsymbol{z}_1, \ldots, \boldsymbol{z}_k) \in \mathbb{Z}^{n \times k}$ *in the homomorphic encryption scheme above satisfy that*

$$r < \frac{1}{20\sqrt{n d_z}},$$

*where* $d_z := \frac{1}{k} \cdot \sum_{i=1}^k \|\boldsymbol{z}_i\|_{\boldsymbol{Q}^{-1}}^2$ *and* $m := n \log_2 q + 1$. *Suppose further that there exists some* $\boldsymbol{Q}' \in S_n^{>0}(\mathbb{Z})$ *such that* $\mathcal{D}_s$-acLIP$^{\boldsymbol{Q},\boldsymbol{Q}'}$ *is hard and* $r \geq \eta_\varepsilon(\boldsymbol{Q}')$ *for some* $\varepsilon < \mathrm{negl}(n)$.

*Then,* (Gen, Enc, Dec, Eval) *is a secure level-L fully homomorphic encryption scheme for any*

$$L \leq \frac{\log\left(\frac{1}{10\sqrt{n d_z} r}\right)}{\log(2m+2)}.$$

### 6.5 Instantiating Our FHE Scheme with Specific Quadratic Forms and Parameters

One possible instantiation of our FHE scheme is to use the quadratic form

$$\boldsymbol{Q} := \begin{pmatrix} g(g+1)\boldsymbol{I}_{n/2} & 0 \\ 0 & \boldsymbol{I}_{n/2} \end{pmatrix},$$

for some large positive integer $g$ to be chosen later. This form was first suggested in a similar context in [33]. The choice of vectors $\boldsymbol{z}_1, \ldots, \boldsymbol{z}_k$ will just be $\boldsymbol{z}_1 := \boldsymbol{e}_1, \ldots, \boldsymbol{z}_{n/2} := \boldsymbol{e}_{n/2}$, with their $\boldsymbol{Q}^{-1}$ norms being

$$\|\boldsymbol{z}_i\|^2_{\boldsymbol{Q}^{-1}} = \frac{1}{g(g+1)},$$

so that $d_{\boldsymbol{z}} = \frac{1}{g(g+1)}$.

For security, again following [33], we can consider

$$\boldsymbol{Q}' := \begin{pmatrix} g\boldsymbol{I}_{n/2} & 0 \\ 0 & (g+1)\boldsymbol{I}_{n/2} \end{pmatrix}.$$

Intuitively, this is a far more "balanced" quadratic form, and in particular it has smoothing parameter roughly proportional to $g$, whereas $\boldsymbol{Q}$ has smoothing parameter roughly proportional to $g^2$. (Note that these are the same choices that we made in Sect. 4.4 except that we have switched the roles of $\boldsymbol{Q}$ and $\boldsymbol{Q}'$. So, at a very high level we end up with effectively the same instance of LIP, since $\mathrm{LIP}^{\boldsymbol{Q},\boldsymbol{Q}'}$ is trivially equivalent to $\mathrm{LIP}^{\boldsymbol{Q}',\boldsymbol{Q}}$. However, as we will soon see, we will consider much larger values of $g$ here—namely subexponentially large $g = 2^{n^\delta}$ for some $\delta > 0$—while in Sect. 4.4 we were able to take $g = \widetilde{\Theta}(n)$.)

From Theorem 11, the security of the scheme follows if $\mathcal{D}_s$-$\mathrm{acLIP}^{\boldsymbol{Q},\boldsymbol{Q}'}$ is hard and

$$r \geq \eta_\varepsilon(\boldsymbol{Q}').$$

See [33] for much more discussion of this particular version of LIP with these particular choices of $\boldsymbol{Q}$ and $\boldsymbol{Q}'$. (See also [16, Section 5] and [29].) Here, we simply observe that, as far as we know, the best algorithms on $\mathcal{D}_s$-$\mathrm{acLIP}^{\boldsymbol{Q},\boldsymbol{Q}'}$ work via a (trivial) reduction to the $g$-approximate Shortest Vector Problem.[17] The best algorithms for this problem run in time $\mathrm{poly}(n) \cdot 2^{\Theta(n \log(n/\log g)/\log g)}$. So, if we take $g < 2^{o(n \log\log n/\log n)}$, then the best known algorithms require superpolynomial time and this problem is plausibly hard. In fact, as we will see, we already get homomorphic operations for polynomial-depth circuits by taking $g = 2^{n^\delta}$ for a small constant $\delta > 0$, in which case the best known algorithm runs in time $2^{\widetilde{\Theta}(n^{1-\delta})}$.

---

[17] One can get slightly faster algorithms by restricting attention to lattices that have dense sublattices, but the improvements are not significant enough to affect the asymptotics as we present them here. Again, see [16,29,33] for more discussion.

Finishing with the parameters, recall that we need to take $r \geq \eta_\varepsilon(\boldsymbol{Q}')$ for negligible $\varepsilon$ in order to have security. With our choice of $\boldsymbol{Q}'$ above, we have that it suffices to take any $r > \omega(\sqrt{g \log n})$, but we can simply take $r = \sqrt{ng}$, as this will not meaningfully harm our parameters. Theorem 11 then tells us that we obtain a level $L$ homomorphic encryption scheme for $L$ up to

$$\frac{\log\left(\frac{1}{10\sqrt{nd_z}r}\right)}{\log(2m+2)} \geq \frac{\log g}{2\log n + 2\log\log q} - O(1) .$$

So, for example, if we take $g = 2^{n^\delta}$ for some constant $\delta > 0$ (and $q \leq 2^{\mathrm{poly}(n)}$), then we can homomorphically evaluate circuits of depth up to $\widetilde{\Omega}(n^\delta)$, for a scheme for which the best known attacks run in time $2^{\widetilde{\Omega}(n^{1-\delta})}$.

Finally, we discuss the parameters $s$ and $q$ (which matter less than the others). The requirement that $r \geq \sqrt{n \log ns}/q$ (which is needed for the sampling step in the encryption algorithm) implies that we must take $q \geq \sqrt{n \log ns}/r = s \cdot \sqrt{\log n/g}$. We also need $s \geq \sqrt{\log(n)}\|\boldsymbol{Q}\| = \mathrm{poly}(n)g$. (In fact, we don't truly need this for our particular choice of $\boldsymbol{Q}$ for which sampling from $\mathcal{D}_s(\boldsymbol{Q})$ is possible even with smaller parameters, but we do not bother to observe this.) So, if we are happy to conjecture that the *average-case* problem $\mathcal{D}_s$-acLIP$^{\boldsymbol{Q},\boldsymbol{Q}'}$ is hard, then we can simply take $s = \mathrm{poly}(n)g$ and $q = \mathrm{poly}(n)\sqrt{g}$.

Taking $q$ and $s$ to be as small as possible makes for a more efficient scheme, since our scheme performs many operations modulo $q$ and since $s$ controls the size of the entries in $\boldsymbol{P}$. However, to invoke the worst-case to average-case reduction in [33], we should take, e.g., $s = 2^n g$. Then, we obtain security under the assumption that wcLIP$^{\boldsymbol{Q},\boldsymbol{Q}'}$ is hard. But, we now must take $q \geq s \cdot \sqrt{\log n/g} = 2^n\sqrt{g \log n}$.

All of the above parameter choices are quite similar to what one obtains for the GSW scheme in [37]. In particular, the best known attacks on LIP$^{\boldsymbol{Q},\boldsymbol{Q}'}$ use essentially the same algorithms as the best known attacks on [37], with nearly identical parameters for the same choice of $L$. However, using sophisticated techniques like those discussed in Sect. 6.6, it is now known how to build leveled FHE from LWE using parameters that are essentially independent of $L$.[18] See [33, Section 7] for more discussion of the best known attacks on LIP$^{\boldsymbol{Q},\boldsymbol{Q}'}$.

### 6.6 A Note on Bootstrapping

We have described our scheme as a *leveled* FHE scheme. To make it truly fully homomorphic, we would need to show how to correctly evaluate arbitrary circuits rather than circuits with bounded depth $L$. The only known way to build such true FHE schemes is via Gentry's *bootstrapping* technique [35]. Indeed, Gentry essentially showed a bootstrapping framework, which proceeds in two steps.

First, one designs a leveled FHE scheme that is capable of homomorphically evaluating its own decryption circuit(!). Specifically, one wishes to homomorphically evaluate circuits computing functions of the form $f_C(\mathsf{sk}) := \mathsf{Dec}(sk, \boldsymbol{C})$,

[18] See the full version [17] for additional discussion of the subtleties involved here.

where notice that the ciphertext $\boldsymbol{C}$ is hard-coded into $f_C$, and the input is the secret key. Notice that our scheme has a rather simple decryption circuit. Indeed, our scheme is closely modeled after the scheme in [37] which is known to have this property. (And, our scheme has some similarity with the scheme in [25], where the authors claim that the decryption circuit can be evaluated homomorphically, though they do not show this formally.) Furthermore, recall from Remark 1 that one can hope to homomorphically evaluate a decryption circuit even if the scheme cannot handle arbitrary circuits whose depth is nearly as large as the decryption circuit's depth, as was done for [37] in [9,24,31]. So, it seems likely that our scheme or a small modification of it would have this property, possibly even with favorable parameters (e.g., $g \leq \text{poly}(n)$ in Sect. 6.5).

Second, one includes as part of the public key additional ciphertexts $\boldsymbol{C}_i \leftarrow \mathsf{Enc}(\mathsf{pk}, \mathsf{sk}_i)$, which are encryptions of the bits of the secret key(!). By taking a given ciphertext $\boldsymbol{C}$ and running $\boldsymbol{C}' \leftarrow \mathsf{Eval}(f_C, \boldsymbol{C}_1, \ldots, \boldsymbol{C}_\ell)$, one obtains a ciphertext $\boldsymbol{C}'$ with the property that $\mathsf{Dec}(\mathsf{sk}, \boldsymbol{C}') = \mathsf{Dec}(\mathsf{sk}, \boldsymbol{C})$, but where the noise size of $\boldsymbol{C}'$ is bounded. So, one can use bootstrapping to "lower the accumulated noise" from the ciphertext $\boldsymbol{C}$.

However, it is not clear whether publishing the ciphertexts $\boldsymbol{C}_i$ can affect security. Schemes with the property that they remain secure even when the adversary is given access to encryptions of the bits of the secret key are called *circularly secure.* As far as we know, standard lattice-based encryption schemes are all circularly secure, but our proofs of security from standard assumptions fail in this setting. The best we know how to do is to show security under *circular* variants of LWE that effectively incorporate such ciphertexts $\boldsymbol{C}_i$ into the assumption.

We imagine that similar ideas work in our setting. However, the authors of the present work are currently quite reluctant to propose a novel assumption of circular security in this setting, since LIP-based cryptography is a new and rapidly developing area.[19]

**Acknowledgments.** The authors thank Chris Peikert for helpful discussion and the anonymous Crypto 2026 reviewers for their useful comments. HB was supported in part by NSF Grant No. CCF-2432132. NSD was supported by NSF Grant No. CCF-2312296, a Packard Foundation Fellowship, and a generous gift from Google.

## References

1. Abdalla, M., De Caro, A., Mochetti, K.: Lattice-based hierarchical inner product encryption, p. Latincrypt (2012)
2. Ackermann, L., Roux-Langlois, A., Wallet, A.: Public-key encryption from the lattice isomorphism problem. WCC (2024)
3. Agrawal, S., Boneh, D., Boyen, X.: Efficient lattice (H)IBE in the standard model. Eurocrypt (2010)

[19] [25] claim that their scheme can be generically converted into a true FHE scheme via bootstrapping. But, they do not seem to address the question of circular security.

4. Agrawal, S., Boyen, X.: Identity-based encryption from lattices in the standard model (2009). https://crypto.stanford.edu/~xb/ab09/latticeibe.pdf
5. Agrawal, S., Freeman, D.M., Vaikuntanathan, V.: Functional encryption for inner product predicates from Learning with Errors. Asiacrypt (2011)
6. Agrawal, S., Libert, B., Stehlé, D.: Fully secure functional encryption for inner products, from standard assumptions. Crypto (2016)
7. Ajtai, M.: Generating hard instances of lattice problems, p. STOC (1996)
8. Allombert, B., Pellet-Mary, A., van Woerden, W.: Cryptanalysis of rank-2 Module-LIP: a single real embedding is all it takes. In: Eurocrypt (2025)
9. Alperin-Sheriff, J., Peikert, C.: Faster bootstrapping with polynomial error. Crypto (2014)
10. Avanzi, R., et al.: CRYSTALS-Kyber (2021). https://pq-crystals.org/kyber/
11. Bai, S., et al.: CRYSTALS-Dilithium (2021). https://pq-crystals.org/dilithium/
12. Bambury, H., Nguyen, P.Q.: Improved provable reduction of NTRU and hypercubic lattices. In: Post-Quantum Cryptography (2024)
13. Bambury, H., Nguyen, P.Q.: Cryptanalysis of an efficient signature based on isotropic quadratic forms. In: Post-Quantum Cryptography (2025)
14. Benčina, B., Budroni, A., Chi-Domínguez, J.J., Kulkarni, M.: Properties of lattice isomorphism as a cryptographic group action. In: Post-Quantum Cryptography (2024)
15. Bennett, H., et al.: Asymptotic improvements to provable algorithms for the code equivalence problem. IEEE Trans. Inf. Theory **72**, 1093–1108 (2026)
16. Bennett, H., Ganju, A., Peetathawatchai, P., Stephens-Davidowitz, N.: Just how hard are rotations of $\mathbb{Z}^n$? Eurocrypt, Algorithms and cryptography with the simplest lattice. In (2023)
17. Bennett, H., Lai, Z., Stephens-Davidowitz, N.: Advanced cryptography from lattice isomorphism—New constructions of IBE and FHE (2026). https://eprint.iacr.org/2026/465, the full version of the present work
18. Bennett, H., Win, K.M.H.: Relating code equivalence to other isomorphism problems. Des. Codes Crypt. **93**, 701–723 (2025)
19. Boneh, D., Freeman, D.M.: Homomorphic signatures for polynomial functions. Eurocrypt (2011)
20. Boneh, D., et al.: Fully key-homomorphic encryption, arithmetic circuit ABE and compact garbled circuits. Eurocrypt (2014)
21. Bos, J.W., et al.: HAWK: a signature scheme inspired by the lattice isomorphism problem (2025). https://hawk-sign.info/
22. Brakerski, Z., Gentry, C., Vaikuntanathan, V.: Leveled) fully homomorphic encryption without bootstrapping, p. ITCS. (2012)
23. Brakerski, Z., Vaikuntanathan, V.: Efficient fully homomorphic encryption from (standard) LWE, p. FOCS (2011)
24. Brakerski, Z., Vaikuntanathan, V.: Lattice-based FHE as secure as PKE, p. ITCS (2014)
25. Branco, P., Malavolta, G., Maradni, Z.: Fully-homomorphic encryption from lattice isomorphism, p. TCC (2025)
26. Cash, D., Hofheinz, D., Kiltz, E., Peikert, C.: Bonsai trees, or how to delegate a lattice basis. Eurocrypt (2010)
27. de Castro Biage, G., Zambonin, G., Idalino, T.B., Panario, D., Custodio, R.: A concrete LIP-based KEM with simple lattices. IEEE Access **12**, 16408–16420 (2024)
28. Chevignard, C., et al.: A reduction from HAWK to the principal ideal problem in a quaternion algebra. Eurocrypt (2025)

29. Ducas, L.: Provable lattice reduction of $\mathbb{Z}^n$ with blocksize $n/2$. Des. Codes Crypt. **92**, 909–916 (2024)
30. Ducas, L., Gibbons, S.: Hull attacks on the lattice isomorphism problem, p. PKC. (2023)
31. Ducas, L., Micciancio, D.: FHEW: bootstrapping homomorphic encryption in less than a second. Eurocrypt (2015)
32. Ducas, L., Postlethwaite, E.W., Pulles, L.N., van Woerden, W.: HAWK: module LIP makes lattice signatures fast, compact and simple. In: Asiacrypt (2023)
33. Ducas, L., van Woerden, W.: On the lattice isomorphism problem, quadratic forms, remarkable lattices, and cryptography. In: Eurocrypt (2022)
34. Fouque, P.A., et al.: FALCON: Fast-Fourier lattice-based compact signatures over NTRU (2020). https://falcon-sign.info/
35. Gentry, C.: Fully homomorphic encryption using ideal lattices, p. STOC (2009)
36. Gentry, C., Peikert, C., Vaikuntanathan, V.: Trapdoors for hard lattices and new cryptographic constructions, p. STOC (2008)
37. Gentry, C., Sahai, A., Waters, B.: Homomorphic encryption from Learning with Errors: Conceptually-simpler, asymptotically-faster, attribute-based. Crypto (2013)
38. Goldwasser, S., Kalai, Y., Popa, R.A., Vaikuntanathan, V., Zeldovich, N.: Reusable garbled circuits and succinct functional encryption, p. STOC (2013)
39. Gorbunov, S., Vaikuntanathan, V., Wee, H.: Attribute-based encryption for circuits, p. STOC (2013)
40. Gorbunov, S., Vaikuntanathan, V., Wichs, D.: Leveled fully homomorphic signatures from standard lattices, p. STOC (2015)
41. Gyawali, M.: Rank-2 module-LIP with special matrices. Inf. Process. Lett. **191**, 106593 (2026)
42. Hoffstein, J., Pipher, J., Silverman, J.H.: NTRU: a ring-based public key cryptosystem, p. ANTS (1998)
43. Jiang, K., et al.: Re-randomize and extract: a novel commitment construction framework based on group actions. In: Eurocrypt (2025)
44. Jiang, K., et al.: Exploiting the symmetry of $\mathbb{Z}^n$: randomization and the automorphism problem. J. Cryptol. **38**, 27 (2025)
45. Kuninets, A., Leevik, A., Malygina, E., Melnichuk, E., Nabokov, D.: On the construction of Barnes-Wall lattices and their application in cryptography (2025). https://eprint.iacr.org/2025/1040
46. Leporati, A., Rovida, L., van Woerden, W.: Beyond LWE: a lattice framework for homomorphic encryption (2025). https://eprint.iacr.org/2025/1171
47. Ling, C., Liu, J., Mendelsohn, A.: On the spinor genus and the distinguishing Lattice Isomorphism Problem. Asiacrypt (2025)
48. Luo, H., Jiang, K., Pan, Y., Wang, A.: Cryptanalysis of rank-2 Module-LIP with symplectic automorphisms. Asiacrypt (2025)
49. Micciancio: Fully homomorphic encryption from the ground up (2019). invited talk at Eurocrypt
50. Micciancio, D., Peikert, C.: Trapdoors for lattices: simpler, tighter, faster, smaller. Eurocrypt (2012)
51. Mureau, G.: Special genera of Hermitian lattices and applications to HAWK, p. TCC (2025)
52. Mureau, G., Pellet-Mary, A., Pliatsok, G., Wallet, A.: Cryptanalysis of rank-2 Module-LIP in totally real number fields. Eurocrypt (2024)

53. Module-lattice-based digital signature standard. In: Federal Information Processing Standards Publications (FIPS) NIST FIPS 204, National Institute of Standards and Technology, U.S. Department of Commerce, Washington, D.C. (2024) Technical Report
54. Module-lattice-based key-encapsulation mechanism standard. In: Federal Information Processing Standards Publications (FIPS) NIST FIPS 203, National Institute of Standards and Technology, U.S. Department of Commerce, Washington, D.C. (2024) Technical Report
55. Peikert, C.: Public-Key cryptosystems from the worst-case Shortest Vector Problem, p. STOC (2009)
56. Peikert, C.: A decade of lattice cryptography. Found. Trends Theor. Comput. Sci. **10**, 283–424 (2016)
57. Regev, O.: On lattices, learning with errors, random linear codes, and cryptography, p. STOC (2005)
58. Silva, F.C., Lie, M., Ling, C.: On hull attacks on the module lattice isomorphism problem (2025). https://eprint.iacr.org/2025/1376
59. Tsabary, R.: Fully secure attribute-based encryption for t-CNF from LWE. Crypto (2019)
60. van Woerden, W.: Dense and smooth lattices in any genus. In: Asiacrypt (2025)
61. Xagawa, K.: Improved (hierarchical) inner-product encryption from lattices, p. PKC (2013)

# Unbounded Broadcast and KP-ABE with Sublinear Ciphertext from Pairings

Junichi Tomida(✉) and Hoeteck Wee

NTT Research, CA, USA
tomida.junichi@gmail.com

**Abstract.** We present the first pairing-based unbounded broadcast encryption and key-policy attribute-based encryption (KP-ABE) with sublinear ciphertext size. Here, unbounded means set-up and the public parameters do not impose a bound on the size of the broadcast set, attribute length, or policy size.

– Our broadcast encryption scheme supports an unbounded number of users, and achieves

$$|\mathsf{mpk}| = O(1), |\mathsf{ct}| = O(\sqrt{N}), |\mathsf{sk}| = O(\sqrt{N})$$

where $N$ denotes an upper bound on the size of the broadcast set.

– Our KP-ABE supports boolean formula and span programs, and achieves

$$|\mathsf{mpk}| = O(1), |\mathsf{ct}| = O(\sqrt{N}), |\mathsf{sk}| = O(\sqrt{N} \cdot |f|)$$

where $N$ is the attribute length and $|f|$ the policy size.

We prove adaptive security for the broadcast encryption and selective security for the KP-ABE, based on the $k$-Lin assumption in the standard model without random oracles.

**Keywords:** Attribute-based encryption · Broadcast encryption · Pairings

## 1 Introduction

In this work, we study broadcast encryption [24] as well as key-policy attribute-based encryption (KP-ABE) schemes [30,38], where ciphertexts $\mathsf{ct}$ and keys $\mathsf{sk}$ are associated with descriptive values which determine whether decryption is possible. In broadcast encryption, ciphertexts are associated with a set $X$ and a message $M$ and key with a value $y$, and decryption returns $M$ when $y \in X$. In KP-ABE, ciphertexts are associated with an attribute $x$ and a message $M$ and keys with a policy $f$, and decryption returns $M$ when $x$ satisfies $f$. Throughout, we require security against unbounded collusions, so that an adversary that sees a ciphertext along with an arbitrary number of secret keys learns nothing about the message as long as none of the keys can decrypt the ciphertext.


N. Heninger and M. Rosulek (Eds.): CRYPTO 2026, LNCS 16800, pp. 477–507, 2026.
https://doi.org/10.1007/978-3-032-35367-2_16

**Unbounded Broadcast and KP-ABE.** Following [34], we consider unbounded broadcast and KP-ABE, where-in set-up and the public parameters $\mathsf{mpk}$ do not impose an a priori bound on the size of the broadcast set, attribute length, or policy size. We note that such unbounded schemes follow from recent constructions of "optimal" broadcast and KP-ABE [2–4,16,42–45]; however these schemes either rely on LWE plus generic groups, or non-standard variants of the LWE assumption. In this work, we focus on schemes based on standard assumptions, and in the standard model without random oracles. Here, we do know unbounded broadcast and KP-ABE from either the standard $k$-Lin assumption in pairing groups [1,6–8,11,19,31–34,36,37], or the LWE assumption [15,21,29], but they all have ciphertext size that is linear in the size of the broadcast set or the attribute length.

### 1.1 Our Results

In this work, we present the first unbounded broadcast encryption and key-policy KP-ABE with sublinear ciphertext size based on standard assumptions.

- Our broadcast encryption scheme supports an unbounded number of users[1], and achieves

$$|\mathsf{mpk}| = O(1), |\mathsf{ct}| = O(\sqrt{N}), |\mathsf{sk}| = O(\sqrt{N})$$

  where $N$ denotes an upper bound on the size of the broadcast set.
- Our KP-ABE supports boolean formula and span programs, and achieves

$$|\mathsf{mpk}| = O(1), |\mathsf{ct}| = O(\sqrt{N}), |\mathsf{sk}| = O(\sqrt{N} \cdot |f|)$$

  where $N$ is the attribute length and $|f|$ the policy size.

We prove adaptive security for the broadcast encryption and selective security for the KP-ABE, based on the $k$-Lin assumption in the standard model without random oracles.

**Comparison with Prior Works.** We provide a brief comparison with prior pairing-based schemes, including constructions based on non-standard assumptions, or even the generic group model.

- All prior pairing-based broadcast encryption e.g. [13,41] requires $|\mathsf{mpk}| \cdot |\mathsf{ct}| = \Omega(N^{2/3})$ (see Fig. 1); we beat this bound, with $|\mathsf{mpk}| \cdot |\mathsf{ct}| = O(\sqrt{N})$. Moreover, the only pairing-based unbounded broadcast is the trivial one that uses an identity-based encryption (IBE) scheme to encrypt to every user in the set, where $|\mathsf{ct}| = O(N)$.[2]

[1] sometimes referred to as identity-based broadcast encryption in the literature.

[2] [8] provided a direct unbounded broadcast construction from pairings, but its asymptotic efficiency is the same as the trivial construction from identity-based encryption.

- All prior pairing-based KP-ABE e.g. [9,10,30] requires $|\mathsf{mpk}| \cdot |\mathsf{ct}| = \Omega(N)$; we beat this bound, with $|\mathsf{mpk}| \cdot |\mathsf{ct}| = O(\sqrt{N})$. Prior unbounded KP-ABE for boolean formula and span programs [1,6–8,11,19,31–34,36,37] achieve $|\mathsf{ct}| = O(N), |\mathsf{sk}| = O(|f|)$.

**Brief Overview.** The main technical novelty of this work lies in the broadcast encryption scheme, notably, one achieving $|\mathsf{mpk}| = O(1), |\mathsf{ct}| = O(\sqrt{N})$. It is helpful to think about the construction abstractly. We adopt the framework of ABE for general predicates $\mathsf{P}$, where ciphertexts are associated with attributes $x$ and keys with policies $y$, and decryption succeeds when $\mathsf{P}(x, y) = 1$. Broadcast encryption corresponds to set membership (with $x$ encoding the recipient set), while KP-ABE captures general satisfiability (where $y$ specifies the policy).

At a high level, we construct a new compiler that transforms a pairing-based ABE scheme from a specific class —namely, those derived from conditional disclosure of secrets (CDS) [6,27,39][3]— into an unbounded ABE for the same predicate with parameters

$$|\mathsf{mpk}'| = O(1), \ |\mathsf{ct}'| = |\mathsf{ct}| + O(|\mathsf{mpk}|), \ |\mathsf{sk}'| = |\mathsf{sk}| + O(|\mathsf{mpk}|)$$

Crucially, this transformation compresses the public parameters to constant size while increasing ciphertext and key sizes only additively in $|\mathsf{mpk}|$. Instantiating this compiler with the broadcast encryption of [35] with $|\mathsf{mpk}| = |\mathsf{ct}| = |\mathsf{sk}| = O(\sqrt{N})$ yields our new unbounded broadcast encryption scheme.

We start with a compiler implicit in prior unbounded KP-ABE [19,34,36]. This compiler preserves the decryption functionality only if we start schemes whose ciphertext structure corresponds to projection "in the exponent". This restriction excludes broadcast encryption schemes where ciphertext components encode more general linear relations. Our main technical advance is overcoming this barrier by developing a compiler that supports all linear functions in the exponent, thereby enabling parameter compression in settings previously out of reach. Our compiler introduces another additive $O(|\mathsf{mpk}|)$ overhead to both the ciphertext and the secret key to facilitate decryption, while preserving security.

## 2 Technical Overview

We use boldface lower case to denote vectors, and boldface upper case to denote matrices. We rely on a bilinear group $(G_1, G_2, G_T, e)$ of prime order $p$ where $e : G_1 \times G_2 \to G_T$. We use $[\cdot]_1, [\cdot]_2, [\cdot]_T$ to denote component-wise exponentiations in respective groups $G_1, G_2, G_T$. The $k$-Lin assumption in $G_1$ asserts that $([\mathbf{A}]_1, [\mathbf{A}\mathbf{s}^\top]_1) \approx_c ([\mathbf{A}]_1, [\mathbf{u}^\top]_1)$ where $\mathbf{s} \leftarrow \mathbb{Z}_p^k, \mathbf{A} \leftarrow \mathbb{Z}_p^{(k+1)\times k}, \mathbf{u} \leftarrow \mathbb{Z}_p^{k+1}$.

### 2.1 Overview of Our Constructions

We provide an overview of our constructions, focusing on the unbounded broadcast encryption.

[3] This does not include the $N^{1/3}$-sized broadcast encryption in [41].

| Scheme | $\vert\mathsf{mpk}\vert$ | $\vert\mathsf{ct}\vert$ | $\vert\mathsf{sk}\vert$ | Assumption | Security |
|---|---|---|---|---|---|
| [13,22,26] | $N$ | 1 | $1^\dagger$ | $q$-type | selective |
| | $\sqrt{N}$ | $\sqrt{N}$ | $1^\dagger$ | | |
| [40,17] | $N$ | 1 | $1^\dagger$ | subgroup decision | selective |
| [25] | $N^2$ | 1 | $1^\dagger$ | $k$-Lin, $k \geq 1$ | adaptive |
| [14,35] | $\sqrt{N}$ | $\sqrt{N}$ | $\sqrt{N}$ | $k$-Lin, $k \geq 1$ | adaptive |
| [41] | $N^{1/3}$ | $N^{1/3}$ | $N^{1/3}$ | bi-$k$-Lin*, $k \geq 2$ | adaptive |
| this work | 1 | $\sqrt{N}$ | $\sqrt{N}$ | $k$-Lin, $k \geq 1$ | adaptive |

**Fig. 1.** Comparison with prior pairing-based broadcast encryption schemes for broadcast sets of size at most $N$, where $|\mathsf{mpk}|, |\mathsf{ct}|, |\mathsf{sk}|$ refer to number of group elements, ignoring $O(1)$ factors. Note that $|\mathsf{ct}|$ ignores the contribution from the set $S$, which is "public". $^\dagger$ Here, decryption requires knowledge of $\mathsf{mpk}$ in addition to $\mathsf{sk}$. $^*$ Here, bi-$k$-Lin (bilateral $k$-Lin) is a strengthening of $k$-Lin.

**ABE from Linear CDS.** We start by describing a broad class of pairing-based ABE derived from conditional disclosure of secrets (CDS) [6,27,39]. A CDS for a predicate $\mathsf{P}$ comprises three functions $c = c_x, k = k_y, d = d_{x,y}$ such that

- for all $x, y$ such that $\mathsf{P}(x, y) = 1$, for all $\mathbf{w}, \alpha$, we have $d(c(\mathbf{w}), k(\alpha, \mathbf{w})) = \alpha$;
- for all $x, y$ such that $\mathsf{P}(x, y) = 0$, the joint distribution $(c(\mathbf{w}), k(\alpha, \mathbf{w}))$ perfectly hide $\alpha$ for a random $\mathbf{w}$.

We say that a CDS is linear, if the three functions $c, k, d$ are linear over $\mathbb{Z}_p$. Starting from a linear CDS with $\mathbf{w} = (w_1, \ldots, w_n) \in \mathbb{Z}_p^n$, we can derive an ABE for the same predicate as follows [6,39]:[4]

$$\begin{aligned} \mathsf{mpk} &= [w_1, \ldots, w_n]_1, [\alpha]_T \\ \mathsf{ct} &= [c(s_0 w_1, \ldots, s_0 w_n),\ s_0]_1, [s_0 \alpha]_T \cdot M \\ \mathsf{sk} &= [k(\alpha, w_1 r_0, \ldots, w_n r_0),\ r_0]_2 \end{aligned} \tag{1}$$

where $c, k$ are linear functions. Decryption recovers $[s_0 \alpha]_T$ using

$$d(\overbrace{[c(s_0 w_1, \ldots, s_0 w_n) \cdot r_0]_T}^{=c(s_0 w_1 r_0, \ldots, s_0 w_n r_0)}, \overbrace{[s_0 \cdot k(\alpha, w_1 r_0, \ldots, w_n r_0)]_T}^{=k(s_0 \alpha, s_0 w_1 r_0, \ldots, s_0 w_n r_0)})$$

where $d$ is computed "in the exponent".

Looking ahead, we show how to construct an unbounded ABE for $\mathsf{P}$ with

$$|\mathsf{mpk}| = O(1),\ |\mathsf{ct}| = O(|c| + n),\ |\mathsf{sk}| = O(|k| + n)$$

where $|c|, |k|$ denote the output lengths of $c, k$ respectively. Combining this with the linear CDS for broadcast in [35] where $|c| = |k| = n = O(\sqrt{N})$ yields our unbounded broadcast encryption.

[4] Readers may interpret a linear CDS as a pair encoding [6,39] if the latter is more familiar.

**Previous Compiler.** The previous works of [19,34,36] show how to reduce the size of mpk to a constant for restricted classes of $c$. The compiler implicit in these works is sufficient for constructing KP-ABE schemes for boolean formula where $c$ is the projection function, but not broadcast encryption where $c$ exploits the full power of linearity to obtain small ciphertexts. The compiler works as follows: replace

$$\begin{aligned}[s_0 w_i]_1 &\mapsto [s_0 v + s_i(u_1 + i u_2)]_1 \\ [w_i r_0]_2 &\mapsto [v r_i]_2\end{aligned}$$

and append $[s_i]_1$ to ct and $[r_i,\ (u_1 + iu_2) r_i]_2$ to sk.

$$\begin{aligned}\mathsf{mpk} &= [v,\ u_1,\ u_2]_1, [\alpha]_T \\ \mathsf{ct} &= [c(s_0 v + s_1(u_1 + u_2), \ldots, s_0 v + s_n(u_1 + n u_2)), s_0,\ s_1, \ldots, s_n]_1, [s_0\alpha]_T \cdot M \\ \mathsf{sk} &= [k(\alpha, v r_1, \ldots, v r_n),\ \{\, r_i,\ (u_1 + i u_2) r_i \,\}_{i\in[n]}]_2\end{aligned}$$

Here, decryption recovers $[s_0\alpha]_T$ using

$$d\big(\, [c(s_0 v r_1, \ldots, s_0 v r_n)]_T, \overbrace{[k(s_0\alpha, s_0 v r_1, \ldots, s_0 v r_n)]_T}^{=e([s_0]_1, [k(\alpha, r_1, \ldots, r_n)]_2)} \,\big)$$

In order to compute the first input to $d$ in the above equation, we need to first compute $[c(\{\, (s_0 v + s_i(u_1 + iu_2)) r_i \,\}_{i\in[n]})]_T$. This steps only works when $c$ is the projection function, so that we can compute $[c(t_1 r_1, \ldots, t_n r_n)]_T$ given just $[c(t_1, \ldots, t_n)]_1, \{\, [r_i]_2 \,\}_{i\in[n]}$, where $t_i = s_0 v + s_i(u_1 + iu_2)$.[5] However, the function $c$ underlying the linear CDS for size $O(\sqrt{N})$ broadcast [35] is not a projection function.

**Our Compiler.** We present a new transformation that works for any linear function $c$. As a warm-up, we present a simple transformation that is insecure: we start with (1) and replace

$$\begin{aligned}[s_0 w_i]_1 &\mapsto [s_i v_1]_1 \\ [w_i r_0]_2 &\mapsto [v_2 r_i]_2\end{aligned}$$

and append $[s_i]_1$ and $[s_0 v]_1$ to ct and $[r_i]_2$ and $[v r_0]_2$ to sk.

$$\begin{aligned}\mathsf{mpk} &= [v_1,\ v_2]_1, [\alpha]_T \\ \mathsf{ct} &= [c(s_1 v_1, \ldots, s_n v_1),\ s_0,\ s_1, \ldots, s_n,\ s_0 v_2]_1, [s_0\alpha]_T \cdot M \\ \mathsf{sk} &= [k(\alpha, v_2 r_1, \ldots, v_2 r_n),\ r_0,\ r_1, \ldots, r_n,\ v_1 r_0]_2\end{aligned}$$

Decryption first computes

$$\begin{aligned}&[c(s_0 v_2 r_1, \ldots, s_0 v_2 r_n)]_T \\ &= e([c(s_1 v_1, \ldots, s_n v_1)]_1,\ [r_0]_2) \cdot c(\{\, [s_0 v_2 \cdot r_i - s_i \cdot v_1 r_0]_T \,\}_{i\in[n]})\end{aligned}$$

[5] As a concrete example, we can compute $(t_1 r_1, t_2 r_2)$ given $(t_1, t_2), r_1, r_2$ but we cannot compute $t_1 r_1 + t_2 r_2$ given $t_1 + t_2, r_1, r_2$.

and then computes $[s_0\alpha]_T = d([c(s_0v_2r_1,\ldots,s_0v_2r_n)]_T,\ [k(s_0\alpha, s_0v_2r_1,\ldots,s_0v_2 r_n)]_T)$. Note that decryption now works for any linear function $c$. However, the scheme is insecure because an adversary can compute the expression on the LHS of the preceding equation for any reordering of the inputs $s_0v_2r_1,\ldots,s_0v_2r_n$ to $c$. The attack arises because an adversary can compute $[s_0v_2 \cdot r_j - s_i \cdot v_1r_0]_T$ for any $i, j$. To prevent this attack, we introduce masking terms similar to the previous compiler where-in we further replace

$$[s_0v_2]_1 \mapsto \{\,[s_0v_2 + s_i(u_1 + iu_2)]_1\,\}_{i\in[n]}$$
$$[v_1r_0]_2 \mapsto \{\,[v_1r_0 + (u_1 + iu_2)r_i]_2\,\}_{i\in[n]}$$

Decryption proceeds as before, except we compute

$$s_0v_2 \cdot r_i - s_iv_1 \cdot r_0 = \overbrace{(s_0v_2 + s_i(u_1 + iu_2))}^{\mathsf{ct}} \cdot \overbrace{r_i}^{\mathsf{sk}} - \overbrace{s_i}^{\mathsf{ct}} \cdot \overbrace{(v_1r_0 + (u_1 + iu_2)r_i)}^{\mathsf{sk}}$$

That is, our new transformation is given by:

$$\begin{aligned} \mathsf{mpk} &= [v_1,\, v_2,\, u_1,\, u_2]_1, [\alpha]_T \\ \mathsf{ct} &= [c(s_1v_1,\ldots,s_nv_1),\, s_0,\, \{\, s_i,\, s_0v_2 + s_i(u_1 + iu_2)\,\}_{i\in[n]}]_1, [s_0\alpha]_T \cdot M \quad (2) \\ \mathsf{sk} &= [k(\alpha, v_2r_1,\ldots,v_2r_n),\, r_0,\, \{\, r_i,\, v_1r_0 + (u_1 + iu_2)r_i\,\}_{i\in[n]}]_2 \end{aligned}$$

Observe that we cannot efficiently compute $[s_0v_2 \cdot r_j - s_iv_1 \cdot r_0]_T$ for $i \neq j$ from the above elements. The underlying security mechanism here is essentially the same as Boneh-Boyen IBE [12] (also used in the previous compiler), where $[s_0\alpha]_T$ is not efficiently computable from,

$$\mathsf{ct} = [s_0,\, s_0(u_1 + iu_2)]_1, \quad \mathsf{sk} = [r_0, \alpha + r_0(u_1 + ju_2)]_2$$

for $i \neq j$. As with the previous compiler, we increase both ciphertext and key size by $O(n)$ group elements. We note that correctness works even if $v_1 = v_2$; the reason we use independent $v_1, v_2$ is for security.

## 2.2 Security Overview

The security proof follows the dual system encryption methodology, which comprises of (i) computational steps that rely on the $k$-Lin assumption and are independent of the linear CDS $c, k, d$, as well as (ii) an information theoretic step that exploits the security guarantee of the linear CDS.[6] We begin by outlining the key computational and information theoretic arguments that are novel in this work.

**Entropy Expansion.** We can start with the proof techniques in [19], where they showed statements of the form:

$$\left\{ \begin{array}{l} [s_0,\, s_i,\, s_0v + s_i(u_1 + iu_2)]_1, \\ [r_i,\, vr_i,\, (u_1 + iu_2)r_i]_2 \end{array} \right\}_{i\in[N]} \approx_c \left\{ \begin{array}{l} [s_0,\, s_i,\, s_0w_i + s_iu_i]_1, \\ [r_i,\, w_ir_i,\, u_ir_i]_2 \end{array} \right\}_{i\in[N]}$$

[6] The reason for working with information-theoretic security here is that (perfect) selective security implies adaptive security.

where on the RHS $u_1, \ldots, u_N, w_1, \ldots, w_N \leftarrow \mathbb{Z}_p$. We note that the distributions $[s_0, \{ s_i, c_i \}_{i\in[n]}]_1, [\{ r_i, d_i', d_i \}_{i\in[n]}]_2$ on both sides satisfy the consistency check $c_i \cdot r_i = s_i \cdot d_i + s_0 \cdot d_i'$ (which can be verified using a pairing).

In our setting, we want a statement with extra terms involving $v_2, r_0$ on the LHS:

$$\left\{ \begin{matrix} [s_0,\, s_i,\, s_i v_1, s_0 v_2 + s_i(u_1 + i u_2)]_1, \\ [r_0,\, r_i,\, v_2 r_i,\, v_1 r_0 + (u_1 + i u_2) r_i]_2 \end{matrix} \right\}_{i\in[N]} \approx_c \left\{ \begin{matrix} [s_0,\, s_i,\, s_i w_i,\, s_0 w_i' + s_i u_i']_1, \\ [r_0,\, r_i,\, w_i' r_i,\, w_i r_0 + u_i' r_i]_2 \end{matrix} \right\}_{i\in[N]} \quad (3)$$

Two remarks to help the reader parse the above statement:

- The distributions $[s_0, \{ s_i, c_i', c_i \}_{i\in[n]}]_1, [r_0, \{ r_i, d_i', d_i \}_{i\in[n]}]_2$ on both sides satisfy the consistency check $c_i \cdot r_i + c_i' \cdot r_0 = s_i \cdot d_i + s_0 \cdot d_i'$.[7]
- Setting $(u_i', w_i, w_i')$ on the RHS to be $(u_1 + i u_2, v_1, v_2)$ yields the LHS.

Applying the original entropy expansion lemma to the LHS of (3), we have:

$$\text{LHS of(3)} \approx_c \left\{ \begin{matrix} [s_0,\, s_i,\, s_i v_1,\, s_0 w_i' + s_i u_i']_1, \\ [r_0,\, r_i,\, w_i' r_i,\, v_1 r_0 + u_i' r_i]_2 \end{matrix} \right\}_{i\in[N]}$$

Next, we have by DDH $[s_i, s_i v_1]_1 \approx_c [s_i, s_i w_i]_1$ to obtain the RHS of (3).

**Information-Theoretic Step.** In order to motivate the information-theoretic step, observe that applying (3) to our scheme in (2) yields:

$$(\mathsf{ct}, \mathsf{sk}) \approx_c \begin{matrix} [c(s_1 w_1, \ldots, s_n w_n),\, s_0,\, \{ s_i,\, s_0 w_i' + s_i u_i' \}_{i\in[n]}]_1, [s_0 \alpha]_T \cdot M \\ [k(\alpha, w_1' r_1, \ldots, w_n' r_n),\, r_0,\, \{ r_i,\, w_i r_0 + u_i' r_i \}_{i\in[n]}]_2 \end{matrix} \quad (4)$$

Note that this above statement holds for any $(\mathsf{ct}, \mathsf{sk})$ pair (even if $\mathsf{P}(x, y) = 1$) and only uses the fact that $c, k$ compute linear functions.

Next, we want to argue that the RHS of (4) perfectly hides $M$ whenever $\mathsf{P}(x, y) = 0$. It suffices to show that for all $s_0, s_1, \ldots, s_n, r_0, r_1, \ldots, r_n \neq 0$, for all $\alpha$ and for all $x, y$ s.t. $\mathsf{P}(x, y) = 0$, the distributions

$$\begin{aligned} &c(s_1 w_1, \ldots, s_n w_n), \{ s_0 w_i' + s_i u_i' \}_{i\in[n]} \\ &k(\alpha, w_1' r_1, \ldots, w_n' r_n),\ \{ w_i r_0 + u_i' r_i \}_{i\in[n]} \\ &w_i, w_i', u_i' \leftarrow \mathbb{Z}_p, i \in [n] \end{aligned}$$

perfectly hide $\alpha$. As a sanity check, observe that if $s_0 = s_1 = \cdots = s_n = r_0 = r_1 = \cdots = r_n = 1$ and $w_i = w_i'$, then the statement follows readily from linear CDS security, since $u_i'$ perfectly masks $w_i = w_i'$. In the more general setting, it is sufficient to show that the following distributions hide $\alpha$:

$$\begin{aligned} &c(s_1 w_1, \ldots, s_n w_n) \cdot r_0, \{ (s_0 w_i' + s_i u_i') \cdot r_i \}_{i\in[n]} \\ &s_0 \cdot k(\alpha, w_1' r_1, \ldots, w_n' r_n),\ \{ s_i \cdot (w_i r_0 + u_i' r_i) \}_{i\in[n]} \end{aligned}$$

[7] If we set $v_1 = v_2 = v$, then there would be $O(n^2)$ additional consistency checks given by $c_i' \cdot r_j = s_i \cdot d_j'$ for all $i, j$, which are violated on the RHS.

With additional linear algebra (similar to that used for decryption), and also using $w_i, u'_i$ to mask $w'_i$, this boils down to arguing that $\alpha$ is perfectly hidden given

$$c(s_0 w'_1 r_1, \ldots, s_0 w'_n r_n)$$
$$k(s_0\alpha, s_0 w'_1 r_1, \ldots, s_0 w'_n r_n)$$

The latter follows readily from linear CDS security.

### 2.3 Instantiation in Prime-Order Groups

Following [18,28], we start with our ABE scheme in (2), sample $\mathbf{A}_1 \leftarrow \mathbb{Z}_p^{3k\times k}, \mathbf{B} \leftarrow \mathbb{Z}_p^{k\times(k+1)}$, and carry out the following substitutions:

$$\begin{array}{llllll} g_1 & \mapsto [\mathbf{A}_1]_1, & h_1 & \mapsto [\mathbf{B}]_2 & & \\ \alpha & \mapsto \mathbf{k} \in \mathbb{Z}_p^{3k} & v_1, v_2, u_1, u_2 & \mapsto \mathbf{V}_1, \mathbf{V}_2, \mathbf{U}_1, \mathbf{U}_2 \in \mathbb{Z}_p^{(k+1)\times 3k} & & \\ s_0, s_i & \mapsto \mathbf{s}_0, \mathbf{s}_i \in \mathbb{Z}_p^k, & r_0, r_i & \mapsto \mathbf{r}_0, \mathbf{r}_i \in \mathbb{Z}_p^k & & \\ [s_i]_1 & \mapsto [\mathbf{A}_1\mathbf{s}_i^\top]_1, & [r_i]_2 & \mapsto [\mathbf{r}_i\mathbf{B}]_2 & & \\ [s_i v_j]_1 & \mapsto [\mathbf{V}_j\mathbf{A}_1\mathbf{s}_i^\top]_1, & [v_j r_i]_2 & \mapsto [\mathbf{r}_i\mathbf{B}\mathbf{V}_j]_2, & [s_0\alpha]_T & \mapsto [\mathbf{k}\mathbf{A}\mathbf{s}_0^\top]_T \end{array} \tag{5}$$

The scheme is as follows:

$$\mathsf{mpk} = ([\mathbf{A}_1, \mathbf{U}_1\mathbf{A}_1, \mathbf{U}_2\mathbf{A}_1, \mathbf{V}_1\mathbf{A}_1, \mathbf{V}_2\mathbf{A}_1]_1, [\mathbf{k}\mathbf{A}_1]_T)$$
$$\mathsf{ct} = \begin{pmatrix} c([\mathbf{V}_1\mathbf{A}_1\mathbf{s}_1^\top, \ldots, \mathbf{V}_1\mathbf{A}_1\mathbf{s}_n^\top]_1) \\ [\mathbf{A}_1\mathbf{s}_0^\top, \{\mathbf{A}_1\mathbf{s}_i^\top, \mathbf{V}_2\mathbf{A}_1\mathbf{s}_0^\top + (\mathbf{U}_1 + i\mathbf{U}_2)\mathbf{A}_1\mathbf{s}_i^\top\}_{i\in[n]}]_1,\ [\mathbf{k}\mathbf{A}\mathbf{s}_0^\top]_T \cdot M \end{pmatrix}$$
$$\mathsf{sk} = (k([\mathbf{k}, \mathbf{r}_1\mathbf{B}\mathbf{V}_2, \ldots, \mathbf{r}_n\mathbf{B}\mathbf{V}_2]_2), [\mathbf{r}_0\mathbf{B}, \{\mathbf{r}_i\mathbf{B}, \mathbf{r}_0\mathbf{B}\mathbf{V}_1 + \mathbf{r}_i\mathbf{B}(\mathbf{U}_1 + i\mathbf{U}_2)\}_{i\in[n]}]_2)$$

**Proof Overview.** The security proof then uses the following sequence of games. We additionally sample $\mathbf{A}_2, \mathbf{A}_2^{\|} \leftarrow \mathbb{Z}_p^{3k\times k}$ conditioned on $\mathbf{A}_2^{\|\top}\mathbf{A}_1 = \mathbf{O}$ and $\mathbf{A}_2^{\|\top}\mathbf{A}_2 = \mathbf{I}_k$.

- $\mathsf{H}_0$: ABE security game where the adversary sees one ciphertext and $Q$ secret keys.
- $\mathsf{H}_1$: we switch the ciphertext and $Q$ secret keys to the "expanded" distribution where we replace

$$\mathbf{A}_1\mathbf{s}_0^\top, \ldots, \mathbf{A}\mathbf{s}_n^\top \mapsto \mathbf{c}_0^\top, \ldots, \mathbf{c}_n^\top \leftarrow \mathrm{span}(\mathbf{A}_1, \mathbf{A}_2)$$
$$\mathbf{U}_1 + i\mathbf{U}_2 \mapsto \mathbf{U}_1 + i\mathbf{U}_2 + \mathbf{U}'_i$$
$$\mathbf{V}_1, \mathbf{V}_2 \mapsto \mathbf{V}_1 + \mathbf{W}_i, \mathbf{V}_2 + \mathbf{W}'_i$$

where $\mathbf{U}'_i, \mathbf{W}_i, \mathbf{W}'_i \leftarrow \mathrm{span}(\mathbf{A}_2^{\|\top})$. That is,

$$\mathsf{ct} = \begin{pmatrix} c([(\mathbf{V}_1 + \mathbf{W}_1)\mathbf{c}_1^\top, \ldots, (\mathbf{V}_1 + \mathbf{W}_n)\mathbf{c}_n^\top]_1) \\ [\mathbf{c}_0^\top, \{\mathbf{c}_i^\top, (\mathbf{V}_2 + \mathbf{W}'_i)\mathbf{c}_0^\top + (\mathbf{U}_1 + i\mathbf{U}_2 + \mathbf{U}'_i)\mathbf{c}_i^\top\}_{i\in[n]}]_1,\ [\mathbf{k}\mathbf{c}_0^\top]_T \cdot M \end{pmatrix}$$
$$\mathsf{sk} = \begin{pmatrix} k([\mathbf{k}, \mathbf{r}_1\mathbf{B}(\mathbf{V}_2 + \mathbf{W}'_1), \ldots, \mathbf{r}_n\mathbf{B}(\mathbf{V}_2 + \mathbf{W}'_n)]_2) \\ [\mathbf{r}_0\mathbf{B}, \{\mathbf{r}_i\mathbf{B}, \mathbf{r}_0\mathbf{B}(\mathbf{V}_1 + \mathbf{W}_i) + \mathbf{r}_i\mathbf{B}(\mathbf{U}_1 + i\mathbf{U}_2 + \mathbf{U}'_i)\}_{i\in[n]}]_2 \end{pmatrix}$$

- $\mathsf{H}_2$: we switch the $Q$ secret keys to the semi-functional distribution where we replace $\mathbf{k}$ in with $\mathbf{k}+\mathbf{z}$ where $\mathbf{z} \leftarrow \mathrm{span}(\mathbf{A}_2^{\|^\top})$ is freshly sampled across all $Q$ keys. That is,

$$\mathsf{sk} = \begin{pmatrix} k([\mathbf{k}+\mathbf{z}, \mathbf{r}_1\mathbf{B}(\mathbf{V}_2+\mathbf{W}'_1), \ldots, \mathbf{r}_n\mathbf{B}(\mathbf{V}_2+\mathbf{W}'_n)]_2) \\ [\mathbf{r}_0\mathbf{B}, \{\mathbf{r}_i\mathbf{B}, \mathbf{r}_0\mathbf{B}(\mathbf{V}_1+\mathbf{W}_i)+\mathbf{r}_i\mathbf{B}(\mathbf{U}_1+i\mathbf{U}_2+\mathbf{U}'_i)\}_{i\in[n]}]_2 \end{pmatrix}$$

$\mathsf{H}_0 \approx_c \mathsf{H}_1$ relies on our new entropy expansion lemma. Then, $\mathsf{H}_1 \approx_c \mathsf{H}_2$ is essentially the proof of the bounded scheme (except we don't need to switch the ciphertext to a "semi-functional" distribution). Concretely, we switch the keys one by one from expanded to semi-functional:

$$\begin{aligned} &\begin{pmatrix} k([\mathbf{k}, \mathbf{r}_1\mathbf{B}(\mathbf{V}_2+\mathbf{W}'_1), \ldots, \mathbf{r}_n\mathbf{B}(\mathbf{V}_2+\mathbf{W}'_n)]_2) \\ [\mathbf{r}_0\mathbf{B}, \{\mathbf{r}_i\mathbf{B}, \mathbf{r}_0\mathbf{B}(\mathbf{V}_1+\mathbf{W}_i)+\mathbf{r}_i\mathbf{B}(\mathbf{U}_1+i\mathbf{U}_2+\mathbf{U}'_i)\}_{i\in[n]}]_2 \end{pmatrix} \\ \approx_c &\begin{pmatrix} k([\mathbf{k}, \mathbf{d}_1(\mathbf{V}_2+\mathbf{W}'_1), \ldots, \mathbf{d}_n(\mathbf{V}_2+\mathbf{W}'_n)]_2) \\ [\mathbf{d}_0, \{\mathbf{d}_i, \mathbf{d}_0(\mathbf{V}_1+\mathbf{W}_i)+\mathbf{d}_i(\mathbf{U}_1+i\mathbf{U}_2+\mathbf{U}'_i)\}_{i\in[n]}]_2 \end{pmatrix} \\ \approx_s &\begin{pmatrix} k([\mathbf{k}+\mathbf{z}, \mathbf{d}_1(\mathbf{V}_2+\mathbf{W}'_1), \ldots, \mathbf{d}_n(\mathbf{V}_2+\mathbf{W}'_n)]_2) \\ [\mathbf{d}_0, \{\mathbf{d}_i, \mathbf{d}_0(\mathbf{V}_1+\mathbf{W}_i)+\mathbf{d}_i(\mathbf{U}_1+i\mathbf{U}_2+\mathbf{U}'_i)\}_{i\in[n]}]_2 \end{pmatrix} \\ \approx_c &\begin{pmatrix} k([\mathbf{k}+\mathbf{z}, \mathbf{r}_1\mathbf{B}(\mathbf{V}_2+\mathbf{W}'_1), \ldots, \mathbf{r}_n\mathbf{B}(\mathbf{V}_2+\mathbf{W}'_n)]_2) \\ [\mathbf{r}_0\mathbf{B}, \{\mathbf{r}_i\mathbf{B}, \mathbf{r}_0\mathbf{B}(\mathbf{V}_1+\mathbf{W}_i)+\mathbf{r}_i\mathbf{B}(\mathbf{U}_1+i\mathbf{U}_2+\mathbf{U}'_i)\}_{i\in[n]}]_2 \end{pmatrix} \\ &\text{where} \mathbf{d}_0, \mathbf{d}_1, \ldots, \mathbf{d}_n \leftarrow \mathbb{Z}_p^{k+1} \end{aligned}$$

The two $\approx_c$ above follows from the $k$-Lin assumption; the $\approx_s$ uses the information-theoretic argument outlined earlier. Finally, we can argue that in $\mathsf{H}_2$, the message $M$ is perfectly hidden.

## 2.4 Unbounded KP-ABE

We construct unbounded KP-ABE for span program following previous schemes, e.g. [30]. Here, we adopt the simpler notation used in Sect. 2.1. The idea is that we will compute shares $\{\alpha_j\}$ of $\alpha$ during key generation, and during decryption, we will first compute $[s_0\alpha_j]_T$ for all authorized shares $\alpha_j$ using our new broadcast encryption, upon which we can recover $[s_0\alpha]_T$.

In more detail, we extend our compiler to obtain unbounded KP-ABE for span program from a linear CDS for broadcast encryption. In the KP-ABE, a ciphertext for an attribute set $X \subseteq [N]$ can be decrypted by a secret key for span program $f = (\mathbf{M}, \rho)$ when $f$ accepts $X$. Recall that $\rho$ maps the rows of $\mathbf{M}$ to $[N]$, and $f$ accepts $X$ when $(1, 0, \ldots, 0)$ lies in the space spanned by all the $i$-th rows of $\mathbf{M}$ such that $\rho(i) \in X$. The KP-ABE from our compiler achieves

$$|\mathsf{mpk}'| = O(1),\ |\mathsf{ct}'| = |\mathsf{ct}| + O(|\mathsf{mpk}|),\ |\mathsf{sk}'| = (|\mathsf{sk}| + O(|\mathsf{mpk}|)) \cdot |f|$$

where $|\mathsf{mpk}|, |\mathsf{ct}|, |\mathsf{sk}|$ are the sizes of the corresponding elements in the underlying ABE scheme from the linear CDS for broadcast. We describe our KP-ABE for span program:

- mpk and ct are the same as those for the original compiler in (2).
- To generate a KP-ABE secret key for $f = (\mathbf{M}, \rho)$, we first compute shares $(\sigma_1, \ldots, \sigma_{|f|})$ of $\alpha$ for the span program $f$ (if $f$ accepts $X$, then we can recover $\alpha$ given the shares $\{\sigma_j\}_{j:\rho(j)\in X}$). The KP-ABE key comprises $|f|$ keys for our compiler in (2) corresponding to master secret key $\sigma_j$ and index $\rho(j)$, for all $j \in [|f|]$.
- Decryption computes $[s_0\sigma_j]_T$ for all $j$ satisfying $\rho(j) \in X$, upon which it can reconstruct $[s_0\alpha]_T$ "in the exponent".

Concretely, we have

$$\begin{aligned}\mathsf{mpk} &= [v_1,\, v_2,\, u_1,\, u_2]_1, [\alpha]_T\\ \mathsf{ct} &= [c_X(s_1v_1, \ldots, s_nv_1), s_0,\, \{\, s_i,\, s_0v_2 + s_i(u_1 + iu_2)\,\}_{i\in[n]}]_1, [s_0\alpha]_T \cdot M\\ \mathsf{sk} &= \{\, [k_{\rho(j)}(\sigma_j, v_2r_{1,j}, \ldots, v_2r_{n,j}),\, \{\, r_{i,j},\, v_1r_{0,j} + (u_1 + iu_2)r_{i,j}\,\}_{i\in[n]}]_2\,\}_{j\in[|f|]}\end{aligned}$$

Instantiating the above scheme with the linear CDS for broadcast with size $O(\sqrt{N})$ by [35] results in our unbounded KP-ABE for span program with

$$|\mathsf{mpk}| = O(1),\ |\mathsf{ct}| = O(\sqrt{N}),\ |\mathsf{sk}| = O(\sqrt{N} \cdot |f|)$$

### 2.5 Paper Organization

Section 3 provides preliminaries, which includes our new bilinear entropy expansion lemma and the definition of linear CDS. Section 4 provides how to compile a linear CDS scheme with unbounded security to an unbounded ABE scheme. Section 5 provides how to convert a linear CDS scheme with bounded security to one with unbounded security. The section also shows how to instantiate our new broadcast encryption scheme:

1. We apply the conversion to the linear CDS scheme for quadratic functions with bounded security by [35] to obtain the linear CDS scheme with unbounded security.
2. Then, we apply the compiler in Sect. 4 to the linear CDS for quadratic functions with unbounded security to achieve the unbounded ABE scheme for quadratic functions.
3. Finally, we achieve our broadcast encryption scheme from the unbounded ABE scheme for quadratic functions by a standard embedding technique.

Section 6 shows how to extend our broadcast encryption scheme to the KP-ABE scheme in a semi-generic way.

## 3 Preliminaries

**Notations.** For integers $m \geq 0, n \geq 1$, $[n]$ denotes $\{1,\ldots,n\}$ and $[m,n]$ denotes $\{m,\ldots,n\}$. For a set of column vectors $\mathbf{v}_1^\top,\ldots,\mathbf{v}_n^\top$ over $\mathbb{Z}_p$, $\mathsf{ColSpan}(\mathbf{v}_1^\top,\ldots,\mathbf{v}_n^\top) = \{\mathbf{v}^\top \mid \exists c_1,\ldots,c_n \in \mathbb{Z}_p, \mathbf{v}^\top = \sum_{i\in[n]} c_i\mathbf{v}_i^\top\}$. We sometimes denote a set of $n$ columns of matrix $\mathbf{V}$ with width $n$ by just $\mathbf{V}$. RowSpan is similarly defined for a set of row vectors. For matrices $\mathbf{M},\mathbf{N}$ over $\mathbb{Z}_p$ such that $\mathbf{NM}$ is defined, $e([\mathbf{M}]_1,[\mathbf{N}]_2)$ is the pairing operation to compute $[\mathbf{NM}]_T$. For distributions $X, Y$ indexed by the security parameter $\lambda$, $X \approx_c Y$ and $X \approx_s Y$ means $X$ and $Y$ are computationally and statistically indistinguishable, respectively. $X \equiv Y$ means $X$ and $Y$ are distributed the same.

**Definition 3.1 (Bilinear Groups).** A description of bilinear groups $\mathbb{G}=(p,G_1,G_2,G_T,g_1,g_2,e)$ consist of a prime $p$, cyclic groups $G_1,G_2,G_T$ of order $p$, generators $g_1$ and $g_2$ of $G_1$ and $G_2$ respectively, and a bilinear map $e: G_1 \times G_2 \to G_T$, which has two properties.

- (Bilinearity): $\forall h_1 \in G_1, h_2 \in G_2, a,b \in \mathbb{Z}_p, e(h_1^a,h_2^b) = e(h_1,h_2)^{ab}$.
- (Non-degeneracy): For generators $g_1$, $g_2$; $g_T = e(g_1,g_2)$ is a generator of $G_T$.

A bilinear group generator $\mathcal{G}_{\mathsf{BG}}(1^\lambda)$ takes a security parameter $1^\lambda$ and outputs a description of bilinear groups $\mathbb{G}$ with a $\Omega(\lambda)$-bit prime $p$.

**Definition 3.2 (MDDH Assumption [23]).** Let $\eta \in \{1,2\}$, $j,k,\ell \in \mathbb{N}$ such that $j > k$. We consider the following distribution: $\mathbb{G} \leftarrow \mathcal{G}_{\mathsf{BG}}(1^\lambda)$, $\mathbf{A} \leftarrow \mathbb{Z}_p^{j\times k}$, $\mathbf{T}_0 \leftarrow \mathsf{ColSpan}(\mathbf{A})^{1\times\ell}$, $\mathbf{T}_1 \leftarrow \mathbb{Z}_p^{j\times\ell}$. We say that the $\mathrm{MDDH}_k$ assumption holds with respect to $\mathcal{G}_{\mathsf{BG}}$ if $(\mathbb{G},[\mathbf{A},\mathbf{T}_0]_\eta) \approx_c (\mathbb{G},[\mathbf{A},\mathbf{T}_1]_\eta)$ for all $\eta, j, \ell$. Throughout the paper, we use $k$ only for the MDDH parameter and often omit $k$, i.e., we just denote the MDDH assumption. The $k$-lin assumption implies the $\mathrm{MDDH}_k$ assumption.

**Definition 3.3 (Unbounded Attribute-Based Encryption).** Let $\mathsf{P} = \{\mathsf{P}_L\}_{L\in\mathcal{L}}$ be a predicate family where $\mathsf{P}_L : \mathcal{X}_L \times \mathcal{Y}_L \to \{0,1\}$, and $\mathcal{L}$ is a parameter space.[8] An unbounded attribute-based encryption (ABE) scheme for a predicate $\mathsf{P}$ consists of the four algorithms:

$\mathsf{Setup}(1^\lambda)$**:** It takes a security parameter $1^\lambda$ and outputs a public key $\mathsf{mpk}$ and a master secret key $\mathsf{msk}$.

$\mathsf{Enc}(\mathsf{mpk},(x,L),M)$**:** It takes $\mathsf{mpk}$, an attribute $x \in \mathcal{X}_L$, the parameter $L$, and a message $M \in \mathcal{M}$ as inputs, and outputs a ciphertext $\mathsf{ct}$. (Note that we let $\mathcal{M}$ be specified in $\mathsf{mpk}$.)

$\mathsf{KeyGen}(\mathsf{mpk},\mathsf{msk},(y,L))$**:** It takes $\mathsf{mpk},\mathsf{msk}$, an attribute $y \in \mathcal{Y}_L$, and $L$ as inputs, and outputs a secret key $\mathsf{sk}$.

$\mathsf{Dec}(\mathsf{mpk},\mathsf{ct},\mathsf{sk},x,y,L)$**:** It takes $\mathsf{mpk},\mathsf{ct},\mathsf{sk},x,y,L$ as inputs, and outputs a message $M'$ or a symbol $\perp$.

[8] $L$ specifies such as the attribute length in ABE for span program, the user set size in broadcast encryption (namely $N$ in Sect. 1.1).

**Correctness.** An ABE scheme is correct if it satisfies the following condition. For all $\lambda \in \mathbb{N}$, $L \in \mathcal{L}$, $x \in \mathcal{X}_L$, $y \in \mathcal{Y}_L$ such that $\mathsf{P}_L(x, y) = 1$, and $M \in \mathcal{M}$, we have

$$\Pr\left[ M = M' : \begin{array}{l} (\mathsf{mpk}, \mathsf{msk}) \leftarrow \mathsf{Setup}(1^\lambda) \\ \mathsf{ct} \leftarrow \mathsf{Enc}(\mathsf{mpk}, (x, L), M) \\ \mathsf{sk} \leftarrow \mathsf{KeyGen}(\mathsf{mpk}, \mathsf{msk}, (y, L)) \\ M' = \mathsf{Dec}(\mathsf{mpk}, \mathsf{ct}, \mathsf{sk}, x, y, L) \end{array} \right] = 1$$

**Security.** An ABE scheme satisfies adaptive unbounded security if it satisfies the following condition. That is, the advantage of $\mathcal{A}$ defined as follows is negligible in $\lambda$ for all stateful PPT adversary $\mathcal{A}$:

$$\mathsf{Adv}_{\mathcal{A}}^{\mathsf{ABE}} = \left| \Pr\left[ \beta = \beta' : \begin{array}{l} \beta \leftarrow \{0,1\} \\ (\mathsf{mpk}, \mathsf{msk}) \leftarrow \mathsf{Setup}(1^\lambda) \\ ((x, L^*), M_0, M_1) \leftarrow \mathcal{A}^{\mathsf{KeyGen}(\mathsf{mpk}, \mathsf{msk}, \cdot)}(\mathsf{mpk}) \\ \mathsf{ct} \leftarrow \mathsf{Enc}(\mathsf{mpk}, (x, L^*), M_\beta) \\ \beta' \leftarrow \mathcal{A}^{\mathsf{KeyGen}(\mathsf{mpk}, \mathsf{msk}, \cdot)}(\mathsf{ct}) \end{array} \right] - \frac{1}{2} \right|$$

where $x \in \mathcal{X}_{L^*}$, and all $(y_j, L_j)_{j \in [Q]}$ on which $\mathcal{A}$ queries $\mathsf{KeyGen}$ must satisfy the following:

- $y_j \in \mathcal{Y}_{L_j}$;
- $L^* \neq L_j$ or $L^* = L_j \wedge \mathsf{P}_{L_j}(x, y_j) = 0$.

Semi-adaptive unbounded security is similarly defined as adaptive unbounded security except that the $\mathsf{KeyGen}$ oracle is not available before $\mathcal{A}$ outputs the challenge $((x, L^*), M_0, M_1)$.[9]

*Remark 3.1.* Definition 3.3 is slightly different from the standard ABE definition (e.g. [6,30]). Specifically, in the standard ABE definition, $\mathsf{Setup}$ takes $L$ and includes it in $\mathsf{mpk}$. $\mathsf{Enc}$ and $\mathsf{KeyGen}$ take only $x \in \mathcal{X}_L$ and $y \in \mathcal{Y}_L$ as attribute, respectively; we then allow the adversary to specify different $L$'s in the security game. That is, we capture unbounded broadcast encryption and KP-ABE wherein the adversary asks for secret keys corresponding to different values of $N$ (i.e., different bounds on the size of the recipient set, or policies with different input lengths), some of which may be incompatible with the value of $N$ specified in the challenge ciphertext. Our definition is more general than the standard definition, and thus an ABE scheme that satisfies Definition 3.3 can be easily converted to the scheme that satisfies the standard ABE definition. We use our definition to capture ABE schemes where $\mathsf{Setup}$ solely depends on $1^\lambda$ but not on $L$.

We define linear conditional disclosure of secrets (linear CDS) [27] as follows, which is essentially the same as predicate encoding [39] and the special case of pair encoding [6].

[9] Semi-adaptive security is slightly stronger than selective security [20,29].

**Definition 3.4 (Linear Conditional Disclosure of Secrets (Linear CDS)).** Let $\mathsf{P} = \{\mathsf{P}_L\}_{L\in\mathcal{L}}$ be a family of predicates $\mathsf{P}_L : \mathcal{X}_L \times \mathcal{Y}_L \to \{0,1\}$ parametrized by $L \in \mathcal{L}$, where $\mathcal{L}$ is a parameter space. A linear CDS for $\mathsf{P}$ consists of a function $\mathsf{p} : \mathcal{L} \to \mathbb{N}$ and the three deterministic polynomial-time algorithms:

- $\mathsf{EncC}(x, L) \to c_x$. On input $x \in \mathcal{X}_L$ and $L \in \mathcal{L}$, $\mathsf{EncC}$ outputs a linear function $c_x : \mathbb{Z}_p^{\mathsf{p}(L)} \to \mathbb{Z}_p^{m_1}$. That is, $c_x$ specifies coefficients $c_{i,j} \in \mathbb{Z}_p$ for $(i, j) \in [\mathsf{p}(L)] \times [m_1]$ such that
$$c_x(\mathbf{w}) = \Big\{ \sum_{i\in[\mathsf{p}(L)]} c_{i,j} w_i \Big\}_{j\in[m_1]}$$
where $\mathbf{w} = (w_1, \ldots, w_{\mathsf{p}(L)}) \in \mathbb{Z}_p^{\mathsf{p}(L)}$.
- $\mathsf{EncK}(y, L) \to k_y$. On input $y \in \mathcal{Y}_L$ and $L$, $\mathsf{EncK}$ outputs a linear function $k_y : \mathbb{Z}_p^{\mathsf{p}(L)+1} \to \mathbb{Z}_p^{m_2}$. That is, $k_y$ specifies coefficients $k_{i,j} \in \mathbb{Z}_p$ for $(i, j) \in [0, \mathsf{p}(L)] \times [m_2]$ such that
$$k_y(\alpha, \mathbf{w}) = \Big\{ k_{0,j}\alpha + \sum_{i\in[\mathsf{p}(L)]} k_{i,j} w_i \Big\}_{j\in[m_2]}$$
where $\alpha \in \mathbb{Z}_p$, $\mathbf{w} \in \mathbb{Z}_p^{\mathsf{p}(L)}$.
- $\mathsf{cRec}(x, y, L) \to d_{x,y}$. On input $L$, $x \in \mathcal{X}_L$, and $y \in \mathcal{Y}_L$, $\mathsf{cRec}$ outputs a linear function $d_{x,y} : \mathbb{Z}_p^{m_1+m_2} \to \mathbb{Z}_p$. That is, $d_{x,y}$ specifies coefficients $d_1, \ldots, d_{m_1}$, $d'_1, \ldots, d'_{m_2} \in \mathbb{Z}_p$, and we have
$$d_{x,y}(\mathbf{c}, \mathbf{k}) = \sum_{i\in[m_1]} d_i c_i + \sum_{i\in[m_2]} d'_i k_i$$
where $\mathbf{c} = (c_1, \ldots, c_{m_1}) \in \mathbb{Z}_p^{m_1}$, $\mathbf{k} = (k_1, \ldots, k_{m_2}) \in \mathbb{Z}_p^{m_2}$.

**Correctness.** For $x \in \mathcal{X}_L$ and $y \in \mathcal{Y}_L$, let $c_x \leftarrow \mathsf{EncC}(x, L)$, $k_y \leftarrow \mathsf{EncK}(y, L)$, and $d_{x,y} \leftarrow \mathsf{cRec}(x, y, L)$. If $\mathsf{P}_L(x, y) = 1$, then it symbolically holds that $d_{x,y}(c_x(\mathbf{w}), k_y(\alpha, \mathbf{w})) = \alpha$.

**Bounded Security.** Let $x, y, c_x, k_y$ be as above. If $\mathsf{P}_L(x, y) = 0$, the following distributions are identical:
$$(c_x(\mathbf{w}), k_y(\alpha, \mathbf{w})) \quad \text{and} \quad (c_x(\mathbf{w}), k_y(0, \mathbf{w}))$$
where $\alpha \leftarrow \mathbb{Z}_p, \mathbf{w} \leftarrow \mathbb{Z}_p^{\mathsf{p}(L)}$.

**Unbounded Security.** For $L, L' \in \mathcal{L}$, $x \in \mathcal{X}_L$ and $y \in \mathcal{Y}_{L'}$, let $c_x \leftarrow \mathsf{EncC}(x, L)$, $k_y \leftarrow \mathsf{EncK}(y, L')$. If $L \neq L'$ or $L = L' \wedge \mathsf{P}_L(x, y) = 0$, the following distributions are identical:
$$(c_x(\mathbf{w}), k_y(\alpha, \mathbf{w}')) \quad \text{and} \quad (c_x(\mathbf{w}), k_y(0, \mathbf{w}'))$$
where $\alpha \leftarrow \mathbb{Z}_p, \mathbf{w} \leftarrow \mathbb{Z}_p^{\mathsf{p}(L)}$, and $\mathbf{w}'$ consists of the first $\mathsf{p}(L')$ elements of $\mathbf{w}$ if $\mathsf{p}(L) \geq \mathsf{p}(L')$, and otherwise, $\alpha \leftarrow \mathbb{Z}_p, \mathbf{w}' \leftarrow \mathbb{Z}_p^{\mathsf{p}(L')}$, and $\mathbf{w}$ consists of the first $\mathsf{p}(L)$ elements of $\mathbf{w}'$.

### 3.1 Bilinear Entropy Expansion Lemma

We recall the bilinear entropy expansion lemma [19] and introduce new variants to make it applicable to our constructions.

**Definition 3.5 (Dual Matrices).** Let $\ell, \ell_1, \ell_2, \ell_3$ be positive integers such that $\ell = \ell_1 + \ell_2 + \ell_3$. Let $\mathbf{A}_1 \in \mathbb{Z}_p^{\ell \times \ell_1}$, $\mathbf{A}_2 \in \mathbb{Z}_p^{\ell \times \ell_2}$, $\mathbf{A}_3 \in \mathbb{Z}_p^{\ell \times \ell_3}$ be matrices such that $\mathbf{A} = (\mathbf{A}_1 || \mathbf{A}_2 || \mathbf{A}_3) \in \mathbb{Z}_p^{\ell \times \ell}$ is invertible. We define $\mathbf{A}_1^{||} \in \mathbb{Z}_p^{\ell \times \ell_1}$, $\mathbf{A}_2^{||} \in \mathbb{Z}_p^{\ell \times \ell_2}$, $\mathbf{A}_3^{||} \in \mathbb{Z}_p^{\ell \times \ell_3}$ as $(\mathbf{A}_1^{||} || \mathbf{A}_2^{||} || \mathbf{A}_3^{||}) = (\mathbf{A}^\top)^{-1}$. Then, we have

$$\mathbf{A}_j^{||^\top} \mathbf{A}_i = \begin{cases} \mathbf{O} & (i \neq j) \\ \mathbf{I}_{\ell_i} & (i = j) \end{cases}$$

**Lemma 3.1 (Bilinear Entropy Expansion Lemma** [19, Lemma 8]**).** *Let $n, \ell_1, \ell_2, \ell_3, \ell_W, \ell$ be positive integers such that $\ell_1, \ell_3, \ell_W \geq k$, and $\ell = \ell_1 + \ell_2 + \ell_3$. Sample $\mathbf{A}_i \leftarrow \mathbb{Z}_p^{\ell \times \ell_i}$ and define $\mathbf{A}_i^{||}$ for $i \in \{1, 2, 3\}$ following Definition 3.5. The original entropy expansion lemma asserts that*

$$\left\{ \begin{array}{l} \mathsf{aux} : \mathbb{G}, [\mathbf{A}_1, \mathbf{U}_1\mathbf{A}_1, \mathbf{U}_2\mathbf{A}_1, \mathbf{V}_2\mathbf{A}_1]_1 \\ \mathsf{ct} : [\mathbf{c}_0^\top]_1, \{[\mathbf{c}_i^\top, \mathbf{V}_2\mathbf{c}_0^\top + (\mathbf{U}_1 + i\mathbf{U}_2)\mathbf{c}_i^\top]_2\}_{i \in [n]} \\ \mathsf{sk} : \{[\mathbf{D}_i, \mathbf{D}_i\mathbf{V}_2, \mathbf{D}_i(\mathbf{U}_1 + i\mathbf{U}_2)]_2\}_{i \in [n]} \end{array} \right\}$$
$$\approx_c \left\{ \begin{array}{l} \mathsf{aux} : \mathbb{G}, [\mathbf{A}_1, \mathbf{U}_1\mathbf{A}_1, \mathbf{U}_2\mathbf{A}_1, \mathbf{V}_2\mathbf{A}_1]_1 \\ \mathsf{ct} : [\mathbf{c}_0^\top]_1, \{[\mathbf{c}_i^\top, (\mathbf{V}_2 + \mathbf{W}_i')\mathbf{c}_0^\top + (\mathbf{U}_1 + i\mathbf{U}_2 + \mathbf{U}_i')\mathbf{c}_i^\top]_1\}_{i \in [n]} \\ \mathsf{sk} : \{[\mathbf{D}_i, \mathbf{D}_i(\mathbf{V}_2 + \mathbf{W}_i'), \mathbf{D}_i(\mathbf{U}_1 + i\mathbf{U}_2 + \mathbf{U}_i')]_2\}_{i \in [n]} \end{array} \right\}$$

*where $\mathbb{G} \leftarrow \mathcal{G}_{\mathsf{BG}}(1^\lambda)$, $\mathbf{U}_1, \mathbf{U}_2, \mathbf{V}_2 \leftarrow \mathbb{Z}_p^{\ell_W \times \ell}$, $\mathbf{D}_i \leftarrow \mathbb{Z}_p^{\ell_W \times \ell_W}$, and $\mathbf{W}_i', \mathbf{U}_i' \leftarrow \mathsf{RowSpan}(\mathbf{A}_2^{||^\top})^{\ell_1 \times 1}$ for $i \in [n]$. In the LHS, $\mathbf{c}_0^\top, \mathbf{c}_i \leftarrow \mathsf{ColSpan}(\mathbf{A}_1)$ while in the RHS, $\mathbf{c}_0^\top, \mathbf{c}_i^\top \leftarrow \mathsf{ColSpan}(\mathbf{A}_1, \mathbf{A}_2)$. This lemma is implied by the MDDH assumption.*

For our compiler, we use the following variant of the entropy expansion lemma.

**Lemma 3.2 (Our Bilinear Entropy Expansion Lemma).** *Let $n, \ell_1, \ell_2, \ell_3, \ell_W, \ell$ be positive integers such that $\ell_1, \ell_2, \ell_3, \ell_W \geq k$, and $\ell = \ell_1 + \ell_2 + \ell_3$. Sample $\mathbf{A}_i \leftarrow \mathbb{Z}_p^{\ell \times \ell_i}$ and define $\mathbf{A}_i^{||}$ for $i \in \{1, 2, 3\}$ following Definition 3.5. Our entropy expansion lemma asserts that*

$$\left\{ \begin{array}{l} \mathsf{aux} : \mathbb{G}, [\mathbf{A}_1, \mathbf{U}_1\mathbf{A}_1, \mathbf{U}_2\mathbf{A}_1, \mathbf{V}_1\mathbf{A}_1, \mathbf{V}_2\mathbf{A}_1]_1 \\ \mathsf{ct} : [\mathbf{c}_0^\top]_1, \{[\mathbf{c}_i^\top, \mathbf{V}_1\mathbf{c}_i^\top, \mathbf{V}_2\mathbf{c}_0^\top + (\mathbf{U}_1 + i\mathbf{U}_2)\mathbf{c}_i^\top]_2\}_{i \in [n]} \\ \mathsf{sk} : [\mathbf{D}_0]_2, \{[\mathbf{D}_i, \mathbf{D}_i\mathbf{V}_2, \mathbf{D}_0\mathbf{V}_1 + \mathbf{D}_i(\mathbf{U}_1 + i\mathbf{U}_2)]_2\}_{i \in [n]} \end{array} \right\}$$
$$\approx_c \left\{ \begin{array}{l} \mathsf{aux} : \mathbb{G}, [\mathbf{A}_1, \mathbf{U}_1\mathbf{A}_1, \mathbf{U}_2\mathbf{A}_1, \mathbf{V}_1\mathbf{A}_1, \mathbf{V}_2\mathbf{A}_1]_1 \\ \mathsf{ct} : [\mathbf{c}_0^\top]_1, \{[\mathbf{c}_i^\top, (\mathbf{V}_1 + \mathbf{W}_i)\mathbf{c}_i^\top, (\mathbf{V}_2 + \mathbf{W}_i')\mathbf{c}_0^\top + (\mathbf{U}_1 + i\mathbf{U}_2 + \mathbf{U}_i')\mathbf{c}_i^\top]_1\}_{i \in [n]} \\ \mathsf{sk} : [\mathbf{D}_0]_2, \{[\mathbf{D}_i, \mathbf{D}_i(\mathbf{V}_2 + \mathbf{W}_i'), \mathbf{D}_0(\mathbf{V}_1 + \mathbf{W}_i) + \mathbf{D}_i(\mathbf{U}_1 + i\mathbf{U}_2 + \mathbf{U}_i')]_2\}_{i \in [n]} \end{array} \right\} \quad (6)$$

*where* $\mathbb{G} \leftarrow \mathcal{G}_{\mathsf{BG}}(1^\lambda)$, $\mathbf{U}_1, \mathbf{U}_2, \mathbf{V}_1, \mathbf{V}_2 \leftarrow \mathbb{Z}_p^{\ell_W \times \ell}$, $\mathbf{D}_0, \mathbf{D}_i \leftarrow \mathbb{Z}_p^{\ell_W \times \ell_W}$, *and* $\mathbf{W}_i, \mathbf{W}'_i, \mathbf{U}'_i \leftarrow \mathsf{RowSpan}(\mathbf{A}_2^{\|\top})^{\ell_1 \times 1}$ *for* $i \in [n]$. *In the LHS,* $\mathbf{c}_0^\top, \mathbf{c}_i \leftarrow \mathsf{ColSpan}(\mathbf{A}_1)$ *while in the RHS,* $\mathbf{c}_0^\top, \mathbf{c}_i^\top \leftarrow \mathsf{ColSpan}(\mathbf{A}_1, \mathbf{A}_2)$. *The lemma is implied by the MDDH assumption.*

We present the proof of Lemma 3.2 in the full version.

In contrast to [19, Lemma 8] (i.e., Lemma 3.1), we need a $Q$-fold version of Lemma 3.2 for our ABE constructions. Intuitively, when we plug the lemma into the dual system proof, the reduction needs to simulate $Q$ secret keys from $\mathsf{sk}$ in the instance of the entropy expansion lemma. In the case of [19, Lemma 8], generating $Q$ sets of random vectors $\{\mathbf{d}_{0,j}, \mathbf{d}_{i,j}\}_{j \in [Q]}$ from $\mathbf{D}_0, \mathbf{D}_i$ is easy by multiplying random vectors $\mathbf{r}_{0,j}, \mathbf{r}_{i,j}$ from the left, respectively, for $j \in [Q]$. In our case, however, this does not work due to the term $[\mathbf{D}_0(\mathbf{V}_1 + \mathbf{W}_i) + \mathbf{D}_i(\mathbf{U}_1 + i\mathbf{U}_2 + \mathbf{U}'_i)]_2$ in $\mathsf{sk}$. This is why we formally define and prove the $Q$-fold version of Lemma 3.2.

**Lemma 3.3 (Our Bilinear Entropy Expansion Lemma ($Q$-fold)).** *Let* $n, \ell_1, \ell_2, \ell_3, \ell_W, \ell, Q$ *be positive integers such that* $\ell_1, \ell_2, \ell_3, \ell_W \geq k$, *and* $\ell = \ell_1 + \ell_2 + \ell_3$. *Sample* $\mathbf{A}_i \leftarrow \mathbb{Z}_p^{\ell \times \ell_i}$ *and define* $\mathbf{A}_i^{\|}$ *for* $i \in \{1, 2, 3\}$ *following Definition crefdef:dualm. The $Q$-fold entropy expansion lemma asserts that*

$$\left\{\begin{array}{l} \mathsf{aux}: \mathbb{G}, [\mathbf{A}_1, \mathbf{U}_1\mathbf{A}_1, \mathbf{U}_2\mathbf{A}_1, \mathbf{V}_1\mathbf{A}_1, \mathbf{V}_2\mathbf{A}_1]_1 \\ \mathsf{ct}: [\mathbf{c}_0^\top]_1, \{[\mathbf{c}_i^\top, \mathbf{V}_1\mathbf{c}_i^\top, \mathbf{V}_2\mathbf{c}_0^\top + (\mathbf{U}_1 + i\mathbf{U}_2)\mathbf{c}_i^\top]_2\}_{i \in [n]} \\ \mathsf{sk}: [\mathbf{D}_0]_2, \{[\mathbf{D}_i, \mathbf{D}_i\mathbf{V}_2, \mathbf{D}_0\mathbf{V}_1 + \mathbf{D}_i(\mathbf{U}_1 + i\mathbf{U}_2)]_2\}_{i \in [n]} \end{array}\right\}$$
$$\approx_c \left\{\begin{array}{l} \mathsf{aux}: \mathbb{G}, [\mathbf{A}_1, \mathbf{U}_1\mathbf{A}_1, \mathbf{U}_2\mathbf{A}_1, \mathbf{V}_1\mathbf{A}_1, \mathbf{V}_2\mathbf{A}_1]_1 \\ \mathsf{ct}: [\mathbf{c}_0^\top]_1, \{[\mathbf{c}_i^\top, (\mathbf{V}_1 + \mathbf{W}_i)\mathbf{c}_i^\top, (\mathbf{V}_2 + \mathbf{W}'_i)\mathbf{c}_0^\top + (\mathbf{U}_1 + i\mathbf{U}_2 + \mathbf{U}'_i)\mathbf{c}_i^\top]_1\}_{i \in [n]} \\ \mathsf{sk}: [\mathbf{D}_0]_2, \{[\mathbf{D}_i, \mathbf{D}_i(\mathbf{V}_2 + \mathbf{W}'_i), \mathbf{D}_0(\mathbf{V}_1 + \mathbf{W}_i) + \mathbf{D}_i(\mathbf{U}_1 + i\mathbf{U}_2 + \mathbf{U}'_i)]_2\}_{i \in [n]} \end{array}\right\} \quad (7)$$

*where* $\mathbb{G} \leftarrow \mathcal{G}_{\mathsf{BG}}(1^\lambda)$, $\mathbf{U}_1, \mathbf{U}_2, \mathbf{V}_1, \mathbf{V}_2 \leftarrow \mathbb{Z}_p^{\ell_W \times \ell}$, $\mathbf{D}_0, \mathbf{D}_i \leftarrow \mathbb{Z}_p^{Q \times \ell_W}$, *and* $\mathbf{W}_i, \mathbf{W}'_i, \mathbf{U}'_i \leftarrow \mathsf{RowSpan}(\mathbf{A}_2^{\|\top})^{\ell_1 \times 1}$ *for* $i \in [n]$. *In the LHS,* $\mathbf{c}_0^\top, \mathbf{c}_i \leftarrow \mathsf{ColSpan}(\mathbf{A}_1)$ *while in the RHS,* $\mathbf{c}_0^\top, \mathbf{c}_i^\top \leftarrow \mathsf{ColSpan}(\mathbf{A}_1, \mathbf{A}_2)$. *The lemma is implied by the MDDH assumption.*

We present the proof of Lemma 3.3 in the full version.

# 4 Unbounded ABE from Linear CDS

In this section, we present our compiler from a linear CDS to an unbounded ABE scheme. Our compiler is generic in a sense that it works with any linear CDS. Our ABE scheme is secure if the underlying linear CDS satisfies unbounded security.

## 4.1 Construction

Let $\mathsf{P} = \{\mathsf{P}_L\}_{L \in \mathcal{L}}$ be a predicate family and $\Gamma = (\mathsf{p}, \mathsf{EncC}, \mathsf{EncK}, \mathsf{cRec})$ be a linear CDS for $\mathsf{P}_L : \mathcal{X}_L \times \mathcal{Y}_L \to \{0, 1\}$ where $L \in \mathcal{L}$.

$\mathsf{Setup}(1^\lambda)$: It outputs mpk and msk as follows.

$$\mathbf{A}_1 \leftarrow \mathbb{Z}_p^{3k\times k},\ \mathbf{B} \leftarrow \mathbb{Z}_p^{k\times(k+1)},\ \mathbf{U}_1, \mathbf{U}_2, \mathbf{V}_1, \mathbf{V}_2 \leftarrow \mathbb{Z}_p^{(k+1)\times 3k},\ \mathbf{k} \leftarrow \mathbb{Z}_p^{3k}$$
$$\mathsf{mpk} = ([\mathbf{A}_1, \mathbf{U}_1\mathbf{A}_1, \mathbf{U}_2\mathbf{A}_1, \mathbf{V}_1\mathbf{A}_1, \mathbf{V}_2\mathbf{A}_1]_1, [\mathbf{k}\mathbf{A}_1]_T)$$
$$\mathsf{msk} = (\mathbf{k}, \mathbf{B}, \mathbf{U}_1, \mathbf{U}_2, \mathbf{V}_1, \mathbf{V}_2)$$

$\mathsf{Enc}(\mathsf{mpk}, (x, L), M)$: It takes mpk, $x \in \mathcal{X}_L$, $L \in \mathcal{L}$, and $M \in G_T$ as inputs, and outputs ct by computing as follows.

$$n = \mathsf{p}(L),\ c \leftarrow \mathsf{EncC}(x, L),\ \mathbf{s}_0, \mathbf{s}_1, \dots, \mathbf{s}_n \leftarrow \mathbb{Z}_p^k$$
$$\mathsf{ct} = \left( \begin{array}{l} \underbrace{c([\mathbf{V}_1\mathbf{A}_1\mathbf{s}_1^\top, \dots, \mathbf{V}_1\mathbf{A}_1\mathbf{s}_n^\top]_1)}_{\mathsf{ct}_1} \\ [\underbrace{\mathbf{A}_1\mathbf{s}_0^\top}_{\mathsf{ct}_2}, \{\underbrace{\mathbf{A}_1\mathbf{s}_i^\top}_{\mathsf{ct}_{3,i}}, \underbrace{\mathbf{V}_2\mathbf{A}_1\mathbf{s}_0^\top + (\mathbf{U}_1 + i\mathbf{U}_2)\mathbf{A}_1\mathbf{s}_i^\top}_{\mathsf{ct}_{4,i}}\}_{i\in[n]}]_1,\ \underbrace{[\mathbf{k}\mathbf{A}\mathbf{s}_0^\top]_T \cdot M}_{\mathsf{ct}_5} \end{array} \right) \tag{8}$$

$\mathsf{KeyGen}(\mathsf{mpk}, \mathsf{msk}, (y, L))$: It takes mpk, msk, $y \in \mathcal{Y}_L$, and $L$ as inputs, and outputs sk by computing as follows.

$$n = \mathsf{p}(L),\ k \leftarrow \mathsf{EncK}(y, L),\ \mathbf{r}_0, \mathbf{r}_1, \dots, \mathbf{r}_n \leftarrow \mathbb{Z}_p^k$$
$$\mathsf{sk} = (\underbrace{k([\mathbf{k}, \mathbf{r}_1\mathbf{B}\mathbf{V}_2, \dots, \mathbf{r}_n\mathbf{B}\mathbf{V}_2]_2)}_{\mathsf{sk}_1}, [\underbrace{\mathbf{r}_0\mathbf{B}}_{\mathsf{sk}_2}, \{\underbrace{\mathbf{r}_i\mathbf{B}}_{\mathsf{sk}_{3,i}}, \underbrace{\mathbf{r}_0\mathbf{B}\mathbf{V}_1 + \mathbf{r}_i\mathbf{B}(\mathbf{U}_1 + i\mathbf{U}_2)}_{\mathsf{sk}_{4,i}}\}_{i\in[n]}]_2) \tag{9}$$

$\mathsf{Dec}(\mathsf{mpk}, \mathsf{ct}, \mathsf{sk}, x, y, L)$: It takes mpk, ct, sk, $x$, $y$, $L$ such that $x \in \mathcal{X}_L$, $y \in \mathcal{Y}_L$, and $\mathsf{P}_L(x, y) = 1$. It computes $c \leftarrow \mathsf{EncC}(x, L)$, $k \leftarrow \mathsf{EncK}(y, L)$, $d \leftarrow \mathsf{cRec}(x, y, L)$ and

$$z_1 = e(\mathsf{ct}_1, \mathsf{sk}_2) - c(e(\mathsf{ct}_{3,1}, \mathsf{sk}_{4,1}), \dots, e(\mathsf{ct}_{3,n}, \mathsf{sk}_{4,n}))$$
$$z_2 = e(\mathsf{ct}_2, \mathsf{sk}_1) - k([0]_T, e(\mathsf{ct}_{4,1}, \mathsf{sk}_{3,1}), \dots, e(\mathsf{ct}_{4,n}, \mathsf{sk}_{3,n}))$$

where the operator $-$ denotes element-wise division of $G_T$ elements. Then outputs $\mathsf{ct}_5/d(z_1, z_2)$.

**Correctness.** Recall $e([\mathbf{M}]_1, [\mathbf{N}]_2) = [\mathbf{N}\mathbf{M}]_T$. In decryption, we have

$$\begin{aligned} e(\mathsf{ct}_1, \mathsf{sk}_2) &= [\mathbf{r}_0\mathbf{B} \cdot c(\mathbf{V}_1\mathbf{A}_1\mathbf{s}_1^\top, \dots, \mathbf{V}_1\mathbf{A}_1\mathbf{s}_n^\top)]_T \\ &= [c(\mathbf{r}_0\mathbf{B}\mathbf{V}_1\mathbf{A}_1\mathbf{s}_1^\top, \dots, \mathbf{r}_0\mathbf{B}\mathbf{V}_1\mathbf{A}_1\mathbf{s}_n^\top)]_T \\ e(\mathsf{ct}_{3,i}, \mathsf{sk}_{4,i}) &= [(\mathbf{r}_0\mathbf{B}\mathbf{V}_1 + \mathbf{r}_i\mathbf{B}(\mathbf{U}_1 + i\mathbf{U}_2))\mathbf{A}_1\mathbf{s}_i^\top]_T \end{aligned}$$

Hence, we have

$$\begin{aligned} z_1 &= \begin{bmatrix} c(\mathbf{r}_0\mathbf{B}\mathbf{V}_1\mathbf{A}_1\mathbf{s}_1^\top, \dots, \mathbf{r}_0\mathbf{B}\mathbf{V}_1\mathbf{A}_1\mathbf{s}_n^\top) \\ - c((\mathbf{r}_0\mathbf{B}\mathbf{V}_1 + \mathbf{r}_1\mathbf{B}(\mathbf{U}_1 + \mathbf{U}_2))\mathbf{A}_1\mathbf{s}_1^\top, \dots, (\mathbf{r}_0\mathbf{B}\mathbf{V}_1 + \mathbf{r}_n\mathbf{B}(\mathbf{U}_1 + n\mathbf{U}_2))\mathbf{A}_1\mathbf{s}_n^\top) \end{bmatrix}_T \\ &= [c(-\mathbf{r}_1\mathbf{B}(\mathbf{U}_1 + \mathbf{U}_2)\mathbf{A}_1\mathbf{s}_1^\top, \dots, -\mathbf{r}_n\mathbf{B}(\mathbf{U}_1 + n\mathbf{U}_2)\mathbf{A}_1\mathbf{s}_n^\top)]_T \end{aligned}$$

which follows from the fact the $c$ is a linear function. Similarly, it also holds that

$$z_2 = [k(\mathbf{k}\mathbf{A}_1\mathbf{s}_0^\top, -\mathbf{r}_1\mathbf{B}(\mathbf{U}_1 + \mathbf{U}_2)\mathbf{A}_1\mathbf{s}_1^\top, \ldots, -\mathbf{r}_n\mathbf{B}(\mathbf{U}_1 + n\mathbf{U}_2)\mathbf{A}_1\mathbf{s}_n^\top)]_T$$

Hence, thanks to the correctness of linear CDS $\Gamma$, we have $d(z_1, z_2) = [\mathbf{k}\mathbf{A}_1\mathbf{s}_0^\top]_T$.

**Parameter Sizes.** In the above construction, the sizes of $\mathsf{mpk}, \mathsf{ct}, \mathsf{sk}$ are as follows:

$$|\mathsf{mpk}| = O(1), \quad |\mathsf{ct}| = O(n + m_1), \quad |\mathsf{sk}| = O(n + m_2)$$

where $n = \mathsf{p}(L)$, $m_1, m_2$ are the number of $\mathbb{Z}_p$ elements in $c(\mathbf{w}), k(\alpha, \mathbf{w})$, respectively. The above sizes hide $\mathsf{poly}(\lambda)$ factors.

### 4.2 Security

**Theorem 4.1.** *Suppose the MDDH assumption holds and the linear CDS $\Gamma$ satisfies unbounded security. Then, our scheme in Sect. 4.1 satisfies adaptive unbounded security as per Definition 3.3.*

*Proof.* We define various distributions of ciphertext and secret key. As global parameters, we sample $\mathbf{A}_2, \mathbf{A}_3 \leftarrow \mathbb{Z}_p^{3k\times k}$, define $\mathbf{A}_1^{\|}, \mathbf{A}_2^{\|}, \mathbf{A}_3^{\|}$ following Definition 3.5, and also sample $\mathbf{W}_i, \mathbf{W}'_i, \mathbf{U}'_i \leftarrow \mathsf{RowSpan}(\mathbf{A}_2^{\|\top})^{(k+1)\times 1}$ for $i \in [n']$ where $n'$ is sufficiently large. Let $\mathbf{a}_{2,1}^{\|\top}$ be the first column of $\mathbf{A}_2^{\|}$. For a ciphertext,

- Normal: As defined in Eq. (8).
- Expanded normal (E-normal): It is generates as

$$n = \mathsf{p}(L),\ c \leftarrow \mathsf{EncC}(x, L),\ \mathbf{c}_0, \mathbf{c}_1, \ldots, \mathbf{c}_n \leftarrow \mathsf{ColSpan}(\mathbf{A}_1, \mathbf{A}_2)$$
$$\mathsf{ct} = \begin{pmatrix} c([(\mathbf{V}_1 + \mathbf{W}_1)\mathbf{c}_1^\top, \ldots, (\mathbf{V}_1 + \mathbf{W}_n)\mathbf{c}_n^\top]_1) \\ [\mathbf{c}_0^\top, \{\mathbf{c}_i^\top, (\mathbf{V}_2 + \mathbf{W}'_i)\mathbf{c}_0^\top + (\mathbf{U}_1 + i\mathbf{U}_2 + \mathbf{U}'_i)\mathbf{c}_i^\top\}_{i\in[n]}]_1,\ [\mathbf{k}\mathbf{c}_0^\top]_T \cdot M \end{pmatrix} \tag{10}$$

For a secret key

- Normal: As defined in Eq. (9).
- E-normal: It is generated as

$$n = \mathsf{p}(L),\ k \leftarrow \mathsf{EncK}(y, L),\ \mathbf{r}_0, \mathbf{r}_1, \ldots, \mathbf{r}_n \leftarrow \mathbb{Z}_p^k$$
$$\mathsf{sk} = \begin{pmatrix} k([\mathbf{k}, \mathbf{r}_1\mathbf{B}(\mathbf{V}_2 + \mathbf{W}'_1), \ldots, \mathbf{r}_n\mathbf{B}(\mathbf{V}_2 + \mathbf{W}'_n)]_2) \\ [\mathbf{r}_0\mathbf{B}, \{\mathbf{r}_i\mathbf{B}, \mathbf{r}_0\mathbf{B}(\mathbf{V}_1 + \mathbf{W}_i) + \mathbf{r}_i\mathbf{B}(\mathbf{U}_1 + i\mathbf{U}_2 + \mathbf{U}'_i)\}_{i\in[n]}]_2 \end{pmatrix} \tag{11}$$

- Pseudo normal (P-normal): It is generated as

$$n = \mathsf{p}(L),\ k \leftarrow \mathsf{EncK}(y, L),\ \mathbf{d}_0, \mathbf{d}_1, \ldots, \mathbf{d}_n \leftarrow \mathbb{Z}_p^{k+1}$$
$$\mathsf{sk} = \begin{pmatrix} k([\mathbf{k}, \mathbf{d}_1(\mathbf{V}_2 + \mathbf{W}'_1), \ldots, \mathbf{d}_n(\mathbf{V}_2 + \mathbf{W}'_n)]_2) \\ [\mathbf{d}_0, \{\mathbf{d}_i, \mathbf{d}_0(\mathbf{V}_1 + \mathbf{W}_i) + \mathbf{d}_i(\mathbf{U}_1 + i\mathbf{U}_2 + \mathbf{U}'_i)\}_{i\in[n]}]_2 \end{pmatrix}$$

– Pseudo semi-functional (P-SF): It is generated as

$$n = \mathsf{p}(L),\ k \leftarrow \mathsf{EncK}(y, L),\ \mathbf{d}_0, \mathbf{d}_1, \ldots, \mathbf{d}_n \leftarrow \mathbb{Z}_p^{k+1},\ \mathbf{z} \leftarrow \mathsf{RowSpan}(\mathbf{a}_{2,1}^{\|})$$

$$\mathsf{sk} = \begin{pmatrix} k([\mathbf{k} + \mathbf{z}, \mathbf{d}_1(\mathbf{V}_2 + \mathbf{W}_1'), \ldots, \mathbf{d}_n(\mathbf{V}_2 + \mathbf{W}_n')]_2) \\ [\mathbf{d}_0, \{\mathbf{d}_i, \mathbf{d}_0(\mathbf{V}_1 + \mathbf{W}_i) + \mathbf{d}_i(\mathbf{U}_1 + i\mathbf{U}_2 + \mathbf{U}_i')\}_{i \in [n]}]_2 \end{pmatrix}$$

– Semi-functional (SF): It is generated as

$$n = \mathsf{p}(L),\ k \leftarrow \mathsf{EncK}(y, L),\ \mathbf{r}_0, \mathbf{r}_1, \ldots, \mathbf{r}_n \leftarrow \mathbb{Z}_p^{k},\ \mathbf{z} \leftarrow \mathsf{RowSpan}(\mathbf{a}_{2,1}^{\|})$$

$$\mathsf{sk} = \begin{pmatrix} k([\mathbf{k} + \mathbf{z}, \mathbf{r}_1\mathbf{B}(\mathbf{V}_2 + \mathbf{W}_1'), \ldots, \mathbf{r}_n\mathbf{B}(\mathbf{V}_2 + \mathbf{W}_n')]_2) \\ [\mathbf{r}_0\mathbf{B}, \{\mathbf{r}_i\mathbf{B}, \mathbf{r}_0\mathbf{B}(\mathbf{V}_1 + \mathbf{W}_i) + \mathbf{r}_i\mathbf{B}(\mathbf{U}_1 + i\mathbf{U}_2 + \mathbf{U}_i')\}_{i \in [n]}]_2 \end{pmatrix} \quad (12)$$

Note that for every P-SF and SF key, we sample a fresh $\mathbf{z}$.

We prove the theorem via a series of hybrids. Let $Q$ be the maximum number of secret key queries by the adversary.

- $\mathsf{H}_0$: The original security game.
- $\mathsf{H}_1$: Same as $\mathsf{H}_0$ except that the challenge ciphertext and all secret keys given to the adversary are E-normal.
- $\mathsf{H}_{2,j,1}$ for $j \in [Q]$: Same as $\mathsf{H}_1$ except that the first $j-1$ keys are SF, the $j$-th key is P-normal (the rest of the keys are E-normal).
- $\mathsf{H}_{2,j,2}$ for $j \in [Q]$: Same as $\mathsf{H}_{2,j,1}$ except that the $j$-th key is P-SF.
- $\mathsf{H}_{2,j,3}$ for $j \in [Q]$: Same as $\mathsf{H}_{2,j,2}$ except that the $j$-th key is SF.
- $\mathsf{H}_3$: Same as $\mathsf{H}_{2,Q,3}$ except that $\mathsf{ct}_5$ in the challenge ciphertext is randomly chosen from $G_T$.

The hybrids proceed as follows:

$$\mathsf{H}_0 \to \mathsf{H}_1 \to \mathsf{H}_{2,1,1} \to \mathsf{H}_{2,1,2} \to \mathsf{H}_{2,1,3} \to \mathsf{H}_{2,2,1} \to \cdots \to \mathsf{H}_{2,Q,3} \to \mathsf{H}_3$$

We prove the indistinguishability of each hybrid transition in the full version. Observe that the adversary's view in $\mathsf{H}_3$ is independent of the challenge bit $\beta$ and its advantage is 0. This concludes the proof. □

## 5 Unbounded Broadcast Encryption

In this section, we present how to instantiate an unbounded (indentity-based) broadcast encryption scheme with new parameters via our compiler in Sect. 4.1. First, we show that any linear CDS for P with bounded security can be converted to a linear CDS for P with unbounded security. Then, we apply the conversion to the linear CDS for non-zero quadratic polynomials with bounded security by [35] to achieve unbounded security. Using the compiler in Sect. 4.1, we can obtain an unbounded ABE scheme for non-zero quadratic polynomials. Finally, we achieve unbounded broadcast encryption with new parameters from the unbounded ABE for non-zero quadratic polynomials with a standard embedding technique. Our unbounded identity-based broadcast encryption can be similarly obtained except that we start with a linear CDS for zero quadratic polynomials.

### 5.1 From Bounded to Unbounded Security

A high level idea of the conversion is the conjunction with the IBE predicate [5] so that only the ciphertext and key encodings for the same $L$ can interact. Given a linear CDS $\Gamma = (\mathsf{p}, \mathsf{EncC}, \mathsf{EncK}, \mathsf{cRec})$ for $\mathsf{P}$ with bounded security, we can generically obtain a linear CDS $\Gamma' = (\mathsf{p}', \mathsf{EncC}', \mathsf{EncK}', \mathsf{cRec}')$ for $\mathsf{P}$ with unbounded security as follows (see Definition 3.4 for the security definition). We require that $L$ is taken from a space $\mathcal{L}^*$ such that $|\mathcal{L}^*| < p$ and can be embedded in $\mathbb{Z}_p$ by an injective map $\phi : \mathcal{L}^* \to \mathbb{Z}_p$.[10]

- $\mathsf{p}'(L) = \mathsf{p}(L) + 2$.
- $\mathsf{EncC}'(x, L) \to c'$: It runs $c \leftarrow \mathsf{EncC}(x, L)$ where $c : \mathbb{Z}_p^{\mathsf{p}(L)} \to \mathbb{Z}_p^{m_1}$. It outputs $c' : \mathbb{Z}_p^{\mathsf{p}(L)+2} \to \mathbb{Z}_p^{m_1+1}$ such that
$$c'(\mathbf{w}, u_1, u_2) = (c(\mathbf{w}), u_1 + \phi(L)u_2)$$
- $\mathsf{EncK}'(y, L) \to k'$: It runs $k \leftarrow \mathsf{EncK}(y, L)$ where $k : \mathbb{Z}_p^{\mathsf{p}(L)+1} \to \mathbb{Z}_p^{m_2}$. It outputs $k' : \mathbb{Z}_p^{\mathsf{p}(L)+3} \to \mathbb{Z}_p^{m_2}$ such that
$$k'(\alpha, \mathbf{w}, u_1, u_2) = k(\alpha - (u_1 + \phi(L)u_2), \mathbf{w})$$
- $\mathsf{cRec}'(x, y, L) \to d'$: It runs $d \leftarrow \mathsf{cRec}(x, y, L)$ and outputs $d' : \mathbb{Z}_p^{m_1+1+m_2+1} \to \mathbb{Z}_p$ such that
$$d'(\mathbf{c}, c_{m_1+1}, \mathbf{k}) = d(\mathbf{c}, \mathbf{k}) + c_{m_1+1}$$

**Lemma 5.1 (From Bounded to Unbounded Security).** *If $\Gamma$ satisfies correctness and bounded security, then $\Gamma'$ satisfies correctness and unbounded security.*

*Proof* Correctness is almost trivial from the definition, i.e.,
$$\begin{aligned} d'(\mathbf{c}, c_{m_1+1}, \mathbf{k}) =& d(\mathbf{c}, \mathbf{k}) + c_{m_1+1} \\ =& \alpha - (u_1 + \phi(L)u_2) + (u_1 + \phi(L)u_2) = \alpha \end{aligned}$$

For security, the unbounded security of $\Gamma'$ for the case $L = L' \wedge \mathsf{P}_L(x, y) = 0$ directly follows from the bounded security of $\Gamma$, so we consider the case $L \neq L'$. What we need to prove is
$$\left\{ \begin{matrix} (c(\mathbf{w}), u_1 + \phi(L)u_2) \\ k(\alpha - (u_1 + \phi(L')u_2), \mathbf{w}') \end{matrix} \right\} \equiv \left\{ \begin{matrix} (c(\mathbf{w}), u_1 + \phi(L)u_2) \\ k(0 - (u_1 + \phi(L')u_2), \mathbf{w}') \end{matrix} \right\}$$
where all variables are randomly taken from $\mathbb{Z}_p$. In this case, we have $\phi(L) \neq \phi(L')$, and thus $(u_1 + \phi(L)u_2, u_1 + \phi(L')u_2)$ is uniformly distributed in $\mathbb{Z}_p^2$. Thus, the above distributions are identical. □

[10] If $|\mathcal{L}| > p$, we can use collision resistant hashing from $\mathcal{L}$ to $\mathcal{L}^*$ such that $|\mathcal{L}^*| < p$ when we instantiate an unbounded ABE scheme from a linear CDS.

### 5.2 Unbounded ABE for Quadratic Polynomials

To construct unbounded ABE for (non-)zero quadratic polynomials, we define the predicate for quadratic polynomials as follows.

**Definition 5.1 (Quadratic Polynomials [35]).** A predicate family $\mathsf{P}^{\mathrm{NQP}} = \{\mathsf{P}_L^{\mathrm{NQP}}\}_{L\in\mathcal{L}}$ where $\mathsf{P}_L : \mathcal{X}_L \times \mathcal{Y}_L \to \{0,1\}$ for non-zero quadratic polynomials is given as follows.

$$\mathcal{L} = \mathbb{N}^2, \quad \mathcal{X}_{N_1,N_2} = \mathbb{Z}_p^{N_1\times N_2}, \quad \mathcal{Y}_{N_1,N_2} = \mathbb{Z}_p^{N_1} \times \mathbb{Z}_p^{N_2}$$
$$\mathsf{P}_{N_1,N_2}^{\mathrm{NQP}}(\mathbf{M},(\mathbf{x},\mathbf{y})) = 1 \Leftrightarrow \mathbf{x}\mathbf{M}\mathbf{y}^\top \neq 0$$

where $N_1, N_2 \in \mathbb{N}$, $\mathbf{M} \in \mathbb{Z}_p^{N_1\times N_2}$, $\mathbf{x} \in \mathbb{Z}_p^{N_1}$, $\mathbf{y} \in \mathbb{Z}_p^{N_2}$. A predicate family $\mathsf{P}^{\mathrm{ZQP}}$ for zero quadratic polynomials is the same as $\mathsf{P}^{\mathrm{NQP}}$ except that

$$\mathsf{P}_{N_1,N_2}^{\mathrm{ZQP}}(\mathbf{M},(\mathbf{x},\mathbf{y})) = 1 \Leftrightarrow \mathbf{x}\mathbf{M}\mathbf{y}^\top = 0$$

**Lemma 5.2 (Linear CDS for $\mathsf{P}^{\mathrm{NQP}}$ [35]).** *A linear CDS $\Gamma = (\mathsf{p}, \mathsf{EncC}, \mathsf{EncK}, \mathsf{cRec})$ for $\mathsf{P}^{NQP}$ was given by [35] as follows. This linear CDS satisfies correctness and bounded security as per Definition 3.4.*

- $\mathsf{p}(N_1,N_2) = N_1 + N_2$.
- $\mathsf{EncC}(\mathbf{M},(N_1,N_2)) \to c$: *Output $c$ such that*

$$c(\mathbf{w}) = \Big\{w_{i_1} + \sum_{i_2\in[N_2]} m_{i_1,i_2} w_{N_1+i_2}\Big\}_{i_1\in[N_1]}$$

  *where $\mathbf{w} = (w_1,\ldots,w_{N_1+N_2}) \in \mathbb{Z}_p^{N_1+N_2}$ and $\mathbf{M} = (m_{i_1,i_2})_{(i_1,i_2)\in[N_1]\times[N_2]}$.*
- $\mathsf{EncK}((\mathbf{x},\mathbf{y}),(N_1,N_2)) \to k$: *Output $k$ such that*

$$k(\alpha,\mathbf{w}) = \Big(\sum_{i_1\in[N_1]} x_{i_1} w_{i_1}, \{y_{i_2}\alpha + w_{N_1+i_2}\}_{i_2\in[N_2]}\Big)$$

  *where $\alpha \in \mathbb{Z}_p$, $\mathbf{x} = (x_1,\ldots,x_{N_1})$, and $\mathbf{y} = (y_1,\ldots,y_{N_2})$.*
- $\mathsf{cRec}(\mathbf{M},(\mathbf{x},\mathbf{y}),(N_1,N_2)) \to d$: *Output $d$ such that*

$$d(\mathbf{c},\mathbf{k}) = \frac{k_0 - \sum_{i_1\in[N_1]} x_{i_1}c_{i_1} + \sum_{(i_1,i_2)\in[N_1]\times[N_2]} x_{i_1} m_{i_1,i_2} k_{i_2}}{\mathbf{x}\mathbf{M}\mathbf{y}^\top}$$

  *where $\mathbf{c} = (c_1,\ldots,c_{N_1})$, $\mathbf{k} = (k_0,\ldots,k_{N_2})$.*

We can generically obtain a linear CDS for $\mathsf{P}^{\mathrm{ZQP}}$ by applying the generic negation [5] to the above linear CDS for $\mathsf{P}^{\mathrm{NQP}}$. However, the parameters of the converted linear CDS with $L = (N_1, N_2)$ will be

$$\mathsf{p}(N_1,N_2) = 2(N_1+N_2), \quad m_1 = N_1 + N_2, \quad m_2 = N_1 + N_2 + 1$$

We directly construct a more efficient linear CDS for $\mathsf{P}^{\mathrm{ZQP}}$ with the following parameters by slightly modifying the above linear CDS:

$$\mathsf{p}(N_1,N_2) = N_1 + N_2 + 1, \quad m_1 = N_1, \quad m_2 = N_2 + 1$$

**Lemma 5.3 (Linear CDS for** $\mathsf{P}^{\mathrm{NQP}}$**).** *A linear CDS* $\Gamma = (\mathsf{p}, \mathsf{EncC}, \mathsf{EncK}, \mathsf{cRec})$ *for* $\mathsf{P}^{ZQP}$ *can be constructed as follows. This linear CDS satisfies correctness and bounded security as per Definition 3.4.*

- $\mathsf{p}(N_1, N_2) = N_1 + N_2 + 1$.
- $\mathsf{EncC}(\mathbf{M}, (N_1, N_2)) \to c$: *Output* $c$ *such that*

$$c(\mathbf{w}) = \left\{ w_{i_1} + \sum_{i_2 \in [N_2]} m_{i_1,i_2} w_{N_1+i_2} \right\}_{i_1 \in [N_1]}$$

*where* $\mathbf{w} = (w_1, \ldots, w_{N_1+N_2+1}) \in \mathbb{Z}_p^{N_1+N_2+1}$ *and* $\mathbf{M} = (m_{i_1,i_2})_{(i_1,i_2)\in[N_1]\times[N_2]}$.
- $\mathsf{EncK}((\mathbf{x}, \mathbf{y}), (N_1, N_2)) \to k$: *Output* $k$ *such that*

$$k(\alpha, \mathbf{w}) = \left( \alpha + \sum_{i_1 \in [N_1]} x_{i_1} w_{i_1}, \{ y_{i_2} w_{N_1+n_2+1} + w_{N_1+i_2} \}_{i_2 \in [N_2]} \right)$$

*where* $\alpha \in \mathbb{Z}_p$, $\mathbf{x} = (x_1, \ldots, x_{N_1})$, *and* $\mathbf{y} = (y_1, \ldots, y_{N_2})$.
- $\mathsf{cRec}(\mathbf{M}, (\mathbf{x}, \mathbf{y}), (N_1, N_2)) \to d$: *Output* $d$ *such that*

$$d(\mathbf{c}, \mathbf{k}) = k_0 - \sum_{i_1 \in [N_1]} x_{i_1} c_{i_1} + \sum_{(i_1,i_2)\in[N_1]\times[N_2]} x_{i_1} m_{i_1,i_2} k_{i_2}$$

*where* $\mathbf{c} = (c_1, \ldots, c_{N_1})$, $\mathbf{k} = (k_0, \ldots, k_{N_2})$.

*proof of Lemma* 5.3. Correctness can be confirmed by doing a simple math. For security, we consider the following programming:

$$w_{N_1+i'_2} = \tilde{w}_{N_1+i'_2} - y_{i'_2} w_{N_1+n_2+1}, \quad w_{i_1} - \tilde{w}_{i_1} - \sum_{i_2 \in [N_2]} m_{i_1,i_2} w_{N_1+i_2}$$

for $(i_1, i'_2) \in [N_1] \times [N_2]$, where $\tilde{w}_{N_1+i'_2}, \tilde{w}_{i_1} \leftarrow \mathbb{Z}_p$. Then, we have

$$\begin{aligned} \{c(\mathbf{w}), k(\alpha, \mathbf{w})\} &= \{ \{\tilde{w}_{i_1}\}_{i_1 \in [N_1]}, (k_0, \{\tilde{w}_{N_1+i_2}\}_{i_2 \in [N_2]}) \ \} \\ &\equiv \{c(\mathbf{w}), k(0, \mathbf{w})\} \end{aligned}$$

where

$$k_0 = \alpha + \sum_{i_1 \in [N_1]} x_{i_1} \tilde{w}_{i_1} - \sum_{(i_1,i_2)\in[N_1]\times[N_2]} x_{i_1} m_{i_1,i_2} (\tilde{w}_{N_1+i_2} - y_{i_2} w_{N_1+n_2+1})$$

The equivalence follows from fact that $\sum_{(i_1,i_2)\in[N_1]\times[N_2]} x_{i_1} m_{i_1,i_2} y_{i_2} \neq 0$ and thus $k_0$ is randomly distributed in $\mathbb{Z}_p$ due to the entropy of $w_{N_1+N_2+1}$. □

We obtain unbounded ABE schemes for $\mathsf{P}^{\mathrm{NQP}}$ and $\mathsf{P}^{\mathrm{ZQP}}$ as follows.

**Corollary 5.1 (Unbounded ABE for $\mathsf{P}^{\mathrm{NQP}}$ and $\mathsf{P}^{\mathrm{ZQP}}$ ).** *We can construct unbounded ABE schemes (Definition 3.3) for $\mathsf{P}^{NQP}$ and $\mathsf{P}^{ZQP}$ (Definition 5.1) that satisfies adaptive unbounded security under the MDDH assumption. Furthermore, the sizes of* mpk, ct *for* $(\mathbf{M}, (N_1, N_2))$, *and* sk *for* $((\mathbf{x}, \mathbf{y}), (N_1, N_2))$ *of both schemes are as follows:*

$$|\mathsf{mpk}| = O(1), \quad |\mathsf{ct}| = O(N_1 + N_2), \quad |\mathsf{sk}| = O(N_1 + N_2)$$

*Proof.* Lemma 5.1 states that we can obtain a linear CDS for $\mathsf{P}$ with unbounded security from a linear CDS for $\mathsf{P}$ with bounded security without changing the asymptotic sizes of $\mathsf{p}(L), m_1, m_2$. By applying the conversion in Sect. 5.1 to the linear CDS schemes in Lemma 5.2 and Lemma 5.3, we obtain linear CDS schemes for $\mathsf{P}^{\mathrm{NQP}}$ and $\mathsf{P}^{\mathrm{ZQP}}$ with unbounded security such that

$$\mathsf{p}(N_1, N_2) = O(N_1 + N_2), \quad m_1 = O(N_1), \quad m_2 = O(N_2)$$

where $m_1$ and $m_2$ refer to the number of $\mathbb{Z}_p$ elements in the output of $c \leftarrow \mathsf{EncC}(\cdot, (N_1, N_2))$ and $k \leftarrow \mathsf{EncK}(\cdot, (N_1, N_2))$, respectively. By instantiating the unbounded ABE schemes in Sect. 4.1 with the linear CDS for $\mathsf{P}^{\mathrm{NQP}}$ and $\mathsf{P}^{\mathrm{ZQP}}$ with unbounded security, we can obtain the ABE schemes for $\mathsf{P}^{\mathrm{NQP}}$ and $\mathsf{P}^{\mathrm{ZQP}}$ described in Corollary 5.1. Unbounded adaptive security of the schemes follows from Theorem 4.1. □

### 5.3 Unbounded Broadcast Encryption

We describe how to construct our (identity-based) broadcast encryption from unbounded ABE for $\mathsf{P}^{\mathrm{NQP}}/\mathsf{P}^{\mathrm{ZQP}}$. We first recall unbounded (identity-based) broadcast encryption.

**Definition 5.2 (Broadcast).** A predicate family $\mathsf{P}^{\mathrm{BE}} = \{\mathsf{P}_L^{\mathrm{BE}}\}_{L \in \mathcal{L}}$ where $\mathsf{P}_L : \mathcal{X}_L \times \mathcal{Y}_L \rightarrow \{0,1\}$ for broadcast is given as follows.

$$\mathcal{L} = \mathbb{N}, \quad \mathcal{X}_N = 2^{[N]}, \quad \mathcal{Y}_N = [N]$$
$$\mathsf{P}_N(X, y) = 1 \Leftrightarrow y \in X$$

where $N \in \mathbb{N}$, $X \in 2^{[N]}$ and $y \in [N]$.

**Definition 5.3 (Identity-Based Broadcast).** A predicate family $\mathsf{P}^{\mathrm{IBBE}} = \{\mathsf{P}_L^{\mathrm{IBBE}}\}_{L \in \mathcal{L}}$ where $\mathsf{P}_L : \mathcal{X}_L \times \mathcal{Y}_L \rightarrow \{0,1\}$ for identity-based broadcast is given as follows.

$$\mathcal{L} = \mathbb{N}, \quad \mathcal{X}_N = \{S \subseteq \mathbb{Z}_p \backslash \{0\} \mid |S| \leq N\}, \quad \mathcal{Y}_N = \mathbb{Z}_p \backslash \{0\}$$
$$\mathsf{P}_N(X, y) = 1 \Leftrightarrow y \in X$$

where $N \in \mathbb{N}$, $p$ is an exponentially large modulus, $X \in \mathcal{X}_N$, and $y \in \mathcal{Y}_N$.[11]

[11] We exclude 0 from $\mathcal{X}_N$ and $\mathcal{Y}_N$ to use it as a dummy attribute for padding when embedding $\mathsf{P}^{\mathrm{IBBE}}$ in $\mathsf{P}^{\mathrm{ZQP}}$.

**Definition 5.4 (Unbounded Broadcast Encryption).** Unbounded broadcast encryption (BE) is defined as unbounded ABE (Definition 3.3) for the predicate $\mathsf{P}^{\mathrm{BE}}$, and identity-based broadcast encryption (IBBE) as unbounded ABE for the predicate $\mathsf{P}^{\mathrm{BE}}$.

**Unbounded Broadcast Encryption.** $\mathsf{P}^{\mathrm{BE}}$ can be embedded in $\mathsf{P}^{\mathrm{NQP}}$ (Definition 5.1), that is, a linear CDS for $\mathsf{P}^{\mathrm{NQP}}$ can also be used for $\mathsf{P}^{\mathrm{BE}}$ as follows. For $N \in \mathbb{N}$, let $g(N) = \lceil \sqrt{N} \rceil$ be the minimum integer that is greater than or equal to $\sqrt{N}$ and $\psi : [N] \to [g(N)]^2$ be any injective function.

- $\mathsf{P}^{\mathrm{BE}}_N$ is embedded in $\mathsf{P}^{\mathrm{NQP}}_{g(N),g(N)}$.
- $X \in \mathcal{X}^{\mathrm{BE}}_N = 2^{[N]}$ is translated to $\mathbf{M} \in \mathcal{X}^{\mathrm{NQP}}_{g(N),g(N)} = \mathbb{Z}_p^{g(N)\times g(N)}$ such that $m_{i,j} = 1$ if $\psi^{-1}(i,j) \in X$ and $m_{i,j} = 0$ otherwise.
- $y \in \mathcal{Y}^{\mathrm{BE}}_N = [N]$ is translated to $(\mathbf{x}, \mathbf{y}) \in \mathcal{Y}^{\mathrm{NQP}}_{g(N),g(N)} \in \mathbb{Z}_p^{g(N)} \times \mathbb{Z}_p^{g(N)}$ such that the $i$-th entry of $\mathbf{x}$ and the $j$-th entry of $\mathbf{y}$ for $\psi^{-1}(i,j) = y$ are 1, and all the other entries are 0.

In the above construction, we can see that $\mathbf{x}\mathbf{M}\mathbf{y}^\top \neq 0$ if and only if $y \in X$. Thanks to Corollary 5.1, we can construct an unbounded BE scheme for $N$ users with the following parameters:

$$|\mathsf{mpk}| = O(1), \quad |\mathsf{ct}| = O(\sqrt{N}), \quad |\mathsf{sk}| = O(\sqrt{N})$$

**Unbounded IBBE.** $\mathsf{P}^{\mathrm{IBBE}}$ can be embedded in $\mathsf{P}^{\mathrm{ZQP}}$ (Definition 5.1), that is, a linear CDS for $\mathsf{P}^{\mathrm{ZQP}}$ can also be used for $\mathsf{P}^{\mathrm{IBBE}}$ as follows. For $N \in \mathbb{N}$, let $g(N) = \lceil \sqrt{N+1} \rceil$ be the minimum integer that is greater than or equal to $\sqrt{N+1}$ and $\psi : [g(N)]^2 \to [0, g(N)^2 - 1]$ be an injective function such that $\psi(i,j) = g(N)(j-1) + i - 1$.

- $\mathsf{P}^{\mathrm{IBBE}}_N$ is embedded in $\mathsf{P}^{\mathrm{ZQP}}_{g(N),g(N)}$.
- $X \in \mathcal{X}^{\mathrm{IBBE}}_N = \{S \subseteq \mathbb{Z}_p \backslash \{0\} \mid |S| \leq N\}$ is translated to $\mathbf{M} = (m_{i,j})_{(i,j)\in[g(N)]^2} \in \mathcal{X}^{\mathrm{ZQP}}_{g(N),g(N)} = \mathbb{Z}_p^{g(N)\times g(N)}$ such that

$$z^{g(N)^2-1-|X|} \prod_{x\in X} (z - x) = \sum_{(i,j)\in[g(N)]^2} m_{i,j} z^{\psi(i,j)}$$

  for a formal variable $z$.
- $y \in \mathcal{Y}^{\mathrm{IBBE}}_N = \mathbb{Z}_p \backslash \{0\}$ is translated to $(\mathbf{x}, \mathbf{y}) \in \mathcal{Y}^{\mathrm{NQP}}_{g(N),g(N)} \in \mathbb{Z}_p^{g(N)} \times \mathbb{Z}_p^{g(N)}$ such that the $i$-th element of $\mathbf{x}$ is $y^{i-1}$ and the $j$-th element of $\mathbf{y}$ is $y^{g(N)(j-1)}$.

In the above construction, we can see that $\mathbf{x}\mathbf{M}\mathbf{y}^\top = 0$ if and only if $y \in X$. Thanks to Corollary 5.1, we can construct an unbounded IBBE scheme with a maximum user set size of $N$ and the following parameters:

$$|\mathsf{mpk}| = O(1), \quad |\mathsf{ct}| = O(\sqrt{N}), \quad |\mathsf{sk}| = O(\sqrt{N})$$

# 6 Our Unbounded KP-ABE for Span Programs from CDS

In this section, we present how to extend our compiler in Sect. 4.1 to construct a KP-ABE scheme for span programs from a linear CDS.

## 6.1 Preliminaries

**Definition 6.1 (Unbounded KP-ABE for Span Programs over $\mathsf{P}$).** Let $\mathsf{P} = \{\mathsf{P}_L\}_{L\in\mathcal{L}}$ be a predicate family where $\mathsf{P}_L : \mathcal{X}_L \times \mathcal{Y}_L \to \{0,1\}$. We define a predicate family $\mathsf{P}^{\mathrm{KP}}[\mathsf{P}] = \{\mathsf{P}^{\mathrm{KP}}_L[\mathsf{P}]\}_{L\in\mathcal{L}}$, where $\mathsf{P}^{\mathrm{KP}}_L[\mathsf{P}] : \mathcal{X}^{\mathrm{KP}}_L \times \mathcal{Y}^{\mathrm{KP}}_L \to \{0,1\}$ as follows:

$$\mathcal{X}^{\mathrm{KP}}_L = \mathcal{X}_L, \quad \mathcal{Y}^{\mathrm{KP}}_L = \{(\mathbf{M},\rho) : d,s \in \mathbb{N},\ \mathbf{M} \in \mathbb{Z}_p^{d\times s},\ \rho : [d] \to \mathcal{Y}_L\}$$
$$\mathsf{P}^{\mathrm{KP}}_L[\mathsf{P}](x,(\mathbf{M},\rho)) = 1 \Leftrightarrow (1,0,\ldots,0) \in \mathsf{RowSpan}(\{\mathbf{m}_h\}_{h:\mathsf{P}(x,\rho(h))=1})$$

The unbounded KP-ABE for span programs over $\mathsf{P}$ refers to the unbounded ABE for $\mathsf{P}^{\mathrm{KP}}[\mathsf{P}]$. We call $f = (\mathbf{M},\rho)$ a span program and say that $f$ accepts $x$ if $\mathsf{P}^{\mathrm{KP}}_L[\mathsf{P}](x,f) = 1$. The size of $f$ is the height of $\mathbf{M}$, i.e., $d$.

In Sect. 6.4, we explain how the above definition captures standard notions of small and large-universe KP-ABE for span programs, namely $\mathsf{P}^{\mathrm{KP}}[\mathsf{P}^{\mathrm{BE}}]$ and $\mathsf{P}^{\mathrm{KP}}[\mathsf{P}^{\mathrm{IBBE}}]$ respectively (Recall $\mathsf{P}^{\mathrm{BE}}, \mathsf{P}^{\mathrm{IBBE}}$ correspond to broadcast and identity-based broadcast, cf Definitions 5.2 and 5.3). Note that span programs capture boolean formula.

**Lemma 6.1 (LSSS for Span Programs).** *Let $\gamma \in \mathbb{N}$. We can construct a linear secret sharing scheme (LSSS) for span programs consisting of a probabilistic algorithm* $\mathsf{Share}$ *and a deterministic algorithm* $\mathsf{sRec}$ *as follows.*

$\mathsf{Share}(\mathbf{M},\mathbf{k};\mathbf{r}_1,\ldots,\mathbf{r}_{s-1})$ *It takes a program $\mathbf{M} \in \mathbb{Z}_p^{d\times s}$, a secret $\mathbf{k} \in \mathbb{Z}_p^{\gamma}$, and randomness $\mathbf{r}_1,\ldots,\mathbf{r}_{s-1} \in \mathbb{Z}_p^{\gamma}$, and outputs shares $\mathbf{k}_1,\ldots,\mathbf{k}_d$ as*

$$\begin{pmatrix}\mathbf{k}_1\\ \vdots\\ \mathbf{k}_d\end{pmatrix} = \mathbf{M}\begin{pmatrix}\mathbf{k}\\ \mathbf{r}_1\\ \vdots\\ \mathbf{r}_{s-1}\end{pmatrix}$$

$\mathsf{sRec}(\mathbf{M},S,\{\mathbf{k}_h\}_{h\in S})$ *It takes $\mathbf{M} \in \mathbb{Z}_p^{d\times s}$, $S \subseteq [d]$ such that $(1,0,\ldots,0) \in \mathsf{RowSpan}(\{\mathbf{m}_h\}_{h\in S})$, and shares $\{\mathbf{k}_h\}_{h\in S}$. It outputs $\mathbf{k}' = \sum_{h\in S} a_h\mathbf{k}_h$ where $\{a_h\}$ are coefficients satisfying $\sum_{h\in S} a_h\mathbf{m}_h = (1,0,\ldots,0)$.*

*The above LSSS satisfies the following properties:*

- **Linearity:** $\mathsf{Share}(\mathbf{M},\mathbf{k};\mathbf{r}_1,\ldots,\mathbf{r}_{s-1})$ *is linear in* $(\mathbf{k},\mathbf{r}_1,\ldots,\mathbf{r}_{s-1})$*, and* $\mathsf{sRec}(\mathbf{M}, S,\{\mathbf{k}_h\}_{h\in S})$ *is linear in* $\{\mathbf{k}_h\}_{h\in S}$.
- **Correctness:** *For all $\mathbf{M} \in \mathbb{Z}_p^{d\times s}$, $S \subseteq [d]$ s.t. $(1,0,\ldots,0) \in \mathsf{RowSpan}(\{\mathbf{m}_h\}_{h\in S})$, and $\mathbf{r}_1,\ldots,\mathbf{r}_{s-1} \in \mathbb{Z}_p^{\gamma}$, we have $\mathsf{sRec}(\mathbf{M},S,\{\mathbf{k}_h\}_{h\in S}) = \mathbf{k}$, where $\mathbf{k}_1,\ldots,\mathbf{k}_d \leftarrow \mathsf{Share}(\mathbf{M},\mathbf{k};\mathbf{r}_1,\ldots,\mathbf{r}_{s-1})$.*

**Security:** *For all* $\mathbf{M} \in \mathbb{Z}_p^{d\times s}$, $S \subseteq [d]$ *s.t.* $(1,0,\ldots,0) \notin \mathsf{RowSpan}(\{\mathbf{m}_h\}_{h\in S})$, *and* $\mathbf{k} \in \mathbb{Z}_p^{\gamma}$, $\{\mathbf{k}_h\}_{h\in S}$ *and* $\{\mathbf{k}'_h\}_{h\in S}$ *are identically distributed, where* $\mathbf{k}_1,\ldots,\mathbf{k}_d \leftarrow \mathsf{Share}(\mathbf{M},\mathbf{k})$ *and* $\mathbf{k}'_1,\ldots,\mathbf{k}'_d \leftarrow \mathsf{Share}(\mathbf{M},\mathbf{0})$ *over the uniform choice of the random vectors.*

### 6.2 Construction

We construct our unbounded KP-ABE scheme for span programs over $\mathsf{P}$, i.e., an unbounded ABE scheme for the predicate $\mathsf{P}_L^{\mathrm{KP}}[\mathsf{P}]$ (Definition 6.1) using the unbounded ABE scheme for $\mathsf{P}$ in Sect. 4.1 in a semi-generic way as follows. Let $(\mathsf{Share},\mathsf{sRec})$ be a LSSS for span programs in Lemma 6.1. Let $(\mathsf{Setup}_0,\mathsf{Enc}_0,\mathsf{KeyGen}_0,\mathsf{Dec}_0)$ be the algorithms of the unbounded ABE scheme for $\mathsf{P}$ in Sect. 4.1 with the following modifications:

- $\mathsf{KeyGen}_0[\mathbf{k}']$ is the same as key generation in the unbounded ABE scheme except that it uses $\mathbf{k}'$ in place of $\mathbf{k}$ in $\mathsf{msk}$;
- $\mathsf{Dec}_0$ is the same as decryption in the unbounded ABE scheme except that it outputs $d(z_1,z_2)$ instead of $\mathsf{ct}_5/d(z_1,z_2)$ (thus $\mathsf{Dec}_0$ works even if $\mathsf{ct}$ does not contain $\mathsf{ct}_5$).

The vector/matrix symbols in the components of $\mathsf{mpk},\mathsf{msk},\mathsf{ct},\mathsf{sk}$ follow Sect. 4.1.

$\mathsf{Setup}(1^\lambda)$**:** It outputs $(\mathsf{mpk},\mathsf{msk}) \leftarrow \mathsf{Setup}_0(1^\lambda)$.
$\mathsf{Enc}(\mathsf{mpk},(x,L),M)$**:** It outputs $\mathsf{ct} = (\mathsf{ct}_0,\mathsf{ct}_5) \leftarrow \mathsf{Enc}_0(\mathsf{mpk},(x,L),M)$ where $\mathsf{ct}_0$ includes all the ciphertext elements except $\mathsf{ct}_5$ as per Eq. (8).
$\mathsf{KeyGen}(\mathsf{mpk},\mathsf{msk},(\mathbf{M},\rho,L))$**:** It extracts $\mathbf{k}$ from $\mathsf{msk}$, runs $\mathbf{k}_1,\ldots,\mathbf{k}_d \leftarrow \mathsf{Share}(\mathbf{M},\mathbf{k})$, and outputs $\mathsf{sk} = \{\mathsf{sk}_h\}_{h\in[d]}$ where

$$\mathsf{sk}_h \leftarrow \mathsf{KeyGen}_0[\mathbf{k}_h](\mathsf{mpk},\mathsf{msk},(\rho(h),L))$$

$\mathsf{Dec}(\mathsf{mpk},\mathsf{ct},\mathsf{sk},x,(\mathbf{M},\rho),L)$**:** It takes $\mathsf{mpk}$, $\mathsf{ct}$, $\mathsf{sk}$, $x$, $(\mathbf{M},\rho)$, $L$ such that $(\mathbf{M},\rho)$ accepts $x$, and parses $\mathsf{ct} = (\mathsf{ct}_0,\mathsf{ct}_5)$. Let $S = \{h \in [d] \mid \mathsf{P}(x,\rho(h)) = 1\}$. It computes

$$[z_h]_T \leftarrow \mathsf{Dec}_0(\mathsf{mpk},\mathsf{ct}_0,\mathsf{sk}_h,x,\rho(h),L) \quad \text{for } h \in S$$

and outputs $\mathsf{ct}_5/\mathsf{sRec}(\mathbf{M},S,\{[z_h]_T\}_{h\in S})$.

**Correctness.** In decryption, we have $z_h = \mathbf{k}_h\mathbf{A}_1\mathbf{s}_0^\top$, which follows from the correctness of the unbounded ABE scheme in Sect. 4.1. Recall that we have $(1,0,\ldots,0) \in \mathsf{RowSpan}(\{\mathbf{m}_h\}_{h\in S})$, which follows from the condition that $(\mathbf{M},\rho)$ accepts $x$. Thus, we have

$$\mathsf{ct}_5/\mathsf{sRec}(\mathbf{M},S,\{[z_h]_T\}_{h\in S}) = [\mathbf{k}\mathbf{A}_1\mathbf{s}_0^\top]_T \cdot M/[\mathbf{k}\mathbf{A}_1\mathbf{s}_0^\top]_T = M$$

where the first equality follows from the correctness and linearity of the LSSS.

**Parameter Sizes.** In the above construction, the sizes of $\mathsf{mpk},\mathsf{ct},\mathsf{sk}$ are as follows:

$$|\mathsf{mpk}| = O(1), \quad |\mathsf{ct}| = O(n+m_1), \quad |\mathsf{sk}| = O(|f|\cdot(n+m_2))$$

where $n = \mathsf{p}(L)$, $m_1,m_2$ are the number of $\mathbb{Z}_p$ elements in $c(\mathbf{w}),k(\alpha,\mathbf{w})$, respectively. The above sizes hide $\mathsf{poly}(\lambda)$ factors.

### 6.3 Security

**Theorem 6.1.** *Suppose the MDDH assumption holds and the linear CDS $\Gamma$ satisfies unbounded security. Then, our scheme in Sect. 6.2 satisfies semi-adaptive unbounded security as per Definition 3.3.*

*Proof.* We define various distributions of ciphertext and secret key. As global parameters, we sample $\mathbf{A}_2, \mathbf{A}_3 \leftarrow \mathbb{Z}_p^{3k\times k}$, define $\mathbf{A}_1^{\|}, \mathbf{A}_2^{\|}, \mathbf{A}_3^{\|}$ following Definition 3.5, and also sample $\mathbf{W}_i, \mathbf{W}'_i, \mathbf{U}'_i \leftarrow \mathsf{RowSpan}(\mathbf{A}_2^{\|^\top})^{(k+1)\times 1}$ for $i \in [n']$ where $n'$ is sufficiently large. Let $\mathbf{a}_{2,1}^{\|^\top}$ be the first column of $\mathbf{A}_2^{\|}$. For ciphertexts, we define Normal$^{\mathrm{KP}}$ and E-normal$^{\mathrm{KP}}$ in the same way as Normal and E-normal in Sect. 4.2. For a secret key on $((\mathbf{M}, \rho), L)$ such that $\mathbf{M} \in \mathbb{Z}_p^{d\times s}$ and $\rho : [d] \to \mathcal{Y}_L$, we consider the following distributions. Since we are considering semi-adaptive security, secret key distributions can depend on the challenge attribute $(x, L^*)$. In the following, let $\mathsf{Cond}^*(L, h)$ be the condition such that $L \neq L^* \vee \mathsf{P}_L(x, \rho(h)) = 0$.

- Normal$^{\mathrm{KP}}$: Same as the output of $\mathsf{KeyGen}$ in Sect. 6.2.
- E-normal$^{\mathrm{KP}}$: Same as the output of $\mathsf{KeyGen}$ in Sect. 6.2 except that $\mathsf{sk}_h$ is generated as

$$\mathsf{sk}_h \leftarrow \mathsf{KeyGen}_0^{\mathrm{EN}}[\mathbf{k}_h](\mathsf{mpk}, \mathsf{msk}, (\rho(h), L)) \tag{13}$$

  for $h \in [d]$ where $\mathsf{KeyGen}_0^{\mathrm{EN}}[\mathbf{k}_h]$ outputs E-normal key distribution (Eq. (11)) with $\mathbf{k}_h$ in place of $\mathbf{k}$.
- Pre-SF$^{\mathrm{KP}}$: It runs $\mathbf{z}_1, \ldots, \mathbf{z}_d \leftarrow \mathsf{RowSpan}(\mathbf{a}_{2,1}^{\|})$, $\mathbf{k}_1, \ldots, \mathbf{k}_d \leftarrow \mathsf{Share}(f, \mathbf{k})$, and outputs $\mathsf{sk} = \{\mathsf{sk}_h\}_{h\in[d]}$ where

$$\mathsf{sk}_h \leftarrow \begin{cases} \mathsf{KeyGen}_0^{\mathrm{EN}}[\mathbf{k}_h + \mathbf{z}_h](\mathsf{mpk}, \mathsf{msk}, (\rho(h), L)) & (\mathsf{Cond}^*(L, h)) \\ \mathsf{KeyGen}_0^{\mathrm{EN}}[\mathbf{k}_h](\mathsf{mpk}, \mathsf{msk}, (\rho(h), L)) & (\text{otherwise}) \end{cases} \tag{14}$$

- SF$^{\mathrm{KP}}$: It runs $\mathbf{z}, \mathbf{z}_1, \ldots, \mathbf{z}_d \leftarrow \mathsf{RowSpan}(\mathbf{a}_{2,1}^{\|})$, $\mathbf{k}_1, \ldots, \mathbf{k}_d \leftarrow \mathsf{Share}(f, \mathbf{k} + \mathbf{z})$, and outputs $\mathsf{sk} = \{\mathsf{sk}_h\}_{h\in[d]}$ where

$$\mathsf{sk}_h \leftarrow \begin{cases} \mathsf{KeyGen}_0^{\mathrm{EN}}[\mathbf{k}_h + \mathbf{z}_h](\mathsf{mpk}, \mathsf{msk}, (\rho(h), L)) & (\mathsf{Cond}^*(L, h)) \\ \mathsf{KeyGen}_0^{\mathrm{EN}}[\mathbf{k}_h](\mathsf{mpk}, \mathsf{msk}, (\rho(h), L)) & (\text{otherwise}) \end{cases} \tag{15}$$

  Note that $\mathbf{z}, \mathbf{z}_1, \ldots, \mathbf{z}_d$ are chosen independently in each key generation for Pre-SF and SF.

We prove the theorem via a series of hybrids. Let $Q$ be the maximum number of secret key queries by the adversary.

- $\mathsf{H}_0$: The original security game.
- $\mathsf{H}_1$: Same as $\mathsf{H}_0$ except that the challenge ciphertext and all the secret keys given to the adversary are E-normal$^{\mathrm{KP}}$.

- $\mathsf{H}_2$: Same as $\mathsf{H}_1$ except that all the secret keys given to the adversary are Pre-SF$^{\text{KP}}$.
- $\mathsf{H}_3$: Same as $\mathsf{H}_2$ except that all the secret keys given to the adversary are SF$^{\text{KP}}$.
- $\mathsf{H}_4$: Same as $\mathsf{H}_3$ except that $\mathsf{ct}_5$ in the challenge ciphertext is randomly chosen from $G_T$.

We prove the indistinguishability of each hybrid transition in the full version. Observe that the adversary's view is independent of the challenge bit $\beta$ and its advantage is 0 in $\mathsf{H}_4$. This concludes the proof. □

### 6.4 Instantiations

We can obtain unbounded KP-ABE schemes for span programs with new parameters from the construction in Sect. 6.2.

**Definition 6.2 (Unbounded KP-ABE for Span Programs).** Small-universe unbounded KP-ABE for span programs is defined as unbounded ABE for $\mathsf{P}^{\text{S-KP}} = \{\mathsf{P}_L\}_{L\in\mathcal{L}}$ where $\mathsf{P}_L : \mathcal{X}_L \times \mathcal{Y}_L \to \{0,1\}$ such that

$$\mathcal{L} = \mathbb{N},\quad \mathcal{X}_N = 2^{[N]},\quad \mathcal{Y}_N = \{(\mathbf{M},\rho) : d,s \in \mathbb{N},\ \mathbf{M} \in \mathbb{Z}_p^{d\times s},\ \rho : [d] \to [N]\}$$
$$\mathsf{P}_N(X,(\mathbf{M},\rho)) = 1 \Leftrightarrow (1,0,\ldots,0) \in \mathsf{RowSpan}(\{\mathbf{m}_h\}_{h:\rho(h)\in X})$$

where $N \in \mathbb{N}$, $X \in \mathcal{X}_N$, $(\mathbf{M},\rho) \in \mathcal{Y}_N$. Similarly, large-universe unbounded KP-ABE for span programs is defined as unbounded ABE for $\mathsf{P}^{\text{L-KP}} = \{\mathsf{P}_L\}_{L\in\mathcal{L}}$ where $\mathsf{P}_L : \mathcal{X}_L \times \mathcal{Y}_L \to \{0,1\}$ such that

$$\mathcal{L} = \mathbb{N},\quad \mathcal{X}_N = \{X \subseteq \mathbb{Z}_p\backslash\{0\} \mid |S| \le N\}$$
$$\mathcal{Y}_N = \{(\mathbf{M},\rho) : d,s \in \mathbb{N},\ \mathbf{M} \in \mathbb{Z}_p^{d\times s},\ \rho : [d] \to \mathbb{Z}_p\backslash\{0\}\}$$
$$\mathsf{P}_N(X,(\mathbf{M},\rho)) = 1 \Leftrightarrow (1,0,\ldots,0) \in \mathsf{RowSpan}(\{\mathbf{m}_h\}_{h:\rho(h)\in X})$$

where $p$ is an exponentially large modulus.

**Our Unbounded KP-ABE for Span Programs.** It is not hard to see that $\mathsf{P}^{\text{S-KP}} = \mathsf{P}^{\text{KP}}[\mathsf{P}^{\text{BE}}]$ and $\mathsf{P}^{\text{L-KP}} = \mathsf{P}^{\text{KP}}[\mathsf{P}^{\text{IBBE}}]$ (see Definitions 5.2, 5.3 and 6.1 for the definitions of these predicates). Thus, we can instantiate small/large-universe unbounded ABE for span programs by applying the linear CDS for $\mathsf{P}^{\text{NQP}}$/ $\mathsf{P}^{\text{ZQP}}$ to the KP-ABE scheme in Sect. 6.2, since we can embed $\mathsf{P}^{\text{BE}}/\mathsf{P}^{\text{IBBE}}$ in $\mathsf{P}^{\text{NQP}}/\mathsf{P}^{\text{ZQP}}$, respectively. The resulting schemes have the following parameters:

$$|\mathsf{mpk}| = O(1),\quad |\mathsf{ct}| = O(\sqrt{N}),\quad |\mathsf{sk}| = O(\sqrt{N}\cdot|f|)$$

where $|f|$ is the height of $\mathbf{M}$ for $f = (\mathbf{M},\rho)$.

## References


1. Agrawal, S., Chase, M.: Simplifying Design and Analysis of Complex Predicate Encryption Schemes. In: Coron, J.-S., Nielsen, J.B. (eds.) EUROCRYPT 2017. LNCS, vol. 10210, pp. 627–656. Springer, Cham (2017). https://doi.org/10.1007/978-3-319-56620-7_22
2. Agrawal, S., Kumari, S., Yamada, S.: Compact pseudorandom functional encryption from evasive LWE. Cryptology ePrint Archive, Paper 2024/1719 (2024). https://eprint.iacr.org/2024/1719
3. Agrawal, S., Wichs, D., Yamada, S.: Optimal Broadcast Encryption from LWE and Pairings in the Standard Model. In: Pass, R., Pietrzak, K. (eds.) TCC 2020. LNCS, vol. 12550, pp. 149–178. Springer, Cham (2020). https://doi.org/10.1007/978-3-030-64375-1_6
4. Agrawal, S., Yamada, S.: Optimal Broadcast Encryption from Pairings and LWE. In: Canteaut, A., Ishai, Y. (eds.) EUROCRYPT 2020. LNCS, vol. 12105, pp. 13–43. Springer, Cham (2020). https://doi.org/10.1007/978-3-030-45721-1_2
5. Ambrona, M., Barthe, G., Schmidt, B.: Generic Transformations of Predicate Encodings: Constructions and Applications. In: Katz, J., Shacham, H. (eds.) CRYPTO 2017. LNCS, vol. 10401, pp. 36–66. Springer, Cham (2017). https://doi.org/10.1007/978-3-319-63688-7_2
6. Attrapadung, N.: Dual System Encryption via Doubly Selective Security: Framework, Fully Secure Functional Encryption for Regular Languages, and More. In: Nguyen, P.Q., Oswald, E. (eds.) EUROCRYPT 2014. LNCS, vol. 8441, pp. 557–577. Springer, Heidelberg (2014). https://doi.org/10.1007/978-3-642-55220-5_31
7. Attrapadung, N.: Dual System Encryption Framework in Prime-Order Groups via Computational Pair Encodings. In: Cheon, J.H., Takagi, T. (eds.) ASIACRYPT 2016. LNCS, vol. 10032, pp. 591–623. Springer, Heidelberg (2016). https://doi.org/10.1007/978-3-662-53890-6_20
8. Attrapadung, N.: Unbounded Dynamic Predicate Compositions in Attribute-Based Encryption. In: Ishai, Y., Rijmen, V. (eds.) EUROCRYPT 2019. LNCS, vol. 11476, pp. 34–67. Springer, Cham (2019). https://doi.org/10.1007/978-3-030-17653-2_2
9. Attrapadung, N., Hanaoka, G., Matsumoto, T., Teruya, T., Yamada, S.: Attribute Based Encryption with Direct Efficiency Tradeoff. In: Manulis, M., Sadeghi, A.-R., Schneider, S. (eds.) ACNS 2016. LNCS, vol. 9696, pp. 249–266. Springer, Cham (2016). https://doi.org/10.1007/978-3-319-39555-5_14
10. Attrapadung, N., Libert, B., de Panafieu, E.: Expressive Key-Policy Attribute-Based Encryption with Constant-Size Ciphertexts. In: Catalano, D., Fazio, N., Gennaro, R., Nicolosi, A. (eds.) PKC 2011. LNCS, vol. 6571, pp. 90–108. Springer, Heidelberg (2011). https://doi.org/10.1007/978-3-642-19379-8_6
11. Attrapadung, N., Tomida, J.: Unbounded Dynamic Predicate Compositions in ABE from Standard Assumptions. In: Moriai, S., Wang, H. (eds.) ASIACRYPT 2020. LNCS, vol. 12493, pp. 405–436. Springer, Cham (2020). https://doi.org/10.1007/978-3-030-64840-4_14
12. Boneh, D., Boyen, X.: Efficient Selective-ID Secure Identity-Based Encryption Without Random Oracles. In: Cachin, C., Camenisch, J.L. (eds.) EUROCRYPT 2004. LNCS, vol. 3027, pp. 223–238. Springer, Heidelberg (2004). https://doi.org/10.1007/978-3-540-24676-3_14
13. Boneh, D., Gentry, C., Waters, B.: Collusion Resistant Broadcast Encryption with Short Ciphertexts and Private Keys. In: Shoup, V. (ed.) CRYPTO 2005. LNCS, vol. 3621, pp. 258–275. Springer, Heidelberg (2005). https://doi.org/10.1007/11535218_16

14. Boneh, D., Waters, B.: A fully collusion resistant broadcast, trace, and revoke system. In: Juels, A., Wright, R.N., De Capitani di Vimercati, S. (eds.) ACM CCS 2006, pp. 211–220. ACM Press (2006). https://doi.org/10.1145/1180405.1180432
15. Brakerski, Z., Vaikuntanathan, V.: Circuit-ABE from LWE: Unbounded Attributes and Semi-adaptive Security. In: Robshaw, M., Katz, J. (eds.) CRYPTO 2016. LNCS, vol. 9816, pp. 363–384. Springer, Heidelberg (2016). https://doi.org/10.1007/978-3-662-53015-3_13
16. Brakerski, Z., Vaikuntanathan, V.: Lattice-inspired broadcast encryption and succinct ciphertext-policy ABE. In: Braverman, M. (ed.) ITCS 2022, vol. 215, pp. 28:1–28:20. LIPIcs (2022). https://doi.org/10.4230/LIPIcs.ITCS.2022.28
17. Chase, M., Maller, M., Meiklejohn, S.: Déjà Q All Over Again: Tighter and Broader Reductions of $q$-Type Assumptions. In: Cheon, J.H., Takagi, T. (eds.) ASIACRYPT 2016. LNCS, vol. 10032, pp. 655–681. Springer, Heidelberg (2016). https://doi.org/10.1007/978-3-662-53890-6_22
18. Chen, J., Gay, R., Wee, H.: Improved Dual System ABE in Prime-Order Groups via Predicate Encodings. In: Oswald, E., Fischlin, M. (eds.) EUROCRYPT 2015. LNCS, vol. 9057, pp. 595–624. Springer, Heidelberg (2015). https://doi.org/10.1007/978-3-662-46803-6_20
19. Chen, J., Gong, J., Kowalczyk, L., Wee, H.: Unbounded ABE via Bilinear Entropy Expansion, Revisited. In: Nielsen, J.B., Rijmen, V. (eds.) EUROCRYPT 2018. LNCS, vol. 10820, pp. 503–534. Springer, Cham (2018). https://doi.org/10.1007/978-3-319-78381-9_19
20. Chen, J., Wee, H.: Semi-adaptive Attribute-Based Encryption and Improved Delegation for Boolean Formula. In: Abdalla, M., De Prisco, R. (eds.) SCN 2014. LNCS, vol. 8642, pp. 277–297. Springer, Cham (2014). https://doi.org/10.1007/978-3-319-10879-7_16
21. Cini, V., Wee, H.: Unbounded ABE for circuits from LWE, revisited. In: Chung, K.M., Sasaki, Y. (eds.) ASIACRYPT 2024, Part IV. LNCS, vol. 15487, pp. 238–267. Springer, Singapore (2024). https://doi.org/10.1007/978-981-96-0894-2_8
22. Delerablée, C.: Identity-Based Broadcast Encryption with Constant Size Ciphertexts and Private Keys. In: Kurosawa, K. (ed.) ASIACRYPT 2007. LNCS, vol. 4833, pp. 200–215. Springer, Heidelberg (2007). https://doi.org/10.1007/978-3-540-76900-2_12
23. Escala, A., Herold, G., Kiltz, E., Ràfols, C., Villar, J.: An Algebraic Framework for Diffie Hellman Assumptions. J. Cryptol. **30**(1), 242–288 (2015). https://doi.org/10.1007/s00145-015-9220-6
24. Fiat, A., Naor, M.: Broadcast Encryption. In: Stinson, D.R. (ed.) CRYPTO 1993. LNCS, vol. 773, pp. 480–491. Springer, Heidelberg (1994). https://doi.org/10.1007/3-540-48329-2_40
25. Gay, R., Kowalczyk, L., Wee, H.: Tight Adaptively Secure Broadcast Encryption with Short Ciphertexts and Keys. In: Catalano, D., De Prisco, R. (eds.) SCN 2018. LNCS, vol. 11035, pp. 123–139. Springer, Cham (2018). https://doi.org/10.1007/978-3-319-98113-0_7
26. Gentry, C., Waters, B.: Adaptive Security in Broadcast Encryption Systems (with Short Ciphertexts). In: Joux, A. (ed.) EUROCRYPT 2009. LNCS, vol. 5479, pp. 171–188. Springer, Heidelberg (2009). https://doi.org/10.1007/978-3-642-01001-9_10
27. Gertner, Y., Ishai, Y., Kushilevitz, E., Malkin, T.: Protecting data privacy in private information retrieval schemes. In: Proceedings of the 30th ACM STOC, pp. 151–160. ACM Press (1998). https://doi.org/10.1145/276698.276723

28. Gong, J., Dong, X., Chen, J., Cao, Z.: Efficient IBE with Tight Reduction to Standard Assumption in the Multi-challenge Setting. In: Cheon, J.H., Takagi, T. (eds.) ASIACRYPT 2016. LNCS, vol. 10032, pp. 624–654. Springer, Heidelberg (2016). https://doi.org/10.1007/978-3-662-53890-6_21
29. Goyal, R., Koppula, V., Waters, B.: Semi-adaptive Security and Bundling Functionalities Made Generic and Easy. In: Hirt, M., Smith, A. (eds.) TCC 2016. LNCS, vol. 9986, pp. 361–388. Springer, Heidelberg (2016). https://doi.org/10.1007/978-3-662-53644-5_14
30. Goyal, V., Pandey, O., Sahai, A., Waters, B.: Attribute-based encryption for fine-grained access control of encrypted data. In: Juels, A., Wright, R.N., De Capitani di Vimercati, S. (eds.) ACM CCS 2006, pp. 89–98. ACM Press (2006). https://doi.org/10.1145/1180405.1180418, available as Cryptology ePrint Archive Report 2006/309
31. Kowalczyk, L., Lewko, A.B.: Bilinear Entropy Expansion from the Decisional Linear Assumption. In: Gennaro, R., Robshaw, M. (eds.) CRYPTO 2015. LNCS, vol. 9216, pp. 524–541. Springer, Heidelberg (2015). https://doi.org/10.1007/978-3-662-48000-7_26
32. Kowalczyk, L., Wee, H.: Compact Adaptively Secure ABE for $\mathsf{NC}^1$ from $k$-Lin. In: Ishai, Y., Rijmen, V. (eds.) EUROCRYPT 2019. LNCS, vol. 11476, pp. 3–33. Springer, Cham (2019). https://doi.org/10.1007/978-3-030-17653-2_1
33. Lewko, A.: Tools for Simulating Features of Composite Order Bilinear Groups in the Prime Order Setting. In: Pointcheval, D., Johansson, T. (eds.) EUROCRYPT 2012. LNCS, vol. 7237, pp. 318–335. Springer, Heidelberg (2012). https://doi.org/10.1007/978-3-642-29011-4_20
34. Lewko, A., Waters, B.: Unbounded HIBE and Attribute-Based Encryption. In: Paterson, K.G. (ed.) EUROCRYPT 2011. LNCS, vol. 6632, pp. 547–567. Springer, Heidelberg (2011). https://doi.org/10.1007/978-3-642-20465-4_30
35. Liu, T., Vaikuntanathan, V., Wee, H.: Conditional Disclosure of Secrets via Non-linear Reconstruction. In: Katz, J., Shacham, H. (eds.) CRYPTO 2017. LNCS, vol. 10401, pp. 758–790. Springer, Cham (2017). https://doi.org/10.1007/978-3-319-63688-7_25
36. Okamoto, T., Takashima, K.: Fully Secure Unbounded Inner-Product and Attribute-Based Encryption. In: Wang, X., Sako, K. (eds.) ASIACRYPT 2012. LNCS, vol. 7658, pp. 349–366. Springer, Heidelberg (2012). https://doi.org/10.1007/978-3-642-34961-4_22
37. Rouselakis, Y., Waters, B.: Practical constructions and new proof methods for large universe attribute-based encryption. In: Sadeghi, A.R., Gligor, V.D., Yung, M. (eds.) ACM CCS 2013, pp. 463–474. ACM Press (2013). https://doi.org/10.1145/2508859.2516672
38. Sahai, A., Waters, B.: Fuzzy Identity-Based Encryption. In: Cramer, R. (ed.) EUROCRYPT 2005. LNCS, vol. 3494, pp. 457–473. Springer, Heidelberg (2005). https://doi.org/10.1007/11426639_27
39. Wee, H.: Dual System Encryption via Predicate Encodings. In: Lindell, Y. (ed.) TCC 2014. LNCS, vol. 8349, pp. 616–637. Springer, Heidelberg (2014). https://doi.org/10.1007/978-3-642-54242-8_26
40. Wee, H.: Déjà Q: Encore! Un Petit IBE. In: Kushilevitz, E., Malkin, T. (eds.) TCC 2016. LNCS, vol. 9563, pp. 237–258. Springer, Heidelberg (2016). https://doi.org/10.1007/978-3-662-49099-0_9
41. Wee, H.: Broadcast Encryption with Size $N^{1/3}$ and More from $k$-Lin. In: Malkin, T., Peikert, C. (eds.) CRYPTO 2021. LNCS, vol. 12828, pp. 155–178. Springer, Cham (2021). https://doi.org/10.1007/978-3-030-84259-8_6

42. Wee, H.: Optimal broadcast encryption and CP-ABE from evasive lattice assumptions. In: Dunkelman, O., Dziembowski, S. (eds.) EUROCRYPT 2022, Part II. LNCS, vol. 13276, pp. 217–241. Springer, Cham (2022). https://doi.org/10.1007/978-3-031-07085-3_8
43. Wee, H.: Circuit ABE with poly(depth, $\lambda$)-sized ciphertexts and keys from lattices. In: Reyzin, L., Stebila, D. (eds.) CRYPTO 2024, Part III. LNCS, vol. 14922, pp. 178–209. Springer, Cham (2024). https://doi.org/10.1007/978-3-031-68382-4_6
44. Wee, H.: Almost optimal KP and CP-ABE for circuits from succinct LWE. In: Fehr, S., Fouque, P.A. (eds.) EUROCRYPT 2025, Part III. LNCS, vol. 15603, pp. 34–62. Springer, Cham (2025). https://doi.org/10.1007/978-3-031-91131-6_2
45. Wee, H., Wu, D.J.: Unbounded distributed broadcast encryption and registered ABE from succinct LWE. In: Kalai, Y.T., Kamara, S.F. (eds.) CRYPTO 2025, Part III. LNCS, vol. 16002, pp. 204–235. Springer, Cham (2025). https://doi.org/10.1007/978-3-032-01881-6_7

# Collusion-Resistant Constrained PRFs for Compute-&-Compare Predicates from LWE

Jiaqi Cheng(✉) and Rishab Goyal

University of Wisconsin–Madison, Madison, WI, USA
{jiaqicheng,rishab}@cs.wisc.edu

**Abstract.** We design the *first collusion-resistant* constrained PRFs (CPRFs) for a non-trivial and expressive class of constraints from *standard LWE*. The two predicate classes for which we design CPRFs are: compute-&-compare and predicated range constraints. We improve our CPRF for compute-&-compare predicates to satisfy *collusion-resistant constraint privacy*. An additional feature of our CPRFs is that they also satisfy (almost-)key-homomorphic property. Prior to this work, we did not have any post-quantum collusion-resistant CPRF beyond prefix-fixing constraints, and collusion-resistant CPRFs for expressive predicates relied on either *code obfuscation or multilinear maps.*

As an immediate application, we obtain a two-sided predicate encryption (PE) and functional encryption (FE) for the compute-&-compare class in the symmetric-key setting. Prior to this work, we did not have any post-quantum construction for 2-sided PE/FE beyond inner product predicates. An important contribution of this work is to introduce a new framework of *purifying functionality.* The main motivation behind our new framework is to systematically eliminate zeroizing attacks, which have been a highly successful cryptanalysis paradigm for breaking various candidates for advanced cryptographic objects.

## 1 Introduction

Constrained pseudorandom functions [23,24,61] (CPRFs) are a powerful advancement of pseudorandom functions (PRFs) [46]. Syntactically, a CPRF is defined nearly identical to a standard PRF, as in it has a Setup algorithm that takes a security parameter $\lambda$, and outputs the (master) PRF key $K$, and an Eval algorithm that takes $K$ and input $x$, and outputs the PRF value $F_K(x)$. The crucial difference between traditional and constrained PRFs is that CPRFs have another special algorithm, Constrain. The Constrain algorithm takes as input, the master key $K$ *and a boolean predicate* $\phi$, and outputs a "constrained" key, $K_\phi$. The desired functionality from $K_\phi$ is that one can compute the PRF output $F_K(x)$ on any $x$ as long as $x$ satisfies the predicate $\phi$ (i.e., $\phi(x) = 1$), yet $K$ is independent of $\phi$ as one wants to choose $\phi$ dynamically, after setup.

*Pseudorandomness.* A critical feature for CPRFs is their ability to maintain pseudorandomness even under a collusion attack. This is formalized as *constrained*


N. Heninger and M. Rosulek (Eds.): CRYPTO 2026, LNCS 16800, pp. 508–538, 2026.
https://doi.org/10.1007/978-3-032-35367-2_17

*pseudorandomness* property. It guarantees that any polytime adversary that corrupts a group of constrained keys $K_{\phi_1}, \ldots, K_{\phi_Q}$, for $Q$ predicates $\{\phi_i\}_i$, cannot distinguish the PRF output on a point $x^*$ as long as none of the predicates satisfy it. Here $Q$ denotes the collusion size, and CPRF is said to be collusion-resistant if $Q$ can be any polynomial.

*Privacy.* Another crucial property for CPRFs is that of *constraint privacy* [19, 24,61]. It states an adversary cannot learn any non-trivial information about the predicates $\{\phi_i\}_i$ from a set of constrained keys $\{K_{\phi_i}\}_i$. The notion of non-trivial information has to be defined carefully as the attacker can pick an input $x$, use every constrained key to evaluate on $x$, and compare the resulting outputs to learn which constraints satisfy $x$ [19].

**Current State of Affairs.** Despite a decade of intensive study, achieving collusion-resistant CPRFs for general predicates remains a formidable challenge. Without leveraging heavy cryptographic machinery (such as indistinguishability obfuscation [9], multilinear maps [21,35,41,43]), our ability to construct collusion-resistant schemes is remarkably limited. Even when constraint privacy is not a requirement, existing collusion-resistant CPRFs are restricted to a narrow class of functions: specifically, prefix-fixing constraints [23,24,46][1] and left-right predicates [23][2]. Neither class provides the expressivity required to support the diverse array of applications envisioned for constrained pseudorandomness. Moreover, if one desires *post-quantum* security, the landscape narrows further; only prefix-fixing PRFs are currently known, as they follow directly from the seminal Goldreich-Goldwasser-Micali (GGM) construction [23,24,46].

More remarkably, designing CPRFs does not get easier even against a 'fixed' collusion size [40,48,49,66]. In the fixed collusion setting, $Q$ is a-priori fixed during setup and security is only guaranteed if no more than $Q$ keys get corrupted. For most primitives, such as encryption, signatures, and even certain forms of obfuscation, restricting to bounded collusion security makes the problem much easier [40,47–49,66]. In sharp contrast, CPRFs supporting a small (e.g., two) number of corrupted keys remain elusive to this day. All prior CPRFs that go beyond inner-product predicates can either resist a single collusion (i.e., $Q = 1$), or require obfuscation [4,5,10,15,16,23,24,26–28,30,36–39,56,61–63,65,69].

**Why are CPRFs so Hard to Design?** On a fundamental level, this large schism between CPRFs and other advanced primitives stems from the fact that CPRFs implicitly enforce a stronger consistency property. Two constrained keys for a CPRF must output *identical* PRF values on a common satisfying input. For other advanced primitives, this consistency property is not as stringent. As an example, consider attribute-based encryption (ABE) [55,68] where two predicate keys only need to recover the plaintext from a ciphertext and nothing else.

[1] A prefix-fixing constraint is defined using a string $P$ such that $x$ satisfies the constraint if $P$ is a prefix of $x$.

[2] A left-right predicate is defined using a half-string $w$ and a 'left/right' flag such that an input $x = (x_{\mathsf{lft}}, x_{\mathsf{rgt}})$ satisfies it if $w = x_{\mathsf{lft}}$ and flag is set to 'left', or vice versa.

This strong consistency requirement raises the technical difficulty in designing CPRFs, which brings us to the central question that we study:

Q1. *Can we design collusion-resistant CPRFs from standard assumptions for any class of constraint predicates that cannot be captured as inner-products?*

Additionally, we ask:

Q2. *Can we design collusion-resistant CPRFs* with constraint privacy *for any non-trivial class of predicates from standard assumptions?*

As two-key constraint privacy for general circuits is known to imply obfuscation [28], thus one must carefully delineate a non-trivial class of predicates that provides meaningful expressivity without inadvertently collapsing into the regime of obfuscation.

### 1.1 Our Results

In this work, we give positive answers to both questions, Q1 and Q2, while emphasizing on realizing post-quantum security. We give the *first* post-quantum collusion-resistant CPRF, that goes beyond prefix-fixing [23,24,46], and also prove it to be constraint private. As a direct application of our CPRFs, we give the *first* post-quantum collusion-resistant 2-sided PE for a non-trivial class of predicates. A key technical contribution of this work is a new framework, that we call *Purified Circuit Class* framework, to eliminate susceptibility to zeroizing attacks [2,8,25,30,31,33,34,57,59] in the context of lattice-based CPRFs. Below we summarize our key results:

1. **Collusion-Resistant *Constraint-Private* CPRF for compute-&-compare predicates from LWE.** We construct a CPRF for compute-&-compare predicates (i.e., equality testing on function output). Each constraint predicate $\mathsf{CC}[f, y]$ is associated with a 'compute' function $f$ (that can be represented by a polynomial-sized circuit) and a function output $y$. A CPRF key for $\mathsf{CC}[f, y]$ can be used to evaluate the PRF on any input $x$ as long as $f(x) = y$.
   We prove our CPRF satisfies collusion-resistant constrained pseudorandomness and constraint privacy, under the Learning With Errors (LWE) assumption [64], as long as the attacker corrupts constrained keys for the same compute function $f$ but many different comparison points $y_1, \ldots, y_Q$. Prior CPRFs were secure as long as an attacker gets *at most one* constrained key and, as we demonstrate in this work, prior lattice-based CPRFs can be easily broken if we corrupt just two keys for compute-&-compare predicates, even with same compute function $f$ and two distinct comparison points.
2. **Collusion-Resistant CPRFs for predicated range from LWE.** We generalize our main CPRF construction to support *predicated range* constraints (i.e., range checking on function output). Each constraint predicate $\mathsf{CC}[f, y, z]$ is associated with a 'compute' function $f$ and an output range $[y, z]$, where an input $x$ satisfies the predicate if $f(x) \in [y, z]$. We prove our CPRF for

predicated range satisfies collusion-resistant constrained pseudorandomness as long as the ranges are pairwise disjoint. We leave it as an interesting open question to prove constraint privacy for this constraint class.

3. **2-Sided Predicate Encryption.** As a direct application of our CPRFs, we construct a collusion-resistant 2-sided (or strongly attribute-hiding) predicate encryption (PE) scheme [22,52,60] for compute-&-compare predicates under standard LWE. Our encryption system is a symmetric-key scheme and also satisfies predicate privacy (i.e., decryption keys hide the predicate). Prior to this work, 2-sided PE could only be built for inner-product predicates [22,60], or by invoking obfuscation and related primitives [3,42,67].

*Key-Homomorphism: an added benefit.* Our CPRF constructions also satisfy (almost-)key-homomorphic property w.r.t. the master key as well as constrained keys [6,17,29,54]. Briefly, (almost-)key-homomorphism states that $F_{K_1}(x) + F_{K_2}(x) \approx F_{K_1+K_2}(x)$, where $K_1, K_2$ are two master keys or two constrained keys for the same predicate. The key-homomorphism property has proven to be extremely valuable for a variety for applications [6,17,29,54] and, to the best of our knowledge, we did not have any collusion-resistant key-homomorphic CPRF for any predicate other than prefix-fixing predicates from standard assumptions.

## 2 Technical Overview

We start with the key technical barrier that deters realizing collusion-resistant CPRFs for circuits from lattices.

**Zeroizing Attacks: A Key Technical Barrier.** Zeroizing attacks are a powerful methodology to cryptanalyze candidates for advanced cryptographic objects [2,8,25,30,31,33,34,57,59]. Abstractly, a zeroizing (colluding) attacker in CPRFs works as follows: (1) corrupt two (or more) constrained keys, (2) evaluate them on an input $x$ that satisfies all constraints (which must give the same output by CPRF correctness), and (3) algebraically combine these keys and outputs, and extract non-trivial (secret) encodings of 'zero'.

Step (3) is the most crucial step and it reveals non-trivial information about the PRF master key $\mathsf{msk}$ in the lattice setting. Basically, each PRF output non-trivially depends on $\mathsf{msk}$, and if two constrained keys can evaluate the PRF on a common point, then they can be used to learn the same $\mathsf{msk}$ encoding in two different ways. In lattice-based CPRFs, being able to compute the same encoding of $\mathsf{msk}$ in two different ways leaks underlying errors, eventually breaking pseudorandomness. Therefore, all prior lattice-based CPRFs [15,26–28,30] succumb to zeroizing attacks. Since zeroizing attacks require at least two keys, thus prior works could prove 1-key constrained pseudorandomness, but fell apart when an attacker corrupts even two.

Our goal is to allow an arbitrary number of key corruptions, while avoiding zeroizing attacks. Towards that goal, we introduce a new notion that we call 'purified circuit classes' to eliminate susceptibility to zeroizing attacks.

**"Purifying" Functionality: Eliminating Zeroizing Attacks.** Our starting observation is that the abstract zeroizing attack methodology no longer works if an attacker corrupts *constraint keys that do not have an overlapping support.* Let $\widehat{\mathcal{C}}$ be a class of predicates where every pair (distinct) predicates have a disjoint support. That is, $\forall C \neq C' \in \widehat{\mathcal{C}},\ \mathsf{Supp}(C) \cap \mathsf{Supp}(C') = \emptyset$.

We call such a predicate class, $\widehat{\mathcal{C}}$, to be a *purified constraint class.* Intuitively, this enforces zero overlap between constraints. Essentially, each constrained key $\mathsf{sk}_C$ controls a unique and disjoint partition of the input space. Our intuition is that if attacker can only acquire secret keys that correspond to a purified class, then zeroizing attack methodology might not work. Basically, the abstract zeroizing attack template stops at step (2) when an adversary cannot evaluate two keys on the same point anymore.

Naturally, moving to this framework invites three fundamental questions:

**Q1 (Utility):** Are there meaningful predicate classes that reside within this 'purified' regime?
**Q2 (Complexity):** Does the restriction to purified classes render the construction of collusion-resistant CPRFs trivial?
**Q3 (Gap Analysis):** Are existing lattice-based CPRFs already implicitly secure for such classes, or can we identify concrete vulnerabilities?

In the following, we address each of these in turn.

**Addressing Q1: The Existence of Expressive Purified Predicates.** We answer in the affirmative by identifying two significant and expressive families of purified predicates.
I. Compute-&-Compare Predicates. Our first example is the class of compute-&-compare circuits. Informally, each circuit in this family checks whether a function $f$ maps an input $x$ to a target value $y$. Formally, for a function $f : \mathcal{X} \to \mathcal{Y}$ and a target $y \in \mathcal{Y}$, we define the circuit $C_{f,y}$ such that:

$$C_{f,y}(x) = 1 \iff f(x) = y$$

For a given $f$, any collection of circuits $\mathcal{F} \subseteq \{C_{f,y} : y \in \mathcal{Y}\}$ constitutes a compute-&-compare class. Notably, any such class is inherently purified: for any two distinct targets $y \neq y'$, the supports of $C_{f,y}$ and $C_{f,y'}$ are disjoint as $f$ is a function (i.e., $\mathrm{supp}(C_{f,y}) \cap \mathrm{supp}(C_{f,y'}) = \emptyset$).
II. Predicated Range Constraints. We further generalize this to the predicated range class. Here, the constraint is satisfied if the function output falls within a specific interval. For a function $f$, we define the range circuit $C_{f,[y,z]}$ as:

$$C_{f,[y,z]}(x) = 1 \iff y \leq f(x) \leq z$$

A collection of such circuits $\{C_{f,[y_i,z_i]}\}$ is a purified predicated range class provided the corresponding intervals $[y_i, z_i]$ in the co-domain $\mathcal{Y}$ are pairwise non-overlapping. This class offers a powerful generalization, allowing for delegated evaluation over partitioned sub-domains of the function's range.

These predicates have been studied in the context of code obfuscation [53,71] and are fairly common in the searchable symmetric encryption (SSE) literature [1,11,12,18]. A more detailed discussion of applications appears in the full version.

**Addressing Q2: The Non-Triviality of Purified Constraints.** The reader might be wondering: does restricting the predicate class to disjoint supports (the "purified" regime) render the construction of collusion-resistant CPRFs trivial? One might consider a naive approach that partitions the input space $\mathcal{X}$ according to the constraints and assigns independent PRF keys to each partition—for instance, defining $\mathsf{Eval}(\mathsf{msk}, x) = F(K_{\mathsf{partition}(x)}, x)$.

However, such an approach fails to satisfy the fundamental requirement of a CPRF: independence of core PRF function and constraints. In a standard CPRF, the Setup and Eval algorithms must remain independent of the specific constraint issued. The master key msk defines a single, consistent pseudorandom function over the entire domain $\{0,1\}^n$, whereas constraints can be selected dynamically via the Constrain algorithm later. A partition-based approach would require "fixing" the constraint (e.g., the function $f$ in a compute-&-compare class) during the Setup phase. This would yield a constraint-specific CPRF rather than a general-purpose CPRF. Our construction maintains a single msk capable of issuing keys for any predicate in the class (and for arbitrary functions $f$) without requiring apriori knowledge of these constraints at setup time.

We emphasize that the requirement of Setup and Eval being independent of the constraining predicates is essential for nearly all applications as well as it ensures the problem does not become trivial. In particular, designing CPRFs even for general constraints (i.e., without the purified restriction) is relatively straightforward if the Setup or Eval algorithm knows the set of constraints $C_1, \ldots, C_Q$ for which a key will be generated. The idea is simple: partition the input space into $2^Q$ disjoint regions based on the validity vector $\mathbf{y} \in \{0,1\}^n$ of the input $\mathbf{x}$ against the constraints (where $\mathbf{y}[i] = C_i(\mathbf{x})$). The system simply assigns an independent standard PRF key $K_{\mathbf{y}}$ for each possible vector $\mathbf{y}$, and a constrained key for $C_i$ corresponds to $\{K_{\mathbf{y}}\}$ for all $\mathbf{y}$ such that $\mathbf{y}[i] = 1$. For completeness, the full version includes the above construction.

**Addressing Q3: The Failure of Existing Lattice-Based CPRFs.** With the introduction of purified circuits, it is natural to ask whether existing lattice-based CPRFs [15,26–29] already satisfy collusion resistance when restricted to such classes. We answer this in the negative. We examine the two dominant algebraic paradigms—the BGG+ approach and the GGH approach—and demonstrate that both are fundamentally insecure against collusion, even in the purified setting.
I. Vulnerability of the BGG+ Approach. The constructions in [15,26,27] utilize the homomorphic properties of the BGG+ framework [14]. In these schemes, the constrained key for a function $f$ is typically an encoding of the form:

$$\mathsf{sk}_f := \mathbf{s}^T \cdot (\mathbf{B} - f \otimes \mathbf{G}) + \mathbf{e}$$

where $\mathbf{s}$ is the LWE secret (serving as the PRF seed), $\mathbf{B}$ is a public matrix, and $\mathbf{G}$ is the gadget matrix. Correctness relies on the fact that for any $x$ such that $f(x) = 0$, one can homomorphically derive $\mathbf{s}^T(\mathbf{B} \cdot \mathbf{H}_x) \approx \mathsf{Eval}(\mathsf{msk}, x)$.
**The Attack:** This design collapses under collusion for the compute-&-Compare class. Consider an adversary who obtains two keys $\mathsf{sk}_{y_0}$ and $\mathsf{sk}_{y_1}$ for the same

function $f$ but distinct targets $y_0, y_1$. The keys take the form:

$$\mathsf{sk}_{y_i} \approx \mathbf{s}^T \cdot (\mathbf{B} - [f \mid y_i] \otimes \mathbf{G})$$

By simply computing the difference $\mathsf{sk}_{y_0} - \mathsf{sk}_{y_1}$, the $\mathbf{s}^T\mathbf{B}$ and $f$-dependent terms cancel out, leaving a term of the form $\mathbf{s}^T \cdot ((y_1 - y_0) \otimes \mathbf{G}) + \mathbf{e}'$. Since $y_0 \neq y_1$, the adversary can use the gadget structure of $\mathbf{G}$ to recover the LWE secret $\mathbf{s}$ in its entirety. This total break of the master secret key demonstrates that the BGG+ framework cannot natively support collusion resistance.
II. Vulnerability of the GGH Approach. The second paradigm, based on GGH-style encodings [43], constructs CPRFs for log-depth or log-space circuits using chains of matrices [28,30]. Here, the constrained key is a sequence of "links" that allow evaluation only if the input $x$ traverses a valid path in a branching program.
**The Attack:** These constructions are susceptible to a mix-and-match attack. Even in the purified setting (e.g., bit-fixing constraints), an adversary holding keys for two disjoint constraints can "splice" the matrix chains together. For example, by combining the first half of a chain from Key A with the second half of Key B, the adversary can evaluate the PRF on inputs that satisfy neither constraint. While this attack can be mitigated for single-key security, the algebraic structure of the GGH encodings inherently allows for the recombination of chain segments across multiple keys, effectively breaking collusion resistance.

The vulnerabilities identified in these two templates reveal a fundamental gap: existing lattice-based CPRFs are susceptible to direct algebraic breaks, even when the adversary is restricted to a purified class of constraints. This demonstrates that existing techniques are insufficient for achieving collusion resistance in this regime. Our construction addresses this gap by effectively immunizing constrained keys against "algebraic combination" attacks. We achieve this by expanding the lattice-based encodings and leveraging the inherent structure of the compute-&-compare and predicated range classes.

## 2.1 Achieving Collusion-Resistance for Compute-&-Compare

We first describe a baseline design that captures the main idea of our approach: algebraically decoupling the function description from the output value by introducing an explicit offset term that depends only on the target output. In the standard BGG+ instantiations for compute-&-compare, the target $y$ is embedded directly into the homomorphic evaluation path (e.g., encoding the circuit $C_{f,y}$ such that $C_{f,y}(x) = 1$ if and only if $f(x) = y$).

Our first idea is to sample a fresh random matrix $\{\mathbf{A}_y\}_y$ for each distinct target value. Given this matrix, we will keep the BGG+ encoding dependent on $f$ only, and move target dependence into a separate offset. A direct way to enforce this is to represent constrained evaluation as a shifted version of master key evaluation:

$$(\mathbf{B} - \mathbf{f}^T \otimes \mathbf{G}) \cdot \mathbf{H}_{\mathcal{U}_{x,f}} = \mathbf{B} \cdot \mathbf{H}_{\mathcal{U}_x} - \mathbf{A}_{f(x)},$$

where $\mathbf{A}_{f(x)}$ is an offset family indexed by the output of target function $f$ on input $x$. For a constrained key for function $f$ and target $y$, the first component remains the standard BGG+ term $\mathsf{sk}_{f,y}^{(1)} = \mathbf{s}^T \cdot (\mathbf{B} - \mathbf{f}^T \otimes \mathbf{G}) + \mathsf{noise}$. Using this component, the evaluator computes

$$\mathsf{sk}_{f,y}^{(1)} \cdot \mathbf{H}_{\mathcal{U}_{x,f}} \cdot \mathbf{G}^{-1}(\mathbf{C}_x) \approx \mathbf{s}^T \cdot (\mathbf{B} - \mathbf{A}_{f(x)}) \cdot \mathbf{H}_{\mathcal{U}_x} \cdot \mathbf{G}^{-1}(\mathbf{C}_x),$$

where $\mathbf{G}^{-1}(\mathbf{C}_x)$ is the standard "bookend" matrix to ensure the output looks pseudorandom, and not just unpredictable. So the baseline constrained evaluation is exactly the master key evaluation minus the offset indexed by $f(x)$. To ensure this offset can be canceled whenever the target matches, we give out a target-specific correction term as the second component of the constrained key: $\mathsf{sk}_{f,y}^{(2)} := \mathbf{s}^T \cdot \mathbf{A}_y + \mathsf{noise}_y$. The evaluator maps it to

$$\mathsf{sk}_{f,y}^{(2)} \cdot \mathbf{G}^{-1}(\mathbf{C}_x) = (\mathbf{s}^T \cdot \mathbf{A}_y + \mathsf{noise}_y) \cdot \mathbf{G}^{-1}(\mathbf{C}_x)$$

and adds this term to the expression above. Hence the final constrained output is

$$\underbrace{\mathbf{s}^T \cdot \mathbf{B} \cdot \mathbf{H}_{\mathcal{U}_x} \cdot \mathbf{G}^{-1}(\mathbf{C}_x)}_{\text{master key evaluation core}} + \underbrace{\mathbf{s}^T \cdot (\mathbf{A}_y - \mathbf{A}_{f(x)}) \cdot \mathbf{G}^{-1}(\mathbf{C}_x)}_{\text{residual offset}} + \text{noise}.$$

If $f(x) = y$, then $\mathbf{A}_y = \mathbf{A}_{f(x)}$, so the residual offset vanishes and we recover the master evaluation value. If $f(x) \neq y$, the residual offset remains and cancellation fails. This is precisely the compute-&-compare behavior we need. We point out that the first term will be (nearly) identical in different constraint keys as long as they encode the same function $f$. Thus, an attacker cannot get any meaningful information from multiple encodings of the same function $f$ it gets from two or more keys. Now while the second component is specialized to the target $y$, it cannot be used to mount a pseudorandomness attack. This is due the fact that $\mathbf{A}_y$ is randomly sampled for each target value $y$, thus looks like an LWE sample.

This separation is the key structural feature that enables many constrained keys for one fixed function without re-encoding targets in the shared BGG+ part. The above design relies on the matrix-valued homomorphic evaluation: the universal circuit $\mathcal{U}_x$ is defined to generate the matrix output, namely $\mathcal{U}_x(f) = \mathbf{A}_{f(x)}$. We remark that the matrix-valued homomorphic evaluation was originally developed in the context of proving constraint privacy for 1-key CPRFs [26], while we use it for homomorphically computing a 'computation-dependent' offset.

**Handling Inefficiency of** Setup**.** In the baseline approach, Setup samples an independent random public matrix $\mathbf{A}_y$ for every $y \in \mathcal{Y}$, and the constrained key for target $y$ includes the noisy linear term $\mathbf{s}^T \mathbf{A}_y + \mathsf{noise}$. While sampling each $\mathbf{A}_y$ matrix randomly substantially helps in proving collusion-resistant constrained pseudorandomness, it makes the CPRF system to be highly inefficient. Note that the universal circuit $\mathcal{U}_x$ is effectively defined with this table hardwired (as this circuit must know which of the offset matrices need to added). Therefore, both parameter size and representation complexity scale with $|\mathcal{Y}|$. Effectively, when $|\mathcal{Y}|$ is exponential, this system becomes infeasible. Thus, we would need the number of targets $|\mathcal{Y}|$ to be polynomially bounded. This is a severe restriction that we would like to avoid.

To remove this bottleneck, we keep exactly the same offset-correction structure and replace only how $\mathbf{A}_y$ is generated. Instead of hardwiring an explicit table $\{\mathbf{A}_y\}_{y\in\mathcal{Y}}$ in $\mathsf{pp}$, we instantiate $\mathbf{A}_y$ using the matrix-generation framework of any of the prior key-homomorphic PRF works such as [7,17]. In this approach, $\mathbf{A}_y$ is efficiently computable from $y$ via a recursive or sequential gadget-based composition, so setup no longer needs to publish one fresh random matrix per target value. The constrained key still contains the same target handle $\mathbf{s}^T\mathbf{A}_y + \mathsf{noise}_y$, and constrained evaluation is unchanged at the algebraic level. Hence correctness continues to follow from the same offset cancellation argument.

This replacement preserves the pseudorandomness argument as well. From the adversary's view, each target handle remains an LWE sample indexed by the queried target. So for polynomially many queries, the joint distribution $\big(\mathbf{s}^T\mathbf{B} + \mathsf{noise}, \mathbf{s}^T\mathbf{A}_{y_i} + \mathsf{noise}_{y_i}\}_{i\in[Q]}\big)$ is still pseudorandom under LWE. Therefore we keep the same collusion-resistant security intuition while eliminating the explicit $|\mathcal{Y}|$-size public table.

We point out that the above construction satisfies *key-homomorphism* property for, both, master keys as well as constrained keys. Key-homomorphism for master key follows the same argument as many prior works [7,17], which is the PRF computation is affine in the master secret key. For key-homomorphism of constrained keys, we can again rely on the same affine property as well as the fact that public-offset matrix $\mathbf{A}_y$ will be common across different systems.

### 2.2 Constraint Privacy for Compute-&-Compare Predicates

Our next goal is to also achieve constraint privacy for our compute-&-compare CPRF scheme. Observe that our previous construction already hides the target value $y$ in each constrained key. In particular, the target-specific component is $\mathbf{s}^T\mathbf{A}_y + \mathsf{noise}_y$, which is an LWE sample and is computationally indistinguishable from random. So the constrained key does not directly reveal the target value. However, this is not sufficient for constraint privacy. The evaluation algorithm still requires the compute function $f$ to compute $\mathbf{H}_{\mathcal{U}_x,f}$, so $f$ must effectively be given to the evaluator. Clearly, this is not constraint private anymore.

To hide $f$, we follow the template of [26,51] and encrypt $f$ under homomorphic encryption (HE) [44]. At a high level, we replace the plaintext evaluation of $f$ with homomorphic evaluation on a ciphertext $\mathsf{ct} = \mathsf{Enc}(f)$, while reusing the same LWE secret $\mathbf{s}$ in both the $\mathsf{BGG+}$ layer and the HE layer. This secret reuse is the standard mechanism that allows the evaluator to combine homomorphic output with the constrained-key term and recover the correct value without learning the underlying circuit.

Our setting requires one additional modification. Prior boolean templates rely on decryption of a bit that directly cancels the gap between constrained and master evaluation. In our construction, that gap is matrix-valued and equals the offset indexed by $f(x)$. So we extend the GSW homomorphic evaluation to matrix outputs as well. Let $\mathcal{U}_x$ be the universal circuit with output $\mathbf{A}_{f(x)}$, and let $\mathsf{MtrxEval}(\mathcal{U}_x, \mathsf{ct})$ denote homomorphic matrix evaluation on encrypted $f$. We use $\mathsf{AllButLastRow}$ and $\mathsf{LastRow}$ for the top and bottom parts of this evaluated ciphertext, respectively. The constrained key is

$$\mathsf{sk}_y = \left(\mathbf{s}^T(\mathbf{B} - \mathsf{ct} \otimes \mathbf{G}) + \mathsf{noise},\ \mathbf{s}^T\mathbf{A}_y + \mathsf{noise}_y\right),$$

and constrained evaluation combines the first term with $\mathsf{LastRow}(\mathcal{U}_x, \mathsf{ct})$ and the target correction term. The crucial algebraic fact is that after extending GSW homomorphic evaluation to matrix outputs, $\mathsf{MtrxEval}(\mathcal{U}_x, \mathsf{ct})$ has the form

$$\begin{bmatrix} \mathbf{C} \\ \mathbf{s}^T\mathbf{C} + \mathsf{noise} \end{bmatrix} \mathbf{R} + \begin{bmatrix} \mathbf{A}_{f(x)} \\ \mathbf{0} \end{bmatrix},$$

so applying $[\mathbf{s}^T \mid -1]$ extracts (up to noise) the matrix offset $\mathbf{s}^T\mathbf{A}_{f(x)}$. Hence the same offset-cancellation argument from the plaintext construction goes through. When $f(x) = y$, the correction $\mathbf{s}^T\mathbf{A}_y + \mathsf{noise}_y$ cancels the extracted offset and constrained evaluation matches master evaluation up to noise tolerance. When $f(x) \neq y$, cancellation fails. Thus, this construction hides, both, the target $y$ and the function $f$ while providing collusion-resistance.

We remark that our above construction only satisfies key-homomorphism property w.r.t. master key, and no longer satisfies key-homomorphism for constrained keys. This is due to the fact that the HE ciphertext computation is randomized, thus does not obey the same additive features that our previous CPRF construction did. We leave the problem of achieving key-homomorphism and collusion-resistant constraint privacy (simultaneously) as an open problem.

**Adaptive Security in the ROM.** Our standard-model proof establishes selective security, where the adversary commits to the relevant compute function before the public parameters are generated. This restriction can be removed in the random oracle model by the standard output-hashing transformation. The variant keeps the same constrained keys and the same algebraic evaluation procedure, but replaces the final output $z_x$ by $H(z_x)$. For an admissible challenge input $x^\star$, the underlying value $z_{x^\star}$ remains hidden from the adversary by the security of the base construction. Thus, except with negligible probability, the adversary never queries $z_{x^\star}$ to the random oracle. Conditioned on this event, $H(z_{x^\star})$ is a fresh random string, and the simulator may program this value as the challenge output. This gives the usual adaptive security upgrade in the ROM, following [4].

## 2.3 CPRFs for Predicated Range Constraints

Next, we generalize our base CPRF construction for compute-&-compare to the class of predicated range circuits. At a high level, our plan is to combine our base CPRF construction with the prefix-fixing CRPF based on GGM [46] PRFs. Essentially, our idea is to ensure that the user of the constrained keys can do partial evaluation over the tree instead of only given the leaf vectors. More concretely, given $\mathbf{s}^T \cdot \mathbf{A}_y + \mathsf{noise}$ as part of the constrained secret key, the user can locally approximate the value of $\mathbf{s}^T \cdot \mathbf{A}_{y|y'}$ for any $y'$. To achieve this, rather than adopting the framework of Banerjee-Peikert [7], we instead follow the approach of Boneh et al. [17]. The issue with [7] is that it computes $\mathbf{A}_y$ using a binary tree structure rather than sequentially. While it improves concrete efficiency, it is unclear whether the prefix-fixing ideas could be applied there. On the other hand, evaluation in [17] proceeds sequentially. In particular, let $\ell$ be the length of $y$, $\mathbf{A}_y$ is defined as

$$\mathbf{A}_y = \mathbf{A}_{y[1]} \cdot \mathbf{G}^{-1}\left(\mathbf{A}_{y[2]}\right) \cdot \mathbf{G}^{-1}\left(\mathbf{A}_{y[3]}\right) \dots \mathbf{G}^{-1}\left(\mathbf{A}_{y[\ell]}\right),$$

which allows the key-constraining algorithm to assign a partial key $\mathbf{s}^T \cdot \mathbf{A}_y + \mathsf{noise}_y$ for arbitrary lengths of $y$, after which the user can independently compute the approximate value of $\mathbf{s}^T \cdot \mathbf{A}_{y|y'}$. By combining the above with the fact that any range constraint (even of exponential size) can be decomposed into polynomially many prefix checks (using the power-of-two trick), we can give out constrained keys for arbitrary range predicates efficiently. To illustrate this, consider the following simple example: let $[y, z]$ be the desired range, where $y = 0010$ and $z = 1011$. The key-constraining algorithm will assign partial keys corresponding to $001\square$, $01\square\square$, and $10\square\square$, where $\square$ denotes a wildcard position. Using this, the constraining algorithm can generate compute-&-compare -style constrained keys for differing length targets.

We highlight that although our collusion-resistant CPRF construction naturally extends our compute-&-compare CPRF scheme, we are unable to generalize it to prove (full) constraint hiding. The issue is that, if we rely on a similar homomorphic-encryption-based constraint hiding template, evaluating $f(x)$ requires explicitly using $f$ to 'select' the partial key corresponding to a prefix of $f(x)$. Thus, the evaluator needs some information about $f(x)$ (which is just the maximum length of the matching prefix as per above decomposition) in order to correctly evaluate the PRF. However, we note that if an evaluator gets this additional information, then we can indeed prove constraint hiding for predicated range circuits. We believe such a weaker notion of constraint hiding might be useful for certain applications, and we leave the problem of constraint hiding for predicated range circuits as an interesting open problem.

### 2.4 Applications to 2-Sided Predicate Encryption

We explore the implications of our construction to 2-sided predicate encryption (PE), contrasting it with the more common 1-sided variant. In a standard PE scheme [22,60], a secret key $\mathsf{sk}_f$ enables the decryption of a ciphertext associated with attribute $x$ if and only if $f(x) = 1$. In the 1-sided setting, attribute-hiding is required only when $f(x) = 0$. In the 2-sided setting, $x$ must remain computationally hidden even from a user who possesses a key that successfully decrypts the ciphertext (i.e., when $f(x) = 1$). Achieving 2-sided security for general predicates is notoriously difficult, as it is essentially equivalent to collusion-resistant Functional Encryption [20,22,60,68].

We introduce a refined security notion termed 2-sided purified security. This notion guarantees attribute-hiding provided that either:

1. **Non-satisfying keys:** All queried keys $\mathsf{sk}_{f_i}$ satisfy $f_i(x) = 0$.
2. **Purified satisfying keys:** Any queried key $\mathsf{sk}_{f_j}$ that satisfies $f_j(x) = 1$ belongs to a purified circuit class (e.g., compute-&-Compare).

Crucially, we do not restrict non-satisfying queries, which may be arbitrary. We demonstrate that any 1-sided PE scheme (instantiable from LWE [51,52,71]) can be generically transformed into a 2-sided purified PE scheme using our collusion-resistant CPRFs.

To encrypt a message $m$ under attribute $x$, the encryptor does the following:

1. **Attribute Encapsulation:** Computes a symmetric-key encryption of $x$ as $\mathsf{ct}_x \leftarrow \mathsf{SKE.Enc}(k, x)$.
2. **Tag Generation:** Derives a tag $\tau \leftarrow \mathsf{CPRF.Eval}(\mathsf{cprf.msk}, \mathsf{ct}_x)$.
3. **1-Sided Encryption:** Encrypts $m$ using a 1-sided PE scheme under the augmented attribute $(\mathsf{ct}_x, \tau)$.

To create a secret key, we first sample a constrained PRF key for a compute-&-compare predicate $(f, y)$ that decrypts $\mathsf{ct}_x$ and checks if $f(\mathsf{Dec}(k, \mathsf{ct}_x)) = y$. Next, we sample a 1-sided PE key that checks if the CPRF evaluation (using the above constrain key) on the ciphertext matches the tag $\tau$. Because the message is "shielded" by the CPRF tag, an adversary learns only the bit representing the success of the evaluation, leaving $x$ hidden even upon successful decryption.

Our scheme only works in the symmetric-key setting as the encryptor needs to evaluate the CPRF for obtaining the 'tag' in the ciphertext. We leave it as an exciting open problem to generalize our construction to the public-key setting.

### 2.5 Discussion and Future Directions

**Boosting to Impure Classes.** A natural question is whether CPRFs for purified constraints can serve as a mechanism to bootstrap to more expressive, "impure" classes. While a jump to general circuits is likely precluded by some complexity theoretic lower bounds, the full version gives partial positive results for "weakly impure" constraints.

We define a circuit class $\mathcal{C}$ as *weakly impure* if any $C \in \mathcal{C}$ can be expressed as a sum of $poly(\lambda)$ purified circuits $C_1, \ldots, C_k$ from a purified class $\mathcal{C}'$. To issue a key for $C \in \mathcal{C}$, the authority generates $k$ independent CPRF keys for the constituent purified circuits. This allows us to handle predicates with *bounded overlaps*. For example, consider a range-based class where two keys might overlap on a small, fixed-length interval. By "purifying" these overlaps during the key-generation phase (i.e., treating the intersection as its own disjoint sub-predicate) we can extend the utility of our construction to non-disjoint settings.

**Open Question: Towards Arbitrary Purified Constraints.** Our result leaves open the problem of designing CPRFs for arbitrary purified circuit classes. Specifically, can we construct collusion-resistant CPRFs for any poly-size constraints where the only guarantee is that their supports are disjoint?

An affirmative answer from standard lattice assumptions would be a major breakthrough, as it would suggest that "zeroizing" attacks are the primary obstacles to collusion resistance. In the full version, we provide a candidate CPRF for log-depth constraints which we conjecture to be secure under purified corruption. We provide a proof under an extremely strong non-falsifiable lattice assumption, and pose the formal proof under a falsifiable lattice assumption (or cryptanalysis) of this candidate as an open problem.

# 3 Purifying Functionality: CPRFs and PE

In this work, we introduce the concept of *purified functionality* in functional cryptography. As discussed earlier, the community currently struggles with designing and proving security of many cryptographic primitives under general adversarial attack strategies. For instance, prior works in CPRFs and PE typically only focus on 1-key security. Our contribution is to get around this shortcoming by proposing a new notion of *purification* across different cryptographic primitives. As our main case study, we start with CPRFs and later extend it to PE as well.

Informally, a *purified* cryptographic object is defined exactly as its traditional counterpart. That is, it is described using the same set of algorithms with identical correctness guarantees. The main difference is that the purified object guarantees (full) collusion-resistant security as long as the adversary corrupts keys for a *purified class of circuits.* For example, in the context of CPRFs, a purified class means that no two constrained keys (for circuits in this class) can be used to evaluate the PRF on the same point. That is, the support for corrupted constrained keys do not overlap. As we demonstrate later via multiple constructions for purified CPRFs with provable security, this purification process enables going beyond the collusion-resistance barrier in CPRFs. Next, we formally introduce the notion of purified constraints, and later incorporate this with CPRFs.

Below, in Fig. 1, we formally define the notion of purified circuits that we refer to throughout the paper.

**Defining purified circuits**

For any $\ell \in \mathbb{N}$, let $\widehat{\mathcal{C}}$ denote a set of circuits that take $\ell$-bits of input. We say $\widehat{\mathcal{C}}$ is a class of *"purified" circuits* if the following holds:

$$\forall\, C \neq C' \in \widehat{\mathcal{C}},\ \mathsf{Supp}(C) \cap \mathsf{Supp}(C') = \emptyset. \tag{1}$$

That is, the supports for every pair of circuits in a purified class are disjoint. In other words, for every input $x \in \{0,1\}^{\ell}$, there exists at most one circuit $C$ in each purified class, $\widehat{\mathcal{C}}$, such that $C(x) = 1$.

**Fig. 1.** Purified Circuits

### 3.1 Collusion-Resistant CPRFs for Purified Constraints

We begin by providing the syntax for a constrained pseudorandom function (CPRF) [23,24,61]. Consider $\{\mathcal{C}_\ell\}_{\ell\in\mathbb{N}}$ denote an ensemble of circuit classes, where $\mathcal{C}_\ell$ consists of circuits that read $\ell$ bits of input. A CPRF for constraint class $\{\mathcal{C}_\ell\}_\ell$ consists of the following four algorithms:

$\mathsf{Setup}(1^\lambda, 1^\ell) \to \mathsf{msk}$. The setup takes the security parameter $\lambda$ and input length $\ell$ as inputs, and outputs a master secret key $\mathsf{msk}$.

$\mathsf{Eval}(\mathsf{msk}, x) \to r$. The master key evaluation algorithm takes as input the $\mathsf{msk}$ and an $\ell$-bit input $x$, and it generates the output $r$.

$\mathsf{Constrain}(\mathsf{msk}, C) \to \mathsf{sk}$. The constrain algorithm takes as input the $\mathsf{msk}$ and a constraint circuit $C \in \mathcal{C}_\ell$, and outputs a constrained key $\mathsf{sk}_C$.

$\mathsf{CEval}(\mathsf{sk}_C, x) \to r$. The constrained evaluation algorithm takes as input a constrained key $\mathsf{sk}_C$ and an input $x$, and generates the output $r$.

We require a CPRF $\mathcal{F} = (\mathsf{Setup}, \mathsf{Eval}, \mathsf{Constrain}, \mathsf{CEval})$ to satisfy the following properties:

**Correctness of constrained evaluation.** For every $\lambda, \ell \in \mathbb{N}$, circuit $C \in \mathcal{C}_\ell$, let $\mathsf{msk} \leftarrow \mathsf{Setup}(1^\lambda, 1^\ell)$ and $\mathsf{sk}_C \leftarrow \mathsf{Constrain}(\mathsf{msk}, C)$. A CPRF $\mathcal{F}$ satisfies correctness if there exists a negligible function $\mathsf{negl}(\cdot)$ such that, for every $x \in \{0,1\}^\ell$, $\Pr[\mathsf{Eval}(\mathsf{msk}, x) = \mathsf{CEval}(\mathsf{sk}, x) : C(x) = 1] \geq 1 - \mathsf{negl}(\lambda)$, where the probability is taken over the randomness of the Setup and Constrain procedures.

**Collusion-Resistant Constrained Pseudorandomness.** Informally, it states that an attacker can not distinguish the CPRF output from random on any input $x^*$ as long as the corrupted constrained keys can not be used to evaluate on $x^*$. In this work, we consider the notion of purified constrained pseudorandomness, which further requires that all constraint queries made by the adversary belong to a purified class. It is formally defined as follows.

**Definition 1** (*Purified* **Constrained Pseudorandomness).** *A CPRF $\mathcal{F}$ satisfies (collusion-resistant) constrained pseudorandomness* for purified constraints *if for every admissible PPT adversary $\mathcal{A}$, there exists a negligible function* $\mathsf{negl}(\cdot)$ *such that for all $\lambda, \ell \in \mathbb{N}$, the following probability is less than or equal to* $1/2 + \mathsf{negl}(\lambda)$:

$$\Pr\left[\mathcal{A}^{\mathsf{Constrain}(\mathsf{msk},\cdot),\mathsf{Eval}(\mathsf{msk},\cdot)}(r_b) = b : \begin{array}{r} \mathsf{msk} \leftarrow \mathsf{Setup}(1^\lambda, 1^\ell);\ b \leftarrow \{0,1\} \\ x^* \leftarrow \mathcal{A}^{\mathsf{Constrain}(\mathsf{msk},\cdot),\mathsf{Eval}(\mathsf{msk},\cdot)}(1^\lambda, 1^\ell) \\ r_0 = \mathsf{Eval}(\mathsf{msk}, x^*);\ r_1 \leftarrow \{0,1\}^{|r_0|} \end{array}\right],$$

*where $\mathcal{A}$ is an admissible adversary if: (i) $C_i(x^*) = 0$ for every circuit $C_i$ that $\mathcal{A}$ queries to the* Constrain *oracle, (ii) $x^*$ is not sent to the* Eval *oracle, and (iii) if $\mathcal{C}_\mathcal{A} = \{C_i\}_i$ denotes all circuits queried by $\mathcal{A}$ to the* Constrain *oracle, $\mathcal{C}_\mathcal{A}$ must be a purified constrain class as per Eq.* (1) *for $\mathcal{A}$ to be admissible.*

**Collusion-Resistant Constraint Hiding.** Informally, constraint hiding security (also called constrained privacy) states that an attacker can not learn nontrivial information about the constrain circuit $C$ from its corresponding constrained key $\mathsf{sk}_C$. As above, we again consider general collusion resistant attackers that can corrupt more than one constrained key. In the purified variant, we additionally require that both query families $\{C_{i,0}\}_i, \{C_{i,1}\}_i$ are purified classes, where these are the two circuit families submitted by $\mathcal{A}$ in its challenge queries. As discussed earlier, this has to be carefully defined. It is formally defined as follows.

**Definition 2 (*Purified* Constraint Privacy).** *A CPRF $\mathcal{F}$ satisfies (collusion-resistant) constrained privacy* for purified constraints *if for any stateful admissible PPT adversary $\mathcal{A}$, there exists a negligible function* $\mathsf{negl}(\cdot)$ *such that for all $\lambda, \ell \in \mathbb{N}$, the following is less than or equal to* $1/2 + \mathsf{negl}(\lambda)$*:*

$$\Pr\left[\mathcal{A}^{O_b(\mathsf{msk},\cdot,\cdot),\mathsf{Eval}(\mathsf{msk},\cdot)}(1^\lambda, 1^\ell) = b \;:\; \mathsf{msk} \leftarrow \mathsf{Setup}(1^\lambda, 1^\ell);\; b \leftarrow \{0,1\}\right],$$

*where $\mathcal{A}$ sends two circuits $C_{i,0}, C_{i,1}$ in each query to oracle $O_b$, and $O_b$ answers it as* $\mathsf{Constrain}(\mathsf{msk}, C_{i,b})$*. That is, $O_b$ generates the constrained key for the b-th circuit in each query. Moreover, $\mathcal{A}$ is an admissible adversary if:*

1. *every evaluation query $x$ is outside the support of all queried circuits. That is, every query $x \notin \bigcup_{i,b} \mathsf{Supp}(C_{i,b})$.*[3]
2. *$\{C_{i,0}\}_i$ and $\{C_{i,1}\}_i$ must both be purified constraint classes, individually, as per Eq.* (1).

*Remark 1 (Indistinguishability vs. Simulation-Based Security.).* Although the above definition only consider an indistinguishability-based notion for constraint privacy, it can be easily generalized to simulation security. While prior works [28] have demonstrated strong barriers to designing collusion-resistant private CPRFs with simulation security due to the known implication to program obfuscation [9], our CPRFs do not imply program obfuscation and thus satisfy simulation security. For the sake of simplicity, we stick to the above indistinguishability-based definition, but highlight that our CPRFs are simulation-secure.

### 3.2 Predicate Encryption for Purified Predicates

A secret-key predicate encryption (SK-PE) scheme [20,22,60], for set of attribute spaces $\mathcal{X} = \{\mathcal{X}_n\}_{n\in\mathbb{N}}$, predicate classes $\mathcal{C} = \{\mathcal{C}_n\}_{n\in\mathbb{N}}$ and message spaces $\mathcal{M} = \{\mathcal{M}_n\}_{n\in\mathbb{N}}$, consists of four polytime algorithms $(\mathsf{Setup}, \mathsf{Enc}, \mathsf{KeyGen}, \mathsf{Dec})$ with the following syntax:

$\mathsf{Setup}(1^\lambda, 1^n) \to \mathsf{msk}$. The setup algorithm takes as input the security parameter $\lambda$ and a functionality index $n$, and outputs the master secret key $\mathsf{msk}$.

$\mathsf{Enc}(\mathsf{msk}, x, m) \to \mathsf{ct}$. The encryption algorithm takes as input master key $\mathsf{msk}$, an attribute $x \in \mathcal{X}_n$ and a message $m \in \mathcal{M}_n$. It outputs a ciphertext $\mathsf{ct}$.

$\mathsf{KeyGen}(\mathsf{msk}, C) \to \mathsf{sk}_C$. The key generation algorithm takes as input master secret key $\mathsf{msk}$ and a predicate $C \in \mathcal{C}_n$. It outputs a secret key $\mathsf{sk}_C$.

[3] One could consider attackers that make evaluation queries on inputs that lie in the intersection of the support of the queried circuits too. We can handle such queries, but do not include these in the definition for simplicity.

$\mathsf{Dec}(\mathsf{sk}_C, \mathsf{ct}) \to m$ **or** $\perp$ . The decryption algorithm takes as input a secret key $\mathsf{sk}_C$ and a ciphertext ct. It outputs either a message $m \in \mathcal{M}_n$ or a special symbol $\perp$.

We require an SK-PE scheme $\mathsf{PE} = (\mathsf{Setup}, \mathsf{Enc}, \mathsf{KeyGen}, \mathsf{Dec})$ to satisfy the following properties:

**Correctness.** An SK-PE scheme PE is said to be correct if there exists s negligible function $\mathsf{negl}(\cdot)$ such that for all $\lambda, n \in \mathbb{N}$, for all $x \in \mathcal{X}_n$, $C \in \mathcal{C}_n$, $m \in \mathcal{M}_n$, the following probability is greater than or equal $1 - \mathsf{negl}(\lambda)$ if $C(x) = 1$:

$$\Pr\left[\mathsf{Dec}(\mathsf{sk}_C, \mathsf{ct}) = m : \begin{array}{c} \mathsf{msk} \leftarrow \mathsf{Setup}(1^\lambda, 1^n); \\ \mathsf{sk}_C \leftarrow \mathsf{KeyGen}(\mathsf{msk}, C); \mathsf{ct} \leftarrow \mathsf{Enc}(\mathsf{msk}, x, m) \end{array}\right].$$

**2-Sided Security.** The standard notion of security for a predicate encryption scheme is that of 2-sided security (or full attribute hiding) [22,52,60]. Informally, it captures two-sided threats– (i) a ciphertext must hide, *both*, message and attribute as long as none of the corrupted keys satisfy the attribute, and (ii) even when a corrupted key can decrypt the challenge ciphertext, ciphertext must hide all non-trivial information about the attribute.

Informally, a *purified* (secret-key) PE system is defined exactly as a regular PE system, i.e. with same syntax and correctness. As for purified CPRFs, we define predicate privacy for PE in a similar manner, which is the predicate keys corrupted by an attacker must correspond to a *purified class of predicates* (as in Fig. 1).

However, unlike purified CPRFs, we define the new purified security properties for PE in a slightly stronger way. A purified PE systems guarantees 2-sided security as long as the attacker either makes arbitrary unsatisfying predicate queries (i.e., do not require queries to correspond to a purified circuit class), or if it makes a satisfying predicate query, then all predicates correspond to a purified circuit class (as in Fig. 1). Thus, a purified PE provides *strictly stronger* security when compared to a regular 1-sided predicate encryption system [53]. We explain it formally below.

**Definition 3 (***Purified* **2-Sided Security).** *An SK-PE scheme* PE *is said to be (fully) purified 2-sided secure if for every stateful admissible PPT adversary $\mathcal{A}$, there exists a negligible function* $\mathsf{negl}(\cdot)$*, such that for every $\lambda \in \mathbb{N}$, the following probability is less than or equal to* $1/2 + \mathsf{negl}(\lambda)$*:*

$$\Pr\left[\begin{array}{c} \mathcal{A}^{\mathsf{KeyGen}(\mathsf{msk},\cdot),\mathsf{Enc}(\mathsf{msk},\cdot,\cdot)}(\mathsf{ct}) = b : \\ 1^n \leftarrow \mathcal{A}(1^\lambda);\ \mathsf{msk} \leftarrow \mathsf{Setup}(1^\lambda, 1^n) \\ ((m_0, m_1), (x_0, x_1)) \leftarrow \mathcal{A}^{\mathsf{KeyGen}(\mathsf{msk},\cdot),\mathsf{Enc}(\mathsf{msk},\cdot,\cdot)} \\ b \leftarrow \{0,1\};\ \mathsf{ct} \leftarrow \mathsf{Enc}(\mathsf{msk}, x_b, m_b) \end{array}\right],$$

*where $\mathcal{A}$ is an admissible adversary if: (i.a)* either *every predicate query $C$, made by adversary $\mathcal{A}$ to the* KeyGen *oracle, satisfies the condition that $C(x_0) = C(x_1) = 0$,* or *(i.b) $m_0 = m_1$ and every predicate query $C$ made by $\mathcal{A}$ is such* *that $C(x_0) = C(x_1)$, and (ii) let $\mathcal{C}_\mathcal{A} = \{C_i\}_i$ denote the set of all circuits queried by $\mathcal{A}$ to the* KeyGen *oracle;* if $C_i(x_0) = C_i(x_1) = 1$ *for some queried circuit $C_i$, then $\mathcal{C}_\mathcal{A}$ must be a purified circuit class as per Eq.* (1).

**Predicate Privacy.** Additionally, we also consider the notion of predicate privacy which states that a secret key must not reveal the associated predicate. Formally, it is defined as follows.

**Definition 4 (*Purified* Predicate Privacy).** *An SK-PE scheme* PE *is said satisfy purified predicate privacy if for every stateful admissible PPT adversary $\mathcal{A}$, there exists a negligible function* $\mathsf{negl}(\cdot)$, *such that for every $\lambda \in \mathbb{N}$ the following holds:*

$$\Pr\left[\mathcal{A}^{O_b(\mathsf{msk},\cdot,\cdot),\mathsf{Enc}(\mathsf{msk},\cdot,\cdot)} = b : \begin{array}{c} 1^n \leftarrow \mathcal{A}(1^\lambda);\ b \leftarrow \{0,1\} \\ \mathsf{msk} \leftarrow \mathsf{Setup}(1^\lambda, 1^n) \end{array}\right] \leq \frac{1}{2} + \mathsf{negl}(\lambda)$$

*where $\mathcal{A}$ sends two circuits $C_{i,0}, C_{i,1}$ in each query to oracle $O_b$, and $O_b$ answers it as* $\mathsf{KeyGen}(\mathsf{msk}, C_{i,b})$. *That is, $O_b$ generates the predicate key for the b-th circuit. Moreover, $\mathcal{A}$ is an admissible adversary if (i) $C_{i,0}(x) = C_{i,1}(x)$ for every attribute $x$ that was queried by $\mathcal{A}$ to the* Enc *oracle, (ii) $\{C_{i,0}\}_i$ and $\{C_{i,1}\}_i$ must both be purified constrain classes, individually, as per Eq.* (1) *for $\mathcal{A}$ to be admissible.*

*Remark 2 (Secret-key functional encryption).* We remark that the above notion of 2-sided (secret-key) predicate encryption implies (secret-key) functional encryption. By setting the plaintext message $m$ to be 1, this would give a secret-key FE scheme with appropriate security.

### 3.3 Examples of Purified Circuits

In this section, we describe two families of purified circuits with increasing expressivity. Looking ahead, we provide new constructions for CPRFs for both purified circuit families – compute-&-compare and predicated range circuits. Below we formally describe them.

**(1) Compute-&-compare** – Each circuit class in this family is associated with a function $f : \mathcal{X} \to \mathcal{Y}$, with domain and co-domain $\mathcal{X}$ and $\mathcal{Y}$. That is, each class $\widehat{\mathcal{C}}_{\mathsf{CC},f}$ is annotated with a function $f$, where $f$ can be represented as an arithmetic circuit of polynomial size.
For any function $f$ and element $y$ in its co-domain $\mathcal{Y}$, let $\mathsf{CC}[f, y]$ correspond to the '*compute-&-compare* ' circuit that, on input $x \in \mathcal{X}$, outputs 1 if and only if $f(x) = y$. In short,

$$\forall x \in \mathcal{X}, \quad \mathsf{CC}[f, y](x) = (f(x) \stackrel{?}{=} y).$$

Now we consider the following class of efficiently enumerable circuits – $\mathsf{CC}_f = \{\mathsf{CC}[f, y] \ :\ y \in \mathcal{Y}\}$. For any fixed $f$, we call any subset of $\mathsf{CC}_f$ as a compute-&-compare family of circuits. It is straightforward to check that every $\widehat{\mathcal{C}} \subseteq$

$\mathsf{CC}_f$ will indeed be a purified circuit family class as per Fig. 1. This is because for any two distinct circuits in $C, C' \in \mathsf{CC}_f$, where $C = \mathsf{CC}[f, y]$ and $C' = \mathsf{CC}[f, y']$ for some $y \neq y' \in \mathcal{Y}$, we have that $\mathsf{Supp}(C) = \{x : x \in f^{-1}(y)\}$ and $\mathsf{Supp}(C') = \{x : x \in f^{-1}(y')\}$. Since $f$ is a function, thus $\mathsf{Supp}(C) \cap \mathsf{Supp}(C')$ will always be $\emptyset$ as long as $C \neq C'$.

**Popular examples of compute-&-compare.** The most basic example of a compute-&-compare class would be if the function $f$ is the identity function, thus $\mathcal{X} = \mathcal{Y}$. Thus, one could view ID-based predicates [13,32,70] as the simplest compute-&-compare circuit class. More generally, compute-&-compare predicates have also been considered in the context of code obfuscation, popularly known as lockable obfuscation [53,71]. Moreover, one could also write down various order-revealing/preserving predicates (used in various searchable encryption systems) [1,11,12,18] as special forms of compute-&-compare predicates.

We emphasize that the setup algorithm of our CPRFs and PE does not depend on the function $f$. The adversary can arbitrarily select any function $f$ of its choice after setup happens.

**(2) Predicated range** – This is a generalization of the compute-&-compare class, wherein every circuit class is again associated with a function $f : \mathcal{X} \rightarrow \mathcal{Y}$. The difference is that instead of a comparison check to a single element, each circuit checks whether the function output lies in a pre-specified range. Concretely, let $y_1 < y_2 \in \mathcal{Y}$ be two co-domain elements.[4] Then a predicated range circuit, denoted as $\mathsf{CR}[f, y_1, y_2]$, is defined as:

$$\forall x \in \mathcal{X}, \quad \mathsf{CR}[f, y_1, y_2](x) = (f(x) \stackrel{?}{\in} [y_1, y_2]).$$

For any function $f$, and any sequence of increasingly ordered pairs $(y_1, y_2)$, $(y_3, y_4), \ldots$ (where $y_i < y_{i+1}$ and $y_i \in Y$ for every $i$), the following class of circuits $\{\mathsf{CR}[f, y_1, y_2], \mathsf{CR}[f, y_3, y_4], \ldots\}$ is referred to as a *'predicated range'* circuit class. In words, a predicated range circuit class is such that any two predicated range circuits (in that class) are associated with two non-overlapping range subsets of the co-domain $\mathcal{Y}$. Again, it is straightforward to check that every predicated range circuit class is indeed a purified circuit family class as per Fig. 1. $C = \mathsf{CR}[f, y_1, y_2]$ and $C' = \mathsf{CC}[f, y_3, y_4]$ have disjoint supports if $y_1, y_2 < y_3, y_4$. This is because $f$ is a function, and $\mathsf{Supp}(C) = \{x : x \in f^{-1}([y_1, y_2])\}$, $\mathsf{Supp}(C') = \{x : x \in f^{-1}([y_3, y_4])\}$ do not intersect.

**Popular Examples of Predicated Range.** In addition to naturally generalizing the compute-&-compare class, it captures various commonly studied circuit classes. For example, it captures fuzzy ID-based predicates [68] if we consider $f$ to be an identity function. Moreover, this also captures range-based search predicates as considered in many searchable encryption systems [1,11,12,18]. Broadly, these can also be further extended to consider hierarchical predicates [14,45,50,58], where a given predicated range circuit could be restricted to define another predicated range circuit or a compute-&-compare circuit.

[4] We are assuming that $\mathcal{Y}$ is a totally ordered set.

# 4 Collusion-Resistant CPRFs for Compute-&-Compare Constraints

In this section, we provide our first construction. We construct collusion-resistant CPRFs for compute-&-compare constraints (see Sect. 3.3). Recall that each compute-&-compare circuit $\mathsf{CC}[f, y]$ is associated with a function $f$ and co-domain element $y$. For any $\ell, \ell', L, d \in \mathbb{N}$, we construct CPRFs for depth-$d$ arithmetic circuits that take $\ell$-bits of input and output $\ell'$-bits, and have a description length $L$. The tools required for this construction are standard lattice preliminaries reviewed in the full version. We start by describing some useful parameters that will be useful for proving correctness and security of our CPRFs.

Let $\chi_0$ and $\chi_1$ be two truncated discrete gaussian distributions set as $\tilde{D}_{\mathbb{Z},\sigma}$ and $\tilde{D}_{\mathbb{Z},\sigma'}$, respectively. Fix any $\epsilon < 1/2$. Let $n, m, q, \sigma, \sigma'$ be parameters with the following constraints:

- $n = \mathsf{poly}(\lambda)$, $q \leq 2^{n^\epsilon}$, $m = \Omega(n \log q)$ (for LWE security)
- $\sigma' \geq \sigma \cdot m^{\ell'+1} \cdot 2^{\Omega(\lambda)}$ (for smudging)
- $\frac{q}{p} \geq \sigma' \cdot (L \cdot m^{\Omega(d)} + m^\ell) \cdot 2^{\Omega(\lambda)}$ (for correctness/smudging)

One possible parameter setting that satisfies the above requirement is as follows:

$$n = 2\lambda(d + \ell + \ell')/\epsilon, m = n \log q, p = 2, q = 2^{n^\epsilon}, \sigma = n, \sigma' = \sigma \cdot m^{\ell'+1} \cdot 2^\lambda.$$

*Notation.* We define function $\mathbf{A}(\mathbf{x})$ as $\mathbf{A}_{\mathbf{x}[1]} \cdot \prod_{i=2}^{\ell} \mathbf{G}^{-1}\left(\mathbf{A}_{\mathbf{x}[i]}\right)$, given matrices $\mathbf{A}_0$, $\mathbf{A}_1$, gadget matrix $\mathbf{G}$, and length $\ell$ of $\mathbf{x}$. In the following construction, $\lceil v \rfloor$ means multiplying $v$ by $p/q$ and rounding to the nearest integer. Unless otherwise specified, these notations apply to the rest of this paper. We will now describe our CPRF algorithms.

$\mathsf{Setup}(1^\lambda, 1^\ell, 1^{\ell'}, 1^L, 1^d)$: It takes as input security parameter $\lambda$, input length $\ell$, output length $\ell'$, description length $L$ of constraint functions, and depth $d$. It samples $\mathbf{B}_1, \ldots, \mathbf{B}_L \leftarrow \mathbb{Z}_q^{n \times m}, \mathbf{s} \leftarrow \mathbb{Z}_q^n, \mathbf{A}_0, \mathbf{A}_1 \leftarrow \mathbb{Z}_q^{n \times m}$. It outputs $\mathsf{pp} := (\mathbf{B}_1, \ldots, \mathbf{B}_L, \mathbf{A}_0, \mathbf{A}_1), \mathsf{msk} := \mathbf{s}$.

$\mathsf{Eval}(\mathsf{msk}, \mathbf{x})$ : It takes as input master secret key $\mathsf{msk}$ and input $\mathbf{x}$. We define circuit $\mathcal{U}_\mathbf{x}$ as the circuit which takes as input a description of a function $f$ and outputs $\mathbf{A}(f(x))$.

$$\mathbf{H}_{\mathcal{U}_\mathbf{x}} := \mathsf{EvalF}(\mathcal{U}_\mathbf{x}, \{\mathbf{B}_i\}_{i \in L}), \mathbf{B}_{\mathcal{U}_\mathbf{x}} := [\mathbf{B}_1 | \ldots | \mathbf{B}_L] \cdot \mathbf{H}_{\mathcal{U}_\mathbf{x}}.$$

The PRF output is $\left\lceil \mathbf{s}^T \cdot \mathbf{B}_{\mathcal{U}_\mathbf{x}} \cdot \mathbf{G}^{-1}(\mathbf{A}(\mathbf{x})) \right\rfloor$.

$\mathsf{Constrain}(\mathsf{msk}, C_{f,\mathbf{y}})$: It takes as input $\mathsf{msk}$ and a compute-&-compare constraint circuit $C_{f,\mathbf{y}}$. It samples $\mathbf{e} \leftarrow \chi_1^{Lm}$ and $\mathbf{e}_\mathbf{y} \leftarrow \chi_1^m$, and outputs

$$\mathsf{sk} := \left(\mathbf{s}^T \cdot [\mathbf{B}_1 - f[1]\mathbf{G} | \ldots | \mathbf{B}_L - f[L]\mathbf{G}] + \mathbf{e}^T, \mathbf{s}^T \cdot \mathbf{A}(\mathbf{y}) + \mathbf{e}_\mathbf{y}^T\right).$$

$\mathsf{CEval}(\mathsf{sk}, \mathbf{x})$: Parse $\mathsf{sk}$ as $\mathbf{b}^T, \mathbf{c}_\mathbf{y}^T$. It computes $\mathbf{H}_{\mathcal{U}_{\mathbf{x},f}} := \mathsf{EvalFX}(\mathcal{U}_\mathbf{x}, f, \{\mathbf{B}_i\}_{i \in [L]})$. The PRF output is $\left\lceil \left(\mathbf{b}^T \cdot \mathbf{H}_{\mathcal{U}_{\mathbf{x},f}} + \mathbf{c}_\mathbf{y}^T\right) \cdot \mathbf{G}^{-1}(\mathbf{A}(\mathbf{x})) \right\rfloor$.

*Proof Sketch.* Due to space constraints, we provide a brief overview here. The full version contains the complete hybrid sequence, the formal pseudorandomness definition, and parameter analysis. We will prove that our construction satisfies semi-adaptive purified constrained pseudorandomness, where the attacker only has to choose function $f$ selectively, and could adaptively select different targets $\mathbf{y}$ for constraint key queries.

The hybrid experiment is as follows: Hybrid 0 corresponds to the original game. Hybrid 1 ensures that any constrained secret key $\mathsf{sk}$ will be independent from the description of function $f$ during constrained key queries, by setting public parameter $\mathsf{pp}$ as $\mathbf{B}_1 + f[1]\mathbf{G}, \ldots, \mathbf{B}_L + f[L]\mathbf{G}$, $\mathbf{A}_0, \mathbf{A}_1$. Hybrid 2 will answer evaluation and challenge queries by generating constrained keys and applying the constrained evaluation algorithm $\mathsf{CEval}$. For example, attacker queries $\mathbf{x}$, the challenger will set $\mathbf{y}$ as $f(\mathbf{x})$ and generate constrained key using $\mathbf{y}$. Constrained keys are in the form $\mathsf{sk} = \left(\mathbf{s}^T \cdot [\mathbf{B}_1| \ldots |\mathbf{B}_L] + \mathbf{e}^T, \mathbf{s}^T \cdot \mathbf{A}(\mathbf{y}) + \mathbf{e}_{\mathbf{y}}^T\right)$, so that answers to all queries are independent from the description of $f$. Hybrid 3 will generate all constrained keys at random. Lastly, Hybrid 4 will answer the challenge query using uniformly random output. We remark that in Hybrid 4, evaluation queries are not generally answered with random strings. The challenger only randomizes those evaluation queries whose target value matches that of the challenge query by guessing such evaluation queries (i.e., for $f(\mathbf{x}) = f(\mathbf{x}^*)$, where $\mathbf{x}$ is an evaluation query and $\mathbf{x}^*$ is the challenge query).

Hybrid 0 is identically distributed to Hybrid 1. By the completeness of our design, Hybrid 1 is statistically close to Hybrid 2. Furthermore, Hybrid 2 is computationally indistinguishable from Hybrid 3, and Hybrid 3 is indistinguishable from Hybrid 4 following from learning with errors and smudging.

*Master-Key Homomorphism.* Recall that $\mathsf{Eval}(\mathbf{s}, \mathbf{x}) = \left\lceil \mathbf{s}^T \cdot \mathbf{B}_{\mathcal{U}_\mathbf{x}} \cdot \mathbf{G}^{-1}(\mathbf{A}(\mathbf{x})) \right\rfloor$, where $\mathbf{B}_{\mathcal{U}_\mathbf{x}}$ depends only on public parameters. For two master keys $\mathbf{s}_1, \mathbf{s}_2$, by linearity of matrix multiplication we have

$$\mathbf{s}_1^T \cdot \mathbf{B}_{\mathcal{U}_\mathbf{x}} \cdot \mathbf{G}^{-1}(\mathbf{A}(\mathbf{x})) + \mathbf{s}_2^T \cdot \mathbf{B}_{\mathcal{U}_\mathbf{x}} \cdot \mathbf{G}^{-1}(\mathbf{A}(\mathbf{x})) = (\mathbf{s}_1 + \mathbf{s}_2)^T \cdot \mathbf{B}_{\mathcal{U}_\mathbf{x}} \cdot \mathbf{G}^{-1}(\mathbf{A}(\mathbf{x})).$$

Therefore, before the rounding step, evaluation under $\mathbf{s}_1 + \mathbf{s}_2$ coincides exactly with the sum of evaluations under $\mathbf{s}_1$ and $\mathbf{s}_2$. The only deviation between $\mathsf{Eval}(\mathbf{s}_1 + \mathbf{s}_2, \mathbf{x})$ and $\mathsf{Eval}(\mathbf{s}_1, \mathbf{x}) + \mathsf{Eval}(\mathbf{s}_2, \mathbf{x})$ comes from the final rounding operation. This rounding error can be analyzed in exactly the same manner as in the correctness proof. In particular, the magnitude of error is negligible compared to $q/p$, and so is the rounding discrepancy. Consequently, we obtain that

$$\mathsf{Eval}(\mathbf{s}_1 + \mathbf{s}_2, \mathbf{x}) \approx \mathsf{Eval}(\mathbf{s}_1, \mathbf{x}) + \mathsf{Eval}(\mathbf{s}_2, \mathbf{x}),$$

which establishes almost key homomorphism for master keys.

*Constrained-Key Homomorphism.* For two master keys $\mathbf{s}_1, \mathbf{s}_2$ and the corresponding constrained keys $\mathsf{sk}_1, \mathsf{sk}_2$ for the same constraint, by adding the two keys gives approximately $\left((\mathbf{s}_1 + \mathbf{s}_2)^T \cdot [\mathbf{B}_1 - f[1]\mathbf{G}|\ldots|\mathbf{B}_L - f[L]\mathbf{G}], (\mathbf{s}_1 + \mathbf{s}_2)^T \cdot \mathbf{A}(\mathbf{y})\right)$. Since $\mathsf{CEval}$ is linear in these two components before the final rounding step, the only deviation again comes from the noise terms. As in the correctness proof, the accumulated error is negligible compared to $q/p$ under our parameter setting.

*Adaptive Security in the Random Oracle Model.* We note that the selective restriction in the above standard-model theorem can be removed in the random oracle model. Let $H : \mathcal{Y}_{\mathsf{PRF}} \rightarrow \{0,1\}^\lambda$ be modeled as a random oracle, where $\mathcal{Y}_{\mathsf{PRF}}$ is the output space of the algebraic PRF value computed above. The ROM variant keeps $\mathsf{Setup}$, $\mathsf{Constrain}$, and $\mathsf{CEval}$ unchanged up to the computation of the original output, and only hashes the final value. Namely, if the adaptive CPRF evaluation algorithm computes $H\left(\lceil \mathbf{s}^T \cdot \mathbf{B}_{\mathcal{U}_\mathbf{x}} \cdot \mathbf{G}^{-1}(\mathbf{A}(\mathbf{x}))\rfloor\right)$. The constrained evaluation algorithm is modified analogously: it first computes the same value as $\mathsf{CEval}$ and then applies $H$.

For an admissible challenge input $\mathbf{x}^*$, let $\mathbf{z}_{\mathbf{x}^*}$ denote the CPRF value computed before applying $H$. In the ROM proof, the simulator answers the challenge query by a fresh random string and programs $H$ at $\mathbf{z}_{\mathbf{x}^*}$. This programming is consistent unless the adversary has already queried $\mathbf{z}_{\mathbf{x}^*}$ to $H$, or obtains the same oracle point through another evaluation query. Thus the only bad events are that the adversary queries $\mathbf{z}_{\mathbf{x}^*}$ to $H$, or finds some evaluation query $\mathbf{x} \neq \mathbf{x}^*$ such that $z_\mathbf{x} = \mathbf{z}_{\mathbf{x}^*}$. The first event is ruled out by the underlying hidden-preimage property of the algebraic construction: for an admissible $\mathbf{x}^*$, the value $\mathbf{z}_{\mathbf{x}^*}$ cannot be computed from the public parameters, evaluation queries, and admissible constrained keys. The second event is ruled out by the standard collision argument for the underlying algebraic evaluation map. Hence, conditioned on these bad events not occurring, the value $H(\mathbf{z}_{\mathbf{x}^*})$ is unseen by the adversary and is distributed as a fresh random string. This gives the ROM adaptive-security upgrade via the standard output-hashing paradigm of [4].

## 5 Constraint-Hiding CPRFs for Compute-&-Compare Constraints

In this section, we additionally achieve constraint-hiding for the constrained PRFs of the above circuit class. The construction relies on the [44] fully homomorphic encryption design and the matrix-evaluation procedures $\mathsf{MtrxEval}$, $\mathsf{AllButLastRow}$, $\mathsf{LastRow}$ reviewed in the full version. The design applies the "dual use" technique in [26] to achieve constraint hiding. We define the algorithms here and additionally define the stateful simulator in the full version for the constraint hiding experiment.

Let $\chi_0$ and $\chi_1$ be two truncated discrete gaussian distributions set as $\tilde{D}_{\mathbb{Z},\sigma}$ and $\tilde{D}_{\mathbb{Z},\sigma'}$, respectively. Fix any $\epsilon < 1/2$. Let $n, m, q, \sigma, \sigma'$ be parameters with the following constraints:

- $n = \mathsf{poly}(\lambda)$, $q \le 2^{n^\epsilon}$, $m = \Omega(n \log q)$ (for LWE security)
- $\sigma' \ge \sigma \cdot m^{\ell'+1} \cdot 2^{\Omega(\lambda)}$ (for smudging)
- $\frac{q}{p} \ge \sigma' \cdot (L \cdot m^{\Omega(d)} + m^{\ell} + m^{\ell'+1}) \cdot 2^{\Omega(\lambda)}$ (for correctness/smudging)

One possible parameter setting is as follows:

$$n = 2\lambda(d + \ell + \ell')/\epsilon, m = n\log q, p = 2, q = 2^{n^\epsilon}, \sigma = n, \sigma' = \sigma \cdot m^{\ell'+1} \cdot 2^{\lambda}.$$

$\mathsf{Setup}(1^\lambda, 1^\ell, 1^{\ell'}, 1^{\ell_f}, 1^d)$: It takes as input security parameter $\lambda$, description length $\ell_f$ of constraint functions, and depth $d$. Let $L = \ell_f \cdot (n+1)^2 \log^2 q$. It samples

$$\mathbf{B}, \mathbf{B}_1, \ldots, \mathbf{B}_L \leftarrow \mathbb{Z}_q^{n\times(m+\log q)}, \mathbf{s} \leftarrow \mathbb{Z}_q^n, \mathbf{A}_0, \mathbf{A}_1 \leftarrow \mathbb{Z}_q^{n\times m},$$

$$\mathbf{R}_1, \ldots, \mathbf{R}_{\ell_f} \leftarrow \{0,1\}^{(m+\log q)\times(m+\log q)}, \mathbf{e}_f \leftarrow \chi_0^{m+\log q}.$$

It outputs

$$\mathsf{pp} := (\mathbf{B}, \mathbf{B}_1, \ldots, \mathbf{B}_L, \mathbf{A}_0, \mathbf{A}_1), \mathsf{msk} := (\mathbf{s}, \mathbf{R}_1, \ldots, \mathbf{R}_{\ell_f}, \mathbf{e}_f).$$

$\mathsf{Eval}(\mathsf{msk}, \mathbf{x})$ : It takes as input master secret key $\mathsf{msk}$ and input $\mathbf{x}$. We define circuit $\mathcal{U}_\mathbf{x}$ as the universal circuit that takes as input a description of a function $f$ and outputs $\begin{bmatrix}\mathbf{A}(f(\mathbf{x}))\\ \mathbf{0}\end{bmatrix} \in \mathbb{Z}_q^{(n+1)\times m}$. Let circuit $\widehat{\mathcal{U}}_\mathbf{x}$ be the circuit that takes as input $\mathsf{ct}_f$ (the encryption of function $f$) and outputs $\mathsf{AllButLastRow}(\mathcal{U}_\mathbf{x}, \mathsf{ct}_f)$ ($\mathsf{AllButLastRow}$ is reviewed in the full version).

$$\mathbf{H}_{\widehat{\mathcal{U}}_\mathbf{x}} := \mathsf{EvalF}(\widehat{\mathcal{U}}_\mathbf{x}, \{\mathbf{B}_i\}_{i\in L}), \mathbf{B}_{\widehat{\mathcal{U}}_\mathbf{x}} := [\mathbf{B}_1|\ldots|\mathbf{B}_L] \cdot \mathbf{H}_{\widehat{\mathcal{U}}_\mathbf{x}}.$$

The PRF output is $\left\lfloor \mathbf{s}^T \cdot \mathbf{B}_{\widehat{\mathcal{U}}_\mathbf{x}} \cdot \mathbf{G}^{-1}(\mathbf{A}(\mathbf{x})) \right\rceil$.

$\mathsf{Constrain}(\mathsf{msk}, C_{f,\mathbf{y}})$ : It takes as input a circuit $C_{f,\mathbf{y}}$ with respect to function $f$ and target $\mathbf{y}$. It then encrypts function $f$ bit by bit using fully homomorphic encryption, such that for all $i \in [\ell_f]$,

$$\mathsf{ct}_i = \begin{bmatrix}\mathbf{B}\\ \mathbf{s}^T\mathbf{B} + \mathbf{e}_f^T\end{bmatrix} \mathbf{R}_i + f_i\mathbf{G}.$$

Let $\mathsf{ct}$ denote $(\mathsf{ct}_1, \ldots, \mathsf{ct}_{\ell_f})$. Next, for all $i \in [L]$, let $\psi_i$ denote the $i$-th bit of the binary representation of $\mathsf{ct}$. It samples $\mathbf{e} \leftarrow \chi_1^{Lm}, \mathbf{e}_\mathbf{y} \leftarrow \chi_1^m$ and outputs

$$\mathsf{sk} := \left(\mathsf{ct}, \mathbf{s}^T \cdot [\mathbf{B}_1 - \psi_1\mathbf{G}|\ldots|\mathbf{B}_L - \psi_L\mathbf{G}] + \mathbf{e}^T, \mathbf{s}^T \cdot \mathbf{A}(\mathbf{y}) + \mathbf{e}_\mathbf{y}^T\right).$$

$\mathsf{CEval}(\mathsf{sk}, \mathbf{x})$: It parses $\mathsf{sk}$ as $(\mathsf{ct}, \mathbf{b}^T, \mathbf{c}_\mathbf{y}^T)$. Again let circuit $\mathcal{U}_\mathbf{x}$ be the circuit which takes as input a description of a function $f$ and outputs $\mathbf{A}(f(x))$. Let circuit $\widehat{\mathcal{U}}_\mathbf{x}$ be the circuit that takes as input $\mathsf{ct}$ (the encryption of function $f$) and outputs $\mathsf{AllButLastRow}(\mathcal{U}_\mathbf{x}, \mathsf{ct})$. It computes $\mathbf{H}_{\widehat{\mathcal{U}}_{\mathbf{x},\mathsf{ct}}} := \mathsf{EvalFX}(\widehat{\mathcal{U}}_\mathbf{x}, \mathsf{ct}, \{\mathbf{B}_i\}_{i\in L})$. Next, it computes the PRF output as

$$\left\lfloor \left(\mathbf{b}^T \cdot \mathbf{H}_{\widehat{\mathcal{U}}_{\mathbf{x},\mathsf{ct}}} + \mathsf{LastRow}(\mathcal{U}_\mathbf{x}, \mathsf{ct}) + \mathbf{c}_\mathbf{y}^T\right) \cdot \mathbf{G}^{-1}(\mathbf{A}(\mathbf{x})) \right\rceil.$$

*Proof Sketch.* Due to space constraints, we provide a brief overview here. The full version gives the formal constraint-hiding definition, complete simulator, and all intermediate hybrids. The pseudorandomness proof is similar to the proof of Sect. 4. We provide a sketch of the proof for constraint-hiding.

In our proof, we show that the answers to constrained key queries are simulatable. Hybrid 0 corresponds to the original game. Challenger of Hybrid 1 will set $\mathsf{pp}$ as $\mathbf{B}_1 + \psi_1\mathbf{G}, \ldots, \mathbf{B}_L + \psi_L\mathbf{G}$, $\mathbf{A}_0, \mathbf{A}_1$, where $(\psi_1, \ldots, \psi_L)$ is the encryption of function $f$. Hybrid 2 will answer evaluation and challenge queries by generating constrained keys. Note that each constrained key $\mathsf{sk}$ is in the form of $\mathsf{sk} = \left(\mathsf{ct}, \mathbf{s}^T \cdot [\mathbf{B}_1|\ldots|\mathbf{B}_L] + \mathbf{e}^T, \mathbf{s}^T \cdot \mathbf{A}(\mathbf{y}) + \mathbf{e}_{\mathbf{y}}^T\right)$. During Hybrid 3, for each constrained key $\mathsf{sk}$, the challenger replaces $\mathbf{s}^T \cdot [\mathbf{B}_1|\ldots|\mathbf{B}_L] + \mathbf{e}^T, \mathbf{s}^T \cdot \mathbf{A}(\mathbf{y}) + \mathbf{e}_{\mathbf{y}}^T$ with uniform random strings, and additionally sets $\mathbf{s}^T\mathbf{B} + \mathbf{e}_f^T$ uniformly at random (an intermediate step of generating $\mathsf{ct}$). Lastly, Hybrid 4 will answer all the evaluation queries using uniformly random output. And it follows from leftover hash lemma that the encryption of function $f$ looks random.

Hybrid 0 is identically distributed to Hybrid 1, which is statistically close to Hybrid 2 by completeness. By LWE and smudging, Hybrids 2, 3, and 4 are computationally indistinguishable. As a remark, the above proof cannot treat the semantic security of [44] homomorphic encryption as a black box, since LWE secret $\mathbf{s}$ is shared across multiple components of $\mathsf{sk}$. Instead, we embed the semantic security proof technique within the hybrid argument.

## 6 Collusion-Resistant CPRFs for Predicated Range Circuits

In this section, we construct our collusion-resistant CPRFs for the predicated range class. (See Sect. 3.3). Due to space constraints, the full version includes the parameters and their complete derivation. For our design, the notations, definition of function $\mathbf{A}(\cdot)$, and algorithms $\mathsf{Setup}, \mathsf{Eval}$ are identical to the design of Sect. 4. The rest of the algorithms are as follows:

$\mathsf{Constrain}(\mathsf{msk}, C_{f,\mathbf{y},\mathbf{z}})$: It takes as input $\mathsf{msk}$ and range constraint circuit $C$ consisting of function $f$ and range bound $\mathbf{y}, \mathbf{z}$. It runs the interval partitioning algorithm $\mathsf{IntervalPartition}(\mathbf{y}, \mathbf{z})$ as defined in Fig. 2, and obtains set $\mathcal{Y}_{\vdash}$. For each $\mathbf{y}_{\vdash} \in \mathcal{Y}_{\vdash}$ and the corresponding $j \in \mathcal{J}$, it samples $\mathbf{e}_{\mathbf{y}_{\vdash}} \leftarrow \chi_1^m$, sets $\mathbf{c}_{\mathbf{y}_{\vdash}}$ such that $\mathbf{c}_{\mathbf{y}_{\vdash}}^T = \mathbf{s}^T \cdot \mathbf{A}(\mathbf{y}_{\vdash}) + \mathbf{e}_{\mathbf{y}_{\vdash}}^T$. It adds $\mathbf{c}_{\mathbf{y}_{\vdash}}$ to the set $\mathcal{C}$. Such $\mathbf{c}_{\mathbf{y}_{\vdash}}$ corresponds to the range between $\mathbf{y}$ and $\mathbf{y} + 2^j - 1$ (including both ends). Next, it samples $\mathbf{e} \leftarrow \chi_1^{Lm}$ and outputs

$$\mathsf{sk} := \left(\mathbf{s}^T \cdot [\mathbf{B}_1 - f[1]\mathbf{G}|\ldots|\mathbf{B}_L - f[L]\mathbf{G}] + \mathbf{e}^T, \mathcal{C}\right).$$

$\mathsf{CEval}(\mathsf{sk}, \mathbf{x})$: Parse $\mathsf{sk}$ as $\mathbf{b}^T, \mathcal{C}$. Let $\mathbf{y}$ be $f(\mathbf{x})$. It takes out the key $\mathbf{c}_{\mathbf{y}_{\vdash}} \in \mathcal{C}$ where $\mathbf{c}_{\mathbf{y}_{\vdash}}$ corresponds to the range of $2^j \cdot \mathbf{y}_{\vdash}$ and $2^j \cdot \mathbf{y}_{\vdash} + 2^j - 1$ for some $j \in \{0, \ldots, \ell'\}$ and $\mathbf{y}_{\vdash}$ as a prefix of $\mathbf{y}$ of length $\ell' - j$. Note that by our design, there must exist such $\mathbf{c}_{\mathbf{y}_{\vdash}}$ corresponding to some prefix of $\mathbf{y}$ as long as the constrained key covers $\mathbf{y}$. Let $\mathbf{y}_{\dashv}$ be the suffix of $\mathbf{y}$ of length $j$. It computes $\mathbf{H}_{\mathcal{U}_{\mathbf{x}},f} := \mathsf{EvalFX}(\mathcal{U}_{\mathbf{x}}, f, \{\mathbf{B}_i\}_{i\in L})$. The PRF output is

$$\left\lfloor \left( \mathbf{b}^T \cdot \mathbf{H}_{\mathcal{U}_{\mathbf{x}},f} + \mathbf{c}_{\mathbf{y}_{\vdash}}^T \cdot \prod_{i=1}^{\ell'-j} \mathbf{G}^{-1}\left(\mathbf{A}_{\mathbf{y}_{\dashv}[i]}\right) \right) \cdot \mathbf{G}^{-1}\left(\mathbf{A}(\mathbf{x})\right) \right\rceil .$$

$\mathsf{IntervalPartition}(\mathbf{y}, \mathbf{z})$

Let $\ell'$ be the length of $\mathbf{y}, \mathbf{z}$. The algorithm follows these steps:

1. If $\mathbf{y} > \mathbf{z}$, the algorithm outputs $\mathcal{Y}_{\vdash}, \mathcal{J}$ and breaks.
2. Let $i$ be the index of the rightmost bit in binary vector $\mathbf{y}$ whose value is 1 ($i = 0$ if $\mathbf{y}$ is all zero), and let $j$ be the largest integer $j$ such that $j \leq \ell' - i$ and $\mathbf{y} + 2^j - 1 \leq \mathbf{z}$.
3. It sets $\mathbf{y}_{\vdash}$ as $\mathbf{y}_{\ell'-j}$ (the prefix of $\mathbf{y}$ of length $\ell' - j$ by our notation). It adds $\mathbf{y}_{\vdash}$ to $\mathcal{Y}_{\vdash}$, and $j$ to $\mathcal{J}$.
4. Then, it updates $\mathbf{y}$ as $\mathbf{y} + 2^j$ and returns to step 1.

**Fig. 2.** The binary interval partitioning algorithm

*Security Analysis.* Due to space constraints, the full version contains the full correctness and pseudorandomness proofs for predicated ranges.

## 7 2-Sided Predicate Encryption for Purified Class

We design predicate encryption for compute-&-compare circuits of the purified class. And our design can also be generalized to the predicated range class. It relies on constrained PRF for compute-&-compare constraints ($\mathsf{CPRF.Setup}$, $\mathsf{CPRF.Eval}$, $\mathsf{CPRF.Constrain}$, $\mathsf{CPRF.CEval}$), and private key encryption scheme ($\mathsf{SKE.Setup}$, $\mathsf{SKE.Enc}$, $\mathsf{SKE.Dec}$), and one-sided secret key predicate encryption ($\mathsf{PE.Setup}$, $\mathsf{PE.Enc}$, $\mathsf{PE.KeyGen}$, $\mathsf{PE.Dec}$).

$\mathsf{Setup}(1^\lambda, 1^{\ell_m}, 1^{\ell_x}, 1^{\ell'}, 1^{L_f}, 1^d)$: It takes as input security parameter $\lambda$, message length $\ell_m$, attribute length $\ell_x$, function output length $\ell'$, description length $L_f$ of the function, and function depth $d$. Let $\ell$ be the length of the SKE ciphertext that encrypts an attribute of length $\ell_x$. Let $L$ be the length of function $\mathsf{CPRF}.f$ where $\mathsf{CPRF}.f$ is as defined in the $\mathsf{KeyGen}$ algorithm. It generates $(\mathsf{cprf.pp}, \mathsf{cprf.msk}) \leftarrow \mathsf{CPRF.Setup}(1^\lambda, 1^\ell, 1^{\ell'}, 1^L, 1^d)$. Next, it generates $\mathsf{ske.sk} \leftarrow \mathsf{SKE.Setup}(1^\lambda)$, $\mathsf{pe.msk} \leftarrow \mathsf{PE.Setup}(1^\lambda)$. It outputs $\mathsf{cprf.pp}$ as $\mathsf{pp}$, and $(\mathsf{cprf.msk}, \mathsf{ske.sk})$ as master secret key $\mathsf{msk}$.

$\mathsf{KeyGen}(\mathsf{msk}, C_{f,\mathbf{y}})$ : It takes as input master secret key $\mathsf{msk}$, and a circuit $C$ defined by function $f$ and $\mathbf{y}$. First define function $\mathsf{CPRF}.f$ as follows: Function $\mathsf{CPRF}.f$ has $\mathsf{ske.sk}$ hardwired and takes as input $\mathsf{ske.ct}$. It outputs $f(\mathsf{Dec}(\mathsf{ske.sk}, \mathsf{ske.ct}))$ and outputs $\mathbf{0}$ if $\mathsf{Dec}(\mathsf{ske.sk}, \mathsf{ske.ct}) = \perp$. The $\mathsf{KeyGen}$ algorithm parses $\mathsf{msk}$ as $(\mathsf{cprf.msk}, \mathsf{ske.sk})$. Let circuit $C$ be the compute-&-compare circuit specified by function $\mathsf{CPRF}.f$ and $\mathbf{y}$. The $\mathsf{KeyGen}$ algorithm sets $\mathsf{cprf.sk}$ as $\mathsf{Constrain}(\mathsf{cprf.msk}, C)$. Next, let $\mathsf{PE}.f$ be the function that takes as input $\mathsf{ske.ct}, \tau$, and has the above $\mathsf{cprf.sk}$ hardwired. It outputs 1 if and only if $\mathsf{CPRF.Eval}(\mathsf{cprf.sk}, \mathsf{ske.ct}) = \tau$. The $\mathsf{KeyGen}$ algorithm generates and outputs $\mathsf{sk} \leftarrow \mathsf{PE.KeyGen}(\mathsf{pe.msk}, \mathsf{PE}.f)$.

$\mathsf{Enc}(\mathsf{msk}, \mathbf{x}, \mathbf{m})$ : It takes as input master secret key $\mathsf{msk}$, attribute $\mathbf{x}$, and message $\mathbf{m}$. It generates $\mathsf{ske.ct} \leftarrow \mathsf{SKE.Enc}(\mathsf{ske.sk}, \mathbf{x})$, $\tau := \mathsf{CPRF.Eval}(\mathsf{cprf.msk}, \mathsf{ske.ct})$, $\mathsf{ct} \leftarrow \mathsf{PE.Enc}(\mathsf{pe.msk}, (\mathsf{ske.ct}, \tau), \mathbf{m})$. It outputs $\mathsf{ct}$.

$\mathsf{Dec}(\mathsf{sk}, \mathsf{ct})$ : It outputs $\mathsf{PE.Dec}(\mathsf{sk}, \mathsf{ct})$.

*Proof Sketch.* Due to space constraints, we provide an overview of the Hybrid experiments and security proof of purified 2-sided security. The full version contains the complete security definitions and the detailed reductions for both attacker types. Hybrid 0 corresponds to the original security experiment. There are two types of attackers:

For type 1 attacker $\mathcal{A}$, both challenge attributes $x_0, x_1$ lie outside the support of the predicate associated with every secret key query. In this case, reduction can simply choose $\tau$ uniformly at random by pseudorandomness of $\mathsf{CPRF}$. By the security guarantee of the underlying one-sided predicate encryption scheme, such attacker cannot have more than $1/2 + \mathsf{negl}(\lambda)$ advantage.

Type 2 attacker corresponds to the case where the challenge messages are identical ($m_0 = m_1$). Let $b$ be the challenger's random bit. We show that even if the adversary is able to decrypt the ciphertext containing $m_b$, the attribute $x_b$ remains hidden. In Hybrid 1, the challenger generates constrained keys for the encryption and challenge queries and computes CPRF output $\tau$ using the constrained evaluation algorithm. Next in Hybrid 2, the constraining function of the underlying compute-&-compare is replaced with a dummy function that always outputs 0. Then, all constrained secret keys generated in this hybrid will be sampled as dummy keys since all possible inputs i.e. outside the supports of the constraints. In Hybrid 3, the challenger instead uses the all-zero attribute to compute $\tau$ during the challenge phase. Hybrid 0 and 1 are indistinguishable by completeness of the underlying $\mathsf{CPRF}$. Hybrid 1 is indistinguishable from Hybrid 2 by the constraint-hiding of the underlying $\mathsf{CPRF}$. Hybrid 2 is indistinguishable from Hybrid 3 by semantic security of $\mathsf{ske}$, since the $\mathsf{CPRF}$ keys are independent of the $\mathsf{ske}$ key. We conclude that both type 1 and type 2 attacker has at most $1/2 + \mathsf{negl}(\lambda)$.

**Disclosure of Interests.** The authors have no competing interests to declare that are relevant to the content of this article.

## References


1. Agrawal, R., Kiernan, J., Srikant, R., Xu, Y.: Order preserving encryption for numeric data. In: Proceedings of the 2004 ACM SIGMOD International Conference on Management of data, pp. 563–574 (2004)
2. Agrawal, S., Pellet-Mary, A.: Indistinguishability obfuscation without maps: attacks and fixes for noisy linear FE. In: Canteaut, A., Ishai, Y. (eds.) EUROCRYPT 2020. LNCS, vol. 12105, pp. 110–140. Springer, Cham (2020). https://doi.org/10.1007/978-3-030-45721-1_5
3. Ananth, P., Brakerski, Z., Segev, G., Vaikuntanathan, V.: From selective to adaptive security in functional encryption. In: Gennaro, R., Robshaw, M. (eds.) CRYPTO 2015. LNCS, vol. 9216, pp. 657–677. Springer, Heidelberg (2015). https://doi.org/10.1007/978-3-662-48000-7_32
4. Attrapadung, N., Matsuda, T., Nishimaki, R., Yamada, S., Yamakawa, T.: Constrained PRFs for NC1 in traditional groups (from crypto 2018). IEICE Technical Report; IEICE Tech. Rep. **118**(212), 61–61 (2018)
5. Attrapadung, N., Matsuda, T., Nishimaki, R., Yamada, S., Yamakawa, T.: Adaptively single-key secure constrained PRFs for $NC^1$. In: Lin, D., Sako, K. (eds.) PKC 2019. LNCS, vol. 11443, pp. 223–253. Springer, Cham (2019). https://doi.org/10.1007/978-3-030-17259-6_8
6. Banerjee, A., Fuchsbauer, G., Peikert, C., Pietrzak, K., Stevens, S.: Key-homomorphic constrained pseudorandom functions. In: Dodis, Y., Nielsen, J.B. (eds.) TCC 2015. LNCS, vol. 9015, pp. 31–60. Springer, Heidelberg (2015). https://doi.org/10.1007/978-3-662-46497-7_2
7. Banerjee, A., Peikert, C.: New and improved key-homomorphic pseudorandom functions. In: Garay, J.A., Gennaro, R. (eds.) CRYPTO 2014. LNCS, vol. 8616, pp. 353–370. Springer, Heidelberg (2014). https://doi.org/10.1007/978-3-662-44371-2_20
8. Barak, B., Brakerski, Z., Komargodski, I., Kothari, P.K.: Limits on low-degree pseudorandom generators (or: Sum-of-squares meets program obfuscation). In: Nielsen, J.B., Rijmen, V. (eds.) EUROCRYPT 2018. LNCS, vol. 10821, pp. 649–679. Springer, Cham (2018). https://doi.org/10.1007/978-3-319-78375-8_21
9. Barak, B., et al.: On the (Im)possibility of obfuscating programs. In: Kilian, J. (ed.) CRYPTO 2001. LNCS, vol. 2139, pp. 1–18. Springer, Heidelberg (2001). https://doi.org/10.1007/3-540-44647-8_1
10. Behera, A.R., Meyer, P., Orlandi, C., Roy, L., Scholl, P.: Privately constrained PRFs from DCR: puncturing and bounded waring rank. Cryptology ePrint Archive, Report 2025/230 (2025). https://eprint.iacr.org/2025/230
11. Boldyreva, A., Chenette, N., Lee, Y., O'Neill, A.: Order-preserving symmetric encryption. In: Joux, A. (ed.) EUROCRYPT 2009. LNCS, vol. 5479, pp. 224–241. Springer, Heidelberg (2009). https://doi.org/10.1007/978-3-642-01001-9_13
12. Boldyreva, A., Chenette, N., O'Neill, A.: Order-preserving encryption revisited: improved security analysis and alternative solutions. In: Rogaway, P. (ed.) CRYPTO 2011. LNCS, vol. 6841, pp. 578–595. Springer, Heidelberg (2011). https://doi.org/10.1007/978-3-642-22792-9_33
13. Boneh, D., Franklin, M.: Identity-based encryption from the Weil pairing. In: Kilian, J. (ed.) CRYPTO 2001. LNCS, vol. 2139, pp. 213–229. Springer, Heidelberg (2001). https://doi.org/10.1007/3-540-44647-8_13
14. Boneh, D., et al.: Fully key-homomorphic encryption, arithmetic circuit ABE and compact garbled circuits. In: Nguyen, P.Q., Oswald, E. (eds.) EUROCRYPT 2014.

LNCS, vol. 8441, pp. 533–556. Springer, Heidelberg (2014). https://doi.org/10.1007/978-3-642-55220-5_30
15. Boneh, D., Kim, S., Montgomery, H.: Private puncturable PRFs from standard lattice assumptions. In: Coron, J.-S., Nielsen, J.B. (eds.) EUROCRYPT 2017. LNCS, vol. 10210, pp. 415–445. Springer, Cham (2017). https://doi.org/10.1007/978-3-319-56620-7_15
16. Boneh, D., Kim, S., Wu, D.J.: Constrained keys for invertible pseudorandom functions. In: Kalai, Y., Reyzin, L. (eds.) TCC 2017. LNCS, vol. 10677, pp. 237–263. Springer, Cham (2017). https://doi.org/10.1007/978-3-319-70500-2_9
17. Boneh, D., Lewi, K., Montgomery, H., Raghunathan, A.: Key homomorphic PRFs and their applications. In: Canetti, R., Garay, J.A. (eds.) CRYPTO 2013. LNCS, vol. 8042, pp. 410–428. Springer, Heidelberg (2013). https://doi.org/10.1007/978-3-642-40041-4_23
18. Boneh, D., Lewi, K., Raykova, M., Sahai, A., Zhandry, M., Zimmerman, J.: Semantically secure order-revealing encryption: multi-input functional encryption without obfuscation. In: Oswald, E., Fischlin, M. (eds.) EUROCRYPT 2015. LNCS, vol. 9057, pp. 563–594. Springer, Heidelberg (2015). https://doi.org/10.1007/978-3-662-46803-6_19
19. Boneh, D., Lewi, K., Wu, D.J.: Constraining pseudorandom functions privately. In: Fehr, S. (ed.) PKC 2017. LNCS, vol. 10175, pp. 494–524. Springer, Heidelberg (2017). https://doi.org/10.1007/978-3-662-54388-7_17
20. Boneh, D., Sahai, A., Waters, B.: Functional encryption: definitions and challenges. In: Ishai, Y. (ed.) TCC 2011. LNCS, vol. 6597, pp. 253–273. Springer, Heidelberg (2011). https://doi.org/10.1007/978-3-642-19571-6_16
21. Boneh, D., Silverberg, A.: Applications of multilinear forms to cryptography. Cryptology ePrint Archive, Report 2002/080 (2002). https://eprint.iacr.org/2002/080
22. Boneh, D., Waters, B.: Conjunctive, subset, and range queries on encrypted data. In: Vadhan, S.P. (ed.) TCC 2007. LNCS, vol. 4392, pp. 535–554. Springer, Heidelberg (2007). https://doi.org/10.1007/978-3-540-70936-7_29
23. Boneh, D., Waters, B.: Constrained pseudorandom functions and their applications. In: Sako, K., Sarkar, P. (eds.) ASIACRYPT 2013. LNCS, vol. 8270, pp. 280–300. Springer, Heidelberg (2013). https://doi.org/10.1007/978-3-642-42045-0_15
24. Boyle, E., Goldwasser, S., Ivan, I.: Functional signatures and pseudorandom functions. In: Krawczyk, H. (ed.) PKC 2014. LNCS, vol. 8383, pp. 501–519. Springer, Heidelberg (2014). https://doi.org/10.1007/978-3-642-54631-0_29
25. Brakerski, Z., Gentry, C., Halevi, S., Lepoint, T., Sahai, A., Tibouchi, M.: Cryptanalysis of the quadratic zero-testing of GGH. Cryptology ePrint Archive, Report 2015/845 (2015). https://eprint.iacr.org/2015/845
26. Brakerski, Z., Tsabary, R., Vaikuntanathan, V., Wee, H.: Private constrained PRFs (and More) from LWE. In: Kalai, Y., Reyzin, L. (eds.) TCC 2017. LNCS, vol. 10677, pp. 264–302. Springer, Cham (2017). https://doi.org/10.1007/978-3-319-70500-2_10
27. Brakerski, Z., Vaikuntanathan, V.: Constrained key-homomorphic PRFs from standard lattice assumptions. In: Dodis, Y., Nielsen, J.B. (eds.) TCC 2015. LNCS, vol. 9015, pp. 1–30. Springer, Heidelberg (2015). https://doi.org/10.1007/978-3-662-46497-7_1
28. Canetti, R., Chen, Y.: Constraint-hiding constrained PRFs for $NC^1$ from LWE. In: Coron, J.-S., Nielsen, J.B. (eds.) EUROCRYPT 2017. LNCS, vol. 10210, pp. 446–476. Springer, Cham (2017). https://doi.org/10.1007/978-3-319-56620-7_16

29. Chen, Y., Vaikuntanathan, V., Waters, B., Wee, H., Wichs, D.: Traitor-tracing from LWE made simple and attribute-based. In: Beimel, A., Dziembowski, S. (eds.) TCC 2018. LNCS, vol. 11240, pp. 341–369. Springer, Cham (2018). https://doi.org/10.1007/978-3-030-03810-6_13
30. Chen, Y., Vaikuntanathan, V., Wee, H.: GGH15 beyond permutation branching programs: proofs, attacks, and candidates. In: Shacham, H., Boldyreva, A. (eds.) CRYPTO 2018. LNCS, vol. 10992, pp. 577–607. Springer, Cham (2018). https://doi.org/10.1007/978-3-319-96881-0_20
31. Cheon, J.H., Han, K., Lee, C., Ryu, H., Stehlé, D.: Cryptanalysis on the multilinear map over the integers and its related problems. Cryptology ePrint Archive (2014)
32. Cocks, C.: An identity based encryption scheme based on quadratic residues. In: Honary, B. (ed.) Cryptography and Coding 2001. LNCS, vol. 2260, pp. 360–363. Springer, Heidelberg (2001). https://doi.org/10.1007/3-540-45325-3_32
33. Coron, J.-S., et al.: Zeroizing without low-level zeroes: new MMAP attacks and their limitations. In: Gennaro, R., Robshaw, M. (eds.) CRYPTO 2015. LNCS, vol. 9215, pp. 247–266. Springer, Heidelberg (2015). https://doi.org/10.1007/978-3-662-47989-6_12
34. Coron, J.S., Lepoint, T., Tibouchi, M.: Cryptanalysis of two candidate fixes of multilinear maps over the integers. Cryptology ePrint Archive, Report 2014/975 (2014). https://eprint.iacr.org/2014/975
35. Coron, J.-S., Lepoint, T., Tibouchi, M.: New multilinear maps over the integers. In: Gennaro, R., Robshaw, M. (eds.) CRYPTO 2015. LNCS, vol. 9215, pp. 267–286. Springer, Heidelberg (2015). https://doi.org/10.1007/978-3-662-47989-6_13
36. Couteau, G., Devadas, L., Devadas, S., Koch, A., Servan-Schreiber, S.: QuietOT: lightweight oblivious transfer with a public-key setup. In: Chung, K.M., Sasaki, Y. (eds.) Advances in Cryptology – ASIACRYPT 2024, Part II. Lecture Notes in Computer Science, vol. 15485, pp. 197–231. Springer, Singapore, Singapore, Kolkata, India (2024). https://doi.org/10.1007/978-981-96-0888-1_7
37. Couteau, G., Meyer, P., Passelègue, A., Riahinia, M.: Constrained pseudorandom functions from homomorphic secret sharing. In: Hazay, C., Stam, M. (eds.) Advances in Cryptology – EUROCRYPT 2023, Part III. Lecture Notes in Computer Science, vol. 14006, pp. 194–224. Springer, Cham, Switzerland, Lyon, France (2023). https://doi.org/10.1007/978-3-031-30620-4_7
38. Davidson, A., Katsumata, S., Nishimaki, R., Yamada, S., Yamakawa, T.: Adaptively secure constrained pseudorandom functions in the standard model. In: Micciancio, D., Ristenpart, T. (eds.) CRYPTO 2020. LNCS, vol. 12170, pp. 559–589. Springer, Cham (2020). https://doi.org/10.1007/978-3-030-56784-2_19
39. Deshpande, A., Koppula, V., Waters, B.: Constrained pseudorandom functions for unconstrained inputs. In: Fischlin, M., Coron, J.-S. (eds.) EUROCRYPT 2016. LNCS, vol. 9666, pp. 124–153. Springer, Heidelberg (2016). https://doi.org/10.1007/978-3-662-49896-5_5
40. Dodis, Y., Katz, J., Xu, S., Yung, M.: Key-insulated public key cryptosystems. In: Knudsen, L.R. (ed.) EUROCRYPT 2002. LNCS, vol. 2332, pp. 65–82. Springer, Heidelberg (2002). https://doi.org/10.1007/3-540-46035-7_5
41. Garg, S., Gentry, C., Halevi, S.: Candidate multilinear maps from ideal lattices. In: Johansson, T., Nguyen, P.Q. (eds.) EUROCRYPT 2013. LNCS, vol. 7881, pp. 1–17. Springer, Heidelberg (2013). https://doi.org/10.1007/978-3-642-38348-9_1
42. Garg, S., Gentry, C., Halevi, S., Raykova, M., Sahai, A., Waters, B.: Candidate indistinguishability obfuscation and functional encryption for all circuits. In: 54th Annual Symposium on Foundations of Computer Science, pp. 40–49. IEEE Computer Society Press, Berkeley (2013). https://doi.org/10.1109/FOCS.2013.13

43. Gentry, C., Gorbunov, S., Halevi, S.: Graph-induced multilinear maps from lattices. In: Dodis, Y., Nielsen, J.B. (eds.) TCC 2015. LNCS, vol. 9015, pp. 498–527. Springer, Heidelberg (2015). https://doi.org/10.1007/978-3-662-46497-7_20
44. Gentry, C., Sahai, A., Waters, B.: Homomorphic encryption from learning with errors: conceptually-simpler, asymptotically-faster, attribute-based. In: Canetti, R., Garay, J.A. (eds.) CRYPTO 2013. LNCS, vol. 8042, pp. 75–92. Springer, Heidelberg (2013). https://doi.org/10.1007/978-3-642-40041-4_5
45. Gentry, C., Silverberg, A.: Hierarchical ID-based cryptography. In: Zheng, Y. (ed.) ASIACRYPT 2002. LNCS, vol. 2501, pp. 548–566. Springer, Heidelberg (2002). https://doi.org/10.1007/3-540-36178-2_34
46. Goldreich, O., Goldwasser, S., Micali, S.: How to construct random functions. J. ACM **33**(4), 792–807 (1986). https://doi.org/10.1145/6490.6503
47. Goldwasser, S., Kalai, Y.T., Popa, R.A., Vaikuntanathan, V., Zeldovich, N.: Reusable garbled circuits and succinct functional encryption. In: Boneh, D., Roughgarden, T., Feigenbaum, J. (eds.) 45th Annual ACM Symposium on Theory of Computing, pp. 555–564. ACM Press, Palo Alto (2013). https://doi.org/10.1145/2488608.2488678
48. Goldwasser, S., Lewko, A., Wilson, D.A.: Bounded-collusion IBE from key homomorphism. In: Cramer, R. (ed.) TCC 2012. LNCS, vol. 7194, pp. 564–581. Springer, Heidelberg (2012). https://doi.org/10.1007/978-3-642-28914-9_32
49. Gorbunov, S., Vaikuntanathan, V., Wee, H.: Functional encryption with bounded collusions via multi-party computation. In: Safavi-Naini, R., Canetti, R. (eds.) CRYPTO 2012. LNCS, vol. 7417, pp. 162–179. Springer, Heidelberg (2012). https://doi.org/10.1007/978-3-642-32009-5_11
50. Gorbunov, S., Vaikuntanathan, V., Wee, H.: Attribute-based encryption for circuits. In: Boneh, D., Roughgarden, T., Feigenbaum, J. (eds.) 45th Annual ACM Symposium on Theory of Computing, pp. 545–554. ACM Press, Palo Alto (2013). https://doi.org/10.1145/2488608.2488677
51. Gorbunov, S., Vaikuntanathan, V., Wee, H.: Predicate encryption for circuits from LWE. In: Gennaro, R., Robshaw, M. (eds.) CRYPTO 2015. LNCS, vol. 9216, pp. 503–523. Springer, Heidelberg (2015). https://doi.org/10.1007/978-3-662-48000-7_25
52. Goyal, R., Koppula, V., Waters, B.: Lockable obfuscation. In: Umans, C. (ed.) 58th Annual Symposium on Foundations of Computer Science, pp. 612–621. IEEE Computer Society Press, Berkeley (2017). https://doi.org/10.1109/FOCS.2017.62
53. Goyal, R., Koppula, V., Waters, B.: Separating semantic and circular security for symmetric-key bit encryption from the learning with errors assumption. In: Coron, J.-S., Nielsen, J.B. (eds.) EUROCRYPT 2017. LNCS, vol. 10211, pp. 528–557. Springer, Cham (2017). https://doi.org/10.1007/978-3-319-56614-6_18
54. Goyal, R., Quach, W., Waters, B., Wichs, D.: Broadcast and trace with $N^{\varepsilon}$ ciphertext size from standard assumptions. In: Boldyreva, A., Micciancio, D. (eds.) CRYPTO 2019. LNCS, vol. 11694, pp. 826–855. Springer, Cham (2019). https://doi.org/10.1007/978-3-030-26954-8_27
55. Goyal, V., Pandey, O., Sahai, A., Waters, B.: Attribute-based encryption for fine-grained access control of encrypted data. In: Juels, A., Wright, R.N., De Capitani di Vimercati, S. (eds.) ACM CCS 2006: 13th Conference on Computer and Communications Security, pp. 89–98. ACM Press, Alexandria (2006). https://doi.org/10.1145/1180405.1180418. available as Cryptology ePrint Archive Report 2006/309
56. Hofheinz, D., Kamath, A., Koppula, V., Waters, B.: Adaptively secure constrained pseudorandom functions. In: Goldberg, I., Moore, T. (eds.) FC 2019. LNCS, vol.

11598, pp. 357–376. Springer, Cham (2019). https://doi.org/10.1007/978-3-030-32101-7_22
57. Hopkins, S., Jain, A., Lin, H.: Counterexamples to new circular security assumptions underlying iO. In: Malkin, T., Peikert, C. (eds.) CRYPTO 2021. LNCS, vol. 12826, pp. 673–700. Springer, Cham (2021). https://doi.org/10.1007/978-3-030-84245-1_23
58. Horwitz, J., Lynn, B.: Toward hierarchical identity-based encryption. In: Knudsen, L.R. (ed.) EUROCRYPT 2002. LNCS, vol. 2332, pp. 466–481. Springer, Heidelberg (2002). https://doi.org/10.1007/3-540-46035-7_31
59. Jain, A., Lin, H., Lou, P., Sahai, A.: Polynomial-time cryptanalysis of the subspace flooding assumption for post-quantum $i\mathcal{O}$. In: Hazay, C., Stam, M. (eds.) Advances in Cryptology – EUROCRYPT 2023, Part I. Lecture Notes in Computer Science, vol. 14004, pp. 205–235. Springer, Cham, Switzerland, Lyon, France (2023). https://doi.org/10.1007/978-3-031-30545-0_8
60. Katz, J., Sahai, A., Waters, B.: Predicate encryption supporting disjunctions, polynomial equations, and inner products. In: Smart, N. (ed.) EUROCRYPT 2008. LNCS, vol. 4965, pp. 146–162. Springer, Heidelberg (2008). https://doi.org/10.1007/978-3-540-78967-3_9
61. Kiayias, A., Papadopoulos, S., Triandopoulos, N., Zacharias, T.: Delegatable pseudorandom functions and applications. In: Sadeghi, A.R., Gligor, V.D., Yung, M. (eds.) ACM CCS 2013: 20th Conference on Computer and Communications Security, pp. 669–684. ACM Press, Berlin (2013). https://doi.org/10.1145/2508859.2516668
62. Koppula, V., Waters, B., Zhandry, M.: Adaptive multiparty NIKE. In: Kiltz, E., Vaikuntanathan, V. (eds.) TCC 2022: 20th Theory of Cryptography Conference, Part II. Lecture Notes in Computer Science, vol. 13748, pp. 244–273. Springer, Cham, Switzerland, Chicago, IL, USA (2022). https://doi.org/10.1007/978-3-031-22365-5_9
63. Peikert, C., Shiehian, S.: Privately constraining and programming PRFs, the LWE way. In: Abdalla, M., Dahab, R. (eds.) PKC 2018. LNCS, vol. 10770, pp. 675–701. Springer, Cham (2018). https://doi.org/10.1007/978-3-319-76581-5_23
64. Regev, O.: On lattices, learning with errors, random linear codes, and cryptography. In: Gabow, H.N., Fagin, R. (eds.) 37th Annual ACM Symposium on Theory of Computing. pp. 84–93. ACM Press, Baltimore (2005). https://doi.org/10.1145/1060590.1060603
65. Riahinia, M.: Constrained pseudorandom functions: new constructions and connections with secure computation. Ph.D. thesis, Ecole normale supérieure de lyon-ENS LYON (2024)
66. Sahai, A., Seyalioglu, H.: Worry-free encryption: functional encryption with public keys. In: Al-Shaer, E., Keromytis, A.D., Shmatikov, V. (eds.) ACM CCS 2010: 17th Conference on Computer and Communications Security, pp. 463–472. ACM Press, Chicago, Illinois, USA (2010). https://doi.org/10.1145/1866307.1866359
67. Sahai, A., Waters, B.: How to use indistinguishability obfuscation: deniable encryption, and more. In: Symposium on Theory of Computing, STOC 2014, New York, NY, USA, May 31 – June 03 2014, pp. 475–484 (2014)
68. Sahai, A., Waters, B.: Fuzzy identity-based encryption. In: Cramer, R. (ed.) EUROCRYPT 2005. LNCS, vol. 3494, pp. 457–473. Springer, Heidelberg (2005). https://doi.org/10.1007/11426639_27
69. Servan-Schreiber, S.: Constrained pseudorandom functions for inner-product predicates from weaker assumptions. In: Chung, K.M., Sasaki, Y. (eds.) Advances in

Cryptology – ASIACRYPT 2024, Part II. Lecture Notes in Computer Science, vol. 15485, pp. 232–265. Springer, Singapore, Singapore, Kolkata, India (2024). https://doi.org/10.1007/978-981-96-0888-1_8
70. Shamir, A.: Identity-based cryptosystems and signature schemes. In: Blakley, G.R., Chaum, D. (eds.) CRYPTO 1984. LNCS, vol. 196, pp. 47–53. Springer, Heidelberg (1985). https://doi.org/10.1007/3-540-39568-7_5
71. Wichs, D., Zirdelis, G.: Obfuscating compute-and-compare programs under LWE. In: Umans, C. (ed.) 58th Annual Symposium on Foundations of Computer Science, pp. 600–611. IEEE Computer Society Press, Berkeley (2017). https://doi.org/10.1109/FOCS.2017.61

# How to Encrypt with Random Reversible Circuits: Functional, Homomorphic and CCA-Secure

Ran Canetti[1(✉)], Ji Luo[2], and Yiding Zhang[1]

[1] Boston University, Boston, USA
{canetti,zyding}@bu.edu
[2] Massachusetts Institute of Technology, Cambridge, USA
luoji@csail.mit.edu

**Abstract.** This paper is a merger of two works.

The first revisits Diffie and Hellman's idea of constructing public-key encryption (PKE) by obfuscating the forward direction of a block cipher. It proves that, when the block cipher is a permutable pseudorandom permutation (PPRP) [Shmueli–Zhandry, Crypto '25], the obfuscation is an indistinguishability obfuscator ($i\mathcal{O}$), and the encryption algorithm is applying the cipher after appending random bits, the resulting PKE scheme has some surprisingly strong security properties.

- *CCA Security.* It is secure under adaptive chosen-ciphertext attacks, without any additional structure or validity checks.
- *Functional Decryption.* For any function $f$, an obfuscated decrypt-then-apply-$f$ circuit can serve as a functional key. The augmented scheme is simulation-secure under chosen-ciphertext attacks.
- *Unary Homomorphisms.* For any length-preserving function $g$ over the plaintexts, the public key can be augmented with an obfuscated decrypt-apply-$g$-reencrypt circuit to support unbounded homomorphic iterations of $g$ over the ciphertexts, while preserving semantic security.

The first part also demonstrates that, under the split-circuit pseudorandomness assumption [Canetti–Chamon–Mucciolo–Ruckenstein, TCC '24], a random reversible circuit with sufficiently many wires and gates is a PRP permutable by reversible circuits. It concludes with instantiating the PKE scheme with reversible circuits in an optimized way.

The second work studies a new and strong cryptographic primitive: encryption schemes that allow both functional decryption and homomorphic evaluation of some functions, while disallowing others. Such a scheme enables providing select recipients with access to limited derivatives of some massive computation performed by an untrusted server, ensuring both secrecy and correctness. This part extends the definition of homomorphic CCA [Prabhakaran–Rosulek, ICALP '08] to capture a strong and versatile security notion combining functional decryption, controlled homomorphisms, and CCA security. It then shows that a slight extension of the scheme from the first work satisfies the new notion, with respect to unbounded homomorphic iterations of any single length-preserving function and unboundedly many functional keys.


N. Heninger and M. Rosulek (Eds.): CRYPTO 2026, LNCS 16800, pp. 539–580, 2026.
https://doi.org/10.1007/978-3-032-35367-2_18

# 1 Introduction

This paper is a merger of two papers that grew out of a single line of research, but ended up with substantially different results and contributions.

It has been long conjectured [21] that random reversible circuits (namely, circuits that consist of a sufficiently large polynomial number of reversible gates, with each gate uniform random from some set of basis gates generating $\mathrm{Alt}(2^n)$) compute strong pseudorandom permutations, or, in other words, are good block ciphers. The initial motivation of this research was to rigorously justify the potential use of such circuits as a basis not only for symmetric encryption, but also as for *public-key* encryption with homomorphic evaluation properties. This goal, in turn, was motivated by the recent heuristic proposals for obfuscating random reversible circuits and using them for symmetric encryption with homomorphic properties [8,13].

As a first step towards such justification, the first work observes that the notion of permutable pseudorandom permutations (PPRP), formalized by Shmueli and Zhandry [33] for very different reasons, captures the properties of random reversible circuits in a clean and powerful way. More specifically, under the split-circuit pseudorandomness (SCP) assumption proposed by [8], random reversible circuits of some fixed polynomial number of gates and wires are PRP permutable by reversible circuits.

Consider the *secret-key* encryption scheme where one encrypts by applying a PRP to the message concatenated with a random nonce—it is CCA-secure. This work proves that its *public-key* version, where the public key is an obfuscated forward evaluation of a permutable PRP, is secure as well. In fact, it is already CCA-secure, without any additional structure or validity checks. This is strong validation of the informal proposal by Diffie and Hellman [16] to do just that!

The first work continues to show that the same scheme can be naturally extended to functional encryption (FE), where the functional decryption key for $f$ is simply an obfuscated decrypt-then-apply-$f$ circuit. This FE scheme achieves *simulation*-based CCA security. The work also shows that the same scheme can be naturally extended to provide unary homomorphisms. For any (single) length-preserving function $g$ over the plaintexts, augmenting the public key by an obfuscated decrypt-apply-$g$-reencrypt circuit preserves semantic security and enables an unbounded number of homomorphic iterations of $g$ over the ciphertexts.

The second work investigates the possibility of meaningfully composing functional decryption and homomorphic evaluation. While the initial impetus was the simple scheme above, it soon became clear that, once properly formalized, the notion (termed *functional homomorphic* encryption) is extremely powerful, supporting functional decryption and homomorphic evaluation of certain computations, while ruling out any other homomorphisms, malleability, and malformed ciphertexts. The main contribution of the second part is a rigorous formulation of this flexible primitive. As a proof of concept, we also show that a natural extension of the above scheme realizes this notion with interesting applications.

Still, much remains to be understood and realized in the context of functional homomorphic encryption.

**Organization.** The rest of the section is divided by the two works.

In Sect. 2, we overview the techniques for PKE from obfuscated block ciphers. In Sect. 3, we overview the definitions and techniques for functional homomorphic encryption. Due to space constraints, we only discuss the formal definitions for SIM-CCA security of FE in Sect. 4 and functional homomorphic encryption in Sect. 5, and refer the readers to the full versions for technical details. The two works will appear on ePrint as [10,11].

### 1.1 Public-Key Encryption from Obfuscated Block Ciphers

We revisit the simplistic idea from [16] of obfuscating a block cipher, instantiated with Shmueli–Zhandry permutable pseudorandom permutation (PPRP)—their work [33] shows that an obfuscated PPRP is a TDP. Specifically, let $\mathsf{Enc}(\widetilde{\pi}, x; r) = \widetilde{\pi}(x\|r)$, where $x \in \{0,1\}^n$ is the message, $r \xleftarrow{\$} \{0,1\}^\lambda$ is the randomness, and $\widetilde{\pi} : \{0,1\}^{n+\lambda} \to \{0,1\}^{n+\lambda}$ is an obfuscated PPRP, i.e., $\widetilde{\pi} \xleftarrow{\$} i\mathcal{O}(\pi)$. To decrypt any $\mathsf{ct} \in \{0,1\}^{n+\lambda}$, simply output the first $n$ bits of $\pi^{-1}(\mathsf{ct})$.

We prove that this construction is semantically secure as long as $n$ (message length) is polynomial in $\lambda$ (security parameter). In fact, we show that the exact same scheme, without any additional encoding or validity checks, is *secure against adaptive chosen-ciphertext attacks.* This demonstrates that the simplistic approach of [16] is viable, at the strongest security level and the highest rate. (We also extend it to a size-optimized key encapsulation mechanism.)

**SIM-CCA Functional Encryption.** We show that the PKE scheme can be augmented in the *natural* way to achieve functional encryption. For a circuit $C : \{0,1\}^n \to \{0,1\}^\star$, its functional key is an obfuscated version of decrypt-then-apply-$C$, i.e., $\pi(x\|r) \mapsto C(x)$, with *zero* integrity verification logic inside. The scheme is *simulation*-secure for semi-adaptive $x$ against *adaptive* chosen-ciphertext attacks.[1] (We also propose this notion, termed SIM-CCA, not having found it in the literature.) It is the first[2] FE scheme for general circuits secure in the presence of adaptive access to the decryption oracle.

**Unary Homomorphic Encryption.** Orthogonally, we show that the same simple scheme maintains semantic security when augmented with a homomorphic evaluation program for any circuit $g : \{0,1\}^n \to \{0,1\}^n$ in the *natural* manner. The program is simply an obfuscated version of decrypt-apply-$g$-reencrypt,

[1] We remark that existing FE schemes where functional keys are obfuscated circuits, such as [17,23,34], do perform cryptographic checks (NIZK, signature, etc.) under obfuscation, yet only enjoy indistinguishability-based security.

[2] The security proof for a previous construction [27] contains an error, unfixed as of the writing of this work (see [28] for details). The notion considered there is $x$-adaptive IND-CCA, which is incomparable to SIM-CCA (see Remark 1) and remains open.

$\pi(x\|r) \mapsto \pi(g(x)\|\sigma'(r))$, where $\sigma'$ is for generating new encryption randomness. This enables everyone to homomorphically apply $g$ on any *single* ciphertext. Following [30], we call such homomorphic encryption schemes *unary*.

It is stressed that $g$ operates on all $n$ bits of the plaintext. Furthermore, the scheme is unleveled, i.e., it supports iterated homomorphic evaluations of $g$ with no *a priori* bound on the number of iterations and the ciphertext remains $(n + \text{poly}(\lambda))$-bit long throughout, with $n$ being an arbitrarily large polynomial in $\lambda$. However, we can only demonstrate semantic security with *one* homomorphic evaluation program per instance of the scheme.

*(Barrier to) Multi-function Unary HE.* The capability of iterating a single unary function already covers many natural use cases, including the original motivation of enabling user-specified remote processing of encrypted data [31]. It is nevertheless an attractive generalization to support multiple unary evaluation programs, each for a different function, with respect to the same decryption key. While we do not have a concrete reason to believe that such an extension is necessarily insecure, there is evidence that existing proof techniques are insufficient. (See more details within.) We leave further analysis of this extension as an intriguing open problem.

**Implementation via Mixed Reversible Circuits.** While the above results may be conceptually pleasing and elegant, so far they arguably are of purely theoretical interest. Indeed, the Shmueli–Zhandry construction of PPRP involves obfuscating general one-way functions using general-purpose indistinguishability obfuscation ($i\mathcal{O}$), which renders it prohibitively complex.

The work of [8] proposed and discussed constructions of reversible-circuit obfuscators (rc$i\mathcal{O}$) via local mixing of reversible circuits. Such an obfuscator preserves the format of reversible circuits, i.e., the obfuscation of an $n$-wire reversible circuit is a functionally equivalent one with *still* $n$ wires (and more gates). We observe that their route provides a potentially viable alternative construction of PPRP. We show that under the *split-circuit pseudorandomness* (SCP) assumption (used in [8] to construct rc$i\mathcal{O}$), for some polynomials $m$, $n$ in $\lambda$, a *random* $n$-wire $m$-gate reversible circuit $\pi$ is a permutable PRP, with the permuted keys being its rc$i\mathcal{O}$. Furthermore, we prove that applying rc$i\mathcal{O}$ to the Toffoli version of $\pi$, i.e., $C(x, y) := (x, y \oplus \pi(x))$ without additional ancillae, yields a TDP (and also PKE and key encapsulation mechanism, KEM).

**New Security Notions for TDP and PRP.** Along the way of obtaining the various advanced encryption schemes, we find a few simple-to-state properties of TDP and PRP satisfied by obfuscated PPRP: multi-mode puncturable TDP (in-)sufficient for CCA-secure PKE; TDP with pseudorandom images for distorted input distributions against chosen-ciphertext attacks; puncturable PRP. We formulate those notions and hope that further research leads to simpler constructions of them.

**Composition of Functional Decryption and Homomorphic Evaluation.** Given the results exhibited so far, one wonders what security properties can be guaranteed if the same PKE is augmented with *both* functional keys *and* homomorphic evaluation programs. Does it retain *any* security, or wishfully, strong security against malleability attacks? If so, how might one capture such security properties? Furthermore, why should the composed capabilities be of interest? This turns to be an intriguing set of questions. Read on!

### 1.2 Functional Homomorphic Encryption

Consider a resource-bounded computational scientist Alice who wants to simulate the computationally intensive evolution of some secret initial state $S_0$ over a long period of time. Furthermore, she wishes to share with her friend-competitor Bob certain partial measurements of the state as soon as the simulation reaches time $t$. In fact, Alice hopes to involve multiple colleagues, all computationally weak, where colleague $B_i$ should learn measurement $f_i$ of the state at any time. In other words, let $T$ be the unit-time evolution operator, then $B_i$ should learn $\{f_i(T^t(S_0))\}_{t \in \mathbb{N}}$.

Can Alice set things up so that she can offload the simulation to a powerful server and have her colleagues obtain the results without her further involvement? Furthermore, can she do so while guaranteeing correctness of all outputs and that nothing about $S_0$ leaks to any coalition of the server and a subset of colleagues, other than the values of their prescribed functions at every time step, even if they deviate from the protocol arbitrarily?

Additionally, the server may demand to be promised that once it computes (an appropriately encrypted version of) $T^m(S_0)$ for some milestone $m$, it will obtain an agreed amount of remuneration, thereby providing built-in incentive to perform the computation correctly.

We would like to design an encryption scheme powerful enough for this setting. It should allow Alice to encrypt $S_0$, provide the server with some information enabling homomorphic evaluation of $T^t$ on encrypted states, and issue to each $B_i$ a functional decryption key $\mathsf{sk}_i$ that yields $f_i(S)$ when applied to a ciphertext $\mathsf{ct}$ encrypting $S$. The scheme should guarantee that all the needed correctness and secrecy requirements hold.

Existing fully homomorphic encryption (FHE) schemes appear ill-suited for this task. In particular, they allow anyone to perform *any* computation over any set of ciphertexts that may have been generated independently of (or for better or for worse, dependent on) each other. Consequently, attestations regarding their *well-formedness* and *provenance* can only be made externally to the encryption scheme. Furthermore, *conditional* decryption that should succeed only for ciphertexts passing certain provenance checks depends on costly cryptographic mechanisms outside of the scheme itself.

The goal of providing encryption schemes that enable *controlled homomorphisms*—namely schemes where some homomorphic computations are possible whereas others are outright prohibited—has proven daunting (see, e.g., [3,29]).

Even the simpler task of constructing FHE schemes with CCA1 security is quite non-trivial [12,35].

Schemes composing functional decryption with homomorphism pose an additional set of challenges. Indeed, recall the basic security guarantee of functional encryption: a functional key $\mathsf{sk}_f$ for function $f$ must not help distinguish encryptions of $x_0$ and $x_1$ whenever $f(x_0) = f(x_1)$. Unrestricted homomorphism inherently undermines this guarantee. Suppose one is given $\mathsf{sk}_f$ and $\mathsf{ct}$ encrypting $x_0$ or $x_1$ with $f(x_0) = f(x_1)$. If the scheme allows unrestricted homomorphism, the plaintext under $\mathsf{ct}$ can be found out by identifying a function $g$ such that $f(g(x_0)) \neq f(g(x_1))$ and homomorphically applying $g$ to $\mathsf{ct}$ then decrypting it with $\mathsf{sk}_f$.

This implies that schemes composing homomorphism and functional decryption must use some mechanism to enable certain homomorphic computations but not others. This is a challenging goal, and the challenge begins at capturing the desired security properties of such schemes with a meaningful definition. This part addresses both components of this challenge.

**Contributions.** The contribution of this part is two-fold. First, we formulate a notion of security for encryption schemes that allow homomorphically applying functions to the plaintexts in any ciphertexts, and at the same time allow generating functional keys that reveal only partial information about the plaintext in any ciphertext. The definition takes into account adversaries capable of both corrupting functional keys and accessing functional decryption boxes on potentially malformed ciphertexts. Second, assuming subexponential $i\mathcal{O}$ and one-way functions, we construct a scheme achieving the above notion and with some additional attractive features.

*Unary Homomorphisms.* Our construction is enabled by confining homomorphisms to *unary* ones. Rather than homomorphically evaluating a small set of basic binary operations over pairs of ciphertexts (encrypting bits), we focus on ciphertexts that encrypt an $n$-bit string, along with one or more homomorphic evaluation programs where each enables the homomorphic application of a circuit with $n$-bit input to the encrypted message in its entirety. As will become evident, the restriction to unary homomorphisms is key to achieving the defined notion of security that accommodates both homomorphic evaluation and functional decryption. At the same time, it still allows for a rich class of applications, including, in particular, the ones in [31].

**Defining Functional Homomorphic Encryption.** Syntactically, the data owner fixes the function(s) supported for homomorphic evaluation upon set-up, and can generate functional keys freely after the set-up.

Our paradigm of security definition builds on that of [29] (which also focuses on unary homomorphisms) with some important differences. In a nutshell, we consider a game among an adversary, an extractor, and the challenger. The adversary's goal is to tell which plaintext (out of $x_0$, $x_1$ chosen by it) is inside the challenge ciphertext $\mathsf{ct}^*$ encrypted by the challenger. For this purpose, it can request functional keys for functions $f$ of its choice, as long as $f(h(x_0)) = f(h(x_1))$ for all $h$ supported as homomorphisms. In addition, the adversary can query (functional) decryptions of ciphertexts $\mathsf{ct}'$ of its choice, even using keys that could distinguish the challenge ciphertext or its homomorphic evaluations, as long as $\mathsf{ct}'$ is *unrelated* to $\mathsf{ct}^*$. The extractor is responsible for *proving provenance* to reject decryption. It is stressed that the adversary is *not responsible* for proving unrelatedness. The scheme is secure if there exists an efficient extractor with correct verdicts making the adversary fail to guess correctly better than random. (See more details below.)

**Construction.** Our construction is an extension of the simplistic PKE scheme. Recall that its encryption algorithm is $\mathsf{Enc}(\widetilde{\pi}, x; r) := \widetilde{\pi}(x\|r)$, where $x \in \{0,1\}^n$ is the message, $r \xleftarrow{\$} \{0,1\}^\lambda$ is the encryption randomness, and $\widetilde{\pi} \xleftarrow{\$} i\mathcal{O}(\pi)$ is PPRP $\pi$ obfuscated. To decrypt $\mathsf{ct} \in \{0,1\}^{n+\lambda}$, simply output the first $n$ bits of $\pi^{-1}(\mathsf{ct})$.

*Functional Decryption.* Given a circuit $f : \{0,1\}^n \to \{0,1\}^n$, a functional key for $f$ is an obfuscated decrypt-then-apply-$f$ circuit $\pi(x\|r) \mapsto f(x)$.

*Homomorphic Evaluation.* Our scheme can support two-way homomorphic iterations of a single permutation $g$. For this purpose, we prepare two programs, one for evaluating $g$ and the other for $g^{-1}$. Each one is an obfuscated decrypt-apply-$g$-reencrypt circuit $\pi(x\|r) \mapsto \pi(g^{(\pm 1)}(x)\|\sigma'_{\pm 1}(r))$.

*Comparison with Schemes in Sect.* 1.1. Other than the fact that the present scheme allows for both functional decryption and homomorphic evaluation to co-exist in the same instance, an important difference here is the specific way of rerandomization via $\sigma'_{\pm 1}$. The implementation here involves more structure to achieve the stronger security. (See details within.)

**Security Analysis.** The security proof extends from those in Sect. 1.1, but is much more challenging. Recall that for the homomorphic encryption scheme, since there are no functional keys (nor access to decryption oracle), the homomorphic evaluation chain starting at the challenge $\mathsf{ct}^*$ can be converted to a default distribution without any information about the plaintext. However, when functional keys exist in the system, this convenient technique is no longer applicable because the adversary could obtain partial information about the plaintext by obtaining functional keys—removing all information about the plaintext would certainly be distinguishable. We thus resort to switching between two possible choices of the plaintexts so as to hide the choice bit. In addition, we must also design an extractor to *precisely* reject decryption of ciphertexts evaluated from $\mathsf{ct}^*$. Carrying out those ideas for two-way evaluation heavily relies on the special structure of our rerandomization method.

## 2 PKE from Obfuscated PRP in More Detail

We start with an *operational characterization* of permutable PRP [33]. Let $i\mathcal{O}$ be an indistinguishability obfuscator. An (input-)permutable PRP family is a distribution over pairs of programs $(\pi, \pi^{-1})$ that compute a permutation over some domain (say, $\{0,1\}^N$) and its inverse, and the distribution satisfies

$$\big(i\mathcal{O}(\pi),\, i\mathcal{O}(\pi^{-1})\big) \approx \big(i\mathcal{O}(\pi \circ \Gamma),\, i\mathcal{O}(\Gamma^{-1} \circ \pi^{-1})\big)$$

for any adversarially chosen permutation $\Gamma$ (from a set of allowed ones) and randomly sampled $(\pi, \pi^{-1})$.

Shmueli and Zhandry showed that if a PPRP family is permutable with respect to all transpositions, then $i\mathcal{O}(\pi)$ is a trapdoor one-way permutation with $\pi^{-1}$ being the trapdoor [33],[3] when $\lambda \le N \le \text{poly}(\lambda)$. It is illuminating to recall their elegant proof.

Consider an adversary that, given $i\mathcal{O}(P)$ (with $P = \pi$) and $y^* = \pi(x^*)$ for a random $x^*$, outputs $x^*$ with non-negligible probability, then... *i)* plant in $P$ a random trigger so that another random point $x'$ collide with $x^*$, i.e., make $P(x') = \pi(x^*)$ and $P(x) = \pi(x)$ for $x \neq x'$; *ii)* invoke PPRP security to swap the roles of $x'$ and $x^*$ within the PPRP itself, i.e., permute $\pi$ by $\Gamma := (x' \;\; x^*)$, which makes $P(x^*) = \pi(x')$ (and $P(x) = \pi(x)$ for $x \neq x^*$) and $y^* = \pi(x')$. After the two steps, $x^*$ is a random trigger—$P$ can be written using any code that decides whether $x = x^*$ and so can the winning condition—so *iii)* remove $x^*$ as a random trigger, which simultaneously reverts $P$ to $\pi$ and makes the winning condition always fail. But all the three transitions are indistinguishable, leading to a contradiction, hence proving one-wayness.

As we shall see, the trigger–permute–untrigger technique can be further exploited to achieve much more than TDP.

### 2.1 Straight-Forward Public-Key Encryption

The mere fact that $\widetilde{\pi} \xleftarrow{\$} i\mathcal{O}(\pi)$ is a TDP does not imply, of course, the security of the simplistic PKE scheme $\mathsf{Enc}(\widetilde{\pi}, x; r) := \widetilde{\pi}(x\|r)$. Indeed, the "textbook" way to build PKE from TDP is significantly less attractive. One needs to find a hardcore function $h$ of the TDP and use them as a key encapsulation mechanism (KEM), i.e., $\mathsf{Enc}(\widetilde{\pi}, x; r) := (\widetilde{\pi}(r),\, h(r) \oplus x)$.

To prove the security of the simplistic scheme, we tweak the above proof to show that if $\pi$ is a PPRP, then $\pi(x)$ is *pseudorandom* given $i\mathcal{O}(\pi)$ as soon as a sufficiently long substring of $x$ is random, even if *the rest of $x$ is fixed.* For any adversarially chosen $v^* \in \{0,1\}^*$, let $r^* \xleftarrow{\$} \{0,1\}^\lambda$, then

$$\big(i\mathcal{O}(\pi),\, \pi(v^*\|r^*)\big) \approx \big(i\mathcal{O}(\pi),\, \text{random}\big), \tag{1}$$

[3] Their original proof uses *output*-permutable PRP, where $\Gamma$ (resp. $\Gamma^{-1}$) is applied after $\pi$ (resp. before $\pi^{-1}$). There is no difference in their feasibility. We find input-permutability cleaner for our expositions.

which implies that the PKE scheme is *selectively* secure (more on this later). Denote by $P\{a \mapsto b\}$ the program $P$ modified to map $a$ to $b$ and suppose that the adversary is always given $\mathsf{pk} \xleftarrow{\$} i\mathcal{O}(P)$ and $\mathsf{ct}^*$. The proof proceeds as follows, with $x' \xleftarrow{\$} \{0,1\}^{|v^*|+\lambda}$:

$$\begin{aligned} & \left(P, \mathsf{ct}^*\right) = \left(\pi,\ \pi(v^*\|r^*)\right) \\ \text{(add random trigger } x'\text{)} \quad & \approx \left(\pi\left\{x' \mapsto \pi(v^*\|r^*)\right\},\ \pi(v^*\|r^*)\right) \\ \text{(permute } \pi \text{ by } (x' \ \ v^*\|r^*)\text{)} \quad & \approx \left(\pi\left\{v^*\|r^* \mapsto \pi(x')\right\},\ \pi(x')\right) \\ \text{(remove random trigger } r^*\text{)} \quad & \approx \left(\pi,\ \pi(x')\right) \equiv \left(\pi,\ \text{random}\right). \end{aligned}$$

Along the hybrids, $i\mathcal{O}$ steps to rewrite programs in equivalent ways are skipped to simplify exposition in this introduction. A key difference from the proof in [33] is that only a portion of the input (corresponding to $r^*$) is used as a trigger in the last step.

**Chosen-Ciphertext Security.** CCA security for PKE is traditionally obtained by adding integrity checks to the ciphertext and during decryption. We show that the simplistic PKE scheme, with no additional structure or checks, is already CCA-secure. Note that if $\pi$ is a (usual) PRP, the *secret*-key encryption scheme $\mathsf{Enc}(\pi, x; r) = \pi(x\|r)$ is indeed CCA-secure. When upgrading to PKE using obfuscation, PPRP security enables retainment of this property.

Indeed, while any $(n+\lambda)$-bit string is a legitimate ciphertext with a well-defined $n$-bit plaintext, the ability to decrypt strings other than the challenge $\mathsf{ct}^*$ is of no help to the adversary in the secret-key version—we show that this also holds for the public-key version. In fact, Eq. (1) holds even in the presence of a *punctured decryption circuit* that decrypts every ciphertext other than $\mathsf{ct}^*$. Let $P \setminus S$ be the program $P$ modified to output $\perp$ on any input in $S$, then for any adversarially chosen $v^*$,

$$\left(i\mathcal{O}(\pi),\ y_0,\ i\mathcal{O}(\pi^{-1} \setminus \{y_0\})\right) \approx \left(i\mathcal{O}(\pi),\ y_1,\ i\mathcal{O}(\pi^{-1} \setminus \{y_1\})\right), \qquad (2)$$

where $r^* \xleftarrow{\$} \{0,1\}^{\lambda}$, $y_0 \leftarrow \pi(v^*\|r^*)$, $y_1 \xleftarrow{\$} \{0,1\}^{|v^*|+\lambda}$.

In the previous proof, we have *underutilized* PPRP security by ignoring $\pi^{-1}$. The trick to prove Eq. (2) is to trigger programs at *correlated* points. Suppose the adversary always receives $(i\mathcal{O}(P), y^*, i\mathcal{O}(Q))$. On the left-hand side, we have

$$P = \pi, \quad y^* = \pi(v^*\|r^*), \quad Q = \pi^{-1} \setminus \{y^*\} = \pi^{-1}\left\{\pi(v^*\|r^*) \mapsto \perp\right\}.$$

First, we plant a trigger $x' \xleftarrow{\$} \{0,1\}^{|v^*|+\lambda}$ into both programs:

$$\begin{aligned} P &= \pi \quad \left\{\ x' \mapsto \pi(v^*\|r^*), \qquad v^*\|r^* \mapsto \pi(v^*\|r^*)\right\}, \quad y^* = \pi(v^*\|r^*), \\ Q &= \pi^{-1}\left\{\pi(x') \mapsto v^*\|r^* \quad , \quad \pi(v^*\|r^*) \mapsto \perp \qquad \right\}. \end{aligned}$$

The redundant branch $v^*\|r^* \mapsto \cdots$ in $P$ is for clarity. Permuting $\pi$ by $(x' \ \ v^*\|r^*)$ leads to

$$\begin{aligned} P &= \pi \quad \left\{ \qquad x' \mapsto \pi(x'), \quad v^*\|r^* \mapsto \pi(x')\right\}, \qquad y^* = \pi(x'), \\ Q &= \pi^{-1}\left\{\pi(v^*\|r^*) \mapsto v^*\|r^*, \quad \pi(x') \mapsto \perp \ \right\}. \end{aligned}$$

Lastly, we remove $r^*$ as a random trigger and reach the right-hand side,

$$P = \pi, \quad y^* = \pi(x'), \quad Q = \pi^{-1}\{\pi(x') \mapsto \bot\} = \pi^{-1} \setminus \{y^*\}.$$

**Adaptive Security.** One caveat of the proofs above is that they only work only when $v^*$ (the challenge plaintext $x^*$) is chosen prior to receiving $\mathsf{pk} \xleftarrow{\$} i\mathcal{O}(\pi)$ and access to the decryption oracle. The scheme can be used as a CCA-secure key encapsulation mechanism (KEM), but we will discuss this point later. Now, we address the issue of adaptive security.

Recall that in the standard definition of CCA security, the adversary sees $\mathsf{pk}$, interacts with the decryption oracle, then chooses the challenge plaintext(s), and further interacts with the decryption oracle before outputting a decision bit. We start by identify two difficulties: *i)* the decryption *oracle* becomes punctured only after choosing the challenge plaintext, but any *program*, once given to the adversary, cannot be retroactively punctured (at least not classically); *ii)* the permutation $\Gamma$ applied to $\pi$ must be chosen prior to seeing $\pi$ in PPRP security, but $\Gamma$ must also somehow "work on" a plaintext chosen dependent on $\pi$.

Our first observation is that the decryption program can be punctured *by encryption randomness*. Namely, we sample $r^* \xleftarrow{\$} \{0,1\}^\lambda$ at the onset of the CCA game, and reject any pre-challenge decryption query $\mathsf{ct}'$ such that $\pi^{-1}(\mathsf{ct}')$ ends with $r^*$. This only leads to a negligible statistical error as the adversary's view is independent of $r^*$ prior to receiving the challenge $\mathsf{ct}^* = y^*$. It removes the apparent capability of decrypting $\mathsf{ct}^*$. Moreover, once $v^*$ is chosen, we reveal another decryption program punctured only at $y^*$. Together, they solve the first difficulty.

To overcome the second difficulty, we design $\Gamma$ to randomize *every possible plaintext* when the encryption randomness is $r^*$. Letting $u^* \xleftarrow{\$} \{0,1\}^{|v^*|}$ and $s^* \xleftarrow{\$} \{0,1\}^\lambda$, we define

$$\Gamma(v\|r) := \begin{cases} (u^* \oplus v)\,\|s^*, & \text{if } r = r^*; \\ v\,\|r^*, & \text{if } r = s^*; \\ v\,\|r, & \text{otherwise.} \end{cases}$$

In other words, $\Gamma$ applies a one-time pad $u^*$ for the challenge and swaps randomness values $r^*$, $s^*$. The PPRP of [33] is permutable by such $\Gamma$.

Roughly speaking, we prove

$$(i\mathcal{O}(P),\, i\mathcal{O}(Q_0),\, y_0,\, i\mathcal{O}(R_0)) \approx (i\mathcal{O}(P),\, i\mathcal{O}(Q_1),\, y_1,\, i\mathcal{O}(R_1)) \tag{3}$$

for $v^*$ adversarially chosen dependent on the first two programs and

$$P = \pi, \qquad Q_0 = \pi^{-1} \setminus \left\{\pi(v\|r^*) \mid v \in \{0,1\}^{|v^*|}\right\},$$

$$y_0 \leftarrow \pi(v^*\|r^*), \qquad y_1 \xleftarrow{\$} \{0,1\}^{|v^*|+\lambda},$$

$$Q_1 = \pi^{-1} \setminus \{y_1\}, \qquad R_\beta(y) = \begin{cases} \bot, & \text{if } y = y_\beta; \\ v, & \text{if } y \neq y_\beta \text{ and } \pi^{-1}(y) = v\|r. \end{cases}$$

Here, we strip the randomness from the output of $R$ due to some technicalities in the proof.

The proof involves two rounds of trigger–permute–untrigger. A general guideline in choosing the functionality on the triggered points is to *(pre-)compose* $\Gamma^{-1}$ *to* $\pi$ *on that branch* so that it reverts to $\pi$ (normal behavior) once $\pi$ is permuted by $\Gamma$. Morphing the hybrids from the left-hand side, for the first round, we first plant trigger $s^*$:

$$P(v\|r) = \begin{cases} \pi(\Gamma^{-1}(v\|r)) = \pi((u^* \oplus v)\|r^*), & \text{if } r = s^*; \\ \pi(v\|r), & \text{otherwise}; \end{cases}$$
$$Q = \pi^{-1} \setminus \left\{ \pi(v\|r^*),\, \pi(v\|s^*) \,\middle|\, v \in \{0,1\}^{|v^*|} \right\},$$

and $R$ is unchanged. Next, we permute $\pi$ by $\Gamma$; then, we remove the trigger $r^*$. The overall effect is to change the components to

$$P = \pi, \qquad Q = \pi^{-1} \setminus \left\{ \pi(v\|s^*) \,\middle|\, v \in \{0,1\}^{|v^*|} \right\},$$
$$y^* = \pi((u^* \oplus v^*)\|s^*), \quad R(y) = \begin{cases} \perp, & \text{if } y = y^*; \\ v \oplus u^*, & \text{else if } \pi^{-1}(y) = v\|s^*; \\ v, & \text{else, } \pi^{-1}(y) = v\|r \text{ for } r \neq s^*. \end{cases}$$

By changing the variable to $w^* \xleftarrow{\$} \{0,1\}^{|v^*|}$ and programming $u^* \leftarrow v^* \oplus w^*$, we write $y^* = \pi(w^*\|s^*)$ without $v^*$, but the code of $R$ leaks information about $v^*$ (due to $u^*$).

The current hybrid is similar to the case of selective security—the "plaintext" inside $y^*$ is chosen independently of $\pi$. Intuitively, we can delete the leaky branch of $R$ because $s^*$, although appearing in $y^*$, should be pseudorandom hence a trigger. Indeed, it can be done by a second round of trigger–permute–untrigger, permuting $\pi$ by $(w^*\|s' \;\; w^*\|s^*)$ for a random $s'$. (It also makes $Q$ punctured only at $y^*$.)

## 2.2 Free Upgrade to Functional Encryption

The simplistic PKE scheme can be easily upgraded to provide functional decryption capability, without changing the encryption key/algorithm at all. In the customary notation for FE, the PKE scheme is cast to $\mathsf{mpk} \xleftarrow{\$} i\mathcal{O}(\pi)$, $\mathsf{msk} = \pi^{-1}$, $\mathsf{ct}(x) = \pi(x\|r)$, and $\mathsf{Dec}(\mathsf{msk}, \mathsf{ct}) = x$ with $x\|r \leftarrow \pi^{-1}(\mathsf{ct})$. A functional key for circuit $C$ is $\mathsf{sk}_C \xleftarrow{\$} i\mathcal{O}(\mathsf{ct} \mapsto C(\mathsf{Dec}(\mathsf{msk}, \mathsf{ct})))$, i.e., an obfuscated decrypt-then-compute program.

The scheme is *simulation*-secure against chosen-ciphertext attacks (SIM-CCA). More precisely, consider the following (real) interaction. The adversary $\mathcal{A}$ receives $\mathsf{mpk}$ and is given access to key creation, key retrieval, and decryption oracles. Here, when a key $\mathsf{sk}_j$ for circuit $C_j$ is created, it is *not* automatically revealed to $\mathcal{A}$. Instead, $\mathcal{A}$ is given a handle (index) to it. It can submit the handle to retrieve the key, or submit $\mathsf{ct}'$ with any index to perform decryption using any key, or query for decryptions adaptively and retrieve keys conditionally, thereby modelling a flexible class of attacks. Prior to the first key retrieval query, the adversary must have chosen a challenge plaintext $x^*$, for which it gets back a ciphertext $\mathsf{ct}^*$.

We construct an efficient simulator such that for any efficient adversary, the real interaction is indistinguishable to the simulation—the simulator is responsible for creating $\mathsf{mpk}$, $\mathsf{ct}^*$, and responding to oracle queries. Upon the challenge, the simulator must output $\mathsf{ct}^*$ without being given $x^*$. All key creation and decryption queries are answered *without* giving $C(x^*)$ to the simulator, regardless of them being pre- or post-challenge. Upon a key retrieval query[4] (to key $j$ for circuit $C_j$), the value $C_j(x^*)$ is provided to the simulator, which responds with $\mathsf{sk}_j$.

The simulator is straight-forward. It generates $\mathsf{mpk}$ normally, keeps $\pi^{-1}$ to itself, and samples a random string $\mathsf{ct}^*$ as the simulated ciphertext. To create key $j$ for circuit $C_j$, it remembers $(j, C_j)$. To decrypt $\mathsf{ct}'$ using key $j$, it outputs $C_j(x)$ for $x \| r \leftarrow \pi^{-1}(\mathsf{ct}')$ if $\mathsf{ct}' \neq \mathsf{ct}^*$, or else $\perp$ if $\mathsf{ct}' = \mathsf{ct}^*$ (including in the pre-challenge phase). When a key is to be retrieved for the first time, the simulator gets $z_j^* = C_j(x^*)$, and it outputs $\mathsf{sk}_j \overset{\$}{\leftarrow} i\mathcal{O}(\widehat{C}_j)$, where $\widehat{C}_j(\mathsf{ct})$ outputs $z_j^*$ if $\mathsf{ct} = \mathsf{ct}^*$ or else $C_j(\mathsf{Dec}(\pi^{-1}, \mathsf{ct}))$—in other words, a simulated key hardwires the decryption result for the simulated ciphertext and otherwise operates normally.

The validity of our simulator is shown using Eq. (3). The program $Q$ is used to answer decryption queries and $R$ is used to generate retrieved keys.

### 2.3 Optimized Key Encapsulation Mechanism

Although simple and powerful for extension, the simplistic PKE does not scale well with the plaintext length—the major overhead would be obfuscating large circuits with long inputs. In practice, public-key encryption is almost always done using hybrid encryption. Any PKE can be used as a KEM, albeit at the cost of ciphertext blow-up on top of *true* entropy in the encapsulated key, i.e., $\mathsf{Enc}(\mathsf{pk}, k; r)$ is necessarily longer than $k$, which has at most $|k|$ bits of true entropy.

We construct a simple *size-optimized* KEM by obfuscating *two* permutation instances. Let $\pi$, $\sigma$ be two PPRP over domain $\{0,1\}^\lambda$. We set $\mathsf{pk} \overset{\$}{\leftarrow} (i\mathcal{O}(\pi), i\mathcal{O}(\sigma))$ and $\mathsf{sk} = (\pi^{-1}, \sigma)$. A ciphertext is $\mathsf{ct} = \pi(r)$ and it encapsulates key $k = \sigma(r) = \sigma(\pi^{-1}(\mathsf{ct}))$. Note that the ciphertext length is $|\mathsf{ct}| = \lambda$ and $k$, marginally, has $\lambda$ bits of entropy, i.e., there is no blow-up at all.

[4] It is stressed that functional keys can be *retrieved* only after the challenge plaintext $x^*$ is chosen. Indeed, if an unbounded number of key retrievals are allowed prior to choosing $x^*$, simulation-secure FE for general circuits is impossible in the standard model [1,6]. On the other hand, they can be (created and) *used for decryption queries* in both pre- and post-challenge phases.

The scheme is CCA-secure, which boils down to

$$\begin{aligned} &\big(i\mathcal{O}(\pi),\, i\mathcal{O}(\sigma),\, \pi(r),\, \sigma(r),\;\; i\mathcal{O}(\pi^{-1} \setminus \{\pi(r)\})\big) \\ \approx\; &\big(i\mathcal{O}(\pi),\, i\mathcal{O}(\sigma),\, \pi(s),\, \sigma(s'),\, i\mathcal{O}(\pi^{-1} \setminus \{\pi(s)\})\big), \end{aligned} \tag{4}$$

where $r$, $s$, $s'$ are independent $\lambda$-bit random strings. Here, the last program (together with $i\mathcal{O}(\sigma)$) is used to answer decryption queries. The proof is a simple extension of PKE selective security: we plant $s$ (resp. $s'$) into $\pi$ and $\pi^{-1}$ (resp. $\sigma$), then permute $\pi$ by $(r\;\; s)$ and $\sigma$ by $(r\;\; s')$.

On top of having full-entropy keys, assuming subexponential $i\mathcal{O}$ and PPRP, the *concrete* computational security of this KEM is *only* limited by the security level of $|\mathsf{ct}|$-bit triggers. Observe that dialing up the security parameters of $i\mathcal{O}$ and PPRP only affects the lengths of $\mathsf{pk}$, $\mathsf{sk}$, not those of $\mathsf{ct}$, $k$.

**Cohardcore Functions.** The KEM result can be phrased as "$i\mathcal{O}(\sigma)$ is a hardcore function for $i\mathcal{O}(\pi)$, even in the presence of punctured $\pi^{-1}$". A consequence of the selective PKE result is that any subset of preimage bits (corresponding to the plaintext) are hardcore as long as the complement subset is large enough. One could ask what other functions $h$ are hardcore for $i\mathcal{O}(\pi)$. We note, however, that a better notion to consider is *cohardcoreness.*

Recall that $h$ is *hardcore* for $f$ if $h(x)$ is pseudorandom given $f(x)$, with the most interesting case being $f(x)$ determining $h(x)$. We say that $h$ is *cohardcore* for $f$ if $f(x)$ is pseudorandom given $h(x)$, with the interesting case *still* being $f(x)$ determining $h(x)$. In this terminology, plaintexts are cohardcore for ciphertexts in PKE. The reason to consider cohardcoreness is that in general, nothing specific can be said about the image distribution of an arbitrary function $h$, yet $i\mathcal{O}(\pi)$ is an obfuscated PPRP, whose image we can expect to be pseudorandom. This dual notion can often be converted to the primal—if $h$ has marginally pseudorandom image distribution and it is cohardcore for $f$, then it is also hardcore for $f$.

We prove that a large class of functions $h$ are cohardcore for obfuscated PPRP $i\mathcal{O}(\pi)$, even for non-uniform input distribution (subject to conditions) and even in the presence of punctured inverse of $\pi$. The condition for $h$ and input $x^*$ is that a public polynomial-size circuit $h'$ exists so that $(h(x^*), h'(x^*))$ has unique preimage $x^*$ under the tuple map $x \mapsto (h(x), h'(x))$ and $h'(x^*)$ is long enough and pseudorandom (given the other information). The function $h'$ will serve the "untrigger" step. This result is general enough to recover KEM and selective PKE, as well as a lemma that will be used for unary homomorphic encryption.

### 2.4 Unary Homomorphic Encryption

Taking another route, we show how to upgrade the same PKE scheme to enable homomorphic evaluation over encrypted data. This is probably quite surprising. More specifically, given any circuit $g : \{0,1\}^n \to \{0,1\}^n$, we augment the public key with an obfuscation of $\mathsf{Ev}_g(\pi(x\|r)) = \pi(g(x)\|\sigma'(r))$ while preserving semantic security. For adversarially chosen $g : \{0,1\}^n \to \{0,1\}^n$ and $x^* \in \{0,1\}^n$, let

$r \xleftarrow{\$} \{0,1\}^\lambda$, we show

$$\big(i\mathcal{O}(\pi),\, i\mathcal{O}(\mathsf{Ev}_g),\, \pi(x^*\|r^*)\big) \approx \big(i\mathcal{O}(\pi),\, i\mathcal{O}(\mathsf{Ev}_g),\, \text{random}\big). \tag{5}$$

We now describe how $\mathsf{Ev}_g$ (in particular, $\sigma'$) works and how security is proven.

For technicalities in the proof, we conceptually split the encryption randomness into two parts, a counter $\ell$ and *the* randomness $r$. For convenience, let each be $\lambda$ bits. We define $\sigma'(\ell\|r) := (\ell+1)\|\sigma(r)$, where "$+1$" is modulo $2^\lambda$ and $\sigma$ is another instance of PPRP for rerandomization.

Spelled out more completely, the public key is $(i\mathcal{O}(\pi), i\mathcal{O}(\mathsf{Ev}_g))$ and a ciphertext is $\mathsf{ct}(x) = \pi(x\|\ell\|r)$. The program $\mathsf{Ev}_g(\mathsf{ct})$ computes $x\|\ell\|r \leftarrow \pi^{-1}(\mathsf{ct})$ and outputs $\pi(g(x)\|(\ell+1)\|\sigma(r))$. To evaluate $g^{(t)}$ on $\mathsf{ct}$, iterate $i\mathcal{O}(\mathsf{Ev}_g)$ for $t$ times on $\mathsf{ct}$. It is stressed that the encryption algorithm remains unchanged—in a fresh ciphertext, both $\ell$ and $r$ are random.

Proving security (Eq. (5)) in the presence of $i\mathcal{O}(\mathsf{Ev}_g)$ is more challenging than the basic case (even with CCA, Eq. (2)). Firstly, $\mathsf{Ev}_g$ is internally capable of decrypting every possible ciphertext, so there is already some flavor of CCA going on. Secondly, the triple $(i\mathcal{O}(\pi), i\mathcal{O}(\mathsf{Ev}_g), \mathsf{ct}^*)$, where $\mathsf{ct}^* = \pi(x^*\|\ell^*\|r^*)$, is in essence the compressed form of a very long chain $\mathsf{ct}^* = \mathsf{ct}^{(0)} \to \mathsf{ct}^{(1)} \to \cdots$ where $\mathsf{ct}^{(t)} = \pi(g^{(t)}(x^*)\|(\ell^*+t)\|\sigma^{(t)}(r^*))$ and its length is not bounded by any polynomial. We are proving security for a *super-polynomial* number of ciphertexts with *correlated* encryption randomness.

Observe that every evaluation chain eventually forms a $\rho$-shaped cycle. We plant a random trigger $\widehat{\ell^*}$ to make $\mathsf{Ev}_g(\mathsf{ct})$ output $\perp$ when $x\|\ell\|r \leftarrow \pi^{-1}(\mathsf{ct})$ has $\ell = \ell^* + \widehat{\ell^*}$. This "cuts" the chain from $\mathsf{ct}^*$ down to a manageable length:

$$\begin{aligned}
&\text{(before) } \mathsf{ct}^* = \mathsf{ct}^{(0)} \to \mathsf{ct}^{(1)} \to \cdots \to \mathsf{ct}^{(\widehat{\ell^*})} \xrightarrow{\mathsf{Ev}_g} \mathsf{ct}^{(\widehat{\ell^*}+1)} \to \cdots \quad \text{(eventually cycles);}\\
&\text{(after) } \mathsf{ct}^* = \mathsf{ct}^{(0)} \to \mathsf{ct}^{(1)} \to \cdots \to \mathsf{ct}^{(\widehat{\ell^*})} \xrightarrow{\mathsf{Ev}_g} \perp \quad \text{(never cycles).}
\end{aligned}$$

We then go through $\widehat{\ell^*}$ hybrids to remove $x^*$ from this chain, by replacing ct's on a longer and longer prefix by pseudorandom values. We use yet another PPRP $\varphi$ to derive the fake ciphertexts. A typical hybrid looks like

$$\mathsf{ct}^* = \varphi(0) \to \varphi(1) \to \cdots \to \boxed{\varphi(\mathsf{t})} \xrightarrow{\mathsf{Ev}_g} \boxed{\mathsf{ct}^{(\mathsf{t}+1)}} \to \cdots \to \mathsf{ct}^{(\widehat{\ell^*})} \to \perp.$$

Here, $\mathsf{Ev}_g$ uses $\varphi^{-1}, \varphi$ to recognize/generate the fake ciphertexts. Advancing t appears a bit more involved, as there is a deep correlation among the $r$'s inside the suffix ct's via $\sigma$. Let $v^*$ be adversarially chosen. We rely on

$$\begin{aligned}
&\big(i\mathcal{O}(\pi),\, i\mathcal{O}(\pi^{-1} \setminus \{y_0\}),\, i\mathcal{O}(\sigma),\, y_0,\, s_0\big)\\
\approx\, &\big(i\mathcal{O}(\pi),\, \underbrace{i\mathcal{O}(\pi^{-1} \setminus \{y_1\}),\, i\mathcal{O}(\sigma)}_{\text{for } \mathsf{Ev}_g},\, \underbrace{y_1,\, s_1}_{\mathsf{ct}^{(\mathsf{t}+1)},\, \mathsf{ct}^{(\mathsf{t}+2)}}\big),
\end{aligned} \tag{6}$$

where $y_0 = \pi(v^* \| r^*)$, $s_0 = \sigma(r^*)$, and $y_1$, $s_1$ are independent and random. This converts $\mathsf{ct}^{(t+1)}$ to random without affecting $\mathsf{ct}^{(t+2)}$. The now-random $\mathsf{ct}^{(t+1)}$ can be switched to pseudorandom $\phi(t+1)$, hence "collected" into the replaced prefix, via

$$\big(i\mathcal{O}(\varphi \setminus \{v^*\}),\, i\mathcal{O}(\varphi^{-1} \setminus \{y_0\}),\, y_0\big) \approx \big(i\mathcal{O}(\varphi \setminus \{v^*\}),\, i\mathcal{O}(\varphi^{-1} \setminus \{y_1\}),\, y_1\big), \quad (7)$$

where $y_0 = \varphi(v^*)$ and $y_1$ is random. The proof completes once the entire chain is replaced.

We note that Eq. (6) is a generalization of Eq. (4)—the latter is the former with $v^*$ being the empty string. Both can be derived from the cohardcoreness result. Moreover, Eq. (7) says that obfuscations of *permutable* PRP with large domain are also *puncturable*, under a suitable definition of puncturable PRP.[5]

*Challenges to Realizing Richer Homomorphisms.* It is tempting to try extending the current scheme by adding homomorphic evaluation gadgets that combine two or more ciphertexts into a single ciphertext, where the corresponding plaintexts are meaningfully correlated, as in traditional binary (or multi-ary) FHE schemes. A less ambitious, yet still interesting, extension is to keep the current unary structure, but allow multiple homomorphic evaluation programs that work with a single public key.

However, while we are not aware of concrete attacks against those extensions, we are unable to assert their security. Let us provide some perspective for this inability, by considering a unary HE scheme with *two* homomorphic evaluation programs $\mathsf{Ev}_{g_0}$ and $\mathsf{Ev}_{g_1}$ for functions $g_0, g_1 : \{0,1\}^n \to \{0,1\}^n$. Such a scheme enables homomorphic evaluation of $g_{b_t} \circ \cdots \circ g_{b_2} \circ g_{b_1}$ for any $b_1, \ldots, b_t \in \{0,1\}$ and for $t$ not *a priori* bounded by any polynomial.[6] This is a significantly more complex requirement than Eq. (5). Instead of having a single chain of $t$ ciphertexts originating from $\mathsf{ct}^*$, we now have a depth-$t$ binary tree rooted at $\mathsf{ct}^*$, of $2^t$ ciphertexts with correlated encryption randomness. Reductions cannot afford to incur loss per each one of them (up to $2^{\lambda^{\omega(1)}}$). Prior works dealt with a similar situation using *lossy* encryption together with leveled homomorphism [9]. Such techniques are incompatible with our unleveled, permutation-based setting.

We further substantiate the gap between single-function and two-function unary HE by demonstrating that proving security for two functions necessarily either relies on primitives other than PPRP and $i\mathcal{O}$ or involves a breakthrough in non-black-box techniques. We prove that unary HE for two-function iterations implies, in black box, primitives known to be unobtainable from black-box usage of $i\mathcal{O}$ and one-way functions. Consider

$$g_b(i^*, i, v) = \begin{cases} (i^*, i+1, b), & \text{if } i+1 = i^*; \\ (i^*, i+1, v), & \text{if } i+1 \neq i^*; \end{cases} \qquad \text{for } b \in \{0,1\},$$

[5] The work of [5] proposed a different definition of puncturable PRP and showed that it cannot be achieved. See discussion in [10] for details.

[6] When $t$ is bounded by a fixed polynomial, or more precisely, when the ciphertext length can grow polynomially in $t$ (and $\lambda$), this is just $i\mathcal{O}$ for compute-and-encrypt.

which implements "read the bit at index $i^*$" in a streaming fashion, i.e.,

$$(g_{b_t} \circ \cdots \circ g_{b_2} \circ g_{b_1})(i^*, 0, 0) = (i^*, t, b_{i^*}).$$

Such a unary HE immediately implies the following.

- *One-Round Private Information Retrieval.* The server stores the database $x_1 \cdots x_t$ and $(\mathsf{pk}, \mathsf{Ev}_{g_0}, \mathsf{Ev}_{g_1})$ from the set-up phase. To query at index $i^*$, the client sends $\mathsf{ct} \xleftarrow{\$} \mathsf{Enc}(\mathsf{pk}, (i^*, 0, 0))$. The server responds with the homomorphically evaluated $\mathsf{Ev}_{g_{x_t}}(\cdots \mathsf{Ev}_{g_{x_2}}(\mathsf{Ev}_{g_{x_1}}(\mathsf{ct}))\cdots)$, which can be decrypted to $x_{i^*}$ by the client.
- *Somewhere Extractable Hash.* Here, $\mathsf{hk} = (\mathsf{pk}, \mathsf{Ev}_{g_0}, \mathsf{Ev}_{g_1}, \mathsf{ct})$ is the hash key and $H_{\mathsf{hk}}(x_1 \cdots x_t) = \mathsf{Ev}_{g_{x_t}}(\cdots \mathsf{Ev}_{g_{x_2}}(\mathsf{Ev}_{g_{x_1}}(\mathsf{ct}))\cdots)$. If $\mathsf{ct} \xleftarrow{\$} \mathsf{Enc}(\mathsf{pk}, (i^*, 0, 0))$, then $x_{i^*}$ is extractable from the hash value using $\mathsf{sk}$.

Neither application can be obtained from just $i\mathcal{O}$ and one-way functions in black box [2,25], so any extension of our scheme to support two-function iterations requires additional primitives or breakthrough non-black-box techniques.

### 2.5 Instantiation with Reversible Circuits

We substantiate an alternative route to PPRP and strong PKE/KEM, based on specific properties of random reversible circuits. Let's start with some background.

Our starting point is the fact that the family of permutations computed by random $n$-wire $m$-gate[7] reversible circuits are $\epsilon$-close to $t$-wise independent ones for some $m = \widetilde{\mathrm{O}}(nt \log(1/\epsilon))$ [21,22]. Furthermore, it has been conjectured that they are in fact a family of strong PRP. Extending from this conjecture, the work of [8] showed that if one could, given a random reversible circuit $C$ of certain polynomial size, come up with a functionally equivalent one that is "sufficiently rerandomized" relative to $C$, then one could also perform general-purpose $i\mathcal{O}$ for all (reversible or not) circuits. They also propose a host of mechanisms for reranodmizing random reversible circuits by way of repeatedly performing local, functionality-preserving perturbations. Two points from [8] are of interest for the present work.

First, their work constructs an $i\mathcal{O}$ that preserves the format of reversible circuits (termed rc$i\mathcal{O}$ by us), i.e., for an $n$-wire reversible circuit $C$, its obfuscation rc$i\mathcal{O}(C)$ is a functionally equivalent $n$-wire reversible circuit, and in particular, allows evaluation of $C^{-1}$. To get $i\mathcal{O}$ for normal circuits, a circuit must be transformed into a reversible one with many ancillae, a somewhat costly process that we would like to avoid.

Second, along the way to rc$i\mathcal{O}$, the work of [8] relies on the so-called *split-circuit pseudorandomness* (SCP) assumption—there exist polynomials $m$, $m^\#$

[7] Each gate is of the form $x_k \leftarrow x_k \oplus f(x_i, x_j)$ for distinct wires $i, j, k \in [n]$ and arbitrary function $f : \{0,1\}^2 \to \{0,1\}$.

such that for any two $n$-wire reversible circuits $C_1$, $C_2$, two versions of "ideally obfuscated" $C_1 \| C_2$ are indistinguishable. The first version is to first sample a random $n$-wire $m$-gate $R$, then produce $\widehat{C}_1 \| \widehat{C}_2$, where $\widehat{C}_1$ (resp. $\widehat{C}_2$) is a uniformly random $(|C_1| + m)m^{\#}$-gate (resp. $(m + |C_2|)m^{\#}$-gate) circuit functionally equivalent to $C_1 \| R$ (resp. $R^{-1} \| C_2$). The second version is a uniformly random $(|C_1| + 2m + |C_2|)m^{\#}$-gate circuit functionally equivalent to $C_1 \| C_2$.

**PPRP from Split-Circuit Pseudorandomness and rc$i\mathcal{O}$.** Assuming SCP and rc$i\mathcal{O}$, we show that a random $n$-wire $m$-gate reversible circuit $R$ is a PRP permutable by polynomial-size $n$-wire reversible circuits, for which a $\Gamma$-permuted key is simply rc$i\mathcal{O}(\Gamma \| R)$ (evaluatable both ways). Essentially, SCP provides that any fixed circuit ($C_1 = \Gamma$) can be smudged into random $m$-gate ones ($R$) given sufficient expansion ($m^{\#}$), but its distributions are not efficiently sampleable. An rc$i\mathcal{O}$ canonicalizes them into efficient ones.

**TDP/PKE/KEM from Reversible-Circuit PPRP and $i\mathcal{O}$.** Due to the format-preserving nature, rc$i\mathcal{O}(R)$ cannot possibly be the $\mathsf{pk}$ of a secure TDP (or PKE or KEM) because it enables efficient inversion of $R$. The simplest fix is to obfuscate its Toffoli version, $\mathsf{TOF}[R](x, y) = (x, y \oplus R(x))$, a $2n$-wire circuit consisting of applying $R$ to the first $n$ wires, applying $\mathsf{CNOT}$'s to XOR the first $n$ wires to the last $n$ wires, and lastly applying $R^{-1}$ to restore the first $n$ wires—$\mathsf{TOF}[R]$ is its own inverse and does not appear to help with inverting $R$. Note that there is no additional ancillae in $\mathsf{TOF}[R]$. It is *a priori* unclear whether the proof of one-wayness or CCA security can go through in this setting, due to complex surgeries applied to the circuits in the hybrids.

We prove that the corresponding KEM is still CCA-secure (and for PKE, plaintext-selectively CCA-secure). Along the way, we develop reversible-circuit triggers and work around the issue of transposition being odd (reversible circuits with at least four wires only compute even permutations).

## 3 Functional Homomorphic Encryption in More Detail

We first overview and motivate our definition of functional homomorphic encryption. Next, we present the construction and provide an overview of the proof of security, including the main challenges addressed.

### 3.1 Developing Definitions

A functional homomorphic encryption scheme composes the capabilities of homomorphic evaluation and functional decryption. The authority sets up the scheme instance and generates a pair of master keys, $\mathsf{mpk}$ and $\mathsf{msk}$.

Using $\mathsf{mpk}$, anyone can encrypt data $x$ into $\mathsf{ct}(x)$. Given $\mathsf{ct}(x)$, anyone can apply $h$ homomorphically to obtain $\mathsf{ct}(h(x))$, where $h$ comes from a set of supported functions. As usual, the evaluator cannot simply offload its work to the decryptor, formulated by requiring the lengths of evaluated ciphertexts to not grow with the complexity of $h$.

The authority can derive functional keys from $\mathsf{msk}$. Each $\mathsf{sk}_f$ is associated with a function $f$. Decrypting $\mathsf{ct}(x)$ using $\mathsf{sk}_f$ yields $f(x)$. Since homomorphic evaluation can be done by anyone, given $\mathsf{ct}(x)$ and $\mathsf{sk}_f$, one can also apply $h$ to $\mathsf{ct}(x)$ then decrypt, obtaining $f(h(x))$.

**Additional Motivating Applications.** Before diving into the security notion, we show two additional applications of the new primitive, on top of the ones given in the introduction. We hope that these applications will help motivate the definitions.

Our first example is homomorphic encryption for Turing machines with *instance-specific* evaluation time, a primitive studied and constructed in [19,20]. The homomorphic evaluation time should grow only with that of cleartext evaluation, which could be much shorter than the worst-case running time, so running, say, the simplex method [14] for linear programming (exponential time in the worst case) homomorphically should complete in reasonable time if a typical input is encrypted in $\mathsf{ct}$. Such HE for TM can be obtained from functional homomorphic encryption—the plaintext $x$ is the TM state and tape, $h$'s include "run the TM for $t$ steps" for all $t$, and $f$ indicates whether the TM has halted. By applying $h$ for $t = 1, 2, 4, 8, \ldots$ and decrypting using $\mathsf{sk}_f$ until the decryption result indicates that computation has halted, the TM evaluation can be done in instance-specific time.

Our other example is randomized encoding for TM with long output. Here, the encoding time and length are much smaller than the computation's running time and output length. We rely on a *multi-hop* functional homomorphic encryption—it is possible to apply another $h$ to a homomorphically evaluated ciphertext. Randomized encoding for TM with long output can be constructed similarly to the first example, except that now $f$ outputs the current-step output of the TM computation.

**Aspects of Security.** By functionality, anyone knowing $\mathsf{ct}(x)$ and $\mathsf{sk}_f$ necessarily knows $f(h(x))$ for all $h$ that can be applied homomorphically. We want to pin down a security definition so that this is the *only* information revealed to an adversary. Multiple axes of strength are to be considered: indistinguishability- or simulation-based; collusion resistance; passive or active attack model; adaptivity. Let's examine each of them.

*Indistinguishability/Simulation.* Our first observation is that simulation security is impossible for any *sufficiently expressive* scheme in the standard model—the schemes we construct will be subject to this lower bound. It is impossible even when the other axes take the weaker requirement, which is vastly different from either FE or HE *on their own*. For HE against chosen-plaintext attacks, simulation security is implied by indistinguishability security (a simulated ciphertext can be an encryption of random/zero). For FE, plaintext-selective simulation is achieved by [15].

For functional homomorphic encryption, simulation security would, at the very least, require a simulator to come up with $\mathsf{mpk}$, $\mathsf{sk}_f$, $\mathsf{ct}$ (the *simulated components*) given $f$ and $\{f(h(x))\}_h$. Suppose $x$ consists of a PRF key and a counter, $h$ increments the counter, and $f$ evaluates the PRF using the counter as input. Clearly, $\{f(h(x))\}_h$ is pseudorandom given the description of $f$. If we tune the counter's range to be larger than the total length of the simulated components, the simulator would have to compress a pseudorandom string, which cannot be done efficiently. We therefore only consider indistinguishability-based security.

*Collusion Resistance.* Collusion-resistant security is a standard requirement for FE schemes, where the adversary can obtain an unbounded number of functional keys $\{\mathsf{sk}_j\}_j$ for $f_j$'s of its choice. Different from FE, the choice is subject to a more strict constraint: $f_j(h(x_0^*)) = f_j(h(x_1^*))$ for all $j$ and supported $h$ (in FE, the only $h$ is the identity function).

*Passive/Active Attacks.* They correspond to chosen-plaintext and -ciphertext attacks, respectively. Homomorphic encryption schemes are malleable by definition, making traditional CCA2 security impossible. We take inspiration from [29], which is to guard the decryption oracle against ciphertexts evaluated from the challenge one(s). We note that the formulation in [29] is only applicable to simulation security and we cannot directly use it.

Some care is needed to properly define a mechanism for identifying "related" ciphertexts. There should be an algorithm deciding whether a ciphertext $\mathsf{ct}'$ "comes from" the challenge one(s). Given a decryption query for $\mathsf{ct}'$, if $\mathsf{ct}'$ is determined to come from the challenge ciphertext(s), the decryption oracle returns $\perp$, and otherwise, it decrypts $\mathsf{ct}'$ and returns the result. However, this simplistic definition does not require the relatedness detection algorithm to be *accurate*. If it simply says that "all ciphertexts are related to each other", then this "CCA" security *degenerates* to CPA.

We overview a simple solution for unary homomorphic functions, corresponding to Sect. 5.4. (The general treatment is in Sect. 5.3.) We require an efficient algorithm, $\mathsf{Link}(\mathsf{mpk}, \mathsf{ct}, \mathsf{ct}')$, to find, not just *whether*, but also *how* $\mathsf{ct}$ and $\mathsf{ct}'$ are related. It outputs either $\perp$ (to indicate that they are unrelated) or a supported $h$ as their relation.

Given a decryption query $\mathsf{ct}'$, we run $\mathsf{Link}(\mathsf{mpk}, \mathsf{ct}^*, \mathsf{ct}')$ to obtain $\mathsf{lnk}$ and decrypt $\mathsf{ct}'$ to $z$. Let $x^*$ be the plaintext inside the challenge ciphertext. If $\mathsf{lnk} = \perp$, simply return $z$ to the adversary. If $\mathsf{lnk} = h \neq \perp$, then check whether $h(x^*) = z$. If not, the relation is incorrect and we let the adversary win. Otherwise, return $\mathsf{lnk}$ and whether $z = \perp$ to the adversary. (This is more information than simply rejecting the decryption query.) The adversary can always win by guessing the correct plaintext (out of two possible ones chosen by it) inside $\mathsf{ct}^*$.

This formulation creates some *healthy tension* for $\mathsf{Link}$, ensuring that the relation identification is accurate, in the sense that the scheme will be considered insecure if $\mathsf{Link}$ faults. On the one hand, it should not output $\perp$ if $\mathsf{ct}'$ does come from $\mathsf{ct}^*$, as that would permit decryption of ciphertexts related to $\mathsf{ct}^*$, which likely reveals which plaintext is under $\mathsf{ct}^*$. On the other hand, it cannot output a *correct* relation if $\mathsf{ct}'$ is indeed unrelated to $\mathsf{ct}^*$. Otherwise, $\mathsf{Link}$ itself would break the scheme because a correct relation is information about the plaintexts under both ciphertexts. Lastly, it must refrain from outputting an *incorrect* relation—we reward the adversary in that case.

A minor point about our definition is that since the scheme is functional, we allow the adversary to query for decryption using any $\mathsf{sk}_f$, even when $\mathsf{sk}_f$ cannot be given to it due to $f(h(x_0^*)) \neq f(h(x_1^*))$ for some supported $h$. This is achieved by separating key creation and retrieval, and the constraint only applies to *retrieved* keys. Decryption using functional keys is guarded the same way as above.

*Adaptivity.* In adaptive security, the adversary's choices (key/decryption queries, challenge plaintexts) can be made in arbitrary order and dependent on all the information received by it so far. In (plaintext-)selective security, the challenge plaintexts must be chosen at the beginning, independent of any component of the instance under attack. (Our schemes are only proven selectively secure.) We note that in both versions, key/decryption queries are always fully adaptive.

**Putting Things Together and Separating Them Again.** Taking everything discussed earlier into account, we define IND-FHCCA in Sect. 5.3. It has many moving parts and is not the easiest to work with. In particular, there are two distinct ways for the adversary to win, causing an inconsistent decryption and guessing the plaintext. Separating those two conditions simplifies both of them, which is done in Sect. 5.4. Below is a quick explainer for the selective version.

The first condition is termed *decryption consistency.* In this game, the adversary wins by finding an incorrect link, and it goes as follows. First, the adversary chooses $x^*$, and gets back $\mathsf{mpk}$ and $\mathsf{ct}^*$. It can then query for functional keys without any constraint (always retrieved) and submit decryption queries. The adversary wins if and only if a decryption query causes $\mathsf{Link}$ to output an incorrect link.

The second condition is termed *ciphertext indistinguishability.* The adversary can only win by guessing which plaintext is encrypted. It first chooses the challenge plaintexts $x_0^*$ and $x_1^*$, and gets back $\mathsf{mpk}$ and $\mathsf{ct}^*$ encrypting $x_\beta^*$. The adversary then makes key creation, key retrieval, decryption queries, subject to the constraint that no retrieved key reveals $\beta$ by evaluate-then-decrypt. For a decryption query, $\mathsf{Link}$ correctness is not tested. Instead, if $\mathsf{Link}$ outputs non-$\perp$, the queried ciphertext is simply not decrypted. Eventually, the adversary guesses $\beta$ and it wins if the guess is correct.

The conjunction of the two conditions implies IND-FHCCA.

### 3.2 Construction and Proof

We give an overview of our functional homomorphic encryption scheme supporting *two-way* iterations of a single permutation, followed by arbitrary circuit for functional decryption. In this scheme, a permutation $g$ is fixed upon set-up, a ciphertext $\mathsf{ct}(x)$ can be homomorphically evaluated into $\mathsf{ct}(g^{(t)}(x))$ for any $t \in \mathbb{Z}$, and decrypting the latter using $\mathsf{sk}_f$ yields $f(g^{(t)}(x))$. We write $g_+$, $g_-$ for the circuits evaluating $g$ in the forward/backward directions.

To set up the scheme, sample two PPRP instances $\pi$, $\sigma$ and output

$$\mathsf{mpk} \xleftarrow{\$} (i\mathcal{O}(\pi), i\mathcal{O}(\mathsf{Ev}_+), i\mathcal{O}(\mathsf{Ev}_-), i\mathcal{O}(\mathsf{Lnk})), \qquad \mathsf{msk} \leftarrow \pi^{-1},$$

where $\mathsf{Ev}_+$ and $\mathsf{Ev}_-$ are the homomorphic evaluation programs and $\mathsf{Lnk}$ is the linking program, both to be specified soon. To encrypt $x$, sample random $\tau$ (tag), $\ell$ (counter), $r$ (encryption randomness) of appropriate lengths and output

$$\mathsf{ct} \leftarrow i\mathcal{O}(\pi)(x\|\tau\|\ell\|r) = \pi(x\|\tau\|\ell\|r).$$

Note that the encryption algorithm and the ciphertext structure remain the same as in Sect. 2, except that the randomness is conceptually split into three portions. With the ciphertext structure spelled out, we can explain how $\mathsf{Ev}_+(\mathsf{ct})$, $\mathsf{Ev}_-(\mathsf{ct})$ (and later, $\mathsf{Lnk}$) work—they compute $x\|\tau\|\ell\|r \leftarrow \pi^{-1}(\mathsf{ct})$ and then output

$$\begin{aligned} &(\text{for } \mathsf{Ev}_+) \qquad \pi(g_+(x)\|\tau\|(\ell+1)\|\sigma(\sigma^{-1}(r)+1)),\\ &(\text{for } \mathsf{Ev}_-) \qquad \pi(g_-(x)\|\tau\|(\ell-1)\|\sigma(\sigma^{-1}(r)-1)),\end{aligned}$$

where "$\pm 1$" are modulo powers of two (the corresponding lengths). In other words, they decrypt $\mathsf{ct}$, apply $g$ in forward/backward direction, then reencrypt the result with the same tag, incremented/decremented counter value, and new randomness. The new randomness is derived by walking one step in the forward/backward direction on a cycle determined by $\sigma$—if $r = \sigma(u)$, the new randomness is $\sigma(u \pm 1)$. To perform a homomorphic evaluation $g^{(t)}$, iterate $\mathsf{Ev}_+$ or $\mathsf{Ev}_-$ for $\mathrm{abs}(t)$ times, depending on the sign of $t$.

$\mathsf{Lnk}(\mathsf{ct}, \mathsf{ct}')$ first recovers the tags and counters $\tau$, $\tau'$, $\ell$, $\ell'$ in $\mathsf{ct}$, $\mathsf{ct}'$. If $\tau \neq \tau'$ or $\ell$ and $\ell'$ are very far away from each other (the threshold is an appropriate subexponential value), it outputs $\perp$ indicating that $\mathsf{ct}$ and $\mathsf{ct}'$ are unrelated. Otherwise, the output is $(\ell' - \ell)$, indicating that $\mathsf{ct}'$ is obtained from $\mathsf{ct}$ via $g^{(\ell'-\ell)}$. The linking algorithm $\mathsf{Link}(\mathsf{mpk}, \mathsf{ct}, \mathsf{ct}')$ simply runs the $i\mathcal{O}(\mathsf{Lnk})$ from $\mathsf{mpk}$ on the two input ciphertexts.

To generate a functional key for a circuit $f$, let $\widehat{f}(\mathsf{ct})$ be a circuit that computes $x\|\tau\|\ell\|r \leftarrow \pi^{-1}(\mathsf{ct})$ and then outputs $f(x)$. The key is $\mathsf{sk}_f \xleftarrow{\$} i\mathcal{O}(\widehat{f})$ and decryption is evaluating $\mathsf{sk}_f$ on $\mathsf{ct}$.

**Proof Sketch of Ciphertext Indistinguishability.** Recall that in ciphertext indistinguishability, the adversary gets a ciphertext $\mathsf{ct}^* = \pi(x^*_\beta\|\tau^*\|\ell^*\|\sigma(u^*))$ plus $\mathsf{mpk}$ and $\mathsf{sk}_f$'s, and it has access to the decryption oracle. The goal is to show that it cannot distinguish between $\beta = 0$ and $\beta = 1$. Write

$$\mathsf{ct}^{(t)}_\beta = \pi(g^{(t)}(x^*_\beta)\|\tau^*\|(\ell^*+t)\|\sigma(u^*+t)),$$

which is the $t^{\text{th}}$ iteration of $\mathsf{ct}_\beta^{(0)}$. The proof should switch $\mathsf{ct}^*$ from $\mathsf{ct}_0^{(0)}$ to $\mathsf{ct}_1^{(0)}$ via hybrids, while keeping the other components unchanged. The security of PPRP allows us to swap out the preimage of $\mathsf{ct}^*$ in a single step, but doing so makes $\mathsf{Ev}_\pm$ "remember" that we have made the swap.

Before elaboration, it helps to depict the current action of $\mathsf{Ev}_\pm$ as follows.

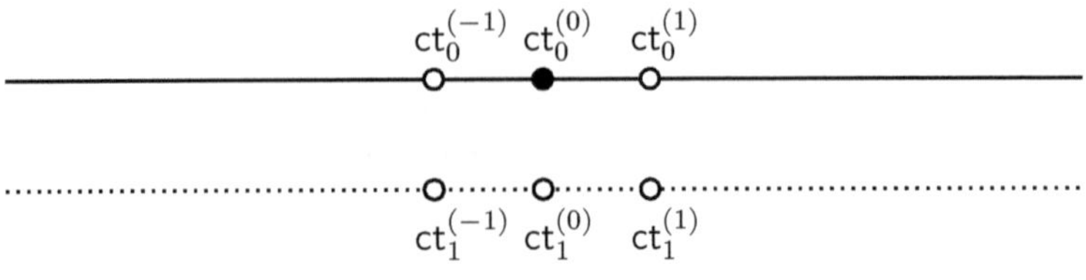


In the diagram above and every diagram below: the solid dot is the challenge $\mathsf{ct}^*$; hollow dots represent the other ciphertexts; every ciphertext on top is evaluated from $x_0^*$ and on bottom, $x_1^*$; a line represents a chain or cycle of $\mathsf{Ev}_\pm$ (currently, cycle), with the solid line having $\mathsf{ct}^*$.

Our first step is to plant a trigger in $\mathsf{Ev}_\pm$ so that evaluation stops when $\ell = \ell^* \pm \widehat{\ell}^*$. This converts the two long cycles into two moderate-length chains.

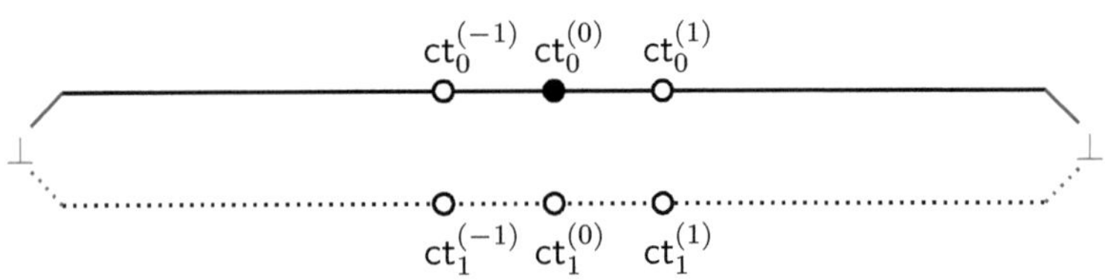


Via a few simple steps, which are the same as a typical hybrid transition and will be explained soon, we change $\mathsf{ct}^*$. This is indeed progress, but $\mathsf{Ev}_\pm$ remembers the swap by evaluating $\mathsf{ct}_\beta^{(0)}$ into $\mathsf{ct}_{1-\beta}^{(\pm 1)}$, i.e., it treats $\mathsf{ct}_\beta^{(0)}$ as an encryption of $x_{1-\beta}^*$ even though $\pi^{-1}(\mathsf{ct}_\beta^{(0)}) = x_\beta^* \| \cdots$:

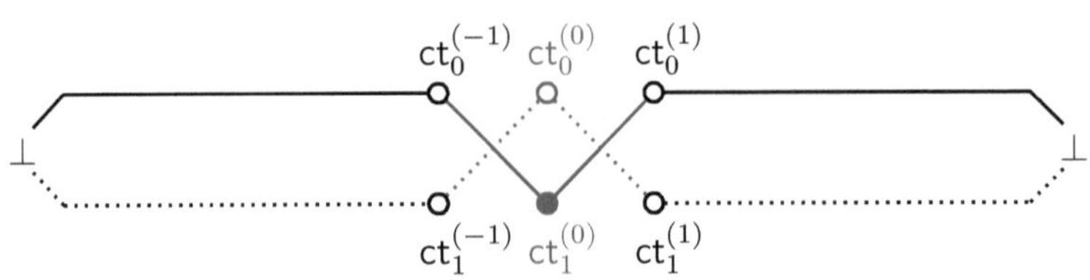


Therefore, the proof is not yet done.

*Typical Hybrid Transition.* We continue swapping ciphertexts, say, symmetrically around 0. A typical transition hence proceeds as follows.

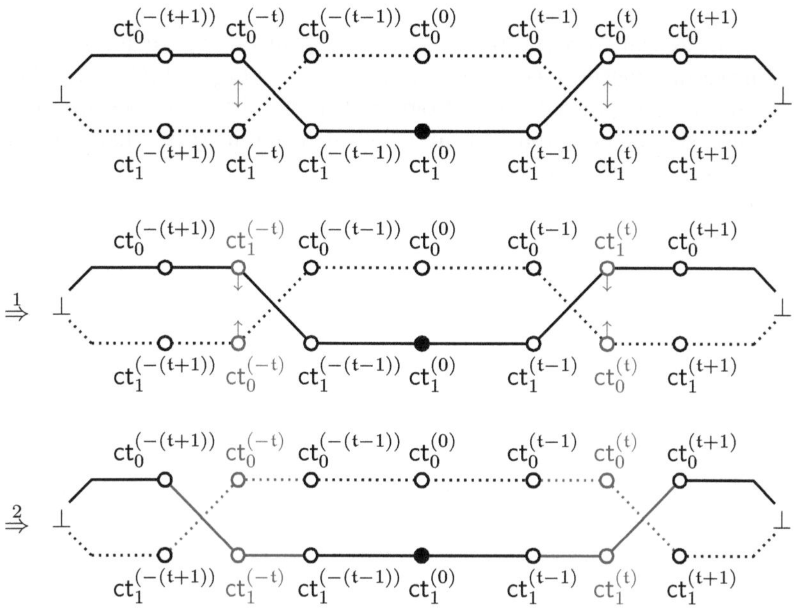

The first transition swaps two ciphertexts, causing them to be temporarily misplaced. The second transition "drags" the two ciphertexts to their intended locations, restoring the order. When $\mathsf{t}$ increases to $\widehat{\ell}^*$, the actions of $\mathsf{Ev}_\pm$ return to normal (modulo the trigger), while the challenge ciphertext is $\mathsf{ct}_1^{(0)}$. The proof is completed by removing the trigger.

The next paragraphs explain how to carry out the steps outlined above.

*Preparation for Swapping Ciphertexts.* Recall that the randomness $r$ in all $\mathsf{ct}_0^{(t)}$'s and $\mathsf{ct}_1^{(t)}$'s are correlated by $\sigma(u^* \mid t)$. When swapping $\mathsf{ct}_0^{(\pm\mathsf{t})}$ and $\mathsf{ct}_1^{(\pm\mathsf{t})}$, the reduction would want to know $u^*$ (for the many ciphertexts on the two chains) and most of $\sigma$, $\sigma^{-1}$ (for creating $\mathsf{Ev}_\pm$). We must therefore first make the randomness in (say) $\mathsf{ct}_0^{(\mathsf{t})}$, $\mathsf{ct}_1^{(\mathsf{t})}$ independent of the other randomness. This can be done using Eq. (7)—for any adversarially chosen $u^*$, $\mathsf{t}$, we have

$$\big(i\mathcal{O}(\sigma \setminus \{u^* + \mathsf{t}\}), i\mathcal{O}(\sigma^{-1} \setminus \{s_0\}), s_0\big) \approx \big(i\mathcal{O}(\sigma \setminus \{u^* + \mathsf{t}\}), i\mathcal{O}(\sigma^{-1} \setminus \{s_1\}), s_1\big),$$

where $s_0 = \sigma(u^* + \mathsf{t})$ and $s_1$ is random.

We note, however, that applying it has the following side effect. Recall that $\mathsf{Ev}_\pm$ use $\sigma$, $\sigma^{-1}$. Puncturing them makes, say, $\mathsf{Ev}_+$ use $s^* \leftarrow s_1$ as the randomness for the output ciphertext when the input ciphertext (not necessarily on the challenge chains) *happens* to use $\sigma(u^* + \mathsf{t} - 1)$ as its randomness. This should be kept in mind for the subsequent steps.

*Swapping Two Ciphertexts.* We show that

$$\big(i\mathcal{O}(P), i\mathcal{O}(Q), i\mathcal{O}(R), \boxed{y_0^*, y_1^*}\big) \approx \big(i\mathcal{O}(P), i\mathcal{O}(Q), i\mathcal{O}(R), \boxed{y_1^*, y_0^*}\big), \quad (8)$$

where $P$, $Q$, $R$ are some programs to be assembled into scheme components and used for answering queries (see below) and $y^*_\beta = \pi(g^{(\mathsf{t})}(x^*_\beta)\|\tau^*\|(\ell^* + \mathsf{t})\|s^*)$ are the two ciphertexts being swapped. Program $P$ is simply $\pi$ for encryption. The adversary also should be given $\mathsf{Ev}_\pm$ and $\mathsf{Lnk}$, can obtain secret keys, and can make decryption queries, which involve $s^*$ and $\pi^{-1}$.

We define

$$Q(v) := \begin{cases} \perp, & \text{if } v \in \{g^{(\mathsf{t})}(x^*_0)\|\tau^*\|(\ell^* + \mathsf{t}),\, g^{(\mathsf{t})}(x^*_1)\|\tau^*\|(\ell^* + \mathsf{t})\}; \\ \pi(v\|s^*), & \text{otherwise.} \end{cases}$$

Recall that due to the previous step, $\mathsf{Ev}_\pm$ must be ready to create ciphertexts with randomness $s^*$ when they see ones with $\sigma(u^* + \mathsf{t} \mp 1)$. Of course, for Eq. (8) to hold, $s^*$ cannot be given in the clear, so instead, $Q$ is used to create ciphertexts without knowing $s^*$. It is punctured at output $y^*_0$, $y^*_1$, again necessary.

Program $R$ is mostly $\pi^{-1}$ plus some surgery. As a starter, it is punctured at input $y^*_0$, $y^*_1$. In addition, $R$ strips the randomness part from its output when that value happens to be $s^*$. Once both surgeries are done, there is no apparent distinguisher, and Eq. (8) can be proven based on PPRP security and $i\mathcal{O}$.

The given $P$, $Q$, $R$ are sufficient. For $\mathsf{Lnk}$, the tags and counters in $y^*_0$, $y^*_1$ are the same and known (as $\tau^*$ and $(\ell^* + \mathsf{t})$), and it can recover the tags/counters of the other ciphertexts using $R$. For $\mathsf{Ev}_\pm$, the swapping of $y^*_0$, $y^*_1$ will achieve the desired transition. For any other ciphertext, $\mathsf{Ev}_\pm$ use $R$ to obtain plaintext, tag, counter, and possibly randomness—when stripped, the next/previous randomness is $\sigma(u^* + \mathsf{t} \pm 1)$—and can produce the output ciphertext using $P$ (or $Q$ if the input ciphertext has randomness $\sigma(u^* + \mathsf{t} \mp 1)$). For a retrieved functional key for $f$, thanks to the constraint of $f(g^{(\mathsf{t})}(x^*_0)) = f(g^{(\mathsf{t})}(x^*_1))$, the intended output on $y^*_0$, $y^*_1$ is this same value, which can be hardwired into the obfuscated program. Otherwise, it can always use $R$ to obtain the plaintext, then compute $f$ and output. For a decryption query, $y^*_0$, $y^*_1$ are always rejected due to their tag and counter values (link identified with $\mathsf{ct}^*$). For the other ciphertexts that are not otherwise rejected, the plaintexts can again be recovered using $R$.

*"Dragging" Ciphertexts to Restore Positioning.* We have to admit that this is a mediocre metaphor. We revert the randomness in $\mathsf{ct}^{(\mathsf{t})}_0$, $\mathsf{ct}^{(\mathsf{t})}_1$ from random back to $\sigma(u^* + \mathsf{t})$ and use $i\mathcal{O}$ to remove special branches in the programs introduced for the previous steps. This advances $\mathsf{t}$ in the typical hybrids.

**Decryption Consistency.** The proof of decryption consistency shares many steps as that of ciphertext indistinguishability. Roughly speaking, we swap the tag instead of the plaintext, to remove information about $\tau^*$—yet the adversary cannot win without knowing $\tau^*$! There are some subtleties in choosing the range of the trigger $\widehat{\ell}^*$ for the two proofs, for which we refer the reader to [11].

# 4 Definition of SIM-CCA for Functional Encryption

We present the definition of plaintext-semi-adaptive simulation security against adaptive chosen-ciphertext attacks for functional encryption, the security notion achieved by our FE scheme.

**Definition 1 (FE for circuits).** *A functional encryption (FE) scheme for circuits consists of four efficient algorithms.*

- $\mathsf{Setup}(1^\lambda, 1^n)$ *takes the message length* $n$ *as input. It outputs a pair* $(\mathsf{mpk}, \mathsf{msk})$ *of master public/secret keys.*
- $\mathsf{KeyGen}(1^\lambda, \mathsf{msk}, C)$ *takes as input* $\mathsf{msk}$ *and a circuit* $C : \{0,1\}^n \to \{0,1\}^\star$. *It outputs a functional key* $\mathsf{sk}_C$.
- $\mathsf{Enc}(1^\lambda, \mathsf{mpk}, x)$ *takes as input* $\mathsf{mpk}$ *and a message* $x \in \{0,1\}^n$. *It outputs a ciphertext* $\mathsf{ct}$.
- $\mathsf{Dec}(1^\lambda, \mathsf{msk}, \mathsf{ct})$ *or* $\mathsf{Dec}(1^\lambda, C, \mathsf{sk}_C, \mathsf{ct})$ *takes as input either* $\mathsf{msk}$ *(first form) or* $C$, $\mathsf{sk}_C$ *(second form), and* $\mathsf{ct}$ *(both forms). It is supposed to recover* $x$ *(first form) or* $C(x)$ *(second form).*

*The scheme must be* correct, *i.e., for all* $\lambda \in \mathbb{N}$, $x \in \{0,1\}^\star$, $C : \{0,1\}^{|x|} \to \{0,1\}^\star$, *it holds that*

$$\Pr\left[\begin{array}{rl} (\mathsf{mpk}, \mathsf{msk}) \xleftarrow{\$} \mathsf{Setup}(1^\lambda, 1^{|x|}) & \mathsf{Dec}(1^\lambda, \mathsf{msk}, \mathsf{ct}) = x \\ \mathsf{sk}_C \xleftarrow{\$} \mathsf{KeyGen}(1^\lambda, \mathsf{msk}, C) : & \text{and} \\ \mathsf{ct} \xleftarrow{\$} \mathsf{Enc}(1^\lambda, \mathsf{mpk}, x) & \mathsf{Dec}(1^\lambda, C, \mathsf{sk}_C, \mathsf{ct}) = C(x) \end{array}\right] = 1.$$

**Definition 2 (SIM-CCA for FE).** *An FE scheme for circuits (Definition 1) can be equipped with a stateful algorithm* $\mathsf{Sim}$ *whose total running time in* $\mathsf{Exp}_{\mathsf{fe}}^{\mathrm{ideal}}$ *is* $\mathrm{poly}\big(\lambda + n + J_+ + \sum_{j'} |C_{j'}|\big)$, *where* $J_+$ *is the total number of queries (of all types). Such a scheme satisfies* SIM-CCA security *if* $\mathsf{Exp}_{\mathsf{fe}}^{\mathrm{real}} \approx \mathsf{Exp}_{\mathsf{fe}}^{\mathrm{ideal}}$, *where the experiments proceed as follows.*

- **Setup.** Launch $\mathcal{A}(1^\lambda)$ and receive $1^n$ from it. In $\mathsf{Exp}_{\mathsf{fe}}^{\mathrm{ideal}}$, launch $\mathsf{Sim}(1^\lambda)$ and maintain its state across the invocations. Run

$$\begin{array}{ll} \text{(real)} & (v, \mathsf{msk}) \xleftarrow{\$} \mathsf{Setup}(1^\lambda, 1^n), \\ \text{(ideal)} & \mathsf{mpk} \xleftarrow{\$} \mathsf{Sim}(\text{“setup”}, 1^n), \end{array}$$

  and send $\mathsf{mpk}$ to $\mathcal{A}$.
- **Query I.** Repeat the following for arbitrarily many rounds determined by $\mathcal{A}$. In each round, $\mathcal{A}$ has two choices (key creation, decryption).
  - $\mathcal{A}$ can submit a circuit $C_J : \{0,1\}^n \to \{0,1\}^\star$ to create a key. Upon such a query, run

$$\begin{array}{ll} \text{(real)} & \mathsf{sk}_J \xleftarrow{\$} \mathsf{KeyGen}(1^\lambda, \mathsf{msk}, C_J), \\ \text{(ideal)} & \mathsf{Sim}(\text{“create”}, C_J), \end{array}$$

    but send nothing to $\mathcal{A}$. Here, $J$ is the total number of key creation queries so far (including this one).

- $\mathcal{A}$ can submit a ciphertext $\mathsf{ct}'$ and an index $j' \in [0, J]$ for decryption, where $J$ is the total number of key creation queries so far. Upon such a query, run

$$z \xleftarrow{\$} \begin{cases} \mathsf{Dec}(1^\lambda, \mathsf{msk}, \mathsf{ct}'), & \text{(real) if} j' = 0; \\ \mathsf{Dec}(1^\lambda, C_{j'}, \mathsf{sk}_{j'}, \mathsf{ct}'), & \text{(real) if} j' \in [J]; \\ \mathsf{Sim}(\text{"decrypt"}, j', \mathsf{ct}'), & \text{(ideal) always;} \end{cases}$$

  and send $z$ to $\mathcal{A}$.

- **Challenge.** $\mathcal{A}$ chooses $x^* \in \{0,1\}^n$. Upon the challenge, run

$$\text{(real)} \qquad \mathsf{ct}^* \xleftarrow{\$} \mathsf{Enc}(1^\lambda, \mathsf{mpk}, x^*),$$
$$\text{(ideal)} \qquad \mathsf{ct}^* \xleftarrow{\$} \mathsf{Sim}(\text{"encrypt"}),$$

  and send $\mathsf{ct}^*$ to $\mathcal{A}$.
- **Query II.** Similar to Query I, except that $\mathcal{A}$ now has *three* choices (key creation, decryption, key retrieval).
  - Key creation remains identical to Query I.
  - For decryption: if $\mathsf{ct}' = \mathsf{ct}^*$, the response is set to $\perp$ in both $\mathsf{Exp}_{\mathsf{fe}}^{\mathrm{real}}$ and $\mathsf{Exp}_{\mathsf{fe}}^{\mathrm{ideal}}$; otherwise, it is identical to Query I. (Note that the simulator could be required to decrypt $\mathsf{ct}' \neq \mathsf{ct}^*$ using $\mathsf{sk}_{j'}$ without knowing $C_{j'}(x^*)$.)
  - $\mathcal{A}$ can submit some $j' \in [J]$ to retrieve a key, where $J$ is the total number of key creation queries so far. If this is the first key retrieval query for $j'$ in $\mathsf{Exp}_{\mathsf{fe}}^{\mathrm{ideal}}$, run

$$\mathsf{sk}_{j'} \xleftarrow{\$} \mathsf{Sim}(\text{"retrieve"}, j', C_{j'}(x^*)).$$

    In any case, $\mathsf{sk}_{j'}$ is now defined. Send $\mathsf{sk}_{j'}$ to $\mathcal{A}$.
- **Guess.** $\mathcal{A}$ outputs a bit $\beta'$, which is the output of the experiment.

*Remark 1.* Security notions of FE can be compared typically along three axes: adaptivity of plaintext ($x^*$), IND/SIM, CPA/CCA. Simulation for fully adaptively chosen $x^*$ is impossible [1,6] in the standard model, even when the other two axes are IND-CPA. Definition 2 is otherwise *maximal* in strength. (The other maximal one is plaintext-adaptive IND-CCA.)

We did not find an existing definition of SIM-CCA for FE. Following [4], key creation and usage (retrieval/decryption) are separated.

## 5 Functional Homomorphic Encryption

In this section, we present the notion of functional homomorphic encryption.

### 5.1 Basic Syntax

**Definition 3 (function homomorphic encryption).** *Let*

$$\mathsf{FH} = \{(D_{\lambda,\mathsf{param}}, H_{\lambda,\mathsf{param}}, F_{\lambda,\mathsf{param}})\}_{\lambda \in \mathbb{N}, \mathsf{param} \in \mathsf{Params}_\lambda}$$

*be a family of domains and two non-empty function sets such that*

- *the domain of every function in* $H_{\lambda,\mathsf{param}}$ *is a union of powers of* $D_{\lambda,\mathsf{param}}$*, and*
- *the domain of every function in* $F_{\lambda,\mathsf{param}}$ *includes the range of every function in* $H_{\lambda,\mathsf{param}}$.

*Let* $T_{0,H}, T_{0,F}$ *be functions with codomain* $\mathbb{N}$. *A* functional homomorphic encryption scheme *for* FH *with cleartext time* $(T_{0,H}, T_{0,F})$ *consists of five algorithms.*

- $\mathsf{Setup}(1^\lambda, \mathsf{param})$ *takes a functionality description* param *as input, and outputs a pair* $(\mathsf{mpk}, \mathsf{msk})$ *of master keys.*
- $\mathsf{KeyGen}(1^\lambda, \mathsf{msk}, f)$ *takes as input* msk *and a functional function* $f \in F_{\lambda,\mathsf{param}}$*, and outputs a functional secret key* $\mathsf{sk}_f$.
- $\mathsf{Enc}(1^\lambda, \mathsf{mpk}, x)$ *takes as input* mpk *and some plaintext* $x \in D_{\lambda,\mathsf{param}}$*, and outputs a ciphertext* ct.
- $\mathsf{Eval}(1^\lambda, \mathsf{mpk}, h, \{\mathsf{ct}_m\}_{m\in[M]})$ *takes as input* mpk*, a homomorphic function* $h \in H_{\lambda,\mathsf{param}}$*, and some ciphertexts. It outputs an evaluated ciphertext* ct′.
- $\mathsf{Dec}(1^\lambda, \mathsf{msk}, \mathsf{ct}')$ *or* $\mathsf{Dec}(1^\lambda, \mathsf{mpk}, f, \mathsf{sk}_f, \mathsf{ct}')$ *takes as input either* msk *(first form) or* mpk, $f$, $\mathsf{sk}_f$ *(second form), and* ct′ *(both forms). It outputs the decryption result.*

*The algorithms* Setup, KeyGen, Enc *must be efficient,* Eval *must halt in time*

$$\mathrm{poly}\Big(\lambda,\ |\mathsf{param}|,\ M,\ |h|,\ \sum_{m\in[M]} |x_m|,\ \ T_{0,H}(\lambda, \mathsf{param}, h, \{|x_m|\}_{m\in[M]})\Big),$$

Dec *(first form) must halt in time* $\mathrm{poly}(\lambda, |\mathsf{param}|, |f|, |y|, |\mathsf{ct}'|)$*, and* Dec *(second form) must halt in time*

$$\mathrm{poly}\Big(\lambda,\ |\mathsf{param}|,\ |f|,\ |y|,\ |\mathsf{ct}'|,\ T_{0,F}(\lambda, \mathsf{param}, f, y)\Big),$$

*where* $y = h(\{x_m\}_{m\in[M]})$.

*The scheme must be* correct*, meaning that for all* $\lambda, M \in \mathbb{N}$, $\mathsf{param} \in \mathsf{Params}_\lambda$, $x_m \in D_{\lambda,\mathsf{param}}$ *for* $m \in [M]$, $h \in H_{\lambda,\mathsf{param}}$, $f \in F_{\lambda,\mathsf{param}}$ *such that the domain of* $h$ *includes* $D^M_{\lambda,\mathsf{param}}$*, it holds that*

$$\Pr\left[\begin{array}{r@{\ }l} (\mathsf{mpk}, \mathsf{msk}) \xleftarrow{\$} & \mathsf{Setup}(1^\lambda, \mathsf{param}) \\ \mathsf{sk}_f \xleftarrow{\$} & \mathsf{KeyGen}(1^\lambda, \mathsf{msk}, f) \\ \{\ \mathsf{ct}_m \xleftarrow{\$} & \mathsf{Enc}(1^\lambda, \mathsf{mpk}, x_m)\ \}_{m\in[M]} \\ \mathsf{ct}' \xleftarrow{\$} & \mathsf{Eval}(1^\lambda, \mathsf{mpk}, h, \{\mathsf{ct}_m\}_{m\in[M]}) \\ y \xleftarrow{\$} & \mathsf{Dec}(1^\lambda, \mathsf{msk}, \mathsf{ct}') \\ z \xleftarrow{\$} & \mathsf{Dec}(1^\lambda, \mathsf{mpk}, f, \mathsf{sk}_f, \mathsf{ct}') \end{array} : \begin{array}{c} y = h(\{x_m\}_{m\in[M]}) \\ \textit{and}\ \ z = f(y) \end{array}\right] = 1.$$

*The scheme is*

- weakly compact *if* $|\mathsf{ct}'| \leq \text{poly}(\lambda, |\mathsf{param}|, |h|, |h(\{x_m\}_{m\in[M]})|)$,
- moderately compact *if* $|\mathsf{ct}'| \leq \text{poly}(\lambda, |\mathsf{param}|, |h(\{x_m\}_{m\in[M]})|)$,
- fully compact *if* $|\mathsf{ct}'| \leq \text{poly}(\lambda, |h(\{x_m\}_{m\in[M]})|)$.

*Remark 2 (FE and HE).* Definition 3 generalizes both functional and homomorphic encryption. By constraining the functional (resp. homomorphic) function set to only contain the identity function, the primitive degenerates down to homomorphic (resp. functional) encryption. Note also that $T_{0,H}$ varies only by input lengths, whereas $T_{0,F}$ is allowed to vary by the specific input. The latter is useful for RAM or TM functional decryption, although not considered in this work.

*Remark 3 (compactness).* The word "compactness" has different meanings in the context of FE and HE. In Definition 3, it is in the context of HE, where *moderate* compactness corresponds to the usual version found in the literature.

In the literature, compactness is often used as a proxy to the desired *time-saving* property, i.e., the computation of $h$ is done by Eval and not Dec. When the function class consists of all circuits (perhaps of *a priori* bounded depth), compactness works well as a proxy. In general, the proxy is not always good. It is difficult to pin down a universal definition of non-triviality (time-saving property) for all kinds of homomorphic function classes. We instead choose to decide whether each scheme is non-trivial as one comes. See Sect. 5.2 for examples.

**Additional FE Features.** For the functional part, one can consider *multi-client* [32] and *multi-input* [18] settings. These features add complexity to the security definition, which, as we shall see later, is already more complex than either FE or HE on their own. We leave their treatment to future work.

**(Additional) HE Features.** A scheme is *multi-ary* if it supports multi-ary homomorphic functions ($M > 1$), i.e., it is possible to apply a joint function using Eval on more than one independently encrypted ciphertexts. In the setting of functional homomorphic encryption, this feature adds complexity to the security definition. In this work, we focus on unary homomorphic functions.

A scheme is *multi-hop* if an arbitrarily evaluated ciphertext can be further evaluated as long as all the (composed) homomorphic functions along the way are in $H$. Our scheme is multi-hop.

### 5.2 Functionality Examples

In this section, we concretize the functionality FH in Definition 3 to demonstrate various interesting schemes to consider whose homomorphic parts are different from (though often weaker than) the usual version of fully homomorphic encryption (FHE).

In [11], we construct schemes supporting Examples 1 and 2.

**Example 1 (homomorphic iterations of a fixed unary function, followed by arbitrary functional circuit).** Each param specifies $D = \{0,1\}^n$ and circuit $g : D \to D$, and

$$H_{\mathsf{param}} = \left\{ g^{(t)} \,|t \in \mathbb{N} \right\}, \qquad T_{0,H}(\mathsf{param}, g^{(t)}, n) = t,$$
$$F_{\mathsf{param}} = \{ f : \{0,1\}^n \to \{0,1\}^\star \,|f \text{ is a circuit} \}, \quad T_{0,F}(\mathsf{param}, f, y) = |f|,$$

with $g^{(t)}$ encoded as $t$ (in binary). The efficiency requirements in Definition 3 translate to the following.

- The algorithm Eval runs in time $\mathrm{poly}(\lambda, |g|, t)$.
- Weak compactness constrains $|\mathsf{ct}'| \le \mathrm{poly}(\lambda, |g|, \log t)$.
- Moderate compactness constrains $|\mathsf{ct}'| \le \mathrm{poly}(\lambda, |g|)$.
- Strong compactness constrains $|\mathsf{ct}'| \le \mathrm{poly}(\lambda, n)$.
- For a moderately compact scheme, Dec runs in time $\mathrm{poly}(\lambda, |g|, |f|)$, independent of $t$.

Such a scheme does not support computing jointly over two ciphertexts.

*Time-Saving and Compactness.* When used as (non-functional) HE, a weakly compact scheme for Example 1 is allowed to have $|\mathsf{ct}'|$ growing polynomially with $|h| = |g| + \Theta(\log t)$. Such a scheme is still meaningful from the first principles of homomorphic encryption, i.e., (*time-saving* property) Dec runs faster (time $\mathrm{poly}(|g|, \log t)$) than the computation being applied homomorphically (time $t$, easily higher order than $\mathrm{poly}(|g|, \log t)$).

**Example 2 (*two-way* homomorphic iterations of a fixed permutation, followed by arbitrary functional circuit).** Each param specifies $D = \{0,1\}^n$ and two circuits $g_+, g_- : D \to D$ such that $g_+$, $g_-$ are each other's inverse. Let $g = g_+$ and

$$H_{\mathsf{param}} = \left\{ g^{(t)} \,|t \in \mathbb{Z} \right\}, \qquad T_{0,H}(\mathsf{param}, g^{(t)}, n) = \mathrm{abs}(t),$$
$$F_{\mathsf{param}} = \{ f : \{0,1\}^n \to \{0,1\}^\star \,|f \text{ is a circuit} \}, \quad T_{0,F}(\mathsf{param}, f, y) = |f|,$$

with $g^{(t)}$ encoded as $t$ (in binary).

*Encoding of* **param's.** In Example 2, the set Params only contains param such that $g_+$, $g_-$ are each other's inverse. If they are written as general circuits, Params is not efficiently decidable.[8] In this case, correctness (and security, as stated in Remark 4) will only hold for valid param's. Another option is to require that param contain a proof that $g_+$, $g_-$ are good. Yet another option is to require that $g_+$ be written as a reversible circuit and that $g_-$ be the literal inverse of $g_+$. Both latter options could constrain the $g$'s allowed for a polynomial-time user (param for the same $g$ could be longer than in the first option).

[8] Pedantically, it would be efficiently decidable if $\mathsf{P} = \mathsf{NP}$, but then there would be no public-key cryptography.

**Example 3 (homomorphic iterations of two fixed unary functions, non-functional).** For bounded number of iterations, each $\mathsf{param}$ specifies a domain $D = \{0,1\}^n$, two circuits $g_0, g_1 : D \to D$, a maximum number $1^{\overline{T}}$ of iterations, and

$$\begin{aligned} H_{\mathsf{param}} &= \left\{ g_{b_t} \circ \cdots \circ g_{b_1} \,\middle|\, t \in [0, \overline{T}],\, b_1, \ldots, b_t \in \{0,1\} \right\}, \\ T_{0,H}(\mathsf{param}, g_{b_t} \circ \cdots \circ g_{b_1}, n) &= t, \\ F_{\mathsf{param}} &= \{\text{identity over } D\}, \qquad T_{0,F}(\mathsf{param}, f, y) = n. \end{aligned}$$

Here, $g_{b_t} \circ \cdots \circ g_{b_1}$ is represented by $(b_1, \ldots, b_t)$. For unbounded number of iterations, $\overline{T}$ is specified in binary.

*Time-Saving and Compactness, Again.* For bounded iterations of two functions (notably $|\mathsf{param}| \geq \overline{T} \geq t$), the trivial scheme appending $b_1, \ldots, b_t$ to $\mathsf{ct}$ in $\mathsf{Eval}$ satisfies efficiency and moderate compactness per Definition 3. Removing the upper bound $\overline{T}$ from the functionality makes a moderately compact scheme non-trivial.

**Example 4 ((L/F)HE for circuits).** In leveled HE for circuits, each $\mathsf{param}$ specifies the maximum depth $1^d$ (in unary), and

$$\begin{aligned} D_{\text{param}} &= \{0,1\}, \qquad\qquad T_{0,H}(\text{param}, C, \{1\}_{m \in [M]}) = |C|, \\ H_{\text{param}} &= \left\{ C : \{0,1\}^M \to \{0,1\}^* \mid \text{depth of circuit } C \text{ does not exceed } d \right\}, \\ F_{\text{param}} &= \left\{ \text{identity function over } \{0,1\}^M \mid M \in \mathbb{N} \right\}, \quad T_{0,F}(\text{param}, f, y) = M. \end{aligned}$$

In FHE for circuits, $\mathsf{param}$ is empty (only one choice) and its functionality is LHE except there is no bound on the circuit depth. Both schemes are multi-ary. For FHE defined above, full compactness is the same as moderate compactness. Typical (circular- or not) LWE-based constructions [7] match efficiency and moderate compactness of Definition 3.

**Two More Existing Examples.** The works of [24,26] studied FHE for RAM, which can be captured by Definition 3 similarly to the above.

In [19,20], the authors considered FHE for TM with instance-specific evaluation time. Since the running time contains information about the plaintext, the Turing machine to evaluate cannot be chosen freely by everyone. Instead, the encryptor prescribes the machine with the input. Their notion is equivalent to randomized encoding of compute-TM-then-encrypt. Moreover, the controlled leakage (of evaluation time) about the plaintext gives the notion a flavor of functional encryption. It turns out that a limited version of this primitive can be *recovered* from functional homomorphic encryption (see Sect. 5.5).

With that said, Definition 3 does not *formulate* the schemes of [19,20], as it only supports instance-specific functional decryption time, but not such homomorphic evaluation time (see Remark 2). We consider this dichotomy a feature, keeping the homomorphic part non-functional (instance-specific evaluation time is "functional") for separation of concerns.

### 5.3 Functional-Homomorphic Chosen-Ciphertext Security

We define the security notion for functional homomorphic encryption schemes, termed functional-homomorphic chosen-ciphertext (FHCCA) security. When the scheme is non-functional (i.e., the only functional function is identity), our notion becomes IND-HCCA. After the definition, we discuss its relation with HCCA in [29], which we shall term as SIM-HCCA.

We will need some notions related to *view*. The view of $\mathcal{A}$ in an experiment $\mathsf{Exp}$ consists of $\mathcal{A}$'s input and randomness and the messages received by $\mathcal{A}$. Given $\rho$ in the format of a view, it is possible to "(re)run" $\mathcal{A}$ deterministically, a process denoted by $\mathsf{rerun}(\rho, \mathcal{A})$. Here, $\rho$ need not come from any execution and its messages might not be fully consumed or sufficient. For example, suppose $\rho$ is from an execution, appending another message to $\rho$ does not affect the rerun. During $\mathsf{rerun}(\rho, \mathcal{A})$, when all of the messages in $\rho$ are consumed, $\mathcal{A}$ is forcibly halted even if it does not choose to do so.

**Definition 4 (IND-FHCCA, extractor).** *For a functional homomorphic encryption scheme (Definition 3), an* (adversary-dependent) extractor *has syntax* $\mathsf{Extract}(1^\lambda, r_{\text{xtrt}}, \rho')$. *It takes as input persistent randomness* $r_{\text{xtrt}}$ *and a view* $\rho'$ *of an adversary up to some point. The algorithm outputs either* $\perp$ *or* $(h, \{\mathsf{ct}_m\}_{m\in[M]})$ *such that* $h \in H_{\lambda,\mathsf{param}}$ *and its domain includes* $D^M_{\lambda,\mathsf{param}}$ *and* $\{\mathsf{ct}^*_i\}_{i\in[I]} \cap \{\mathsf{ct}_m\}_{m\in[M]} \neq \varnothing$, *where* $\mathsf{param}$, $\mathsf{ct}^*_i$*'s (and* $\mathsf{mpk}$, $\mathsf{ct}'$*) are determined by* $\rho'$ *as in Definition 5. (When the output is non-*$\perp$*, supposedly* $\mathsf{ct}'$ *is obtained from* $\mathsf{Eval}(1^\lambda, \mathsf{mpk}, h, \{\mathsf{ct}_m\}_{m\in[M]})$*.)*

**Definition 5 (IND-FHCCA).** *A functional homomorphic encryption scheme (Definition 3) satisfies* IND-FHCCA security *if for all* admissible *(defined below) efficient* $\mathcal{A}$, *there exists an efficient* $\mathsf{Extract}$ *(Definition 4) such that*

$$\{\rho(1^\lambda, \mathsf{Exp}^0_{\text{fhcca}}, \mathcal{A}, \mathsf{Extract})\}_{\lambda\in\mathbb{N}} \approx \{\rho(1^\lambda, \mathsf{Exp}^1_{\text{fhcca}}, \mathcal{A}, \mathsf{Extract})\}_{\lambda\in\mathbb{N}},$$

*where* $\rho(1^\lambda, \mathsf{Exp}^\beta_{\text{fhcca}}, \mathcal{A}, \mathsf{Extract})$ *is the view of* $\mathcal{A}$ *in* $\mathsf{Exp}^\beta_{\text{fhcca}}(1^\lambda, \mathcal{A}, \mathsf{Extract})$. *The experiment proceeds as follows.*

- **Setup.** Launch $\mathcal{A}(1^\lambda)$ and receive from it $\mathsf{param} \in \mathsf{Params}_\lambda$. Run

$$(\mathsf{mpk}, \mathsf{msk}) \xleftarrow{\$} \mathsf{Setup}(1^\lambda, \mathsf{param})$$

  and send $\mathsf{mpk}$ to $\mathcal{A}$. Sample $r_{\text{xtrt}}$ and keep it.
- **Query/Challenge.** Repeat the following for arbitrarily many rounds determined by $\mathcal{A}$. In each round, $\mathcal{A}$ has four choices (key creation, key retrieval, ciphertext challenge, decryption).
  - $\mathcal{A}$ can submit some $f_J \in F_{\lambda,\mathsf{param}}$ to create a functional key. Upon such a query, run

$$\mathsf{sk}_J \xleftarrow{\$} \mathsf{KeyGen}(1^\lambda, \mathsf{msk}, f_J)$$

    but send nothing to $\mathcal{A}$. Here, $J$ is the total number of key creation queries so far (including this one).

- $\mathcal{A}$ can submit some $j' \in [J]$ to retrieve a functional key, where $J$ is the total number of key creation queries so far. Upon such a query, send $\mathsf{sk}_{j'}$ to $\mathcal{A}$.
- $\mathcal{A}$ can submit $x^*_{I,0}, x^*_{I,1} \in D_{\lambda,\mathsf{param}}$ of equal length for a challenge ciphertext. Upon such a challenge, run

$$\mathsf{ct}^*_I \xleftarrow{\$} \mathsf{Enc}(1^\lambda, \mathsf{mpk}, x^*_{I,\beta})$$

and send $\mathsf{ct}^*_I$ to $\mathcal{A}$. Here, $I$ is the total number of ciphertext challenges so far (including this one).
- $\mathcal{A}$ can submit a ciphertext $\mathsf{ct}'$ and an index $j' \in [0, J]$ for decryption, where $J$ is the total number of key creation queries so far. Upon such a query, let $\rho'$ be the view of $\mathcal{A}$ up to this point and $I$ the total number of ciphertext challenges so far. Run

$$\mathsf{lnk} \xleftarrow{\$} \mathsf{Extract}(1^\lambda, r_{\mathrm{xtrt}}, \rho'), \quad z \xleftarrow{\$} \begin{cases} \mathsf{Dec}(1^\lambda, \mathsf{msk}, \mathsf{ct}'), & \text{if } j' = 0; \\ \mathsf{Dec}(1^\lambda, \mathsf{mpk}, f_{j'}, \mathsf{sk}_{j'}, \mathsf{ct}'), & \text{if } j' \in [J]. \end{cases}$$

If $\mathsf{lnk} = \bot$, send $(\mathsf{lnk}, z)$ to $\mathcal{A}$ and the round ends. Otherwise, parse $\mathsf{lnk}$ into $(h, \{\mathsf{ct}_m\}_{m\in[M]})$[9] and run

$$x_m \xleftarrow{\$} \mathsf{Dec}(1^\lambda, \mathsf{msk}, \mathsf{ct}_m) \quad \text{for all } m \in [M].$$

If $x_m = \bot$ for some $m \in [M]$, send $\beta$ to $\mathcal{A}$ and the round ends. Otherwise, compute

$$z' \leftarrow \begin{cases} h(\{x_m\}_{m\in[M]}), & \text{if } j' = 0; \\ f_{j'}(h(\{x_m\}_{m\in[M]})), & \text{if } j' \in [J]. \end{cases}$$

If $z' \neq z$, send $\beta$ to $\mathcal{A}$ and the round ends. Otherwise, compute

$$z'' \leftarrow \begin{cases} \bot, & \text{if } z = \bot; \\ \top, & \text{if } z \neq \bot; \end{cases} \qquad (m \in [M]) \;\; x'_m \leftarrow \begin{cases} x_m, & \text{if } \mathsf{ct}_m \notin \{\mathsf{ct}^*_i\}_{i\in[I]}; \\ \top, & \text{if } \mathsf{ct}_m \in \{\mathsf{ct}^*_i\}_{i\in[I]}; \end{cases}$$

send $(\mathsf{lnk}, \{x'_m\}_{m\in[M]}, z'')$ to $\mathcal{A}$, and the round ends.

*Let $\rho'$ be in the format of a view. If, after $\mathsf{rerun}(\rho', \mathcal{A})$, there exists $i' \in [I]$, $j' \in [J]$, $h \in H_{\lambda,\mathsf{param}}$, $M \in \mathbb{N}$, $m' \in [M]$, $x'_1, \ldots, x'_M \in D_{\lambda,\mathsf{param}}$ such that the domain of $h$ includes $D^M_{\lambda,\mathsf{param}}$ and $\mathcal{A}$ submits a key retrieval query for $j'$ and*

$$\begin{aligned} & f_{j'}(h(x'_1, \ldots, x'_{m'-1}, \boxed{x^*_{i',0}}, x'_{m'+1}, \ldots, x'_M)) \\ & \quad \neq f_{j'}(h(x'_1, \ldots, x'_{m'-1}, \boxed{x^*_{i',1}}, x'_{m'+1}, \ldots, x'_M)) \\ \text{or} \quad & T_{0,F}(\lambda, \mathsf{param}, f_{j'}, h(x'_1, \ldots, x'_{m'-1}, \boxed{x^*_{i',0}}, x'_{m'+1}, \ldots, x'_M)) \\ & \quad \neq T_{0,F}(\cdots, \boxed{x^*_{i',1}}, \cdots), \end{aligned}$$

9 Recall that it is syntactically required that $h \in H_{\lambda,\mathsf{param}}$ and its domain must include $D^M_{\mathsf{param},\lambda}$ and at least one challenge ciphertext must appear in $\mathsf{ct}_m$'s.

*then* $\mathcal{A}$ violates the constraint *in* $\mathsf{rerun}(\rho', \mathcal{A})$. *An adversary* $\mathcal{A}$ *is* admissible *if for all* $\rho'$ *in the format of a view (not necessarily from any execution of* $\mathsf{Exp}_{\mathsf{fhcca}}$*), it does not violate the constraint in* $\mathsf{rerun}(\rho', \mathcal{A})$.

*Remark 4 (admissibility and output discarding).* Definition 5 is unusual in that it does not consider the advantage function of an inadmissible adversary *at all.* The more common approach to constrained experiments is to discard the distinguisher's output when the adversary violates the constraint in a particular execution, e.g., if $\mathcal{A}$ violates the constraint with probability 1/3, the advantage is simply reduced by 1/3, but the scheme must otherwise be secure against $\mathcal{A}$. Let's call the usual approach "output discarding".

When the constraint can be checked efficiently, there is no difference between the two. In general, output discarding is preferred as it is stronger, but proving security in this setting requires the reduction algorithms be able to efficiently catch violation (or by reduction only to experiments capable of discarding output). For example, for $i\mathcal{O}$, a reduction can do so by enumerating all the input, incurring an exponential loss. For our specific scheme, we could not prove the output-discarding version of security, so we settled by requiring admissibility.

Furthermore, the definition of admissibility is rather strict. The adversary must not violate the constraint even if the replies it receives are pure nonsense (e.g., incorrect format) or worse, "hidden traps" (i.e., indistinguishable but not possible in a real execution). The reason is technical. Suppose we only require the constraint in $\mathsf{Exp}_{\mathsf{fhcca}}$ (for all $\mathsf{Extract}'$), it is not immediate that the constraint would hold (even just with overwhelming probability) in the hybrids—computational indistinguishability only transfers efficiently checkable properties and the constraint is not such. Inspecting our proofs, it turns out that we will rely on part of the constraint verifiable in a long time but the indistinguishability between $\mathsf{Exp}_{\mathsf{fhcca}}$ and the hybrid *does not hold* against general adversaries taking so much time. Nevertheless, the strict admissibility still covers some interesting scenarios, such as when the choice of challenge plaintexts and functions for keys is static, independent of any components of the scheme instance (decryption queries can still be made adaptively)—in this case, constraint satisfaction does not vary by hybrids.

Note that an adversary choosing $\mathsf{param} \notin \mathsf{Params}_\lambda$ with positive probability is also not considered at all. For uniform security, this restriction can be significant if $\mathsf{Params}$ is not efficiently decidable. (See Example 2)

**Plaintext Selectivity.** The aforementioned definition is fully adaptive. Usually, it is easy to allow challenge plaintexts to be fully adaptive, yet difficult to handle post-challenge queries, so in the standard terminology, *non-adaptive* CCA (CCA1) means that decryption queries cannot be made adaptively based on the challenge ciphertexts. In our schemes, the situation is different—handling post-challenge queries is simple but allowing adaptive plaintexts is difficult. We consider *plaintext-selective* security.

**Definition 6 (plaintext-selective security).** *For* plaintext-selective *security, the experiment in Definition 5 (as well as those later in Definitions 8 and 9) is modified to require that $\mathcal{A}$ choose $\{x^*_{i,0}, x^*_{i,1}\}_{i\in[I]}$ (resp. $x^*$ or $x^*_0, x^*_1$) together with* $\mathsf{param}$*, before seeing* $\mathsf{mpk}$*. Each challenge ciphertext is only given when requested (using the "ciphertext challenge" choice or in the Challenge phase), so that $\mathcal{A}$ can make (less restricted or unrestricted) decryption queries before opting to receive them.*

**(SIM-)HCCA** [29] **and IND-FHCCA.** In HCCA as defined by [29], the real world is compared with an ideal world where the challenge $\mathsf{ct}^*$ is fake-encrypted (without information of the challenge plaintext) and the decryption queries related to $\mathsf{ct}^*$ (as identified by, in our parlance, $\mathsf{Extract}$, or $\mathsf{Link}$ later on) are rerouted to the relation homomorphism. This makes it a simulation-based security, hence SIM-HCCA.

We consider indistinguishability-based security, because no sufficiently expressive functional homomorphic encryption can achieve a simulation-based definition in the standard model, even just for very selective security (in stark contrast with either FE [15] or HE on their own), for the following reason. Given $\mathsf{ct}^*$, $\mathsf{sk}_f$, an adversary can homomorphically apply $h$ to $\mathsf{ct}^*$ then decrypt it using $\mathsf{sk}_f$. A would-be simulator has to come up with $\mathsf{mpk}$, $\mathsf{ct}^*$, $\mathsf{sk}_f$ given $\{f(h(x^*))\}_{h\in H}$. In general, the latter could contain an excessive amount of false entropy, making efficient simulation impossible, since pseudorandomness cannot be efficiently compressed.

Our definition can be regarded as a natural indistinguishability-based version of HCCA taking functional decryption into consideration. In indistinguishability-based security, the adversary always receives a ("real") ciphertext produced by $\mathsf{Enc}$. This naturally requires $\mathsf{Extract}$ to work with real ciphertexts and does away with a fake encryption algorithm. We further allow $\mathsf{Extract}$ to be adversary-dependent, prompting a multi-challenge formulation—it is unclear whether Definition 5 is implied by its single-challenge version.

**Nuances of $\mathsf{Exp}_{\mathsf{fhcca}}$.** We want $\mathsf{Extract}$ to accurately identify related ciphertexts. This is captured by how a distinguisher can succeed. By giving $\beta$ to $\mathcal{A}$ (part of the view $\rho$ given to the distinguisher) whenever $\mathsf{Extract}$ outputs an incorrect relation, Definition 5 guards against false positives. On the other hand, if $\mathsf{Extract}$ outputs $\bot$ when $\mathsf{ct}'$ is in fact related to the challenge ciphertexts (false negatives), then $\mathcal{A}$ will see the decryption result, which likely[10] reveals $\beta$ when cross-checked with the challenge plaintexts. The definition also takes trivial relations into consideration, e.g., $\mathsf{lnk} = (h^*, \mathsf{ct}^*_1, \mathsf{ct}')$ with $h^* : (x_1, x_2) \mapsto x_2$,[11] by giving $\mathcal{A}$

[10] On the contrary, for example, if a constant function is applied to a challenge ciphertext, decrypting the homomorphic ciphertext does not enable trivial distinguishing, in which case it is permissible for $\mathsf{Extract}$ to output $\bot$.

[11] This relation effectively says "$\mathsf{ct}'$ is obtained from $\mathsf{ct}'$". It should be prevented in general, although it does not apply to our scheme—in our scheme, $h$ must be unary and at least one challenge ciphertext is required to be *a* (hence *the only*) underlying ciphertext.

the decryptions of all the ciphertexts in $\mathsf{lnk}$ except the challenge ones—in this example, $\mathsf{Extract}$ cannot "help $\mathsf{ct}'$ evade decryption" to trivialize the decryption oracle.

There is another subtlety. When $\mathsf{Extract}$ identifies a relation, we cannot give the adversary $f(h(\{x_m\}_{m\in[M]}))$ *even if* this value happens to not depend on $\beta \in \{0,1\}$—we do not know how to prove security if this is allowed. If the adversary wants to obtain the possible homomorphic evaluation results, it can apply $h$ by itself (together with the challenge plaintexts), using the decryptions of $\mathsf{ct}_m$'s (excluding the challenge ones) it receives back from the decryption query.

### 5.4 Simpler Security Definitions with Universal Unary Linking

Definition 5 captures the desired security with a single, intuitive experiment, but it is not ergonomic to work with in proofs. The definition is multi-stage due to adversary-dependent $\mathsf{Extract}$, it is multi-challenge, and its logic in handling decryption queries is quite complex. For our specific constructions, $\mathsf{Extract}$ is universal (renamed to $\mathsf{Link}$ in this case) and unary, it does not need persistent randomness, a single challenge suffices, and it is easier to consider the two ways of breaking security separately—finding incorrect relations (one-wayness) or guessing the secret bit inside the challenge ciphertext (indistinguishability)—as we will employ different strategies to prove that the adversary/distinguisher cannot do either. We formulate the simpler definitions, whose conjunction implies IND-FHCCA.

**Definition 7 (IND-FHCCA, universal unary linking).** *A functional homomorphic encryption scheme (Definition 3) can be equipped with an efficient* (universal unary) linking algorithm $\mathsf{Link}(1^\lambda, \mathsf{mpk}, \mathsf{ct}, \mathsf{ct}')$. *It takes as input* $\mathsf{mpk}$, $\mathsf{ct}$, $\mathsf{ct}'$, *and outputs either* $\perp$ *or* $h$ *such that* $h \in H_{\lambda,\mathsf{param}}$ *and its domain includes* $D_{\lambda,\mathsf{param}}$. *(When the output is non-*$\perp$*, supposedly* $\mathsf{ct}'$ *is obtained from* $\mathsf{Eval}(1^\lambda, \mathsf{mpk}, h, \mathsf{ct})$*.)*

**Definition 8 (IND-FHCCA, decryption consistency).** *A functional homomorphic encryption scheme equipped with* $\mathsf{Link}$ *(Definitions 3 and 7) satisfies* decryption consistency *against FHCCA if* $\Pr[\mathsf{Exp}^{\mathrm{dec}}_{\mathrm{fhcca}}(1^\lambda, \mathcal{A}) \to 1]$ *is negligible for all efficient adversary* $\mathcal{A}$*, where the experiment proceeds as follows.*

- **Setup.** Launch $\mathcal{A}(1^\lambda)$ and receive from it $\mathsf{param} \in \mathsf{Params}_\lambda$. Run
$$(\mathsf{mpk}, \mathsf{msk}) \xleftarrow{\$} \mathsf{Setup}(1^\lambda, \mathsf{param})$$
and send $\mathsf{mpk}$ to $\mathcal{A}$.
- **Query I.** Repeat the following for arbitrarily many rounds determined by $\mathcal{A}$. In each round, $\mathcal{A}$ has two choices.
  - $\mathcal{A}$ can submit some $f_J \in F_{\lambda,\mathsf{param}}$ for a functional key. Upon such a query, run
$$\mathsf{sk}_J \xleftarrow{\$} \mathsf{KeyGen}(1^\lambda, \mathsf{msk}, f_J)$$
and send $\mathsf{sk}_J$ to $\mathcal{A}$. Here, $J$ is the total number of key queries so far (including this one).

- $\mathcal{A}$ can submit a ciphertext $\mathsf{ct}'$ for decryption. Upon such a query, run

$$z \xleftarrow{\$} \mathsf{Dec}(1^\lambda, \mathsf{msk}, \mathsf{ct}')$$

and send $z$ to $\mathcal{A}$.

– **Challenge.** $\mathcal{A}$ submits $x^* \in D_{\lambda,\mathsf{param}}$. Upon the challenge, run

$$\mathsf{ct}^* \xleftarrow{\$} \mathsf{Enc}(1^\lambda, \mathsf{mpk}, x^*)$$

and send $\mathsf{ct}^*$ to $\mathcal{A}$.

– **Query II.** Same as Query I, except that decryption queries are different. For each decryption query, together with $\mathsf{ct}'$, the adversary submits an index $j' \in [0, J]$, where $J$ is the total number of key queries so far. Upon such a query, run

$$\mathsf{lnk} \xleftarrow{\$} \mathsf{Link}(1^\lambda, \mathsf{mpk}, \mathsf{ct}^*, \mathsf{ct}'), \quad z \xleftarrow{\$} \begin{cases} \mathsf{Dec}(1^\lambda, \mathsf{msk}, \mathsf{ct}'), & \text{if } j' = 0; \\ \mathsf{Dec}(1^\lambda, \mathsf{mpk}, f_{j'}, \mathsf{sk}_{j'}, \mathsf{ct}'), & \text{if } j' \in [J]. \end{cases}$$

If $\mathsf{lnk} = \bot$, send $(\mathsf{lnk}, z)$ to $\mathcal{A}$ and the round ends. Otherwise, $\mathsf{lnk} = h$, compute

$$z' \leftarrow \begin{cases} h(x^*), & \text{if } j' = 0; \\ f_{j'}(h(x^*)), & \text{if } j' \in [J]. \end{cases}$$

If $z' \neq z$, the experiment outputs 1 and terminates. Otherwise, send $(\mathsf{lnk}, z)$[12] to $\mathcal{A}$ and the round ends.

– **End.** The experiment outputs 0 and terminates.

**Definition 9 (IND-FHCCA, ciphertext indistinguishability).** *A functional homomorphic encryption scheme equipped with* Link *(Definitions 3 and 7) satisfies* ciphertext indistinguishability *against FHCCA if* $\mathsf{Exp}^0_{\mathrm{fhcca}} \approx \mathsf{Exp}^1_{\mathrm{fhcca}}$ *against all* admissible *(defined below) efficient adversaries, where* $\mathsf{Exp}^\beta_{\mathrm{fhcca}}(1^\lambda, \mathcal{A})$ *proceeds as follows.*

– **Setup.** Launch $\mathcal{A}(1^\lambda)$ and receive from it $\mathsf{param} \in \mathsf{Params}_\lambda$. Run

$$(\mathsf{mpk}, \mathsf{msk}) \xleftarrow{\$} \mathsf{Setup}(1^\lambda, \mathsf{param})$$

and send $\mathsf{mpk}$ to $\mathcal{A}$.

– **Query I.** Repeat the following for arbitrarily many rounds determined by $\mathcal{A}$. In each round, $\mathcal{A}$ has three choices.
  - $\mathcal{A}$ can submit some $f_J \in F_{\lambda,\mathsf{param}}$ to create a functional key. Upon such a query, run

$$\mathsf{sk}_J \xleftarrow{\$} \mathsf{KeyGen}(1^\lambda, \mathsf{msk}, f_J)$$

but send nothing to $\mathcal{A}$. Here, $J$ is the total number of key creation queries so far (including this one).

[12] Unlike in Definition 5, the value $z$ is not reset to $\top$ (in this case, $\mathsf{lnk} \neq \bot$). This is a strengthening orthogonal to the universality of Link.

- $\mathcal{A}$ can submit some $j' \in [J]$ to retrieve a functional key, where $J$ is the total number of key creation queries so far. Upon such a query, send $\mathsf{sk}_{j'}$ to $\mathcal{A}$.
- $\mathcal{A}$ can submit a ciphertext $\mathsf{ct}'$ and an index $j' \in [0, J]$ for decryption, where $J$ is the total number of key creation queries so far. Upon such a query, run

$$z \xleftarrow{\$} \begin{cases} \mathsf{Dec}(1^\lambda, \mathsf{msk}, \mathsf{ct}'), & \text{if } j' = 0; \\ \mathsf{Dec}(1^\lambda, \mathsf{mpk}, f_{j'}, \mathsf{sk}_{j'}, \mathsf{ct}'), & \text{if } j' \in [J]; \end{cases}$$

and send $z$ to $\mathcal{A}$.

– **Challenge.** $\mathcal{A}$ submits $x_0^*, x_1^* \in D_{\lambda,\mathsf{param}}$. Upon the challenge, run

$$\mathsf{ct}^* \xleftarrow{\$} \mathsf{Enc}(1^\lambda, \mathsf{mpk}, x_\beta^*)$$

and send $\mathsf{ct}^*$ to $\mathcal{A}$.

– **Query II.** Same as Query I, except that decryption queries are handled differently. Upon a decryption query for $(\mathsf{ct}', j')$, run

$$\mathsf{lnk} \xleftarrow{\$} \mathsf{Link}(1^\lambda, \mathsf{mpk}, \mathsf{ct}^*, \mathsf{ct}'), \qquad z \xleftarrow{\$} \begin{cases} \mathsf{Dec}(1^\lambda, \mathsf{msk}, \mathsf{ct}'), & \text{if } j' = 0; \\ \mathsf{Dec}(1^\lambda, \mathsf{mpk}, f_{j'}, \mathsf{sk}_{j'}, \mathsf{ct}'), & \text{if } j' \in [J]; \end{cases}$$

$$z'' \leftarrow \begin{cases} z, & \text{if } \mathsf{lnk} = \bot; \\ \bot, & \text{if } \mathsf{lnk} \neq \bot \text{ and } z = \bot; \\ \top, & \text{if } \mathsf{lnk} \neq \bot \text{ and } z \neq \bot; \end{cases}$$

and send $(\mathsf{lnk}, z'')$ to $\mathcal{A}$.

– **Guess.** $\mathcal{A}$ outputs a bit $\beta'$, the output of this experiment.

*Let $\rho'$ be in the format of a view. If, after $\mathsf{rerun}(\rho', \mathcal{A})$, there exists $j' \in [J]$, $h \in H_{\lambda,\mathsf{param}}$, $M \in \mathbb{N}$, $m' \in [M]$, $x'_1, \ldots, x'_M \in D_{\lambda,\mathsf{param}}$ such that the domain of $h$ includes $D^M_{\lambda,\mathsf{param}}$ and $\mathcal{A}$ submits a key retrieval query for $j'$ and*

$$\begin{aligned} & f_{j'}(h(x'_1, \ldots, x'_{m'-1}, \boxed{x_0^*}, x'_{m'+1}, \ldots, x'_M)) \\ & \quad \neq f_{j'}(h(x'_1, \ldots, x'_{m'-1}, \boxed{x_1^*}, x'_{m'+1}, \ldots, x'_M)) \\ \text{or} \quad & T_{0,F}(\lambda, \mathsf{param}, f_{j'}, h(x'_1, \ldots, x'_{m'-1}, \boxed{x_0^*}, x'_{m'+1}, \ldots, x'_M)) \\ & \quad \neq T_{0,F}(\cdots, \boxed{x_1^*}, \cdots), \end{aligned}$$

*then $\mathcal{A}$* violates the constraint *in $\mathsf{rerun}(\rho', \mathcal{A})$. An adversary $\mathcal{A}$ is* admissible *if for all $\rho'$ in the format of a view (not necessarily from any execution of $\mathsf{Exp}^\beta_{\text{fhcca}}$), it does not violate the constraint in $\mathsf{rerun}(\rho', \mathcal{A})$.*

**Lemma 1.** *If a functional homomorphic encryption scheme equipped with* Link *(Definitions 3 and 7) satisfies* decryption consistency *and* ciphertext indistinguishability *against FHCCA (Definitions 8 and 9), then it is* IND-FHCCA *(Definition 5). The same holds for* plaintext-selective *variants (Definition 6).*

We note that the universal Link is equipped to a *scheme*, not *quantified* in a security notion (the latter *is* the case for adversary-dependent extractors). This means that decryption consistency and ciphertext indistinguishability must be satisfied with the same Link.

### 5.5 Applications

Part of our results is the construction of a functional homomorphic encryption scheme for homomorphic iterations of a fixed unary function followed by arbitrary functional circuit (i.e., Example 1). It directly implies limited versions of two existing primitives, as shown below. We remark that both are implied by obfuscation. Since our construction relies on obfuscation, the implications are not very exciting in terms of *feasibility*. Instead, it is evidence that the *abstraction* of functional homomorphic encryption is interesting and powerful.

After the two functionality applications, we also discuss a possible usage of (universal) Link outside of security definition.

**Instance-Specific FHE for TM.** At the end of Sect. 5.2, we noted that the works of [19,20] proposed FHE for Turing machines with instance-specific evaluation time, i.e., the time of Eval grows only with that of running the machine on the specific input, not with the worst-case running time. Since the evaluation time leaks information about the input, it is necessary to forbid arbitrary choice of machine for evaluation. This already gives the primitive a functional-encryption flavor on top of being homomorphic. It is hence expected that functional homomorphic encryption can be used to implement such a primitive.

In [19,20], the machine is specified as part of the plaintext and only that machine can be evaluated. Example 1 achieves it for *space-bounded* computation. Concretely, set

$$\begin{aligned} x &= \text{a Turing machine and its state and tape,} \\ g &= \text{one step of universal Turing machine,} \\ f &= \text{whether evaluation has halted.} \end{aligned}$$

Given a ciphertext ct, the evaluator[13] homomorphically applies $g^{(1)}, g^{(2)}, g^{(4)}, g^{(8)}, \dots$ to obtain $\mathsf{ct}'_0, \mathsf{ct}'_1, \mathsf{ct}'_2, \mathsf{ct}'_3, \dots$, and outputs $\mathsf{ct}'_t$ with the smallest $t$ such that evaluation has halted as indicated by functional decryption using $\mathsf{sk}_f$.

**Randomized Encoding for Computation with Long Output.** As a generalization of the previous application, using a *multi-hop* functional homomorphic encryption supporting Example 1, we can easily obtain a randomized encoding for *space-bounded* TM with long output. The encoding time and length are much shorter than the evaluation time and the output length could be as large as the

[13] Our functional homomorphic encryption scheme is multi-hop, so alternatively, the evaluator can repeatedly apply $g$ until decryption indicates halting.

evaluation time. (Such an RE can only enjoy indistinguishability-based security.) Concretely, let

$$x = \text{the state and tape}, \qquad g = \text{one step of the machine},$$
$$f(y) = \begin{cases} \text{output from current step}, & \text{if computation is on-going;} \\ \top, & \text{if computation has halted;} \end{cases}$$

and let the RE be $(\mathsf{mpk}, \mathsf{sk}_f, \mathsf{ct})$. To evaluate, repeatedly homomorphically apply $g$ to $\mathsf{ct}$, decrypt using $\mathsf{sk}_f$, and collect the output, until decryption indicates that computation has halted.

**(Universal) Linking Beyond Security Definition.** Though Link (Definition 7) is defined for the purpose of IND-FHCCA security, it can also be useful to users. In Example 1, suppose $x$ (plaintext, input/output to $g$) has a counter inside and $g$ increments it (unless it is about to overflow an exponentially large range), then for a scheme with IND-FHCCA security, Link will accurately identify the number of $g$-iterations applied to a ciphertext. Say $\mathsf{ct}'$ is obtained from $\mathsf{ct}^*$ by applying $g^{(t)}$, then $\mathsf{Link}(\mathsf{mpk}, \mathsf{ct}^*, \mathsf{ct}')$ must output $g^{(t)}$. It cannot output $\perp$ as that would permit decryption of IND-FHCCA challenge ciphertext. It also cannot output any function other than $g^{(t)}$ as that would let the adversary win the IND-FHCCA game by finding an inconsistent decryption.

In the scenario of delegated computation, the client can use Link to verify that the specified computation has been done by the server. Since Link is public-key, it can further serve as proof (for the server's benefit) that the computation is done correctly.

We remark that our scheme supporting Example 1 uses a counter *outside of* $x$ as an implementation detail (let's call it the "internal counter"). The counter in $x$ for this application is separate ("dedicated counter"). For a general scheme, Link could under- or over-report $t$ as $t'$ if it is hard to find $x$ such that $g^{(t)}(x) \neq g^{(t')}(x)$, in which case an honest server could be judged as under-performing. The dedicated counter removes such possibility (overflow detection plays an important role in this argument) and makes linking accurate in general. It is not immediately clear whether our specific scheme's internal counter can be double-purposed to eliminate the dedicated one.

For a general two-way scheme (Example 2), the counter overflow logic is non-invertible, rendering the transformation syntactically invalid. For our specific two-way scheme, its security actually holds (with a more careful proof) if $g_+$, $g_-$ are each other's inverse *starting from* the challenge plaintexts *within sufficiently many* iterations (much larger than the upper bound of Link output), so the transformation would work given an appropriate counter range.

*Remark 5 (refuting triviality argument of* [29]**).** The work of [29] defines (SIM-)HCCA (see discussion in Sect. 5.3) and unlinkability. The authors argue that HCCA without unlinkability is trivial for unary homomorphisms. A unary scheme satisfying Definitions 7, 8, and 9 is never unlinkable.

Their argument is that without unlinkability, the trivial scheme—appending the homomorphic function to a CCA-secure encryption and pushing the evaluator's work to decryption—is HCCA. This argument carries over to the functional case, but it *only* applies when the homomorphic functions can be computed in time $\mathrm{poly}(\lambda, |\mathsf{param}|)$. In Examples 1 and 2, the trivial schemes fail the efficiency requirement of $\mathsf{Dec}$. Therefore, the notion of (F)HCCA can be non-trivial even without unlinkability.

**Acknowledgments.** The authors thank Claudio Chamon, Eduardo Mucciolo, and Andrei Ruckenstein for many enlightening discussions, including the idea of homomorphically evaluating a permutation $f$ over encrypted data using the conjugation of $f$ by the encryption permutation. We appreciate the anonymous reviewers of Crypto 2026 for their constructive feedback. Part of this work was done when Ji Luo was at Boston University. The authors were supported by NSF Grant GCR-2428487. Ji Luo also received support from a Simons Investigator Award and a Ford Foundation Chair.

## References

1. Agrawal, S., Gorbunov, S., Vaikuntanathan, V., Wee, H.: Functional encryption: new perspectives and lower bounds. In: Canetti, R., Garay, J.A. (eds.) CRYPTO 2013, Part II. LNCS, vol. 8043, pp. 500–518. Springer, Heidelberg (2013). https://doi.org/10.1007/978-3-642-40084-1_28
2. Asharov, G., Segev, G.: Limits on the power of indistinguishability obfuscation and functional encryption. In: Guruswami, V. (ed.) 56th FOCS, pp. 191–209. IEEE Computer Society Press (2015). https://doi.org/10.1109/FOCS.2015.21
3. Bitansky, N., Chiesa, A.: Succinct arguments from multi-prover interactive proofs and their efficiency benefits. In: Safavi-Naini, R., Canetti, R. (eds.) CRYPTO 2012. LNCS, vol. 7417, pp. 255–272. Springer, Heidelberg (2012). https://doi.org/10.1007/978-3-642-32009-5_16
4. Blömer, J., Liske, G.: Subtleties in security definitions for predicate encryption with public index. In: Blömer, J., Kotsireas, I.S., Kutsia, T., Simos, D.E. (eds.) Mathematical Aspects of Computer and Information Sciences, pp. 438–453. Springer (2017). https://doi.org/10.1007/978-3-319-72453-9_35
5. Boneh, D., Kim, S., Wu, D.J.: Constrained keys for invertible pseudorandom functions. In: Kalai, Y., Reyzin, L. (eds.) TCC 2017, Part I. LNCS, vol. 10677, pp. 237–263. Springer, Cham (2017). https://doi.org/10.1007/978-3-319-70500-2_9
6. Boneh, D., Sahai, A., Waters, B.: Functional encryption: definitions and challenges. In: Ishai, Y. (ed.) TCC 2011. LNCS, vol. 6597, pp. 253–273. Springer, Heidelberg (2011). https://doi.org/10.1007/978-3-642-19571-6_16
7. Brakerski, Z., Vaikuntanathan, V.: Efficient fully homomorphic encryption from (standard) LWE. In: Ostrovsky, R. (ed.) 52nd FOCS, pp. 97–106. IEEE Computer Society Press (2011). https://doi.org/10.1109/FOCS.2011.12
8. Canetti, R., Chamon, C., Mucciolo, E.R., Ruckenstein, A.E.: Towards general-purpose program obfuscation via local mixing. In: Boyle, E., Mahmoody, M. (eds.) TCC 2024, Part IV. LNCS, vol. 15367, pp. 37–70. Springer, Cham (2024). https://doi.org/10.1007/978-3-031-78023-3_2

9. Canetti, R., Lin, H., Tessaro, S., Vaikuntanathan, V.: Obfuscation of probabilistic circuits and applications. In: Dodis, Y., Nielsen, J.B. (eds.) TCC 2015, Part II. LNCS, vol. 9015, pp. 468–497. Springer, Heidelberg (2015). https://doi.org/10.1007/978-3-662-46497-7_19
10. Canetti, R., Luo, J., Zhang, Y.: How to encrypt with random reversible circuits. To appear in Cryptology ePrint Archive (2026)
11. Canetti, R., Luo, J., Zhang, Y.: Functional homomorphic encryption. To appear in Cryptology ePrint Archive (2026)
12. Canetti, R., Raghuraman, S., Richelson, S., Vaikuntanathan, V.: Chosen-ciphertext secure fully homomorphic encryption. In: Fehr, S. (ed.) PKC 2017, Part II. LNCS, vol. 10175, pp. 213–240. Springer, Heidelberg (2017). https://doi.org/10.1007/978-3-662-54388-7_8
13. Chamon, C., Jakes-Schauer, J., Mucciolo, E.R., Ruckenstein, A.E.: Encrypted operator computing: A novel scheme for computation on encrypted data. arXiv:2203.08876 (2022). https://doi.org/10.48550/arXiv.2203.08876
14. Dantzig, G.B.: Linear programming and extensions. Report R-366-PR, RAND Corporation (1963). https://doi.org/10.7249/R366
15. De Caro, A., Iovino, V., Jain, A., O'Neill, A., Paneth, O., Persiano, G.: On the achievability of simulation-based security for functional encryption. In: Canetti, R., Garay, J.A. (eds.) CRYPTO 2013, Part II. LNCS, vol. 8043, pp. 519–535. Springer, Heidelberg (2013). https://doi.org/10.1007/978-3-642-40084-1_29
16. Diffie, W., Hellman, M.E.: New directions in cryptography. IEEE Trans. Inf. Theory **22**(6), 644–654 (1976). https://doi.org/10.1109/TIT.1976.1055638
17. Garg, S., Gentry, C., Halevi, S., Raykova, M., Sahai, A., Waters, B.: Candidate indistinguishability obfuscation and functional encryption for all circuits. In: 54th FOCS, pp. 40–49. IEEE Computer Society Press (2013). https://doi.org/10.1109/FOCS.2013.13
18. Goldwasser, S., et al.: Multi-input functional encryption. In: Nguyen, P.Q., Oswald, E. (eds.) EUROCRYPT 2014. LNCS, vol. 8441, pp. 578–602. Springer, Heidelberg (2014). https://doi.org/10.1007/978-3-642-55220-5_32
19. Goldwasser, S., Kalai, Y.T., Popa, R.A., Vaikuntanathan, V., Zeldovich, N.: How to run Turing machines on encrypted data. In: Canetti, R., Garay, J.A. (eds.) CRYPTO 2013, Part II. LNCS, vol. 8043, pp. 536–553. Springer, Heidelberg (2013). https://doi.org/10.1007/978-3-642-40084-1_30
20. Goldwasser, S., Kalai, Y.T., Popa, R.A., Vaikuntanathan, V., Zeldovich, N.: Reusable garbled circuits and succinct functional encryption. In: Boneh, D., Roughgarden, T., Feigenbaum, J. (eds.) 45th ACM STOC, pp. 555–564. ACM Press (2013). https://doi.org/10.1145/2488608.2488678
21. Gowers, W.T.: An almost $m$-wise independent random permutation of the cube. Comb. Probab. Comput. **5**(2), 119–130 (1996). https://doi.org/10.1017/S0963548300001917
22. Gretta, L., He, W., Pelecanos, A.: More efficient approximate $k$-wise independent permutations from random reversible circuits via log-sobolev inequalities. In: Azar, Y., Panigrahi, D. (eds.) 36th SODA, pp. 5582–5598. ACM-SIAM (2025). https://doi.org/10.1137/1.9781611978322.191
23. Guan, J., Wichs, D., Zhandry, M.: Incompressible cryptography. In: Dunkelman, O., Dziembowski, S. (eds.) EUROCRYPT 2022, Part I. LNCS, vol. 13275, pp. 700–730. Springer, Cham (2022). https://doi.org/10.1007/978-3-031-06944-4_24
24. Hamlin, A., Holmgren, J., Weiss, M., Wichs, D.: On the plausibility of fully homomorphic encryption for RAMs. In: Boldyreva, A., Micciancio, D. (eds.)

CRYPTO 2019, Part I. LNCS, vol. 11692, pp. 589–619. Springer, Cham (2019). https://doi.org/10.1007/978-3-030-26948-7_21
25. Ishai, Y., Kushilevitz, E., Ostrovsky, R.: Sufficient conditions for collision-resistant hashing. In: Kilian, J. (ed.) TCC 2005. LNCS, vol. 3378, pp. 445–456. Springer, Heidelberg (2005). https://doi.org/10.1007/978-3-540-30576-7_24
26. Lin, W.K., Mook, E., Wichs, D.: Doubly efficient private information retrieval and fully homomorphic RAM computation from ring LWE. In: Saha, B., Servedio, R.A. (eds.) 55th ACM STOC, pp. 595–608. ACM Press (2023). https://doi.org/10.1145/3564246.3585175
27. Pal, T., Dutta, R.: Chosen ciphertext secure functional encryption from constrained witness PRF. In: Baek, J., Ruj, S. (eds.) ACISP 21. LNCS, vol. 13083, pp. 24–45. Springer, Cham (2021). https://doi.org/10.1007/978-3-030-90567-5_2
28. Pal, T., Dutta, R.: Chosen ciphertext secure functional encryption from constrained witness PRF. Cryptology ePrint Archive, Report 2021/512, version 20260415:061416
29. Prabhakaran, M., Rosulek, M.: Homomorphic encryption with CCA security. In: Aceto, L., Damgård, I., Goldberg, L.A., Halldórsson, M.M., Ingólfsdóttir, A., Walukiewicz, I. (eds.) ICALP 2008, Part II. LNCS, vol. 5126, pp. 667–678. Springer, Heidelberg (2008). https://doi.org/10.1007/978-3-540-70583-3_54
30. Prabhakaran, M., Rosulek, M.: Towards robust computation on encrypted data. In: Pieprzyk, J. (ed.) ASIACRYPT 2008. LNCS, vol. 5350, pp. 216–233. Springer, Heidelberg (2008). https://doi.org/10.1007/978-3-540-89255-7_14
31. Rivest, R.L., Adleman, L., Dertouzos, M.L.: On data banks and privacy homomorphisms. Found. Secure Comput. 169–180 (1978)
32. Shi, E., Chan, T.H.H., Rieffel, E.G., Chow, R., Song, D.: Privacy-preserving aggregation of time-series data. In: NDSS 2011. The Internet Society (2011)
33. Shmueli, O., Zhandry, M.: On one-shot signatures, quantum vs. classical binding, and obfuscating permutations. In: Kalai, Y.T., Kamara, S.F. (eds.) CRYPTO 2025, Part II. LNCS, vol. 16001, pp. 350–383. Springer, Cham (2025). https://doi.org/10.1007/978-3-032-01878-6_12
34. Waters, B.: A punctured programming approach to adaptively secure functional encryption. In: Gennaro, R., Robshaw, M.J.B. (eds.) CRYPTO 2015, Part II. LNCS, vol. 9216, pp. 678–697. Springer, Heidelberg (2015). https://doi.org/10.1007/978-3-662-48000-7_33
35. Yang, R., Yu, Z., Susilo, W.: Fully homomorphic encryption with chosen-ciphertext security from LWE. In: Kalai, Y.T., Kamara, S.F. (eds.) CRYPTO 2025, Part III. LNCS, vol. 16002, pp. 371–405. Springer, Cham (2025). https://doi.org/10.1007/978-3-032-01881-6_12

# Generic-Group Barriers for Function-Hiding and Multi-input Functional Encryption

Mohammad Hajiabadi[1], Roman Langrehr[1(✉)], and Mingyuan Wang[2]

[1] University of Waterloo, Waterloo, Canada
{mdhajiabadi,roman.langrehr}@uwaterloo.ca
[2] NYU Shanghai, Shanghai, China
mingyuan.wang@nyu.edu

**Abstract.** We show that private-key function-hiding inner-product functional encryption (FH-IPFE) is impossible in the generic group model (GGM). This impossibility extends to (non-compact) two-input quadratic functional encryption (QFE) under a weak security notion that allows only a single key corruption. Our results apply both to the variant where decryption outputs the result directly, and to the variant where the result is encoded in the exponent of a group element.

Our results hold in both Maurer's and Shoup's model, with different tradeoffs. In Maurer's model, we prove that FH-IPFE over $\mathbb{Z}_q^n$ cannot be realized even when $q^n$ is polynomially bounded. Here, $q$ denotes the modulus of the inner-product functionality, not the order of the underlying group. This stands in sharp contrast to non-function-hiding FE, which can be constructed from minimal assumptions (one-way functions in the private-key setting and public-key encryption in the public-key setting) whenever the set of functions is polynomially bounded. We extend this impossibility to Shoup's model when $q^n$ is super-polynomial. Conceptually, our proof simulates any construction in Shoup's model as one in Maurer's model equipped with a random oracle. Our techniques may be of independent interest, offering a *general* method for upgrading other impossibility results from Maurer's model to Shoup's model.

We match these negative results with two positive ones. First, we show that *one-sided bounded* FH-IPFE (i.e., either the number of key queries or the number of encryption queries is bounded) can be realized from one-way functions. Second, when both the number of key queries and encryption queries are bounded, we show the resulting notion of FH-IPFE can be achieved information-theoretically. These positive results show that our impossibility precisely characterizes the threshold for FH-IPFE.

**Keywords:** Black-box impossibility · Functional encryption

---

R. Langrehr—Part of the work was done while the author was affiliated with ETH Zurich.


N. Heninger and M. Rosulek (Eds.): CRYPTO 2026, LNCS 16800, pp. 581–613, 2026.
https://doi.org/10.1007/978-3-032-35367-2_19

# 1 Introduction

Functional Encryption (FE) [19,33,36] is an advanced encryption paradigm that enables controlled access to encrypted data. In particular, a secret key $\mathsf{sk}_f$ is associated with a function $f$ so that, given a ciphertext $\mathsf{ct}$ encrypting a message $x$, the keyholder can decrypt to learn $f(x)$ but nothing else. In the private-key setting, an important and desirable property is function-hiding (FH-FE) [38], which requires the secret key $\mathsf{sk}_f$ to reveal no information about $f$. Function-hiding is generally impossible in the public-key setting, as $\mathsf{sk}_f$ effectively grants oracle access to the function $f(\cdot)$. Such a notion enables secure delegation of function evaluation and has found real-world applications, including privacy-preserving machine learning and computation of statistics [6,29], biometric authentication [29], DNA similarity testing [41], and keyword search [15].

Despite being a natural extension to functional encryption, function-hiding functional encryption remains elusive to construct. To the best of our knowledge, the only known constructions of FH-FE from 'standard assumptions' are for the inner-product function family. For more powerful functionalities, only constructions based on FE for general circuits are known [20] (which, in turn, requires heavy assumptions such as indistinguishability obfuscation). In FH-IPFE, both the function $f$ and the message $x$ are vectors in $\mathbb{Z}_q^n$, and decryption reveals only the inner product $\langle f, x\rangle \in \mathbb{Z}_q$. Even for this seemingly simple family, the only known constructions of FH-IPFE rely on pairing-based assumptions [3,16,23,29,41,43]. This is in sharp contrast to its non-function-hiding variant, which can be built from various assumptions, including Decisional Diffie-Hellman (DDH) [1–5,8,11,14,16,21,26,41], Learning With Errors (LWE) [10,11] and Decision Composite Residuosity (DCR) [11].

Given this lack of progress, several recent works [40,44] attempted to understand the difficulties in constructing FH-IPFE. However, these works have focused exclusively on the lattice setting. Consequently, the current state-of-the-art leaves the following natural question completely unexplored.

*Is Function-Hiding Inner-Product Functional Encryption possible from pairing-free groups?*

**Dimensions to FE.** FE schemes can be analyzed along several dimensions—such as bounded vs. unbounded key corruptions/collusions, polynomial vs. exponential function families, and compact vs. non-compact ciphertexts, to name a few. Bounded collusions mean the number of adversary's secret-key queries is fixed in advance. Compactness requires that the ciphertext size grows only with the plaintext length, and not with $|f|$ of the underlying function $f \in \mathcal{F}$. Polynomial vs exponential-sized function families refer to the number of all possible functions. It is known that non-compact, bounded-collusion FE for all circuits can be constructed from minimal assumptions. Regarding compactness, non-compact quadratic FE (QFE) schemes can be built from DDH via a reduction to IPFE by linearizing the QFE function. However, compact QFE constructions are only known under stronger assumptions such as pairings [9,14,42,45].

A fundamental question is whether seemingly "easy" properties—such as bounded collusions, non-compactness, or polynomial-sized function families—remain trivial for non-vanilla FE, like function-hiding or multi-input FE.

### 1.1 Our Contributions

We show that private-key FH-IPFE is impossible in the generic group model (GGM). We prove this impossibility in both Maurer's model [32] and Shoup's model [39] with different tradeoffs. Furthermore, we establish a new connection: Any non-compact, two-input QFE scheme that is secure against only a single-key corruption implies the existence of FH-IPFE. This implication allows us to rule out such QFE schemes in the GGM as well. To the best of our knowledge, this connection has never been observed previously. Finally, we match our negative FH-IPFE with positive results for bounded collusions in FH-IPFE.

**New Insights on FE.** By studying FH-IPFE, we uncover subtle interactions involving the most permissive variants of required FE dimensions: bounded collusions, non-compactness, and polynomial-sized function families. Our results show that even in this highly relaxed regime, adding non-vanilla capabilities such as function-hiding or multi-input functionality leads to fundamental obstacles, even in the GGM. While it is known that for FE for general circuits some of these properties become non-trivial when combined with advanced capabilities [12,17,25,30], our work demonstrates that such tensions already arise in significantly simpler settings. We elaborate below.

*Impossibility in Maurer's model.* We first prove that FH-IPFE is impossible in Maurer's GGM in the strongest sense.

*Informal Theorem 1.* There is no unbounded collusion FH-IPFE over $\mathbb{Z}_q^n$ in Maurer's GGM for any $n, q \geqslant 2$ with $(n, q) \neq (2, 2)$, achieving correctness probability $\frac{1}{2} + \frac{1}{\mathsf{poly}}$ or $\frac{2}{q} + \frac{1}{q^{n-1}} + \frac{1}{\mathsf{poly}}$ for a polynomial $\mathsf{poly}$.[1]

Perhaps surprisingly, our theorem holds even if $q^n$ is only polynomially large. Note that, when the function family is polynomial sized, one can generically build private-key FE by letting each functional key $\mathsf{sk}_f$ be a secret key for a standard encryption scheme, and the master secret key $\mathsf{msk}$ contain all such $\mathsf{sk}_f$. Encrypting a message $x$ under $\mathsf{msk}$ outputs all the ciphertexts $\{\mathrm{Enc}(\mathsf{sk}_f, f(x))\}_f$.

At first glance, this may suggest function-hiding is trivial for polynomial-size families, since $\mathsf{sk}_f$ appears independent of $f$, seemingly supporting function privacy. However, this intuition is flawed. A function-hiding FE scheme must satisfy semantic security for functional keys, requiring the key generation process to be randomized. The above scheme is trivially broken if an adversary can query the same function key twice. Our result shows that this limitation is not merely an artifact of this naïve construction but is, in fact, inherent, even in the GGM.

[1] Our impossibility results rule out both regimes of correctness. When $q$ is very large (e.g., exponential), the bound $\frac{2}{q} + \frac{1}{q^{n-1}} + \frac{1}{\mathsf{poly}}$ yields a stronger impossibility. However, this bound becomes vacuous for $q = 2$, in which case the alternative bound $\frac{1}{2} + \frac{1}{\mathsf{poly}}$ provides a meaningful guarantee.

*Shoup Impossibility.* We further extend our impossibility to Shoup's model [39].

*Informal Theorem 2.* For any $q \geqslant 3$, $n \geqslant 4$ where $q^{-n}$ is negligible, no unbounded collusion FH-IPFE over $\mathbb{Z}_q^n$ exists in Shoup's GGM with correctness $\frac{3}{q} + \frac{1}{\mathsf{poly}}$ for a polynomial $\mathsf{poly}$.

An (FH)-IPFE with correctness probability $\frac{1}{q}$ is trivial to build, so we must assume correctness at least $\frac{1}{q} + \frac{1}{\mathsf{poly}}$ for a polynomial $\mathsf{poly}$. Our result in Shoup's model nearly matches this threshold by ruling out correctness probabilities as low as $\frac{3}{q} + \frac{1}{\mathsf{poly}}$. Also, note that when correctness is at least $\frac{1}{2} + \frac{1}{\mathsf{poly}}$, it can be amplified arbitrarily close to 1 via parallel repetition.

*A Conceptual Framework for Shoup Impossibilities.* Proving impossibility results in Shoup's model is notoriously challenging, and as a result, nearly all prior results have been limited to Maurer's model (see [46]). Our proof introduces a novel strategy: We simulate any IPFE construction in Shoup's model within an augmented version of Maurer's model, which enhances Maurer's with access to a random oracle (RO). This modular perspective enables us to decouple the two idealized models—Maurer's GGM and the RO—and apply our existing techniques for Maurer's model in conjunction with a recent combinatorial lemma used to prove the impossibility of IPFE in the RO model [27]. The main limitation of our approach—namely, the requirement that $q^n$ be super-polynomial—arises directly from the bounds inherent to that combinatorial lemma.

Because no modular framework for Shoup-style lower bounds existed previously, most existing impossibility results were proved only in the more limited Maurer model, e.g., [7,18,22,35,37]. We believe the modular framework formalized in this work can facilitate lifting some of these results to Shoup's model.

*Implications for Multi-input Quadratic FE.* We observe that multi-input quadratic functional encryption (MI-QFE) [9] implies FH-IPFE. Given an MI-QFE scheme, one can embed the FH-IPFE's secret-key vectors $f$ and the plaintext vector $x$ as two different MI-QFE inputs and set the quadratic function $F$ to compute their inner product (i.e., $F(f, x) = \langle f, x \rangle$). Concretely, $(\mathsf{sk}_F, \mathsf{ct}_f)$ becomes the functional secret key and $\mathsf{ct}_x$ the ciphertext in the FH-IPFE scheme. The semantic security of MI-QFE ensures that the resulting IPFE is function-hiding (see full version). Therefore, our impossibility result for FH-IPFE directly yields the following:

*Informal Theorem 3.* There does not exist a 2-input single-corruption non-compact quadratic functional encryption over $\mathbb{Z}_q^n$ with correctness probability $\nu$ in

(a) Maurer's GGM for the same restrictions on $n$, $q$ and $\nu$ as in Informal Theorem 1, and
(b) Shoup's GGM for the same restrictions on $n$, $q$ and $\nu$ as in Informal Theorem 2.

This result rules out the weakest possible form of MI-QFE: 2 inputs, a single corruption and no compactness requirements. Moreover, our result implies a separation between non-compact QFE and non-compact MI-QFE. The former (equivalent to non-function-hiding IPFE) can be constructed in the GGM, while we show the latter is GGM impossible. The above result shows that even the weakest variant of non-compact MI-QFE cannot be built from non-compact QFE in a black-box way. This is in contrast to the equivalence of IPFE and MI-IPFE [3]. Thus, our result also shows a separation between MI-IPFE and non-compact MI-QFE, which is in contrast to the equivalence of IPFE and non-compact QFE (Fig. 1).

*Implications for FE with Polynomially Many Functions.* When the set of supported functions $\mathcal{F}$ is of polynomial size, one can build 'vanilla' FE from minimal assumptions. We showed that this fails for function-hiding IPFE in Maurer's GGM. Moreover, this limitation is not confined to function hiding. By combining the above impossibility with Informal Theorem 3, we identify a second regime where the same obstruction arises, namely single-corruption 2-input QFE for arbitrary polynomial size functions is also impossible in Maurer's GGM.

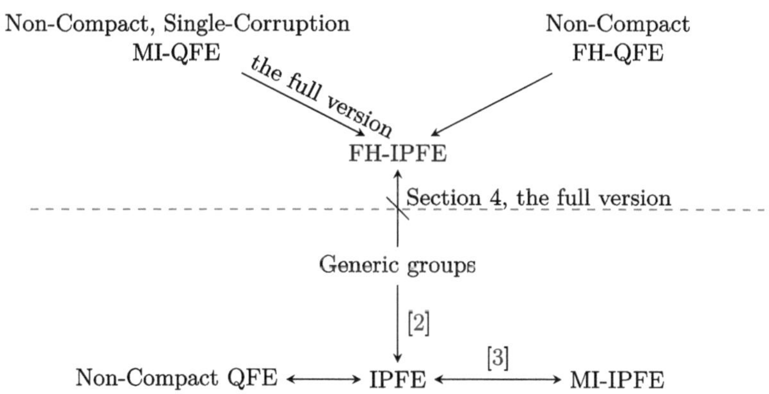


**Fig. 1.** The relation between generic groups, IPFE, non-compact QFE, and its function-hiding and multi-input variants. Our main result is the separation of FH-IPFE from generic groups, which implies separations for all primitives above the dashed line from all primitives below the dashed line.

*Positive Results for Bounded Collusion.* Motivated by our negative results and by our demonstration of the non-triviality of *bounded collusions* in 2-input QFE, we investigate FH-IPFE under one-sided bounded collusions. Here, the adversary may obtain arbitrarily many ciphertexts, but the number of keys that can be corrupted is bounded by a fixed $Q$.[2] One can also define the dual notion, where

[2] Since FH-IPFE is defined in the private-key setting, the adversary obtains ciphertexts via an encryption oracle.

only the number of encryption queries is bounded. In this one-sided bounded model, we obtain the following result.

*Informal Theorem 4.* There exists a generic construction of one-sided bounded-collusion FH-IPFE from bounded-collusion (non-function-hiding) private-key IPFE, and hence from one-way functions.

Previously, it was only known how to boost an FE to its function-hiding variant if the original FE supports all functions computable by bounded-size circuits [20]. Notably, our reduction is both simple and concretely efficient. Combined with the generic construction of bounded-collusion private-key FE from OWFs [13], this yields a one-sided bounded-collusion FH-IPFE from OWFs. Alternatively, one can instantiate our reduction using DDH-based (unbounded collusion) IPFE, which may offer better concrete efficiency.

We also consider the two-sided bounded-collusion model, where both the number of functional secret keys and the number of ciphertexts are bounded. This weaker model suffices for several applications of FH-IPFE, such as bounded-collusion inner-product revealing encryption [6]. In this setting, we obtain:

*Informal Theorem 5.* There exists an information-theoretic FH-IPFE in the two-sided bounded-collusion model.

## 2 Technical Overview

An oracle-aided private-key IPFE for $\mathbb{Z}_q^n$ is described by $\mathcal{E}^O = (\mathrm{Setup}^O, \mathrm{KGen}^O, \mathrm{Enc}^O, \mathrm{Dec}^O)$. The setup algorithm $\mathrm{Setup}^O(1^\kappa)$ outputs a master secret key $\mathsf{msk}$. The algorithms $\mathrm{KGen}^O$ and $\mathrm{Enc}^O$ on input $(\mathsf{msk}, \mathbf{x} \in \mathbb{Z}_q^n)$ output, respectively, a functional key $\mathsf{sk}[\mathbf{x}]$ and a ciphertext $\mathsf{ct}[\mathbf{x}]$. The decryption algorithm $\mathrm{Dec}^O$ inputs $\mathsf{pp}$, a functional key $\mathsf{sk}[\mathbf{y}]$, and a ciphertext $\mathsf{ct}[\mathbf{x}]$, and outputs the inner product $\langle \mathbf{y}, \mathbf{x} \rangle$.

The standard indistinguishability (FH-IND-CPA) notion says that a PPT adversary who makes LoR key-corruption queries $\{(\mathbf{y}_i, \mathbf{y}'_i)\}_i$ and LoR encryption queries $\{(\mathbf{x}_h, \mathbf{x}'_h)\}_h$, under the restriction that $\langle \mathbf{y}_i, \mathbf{x}_h \rangle = \langle \mathbf{y}'_i, \mathbf{x}'_h \rangle$ for all values of $i$ and $h$, should not be able to distinguish if the received responses correspond to the first component or the second one.

### 2.1 Impossibility in Maurer's GGM

We first present our impossibility result in Maurer's GGM.

*Big Picture:* In a FH-IPFE, both ciphertexts $\mathsf{ct}[\mathbf{x}]$ and secret keys $\mathsf{sk}[\mathbf{y}]$ need to hide the vectors $\mathbf{x}$ and $\mathbf{y}$. In all existing pairing-based constructions, $\mathsf{ct}[\mathbf{x}]$ and $\mathsf{sk}[\mathbf{y}]$ contain group-based encryptions of $\mathbf{x}$ and $\mathbf{y}$, subsequently combined via pairings in decryption to recover $\langle \mathbf{x}, \mathbf{y} \rangle$.

We show that in the absence of pairings, not *both* $\mathrm{Enc}^{\mathbb{G}}$ and $\mathrm{KGen}^{\mathbb{G}}$ can use the group in a meaningful way to encrypt the vectors $\mathbf{x}$ and $\mathbf{y}$. More concretely,

1. We show how to compile a given GGM-based FH-IND-CPA IPFE $\mathcal{E}^{\mathbb{G}} = (\text{Setup}^{\mathbb{G}}, \text{KGen}^{\mathbb{G}}, \text{Enc}^{\mathbb{G}}, \text{Dec}^{\mathbb{G}})$ into $\overline{\mathcal{E}}^{\mathbb{G}} = (\overline{\text{Setup}}^{\mathbb{G}}, \overline{\text{KGen}}, \overline{\text{Enc}}^{\mathbb{G}}, \overline{\text{Dec}}^{\mathbb{G}})$ with 'comparable security and correctness', such that $\overline{\text{KGen}}$ makes no $\mathbb{G}$ queries.

Intuitively, if $\overline{\text{KGen}}$ does not use the generic group, it cannot encrypt the vector $\mathbf{y}$ in the GGM. We formalize this as follows.

2. We give a generic, information-theoretic attack against any FH-IPFE whose $\overline{\text{KGen}}$ algorithm makes no oracle queries. Our attack works for every oracle, and not just a GGM oracle.

*Challenges:* Both Steps 1 and 2 above involve significant challenges. The main challenge in Step 1 is that we deal with a private-key IPFE scheme (as opposed to a public-key one), in which encryptions are made using msk, not known to the adversary. In the public-key setting (in which encryptions are made with a public mpk) there are compilation techniques [34,37] that allow one to implement something similar to Step 1 for primitives such as Identity-Based Encryption (IBE). Those techniques rely crucially on an adversary seeing encryptions of many random plaintexts, a property inherent to public-key schemes but absent in the private-key setting. We introduce techniques for a compilation strategy adaptable to the private-key setting that preserves both correctness and a security property weaker than FH-IND-CPA, which nonetheless suffices for Step 2. Our novelty involves formalizing these new security definitions that will allow us to preserve both security and correctness. We elaborate more in Sect. 2.1.

The challenge behind Step 2 is that the FH-IPFE scheme may have a decryption error. Even starting from a perfectly correct scheme, the Step 1 compilation introduces a small error. It is relatively easy to do Step 2 for perfectly-correct schemes. But the strategy employed fails completely when we have decryption errors. We develop techniques to handle these errors (Sect. 2.1).

**Step 1: The Compiler.** To describe the challenges and our techniques, let us review the compilation strategy of [34,37], adapted to **public-key** IPFE and for non-FH IND-CPA. The latter is defined as in FH-IND-CPA (Sect. 2) except that for LoR key-corruption queries $(\mathbf{y}_i, \mathbf{y}'_i)$ we must always have $\mathbf{y}_i = \mathbf{y}'_i$.

Before describing this previous compilation, let us review the GGM model. In Maurer's GGM, the algorithms do not have explicit access to group elements. Instead, they get 'pointers' to group elements and can perform operations with the following two oracles: The Add oracle adds two group elements and gives a 'pointer' to the new group element. The Eql oracle compares two group elements for equality. An algorithm that outputs group elements simply outputs pointers to group elements. If an algorithm outputs no such pointers, we say its output contains no group elements.

For algorithms $\mathsf{Alg}^{\mathsf{Add},\mathsf{Eql}}(g_1, \ldots, g_m)$ that do not output any group elements, we can remove access to both Add and Eql oracles if we provide a stronger Eql oracle, called Eql*. An Eql* query takes $(a_1, \ldots, a_m, g_1, \ldots, g_m)$ and outputs 1 iff $a_1 g_1 + \cdots + a_m g_m = 0$. Now we can simulate Add queries of Alg as follows. We return to $\mathsf{A}$ a new 'virtual' group element, which is a pointer to a 'dummy' group element. For each virtual group element we store the inputs of the $\mathsf{Add}$ query. This way we know for every virtual group element $g$ coefficients $a_1, \ldots, a_m$ such that $g = a_1 \cdot g + \cdots + a_m g_m$, where $g_1, \ldots, g_m$ are the group elements given to $\mathsf{Alg}$ as input. When the virtual group element is later used in an $\mathsf{Eql}$ query, we can replace it with its linear combination of input group elements and make an equivalent $\mathsf{Eql}^*$ query. Note that introducing virtual group elements works precisely because $\mathsf{Alg}$ does not output any group elements itself.

*Compilation of* [34,37]*:* These compilers, discussed here for non-function-hiding **public-key** IPFE, start by removing all group elements from functional keys, while preserving (a form of) correctness and security. Once this is done, it is easy to eliminate any $\mathbb{G}$ queries made during KGen.

We describe this latter step first. Since KGen does not output any group elements (as functional keys contain no group elements), by the discussion above, we may assume KGen makes only $\mathsf{Eql}^*$ queries. We can let $\mathsf{msk}$ store the discrete logarithms of all group elements generated during Setup. Since KGen takes $\mathsf{msk}$ as input, knowledge of these stored discrete logarithms allows KGen to answer all issued $\mathsf{Eql}^*$ queries without calling the $\mathsf{Eql}^*$ oracle. Because $\mathsf{msk}$ is never given to the adversary, this does not compromise security.

We now discuss removing group elements from functional keys by recalling the compilations of [34,37] adapted to *public key, non-function hiding* IPFE. Let $\mathsf{sk}[\mathbf{y}] := (s \in \{0,1\}^*, g_1, \ldots, g_t)$ be a functional key with group elements $g_1, \ldots, g_t$. We describe how to obtain a key $\overline{\mathsf{sk}[\mathbf{y}]}$ from $\mathsf{sk}[\mathbf{y}]$ that does not contain any group elements.

To have fewer variables, suppose each $\mathsf{mpk}$ and $\mathsf{sk}$ have $t$ group elements. Also, suppose $\mathrm{Dec}(\mathsf{sk}[\mathbf{y}], \mathsf{ct}[\mathbf{x}])$ outputs the inner product $\langle \mathbf{x}, \mathbf{y} \rangle$ directly. We sketch at the end of this section how to handle IPFE schemes where Dec just outputs $(\langle \mathbf{x}, \mathbf{y} \rangle) \cdot g$, which is typically the case for group-based (FH-)IPFE schemes.

1. For $i \in [\ell]$, sample $\mathbf{x}_i \leftarrow \mathbb{Z}_q^n$, and run $\mathrm{Dec}(\mathsf{sk}[\mathbf{y}], \mathsf{ct}_i := \mathrm{Enc}(\mathsf{mpk}, \mathbf{x}_i))$. Let $u_1, \ldots, u_t$ be the group elements of $\mathsf{mpk}$. Since running Enc and then Dec together does not output any group elements, we can remove all $\mathsf{Add}$ queries and accept instead $\mathsf{Eql}^*$ queries, which are always over $(g_1, \ldots, g_t, u_1, \ldots, u_t)$, as described above. For each positively answered $\mathsf{Eql}^*$ query, i.e., $\sum_{i=1}^t a_i \cdot g_i + \sum_{i=1}^t a'_i u_i = 0$, we add the coefficients $(a_1, \ldots, a_t, a'_1, \ldots, a'_t)$ as a new row to a matrix $R$. The compiled secret key $\overline{\mathsf{sk}[\mathbf{y}]} = (s, R)$ is then obtained by removing all the group elements from $\mathsf{sk}[\mathbf{y}]$, and augmenting it with $R$.
2. For a given ciphertext $\mathsf{ct} = (w \in \{0,1\}^*, z_1, \ldots, z_t)$, we simulate the execution of $\mathrm{Dec}^{\mathbb{G}}(\mathsf{sk}[\mathbf{y}], \mathsf{ct})$ using $\overline{\mathsf{sk}[\mathbf{y}]}$ as follows. Since Dec outputs no group element (but only an element in $\mathbb{Z}_q$) we may assume it only makes $\mathsf{Eql}^*$ queries. For a given such query

$$\sum_{i=1}^{t} a_i g_i + \sum_{i=1}^{t} a'_i u_i + \sum_{i=1}^{t} a''_i z_i \stackrel{?}{=} 0, \tag{1}$$

the compiled $\overline{\mathsf{sk}[\mathbf{y}]}$ does not have explicit access to $(g_1, \ldots, g_t)$, since those group elements where remove from $\overline{\mathsf{sk}[\mathbf{y}]}$. Instead, $\overline{\mathsf{Dec}}$ attempts reducing the relation check of Eq. 1 into an equivalent one involving only $\{u_i\}$ and $\{z_i\}$, both of which it has explicit access to. To this end, $\overline{\mathsf{Dec}}$ checks if $(a_1, \ldots, a_t) \in \mathsf{Span}(R')$, where $R'$ is the submatrix of $R$ that contains only those columns corresponding to $(g_1, \ldots, g_t)$. If $(a_1, \ldots, a_t) \notin \mathsf{Span}(R')$ (call this Condition (*)), then $\overline{\mathsf{Dec}}$ responds to Eq. 1 with 0. Else, $\overline{\mathsf{Dec}}$ obtains an equivalent relation that involves only $\{u_i\}$ and $\{z_i\}$, which it can query $\mathsf{Eql}^*$ on.

Correctness follows by setting $\ell$ large enough. Specifically, $\overline{\mathsf{Dec}}$ makes a mistake only when Condition (*) occurs but the answer to Eq. 1 is 1. Call this the bad case. By using the Chernoff bound and the fact that each $\mathbf{x}_i$ is chosen uniformly at random, one may argue that when decrypting the encryption of a random $\mathbf{x}$ with $\overline{\mathsf{sk}[\mathbf{y}]}$, the probability that the bad case happens is small.

For non-FH IND-CPA, one should argue $\overline{\mathsf{sk}[\mathbf{y}]}$ can be simulated from $\mathsf{sk}[\mathbf{y}]$ by an adversary with full access to $\mathbb{G}$. This follows immediately, since the augmentation involves sampling many ciphertexts of random vectors, which can be simulated knowing only $\mathsf{mpk}$. This is where things break down in the private-key setting.

*Take-Home Summary:* What makes the above compilation [34,37] possible is that each secret key $\mathsf{sk}[\mathbf{y}]$ is compiled against a list $(\mathsf{ct}_1, \ldots, \mathsf{ct}_\ell)$ of ciphertexts each encrypting a **uniformly random vector**. This is needed for correctness. And the resulting augmentation does not harm security because all those encryptions can be obtained for free (i.e., from $\mathsf{mpk}$).

*The Compiler* [34,37] *for FH-IPFE?* The main issue in applying the above compiler to FH-IPFE is that it destroys FH-IND-CPA security. To see this, note that a given $\mathsf{sk}[\mathbf{y}]$ is compiled by performing many encryptions of random vectors $\mathbf{x} \leftarrow \mathbb{Z}_q^n$. To ensure security is preserved, we have to show that an adversary can simulate $\overline{\mathsf{sk}[\mathbf{y}]}$ from $\mathsf{sk}[\mathbf{y}]$. To do this, the adversary should be given many encryptions of random plaintexts $\mathbf{x}$ from $\mathbb{Z}_q^n$. But this cannot be provided in general under the FH-IND-CPA game for private-key IPFE. In particular, imagine an adversary $\overline{\mathcal{A}}$ against the compiled scheme that makes a single LoR key corruption query for $(0^n, 1^n)$, and no other queries. To simulate the view of $\overline{\mathcal{A}}$ by an adversary $\mathcal{A}$ against the base scheme, $\mathcal{A}$ must also make the same query to get a secret key $\mathsf{sk}$ encoding either $0^n$ and $1^n$. To compile this key $\mathsf{sk}$, $\mathcal{A}$ must be given many encryptions of random vectors $\mathbf{x}$ from $\mathbb{Z}_q^n$. However, $\mathcal{A}$ cannot obtain these ciphertexts via encryption queries, because $\mathcal{A}$'s queries will become inadmissible (i.e., w.h.p. $\langle 0^n, \mathbf{x}\rangle \neq \langle 1^n, \mathbf{x}\rangle$ for a random $\mathbf{x}$). This was not an issue for public-key IPFE with non-FH IND-CPA because encryptions there were free.

The above compiler, which preserves correctness but not security, illustrates the challenges in getting both correctness and security. Looking ahead, our solution is a careful weakening of FH IND-CPA and a modified compilation such that (1) both security and correctness are preserved and (b) the new security notion is still strong enough to be broken information-theoretically for schemes where KGen makes no queries.

*First Attempt.* To give intuition about our final compilation, let us give a procedure which preserves a weaker security notion, but not correctness—the opposite of the above situation. Our weakened security notion (call it key hiding, formalized in Definition 2) is defined with respect to an $(n-1)$-dimensional subspace $\mathbf{V}$. The adversary may make key-corruption and encryption queries, but the adversary does not provide an inputs for any query. In response to a key-corruption query, the challenger samples $\mathbf{y} \leftarrow \mathbb{Z}_q^n$ and $\mathbf{w} \leftarrow \mathsf{V}^\perp$, and returns $(\mathbf{y}, \mathbf{y}+\mathbf{w}, \mathsf{sk}[\mathbf{y}+b\mathbf{w}])$ to the adversary, where $b$ is the challenge bit and $\mathsf{V}^\perp$ is the orthogonal complement of $\mathsf{V}$. In response to an encryption query, the challenger returns $(\mathbf{x}, \mathsf{ct}[\mathbf{x}])$, where $\mathbf{x} \leftarrow \mathsf{V}$ and $\mathsf{ct}[\mathbf{x}]$ is an encryption of $\mathbf{x}$.

We slightly modify the previous compilation as follows. To compile a secret key $\mathsf{sk} := (s, g_1, \ldots, g_m)$ into $\overline{\mathsf{sk}}$, and specifically to learn an underlying relation $R$ among $\{g_i\}$ to be included in $\overline{\mathsf{sk}}$, we proceed as before by performing decryptions of many ciphertexts but now each ciphertext $\mathsf{ct}_i$ is encrypting a random vector from $\mathsf{V}$, as opposed to from $\mathbb{Z}_q^n$. Namely, during decryption of each $\mathsf{ct}_i$, we add to $R$ all positively-answered equality relations. It is easy to argue that this transformation preserves key-hiding security because any adversary $\overline{\mathcal{A}}$ against the key-hiding of the compiled scheme can be simulated by an $\mathcal{A}$ against the base scheme. This is because encryption queries can be relayed from $\overline{\mathcal{A}}$ to $\mathcal{A}$. Moreover, for any key-corruption query of $\overline{\mathcal{A}}$, $\mathcal{A}$ may make a key-corruption query to get $(\mathbf{y}, \mathbf{y}+b\mathbf{w}, \mathsf{sk}[\mathbf{y}+b\mathbf{w}])$ and augment $\mathsf{sk}[\mathbf{y}+b\mathbf{w}]$ by requesting many encryption queries (resulting in ciphertexts encrypting random vectors in $\mathsf{V}$) and decrypting them with $\mathsf{sk}[\mathbf{y}+b\mathbf{w}]$. Moreover, it is easy to argue correctness as long as plaintext vectors are chosen uniformly at random from $\mathsf{V}$, as opposed to the entire space $\mathbb{Z}_q^n$. Call this weak correctness.

We may hope that the key-hiding property of any SK-IPFE whose KGen algorithm makes no $\mathbb{G}$ queries (as the compiled scheme above) and which provides weak correctness can be broken information-theoretically, so to reach a contradiction. However, this intuition is completely false. In fact, it is possible to build SK-IPFE which provides weak correctness as above and key hiding, information theoretically! Let KGen$(\mathsf{msk}, \mathbf{y})$ output $\mathbf{w}+\mathbf{y}$ for a random $\mathbf{w} \leftarrow \mathsf{V}^\perp$. Let Enc$(\mathsf{msk}, \mathbf{x})$ return $\mathbf{x}$. The decryption algorithm simply outputs the inner product. It is easy to argue that this trivial scheme satisfies both weak correctness and key hiding.

*Fixing the Above Issue.* We point out another issue with the above approach. Note that our key-hiding definition says nothing about plaintext hiding, and so it can be realized from the DDH assumption (even) with perfect correctness. (If we require weak correctness in the sense of above as opposed to perfect correctness, then as argued above, the notion can be realized information theoretically.) Specifically, the dual of any non-FH IND-CPA IPFE (e.g., [2]) satisfies key hiding, where by dual we mean swapping the roles of KGen and Enc. Thus, we cannot rule out perfectly-correct key-hiding SK-IPFE schemes in the GGM model. Note, however, that we have not yet made use of any plaintext hiding properties, which must also be satisfied by FH-IPFE schemes. We formalize a plaintext-hiding property and show that any perfectly-correct (or even $(1-\text{negl})$ correct) SK-IPFE with both plaintext hiding and key hiding properties can be transformed into a SK-IPFE $\overline{\mathcal{E}}$ which is almost as correct, and satisfies the key-hiding property and whose $\overline{\text{KGen}}$ makes no $\mathbb{G}$ queries. We then break such schemes information theoretically. Note that breaking such SK-IPFE schemes with key hiding does not contradict the above positive result, because the above positive result (the dual of [2]) results in KGen making $\mathbb{G}$ calls.

The plaintext hiding property (formalized in Definition 3) is defined as follows. Imagine an adversary $\mathcal{A}$ that is given $\mathsf{sk}[\mathbf{y}]$ for an arbitrary $\mathbf{y} \notin \mathsf{V}^{\perp}$, and is given $\ell$ ciphertexts $\mathsf{ct}_1, \ldots, \mathsf{ct}_\ell$, where each $\mathsf{ct}_i$ is either encrypting a random vector from $\mathbf{V}$ (if $b = 0$) or from $\mathbb{Z}_q^n$ (if $b = 1$). Suppose $\mathcal{A}$ is also given an encryption of a random vector $\mathbf{x}$ from $\mathbb{Z}_q^n$, together with $\langle \mathbf{y}, \mathbf{x} \rangle$. We show that FH-IND-CPA implies the challenge bit remains hidden. Suppose the original scheme $\mathcal{E}$ is perfectly correct, and provides plaintext hiding. (Again we can relax this to $(1-\text{negl})$ correctness.) We will show that the compiled scheme has $(1 - \frac{1}{\mathsf{poly}})$ correctness for every choice of a secret key vector $\mathbf{y} \notin \mathsf{V}^{\perp}$ (i.e., for every such $\mathbf{y} \notin \mathsf{V}^{\perp}$, if we sample $\overline{\mathsf{sk}[\mathbf{y}]}$ and $\mathsf{ct}[\mathbf{x}]$ for a random $\mathbf{x}$, $\overline{\text{Dec}}(\mathsf{sk}[\mathbf{y}], \mathsf{ct}[\mathbf{x}])$ outputs $\langle \mathbf{y}, \mathbf{x} \rangle$ with probability close to one). This implies almost-always correctness because $\mathsf{V}^{\perp}$ has a small weight over $\mathbb{Z}_q^n$. Fix $\mathbf{y} \notin \mathsf{V}^{\perp}$ and let $\alpha$ be the probability of correctness under $\mathbf{y}$ for the compiled scheme, as defined above. Suppose $\mathsf{ct}_1, \ldots, \mathsf{ct}_\ell$ given above are used for the compilation procedure.

1. If $b = 0$, namely all $\mathsf{ct}_i$ are encrypting $\mathsf{V}$-vectors, then the probability that $\overline{\text{Dec}}$ correctly decrypts $\mathsf{ct}$ to $\langle \mathbf{y}, \mathbf{x} \rangle$ is $\alpha$. This follows because in our compilation above, we compile secret keys against $\mathsf{V}$ ciphertexts.
2. If $b = 1$, namely all $\mathsf{ct}_i$ are encrypting fully-random vectors, then the probability that $\overline{\text{Dec}}$ correctly decrypts $\mathsf{ct}$ to $\langle \mathbf{y}, \mathbf{x} \rangle$ is $\beta \approx 1$. This follows from the techniques of [34,37], explained before.
3. By plaintext hiding $\alpha \approx \beta$, because otherwise an adversary can distinguish $b = 0$ from $b = 1$; i.e., compile $\mathsf{sk}[\mathbf{y}]$ against $\mathsf{ct}_1, \ldots, \mathsf{ct}_\ell$, decrypt $\mathsf{ct}$ using the compiled secret key and output 1 iff the result equals $\langle \mathbf{y}, \mathbf{x} \rangle$.

We have now argued the compiled scheme has key hiding, has correctness $\approx 1$, and has a $\overline{\text{KGen}}$ algorithm that makes no oracle queries. We break such schemes in Sect. 2.1.

*Learning the Inner Product in the Exponent.* So far, we have assumed that the decryption algorithm $\text{Dec}^{\mathbb{G}}$ outputs the inner product in the clear, i.e., as a $\mathbb{Z}_p$ element. Accordingly, we assumed that $\text{Dec}^{\mathbb{G}}$ makes no $\mathsf{Add}$ queries and only issues $\mathsf{Eql}$ queries. However, decryption in existing GGM-based IPFE schemes (e.g., [2]) does not output the inner product itself, but rather an encoding of it, such as $(\langle \mathbf{y}, \mathbf{x} \rangle) \cdot g$, where $g$ is a generator of the group. To capture this setting, we modify our model by allowing $\text{Dec}^{\mathbb{G}}$ to take as input a candidate inner product value $z$ and output 0/1. Concretely, we view Dec as operating in two phases. In the first phase, $\mathrm{Dec}_0^{\mathbb{G}}(\mathsf{sk}[\mathbf{y}], \mathsf{ct}[\mathbf{x}])$ outputs a single group element $\widetilde{g}$. In the second phase, $\mathrm{Dec}_1(g, \widetilde{g}, z)$ outputs 0/1, corresponding to the equality test $z \cdot g =^? \widetilde{g}$. We show how to extend our compilation to handle this more general setting. More generally, one could define richer variants of $(\mathrm{Dec}_0, \mathrm{Dec}_1)$ in which, for example, $\mathrm{Dec}_0$ outputs multiple group elements and $\mathrm{Dec}_1$ performs equality checks on linear combinations of these elements together with $z \cdot g$. For clarity of exposition, however, we restrict attention to the above $(\mathrm{Dec}_0, \mathrm{Dec}_1)$ formulation.

**Step 2: The Information-Theoretic Attack.** We now prove Step 2. Specifically, we show how to break the key-hiding property of any $\mathcal{E}^O = (\mathrm{Setup}^O, \mathrm{KGen}, \mathrm{Enc}^O, \mathrm{Dec}^O)$, with an $O$-free algorithm KGen, which has correctness $\approx 1$. Interestingly, our attacker $\mathcal{A}$ does not need to make any $O$ queries at all. Recall that under the key-hiding game, $\mathcal{A}$ has to guess the challenge bit $b$, where $\mathcal{A}$ is given $(\mathbf{y}_i, \mathbf{z}_i = \mathbf{y}_i + \mathbf{w}_i, \mathsf{sk}[\mathbf{y}_i + b\mathbf{w}_i])$ for $i \in [\ell]$, where $\mathbf{y}_i \leftarrow \mathbb{Z}_q^n$, $\mathbf{w}_i \leftarrow \mathsf{V}^\perp$ and $\mathsf{V}$ is an $(n-1)$ dimensional subspace. Also, $\ell$ is an arbitrary polynomial. The key-hiding game also allows for encryption queries, but $\mathcal{A}$ does not need to make such queries.

As a warm-up assume $\mathcal{E}^O$ is perfectly correct. The attack in this case is simple. But it is not sufficient for our general purpose because our compilation induces a small decryption error.

In a perfectly correct IPFE $\mathcal{E}^O$, given a fixed master secret key $\mathsf{msk}$ generated by $\mathrm{Setup}^O$, each $\mathsf{sk}[\mathbf{y}]$ is a perfect commitment to $\mathbf{y}$; i.e., there does not exist $\mathbf{y}$ and $\mathbf{z}$ such that $\mathbf{y} \neq \mathbf{z}$ but a secret key $\mathsf{sk}$ is in the image of both $\mathrm{KGen}(\mathsf{msk}, \mathbf{y})$ and $\mathrm{KGen}(\mathsf{msk}, \mathbf{z})$. With this intuition in mind, $\mathcal{A}$ determines the value of $b$ from $\{(\mathbf{y}_i, \mathbf{z}_i = \mathbf{y}_i + \mathbf{w}_i, \mathsf{sk}_i)\}$ as follows. We will write $x \in \mathcal{D}$ for a distribution $\mathcal{D}$ to mean $x$ is in the support of $\mathcal{D}$.

- If there exists $\widetilde{\mathsf{msk}}$ such that $\mathrm{Recover}(\widetilde{\mathsf{msk}}, \mathsf{sk}_1, \ldots, \mathsf{sk}_\ell) = (\mathbf{y}_1, \ldots, \mathbf{y}_\ell)$, return 0. (We define the procedure Recover momentarily.) Else, return 1.

The procedure $\mathrm{Recover}(\widetilde{\mathsf{msk}}, \mathsf{sk}_1, \ldots, \mathsf{sk}_\ell)$ works as follows: if there exists $(\mathbf{f}_1, \ldots, \mathbf{f}_\ell)$ such that for all $i \in [\ell]$, $\mathsf{sk}_i \in \mathrm{KGen}(\widetilde{\mathsf{msk}}, \mathbf{f}_i)$ and $\mathsf{sk}_i \notin \mathrm{KGen}(\widetilde{\mathsf{msk}}, \mathbf{f}'_i)$ for all $\mathbf{f}'_i \neq \mathbf{f}_i$, return $(\mathbf{f}_1, \ldots, \mathbf{f}_\ell)$. Else, return $\perp$.

Note that $\mathcal{A}$ makes no $O$ queries; in particular, the procedure Recover involves making no $O$ queries.

It is easy to see that whenever $b = 0$, $\mathcal{A}$ outputs 0 with probability one. We now argue that if $b = 1$, then $\mathcal{A}$ outputs 0 with negligible probability, assuming $\ell$ is large enough. This will complete the proof.

Suppose $b = 1$, meaning that each $\mathsf{sk}_i$ is encoding $\mathbf{z}_i = \mathbf{y}_i + \mathbf{w}_i$. Given $\mathbf{z}_i$ the probability one can guess the value of $\mathbf{y}_i$ is at most $\frac{1}{|\mathsf{V}^\perp|} = \frac{1}{q}$. Thus, for any fixed $\widetilde{\mathsf{msk}}$, the probability that $\mathrm{Recover}(\widetilde{\mathsf{msk}}, \mathsf{sk}_1, \ldots, \mathsf{sk}_\ell)$ outputs $(\mathbf{y}_1, \ldots, \mathbf{y}_\ell)$ is at most $\frac{1}{q^\ell}$. Assuming $m = |\mathsf{msk}|$, by choosing $\ell$ such that $\frac{2^m}{q^\ell} = \mathrm{negl}(\kappa)$, we get the desired result.

*Going Beyond Perfect Correctness.* If $\mathcal{E}^O$ has even a negligible correctness error, the above attack completely fails. In fact, not a single functional key might be perfectly binding in the above sense. To see why, change a perfectly-correct IPFE as follows: when generating a key for $\mathbf{y}$ under $\mathsf{msk}$, with probability $1 - \frac{1}{q^n}$, generate a key for $\mathbf{y}$ itself, and with probability $\frac{1}{q^n(q^n-1)}$ generate a key for $\mathbf{y} + \mathbf{s}$ for any non-zero shift $\mathbf{s}$. Here for every functional secret key we will have exponentially many pre-images. As such, designing an attack in this case is delicate, requiring one to come up with the right notion of 'binding'.

We define the new binding probability as follows. We say $(\mathsf{msk}, \mathsf{sk})$ is binding to $\mathbf{y}$ if by reverse sampling a secret-key vector based on pre-images of $\mathsf{sk}$ we get $\mathbf{y}$ with a probability strictly greater than 1/2. That is,

$$\Pr_{\mathbf{x} \leftarrow \mathbb{Z}_q^n}[\mathbf{x} = \mathbf{y} \mid \mathrm{KGen}(\mathsf{msk}, \mathbf{x}) = \mathsf{sk}] > \frac{1}{2}. \tag{2}$$

Note that given $\mathsf{msk}$, each $\mathsf{sk}$ binds itself to at most one secret-key vector. And note that, since KGen is oracle free, one can find the vector $\mathbf{y}$ (if any) to which $\mathsf{sk}$ is binding, without making any $O$ queries.

Suppose for simplicity that every $\mathsf{msk}$ output by Setup induces a decryption error of at most 0.001. (Our actual proof will relax this assumption.) We will show that with high probability (greater than 33/60), $(\mathsf{msk}, \mathsf{sk}[\mathbf{y}])$ will be a binding to $\mathbf{y}$ (Eq. 2), where $\mathbf{y}$ is a random vector and $\mathsf{sk}[\mathbf{y}]$ is a random secret key for $\mathbf{y}$. We will prove this by showing that if this does not hold, the probability of correctness will be strictly less than 0.999. With this in mind, we may then change the procedure Recover above so that for a given $\widetilde{\mathsf{msk}}$ and for each component $i$, it recovers the unique vector $\mathbf{h}_i$ to which $\mathsf{sk}_i$ is binding (if any), and outputs 0 if $(\mathbf{h}_1, \ldots, \mathbf{h}_\ell)$ agrees with $(\mathbf{y}_1, \ldots, \mathbf{y}_\ell)$ on a large fraction of coordinates (close to 33/60 above).

Our final proof is delicate, formalizing all of the above probability conditions.

## 2.2 Impossibility in Shoup's GGM

Maurer's GGM is restrictive, and several cryptographic primitives, such as delay functions [35], signatures [24], compact encryption, and several other primitives [46] are impossible in Maurer's GGM, even though they can be realized from concrete groups. Informally, the lack of a bit representation for group elements is what makes Maurer's GGM restrictive.

In contrast, Shoup's GGM [39], where each group element is represented by a unique random bitstring (the "label"), does not suffer from this lack of expressiveness. In fact, all the primitives mentioned above can be realized in Shoup's model. Thus, an impossibility result in Shoup's model is a much stronger indication that a primitive cannot be built from concrete groups, such as elliptic curves. Unfortunately, proving impossibility results in Shoup's model is also much more challenging, and as such almost all existing impossibility results were proved only in Maurer's model (e.g. [7,18,22,24,35,37,46]). For example, the impossibility of IBE in Maurer's GGM [34,37] was only generalized recently to Shoup's model [46], using very different techniques.[3]

For our impossibility result for FH-IPFE in Maurer's GGM, outlined earlier, it may seem the techniques cannot be applied in Shoup's model. Recall that our techniques relied on removing group elements from the secret key while keeping the bitstring part. In Shoup's model, however, each group element has a bit representation, so it is not even well-defined which part of a secret key is a group element and which part is a bitstring that does not encode a group element.

Nevertheless, we show that our impossibility result in Maurer's GGM can in fact be extended to Shoup's GGM *in a modular way*. We believe that our techniques can be adapted to lift other impossibility results from Maurer's GGM to Shoup's GGM in a similarly modular fashion.

**Maurer's GGM with Random Representations.** For our modular approach we introduce a new model that we call *Maurer's GGM with random representations*. This model is defined like Maurer's GGM model with the oracles $\mathbb{G} = (\mathsf{Add}, \mathsf{Eql})$, but additionally each group element is assigned a random bitstring label, from a set $\mathsf{LB} \subseteq \{0,1\}^*$. Concretely, we add an oracle $\mathsf{PointerToLabel}$ that inputs a group element, which is represented via a pointer, as in Maurer's model, and outputs its assigned label as an ordinary bitstring. We also add an oracle $\mathsf{LabelToPointer}$ that is the inverse of $\mathsf{PointerToLabel}$: It inputs a bitstring label and returns the group element that was assigned this label, represented as pointer, or a failure symbol $\perp$ if the bitstring is not a valid label of any group element. We use $\mathbb{L} := (\mathsf{PointerToLabel}, \mathsf{LabelToPointer})$ to denote both of these oracles. We call this model the random label Maurer GGM (RL-MGGM) model and an algorithm in this model has oracle access to both $\mathbb{G}$ and $\mathbb{L}$ (see full version).

In this model it is easy to simulate Shoup's generic group model, because we can use the $\mathbb{L}$ oracle to obtain a random bit representation for each group element and also convert these bit representations back to 'pointer-type' group elements. More specifically, Shoup's model can be described by a single oracle $\mathsf{SAdd}$ that inputs two labels of group elements and outputs the label of the sum of these group elements. We can simulate this by converting these labels to pointers to group elements via the $\mathsf{LabelToPointer}$ oracle, compute their sum with the $\mathsf{Add}$ oracle of Maurer's model, and convert the resulting group element pointer back to a label with the $\mathsf{PointerToLabel}$ oracle.

This model might seem like an overly complicated description of Shoup's GGM. However, it has the advantage that it separates the algebraic structure of groups from the random labels. On a high level, we will use the technique for the separation in Maurer's model to handle the $\mathbb{G}$ queries of the RL-MGGM model. The $\mathbb{L}$ oracle is essentially a random permutation, that can be handled

[3] The work [34] claims that their impossibility is in Shoup's model. However, as noted in [46], they impose GGM restrictions that are only allowed in Maurer's model.

using techniques to separate SK-IPFE from random permutations from prior work [27,28].

However, even with this model and these techniques the problem is still non-trivial. Remember that the first step of our impossibility result is to remove all oracle queries from KGen. To achieve this, we remove group elements from functional keys and ensure that KGen knows the discrete log of every group element in its input. Then, KGen can be simulated without ever obtaining a pointer to a group element and therefore without any oracle queries. This argument completely fails in this new model, because KGen might use pointers to group elements as input to the PointerToLabel oracle. Concretely, imagine that KGen samples $z \leftarrow \mathbb{Z}_q$ and includes $(z, \mathsf{Label} := \mathsf{PointerToLabel}(z \cdot g))$ in the functional key. Dec checks if $\mathsf{Label} := \mathsf{PointerToLabel}(z \cdot g)$ holds and outputs a failure symbol if this check does not pass. If KGen has no oracle access, it is impossible to produce a pair $(z, \mathsf{Label})$ that passes this check.

**Challenge 1:** KGen needs pointers to group elements (and therefore access to the oracle $\mathbb{G}$) to compute bit representations via the PointerToLabel oracle.

However, even if we would successfully remove all $\mathbb{G}$ queries from KGen (and, for example, would allow KGen retrieving the random representations providing just the exponent of the group element), we cannot use the information-theoretic attack outlined above, because this attack relies on KGen making no queries at all, and KGen still has oracle access to $\mathbb{L}$. A natural idea would be to remove the oracle $\mathbb{L}$ from KGen, too. However, this seems to be impossible. For example, consider an IPFE that stores a random exponent $z$ in the master secret key. The $\mathrm{Enc}(\mathsf{msk}, \mathbf{x})$ algorithm first creates an IPFE ciphertext $\mathsf{ct}[\mathbf{x}]$ for $\mathbf{x}$ and then additionally secret-key encrypts $\mathsf{ct}[\mathbf{x}]$ using the bit representation of $z \cdot g$ as secret key. Moreover, it adds a secret key encryption of the entire plaintext $\mathbf{x}$ under the secret key $z$ to the ciphertext. All functional secret keys of this IPFE contain the bit representation of $z \cdot g$, so that decryption can recover the actual IPFE ciphertext $\mathsf{ct}[\mathbf{x}]$ from the SKE ciphertext. In this example, it is unclear how we can remove the $\mathbb{L}$ oracle from KGen. Adding the exponent $z$ to the secret keys would violate security, because they can be used to recover the entire plaintext. But without adding any information about $z$, Dec will not be able to recover the IPFE ciphertext $\mathsf{ct}[\mathbf{x}]$, and thus we would violate correctness.

**Challenge 2:** It seems impossible to remove $\mathbb{L}$ queries from KGen.

*Our Proof Strategy.* To overcome Challenge 2, we introduce an alternative information-theoretic attack to the one outlined above. This alternative information-theoretic attack does not require us to remove all queries from KGen. Instead, it only requires that KGen and Dec each get access to different, independent oracles. This provides an alternative path to solve the second challenge.

**Alternative challenge 2:** Remove $\mathbb{L}$ queries from Dec.

The first step of our proof solves Alternative Challenge 2 by introducing a generic compiler that removes $\mathbb{L}$ queries from Dec. The second step of our proof solves Challenge 1 by replacing the $\mathbb{L}$ oracle with an ordinary random oracle. After these two compilation steps, we can use the compiler we have introduced for the Maurer impossibility result to remove $\mathbb{G}$ queries from KGen. Finally, we apply our new information-theoretic attack.

**Step 1: Removing $\mathbb{L}$ Queries from Dec.** The idea to remove $\mathbb{L}$ queries from Dec is to simulate the random labels of group elements. Concretely, Dec keeps a table of group element handles and their corresponding label. Whenever a random representation for a group element is queried, we look for this group element in the table and return its label, if we found it. If the table has no matching entry, we sample a new label (that is also stored in the table) and return it. Queries to convert random representations back to handles are handled similarly.

The obvious difficulty with that approach is that we need to ensure that we answer these queries consistently with those queries already made during generation of the ciphertext and the functional key. We cannot simply include the handle/label pairs that were used during encryption or key generation in the ciphertext or key, because that might violate security (for example, Enc and KGen could query a group element whose random representation matches the master secret key). Instead, we generate in KGen queries many ciphertexts $\mathsf{ct}_1, \ldots, \mathsf{ct}_{\ell_e}$ that we decrypt and append the handle/label pairs that we collect during these decryptions to the secret keys. For Enc, we proceed analogously with many random functional keys $\mathsf{sk}_1, \ldots, \mathsf{sk}_{\ell_k}$.

Now we face a similar challenge to the compiler for Maurer's GGM. To preserve correctness (for uniformly random vectors), we should sample the plaintexts for the ciphertexts uniformly at random from the entire space $\mathbb{Z}_q^n$. However, to argue security, we can only afford to sample them from a subspace $\mathsf{V} \subsetneq \mathbb{Z}_q^n$. In the compiler for Maurer's GGM we solved this by leveraging the plaintext hiding property of the scheme to argue that correctness is still preserved, when the ciphertexts come only from a subspace. While this argument worked for learning the relations among group elements, it does not work for learning group element labels.

To overcome this problem, we use a combinatorial trick that was introduced in [27] that essentially shows that we can learn the same query-answer pairs (for any oracle) if the vectors are sampled from a subspace (instead of the entire space). However, using this lemma comes at the price that we have to assume that $q^n$ is superpolynomial (and $n \geqslant 4$). We leave it as an open problem to provide a positive or negative result for FH-IPFE in Shoup's GGM when $q^n$ is only of polynomial size.

**Step 2: Replacing $\mathbb{L}$ by a Random Oracle.** The above compilation is not only a necessity for the final information-theoretic attack on the scheme, it also makes the second step, replacing $\mathbb{L}$ by a random oracle, easy. We can assume that during Enc and KGen we know the discrete log of every group element. Thus, we can use the random oracle to build a pseudorandom permutation (PRP) [31]. We can then apply the PRP to the exponent of a group element to get the label and the inverse to get from a label the exponent.[4] This way, we can ensure that KGen and Enc generate all labels consistently. Since Dec makes no queries, correctness is preserved, even when the labels no longer match the labels of the oracle $\mathbb{L}$.

To argue that this compiler preserves security, we just have to reduce an adversary for the FH-IPFE where labels in Enc and KGen are inconsistent with the oracle $\mathbb{L}$ to one where they are consistent with the oracle $\mathbb{L}$. This can be achieved by a reduction that simulates the oracle $\mathbb{L}$ for the adversary independently of the real $\mathbb{L}$ and forwards all other queries.

**Step 3: Remove $\mathbb{G}$ queries from KGen.** The next step is to run the compiler we already used for the impossibility result in Maurer's GGM to remove $\mathbb{G}$ queries from KGen.

Recall that this compiler relies on the plaintext hiding property of the FH-IPFE to argue that it preserves correctness. One difficulty is that the plaintext hiding notion we can preserve in the previous step is weaker than the one we used for the impossibility result in Maurer's model, because we have to make sure that our notion allows us to generate keys from a subspace $\mathsf{U} \subseteq \mathbb{Z}_q^n$ to be preserved in Step 1. This makes arguing correctness more challenging, and we provide an alternative proof that this notion still sufficient to guarantee that correctness is preserved in the compilation.

An advantage of this, more involved, argument, compared to the previous one, is that we can tune the decryption failures to an arbitrary small polynomial, which even improves our result for Maurer's model.

**Step 4: Alternative Information-Theoretic Attack.** After executing the compiler from step 1, 2, and 3 we end up with an FH-IPFE scheme where KGen makes no $\mathbb{G}$ queries, but it can still make random oracle queries. As mentioned above, this prevents us to use the previous, information-theoretic attack.

Instead, we leverage that KGen makes random oracle queries, but no $\mathbb{G}$ queries and Dec makes $\mathbb{G}$ queries, but not random oracle queries.

Our information-theoretic attack makes many secret key queries that return $(\mathbf{y}_i, \mathbf{y}'_i = \mathbf{y}_i + \mathbf{v}_i, \mathsf{sk}_i)$, where $\mathbf{y}_i \leftarrow \mathbb{Z}_q^n$, $\mathbf{v}_i \in \mathsf{V}^\perp$ and $\mathsf{sk}_i$ is a secret key for $\mathbf{y}_i + b\mathbf{v}_i$, where $b \leftarrow \{0,1\}$ is a challenge bit sampled once for all queries. The attack will make a brute force search for a master secret key $\mathsf{msk}$, a vector $\mathbf{x} \notin \mathsf{V}$, a ciphertext $\mathsf{ct}[\mathbf{x}]$ encrypting $\mathbf{x}$ and a set of query-answer pairs of all queries made during the generation of $\mathsf{msk}$ and $\mathsf{ct}[\mathbf{x}]$. If decrypting $\mathsf{ct}[\mathbf{x}]$ with $\mathsf{sk}_i$ results in $\langle \mathbf{x}, \mathbf{y}_i \rangle$ for a large enough fraction of indices $i$, the adversary guesses $b = 0$ and otherwise $b = 1$. All queries made during decryption are simulated, which is possible for the adversary, since it knows the discrete log of every group element. Note that this simulation is faithful, because no $\mathbb{G}$ queries where made during the generation of the secret keys $\mathsf{sk}_i$.

[4] If we want the labels to be sparse, we interpret all labels that are mapped to an exponent larger than the group order as invalid labels.

By carefully tuning the threshold of the number of indices for which decryption resulted in $\langle \mathbf{x}, \mathbf{y}_i \rangle$ and making the number of secret keys large enough, we can guarantee that this adversary wins with high probability.

For this information-theoretic attack, we need at least $q \geqslant 3$, but for $q \geqslant 5$ it even rules out FH-IPFE schemes with correctness probability less than 1/2, which strengthens our impossibility result also in Maurer's model.

## 3 Preliminaries

*Notation.* We use $\kappa$ to denote the security parameter. We use $[n] := \{1, \ldots, n\}$ for $n \in \mathbb{N}$. For two functions $f, g \colon \mathbb{N} \to \mathbb{R}$, when we say $f \geqslant g$, we mean that this holds asymptotically; i.e., there exists $c \in \mathbb{N}$ such that for all $x \geqslant c$, $f(x) \geqslant g(x)$. For a discrete distribution $\mathsf{D}$, we use $\mathsf{D}(a)$ to mean the output of the probability mass function of $\mathsf{D}$ on point $a$; i.e., $\mathsf{D}(a) = \Pr_{x \leftarrow \mathsf{D}}[x = a]$. We write $x \leftarrow \mathsf{D}$ to denote sampling $x$ from $\mathsf{D}$ and write $x \in \mathsf{D}$ to indicate $x$ is in the support of $\mathsf{D}$.

We use $\mathsf{Span}(\mathsf{S})$ to denote the linear span of a set of vectors $\mathsf{S} \subseteq \mathbb{Z}_q^n$ or the column vectors of a matrix $\mathsf{S} \in \mathbb{Z}_q^{n \times m}$. For a $\mathbb{Z}_q$ module $\mathsf{V} \subseteq \mathbb{Z}_q^n$ we write $\mathsf{V}^\perp := \{\mathbf{w} \in \mathbb{Z}_q^n \mid \forall \mathbf{v} \in \mathsf{V} : \langle \mathbf{w}, \mathbf{v} \rangle = 0\}$ and similarly for a vector $\mathbf{x} \in \mathbb{Z}_q^n$ we write $\mathbf{x}^\perp := \{\mathbf{w} \in \mathbb{Z}_q^n \mid \langle \mathbf{w}, \mathbf{x} \rangle = 0\}$.

**Lemma 1 (Chernoff bound).** *Let $X_1, \ldots, X_m$ be i.i.d. Bernoulli random variables where $\mu = \Pr[X_1 = 1]$. Let $X = \frac{X_1 + \cdots + X_m}{m}$. Then*

$$\Pr[|X - \mu| \geqslant \epsilon] \leqslant 2 \cdot e^{-\frac{m\epsilon^2}{4}}.$$

### 3.1 Inner-Product Functional Encryption

We define private-key IPFE schemes relative to an oracle. Later on, we define a GGM-based definition of IPFE to capture the scenario where the decryption algorithm learns the inner product in the exponent (Definition 4).

**Definition 1 (IPFE).** *A private-key IPFE scheme $\mathcal{E}^O = (\mathrm{Setup}^O, \mathrm{KGen}^O, \mathrm{Enc}^O, \mathrm{Dec}^O)$ relative to an oracle $O$ for $\mathbb{Z}_q^n$ with dimension $n = n(\kappa)$ and modulus $q = q(\kappa)$ is given by the following oracle-aided PPT algorithms.*

- $\mathrm{Setup}^O(1^\kappa)$: *On input a unary encoded security parameter, it outputs a master secret key* $\mathsf{msk}$.
- $\mathrm{KGen}^O(\mathsf{msk}, \mathbf{y})$: *On input a master secret key* $\mathsf{msk}$ *and a vector* $\mathbf{y} \in \mathbb{Z}_q^n$, *the key generation algorithm outputs a secret key* $\mathsf{sk}[\mathbf{y}]$.
- $\mathrm{Enc}^O(\mathsf{msk}, \mathbf{x})$: *On input a master secret key* $\mathsf{msk}$ *and a vector* $\mathbf{x} \in \mathbb{Z}_q^n$, *the encryption algorithm outputs a ciphertext* $\mathsf{ct}$.
- $\mathrm{Dec}^O(\mathsf{sk}[\mathbf{y}], \mathsf{ct})$: *On input a secret key* $\mathsf{sk}[\mathbf{y}]$ *and a ciphertext* $\mathsf{ct}$, *the decryption algorithm outputs* $z \in \mathbb{Z}_q$.
- ***$\nu$-correctness:*** *We say $\mathcal{E}^O$ is $\nu$-correct if the following experiment outputs one with probability at least $\nu$. Sample* $\mathsf{msk} \leftarrow \mathrm{Setup}^O(1^\kappa)$, $\mathbf{y} \leftarrow \mathbb{Z}_q^n$, $\mathsf{sk}[\mathbf{y}] \leftarrow \mathrm{KGen}^O(\mathsf{msk}, \mathbf{y})$, $\mathbf{x} \leftarrow \mathbb{Z}_q^n$ *and* $\mathsf{ct} \leftarrow \mathrm{Enc}^O(\mathsf{msk}, \mathbf{x})$. *The experiment outputs one if* $\mathrm{Dec}^O(\mathsf{sk}[\mathbf{y}, \mathsf{ct}) = \langle \mathbf{y}, \mathbf{x} \rangle$. *If the oracle $O$ is randomized, the probability is taken also over the random coins of the oracle.*

*Definitions for the Impossibility Result.* We introduce two new security notions that are parameterized by a fixed $(n-1)$-dimensional subspace $\mathsf{V}$. In the full version we show that the standard FH-IND-CPA security notion implies both of these notions for any $\mathsf{V}$.

**Definition 2 ($\mathsf{V}$-key hiding ).** *Let $\mathsf{V} \subseteq \mathbb{Z}_q^n$ be an $(n-1)$-dimensional subspace of $\mathbb{Z}_q^n$ and $\mathcal{E}^O = (\mathrm{Setup}^O, \mathrm{KGen}^O, \mathrm{Enc}^O, \mathrm{Dec}^O)$ be an IPFE over $\mathbb{Z}_q^n$. The game is defined over a PPT adversary $\mathcal{A}$ and a challenger. The challenger samples a master secret key $\mathsf{msk} \leftarrow \mathrm{Setup}^O(1^\kappa)$ and a challenge bit $b \leftarrow \{0,1\}$. The adversary $\mathcal{A}$, who has the description of $\mathsf{V}$, can make queries of the following types, where neither type requires an input from $\mathcal{A}$, and where all the queries must be made non-adaptively at once.*

- ***Key corruption queries:*** *For any such query, $\mathcal{A}$ receives $(\mathbf{y}, \mathbf{y}+\mathbf{w}, \mathrm{KGen}(\mathsf{msk}, \mathbf{y}+b\mathbf{w}))$, where $\mathbf{y} \leftarrow \mathbb{Z}_q^n$ and $\mathbf{w} \leftarrow \mathsf{V}^\perp$. Here $\mathsf{V}^\perp$ denotes the orthogonal complement of $\mathsf{V}$; i.e., $\mathsf{V}^\perp = \{\mathbf{w} \in \mathbb{Z}_q^n \mid \forall \mathbf{v} \in \mathsf{V} : \langle \mathbf{w}, \mathbf{v} \rangle = 0\}$.*
- ***Encryption queries:*** *For any such query, $\mathcal{A}$ receives $(\mathbf{v}, \mathrm{Enc}(\mathsf{msk}, \mathbf{v}))$, where $\mathbf{v} \leftarrow \mathsf{V}$.*

*At the end, $\mathcal{A}$ outputs a bit $b'$ and wins if $b = b'$. We say $\mathcal{A}$ is admissible if all of $\mathcal{A}$'s queries are made non-adaptively at once. We say $\mathcal{E}$ is $\mathsf{V}$-key hiding if any admissible PPT $\mathcal{A}$ wins the game with probability at most $1/2 + \mathrm{negl}(\kappa)$.*

Note that the above definition can be realized under the DDH assumption, since it only concerns key hiding, and not plaintext hiding. In particular, the dual version of any IPFE that satisfies the standard notion of IND-CPA security satisfies the above notion (e.g., [2]). Dual means swapping the roles of the key-generation and encryption algorithms. Thus, the above definition, in isolation, cannot be ruled out in the GGM. Thus, we give a definition for plaintext hiding below, and will show that these two definitions cannot be simultaneously realized in the GGM.

**Definition 3 ($\mathsf{V}$-plaintext hiding ).** *Let $\mathsf{V} \subseteq \mathbb{Z}_q^n$ be an $(n-1)$-dimensional subspace of $\mathbb{Z}_q^n$ and $\mathcal{E}^O = (\mathrm{Setup}^O, \mathrm{KGen}^O, \mathrm{Enc}^O, \mathrm{Dec}^O)$ be an IPFE over $\mathbb{Z}_q^n$. Let $\mathsf{msk}$ and bit $b$ be sampled as in Definition 2. The adversary $\mathcal{A}$ may make queries of the following types, all made non-adaptively at once.*

- ***Key corruption queries:*** *The adversary $\mathcal{A}$ submits $\mathbf{y}$ subject to the restriction that $\mathbf{y} \notin \mathsf{V}^\perp$ and receives $\mathrm{KGen}(\mathsf{msk}, \mathbf{y})$. The adversary may make this query only once.*
- ***LoR encryption queries:*** *For any such query, $\mathcal{A}$ receives $(\langle \mathbf{y}, \mathbf{x} \rangle, \mathrm{Enc}(\mathsf{msk}, \mathbf{x}))$, where $\mathbf{x} = \mathbf{v} + b\mathbf{x}'$ for $\mathbf{v} \leftarrow \mathsf{V}$ and $\mathbf{x}' \leftarrow \mathbb{Z}_q^n$.*
- ***Straight encryption queries:*** *For any such query, $\mathcal{A}$ receives $(\mathbf{x}, \mathrm{Enc}(\mathsf{msk}, \mathbf{x}))$, where $\mathbf{x} \leftarrow \mathbb{Z}_q^n$.*

*At the end, $\mathcal{A}$ outputs a bit $b'$ and wins if $b = b'$. We say that $\mathcal{A}$ is admissible if $\mathcal{A}$ makes at most one key corruption query and if all of $\mathcal{A}$'s queries are made non-adaptively at once. We say that $\mathcal{E}$ is $V$-plaintext hiding if any admissible PPT $\mathcal{A}$ wins the game with probability at most $1/2 + \mathrm{negl}(\kappa)$.*

We now give an adaptation of the IPFE notion of Definition 1 to the GGM setting, capturing the common scenario where the decryption algorithm learns the inner product only in the exponent. Here $\mathbb{G}$ is the generic group oracle (in Maurer's or Shoup's variant) that we describe in more detail in the full version.

**Definition 4 (IPFE in GGM).** *The algorithms* $\text{Setup}^{\mathbb{G}}$, $\text{KGen}^{\mathbb{G}}$ *and* $\text{Enc}^{\mathbb{G}}$ *are the same as in Definition 1. We define* $\text{Dec}^{\mathbb{G}}$ *as follows: it takes in* $(\mathsf{sk}[\mathbf{y}], \mathsf{ct}[\mathbf{x}], z)$, *where* $z$ *is a candidate inner product value, and* $\text{Dec}^{\mathbb{G}}$ *outputs* $\{0, 1\}$ *while having the following structure:* $\text{Dec}^{\mathbb{G}} = (\text{Dec}_0^{\mathbb{G}}, \text{Dec}_1^{\mathbb{G}})$, *where* $\text{Dec}_0^{\mathbb{G}}(\mathsf{sk}[\mathbf{y}], \mathsf{ct}[\mathbf{x}])$ *outputs a group element* $\widetilde{g}$, *and* $\text{Dec}_1^{\mathbb{G}}$ *outputs the result of an equality query on* $(\widetilde{g}, zg)$, *where* $g$ *is the generator.*[5] *The output of* Dec *is the output of* $\text{Dec}_1$. *Also, note that* $\text{Dec}_0$ *does not take in* $z$. *For* $\nu$*-correctness we require for* $\mathsf{msk} \leftarrow \text{Setup}^{\mathbb{G}}(1^{\kappa})$, *for* $\mathbf{y}, \mathbf{x} \leftarrow \mathbb{Z}_q^n$, $\mathsf{sk}[\mathbf{y}] \leftarrow \text{KGen}^{\mathbb{G}}(\mathsf{msk}, \mathbf{y})$ *and* $\mathsf{ct}[\mathbf{x}] \leftarrow \text{Enc}^{\mathbb{G}}(\mathsf{msk}, \mathbf{x})$, *the probability that* $\text{Dec}^{\mathbb{G}}(\mathsf{sk}[\mathbf{y}], \mathsf{ct}[\mathbf{x}], \langle \mathbf{y}, \mathbf{x} \rangle)$ *outputs 1 is at least* $\nu$.

# 4 Impossibility of FH-IPFE in Maurer's GGM

In this section, we present our impossibility result in Maurer's GGM. We refer the reader to the full version for a definition of Maurer's GGM.

For simplicity, we assume for our impossibility results that $q$ is a prime and thus $\mathbb{Z}_q^n$ is a vector space and not just a module. This is without loss of generality, because an IPFE for a composite modulus $q$ can be transformed into an IPFE for any prime modulus $p \mid q$. The transformation simply multiplies in key generation the input vector with $q/p$ and the decryption algorithm divides the result by $q/p$.

## 4.1 Step 1: Removing Oracle Queries from KGen

**Lemma 2.** *Assume* $(\text{Setup}^{\mathbb{G}}, \text{KGen}^{\mathbb{G}}, \text{Enc}^{\mathbb{G}}, \text{Dec}^{\mathbb{G}})$ *is* $\nu$*-correct and satisfies both* $\mathsf{V}$*-key hiding (Definition 2) and* $\mathsf{V}$*-plaintext hiding (Definition 3) for every* $(n-1)$*-dimensional subspace* $\mathsf{V}$. *The compiled scheme* $\overline{\mathcal{E}}^{\mathbb{G}} := (\overline{\text{Setup}}^{\mathbb{G}}, \overline{\text{KGen}}, \overline{\text{Enc}}^{\mathbb{G}}, \overline{\text{Dec}}^{\mathbb{G}})$, *defined for any given* $\mathsf{V}$, *has the property that* $\overline{\text{KGen}}$ *makes no* $\mathbb{G}$ *queries, and* $\overline{\text{Setup}}^{\mathbb{G}}, \overline{\text{KGen}}, \overline{\text{Enc}}^{\mathbb{G}}, \overline{\text{Dec}}^{\mathbb{G}}$ *continue to be PPT algorithms, and*

1. $\overline{\mathcal{E}}^{\mathbb{G}}$ *is* $((3\nu - 2) - 1/q^{n-1} - 1/\mathsf{poly}(\kappa))$*-correct for an arbitrarily chosen polynomial* $\mathsf{poly}(\kappa)$ *and for some subspace* $\mathsf{V}$.[6]
2. $\overline{\mathcal{E}}^{\mathbb{G}}$ *provides* $\mathsf{V}$*-key hiding (Definition 2) for any subspace* $\mathsf{V}$.

[5] Technically, this means making a sequence of $\mathsf{Add}$ queries to compute $xg$ from $g$ and comparing it against $\widetilde{g}$.

[6] Note that $q$ represents the modulus of the IPFE, which does not necessarily agree with the order of the group $p$.

**Proof of Lemma 2.** Our compiler is presented in Fig. 2. It is parametrized by an $(n-1)$-dimensional subspace $\mathsf{V} \subseteq \mathbb{Z}_q^n$, and compiles $(\mathrm{Setup}^{\mathbb{G}}, \mathrm{KGen}^{\mathbb{G}}, \mathrm{Enc}^{\mathbb{G}}, \mathrm{Dec}^{\mathbb{G}})$ into $\overline{\mathcal{E}}^{\mathbb{G}} := (\overline{\mathrm{Setup}}^{\mathbb{G}}, \overline{\mathrm{KGen}}, \overline{\mathrm{Enc}}^{\mathbb{G}}, \overline{\mathrm{Dec}}^{\mathbb{G}})$.

*Remark 1.* For a GGM algorithm $A^{\mathbb{G}}(g_1, \ldots, g_m)$ with initial input group elements $g_1, \ldots, g_m$, we define a notion of positively-answered equality relations. In particular, for any equality query $\mathsf{Eql}(g', g'')$ answered with 1, the algorithm $A$ may map each $g'$ and $g''$ to a linear combination over $(g_1, \ldots, g_m)$, hence obtaining a satisfying relation $(a_1, \ldots, a_m)$ over $(g_1, \ldots, g_m)$; i.e., $a_1 g_1 + \cdots + a_m g_m = 0$.

$\overline{\mathrm{Setup}}^{\mathbb{G}}(1^\kappa)$: Sample $\mathsf{msk}$ according to $\mathrm{Setup}^{\mathbb{G}}(1^\kappa)$. Let $\ell$ be an integer which will be instantiated later (in the proof for correctness). For $i \in [\ell]$, sample $\mathbf{v}_i \leftarrow \mathsf{V}$ and $\mathsf{ct}_i \leftarrow \mathrm{Enc}^{\mathbb{G}}(\mathsf{msk}, \mathbf{v}_i)$. Let the resulting master secret key $\overline{\mathsf{msk}}$ contain $\mathsf{msk}$ and $\mathsf{pp} := (\mathbf{v}_1, \mathsf{ct}_1, \ldots, \mathbf{v}_\ell, \mathsf{ct}_\ell)$, as well as $\mathsf{aux}$, which contains all the randomness and the underlying query-answer (Q-A) pairs (i.e., all the discrete log values) made throughout. For $i \in [\ell]$, let $(g_{i,1}, \ldots, g_{i,t})$ denote the group elements in $\mathsf{ct}_i$. $\overline{\mathrm{KGen}}(\overline{\mathsf{msk}} := (\mathsf{msk}, \mathsf{pp}, \mathsf{aux}), \mathbf{y})$: Sample $\mathsf{sk}[\mathbf{y}] := (s, g_1, \ldots, g_m) \leftarrow \mathrm{KGen}^{\mathbb{G}}(\mathsf{msk}, \mathbf{y})$, where $s$ is a bit string and $g_i$'s are group elements. The oracle $\mathbb{G}$ is simulated using $\mathsf{aux}$ without making any queries to the real oracle. Let the compiled key be $\overline{\mathsf{sk}[\mathbf{y}]} := (s, \mathsf{pp}, \mathsf{R})$, where $\mathsf{R}$ is a set of relations over $(g_1, \ldots, g_m, \{g_{i,j}\}_{i \in [\ell], j \in [t]})$, formed as follows.

1. For all $h \in [\ell]$, perform $\mathrm{Dec}^{\mathbb{G}}(\mathsf{sk}[\mathbf{y}], \mathsf{ct}_h, \langle \mathbf{y}, \mathbf{v}_h \rangle)$. For any positively-answered equality query $\sum_{i=1}^m a_i \cdot g_i + \sum_{i=1}^t a'_{h,i} \cdot g_{h,i} = 0$, add the corresponding coefficients (i.e., $(a_1, \ldots, a_m,\ a'_{h,1}, \ldots, a'_{h,t})$) to $\mathsf{R}$ (Remark 1).

$\overline{\mathrm{Enc}}^{\mathbb{G}}(\overline{\mathsf{msk}} := (\mathsf{msk}, \mathsf{pp}, \mathsf{aux}), \mathbf{x})$: output $\mathrm{Enc}^{\mathbb{G}}(\mathsf{msk}, \mathbf{x})$.
$\overline{\mathrm{Dec}}^{\mathbb{G}}(\overline{\mathsf{sk}[\mathbf{y}]} := (s, \mathsf{pp}, \mathsf{R}), \mathsf{ct} := (s', u_1, \ldots, u_t), z)$: To decrypt a ciphertext $\mathsf{ct} := (s', u_1, \ldots, u_t)$, where $s'$ is a bit string and $u_i$'s are the group elements, perform $\mathrm{Dec}^{\mathbb{G}}(\mathsf{sk}[\mathbf{y}], \mathsf{ct}, z)$. The decryptor can perform all operations except for equality queries (since the secret key no longer contains the group elements $(g_1, \ldots, g_m)$, but only contains the relations $\mathsf{R}$). Instead, $\overline{\mathrm{Dec}}^{\mathbb{G}}$ answers such equality queries as follows.

(a) Any equality query must be of the form $\sum_{i=1}^m z_i \cdot g_i + \sum_{i=1}^t c_i \cdot u_i = 0$. Now, if $(z_1, \ldots, z_m) \notin \mathsf{Span}((\mathsf{R}')^\top)$, where $\mathsf{R}'$ is the submatrix of $\mathsf{R}$ that contains the columns that correspond to $(g_1, \ldots, g_m)$, answer the equality query with 0. Otherwise, cancel out $g_i$'s using the relations in $\mathsf{R}$ and obtain an equivalent equality query that involves instead $\{g_{i,j}\}_{i \in [\ell], j \in [t]}$ and $\{u_i\}_{i \in [t]}$. We can ask $\mathbb{G}$ on this relation.

We remind the reader that, without loss of generality, we may assume that $\mathrm{Dec}^{\mathbb{G}}$ does not make any Add queries (see full version) and, hence, we only need to worry about equality queries.

**Fig. 2.** The compiler for Lemma 2, parameterized by a subspace $\mathsf{V} \subseteq \mathbb{Z}_q^n$.

$\overline{\text{KGen}}$ *makes no* $\mathbb{G}$ *queries.* We note that $\overline{\text{KGen}}$ indeed does not require making any $\mathbb{G}$ queries. Firstly, $\overline{\text{KGen}}$ does not need to output any group elements beyond $\mathsf{pp}$, which is already prepared in $\overline{\mathsf{msk}}$ by $\overline{\text{Setup}}^{\mathbb{G}}$. Secondly, for a given $\mathsf{Add}$ query, $\overline{\text{KGen}}$ may create a 'dummy' entry in the table and give a pointer to that dummy cell. This creates no issues because $\overline{\text{KGen}}$ is not supposed to output any of such dummy entries (only those in $\mathsf{pp}$ are output). Finally, for an equality query asked during the invocation of $\text{KGen}^{\mathbb{G}}$ or during the preparation of $\mathsf{R}$, $\overline{\text{KGen}}$ may simulate the response itself. $\overline{\text{KGen}}$ is capable of doing this because it takes $\overline{\mathsf{msk}}$ as input and, hence, it knows the discrete logs (i.e., $T(i)$) for all the group elements created during $\overline{\text{Setup}}$ (given in $\mathsf{aux}$) and also during $\overline{\text{KGen}}$'s execution so far. Consequently, $\overline{\text{KGen}}$ can answer all the equality queries by examining the underlying discrete log values.

$\mathsf{V}$-*key hiding.* Next, we argue the compiled scheme satisfies $\mathsf{V}$-key hiding. We do so by showing that, if there is an adversary $\mathcal{A}$ that breaks the $\mathsf{V}$-key hiding property, we can build another adversary $\mathcal{A}^*$ that breaks the $\mathsf{V}$-key hiding property of the base scheme.

In particular, $\mathcal{A}^*$ will first make $\ell$ encryption queries and obtain the $\mathsf{pp} = (\mathsf{ct}_1, \dots, \mathsf{ct}_\ell)$ in the compiled scheme, together with the underlying plaintexts $\mathbf{v}_1, \mathbf{v}_2, \dots, \mathbf{v}_\ell$. Then, $\mathcal{A}^*$ proceeds to simulate the view of $\mathcal{A}$ for the key hiding game for the compiled scheme. For each encryption query, $\mathcal{A}^*$ simply relays the query to $\mathcal{A}^*$'s own external challenger and responds to $\mathcal{A}$ whatever it receives from the challenger. For each key corruption query, $\mathcal{A}^*$ will first relay this query to its own external challenger to receive $\mathsf{sk}$. Next, it proceeds to augment its received $\mathsf{sk}$ in the same way the compiler does. Note that $\mathcal{A}^*$ is able to do so since it holds $\mathsf{pp}$ which contains $(\mathbf{v}_i, \mathsf{ct}_i)$ for all $i \in [\ell]$—which, in turn, means that $\mathcal{A}^*$ knows the inner product used as input to Dec. $\mathcal{A}^*$ then gives the compiled key to $\mathcal{A}$.

Clearly, $\mathcal{A}^*$ perfectly simulates the view of $\mathcal{A}$ and the $\mathsf{V}$-key hiding of the original scheme implies the $\mathsf{V}$-key hiding of the compiled scheme. □

*Correctness.* Next, we argue correctness. When we invoke the our compiler using a subspace $\mathsf{V}$, define the correctness specific to $\mathsf{V}$ as

$$\mathsf{Correct}_{\mathsf{V}} := \Pr\left[\overline{\text{Dec}}^{\mathbb{G}}(\mathsf{sk}[\mathbf{y}], \mathsf{ct}, \langle \mathbf{y}, \mathbf{x}\rangle) = 1 \;\middle|\; \begin{array}{c} \overline{\mathsf{msk}} \leftarrow \overline{\text{Setup}}^{\mathbb{G}}(1^\kappa) \\ \mathbf{y} \leftarrow \mathbb{Z}_q^n,\ \mathbf{x} \leftarrow \mathbb{Z}_q^n \\ \overline{\mathsf{sk}[\mathbf{y}]} \leftarrow \overline{\text{KGen}}(\overline{\mathsf{msk}}, \mathbf{y}) \\ \mathsf{ct} \leftarrow \overline{\text{Enc}}^{\mathbb{G}}(\overline{\mathsf{msk}}, \mathbf{x}) \end{array}\right].$$

We are going to prove that

$$\mathop{\mathrm{E}}_{\mathsf{V}}[\mathsf{Correct}_{\mathsf{V}}] \geqslant (3\nu - 2) - 1/q^{n-1} - 3m/(\ell+1) - \text{negl}(\kappa). \tag{3}$$

This suffices to prove Lemma 2 since Eq. 3 states that the correctness of the compile scheme with respect to a random parameter $\mathsf{V}$ is sufficiently high, which implies the existence of a subspace $\mathsf{V}$ such that the compilation using this particular $\mathsf{V}$ satisfies the above bound. Henceforth, the requirement of Lemma 2 is met by setting $\ell$ to be a sufficiently large polynomial.

For this proof, let us consider a slightly different compiled scheme, where the only difference lies in the choice of $\mathsf{V}$ (within $\overline{\text{Setup}}^{\mathbb{G}}$) for the compiler. Instead of picking $\mathsf{V}$ as a subspace of dimension $n-1$, we pick $\mathsf{V}$ to be the *entire space.* Our proof breaks into the following two steps.

1. For this slightly different compiled scheme, where $\mathsf{V}$ is the entire space, its correctness $\geqslant \nu - \frac{m}{\ell+1}$.
2. When we switch $\mathsf{V}$ from the entire space to a random dimension-$(n-1)$ subspace, the correctness will not drop significantly.

**Proof of Step** 1. For this step, let us first import a result from [37].

**Lemma 3 (Lemma 3.2 of** *[37]***).** *Let $X_1, X_2, \ldots, X_k$ be i.i.d. random variables over subsets of a linear vector space* $\mathsf{V}$ *of dimension* $\mathsf{dim}(\mathsf{V})$*. Then*

$$\Pr\left[X_k \not\subseteq \mathsf{span}(X_1 \cup X_2 \cup \cdots \cup X_{k-1})\right] \leqslant \frac{\mathsf{dim}(\mathsf{V})}{k}.$$

By the correctness of the base scheme,

$$\Pr\left[\text{Dec}^{\mathbb{G}}(\mathsf{sk}[\mathbf{y}], \mathsf{ct}, \langle \mathbf{y}, \mathbf{x}\rangle) = 1 \;\middle|\; \begin{array}{c} \mathsf{msk} \leftarrow \text{Setup}^{\mathbb{G}}(1^{\kappa}) \\ \mathbf{y} \leftarrow \mathbb{Z}_q^n,\ \mathbf{x} \leftarrow \mathbb{Z}_q^n \\ \mathsf{sk}[\mathbf{y}] \leftarrow \text{KGen}(\mathsf{msk}, \mathbf{y}) \\ \mathsf{ct} \leftarrow \text{Enc}^{\mathbb{G}}(\mathsf{msk}, \mathbf{x}) \end{array}\right] \geqslant \nu. \tag{4}$$

The compiled scheme has the same encryption process and "almost" the same decryption process except for when an equality query is issued. For $\text{Dec}^{\mathbb{G}}$, such equality queries are answered by the GGM oracle. For $\overline{\text{Dec}}^{\mathbb{G}}$, such equality queries are answered by the linear relation $\mathsf{R}$ made by the compiler.

For Eqs. 3 and 4 let $\mathsf{sk}[\mathbf{y}] = (s, g_1, \ldots, g_m)$ be the base secret key and $\overline{\mathsf{sk}[\mathbf{y}]} := (s, \mathsf{pp}, R)$ be the compiled secret key. The only time that the random process in Eq. 3 and Eq. 4 might produce different outputs is when equality queries asked during the two decryption processes result in different outputs. That is,

$$\overline{\text{Dec}}^{\mathbb{G}}(\overline{\mathsf{sk}[\mathbf{y}]}, \mathsf{ct}, \langle \mathbf{y}, \mathbf{x}\rangle) \neq \text{Dec}^{\mathbb{G}}(\mathsf{sk}[\mathbf{y}], \mathsf{ct}, \langle \mathbf{y}, \mathbf{x}\rangle)$$

only when some equality query is answered differently between $\overline{\text{Dec}}^{\mathbb{G}}$ and $\text{Dec}^{\mathbb{G}}$. We are going to argue that this can only happen with probability at most $\frac{m}{\ell+1}$, which would conclude the proof of Step 1.

We define the following variables.

- $X_h$ for $h \in [\ell]$: for any positively-answered relation $\sum_{i=1}^{m} a_i \cdot g_i + \sum_{i=1}^{t} a'_{h,i} \cdot g_{h,i} = 0$ during the execution of $\mathrm{Dec}^{\mathbb{G}}(\mathsf{sk}[\mathbf{y}], \mathsf{ct}_h)$ performed by $\overline{\mathrm{KGen}}$ (Step 1. of Fig. 2), add the vector $(a_1, \ldots, a_m)$ to $X_h$, the corresponding coefficients underlying $(g_1, \ldots, g_m)$.
- $X_{\ell+1}$: Let $u_1, \ldots, u_t$ be the group elements in the ciphertext $\mathsf{ct}$ (Eqs. 3 and 4). For any positively-answered relation $\sum_{i=1}^{m} a_i \cdot g_i + \sum_{i=1}^{t} a'_i \cdot u_i = 0$ during the execution of $\mathrm{Dec}^{\mathbb{G}}(\mathsf{sk}[\mathbf{y}], \mathsf{ct})$, add the vector $(a_1, \ldots, a_m)$ to $X_{\ell+1}$, the corresponding coefficients underlying $(g_1, \ldots, g_m)$.

Let $\mathsf{Good}$ be the event that $X_{\ell+1} \subseteq \mathsf{span}(X_1 \cup X_2 \cup \cdots \cup X_\ell)$. By Lemma 3, $\Pr[\overline{\mathsf{Good}}] \leqslant \frac{m}{\ell+1}$. Moreover, we claim (*) that whenever $\mathsf{Good}$ holds, then the decryption outputs will be consistent, namely $\overline{\mathrm{Dec}}^{\mathbb{G}}(\mathsf{sk}[\mathbf{y}], \mathsf{ct}, \langle \mathbf{y}, \mathbf{x} \rangle) = \mathrm{Dec}^{\mathbb{G}}(\mathsf{sk}[\mathbf{y}], \mathsf{ct}, \langle \mathbf{y}, \mathbf{x} \rangle)$. This will conclude the proof of Step 1. Claim (*) follows because as we will show if $\mathsf{Good}$ holds, $\overline{\mathrm{Dec}}^{\mathbb{G}}$ will simulate correctly the response to any equality query of the form

$$\sum_{i=1}^{m} z_i \cdot g_i + \sum_{i=1}^{t} c_i \cdot u_i = 0. \tag{5}$$

Note that $\overline{\mathrm{Dec}}^{\mathbb{G}}$ does not have explicit access to the group elements $(g_1, \ldots, g_m)$, which are those in the secret key $\mathsf{sk}[\mathbf{y}]$, and should make up for its lack of access via the prepared matrix $R$. Let $R'$ be the submatrix of $R$ that contains only the columns that correspond to $(g_1, \ldots, g_m)$ (Step (a) of Fig. 2). We consider all possible cases.

- $(z_1, \ldots, z_m) \in \mathsf{Span}(X_1 \cup \cdots \cup X_\ell)$: In this case $\overline{\mathrm{Dec}}$ reduces the relation to an equivalent relation involving group elements $\{u_i\}$ and $\{g_{i,j}\}$ that it has explicit access to, and so $\overline{\mathrm{Dec}}$ will return a consistent response (Step (a) of Fig. 2).
- $(z_1, \ldots, z_m) \notin \mathsf{Span}(X_1 \cup \cdots \cup X_\ell)$ and the relation of Eq. 5 does not hold: In this case both Dec and $\overline{\mathrm{Dec}}$ respond to the query with 0.
- $(z_1, \ldots, z_m) \notin \mathsf{Span}(X_1 \cup \cdots \cup X_\ell)$ and the relation of Eq. 5 holds: This case cannot happen because we assumed $\mathsf{Good}$ holds.

The proof of Step 1 is now complete. □

**Proof of Step 2.** In this step, we argue that the correctness does not drop by too much when we switch from the entire space to a random $(n-1)$-dimensional subspace. For ease of presentation, let us introduce some notations. Let $\mathsf{Corr}$ be the following randomized process.

$$\mathsf{Corr} := \left\{ \begin{array}{c} \mathsf{msk} \leftarrow \mathrm{Setup}^{\mathbb{G}}(1^\kappa) \\ \mathbf{y} \leftarrow \mathbb{Z}_q^n,\ \mathbf{x} \leftarrow \mathbb{Z}_q^n \\ \mathsf{sk}[\mathbf{y}] \leftarrow \mathrm{KGen}^{\mathbb{G}}(\mathsf{msk}, \mathbf{y}) \\ \mathsf{ct} \leftarrow \mathrm{Enc}^{\mathbb{G}}(\mathsf{msk}, \mathbf{x}) \end{array} \right\}.$$

Note that $\mathsf{Corr}$ is defined using the base IPFE scheme. In the rest of the analysis, all the probabilities we consider are computed over the sampling of $\mathsf{Corr}$. Let $\mathrm{SubDec}_{\mathsf{V}}$ denote the following process.

1. Sample $\ell$ ciphertexts $(\mathsf{ct}_1, \ldots, \mathsf{ct}_\ell)$ encrypting random vectors from $\mathsf{V}$, using $\mathsf{msk}$ of $\mathsf{Corr}$.
2. Compile $\mathsf{sk}[\mathbf{y}]$, given in $\mathsf{Corr}$, by learning the relation $\mathsf{R}$ just as in the compiler of Fig. 2 (Step 1.). To do this step, we make use of the oracle $\mathbb{G}$. Let the compiled secret key be $\overline{\mathsf{sk}[\mathbf{y}]}$.
3. Run $\overline{\mathrm{Dec}}^{\mathbb{G}}(\overline{\mathsf{sk}[\mathbf{y}]}, \mathsf{ct}, \langle \mathbf{y}, \mathbf{x} \rangle)$, where recall that $\mathsf{ct}$ was defined in $\mathsf{Corr}$.

Let FullDec denote the similar process except $\mathsf{V}$ is the entire space. Under this notation, what we have proved in Step 1 is

$$\Pr[\mathrm{FullDec} = 1] \geqslant \nu - \frac{m}{\ell + 1}.$$

We need to argue that $\Pr[\mathrm{SubDec}_{\mathsf{V}} \neq 1]$ is small. Consider the following derivation.

$$\begin{aligned}
&\Pr[\mathrm{SubDec}_{\mathsf{V}} \neq 1] \\
&\leqslant \Pr[\mathrm{SubDec}_{\mathsf{V}} \neq \mathrm{FullDec}] + \Pr[\mathrm{FullDec} \neq 1] \\
&\leqslant \Pr[\mathbf{y} \in \mathsf{V}^{\perp}] + \Pr\left[\mathrm{SubDec}_{\mathsf{V}} \neq \mathrm{FullDec} \mid \mathbf{y} \notin \mathsf{V}^{\perp}\right] + \left(1 - \nu + \frac{m}{\ell + 1}\right) \\
&\leqslant \frac{1}{q^{n-1}} + \Pr\left[\mathrm{SubDec}_{\mathsf{V}} \neq \mathrm{FullDec} \mid \mathbf{y} \notin \mathsf{V}^{\perp}\right] + \left(1 - \nu + \frac{m}{\ell + 1}\right).
\end{aligned}$$

We complete the proof of correctness by proving that, due to $\mathsf{V}$-plaintext hiding (Definition 3) property, we have

$$\mathop{\mathrm{E}}_{\mathsf{V}}\left[\Pr\left[\mathrm{SubDec}_{\mathsf{V}} \neq \mathrm{FullDec} \mid \mathbf{y} \notin \mathsf{V}^{\perp}\right]\right] \leqslant 2 \cdot \left(1 - \nu + \frac{m}{\ell + 1}\right) + \mathrm{negl}(\kappa).$$

This suffices because

$$\begin{aligned}
&\mathop{\mathrm{E}}_{\mathsf{V}}\left[\Pr[\mathrm{SubDec}_{\mathsf{V}} \neq 1]\right] \\
&\leqslant \mathop{\mathrm{E}}_{\mathsf{V}}\left[\frac{1}{q^{n-1}} + \Pr\left[\mathrm{SubDec}_{\mathsf{V}} \neq \mathrm{FullDec} \mid \mathbf{y} \notin \mathsf{V}^{\perp}\right] + \left(1 - \nu + \frac{m}{\ell + 1}\right)\right] \\
&\leqslant \frac{1}{q^{n-1}} + \mathop{\mathrm{E}}_{\mathsf{V}}\left[\Pr\left[\mathrm{SubDec}_{\mathsf{V}} \neq \mathrm{FullDec} \mid \mathbf{y} \notin \mathsf{V}^{\perp}\right]\right] + \left(1 - \nu + \frac{m}{\ell + 1}\right) \\
&\leqslant \frac{1}{q^{n-1}} + 2 \cdot \left(1 - \nu + \frac{m}{\ell + 1}\right) + \mathrm{negl}(\kappa) + \left(1 - \nu + \frac{m}{\ell + 1}\right),
\end{aligned}$$

which proves Eq. 3 and, henceforth, the correctness guarantee.

Let us run the V-plaintext hiding game, where the adversary makes one key corruption query (on the vector $\mathbf{y}$) to receive $\mathsf{sk}[\mathbf{y}]$, and makes both (a) $\ell$ many LoR queries and (b) $\ell$ many straight encryption queries. Now we can run the compiler twice on $\mathsf{sk}[\mathbf{y}]$: (a) once using the $\ell$ ciphertexts from the LoR queries and (b) once using the $\ell$ ciphertexts from the straight encryption queries. Note that we can run the compiler since we always know *the inner product between the secret key vector* $\mathbf{y}$ *and the plaintext vector that the ciphertext encrypts* (refer to Definition 3 that we can either compute this inner product ourselves or receive it from the oracle). This information is used in the compiler to run decryption $\mathrm{Dec}^{\mathbb{G}}$.

Finally, we ask for one more random ciphertext $\mathsf{ct}$ from the straight encryption query and try to decrypt $\mathsf{ct}$ using the two compiled secret keys to see if they result in the same decryption or not. When the bit $b = 1$, this corresponds to the probability

$$\Pr\left[\mathrm{FullDec} \neq \mathrm{FullDec} \mid \mathbf{y} \notin \mathsf{V}^{\perp}\right], \tag{6}$$

where the two FullDec are two independent runs of FullDec with fresh randomness (but under the same $\mathsf{sk}[\mathbf{y}]$ and $\mathsf{ct}$). On the other hand, when the bit $b = 0$, the probability is exactly

$$\Pr\left[\mathrm{SubDec}_{\mathsf{V}} \neq \mathrm{FullDec} \mid \mathbf{y} \notin \mathsf{V}^{\perp}\right]. \tag{7}$$

By the plaintext hiding property, we know that the two probabilities in Eq. 6 and Eq. 7 should only differ by $\mathrm{negl}(\kappa)$. Finally, when we run FullDec twice, the probability that these two decryptions are different is upper-bounded by twice the correctness error (i.e., $2 \cdot (1 - \nu + \frac{m}{\ell+1})$). Note that the conditioning on $\mathbf{y} \notin \mathsf{V}^{\perp}$ does not change the correctness error when we average over the choice of $\mathsf{V}$ because $\mathsf{V}$ is a random subspace independent of all other randomness. That is,

$$\mathop{\mathrm{E}}_{\mathsf{V}}\left[\Pr\left[\mathrm{FullDec} \neq \mathrm{FullDec} \mid \mathbf{y} \notin \mathsf{V}^{\perp}\right]\right] \leqslant 2 \cdot \left(1 - \nu + \frac{m}{\ell+1}\right)$$

This concludes the proof since we now obtain

$$\mathop{\mathrm{E}}_{\mathsf{V}}\left[\Pr\left[\mathrm{SubDec}_{\mathsf{V}} \neq \mathrm{FullDec} \mid \mathbf{y} \notin \mathsf{V}^{\perp}\right]\right] \leqslant 2 \cdot \left(1 - \nu + \frac{m}{\ell+1}\right) + \mathrm{negl}(\kappa).$$

### 4.2 Step 2: Breaking Key Hiding for Oracle-Free KGen

In this section we show how to break the V-key hiding of any given IPFE, for which KGen makes no oracle queries. Our attack is general and applies to any oracle $O$. The described attacker does not make any queries to $O$ at all, and in fact breaks even *weak* V-key-hiding: defined as in Definition 2, where the adversary is not allowed to make any encryption queries, and can only make key-corruption queries. Also, we give the attack for the general IPFE schemes of Definition 1. We explain in the full version the changes we need to make to the proof to adapt it to the two-phase decryption algorithms as in Definition 4.

**Lemma 4.** *Let* $\mathcal{E}^O := (\text{Setup}^O, \text{KGen}, \text{Enc}^O, \text{Dec}^O)$ *be an IPFE over* $\mathbb{Z}_q^n$ *with correctness of at least* 0.999, *where* KGen *makes no oracle queries. Suppose* $n \geqslant 2$. *Then, there exists an attacker* $\mathcal{A}$ *that makes no* $O$ *queries and wins the weak* $\mathsf{V}$*-key hiding game, for any given* $\mathsf{V}$, *with probability* $1/2 + \frac{1}{\mathsf{poly}(\kappa)}$ *for some polynomial* $\mathsf{poly}$.

*Proof.* We give the description of the attacker. Suppose $|\mathsf{msk}| = \rho$. Let $m = 16(\kappa + \rho)\kappa^2$. The adversary $\mathcal{A}$ makes $m$ key-corruption queries to receive $(\mathbf{w}_1, \mathbf{u}_1 := \mathbf{w}_1 + \mathbf{v}_1, \mathsf{sk}_1), \ldots (\mathbf{w}_m, \mathbf{u}_m := \mathbf{w}_m + \mathbf{v}_m, \mathsf{sk}_m)$. Recall that for all $i \in [m]$: $\mathbf{w}_i \leftarrow \mathbb{Z}_q^n$, $\mathbf{v}_i \leftarrow \mathsf{V}^\perp$. The adversary attempts decoding the $m$ given secret keys via a procedure Recover, defined momentarily, to obtain $m$ recovered vectors, one for each coordinate $i \in [m]$. Specifically, $\mathcal{A}$ works as follows.

1. If $\exists \widetilde{\mathsf{msk}} \in \{0,1\}^\rho$ such that for at least $m(\frac{1}{q} + \frac{1}{2\kappa})$ coordinates $i$, $\mathbf{w}_i = \mathbf{h}_i$, where $(\mathbf{h}_1, \ldots, \mathbf{h}_m) := \text{Recover}(\widetilde{\mathsf{msk}}, \mathsf{sk}_1, \ldots, \mathsf{sk}_m)$, return $b' = 0$. Else, return $b' = 1$.

The procedure Recover recovers the $i$th vector by examining the distribution over vectors obtained by reverse sampling a vector based on $(\widetilde{\mathsf{msk}}, \mathsf{sk}_i)$. Then, it outputs the vector with weight strictly greater than 1/2 (if any). Details follow.

*Procedure* $\text{Recover}(\widetilde{\mathsf{msk}}, \mathsf{sk}_1, \ldots, \mathsf{sk}_m)$*:*

1. For $i \in [m]$, form the vector $\mathbf{h}_i$ as follows.
   (a) Let $\mathsf{D}_i$ be the induced distribution over uniformly-random vectors conditioned on $(\widetilde{\mathsf{msk}}, \mathsf{sk}_i)$:
$$\mathsf{D}_i(\mathbf{v}) = \Pr_{\mathbf{x} \leftarrow \mathbb{Z}_q^n}[\mathbf{x} = \mathbf{v} \mid \mathsf{sk}_i = \text{KGen}(\widetilde{\mathsf{msk}}, \mathbf{x})]. \tag{8}$$
   (b) If there exists a vector $\mathbf{v}$ such that $\mathsf{D}_i(\mathbf{v}) > \frac{1}{2}$, set $\mathbf{h}_i = \mathbf{v}$. Else, set $\mathbf{h}_i = \perp$.
2. Return $(\mathbf{h}_1, \ldots, \mathbf{h}_m)$.

First, note that the above computation, especially that of Recover, involves no oracle queries. This is where we make use of the fact that KGen makes no oracle calls. Moreover, $\mathcal{A}$ makes no encryption queries in the key-hiding game (Definition 2), so $\mathcal{A}$ indeed breaks *weak* $\mathsf{V}$-key hiding.

The proof of Lemma 4 follows immediately from the following two lemmas. In the following $b$ denotes the challenge bit. □

**Lemma 5.** *We have* $\Pr[b' = 0 \mid b = 0] \geqslant \frac{1}{\mathsf{poly}(\kappa)}$, *for some polynomial* $\mathsf{poly}$.

**Lemma 6.** *We have* $\Pr[b' = 0 \mid b = 1] \leqslant \text{negl}(\kappa)$.

**Proof of Lemma 5.** To have a compact way to refer to Eq. 8, for a given $(\mathsf{msk}, \mathsf{sk})$ let $\mathrm{Vect}(\mathsf{msk}, \mathsf{sk})$ denote the distribution over secret-key vectors induced by $(\mathsf{msk}, \mathsf{sk})$, namely letting $\mathcal{D} := \mathrm{Vect}(\mathsf{msk}, \mathsf{sk})$,

$$\mathcal{D}(\mathbf{v}) := \Pr_{\mathbf{x} \leftarrow \mathbb{Z}_q^n}[\mathbf{x} = \mathbf{v} \mid \mathsf{sk} = \mathrm{KGen}(\mathsf{msk}, \mathbf{x})]. \tag{9}$$

Say $\mathsf{msk}$ is $\mathsf{good}$ if the probability of decryption correctness under $\mathsf{msk}$ is at least $\frac{47}{48}$. To have a compact way to denote this, let $\mathrm{PCorrect}(\mathsf{msk})$ denote the probability of correctness when all the parameters but $\mathsf{msk}$ are chosen at random.

$$\mathrm{PCorrect}(\mathsf{msk}) = \Pr_{\mathbf{u}, \mathsf{sk}, \mathbf{x}}[\mathrm{Dec}^{O}(\mathsf{sk}, \mathrm{Enc}^{O}(\mathsf{msk}, \mathbf{x})) = \langle \mathbf{u}, \mathbf{x} \rangle], \tag{10}$$

where $\mathbf{u}, \mathbf{x} \leftarrow \mathbb{Z}_q^n$ and $\mathsf{sk} \leftarrow \mathrm{KGen}(\mathsf{msk}, \mathbf{u})$. We may extend this notation when additional parameters besides $\mathsf{msk}$ are fixed (e.g., $\mathrm{PCorrect}(\mathsf{msk}, \mathbf{u}, \mathsf{sk})$).

Equipped with this notation, we say $\mathsf{msk}$ is $\mathsf{good}$ if $\mathrm{PCorrect}(\mathsf{msk}) \geqslant \frac{47}{48}$. We make two claims and then show how to derive Lemma 5 from these two claims.

*Claim 6.* $\Pr_{\mathsf{msk} \leftarrow \mathsf{Setup}(1^{\kappa})}[\mathsf{msk} \text{ is good}] \geqslant \frac{118}{6000}$.

*Claim 7.* Fix a $\mathsf{good}$ $\mathsf{msk}$. For at least a $\frac{33}{60}$-fraction of $(\mathbf{u}, \mathsf{sk}[\mathbf{u}])$ produced under $\mathsf{msk}$, the pair $(\mathsf{msk}, \mathsf{sk}[\mathbf{u}])$ is a binding to $\mathbf{u}$:

$$\Pr_{\mathbf{u}, \mathsf{sk}[\mathbf{u}]}[\mathcal{D}(\mathbf{u}) > \frac{1}{2}] \geqslant \frac{33}{60}, \tag{11}$$

where $\mathbf{u} \leftarrow \mathbb{Z}_q^n$ and $\mathsf{sk}[\mathbf{u}] \leftarrow \mathrm{KGen}(\mathsf{msk}, \mathbf{u})$ and $\mathcal{D} := \mathrm{Vect}(\mathsf{msk}, \mathsf{sk}[\mathbf{u}])$.

*Proof of Lemma 5 via Claims 6 and 7.* Let $\mathsf{msk}$ be the master secret key picked by the challenger to generate $\mathsf{sk}_i \leftarrow \mathrm{KGen}(\mathsf{msk}, \mathbf{w}_i)$ for $i \in [m]$. Since the challenge bit $b$ is zero, each $\mathsf{sk}_i$ is indeed a secret key for $\mathbf{w}_i$ (as opposed to $\mathbf{u}_i$). Note that this $\mathsf{msk}$ is eventually picked by the adversary $\mathcal{A}$ because of the brute-force search in Step 1 of $\mathcal{A}$'s execution (i.e., $\mathcal{A}$ will eventually set $\widetilde{\mathsf{msk}} := \mathsf{msk}$ if it has not already output 0). Conditioned on $\mathsf{msk}$ being $\mathsf{good}$, we show the probability that $\mathcal{A}$ outputs 0 is $1 - \mathrm{negl}(\kappa)$. Specifically, setting $\widetilde{\mathsf{msk}}$ to $\mathsf{msk}$ in Step 1's execution will make $\mathcal{A}$ output 0 with all but negligible probability, assuming $\mathsf{msk}$ is $\mathsf{good}$. This will prove the lemma because

$$\begin{aligned}
\Pr[b' = 0 \mid b = 0] &\geqslant \Pr[b' = 0 \wedge (\mathsf{msk} \text{ is good}) \mid b = 0] \\
&= \Pr[b' = 0 \mid (b = 0) \wedge (\mathsf{msk} \text{ is good})] \Pr[\mathsf{msk} \text{ is good} \mid b = 0] \\
&= \Pr[b' = 0 \mid (b = 0) \wedge (\mathsf{msk} \text{ is good})] \Pr[\mathsf{msk} \text{ is good}] \\
&\geqslant (1 - \mathrm{negl}(\kappa)) \times \frac{118}{6000}, \qquad \text{Claims 6}
\end{aligned}$$

which is at least $1/\mathsf{poly}(\kappa)$ for some polynomial $\mathsf{poly}$.

Let $\mathsf{msk}$ be the challenge master secret key picked by the challenger and suppose $\mathsf{msk}$ is $\mathsf{good}$. Recall that for all $i$, $\mathsf{sk}_i \leftarrow \mathrm{KGen}(\mathsf{msk}, \mathbf{w}_i)$. Say $(\mathsf{msk}, \mathsf{sk})$ is a binding to $\mathbf{v}$ if $\mathcal{D}(\mathbf{v}) > \frac{1}{2}$, where $\mathcal{D} := \text{Vect}(\mathsf{msk}, \mathsf{sk})$ (Eq. 9). For $i \in [m]$, define a Bernoulli random variable $X_i$ as follows: $X_i = 1$ iff $(\mathsf{msk}, \mathsf{sk}_i)$ is a binding to $\mathbf{w}_i$. Since each $\mathbf{w}_i$ is chosen uniformly at random from $\mathbb{Z}_q^n$ we have:

1. $X_i$'s are i.i.d random variables.
2. $\mu := \Pr[X_1 = 1] \geqslant \frac{33}{60} \geqslant \frac{1}{q} + \frac{1}{\kappa}$ for all $q \geqslant 2$. This follows from Claim 7.

Let $X = \frac{X_1 + \cdots + X_m}{m}$. If $X \geqslant \frac{1}{q} + \frac{1}{2\kappa}$, then $\mathcal{A}$ will output 0. Let $\epsilon = \frac{1}{2\kappa}$. Since $m = 16(\kappa+\rho)\kappa^2$, we have $\frac{m\epsilon^2}{4} = \kappa+\rho$. Invoking the Chernoff bound (Lemma 1), the probability that $\mathcal{A}$ outputs 1 is at most

$$\Pr[X < \frac{1}{q} + \frac{1}{2\kappa}] \leqslant \Pr[|X - \mu| \geqslant \frac{1}{2\kappa}] \leqslant \frac{2}{e^{\frac{m\epsilon^2}{4}}} = \frac{2}{e^{\kappa+\rho}} = \text{negl}(\kappa), \tag{12}$$

as desired. □

The proofs of Claim 6 and Claim 7 are deferred to the full version.

*Proof.* (Proof of Lemma 6. Suppose $b = 1$ as in the lemma. We prove that for any fixed $\widetilde{\mathsf{msk}}$, the probability that that fixed $\widetilde{\mathsf{msk}}$ makes $\mathcal{A}$ output 0 is at most $\frac{2}{e^{\kappa+\rho}}$. The proof then follows by a union bound over all $\mathsf{msk} \in \{0,1\}^\rho$. Fix $\widetilde{\mathsf{msk}}$. Let $(\mathbf{h}_1, \ldots, \mathbf{h}_m) = \text{Recover}(\widetilde{\mathsf{msk}}, \mathsf{sk}_1, \ldots, \mathsf{sk}_m)$. Note that:

1. $(\mathbf{h}_1, \ldots, \mathbf{h}_m)$ is solely picked based on $(\mathbf{u}_1, \ldots, \mathbf{u}_m)$ (since $b = 1$), and not based on $(\mathbf{w}_1, \ldots, \mathbf{w}_m)$.
2. The Bernoulli random variables $(X_1, \ldots, X_m)$ are i.i.d, where $X_i = 1$ iff $\mathbf{w}_i = \mathbf{h}_i$.
3. For all $i \in [m]$, $\mu := \Pr[X_i = 1] \leqslant \frac{1}{q}$. This is because $|\mathsf{V}^\perp| = q$.

$\mathcal{A}$ outputs 0 iff $X := \frac{X_1 + \cdots + X_m}{m} \geqslant \frac{1}{q} + \frac{1}{2\kappa}$. Let $\epsilon = \frac{1}{2\kappa}$. Since $m = 16(\kappa+\rho)\kappa^2$, we have $\frac{m\epsilon^2}{4} = k + \rho$. Invoking the Chernoff bound (Lemma 1),

$$\Pr[X \geqslant \frac{1}{q} + \frac{1}{2\kappa}] \leqslant \Pr[|X - \mu| \geqslant \frac{1}{2\kappa}] \leqslant \frac{2}{e^{\frac{m\epsilon^2}{4}}} = \frac{2}{e^{\kappa+\rho}}, \tag{13}$$

as desired. □

**Acknowledgments.** Mohammad Hajiabadi was supported in part by the NSERC Discovery Grant RGPIN-2022-03270 and a Meta research award. Roman Langrehr was supported by SNSF Postdoc.Mobility grant no. 235425. Mingyuan Wang is supported in part by a research grant from Open Philanthropy.

## References

1. Abdalla, M., Benhamouda, F., Gay, R.: From Single-Input to Multi-client Inner-Product Functional Encryption. In: Galbraith, S.D., Moriai, S. (eds.) ASIACRYPT 2019. LNCS, vol. 11923, pp. 552–582. Springer, Cham (2019). https://doi.org/10.1007/978-3-030-34618-8_19

2. Abdalla, M., Bourse, F., De Caro, A., Pointcheval, D.: Simple Functional Encryption Schemes for Inner Products. In: Katz, J. (ed.) PKC 2015. LNCS, vol. 9020, pp. 733–751. Springer, Heidelberg (2015). https://doi.org/10.1007/978-3-662-46447-2_33
3. Abdalla, M., Catalano, D., Fiore, D., Gay, R., Ursu, B.: Multi-Input Functional Encryption for Inner Products: Function-Hiding Realizations and Constructions Without Pairings. In: Shacham, H., Boldyreva, A. (eds.) CRYPTO 2018. LNCS, vol. 10991, pp. 597–627. Springer, Cham (2018). https://doi.org/10.1007/978-3-319-96884-1_20
4. Abdalla, M., Catalano, D., Gay, R., Ursu, B.: Inner-Product Functional Encryption with Fine-Grained Access Control. In: Moriai, S., Wang, H. (eds.) ASIACRYPT 2020. LNCS, vol. 12493, pp. 467–497. Springer, Cham (2020). https://doi.org/10.1007/978-3-030-64840-4_16
5. Abdalla, M., Gay, R., Raykova, M., Wee, H.: Multi-input Inner-Product Functional Encryption from Pairings. In: Coron, J.-S., Nielsen, J.B. (eds.) EUROCRYPT 2017. LNCS, vol. 10210, pp. 601–626. Springer, Cham (2017). https://doi.org/10.1007/978-3-319-56620-7_21
6. Acharya, O., Feng, W., Langrehr, R., O'Neill, A.: Access-controlled inner product function-revealing encryption. CiC **2**(3), 7 (2025). https://doi.org/10.62056/abe0zo-3y
7. Afshar, A., Couteau, G., Mahmoody, M., Sadeghi, E.: Fine-grained non-interactive key-exchange: Constructions and lower bounds. In: Hazay, C., Stam, M. (eds.) EUROCRYPT 2023, Part I. LNCS, vol. 14004, pp. 55–85. Springer, Cham (2023). https://doi.org/10.1007/978-3-031-30545-0_3
8. Agrawal, S., Clear, M., Frieder, O., Garg, S., O'Neill, A., Thaler, J.: Ad hoc multi-input functional encryption. In: Vidick, T. (ed.) ITCS 2020. vol. 151, pp. 40:1–40:41. LIPIcs (2020). https://doi.org/10.4230/LIPIcs.ITCS.2020.40
9. Agrawal, S., Goyal, R., Tomida, J.: Multi-input Quadratic Functional Encryption from Pairings. In: Malkin, T., Peikert, C. (eds.) CRYPTO 2021. LNCS, vol. 12828, pp. 208–238. Springer, Cham (2021). https://doi.org/10.1007/978-3-030-84259-8_8
10. Agrawal, S., Libert, B., Maitra, M., Titiu, R.: Adaptive Simulation Security for Inner Product Functional Encryption. In: Kiayias, A., Kohlweiss, M., Wallden, P., Zikas, V. (eds.) PKC 2020. LNCS, vol. 12110, pp. 34–64. Springer, Cham (2020). https://doi.org/10.1007/978-3-030-45374-9_2
11. Agrawal, S., Libert, B., Stehlé, D.: Fully Secure Functional Encryption for Inner Products, from Standard Assumptions. In: Robshaw, M., Katz, J. (eds.) CRYPTO 2016. LNCS, vol. 9816, pp. 333–362. Springer, Heidelberg (2016). https://doi.org/10.1007/978-3-662-53015-3_12
12. Ananth, P., Jain, A.: Indistinguishability Obfuscation from Compact Functional Encryption. In: Gennaro, R., Robshaw, M. (eds.) CRYPTO 2015. LNCS, vol. 9215, pp. 308–326. Springer, Heidelberg (2015). https://doi.org/10.1007/978-3-662-47989-6_15
13. Ananth, P., Vaikuntanathan, V.: Optimal Bounded-Collusion Secure Functional Encryption. In: Hofheinz, D., Rosen, A. (eds.) TCC 2019. LNCS, vol. 11891, pp. 174–198. Springer, Cham (2019). https://doi.org/10.1007/978-3-030-36030-6_8
14. Baltico, C.E.Z., Catalano, D., Fiore, D., Gay, R.: Practical Functional Encryption for Quadratic Functions with Applications to Predicate Encryption. In: Katz, J., Shacham, H. (eds.) CRYPTO 2017. LNCS, vol. 10401, pp. 67–98. Springer, Cham (2017). https://doi.org/10.1007/978-3-319-63688-7_3

15. Barbosa, M., Catalano, D., Soleimanian, A., Warinschi, B.: Efficient Function-Hiding Functional Encryption: From Inner-Products to Orthogonality. In: Matsui, M. (ed.) CT-RSA 2019. LNCS, vol. 11405, pp. 127–148. Springer, Cham (2019). https://doi.org/10.1007/978-3-030-12612-4_7
16. Bishop, A., Jain, A., Kowalczyk, L.: Function-Hiding Inner Product Encryption. In: Iwata, T., Cheon, J.H. (eds.) ASIACRYPT 2015. LNCS, vol. 9452, pp. 470–491. Springer, Heidelberg (2015). https://doi.org/10.1007/978-3-662-48797-6_20
17. Bitansky, N., Vaikuntanathan, V.: Indistinguishability obfuscation from functional encryption. In: Guruswami, V. (ed.) 56th FOCS. pp. 171–190. IEEE Computer Society Press (2015). https://doi.org/10.1109/FOCS.2015.20
18. Boneh, D., Guan, J., Zhandry, M.: A lower bound on the length of signatures based on group actions and generic isogenies. In: Hazay, C., Stam, M. (eds.) EUROCRYPT 2023, Part V. LNCS, vol. 14008, pp. 507–531. Springer, Cham (2023). https://doi.org/10.1007/978-3-031-30589-4_18
19. Boneh, D., Sahai, A., Waters, B.: Functional Encryption: Definitions and Challenges. In: Ishai, Y. (ed.) TCC 2011. LNCS, vol. 6597, pp. 253–273. Springer, Heidelberg (2011). https://doi.org/10.1007/978-3-642-19571-6_16
20. Brakerski, Z., Segev, G.: Function-Private Functional Encryption in the Private-Key Setting. In: Dodis, Y., Nielsen, J.B. (eds.) TCC 2015. LNCS, vol. 9015, pp. 306–324. Springer, Heidelberg (2015). https://doi.org/10.1007/978-3-662-46497-7_12
21. Castagnos, G., Laguillaumie, F., Tucker, I.: Practical Fully Secure Unrestricted Inner Product Functional Encryption Modulo $p$. In: Peyrin, T., Galbraith, S. (eds.) ASIACRYPT 2018. LNCS, vol. 11273, pp. 733–764. Springer, Cham (2018). https://doi.org/10.1007/978-3-030-03329-3_25
22. Catalano, D., Fiore, D., Gennaro, R., Giunta, E.: On the impossibility of algebraic vector commitments in pairing-free groups. In: Kiltz, E., Vaikuntanathan, V. (eds.) TCC 2022, Part II. LNCS, vol. 13748, pp. 274–299. Springer, Cham (2022). https://doi.org/10.1007/978-3-031-22365-5_10
23. Datta, P., Dutta, R., Mukhopadhyay, S.: Functional Encryption for Inner Product with Full Function Privacy. In: Cheng, C.-M., Chung, K.-M., Persiano, G., Yang, B.-Y. (eds.) PKC 2016. LNCS, vol. 9614, pp. 164–195. Springer, Heidelberg (2016). https://doi.org/10.1007/978-3-662-49384-7_7
24. Döttling, N., Hartmann, D., Hofheinz, D., Kiltz, E., Schäge, S., Ursu, B.: On the Impossibility of Purely Algebraic Signatures. In: Nissim, K., Waters, B. (eds.) TCC 2021. LNCS, vol. 13044, pp. 317–349. Springer, Cham (2021). https://doi.org/10.1007/978-3-030-90456-2_11
25. Garg, S., Srinivasan, A.: Single-Key to Multi-Key Functional Encryption with Polynomial Loss. In: Hirt, M., Smith, A. (eds.) TCC 2016. LNCS, vol. 9986, pp. 419–442. Springer, Heidelberg (2016). https://doi.org/10.1007/978-3-662-53644-5_16
26. Gay, R.: A New Paradigm for Public-Key Functional Encryption for Degree-2 Polynomials. In: Kiayias, A., Kohlweiss, M., Wallden, P., Zikas, V. (eds.) PKC 2020. LNCS, vol. 12110, pp. 95–120. Springer, Cham (2020). https://doi.org/10.1007/978-3-030-45374-9_4
27. Hajiabadi, M., Langrehr, R., O'Neill, A., Wang, M.: On the black-box complexity of private-key inner-product functional encryption. In: Boyle, E., Mahmoody, M. (eds.) TCC 2024, Part III. LNCS, vol. 15366, pp. 318–343. Springer, Cham (2024). https://doi.org/10.1007/978-3-031-78020-2_11

28. He, J., Li, S., Lin, W.K.: Lower bounds on inner-product functional encryption from all-or-nothing encryption primitives. In: Applebaum, B., Lin, H.R. (eds.) TCC 2025, Part II. LNCS, vol. 16269, pp. 123–152. Springer, Cham (2025). https://doi.org/10.1007/978-3-032-12293-3_5
29. Kim, S., Lewi, K., Mandal, A., Montgomery, H., Roy, A., Wu, D.J.: Function-Hiding Inner Product Encryption Is Practical. In: Catalano, D., De Prisco, R. (eds.) SCN 2018. LNCS, vol. 11035, pp. 544–562. Springer, Cham (2018). https://doi.org/10.1007/978-3-319-98113-0_29
30. Li, B., Micciancio, D.: Compactness vs Collusion Resistance in Functional Encryption. In: Hirt, M., Smith, A. (eds.) TCC 2016. LNCS, vol. 9986, pp. 443–468. Springer, Heidelberg (2016). https://doi.org/10.1007/978-3-662-53644-5_17
31. Luby, M., Rackoff, C.: How to Construct Pseudo-random Permutations from Pseudo-random Functions. In: Williams, H.C. (ed.) CRYPTO 1985. LNCS, vol. 218, pp. 447–447. Springer, Heidelberg (1986). https://doi.org/10.1007/3-540-39799-X_34
32. Maurer, U.: Abstract Models of Computation in Cryptography. In: Smart, N.P. (ed.) Cryptography and Coding 2005. LNCS, vol. 3796, pp. 1–12. Springer, Heidelberg (2005). https://doi.org/10.1007/11586821_1
33. O'Neill, A.: Definitional issues in functional encryption. Cryptology ePrint Archive, Report 2010/556 (2010). https://eprint.iacr.org/2010/556
34. Papakonstantinou, P.A., Rackoff, C.W., Vahlis, Y.: How powerful are the DDH hard groups? Cryptology ePrint Archive, Report 2012/653 (2012). https://eprint.iacr.org/2012/653
35. Rotem, L., Segev, G., Shahaf, I.: Generic-Group Delay Functions Require Hidden-Order Groups. In: Canteaut, A., Ishai, Y. (eds.) EUROCRYPT 2020. LNCS, vol. 12107, pp. 155–180. Springer, Cham (2020). https://doi.org/10.1007/978-3-030-45727-3_6
36. Sahai, A., Waters, B.: Fuzzy Identity-Based Encryption. In: Cramer, R. (ed.) EUROCRYPT 2005. LNCS, vol. 3494, pp. 457–473. Springer, Heidelberg (2005). https://doi.org/10.1007/11426639_27
37. Schul-Ganz, G., Segev, G.: Generic-group identity-based encryption: A tight impossibility result. In: Tessaro, S. (ed.) ITC 2021. LIPIcs, vol. 199, pp. 26:1–26:23. Schloss Dagstuhl (2021). https://doi.org/10.4230/LIPIcs.ITC.2021.26
38. Shen, E., Shi, E., Waters, B.: Predicate Privacy in Encryption Systems. In: Reingold, O. (ed.) TCC 2009. LNCS, vol. 5444, pp. 457–473. Springer, Heidelberg (2009). https://doi.org/10.1007/978-3-642-00457-5_27
39. Shoup, V.: Lower Bounds for Discrete Logarithms and Related Problems. In: Fumy, W. (ed.) EUROCRYPT 1997. LNCS, vol. 1233, pp. 256–266. Springer, Heidelberg (1997). https://doi.org/10.1007/3-540-69053-0_18
40. Tairi, E., Ünal, A.: Lower bounds for lattice-based compact functional encryption. In: Joye, M., Leander, G. (eds.) EUROCRYPT 2024, Part II. LNCS, vol. 14652, pp. 249–279. Springer, Cham (2024). https://doi.org/10.1007/978-3-031-58723-8_9
41. Tomida, J.: Tightly Secure Inner Product Functional Encryption: Multi-input and Function-Hiding Constructions. In: Galbraith, S.D., Moriai, S. (eds.) ASIACRYPT 2019. LNCS, vol. 11923, pp. 459–488. Springer, Cham (2019). https://doi.org/10.1007/978-3-030-34618-8_16
42. Tomida, J.: Unbounded quadratic functional encryption and more from pairings. In: Hazay, C., Stam, M. (eds.) EUROCRYPT 2023, Part III. LNCS, vol. 14006, pp. 543–572. Springer, Cham (2023). https://doi.org/10.1007/978-3-031-30620-4_18

43. Tomida, J., Abe, M., Okamoto, T.: Efficient Functional Encryption for Inner-Product Values with Full-Hiding Security. In: Bishop, M., Nascimento, A.C.A. (eds.) ISC 2016. LNCS, vol. 9866, pp. 408–425. Springer, Cham (2016). https://doi.org/10.1007/978-3-319-45871-7_24
44. Ünal, A.: Impossibility Results for Lattice-Based Functional Encryption Schemes. In: Canteaut, A., Ishai, Y. (eds.) EUROCRYPT 2020. LNCS, vol. 12105, pp. 169–199. Springer, Cham (2020). https://doi.org/10.1007/978-3-030-45721-1_7
45. Wee, H.: Functional Encryption for Quadratic Functions from $k$-Lin, Revisited. In: Pass, R., Pietrzak, K. (eds.) TCC 2020. LNCS, vol. 12550, pp. 210–228. Springer, Cham (2020). https://doi.org/10.1007/978-3-030-64375-1_8
46. Zhandry, M.: To label, or not to label (in generic groups). In: Dodis, Y., Shrimpton, T. (eds.) CRYPTO 2022, Part III. LNCS, vol. 13509, pp. 66–96. Springer, Cham (2022). https://doi.org/10.1007/978-3-031-15982-4_3

# Author Index





N. Heninger and M. Rosulek (Eds.): CRYPTO 2026, LNCS 16800, pp. 615–616, 2026.
https://doi.org/10.1007/978-3-032-35367-2

MIX
Papier aus verantwortungsvollen Quellen
Paper from responsible sources
FSC® C105338

If you have any concerns about our products,
you can contact us on
**ProductSafety@springernature.com**

In case Publisher is established outside the EU,
the EU authorized representative is:
**Springer Nature Customer Service Center GmbH**
**Europaplatz 3, 69115 Heidelberg, Germany**

Printed by Libri Plureos GmbH
in Hamburg, Germany